AMERICAN
AURORA

View of Philadelphia in 1798, from the north,
along the Delaware.[1]

AMERICAN AURORA

A DEMOCRATIC-REPUBLICAN RETURNS

SURGO UT PROSIM.

THE SUPPRESSED HISTORY OF OUR NATION'S
BEGINNINGS AND THE HEROIC NEWSPAPER
THAT TRIED TO REPORT IT

RICHARD N. ROSENFELD

FOREWORD BY EDMUND S. MORGAN

ST. MARTIN'S PRESS ❧ NEW YORK

Library of Congress Cataloging-in-Publication Data

Rosenfeld, Richard N.
American Aurora : a Democratic-Republican returns : the suppressed history of our nation's beginnings and the heroic newspaper that tried to report it / Richard N. Rosenfeld : foreword by Edmund S. Morgan.
— 1st ed.
    p. cm.
Text written by Richard N. Rosenfeld as if he were the Aurora publisher/editor William Duane, interwoven with excerpts from the Aurora general advertiser (published in Philadelphia) and from other sources.
Includes bibliographical references and index.
ISBN 0–312–15052–0
1. Aurora General Advertiser. 2. Press and politics—United States—History—18th century. 3. United States—Politics and government—1783–1809. 4. United States—Politics and government—1775–1783. 5. United States—Politics and government—To 1775. I. Duane, William, 1760–1835. II. Aurora general advertiser. III. Title.
PN4899.P5A977   1997
071'.3'09033—dc20   96–30680
                                                                 CIP

First Edition: May 1997

10   9   8   7   6   5   4

The red-brick townhouses and walking pavements of High-street, also known as Market-street, in Philadelphia, 1798.[2]

CONTENTS

Promenading on Third-street, in Philadelphia, 1798.[3]

FOREWORD

Political passions fade with time, leaving their pale shadows to be recovered by historians who usually affect an objective, if not an amused, detachment from them. American politics have seldom generated the fierceness of passion that they did in their first decade. The extravagant exchanges in the contests between Federalists and Republicans in the late 1790s seem today so to exceed the issues as to merit the patronizing dismissal that scholars have generally given them. After all, the nation survived, President John Adams did not secure the crown to which he allegedly aspired, and President Thomas Jefferson succeeded him without bloodshed. Accordingly the dire predictions of tyranny by journalists like Benjamin Franklin Bache and William Duane in their notorious newspaper, the *Aurora,* have become mere curiosities, extreme examples of the bad manners that political contests so often provoke.

Not so fast, Richard Rosenfeld warns us. He has studied the newspapers and politics of the 1790s afresh and found the issues to justify all the passion they generated. Scorning the usual detachment, he has embraced as his own the outrage of the men who saw the republic threatened by the thrust for power of those entrusted with running it. He stands up for Benjamin Bache, the beloved grandson of Benjamin Franklin, and he literally and literarily becomes William Duane, Bache's successor as publisher of the *Aurora.* He invites us to join him in living through the events that so alarmed these men and to share their alarm in their own words. If we see what was happening as these men saw it, we may emerge with a less complacent view of what it was that the country survived in the 1790s, with a different perspective of what the founding fathers accomplished, even with a new view of who the true founding fathers were.

This is not a typical history, nor does it pretend to be. It is an indictment of some of our customary heroes and a salute to some of our customary villains. It is a piece of historical heresy, written by heretics of the time with the assistance of a kindred spirit who now appeals the sentence of irrelevance that orthodox history has imposed on them. If eternal vigilance is the price of liberty, its vigilant defenders of an earlier time may still have a message for the republic they cherished. That message resounds through these pages.

EDMUND S. MORGAN

AUTHOR'S NOTE

American Aurora was born of some curiosity I had about the Sedition Act of 1798. How, I wondered, could America's second President, John Adams, possibly sign—and its first President, George Washington, possibly support—a law that prohibited newspaper criticism of the President? After all, the Bill of Rights, with its guarantee of press freedom, was already seven years old in 1798.

The official answer, I soon learned, was national security. America was preparing for war with France. Press restrictions are upheld in times of war.

Yet something I read greatly troubled me. The *Philadelphia Aurora,* the principal newspaper that Adams and Washington wanted to silence—a paper that reportedly had driven Washington from the presidency the year before—was being published by Benjamin Franklin's grandson (who began the paper shortly after Franklin's death). Why, I wondered, would this grandson, Benjamin Bache, want to criticize his grandfather's most famous colleagues? Why wouldn't he want to stand in Franklin's shoes?

I was flabbergasted when I read John Adams' explanation:

> *I knew [Benjamin Franklin] had conceived an irreconcilable hatred to me and that he had propagated and would continue to propagate prejudices, if nothing worse, against me in America from one end of it to the other. Look into Bache's* Aurora *and Duane's* Aurora *for twenty years and see whether my expectations have not been verified.*[4]

Did Adams see the ghost of Franklin at the *Philadelphia Aurora?* Did he want a sedition act, I wondered, to silence Franklin's ghost?

I decided to take Adams' advice and look into Bache's *Aurora* and his successor William Duane's *Aurora* to see what old "prejudices" Franklin's ghost was propagating, what old coals Bache and Duane had rekindled that might provoke Adams and Washington to suspend the Bill of Rights, cause them to urge the arrest and prosecution of these editors, incite mobs of their supporters to attack the *Aurora's* offices and to assault and nearly kill these editors, and justify the sacrifice of Bache's life and Duane's editorship in hiding.

Heresies! Charges that Washington and Adams were warring against the French Revolution because they were enemies to democracy, and had been even during the American Revolution; that Washington was not the "father of his country," but an inept general who would have lost the American Revolution had Benjamin Franklin not gotten France to intervene; that Washington, Adams, Hamilton, and other founding fathers had denied Franklin his credit (partly by understating France's), had mythologized Washington's, and had adopted a British-style constitution to avoid Franklin's design (and many Americans' hopes) for a democracy; and that Adams, Hamilton, and other "Federalists" really wanted an American king.

The more I read, the more I wondered. The more I wondered, the more I read. Finally, the curtain of time seemed to lift, and I saw the America these editors saw. It was then that I shared their fears.

American Aurora is the story of Bache and Duane, the story of their newspaper, and the story of America's beginnings that these editors wanted us to know. It is written from Duane's radical Democratic-Republican point of view.

A word about methodology. William Duane, himself an historian, found great difficulty in writing a history of his time. He cited the following:

> The epoch of a great revolution is never the eligible time to write its history. Those memorable recitals to which the opinions of ages should remain attached cannot obtain confidence or present a character of impartiality if they are undertaken in the midst of animosities and during the tumult of passions; and yet, were there to exist a man so detached from the spirit of party or so master of himself as calmly to describe the storms of which he has been a witness, we should be dissatisfied with his tranquillity and should apprehend that he had not a soul capable of preserving the impressions of all the sentiments we might be desirous of receiving.[5]

Today's historian who writes of Duane's times is on the other horn of Duane's dilemma. He or she gains from the passage of time but loses from not having experienced the "animosities . . . the tumult of passions . . . the spirit of party . . . the storms." How can he or she convey "the impressions of all the sentiments we might be desirous of receiving"? Won't readers be "dissatisfied with his [or her] tranquillity"? The dilemma poses important questions about historical writing as reality, narrative, drama, literature, and more.

To resolve William Duane's dilemma and reanimate his time, *American Aurora* allows the *Philadelphia Aurora* to report its own story, its own times, its own trials and tribulations, through day-to-day excerpts from the paper, same-day responses from opposing (evening) gazettes, same-day reactions from such avid *Aurora* readers as Washington, Adams, Hamilton, Jefferson, Madison, and Monroe, and same-day writings of other government officials, legislative and court reporters, neighbors, friends, etc. To provide background, where needed, for this firsthand testimony (and to provide *leitmotif* reminders that *American Aurora* embodies Duane's point of view), *American Aurora* imagines William Duane to be its narrator and its historian (chooser-of-fact), granting him the advantage of these intervening years but grounding his narrative assertions (which can be read as the author's) in endnoted sources. At the midpoint of this work, William Duane becomes the editor of and speaks through the *Philadelphia Aurora* and thus becomes (as much as possible) the actual narrator of and speaks through this work. From that point, readers can compare Duane's actual voice with the posited one, traveling the path of free inquiry from the imagined to the real, from the given to the tested, which lies at the heart of our First Amendment and which survived its most formidable test at the time of the *American Aurora*.

RICHARD N. ROSENFELD

The Library at Philadelphia in 1798.[6] Founded in 1730
by Dr. Benjamin Franklin.

THURSDAY, JUNE 10, 1731

✣ The Pennsylvania Gazette ✣

Being frequently censur'd and condemn'd by different Persons for printing Things which they say ought not to be printed, I have sometimes thought it might be necessary to make a standing Apology for myself and publish it once a Year to be read upon all Occasions of that Nature . . .

I request all who are angry with me on Account of printing things they don't like calmly to consider these following Particulars

1. That the Opinions of Men are almost always as various as their Faces . . .

2. That the Business of Printing has chiefly to do with Men's Opinions; most things that are printed tending to promote some, or opposite others . . .

4. That it is unreasonable in any one Man or Set of Men to expect to be pleas'd with every thing that is printed . . .

5. Printers are educated in the Belief that when Men differ in Opinion, both Sides ought equally to have the Advantage of being heard by the Publick; and that when Truth and Error have fair Play, the former is always an overmatch for the latter . . .

8. That if all Printers were determin'd not to print anything till they were sure it would offend nobody, there would be very little printed . . .

DR. BENJAMIN FRANKLIN, EDITOR,
THE PENNSYLVANIA GAZETTE, 1729–1748

Aurora General Advertiser (Philadelphia) in 1798.

*If you read the Aurora of this City . . . you cannot but have perceived
with what malignant industry and persevering falsehoods
I am assailed in order to weaken, if not destroy,
the confidence of the Public.*

GEORGE WASHINGTON,
PRESIDENT OF THE UNITED STATES, 1789–1797[7]

*[George Washington] is very jealous of Dr. Franklin & those who are
governed by Republican Principles from which he is very averse.*

PAUL WENTWORTH, BRITISH SPY[8]

*I knew [Benjamin Franklin] had conceived an irreconcilable hatred to
me and that he had propagated and would continue to propagate
prejudices, if nothing worse, against me in America from one end of it
to the other. Look into Bache's Aurora and Duane's Aurora for twenty
years and see whether my expectations have not been verified.*

JOHN ADAMS,
PRESIDENT OF THE UNITED STATES, 1797–1801[9]

High-street *(to the left)* crossing Third-street,
in Philadelphia, 1798.[10]

BOOK ONE

AURORA

This country should not forget, either for the country's honor, for the
honor of republican justice, or for an example to others . . . the
free and manfully conducted Press [of the Aurora] in the
hands of Benjamin Franklin Bache . . .
[W]hen to take this paper was denounced by the administration and
their partizans as sufficient cause for persecution and proscription;
when men who professed to be republicans and applauded the virtue of
Benjamin Franklin Bache dared not or feared to stand by him and their
common country whose cause he espoused; when the menaces of power
and the money of the country were employed to overwhelm him; . . .
when bodily injury done on him was countenanced and rewarded;
when few men had courage enough to read free opinion in a country
where the Constitution guaranteed its freedom; . . . when those readers
were so few as by their subscription not to afford means adequate to the
ordinary expences for the support of this Paper; . . . [t]hen and thus
circumstanced, upheld by conscious virtue alone, he stood forward and
. . . upheld the drooping liberties of America . . .
Under persecution and desertion of friends—under the sacrifice
of fortune and the menaces of assassins and even on the bed of
death—the same spirit actuated and the constant assurance was
impressed on his mind, that by perseverance the cause of virtue
must at length prevail.

WILLIAM DUANE, EDITOR, 1798–1822,
AURORA GENERAL ADVERTISER[11]

High-street (*to the left*) crossing Second-street, 1798,
with one of the market buildings (an old courthouse)
immediately to the left.[12]

CHAPTER ONE

REIGN OF WITCHES

It was a special time in the history of America. The Vice President of the United States, Thomas Jefferson, called it a *"reign of witches."*[13]

A short, fat man who puffed at "seegars" and believed in monarchy[14] was President of the United States. At incautious moments, he predicted the nation's conversion to a kingdom with a titled nobility to oversee Congress.[15] Presumably, he would be king.

When the U.S. Senate considered titles for the President, this man favored *"His Highness The President of The United States and Protector of the Rights of the Same."*[16] His hauteur failed of adoption, however, and many of us soon mocked him with the title *"His Rotundity."*[17]

People who supported His Rotundity wore black cockades, most often as decoration for their hats. These inky circles of folded ribbon[18] identified them with the patriotic fulminations of this irascible President, with his plans to wage war against the French Revolution, and with his notion that those who own this country ought to govern it.

People like me[19] wore tricolor cockades. Our colors shone red, white, and blue.

I don't like monarchs. I was born the year King George III became monarch of the British Empire, and I suffered all my years fighting or fleeing him. In his Ireland, I was a dirty Catholic; in his India, I teetered at the edge of Calcutta's "Black Hole"; in his England, I was a possible assassin; and, in the American breakaway, I was a *sans-culotte.* Through it all, I was a newspaperman, a "scribbler" they called me. *The fact is that my pen and press are the only formidable weapons I have ever used.*[20]

When I look back on my life with the advantage of these intervening years, I see my greatest battle with monarchy was fought in the last three years of the eighteenth century. I was working for my last newspaper and for my final publisher.

I had fled London's Copenhagen Field and, accompanied by my wife, Catherine, our sixteen-year-old son, William John, our daughter, Kate, and our youngest child, Patrick, shipped to America aboard the *Chatham* under Captain Sammis. Throughout the journey, I anticipated a place ruled neither by George III nor by any other monarch. Though I had no money and no job awaiting me, I expected my life in America to be free and independent as the American nation, as new as her Constitution. The *Chatham* arrived in America on the

The New Theatre in Chestnut-street at
Philadelphia, 1798.[21]

Fourth of July, America's Independence Day, 1796. It was as though the Lord himself had said, "William Duane, your freedom and America's are now intertwined."[22]

This history begins twenty months later when I am living in Philadelphia and working part-time for Benjamin Bache (pronounced "Beech") and his *Philadelphia Aurora.*[23] Had I kept a daily journal of this time and been able to quote from private letters and other documents that came to light only much later, I would offer you this history, day by day, in the words of those who lived it and in the writings of gazettes that reported it. I would start each day's entry with a report from the *Aurora,* and I would let you tremble, with Thomas Jefferson and me, at *"the rapid march of our government toward monarchy."*[24] Such a journal would read like this . . .

THURSDAY, MARCH 1, 1798

GENERAL ★ AURORA ★ ADVERTISER

NEW THEATRE.
—On FRIDAY EVENING March 2.—
Will be Presented, a Comedy, Called,
THE ROAD TO RUIN
To which will be added a COMIC OPERA
(never Performed in America) Called
THE SHIP WRECK

BOX—One Dollar, PIT—Three-Quarters of a Dollar. GALLERY—Half a Dollar. The Doors of the Theatre will open at HALF past FIVE, and the Curtain rise precisely at HALF past SIX . . . Tickets to be had at H. & P. Rice's Bookstore, No. 40 Market street and at the Office adjoining the Theatre.

AN EXHIBITION OF Elegant Figures In Wax, Equal in Nature to life, and lately arrived from France. By JOSEPH PROVINI, No. 107 North Second Street—WHERE the SPECTATOR will be delighted with a well executed Wax representation of all the late ROYAL FAMILY OF FRANCE . . . the great GENERAL BUONAPARTE, with many ANCIENT PHILOSOPHERS among whom the striking likenesses of VOLTAIRE and ROUSSEAU . . . at the low price of a QUARTER OF A DOLLAR . . .

JUST PUBLISHED—And to be sold at the AURORA (Price One Dollar, neatly bound and lettered) AN ENQUIRY into the DUTIES of the FEMALE SEX. By THOMAS CISBORNE . . .

—PEALE'S MUSEUM—

This valuable Repository of the works of Nature . . . is open daily as usual . . . Many interesting additions have been lately made to this Museum: even the feathered tribe . . . Waxen figures often large as life . . . the North American Savage and the Savage of South America—a

The covered country marketplace (*to left*) in the
middle lane of High-street, 1798.[25] (The market opens on
Wednesdays and Saturdays.)

labouring Chinese and the Chinese Gentleman—the sooty African and the Kamischadle, with some Natives of the South Sea Islands. Admittance only 1/4 of a dollar.

LAILSON'S CIRCUS—MR. LAILSON has the honour of informing the Public, that . . . his Circus . . . will open . . . on the first Tuesday of next month—By the Novelty and Variety of Equestrian Exercises, as well as by the other representations which will be given, he hopes to deserve the approbation and patronage with which his Public has already honoured him.

For the Relief & Cure—OF COUGHS, ASTHMAS, and CONSUMPTIONS—CHURCH's COUGH DROPS, AFTER a trial of Six Years, prove to be unequaled by any other Medicine in the world, Prepared by the INVENTOR and SOLE PROPRIETOR, DR. JAMES CHURCH, At his Medicine Store, No. 1, South Third street, Philadelphia . . .

It's the first day of March, 1798. I am living in Philadelphia and writing part-time for Benjamin Bache and the *Philadelphia Aurora* at a salary of $10 a week.[26]

I choose these advertisements from this morning's *Aurora* to illustrate why a visitor says, *"Philadelphia is . . . the finest city of the United States."*[27] They also show some features of our time.

The government of these United States is less than a decade old. Pending completion of a new federal city on the banks of the Potomac River, this government rests in Philadelphia, a town of some 55,000 people occupying a grid of cobblestone streets and red-bricked town houses, ten blocks square, which slopes west to higher ground from the docks and ships of the Delaware River.

The Delaware connects this town with the farmlands and fisheries which feed its stomach and with the trade routes of the Atlantic which feed its purse. At each favorable tide, numerous square-rigged vessels as well as sloops and schooners, coasters and foreign, negotiate the Delaware to deposit hooped barrels of beef and pork, casks of shad, herring, rye flour, and flax seed, kegs of rum, Madeira wine, and butter, bundles of shingles and lumber, carts of vegetables, and every other object of desire on the congested wharves along Waterstreet. From the riverfront and perpendicular to it, a covered country market occupies the middle of High-street (the city's broadest avenue) in its gradual ascent to the city's center. Sheltered by a series of old market buildings, this country market accommodates hundreds of vendors in a range of open wooden stalls, separated from each other by brick and wooden pillars and overhung by crossbeams and iron provision hooks.

During the course of this century, the covered market along High-street has extended itself, block by block, from the riverfront toward the city's center, so that "High-street" is becoming known as "Market-street." Today, half call it "High"; half, "Market."

Facing the covered market on the south side of High, between Third- and Fourth-streets, is No. 112, the publishing office of the *Philadelphia Aurora*. A

7

Congress Hall at Philadelphia, 1798.
U.S. House of Representatives on the first floor,
U.S. Senate on the second.[28]

block and a half farther up High, on the same side of the street, is No. 190, the Executive House of the President of the United States.

FRIDAY, MARCH 2, 1798

GENERAL ★ AURORA ★ ADVERTISER

FEDERAL LEGISLATURE

HOUSE OF REPRESENTATIVES

The bill for erecting a light house & placing certain Buoys in places therein mentioned was read the third time and passed . . .

March, the 2nd. Today's *Aurora* carries its usual measure of Congressional news . . .

The Congress of these sixteen[29] United States of America meet a block and a half southwest of the *Aurora* in the City Hall of Philadelphia, commonly called the State-house of Pennsylvania, a range of attached brick buildings occupying the entire south side of Chestnut-street (parallel to and one block south of High) between Fifth- and Sixth-streets. The House and Senate chambers occupy a wing, commonly called Congress Hall, on the west (away from the Delaware) side of the State-house.[30] The U.S. House of Representatives sits on the first floor, the U.S. Senate on the second. A visitor to the city describes the House and Senate chambers as follows:

> *The hall for the Representatives is spacious. The Galleries above and below could hold perhaps four hundred spectators each. They are nearly always filled . . . The members have the privilege of introducing into the chamber itself all those [including the press] whom they wish; these persons must then remain behind the bar. Four rows of chairs placed in a semi-circle and protected by a semicircular enclosure are made ready for the members. Behind these . . . one sees as many benches or desks in a semi-circle in such a way that each member has an inkstand, a sandbox, some pens, a wafer, and some papers to make notes and comments, and even for writing letters. Before the center of this circle there is a raised platform on which is the Speaker's chair, in front of two tables on which are placed the volumes of law . . . Four great stoves warm the chamber . . .*
>
> *The chamber where the Senate assembles is above. It resembles more the rooms of a society than a sanctuary of laws. Thirty-two senators are likewise seated in a semicircle. The . . . Vice President of the United States performs the function of a Speaker. A small Gallery above can hold 50 spectators; they withdraw when the Senate is concerned with executive business.[31]*

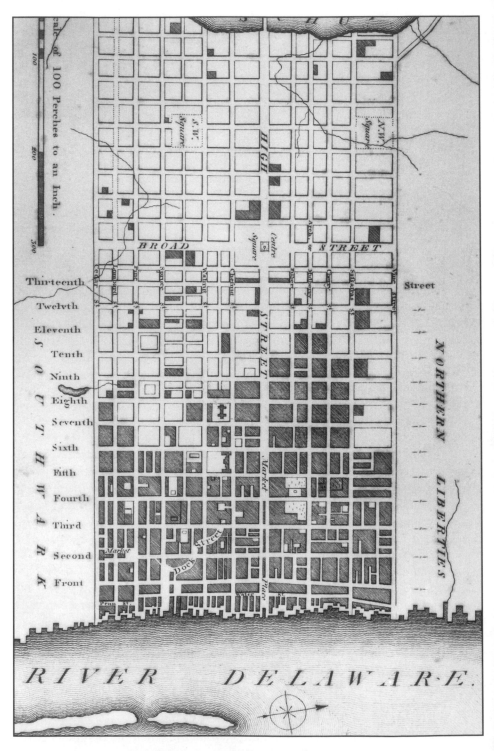

Plan of the City of Philadelphia in 1798.[32]

All Philadelphia newspapers report the affairs of Congress, although the *Aurora*'s publisher, Benjamin Bache, was barred, as of three weeks ago, from taking notes on the floor of the House of Representatives.

The banishment of Benjamin Bache arose from a bizarre incident which occurred in the House chamber on the last and very icy Tuesday of January, the 30th. Several members were warming themselves by the great stoves which heat the House chamber when, in idle conversation, a Republican congressman from Vermont (an Irish newspaper publisher) posed the possibility of starting an opposition newspaper in Federalist Connecticut. (President John Adams' Federalist party controls each of the New England states and holds a commanding majority in both the U.S. House of Representatives and the U.S. Senate.) The Report of the House Committee on Privileges reads as follows:

> Mr. Lyon [the Vermont Republican] was . . . holding a conversation with the Speaker [Mr. Jonathan Dayton] . . . loud enough to be heard . . . On Mr. Lyon's observing that, if he should go into Connecticut and manage a press there six months . . . he could effect a revolution and turn out the present [Federalist] Representatives—Mr. Griswold [a Federalist representative from Connecticut] replied . . . "you had better wear your wooden sword" or words to that effect, alluding to Mr. Lyon's having been cashiered in the army . . . Mr. Lyon spat in his face.[33]

Personal insults! Spitting! At a time when political etiquette and the hardship of overland travel force politicians to wait at home for the call to office[34] rather than travel some campaign trail in pursuit of it, the newspaper is a mighty force in the political life of America. As this bizarre event suggests, even the threat of an "opposition press" can lead to violence.

During the next three weeks, Congress held hearings on the spitting incident, and the Federalist Speaker of the House, Jonathan Dayton of New Jersey, tried to impose restrictions on newspaper coverage of embarrassing testimony. The Annals of Congress report:

> The SPEAKER said . . . [h]e thought it improper that persons attending in the House to take notes . . . should publish the evidence [i.e., testimony] of members before [the members] had the opportunity of correcting it . . . The SPEAKER said, until the House should make an order . . . he did himself prohibit the publication of evidence in the future until it should be corrected by the members themselves . . .[35]

A gag rule! This was the federal government's first attempt to restrict press freedom since the First Amendment of the U.S. Constitution (guaranteeing freedom of the press) was ratified in December of 1791. Benjamin Bache refused to comply, even after Thursday morning, February 15th, when Lyon and Griswold fell upon each other with stick and tong. The Annals of Congress report:

FRACAS IN THE HOUSE.

About a quarter past eleven o'clock, after prayers, whilst the SPEAKER was in his chair . . . Mr. GRISWOLD [Federalist, Connecticut] entered the

The State-house Park behind Congress Hall, 1798.[36]

House and observing Mr. LYON [Republican, Vermont] in his place (who was writing), he went up to him with a pretty strong walking stick in his hand with which he immediately began to beat him with great violence . . . At length, getting behind the SPEAKER'S chair, Mr. L[YON] snatched up the tongs from the fire; the combatants then closed and came down together upon the floor, Mr. G[RISWOLD] being uppermost. The members of the House . . . got round the parties and separated them but not before Mr. L[YON] had aimed a blow at Mr. G[RISWOLD]'s head with the tongs but which he parried off.[37]

From the initial encounter to the latest fracas, Benjamin Bache reported details and testimony of congressional misbehavior without prior clearance by Speaker Dayton. For this disregard, Speaker Dayton barred Benjamin Bache, as of February 12th, from reporting on the House floor. Instead, the *Aurora's* representative would take notes from the spectators' gallery, where debate is less audible, less visible (Quaker spectators don't remove their hats!), and thus more difficult to discern.[38]

Two days after his banishment, Benjamin Bache reported, in the *Philadelphia Aurora,* as follows:

> The right of the people of the United States to listen to the sentiments of their representatives . . . was acknowledged by the first agents whom they appointed to express their voice in that assembly . . . It was never attempted to restrain reporters from publishing the proceedings of Congress till last week when the Speaker declared that if [reporters] continued to report the oral testimony . . . he would send them into the crowded gallery . . . [T]he threat was executed against one (The Editor of the *Aurora*) who was desired by the Speaker to leave . . .[39]

That's where things stand today. The *Aurora's* reporter takes notes from the crowded House gallery, but the paper continues to report without Congress' prior review.[40]

One last word about Congress . . . A recent visitor claimed, "Philadelphia is not only the finest city of the United States, but may be deemed one of the most beautiful cities in the world."[41] The State-house Park behind Congress Hall supports this view. A current issue of the *Philadelphia Monthly Magazine* describes the park in these words:

> *On the south of [the State-house] buildings is a large area . . . enclosed with a brick wall and commanding an elegant front view of the [Walnut-street] jail, Philadelphia Library and Philosophical hall with the valuable Museum of the ingenious Mr. Peale. This garden is appropriated as a public walk for the use of the Citizens . . . [I]t is laid down in a grass platt, divided in the middle by a spacious gravel walk, lined with a double row of large native and exotic elms, which form a cool shadowy retreat, and is plentifully supplied with benches for the accommodation of visitors. As this is the only spot in this populous city appropriated to*

The City Hall Clock Tower at the State-house, 1798.[42]
(Its chime foretells each market day.)

the necessary and refreshing uses of exercise and air, it is usually thronged with company . . . and on days of festivity, exhibits a lively scene of busy gaiety.[43]

Today, being a Friday, is the day before a market day. The covered market in High-street is open each Saturday and Wednesday. To remind Philadelphians that tomorrow is a provisioning day, a bell in the City Hall's clock tower tolls this evening from dusk until nine, and, as custom dictates, Philadelphians emerge from their homes in fancy dress, meander the brick walking pavements of High, imbibe brandy, whiskey, and Madeira at their favorite taverns, and dance their legs away. At nine, the complexion of the town perceptibly darkens, the crowd of revelers thins, and an occasional streetwalker is the only newcomer to the night's activities. By ten, the wailing oystermen with their barrows of mollusks are gone, and, by eleven, only the flickering of double-branched oil lamps on sidewalk posts and patrolling watchmen (no longer crying hour or weather) animate otherwise motionless streets.[44]

One last item . . . A newsworthy event occurs this Friday evening, March 2nd, though too late for inclusion in tomorrow's *Aurora* (Monday's will report it). Some angry citizen or citizens hurl large rocks at the windows of the *Aurora's* office at 112 High-street, shattering a number of panes. This has happened several times before . . .[45]

SATURDAY, MARCH 3, 1798

GENERAL   ★ AURORA ★   ADVERTISER

What were the merchants of the United States to expect from France when Great Britain continued to [attack American shipping to France, even] after our treaty with [Britain]? Our country and trade will never be placed upon a safe and respectable footing until our Executive and Legislative authorities display a vigilant and intelligent observation of the misconduct of every foreign nation . . . whether English, French or Spanish . . .

The War of the French Revolution between Britain and France continues in its fifth year. The issues and conduct of that war occupy the pages of the *Philadelphia Aurora* this and every morning.

Five winters ago (which was almost four years after the French Revolution began), Frenchmen guillotined their king, Louis XVI, declared an end to kingly government, and founded France's first democratic republic. As King Louis XVI passed through "the little door to heaven," Europe's other monarchs trembled at the thought that their own populations, inspired by the French example, might send them on a similar journey. Britain's King George III was quick to respond, joining other European monarchs in a war to crush the French Revolution, to restore the French monarchy, and to prove the invincibility of monarchy in general.

This War of the French Revolution between Britain and France still rages. America claims neutrality in this war, but Britain and France continue to seize American shipping to each other's ports. Needless to say, America's merchant-traders are suffering.

Today is Saturday and so a market day. The covered market along High-street is open from daylight till three. A French visitor describes the congestion:

> The principal market in Philadelphia excites the attention of every visitor. It is a long building [and] . . . greatly crowded . . . [T]he passages sometimes are almost choked up with people . . . [P]rovisions are so abundant, and the vendors so numerous, that the purchaser who is dissatisfied has but a step or two to make to consult his caprice, or to endeavor to take a better bargain . . . A great quantity of the provisions sold at Philadelphia is . . . conveyed in covered waggons that arrive in the night. The horses are unharnessed, and stand round the carts, with hay before them, which the farmer always brings with him, to save expenses at the inns. Sometimes there are more than a hundred of these waggons standing at the upper part of the street in which the great market is situated. Sometimes the farmers retail their provisions themselves, from their carts, which bring veal, pork, poultry, game, butter and cheese, as well as articles of agriculture and even the products of industry. Jersey furnishes the markets of Philadelphia with many articles, particularly hams, poultry, butter, and vegetables . . .[46]

The market exudes quality. Another European claims, *"for beef, veal and mutton, the big market of Philadelphia is only second to that of London-hall, and, for fish, it only yields to that of New York."*[47]

The covered country market is a great distraction. Neither the *Aurora's* office workers nor the President of the United States can ignore the hawkers and bell ringers, horses and hand-carts, and the babel of Philadelphia's German, French, Dutch, English, and Gaelic tongues. The *Aurora's* subscription office directly faces the boisterous High-street market, but the paper's two-story print shop is located in a courtyard behind 112, through a vaulted carriageway which separates 106 from 108.[48] Office workers suffer market distractions; pressmen and compositors don't.

Though the High-street country market and a weekly horse auction on Seventh-street are two important Saturday events, Saturday morning is also the time when Philadelphians wash doors, walking pavements, and window ledges, even during the freezing weather of deepest winter. Water for the task is provided by long-handled, black wooden pumps which border Philadelphia's walking pavements every eighty-five yards or so, on alternate sides of the street.[49] Obviously, the *Aurora* waits till three (when the market closes) before cleaning the brickwork at 112 High.

[T]he front window of the office of the *Aurora* was, on Friday evening, successfully assailed by three stones of the size of a man's fist or larger. Several panes of glass were consequently broken, and this is the third attack of the kind for which Mr. Bache has been indebted to the friends of *regular government*.

Mr. Adams, before taking his oath of office, made a long exordium . . . that, although the constitution makes no distinction in favour of the Christian religion, yet that he (Mr. Adams) in nominating to public offices would always have a special eye to that point. This truth was thereafter sent to the press. In July or August last . . . in plain terms, when [former Secretary of the Treasury Mr. Alexander] Hamilton came to Philadelphia to vindicate his character by a confession of adultery, this identical and most Christian president invited him to a family dinner with Mrs. Adams. Such is his selection of company for the entertainment of his wife! Oh, Johnny! Johnny!

[O]ne of the members . . . read in Congress the far famed letter said to be written by Mr. [Thomas] Jefferson to Mr. Mazzei . . . The substance of it is a complaint [by Mr. Jefferson] of an American aristocracy and of the growth of the principle of monarchy . . .

A word of explanation about each of these items from this morning's *Philadelphia Aurora*:

On the breaking of the Aurora's windows . . .

Public anger against the *Philadelphia Aurora* and Benjamin Bache really began last May 16th. That's when President Adams warned Americans that French sympathizers were a threat to the nation's security. President Adams was addressing an extraordinary session of the current U.S. Congress (the Fifth) which he had convened to consider relations with France.

Relations with France first began to deteriorate under the presidency of George Washington, who, having declared neutrality in the war between Britain and France, sought to end British interference with American shipping by signing the pro-British (and anti-French) Jay Treaty of 1795, and by firing America's friendly Ambassador to France, James Monroe, who had publicly criticized Washington's anti-French actions. These events upset France, provoking her to increase her seizures of U.S. shipping and not to accept James Monroe's ambassadorial replacement, Federalist Charles Cotesworth Pinckney.

In his speech to Congress of May 16th—a speech that France found very insulting—the President's *"rage almost choked his utterance,"*[50] as he excoriated the French for rejecting his ambassador, urged defensive measures against French dangers from abroad, and warned about French dangers at home. He cautioned,

[France] evinces a disposition to separate the people of the United States from the [American] Government, to persuade them that they have different affections, principles, and interests from those of their fellow-citizens whom they themselves have chosen to manage their common concerns, and thus to produce divisions fatal to our peace. Such attempts ought to be repelled with a decision which shall convince France and the world that we are not a degraded people, humiliated under a colonial spirit of fear and sense of inferiority, fitted to be the miserable instruments of foreign influence, and regardless of national honor, character, and interest.[51]

Following that May 16th diatribe, the President's supporters saw his critics as the *"miserable instruments of foreign influence"* producing *"divisions fatal to our peace."* They saw French sympathizers such as Benjamin Bache and even Vice President Thomas Jefferson as *"degraded people."* Thomas Jefferson himself remarked, *"Men who have been intimate all their lives cross the street to avoid meeting and turn their heads another way lest they be obliged to touch their hats."*[52] A friend of Ben Bache wrote, "What a pity . . . At the time of Dr. F[ranklin]'s death, Benjamin [Bache] was universally beloved and esteemed, and now he is as much despised, even by some who are warm Democrats."[53] Now, the President's supporters break Benjamin Bache's windows.

That presidential speech was almost a year ago. Since then, Adams has sent a new three-man delegation (including the rejected Pinckney) to meet with French Foreign Minister Talleyrand in Paris. Last night, Mr. Adams received his first dispatches from those envoys. The news is not good.

On Mr. Alexander Hamilton's adultery . . .

Lawyer Alexander Hamilton, who was George Washington's first Treasury Secretary, founded the Federalist party and still leads it from the relative anonymity of his private New York life. To the chagrin of his party, however, Mr. Hamilton publicly confessed last August to some adultery he had committed several summers earlier with one Maria Reynolds, wife of a convicted securities swindler. The liaison included several libidinous encounters in Hamilton's own home while his wife, Betsy, and the Hamilton children were in upstate New York visiting Betsy's father.[54] The article in this morning's *Philadelphia Aurora* connects Mr. Hamilton's adultery to President and Mrs. Adams and can only anger our very prudish and very Christian President of the United States.

On Vice President Jefferson's letter to Mr. Mazzei . . .

Last spring, the American press published a private letter that Vice President Thomas Jefferson had written a year earlier to his Italian friend and former neighbor Philip Mazzei. This letter claimed that George Washington and John Adams' Federalist party preferred monarchy and aristocracy to American democracy and, therefore, were returning America to British influence.[55] Mr. Jefferson never dreamt the following of his words would be made public:

The aspect of our politics has wonderfully changed since you left us. In place of that noble love of liberty & republican government which carried us triumphantly thro' the war, an Anglican monarchical & aristocratical party has sprung up whose avowed object is to draw over us the substance, as they have already done the forms, of the British government . . . Against us [Republicans] are the [Federalist-controlled] Executive, the Judiciary, two out of three . . . of the legislature, all the officers of the government, all who want to be officers, all timid men who prefer the calm of despotism to the boisterous sea of liberty, British merchants & Americans trading on British capitals, speculators, & holders in the banks & public funds, a contrivance invented for the purposes of corruption & for assimilating us in all things to the rotten as well as the sound parts of the British model. It would give you a fever were I to name to you the apostates who have gone over to these heresies, men who were Samsons in the field & Solomons in the council, but who have had their heads shorn by the harlot England. In short, we are likely to preserve the liberty we have obtained only by unremitting labors & perils.[56]

Jefferson's letter to Philip Mazzei rebukes Federalist party leaders like Alexander Hamilton and John Adams for their monarchical, aristocratic, and pro-British sympathies. More shockingly, the letter's charge of apostasy to *"men who were Samsons in the field and Solomons in the council"* clearly aims at George Washington!

Today, President John Adams sends a message to the Congress of the United States. The Annals of Congress report:

RELATIONS WITH FRANCE.

The following Message, with the documents accompanying it, were received from the President of the United States:

Gentlemen of the Senate and Gentlemen of the House of Representatives,

The first dispatches from our envoys extraordinary [to France] since their arrival in Paris were received at the Secretary of State's office at a late hour the last evening—They are all in a character, which will require some days to be decyphered, except the last which is dated the 8th of January, 1798. The contents of this letter are of so much importance to be immediately made known to the Congress, and to the public, especially to the mercantile part of our fellow citizens, that I have thought it my duty to communicate them to both houses without loss of time.

JOHN ADAMS
UNITED STATES, March 5, 1798

PARIS, January 8, 1798
[To U.S. Secretary of State Timothy Pickering]
DEAR SIR: We embrace the unexpected opportunity to send you the

"Redacteur" [a Paris newspaper] of the fifth instant, containing the Message of the Directory [France's five-man executive council] . . .

We can only repeat that there exists no hope of our being officially received by this Government or that the objects of our mission will be in any way accomplished . . .

CHARLES C. PINCKNEY
J[OHN] MARSHALL
E[LBRIDGE] GERRY

[TRANSLATION of the *Le Redacteur* report]
Message of the Executive Directory to the Council of Five Hundred [the larger chamber of France's legislature].

4th January, 1798

Citizen Representatives: . . . The English Government . . . has violated . . . the law of . . . neutral powers. It has caused to be seized the provisions, grain, and commodities which it supposed to be destined for France. It has declared contraband [not just military supplies as permitted under the law of neutral powers but] everything which it thought useful to the [French] Republic. It desired to starve it. All the citizens demand vengeance upon it . . .

The Directory thinks it urgent and necessary to pass a law declaring that the condition of [vessels as] . . . neutral or enemy shall be determined [no longer by their national flag but] by their cargo . . . In consequence, every vessel found at sea having on board English merchandise and commodities as her cargo, in whole or in part, shall be declared to be good prize . . .

P. BARRAS, *President.*[57]

By these documents, the *"mercantile part of our fellow citizens"* knows that, under the proposed French decree, France will seize and confiscate any ship carrying British goods, whether or not it flies the American flag and regardless of its destination. American merchant-traders will want to arm their merchantmen.

TUESDAY, MARCH 6, 1798

GENERAL ★ AURORA ★ ADVERTISER

The prejudices which have been excited against *France* . . . have greatly deceived the American public. It is believed that the French deserve to be viewed in a light very different [and more favorable] from what was lately pretended to be just . . .

From the beginning of the present war [between Britain and France] down to this time, the conduct of our executive [the President] has been a series of ill offices toward France . . .

Benjamin Bache's *Philadelphia Aurora* is the leading opposition paper in the United States.[58] Its location in the nation's capital provides immediate access to national and international news.

Readership of the *Aurora* is perhaps the largest in the country, far larger than its subscriber base of 1,700 might suggest. With newspaper franking privileges to mail the *Aurora* cost-free to fellow publishers, the *Aurora* inflates its readership by a network of papers throughout the nation which share its views and reprint its news and opinion as part of their daily fare. The *Aurora*'s popularity among the lower classes also multiplies its readership, because such people tend to pass a newspaper from hand to hand, and family to family, and leave it in local taverns, which serve as libraries for the poor.[59]

The *Aurora* is manufactured six days a week in a two-story wooden print shop in the courtyard behind 112 High. Compositors and binders work on the first floor; pressmen on the second. Though the newspaper owns type fonts from Baskerville, Caslon, Fournier, and Didot (specimen books display sixty different fonts),[60] the *Aurora* emphasizes simple Petite Texte-Romain as its standard face.

American newspapers are printed on the English common press,[61] with its vintage profile of two upright pieces of timber, seven feet tall and four feet apart, joined at their upper ends by a heavy crossbeam from which the square wooden platen (plate) descends to force paper against type and joined at their midpoint by a long horizontal carriageway on which paper and type travel to their proper place beneath the platen's descent.

To print a daily *Aurora,* platens have to descend about eight thousand times, and the *Aurora*'s pressmen dance and wrestle in a bath of perspiration to achieve that production. To make an imprint on one side of a newspaper sheet, two pressman have to coordinate thirteen steps in agreed roles as *Puller* and *Beater.*

The *Puller* takes a sheet from the heap of paper and lays it on top of a parchment, of equal size, stretched across a wooden frame (the tympan), which is hinged to the end of the press. To hold the edges of the paper to the edges of the tympan, the Puller overlays a metal frame (the frisket), which is hinged to the other end of the tympan. He then lowers the paper (sandwiched between the tympan and the frisket) onto the locked bed of metal type (the form), which resides on a large flat stone within a wooden box (the coffin) on the carriageway. The Puller then pulls a three-and-a-half-foot overhead iron bar across the press, lowering the platen to force half a side of paper against half of the inked type form. He then returns the overhead bar to raise the platen, rotates a sidehandle (the rounce) to position the remaining half sheet beneath the platen, pulls the overhead bar to imprint the remaining half sheet, and returns the bar to raise the platen. Next, he rotates the rounce to remove the carriage, paper, and form from beneath the platen, raises the printed sheet (still sandwiched between frisket and tympan) off the form, hinges the frisket back from the tympan to release the sheet, removes the sheet from the tympan, places it onto a heap, and examines the form for problems of registration and foreign particles.

While the *Puller* is performing this list of tasks and in close coordination with him, the other pressman, as *Beater,* mixes (rubs) a mound of lampblack (soot from burning oil) and varnish (linseed oil thickened by boiling), which together compose printer's ink, slices away any film that has dried on the surface of the ink, dips two wooden-handled, leather-covered balls of wool into the ink, presses (beats) the inked leather-balls along the form of type for uniform ink distribution, and reviews the latest printed sheet for imperfections (picks) in inking.

Though Puller and Beater exchange roles every two or three tokens (a token being 250 sheets), each pressman performs the entire series of described procedures in fewer than fifteen seconds, thousands of times each day, six days a week.[62]

THURSDAY, MARCH 8, 1798

GENERAL ★ AURORA ★ ADVERTISER

A custom has crept into the United States of publishing toasts. A club of any tolerable number can hardly meet and get drunk without incumbering the newspapers of the next morning by a long string . . . [I]n the Concert Hall in Boston, on Mr. Washington's late birthday . . . toasts were drank to the bottom of the glass. Thirty-five glassfuls . . . [T]he majority must have been in a beastly pickle before the end of the entertainment. Even of Yankee rum diluted into grog, so many cubic inches would make an enormous belly full. It is no wonder that the toasts . . . leave room for criticism . . .

Mr. Dawson [Republican, Virginia] proposed a resolution for amending the rules of the house [of representatives] . . . "Resolved, That . . . persons attending this house to take down its debates and proceedings for the purpose of publication shall be permitted to take their seats within the bar of the house." The Speaker [Mr. Dayton] said he would state to the house that this was the case except as to one person who had abused the privilege . . . Mr. Bache having been driven from his place within the bar of the house by the single mandate of the Speaker, Mr. Dawson moved the above resolution that he might be admitted there . . .

Many charges and much abuse have issued from the *Gazette of the United States* and *Porcupine's Gazette* . . . To charges so general and so vague, however, it is impossible to give any other than a general answer which may be effectually done by these two words: *prove them!*

No. V.

[I]n the [French] decree proposed in [this] January 1798, the unwarrantable proceedings of the English government are the avowed foundations of the French measures . . . It is really time . . . to acknowledge and admit the extravagance and unwarrantableness of the . . . British . . . [and to] take a correct and candid view of the course of English proceedings from 1792 to 1797 which have contributed to bring on the measures of the French Government.

Today, Thomas Jefferson writes former U.S. Minister to France James Monroe:

At length the charm is broke, and letters have been received from our envoys at Paris. Only one of them has been communicated, of which I enclose you a copy with the documents accompanying it. The decree therein proposed to be passed has struck the greatest alarm through the merchants . . . You will see in Bache's paper of this morning the 5th. number of some pieces . . . in which the proposed decree is well viewed. [63]

Thomas Jefferson praises the *Philadelphia Aurora*. Federalist gazettes hurl charges and abuse.

John Fenno's well-established and quasi-official *Gazette of the United States* and William Cobbett's new and reactionary *Porcupine's Gazette* are the two leading papers for the views of John Adams' Federalist administration. Like the *Aurora*, these papers are published in Philadelphia six days each week and copied by like-minded publishers throughout the country. Unlike the *Philadelphia Aurora*, these papers serve highborn readers and, as late-afternoon papers, enjoy the last journalistic word each day.

John Fenno, publisher of the *Gazette of the United States*, is a former Boston merchant of pure English ancestry who, following a business failure, moved to New York in January of 1789 to undertake a new life and a new newspaper when the federal government was beginning its operations, initially at New York. Accompanying John Fenno were his wife, Mary (he calls her "Polly"), their then-eleven-year-old son, John Ward (the family calls him "Jack"), and the other Fenno children. With financial help from fellow Bostonian and then Vice President–elect John Adams, and from New Yorker and then U.S. Senator Rufus King,[64] John Fenno started the *Gazette of the United States* in mid-April of that year. He has published that paper ever since.

In the autumn of 1790 when the federal government moved to Philadelphia, John Fenno, his family, and his newspaper followed, becoming a Philadelphia institution (Mary alone would justify this with her birthing of fourteen children). Fenno gets the lion's share of federal government printing, is printer to the United States Senate,[65] and, when problems arise, gets help from Federalists like Rufus King, Alexander Hamilton,[66] and his confidential friend John Adams.[67] This support upsets Benjamin Bache,[68] but not nearly so much as John Fenno's strict adherence to the ideology of his government sponsors.

William Cobbett, publisher of the *Porcupine's Gazette*, has, in one short and vitriolic year, made his radically conservative paper more popular and influential than any Federalist journal in the country except perhaps John Fenno's *Gazette of the United States*. William Cobbett started *Porcupine's Gazette* on the day John Adams took the presidential oath, and, from that day to this,

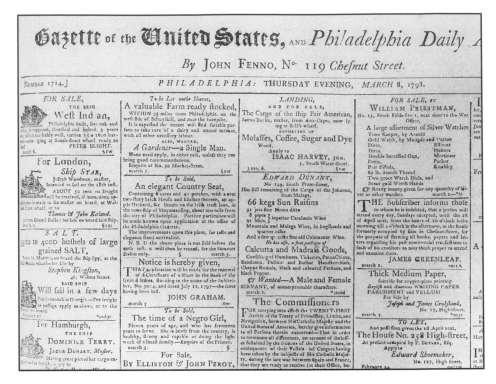

John Fenno's *Gazette of the United States*, 1798.

William Cobbett's *Porcupine's Gazette*, 1798.

"Peter Porcupine" (as Cobbett often signs his articles) has defended Mr. Adams with a knifelike quill his opponents are loath to match.

William Cobbett is a powerful man, six feet in height, of heavy build, fair-complected, gray-eyed, and possessing, as he says, "a plump and red and smiling face."[69] Perhaps because he endured seven years as a British corporal in the backwoods of Canada, William Cobbett is dogged in his pursuits and intense in his anger. He is also British, very royalist, and possibly crazy.

Crazy! How else can one explain an Englishman—and he is an Englishman—who, eight months before starting an American newspaper, opened a bookstore opposite Philadelphia's Christ Church (the "English" church) on Second-street to sell loyalist, royalist, and Federalist propaganda, removed the building's shutters, painted its facade a bright blue, and decorated its front windows with portraits of royalty like Britain's King George III (from whom Americans won their independence) and France's King Louis XVI (whom the French Revolution had overthrown)?[70]

In the first issue of *Porcupine's Gazette,* William Cobbett declared Benjamin Bache and the *Philadelphia Aurora* his enemies. Calling the *Aurora* a "vehicle of lies and sedition," the first *Porcupine's Gazette* opened with a letter to Benjamin Bache:

> I assert that you are a liar and an infamous scoundrel . . . Do you dread the effects of my paper? . . . We are, to be sure, both of us news-mongers by profession, but then the articles you have for sale are very different from mine . . . I tell you what, Mr. Bache, you will get nothing by me in a war of words, and so you may as well abandon the contest while you can do it with good grace . . . I am getting up in the world, and you are going down. [F]or this reason it is that you hate me and that I despise you; and that you will preserve your hatred and I my contempt till fortune gives her wheel another turn or till death snatches one or the other of us from the scene. It is therefore useless, my dear Bache, to say any more about the matter . . .[71]

Nearly every day, John Fenno's *Gazette of the United States* and William Cobbett's *Porcupine's Gazette* assail the *Philadelphia Aurora,* and, with equal frequency, the *Aurora* reviles them. Their angry colloquy ripples across the pages of America's newspapers and infuses the nation's opinions.

Tonight, March 8th, for example, John Fenno's *Gazette of the United States* attacks *Aurora* writer Jimmy Callender, who is in charge of the *Aurora* when Benjamin Bache is away. The *Gazette* calls Callender a "renegade":

> The Scotch renegade Callender is at present in the pay of *Surgo ut Prosim*, for the purpose of traducing the people of this country.

"*Surgo ut Prosim*" is the *Philadelphia Aurora's* masthead motto: "I rise so that I may be useful."

Tonight, for another example, in the *Porcupine's Gazette*, publisher William Cobbett attacks the *Aurora's* publisher, Benjamin Bache:

> In this morning's *Aurora,* Young Lightening-Rod has justified the conduct of his [French] friends even in their last nefarious measures against the commerce of this country . . . I look upon the fellow as a sort of bedlamite, or I must insist that he looks upon himself as talking to nobody but fools and idiots . . .

"Young Lightening-Rod" is a nickname for Benjamin Bache. It derives from a Latin epigram that France's onetime Comptroller General of Finance, Anne-Robert-Jacques Turgot, wrote to honor Benjamin Franklin: *"Eripuit caelo fulmen, sceptrumque tyrannis."* Translation: "He snatched the lightning from the sky and the scepter from tyrants."[72]

Benjamin Franklin Bache is the grandson of Benjamin Franklin. He was born August 12, 1769, in Franklin's home at the rear of Franklin Court, only a few yards from where the *Aurora's* printshop now stands. Poor Richard[73] designed and built that two-story printshop. Poor Richard bought the *Aurora's* presses. He bought its very printing fonts. At his death, Benjamin Franklin bequeathed the *Aurora's* presses and other equipment to his twenty-year-old grandson, "Benny" (as his grandfather called him),[74] who, six months later, started the *Aurora,* with a public acknowledgment of **"the advice the Publisher had received from his late Grand Father."**[75]

Benjamin Franklin's wife, Deborah Read Franklin, bore him only one son. That was "Franky," who died at the age of four. When their only daughter, Sarah, and her husband, Richard Bache, named their first son after his grandfather, Ben Franklin quickly identified the dark-haired child with the "Franky" he had lost long before. Though Ben Franklin was in London when Benny turned two, Poor Richard celebrated his grandson's birthday, reporting:

> *The Bishop's Lady knows what Children and Grandchildren I have, their Ages, &c. So when I was to come away on Monday the 12th [of August] in the Morning, she insisted on my staying that one Day longer that we might together keep my Grandson's Birthday . . . The chief Toast of the Day was Master Benjamin Bache, which the venerable old Lady began in a Bumper of Mountain [a Malaga wine]. The Bishop's Lady politely added, "And that he may be as good a Man as his Grandfather." I said I hop'd he would be much better.*[76]

As Benny himself approached the age of four, Ben Franklin confessed that Benny brought *"often afresh to my Mind the Idea of my Son Franky, tho' now dead 36 Years, whom I have seldom since seen equal'd in every thing, and whom to this Day I cannot think of without a Sigh,"*[77] and when Benny turned fifteen, Poor Richard began to teach him the printing business, noting,

> *Benny continues well, and grows amazingly. He is a very sensible and a very good Lad, and I love him much. I had Thoughts of . . . fitting him for Public Business, thinking he might be of Service hereafter to*

his Country; but being now convinc'd that Service is no Inheritance, as the Proverb says, I have determin'd to give him a Trade [in printing and letter founding] that he may have something to depend on . . . He has already begun to learn the business from Masters who come to my House, and is very diligent in working and quick in learning . . .[78]

The sight of them was wonderful, as a family friend observed:

With Franklin, there is a youth of sixteen years, bright and intelligent, who looks like him physically and who, having decided to become a printer, is working to that end. There is something very imposing in the sight of the American Legislator's grandson taking part in so simple a task.[79]

So Franklin treated this grandson like his own son, and the grandson was at Poor Richard's bedside when he died. Of that last day, Benny wrote, "*Whenever I approached his bed, he held out his Hand & having given him mine he would take & hold it for some time.*"[80]

Strange the *Aurora* should rise in 1790, the year of Franklin's death! Strange that Franklin's namesake should start work on a Philadelphia newspaper at about the same age Franklin did![81] Strange that Franklin's old printing equipment should still publish his philosophy! Strangest of all, how Poor Richard still lives, in the minds of everyone, through a twenty-eight-year-old giant-killer we all view as "Young Lightening-Rod"!

CHAPTER TWO

YOUNG LIGHTENING-ROD

*I sometimes received visits from Mr. Bache . . . always with pleasure,
because [he is a man] . . . of abilities and of principles the most
friendly to liberty & our present form of government. Mr. Bache has
another claim on my respect, as being the grandson of Dr. Franklin,
the greatest man & ornament of the age and country in which he lived.*

THOMAS JEFFERSON,
PRESIDENT OF THE UNITED STATES, 1801–1809[82]

[Benjamin Bache's Philadelphia Aurora*] is the highest and, in my
opinion, best political paper.
He is the grandson of Dr. Franklin and a republican . . .*

JAMES MONROE,
PRESIDENT OF THE UNITED STATES, 1817–1825[83]

FRIDAY, MARCH 9, 1798

GENERAL ★ AURORA ★ ADVERTISER

JUST PUBLISHED and for sale at the office of the AURORA (Price
one-eighth of a dollar.) An Expostulatory letter, TO GEN. WASHING-
TON (Late President of the United States) ON THE SUBJECT OF HIS
CONTINUING A PROPRIETOR OF SLAVES. Written by a citizen of Liv-
erpool . . .

George Washington reads the *Philadelphia Aurora*, and George Washington
absolutely detests it. If he sees this advertisement for a pamphlet against his
slaveholding, he can recall several *Aurora* editorials on the same subject,[84] one
of which, according to Thomas Jefferson, made Washington slam the paper on
the floor with a "damn."[85]

The *Aurora* published its first series of anti-Washington articles around the
beginning of 1793 (the year Washington declared American neutrality in the
war between Britain and France). Washington's birthday was to be celebrated

on February 21, and on January 2nd the *Aurora* published a mock advertisement for an American poet laureate. The humor was bitter:

TO THE NOBLESSE AND COURTIERS
OF THE UNITED STATES . . .

WANTED against the 21st of February, a person . . . who is willing to offer up his services to government as *Poet laureate* . . . One thing . . . will be certainly required, a dexterity in composing birthday odes . . . [C]ertain monarchical prettiness must be highly extolled, such as LEVIES, DRAWING ROOMS, STATELY NODS INSTEAD OF SHAKING HANDS, TITLES OF OFFICE, SECLUSION FROM THE PEOPLE, &C . . .[86]

Benny contrasted the pomp and pretentiousness of George Washington with the simplicity and modesty of his grandfather and with the egalitarianism of the French Revolution. Why not celebrate Ben Franklin's birthday?

> [I]n ascribing all the honors and glory to *one man*, you deprive . . . others . . . of *their portion* . . . Shall that venerable sage (who has since gained another immortality) . . . who . . . tamed the rage of thunder and of despotism, shall that philosopher who most contributed to extend the conquests of liberty over the whole earth, shall he be assigned to oblivion? . . . [S]hall his shade bear witness to our ingratitude? No, illustrious FRANKLIN . . . freemen cannot drop the curtain of indifference upon your services . . .
>
> Turn your eyes, me brethren, to France . . . [Y]ou will see none but [equal] citizens, nothing but equality, the substance and not the shadow of democratic spirit—[A]re there any levees [audiences] in France since the downfall of monarchy? Are there any birthday celebrations and titles of office there? Does any officer of her government refuse to mix with the citizens? Does the pomp and splendour and distance of royalty cloath any officer acting under the republic?[87]

Shortly before the celebration of Washington's birthday, the *Aurora* published a letter to Benny Bache which included:

> Will this monarchical farce never end? . . . Could your venerable grandfather view from his celestial residence the mockery of royalty which is already acting among us? . . . No man ever deserved better of his country than Dr. Franklin, and yet the laurels which he nobly won are torn from his brow and entwined around the brow of another, who, if not second, is at most not more than his equal in fame and desert . . .[88]

For the remainder of Washington's time as President, Benny described Washington's comportment as "that of a monarch,"[89] his governance as the "apish mimickry of Kingship,"[90] citing his formal Tuesday-afternoon court-style public receptions ("levees") at the President's House,[91] his "pompous carriages, splendid feasts, and tawdry gowns,"[92] his "creamed coloured coach, drawn by six bay horses . . . attended by a wond'rous number of servants in livery,"[93] and his encouragement of the public celebration of his birthday.[94]

In 1795, after Washington signed the Jay Treaty with England (which Thomas Jefferson described as an *"infamous act which is really nothing more than a treaty of alliance between England & the Anglomen of this country against the legislature & people of the United States"*[95]), the *Aurora* widened the accusations.

With the observation that Washington's "new character ought to . . . shake off the fetters that his name has hitherto imposed on the minds of freemen,"[96] the *Aurora* characterized Washington as anti-French and pro-British,[97] charged that "[t]he administration of our government has been a series of errors or of crimes,"[98] revealed that the U.S. Treasury had unlawfully advanced "expense" monies to Washington far exceeding the presidential salary he had supposedly waived ("the world was led to believe that, as President, he received no compensation; they are now permitted to suspect . . ."),[99] urged the President's immediate resignation ("let no flatterer persuade you to rest one hour longer at the helm of state"[100]), and published repeated calls for his impeachment.[101]

Not content merely to criticize Washington's presidency, the *Aurora* attacked his leadership during the American Revolution, describing his mental faculties as "unadorned by extraordinary features or uncommon capacity," his politics as an "inoffensive newtrality," and his elevation to revolutionary war commander as an act of compromise ("because you were in principle neither a Briton nor an American, a whig nor a tory").[102] It portrayed Washington as lukewarm toward independence ("I ask you, sir, to point out ONE SINGLE ACT which *unequivocally* proves you a FRIEND to the INDEPENDENCE OF AMERICA"), incompetent as a military leader ("[T]here is scarcely an action which stamps your character as a consummate General"), and deserving little credit for the final outcome of the war.[103] It questioned how the owner of a thousand slaves could be the symbol of freedom ("[I]t must appear a little incongruous then that Liberty's Apostle should been seen with chains in his hands, holding men in bondage")[104] and republished some wartime correspondence (*"I love my king; you know I do . . ."*) which purportedly discredited his patriotism.[105]

Benjamin Bache and his *Philadelphia Aurora* led the journalistic assault on Washington. Other newspapers merely copied. As one historian has written, *"[I]t is unnecessary to investigate the motives of dozens of independent journalists and critics in order to reach some understanding of the nature of the assault on Washington. It is unnecessary, because one man alone —Benjamin Franklin Bache—either wrote or published a vast majority of the attacks."*[106]

George Washington suffered from the *Aurora*'s verbal onslaught, protesting that *"[Bache's] papers are outrages on common decency,"*[107] and *"void of truth and fairness."*[108] He complained

> *[i]f you read the Aurora of this City . . . you cannot but have perceived with what malignant industry, and persevering falsehoods I am assailed, in order to weaken, if not destroy, the confidence of the Public.*[109]

But the attacks took their toll.

By the end of the winter of 1795/96, Washington suggested to then Vice President John Adams that he would not seek the presidency in the coming autumn election.[110] Washington explained his readiness to leave office as a *"disinclination to be longer buffited in the public prints by a set of infamous scribblers."*[111] Early in May, preparing a first draft of his Farewell Address, Washington included some words (deleted from the final text on Alexander Hamilton's advice) bemoaning that

> *some of the gazettes of the United States have teemed with all the Invective that disappointment, ignorance of facts, and malicious falsehoods could invent to misrepresent my politics and affections; to wound my reputation and feelings; and to weaken, if not entirely destroy the confidence you have been pleased to repose in me.*[112]

Washington feared a loss of reputation and observed (at the beginning of July),

> *That Mr. Bache will continue his attacks on the Government, there can be no doubt, but that they will make no Impression on the public mind is not so certain, for drops of Water will Impress (in time) the hardest Marble.*[113]

On July 18, Washington wrote his Secretary of State, Timothy Pickering,

> *The continual attacks which have been made and are still making on the administration, in Bache's [paper are as] . . . indecent as they are devoid of truth and fairness . . . Under these circumstances, it would be wished that the enlightened public could have a clear and comprehensive view of facts. But how to give it lies the difficulty . . . I see no method at present . . .*[114]

On September 17, Washington signed a public announcement he would leave the presidency. Two days later, a Philadelphia newspaper carried this Farewell Address.[115] When he actually left office the following March, the *Philadelphia Aurora* proclaimed,

> If ever there was a period for rejoicing, this is the moment—every heart, in unison with the freedom and happiness of the people, ought to beat high with exultation that the name of WASHINGTON from this day ceases to give currency to political inequity and to legalize corruption . . .[116]

The same day, George Washington exploded,

> *Mr. Bache has . . . celebrity in a certain way, for his Calumnies are to be exceeded only by his Impudence, and both stand unrivalled.*[117]

And the following day, in the *Gazette of the United States*, John Fenno wrote,

> [W]hat pain must the shade of the immortal Franklin experience in beholding the apostasy of his grandson . . . Mr. Bache . . . seems to take a kind of hellish pleasure in defaming the name of WASHINGTON. That a

man who was born in America and is part of the great family of the United States could thus basely aim his poisoned dagger at the FATHER OF HIS COUNTRY is sorely to be lamented.[118]

By then, "the FATHER OF HIS COUNTRY" was gone.

What part did the *Aurora* play in Washington's decision to leave the presidency? Dr. Benjamin Rush (a signer of the Declaration of Independence, a confidant of John Adams, and a highly respected Philadelphian) reports:

> *It is even said that [Bache's] paper induced [Washington] to retire from the president's chair of the United States.*[119]

So, today, this 9th day of March in 1798, George Washington is in retirement "under his vine and fig tree" at Mount Vernon, though, even out of office, he claims *"Mr. Bache . . . is no more than the Agent or tool of those who are endeavouring to destroy the confidence of the people in the officers of Government,"*[120] and, only a month ago, he described the *Aurora* as *"cowardly, illiberal and assassin-like,"* as offering *"malignant falsehood,"* and as attempting to *"destroy all confidence in those who are entrusted with the Administration . . ."*[121]

Despite it all, George Washington continues to read the *Aurora,* and, today as every day, he can find advertisements for works which disparage his administration. Others from today's *Aurora* are:

THIS DAY IS PUBLISHED—BY SNOWDEN & McCORKLE, N. 47, North Fourth-street—CALLENDER's Sketches of the History of America. They have Likewise for Sale, a few Copies of the HISTORY OF THE UNITED STATES FOR 1796—The SUBSCRIBERS to the latter Volume are informed that in a few days, they will be waited on with the former; which is not doubted will meet equally with their approbation.

With a bit of help from Thomas Jefferson,[122] *Aurora* writer Jimmy Callender (the "renegade") published last June his *History of the United States for 1796*[123] and more recently his *Sketches of the History of America,* two works which completely shattered the image of Washington's most important cabinet member, Secretary of the Treasury Alexander Hamilton.

In his *History of the United States for 1796,* Jimmy revealed that, while Secretary of the Treasury, Hamilton transferred sizable sums to a convicted securities swindler, James Reynolds, suggesting that Hamilton used Reynolds to speculate in the very treasury certificates that Hamilton was supposed to be regulating.[124] The public outcry demanded an answer, so Hamilton gave two, first in July through John Fenno's *Gazette of the United States*[125] and then in August through his own pamphlet,[126] admitting he had paid money to James Reynolds but claiming the money was not to speculate in treasury certificates but rather to pay James Reynolds' blackmail demands for adultery Hamilton had committed with James Reynolds' wife.

To the Federalists' dismay, Hamilton's confession of marital infidelity precluded their party leader from ever seeking high elective office, but what was even more distressing, the confession didn't vindicate the former secretary. The wife in question, Maria Reynolds, insisted her honor was quite intact and that Hamilton's confession merely reflected an ongoing conspiracy between Hamilton and her husband, James (whom she divorced). As Thomas Jefferson observed of Hamilton, *"his willingness to plead guilty to adultery seems rather to have strengthened than weakened the suspicions that he was in truth guilty of the speculations."*[127] As Jimmy Callender argued, "So much correspondence could not refer exclusively to wenching . . . No man of common sense will believe that it did. Hence it must have implicated some connection still more dishonourable, in Mr. Hamilton's eyes, than that of incontinency . . . [I]t respected certificate speculations."[128]

In all events, Jimmy would not go away. Last month, he published his *Sketches of the History of America,* including an analysis of Hamilton's pamphlet and the infallible conclusion:

> *The whole proof in this pamphlet rests upon an illusion. "I am a rake, and for that reason I cannot be a swindler . . ." This is an edifying and convenient system of logic.*[129]

So was Hamilton fooling with the wife or the money? Difficult to say. Hamilton would best have heeded Poor Richard's advice:

> *Dally not with other Folks' Women or Money.*[130]

T. Paine to G. Washington. THIS DAY IS PUBLISHED, at the Office of the Aurora. Price 25 Cents. A LETTER from THOMAS PAINE to GEORGE WASHINGTON, PRESIDENT OF THE UNITED STATES, on affairs Public and Private. [Copy Right secured.] The usual allowance will be made to Book Sellers, and Political works of approved merit taken in exchange.

Benny Bache is Tom Paine's publisher in America, including Tom Paine's thirty-six-page *Letter to George Washington.* In this "letter," the great pamphleteer of the American Revolution charges that George Washington was an incompetent commander in chief of the American Revolution and that America owes its independence to the intervention of France:

> *[H]ad it not been for the aid received from France in men, money and ships, your cold and unmilitary conduct, as I shall show in the course of this letter, would in all probability have lost America; at least she would not have been the independent nation she now is. You slept away your time in the field till the finances of the country were completely exhausted, and you have little share in the glory of the final event. It is time, sir, to speak the undisguised language of historical truth.*[131]

Washington told John Adams that Paine's "letter" was the most insulting letter he ever received. *"He must have been insane to write so,"* John Adams wrote his wife, Abigail.[132]

> THIS DAY IS PUBLISHED,—At the Office of the Aurora, Price One dollar
> and a Half. MONROE'S VIEW of the CONDUCT OF THE EXECUTIVE.
> A very liberal allowance to those who buy to sell again.

Benny Bache also publishes former U.S. Minister to France James Monroe's
407–page book, *A View of the Conduct of the Executive* . . .[133] This book argues
that once George Washington became President, he turned his back on America's French ally by signing the infamous Jay Treaty of 1795, which gave Britain
many privileges at the expense of France. As Washington's Ambassador to
France, James Monroe became so incensed with Washington's anti-French behavior that he wrote some critical articles for Benny Bache to publish in the
Philadelphia Aurora. Benny tried to mask Monroe's authorship behind the
anonymous heading "From a Gentlemen in Paris to His Friend in the City,"[134]
but Washington uncovered the truth and fired James Monroe.[135] Monroe's *View
of the Conduct of the Executive* is a public response to George Washington. It
is also a powerful retaliation.

> THIS DAY IS PUBLISHED,—At the Office of the Aurora . . . Price 25
> Cents. A letter to GEORGE WASHINGTON, PRESIDENT OF THE
> UNITED STATES: containing STRICTURES on his ADDRESS of the 17th
> Sept. 1796, notifying his relinquishment of the Presidential office. By
> JASPER DWIGHT of Vermont.

Another Benny Bache publication is *A Letter to George Washington* . . . by Jasper Dwight of Vermont.[136] This forty-eight-page pamphlet argues that George
Washington's Farewell Address offered warnings against dissent ("faction") and
against foreign entanglements merely to forestall criticism of Washington's
treaty relations with Britain and France.

Washington's Farewell Address suggested, *"[T]he common and continual mis-
chiefs of the spirit of party are sufficient to make it in the interest and duty of a
wise people to discourage and restrain it."* In it, Washington warned, *"[B]e deaf
to such as would sever you from your brethren and connect you with aliens."*

Jasper Dwight of Vermont answers, *"[Y]ou pronounced an anathema
against all combination and association because a few . . . dared to assert
their own opinions in opposition to yours . . ."* Dwight asks, *"Are men to remain silent until called upon by their government agents? Who are they that
the constitution appoints to restrain private deliberation and mark the line
beyond which freedom becomes sedition? Where is the law that forbids the
exercise of opinion and restrains the conscience from its honesty?"*

Washington's Farewell Address asks, *"Why, by interweaving our destiny
with any part of Europe, entangle our peace and prosperity in the toils of
European ambition, rivalship, interest humor or caprice? 'Tis our true policy
to steer clear of permanent alliances with any portion of the foreign world . . ."*

Jasper Dwight of Vermont answers that Washington himself executed the
infamous Jay Treaty with England; *"Whatever may have stimulated you to*

the execution of such a treaty, it is evident the advice you have here of-
fered to your fellow citizens, with regard to foreign connections, conveys a
tacit condemnation of that measure . . . [A] short time prior to the agitation
of the British Treaty [the Jay Treaty], it should not be forgotten that the
British Cabinet ha[d] issued a secret order to their cruisers to seize all
American vessels which they should meet bound for France, that some
hundreds of them were actually seized . . . The British Treaty . . . was the
price [America paid for] your fears . . . and the sacrifice of our relations
with France was the return [quid pro quo] for the repeal of the British or-
der . . . When we fought for our Freedom . . . France fought for us; we had
her navy to protect us, her valorous generals to direct us . . . [W]e have de-
rived the most signal advantages from the alliance of France . . . [T]hat ob-
ligation has never been repaid . . ."

A word about me . . .

Jasper Dwight and I are the same. That is, "Jasper Dwight" is a pen name for William Duane. "Of Vermont" is almost true, but Vermont was not a state when I was born there in 1760 and during the time I lived there (until I was five).

My father, John Duane, fled the miserable life of the Catholic in British-ruled Ireland in order to settle with my mother on the American frontier near Lake Champlain. This area later became part of Vermont.

My father was a farmer and a surveyor who came to America for a better life but found himself fighting the British monarch on the American frontier, defending French claims to land and trapping rights. That was the French and Indian War which ended in 1763.[137]

It was an "Indian" war because both sides stirred up the Indians, and, one day in 1765, some of those Indians ambushed and killed my father. Mother and I fled to New York and Philadelphia. Six years later, when I was eleven, we returned to Ireland.[138]

Two summers ago, at the age of thirty-six, now married with children, I returned to America with my wife, Catherine, our now fifteen-year-old son, William John, our daughter, Kate, and our youngest child, Patrick. I take work where I can get it, and I am writing part-time for Benny Bache and his *Phila-delphia Aurora*. But it isn't easy. No one forgets my Washington criticism, and Federalists denounce me as "Jasper Dwight."

One more word about the French and Indian War and about the death of my father at the hands of the Indians . . . Just about a year ago, Benny Bache's *Philadelphia Aurora* accused George Washington of a heinous crime back in 1754:

The accusation in question is no less than of having, while commanding a party of American troops, fired on a flag of truce; killed the officer in the act of reading a summons under the sanction of such a flag; of having attempted to vindicate the act, and yet of having signed a capitulation, in which the killing of that officer and his men was acknowledged as an act of *assassination*.[139]

Two decades before the American Revolution (in the spring of 1754), George Washington was a twenty-two-year-old lieutenant colonel of Virginia militia, leading his men along the colony's western frontier to protect Virginian land claims (including his own) from the encroachment of French Canadian trappers. Hearing some Frenchmen were in his vicinity and ignoring the fact that France and Britain were then at peace, young Colonel Washington led an early-morning ambush of what proved to be a peaceful ambassadorial delegation from the French governor of Quebec (to warn Americans off the disputed land). On that morning of May 28th, George Washington killed the Governor's emissary, a lieutenant named Jumonville, as he was reading the governor's message, and Washington allowed his Indian guides to scalp several Frenchmen who had accompanied the ambassador.

Young George Washington's attack on this peaceable French delegation and his acquiescence to the butchering of French soldiers were atrocities that started America's French and Indian War, drawing French and British soldiers to the American frontier and inflaming the Indians who ultimately killed my father.[140]

Not long after Lieutenant Jumonville's murder, his half brother, Captain Coulon de Villiers, led French soldiers in an assault on Washington's forces at Fort Necessity. The troops surrounded the fort and only agreed to release Washington after he signed a confession—for all the world to see—admitting to the "assassination" of the French governor's peaceful emissary. This was "the Jumonville murder"![141]

SATURDAY, MARCH 10, 1798

GENERAL ★ AURORA ★ ADVERTISER

In Thursday's Gazette of the U. States, Mr. John Fenno applied the epithet of *Renegade* to one of the Correspondents [Jimmy Callender] in the Aurora whose name he inserted at full length and who is supposed to have recently bestowed upon him some decent drubbing in this paper. For *this time*, no personal retort shall be made on Mr. Fenno himself, unless in his editorial capacity where he is undoubtedly fair game. But we are determined to return blow for blow and to stick closely by his Gazette . . . [W]e beg leave to ask him this plain question: Whether one of his principal correspondents, if not *the* principal of his correspondents, is not an infamous, swindling jobber in lottery tickets, a wretch who has cheated every one who would trust him and who is equally divested of reputation and of probity.

Though Benny Bache won't admit it, "renegade" is a good word for forty-year-old Jimmy Callender. A poet whose passions often end in anger, a family man with too much love for the bottle, this Scotsman is caught between political writing that doesn't pay and a wife and four children he can no longer support.[142] Yet there's no denying the power of his pen.

Jimmy first used that pen in Edinburgh, Scotland, in the early 1790s, to rebuke British tax collectors for abusing Scottish brewers, but he crossed the line in 1792 (the year George III issued royal proclamations against seditious writings) with his eighty-page pamphlet *Political Progress of Britain*, condemning British rule in Scotland and lauding America for choosing to revolt.[143] His words struck with a power only equaled by Tom Paine's *Rights of Man*.

Two weeks after those royal proclamations, the British Lord Advocate and the Edinburgh deputy sheriff were fast on Jimmy's trail, charging him with sedition and scheduling a trial that Jimmy failed to attend. The court then outlawed him, and, by April of 1793, Jimmy was aboard the ship *Mary John*, in full retreat toward the Delaware River.[144]

Today, Jimmy Callender writes for the *Philadelphia Aurora*, but the pay simply isn't enough.[145] Jimmy has moved his family onto Philadelphia's docks,[146] drinks too heavily, and asks friends for handouts.[147] As Poor Richard said,

> *Kings have long Arms, but Misfortune longer;*
> *Let none think themselves out of her Reach.*[148]

MONDAY, MARCH 12, 1798

GENERAL ★ AURORA ★ ADVERTISER

We are convinced that . . . people begin to see their madness in preferring *John Adams* and a *French war* to *Thomas Jefferson with a French peace.*

Some family matters . . . Today, in the U.S. Senate, John Adams puts forth the nomination of his son, John Quincy Adams,

> *to be a commissioner with full powers to negotiate a treaty of amity and commerce with His Majesty the King of Sweden.*[149]

Formerly U.S. Minister to The Hague (Netherlands), John Quincy Adams is currently U.S. Minister to Berlin (Prussia).

More family matters . . . Benny's wife, Peggy,[150] is pregnant. This will be their fourth. The first three are boys, Franklin, six, Richard, four, and Benjamin, two. Poor Richard said,

> *A Good Wife & Health is a Man's best Wealth.*[151]

In Peggy Bache, Benny has found his fortune.

Benny Bache first met Peggy Bache (née Markoe) in the spring of 1788, following his graduation (1787)[152] from the University of the State of Pennsylvania. He was eighteen. She was seventeen. Peggy's parents were Danes who had farmed a sugar plantation on the island of St. Croix in the West Indies. Her father died when she was a child, so her mother moved Peggy and one of her two brothers, Peter, to Philadelphia, where, in 1780, her mother married Adam Kuhn, a prominent Philadelphia physician.[153]

Benny and Peggy courted for almost two years when Peggy's mother took ill and asked Peggy to return with her to St. Croix. The separation proved affecting.[154] During it, Peggy attended her mother and Benny attended his grandfather until their respective deaths. Peggy returned in June of 1790; Benny started the *Aurora* in October; and in November of the following year, they were married. At first they lived with Benny's parents in Franklin Court, but, in 1792 when their first son, Franklin, was born, they moved above the *Aurora*'s offices at 112 High.[155] At that time, Benny wrote a friend,

> *I am no longer little Benjamin, I am the large bearded Benjamin, and what is worse—married. Yes, at 22 . . . to my taste and to the taste of my friends, too. If you know her, you will like her very much . . .*[156]

Peggy has endured difficult times with Benny Bache. She also has shared heroic moments. In July of 1795, when the *Aurora* published (in America's first journalistic "scoop") the text of the infamous Jay Treaty (which Washington and the Senate were trying to keep secret), Benny set out by stagecoach to spread copies of the treaty throughout the country. Like Paul Revere, Benny traveled from city to city, warning, in effect, that "the British are coming." While Benny generated large anti-treaty rallies in each city he visited, Peggy Bache remained at home, publishing the *Aurora* herself, with the help of her brother, Peter.[157]

Things have intensified since then. After John Adams' "miserable instruments of foreign influence" speech last May 16th, a friend wrote of Peggy Bache,

> *Poor woman, her old acquaintances have almost all deserted her. She is luckily of the opinion that her husband is quite in the right. She does not therefore suffer the pain of entertaining a mean opinion of him which I am sorry to say most people do.*[158]

That's where things stand at this time. Benny finds strength in Peggy. As Poor Richard said,

> *Prosperity discovers Vice, Adversity Virtue.*[159]

Tonight, the *Porcupine's Gazette* resumes the attack on Benny Bache:

> [T]he notorious Jacobin BACHE, Editor of the *Aurora*, [is] Printer to the French Directory [France's executive council], General of the Principles of Insurrection, Anarchy and confusion; the greatest fool and most stubborn sans culotte in the United States . . . No sooner had this chief of anarchy given the signal for attack . . . than to work went all his understrappers in the different parts of the United States.[160]

Though Federalists call Republicans like Benny and me "democrats" and "demos," they use the particular words *"Jacobin"* and *"sans-culotte"* to associate us with lower-class Paris street radicals who catapulted Maximilien François Marie Isidore de Robespierre to the leadership of the French Revolution for a ten-month "Reign of Terror" (from September 17, 1793, until Robespierre was guillotined on July 28, 1794).

Robespierre's violence actually caused many French democrats to leave France. Two good examples are Philadelphians Médéric-Louis-Elie Moreau de St. Méry and Constantin-François Volney.[161] Moreau de St. Méry, a tall man of good proportions and quick wit, was active in Parisian politics but now dispenses French books, contraceptives, and a variety of other items from a Front-street (from "river front") shop.[162] Constantin Volney, the handsome, wispy-haired political-philosopher and friend of Benjamin Franklin, enjoyed great fame in revolutionary France for his 1791 French masterwork, *The Ruins of Empires . . . ,"* which attributed the fall of diverse societies to monarchical and aristocratic governments and to state-sanctioned religious establishments. Today, Volney is writing an English translation of his *Ruins,* which is the most popular French book in America.[163]

Like the many other Frenchmen who came to America, Moreau de St. Méry and Constantin-François Volney are well-accepted members of the community. They are even members of Philadelphia's (and America's) oldest and most revered intellectual forum, the American Philosophical Society.[164]

In the ten years of the French Revolution, Robespierre's ten-month "Reign of Terror" was actually a brief episode. Besides, the time of Robespierre is four years past.[165] Today's France, even in wartime, has a more moderate government, consisting of a plural executive (France's five-man "Executive Directory") and a bicameral legislature (the Council of Ancients and the Council of Five Hundred). But Federalists speak as though Robespierre still rules. One might ask, as Poor Richard,

> *What signifies knowing the Names,*
> *if you know not the Natures of Things.*[166]

Tonight, in the *Gazette of the United States*, John Fenno continues his attack on Jimmy Callender:

> The following paragraph which appeared in the *Aurora* of the 6th instant is evidently the production of a bitter enemy to the honor and independence of the United States. No American can be the author, it is the work of some *imported* felon . . .
>
> "From the beginning of the present war down to this time, the conduct of our executive has been a series of ill offices toward France . . ."
>
> > *Scotland take back thy gallows son,*
> > *And let the halter have its own;*
> > *On prior right, Bache can't refuse*
> > *His lying cat'rer to the noose—*

GENERAL ★ AURORA ★ ADVERTISER

[T]he French decree of January 1798 is not particularly intended to incommode and injure America . . . It is a great infraction of our neutral rights, [but] so were the British detentions of neutral vessels . . .

Mr. Fenno can neither be reasoned nor ridiculed out of his practice of scolding at the French republic. In this he undoubtedly acts by *orders of his superiors*, and therefore the less blame can rest on him.

John Fenno and his *Gazette of the United States* are predictable. Peter Porcupine (William Cobbett) and his *Porcupine's Gazette* are wild! George Washington thinks Peter Porcupine "not a bad thing."[167] The Adamses seem to adore him.[168] Today, Abigail Adams writes her sister,

Peter says many good things, and he is the only thorn in Bache's side. He [Bache] is really afraid to encounter him . . .[169]

GENERAL ★ AURORA ★ ADVERTISER

John Fenno, in his paper of Monday attacks a paragraph in the *Aurora* of the 6th . . . which begins in these words:
"From the beginning of the present war down to this time, the conduct of our executive has been a series of ill offices towards France." . . . Yet John . . . says that this must have been the work of some *imported felon* and . . . alludes to *some gallows son of Scotland.*
This Scot [Jimmy Callender] is paid a very high compliment . . . The truth is that this editor [John Fenno] has of late been detected in a multitude of fibs . . . He is therefore an object rather of pity than resentment and is personally of too little consequence to occupy much room in the *Aurora.*

Tonight, the *Gazette of the United States* broadens its attack on scribblers who have fled the British monarch:

Burk, the "Wild Irishman," is employed . . . writing sedition.—*Callender*, a Scotch vagrant, has written a libel on General Washington.—It seems then our revolution has not secured us from the importation of Foreign Convicts who abuse our Government [and] traduce our worthies . . .

"Burk" is John Daly Burk, a twenty-two-year-old Irish scribbler who, like me, escaped the British sedition act by fleeing to America. Burk's crime was trying to stir up fellow students at Dublin's Trinity College to prevent British soldiers from executing an Irish detainee. The British soldiers chased Burk into a Dublin bookshop, where he charmed a Miss Daly, escaped with her clothing as a disguise, and adopted "Daly" as his middle name to express eternal gratitude. John Daly Burk fled to America, arrived some eighteen months ago, acquired a new wife, Christiana, and is working as a scribbler for Republican journals in New York.[170]

An OX was paraded thro' our streets yesterday [the Wednesday market day], weighing about 2000 lb. gross weight. The beef will be exposed to sale on Saturday [the next market day] by Jacob Lounslaer, No 48 in the Market. This ox was raised in Jersey by John Pissant, on the Farm of Jno. Lardner, Esq.

On market days, animals file and obstruct passage between the *Philadelphia Aurora's* entryway and the covered country marketplace in the center lane of High-street. It's a problem.

Today, President Adams works on a speech he will deliver on Monday to a joint session of the Congress. His first instincts are to declare war. From one draft:

> *[The actions of France] demand an immediate Declaration that all the Treaties and Conventions between the United States and France are null . . . and, in my opinion, they demand on the part of Congress an immediate Declaration of War against France.*

From another:

> *To me there appears no alternative between actual hostilities and national ruin. The former, no American will hesitate to prefer: and all Men will think it more honourable and glorious to the national Character, when its existence as an independent nation is at Stake, that Hostilities should be avowed in a formal Declaration of War.*[171]

Adams' final draft won't include these requests. The President's Lady Abigail Adams observes:

> *[K]nowing what he thinks ought to be done, yet not certain whether the people are sufficiently determined to second the Government is a situation very painfull . . . .*[172]

When JOHN Q. ADAMS, the son of the President, was taken from the Hague and sent to Berlin on a new appointment with a *new* outfit [sti-

pend], we suggested that he would be made to perform the circuit thro'
the Northern Courts of Europe with a *new* outfit at each removal, as
such business would be found more profitable than any he could follow
at home and as it was the duty of every father to provide handsomely for
his son, especially when it can be done at public expense. Our hint has
been taken, and JOHN Q. ADAMS has been appointed for Stockholm . . .
an appointment so repugnant to every idea of propriety . . .

Tonight, in John Fenno's *Gazette of the United States*:

A more infamous attempt to deceive the public was never made than
was made in Bache's *Aurora* of this morning—The story . . . is a falsehood
from beginning to end . . . Mr. Adams is appointed a commissioner for the
particular purpose of renewing with Sweden a very valuable commercial
treaty which is about expiring—He has no salary or pay annexed to his
appointment—It is not probable he will leave Berlin to transact the business but will renew the treaty with the Swedish minister at Berlin.

A MEMBER OF THE SENATE

[W]hen J. Q. Adams was appointed to Berlin, he had not a new outfit
other than a small sum . . . Mr. Bache very well knows an outfit to a minister is generally understood to be one year's salary, and the law of the
United States sanctions such an outfit—this was not given, and Mr. Bache
knows the fact.   JUNIUS

SATURDAY, MARCH 17, 1798

GENERAL ★ AURORA ★ ADVERTISER

Two of Mr. Fenno's correspondents in last evening's paper attempt to
controvert the statement which appeared in our last, respecting the new
appointment which JOHN Q. ADAMS has received to the Court of Sweden. One . . . a member of the Senate . . . proceeds to say "that it is probable he will renew the treaty with the Swedish minister at Berlin" . . .
[I]t cannot be believed, upon the Senator's anonymous assertion, that
Mr. Adams is to have no pay or salary; nor is it probable that he will
transact our affairs with the Court of Sweden at Berlin.

Citizen Fenno, in last Wednesday night's paper, says that "*Burk, the
wild Irishman*, is employed . . . writing Sedition. *Callender*, a Scotch vagrant, has written a libel on General Washington." What can ail the six per
cent [federal debt interest] people at Irishmen? Their own Grand Lama,
the truly illustrious Alexander Hamilton, as far as his maternal descent can
be traced, was the son of an IRISH CAMP GIRL . . . Reflections upon a
whole people in the mass are . . . stupid . . . The people of New England

are [themselves] sprung from a set of dissenters whom the Government of England had proscribed as either rebels or nothing better.

Federalists, especially New England Federalists like Boston-born John Fenno and influential congressman Harrison Gray Otis of Boston, are very hard on the Irish. Many Irish refugees from the British monarch (especially Irish Catholics) avoid Federalist (and Congregationalist) New England to settle farther south in states like Pennsylvania and Maryland. Last July, Bostonian Otis stood up on the floor of the U.S. House of Representatives and proclaimed that America should no longer, in his words,

> *wish to invite hordes of Wild Irishmen, nor the turbulent and disorderly of all parts of the world, to come here with a view to disturb our tranquillity, after having succeeded in the overthrow of their own Governments.*[173]

This "Wild Irish" speech achieved great circulation and approval among the Federalists.[174]

With Federalists so anti-Irish and the Irish so anti-British, it is hardly surprising that Irish scribblers like John Daly Burk and me lend our pens to the Republican cause. Others are Matthew Lyon, the Vermont congressman and newspaper publisher of "spitting" fame, and Mathew Carey, a Philadelphia newspaper and magazine publisher who worked for Ben Franklin in Paris, gave Jimmy Callender one of his first jobs in Philadelphia,[175] serves as secretary for the Hibernian Society for the relief of Irish Emigrants,[176] and runs a bookshop and publishing firm only two doors from the *Aurora* at 118 High.[177]

Two Irish scribblers whom the British imprisoned are Dr. James Reynolds[178] and Thomas "Newgate" Lloyd. Jimmy Reynolds now practices medicine in Philadelphia, volunteers it at the Philadelphia Dispensary,[179] leads Philadelphia's Society of United Irishmen,[180] and writes occasionally for the *Philadelphia Aurora*.[181] "Newgate" Lloyd befriended me in London, paid for my family and me to travel with him to America, and co-edited a newspaper with me when we first arrived.[182] "Newgate" (nicknamed for the British prison where he was incarcerated) and I are good friends.

Today, the *Philadelphia Aurora* receives a "Letter to the Editor" from Mrs. Abigail Adams, wife of the President of the United States:

> *Sir Taking up your paper yesterday morning, I was shocked at the misrepresentation a writer in your paper has given the nomination and appointment of J. Q. Adams . . . I could not reflect upon the different feelings which must actuate your mind and [those of J. Q. Adams,] the writer of the following paragraph, written last October . . .*
>
> *"As for Mr. Bache, he was once my schoolmate; one of the companions of those infant years when the Heart should be open to strong and*

deep impressions of attachment . . . Mr. Bache must have lost those
feelings . . ."

Mr. Bache is left to his own reflections. This communication is only
to his own Heart, being confident that the writer [J. Q. Adams] never
expected it would meet his Eye.

[Mrs. Abigail Adams][183]

Benny won't answer (let alone publish) this letter. How could Abigail Adams
refer to Benny's school years with John Quincy? How could she mention 1778?
The only reason J.Q. and Benny were schoolmates at Le Coeur's boarding
school was that J.Q.'s father and Benny's grandfather were diplomats together
in Paris. As Poor Richard said,

Let our Fathers and Grandfathers be valued for
their Goodness, ourselves for our own.[184]

Tonight, in the *Porcupine's Gazette,* William Cobbett attacks Benny Bache (as
well as Turks, Jews, &c.):

Nobody, or, at least, nobody worth notice ever believes [BACHE]; and
to contradict him seems to imply that he is sometimes a credible person
which is admitting what never ought, even for argument's sake, to be
admitted. He knows that all the world knows and says he is a liar; a fallen
wretch, a vessel formed for reprobation; and, therefore, we should always
treat him as we would a TURK, a JEW, a JACOBIN, or a DOG.

MONDAY, MARCH 19, 1798

GENERAL ★ AURORA ★ ADVERTISER

The pith of the objection to the appointment [of J. Q. Adams] is . . . that
it is heaping honor and profit with a partial hand upon a young man who
has never done anything for this Country except writing Publicola . . .

"Publicola" is the pseudonym John Quincy Adams used seven years ago in
anonymous letters that Benny published in the mistaken belief that J.Q.'s father, John Adams, had authored them. "Publicola" responded to Benny's publication (first American edition) of Tom Paine's *Rights of Man,* a work that
praised the French Revolution as a progressive and democratic solution to the
inherent failings of monarchy. In attacking Paine's work, "Publicola" argued
that the disruptive behavior of the French Revolution demonstrated the dangers of pure democracy and that Britain's mixed form of government with its
strong executive (the king) and upper legislative chamber (the propertied,
hereditary, and titled House of Lords) imposed important checks on the dangers of pure democracy which threaten from such "lower" people's chambers
as the British House of Commons or the American House of Representatives.[185]

Benny Bache sees the Adamses as monarchists. During John Adams' campaign for President, the *Aurora* recalled that, as a lawyer, Adams defended and

acquitted the British soldiers who committed the Boston Massacre,[186] describing Adams as "the friend of monarchic and aristocratic government."[187] Adams, the paper said, was

> one who has no faith, no confidence in representative or elective government, who believes, with the jealous enemies of our Constitution abroad, that a Monarchical Constitution is not only better than a Federal Constitution, but that a mixed Monarchy is the "best of all possible governments."[188]

Specifically, the *Aurora* charged,

> JOHN ADAMS [is] the advocate of a kingly government and of a titled nobility to form an upper house and to keep down the swinish multitude . . . JOHN ADAMS . . . would deprive you of a voice in chusing your president and senate, and make both hereditary—this champion for kings, ranks, and titles is to be your president.[189]

To prove its point, the *Aurora* demonstrated that "MR. ADAMS has written in favor of monarchy,"[190] quoting his historical treatises on government:

> I.   *"The Lacedemonian Republic . . . had the three essential parts of the best possible government; it was a mixture of monarchy, aristocracy, and democracy."*[191]
>
> II.   *"Instead of projects [in Britain] to abolish the kings and lords, if the House of Commons had been attended to . . . [there would not] have remained an imperfection perhaps in the English constitution."*[192]
>
> III.   *"First magistrates and senators had better be made hereditary at once [rather] than that the people be universally debauched and bribed, go to loggerheads, and fly to arms every year."*[193]

Most embarrassingly, the *Aurora* recalled and ridiculed Adams' attire at the opening sessions of the U.S. Senate in the autumn of 1789,

> a sword at his side, his hat under his arm, his wig frizzed a la mode de noblesse, and his coat buttoned down to his waistband.

The *Aurora* remembered that, at those opening sessions, Adams advocated titles of nobility for government officials, prompting one unmannered senator to propose a title for Adams himself: "We will dub him his rotundity by g——d."[194] The *Aurora's* article might remind us of Poor Richard's saying,

> *Poverty, poetry, and new Titles of Honour,*
> *make Men ridiculous.*[195]

Today, the monarchist is President, and, today, he delivers his address to a joint session of the Congress of these United States. The Journals of Congress report:

> The following Message was received from the PRESIDENT OF THE UNITED STATES:

Gentlemen of the Senate, and Gentlemen of the House of Representatives

The Dispatches from the Envoys Extraordinary of the United States to the French Republic . . . have been examined and maturely considered . . .

I perceive no ground of expectation that the . . . mission can be accomplished on terms compatible with the safety, honor, or the essential interests of the nation . . .

Under these circumstances, I cannot forbear to reiterate the recommendations which have been formerly made . . . for the protection of our seafaring and commercial citizens, for the defense of the exposed portions of our territory, for replenishing our arsenals, establishing foundries and military manufactures and to provide such efficient revenue as will be necessary . . .

[I]nstructions were given . . . to restrain vessels of the United States from sailing in armed condition . . . I no longer conceive myself justifiable in continuing [these instructions] . . .

JOHN ADAMS.[196]

John Adams has not asked for a Declaration of War, but he has certainly delivered a war speech. Thomas Jefferson calls it "almost insane."[197]

Tonight, in the *Porcupine's Gazette*, William Cobbett answers a Jew who objected to his remarks on Saturday:

A JEW writes me to "be more lenient in the future" (respecting his *nation*, as he calls it) or "to blot his name out" of my list.—I do the latter with pleasure. I am sure I never solicited his name, and am only sorry I did not know before, that it was the name of A JEW.

TUESDAY, MARCH 20, 1798

GENERAL ★ AURORA ★ ADVERTISER

REMARKS on the PRESIDENT'S MESSAGE.

The time is then come which *(in the opinion of the Executive)* calls on Americans to draw the sword. If our legislative councils are to be actuated by the impressions made on his mind, then the United States are to join in the European War on the side of the tottering *government* of Britain and against the French Republic . . . From the . . . President's address, it would appear that, however he may acknowledge a right in the Legislature to *declare* war, he conceives he has that of *making* it . . . If our merchantmen may now arm . . . we are at war . . . [I]f our legislature does not interpose and prevent the arming, we shall be dragged into a war. Indeed the whole tenor of the president's message bears an aspect extremely threatening to our peace . . . [D]oes not the crisis call upon the PEOPLE to step forward . . . [?]

Today, the President's Lady, Abigail Adams, writes her sister,

> *I expect the President will be represented as declaring War by tak-*
> *ing off the restrictions which prevented Merchantmen from Arming . . .*
> *[Y]ou see by the papers that Bache has begun his old billingsgate*
> *[slander] again, because Mr. J. Q. Adams is directed to renew the*
> *treaty with Sweden [from his post in Berlin] . . . [T]his lying wretch of*
> *a Bache reports that no treaties were ever made without going to the*
> *courts to negotiate them . . . [B]ut there is no end to their audacious-*
> *ness, and you will see that French emissaries are in every corner of*
> *the union sowing and spreading their Sedition. We have renewed in-*
> *formation that their System is to calumniate [defame] the president,*
> *his family, his administration until they oblige him to resign, and then*
> *they will Reign triumphant, headed by the Man of the People [Jeffer-*
> *son]. It behooves every pen and press to counteract them. We are come*
> *to a crisis too important to be languid, too dangerous to slumber . . .*[198]

Tonight, in the *Porcupine's Gazette*:

Mr. COBBETT,

I have often observed, in looking over Bache's paper, that he never has any advertisements in his paper relating to mercantile business. I cannot account for the reason of this, unless it is that merchants are ashamed to have their names seen in so scandalous a paper or think that it would be of little or no use to advertise in it on account of their being so few—except the poor, ignorant, low-bred jacobins—who take pains enough to read it . . .

If, Sir, you will be so good as to give me your sentiments on the above, you will much oblige . . .   VERITAS

(My sentiments, Mr. Veritas, are [that] if you wish to continue to de-
serve your name, you should immediately cease to read BACHE; for if you
have the virtue of an angel, frequent converse with him will corrupt you.)

WEDNESDAY, MARCH 21, 1798

GENERAL   ★ AURORA ★   ADVERTISER

THE message . . . from the President of the United States to Congress is fatal and destructive to the peace of the United States . . . Are the people of the United States prepared to draw the sword . . . against the French Republic at this presidential call without knowing either the necessity or the object to be obtained[?] . . . His harpies say it is not a declaration of war, although they know it amounts to the same thing . . .

Mr. Adams has it now in his power to do a most acceptable service to his country by retiring from . . . public life . . . He must be sensible himself that at this time he is unfit to be trusted with the interests of a peaceful nation. His personal pride has been wounded . . . and this leads him to do what it can never be the interests of his country to suffer. Let him manage his own passions on the occasion, and, without him, our councils will manage our differences with France.

At its commencement, about as many papers left this city from [*Porcupine's Gazette*] . . . as from all other Philadelphia presses put together. But this extensive circulation does not rest upon a list of *bona fide* subscribers. The paper was scattered . . . without any expectation of remuneration from most of those who received it. Whence its support was derived was no difficult matter to conjecture . . . The late declaration of the editor of that paper that he was and was proud to be "a British subject" has opened the eyes of many . . .

Today, in the *Porcupine's Gazette,* Peter Porcupine responds:

BACHE'S infernal Farrago [mixture] of this morning shall have its due in due time.

On the prospect of
WAR WITH FRANCE
MY COUNTRYMEN, THE die is cast—compromise is at an end—there is now no retreat—now no other alternative but instantly to assert the spirit which was once the boast of Americans . . . You have no other choice but either to submit to the detested and once despised yoke of France or else to open the armory of your ancestors . . .

Today, U.S. Secretary of the Treasury Oliver Wolcott issues a directive:

(CIRCULAR to the COLLECTORS of the CUSTOMS.)
Treasury Department, March 21.
SIR, IT has been determined by the President of the United States . . . to modify the instructions issued from this department on the 8th day of April 1797 in such a manner as no longer to restrain vessels of the United States from sailing in an armed condition . . . [Y]ou are to consider the general prohibition as no longer remaining in force . . .
OLIVER WOLCOTT
Secretary of the Treasury[199]

Today, Vice President Thomas Jefferson writes former U.S. Minister to France James Monroe:

The public papers will present to you the almost insane message sent to both houses of Congress 2. or 3. days ago. This has added to the alarm . . . The effect of the French decree on the representatives had been to render the war party inveterate & more firm in their purpose . . . We had reposed great confidence in that provision of the Constitution which requires 2/3 of the Legislature to declare war. Yet it can be entirely eluded by a majority's taking such measures as will bring on war.[200]

Today, Thomas Jefferson also writes James Madison:

> *The French decree . . . excited indignation highly in the war party . . . the insane message which you will see in the public papers has had great effect. Exultation on the one side, & a certainty of victory; while the other is petrified with astonishment . . . We see a new instance of the inefficiency of Constitutional guards. We had relied with great security on that provision which requires two-thirds of the Legislature to declare war. But this is completely eluded by a majority's taking war measures which will be sure to produce war.*[201]

Today, the U.S. House of Representatives considers the power of the Speaker to expel Benny Bache or any other reporter from the House floor. The Annals of Congress report:

> Mr. NICHOLAS [Republican, Virginia] said that . . . he wished . . . not to ascertain whether the Speaker had done his duty heretofore, but whether the power of discharging short-hand writers from the House should be vested in the Speaker . . .
>
> Mr. LYON [Republican, Vermont] . . . thought it of great importance . . . When he first took his seat in the House, there were six persons who attended to take down notes; now, he said, there is only one . . . and he wished the regulation to be adopted, lest that one should be driven away by the same power which had sent off the others.
>
> The SPEAKER said the remark of the member from Vermont was very improper and indecent . . .

Federalists vote to retain the Speaker's power, 50 to 36.[202]

FRIDAY, MARCH 23, 1798

GENERAL ★ AURORA ★ ADVERTISER

Every act of our government has shewn their partiality for Britain in preference to France; and tho' the latter has claims on our gratitude [for her help with our American Revolution] and was engaged [by her French Revolution] in a contest for the liberty of mankind, yet even in such a cause, every unfair advantage was taken of her situation, and, as far as it was possible without actual hostility, we assisted her [British] Enemy . . . Madness itself is the order of the day [!]

Today, President Adams issues a proclamation:

> *By Authority*
> OF THE
> *President of The United States.*
> A PROCLAMATION
> *As the safety and prosperity of nations ultimately and essentially depend on the protection and the blessing of almighty God . . . and as the*

United States of America are at present placed in a hazardous and af-
flictive situation by the unfriendly disposition, conduct, and demands
of a foreign power . . . I do hereby recommend that Wednesday, the 9th
day of May next, be observed throughout the United States as a day of
solemn humiliation, fasting, and prayer . . .[203]

> JOHN ADAMS *By the President,*
> TIMOTHY PICKERING, *Secretary of State.*

Today, Quaker leaders Samuel Weatherill and Dr. George Logan circulate a petition urging the President and Congress to maintain the peace.[204]

Tonight, in the *Porcupine's Gazette*:

> TO BACHE. *Downlooking Caitiff,* What has given thee courage? What has led to this imprudent attack [the day before yesterday]? . . . As to my sending papers *without payment* . . . wretch as you are, come yourself and look at these books . . . You affect to believe that my paper had produced no effect . . . You know better. You stinking, chop-fallen mortal, you know better. You know that the first moment of my rise was the first moment of your decline and fall. You and your whole party feels its effects daily and hourly and minutely . . .
>
> Perverted BACHE! . . . [I]t is useless for you to say anything against me, or I against you. People are well satisfied that I am descended from honest parents; they know (whatever some of them may think, or say) that I am sincere in my attachment to my adopted country and its government. All who have ever had concerns with me know me to be a punctual, honest man; and, as to you, every body knows that you are BACHE, the grand-son of old Franklin, and that's enough. To be BACHE is all I wish to see my enemy. Wm. COBBETT.

SATURDAY, MARCH 24, 1798

GENERAL ★ AURORA ★ ADVERTISER

Let me ask for what cause does the President desire war with France? Is it to protect British trade and commerce with the United States . . . ? Or is it to produce an alliance offensive and defensive between Great Britain and the United States, the more effectually to defeat and destroy republicanism in France and reestablish monarchy and thereby maintain that favorite government which Mr. Adams . . . declared "is the most stupendous fabric of human invention"?

Mr. BACHE, The house of representatives having decided the question concerning Stenographers in such a manner as to leave their admission or expulsion at the arbitrary discretion of the Speaker, I think it proper to state some facts . . .

Mr. Dayton said the exclusion of reporters had not been exercised but on one person, meaning the Editor of the *Aurora* . . . This assertion [is] . . . incorrect . . . I was engaged during the extraordinary session of Congress to report for a daily paper of which I was also the editor. A [Federalist] member wished me to alter a speech which had been delivered in the house . . . [T]his I refused to do . . .

[T]he sergeant at arms delivered to me the following message—*"Sir, the Speaker has directed me to inform you that . . . you must not write shorthand in this house any more—you must go; if you do not, I must use force."*

It has been a constant trick with some members of the house to speak a speech calculated to make an impression in the house and to publish another containing different sentiments for . . . their constituents . . . I have lost an engagement . . . because I would not retract the truth . . .

A REPORTER

I, William Duane, wrote this morning's anonymous letter by "A REPORTER." Dayton barred me from the House floor,[205] costing me the job and the revenue ($800) it entailed.[206] Benny may have given me a job from empathy with my injury.

John Adams knows that Benny Bache is secretly meeting with Thomas Jefferson. Today, the President's wife writes,

> *How different is the situation of the President from that of Washington? The Vice President never combined with a party against him. He never made Bache his companion and counselor.*[207]

True, but Thomas Jefferson hasn't changed. Before he resigned as George Washington's Secretary of State, he held many private meetings with Benny Bache, encouraging Benny to publish a condensed "country" edition of the *Aurora*[208] and once admitting to Washington that the *Aurora* publisher *"tried, at my request, the plan of a weekly paper . . ."*[209] Jefferson knew Benny Bache made George Washington sick,[210] and, as earlier mentioned, he once saw Washington slam the paper on the floor with a "damn."[211] Whether Washington spelled Benny's name accurately or phonetically, his opinion was the same: *"Beeche's papers are outrages on common decency."*[212]

MONDAY, MARCH 26, 1798

GENERAL   ★ AURORA ★   ADVERTISER

[Reprint] FROM THE MIDDLESEX GAZETTE
[A Connecticut Paper].
Friends and fellow citizens:
You engaged in a long and bloody war with Great Britain—for what? To secure the fruits of your labours to yourselves and equal rights . . . At

the close of the revolution, the image of liberty was enstamped on every heart; we looked with a kind of horror on the British plans of oppression. Is not the case far different now? have we not adopted in almost every instance, the spirit, if not the forms, of their oppression . . . [Our government] have taught the people *that the President can do no wrong;* and that all are jacobins, democrats, disorganizers, and enemies to their country who dare to doubt this doctrine . . . [They] detach our government from France; and join it in close league with Great Britain . . . Have not all the governmental papers abused and villified the French? Has not our [revolutionary war] treaty with them been so construed as to deprive them of almost all the advantages . . . meant to be secured to them by it? . . . We are now about entering on a war; not with a natural, not with an ordinary enemy; but with a nation which saved us from the rapacious jaws of Britain, now become a republic like our own . . .

A fellow citizen who does not
believe in executive infallibility.

Tonight, in the *Gazette of the United States*:

A turgid libeller in a jacobin Connecticut print, whose production is copied into the *Aurora* of today, repeats the hackneyed assertion that the *old soldiers* [of the American Revolution] are enemies to government[al war measures] . . . It may be boldly proclaimed that not an officer of the least credit or respectability or whose conduct during the revolutionary struggle will bear scrutiny is now to be found amongst the hireling crew of calumniating jacobins.

Today, James Monroe answers Thomas Jefferson's letter of last Wednesday:

The want of light . . . will not be remedied till more pens are put to work. It occurred to me it [would] be proper for my narrative [the retaliatory "A View of the Conduct of the Executive . . ."] to be inserted in the gazettes. I should suppose Bache would not object to it since it would most probably promote his interest by promoting the sale of the book . . .

It seems to me that the line of propriety on my part is to rest quiet . . . The book ["A View of the Conduct of the Executive . . ."] will remain & be read in the course of 50 years, if not sooner, and I think the facts it contains will settle or contribute to settle the opinion of posterity in the character of the administration, however indifferent to it the present race may be. And it will be some consolation to me to . . . do justice to them with posterity, since a gang of greater scoundrels never lived. We are to dance on [Washington's] birth night, forsooth, and say they are great & good men, when we know they are little people. I think the spirit of that idle propensity is dying away & that the good sense of the people is breaking thro' the prejudice which has long chained them down.[213]

Tonight, in the *Porcupine's Gazette,* Peter Porcupine writes:

A TIMELY CAUTION TO THE QUAKERS of *The City and County of Philadelphia.*—Gentlemen: Having been informed that there is a petition to the HOUSE OF REPRESENTATIVES hawking about by [Quaker] Samuel Weatherill . . . against the horrors of war . . . I trust it will be easy to convince you that this PETITION is an insidious appeal to . . . your well known and amiable principles [of non-violence] . . . What would you say if it should appear that the palavering paper was drawn up by BACHE! . . . Mortified as you must feel at being thus ranked with the Democrats, with disorganizers and atheists; yet that mortification will be nothing compared to the odium, the keen and well grounded reproach, that this factious petition must bring on you from all the friends of government . . . Do not excite disgust and contempt in your friends, and render the name of Quaker a reproach . . . [D]o not dishonour your names by placing it at the bottom of a petition . . . which will be extolled by the *Aurora* . . .

TUESDAY, MARCH 27, 1798

GENERAL ★ AURORA ★ ADVERTISER

John Fenno [in the *Gazette of the U.S.*] is very angry at the *Aurora* for having yesterday copied an article from a Connecticut newspaper hinting that the old soldiers were not fond of a French war. He affirms, on the contrary, that there is not one officer whose conduct in the late war will bear scrutiny, who is to be found among the "base hireling crew of calumniating Jacobins."

Looking into Congress, we find many respectable military characters opposed to the present plan for war, such as General Smith of Baltimore, Colonel Parker of Virginia, Gen. M'Dowell and Col. Gillespie, of North Carolina. It is needless to multiply further examples.

War measures . . . Today, John Adams approves and signs into law the first piece of war legislation against France:

AN ACT
*For an additional appropriation to provide
and support a Naval Armament.*
Be it enacted. &c. That there be, and there hereby is, appropriated a further sum, not exceeding one hundred and fifteen thousand, eight hundred and thirty-three dollars to complete and equip for sea, with all convenient speed, the [armed] frigates, the *United States*, the *Constitution*, and the *Constellation*.[214]

Today, in the U.S. House of Representatives, Republicans try to thwart the move toward war. The Annals of Congress report:

RELATIONS WITH FRANCE

Mr. SPRIGG [Republican, Maryland] rose and observed . . . he should offer the following resolutions . . .

Resolved, That . . . under existing circumstances it is not expedient for the United States to resort to war against the French Republic.

Resolved, &., That provision ought to be made by law for restricting the arming of merchant vessels . . .

Mr. GALLATIN [Republican, Western Pennsylvania] said . . . the United States had arrived at a crisis . . . in which it was necessary for Congress to say whether they will resort to war or preserve peace . . . [B]efore measures are taken which will lead to war, the House ought to decide whether it is their intention at present to go to war . . .

Mr. J. WILLIAMS [Federalist, New York] . . . thought it very extraordinary, as no one was found to bring forward a resolution to declare war, that a gentleman would introduce a resolution of its being inexpedient so to do. He was persuaded that this negative mode of proceeding was calculated to draw on a debate, to set the people against the Executive . . . He had himself seen gentlemen write upon the late Message of the President, for the purpose of sending to their constituents, *"A war message against France"* . . .

A call to order took place; and a motion was made . . . to rise [adjourn], and carried.[215]

Today, in Philadelphia's Northern Liberties district (which is north, along the Delaware), Federalists are recruiting young men into a private militia, the Macpherson's Blues, to combat what they call America's *"false, perfidious friends, both at home and abroad."* Their notice calls young men *"to arms."*[216]

Tonight, in the *Gazette of the United States*:

Callender, in the *Aurora* of this morning, has printed . . . "Looking into Congress, we find many respectable military characters opposed to the present plan of war, such as General Smith [&c] . . ." Has Callender the audacity to insinuate that . . . the above gentlemen are Jacobins? Or is it a "precious confession" of his employer Bache?

Tonight, in the *Porcupine's Gazette*:

The peace-makers, WEATHERILL, the *fighting Quaker,* and Dr. [George] LOGAN, the particular friend of Monroe . . . [and] Bache . . . were yesterday employed in handing out their factious [peace] petition. They generally met with a very cold and sometimes with a very rough reception . . . They have got the names of a number of Democrats, and they will get as many of them as they like; but this is not what they wanted. They wanted respectable names; and these they will not get . . .

A word about Quaker peace-petitioner George Logan . . . George Logan and Benny Bache share old family ties. George's grandfather, James, was secretary to Pennsylvania's founder, William Penn, and helped Benny's grandfather found the Library Company of Philadelphia about seventy years ago. At forty, George Logan still lives on an old family farm, Stenton, that his grandfather built in Germantown (northwest of Philadelphia) back in 1728.[217]

Despite the prestige of his old family name, George Logan maintains a very simple Quaker lifestyle, once chastising his attractive wife, Deborah, for serving George Washington a fancy dessert,[218] championing the small farmer (the "yeomanry") against Federalist schemes of big government and big taxation,[219] and generally sympathizing with Republican causes. He resented the Jay Treaty and Washington's treatment of France,[220] organized a welcome dinner for James Monroe when the ambassador was recalled,[221] and, now that war has become the question, finds equal determination in his Quakerism and his Republicanism that there must be no war with France.

WEDNESDAY, MARCH 28, 1798

GENERAL ★ AURORA ★ ADVERTISER

A petition to be presented to Congress is in circulation for signatures in this city, praying that every honorable and possible means may be used to prevent the country from being involved in the calamities of war.

Today, in the U.S. House of Representatives, Republicans vainly attempt to stop the push toward war. The Annals of Congress report:

RELATIONS WITH FRANCE

The House again resolved itself into a committee of the Whole . . . propositions as to the inexpediency or resorting to war against the French Republic being under consideration . . .

Mr. PINCKNEY [Federalist, South Carolina] rose and said . . . [t]he gentleman from Pennsylvania (Mr. GALLATIN) . . . says the adoption of the resolution will go to prevent the taking of any measures which may, in their tendency, lead to war . . . [T]he adoption of the resolution would not only declare that we will not go to war but that we will not take any measures for the defence of our property . . .[222]

A word about "Mr. GALLATIN" . . . Since last year, when James Madison (Republican, Virginia) retired from Congress and took his young Quaker wife, Dolley, back to Virginia, Albert Gallatin (Republican, Western Pennsylvania) has emerged as undisputed Republican leader in the U.S. House of Representatives.[223] One might think, on reading Peter Porcupine, that Al Gallatin arrived just yesterday from Geneva, Switzerland. He's actually been here eighteen years. He hasn't lost his French accent,[224] however, so Porcupine mocks him, for example, as follows:

*When Mr. Gallatin rose from his seat . . . there was an old farmer
sitting beside me . . ."Ah, ah!" says he, "what's little Moses in Congress?" I sharply reprimanded him for taking one of our representatives for a Jew: but to confess a truth, the Gentleman from Geneva has
an accent not unlike that of a wandering Israelite.*[225]

In a similar vein, Porcupine has popularized the taunting accusation that, in
leading congressional Republicans, Al Gallatin wants to, *"stop de wheels of de
gouverment."*[226]

THURSDAY, MARCH 29, 1798

GENERAL   ★ AURORA ★   ADVERTISER

[O]ur president has issued a proclamation for a fast and thanksgiving
both in one day [May 9th] . . . Mr. Adams wants to have . . . every pulpit
resound with declamations against France. He chuses to take for granted
. . . that Mr. Adams is exactly in the right and the French Directory are
entirely in the wrong . . . While John Fenno continues to publish his daily
libels against France, nobody in consistency with common sense can
believe that his patron, Mr. Adams, is desirous of soliciting the good will
of the [French] Republic.

[F]or refusing to suffer this press being muzzled by order of the Speaker
[of the House of Representatives], the Editor . . . was directed by the
Speaker to leave the place actually allotted to the reporters. The . . .
question was brought up to decide whether the Speaker should retain
this power . . . Had the grievance of which the Editor (in common with
other reporters) complains been clearly and directly before the committee . . . [t]hey never would have countenanced their Speaker . . . to be
indulged at the expense of the most valuable right of freemen—the liberty of the Press.

Today, President Adams confers a special honor on someone who is well
known[227] for having brutally assaulted Benjamin Bache less than a year ago.
The assault put Benny in bed for two days.[228] Secretary of State Timothy Pickering writes Clement Humphreys of Philadelphia:

*SIR, The President of the United States having directed that a spe-
cial messenger should be engaged to carry a letter to the Envoys from
the United States to the French Republic, you have been selected for
that service. You are to embark forthwith in the United States brigantine Sophia, whereof Captain Henry Geddes is master.*[229]

Clement Humphreys led shipyard workers to attack Benny Bache while Benny
was inspecting the 175–foot, forty-four-gun U.S. Navy frigate *United States*,
then under construction in the Humphreys family shipyard which is along the

The Humphreys' shipyard in Southwark, Philadelphia's southern district, with a U.S. frigate under construction.[230]

Delaware in Southwark (Philadelphia's southern district). Benny describes the attack:

I took a walk with two friends into Southwark. It was proposed by one of them that we should step on board the frigate which we did, having first obtained leave from the guard. The workmen were at their dinner. While we were looking at the river from the windows of the upper cabin, we perceived some pieces of cork thrown toward us thro' the hatchway from below. We concluded that they were thrown out of playfulness by some acquaintance or perhaps by some persons belonging to the frigate who might have mistaken us for acquaintances. The intention, however, was probably to provoke us to an altercation or induce us below on the main deck. We took no notice of the throwing, several minutes elapsed without it being repeated, and I had quite forgotten it.

The bell on the upper deck was struck. My friends walked toward it. I stood on the gangway looking at it. Immediately some 12 or 15 of the workmen came upon the deck from the stage and stood along the gunwale. I supposed at the time that the bell was to summon them to their work, but probably it was struck to get them on deck to stand by the assassin in case of need.

I was thus standing, alone as I thought, still looking at the bell, when I felt a violent blow on my head. My first thought was that something had fallen on me; I then received a second blow, and immediately after, perceived the cowardly ruffian before me in a menacing attitude. Stunned as I was with the violence of the two blows, which must have struck from behind, I was unable to defend myself against a third, much less to return them. About this period in the assault, I heard several broken sentences uttered such as that I had, in my paper . . . "abused the President on the day of his resignation . . ." . . . The perpetrator of this act of cowardly assassination, I have been since informed, is HUMPHREYS, son of the builder of the frigate.[231]

It is too dangerous for Benny to wander unprotected. Poor Richard advised,

> *He that scatters Thorns,*
> *let him not go barefoot.*[232]

John Adams' appointment of Clement Humphreys promises presidential rewards for anyone who attempts to silence Benjamin Bache!

Today, the Common Council of Philadelphia enacts the following:

AN ORDINANCE FOR THE
Regulation of the Market
HELD IN HIGH-STREET

Be it therefore ordained . . . that within half an hour after the time of sun rising, on every market day, strong chains, well secured, shall be stretched across the passages [onto High street] . . . to prevent any horses, cattle, carts or carriages from entering or passing . . . leaving nevertheless intervals in proper and convenient places for the passage of persons on foot . . .[233]

At last Benny and the rest of us in the lower part of High-street will be protected from the market day animals.

In [Tuesday's] Aurora, a reply was made to one of Fenno's Snip-snap paragraphs wherein he said that no officer whose conduct in the late war will bear scrutiny is to be found among "the base hireling crew of calumniating *Jacobins.*" Not knowing precisely what John meant by Jacobins, we ventured only to say that "many respectable military characters opposed the present plan of war." We named four members of Congress . . . John replies [on Tuesday] with great spirit: "Has Callender," says he, "the audacity to insinuate that either of the above Gentlemen are Jacobins, or is it a *precious confession* of his employer Bache." . . . John . . . speaks of *precious confessions* . . . When Hamilton printed his PRECIOUS CONFESSION [of adultery], a pamphlet the most infamous and even one of the most stupid that ever disgraced any age or nation, John Fenno secured *the copy right!*

At a legal meeting of the Freeholders and other
Inhabitants of the TOWN of ROXBURY [MASS.] . . .
The following motion was regularly made and seconded . . .
The inhabitants of this Town . . . hear with deepest concern that it has been proposed to allow the Merchants to Arm their vessels . . . [W]hen it is obvious that between Arms in the hands & the commencement of Hostilities there is but a [short] span, we deprecate . . . the prospect of the Peace . . . being suspended on so precarious a tenure . . . [This is] confiding the decision . . . not to the cool deliberate determination of Congress; but to the Pride, Caprice or Passion of an individual . . .

A true copy.– Attest,   STEVEN WILLIAMS,
                             Town Clerk [Roxbury, Massachusetts].

Mr. Bache, I have been much edified by reading the Proclamation of the President, appointing the 9th of May as a day of general fast throughout the United States . . . [T]he dangers which threaten [our country] have principally arisen from our Administration and . . . it is it that ought to *fast, reform, and repent* . . . The good American people are only guilty of one fault which, although light and trifling if the intention is weighed, has been dreadful in its consequences, *it is that of having elected Mr. Adams their President . . .*   *A good Christian . . .*

Poor Richard wrote,

The Bell calls others to Church,
but itself never minds the Sermon.[234]

Today, in the U.S. House of Representatives, the Annals of Congress report:

RELATIONS WITH FRANCE

MR. ALLEN [Federalist, Connecticut] . . . proposed the following resolution, to which he hoped there would be no objection:

Resolved, that the President of the United States be requested to communicate to this house the dispatches from the envoys extraordinary of the United States to the French republic, mentioned in his message of the 19th inst . . .

Mr. GALLATIN [Republican, Pennsylvania] could not see how the information . . . could influence the vote . . . [T]he Message of the President had produced . . . the effect of a declaration of war . . .[235]

Tonight, William Cobbett in the *Porcupine's Gazette*:

Being yesterday in the *Northern Liberties,* I accidentally saw, lying on a table, "An *address to the Youth"* . . . proposing to them to form *a company of infantry* and *another of artillery;* to disciple themselves and to be ready to march at the command of the government.—I am sorry I have not room for this address today; but it shall have a place tomorrow.

Tonight, in the *Gazette of the United States*:

The acknowledgment of a Deity and a superintending providence is so contrary to the practice of the rulers of France, Tom Paine . . . Bache and Callender that blasphemy and slander respecting the President's proclamation [for a day of prayer] from these foreign agents was a thing of course.

Bache . . . tells Callender to dub the friends of the constitution and government of the United States—Tories [supporters of monarchy]—but I would ask . . . if they . . . suppose the people of the United States will ever believe that the present or late President of the United States . . . who effected the independence of this Country are Tories?

SATURDAY, MARCH 31, 1798

GENERAL ★ AURORA ★ ADVERTISER

In yesterday's *Aurora* there appeared the copy of resolutions entered into by the town of Roxbury in Massachusetts . . . against arming our merchantmen . . .

We would ask . . . whether the conduct of the townsmen of Roxbury does not show that, even in the native state of our president, there is a numerous party who entirely disapprove of his harangues in favor of war.

A few weeks ago, we published a short statement of the amount charged the United States for building and equipping the three frigates *United States, Constitution* and *Constellation*. [T]hese frigates were in '94 ordered to be built in order to protect our trade against the Algerines [Barbary pirates] . . . The delay [in completing the ships] . . . rendered it necessary, in order to have a treaty, to promise the [Algiers] Dey's *daughter* a FRIGATE by way of *douceur* [bribe] . . . Here we have then the whole cost . . . 9,878,362.53.

Today, Abigail Adams writes her sister,

> *Bache you see is striving to render the Proclamation [for a May 9th prayer day] ridiculous and, with his Atheistical doctrines, spreading the French principles far and wide. But I trust and hope we may as a people . . . never forget that it is Righteousness which exalteth a Nation, whilst Sin is their Reproach.*[236]

Tonight, in the *Porcupine's Gazette*:

AN ADDRESS
To The Young Men of the Northern Liberties
[District of Philadelphia].

> *YOUR country calls for your assistance—the hour of danger is arrived . . . The mask is taken from the face of our false, perfidious friends, both at home and abroad . . . Shall the youthful arm of America be unnerved in the hour of danger . . . ? No, rise up, gird on the armour of defence . . .*

A number of persons having enrolled themselves for the purpose of forming a complete company of infantry, or artillery, as a majority deem most beneficial, invite their brethren of the Northern Liberties to follow their example . . . Information will be given to Mr. Samuel Gano, at the sign of the President of the United States, in Second-street, below the Court House.

SUNDAY, APRIL 1, 1798

Today, alarmed by the Federalist effort to organize their own private army (the Macpherson's Blues) and to arm "young men" against "perfidious friends . . . at home," Dr. George Logan meets with other Republican leaders in Germantown, outside Philadelphia.[237]

MONDAY, APRIL 2, 1798

GENERAL ★ AURORA ★ ADVERTISER

Mr. Adams . . . was careful in his extraordinary speech [of last May 16th] to make use of such indecent and provoking language to a [French] nation . . . as would banish every prospect of an immediate settlement.

The French nation, in order to make [Adams] appear perfectly ridiculous, have taken no notice either of him or his Commissioners [envoys] but have left him to put his great swelling words into execution.

Today, in the U.S. House of Representatives, the Annals of Congress report:

RELATIONS WITH FRANCE

Mr. VARNUM [Federalist, Massachusetts] presented a petition from the inhabitants of Milton, in Massachusetts, stating their alarm at the idea of the peace of the United States being placed in the hands of . . . the masters of merchant vessels, many of whom were formerly British subjects and . . . retain all their English prejudices against the French and may exert them in a manner which leads to war . . .

Mr. ALLEN [Federalist, Connecticut] called up for decision the resolution for certain papers [the Paris dispatches] from the President of the United States . . .

The question was taken, and decided in the affirmative—yeas 65, nays 27 . . .[238]

Today, James Madison writes Thomas Jefferson,

The President's message is only a further development to the public of the violent passions & heretical politics which have been long privately known to govern [John Adams]. It is to be hoped however the House of Representatives will not hastily echo them . . . Congress ought clearly to prohibit arming, & the President ought to be brought to declare on what ground he undertook to grant an indirect license to arm . . .[239]

Today, in Philadelphia, Polish author and poet Julien Niemcewicz notes in his diary:

The Barbary treaty [bribing the Barbary pirates to cease their attacks on American vessels] cost the United States 9 million doll[ars] . . . It is the journalist Beach [Bache] who has made public disclosure of this. This is one of the advantages of the freedom of the press: the government does not commit a fault but it is immediately criticized and denounced in the terrible tribunal of public opinion. Of all the means of enlightening a nation, that of public newspapers seems to me the best and the most easily accomplished.[240]

Julien Niemcewicz came to America last August with a Polish hero of the American Revolution, General Tadeusz Kosciuszko. Like Irishmen and Scotchmen, Poles flee despotism in their homeland to find freedom in America.

Kosciuszko fought without pay in America's revolution, returning to fight for Poland's independence from czarist Russia. Kosciuszko was captured, as was his adjutant, Niemcewicz, in 1794, released two years later by Russian Czar Paul I, and allowed to leave Poland in 1796, traveling first to Sweden and then to the United States.

Kosciuszko and Niemcewicz are settled in Philadelphia, where Niemcewicz makes note of America's interesting people and places. He has authored two travel books in Europe.[241]

Tonight, in the *Gazette of the United States*:

> You [Republicans] say the Tories have for many years been anxious to destroy the friendship between France and the United States . . . mentioning WASHINGTON and ADAMS . . . You say, Mr. ADAMS was tainted with the glare and pomp of [the British Royal Court of] St. James [when he was the American ambassador there] . . . Why was he not tainted with the much greater glare of the court of Versailles [in France]? We see him there with his excellent colleague Mr. JAY [during the American Revolution], baffling the intrigues of the [French Foreign Minister] Count de Vergennes and the more dangerous opposition of Dr. [Benjamin] Franklin until, by their firmness alone, we obtained the acknowledgment of our independence . . .   MARCUS

TUESDAY, APRIL 3, 1798

GENERAL ★ AURORA ★ ADVERTISER

The Tory newspapers of New England are crowded with invectives . . . against the late meeting in Roxbury to prevent the arming of merchantmen. They have met, however, with a spirited reception . . . The Resolutions of the freemen of Milton . . .

A hand bill has been circulated in the city recommending to the citizens immediately to arm themselves to crush their domestic foes. As we understand that this paper will probably be an object of legal prosecution, it is perhaps improper to say, in this place, any more concerning it.

Today, in Congress, the Annals report:

> A Message was announced from the PRESIDENT OF THE UNITED STATES . . .
>
> *Gentlemen of the Senate, and Gentlemen of the House of Representatives*
>
> In compliance with the request of the House of Representatives, expressed in their resolution of the 2nd of this month, I transmit to both Houses the instructions to and despatches from the Envoys Extraordinary of the United States to the French Republic which were mentioned in my Message of March 19th last, omitting only some names . . .
>
> UNITED STATES, *April 3, 1798.*   JOHN ADAMS

The above Message having been read, the galleries and House were cleared of strangers, and the House was occupied in reading the papers accompanying until past 3 o'clock, when they adjourned, without making any order respecting them.[242]

WEDNESDAY, APRIL 4, 1798

GENERAL ★ AURORA ★ ADVERTISER

A short view of the Question, whether it is advisable for the United States to enter into a war with France.

[T]he advocates for a war with France [say] . . . that our national honor hath been insulted . . . Those who speak . . . seem to forget that the existence of the United States as a nation is but of yesterday . . . Our late contest [the War of Independence] with Great Britain might have made us remember our imbecility and inaptitude for war. Defenceless on every side, the enemy changed the point of attack at every moment, and everywhere found us vulnerable and weak. The alliance of France . . . saved us from perdition. Have we forgot the portentous year when one half the United States was overrun by our enemy, when we were almost without an army, and that army [was] without money to subsist it? Have we forgotten the mission . . . to France, the object of the mission [being] the deplorable and just picture . . . to present [to France] of our distress, the relief we obtained, and its consequences? If we have not [forgotten], must we not be astonished that there are men among us who would hurry us into war with that very power whose succour alone saved us from perdition? And for what is such a state of danger to be hazarded? Truly, to compel France to receive our ambassadors!! . . .

JOHN FENNO has long been in the habit of harping upon the immense sums received by the Editor of the *Aurora* from the French Directory. His evidence of the fact we should be very glad to hear; and also what sums he himself gets from land jobbers, lottery ticket mongers, and British agents.

Report has been busy for these few days past in *decyphering* the dispatches lately received from our commissioners . . . They are said to contain information that the French had taken great exception at some of the speeches of our administration . . . as evidencing too much of a partiality for Britain . . . The dispatches are further said to contain overtures, on the part of some unacknowledged agents of the French, for money for themselves to smooth the way to reconciliation . . . We are . . . unable to state the contents of the dispatches except from report.

Tonight, John Fenno in the *Gazette of the United States*:

Bache, in the *Aurora* of this morning, has from *report* given to the public the contents of the dispatches from our commissioners which were yesterday laid before the two houses of Congress by the President as a confidential communication. Whether Mr. Bache received this information from *report* as he states or whether through the channel of some confidential friend, we shall probably be able to decide when those dispatches shall receive an official publication . . .

The chance of truth in the *Aurora* was always bad, but its editor has recently taken into employ some assistants which afford it no chance at all . . .

DEMOCRATS ALL IN AN UPROAR.

So alarmed are they at the proposal of some of the Young Men of the *Northern Liberties [District of Philadelphia]* associating, training themselves in the military exercise for the express purpose of supporting government that Doctor [George] L.[ogan] . . . went off to the Governor to endeavor to prevail on him to issue a proclamation to prevent the youth from holding such unprofitable associations . . .

THURSDAY, APRIL 5, 1798

GENERAL ★ AURORA ★ ADVERTISER

The Federal House of Representatives were yesterday debating, within closed doors, the propriety of publishing the papers received the day before from the President. There was no decision.

Today, the Senate votes to publish 500 copies of the dispatches.[243]

Tonight, in the *Porcupine's Gazette*:

TO THE AMERICAN YOUTH . . .

I can scarcely repress the indignation which rises in my bosom when I think of the manner we have been treated by France . . . Let us be united in assisting our government to obtain satisfaction for the insults . . . and evince to the world that . . . we possess the means . . . to punish the internal and external foes of our honour, freedom, and independence. J.

FRIDAY, APRIL 6, 1798

GENERAL ★ AURORA ★ ADVERTISER

The senate have resolved to publish the communication [of the dispatches] received from the president . . . This vote had a majority of *two* . . .

Tonight, in the *Gazette of the United States*:

Why, what sort of a man must this B. F. Bache be? His grand daddy was a dealer in almanacs, if I don't mistake . . . PLOUGHSHARE

THEATRE

A very crowded and splendid theatre assembled last evening . . . A general clamour was made for the PRESIDENT'S MARCH. When the tune was played, the uproar and applause from all quarters of the house were so general, so loud, and so incessant that very little of the tune was heard. Thus as our affections are withdrawn from foreign influence, the warmth of the public love and gratitude for our own worthy and real benefactors will return with redoubled vigour.

Tonight, in the *Porcupine's Gazette,* Peter Porcupine advertises a book he has co-published:

JUST PUBLISHED BY T. DOBSON & W. COBBETT
"PROOFS OF A CONSPIRACY AGAINST ALL
Religions And Governments OF EUROPE CARRIED ON IN THE
SECRET MEETINGS OF *FREE MASONS, ILLUMINATI,*
AND READING SOCIETIES."
COLLECTED FROM GOOD AUTHORITIES,
BY JOHN ROBISON, A.M. Professor of Natural Philosophy, and
Secretary to the Royal Society of Edinburgh . . . Price One Dollar and
Three Quarters in boards, and Two Dollars neatly bound and lettered.
The design of the work is to exhibit to the public the dangerous machi-
nations which, for many years, have been carried on . . . for debauching
the morals of the people and subverting their respect for religion to pave
the way for overturning the governments of Europe in order that, in the
state of anarchy which should succeed, the leaders of these secret cabals
might seize on the property and destroy the persons of their more opulent
neighbors . . .

With this view, their emissaries have spread far and wide over Ger-
many, France, England and America . . . and the Revolution in France,
. . . under the direction of those very individuals who are leaders of the
order, mark with distinguishing energy its peculiar features.

SATURDAY, APRIL 7, 1798

GENERAL ★ AURORA ★ ADVERTISER

Dispatches from the Envoys.

Until we are able to publish them in detail, we offer the following as a correct outline of their content . . . The Envoys had no regular inter-course with the French government . . . [T]hey were told that it would be necessary to . . . deposit . . . the sum of £50,000 sterling for . . . [French Foreign Minister] Talleyrand . . . [and] some members of the directory . . . The irritation occasioned by the President's speech [of last May 16th] was repeated . . . Mr. Talleyrand himself wrote some proposals . . . that the United States should lend a sum of money to France . . .

Remarks on the above.

We think it will appear from the above statement of facts that the negotiation ought not be considered as at an end . . . [I]f there was proof of the directory being concerned in the swindling of our commissioners (of which there is none) . . . it must leave opinion where it was;— That Mr. Talleyrand is notoriously anti-republican; that he was the intimate friend of Mr. Hamilton . . . and other great Federalists, and that it is probably owing to the determined hostility which he discovered in them towards France that the Government of that country consider us only as objects of plunder . . .

Today, Abigail Adams writes her sister,

The Senate on Thursday voted to have the dispatches from our Envoys made publick . . . [T]he President forbore to communicate them . . . But such lies and falsehoods were continually circulated and incendiary Letters sent to the house addrest to him that I have been allarmed for his Personal Safety, tho I have never before expressed it. With this temper in a city like this, materials for a mob might be brought together in 10 minuts. When the Language in Baches paper has been of the most insolent and abusive kind . . . and a call upon the people to Humble themselves before their Maker treated with such open contempt and Ridicule, had I not cause for allarm?[244]

MONDAY, APRIL 9, 1798

GENERAL ★ AURORA ★ ADVERTISER

The bulk of the dispatches relate to informal conferences held by unofficial agents of the department of foreign affairs with our commissioners in which the sum of £50,000 sterling was asked for as douceurs [bribes] to insure a reception . . .

Curiosity next seeks . . . whether these persons were agents of [French Foreign Minister] Talleyrand; and, if they were, whether they were authorized by Talleyrand to demand the £50,000 [bribe] . . .

It will be remembered that, not long since it was said in this paper that, in the office of the [U.S.] Secretary of State, money had been taken for passports which ought to have been given gratis. Mr. Pickering was very angry at being implicated and shewed that one of his clerks improperly took the money. Does not that case resemble the present one; and will not Talleyrand and the Directory be justifiable in shewing some resentment for having been suspected for the mis-doings of their inferior agents?[245]

War measures . . . Today, U.S. Secretary of War James McHenry writes the House Committee for the Protection of the Commerce, &c.:

War Department, April 9, 1798 . . .

France . . . prepares us for the last degree of humiliation and subjection. To forebear . . . from undertaking naval and military measures . . . would be to offer up the United States a certain prey to France . . .

The measures which appear indispensably necessary for Congress to take are as follows:

1st. An increase of the naval force . . . 2nd. An augmentation of the present military establishment. 3rd. Arrangements which in case of emergency will give the President . . . a further and efficacious military force. 4th. The more complete defence of our principal ports by fortifications. 5th. A supply of ordinance, small arms, powder, salt petre, copper, and military stores. 6th. Additional Revenue . . .

JAMES McHENRY[246]

Today, U.S. Secretary of State Timothy Pickering writes Federalist party leader Alexander Hamilton,

You will readily imagine what apologies our internal enemies make for the French Government. Jefferson says that the Directory are not implicated in the villainy and corruption displayed in these dispatches— or at least that these offer no proof against them. Bache's paper of last Saturday says "That M. Talleyrand is notoriously anti republican; that he was the intimate friend of Mr. Hamilton . . . and other great Federalists, and that it is probably owing to the determined hostility which he discovered in them towards France that the Government of that country consider us only as objects of plunder."[247]

TUESDAY, APRIL 10, 1798

GENERAL ★ AURORA ★ ADVERTISER

DISPATCHES
From our Envoys Extraordinary to France,
ordered to be published by the Senate . . .
[Excerpts] (No. 1)
PARIS, October 22, 1797

Dear Sir: ALL of us having arrived in Paris on the evening of the 4th instant . . . In the evening of [October the 18th], Mr. X called, and . . . whispered . . . that he had a message from M. Talleyrand . . . that the Directory . . . were exceedingly irritated at some passages of the President's [May 16th] Speech and desired that they should be softened, and that this step would be necessary previous to our reception. That, besides this, a sum of money was required for the pocket of the Directory and Ministers, which would be at the disposal of Mr. Talleyrand; and that a loan [to France] would be insisted on . . . On inquiry Mr. X . . . mentioned that the *douceur* [bribe] for the pocket was twelve thousand livres, about fifty thousand pounds sterling . . .

October the 21st, Mr. X came before nine o'clock; Mr. Y did not come until ten: he had passed the morning with Mr. Talleyrand . . . [H]e proceeded to state . . . the measure would be an advance by us to France of thirty-two millions [Dutch florins] . . . We asked him whether the fifty thousand pounds sterling, as a *douceur* to the Directory, must be in addition to this sum. He answered in the affirmative . . .

(No. 2) October 27th, 1797

About twelve we received another visit from Mr. X . . . He told us that we [the United States] had paid money to obtain peace with the Algerines [the Barbary pirates] and with the Indians; and that it was doing no more to pay France for peace . . . He said that France had lent us money during our revolution war and only required that we should now exhibit the same friendship . . . He said he would communicate as nearly as he could our conversation to the Minister or to Mr. Z . . .

(The remainder in our next.)

The French will not formally receive Adams' envoys without a recanting of his anti-French speech of last May 16th, without a U.S. loan to France, and without a U.S. *douceur* to calm the French Directory. In the meantime, French Foreign Minister Talleyrand deals with our envoys through informal intermediaries whose identities are concealed as X, Y, and Z in the dispatches presented to Congress.[248]

Today, President Adams writes Federalist party leader Alexander Hamilton:

> *The papers relative to the negotiation which has been attempted with France have been laid before Congress . . . The dose will kill or cure, and I wish I was not uncertain which. Not that I doubt the expediency of what the government has done or attempted, but because I believe faction and Jacobinism to be the natural and immortal enemies of our system.*[249]

Public excitement about the dispatches brings crowds to this afternoon's presidential "levee" (audience). Peter Porcupine reports,

> [T]he PRESIDENT'S LEVEE . . . was by far the most crowded that has ever been since the commencement of the Federal government . . .[250]

Not everyone is so enthusiastic. Today, Julien Niemcewicz, the Polish writer, visits Stenton, the 450–acre farm that peace petitioner and Quaker leader George Logan owns in Germantown, outside Philadelphia. The visit is short, as Poor Richard suggested:

> *Visits should be short, like a winters day,*
> *Lest you're too troublesome, hasten away.*[251]

Julien Niemcewicz notes in his diary:

> [W]e left . . . in a cabriolet [two-wheeled carriage] to see Dr. Logan,
> the celebrated farmer and celebrated fanatic, living near Germantown
> . . . [H]is house . . . is of brick, large and well kept. A smooth lawn like
> a green carpet, sown with groups of cedars and Hemlocks extended
> before one's eye.
>   Doctor Logan received us civilly but with an air of preoccupation
> and pain. We did not wait long to discover the source of his ills. It was
> a preoccupation, a fixation, indeed a madness. He was convinced that
> his country was the most unhappy on earth, that it was menaced by
> the greatest dangers, that is to say, by total destruction. The authors of
> all these . . . calamities were the English; they had bought and cor-
> rupted the government . . . This was the subject of the conversation be-
> fore dinner. Mrs. Logan, pale, with a rather good figure, has caught the
> same disease . . . [H]er discourses carried indeed more vehemence
> than those of her husband. The dinner was frugal but good . . .
>   After . . . , they began to sing the praises of, to render homage to the
> virtues of the nation which has revenged humanity so long oppressed
> . . . They began to praise the French up to the skies . . .
>   Madman, I said to myself, You do not know what you want . . . But
> go to France; go to Europe; see what goes on there and you will return
> cured of your madness.[252]

What Julien Niemcewicz doesn't know is that George Logan is going to France.
If Adams can't make peace, George Logan will! Poor Richard wrote,

> *God helps them that helps themselves.*[253]

Tonight, in the *Porcupine's Gazette*, Peter Porcupine writes:

> I said that not even the damning proofs . . . in the DISPATCHES would
> operate any material change in the politics or the conduct of the French
> faction here. BACHE, who is the mouthpiece of that infernal crew, has
> proved the assertion true [in yesterday's *Aurora*]. He denies not the au-
> thenticity of the DISPATCHES; he *dares* not do that: but he denies that
> the persons who made the insolent overtures to the envoys were author-
> ized by the French government . . .
>   BACHE publishes to *rogues* and *fools*. The former are the approbators,
> the supports, and sometimes the authors of his shameless misrepresen-
> tations and infamous falsehoods; the latter, he well knows, have not the
> capacity to detect him . . . Bache has amply proved the Jacobins will still
> remain the same; yet . . . [t]his is a dreadful stroke to the French Faction.

[H]aving completely sailed round the world of sedition, [CALLENDER]
has hove his shattered and disfigured bark into the harbour of Citizen
Benjamin Franklin Bache, the Grandson of Old Ben and the ample inher-
itor of all his factious principles. This BACHE . . . is the sworn enemy of

this government and the notorious hireling of France . . . [T]he wretch had the audacity openly to call GENERAL WASHINGTON a *legalizer of corruption* and an *assassin*; . . . he has *justified* the French in all their depredations, their robberies, their cruelties, and their insults heaped on America . . . [and] he has now the infamy to *justify* the last instance of their turpitude and perfidy, as exposed in the *Dispatches* just received from our envoys in Paris.

WEDNESDAY, APRIL 11, 1798

GENERAL ★ AURORA ★ ADVERTISER

DISPATCHES
From our Envoys Extraordinary to France,
ordered to be published by the Senate . . .

(concluded from our last.)

October 30th [1797] . . .

Mr. Y then called our attention to our own situation . . . Perhaps, said he, that you believe that, in returning and exposing to your countrymen the unreasonableness of the demands of this government, you will unite them in their resistance to those demands: you are mistaken: you ought to know that the diplomatic skill of France and the means she possesses in your country are sufficient to enable her, with the French party in America, to throw the blame which will attend the rupture of the nego-ciations on the federalists, as you term yourselves, but on the British party as France terms you . . .

The dispatches from France fully occupy today's *Philadelphia Aurora, Gazette of the United States*, and *Porcupine's Gazette*.

THURSDAY, APRIL 12, 1798

GENERAL ★ AURORA ★ ADVERTISER

[Adv.] TO THE CURIOUS.
A Beautiful African
L I Ö N.

To be seen everyday (Sundays excepted) at Mr. I. Chambers, Sign of the Plough, in Third-street, near Market street . . . Great attention has been paid in providing a strong and substantial cage and to have the L I O N under very good command . . . [I]t is said by those who have seen LIONS in the Tower of London and many other parts that he is really worth the contemplation of the curious. Admittance for Ladies and Gentlemen, One Q U A R T E R of a DOLLAR and Children, Half Price.

Poor Richard said,

Kings & Bears often worry their keepers.[254]

What did he think about lions? The lion's cage is around the corner from the *Aurora*!

War measures . . . Today, in the U.S. House of Representatives, the Annals of Congress report:

ADDITIONAL ARTILLERY, &c . . .

Mr. GALLATIN [Republican, Pennsylvania]: He agreed that the probability of a war is greater than it has been at any former period. He would not make any remarks on what has drawn us into this situation. But, among the causes, he would beg leave to mention the publication of the late despatches . . . (The CHAIRMAN said this remark was not in order.) Mr. G. said . . . he meant to state only that the publication of these papers had destroyed the hope . . . (A cry of order.) Mr. G. wished to know what was in order . . . [H]e contended that it was the duty of the House to be cautious . . . [T]o increase the artillery corps sixteen companies instead of eight . . . he did not think necessary. Is there, said Mr. G., any person on this floor seriously afraid of an invasion. He was sure there was not . . .

Mr. DAYTON (the speaker) [Federalist, New Jersey] said that the speech of the member from Pennsylvania (Mr. GALLATIN) in opposition to the amendment of increasing the corps of artillerists and engineers must be considered as the exhibition of another leaf of that favorite book in which was written the system of his uniform opposition to all measures of the Administration . . .[255]

Tonight, in the *Gazette of the United States*:

The late French faction has died . . . The recent exposure . . . has proved to them like the shock of some vast explosion . . . Mazzei [i.e., Jefferson] may still remain Vice-President of the turbulent and factious; but, his adherents cut off . . . he stands an awkward and misplaced Colossus . . .

Tonight, Federalists meet at John Dunwoody's tavern, several squares west of the *Aurora* (that is, away from the Delaware) on the opposite side of High-street.[256] Joseph Thomas, a prominent lawyer and Philadelphia Federalist leader who lives in Third-street,[257] is among the organizers of the meeting. The meeting issues a notice:

At a numerous and respectable meeting of the citizens of the city of Philadelphia, District of Southwark, and Northern Liberties, held in Dunwoody's tavern on the evening of the 12th of April, 1798,
Colonel GURNEY in the chair,
It was *Resolved Unanimously,* as the sense of this meeting, that the information contained in the Dispatches . . . is of a nature to excite universal alarm throughout America . . .

Resolved Unanimously, That the measures pursued by the President of the United States . . . have been wise . . .

Resolved Unanimously, That an Address and Memorial expressive of the sentiments . . . be presented to the President . . .

Resolved, that the following gentlemen be a committee to prepare the address . . . [Philadelphia Federalist leader] Joseph Thomas . . . [Federalist ship builder and defense contractor] Joshua Humphreys . . . [&c.]"—[258]

This is not a gathering of Benny's friends. Joshua Humphreys' son, Clement Humphreys, attacked Benny in the family shipyard last year. Joseph Thomas is John Fenno's friend[259] and someone not to be trusted. As Poor Richard said,

> *Don't judge of Mens Wealth or Piety,*
> *by their Sunday Appearances.*[260]

FRIDAY, APRIL 13, 1798

GENERAL ★ AURORA ★ ADVERTISER

I feel sensibly both the injury and the insults in the refusal [of the French] to receive and treat [negotiate] with our ambassadors . . . though I think it probable that both proceeded from our having abandoned our neutral station by the British Treaty [the Jay Treaty of 1795] . . . To arm our merchant ships for defence would undoubtedly be proper if we could secure against their acting offensively and bringing on a war which it is supposed they would do. But there is another difficulty. To permit the arming against France when Britain is also daily taking our vessels would be strange, and yet, is it intended to arm against Great Britain? . . .

The Citizens of Dorchester in Massachusetts have had a meeting on the present critical state of affairs, and have entered into spirited resolutions *against arming.* Number of votes 110, of whom 101 were for the resolution.

The Citizens of Cambridge in Massachusetts have also had a meeting; when it was declared the sense of the town that there is now more need than ever of restrictions upon arming.

Today, Thomas Jefferson notes in his journal:

> *The Presidt. has sent a govmt brig to France, probably to carry despatches. He has chosen as the bearer of these one Humphreys, the son of a ship carpenter, ignorant, under age, not speaking a word of French, most abusive of that nation, whose only merit is having mobbed & beaten Bache on board the frigate built here, for which he was indicted & punished by fine.*[261]

Today, Grand Jurors of Pennsylvania's U.S. District Court address the President of the United States:

Sir, we hesitate not to declare it is our firm belief, notwithstanding the opinion of the enemies of America, that the great mass of our fellow citizens approve of your administration . . .

JOHN LARDNER, Foreman[262]

Tonight, in the *Porcupine's Gazette*:

Much conjecture has been afloat respecting the famous peace petition that this preaching Apothecary [Quaker Samuel Weatherill] was hawking about some days ago. According to the best accounts I have been able to gather, SAMMY was busy amongst his chemical matters when a bottle of oil of vitriol broke; some of it got into his pocket and burnt up the petition: and thus came to a timely end the darling hopes of . . . Callender, Dr. Logan, Bache, ["Newgate"] Lloyd, and Company.

Tonight, in the *Gazette of the United States*:

At a numerous and respectable meeting of the citizens of the city of Philadelphia, District of Southwark and Northern Liberties, held in Dunwoody's tavern [last evening] . . . citizens of almost every profession attended . . . [O]ne sentiment appeared to animate every mind—a firm resolution to rally round the government . . . Many were present who have heretofore greatly differed in political opinions. Upon this important occasion, laying aside all local politics and party views, they came forward and joined in the unanimous vote. May Americans ever thus rally round their own *standard when their country calls.*

MONDAY, APRIL 16, 1798

GENERAL ★ AURORA ★ ADVERTISER

[T]here has been a systematic effort in the part of the administration to alienate this country from France and to attach it to Great Britain . . . Evidence cannot be stronger . . . The memorable declaration of the late President [Washington] that the friends of France were *"the partisans of war and confusion"* [is] . . . proof of this position . . .

Today, George Washington writes Secretary of State Timothy Pickering,

One would think that the measure of infamy was filled and the profligacy of and the corruption of the system pursued by the French Directory required no further disclosure of the principles by which it is actuated than what is contained in the above Dispatches, to open the eyes of the blindest; and yet I am persuaded that those communications will produce no change in the leaders of the opposition unless there should appear a manifest desertion of their followers. There is sufficient evidence already, in the Aurora, of the turn they intend to give the business and of the ground they mean to occupy; but I do not believe they will be able to maintain that or any other much longer."[263]

Tonight, in the *Gazette of the United States*:

A new edition of jacobin lies is now running through the *Aurora* . . . *Publicity* is all the cry with the anti-american gallic [French] faction . . . It is not known that the United States have a press in France devoted to the cause of this country, but that France has presses in the United States devoted to her interest is most true. This is not fair play; the French papers in this country ought to be silent till we get one at least established in France.

Tonight, in the *Porcupine's Gazette*:

BACHE (old Franklin's grandson) was sued some time ago for [import] duties to the amount of about forty dollars, and judgment has been taken out during this present Federal court.—*Question*—Were not these duties for the edition of [Tom] Paine's *Age of Reason* [against established religion] which was imported from Paris ?

The merchants, underwriters, and traders of this city will meet at the Coffee House to-morrow at 12 o'clock for the purpose of presenting their address to the President of the United States.

TUESDAY, APRIL 17, 1798

GENERAL ★ AURORA ★ ADVERTISER

The spirit of opposition to the arming of our merchantmen is gradually augmenting. Several memorials on that head . . . were yesterday presented to Congress. For some days past, Mr. Fenno has been more than usually elated and abusive. The extreme length of the public papers [the *Aurora* has been publishing] . . . hath suspended our paragraphical rejoinders. But the people of Massachusetts are coming round to the right point of the Political Compass with so much haste that our efforts may well be spared. The respective town meetings of Roxbury, Milton, Cambridge, Arlington, Bridgewater and Randolph have reprobated in the strongest terms the proposal of arming the merchant vessels . . .

Today, at noon, Philadelphia's merchants and traders present an address, with five hundred signatures, to the President:

To the President of the United States . . . —The address of the Merchants, Underwriters and Traders of the city of Philadelphia.

RESPECTFULLY SHEWETH,

That the Merchants, Underwriters and traders of Philadelphia . . . cannot but express their deep regret at the failure of the late attempt to negotiate with [the French Republic] . . .

As Americans, jealous of the honor and attached to the freedom of our country, we repel with indignation every attempt to separate us from the government of our choice . . .

Under the impulse of these sentiments, we come forward to . . . give our sincere firm support to the measures which may be adopted . . .[264]

Today, Abigail Adams writes her sister,

The publick opinion is changeing here very fast . . . I am told that the [tri-colour] French Cockade, so frequent in the streets here, is not now to be seen, and the Common People say if J.[efferson] had been our President . . . we should all have been sold to the French . . .[265]

Today, in the U.S. House of Representatives, the Annals of Congress report:

NATURALIZATION OF FOREIGNERS

Mr. COIT [Federalist, Connecticut] . . . proposed a resolution to the following effect: *Resolved,* That the committee appointed for the protection of commerce and the defence of our country be directed to inquire and report whether it be not expedient to suspend . . . the act establishing a uniform rule of naturalization.[266]

Under current law, immigrants can be naturalized as American citizens after five years' residency, and it has been five years since the war between Britain and France propelled European democrats to seek refuge in America from King George III's Alien and Sedition Acts and French leader Robespierre's temporary Reign of Terror. These refugees are Irish dissidents like John Daly Burk, Dr. Jimmy Reynolds, "Newgate" Lloyd, and me, Scotch dissenters like Jimmy Callender, true French democrats like Moreau de St. Méry and Constantin Volney. Will the Federalists deny them citizenship?

Tonight, in the *Gazette of the United States*:

THE MANAGERS OF THE THEATRE—

Should pay some respect to the public feeling in the selection of their music—The enthusiastic clamors and applause with which the President's March has been called for and received for some time past should have taught the managers the impropriety of refusing it to the people until absolutely compelled to give it. As the patriotic enthusiasm increases, such an unwillingness to gratify it may be dangerous to the fiddles and the fiddlers. For the same reason it is to be hoped no more attempts will be made to grate and torture the public ear with those shouts [for] *Ca Ira* . . .

"Ça Ira" is the great song of the French Revolution which honors Benjamin Franklin. Frenchmen remember that, when asked how America's revolution was going, Ben Franklin frequently replied, "*Ça ira. Ça ira.*" (*It will work out! It will work out!*)[267]

"*To the Congress of the United States, the subscribers, people of the county of Caroline and State of Virginia, beg leave to represent . . .*

That war is an evil . . . The refusal of a government to regard the invocation of the people for averting war would be sufficient to excite a suspicion that it is guided by other views than the public good, especially as though a nation seldom makes an advantage by war, a government often does. Soldiers and money, to the people the expense, to a government are the fruits of war . . ."

Today, an anonymous party writes President Adams that his May 9th prayer and fasting day will be a day of murder and mayhem:

Much respected Sir,

There is generally so little attention paid to anonymous letters that I have little to hope, but the present occasion is so unprecedented that I cannot avoid giving way to the impulse of the moment and have therefore acted accordingly. Conscious of the rectitude of my intentions and convinced that I am barely doing my duty, I feel little repugnance at betraying the horrid designs of a barbarous set of wretches who are unworthy of the names of human beings. Know Sir, that it is the fix'd resolve of a very numerous party of Frenchmen (in conjunction with a few other unsuspected Characters) to set fire to several different parts of this City on the night of that day (in May next) which is set apart by you as a day of solemn fasting & prayer, and when the whole attention of the devoted Citizens is engaged, they intend to massacre Man, Woman & Child, save those who are friendly to their interests. More I dare not write, but let it suffice, that my information is genuine. How I came by it must for ever remain an inviolable secret, my honour is partly pledged and that will plead my excuse . . .

> *An unfortunate misled Man*
> *but a real friend to America*[268]

Tonight, in the *Gazette of the United States*:

Yesterday at noon a large and respectable body of the Merchants of this city waited on the President of the United States . . .

ANSWER.

To the Merchants, Underwriters, and Traders of the City of Philadelphia.

If the sincere sentiments of my heart toward France, which are now open before the public, had met with a similar disposition in the government of that country, we should still have pursued our neutral, impartial, and pacific course. But unhappily they have met with nothing that I can discern but a determined, though insidious spirit of hostility. The consequences are not for me to anticipate.

JOHN ADAMS

The Gallic Editor of the *Aurora* is known to be in daily and secret conference with a certain high officer in the Government (infamous for his *foreign correspondence*). It is supposed the fruits of this republican connection will be thrown on the parish before long for public maintenance. The brat may gasp, but it will surely die in the infamy of its parents.

Benny Bache is meeting with Thomas Jefferson who is *"infamous"* for his correspondence with Philip Mazzei in Italy.

The drama of Philadelphia is expressed in meetings. Poor Richard noted,

Men meet, mountains never.[269]

THURSDAY, APRIL 19, 1798

GENERAL ★ AURORA ★ ADVERTISER

John Fenno, in his paper of last evening, says that "the Gallic Editor of the *Aurora* is known to be in daily and secret conference with a certain high officer in government, *infamous for his foreign correspondence*.

Mr. Bache has been for some days in the country. As for the officer of government, we do not pretend to know who is meant; but, as John abuses him, we presume that he must be some character eminently respectable in the eyes of honest men.

It cannot be that John Fenno who, at an early period of life stopt payment and defrauded his creditors in Boston and who, ever since, has been the dirty tool of a dirty faction should know what the word *infamy* means.

We are informed that ten memorials were on Monday read in congress against the arming of our merchantmen . . . Poor Johnny Fenno vilifies the subscribers of the New England memorials as Jacobins. He says that the town meetings were not *regularly called*, &c. &c. Let the friends of order call counter meetings and try, if they can, [to] get counter memorials.

An address has been presented [April 13] by a Grand Jury of the District Court of the United States to the President . . . [T]hey neglected to inform the public . . . that [the grand jurors] are the creatures of the Marshall of the district and that the Marshall is the creature of the President. The address must then be viewed as an address of the President to himself. Whether such a grand jury was selected for *party purposes* is not mentioned . . . We have already seen judges [who were] appointed by the President turn preachers of certain political opinions, and now we see Grand Juries converted into party apostles.

Benny is at Settle, the beautiful farm his father owns, about sixteen miles south of Philadelphia along the Delaware River.[270] Today, Polish writer Julien Niemcewicz travels downriver with Benny's twenty-five-year-old doctor brother, William, for a visit to the Bache farm. Niemcewicz makes note in his diary:

> *I embarked with Dr. Bache on a boat which performed the office of a carriage and leaves at each flood tide for Burlington . . . The weather was rather fine, but the wind very weak. We enjoyed the beauty of both banks of Jersey and Pennsylvania completely at our ease . . . After three and a half hours we arrived at the farm of Mr. [Richard] Bache, the father. He is the husband of the daughter of [Benjamin] Franklin, celebrated American philosopher and patriot.*
>
> *Mr. [Richard] Bache has completely the air of a Country Esquire, frank countenance and with a rather jovial humor. Madame by her natural wit and her conversation does not belie the origin from which she descends. We found there the whole family assembled with the exception of a little boy who was at school in Burlington. It consisted of three sons, of whom the first, Benjamin is the printer known for his opposition newspaper . . . The second son was the doctor [William] with whom I came, an interesting young man. The third, Louis [age nineteen], was destined to be a farmer; three girls, one of ten [Sarah] and two of marriageable age [Elizabeth, twenty-one, and Deborah, seventeen or eighteen]. They were very pretty and were neatly dressed, and nothing was more natural nor more touching than their behavior toward their parents. While one was holding his hand and leaning on her father (seated in an armchair at one time belonging to Dr. [Ben] Franklin), she was caressing him; the other was singing very well, accompanying herself on the harpsichord. The good old man joined at times his bass voice to the piping voice of his daughter . . .*
>
> *Mr. Bache has a farm of 270 acres divided into meadows, cultivated ground and woodland. He has five men to work it and a gardener; a Negro and one girl do the domestic service . . . Fish, salt beef with all sorts of vegetables made up the dinner. The mush, a kind of gruel [porridge] from Indian Corn with milk added made a healthy and frugal supper.[271]*

Today, Thomas Jefferson writes James Madison,

> *[P]etitions to Congress against arming from the towns of Massachusetts were multiplying. They will no doubt have been immediately checked. The P.[resident]'s answer to the address of the merchants here you will see in Fenno of yesterday. It is a pretty strong declaration that a neutral & pacific conduct on our part is no longer the existing state of things. The vibraters in the H.[ouse] of R.[epresentatives] have chiefly gone over to the war party.[272]*

Tonight, in the *Gazette of the United States:*

MR. FENNO, The observations of Bache in the *Aurora* of this morning respecting the Grand Jury are worthy of himself. The wretch cannot write but to abuse—nor speak but to vilify. I would advise him not to leave his Press, for he may be assured there will be as much business shortly as he and his friend Callender can attend to. Addresses from all parts of the Union are coming forward, and it is his DUTY to attack them because they express the determination of the People to support the government—"The Grand Jury, he observes, are the creatures of the Marshall." I was one of that body, and I assert he is a *Liar*.

It would be degrading indeed if there should be a man in the United States who would hesitate for a moment [as] to whose assertion to attach the most credit, to that of any one of the late Jury or that of Benjamin Franklin Bache. I have not time just now to say as much to this man as I could wish. I will, however, recommend to him to discharge the Notes which he gave to his paper makers and which, since last October, have been laying protested in one of the Banks of this city before he says anything about Credit.　　　　　ONE OF THE LATE GRAND JURY.

Is it not high time to enquire who are these traitors, who have sold their country and are ready to deliver it to the French? . . . Look around you to those who have been the associates of these French incendiaries, their agents at meetings, at clubs, their news-writers and panegyrists . . . Whose houses are the resort of Frenchmen, and who are always in French company? Mark the public men who go hand in hand with French agents, who declaim against the purity of their own government and its measures, while on the other hand they set up corrupt France as a pattern of all that is excellent. These men cannot be all honest. Some of them have Judas-like accepted the price of the blood of their friends and are preparing to betray them. Let us watch them closely for when our country is at stake, when we are told by our enemies that it is already sold, suspicion becomes a virtue.

Extract of a letter from Massachusetts . . . Communications from Phila-delphia mention we may expect a list of *traitors* will soon be published . . . It certainly would not wound our humane feelings so much to see *such* criminals go to execution as the petty robber or house breaker . . .

Federalist "committees of surveillance" are spying on leading Republicans such as Thomas Jefferson, Benny Bache, and George Logan.[273] George Logan's wife, Deborah, will recall,

> *The dominant party scorned any longer to affect even the appear-*
> *ance of moderation toward their opponents. Not only the public acts of*
> *the Legislature were framed to keep them in awe . . . Friendships were*
> *dissolved, tradesmen dismissed, and custom withdrawn from the Re-*
> *publican party, the heads of which, as object of the most injurious sus-*

picion, were recommended to be closely watched, and committees of Federalists were appointed for that purpose.

Many gentlemen went armed that they might be ready to resent any personal aggression. In the midst of this state of things, my husband formed the project of his visit to France . . .[274]

Republicans know their neighbors are spying on them. As Poor Richard said,

Love thy Neighbour; yet don't pull down your Hedge.[275]

Tonight, in the *Porcupine's Gazette*:

Some musicians last night and the evening before had the audacious impudence to refuse playing the President's March [at the New Theatre] although requested by the box and the greater part of the house. [I r]eprobate strongly the action of pelting the musicians, but [I] would have preferred the . . . dignified conduct of leaving the theatre and refrain going thither until the managers positively declared the President's March should be for the future the first tune played in the house and further give assurance that those Gallic murder-shouts, Ça Ira . . . shall no more grate our ears.

FRIDAY, APRIL 20, 1798

GENERAL   ★ AURORA ★   ADVERTISER

The short administration of the present chief magistrate [Mr. Adams] . . . has added considerably in producing the present catastrophe . . . It was this speech [to Congress on last May 16th] which interposed the barrier to an adjustment of our differences with the French Republic. It was this speech which prevented the recognition of our envoys by the [French] Directory . . . The impolicy and intemperance of Mr. Adams may yet entail great evils upon the United States.

Today, in the U.S. House of Representatives, a Federalist congressman attacks the *Aurora*. The Annals of Congress report:

Mr. ALLEN [Federalist, Connecticut], Let me add, as no contemptible engine in this business of sowing discord, dissension, and distrust of the Government, a vile incendiary paper published in this city, which constantly teems with the most atrocious abuse of all measures of the Government and its administrators. A flood of calumny is constantly poured forth against those whom the people have chosen as the guardians of the nation. The privilege of franking letters is abused in sending this paper into all parts of the country; and the purest characters are, through this medium, prostrated and laid low in the view of the people. No nation, no Government was ever so insulted. In another country, this printer and his supporters would long ago have found a *fourth of September* [day of judgment and execution]; and this paper is well known always to speak the

81

sentiments of, and to be supported by, certain gentlemen in this House. These, sir, are the fruits of "the diplomatic skill of France"—these are the effects of her "means"—these are the effects of "her party in this country."[276]

As Poor Richard said,

> At this Season 'tis no wonder
> if we have clouds, hail, rain and thunder.[277]

And so we do. A visitor describes today's weather:

> [W]e had a thunderstorm, lightening, and a deluge of rain. The thunder is more terrible here than in Europe. Its rolls spread out through the whole heaven with a din which at times imitates cannon fire, at times the rolling fire which passes from one flank to another of a large army. The whole firmament was covered with streaks of lightning; it all finished with a deluge of rain and hail.[278]

Tonight, in the *Porcupine's Gazette,* Peter Porcupine writes:

> No man is bound to pay the least respect to the feelings of *Bache.* He has outraged every principle of decency, of morality, of religion and of nature. I should have no objection to the boys' spitting on him as he goes along the street, if it were not that I think they would confer on him too much honour . . .

Tonight, in the *Gazette of the United States*:

> In that detestable sink of pollution, Bache's paper, the thermometer of the [Jacobin] faction, we already see apologies for French enormities . . . [The French] tell us . . . they have the "means" and the skill to prevent our making one generous effort for independence . . . The first attempt to exhibit their skill is displayed by their creature Bache. He has undertaken to prove that Talleyrand . . . was not authorized by his government to make the corrupt proposals . . .
>
> ---
>
> It is highly probable that this expatriated Scot [Callender], this fugitive from the pillory . . . has fixed his residence in Pennsylvania . . . for the mildness of her penal code. But let this miscreant reflect, if war is approaching . . . that the conduct of traitors will then be closely scrutinized.—That in this case, his worthless carcass may be destined to swell the measure of Federal despotism, as that government has not yet evinced its philanthropy by the abolition of the gallows . . . Mr. Adams will not *retire from office* . . . He will proceed as he has begun, and he will be supported too by all that deserve the name of Americans . . .
>
> THE FEDERALIST

Tonight, Vice President Thomas Jefferson finds solace in the capacious rooms of Philosophical Hall, home of the American Philosophical Society.[279] On the east side of the State-house park, Philosophical Hall overlooks Fifth-street, the Court House, and the Philadelphia Library. The society and the library owe their founding to Benjamin Franklin. Moreau de St. Méry observes:

> In a niche above the entrance on the front of the Philadelphia Library (opposite the Philosophical Society) is a white marble statue of Benjamin Franklin a little larger than life size. He wears a Roman robe, and his left arm rests on several books piled on top of a column . . .[280]
>
> [The Philosophical] Society occupies several rooms on the first floor of a building south of the Court House. The room for meetings has a long table on the south side of which the president sits alone in a shabby armchair which Franklin had long used as a desk chair and which he himself had occupied when president of the society. On the wall behind the president is an oil painting of this venerable philosopher . . .[281]

The American Philosophical Society meets two to four times each month. Thomas Jefferson, its president, presides. Tonight's meeting agrees to refinance a loan originally made to the society by Benjamin Franklin and now held by Benny's father, Richard Bache. The meeting also elects four new members, including Polish writer Julien Niemcewicz, who visited Richard Bache's farm just yesterday.[282]

SATURDAY, APRIL 21, 1798

GENERAL ★ AURORA ★ ADVERTISER

The following circumstance which took place at the Theatre on Wednesday Evening last may be depended on as a fact . . . Mr.****, a member of the Federalist Legislature from New Jersey, accompanied by some other *gentlemen,* left their seats in the boxes, came into the gallery and began to vociferate for the President's March. The horrid noise . . . created some alarm in the citizens in every part of the house, who imagined these men had broken out of the Lunatic Hospital . . . *These are Federalists, the supporters of Order and Good Government!!*

The managers of the Theatre ought to beware how they suffer the theatre to be converted to a political engine. Men of all political creeds resort there . . . Besides, Mr. Adams was not the choice of the people there, and to aim at thrusting him down their throats will produce something like resistance . . .

Extract of a letter . . . I find most good men look on the President's Proclamation for Fasting, Humiliation and Prayer throughout the States as one of those apparently humble, hypocritical and delusive methods Tyrants have universally began the foundation for oppressing the people with . . .

The *federalists* . . . are giving daily proof of their love of order, decency, unanimity, &c. &c. In the Gazette of the United States, a paper patronized by Mr. Adams, Mr. Jefferson is spoken of as a man *"infamous for his foreign correspondence."* Is this a stile suited to the second officer in the government . . . ? Is this a language suited to this moment when the calls are so loud for union?

The Federalist mob is calling Young Men into their private army. They are vociferating at the theatre. Poor Richard feared the mob:

> *A Mob's a Monster; Heads enough, but no brains.*[283]

The President's wife, Abigail, endorses the call for presidential music. Today, she fumes,

> *Bache has the malice & falshood of Satin . . . But the wretched will provoke to measures which will silence them e'er long. An abused and insulted publick cannot tollerate them much longer. In short they are so criminal that they ought to be Presented by the grand jurors.*[284]

Tonight, in the *Porcupine's Gazette*:

> Bache's observations on the call for the President's March at the theatre is perfectly consistent with himself. Any expression indicative of attachment to the federal government is certain of his disapprobation & always serves to excite the corrosion that is destroying his malignant heart, where envy, baseness, and every passion which render a mortal detestable to those who have the slightest attachment to truth and virtue, have fixed their abode. Continue, base lying wretch; you cannot offer the public a more efficacious antidote to the poison you have disseminated than by publishing your remarks on the government and its friends.

Tonight, in the *Gazette of the United States*:

> THE UNGUARDED CONFESSION.
> Bache a few days past affected entire ignorance of the *"high officer"* alluded to in Mr. Fenno's paper as *"infamous for his foreign correspondence."* And this morning, by sudden illumination, he asserts and takes it for granted that *Jefferson* is the man.—Pray did Mr. Fenno tell him so, or has Mr. Jefferson been complaining to him of the blow? In either case, the application of the charge rests not with Mr. Fenno. Bache himself is the author of the slander (if such he deems it) against his beloved Vice President.

Tonight, Federalists are at Jim Cameron's Tavern in Southwark for a dinner arranged by naval contractor Joshua Humphreys (whose son, Clement, assaulted Benny Bache last April), by Peter Miercken (who will someday assault me), and by Philadelphia Federalist leader and attorney Joseph Thomas,[285] who reports, *"the glow of enthusiasm . . . caught from man to man, and gave to the ears of Southwark a sound to which she had been too long unaccustomed!"*[286] The *Gazette of the United States* reports:

[N]ear a hundred staunch Federalists assembled at James Cameron's tavern, Shippen-street, in the district of Southwark, to partake of an elegant dinner . . . For the convenience of accommodating so large a group, the tables were laid out in the Ball Alley, sheltered from the weather by two large sails extending from end to end. Over the head of the President waved . . . the banner of Freedom, the Eagle of the United States . . . During the intervals of the following toasts, several songs composed for the occasion were sung. The incessant huzzas gave . . . hearty acclamations of genuine Patriotism:

T O A S T S.

1. The Constitution of the United States . . . 9 cheers . . . 2. The President of the United States . . . 9 cheers . . . 3. George Washington . . . 9 cheers . . . 5. The American people—May they banish . . . those who have shown a disposition to degrade their country—9 cheers . . . 9. Death to Jacobin principles throughout the world . . . 9 cheers. 10. May France soon learn . . . that we are not a divided people in the cause of our country . . . 9 cheers . . . 14. May the wretches among us on whom France calculates for our destruction be speedily detected and punished . . . 9 cheers . . . 19. May all men detest the wretch who would justify foreign depravity at the expense of his own country . . . 9 cheers . . .

VOLUNTEERS.

By . . . William Clifton, jun. Joseph Thomas . . . without whose patriotic exertions . . . the pleasures of this meeting would never have been enjoyed—9 cheers

After the President withdrew

Joshua Humphries [Federalist navy contractor] —9 cheers.[287]

At this dinner, Federalists sing some new words to an old tune, "The Sages of Old." Its second verse includes:

> *Benny Bache and his crew*
> *To the Devil we'll throw . . .*
> *Then Rebellion will cease*
> *And the world be at peace*
> *No longer we'll fear the "dread nation."*[288]

From such songs and such dinners bad things can come, but, as Poor Richard said,

Tis easy to see, hard to foresee.[289]

If the sincerity of Mr. Adams to restore harmony among the two Republics had been equal to his professions, it would not have displayed itself in bustle and heat . . . Instead of listening to the voice of reason or the suggestions of sound policy, he girded on his sword, mounted his mighty [black] cockade, and stalked the hero. In pronouncing his war speech, rage almost choked his utterance, and if the combustibility of the people had been equal to his own, all America would have been in a flame.

Tonight, in the *Porcupine's Gazette*:

A public dinner was given at Baltimore on the 19th inst. *"in honour of JOHN ADAMS, our worthy President."*
—Now, BACHE, what will you say to this?

Much has been said by BACHE, the printer, and other hirelings of France to deceive the people of this country with respect to the late infamous decree by which the French plunderers are authorized to seize and condemn the property of this country.

Tonight, in the *Gazette of the United States*:

Mr. Bache has issued a threat at the managers of the Theatre, stating that their . . . national music may occasion the jacobins to withdraw . . . [T]he enemies of the country should be driven out of all respectable places and associations, and it is also a fact that the creditors of these reprobates are frequently in want of the money thus expended.

It is rather hard upon the people that they should be driven into a war and be loaded with an expense . . . in support of Mr. Adams's speech [against France on May 16th of last year]. The true ground of the non reception of our envoys was the *speech* . . .

Tonight, in the *Gazette of the United States*:

In the *Aurora* of [Saturday], of which in the absence of Bache it is presumed [Callender] is the sole editor, he . . . says, "most good men look on the President's late Proclamation for fasting humiliation, and prayer, as one of those . . . methods tyrants have began the foundation for oppressing the people with." . . . Do not the times approach when it must and *ought to be* dangerous for this wretch, or any other, thus to vilify our country and government . . . ?

PATRIOTIC SONG

We understand the Public will be gratified at Mr. Fox's Benefit with a Patriotic Song—A NATIVE AMERICAN, and glowing with the true love of *our own* country. It is hoped this first attempt to introduce a *National Song* will be encouraged.

Tonight, in the *Porcupine's Gazette*:

> Now is the time . . . to set a mark upon the enemies of their country . . . He, therefore, who still perseveres in his attachment to [the French] and in his justification of their abominable measures ought to be branded as a hired villain or a natural seeker of pillage and blood. Let, therefore, a mark be set upon the miscreant; let all men stand aloof from him; let him be banished from the converse of honesty and virtue; let him associate with BACHE, the Printer, and his patricide crew, and with them let him sink through the vault of poverty into oblivion with the curse of the country on his head.

It is not often I interest myself in the success of Theatrical Representations; but, I cannot help bestowing a word or two in approbation of what is advertised for tomorrow night. Mr. Fox has, with singular propriety, admitted a SONG, written by a gentleman of Philadelphia, adapted to the PRESIDENT'S MARCH, which has long been the national and is now the popular tune. Long, much too long, have the lovers of the drama been shocked and insulted with the sacrilegious hymns of atheism and murder [like "The Marseillaise"] . . .

WEDNESDAY, APRIL 25, 1798

GENERAL ★ AURORA ★ ADVERTISER

NEW THEATRE
—Mr. Fox's Night.—
THIS EVENING, April 25,
(BY DESIRE)
Will be presented (for the second time in
America) a Play interspersed with
songs, in 3 acts called
THE ITALIAN MONK.

Today, handbills for the New Theatre announce that, at the conclusion of this evening's performance, Gilbert Fox will sing a new patriotic song, "Hail Columbia," which young Philadelphian lawyer Joseph Hopkinson (son of John Adams' friend Francis Hopkinson) has written to the tune of the traditional "President's March."[290]

War measures . . . Today, in the U.S. Senate, the Annals report:

A motion was made by Mr. HILLHOUSE [Federalist, Connecticut].

That a committee be appointed to consider . . . removing from the territory of the United States such aliens . . . as may be dangerous to its peace and safety . . .[291]

War measures . . . Today, in the U.S. House of Representatives, the Annals of Congress report:

DEPARTMENT OF THE NAVY

Mr. HARPER [Federalist, South Carolina]: called for the order of the day on the bill for establishing an Executive Department, to be denominated The Department of the Navy . . .

Mr. GALLATIN [Republican, Pennsylvania]: He did not think it necessary to establish a Navy Department . . . He called for the yeas and nays upon the question . . . The yeas and nays were taken upon this bill . . . and decided in the affirmative—yeas 47, nays 41 . . .[292]

Many Republicans have abandoned the effort to stop John Adams' war measures. Tonight, in the *Gazette of the United States*:

ALARMING DESERTION.

"[S]trange to tell, never has there been such a general and early desertion from Congress as at this time—Upon a call of yeas and nays a few days since in the House of Representatives, it appeared that one fourth of the whole house was absent—They are daily dropping off."

Tonight, in the *Porcupine's Gazette*:

> Sure ne'er was paper better call'd
> Than the *Aurora* is,
> The sun hast ris'n half enthral'd
> Twixt light and darkness 'tis.
>
> Now six years since it began
> To *light* the fed'ral morn,
> Yet not advanced a single span
> From where it first was born.
>
> 'Midst democratic fogs and clouds
> Its course it first begun;
> In scandal's drab its face it shrouds
> And sets a rising sun!

Tonight, the President's Lady, Abigail Adams, attends Philadelphia's New Theatre to hear the new patriotic song "Hail Columbia." An *Aurora* reporter also attends.[293] Moreau de St. Méry describes the theatre:

The interior is pretty, and three tiers of boxes are pleasingly arranged in a semi-ellipse . . . The seats in the pit descend . . . from the bottom tier of boxes to the orchestra . . .

The hall is painted gray with gilded scrolls and carvings. The upper tier of boxes has small gilded balustrades which are quite elegant . . . separated in the front by small columns [and] . . . papered with red paper in extremely bad taste. The theater is lighted by small four-branched chandeliers placed on every second box . . . They are supported by gilded iron S's . . .

The orchestra holds thirty musicians in two rows facing each other. The front of the stage is huge. Its wings represent portions of facades of beautiful houses . . . The stage, which is large, is lighted by oil lamps, as in France. These can be changed from high to low for night scenes and those that require dimness. The wings have illumination lamps . . .

Women go in the pit like men; but these are not women of any social standing. The upper gallery admits women and colored people who can't sit anywhere else . . .

The performance is boisterous, and the interludes are even indecent. It is not unusual to hear such words as Goddamn, Bastard, Rascal, Son of a Bitch. Women turn their backs to the performance during the interludes . . .

People eat and drink in the pit. The refreshments, of which there is a store in a pretty little shop in the lobby . . . cost fifty per cent more than in the city which is the natural result of the rental cost of the shop.[294]

The President's Lady describes her evening:

I had a Great curiosity to see for myself the Effect. I got Mr. Otis to take a Box . . . I meant now to be perfectly in cogg [incognito], so [I] did not sit in what is calld the President's Box. After the principle peice was perfor[m]ed, Mr. Fox came upon the stage to sing the song. He was welcomed by applause. The House was very full, and, at every Choruss, the most unbounded applause ensued. In short it was enough to stund one. They had the song repeated—After this, Rossina was acted. When Fox came upon the stage, after the Curtain dropt, to announce the peice for fryday, they calld again for the song and made him repeat it to the fourth time. And the last time, the whole Audience broke forth in the Chorus whilst the thunder from their Hands was incessant, and, at the close, they rose, gave three Huzzas that you might have heard a mile—My Head aches in consequence of it.[295]

The last of four verses and the refrain:

> Behold, THE CHIEF WHO NOW COMMANDS,
> Once more to serve his country, stands
> The Rock on which the storm will beat,
> The Rock on which the storm will beat,
> But arm'd in virtue, firm and true,

"Hail Columbia" (1798)[296]

Hail Co-lum-bia, hap-py land, Hail ye He-roes Heav'n born band, Who

Fought and Bled in Free-dom's cause, Who Fought and Bled in

Free-dom's cause, And when the storm of War was gone, En-

joy'd the Peace your Va-lor won, Let In-de-pen-dence

be our boast, E-ver mind-ful what it cost,

E-ver grate-ful for the Prize, Let its al-tar reach the skies

Firm, u-ni-ted, let us be, Rall-ying round our

Li-ber-ty, As a band of Bro-thers Join'd,

Peace and safe-ty we shall find.

2

Immortal Patriots, rise once more,
Defend your rights, defend your shore,
  Let no rude foe with Impious hand,
  Let no rude foe with Impious hand,
Invade the shrine where sacred lies,
Of toil and blood the well earn'd prize,
  While offering Peace sincere and just,
  In Heav'n we place a manly trust,
That truth and Justice may prevail,
And ev'ry scheme of bondage fail.
  Firm, united, &c.

3

Sound, Sound, the trump of fame,
Let Washington's Great Name,
  Ring through the world with loud applause,
  Ring through the world with loud applause,
Let ev'ry clime to freedom dear,
Listen with a Joyful ear,

With equal skill, with god-like pow'r,
He governs in the fearful hour,
Of horrid war, or guides with ease,
The happier time of honest peace.
  Firm, united, &c.

4

Behold, the Chief who now Commands,
Once more to serve his Country, stands,
  The Rock on which the storm will beat,
  The Rock on which the storm will beat,
But arm'd in virtue, firm and true,
His hopes are fix'd on Heav'n and You.
  When Hope was sinking in dismay,
  When glooms obscur'd Columbia's day,
His steady mind, from changes free,
Resolv'd on Death or LIBERTY.
  Firm, united, &c.

His hopes are fix'd on Heav'n and YOU.
When Hope was sinking in dismay,
When glooms obscur'd Columbia's day
His steady mind, from changes free,
Resolv'd on Death or Liberty.
[and chorus] *Firm—united—let us be,*
Rallying round our liberty,
As a band of Brothers join'd,
Peace and safety we shall find.[297]

TO THE PRESIDENT OF THE UNITED STATES

SIR . . . You had an active part in bringing about that glorious revolution that made us an independent nation.—But . . . your ideas of government and policy have become warped . . . You left this country [to get French help during the American Revolution], Sir, with the warm affections of the people of America & with violent prejudices in your favor. The first public act which induced them to doubt the sincerity of your principles was your book, entitled *"A [D]efence of the [C]onstitutions of America."* In this book, an aristocratical form of government . . . you boldly avow . . . is the only one conducive to the happiness of the people . . . [Y]ou may remember . . . [t]he universal acclamation . . . that you were an enemy of equal rights, and sorry am I to acknowledge that your subsequent conduct has evinced the truth of this assertion . . .   VALERIUS

Today, President Adams answers the address from the Philadelphia Federalists who met at Dunwoody's Tavern on April 12th:

To the Citizens of Philadelphia, The District of Southwark, and the Northern Liberties.
G E N T L E M E N, [Y]our implicit approbation of the general system and the particular measures of the government; your generous feelings of resentment at the Wrongs and Offences committed against it and at the menaces of others still more intolerable . . . do you great honour as patriots and citizens . . .

     JOHN ADAMS[298]

As John Adams answers laudatory addresses from various parts of the country, he might remember Poor Richard's warning,

     He that falls in love with himself will have no Rivals.[299]

Today, the President's Lady, Abigail Adams, writes:

     Their have been six different addresses presented from this city alone, all expressive of the Approbation of the measures of the Execu-

tive. Yet daringly do the vile incendiaries keep up in Bache's paper the most wicked and base, violent & calumniating abuse—It was formerly considered as leveld against the Government, but now it is contrary to their declared sentiments daily manifested, so that it insults the Majesty of the Sovereign People. But nothing will have an Effect untill Congress pass a Sedition Bill which I presume they will do before they rise—Not a paper from Bache's press issues . . . but what might have been prossecuted as libels upon the President and Congress. For a long time they seem as if they were now desperate—The wrath of the public ought to fall upon their devoted Heads.[300]

Today, Thomas Jefferson writes James Madison:

One of the war party, in a fit of unguarded passion, declared some time ago they would pass a citizen bill, an alien bill, & a sedition bill; accordingly, some days ago, Coit laid a motion on the table of the H.[ouse] of R.[epresentatives] for modifying the citizen law. Their threats point at Gallatin, & it is believed they will endeavor to reach him by this bill. Yesterday mr. Hillhouse laid on the table of the senate a motion for [an alien bill] giving power to send away suspected aliens. This is understood to be meant for Volney . . . But it will not stop there when it gets into a course of execution. There is now only wanting to accomplish the whole declaration before mentioned, a sedition bill which we shall certainly soon see proposed. The object of that is the suppression of the Whig presses. Bache's had been particularly named . . . [I]f these papers fail, republicanism will be entirely brow beaten . . . At present, the war hawks talk of septembrizing [massacring], Deportation, and the examples for quelling sedition set by the French Executive. All the firmness of the human mind is now in a state of requisition.[301]

Tonight, in the *Porcupine's Gazette*:

From rascal Bache's Paper.
"Most good men look on the President's late Proclamation for fasting, humiliation, and prayer, as one of those apparently humble, hypocritical and delusive methods tyrants have universally began the foundation of oppressing the people with . . ."

It is said that BACHE is absent, very likely to avoid importunate visitors . . .

CHAPTER THREE

BLACK COCKADES

Their rise [as a Federalist militia, the Macpherson's Blues] was at a season of alarm and political ferment . . . [A]n advertisement calling upon the YOUTH of Philadelphia to meet at a public tavern . . . was couched in singular form, for the youth were explained to comprehend those between 16 and 23 years of age . . . [E]ffects not to be then foreseen arose from the example set by Philadelphia, for all the continent was taught, and the eulogy bestowed by the president on these youths of 23 gave our nether world a high opinion of this queer begotten association, and the example was followed as we have seen . . .

Never was l'esprit de corps more strongly manifested than in the first months of its institution by this body . . . [M]en of sound republican principles but weak minds were seen enrolling themselves in ranks under the apprehension of their growing power and the consequent danger; and men . . . were seen disgracing the memories of their fathers and the independence of their country by the elevation of the black British cockade! . . .

This corps, sanctioned by the President . . . gave a species of law to the public of this city.—Weak men feared them . . . The theatre—the public streets—and even the domestic sanctuary was infested with their folly or their violence . . .

**WILLIAM DUANE, EDITOR,
AURORA GENERAL ADVERTISER, 1798–1822**[302]

A great riot happened . . . and hints thrown out of a design to fire the city; the light horse were out all night, and the militia and private citizens were on guard, patrolling also, but it was passed in quiet, but we are still suspicious that the evil spirit is not wholly at rest, only lulled asleep. "Young Lightning Rod" had his house guarded by armed men, within and without, being fearful of having it pulled down. I think I never saw so many people at one time in my life as on that evening. What a world we live in, and what tumultuous times!

MARGARET MORRIS OF PHILADELPHIA, MAY 11, 1798[303]

For some days past, the Anglo Monarchical Tory party have appeared at the [New] Theatre in full triumph—and the President's March and other aristocratical tunes have been . . . vehemently applauded.—

A few evenings ago, a drunken-Bravo with some valiant associates called upon the Democrats to [dare] hold up their hands, but he and his comrades were soon silenced by the spirited conduct of ONE gentleman in the Boxes, when they prudently retired. On Wednesday evening, however, the admirers of British tyranny again assembled in consequence of the managers having announced in the bills of the day that there would be given a *Patriotic song* to the tune of the President's March. All the British merchants, British agents, and many of our congress tories attended to do honor to the occasion. When the wished-for song came—which contained, amidst the most ridiculous bombast, the vilest adulation to the Anglo Monarchical Party and the two Presidents, the extacy of the party knew no bounds; they encored, they shouted, they became

Mad as the Priests of the Delphic God,

And in the fury of their exultation threatened to throw over or otherwise ill treat every person who did not join heartily in the applause.

The rapture of the moment was as great as if . . . John Adams had been proclaimed king of America, and the loyalty was so impressive that even the excellent Lady of his Excellency (who was present) shed tears of sensibility and delight.

For what reason the managers presume to offend a great body of the citizens of Philadelphia by devoting their theatre to party purposes we are at a loss to determine; or why the orchestra who had so readily gratified one party, should refuse to play *Ca Ira* when repeatedly called for, unless the managers wish to drive from the Theatre every friend to plain republican principles and depend alone upon the tories for support . . . The Republican party would do well therefore to absent themselves from the Theatre, unless they wish to have their noses pulled by the Tories and it is even possible their ears will be offended . . . If however any should be rash enough to enter that Temple of Aristocracy called the New Theatre, let them at least go in a party sufficiently strong to protect themselves from outrage, from insult, and degradation.

The aspect of affairs in America is . . . mysterious and alarming . . . [I]t would be ludicrous to suppose that the querulous and cankered murmurs of blind, bald, crippled, toothless Adams . . . can have any other effect than to afford additional and experimental proof of the folly of trusting such men with power.

Later today, the President's Lady, Abigail Adams, writes her sister:

I inclose to you a National Song composed by this same Mr. Hopkinson. French tunes have for a long time usurped an uncontrould sway. Since the Change in the publick opinion respecting France, the people begin to lose their relish for them, and what had been harmony now becomes discord. Accordingly their had been for several Evenings at the Theatre something like disorder, one party crying out for the Presidents March and Yankee Doodle, while Ciera ["Ça Ira"] was vociferated from the other. It was hisst off repeatedly. The managers were blamed. Their excuse was that they had not any words for the Presidents March—Mr. Hopkinson accordingly composed these to the tune. Last Eve'ng they were sung for the first time . . .

Bache says this morning among other impudence that the excellent Lady of the Excellent President was present and shed Tears of sensibility upon the occasion. That was a lie. However I should not have been ashamed if it had been so. I laughed at one scene which was playd [to] be sure, untill the tears ran down, I believe. But the song, by the manner in which it is received, is death to their Party. The House was really crowded and by the most respectable people in the city.[304]

War measures . . . Today, John Adams approves and signs into law:

AN ACT
*To provide an additional armament for the
further protection of the trade of the United States,
and for other purposes.*
Be it enacted, &c. That the President of the United States shall be, and is hereby, authorized and empowered to cause to be built, purchased or hired a number of vessels, not exceeding twelve, not carrying more than twenty-two guns each, to be armed, fitted out, and manned under his direction."[305]

President Adams also approves and signs into law,

AN ACT
*To provide an additional regiment of
artillerists and Engineers.*
Be it enacted, &c., That an additional regiment of artillerists and engineers shall and may be engaged by voluntary enlistments [and] . . . shall be considered as part of the Military Establishment of the United States . . .[306]

Tonight, in the *Gazette of the United States*:

EXTRACT OF LYING
"Firm—united—let us be," &c.
Bache, finding this sentiment of union and patriotism spreading rapidly throughout the United States . . . attacks it with wickedness and virulence

wherever he finds it. The song, sung with the enthusiastic applause of every American at the Theatre on Wednesday last, has excited his keenest resentment and called for an exertion of his *Lying faculty* . . . The song is now before the public, and they will see there is not throughout a single allusion to any party or any party principle or question . . . But the two Presidents are spoken of with respect, and this offends the delicacy of Bache. And if I shall ever see the day when my countrymen shall forget the services of a WASHINGTON or an ADAMS . . . I shall see the day when American virtue and gratitude are buried and extinct . . .

AN AMERICAN

Tonight, in the *Porcupine's Gazette*:

BACHE is said to be—*not at home;* so that it is probable that everything . . . ought to be attributed immediately to CALLENDER, a wretch who boasted of having fled hither *to escape the hands of justice* . . . a runaway and incendiary, a vagabond, and a pauper.

SATURDAY, APRIL 28, 1798

GENERAL ★ AURORA ★ ADVERTISER

SUMMER CIRCUS
Corner of Market and Thirteenth street.

WILL open on TUESDAY next, the FIRST of MAY—The details of the Performance of the Evening, which are very ENTERTAINING, will be given in a New Advertisement.

Today, another anonymous letter warns President Adams that his Fast Day will be a day of murder and mayhem:

Much respected Sir,
To warn a worthy people of impending danger is surely laudable. Permit me therefore to warn you against the Ninth of May. Be prepared, be courageous, for you will then stand in need of all your fortitude to repel the insidious attacks of domestic enemies. There is a vile plot laid. The prime movers of it are Frenchmen. They imagine themselves secure in their villainy, and thus will (on that day which is fixed on for fasting & prayer) perpetrate such [deeds] as all good men will shudder at. They will [murder] man, woman & Child, set fire to all your [offices] &c. &c. unless timely steps are taken to prevent it. Do not sleep in fearless security. The hour of danger is near . . .

A Friend to America & Truth[307]

Poor Richard wrote,

Happy that nation, fortunate that age,
whose history is not diverting.[308]

This is not that nation. This is not that age.

Tonight, in the *Gazette of the United States*:

> Although Bache called his myrmidons to arms and requested the republican party (as he called it) to go to the Theatre in a strong body for the purpose of exciting riot and tumult, yet the PATRIOTIC SONG was received last evening with more enthusiastic applause than before. It was again *encored and sung four times,* and called for oftener . . .

Tonight, in the *Porcupine's Gazette*:

> THE THEATRE was very full last night . . . [W]hat gave life to everything was the SONG . . . At every repetition it was received with additional enthusiasm, till towards the last, [the] great part of the audience, pit, box, and gallery, actually joined in the chorus.—It was very pleasing to observe that the last stanza received particular marks of approbation. Every one was closed with long and loud clapping and huzzas, but no sooner were the words,
> "BEHOLD THE CHIEF WHO NOW COMMANDS"
> pronounced than the house shook to its very center; the song and the whole were drowned in the enthusiastic peals of applause, and were obliged to stop and begin again and again in order to gain a hearing.

Today, Abigail Adams delights in the public response:

> *[W]herever I past, I received a marked notice of Bows . . . & the Friends [Quakers] in the Street in their way noticed me. I thought nothing of it untill my attention was caught by a Bunch of Tradesmen, they lookt like, who at the corners of the Street saluted me as I past with their Hats—*
> *In short, we are now wonderfully popular except with Bache & Co who in his paper calls the President old, querilous, Bald, blind, cripled, Toothless Adams. Thus in scripture was the Prophet mocked, and tho no Bears may devour the wretch, the wrath of an insulted people will by & by break upon him.*[309]

Tonight, in Philadelphia's Southwark district, Samuel Relf (who is recruiting for the private Federalist militia, the Macpherson's Blues) presides over a boisterous meeting of "Young Men" at James Cameron's Tavern on Shippen-street. The meeting chooses a committee to draft an address to the President and agrees to reconvene on Monday to approve the address. Before adjourning, all sing Joseph Hopkinson's new song, "Hail Columbia."[310]

Some days ago, it was noticed in the *Aurora* that the friends of order in this city were beginning to threaten the *disorganizers*, that is to say, such people as do not wish to get into war in defence of two presidential speeches, with *a trial of your own guillotine*. We expected to see this menace denied in the anglo presidential gazette of Chestnut street [the *Gazette of the United States*]. Instead of that, how great was our surprize to see the threatening repeated . . .

Mr. Fenno, in some late numbers, has reproached Callender as the author of several pieces printed in the *Aurora* which the latter had never seen or heard of . . . [N]othing shall be said but simply that he *knew nothing about the*m; that he writes but little for the *Aurora*, and that he neither has nor ever had any concern whatever in the editorship of the paper.

Jimmy Callender can't write for the *Aurora* unless Benny pays him more. The issue is distancing them, and Benny wants me to give up my paltry salary to keep Jimmy on the payroll.[311]

Tonight, in the *Gazette of the United States*:

CALLENDER TURN'D OFF
Bache begins to be ashamed or rather tired of his scald-headed associate—In the *Aurora* of this morning, we find Callender disavowed as a contributor to the elegancies of that repository or as having any participation in its editorship—It is possible that the scald-headed Pauper has been asking for some of those broken victuals which his employer is not so well able to spare as when *his* employers were on the spot.

Tonight, at seven o'clock, almost a thousand "Young Men of Philadelphia" cram into James Cameron's Tavern in Southwark to approve, paragraph by paragraph and by acclamation, an address to be presented next Monday to the President of the United States.[312]

Tonight, in the *Porcupine's Gazette*:

THE THEATRE is tomorrow Evening to be honored with the company of THE PRESIDENT and his LADY, and also of the OFFICERS OF THE FEDERAL GOVERNMENT.

It is difficult to give a distinct account of the proceedings of the meeting held [at Cameron's] on Saturday evening by the *half-fledged friends of order* . . . [F]rom beginning to end, the whole (according to a correspondent) exhibited a scene of puerile hurly-burly confusion . . . The young gentlemen wished to do something, but they could not express what . . . The laws require the full age of 21 before a citizen shall have the right of voting; is it not absurd that young men under that age should attempt to instruct representatives on their own . . .

Certain unknown incendiaries intend to set fire to this city on the ninth of May, and in order to facilitate the execution of this infernal design, they thought fit to inform his excellency the President Adams by three successive letters of the exact day and time they intend to attempt it . . . These incendiaries, it would appear, express great confidence in the President, and if the scheme for setting fire is not a mere silly fiction, they must have looked upon him as a faithful accomplice in setting not only the city but the whole country on fire.

We are requested to say the President attends the Theatre this evening.

Tonight, in the *Gazette of the United States*:

Bache's account of the meeting [of Philadelphia's "Young Men"] at Cameron's is totally false . . . This contemptible foreign tool goes on to say that young men between eighteen and twenty-one are not entitled to the rights of citizens and that therefore it is improper in them to give instructions to the government . . .

The young men between the age of eighteen and twenty-one are liable to be called into actual service; there can be no impropriety in declaring their determination not to shrink from the task in the eyes of any other than an infamous miscreant who wishes the destruction of his country in order that France may rise on the ruins of its greatness.

ONE OF THE MEETING

THE YOUNG MEN

of this city and suburbs . . . will not feel themselves debased or suffer their ardor to be abated by the low abuse and affected contempt of such a *thing* as Bache. This poor creature whose register of infamy and falsehood is rapidly sinking to its dissolution: who is himself as deep in ruin as he is in dishonor, and will shortly exhibit an awful picture of the contempt and misery into which that man must fall who devotes himself to the interests of a foreign country, to the destruction of his own; whose disgrace and sufferings will furnish a memento of the indignation which *Americans* feel against those who dare to vilify their country, and express a wish to prostrate her at the feet of foreign insolence, ought not to excite any resentment even in the ardent breasts of youthful patriots—Let them pursue their course of honor and independence and pass this harmless, hissing snake in contempt.

Nothing can display, in a more strong or pleasing view, the spirit of national honor . . . than the associations of young men similar to that now set on foot. I am informed that between three and four hundred attended the first meeting . . . There are few *young traitors*; ones that have spent their early years in France [like Benjamin Franklin Bache]; and been reared and educated under examples of *cunning* prudence; and in the maxims of hypocrisy and the wisdom of *fair appearances*.

Tonight, in the *Porcupine's Gazette*:

Mr. B. F. BACHE. As a member of the meeting held at Cameron's on Saturday evening last, I thank you for the colouring you have attempted to give their proceedings; you could not have imagined a panegyric more pleasing to the feelings of the youth of Philadelphia . . . Holding you as the tool of a disorganizing faction and as a *full fledged scoundrel*, they consider [that] your countenance to their measures would disgrace them . . .

A Member of the Committee.

Bache must soon wind up his business here, and he will doubtless take his flight to France, that land of liberty and equality, which he is so well fitted to become a subject of . . . [Bache] is poor, very poor; has not the money he has advanced and the protested notes which are unpaid place him in critical circumstances? Does he not owe his papermakers, his journeymen, &c. &c. &c.? and as for Callender, his demi-devil . . . to keep his family from starving . . . , I would here recommend to the smoaky wig'd *pauper* to accept of Bache's *valuable* copy rights in part pay . . .

The raucous Federalist dinners and recruitment of young men into the Macpherson's Blues have disquieted Republicans.[313] Tonight, Republicans hold their own dinner in the Northern Liberties district of Philadelphia.[314]

Tonight, the President of the United States and *entourage* attend Philadelphia's New Theatre to hear the patriotic song "Hail Columbia." *Porcupine's Gazette* reports:

THE PRESIDENT, accompanied by his LADY and the OFFICERS OF THE GOVERNMENT, honoured the theater with his Presence. The reception he met with cannot be so well described as by saying that it was such as he merits and has a right to expect from a grateful people. The moment he entered the box, the whole audience rose and expressed their affection for him in enthusiastic acclamations that did honour to their hearts. Mr. HOPKINSON's song was repeatedly sung, the *last stanza* was every time encored, and the audience, men and women, joined aloud in the chorus . . .[315]

President Adams will now appoint Joseph Hopkinson to a federal position.

WEDNESDAY, MAY 2, 1798

GENERAL ★ AURORA ★ ADVERTISER

A citizen, being asked whether he would keep the 9th of May as a day of fasting, answered dryly: *"I am not of the opinion that in Adams' fall, we sinned all."*

Today, President Adams answers an address from the citizens of Baltimore, Maryland:

[D]ivisions are generally harmless, often salutary, and seldom very hurtful, except when foreign nations interfere and by their arts and agents excite and ferment them into parties and factions . . . Such interference and influence must be resisted and exterminated, or it will end in America, as it did anciently in Greece and in our own time in Europe, in our total destruction as a republican government and independent power.[316]

Tonight, in the *Porcupine's Gazette*:

THE PROCEEDINGS OF
The Young Men of Philadelphia.
At a general meeting of the young men of Philadelphia, of the District of Southwark and the Northern Liberties, convened by public notice at the house of Mr. Cameron, Shippen-street, . . . the following resolutions were proposed and unanimously adopted, viz . . .
2d . . . [W]e cheerfully *pledge ourselves to obey with alacrity the first summons of our country in resisting the invasion of a foreign enemy* . . .
Samuel Relph, Chairman
(Let BACHE and his French clan growl at this. I can very well excuse the wretches; for if anything can convince them of the ruin of their cause, it is the generous enthusiasm that has here made its appearance. The pledge of the young men of the capital of the Union to fly, on the first summons, to the defence of this country is not a vain and empty boast . . .)

Tonight, in the *Gazette of the United States*:

THE MANAGERS of the Theatre deserve much credit for the honourable and splendid manner in which they received the President last evening . . . [N]o man who was not there can have an idea of the loud bursting enthusiasm, the heartfelt rapture with which they received their respected President, and the constant shouts and huzzahs which rang through the house in honour of him through the whole evening. The National Songs met with unbounded applause. *"Firm—united—let us be"* was the universal sentiment; and this chorus was joined in by the audience with general enthusiasm and great effect. If I hated Bache and some others even more than they hate the country and government, I could not wish them a greater punishment than to have obliged them to be at the Theatre last evening and to have witnessed the joyful return of American feelings . . . In the course of the night . . . a great number of gentlemen, accompanied with a Band of Music, serenaded the President and the Heads of the Departments and the author of the Song, with the new Song "HAIL COLUMBIA! happy land." The spirit of America is aroused—Let its enemies beware . . .[317]

To the Citizens of Newark, in the State of New-Jersey,

GENTLEMEN . . . I know of no further measures that can be pursued to produce an amicable adjustment of differences with the French Republic. THE delusions and misrepresentations which have misled so many citizens are very serious evils and must be discountenanced by authority as well as by citizens at large, or they will soon produce all kinds of calamities in this country . . .

JOHN ADAMS

☞ The Youth of Philadelphia and Liberties are informed that a copy of the address to the President is deposited at the Library, to which, between the hours of two and six P.M., they may place their signatures if they think proper—Also at the City Tavern.

THURSDAY, MAY 3, 1798

GENERAL ★ AURORA ★ ADVERTISER

On Saturday, the 21st instant, "near a hundred *staunch federalists*" (to use their own words) "assembled at James Cameron's tavern, in the district of Southwark . . . " [I]t appeared a perfect scene of riot and confusion. These *hundred staunch federalists* drank no less than *thirty-two staunch toasts* to each of which they gave exactly 9 cheers . . . [T]hese hundred *staunch federalists* roared like a hundred bulls . . .

Today, Thomas Jefferson notes in his journal:

The Presid[en]t has . . . app[ointe]d Joseph Hopkinson Comm[issione]r to make a treaty with the Oneida Ind[ia]ns. He is a youth of about 22 or 23 and has no other merit than extreme toryism & having made a poor song to the tune of the President's March.[318]

Today, Thomas Jefferson writes James Madison:

These [towns] and N[ew] Jersey are pouring in their addresses, offering life & fortune. Even these addresses are not the worst things . . . Whatever chance for peace . . . is compleatly lost by these answers [of John Adams].

Nor is it France alone but his own fellow citizens against whom his threats are uttered. In Fenno of yesterday, you will see one wherein he

says to the address from Newark, "The delusions and misrepresenta-
tions which have misled so many citizens must be discountenanced by
authority as well as by the citizens at large." . . . What new law they
will propose on this subject has not yet leaked out . . .

   The threatening appearances from the Alien bills have so alarmed
the French who are among us that they are going off. A ship, chartered
by themselves for this purpose, will sail within about a fortnight for
France, with as many as she can carry . . .

   Perhaps the Pr.[esident]'s expression before quoted may look to the
Sedition bill which has been spoken of and which may be meant to put
the Printing presses under the Imprimatur of the executive. Bache is
thought a main object of it.[319]

Republicans are afraid. Tonight, there is a meeting of Republicans at John Shnyder's at the sign of Robinhood.[320]

Today, in the U.S. House of Representatives, the Annals of Congress report:

NATURALIZATION LAW.

   Mr. ALLEN [Federalist, Connecticut] . . . [T]here are citizens of several other countries who . . . have dispositions equally hostile to this country as the French . . . Mr. A. alluded to the vast number of naturalizations which lately took place in this city to support a particular party [the Republican party] in a particular election. It did not appear to him necessary to have the exercise of this power [to expel aliens] depend on any contingency, such as a threatening of invasion, or war, before it could be exercised. He wished the President to have it at all times . . . to remove at any time the citizen of any foreign country whatever . . .[321]

Tonight, the *Porcupine's Gazette* publishes a death threat from the "Young Men" who gathered at Cameron's:

   That Child of infamy *Bache* or his clipt and pauper associate *Callender* affects to despise the young men who have agreed to offer their personal services in defence of their country if necessary and calls them *half fledged men*. It appears to me who am one of the *half fledged men* that the dastardly vagabond trembled as he wrote . . .

   You may inform him, Sir, . . . that although there is not one of the half-fledged men who would be backward in conferring upon him such chastisement that he not long since received from Mr. Humphreys or such as his beastly *franking* friend suffered in the Hall of Congress, . . . it would be unfair to deprive a *very useful man* of the fee which he may expect shortly to receive for doing the last kind office to the grandson of a Philosopher, and it is a disgraceful thing to see the miscreant riding to his long home with a pair of *black eyes* . . . So wishing him a happy and speedy deliverance from all his afflictions, I remain.

                                                          A Half Fledged Man

☞ As Wednesday the 9th instant is appointed by the President of the United States as a day of solemn humiliation, fasting, and prayer, notice is hereby given that the Bank of Pennsylvania will be shut on that day, and that all payments . . . must be made on the day preceding.

By order of the Board.
Jonathan Smith, *Cashier.*

Tonight, in the *Gazette of the United States*:

LOST—by the Editor of the Aurora.
THE PEOPLE.

FRIDAY, MAY 4, 1798

GENERAL ★ AURORA ★ ADVERTISER

Mr. Allen [Federalist, Connecticut] on the 20th [of April] ult. made the following observations in the Federal House of Representatives:— "Let me add, as no contemptible engine in this business of sowing discord, dissension, and distrust of the Government, a vile incendiary paper published in this city . . ." [&c., &c.]

[*Congressman Allen's remarks on the Aurora follow.*]

Remarks on the Above by the EDITOR OF THE AURORA

Mr. Allen's speech is in the hackneyed style of the abuse which has been unceasingly poured on the *Aurora* . . . The opposers of any measures of administration will always be called . . . "incendiaries, sowers of discord, dissentious, and distrust of government . . ."

Mr. Allen should never mention the words "discord, dissension, and distrust of the government, &c.." This is the very man who the other day in Litchfield in Connecticut, expressed strong doubts as to the permanency of the Federal government; spoke of his political opponents as *rascals*; and rounded his . . . speech with the remark that if those *"rascals"* could not be put down, the government is not worth preserving, &c . . .

We want no *"septembrizing"* [*massacring*] to get rid of men such as Mr. Allen. It is only necessary that the People should be acquainted with the truth to throw them in the back ground . . .

We have as much stake in this country at least as this very Mr. Allen. If he is a native of it; so are we. Does he plume himself upon the *foolish pride of ancestry;* let him make the comparison [with *our roots in Dr. Franklin.*] Has he a family to attach him to the country; and so have we; one as dear to us as his can be to him: We have something more to attach us here: it is that very constitution which he has talked of subverting; those principles which he is endeavoring to sap.

As to the dark insinuations of this paper's receiving foreign support, it is scandalous and false. The *Aurora* is bottomed upon the support of

104

the persons who individually subscribe for it, & of those who advertise in it. It has never been upheld by the donations of private individuals, much less by foreign aid.

Today, President Adams writes the inhabitants of Chester County, Pennsylvania:

> *Those lovers of themselves, who withdraw their confidence from their own legitimate government and place it on a foreign nation or domestic faction or both in alliance, deserve all your contempt and abhorrence.*[322]

War measures . . . Today, John Adams approves and signs into law:

AN ACT
*To enable the President of the United States
to procure cannon, arms, and ammunition
and for other purposes.*

Be it enacted, &c, That a sum not exceeding eight hundred thousand dollars shall be, and hereby is appropriated . . . to purchase as soon as may be, a sufficient number of cannon; also, a supply of small arms, and of ammunition and military stores to be deposited and used as will be most conducive to the public safety and defence, at the discretion of the President of the United States.[323]

John Adams also approves and signs into law:

AN ACT
*To authorize the President of the United States
to cause to be purchased, or built, a number of
small vessels, to be equipped as Gallies, or otherwise.*

Be it enacted, &c, That the President of the United States be, and he is hereby, authorized . . . to cause a number of small vessels, not exceeding ten, to be built or purchased, and to be fitted out, manned, armed and equipped as galleys or otherwise in the service of the United States . . . [and t]hat there be appropriated for the purpose aforesaid the sum of eighty thousand dollars . . .[324]

Tonight, William Cobbett in the *Porcupine's Gazette*:

> I am happy to inform my readers that the *Young Men* of New York are following the example of those at Philadelphia. A correspondent proposes that the young men [of Philadelphia] who sign the address . . . should, when the address is delivered, assume the [black] *American Cockade* and never leave it off till the haughty and insolent foe is reduced to reason. This is, I observe, already adopted at New York; and it is certainly proper. The hand writing at the bottom of the address is seen but by few persons; whereas a cockade will been seen by the whole city . . .

Tonight, Thomas Jefferson presents letters on the discovery of mammoth bones to a meeting of the American Philosophical Society. Eight members of the society attend, including the newly elected Polish writer Julien Niemcewicz.[325] The meeting breaks up about ten-thirty, though Jefferson and Niemcewicz will remain awake for many hours. Niemcewicz:

> *On my return from this meeting at half past ten in the evening . . . General [Kosciuszko]'s servant told me that his master asked to speak with me . . . [W]hen we were alone, [the Polish General Kosciuszko] said, "I leave this night for Europe. I leave alone . . . I beseech you to tell everyone that I have gone to take the waters in Virginia. You will leave Philadelphia in three days and you will go in that direction saying it is to rejoin me."*
>
> *Too moved, too agitated by all that I had just heard, I could not close an eye. At one o'clock in the morning, I left and roamed the streets . . . At 4 o'clock a covered carriage arrived with Mr. J[efferson] inside. K[osciuszko] got in . . . With my eyes I followed the carriage as far as I could. They took a route completely opposite from that to the harbor. I do not know for whom this precaution was taken, for all the world slept. I learned later that they had gone by land up to New Castel where a boat awaited him . . . This departure, so precipitous, so concealed, so stealthy, caused general astonishment . . . How in this time of mistrust and suspicion is one to explain this clandestine voyage . . . ?[326]*

Tadeusz Kosciuszko has departed for France to join any French effort to liberate his native Poland from czarist Russia. He has entrusted his last will and testament to Thomas Jefferson.[327]

SATURDAY, MAY 5, 1798

GENERAL ★ AURORA ★ ADVERTISER

On Friday night last, a Club of Jovial citizens attacked the sign of Citizen *Julien* on which was wrote "a perpetual Alliance between France & the United States." These formidable patriots conveyed it to the place of execution and demolished it *sans ceremonie* . . . This is emblematical of the disposition of the British faction . . .

On Thursday, the "true Republican Society," composed of between eighty and one hundred members, assembled at John Shnyder's at the sign of the Robinhood. A handsome dinner was provided . . .

Republicans are organizing. Benny will need their help.

Tonight, in the *Porcupine's Gazette:*

SIR, In a letter to the committee . . . I requested them to call on every one who may sign the address to wear the [black] cockade in order that they may be known, and as the propriety of this cannot be called in question but by cowards, I have not a doubt when they notify the addressers to meet, that they will make known that request . . . I am, &c.

A Young Man

P. S. With respect to Bache and his "half fledged men," more hereafter.

The concourse of spectators, to see the YOUNG MEN of this city march to the President's on Monday will doubtless be very numerous; and I think they may promise themselves the countenance of all the fair sex. The committee have very properly left it to every one to put a [BLACK] COCK-ADE in his hat or not; because, by this, the PRESIDENT will know whom he can depend upon and whom he cannot. The man who is afraid to be known at all times and in all places as the friend of his country will most certainly be afraid to expose his life in its defence . . .

N O T I C E.

☞ The YOUTH of the City of Philadelphia, the Northern Liberties, and the district of Southwark are requested to meet at the City Tavern on Monday morning next at 11 o'clock precisely; from thence to wait upon the President of the United States with their Address.   *Samuel Relf*

SUNDAY, MAY 6, 1798

Today, at Mount Vernon, George Washington writes:

The Demo's seem to be lifting up their heads again according to Mr. Bache. They were a little crest fallen; or one might say, thunder stricken on the publication of the ["X, Y, Z"] Dispatches from our Envoys [in Paris], but the contents of them are now resolved into harmless chit-chat and trifles . . .[328]

MONDAY, MAY 7, 1798

GENERAL   ★ AURORA ★   ADVERTISER

Plots, Conspiracy, and Conflagration!

Some wag or modern Titus Oates has taken it into his head to amuse himself by writing incendiary letters to the President, threatening to lay this city in ashes! and for this *silly business* the weak and ignorant are *seriously* called on to use their utmost vigilance to avert the impending calamity . . . [I]ndeed have the citizens, not of Philadelphia only but of America in general, a right to be on their guard, for history informs us that plots like standing armies have ever been found fit instruments to strengthen the bands of government and curtail the liberties of the people.

This morning, the President's Lady, Abigail Adams, writes:

We are today to have a moveing and strikng spectacle, no less than between 7 & 8 Hundred young Men from 18–23 in a Body to present an address. Upon this occasion the President puts on his uniform, and the whole House will be thrown open to receive them. A number of ladies will be present upon the occasion with me . . .[329]

John Fenno:

This day, at 12 o'clock, the YOUNG MEN of this City assembled at the Merchants' Coffee House, from whence they marched in a body, attended by an immense concourse of their fellow citizens, to the House of the President of the United States . . .[330]

William Cobbett (Peter Porcupine):

The concourse of people, as spectators of the march to the PRESIDENT'S was immense. There could not be less than ten thousand. Every female in the city, whose face is worth looking at, gladdened the way with her smiles; and they certainly were well bestowed, for an assemblage of finer or more worthy young men, has seldom been seen in this city or in any other. It has been a proud day for Philadelphia, to see the flower of its youth thus voluntarily collected, hoisting the [BLACK] COCKADE, and proceeding to deposit in the hands of the common Father a solemn pledge of their attachment to their country and of their resolution to defend its laws, liberties, and religion, or to perish in the struggle . . . They were about twelve hundred in number, The procession was formed, or rather the battalion was drawn up, opposite the City Tavern, from whence they marched to the PRESIDENT'S HOUSE, in person who [bore] . . . a countenance expressive of the pleasure he felt . . .[331]

Abigail Adams:

The Young Men of the City . . . to the amount of near Eleven Hundred came at 12 oclock at procession two and two. There was assembled on the occasion it is said ten thousand Persons. One might have walkd upon their Heads besides the houses, windows & even tops of Houses. In great order & decorum the Young Men, with each a black cockade, marchd through the Multitude and all of them entered the House preceeded by their committe. When a young gentleman by the name of Hare, a nephew of Mrs. Binghams, read the address, the President received them in his Levee Room drest in his uniform, and as usual upon such occasions, read his answer to them . . .[332]

John Adams is pleased with the address. As Poor Richard says,

> *A Flatterer never seems absurd:*
> *The Flatter'd always takes his Word.*[333]

President Adams speaks:

> *For a long course of years, my amiable young friends, before the*
> *birth of the oldest of you, I was called upon to act with your fathers in*
> *concerting measures the most disagreeable and dangerous, not from a*
> *desire of innovation, not from discontent with the government under*
> *which we were born and bred, but to preserve the honor of our coun-*
> *try, and vindicate the immemorial liberties of our ancestors . . . I sin-*
> *cerely wish that none of you . . . [&c, &c]*[334]

Abigail Adams:

> *The Multitude gave three Cheers, & followed them to the State House*
> *Yard, where the answer [by the President] was again read by the*
> *Chairman of the committee, with acclamations.*[335]

Later today, the *Gazette of The United States* prints the "Young Men's" noontime address to the President, the President's answer to the "Young Men," and a song for wandering crowds to sing about Benny Bache and his "grand pap," Benjamin Franklin:

> To be sung or said in all the lanes, alleys and streets, public houses and
> private parties in Philadelphia and elsewhere . . . to the tune of YANKEE
> DOODLE.
>
> > Tom Callender's a nasty beast,
> >   Ben Bache a dirty fellow;
> > They curse our country day and night,
> >   And to the French would sell her.
> >   *Fire and murder, keep it up,*
> >   *Plunder is the dandy;*
> >   *When some folks get the upper hand,*
> >   *With heads they'll be so handy*
> > When Benny was a little brat,
> >   He whipt his top in France, sir,
> > They taught him how to shape a lie,
> >   As well as how to dance, sir.
> >   *Fire and murder, &c.*
> > The little dog was also taught,
> >   That laws are human scourges;
> > That war and murder now and then
> >   Are naught but wholesome purges.
> >   *Fire and murder, &c. . . .*
> > That precept might not lose its force,

For want of good example:
Of every vice which *cunning hides,*
  His *grandpap* gave a sample.
    Fire and murder, &c.
He shew'd him how to seem most learn'd
  Without an education;
And how, with wond'rous skill to steal
  Another's reputation.
    Fire and murder, &c. . . .
Behold, he cried, how long my life,
  How great my reputation;
In time of trouble and of strife;
  I chose the strongest station . . .
    Fire and murder, &c. . . .
So deep I played the hypocrite,
  So simple were my manners,
That all admir'd the artless man—
  Who bore deception's banners.
    Fire and murder, &c. . . .
A patriot's honor too I claim'd,
  Without a patriot's heart, sir;
For, Pope declares, all honor lies
  In acting well your part, sir.
    Fire and murder, &c.
When Benny's mind had well imbib'd,
  This precious education;
Tis plain he was prepared to be
  The curse of any nation.
    Fire and murder, &c. . . .

Tonight (too late for inclusion in tomorrow's *Aurora),* a crowd of young men attacks Benny's house. Benny:

> [B]*etween ten and eleven, my house was assailed by a party of young men who in the morning had addressed the President . . . They honored me with imprecations and threats . . . My doors and windows were battered, and the women and children in the house (I happened to be from home) [were] somewhat terrified. They were prevented from going to more unjustifiable lengths by some citizens who happened to be passing at the time and by the neighbors . . .*[336]
>
>   *The attack of a loyal mob on this house [was] . . . the most unfortunate for the abbettors of it. It served only to convince the Editor of the number and spirit of his friends; who shewed themselves, in consequence of that outrage, determined, if violence was offered to his person or property, to assist him in repelling force by force.*[337]

Julien Niemcewicz is a witness:

Since these youths have begun to gather, the peace of the night is disturbed by their cries and chants. Drunk with wine they go to serenade at the windows of the President; they then go to break those of the printer Bache; they have hoisted the black cockade . . . It is these same means that provoke divisions. Alas, how many times have we not seen pools of blood spilled for a half a yard of ribbon?[338]

Abigail Adams:

They then closed the scene by singing the new song ["Hail Columbia"], which at 12 oclock at night was sung by them under our windows, they having dined together or rather a part of them.[339]

TUESDAY, MAY 8, 1798

GENERAL   ★ AURORA ★   ADVERTISER

Where are we! when the president makes the avowal [in his answer yesterday to the Young Men assembled in his House] . . . that he was not induced to join our revolutionary war from any discontentment with the form of *kingly government* established in Britain and that independence was then not an object of *predilection* and *choice* but of indispensable necessity? Is it not avowing, in fact, that he would have no objection to the establishment of a monarchy here and that if we had been admitted to the privileges of British subjects in the then mother country, he would not have wanted independence? . . .

The "friends of order" at the meeting for free debate on Thursday evening *menaced* the Republicans, broke the *banisters* and *benches* in the gallery and some of the *glass* in the neighboring doors. All this is well; the practical effect of that good order with which their mouths are filled, and a good criterion by which to judge of their profession, that they *wish to maintain* PEACE in our once happy COUNTRY.

Today, in reaction to the Federalist attack on Benny's home, groups of Republicans appear on High-street to defend the *Aurora*. They wear the tricolor cockade of red, white, and blue.[340]

Today, President Adams writes some admirers,

There is nothing in the conduct of our enemies more remarkable than their total contempt of the people . . . [T]he people are represented as in opposition, in enmity, and on the point of hostility against the government of their own institution and the administration of their own choice. If this were true, what would be the consequence? Nothing more or less than that they are ripe for a military despotism under the domination of a foreign power. It is to me no wonder that American blood boils at these ideas..[341]

111

War measures . . . Today, the U.S. House of Representatives opens debate on a bill *"authorizing the President of the United States to raise a provisional army"* of ten thousand volunteers. This bill would allow Federalist militias, like the black-cockaded Macpherson's Blues, to become, in effect, the federal army! From today's debate, as reported in the Annals of Congress:

PROVISIONAL ARMY . . .

Mr. GALLATIN [Republican, Pennsylvania] said . . . He must confess he looked upon all that was said of an invasion by France as a mere *bugbear.* He did not believe any attempt would ever be made . . .

Mr. BRENT [Republican, Virginia] said he knew that one of the more cogent reasons urged in favor of this army was that the southern states stood in need of them in order to quell any insurrection . . . Let us, said he, go on and make the people salutary laws; let the people experience the blessings of good government . . . and you will not require a standing army either to defend the country against internal or external enemies . . .

Mr. OTIS [Federalist, Massachusetts] . . . Could there be any fear that the President would raise these men if no danger threatened the country?[342]

Everyone senses the growing hostility to foreigners. Polish writer Julien Niemcewicz notes in his diary:

[T]he Alien bill, conceived in a truly Turkish spirit, shows to what point the administration attempts to adopt and imitate the arbitrary means of despots. There is nothing more proper than to be on guard against troublesome and dangerous foreigners, but indiscriminately to place under suspicion all foreigners comes from a desire more to rule than to protect.[343]

Tonight, in the *Porcupine's Gazette,* William Cobbett writes:

DETECTION OF A CONSPIRACY FORMED BY THE UNITED IRISH-MEN, For the Evident Purpose Of Aiding the Views of France In Subverting the Government OF THE UNITED STATES OF AMERICA— . . .

I have long thought that the French have formed a regular plan for organizing an active and effective force within these States . . . [W]here could they have sought them with such certainty of success as amongst that restless rebellious tribe, the emigrated UNITED IRISHMEN?

The first I heard of the existence of a Society of United Irishmen *here* was by a printed paper . . . signed Js. REYNOLDS . . . and about three weeks afterwards, the plan of the conspiracy was conveyed to me . . .

The *plan*, which is called a *constitution,* is printed in a small octavo pamphlet . . .[344]

The gallant youth of the city . . . should reflect that . . . [i]t is not hoisting a [black] COCKADE merely to pass in review and then *cramming it in the pocket* that will merit the applause of the nation . . . [A]ll those, in short, who are not afraid to meet the sans-culottes will wear the sign of their determination to oppose them.

That the PRESIDENT highly approves of *this* is clear from his conduct of yesterday. He not only put on *his* [black] cockade but his whole *military uniform.* It was not in this dress that he received the address of the merchants . . . [Y]esterday he had to receive those whom he looked upon as *soldiers;* and therefore as soldiers he met them.

I have heard that a few . . . sunshine soldiers have laid up the [black] cockade . . . [T]hey must not only wear [black] cockades, but must begin to wear a musket against their shoulder, or . . . that Government would be very foolish that should place any reliance on their efforts.

Tomorrow is President Adams' day for prayer and fasting. Everyone prepares for violence. Thomas Jefferson will recall,

> *The President received 3. anonymous letters . . . announcing plots to burn the city on the fast-day. He thought them worth being made known, and great preparations were proposed by way of caution, and some were yielded to by the Governor. Many . . . packed their most valuable moveables to be ready for transportation.*[345]

Tonight, the Macpherson's Blues appear in the city, pledging to support the government. "Citizen Volunteers" guard the Mint and the Arsenal. Troops of cavalry clatter throughout the streets.[346]

WEDNESDAY, MAY 9, 1798

GENERAL ★ AURORA ★ ADVERTISER

The other papers of this city have chosen to be silent this day, because the President has recommended a fast. We do not follow their example: Because there is nothing in the constitution giving authority to proclaim fasts . . . Because prayer, fasting, and humiliation are matters of religion and conscience, with which government has nothing to do . . . And Because we consider a connection between state and church affairs as dangerous to religious and political freedom and that, therefore, every approach towards it should be discouraged . . .

On Monday evening, between ten and eleven, my house was assailed by a party of young men who, in the morning, had addressed the President. They had dined together and were more than gay; but this is no excuse for the outrage. They honored me with imprecations and threats, the only notice I could be proud to receive from them. My doors and windows were battered . . .

It has been wrong from the beginning to encourage young men, not of age, to meddle in politics . . . We see how early they dive in excesses. They are now called upon to arm themselves; what are we to expect from them? The sincere friends to order and laws should look to those things.

It might, indeed, be a gratification to some that I should have my throat cut without the trouble of going through the tedious and uncertain forms of law. To be sure this in itself would be no very mighty matter, but the work of blood once begun, who will say where it would stop?

If the proceeding I have thought it my duty to notice is by way of intimidation, I pledge myself [that it] shall not produce the effect. While I respect and obey the laws of my country, I shall not be unmindful of the voice of my conscience which tells me it is my duty to remain at my post when the liberties of my country are endangered.

BENJAMIN FRANKLIN BACHE

[Yesterday] morning, about 3 or 4 o'clock, the peaceful and industrious inhabitants of Carter's alley were disturbed by a youthful "band of brothers," singing and playing Mr. Hopkinson's new song . . . and afterwards made some feeble attempts at *Yankee Doodle* . . .

However fond some of the inhabitants of that part of the city may be of the "concord of sweet sounds" in general, or partial to the President's March in particular, . . . '[t]is . . . to be hoped that these nocturnal revellers will hereafter choose some other scene to "warble their wood notes wild."

Today is the day John Adams set aside for humiliation, prayer, and fasting. It is also the day, by anonymous threat, Philadelphia is to burn!

Today, lawyer Joseph Hopkinson sends George Washington a copy of his new patriotic song, "Hail Columbia," as well as a pamphlet he has written which includes:

> *The opposition to government has been remarkable . . . Even the public acts of government, the votes of the legislature . . . undergo some distortion under the press of the Aurora . . . Even WASHINGTON, the noblest fabrick of humanity that ever came from the hands of the creator . . . has not withered the tongue of slander . . .*
>
> *Believe me. Americans, the object of this faction is not to correct the abuses of government or defend your liberties: Your government despises such monitors and you need no such defenders . . .*[347]

Today, Thomas Jefferson observes:

> *Party passions are indeed high. Nobody has more reason to know it than myself. I receive daily bitter proofs of it from people who never saw me, nor know anything of me but through Porcupine & Fenno. At this moment all the passions are boiling over, and one who keeps himself cool and clear of the contagion is so far below the point of ordinary conversation that he finds himself isolated in every society.*[348]

Today, as the President requested, churches hold special prayer services. William Cobbett observes:

> *The churches were, perhaps, never so crowded on any Sunday for years past. The sermons preached by Mr. [James] ABERCROMBY . . . were the most animated and awful discourses ever delivered in this city . . .*[349]

From his pulpit in Philadelphia's Christ Church (across from Porcupine's offices on Second-street), Porcupine's friend and constant associate[350] the Reverend James Abercrombie, A.M., intones:

> *That frantic and licentious spirit of disorder and desolation . . . originated in the infidelity of [France's] Philosophers . . . a Voltaire . . . a Diderot, a Helvetius, a Rousseau . . .*
>
> *How so infatuated an attachment to French politics and principle should so long have captivated . . . Americans is truly surprising . . . "The God whom we profess to serve is able to deliver us, and he will deliver us . . ." . . .*
>
> *As the Jews of old . . . we are in like manner now called upon by THE FATHER AND GUARDIAN OF OUR COUNTRY, who . . . will continue to be, "the minister of God to us for good." Justly elevated by the gratitude of his country . . . to the honorable station of CHIEF MAGISTRATE, the reiterated tributes of applause which now resound thro' our immense Continent incontestably prove that, during his administration of the adopted government, "he hath done all things well." . . .*
>
> *Now to God the Father &c.*[351]

The *Aurora's* name is not omitted from today's worship. A congregation in Medford, Massachusetts, not far from Boston, hears the Rev. David Osgood preach:

> *Having no other prey at present at hand, the arms of the French Republic are now stretched toward us . . . [T]he Aurora of Philadelphia and some other ignes fatui are so many decoys to draw us within reach of her fraternal embrace. If you would not be ravished by the monster, drive her panders from among you. The editors, patrons, and abettors of those vehicles of slander upon our government . . . have no longer any cloak for their guilt . . . Brethren, mark them who cause such dangerous divisions among us, and let them wear the stigma of reproach due to the perfidious betrayer of their country . . . So, O Lord God of Israel, let our enemies be turned back, disappointed and ashamed; and to thee shall be glory!* A M E N.[352]

Everyone is braced for violence. Tonight, it occurs. Abigail Adams:

> *The purport of the [two anonymous] letters was to inform the President that the French people who were in this city had formed a con-*

spiracy with some unsuspected Americans, on the Evening of the day appointed for the fast, to set fire to the city in various parts and to Massacre the inhabitants, intreating the President not to neglect the information & the warning given . . . Another Letter of the same purport was sent ten days after, thrust under the door of Mr. Otis's office. These with some Rumours of combinations got abroad, and the Mayor, Aldermen &c kept some persons upon the watch through all parts of the city, & the Governor gave orders privately to have a troop of Horse in case of need.[353]

Jimmy Callender:

The British gang wanted to burn [Bache's home] . . . They were headed by [Federalist Joseph Thomas, who led the crowds at Dunwoody's and James Cameron's]; and truly the head and the tail were worthy of each other. The fast day of May 9th, 1798 was chosen for the design . . . Bache heard of his danger, and informed [Mr.] Hilary Baker, then mayor of the city. No notice was taken of this intimation. The jacobin [Bache], the French pensioner, was left to his fate.[354]

Tonight, Philadelphia Federalist leader and lawyer Joseph Thomas, brandishing a sword above his head, leads a phalanx of sword-waving Federalists toward the *Aurora*'s offices.[355] Learning that a corps of Republican volunteers has prepared for its arrival, the mob limits itself to breaking windows in Benny's house. Jimmy Callender:

Bache collected and armed some of his friends. The six per cent myrmidons [the Federalists] heard of his preparations, and fortunately desisted from their plan. They filled the streets with noise and alarm; but they did not hazard an attack . . . It was affirmed, at the time, that a large quantity of arms was lodged by the government faction in a house near the hall of congress and that, in case of disturbance, muskets and ball were to be distributed to the young citizens, as the attorney's mob chose to call themselves . . .[356]

Philadelphian Margaret Morris, who lives near the State-house, will recall,

A great riot happened on . . . [that] evening, and hints thrown out of a design to fire the city; the light-horse were out all night, and the militia and private citizens were on guard, patrolling also, but it was passed in quiet, but we are still suspicious that the evil spirit is not wholly at rest, only lulled asleep. "Young Lightning Rod" had his house guarded by armed men, within and without, being fearful of having it pulled down. I think I never saw so many people at one time in my life as on that evening. What a world we live in, and what tumultuous times![357]

From Benny's house, the Federalist "Young Men" march toward the State-house yard, knocking down lampposts, breaking windows, and smearing mud on the statue of Benjamin Franklin at the Philadelphia Library.[358] A group of thirty or forty Republicans, wearing red and blue cockades, also march toward the State-house, and, as the *Gazette of the United States* reports, "*riots*" occur between opposing groups about 6 P.M.,

> the magistry sending to prison as many of those persons who did not escape either by flight or taking the [red & blue] cockades out of their hats . . .[359]

Abigail Adams:

> [I]t was in the State House Garden . . . [T]here they had their contest which terminated by sending half a dozen to prison . . .[360] [The encounter] was sufficient to allarm the inhabitants, and there were every where large collections of people. The light Horse were calld out & patrold the streets all night. A guard was placed before this [Presidential] House . . . A foreign attempt to try their strength & to awe the inhabitants was no doubt at bottom. Congress are upon an Allien Bill.[361]

President John Adams:

> [T]he night of the fast day, the streets were crowded with multitudinous assemblies of the people, especially that before my door, and kept in order only, as many people thought, by a military patrol, ordered, I believe, by the Governor of Pennsylvania.[362]

Jimmy Callender:

> [T]hirty lads appeared in a body in Philadelphia with French cockades . . . They were dispersed by the magistrates who committed some of them to prison. The federal mob were by far more numerous, more noisy, and more apparently dangerous. No attempt was made by the magistrates to reduce them to quiet . . .[363]

An anonymous eyewitness:

> [U]nder color of a danger of the city being set on fire . . . the independent horse and light infantry companies were put in a state of requisition under the command of the militia brigadier general M'Pherson (who is also a naval officer). In the evening forty draymen and butcher boys, angry at the arrogance of the black cockades, paraded the town with blue and red cockades . . . In the mean while, 7 or 800 black cockades, without any orders whatsoever, collected, some with guns, others with bludgeons, with the design, as they said, of suppressing mobs, while the greatest appearance of mob was among themselves and no danger except what they might create. They were persuaded to parade by the mayor's door as waiting for orders and from thence sent detachments to the suburbs, &c. It was two o'clock in the morning before they were persuaded finally to disperse.[364]

Our city yesterday bore a very disquieting appearance. The passions of our citizens which have been artfully inflamed by war speeches and addresses, as well as threats and denunciations against the Republicans, burst out in such a manner as to endanger the peace of the city. It was early foretold that the insidious recommendation of [Porcupine] a British printer to the youths of this city to wear a [black] cockade would be attended with disagreeable consequences. The prediction has been in a degree verified; tumultuous meetings and riots took place towards dark . . . The scenes of yesterday should be a warning . . . Another step and the yawning gulph may swallow up in inevitable ruin the fabricators of this scheme of arraying our citizens against each other as well as those against whom the destruction is intended.

It is true and lamentably true that endeavors are making to silence the freedom of opinions and the freedom of the press. The President of the United States has publicly denounced the freedom of opinion . . . In his answer to the address of the citizens of Newark may be found this remarkable sentence, "the delusions and misrepresentations . . . *must be discountenanced by authority as well as by citizens at large*, or they will soon produce all kinds of calamities in this Country." . . . Cannot public measures bear public viewing? . . . [Has t]he genius of freedom mingled itself in the dust with the ashes of Franklin . . . ? Was it to be made subservient to the will of an individual . . . ?

Today, John Adams answers an address from Hartford, Connecticut:

If the designs of foreign hostility and the views of domestic treachery are now fully disclosed; . . . if the spirit of independent freemen is again awakened and its force is combined . . . it will be irresistible.[365]

Today, the President also answers citizens from the vicinity of Shepherd's Town in Berkeley County, Virginia:

I had never until lately any expectation that I should live to see . . . the Executive authority vilified and our very existence threatened through the means of our citizens or any other with impunity . . .[366]

Today, Thomas Jefferson writes James Madison:

No bill has passed since my last [letter]. The alien bill, now before the Senate, you will see in Bache [May 8 issue] . . . Some of the young men who addressed the President on Monday mounted the black (or English) cockade. The next day numbers of people appeared with the tricolored (or French) cockade. Yesterday, being the fast day, the black cockade again appeared, on which the tricolour also showed itself. A fray ensued, the light horse were called in, & the city was so filled with confusion from about 6. to 10. o'clock last night that it was dangerous going out . . .[367]

Today, Abigail Adams writes her sister,

> *Bache is cursing and abusing daily. If that fellow . . . is not surpressed, we shall come to a civil war. I hope the Gen'll Court of our State will take the subject up &, if they have not a strong Sedition Bill, make one.*[368]

Today, Liz Hewson, Benny's friend, writes:

> *[Benny is] very much embarrassed in his circumstance . . . [and] going fast to destruction.*[369]

War measures . . . Today, the U.S. House of Representatives debates the bill that allows John Adams to enlist the new Federalist militias into his "provisional" army. The Annals of Congress report:

PROVISIONAL ARMY.

Mr. GALLATIN [Republican, Pennsylvania]: [said that] one of the most important powers that could be vested in Congress, viz: the power of raising an army is, by this bill, proposed to be transferred from Congress to the President. This he considered a dangerous principle . . .

Mr. DAYTON [Federalist, New Jersey]: The gentleman from Pennsylvania (Mr. GALLATIN) had now boldly erected his . . . opposition, not merely to the Administration or to the Government, but to all effectual measures of protection, defence, and preservation; and what was the motto . . . ? "Weakness and Submission" . . .

[T]he power and means of invasion . . . was known . . . [T]here were already collected upon the coasts of France, bordering upon the English channel, a numerous army . . . The same soldiers who were prepared to invade an island might certainly be employed [toward us] upon the Main and the same bayonets would pierce the breasts of the people inhabiting the latter as the former. Their larger transports . . . might transport a considerable part of them across the Atlantic and land them upon our shores . . . But the member from Pennsylvania [Mr. GALLATIN], aware of the possibility of the attempt, has attempted to divert the country from immediate preparation . . .[370]

Tonight, in the *Porcupine's Gazette*:

THE FAST

Was yesterday observed in this city with all the Solemnity of a Sabbath . . . The spirit of faction is not, however, quite killed. Towards evening, about twenty fellows, the greatest part of them foreigners, had the impudence to go to the State House yard with French cockades in their hats . . . The conduct of the *Associated Youth* was highly praiseworthy. They all assembled with alacrity . . . They should now lose no time in forming themselves into companies, procuring themselves arms, and appointing commanders. It has been stupidly asserted that their hoisting of the [BLACK] COCKADE was the occasion of the fracas! Monstrous!—What! are men to carry about them no sign of their devotion to the cause of their own country . . . for fear of giving offence and exciting tumults!

The Youth of Lancaster have mounted the BLACK COCKADE—Bravo!— Either it must stand, or the Country falls.

VOLUNTEER CORPS.
The Youth of North and South Mulberry Ward who are desirous of forming themselves into a Uniform Volunteer Corps, are requested to meet on Friday evening, the 11th instant, at the house of J. Hardy, Swan tavern, Third-street.

CONSPIRACY OF THE UNITED IRISHMEN
(Continued from Tuesday's paper.)

In my last, it was amply proved that this conspiracy had for its object something highly criminal . . . That this conspiracy is intended to aid the cause of France . . . [O]bserve that the closest intimacy exists between the sans-culotte French who are here, the most distinguished of the emigrated United Irishmen, and a base American printer, notoriously in the service of France . . . [A]ny ALIEN LAW which extends only to ALIENS of a *nation committing hostilities on the United States* will not reach the members of this affiliation.

FRIDAY, MAY 11, 1798

GENERAL ★ AURORA ★ ADVERTISER

Several persons, it is said, have been . . . committed for wearing in their hats a red and blue ribbon . . . cockade. If these persons appeared disposed to be riotous or if the magistracy feared that the wearing of those ribbons might be productive of disorder, those who refused to put them by were proper subjects of the notice of the police; but so are many of those also who wear black cockades in their hats, who have indeed proceeded to actual violence by attacking the house of a citizen [the Editor] at the dead of night, threatening those whom they have been taught to consider as obnoxious . . .

It will no doubt be attempted to make a distinction between the two sorts of badges, the one will be called French because it bears some resemblance to it; the other American tho' it is exactly like the British; but if the wearing of one of the cockades is permitted, the incitement to disorder will still exist, as still a distinction will be marked between our citizens—those with and those without the cockade. [T]he black cockade has been mounted on the express recommendation of [Porcupine] a printer in this city who avows himself a *British subject* and a *royalist*, and glories in their titles . . .

The proposals for embodying the youth of the City . . . is another egg from the same nest. The Adamites are not, it seems, contented with plunging their Country into foreign war, unless they can superadd a military government at home. The present proceedings of the faction are so monstrous that they must completely open the eyes of every one who is not absolutely blinded. The assertion of the President that he was not discontented with the British government before the Revolution ought to have been made more than twenty years ago, that America might have been on her guard against him.

We shall be in a precious plight if the Aristocrats in Congress get their bill past for a *provisional* standing army of ten thousand men: *provisional*, that is to say, if the President shall see them necessary, and this he infallibly will do. He wants, as he has kindly told us, to suppress opinions by authority which, without force, is a shadow, and so, when he has got the standing army, he will then have force . . . This standing army, of which the black cockade men have on Monday & on Wednesday evening last given so desirable a specimen, will cost at least fifteen thousand dollars a day . . .

The fast [day] puzzled the Printers not a little. Most of them did not publish on that day . . . For our part, determined to maintain our conscience free from political fetters, we published our paper as usual; but Mr. Adams resolved not to be broken in upon and sent it to us back . . . He was the only one of our subscribers who so scrupulously observed the fast to send back our paper. He was determined to shew a proper respect to his own recommendation—and, who had a better right ?

Word is out that Republicans are raising a private militia and that Benny has gone to the Northern Liberties to encourage attendance at Saturday's gathering of the Tammany Society on the banks of the Schuylkill River.[371]

Today, John Adams writes some citizens,

> *I trust with you that the spirit of disunion is much diminished . . . but unless the spirit of libelling and sedition shall be controlled by an execution of the laws, that spirit will again increase.*[372]

Tonight, in the *Gazette of the United States*:

Bache, whilst other people were observing the Fast Day yesterday (except a few Jacobins) as every good man ought to, was circulating his vehicle of lies and sedition . . .

Bache in his newspaper of this morning says, "it was early foretold that the insidious recommendation of a British Printer to the Youth of this city to wear a cockade would be attended with disagreeable consequences . . ." Bache, with his usual effrontery, ascribes to the [black cockade] badge which distinguishes Americans the tumult of Wednesday evening, when he knows that what took place was begun by persons wearing French cockades . . . Yet with respect to their badge he would have been silent.— No, he means that we should discard the badge which distinguishes Americans from the enemies of America. But why discard this badge? . . . [I]t is essential . . . that true Americans be distinguished from the partizans of France . . . Bache disseminates the atheistical principles of Paine— publishes forged letters of general Washington . . . endeavors to ridicule the age of our President. This same Bache . . . has the front to talk of the good of his country whose peace and happiness he has labored to destroy. He has sounded the lowest depth of human depravity and now exhibits to the world an example of wickedness that no man of his years ever arrived at before. Let none attempt to describe him—language is too weak—no combination of words will come so near to expressing everything that is monstrous in human nature as BENJAMIN FRANKLIN BACHE . . .

We hear the vile incendiary Bache . . . was disseminating his political poison among the citizens of the Northern Liberties, and announced his intention of having a Jacobinian festival at the Falls of Schuylkill [River] on Saturday, where he intended to descant [discourse] upon the answer of the President to the address of the Youth of the City—You may therefore expect to see a long list of hellish toasts . . . on Monday [or Tuesday] next inserted in his shameless *Aurora*.

Tonight, in the *Porcupine's Gazette*:

The adoption of the American [black] cockade will at once point out the friends of good order . . . and demonstrate to Bache and his cut throat abettors that the Fable of the LYON and the BULLS will not be verified in the conduct of the American people . . .

SIR, How the tumult originated yesterday afternoon that disturbed the peace of the city I now know . . . It was the French cockade . . . To . . . prevent future riots on the same account, it will not be amiss for the Mayor and Corporation, or some other authority, immediately to issue a proclamation, forbidding all men to wear the French cockade in Philadelphia . . .   *A HINT*

The black cockade is the military cockade of this country. [I]t has been so settled by the Federal government. It is earnestly recommended to Republicans, the real friends of order, not to think of assuming any badge liable to misconstruction. This . . . might be attended with mischief.

The *Gazette of the United States* is constantly harping on the assertion that the editor of the *Aurora* is in French pay. We are tired of giving the lie to this falsehood.

In a paper published under the immediate direction and constant inspection of the English Agent in this city, a publication has been recently made concerning *The United Irishmen*. It is not at all surprising . . . [I]f nationality proceeds to the length of supporting tyranny . . . then is nationality the most execrable of all human propensities. Of the latter character is the [British] nationality which attacks the unfortunate and long oppressed Irish. Of that character are the . . . two [Porcupine] papers of this week by the organ of the English Government, William Cobbett, formerly a corporal in the English regiment of foot, still remaining a British subject and a professed royalist.

Today, Benny Bache and other leading Republicans[373] attend the Annual Festival of the Republican Tammany Society at the Columbia Wigwam on the banks of the River Schuylkill. The society is a center for radical Republicanism, particularly among the newly arrived Irish.[374] Benny's Quaker friend Dr. George Logan of Stenton speaks:

> [A]ssisted by the blood and treasure of that brave and generous people, the French, we became a free, independent republic . . .
>
> The present gloomy appearance of our public affairs has no doubt been occasioned by the Citizens of the United States having too much neglected the representative principles of the federal government and looking up to one man for the salvation of our country . . .
>
> The kingly power, after having been a scourge to Europe for ages, is now, by the light of the American and French revolutions, coming to an end. It is devoutly to be wished that the citizens of the United States may be upon their guard not to suffer even the appearance of kingly authority to return amongst us to blast the fair prospects of our revolution . . .[375]

Tonight, in the *Gazette of the United States*:

APPOINTMENTS—BY AUTHORITY

JOSEPH HOPKINSON, of Pennsylvania, Commissioner for holding a treaty with the Oneida Indians.

GENERAL ★ AURORA ★ ADVERTISER

The alarms and disorders which have taken place within these few days . . . will, if not speedily checked, end in blood . . . The partizans of war . . . [i]nstead of resorting to reason . . . have recourse to threat, and instead of endeavoring to convince, they endeavor to enforce . . . Are free men to be bullied into certain opinions? . . .

To evince their zeal, a number of young men [on May 7] addressed the president . . . If, after the address was presented, the black cockade recommended by Porcupine had been laid aside, all might have been well; but this was not done, and the consequences are now unfolding themselves. The Day which was to have been set aside to implore the Deity in behalf of our country and to prostrate ourselves before him in humility and meekness became a day of riot and disorder . . . Our city never was in such alarm as on the evening of the fast day—the causes must be obvious to every one.

If proceedings like these are not discountenanced, my fellow citizens, where will they end? . . . Already it is said . . . that opposition is maturing itself. If hostile corps thus rise up among us, who can say that he will be safe. The consequences are to be deprecated, and an immediate check ought to be given to proceedings which are pregnant with ruin and murder. Before it is too late, my fellow-citizens, interpose your counsel and your influence, for if we are to have war, heaven guard us against a civil war.

Tonight, in the *Porcupine's Gazette*:

Many of the *Young Men* here have gotten themselves *arms* and are forming themselves into companies.

GENERAL ★ AURORA ★ ADVERTISER

On Saturday, the Tammany Society met . . . A long talk was . . . delivered by DR.[GEORGE] LOGAN. After dinner the following [16] toasts were drank: . . . 5. The chief of one of the Councils Thomas Jefferson . . . Two guns and three cheers . . . 10. The freedom of talk—May he who aims at interrupting it be branded by the tribes as a traitor, monster, and tyrant.— Three guns and six cheers. 11. The memory of our great and good father Dr. Franklin.—May the children of Pennsylvania cherish at every hazard the great legacy of freedom which he bequeathed.—Two guns. 12. The warriors of 76—May those only who fought from *choice* & not *necessity*, for *liberty* as well as *independence*, be entitled to the honors and rewards of the sixteen tribes.—Three guns and six cheers . . .

Tonight, in the *Porcupine's Gazette,* William Cobbett writes:

From various causes, these United States have become the resting place of ninety-nine hundredths of the factious villains which Great Britain and Ireland have vomited from their shores. They are all schooled in sedition, are adept at their trade, and they most certainly bear as cordial a hatred to this government as they did to their own . . . [A] paragraph . . . appeared a few days ago in the paper of that well-known scoundrel, the grand son of old Franklin. This wretch attempts to impose on the public a belief that, in every thing I say against the UNITED IRISHMEN, I aim at the whole Irish nation . . . [H]e lies from the bottom of his heart.

Wear the [black] *American cockade* . . . It is not sufficient that a man view unconcerned the progress of vice; if he makes no attempt to impede it, he gives it countenance . . . And is this not analogous to the *Aurora con-federation* . . . [C]an any man who has eyes and ears plead ignorance of the wishes and designs of that hydra of iniquity ? No . . . Wear the *American cockade* . . .

WEDNESDAY, MAY 16, 1798

GENERAL ★ AURORA ★ ADVERTISER

[In] the constitution alleged to be that of the United Irishmen, I find . . . *That* ALL *men are created equal* . . . But let me ask, in what respect do the circumstances of Ireland in 1798 differ from those of America in 1776?

Mr. Adams . . . proclaimed a *fast* and, but a few days before that fast, he attended the *play house* [to hear the Federalist song]. He first endeavors to ingratiate himself with the powers of darkness by going to the *play house* and then with the source of light by going to *church.*

Today, in the U. S. House of Representatives, the Annals of Congress report:

PROVISIONAL ARMY . . .

Mr. GALLATIN [Republican, Pennsylvania] said . . . The committee was told the other day that, by virtue of this bill, a number of volunteer corps would be raised who would associate themselves for the purpose of learning the military art . . . To consist of whom? Of those persons who, from their situation in life, are able to arm, clothe and equip themselves at their own expense. It was therefore giving an exclusive privilege to a certain class of men (young merchants, lawyers, and others) who are possessed of more wealth than their poorer neighbors to form a Military Association. And for what purpose? . . . [T]o do military duty in any manner that the President may think proper . . . The President is also to accept whom and reject whom he pleases . . .

[I]t would be impossible to form a standing army more dangerous than this . . . Upon the whole, Mr. G.[allatin] said, it appeared to him . . . a plan to arm one description of men exclusively of others and give them to the President of the United States to be used as he pleased, and what security had they that they would not be used for dangerous purposes?[376]

Mr. DAYTON [Federalist, New Jersey] . . . then replied to the member from Pennsylvania (Mr. GALLATIN) who had called these volunteer corps a most formidable force to be put into the hands of the President . . . [T]o whom, he asked, would they be truly formidable? To the invaders of our country—to the turbulent and seditious—to insurgents—to the daring infractors of the laws . . . [T]hese volunteers would be the first . . . to suppress seditious and disaffected persons, insurgents, or any daring infractors of the law . . .[377]

Mr. GALLATIN [Republican, Pennsylvania, answered] . . . we have seen differences of political opinion but no symptom of any infraction of the laws . . . Why then is the House told, not only today, but on former occasions, of seditious and disaffected persons—of dangers threatened to this country from insurrections? . . .[378]

Mr. HARPER [Federalist, South Carolina] said he should not employ a great deal of time in answering what had fallen from the gentleman from Pennsylvania (Mr. GALLATIN) . . . Certain gentlemen are alarmed to see this corps of generous youth and represent them as a force not to be trusted. Why? Because it will prove dangerous to liberty. To the liberty of insurgents and the seditious . . .[379]

Mr. GALLATIN [Republican, Pennsylvania] . . . The gentleman from South Carolina had said there were disorganizers and seditious persons . . . and yet he has not shown where these disorganizers and perturbators exist . . . A gentleman rises from his seat and tells the committee he saw five or six men in the streets of this city with French cockades . . . that some one had reported that it was said that somebody had heard that one of them had said he would join the French if they landed here; the gentleman immediately concluded that there is a deep conspiracy in the country . . .[380]

Mr. ALLEN [Federalist, Connecticut] . . . What the committee had heard from the Gentlemen from Pennsylvania, of this being a plan to arm the rich against the poor, was said to raise a popular clamour against it . . . While the people . . . are addressing the Government with offers of their lives and fortunes in support of our measures against France, the gentleman from Pennsylvania wishes to take no measures for our security. There is something very extraordinary in this. But the young men of our country possess a different spirit; they are resolved to unite in their country's cause; and they will be able effectually to prevent insurrections and insults from taking place in large cities which are the most subject to them . . .[381]

Tonight, in the *Porcupine's Gazette*:

The imps of the infernal Paris monster . . . are endeavoring to persuade the young men that the *black* is not the American cockade but the *British* . . . [I]s it not now worn by all the officers, land and sea, and by the PRESIDENT himself?

SPITTING RECORD, BE IT REMEMBERED. THAT . . . ONE MATTHEW LYON, an Irishman and a furious Democrat . . . did, in Congress Hall, while the House was in actual session, *spit* the nauseous slime from his jaws into the face of Roger Griswold, a member from Connecticut . . .

THURSDAY, MAY 17, 1798

GENERAL ★ AURORA ★ ADVERTISER

Citizens of America, you are called upon to unite and for what? In support of a man who openly avows his predilection for monarchical government and who has openly declared that it was not from discontent with the British government that he espoused the cause of your country—That there is cause for alarm no one can deny; but that this cause is domestic and not foreign is too palpable to be questioned . . . [W]hile you are [busied] in preparing for an imagined enemy, the real enemy is assaulting the citadel of your dearest privileges . . . and ere long you will be convinced to your sorrow that it was for *independence* and not for *liberty* that the present President of the United States contended.

Tonight, in the *Porcupine's Gazette,* Peter Porcupine writes:

I informed my readers that there was a section in the *provisional army bill,* authorizing the President to accept the services of volunteers corps . . . Gallatin said there was no occasion for the volunteer corps, as there was "no fear of war." . . . He was told that he feared the existence of volunteer corps, because he well knew from experience their efficacy *"in SUPPRESSING INSURRECTIONS."*

FRIDAY, MAY 18, 1798

GENERAL ★ AURORA ★ ADVERTISER

The French had assisted us very materially in our own revolutionary war, even before they openly joined us, with not only loans of money but with gratuitous donations to a large amount. Was it not natural when they, in their turn, were struggling under the burdens of a revolution, that they should look to us for some aid at least in the way of a loan?

War measures . . . Today, the U.S. House of Representatives approves, 51 to 40, the bill for a new provisional army of ten thousand volunteers.[382] The U.S. Senate resumes a second reading of the bill concerning aliens.[383]

Republicans are abandoning Congress.[384] Today, Republican House leader Al Gallatin writes his brother-in-law:

> I remain almost alone to bear the irksome burthen of opposition against a dozen or two speakers, several of whom [are] exceedingly deficient in talents but supplying their room by blackguardism and impudence . . . I consider it my sacred duty to remain firm to the post assigned to me by my constituents, however ungrateful the task.[385]

Thomas Jefferson explains:

> The Federalists' usurpations and violations of the Constitution at that period and their majority in both Houses of Congress were so great, so decided, and so daring that, after combatting their aggressions inch by inch without being able in the least to check their career, the Republican leaders thought it would be best for them to give up their useless efforts there, go home, get into their respective legislatures, embody whatever of resistance they could be formed into, and, if ineffectual, to perish there as in the last ditch. All therefore retired, leaving Mr. Gallatin alone in the House of Representatives, and myself in the Senate, where I then presided as Vice President . . . No one who was not a witness to the scene of that gloomy period can form any idea of the afflicting persecutions and personal indignities we had to brook.[386]

SUNDAY, MAY 20, 1798

Today, James Madison writes Thomas Jefferson:

> The Alien bill proposed in the Senate is a monster that must forever disgrace its parents. I should not have supposed it possible that such a one could have been engendered in either House & still persuade myself that it cannot be fathered by both . . . These addresses to the feelings of the people from their enemies may have more effect in opening their eyes than all the arguments addressed to their understandings by their friends. The President also seems to be co-operating for the same purpose. Every answer he gives to his addressers unmasks more and more his principles & views. His language to the young men at Ph[iladelphia] is the most abominable & degrading that could fall from the lips of the first magistrate of an independent people . . . It throws some light on his meaning when he remarked to me "that there was not a single principle the same in the American & French Revolutions;" . . . The abolition of Royalty was, it seems, not one of his Revolutionary principles . . .[387]

Today, President Adams' nephew, William Shaw, writes his aunt, Abigail Adams:

I believe the grand cause of all our present difficulties may be traced to this source—too many hordes of Foreigners to America. I believe the English government will not allow any alien to be capable of receiving any office what ever. We shall not, I am afraid, continue long independent as citizens and as a nation, unless we speedily enact some-such law. Let us no longer pray that America may become an asylum to all nations, but let us encourage our own men & cultivate our simple manners.[388]

The President will shortly make William Shaw his private secretary.

MONDAY, MAY 21, 1798

GENERAL ★ AURORA ★ ADVERTISER

The United States ship the *Ganges*, capt. Dale, of 20 guns (nine pounders), having completed her preparations for sea, is now lying at anchor in the cove with a full complement of men. The Cutter *General Greene* is also completely armed and manned.

Tonight, in the *Porcupine's Gazette*:

[The President] has the happiness never to have approved of the principles of the French Revolution, directly or indirectly.

TUESDAY, MAY 22, 1798

GENERAL ★ AURORA ★ ADVERTISER

The armed cutter Gen. Greene, captain Price, sailed from hence yesterday on a cruise.

Today, John Adams calls another group of young men to arms:

To arms, then, my young friends,—to arms . . . For safety against dangers which we now see and feel, cannot be averted by truth, reason, or justice . . . I ought not to forget the worst enemy we have, that obloquy [slandering] which you have observed, it is the worst enemy to virtue and the best friend to vice; it strives to destroy all distinction between right and wrong; it leads to divisions, sedition, civil war, and military despotism. I need say no more. JOHN ADAMS[389]

Tonight, in the *Gazette of the United States*:

I am one of the young men . . . [W]hy does our wearing the [black] American cockade excite the warmest sensibility of the corrupt *Aurora* man and his *virtuous friends*? Why have they raised a villainous mob to insult and intimidate those who had courage and patriotism to wear it? Because it shews who are friends of this country . . . because it has a tendency to check the spreading of the baneful principles which have been industriously disseminated for the purpose of rearing the hideous head of anarchy. The panic with which the American cockade strikes the French faction is an undeniable proof of the absolute necessity of wearing it . . .

Tonight, in the *Porcupine's Gazette*:

> *Robison's Proofs of a Conspiracy* . . . contains an exposure of such deep-laid villainy . . . The French Revolution with all its abominations are traced to . . . [the] ILLUMINATI . . .
>
> While a pupil is under trial and before he is admitted into this infernal society, many questions are put . . . For instance: *"How far is the proposition true that WICKED MEANS may be used for a GOOD PURPOSE?"*
>
> In one of the answers to this question, the example of a great philosopher and Cosmopolite is adduced, who *betrayed a private correspondence entrusted to him,* for the service of Freedom: the case was DOCTOR FRANKLIN!!!!!—This is excellent! DOCTOR FRANKLIN is held up as an example to the pupils of a society, surpassing if possible hell itself in perfidy and every species of wickedness !! The *illuminati* understood the merits of Doctor Franklin . . .

As Jimmy Callender has observed, *"Abuse on the memory of Dr. Franklin has, for some time, been an essential ingredient in every federal pamphlet."*[390]

WEDNESDAY, MAY 23, 1798

GENERAL ★ AURORA ★ ADVERTISER

Mr. Adams, in his answer to the address from Burlington, declares the French nation to be *"our enemies."* Query, has the President the power of declaring war? If he has not, by what authority does he presume to stile a nation our enemy with whom we are at peace?

THURSDAY, MAY 24, 1798

GENERAL ★ AURORA ★ ADVERTISER

PORCUPINE AND THE PRESIDENT

Amongst the numerous and fulsome praise which issue from Cobbett's press to daub and flatter the President, we cannot help noticing one . . . for [his] having *never approved of the principles of the French Revolution, either directly or indirectly!*— This indeed we required no ghost to inform us of: for the American who could not approve of the principles which gave freedom and independence to his own country could certainly not view the emancipation of a foreign and distant nation in any favourable point for view.

War . . . This morning at eleven o'clock, the Secretary of War, accompanied by Captain Barry of the frigate *United States,* boards the U.S. ship-of-war *Ganges* and delivers sailing orders to Captain Dale. This afternoon, the *Gazette of the United States* reports,

On the Secretary's leaving the ship, a salute was fired, immediately after which she weighed anchor to proceed to her cruising station.

War . . . At about five o'clock this afternoon, between Norfolk, Virginia and Philadelphia, the American schooner *Liberty* has an encounter with a French privateer. Captain Joseph Canby reports:

I was chased by a privateer without colours but whose crew wore the National Cockade of France. When she overhaled me and came alongside, within about thirty yards, she ordered me to hoist out my boat, and go aboard her, but before I could do it, the man at the masthead called out . . . "a Sail," upon which the privateer left me . . . The privateer carried twelve guns . . .[391]

SATURDAY, MAY 26, 1798

Hopkinson, the author of the late Federal Song ["Hail Columbia"] to the tune of the President's March . . . has been nominated [by the President] a commissioner to transact some business with some Indians. He has written his song to *some* tune, and to the *right* tune—that's clear.

[Clement] Humphries, who attempted to assassinate Mr. Bache, of which he was convicted, on going to pay his penalty received notice it had been paid already; and he has since been selected to carry dispatches to the three envoys at Paris! pause, reader, and reflect on conduct that beggars all commentary. The next conspirator for the murder of Mr. Bache ought not to complain for the want of previous engagement. If the writing of adulatory songs to the president and the assassinating of men who have firmness to expose the improper measures of our government are to recommend them to executive appointments, to what an alarming pass has our government arrived.

HIGHLY ALARMING!

It is said, that there are six French privateer Cruisers now on our coast to take all American vessels with British property on board!

HIGHLY ALARMING, AGAIN.

It is said that there are ten sail of British Ships of war on the American coast to [take] . . . all American vessels bound to or from the ports of France . . . having the produce of those countries on board.

A pretty pickle of fish for the United States to digest!

The object of the late political fast [May 9th] is every day better and better understood. Instead of a day devoted to solemn prayer and humiliation, rancorous fulminations and party invectives issued from most of the pulpits. Many ministers of religion . . . were wonderfully uniform . . . They moved with an exactness which proved that there existed a main spring somewhere. The mystery is unraveled when the reader is informed that some weeks before the fast day, circulars were issuing from a certain public office in this city to these select Reverends throughout the Union.

Today, The President's Lady, Abigail Adams, writes her sister:

> *I wish the Laws of our Country were competent to punish the stirrer up of sedition, the writer and Printer of base and unfounded calumny. This would contribute much to the Peace and harmony of our Country as any measure, and in times like the present, a more carefull and attentive watch ought to be kept over foreigners. This will be done in the future if the Alien Bill passes, without being curtaild & clipt untill it is made nearly useless. The Volunteer Corps which are forming not only of young Men but others will keep in check these people, I trust . . .*[392]

SUNDAY, MAY 27, 1798

Today, George Washington answers Joseph Hopkinson's letter of May 9th:

> *I pray you now, my good Sir, to accept my thanks for the Pamphlet and Song which accompanied it . . . To expect that all men should think alike upon political, more than on religious or other subjects, would be to look for a change in the order of things; but at so dangerous a crisis as the present, when everything dear to Independence is at stake, the well disposed part of them might, one would think, act more alike; Opposition therefore to the major will and to that self respect which is due to the National character cannot but seem strange!*
>
> *But I will unite with you in a fervent wish and hope that greater unanimity than heretofore will prevail . . . and that the young men of the present day will not suffer the liberty for which their fore fathers fought . . . [to] be lost by them either by supineness or divisions among themselves disgraceful to the Country . . .*[393]

MONDAY, MAY 28, 1798

GENERAL ★ AURORA ★ ADVERTISER

The westerly winds that have prevailed for some days past compelled the English frigates to retire from our coasts, and several vessels have in consequence entered port.

There are now French vessels of war within the capes of Delaware, and there is a treaty [of 1778] still in existence between the United States and France . . . [B]y that treaty, not only armed French vessels may come into our ports and bring in their prizes; but they may also sail out of our ports at any time unmolested, and we are bound not to give them hindrance.

War measures . . . Today, John Adams approves and signs into law,

AN ACT
*More effectually to protect the commerce
of the United States.*

WHEREAS armed vessels . . . of France have committed depredations on the commerce of the United States . . .

Be it Enacted . . . That . . . the President . . . is hereby authorized to instruct and direct the armed vessels belonging to the United States to seize, take and bring into any port of the United States . . . any such armed vessel which shall have committed, or which shall be found hovering on the coast for the purpose of committing, depredations . . .[394]

War measures . . . Today, John Adams approves and signs into law,

AN ACT
*Authorizing the President of the United States
to raise a Provisional Army.*

Sec. 1. *Be it enacted . . .* That the President . . . is hereby authorized in the event of a declaration of war against the United States, or of actual invasion, . . . or of imminent danger of such invasion discovered in his opinion to exist, to cause to be inlisted . . . a number of troops not exceeding ten thousand . . .

Sec. 3. *And be it further enacted . . .* That . . . the President is hereby empowered, at any time within three years after the passing of this act, if in his opinion the public interest shall require, to accept of any company or companies of volunteers . . . who may associate and offer themselves for the service, who shall be armed, clothed and equipped at their own expense . . .[395]

John Adams will now invest Macpherson's Blues and other Federalist militias with the authority of the U.S. government.

Today, President Adams warns some citizens,

[Y]our tranquillity has been disturbed by incessant appeals to the passions and prejudices of the people by designing men and by audacious attempts to separate the people from the government . . .[396]

Tonight, in the *Gazette of the United States*:

It would be an endless labor to notice all the lies and misrepresentations that crowd the pages of Bache's papers. In the *Aurora* of [Saturday morning], he pretends to account for the unanimity of the sentiments expressed by the ministers of religion on the late [May 9th] fast day by suggesting that they were prompted to do this by "circulars issued some weeks before by a certain public office to the select reverends throughout the union." The office alluded to is certainly the Department of State, and the facts were simply these—Proclamations were printed for the information of all the clergy in the United States. [T]hey were formed into packages and addressed to the marshals and, to facilitate their distribution by the aid of the public mails, they were separately folded and packed up at the Department of State without the name of one clergy superscribed, it being left to the marshal to add to the superscription of *Reverend* the name of each minister in his district . . . Bache . . . says that "rancorous fulminations and party invectives issued from most of the pulpits." . . . [This fact] proves that most of the clergy in the United States, and thence we can conclude most of the people, detest the conduct of the French and are ready to oppose their attempts to control our government.

Several volunteer companies are now forming in this city. The Troops of Horse have increased their number. M'Pherson's Blues are organizing themselves anew . . . A company of Grenadiers has likewise been established . . . Let the youthful signers of the late address to the President now come forward and join . . . Their country does now call for their assistance, and Congress has prescribed the mode in which it shall be rendered by authorizing the President to accept their services as volunteers . . .

Tonight, in the *Porcupine's Gazette*:

The YOUNG MEN who pledged themselves to the president will take notice that the committee will wait this evening (only) at the City Tavern, from 6 till 9 o'clock, to receive signatures of those who wish to join themselves to Macpherson's Blues.

TUESDAY, MAY 29, 1798

GENERAL   ★ AURORA ★   ADVERTISER

We are now, by the mad measures of our administration, on the eve of war, if not actually at war with the French Republic; our legislature it is hoped will not separate without further provision for the defence of our sea port towns and harbours. As government have determined that we should come to an open rupture with the French, we must expect to be treated as enemies.

Tonight, in the *Gazette of the United States*:

> The vapourings of poor *Surgo Ut Prosim* and his party remind one of the Balloonist who, after ascending in his machine with the pompous motto *"sic itur ad astra"* [thus may you go to the stars] was presently dropped upon the *earth* and shattered to pieces.

> "Rise," cries Bache, "ere it be too late"—Rise, and redress your wrongs: But ah! he cries in vain. The cruel state of his party resembles that of a wounded serpent . . .

WEDNESDAY, MAY 30, 1798

GENERAL ★ AURORA ★ ADVERTISER

TO JOHN ADAMS, PRESIDENT OF THE UNITED STATES. SIR . . . [T]he many addresses from different parts of the union approbating your conduct . . . are founded upon th[e] supposition that you have been sincere in your attempts at negociation with the French Republic . . . [Others] have said you secretly wished for a rupture with France and for a closer connection with Great-Britain whose government was more consonant with your feelings and with your ideas of perfection . . . [Should the people] hereafter be convinced that your secret movements spoke a different language from your public declarations . . . that by stirring upon the Americans to hate the French, it was intended they should hate . . . both Frenchmen and Republicanism . . . the public resentment will recoil with redoubled vengeance upon the heads of those who are its proper objects . . .

Today, Benny's brother, William, and four other doctors at the Philadelphia Dispensary urge the dispensary's managers not to dismiss Dr. Jimmy Reynolds, leader of Philadelphia's Society of United Irishmen:

> *GENTLEMEN, The Physicians of the Philadelphia Dispensary have been informed that some of the contributors have applied to you for the removal of one of their associates, against whom nothing is urged but difference in political opinion, while all agree that his attentions to the duty annexed to the appointment have been useful to the sick and honorable to himself.*

> *We place too much reliance on the candor and liberality of the Managers to believe that they will be the instruments of introducing into a charitable association the distinctions of party and are persuaded they will never consent to render a valuable institution an engine of oppression.*

> *WILLIAM BACHE [et al]*[397]

GENERAL ★ AURORA ★ ADVERTISER

BOSTON, MAY 24. Yesterday between 2 and 3 o'clock, P. M. was experienced a very violent storm . . . declared to be a damn'd jacobin storm, by a noted major, for destroying a picture of George Washington and striking the mast of the schooner FEDERAL GEORGE. This is as conclusive reasoning as perhaps can be had that the operation of nature is highly anti-federal and ought, if possible, to be arrested in its progress.

Today, Thomas Jefferson writes James Madison:

The Alien bill will be ready today, probably, for its 3rd reading in the senate . . . [I]t is a most detestable thing . . . This bill will unquestionably pass the H of R, the majority there being decisive, consolidated, and bold enough to do anything. I have no doubt from the hints dropped they will pass a bill to declare the French treaty void . . .

Volney & a ship-load of others sail on Sunday next. Another ship-load will go off in about 3 weeks.[398]

Tonight, in the *Gazette of the United States*:

It is currently reported that the itinerant philosopher VOLNEY has determined shortly to embark for Europe . . . [T]he day is just at hand when he and other emissaries must quit this land of toleration for the regions of directorial tyranny.

GENERAL ★ AURORA ★ ADVERTISER

We believe nothing will so much endanger the liberties of the people of any country as frequent wars. They produce a vast accumulation of debt, an immense patronage in the hands of the executive, a great increase in fiscal influence (at all times unfavorable to liberties) and by harassing the people, induce them to trust the defence of their country to standing armies who will soon make some bold and aspiring man the tyrant of his country.

☞ A special meeting of the AMERICAN PHILOSOPHICAL SOCIETY will be held at their Hall at 7 o'clock this evening.

Today, Thomas Jefferson writes fellow Virginian John Taylor:

A little patience, and we shall see the reign of witches pass over, their spells dissolved, and the people recovering their true sight, restoring their government to its true principles . . . It is hardly necessary to caution you to let nothing of mine get before the public; a single sen-

tence got hold of by the Porcupines will suffice to abuse and persecute me in their papers for months.[399]

Tonight, the Rev. James Abercrombie of Philadelphia's Christ Church repeats his anti-French Fast Day sermon before a meeting of the American Philosophical Society. Thomas Jefferson, who has been at every meeting of the society since March, does not attend. The minutes read:

Abercrombie's Sermon on fast day, May 9, was presented by him. Thanks voted.
Adjourned to this day week.[400]

Tonight, in the *Gazette of the United States*:

To the citizens of Queen Anne's County in . . . Maryland . . .
I cannot profess my attachment to the principles of the French Revolution . . . An anxiety for the establishment of a government in France on the basis of the equal rights of mankind . . . I feel in common with you . . .
JOHN ADAMS

Tonight, in the *Porcupine's Gazette*:

LONDON [England] . . . [I]n consequence of the order issued by the House of Peers [Lords] for the apprehension of the proprietor and printer of the *Morning Chronicle*, Mr. Perry and Mr. Lambert . . . were . . . conveyed to Newgate [Prison] by two doorkeepers of the House of Lords.
Take care Bache !—Take care, child of Old Franklin !

SATURDAY, JUNE 2, 1798

GENERAL ★ AURORA ★ ADVERTISER

From the accounts brought by the packet, it appears that Ireland is in a very unsettled, distracted state; and declared in a state of rebellion.

SHIP NEWS.
PORT OF PHILADELPHIA
Cleared. Brig. Benjamin Franklin, Jones, Bourdeaux.

The ship *Benjamin Franklin* is preparing to take would-be Americans back to France.

Today, Abigail Adams writes her nephew, William Shaw:

France has Settled her plan of subjugating America. [H]er system is fully known . . . [S]he can pour in her armies upon us. [S]he can, as she has Done, Arm the Slave against his master, and continue by her Agents and emissaries whom . . . she boasts of having thickly Scattered through our Country, serving her principles, her depravity of manners, her Atheism, in every part of the United States. [B]y these

means she will seduce the mind & sap the foundation of our strongest
pillars, religion & Government. These are not visionary ideas of future
events. They are now active. They have already proceeded to a most
alarming height. It becomes every individual to rise and unite, to stop
the progress, to resist the poison before it contaminates our vitals.
[L]et not the question be asked what can I do? but what may I do ?
unite, unite
　　　　　　　"As a band of Brothers joined,
　　　　　　　peace and safety we shall find"
Form voluntary corps—let every citizen become a soldier and deter-
mine, as formerly, on Liberty or Death![401]

Tonight, in the *Porcupine's Gazette*:

> DUPONT, the French consul, who came from Charleston to replace
> MONS[IEUR] LE TOMBE as [Philadelphia's French] Consul General has
> been refused to be received by the President; and, I understand he is going
> off for France, having obtained a passport for that purpose . . .

Tonight, in the *Gazette of the United States*:

> The propriety of wearing some badge of distinction is suggested to the
> different volunteer corps now forming in this city . . . It has now become
> necessary to give a military appearance to the United States . . . Upon the
> bulk of mankind, parade and even ostentation most forcibly operate, and
> the sign of a feather or a uniform may give greater aid than could at first
> be imagined to motives of duty and patriotism . . . It is not sufficient for
> this purpose to wear only the [black] cockade, since it is worn by persons
> who neither are nor mean to become soldiers . . . Actuated by these opin-
> ions, the volunteer company of Philadelphia Grenadiers have entered into
> a resolution to wear at all times a black feather in their hats and to appear
> upon Sundays in full uniform . . .

John Fenno's twenty-year-old son, John Ward ("Jack") Fenno, helped to organize the Philadelphia Grenadiers,[402] who are joined with the Macpherson's
Blues.[403]

SUNDAY, JUNE 3, 1798

Today, George Washington writes Judge Alexander Addison of the U.S. District
Court of Pennsylvania:

> *[M]uch good may, and I am persuaded will, result from the investi-*
> *gation of Political heresies when the propagation of them is intended*
> *evidently to mislead the multitude who . . . only require correct infor-*
> *mation to enable them to decide justly upon all National matters . . .*
> *not like the Demagogues that attempt to impose upon their under-*
> *standings and . . . embarrass them more in the prosecution of their*

system of opposition to the Wheels of Government which they have adopted, and at all events, it would seem, are determined to adhere to . . .[404]

Today, James Madison writes Thomas Jefferson:

Whilst it was expected that the unrelenting temper of France would bring on war, the mask of peace was worn by the [Federalist] war party. Now that a contrary appearance on the side of France is intimated, the mask is dropped and the lye openly given to their own professions by [their] pressing measures which must force France into War.[405]

MONDAY, JUNE 4, 1798

GENERAL ★ AURORA ★ ADVERTISER

REPUBLICAN BLUES

☞ Citizens desirous to attach themselves to this Company are requested to apply to a Committee of the Company who will sit at the house of Abraham Morrow, Chestnut-street on Tuesday, Thursday & Sunday; or at the sign of the Cock and Lion, corner of Coates' and Second-streets, on Wednesday and Friday evenings, between the hours of 7 & 9 o'clock.

Today, the Philadelphia Infirmary dismisses not only my Irish friend Dr. Jimmy Reynolds,[406] but also Benny's brother, William, and the other four doctors who wrote in Jimmy Reynolds' defense.[407]

Fearing Federalist militias, friends of the *Aurora* are forming their own private militia, the "Republican Blues," which Benny's brother, William, will lead.[408]

Today, Thomas Jefferson writes a letter of introduction for Quaker George Logan, who is getting ready to leave for France:

I, Thomas Jefferson, do hereby certify that George Logan . . . is a citizen of the commonwealth of Pennsylvania and of the United States, of one of the most ancient and respectable families of the said commonwealth, of independent fortune, good morals, irreproachable conduct, and true civism . . .[409]

Today, French philosopher Constantin-François Volney announces his plans to leave:

Determined to leave this country immediately, I inform the public that the translation of my book, the RUINS, announced two years ago, and which I was to direct, is stopped and cannot take place . . .[410]

Today, in the U.S. House of Representatives, the Annals report:

SEDITIOUS PRACTICES

MR. SEWALL [Federalist, Massachusetts], from the Committee for the Protection of Commerce and the Defence of the Country reported a bill

. . . that any alien resident . . . who shall be a *notorious fugitive from justice* upon the charge of treasonable practices in any foreign State or country or whose continuance within the United States shall be, in the opinion of the President, injurious to the public peace . . . may be required to depart from the country . . .

And if any person, whether alien or citizen . . . discourage any person . . . under the Government . . . from undertaking his trust . . . by any writing, printing, or advised speaking . . . [such person] may be punished . . . by imprisonment . . .[411]

Today, Jimmy Callender, a "notorious fugitive" from Scottish "justice," who arrived in America just five years and one week ago, rushes to take his citizenship oath at Pennsylvania's Court of Common Pleas.[412]

Tonight, the *Gazette of the United States* reveals that Thomas Jefferson is helping the *Aurora*:

HELP! OH! HELP! . . .
We have it from good authority that a certain gentleman of high station in our Government has written on to Virginia *"earnestly soliciting his partizans and all their influential men in his part of the country to exert themselves to procure subscriptions to the A U R O R A, or the paper must fall, many Subscribers having lately withdrawn."* Strange Revolution!

Aurora about to set, to rise no more !
Aurora, that rose to profit all, should fail to profit herself !

TUESDAY, JUNE 5, 1798

GENERAL ★ AURORA ★ ADVERTISER

Mr. Fenno, in last evening's paper, states that a certain gentleman of high station in our government has written to Virginia, recommending to his friends to exert themselves in procuring subscriptions to the Aurora, *or the paper must fall, many subscriptions having lately withdrawn.* We can readily believe that there are persons high in office, even in the federal government, friendly to the cause of liberty and equal rights, & to the genuine principles of the constitution . . . who would, therefore, be ready to promote the circulation of the Aurora. But the inference therefrom that the paper must fall without additional support or that many subscribers have lately withdrawn is FALSE. The paper never brought in more money than it does now. It had never a more extensive circulation than at present, and its circulation is as extensive, at least, as that of the Gazette of the United States. It is true, nevertheless, that it has never been a very lucrative establishment; but it may become so, and, in the meantime it is reasonable to support itself and the proprietor of it without *"benefactions"* from any individual whatever.

As Poor Richard advised,

Let thy Discontents be Secrets.[413]

Tonight, in the *Gazette of the United States*:

OF REPUBLICAN MODESTY

Take the following sample from the dying lips of the Jacobin *Aurora*. *"We can readily believe that there are persons high in office . . . ready to promote the circulation of the Aurora."*

Tonight, in the *Porcupine's Gazette,* Peter Porcupine writes:

In order to avoid the operation of the . . . law with respect to *fugitive* ALIENS, the CAITIFF CALLENDER went yesterday and offered himself as a *Citizen of the United States* and was *admitted.*

Tonight, a bad omen . . . Benjamin Jones, a tailor in Fromberger's court, dies a horrible death. A report:

Mr. Jones had been but six or seven weeks resident in Philadelphia. About seven or eight months previous, he had been bit by a dog supposed to be mad. He was delirious and attempted to bite his attendants. These circumstances produced suspicion that he had the hydrophobia; but his physician, Dr. Physick, who opened his body after death, asserted it to be the yellow fever.[414]

WEDNESDAY, JUNE 6, 1798

GENERAL ★ AURORA ★ ADVERTISER

TEXT

"Congress shall make no law abridging the freedom of Speech or of the press . . ."

COMMENTARY

A BILL

For the prevention and restraint of dangerous
and seditious persons . . .

Sec. 2. *And be it further enacted,* . . . if any person . . . shall, by any writing, printing or advised speaking, threaten *[a public official]* . . . with any damage to his character . . . shall and may be punished . . .

The above Bill is to be debated in committee of the whole house [of representatives] this day.

Tonight, in the *Porcupine's Gazette*:

A few days ago, a committee of the House of Representatives reported a bill [that] . . . proposes that "any alien resident . . . who shall be a notorious fugitive from justice . . . in any foreign state or country . . . may be required to depart the country . . ." The miscreant CALLENDER saw that this bill would very soon send him back to Britain . . . [T]o avoid this long and disagreeable journey, he flew to the shelter of *citizenship.* He went on Monday last into the court of *Nisi Prius* . . . Here *Thomas Leiper,* a snuff-grinder [tobacconist], swore that he had known Callender for upwards of four years; that during that time he had been . . . *attached to the constitution of the United States* . . . [T]his we have it in our power to prove to be false . . . In his [Callender's] *History of the United States for 1796,* he says . . ."the *Federal Constitution was framed in darkness."* He represents the proceedings of the [FEDERAL CONSTITUTIONAL] CONVENTION as *"clandestine"*. . . In his *Sketches of the History of America,* . . . on the power which the constitution gives to the President and the Senate, he concludes thus: "This may be *called REPRESENTATIVE GOVERNMENT,* but is evidently the *dregs of Monarchy and Aristocracy."*

Tonight, in the *Gazette of the United States*:

The Editor of the *Aurora,* to keep his readers in the dark as much as possible . . . omits the publication of the [laudatory] addresses to the government from almost every part of the Union . . .

THURSDAY, JUNE 7, 1798

GENERAL   ★ AURORA ★   ADVERTISER

The Tories are . . . determined on war; they know that the conduct and language of the Executive make war *unavoidable*; they are therefore resolved to be . . . the first to strike a blow . . . The present is really a crisis in our affairs. Those members of the legislature who are absent should instantly repair to their posts, & the People, as they value the blessings of peace and their liberties (for their rights will always be more or less endangered in the turmoil of war), should meet and, by firm and manly remonstrances to their Representatives, avert the evils that threaten.

Regrettably, Republicans won't return.

War . . . This morning, by report, the second of the navy's new warships is at sea against France:

[T]he frigate *United States,* John Barry Esq. commander, weighed anchor and sailed down river. She reached the fort and came to about noon.[415]

Today, Thomas Jefferson writes James Madison:

> [T]hey have brought into the lower house a sedition bill which,
> among other enormities, undertakes to make printing certain matters
> criminal, though one of the amendments to the Constitution has so ex-
> pressly taken religion, printing presses, &c. out of their coercion. In-
> deed this bill and the alien bill both are so palpably in the teeth of the
> Constitution as to show they mean to pay no respect to it. The citizen
> bill passed by the lower house sleeps in a Committee of the Senate. In
> the meantime, Callender, a principal object of it, has eluded it by get-
> ting himself made a citizen. Volney is gone. So is Dupont, the rejected
> consul . . .[416]

Today, the brig *Benjamin Franklin* departs Philadelphia for France. Chartered
by Frenchmen who now seek refuge from America and cleared for departure
by U.S. Secretary of State Pickering, the *Benjamin Franklin* carries, among
others, Constantin-François Volney (the great literary figure of the Enlightenment) and Victor Marie Dupont (the new consul general from France that John
Adams has refused to receive).[417] Fifteen such shiploads will flee America this
year.[418]

Today, Federalist party leader Alexander Hamilton urges Secretary of State
Pickering to expel French nationals:

> If an alien Bill passes I should like to know what policy on exequa-
> turs is likely to govern the Executive. My opinion is that while the
> mass ought to be obliged to leave the Country, the provisions in our
> Treaties in favor of Merchants ought to be observed & there ought to be
> guarded exceptions of characters whose situations would expose them
> too much if sent away . . . There are a few such.[419]

Tonight, in the *Porcupine's Gazette,* Peter Porcupine writes:

> THE [MOST RECENT] DISPATCHES from our envoys at Paris . . . pre-
> sent us nothing new. They only place all the propositions of X, Y, Z to the
> account of the [French] minister of Foreign Affairs. Infamous BACHE can
> therefore no longer impute the insolent demands to *"unauthorized
> agents."* Talleyrand . . . is no unauthorized agent..
>
> ---
>
> How [Dr. James Reynolds] ever came to be admitted as a Physician to so
> respectable an institution as the Philadelphia Dispensary, I know not; but
> I know that several of the most liberal contributors lately expressed their
> determination to withdraw their aid from it if he was suffered to remain.
> In consequence of which, he was, last Monday, *turned out* by the Man-
> agers. His colleagues (amongst whom was *Bache the printer's Brother*)
> had the impertinence to resent the measure, in consequence of which the
> Managers very politely informed them that their services also were dis-
> pensed with!!!
>   This is worthy . . . [of] imitation, not only of every institution of this
> kind, but of every department of government. It is time that the foes of

the nation should feel its resentment—If they love France, to France let them go. It is mere nonsense to say that the politics of a man ought to be no exception to him in the common concerns of life. A man's politics, at this time, are every thing. I would sooner have my wounds dressed by a dog than a democrat.

A personal note . . . Today, my rent is one week overdue, so my landlady, *an unconscionable foul mouthed Dutch woman, seized on my goods*, notwithstanding that my wife, Catherine, is very ill and I have to ransom my possessions *that I may go to business*. Yet I know Benny can't pay me more.[120]

FRIDAY, JUNE 8, 1798

GENERAL ★ AURORA ★ ADVERTISER

TO HIS SERENE HIGHNESS JOHN ADAMS—
PRESIDENT OF THE UNITED STATES—
SIRE . . . As the present moment is the rage for Addresses, . . . I have . . . yielded . . .

In common with those who detest *mob government*, I beheld your election . . . with inexpressible rapture . . . [T]he people would enjoy the happy tranquillity of being *"well governed"* without the trouble of governing themselves.—Every reasonable man must admit the truth of your opinion that governments of the people are governments of disorder and anarchy and that checks and balances of monarchy and aristocracy ought to be engrafted on every well regulated constitution . . . Away, sir, with those Frenchified doctrines that teach men to believe they are all created equal and that God has dispensed to all the same rights—they are atheistical . . .

The factions and *"unprincipled mercenaries"* who opposed your election compose no part of the American citizens . . . Sir, the very attempt to keep you from the presidency is proof of their alliance with a foreign nation and of their love of faction!!! What, could men who had their country's good at heart have aided in opposition to *you*! To *you*, who are the oracle of all wisdom and the fountain of all patriotism! . . .

DEMOCRITUS

War measures . . . Today, the U.S. Senate passes the alien bill.

Today, Benny Bache writes an *Aurora* subscriber who wants to cancel his subscription:

> *Dear Sir . . . [Y]ou are backed in your determination to withdraw your support by no less a man than the President of the United States who has also lately decided my paper is no longer to be sent him, and if he should be able to discover—from the clue given by this letter—your name, it may probably recommend you to his good graces.*

Any thing in the shape of persecution against the cause which I have espoused . . . will meet with the countenance of our federal executive . . .

You may have . . . heard me speak of an unprovoked, premeditated, assassin-like, and cowardly assault upon my person on board the Frigate United States. The perpetrator of that foul deed has been taken by the hand by the Executive and has been sent the bearer of special dispatches to France . . .

To take this marked notice of a man who was yet under penalty of the law . . . is giving direct encouragement to assassination and setting a price upon my head. You may suppose that, in writing thus freely, I may expose myself to further outrage.[421]

The President's appointment of Clement Humphreys might remind us of Poor Richard's adage:

Pardoning the Bad is injuring the Good.[422]

Jimmy Callender:

[T]he case of Humphries demonstrates how gladly those who professed to applaud his intended murder and who paid his fine would butcher if they dared.[423]

Today, Abigail Adams writes her sister:

I was out yesterday at the Farm of Judge Peters calld Belmont. It is in all its Glory. I have been twice there . . . The Judge is an old friend and acquaintance of the President . . .

We have just got a Pamphlet from France, abusive as Thom. Paines against Washington, part Prose & part Poetry, the very language of their Party here, the very words of Bache & Volney in some parts of it . . .[424]

SUNDAY, JUNE 10, 1798

Today, James Madison writes Thomas Jefferson:

The law for capturing French privateers may certainly be deemed a formal commencement of hostilities and renders all hope of peace vain, unless a progress in amicable arrangements at Paris, not to be expected, should have secured it against the designs of our Gover[nment] . . .

The answers of Mr. Adams to his addressers form the most grotesque scene in the tragicomedy acting by the Gover[nment] . . . He is verifying compleatly the last feature in the character drawn of him by Dr. F.[ranklin] . . . "Always an honest man, often a wise one, but sometimes wholly out of his senses."[425]

Poor Richard also said,

A Man in a Passion rides a mad Horse.[426]

MONDAY, JUNE 11, 1798

GENERAL ★ AURORA ★ ADVERTISER

It has been surmised that the editors of well affected papers are about forming themselves into a corps to be armed in the Parthian [defensive] manner . . .

CHAPTER FOUR

AMERICAN TERROR

I received a visit from Thomas Jefferson who told me he had been greatly concerned for me . . . He said . . . he was himself dogged and watched in the most extraordinary manner; and he apologized for the lateness of his visit (for we were at tea when he arrived) by saying that, in order to elude the curiosity of his spies, he had not taken the direct road but had come by a circuitous route by the Falls of Schuylkill . . . He spoke of the temper of the times and of the late acts of the Legislature with a sort of despair, but said he thought even the shadows of our liberties must be gone if they attempted anything that would injure me . . .

DEBORAH LOGAN[427]

TUESDAY, JUNE 12, 1798

GENERAL ★ AURORA ★ ADVERTISER

Attached by education, example & principle to my native country; unconscious of a single sentiment that is not devoted to her welfare, I have watched with tremendous anxiety the progress of those events which threatened to interrupt her tranquillity . . . [&c, &c]   APPREHENSION

Today, the Quaker peace petitioner Dr. George Logan departs on his private peace mission to France. His wife, Deborah, explains.

At length, after having disposed of two parcels of real estate very cheaply in order to obtain funds to undertake the voyage and . . . pay off all his debts, on the 12th of June, 1798, he left me and his children, and his pleasant home at Stenton, and embarked on board the "Iris" a neutral vessel bound for Hamburg . . . When he left me, indeed I was as completely miserable as I could be, whilst innocent myself and united to a man whose honor I knew to be without stain. But I found it necessary, by a strong effort, to control my feelings. As soon as his [Federalist] committee of surveillance missed their charge, there was

a prodigious stir in the city; they looked upon each other with blank
faces as having suffered an adroit enemy to escape their vigilance.
Some idea may be formed of the temper of the time when I add that . . .
Dr. Rush . . . suffered himself to be one of this committee . . .[428]

The loss of subscribers has worsened the *Aurora's* financial condition. Tonight, in the *Porcupine's Gazette*:

> *To the Generous, Humane, and Charitable . . .*
> Ben Surgo, the Grandson of the great Philosopher "qui eripuit coelo fulmen, sceptrumque tyrannis" . . . [is] suffering from the obstinacy of the Federal Government . . . It is useless to dwell on the merits of the [Gazette] published by the aforesaid Citizen . . . [T]o the Grandson of the reknowned Lightening-catcher, we are indebted for early and large-editions of those excellent works, [Tom Paine's writing against established religion,] the *Age of Reason*, [Tom Paine's] *Letter to George Washington*, and a string of et ceteras . . . The immortal Paine . . . is employed in writing a book to be entitled *"Treachery a Virtue."* . . . Surgo, the correspondent of the celebrated and virtuous Paine, will undoubtedly have it first in America. With such powerful claims on your purses, is there a man who can refuse some assistance . . . ? Surgo's butcher's bill unpaid, he has not credit for a shin of beef . . . —Alas ! alas ! If this pathetic narrative should not have the desired effect, the shade of the great Franklin . . . will view with the deepest afflictions our degeneracy and apathy with respect to his meritorious grandson.

WEDNESDAY, JUNE 13, 1798

GENERAL ★ AURORA ★ ADVERTISER

> The name of that man who proposed to make our constitution a nullity by retraining the liberty of speech and the press ought to possess that species of immortality attached to the ruffian who burnt the temple of the Ephesian Diana.— We ring the alarm. Papers of freedom, you that have not sold yourselves, you that forget not your revolution and the constitution . . . —take up the sound before it dies, and let the peal rouse the spirit and reflection of the land . . .

Today, my fellow Irish scribbler John Daly Burk becomes co-editor of the New York *Time Piece*, a thrice-weekly newspaper published in New York City.[429] In today's paper, he explains his editorial policy:

> The spirit of the Paper shall be wholly Republican. It will support the Federal Constitution. But its Federalism will not be of that kind which displays itself in mean sycophantic compliance with every act of Administration, in clamouring for . . . a government of terror in efforts to sup-

press liberty of speech and the press. It will love the Constitution as it ought to be loved, for its excellence, for its republicanism; and will hold up to public abhorrence those who attempt to violate it, whatever be their professions.—This is our Federalism.

War measures . . . Today, John Adams approves and signs into law,

AN ACT
*To suspend the commercial intercourse between the
United States and France, and the dependencies thereof.*
Be it enacted, &c., That no ship or vessel owned, hired, or employed, wholly or in part, by any person resident in the United States . . . shall be allowed to proceed . . . to any port or place within the territory of the French Republic or the dependencies thereof . . . or shall be employed in any traffic or commerce with, or for any person resident within the jurisdiction, or under the authority of the French Republic . . .[430]

FRIDAY, JUNE 15, 1798

GENERAL ★ AURORA ★ ADVERTISER

In this state of things—when some of the tories are for committing the people by declaring war . . . it is greatly to be lamented that so many of the Whigs [Republicans] have absented themselves . . . Although his excellency of Braintree has said to our youth, "To arms! To arms my young friends!" yet it may be possible to prevent the use of them if the republican absentees will but return to their seats.

All that Callender has alleged against the conduct of government never mounted to the oddity of the *four* alien bills now depending in congress and which, as I am informed by members of both houses, were principally and confessedly framed for Callender's destruction. His having stolen a march upon the party by becoming a citizen was received in the upper house with infinite mortification. This I heard a very distinguished senator declaring to Callender himself.

Today, in the *Gazette of the United States*:

Bache . . . would be well to recollect that though he has not nominally renounced his allegiance to the United States and therefore is yet entitled to the privileges of a Citizen, it is no part of those privileges to misrepresent the proceedings of either branch of the legislature or to calumniate its members—that both houses are in duty bound to protect their members, and that he owes his impunity to their forbearance and his own insignificance.—He ought not to presume too far.

We hasten to communicate to our Readers the following very
IMPORTANT STATE PAPER
From the French Minister of Foreign Affairs
to the American Commissioners
Paris, . . . *18th March 1798* . . .
It is an incontestable truth . . . that France is entitled to a priority
of complaints and of grievances . . . *before the United States had
the least foundation for either* . . . [A]ll the grievances exhibited
by the [American] commissioners and envoys extraordinary, with
some exceptions that the undersigned *was ready to discuss*, are
a necessary consequence of the measures which the prior conduct
of the United States has rendered justifiable on the part of the
French Republic . . .

Complaint was made [by France] . . . of the non-execution of
the only clauses of the treaties concluded in 1778 in which France
has stipulated some advantages in return for the efforts she had
engaged [to win America's independence]. [C]ontrary to the letter
of the Treaty of Commerce of 1778 . . . the French were entirely
discouraged from cruising in the American seas against an enemy
. . . The French government endeavored in vain to . . . procure
. . . privileges to our commerce and navigation the principle of
which was well established by the treaties of 1778 . . .

What has been, till [recently], the conduct of the French government toward the United States? . . . Scarcely was the Republic
[of France] constituted when we sent a minister [Edmund Genêt]
to Philadelphia whose first step was to declare to the United States
that they should not be urged to carry into execution the defensive
clauses of the Treaty of alliance [requiring the United States to
defend the French West Indies islands against the British] . . .

Yet it will hardly be believed that the French Republic and her
[American] alliance were *actually sacrificed* at the very moment
she was giving to her ally increased proof of her attention . . . Mr.
[John] Jay . . . signing a Treaty [with Britain] . . . to make the
neutrality of the United States operate to the disadvantage of the
French Republic and to the advantage of England . . . French
cruisers were notified . . . they could not longer . . . sell their
prizes in the ports of the United States. This decision was
grounded . . . on the treaty concluded between the United States
and Great Britain . . .

Such are the motives which have prompted the *arretes* [de-
crees] of the Directory of which the United States complain, as
well as the conduct of its agents in the West Indies [seizing Amer-

ican shipping]. All those measures are founded on the Article II of the treaty of 1778 [between the U.S. and France] which provides that, as to navigation and commerce, France shall always stand in relation to the United States on the footing of the most favored nation. The Executive Directory cannot be blamed if . . . this clause has produced some inconveniences to the American flag. As to abuses which may have arisen under the operation of that principle, the undersigned again repeats—*that he was ready to discuss them in the most amicable manner . . .*

(Signed) CH. MAU. TALLEYRAND

We have good reason to believe that [the] administration have been for more than a week in possession of the important State Paper which we this day communicate. Is it not astonishing that it should so long have been kept secret[?] Surely, while Congress are engaged in determining on the awful alternative of peace or war, they should be possessed of the fullest and earliest information . . . or are they to be the mere puppets of the Executive[?] We shall strike off an extra number of our paper this day . . .

Today's publication of the Talleyrand letter is the scoop of the year. It should give the lie to those who say France doesn't want to negotiate.

Benny and I share Talleyrand's perspective.[431] During the American Revolution while Washington was leading American forces against Britain, the Continental Congress dispatched Ben Franklin and John Adams to get French help. In February of 1778, a Treaty of Alliance and a Treaty of Amity and Commerce were signed with France, providing that, in exchange for France's entering the war on America's side, America would always defend France's islands in the West Indies (Caribbean), would always let France take *prizes* (i.e., ships France captures from her enemies) into American ports, and would not allow any nation except France to outfit *privateers* (privately commissioned vessels of war) in American ports. By these treaties, France and America pledged to honor each other's freedom of the seas, meaning the freedom to carry trade anywhere, even to the ports of the other's enemies during wartime (with the obvious exception of military contraband). Finally, America promised to treat France, in commerce and navigation, as favorably as America treated her most favored of other nations.

Fifteen years later, France called for help under these treaties. Ben Franklin was dead. George Washington and John Adams were governing America.

In early 1793, two weeks after the French Revolution guillotined the King of France, Britain's King George III went to war against the new French Republic to end French democracy and to restore monarchical rule. Two weeks thereafter, the French Republic dispatched its first American ambassador, Edmond Genêt, to ask for American help.

Genêt would make clear that France was not asking—as well she might— for America to defend France's islands in the West Indies, but France did want to sell French prizes and outfit privateers in American ports. Suddenly, Washington and Adams had to decide how to treat America's old and only ally.

As "an Old French Soldier" asked in the pages of the *Philadelphia Aurora*, "Who would have thought, when the blood of Frenchmen drenched the foundation of the temple of your [American] liberty, that a day would come when the interests of your former tyrants and those of your allies should be weighed in the same balance . . . ?"[432]

But that day had come. Within twenty-four hours of Genêt's arrival in Philadelphia and even before he met with the President, George Washington issued his Neutrality Proclamation of 1793, declaring, in effect, that America would not help France. When the French ambassador threatened to appeal to the American people, Washington asked France to recall Edmond Genêt.

As America was abandoning its old French ally, its old enemy, Great Britain, continued to seize American shipping to French ports, abducting (impressing) into the British navy large numbers of American seaman whose American citizenship Britain refused to recognize. In 1794, under pressure from these attacks, Washington dispatched Federalist John Jay to conciliate Britain, whereupon Jay negotiated and Washington signed the so-called Jay Treaty of 1795 (also known as the "British treaty"), which promised Britain that America would not permit France to sell prizes or outfit privateers in American ports (Articles XXIV and XXV) and which recognized Britain's right to seize any American shipments—even nonmilitary shipments like food—to French ports, even to ports in the French islands America had promised to defend (Article XVII).

John Jay was familiar with America's obligations to France. Jay had also gone to France during America's Revolution and, with Ben Franklin and John Adams, negotiated the treaty that ended America's Revolutionary War. Yet, ten years later, Jay negotiated this shameful treaty.

That's what brings America to the crisis of 1798. French reaction to the Jay Treaty has been to treat American shipping on the same unfavorable basis ("as favorably") as Jay and Washington agreed Britain could treat it. That's what January's decree promises to do. Despite America's proclamation of neutrality, France will seize any American ship with a British product on board. How could France do otherwise? How could America permit Britain to seize American food and other nonmilitary shipments to France while France was obligated, by her American treaties, not to impede such American shipments to Britain? France has every right to be outraged, and France is doing no more than what America permits Britain to do.[433] Freedom of the seas is gone.

Last year, Benny addressed Washington's conduct in a powerful pamphlet, *Remarks Occasioned by the Late Conduct of Mr. Washington, President of the United States,* including,

> *Such however is the fate of America that, after having kept the world in flames for above seven years to save her own liberties; yet, before twice seven years are expired, she makes herself an instrument to undo the liberties of [France] her great benefactor; to increase the power of [Brit-*

ain] her only persecutor; to surrender the rights of neutral nations . . . finally to enter into stipulations for spreading famine among mankind during war . . . This pursuit of the new friendship of [Britain,] an arbitrary court, and this rejection of the old alliance of [France,] a freed nation, speak for themselves.—Let each American take this subject to his pillow . . .[434]

Today, James Monroe writes Thomas Jefferson:

[N]othing is more obvious than that France intends not to make war on us, so that our administration has the merit exclusively of precipitating us into that state . . . France has been roused against us by the administration who have never lost a moment to keep her [France's] resentment at the height by multiplying the causes of irritation daily . . .[435]

Today, volunteers swell the ranks of the Macpherson's Blues to six hundred men. Macpherson's Blues now controls the First Troop of City Cavalry, the Second Troop of City Cavalry, separate companies of Grenadiers, Artillery, and Riflemen, four companies of Infantry (Blues), and a Germantown infantry company.[436]

Tonight, in the *Porcupine's Gazette*:

The hireling *Bache* has this morning published a letter from the French Minister of Foreign Affairs to our envoys in Paris, dated the 18th of March last . . . Talleyrand says the Directory were astonished to hear America complain, when the grievances were all on the side of France!—He then goes over the old hackneyed topics of . . . BACHE, respecting the British Treaty . . . [I]t is certain that BACHE has received this letter from France or from some French agent here for the express purpose of *drawing off the people from the Government*, of exciting discontents, and to procure a *fatal DELAY of preparation for war*. The prostitute printer has announced that he has struck off an *extraordinary number* of the gazette . . . Ought not Bache to be regarded as an organ of the *diplomatic skill* of France? And ought such a wretch be tolerated at this time?

Tonight, in the *Gazette of the United States*:

Whether the Editor of the *Aurora* is an *official* agent of the French Directory or not, time will elucidate. There is, however, not a doubt that he was furnished with the State Paper published in the *Aurora* this morning before it was received by the Executive of the United States . . . —By what means can it be supposed such a paper, if it be genuine, could come into the hands of any individual in his private capacity unless by transmission from the government of France itself or from our envoys? . . . Can the latter be supposed to hold correspondence with Bache or his office?

MR. FENNO, What better proof do we want of the diplomatic skill of France—The document this day published in the *Aurora* was received the day before yesterday, in French, together with an answer from our commissioners which is voluminous. The clerks have been engaged in translating one and copying the other—But behold master Ben has a translation cut and dried . . .

MONDAY, JUNE 18, 1798

GENERAL   ★ AURORA ★   ADVERTISER

The *official answer* of the minister of foreign affairs, Talleyrand, to the long memorial of our commissioners [envoys], which was published in the last number of the Aurora plainly shews that . . . Mr. Adams was highly mistaken that negotiation was at an end . . .

Communicated for publication in the AURORA— *GENTLEMEN,* The students of William and Mary [College] regard the brooding hostilities . . . as forming a crisis in our political affairs which involves the future destiny of our country. Although we do not yet, by the laws of this state, possess the full power of constituents, yet . . . we conceive it but reasonable and just that our opinions be heard . . . Our wishes for a temper of pacification on the part of our government are grounded not in any juvenile predilections . . . but on a conviction of the injuries which would result . . .

Today, one of America's three envoys to France, John Marshall, arrives back in Philadelphia. John Fenno describes his reception:

The three corps [of Philadelphia cavalry] . . . turned out in full uniform. The concourse of citizens in carriages, on horseback, and on foot was immense . . . Mr. Marshall was met by his applauding fellow-citizens about 6 miles from the city and escorted through the principal streets to the City Tavern amidst the ringing of bells and the shouts of the exulting multitude. Even in the Northern Liberties where the demos of anarchy and confusion are attempting to organize treason and death, repeated shouts of applause were given as the cavalcade approached and passed along.[437]

War measures . . . Today, at midday, President Adams receives the Macpherson's Blues and their commandant, William Macpherson. The President addresses the assemblage:

THIS dedication of yours, in the presence of God and the world, to defend—against the attacks of arrogance, injustice, and lawless ambition—that happy system of government you have inherited from your fathers, cemented by the best blood of America and sanctioned by your own approbation, is very solemn and affecting . . . I am fully convinced

*that America must reassume the warlike character . . . I accept with
pleasure your services . . .*[438]

War measures . . . Today, John Adams approves and signs into law

AN ACT
*Supplementary to and to amend an act, entitled
"An Act to establish an uniform rule of Naturalization,"
and to repeal the act heretofore passed on that subject.*
Be it enacted, &c., That no alien shall be admitted to become a citizen
of the United States or any State unless . . . he has resided within the
United States fourteen years at least . . .[439]

By prolonging the residency requirement from five to fourteen years, John Adams keeps those who are refugees from the British monarch or Robespierre's despotism from following Jimmy Callender's route to American citizenship. Such European democrats will remain aliens and will soon be subject to Adams' arbitrary control.[440] Adams forgets Poor Richard's admonition,

> *No longer virtuous no longer free is a Maxim as true
> with regard to a private Person as a Common-wealth.*[441]

Today, John Adams delivers to Congress Dispatch No. 8 from the Paris envoys, including the Talleyrand letter that Benny published two days ago.[442] In the House of Representatives, the Annals of Congress report:

MR. THATCHER [Federalist, Massachusetts] stated . . . It was well known that the letter of Mr. Talleyrand had already been printed in the French paper of this city, and he believed by order of the Executive Directory . . . [H]e saw . . . the Executive Directory and its agents taking extraordinary means to spread that letter . . .

Mr. T. CLAIBORNE [Republican, Virginia] did not understand what the gentleman meant in saying he believed certain persons are French agents.

Mr. THATCHER [Federalist, Massachusetts] said he considered the printer of the paper to which he had alluded as an agent of the French Directory, and he hoped soon to lay before the House satisfactory evidence of the fact.

Mr. HARPER [Federalist, S. Carolina] . . . It had long been manifest to him that France had her secret agents in this country . . . and the act of Saturday was only one of the ramifications of the scheme.[443]

Today, Federalist U.S. Senator James Lloyd of Maryland writes George Washington,

> *You will, before this reaches you, have seen Talleyrand's puny performance which was first published by Bache . . . Bache was in possession of Talleyrand's note before the dispatches were received by our government but it was not known how he came by them 'till Saturday when a Mr. Keeder told a number of Gazette men at the City Tavern*

that he had received a packet for Bache sealed with the seal of the minister of exterior relations . . . and that he had delivered the packet to Bache . . .   *Your most obedt Servant,*
                                                                    James Lloyd

P.S. We shall soon declare the Treaty with France void and pass a strong act to punish Sedition. Doctor Logan left the City this morning for France. This Gov't had information of his intentions but . . . we have no law by which he could be laid hold of.[444]

Tonight, in the *Porcupine's Gazette*:

The letter was without any doubt sent to Bache from Talleyrand himself, and its object, it is very clear, was to deceive the people . . . and to prepare the way for an invasion . . .

Doctor LOGAN is just departed for *France !* Recollect his connections; recollect that seditious envoys from all the Republics that France has subjugated first went to Paris and *concerted measures* with the despots . . . The whole of this business is not come to light yet . . . In the mean time, watch, Philadelphians, or the fire is in your houses and the *couteau [knife] at your throats.*—A *guard* should be mounted every night in this city.— Take care; or, when your blood runs down the gutters, don't say you were not forewarned of the danger!

Tonight, in the *Gazette of the United States*:

In the beginning of last week arrived in this city Mr. Keeder from Paris, with dispatches from the French Directory to Benjamin Bache, Printer of the *Aurora*, under the seal of Mr. Talleyrand . . .

TUESDAY, JUNE 19, 1798

GENERAL   ★ AURORA ★   ADVERTISER

Mr. Harper, in the House yesterday, spoke obscurely of conspiracies . . . Mr. Thatcher [observed] . . . "that he considered the French paper of this city, who had published his letter of Talleyrand, *as agent of the French Directory, and he hoped soon to be able to convince the house of the fact by satisfactory evidence.*" . . . This attack is a link in the chain of persecution by which it is attempted to injure the *Aurora* and muzzle the press . . . Mr. Thatcher's charge against us, we say, is a base calumny; — it is false. He has promised proof in support of it . . . We dare him . . .

In conversation a few days ago, a federalist made use of this declaration: "*wait,* said he, *'till the sedition bill is passed and then we shall show you what we will do—we will begin first with* JEFFERSON *and* GALLATIN, *banish them and then we will take the others one by one.*" This declaration ought to be proclaimed from the house top that the people may be made acquainted with the true designs of federalism.

On Saturday morning, before the House of Representatives met, the friends of order as they call themselves met in groups in different parts of the hall: "where did this Bache get the State Paper he published this morning?" No one can tell . . . Mr. Otis trudged away to the Secretary of State to advise him to [send] . . . Talleyrand's note and our commissioners' answer . . . to Porcupine and Fenno to appear in their papers of that evening. Timothy [Pickering] did not like this and observed, with a cunning look, that it would be better to give it out that the communications had been *just received* in cypher . . .

So much for Bache's printing Talleyrand's letter: if it had not been for this free press which is not under the direction of his Excellency, the People of America would not have known of Mr. Talleyrand's dispatch until after they had been "committed by a declaration of war" which a Federal Representative has said they ought to be.   Z.

How did the Editor of the *Aurora* get M. Talleyrand's letter[?] . . . (In answer . . . we can only at present say that it is a *lie* that we received the letter of Talleyrand from France. More of this in our next.)

Last Saturday afternoon, we could not avoid an immoderate fit of laughter on casting a first glance at that thing which *pensioner* Fenno calls *the* Gazette. He had been obliged . . . to borrow from a hostile, we scorn to say rival, print the most interesting state paper [from French Foreign Minister Talleyrand] . . .

Fenno . . . lost his patience . . . He [had] no less than four pieces . . . reviling *Ben* for doing himself on Saturday last what Mr. Adams could and should have done a week or ten days before.

To be sure it was a very jacobinical, democratical, anti-presidential, unconstitutional trick in the said Editor of the *Aurora* to let Congress and the American people into their own business. Who knows but what this production may stop or check the stream of warlike addresses and most warlike answers. It may clog the maturity of the war bills and give our hen-hearted Republican Representatives a fillip of courage in their replies . . .

Today, Abigail Adams writes,

> [I]n any other Country, Bache & all his papers would have been seazd and ought to be here, but congress are dilly dallying about passing a Bill enabling the President to seize suspicious persons and their papers . . . I am weary of conjectures, so I shall say nothing of when it is probable Congress will rise. I believe they will declare war against the French first.[445]

Today, Benny Bache is meeting with Thomas Jefferson.[446]

Tonight, in the *Porcupine's Gazette*:

THE TRAITOR-TRAP.

I have long said (and I have been joined by the public voice) that the infamous Lightening-Rod, Jun. was a *hireling* of and *in correspondence with* the Despots of France. The fact is now PROVED beyond all contradiction, and it is with infinite satisfaction that I lay the proof of it before the people of America.

[Affidavit]

AT Paris, on the 19th or 20th of March last, or soon after at Bordeaux, Mr. LEE, the gentleman who brought dispatches to government, desired me to take charge of letters addressed to different persons in America, among others one to Ben. Bache . . . Their size and the seal of the [French] *Minister of Foreign Affairs attracted my notice . . . I delivered the letters at the Post Office without even suspecting their contents.*

June 18, 1798
JOHN KIDDER.

Thus is the traitor caught at last! This discovery accounts for all the villain's conduct and for the continual connection that has been kept up with him by many persons in this country. JEFFERSON was seen going into his house on the very day that the dispatches appeared . . . [S]hall this atrocious villain, BACHE, be tolerated? Shall he be suffered to proceed in his career of defaming the government, misleading the people, exciting them to insurrection, when it is known, when it is *proved,* that he acts in concert with the *foreign* as well as domestic enemies of his country?—My God, can any such thing as law or government exist if this is to be suffered with impunity? It may for a little while; but be assured it will not long. The French faction must be crushed, or the government here MUST FALL; choose which you please . . .

Tonight, in the *Gazette of the United States*:

AMERICANS—*Beware of French Intrigue! and Of your own CITIZENS who are agents for the French !!!*

WEDNESDAY, JUNE 20, 1798

GENERAL ★ AURORA ★ ADVERTISER

We are obliged to postpone our answer to JOHN KIDDER & to the stupid columns of the Tory prints . . . We wait till tomorrow to lay the whole before our readers . . .

George Thatcher, a member of the House . . . did say on the 18th inst. that he would bring . . . evidence that the Editor of the *Aurora* is a French agent; which he did not do on the 19th . . .

Today, Benny's good friend Elizabeth Hewson writes her brother:

*[Benny is] going fast to destruction . . . I am afraid very fatal conse-
quences will attend his publishing the pieces he does.*[447]

Tonight, in the *Gazette of the United States*:

> Monsieur Bache . . . affects to be mightily offended at being called a
> French Agent . . . There can be no doubt but that, to the extent of his poor
> abilities, he is a French agent . . .

> He is but a luke-warm friend who waivers in the cause of his country . . .
> *"He that is not for us is against us."*

Tonight, in the *Porcupine's Gazette,* Peter Porcupine:

> BACHE (the grandson of Old Franklin) published a LETTER . . . sent off
> from Paris the moment TALLEYRAND'S letter was delivered to our envoys
> there . . . BACHE was able to get his out first; but learning that those of
> the government were about to appear . . . he then accused the govern-
> ment of having had an *intention to keep the dispatches a secret* in order
> to blind the people and betray them into war !

THURSDAY, JUNE 21, 1798

GENERAL ★ AURORA ★ ADVERTISER

TALLEYRAND'S LETTER.
The following affidavit will save those that know the Editor the trouble
of wading through the subjoined legal detail.
—*City of Philadelphia, ſſ.* On the 20th of June, 1798, personally
appeared before me, Hilary Baker, Mayor of the city of Philadelphia, Benjamin Franklin Bache; who, being duly sworn, deposed and said: That
the letter signed Ch. Mau. Talleyrand and, which appeared in his newspaper, the *Aurora*, on Saturday last, was not received by him from
France; that it was delivered to him for publication by a gentleman of
this city; that he never received the letter said to have been put into the
post office for him, in a piece signed John Kidder . . .
BENJ. FRANKLIN BACHE.—
Sworn before me, HILARY BAKER, Mayor.

> I have gone through this . . . to show . . . the groundlessness of the cal-
> umnies . . . and to avoid satisfying them as to the source from which I
> really had the letter. The administration, however—we doubt not—by
> this time have discovered whence [and] . . . can inform me where I shall
> find my [other undelivered] letter, said to be sealed with the seal of the
> French department of Foreign Affairs . . . Even if the seal should be bro-
> ken or the letter defaced, I shall attribute it to accident, & never suspect
> them of having done either. Provided the pamphlet be whole, they will
> receive the thanks of   THE EDITOR OF THE AURORA.

War measures . . . Today, in the U.S. House of Representatives, Republican Edward Livingston of New York speaks against an alien bill that would allow John

Adams to expel, without notice and without a hearing, any non-citizen who excites the President's suspicions. The Annals of Congress report:

ALIENS . . .

Mr. [Edward] LIVINGSTON [Republican, New York], [stated that] the crime is "exciting the suspicions of the President," but no man can tell what conduct will avoid that suspicion—a careless word, perhaps misrepresented or never spoken may be sufficient evidence; a look may destroy; an idle gesture may insure punishment . . .

Judiciary power is taken from the courts and given to the executive . . . ; the trial by jury is abolished; the "public trial" required by the Constitution is changed into a secret and worse than inquisitorial tribunal . . . No indictment; no jury; no trial; no public procedure; no statement of the accusation; no examination of witnesses in its support; no counsel for defence; all is dark, silence, mystery, and suspicion . . .

If we are ready to violate the constitution we have sworn to defend—will the people submit to our unauthorized acts? . . . Sir, they ought not to submit . . . For let no man vainly imagine that the evil is to stop here, that a few unprotected aliens are only to be affected by this inquisitorial power. The same arguments which enforce these provisions against aliens apply with equal strength to enacting them in the case of citizens . . . You have already been told of plots and conspiracies; and all the frightful images that were necessary to keep up the present system of terror and alarm were presented to you. But who were implicated by these dark hints—these mysterious allusions? They were our own citizens, sir, not aliens. If there is then any necessity for the system now proposed, it is more necessary to be enforced against our own citizens than against strangers; and I have no doubt that, either in this or some other shape, it will be attempted. I must ask, sir, whether the people of America are prepared for this? . . . Whether they are ready to submit to imprisonment or exile whenever suspicion, calumny or vengeance shall mark them for ruin? Are they base enough to be prepared for this? No sir; they will, I repeat it, they will resist this tyrannic system; the people will oppose it . . .

Mr. KITTERA [Federalist, Pennsylvania] said he hoped that this bill . . . would be followed by a strong sedition bill; and that they would, together, preserve us from the dangers with which we are threatened from internal enemies . . .[448]

Today, John Adams delivers a message to Congress:

UNITED STATES. June 21, 1798.
Gentlemen of the Senate and
Gentlemen of the House of Representatives: . . .
[T]he negotiation may be considered at an end.
I will never send another minister to France without assurances that

he will be received, respected, and honored as the representative of a great, free, powerful, and independent nation.

JOHN ADAMS.[449]

Today, Thomas Jefferson writes James Madison:

> *Dr. Logan, about a fortnight ago, sailed for Hamburg, tho' for a twelve month past he had been intending to go to Europe as soon as he could get money enough to carry him there. Yet when he had accomplished this and fixed a time for going, he very unwisely made a mystery of it: so that his disappearance without notice excited conversations. This was seized by the war hawks and given out as a secret mission for the Jacobins here to solicit an army for France, instruct them as to their landing, &c. This extravagance produced a real panic among the citizens; & happening just when Bache published Talleyrand's letter, Harper, on the 18th, gravely announced to the H[ouse] of R[epresentatives], that a traitorous correspondence between the Jacobins here and the French Directory; that he had got hold of some threads & clues of it, and would soon be able to develop the whole. This increased the alarm; their libelists immediately set to work, directly & indirectly to implicate whom they pleased. Porcupine gave me a principal share in it, as I am told, for I never read his papers. This state of things added to my reasons for not departing at the time I intended. These follies seem to have died away in some degree already. Perhaps I may renew my purpose [to return to Virginia] by the 25th.[450]*

Tonight, John Fenno in the *Gazette of the United States*:

> Bache says he never has and never will wittingly deceive the public. I ask him if he has not published a vile falsehood when he charges our government with keeping back the last dispatches from our Envoys . . . ? It is to be remembered that few persons who take the *Aurora* ever see any other paper.
>
> ---
>
> It is evident from the Statement published by the Editor of the *Aurora* that he has a Correspondent in the Office of Foreign Affairs at Paris. It is undoubtedly fact also that the correspondence relates to public affairs, as it appears the packets directed to that Editor ARE SEALED WITH THE SEAL OF OFFICE.

Tonight, in the *Porcupine's Gazette*:

> BACHE, in his infamous paper of this morning, has published a copy of *an affidavit* which he has made before the Mayor, denying that TALLEYRAND'S LETTER was sent *to him* from France. On this subject, I would first ask: WHAT BOOK did Bache swear on? . . . [T]he reader will recollect that this same BACHE has for several years past been engaged in the cause of *Infidelity* and *Blasphemy*: that is, in inculcating a disbelief

of and *in villifying* the Holy Scriptures *on which he has now sworn . . .* If I were to swear on *Bache's paper,* would such an oath add any thing to the credibility of what I should assert on my bear word?

FRIDAY, JUNE 22, 1798

GENERAL ★ AURORA ★ ADVERTISER

Let it not be forgotten that George Thatcher declared in Congress that the Editor of this paper is an agent of the French Directory and said he would bring evidence of it before the house; which if he does not do, he must be considered as guilty of misprision of treason, as concealing treason. This Thatcher was called on yesterday in the house for his proofs. He had not a word to offer in answer.

Could Benny's publication of the Talleyrand letter deny John Adams his congressional majority for a declaration of war? Talleyrand appears ready to negotiate!

Today is the last day Jimmy Callender will write for the *Aurora*.[451] He must leave Philadelphia. Federalists are threatening his life. His wife died this spring. He can't support the children.

War measures . . . Today, the President approves and signs into law:

AN ACT
Supplementary to, and to amend the act, entitled
"an act authorizing the President of the United States
to raise a provisional army."
Be it enacted, &c., That the companies of volunteers and the members of each company who shall be duly engaged and accepted by the President of the United States [in the] . . . provisional army shall submit to and observe such rules [as] . . . the President of the United States is hereby authorized to make . . . *And it be further enacted,* That the President of the United States may proceed to appoint and commission . . . so many of the officers . . . for the raising, organizing, and commanding the provisional army of ten thousand men, as, in his opinion, the public service shall more immediately require . . .[452]

Today, President John Adams writes George Washington:

Dear Sir . . .
The prosperity of [my Administration] to the Country will depend upon Heaven and very little on anything in my Power . . . I have no qualifications for the martial part of it, which is like[ly] to be the most essential. If the Constitution and your Convenience would admit of my Changing Places with you, or of my taking my old station as your Lieutenant civil, I shall have no doubts of the Ultimate Prosperity and Glory of this Country.

In forming an Army, whenever I must come to that extremity, I am at an immense Loss whether to call out all the old Generals or to appoint a young List . . . I must have you sometimes for Advice . . . We must have your Name, if you in any case will permit us to use it. There will be more efficacy in it than in many an Army . . .

[JOHN ADAMS][453]

Today, in the *Gazette of the United States*:

The falling *Surgo* has filled up two columns of his paper with a vain and futile attempt to demonstrate his innocence . . . Whether he received the treasonable communication directly from his master or whether it was put into his hands indirectly by any of their secret or open agents in this country is a point of no consequence at all. It is sufficient that he received it in an improper manner. But until some more creditable testimony is opposed to the respectable testimony of Mr. Kidder . . . it will be impossible to doubt that there was received from the office of the old hobbling cut-throat apostate [French Foreign Minister Talleyrand] a communication for his humble servant and tool in this country . . .

Bache has published that our Executive, to answer the most nefarious and villainous purposes, kept back for a number of days Talleyrand's letter to the Envoys and that he the said Bache extorted the publication at last. This is one of the most atrocious libels ever uttered by him or any of his gang; and if there is not vigor in the laws to punish him, the existence of society in the United States is a mere cobweb existence.

Tonight, in the *Porcupine's Gazette*:

In times so alarming as the present, the residence of Volney [a French democrat] and other foreigners who, by a certain line of conduct, made themselves conspicuous strongly attracts the attention of every virtuous American . . . Americans now have everything in danger, morals, religion, independence, liberty, civil and religious, everything that can be dear to man as a social animal. Our country has been the resort of almost all seditious foreigners of every distinction . . . It is a matter of the most serious consideration in times so alarming; what is to be done with those vile miscreants . . . ?

Returning to France aboard the chartered ship *Benjamin Franklin,* Volney, the French philosopher, is two weeks at sea.

SATURDAY, JUNE 23, 1798

GENERAL ★ AURORA ★ ADVERTISER

> whether in French or in English may be undertaken at the same time . . .
> The remnant of his assortment of books . . .
> Moveables, and other articles too tedious to enumerate.
> MOREAU de St. MERY lives at the corner
> of Front and Callowhill-street.

It is said by some tory papers that Dr. G.[eorge] Logan is gone to Europe . . . [I]t is said he is gone to persuade those terrible sans-culottes, the French, to come . . . and prevent us from *fasting* . . . But if he is really gone to Europe, how came he to let all those cunning rogues into his secrets?

[Fine-made Italian, that is, foreign] Cremona fiddles are to be ordered out of the kingdom under the *Alien Bill;* their [tones] being calculated to bring the constitutional music of *organs* and *kettle-drums* into contempt.

This morning's "Cremona fiddles" satire proves Poor Richard's observation,

The muses love the Morning.[454]

Today, Abigail Adams writes,

I wish our Legislature would set the example & make a sedition act to hold in order the base Newspaper calumniators.[455]

Tonight, in the *Gazette of the United States*:

It is hardly worthwhile to notice *that* "skunk of scurrility" *Bache* . . . [H]is question of this forenoon—"How came the doctor (Logan) to let all these cunning rogues into his secrets?" . . . I will tell you Bache that the low cunning of the unsteady doctor prudently secreted his errand to Europe from the federalists, but did not the C[hie]f J[ustic]e [of Pennsylvania, Republican Thomas McKean] know it . . . ? Yes, Bache, he did . . . Do you remember what your grand father Franklin wrote, that *"part of the truth is worse than the whole truth"?* . . .

This evening, prominent members of the Adams administration and other leading Federalists attend a rousing 120–person banquet dinner at Philadelphia's fashionable O'Ellers' Hotel in Chestnut-street for returning envoy John Marshall. The thirteenth toast is encored with particular enthusiasm:

"Millions for Defence, but not a Cent for Tribute."[456]

Tonight, the leading merchants of Baltimore, Maryland hold a public dinner for Maryland's Federalist U.S. Senator John Howard. The third toast volunteered:

A halter of strong hemp, in the place of a French pension, to Bache, printer of the Aurora.[457]

Tonight, in the *Porcupine's Gazette*:

SHORT ADVICE TO BACHE,
In the words of the king of Prussia to the factious Baron Trenck.
"The thunder begins to roll, young man. Take care, for *the [lightning]
bolt may fall.*"

MONDAY, JUNE 25, 1798

GENERAL   ★ AURORA ★   ADVERTISER

The *ire* of the ministerialists at Philadelphia is roused at BACHE
for having *let the cat out of the bag*—they can now fully establish
their charges of "*jacobinical, democratical, disorganizing, anti-
presidential;*" for doubtless it was all this, and even *unconstitutional*, to
inform *Congress* and *the people* of their own business—but how to make
it "*Conspiracy*" will puzzle . . .

THE PLOT UNRAVELLED

The latest artifice employed by the Tory faction to injure the *Aurora*
has been the accusation directed against its Editor . . . that he was a
French agent . . . It will be remembered that we were said to have received a letter of the French Minister of Foreign Affairs in a packet
through Kidder, and when we proved that we did not, it was contended
that there was in existence such a letter as Kidder described and that, as
it was sealed with a French official seal, it must contain something treasonable. This mysterious packet . . . we at length received on Saturday
from [Secretary of State Timothy] Pickering, the seal in appearance intact. We detained his messenger and kept [the packet] in his view till
two gentlemen could be called in to be witnesses at its being opened, and
the following is the result of the examination they made of its contents.

CERTIFICATE

*We do hereby certify that, at the request of BENJAMIN FRANKLIN
BACHE, we were present at the opening of a Packet . . . with a seal
round which were inscribed the words "REPUBLIQUE FRANÇAISE"
and at the bottom "Relations Extérieures" which packet was delivered
to Mr. Bache by a messenger from the Secretary of State of the United
States. The only things contained in the said Packet were two pamphlets . . . and, excepting the directions (and the receipts on the cover
signed "Oliv. Wolcott" [Secretary of the Treasury] and "T. Pickering"
[Secretary of State]), there was not a single word in manuscript . . .*

MATHEW CAREY, JAMES CLAY

While this business of espionage was pursuing, another method was
attempted to confound the Editor. Reports were industriously spread
that he was arrested,—that he was in jail, that he had fled. Thro' a channel, almost official, he learnt that the order was actually signed for his
arrestation.

165

What was the object of these reports? It was hoped that they might intimidate; that . . . he would be induced to fly. But what was his conduct? . . . [H]e braved their most envenomed malice. When denounced on the floor of Congress, he did not truckle . . . Neither was the spirit of his paper cowed. His readers will testify that, from the dawn of this week's presentation, it rose in its spirit—and so it ever shall; persecution shall only fan the flame of his detestation for those whom he considers the enemies of his country. They shall not make him abandon his post for fear of a trial before their tribunals. He will ever prefer death . . .

The letter directed to the Editor was his property. What right had [Secretary of Treasury] Oliver Wolcott to receive it? and then to send it to a third person [Secretary of State Timothy Pickering]? . . . And who are the persons who have taken upon themselves thus to violate and injure the rights and character of the Editor? They are officers not even known to the constitution; mere creatures of the executive, subject to his will and pleasure . . .[458]

Jimmy Callender will write:

Mr. Adams may . . . explain the creed of a cabinet faction that vindicates the principle . . . of intercepting letters. Wolcott and Pickering stopt one, addressed to Bache, and while it was in their own custody, while they knew that its contents were strictly innocent, the newspapers under their direction resounded all over America with charges of a treasonable correspondence between Bache and France . . .[459]

Philadelphia is hot and putrid. Today, Abigail Adams writes,

[T]he weather is so Hot and close, and the flies so tormenting that I cannot have any comfort. The mornings . . . are stagnant. Not a leaf stirs till nine or ten oclock I get up & drop in my chair; without spirits or vigor, breath a sigh for Quincy, and regret that necessity obliges us to remain here. It grows sickly, the city noisome . . . We have began the use of the cold Bath, and hope it will in some measure compensate for want of braceing air.[460]

Today, at Mount Vernon, George Washington responds to Senator James Lloyd's June 18th letter concerning Bache's Talleyrand letter:

I wonder the French Government has not more pride than to expose to the world such flimsy performances as the ministers of it exhibit by way of complaint and argument [in Bache's Talleyrand letter]. But it is still more to be wondered at that these charges which have been refuted over and over again should find men . . . [illegible] The Editor of the Aurora . . . [illegible] and bolder! Whence his support?[461]

War measures . . . Today, John Adams approves and signs into law:

AN ACT
CONCERNING ALIENS

Be it enacted, &c., That it shall be lawful for the President of the United States, at any time during the continuance of this act, to order all such aliens as he shall judge dangerous to the peace and safety of the United States, or shall have reasonable grounds to suspect are concerned in any treasonable or secret machinations against the government hereof, to depart out of the territory of the United States within such time as shall be expressed in that order . . .

SEC. 6. *And it be further enacted,* That this act shall continue and be in force for and during the term of two years from the passing thereof.[462]

First, John Adams makes it impossible for those who have fled despotism to become citizens, and now he gives himself a despotic right to expel them without notice, without a hearing, and for no better reason than that he "suspects" a "secret machination"! Like the coming sedition act, this alien act will intimidate people into silence. What non-citizen will criticize Adams when Adams can expel him on a whim?

War measures . . . Today, John Adams approves and signs into law:

AN ACT
*To authorize the defence of the merchant vessels
of the United States against French depredations.*

Be it enacted, &c. That the commander and crew of any merchant vessel of the United States . . . may oppose and defend against any search . . . [by] any armed vessel sailing under French colors . . . and may subdue and capture the same . . .

SEC. 2. *And be it further enacted,* That . . . such [captured] armed vessel . . . shall accrue one half to the owner or owners of the merchant vessel of the United States and the other half to the captors . . . in any court to which such captured vessel shall be brought . . .[463]

Today, John Adams writes the Students of Dickinson College:

If there are any who plead the cause of France and attempt to paralyse the efforts of your government, I agree with you they ought to be esteemed our greatest enemies.[464]

Tonight, in the *Gazette of the United States*:

[T]he *"wayward splinter of old Lightening Rod"* . . . Bache . . . has been an admirer of French politics—the organ of sedition—and the calumniator of WASHINGTON; in fact, the *Aurora* has been the focus where all productions inimical to the peace, happiness, and above all, the Independence of America centered.

Bache informs his readers that he has at last received a packet with Talleyrand's seal of office! This packet . . . contained, they say, two pamphlets . . . Thus the fact of a correspondence with the enemies of the United States is fully ascertained. It yet remains to satisfy the public how the letter of Talleyrand got to Bache's hands . . .

What can be a more complete refutation of all the charges against the sincerity and integrity of our government by Talleyrand, Bache, and Co. than the admirable answer of our ministers?

TUESDAY, JUNE 26, 1798

GENERAL   ★ AURORA ★   ADVERTISER

Fenno senselessly asserts that our receiving two printed pamphlets is a proof of our being in correspondence with the enemies of our country . . . The fellow is a fool . . . He wants very much yet to know where we got Talleyrand's letter. We are at liberty to tell but will not gratify his curiosity so far. He asserted that we received it from France; we have proved we did not: Now let him guess again.

John Fenno begs the questions—What can be a more effectual answer to the letter of Talleyrand, &c. than the reply of our commissioners? The question will be answered some time in the [presidential election] year 1800—by the People of the United States.

Today, the U.S. District of Pennsylvania's federal marshal, William Nichols (whose son was among those who broke windows at the *Aurora's* offices),[465] enters the offices of the *Philadelphia Aurora* and, on behalf of the United States of America, arrests Benjamin Franklin Bache for the crime of sedition. He takes Benny to Philadelphia's Federal District Court to answer an indictment for *"libelling the President & the Executive Government in a manner tending to excite sedition and opposition to the laws, by sundry publications and republications."* John Adams hasn't waited for a federal sedition law to pass. The government has based the indictment on Pennsylvania's common criminal law of sedition, arguing that the U.S. Constitution has adopted Pennsylvania law as a "federal common law." Benny's lawyers believe no such "federal common law" exists, and Benny sees his primary defence as the First Amendment's freedom of the press. Poor Richard believed,

Innocence is its own Defence.[466]

Judge Peters grants a delay until Friday and paroles Benny to the district marshal.[467]

This afternoon, in the *Porcupine's Gazette*:

The notorious BACHE, it is said, is at this moment before the honourable Judge Peters.

This afternoon, in the *Gazette of the United States*:

The President with good intent,
  Three Envoys sent to Paris,
But cinq Tetes would not with 'em treat,
  Of honor France so bare is . . .
      Chorus   Yankee doodle (mind the tune)
        Yankee doodle dandy,
      If Frenchmen come with naked bum,
        We'll spank 'em hard and handy . . .
That Talleyrand might us trappan,
  And o'er the country sound it;
He sent his pill, t' *Aurora*'s mill,
  And Benny Faction ground it.
        Yankee doodle, &c . . .
Bold ADAMS did in seventy-six,
  Our Independence sign, Sir:
And he will not, give up a jot,
  Tho' all the world combine, Sir.
        Yankee doodle, &c . . .

[E]very native of the United States who now stands opposed to the government thereof must be either a fool or a knave . . . I believe it will be readily granted that Mr. Bache is bad enough . . . [N]o doubt he is of the greatest use to [French] leaders in disseminating their poison. He works the most noted engine for throwing filth and spreads it over the continent like a blasting mildew in the pestilential pages of the *Aurora* which has been prostituted to the vilest purposes . . . I have no doubt that he will hereafter be execrated by the French as heartily as ever any of our internal traitors were by the English in the American war. They both, more or less, encourage the treason and, alike, despise the traitor. Like all true Americans, I am,   *An enemy to Traitors*

WEDNESDAY, JUNE 27, 1798

GENERAL   ★ AURORA ★   ADVERTISER

The Editor of the *Aurora* was yesterday arrested on a warrant from Judge Peters of the Federal Circuit Court on the charge of libelling the President & the Executive Government in a manner tending to excite sedition and opposition to the laws by sundry publications and *re*-publications. At the request of his counsel (who were not applied to till the very moment fixed for attendance at the Judge's), the proceedings were postponed till Friday next, and the Marshall of the district held him upon his parole then to appear. So much may be stated, we presume with propriety, to satisfy the anxiety of the Public, and, for the same purpose, the Editor adds:

That the present prosecution cannot be supported in the Federal Court, according to the recent opinion of Judge CHASE against the opinion of Judge PETERS. He trusts, however, the ultimate decision will turn, not on the right of jurisdiction, but on THE LIBERTY OF THE PRESS.

We hope sincerely for the honor of our country and the safety of the *Aurora* that, if [Mr. Bache] is innocent, he may *most cordially* prove himself so . . . We cannot be persuaded to believe that . . . any native American, much less a descendant of the illustrious Franklin . . . that HIS grandson has turned assassin and conspirator and aimed the *first* dagger at our vitals.—But time, we trust, will ere long develop the truth . . .   Daily Adv.
(We thank the editor of the Daily Advertiser that he was not so far led away by party spirit to condemn the Editor of the Aurora . . .)

Benny will return to court in two days. Republicans are frightened. Jimmy Callender will soon be gone. Many Republican senators and congressmen have already left. Non-citizens are leaving. Today, Thomas Jefferson leaves for Virginia.[468]

This afternoon, in the *Gazette of the United States:*

To THOMAS JEFFERSON, Esq.
SIR, I have accidentally heard today that you are about to return to Virginia immediately; pray stay a little longer . . . leave not your country at this critical period when it is seeking the most effectual means of self-preservation. But if considerations of this kind will not persuade you to tarry a day or two, recollect that your friend Bache is just now prosecuted for some of his false and scandalous stories concerning the Government of the United States which he has published in the *Aurora*—the same newspaper which you have seditiously endeavored to circulate among your countrymen and for which *you have condescended to solicit subscriptions*—the same which your fellow laborers on the iniquitous work of alienating the affections and confidence of the people from the administration of their government have used for their engine . . . &c.—Let me entreat you not to leave the city at a time so interesting to your friend, who you know is also a friend of Monroe, the friend of Logan the implacable enemy to the measures of America, and the *devoted friend of France.* I beg, I pray, I beseech you not to forsake him, but stay and assist him with your best advice—A friend in need is a friend indeed.   PLINY.

This afternoon's *Porcupine's Gazette* chronicles other occasions when Thomas Jefferson avoided danger:

MUCH has been said of MR. JEFFERSON'S celebrity as a *philosopher* . . . [I]t comes to shew . . . the use he has made of his philosophy, or rather, the manner in which it has operated upon him.

In the latter part of 1776 [during the American Revolution], Mr. Jefferson was elected . . . to go to Europe in order to solicit foreign alliances; the ocean was at this time covered with the British cruisers . . . [H]e declined the office.

In 1781, while he was governor of Virginia, the state was invaded by the [British] enemy, and the post of honor became a post of considerable danger . . . [H]e abandoned it . . . [T]he state of Virginia suffered very materially by the confusion, loss, and distress which such a sudden resignation produced.

At the close of the American war [of Independence], he obtained the appointment of minister plenipotentiary [to France] . . . But as soon as the French Revolution began to break out, the times grew too turbulent for his repose, and he returned to America . . .

[In the Washington administration, S]ecretary of State [Jefferson] . . . was obliged to speak [on the question of helping France] . . . ; the office became irksome, and Mr. Jefferson most philosophically retreated from it at a period of the greatest difficulty and danger . . .[469]

Fenno and Porcupine have their point! Mr. Jefferson is an intellectual, not a fighter. Scribblers like Benny and me must take the risks. *The general fault which Mr. Jefferson's friends impute to him is that he is a quiescent and indifferent spectator of public measures . . . [H]is own friends blame him for too much inactivity, and with justice too . . . [W]hether Mr. Jefferson thinks his situation as Vice President precludes him from an active concern in politics or that he thinks the evil will work its own cure, he is censured by his most steadfast friends for his coldness and reserve on political issues.*[470] Jefferson won't even write a "Letter to the Editor."[471]

Benny is frightened, but he'll do what's right. Today, he writes a childhood friend who wants to leave Switzerland and seek his fortune in America:

> *You are better where you are . . . At this moment, Frenchmen are leaving America in a crowd . . .*
>
> *For my part, I have worked nearly eight years for what I believed was the good of my country, but I made no fortune. I have been exposed to political persecutions of every kind. I will triumph, I hope. Meantime, it's a day of every difficulty. But I am determined to pay whatever the price of doing what I believe to be my duty as a printer who is a zealous friend to liberty.*[472]

Poor Richard advised:

> *The nearest way to come at glory
> is to do that for conscience which we do for glory.*[473]

Today, Benny's French friend, Moreau de St. Méry, receives a letter from the French vice-consul in New York:

I am told your departure for France is at hand. I envy your lot . . . I had hoped to see you and say good-bye, but I must give that up. This disappointment is an added reason for me to damn all these busybodies, all these rascals, who are trying to throw this country into turmoil. All those who have no love for Robespierism [despotism] had better get out and get out quick![474]

Today, Moreau de St. Méry writes in his diary:

People acted as though a French invasion force might land in America at any moment. Everybody was suspicious of everybody else: everywhere one saw murderous glances.[475]

Today, a Philadelphia doctor by the name of Currie records:

June 27th, cool, thermometer only 76°, at two P.M. Mark Miller died to-day under the care of Drs. Wistar and Hodge with symptoms of the yellow fever at Mrs. Reeves's in Callowhill-street. He had been much fatigued and debilitated from loading a vessel at Almond-street wharf, a mile from his lodgings, in the heat of the day, to which he had walked daily for sometime.[476]

An independent report affirms:

Drs. Hodge and Wistars who attended him declared it to have been a true case of yellow fever: the black vomit, one of its most sure and violent characteristics, appeared previous to death.[477]

THURSDAY, JUNE 28, 1798

GENERAL ★ AURORA ★ ADVERTISER

A BILL . . .

Be it enacted . . . That the government and people of France . . . are declared to be enemies to the United States and the people thereof; and any person . . . giving them aid and comfort . . . shall suffer death . . .

And be it further enacted. That if any person shall, by writing, printing, publishing, or speaking, attempt to defame or weaken the government . . . or to defame the President of the United States . . . [he] shall be punished by fine . . . and imprisonment . . .

The foregoing bill was brought into the Senate by Mr. Lloyd [Federalist, Maryland] . . .

Under the late emanation of superlative wisdom making it high treason to aid, abet or *comfort* persons from France, will it be considered high treason to cure a Frenchman of the *cholic?*

The people may be gagged by alien and sedition bills; but at elections they will make their voice heard.

It is a curious fact, America is making war with France for not treating [negotiating] at the very moment the [French] minister for foreign affairs fixes . . . for opening negotiation with Mr. Gerry [the remaining American envoy in Paris].

"What" says a writer in the Daily Gazette, "are the heads of C.[allender] and B.[ache] . . . ? [T]hey are far lighter (continues he) than smoke"—That is, in plain English, it would be as easy to *assassinate* them as for smoke to ascend! This tory, federalist . . . or terrorist (which are now become synonymous terms) is hereby informed that the heads of these respectable printers are of more worth, in the estimation of every honest man, than those of all the ministerial hirelings and tories on the continent.— Let this cowardly cutthroat or any other of the British faction touch a hair of their head, and the swift vengeance of the Republicans would fall like lightning on every pensioned [Federalist] printer in the United States—This should be another hint to the republicans to be armed against personal violence. A man must be blind indeed not to perceive that the leaders of the federalists meditate a blow against them . . .

It is highly interesting to see a nation, after invoking heaven in a solemn manner, a nation boasting of knowledge and religion, opening without any one visible motive a career of tyranny which blushes before high heaven and that must stink in the nose of all posterity !

[Adv.]   SOUTHWARK LIGHT INFANTRY
CITIZENS of Philadelphia . . . are informed that the Committee of Election for the above Company meet every WEDNESDAY and SATURDAY evening, between 6 & 9 o'clock at No. 299, South Front-street, to receive applications from such as propose to become Members.
      N. B. REPUBLICANS ONLY, are admitted.——

Five advertisements for Republican militias appear in today's *Aurora.* Benny carries a cane for personal protection.[478] Republicans are in fear. So are their families.

Six months pregnant with her fourth child, Peggy Bache suffered mob attacks on her home in May, the arrest of her husband two days ago, and continuing threats of violence.[479] Today, she writes her brother, Francis Markoe, on the family estate in St. Croix. Her brother will advise Peggy to abandon Benny Bache and come to St. Croix with the children![480]

Whatever Peggy Bache does, Benny won't leave Philadelphia. Perhaps he hears the whisper of his grandfather, Poor Richard,

> *Fear not Death; for the sooner we die,*
> *the longer shall we be immortal.*[481]

Tonight, in the *Gazette of the United States:*

Bache is desirous of knowing whether it would be high treason to cure a Frenchmen of *cholic*. This is a very pertinent question; the [Republican] party being at present violently convulsed with the *gripes*.

The Constitution is ever in the mouth of the federalists . . . Mr. Lloyd introduced a bill into the Senate defining treason and sedition. The constitution declares that "Congress *shall make no law abridging the freedom of speech nor of the press*"—the same constitution declares that every member of the Senate shall take an oath or affirmation to support the constitution. *Quere*, was Mr. Lloyd exempted from this oath?

The period is now at hand when it will be a question difficult to determine, *Whether there is more safety and liberty to be enjoyed at Constantinople or Philadelphia?*

This morning, at ten o'clock, Benny Bache appears before Pennsylvania's Federal District Court Judge Richard Peters. Benny's lawyers are Moses Levy, a Republican lawyer of Jewish ancestry,[482] and Alexander James Dallas, a Republican lawyer of Scottish ancestry who is Pennsylvania's state secretary. Mr. William Rawle, the federal district attorney, appears for the federal government.

Judge Peters sets bail at the extraordinary sum of $2,000 and demands two sureties of $1,000 each to guarantee Benny's appearance on October 11th (when Federal Circuit Court reconvenes).[483] Benny's bail is put up by Philadelphia tobacconist Thomas Leiper (Jimmy Callender's good friend) and by Israel Israel, a Philadelphia tavernkeeper and stableowner, also of Jewish extraction.[484] (Benny defended Israel Israel, in February, against lawyer Joseph Thomas and other Federalists who wrongfully denied him a seat in the Pennsylvania state senate.)[485] Two other friends of Benny, Robert Smith, a hatter, and Colonel Barker, a tailor, also appear.[486] Jimmy Callender:

> *If Bache had not been able to give surety, he must have remained in jail for probably six months before he was brought to trial. The interval is sufficient for bringing many people to ruin.*[487]

Tonight, in the *Gazette of the United States*, John Fenno ridicules Benny's friends:

> What a group! What a concatenation of characters! How . . . birds of a feather flock together! I question whether a *farrago* of such pure, genuine jacobinical democratical spirits could be selected and collected, as was exemplified at the Judge's—and are seen held up to public observation as the *anti-federal Printer*, the *two Law-ware men*, the *Scottish Quarrier alias quarrelsome man*, the *Synagogue stabler*, and would-be Senator, the warlike Taylor and the Don Quixote Hatter. Reader! bless thyself that

thou art not like one of these men but one who believeth that justice and truth will always be an over match for treason and rebellion.

Tonight, in the *Porcupine's Gazette*:

LIBERTY OF THE PRESS . . . The French faction are working like devils to persuade the people that the federal government is acting against them with *rigour* and with *partiality*. I shall therefore remind the public . . .

As to [Tom Paine's book against established religion,] *AGE OF REASON*, its publication by *BACHE* . . . is too notorious a fact to be for a moment dwelt on . . . *Christianity* is part of *the law of the land* . . . [T]o deride and blaspheme it is punishable by the common law . . .

BACHE, in his paper No. 1460, calls the Honourable John Jay . . . "that *damned arch traitor* JOHN JAY" . . . I could name here at least one hundred of the greatest and best men that this country ever produced who have been vilified by this reprobate descendant of Old Franklin, but . . . I shall forbear the enumerations and content myself with the instance of two of his attacks on the character of GENERAL WASHINGTON for which every good man, in every part of the world, must and will execrate the libeller and his supporters.

He published PAINE'S letter to the GENERAL of which he claimed an exclusive copyright . . . In this work, GENERAL WASHINGTON . . . is called, *"the patron of fraud,"*—an *"impostor,"* or an *"apostate."*— Yet the vile printer was never *"bound over."*

The day the GENERAL closed his public labours (the 4th of March, 1797), BACHE, after announcing his retirement from the office of President, says: "If there ever was a period for rejoicing, this is the moment . . ."

Yet, we are not all the worst: for on the 13th of March 1797, this viperous Grand Son of Old Franklin, accused the same eminent person of *murder!* brought forward a long, formal, and circumstantial charge of cool, deliberate *assassination, "committed by GENERAL WASHINGTON, late President of the United States."*

SATURDAY, JUNE 30, 1798

GENERAL ★ AURORA ★ ADVERTISER

Yesterday at 10 o'clock, Mr. Bache, attended by Messrs. Levy and Dallas as his counsel, appeared before Judge Peters at his chambers, when Mr. Rawle, the Attorney of the district, attended on behalf of the United States to support the warrant issued against Mr. Bache for publications alleged to be libellous in relation to the President and the Executive government of the United States. Mr. Bache's counsel stated . . . that the Federal Courts had no common law jurisdiction in criminal cases . . . Judge PETERS observed that . . . his mind was confirmed . . . He proposed that Mr. Bache should give security in 2000 dollars himself, with two sureties in 1000 dollars each, to appear and answer. The security was immediately given.

Tonight, in the *Gazette of the United States*:

> The *Aurora*, after having attacked both Presidents of the United States in succession, and the majorities of both Houses of Congress for several years past, pretending all the time to the most violent Republicanism, has at last attacked the whole American people. The following libel is proof in point and is copied from the *Aurora* of Thursday last.
> "It is highly interesting to see a nation . . . opening, without any visible motive, a career of tyranny . . ."

SUNDAY, JULY 1, 1798

Tonight, congressional Federalists caucus at U.S. Senator William Bingham's mansion at the corner of Spruce- and Third-streets in Philadelphia. The subject: a Declaration of War against France.[488]

MONDAY, JULY 2, 1798

GENERAL　　★ AURORA ★　　ADVERTISER

(We are happy to lay the following speech of Mr. [Edward] Livingston on the third reading of the alien bill before our readers . . .)

Edward Livingston's June 21st speech in Congress occupies most of the editorial space in today's *Aurora*.

Today, President Adams informs the Senate,

> *I nominate George Washington, of Mount Vernon, to be Lieutenant-General and Commander in Chief of all the armies raised or to be raised in the United States.*[489]

George Washington will lead America's new federal army against our former French ally!

Today, Federalists caucus again on passing a formal Declaration of War against France.[490]

TUESDAY, JULY 3, 1798

GENERAL　　★ AURORA ★　　ADVERTISER

John Fenno appears very angry because the friends of the Printer of the *Aurora* are *tradesmen—mere simple men*, none of your high-flying *well borns* . . . [T]hey are only plain, simple, unaffected Republicans, and this is indeed a *heinous fault !*

Tonight, in the *Gazette of the United States*:

> *To the . . . Inhabitants of the town of Rutland, in . . . Vermont.*
> GENTLEMEN, I THANK you for this address . . . The words "Republican
> Government" have imposed on many who had very imperfect ideas under
> them—as there are none in our language more indeterminate, they may
> be interpreted to mean anything . . .
>
> JOHN ADAMS

☞ To-morrow being the Anniversary of INDEPENDENCE, the next publication of this Gazette will not take place till Thursday.

The union of the People of the United States in support of their Independence and Government at the present crisis is greater than it
was in the year 1775— and the preparations and provision to defend all
that is dear and sacred much more extensive; and yet, monstrous impudence ! a few desperadoes vomit thro' the medium of the *Aurora* a perpetual cascade of abuse against the people, their government and its
administration.

WEDNESDAY, JULY 4, 1798

GENERAL ★ AURORA ★ ADVERTISER

This day will be celebrated as the Great Jubilee of Americans. We ask
a Holiday; in consequence of which the next number of the AURORA will
appear on Friday.

In a republican government, freedom of sentiments and a right to deliver such sentiments on every subject has been held essential to true
liberty, but when that freedom is by whatever means restrained, despotism will most probably be the consequence.

*TO IRISH EMIGRANTS AND PARTICULARLY
THAT CLASS DENOMINATED ALIENS—*

A Bill respecting Naturalization is passed into a law. By this law, fourteen years residence in the United States are necessary to obtain the
rights of citizenship . . . An alien bill is on its passage . . . By this law the
President of the U.S. is vested with a discretionary power of seizing on,
confining or transporting your persons beyond the territories of the
United States . . .

The United States are largely indebted for their independence to
the exertions of the Irish both in Europe and America. The Pennsylvania, Maryland, and Delaware Lines were almost entirely composed
of natives of Ireland . . . And what is the return they have met with?
A Naturalization Law, an alien law, a sedition law topped off with
the most opprobrious obloquy and abuse that ever disgraced a legislative
body.

Today, America celebrates its independence. At Hartford in Connecticut, Thomas Day delivers an oration to Revolutionary War veterans on the dangers of faction ("party spirit"):

> *Among those means which are calculated to destroy a free government, none will be found more efficient than PARTY SPIRIT . . .*
>
> *[T][he present Vice President of the United States . . . has ever been the great Manager of the Gallico-Anarchic-Democratic Force . . . [H]e has countenanced and recommended a Gazette Edited by Bache, teeming with all that is virulent and abusive against the government and its administration . . .*[491]

Theodore Dwight addresses another Hartford audience:

> *Mr. Jefferson's celebrated letter to Mazzei made its . . . first charge . . . that "a party has arisen . . . to impose on the people the substance of the British government." This assertion has often been boldly made by the profligate printer of the Aurora . . .*
>
> *[I]f the French Councils, by any means whatever, should gain an ascendency over our government . . . our Independence will be at an end.*[492]

Augustus Pettibone speaks at Norfolk, Connecticut:

> *O Liberty ! how has thy name been perverted by our Democratic disorganizers . . . May they, with Bache, that secret emissary, whose press has teemed with abuse and poured forth a flood of calumny against the guardians of our nation, be learnt and learn . . . that our federal soil will not nourish their felonious practices . . .*
>
> *What nation, what kingdom, what empire, can boast of a better Executive Department than the United States of America? Great ADAMS, the illustrious Chief of that noble order, faires like a star of the first magnitude and may be justly compared with the Sun in the political world . . .*[493]

At the Presbyterian Church in Newark, New Jersey, David Ogden speaks to an "Association of Young Men":

> *Suspect the motives of those who would persuade you [the President] is not the friend of his country. Your fathers, in their glorious struggle for Independence, entrusted him with the management of some of their dearest interests.*[494]

In Philadelphia, the "Young Men" of the Macpherson's Blues parade. The *Gazette of the United States* reports:

> The military assembled on the occasion consisted of some small detachments of a few of the militia companies, infantry and artillery, and of the whole body of newly formed volunteer corps in full uniform—These, with the several troops of horse, formed a most brilliant military procession.
>
> From the center square, the whole marched down High-street and

passed in review of the President of the United States, the officers paying the proper marching salute. The President appeared greatly delighted . . .

At noon a federal salute was fired by Guy's Artillery. The bells of Christ Church were rung at intervals thro' the day . . .[495]

Abigail Adams expresses her pleasure:

> *[A] Glorious sight . . . 400 Young Men all in uniform and 60 Grenadiers none of whom exceeded 22 years marching in review as volunteers whose services had been tendered to their Country in a free will offering to the Chief Executive . . . To the committee of young men . . . I presented a cockade in the middle of which is a small Silver Eagle, being the arms of the United States . . . [T]he whole volunteer corps have adopted them.*[496]

There are disturbances. *Porcupine's Gazette*:

> [T]here were some turbulent malicious spirits . . . The splendid and military appearance of the Volunteer Horse and foot was what mortified them most. As a force ready to support government and to oppose all its intestine as well as foreign enemies, it was a galling spectacle to the eyes of a Jacobin.
>
> Several fellows of this description, but two more particularly, attempted to insult the first troop of Light Horse, commanded by Capt. Dunlap, as they were returning up High-street in the evening. The horses were moving remarkably slow, four abreast, and of course filled most of the ground between the butchers shambles [of the covered market] and the foot pavement. One of the fellows had been daringly insolent, but both became outrageous . . . poured out torrents of abusive language, advanced up to the horsemen, flourished their bludgeons, and at length struck one of the horses several heavy strokes. This provoked one of the riders to draw and to strike the aggressor with the flat of his sword . . . I expected to see both of them cut down . . .[497]

At Williamsburg in Virginia, William and Mary College students burn John Adams in effigy. Peter Porcupine reports:

> [T]he burning of the President's effigy at Williamsburg was not the work of the mob, nor of the inhabitants of the place in general; but of the learned, polite, and patriotic *students of William and Mary College*. A precious seminary! I wonder who is at the head of it! Some bitter, factious, envious wretch, I will answer for it; if not some philosopher of the infamous tribe of the *illuminati*. One of the great objects of these plotting villains was to thrust their members into all places of education in order to be enabled to corrupt the youth. They have succeeded at William and Mary clear enough. I would sooner put a child of mine under the tuition of a common thief than send him amongst this rascally seditious crew.— I shall once more remind my readers that these base blackguards, who now insult their president, actually had the courage a few years ago to

behead the statue of the founder of their college because he was an aristocrat.[498]

Senate Federalists want to associate the sedition act with the nation's independence and, therefore, to pass a bill today. Republican Senator Stevens T. Mason of Virginia:

[T]here seemed to be a particular solicitude to pass it on that day . . . The drums, Trumpets and other martial music which surrounded us drown'd the voices of those who spoke on the Question. The military parade so attracted the attention of the majority that much the greater part of them stood with their bodies out of the windows and could not be kept to order. To get rid of such a scene of uproar and confusion, an attempt was made at adjournment and then of a postponement of that question. These were both overruled and the final decision taken . . .[499]

Today, with Senator Theodore Sedgwick (Federalist, Massachusetts) acting as U.S. Senate president for the absent Thomas Jefferson and with more than one third of Republican senators also absent, the United States Senate passes a sedition bill, 18 ayes to 6 nays, including a provision,

That if any person shall, by . . . writing, printing, publishing, or speaking . . . create a belief [that] . . . the said Legislature, in enacting any law, was induced thereto by motives hostile to the Constitution . . . the person so offending . . . shall be punished by a fine, not exceeding two thousand dollars, and by imprisonment not exceeding two years."[500]

Later today, the sponsor of the Senate's sedition bill, U.S. Senator James Lloyd (Federalist, Maryland), writes George Washington:

Sir . . . You will have heard before this reaches you that you were . . . by the unanimous vote of the senate, appointed Lieutenant General & Commander in Chief of the Armies of America . . .

The packet for Bache, sealed with the seal of the minister of foreign relations fell into the hands of Government and I believe it is pretty certain [that it] did not contain Talleyrand's letter to our Envoys. Whether he received it immediately from Talleyrand or from Letombe, the consul [general of France at Philadelphia], or from one of our French-Americans is uncertain.

Your Excellency has probably seen in the papers a bill which was introduced into the Senate, to define & punish the crimes of Treason & Sedition. This bill . . . passed the Senate . . . 18 to five, & will certainly pass the ho. of Representatives. I enclose the bill as amended . . .

I fear that Congress will close the session without a Declaration of War, which I look upon as necessary to enable us to lay our hands on traitors . . .[501]

Today, George Washington writes President John Adams:

[The French] have been led to believe by their Agents and Partisans amongst Us that we are a divided People, that the latter are opposed to their own Government, and that a show of a small force would occasion a revolt, I have no doubt; and how far these men (grown desperate) will further attempt to deceive and may succeed in keeping up the deception is problematical . . .[502]

Today, George Washington also writes Secretary of War James McHenry:

[My principles] would not suffer me in any great emergency to withhold any services I could render, required by my Country, especially in a case where its dearest rights are assailed by lawless ambition . . . with obvious intent to sow thick the Seeds of disunion for the purpose of subjugating the Government and destroying our Independence and happiness . . .[503]

Today, another Federalist caucus on a Declaration of War.[504]

It was Poor Richard who wrote,

The Golden Age never was the present age.[505]

THURSDAY, JULY 5, 1798

**[As announced yesterday,
there is no edition of the Aurora.]**

Today, the House of Representatives considers the sedition bill that the Senate passed yesterday. The Annals of Congress report:

PUNISHMENT OF CRIME
A bill was received from the Senate . . .
Mr. ALLEN [Federalist, Connecticut]. Let gentlemen look at certain papers printed in this city and elsewhere, and ask ourselves whether an unwarrantable and dangerous combination does not exist to overturn and ruin the Government by publishing the most shameful falsehoods . . .
In the *Aurora* of the 28th of June last, we see this paragraph "It is a curious fact, America is making war with France for *not* treating, at the very moment the Minister for Foreign Affairs fixes upon the very day for opening a negotiation with Mr. Gerry. What do you think of this, Americans!"
Such paragraphs need but little comment . . .
I will take the liberty of reading to the House another paragraph from the same paper [on July 2d] . . . published as the speech of the same gentleman (Mr. [Edward] LIVINGSTON) when we were discussing the Alien bill . . . "If there is, then, any necessity for the system now proposed, it is more necessary to be enforced against our own citizens than against strangers; and I have no doubt that either in this, or some other shape, this will be attempted. I now ask, sir, whether the people of America are

prepared for this? . . . Whether they are ready to submit to imprisonment or exile, whenever suspicion, calumny or vengeance, shall mark them for ruin? No sir, they will, I repeat it they will resist this tyrannic system! . . ."

Sir, is this a just picture? The gentleman attempted, in this instance, to persuade the people . . . that opposition to the laws, that insurrection is a duty whenever they think we exceed our constitutional powers . . .

In the *Aurora* of last Friday, we read the following:

"The period is now at hand when it will be a question difficult to determine, whether there is more safety to be enjoyed at Constantinople or Philadelphia!"

This, sir, is . . . announcing to the poor deluded readers of the factious prints the rapid approach of Turkish slavery in this country . . .

At the commencement of the Revolution in France those loud and enthusiastic advocates for liberty and equality took special care to occupy and command all the presses in the nation; they well knew the powerful influence to be obtained on the public mind by that engine; its operations are on the poor, the ignorant, the passionate, and the vicious . . . The Jacobins in our country, too, sir, are determined to preserve in their hands the same weapon; it is our business to wrest it from them . . .

This paper (the *Aurora*) is the great engine of all these treasonable combinations, and must be strongly supported, or it would fall long ago.

Mr. W.[illiam] CLAIBORNE [Republican, Tennessee] interrupted Mr. A.[llen] and asked him whether he did not subscribe for it, and so become one of its supporters?

I do, said Mr. A.[llen]. I take it under the rule of the House at the public expense. I take it for the purpose of seeing what abominable things can issue from a genuine Jacobinic press but this is not supporting it with my name and influence [as Thomas Jefferson does]; this is not giving it the authority of my opinions; I do not walk the streets arm-in-arm. I hold no mid-night conference. I am not daily and nightly closeted with its editor. I may say, sir, this paper must necessarily, in the nature of things, be supported by . . . certain great men.[506]

Mr. GALLATIN [Republican, Pennsylvania]: . . . The Gentleman from Connecticut (Mr. ALLEN) . . . had communicated to the House—what? . . . a number of newspaper paragraphs . . . His idea was to punish men for stating facts which he happened to disbelieve, or for enacting and avowing opinions, not criminal, but perhaps erroneous . . . The gentleman from Connecticut had also quoted an extract of a letter . . . published in last Saturday's *Aurora*. The style and composition of that letter did the highest honor to its writer. It contained more information and more sense and gave more proofs than ever the Gentleman from Connecticut had displayed or could display on this floor . . .

This bill and its supporters suppose, in fact, that whoever dislikes the measures of the administration and of a temporary majority in Congress and shall either by speaking or writing, express his disapprobation and his want of confidence in the men now in power is seditious, is an enemy, not of Administration, but of the Constitution, and is liable to punishment. That principle, Mr. G[allatin] said, was subversive of the Constitution itself. If you put the press under any restraint in respect to the measures of the members of Government; if you thus deprive the people of the means of obtaining information of their conduct, you render in fact the right of electing nugatory; and this bill must be considered only as a weapon used by a party now in power in order to perpetuate their authority and preserve their present places . . .[507]

The House next considers a Declaration of War. The Annals report:

Mr. ALLEN [Federalist, Connecticut] laid a resolution upon the table to the following effect,

"*Resolved,* That a committee be appointed to consider upon the expediency of declaring, by Legislative act, the state and relation subsisting between the United States and the French Republic."[508]

Today, George Washington writes a secret letter to the U.S. Secretary of War:

I do not . . . conceive that a desirable set [of officers for the new army] could be formed from the old Generals, some . . . from their opposition to the Government or their predilection to French measures . . .[509]

Tonight, in the *Porcupine's Gazette,* William Cobbett writes:

It is with great satisfaction that I announce to my readers the appointment of GENERAL WASHINGTON TO BE LIEUT-GENERAL AND COMMANDER IN CHIEF of the Armies of the United States. I understand that he *offered his services* to his country at this trying moment.

FRIDAY, JULY 6, 1798

GENERAL ★ AURORA ★ ADVERTISER

We are informed from New Jersey that a number of citizens were last week remanded before the Judge of the District Court of the United States for having spoken their sentiments on the subject of the President.

Johnny Fenno, the well paid tool of the anti-republican Partizans, now takes courage and says we must declare war at once.

Today, the House of Representatives continues to consider a Declaration of War. The Annals of Congress:

Mr. ALLEN [Federalist, Connecticut] then called up his resolution . . .
Mr. HARRISON [Republican, Virginia] . . . He hoped gentlemen would bring forward their declaration of War at once. He had always been and should now be opposed to war, but he wanted to put his negative upon it . . . Seeing, however, that no member is ready to make the declaration

which has been so often spoken of, [Mr. ALLEN] should withdraw his motion . . .

Mr. SITGREAVES [Federalist, Pennsylvania] thought it would be proper first to go into a consideration of this resolution. We are, said he, now in a state of war . . .

The question on the resolution was put and negatived without a division [roll call].[510]

There will be no Declaration of War! Abigail Adams:

T]he people throughout the United States . . . called for the declaration to be made from various quarters of the union, but the majority in Congress did not possess firmness and decision enough to boldly make it . . .[511]

Did publication of Talleyrand's letter make the difference? Is it important? With or without a Declaration of War, John Adams will have his war against France!

War measures . . . Today, John Adams approves and signs into law:

AN ACT
Respecting Alien Enemies
Be it enacted, &c., That whenever there shall be a declared war . . . or an invasion or predatory incursion . . . shall be perpetrated, attempted or threatened . . . and the President shall make a public proclamation of the event, [then] all natives, citizens, denizens, or subjects of the hostile nation or government being males of the age of fourteen years and upwards . . . shall be liable to be apprehended, retrained, secured and removed as alien enemies . . .[512]

More war measures . . . Today, John Adams approves and signs into law,

AN ACT
Providing arms for the Militia
throughout the United States.
Be it enacted, &c., That there shall be provided at the charge and expense of the Government of the United States thirty thousand stand of arms which shall be deposited by order of the President of the United States at suitable places . . .[513]

Today, two Federal marshals enter the offices of the New York *Time Piece* and arrest its editor and co-proprietor, John Daly Burk. He is charged with seditious utterances against the President of the United States. The other *Time Piece* owner, Dr. James Smith, is also taken into custody. After the newsmen post bail of 2,000 dollars and provide sureties of 1,000 dollars each, Judge Hobarton frees the newsmen, pending trial. New York Republican leader Aaron Burr and Colonel Henry Rutgers are the sureties.[514]

Tonight, in the *Porcupine's Gazette*:

> The *Aurora* Printer has been so hard pressed . . . that he has at length been obliged to *confess* that he is in frequent correspondence with the office of foreign affairs in France. It is said, however, by some that he will not BE HANGED.

VOLUNTEER TOASTS [ON JULY 4TH] . . .
Republican Printers in the United States—when arraigned by the voice of calumny, may they find impartial judges and honest Jurors . . .

Today, unaware that John Daly Burk of the New York *Time Piece* was arrested yesterday, U.S. Secretary of State Timothy Pickering writes New York Federal District Attorney Richard Harrison:

> It appears that the Editor of Time Piece is an Irishman and alien . . .
> If Burk be an alien, no man is a fitter object for the operation of the alien act.[515]

War measures . . . Today, John Adams approves and signs into law,

AN ACT
*To declare the Treaties heretofore concluded with
France no longer obligatory on the United States . . .*
Be it enacted &c. That the United States are of right, freed and exonerated from the stipulations of the treaties and of the consular conventions heretofore concluded between the United States and France . . .[516]

By signing this law which abrogates the Franco-American Treaty of Alliance of 1778 and the Franco-American Treaty of Amity and Commerce of 1778, John Adams commits an act of war against the Republic of France. Even without a formal Declaration of War, Adams has us at war with France![517]

War . . . Tonight, the fighting begins! Just off Egg Harbour, New Jersey, the United States Navy's twenty-gun, 180–man Sloop of War *Delaware,* under Navy Captain Stephen Decatur, fires on, pursues, and captures a twelve-gun, seventy-man privateer schooner, *La Croyable*, which flies the flag of the French Republic. Captain Decatur brings his prize into the Port of Philadelphia.[518] A report:

> The Captain of the French privateer . . . seemed astonished, when he
> went on board of Capt. Decatur's sloop of war, at his being taken by
> an American vessel, and said he knew of no war between the two re-
> publics . . . The Frenchman seemed to be vastly mortified at seeing his
> Colours hauled down and wished he had been sunk.[519]

The *alarm* system is kept up with great spirit,—We learn from *John Fenno* (& for executive measures and sentiments, he stands next in authenticity to Porcupine) that John D. Burk and Dr. J. Smith [co-publishers of the *Time Piece]* have been arrested at New York . . .

War measures . . . Today, John Adams approves and signs into law an act which anticipates the imposition of war taxes:

AN ACT
*To provide for the valuation of land and dwelling-houses
and the enumeration of slaves, within the United States.*

There will be a property tax, so each state must value and list the property of its inhabitants, evaluating homes, for example, on *"their situation, their dimensions or area, their number of stories, the number and dimensions of their windows, the materials whereof they are built, whether wood, brick or stone, the number, description, and dimensions of the outhouses . . . [&c.]"*[520]

War measures . . . John Adams also approves and signs into law,

AN ACT
Further to protect the commerce of the United States
Be it enacted, That the President . . . is hereby authorized to instruct the commanders of the public armed vessels . . . to subdue, seize, and take any armed French vessel . . . on the high seas . . .
Sec 2. *And be it further enacted,* That the President . . . is hereby authorized to grant to owners of private armed ships and vessels of the United States . . . authority for the subduing, seizing, and capturing [of] any French armed vessel . . .
Sec 5. *And be it further enacted,* That all armed French vessels . . . shall be forfeited and shall accrue to the owners . . . officers, and crew by whom such captures are made . . .[521]

We don't have to wait for France to land soldiers on American shores! The President will commission, within the next eight months, more than 350 American privateers, carrying more than 2,700 guns, to seek out, attack, seize, and sell for profit any French merchant ship which has the misfortune to be armed.[522] By year's end, America will have more than four hundred armed vessels at sea.[523]

Today, Abigail Adams writes her sister,

Let the vipers cease to hiss. They will be destroyd with their own poison. Bache is in duress here . . .[524]

Tonight, in the *Gazette of the United States*:

> [T]he *Delaware* sloop of war, Capt. Decatur . . . captured a French privateer schooner of 12 guns and 70 men, close in with Egg-Harbour [New Jersey] . . . [S]he was obliged to surrender after a pretty long chase to the Delaware and several shot being fired at her . . .

Tonight, in the *Porcupine's Gazette*:

> The Historian, who is to record the events of the present times, after relating the long suffering of America; the injuries and insults and cruelties she has received at hands of the perfidious French . . . will then say . . . "on the 7th of July, 1798, the *first blow* of that conflict, *which preserved the independence of America and finally brought France to her feet,* was struck by Captain STEPHEN DECATUR, who, in the sloop of War DELAWARE, attacked and brought into the Port of Philadelphia, a French privateer of 12 guns and 70 men."—This, I hope, will be the language of History.

TUESDAY, JULY 10, 1798

GENERAL ★ AURORA ★ ADVERTISER

Yesterday morning was ushered in with the ringing of bells and other demonstrations of joy; great numbers of the opulent mercantile interest of this flourishing city assembled at the Coffee house to reciprocate their congratulations on the occasion—the *taking of a French schooner* after a desperate action of *one gun* . . . The captured schooner, it appears, mistook the Delaware for a British ship of war and, being an inferior force, took refuge in Egg Harbour . . . The French schooner, it appears did not fire on the Delaware . . .

Today, John Adams issues instructions, through his Navy Secretary, to commanders of all armed vessels belonging to the United States:

> *You are hereby authorized, instructed, and directed to subdue, seize and take any armed French Vessel or Vessels sailing under Authority or Pretence of Authority from the French Republic which shall be found within the Jurisdictional Limits of the United States or elsewhere on the high Seas: and such captured Vessel . . . to bring within some Port of the United States . . .*[525]

Today, the U.S. House of Representatives passes the sedition act, 44 ayes to 41 nays. To become law, the bill only requires John Adams' signature. This can hardly be in doubt. Confirming Republican suspicions that the sedition act serves John Adams' party purposes rather than any national emergency, the bill is written to expire at the end of John Adams' term of office![526]

GENERAL ★ AURORA ★ ADVERTISER

The Libel and Sedition Bill yesterday passed the House, 44 to 41 . . . [T]he good citizens of these States had better hold their tongues and make tooth picks of their pens.

Mr. Adams, in his answer to four companies of militia in New Jersey, insinuates that the Government is not a party. He certainly must have forgotten that he was elected by a party, that he is supported by a party, and that he supports none but a party. Who are the persons delegated to public office? None but men of a particular mode of thinking.

War . . . Today, John Adams approves and signs into law:

AN ACT
For establishing and organizing a Marine Corps.
Be it enacted, &c., That in addition to the Present military establishment, there shall be raised and organized a corps of marines . . . to do duty in the forts and garrisons of the United States, on the sea coast, or any other duty on shore, as the President, at his discretion, shall direct.[527]

Tonight, in the *Gazette of the United States*:

The *Aurora* of this morning, (a thing quite new) calls the government a party and says the President is supported by a party, &c. Verily, these words must be true; for they proceed from the pen of a man who never told a *lie* !! All America is, however, *at this moment* testifying to the contrary.

GENERAL ★ AURORA ★ ADVERTISER

Communication.
"The conduct of Mr. Bache is particularly meritorious. Unawed by a denunciation . . . on the floor of Congress or by threats which were industriously circulated out of doors . . . he has exhibited more than his wonted firmness . . . and bid defiance to a host of foes leagued for his destruction. It is hoped that the republicans . . . will, in every part of the union, countenance his virtuous exertions. Although his paper already has a general circulation, no republican who can afford it should neglect becoming a subscriber. It is by the dissemination of such salutary truths as are contained in the Aurora and a few other Republican papers that the eyes of the people will be opened . . ."

Today, President Adams revokes U.S. government recognition *(exequaturs)* for French Consul General Joseph Philippe Létombe (Philadelphia), for French

Vice-Consuls Rosier (New York) and Arcambal (Newport), and for French Consul Charles Mozard (New Hampshire, Massachusetts, and Rhode Island).[528]

Today, from Mount Vernon, George Washington writes John Adams,

> *It was not possible for me to remain ignorant of, or indifferent to, recent transactions. The conduct of the Directory of France towards our Country . . . their various practices to withdraw the affections of the people from it; the evident tendency of their Arts and those of their agents to countenance and invigorate opposition; . . . could not fail to excite in me corresponding sentiments with those my countrymen have so generally expressed in their Affectionate addresses to you. Believe me, sir, no one can more cordially approve of the wise and prudent measures of your Administration.*[529]

Today, at this dark hour in our country's history, a great personal tragedy befalls my family. Today, in our meager living quarters next to a hot, smoke-filled alley, my wife, Catherine, dies of cholera.[530] Three of us got cholera this year, Catherine, William John, and I.[531] Now Catherine has died from it, and I must be father and mother to the children. When we married in Ireland twenty years ago, Catherine was only seventeen, and I was nineteen. She was Protestant; I was Catholic. After our wedding, my mother shunned Catherine and disinherited me. Mother died a few years later.[532] During nine of the last twelve years, Catherine and I lived apart, she remaining in Ireland while I worked for newspapers in India and England. We reunited for the trip to America, but it hasn't turned out well for Catherine.[533] As Poor Richard said,

> *A good Wife lost is God's Gift lost.*[534]

My son, William John, now 18, can help with the other children, and William John has a job with Benny Bache as a clerk at the *Aurora* (where I am now working full-time).[535] The Baches are good friends to the Duanes, and the Duanes will be good friends to them. Especially in times like these, as Poor Richard wrote,

> *No better relation than a prudent & faithful Friend.*[536]

Jimmy Callender is gone. Though Jimmy Callender has insulated himself from the Alien Acts by citizenship, President Adams will sign the Sedition Act tomorrow. Jimmy has said his "good-byes," left his four children in the care of his tobacconist friend Thomas Leiper, and is the first Republican scribbler to flee the federal government.[537]

Tonight, in the *Gazette of the United States*:

ENVOY CALLENDER

Left this city on a tour to the westward. His business or destination is not known. But he was seen a few days since, near the 22d mile stone, on the Lancaster road . . . DRUNK.

Tonight, in the *Porcupine's Gazette:*

Three French frigates are said to be on their way towards the American coast.

GENERAL ★ AURORA ★ ADVERTISER

FOR THE AURORA
ADVERTISEMENT EXTRAORDINARY ! ! !
Orator M u m takes this *very orderly* method of announcing that a T H I N K I N G CLUB will be established in a few days at the sign of the *MUZZLE* in *Gag* street. The first subject for cogitation will be
"Ought a Free People to obey laws which violate the constitution they have sworn to support?"

N. B. No member will be permitted to think longer than fifteen minutes.

*** The Editors of newspapers in this city are requested to insert this important information.

The Constitution of the United States says that "Congress shall make no law abridging the freedom of speech or of the press," but Congress have passed a law abridging the freedom of the press and therefore the Constitution is infracted. Quere, of what efficacy is a law made in direct contravention of the Constitution?

Today, John Adams approves and signs into law the federal Sedition Act:

AN ACT
In addition to the act entitled
"An act for the punishment of certain crimes
against the United States."
Be it enacted, &c., That if any persons shall unlawfully combine or conspire together with intent to oppose any measure or measures of the government of the United States . . . [&c.]

Sec.2. *And be it further enacted,* That if any person shall write, print, utter, or publish . . . any false, scandalous, and malicious writing or writings against the Government of the United States, or either House of the Congress of the United States, or the President of the United States with intent to defame . . . or bring them, or either of them, into contempt or disrepute; or to excite against them, or either or any of them, the hatred of the good people of the United States . . . or to impede the operation of any law of the United States . . . or to resist, oppose or defeat any such law or act . . . then such persons, being thereof convicted, before any court of the United States having jurisdiction thereof, shall be punished by a fine not exceeding two thousand dollars and by imprisonment not exceeding two years . . .[538]

With Adams' signature, it becomes a federal crime for any American to print, write, or speak criticism of the President, the federal government, or the Congress (though one can still criticize the Vice President!).[539] Like the British monarch, John Adams now has Alien and Sedition Acts to silence his critics. John Adams:

> *I knew there was need enough of both, and therefore I consented to them . . .*[540]

U.S. Secretary of State Timothy Pickering will be the enforcer.

War Measures . . . Today, John Adams approves and signs into law

AN ACT
*To lay and collect a direct
tax within the United States.*

Be it enacted, &c., That a direct tax of two millions of dollars shall be, and hereby is, laid upon the United States . . . under the direction of the Secretary of the Treasury . . . assessed upon dwelling-houses, lands, and slaves, according to the valuations and enumerations to be made pursuant to the act, entitled "An act to provide for the valuation of lands and dwelling-houses, and the enumeration of slaves, within the United States" [signed by the President on July 9th].[541]

Today, Moreau de St. Méry writes in his diary,

> *I received a passport for myself, my wife and the children.*
> *Antagonism against the French increased daily.*
> *I was the only person in Philadelphia who continued to wear a French cockade.*
> *Soon thereafter the Republicans, fearing acts of violence on the part of the Federalists, met secretly and took steps to defend themselves. Since I was a party to these meetings, I was given keys to two shelters in which I and my family could take refuge in case my own house should be attacked.*[542]

Tonight, in the *Porcupine's Gazette*:

> "Envoy Callender" is gone to the Westward; and Fenno says he was met a few days ago near the 22 mile stone, DRUNK . . . [T]o do historical justice, he must bring himself under the gallows tree; and in that case, I hereby promise to put a finishing hand to the performance and publish it for the benefit of his friend BACHE, the Grandson of Old Franklin.

Have the government the right or power to send the *Federal Constitution* out of the country as an *Alien* ?

War measures . . . More warships. Today, John Adams approves and signs into law,

AN ACT
To make a further appropriation for
the additional naval armament.
Be it enacted, &c., That the sum of six hundred thousand dollars shall be, and hereby is, appropriated . . . to cause to be built and equipped three ships or vessels, to be of a force not less than thirty-two guns each . . .

More war measures . . . Today, Adams also approves and signs into law,

AN ACT
To augment the Army of the United States,
and for other purposes.
Be it enacted, &c., . . . That the President of the United States be and he is hereby authorized to raise, in addition to the present Military Establishment, twelve regiments of infantry and six troops of light dragoons, to be enlisted for and during the continuance of the existing differences between the United States and the French Republic . . .[543]

Today, the Second Session of the Fifth Congress of the United States of America adjourns (though the Senate will remain in executive session for three days to receive the President's nominations of army officers). Republican congressmen who have remained at their posts, such as Edward Livingston (New York), Matthew Lyon (Vermont), and Albert Gallatin (Western Pennsylvania), will now depart.[544] President and Mrs. Adams will also leave. Benny and I will remain.

Tonight, the *Gazette of the United States* reports restlessness in Virginia:

From a Gentleman in Virginia
TO the disgrace of our state, the spirit of opposition still runs high. The anti-governmental party . . . revives the animosity against our government. To accomplish these objects, our members of Congress have deluged the state with *Auroras* . . . Through the same channels of calumny, we have lately been informed that "JOHN ADAMS WAS AT THE HEAD OF THE MOB WHO ATTACKED BACHE'S HOUSE." . . .

A VIRGINIAN

GENERAL ★ AURORA ★ ADVERTISER

The Legislature of the United States closed yesterday a very long and important session . . .

The misunderstanding between the United States and the French Republic is made use of to justify the enaction of odious laws. But what has this misunderstanding to do with a sedition or an alien bill? Will a sedition bill repress French aggressions or an alien bill make the Directory listen to our terms? . . . What has their conduct to do with our constitutional or our republican principles? . . . Let us not forget ourselves in our attention to others, and while our eyes are fixed upon distant dangers, let us not omit to turn them likewise to those which may menace us nearer home . . .

Persons pretending to the utmost liberality, professing the most unbounded toleration, and perpetually blubbering out praises on *liberty, justice,* and the rights of *private opinion,* are yet hourly supporting persecution for *opinion's sake* . . . Dr. Franklin, in his celebrated examination, briefly told the English parliament that *men's opinions are not to be conquered !*

Today, U.S. marshals arrest William Durrell, Republican editor of the *Mount Pleasant Register* in upstate New York, for criticizing the President of the United States. After posting a $4,000 bail, Durrell is released pending trial. Today's edition of the *Mount Pleasant Register* is the last that will ever appear.[545]

GENERAL ★ AURORA ★ ADVERTISER

NEWBURGH [New York] . . . A Liberty Pole is erected in this town with the following inscription thereon:
LIBERTY 1776 JUSTICE
THE CONSTITUTION INVIOLATE . . .
NO SEDITION ACT.
We hear that others have been erected at Blooming Grove, Montgomery, Goshen, Fish-kill, &c.

The ensuing trials for libels will determine whether the press is to be the *palladium* and *centinel* of *liberty* or the mere vehicle of *madrigals, rhebus' [pictures]* and *lampoons* on the people . . .

[Adv.]   PARLIAMENT SHIP FOR BORDEAUX

THE naval vessel *ADRASTUS* . . . currently at BRIGHT's WHARF, between Sassafras and Vine streets, will depart for BORDEAUX [France] during the course of this month. Its construction is very solid . . . very appropriate for these crossings. Those who wish to profit from this favorable occasion will wish to act and engage passage at MESSRS. BOUSQUET Bros., No. 117 South First Street

Today, Moreau de St. Méry writes:

I engaged a passage on the Adrastes. Shortly afterwards, we learned that Mr. Adams, the President of the United States, has made a list of French people to be deported and that the list was headed by Volney . . . myself, etc., etc. I was sufficiently curious to question Mr. Adams through Mr. Langdon, [U.S.] senator from New Hampshire, to find out what I was charged with. He replied, "Nothing in particular, but he's too French." Now Mr. Adams had often come to my house, to my study and to my shop during his term as Vice President, and we had exchanged our books as gifts. But after he became President, I never saw him. [546]

Today, in the U.S. Senate, the Annals of Congress report:

The following Message was received from the PRESIDENT OF THE UNITED STATES:

Gentlemen of the Senate:
    Believing the letter received this morning from General Washington will give high satisfaction to the Senate, I transmit them a copy of it . . .
JOHN ADAMS
UNITED STATES, July 17, 1798

MOUNT VERNON, July 13, 1798
DEAR SIR: . . .[W]hen everything we hold dear and sacred is so seriously threatened, I have finally determined to accept the commission of Commander-in-Chief of the Armies of The United States . . .
Go: WASHINGTON . . . [547]

The following Message was received from the PRESIDENT OF THE UNITED STATES:

Gentlemen of the Senate:
    I nominate Alexander Hamilton, of New York, to be Inspector General of the Army, with the rank of Major General.
    Charles Cotesworth Pinckney, of South Carolina, to be a Major General . . .
    Jonathan Dayton, of New Jersey, to be a Brigadier General . . .

William Stevens Smith, of New York, to be adjutant General . . . [&c.]

JOHN ADAMS[548]

John Adams is nominating leading Federalists to command the new federal army. Alexander Hamilton, founder of the Federalist party, will be second in command (behind Washington). C. C. Pinckney is the Federalist whom Washington appointed and France rejected as James Monroe's successor as minister to France. Jonathan Dayton is the Federalist Speaker of the House, who expelled Benny Bache and me from the House floor. William Smith is John Adams' son-in-law.

Today, John Adams writes some citizens:

> *No light or trivial cause would have given you the opportunity of beholding your WASHINGTON again relinquishing the tranquil scene in delicious shades.—To complete the character of French philosophy and French policy at the end of the eighteenth century, it seemed to be necessary to combat this PATRIOT and HERO.*[549]

Tonight, in the *Porcupine's Gazette*:

> On *Monday* last, in consequence of an order from the PRESIDENT to the French Consul in New York to cease his functions, the arms of the *Grande Nation* were taken off from over his door.

Tonight, in the *Gazette of the United States*:

> The Secretary of War arrived in town yesterday morning from Mount Vernon.

THURSDAY, JULY 19, 1798

GENERAL ★ AURORA ★ ADVERTISER

Something like treason by the new bill.
Some time ago, there were people so wicked as to think America could not have a worse man for President than Gen. Washington; but we learn that they have since, from the most complete conviction, acknowledged the error of their opinion.

FOURTH OF JULY. SELECTION OF TOASTS . . .
Celebration in Montgomery (N.Y.) . . . *Benjamin Franklin Bache and the Republican Printers throughout the United States.* [M]ay their virtues be rewarded with the applause of their country and may they never bow to Baal or worship the Golden Calf.

Benny will neither bow nor run. Not so with New York *Time Piece* publisher James Smith. Tonight, in the *Gazette of the United States*:

Doctor Smith and Burk. The two editors of the Time Piece it seems have had a squabble . . . Last Friday morning, it seems Burk had written for one of the papers a most violent invective against the President, had got it set in type, and was proceeding to correct the proof sheet when Dr. Smith came into the office. Burk, being delighted with the production began to read it aloud to his coadjutor, but he had not more than finished the first paragraph before Smith interrupted and told him it *would not do*, it was going too far and would even work a forfeiture of their recognizance [guarantee to the court of their good behavior]. Burk flushed up in the face and told him his fears were childish, that as to the forfeiture of their recognizance, suppose it did, it was nothing to them, it would not be left for them to pay, that the piece was well written . . . Smith shook his head and said it was indeed going too far . . . in short that it should not appear in the paper . . . Burk . . . swore by G-d the piece should appear. Smith pulled off his spectacles and called Burk a dam'd rascal and an unprincipled alien . . . Burk gnashed his teeth and retorted the language with tenfold recrimination . . . On this Smith laid hold of a handful of types all covered with ink and threw them dab into Burk's face—Burk returned the compliment with the same ammunition . . . Burk in his zeal to defend himself had not once thought of his piece which in the end he found scattered all over the office and was irretrievably distributed; it became necessary instantly to repair the loss with other matter, and this accounts for the late hour at which the Time Piece was delivered last Friday morning.

The government's prosecution of James Smith has intimidated him. As Poor Richard observed,

Without justice, courage is weak.[550]

FRIDAY, JULY 20, 1798

GENERAL ★ AURORA ★ ADVERTISER

Extract of a letter from Norfolk . . . "Our noble president was burnt in effigy in Williamsburgh on the 4th of July by the students of William and Mary College and a troop of cavalry—He was exhibited in the act of receiving a *loyal* address and looking among a budget of ready-made answers for one in return."

A Federal fire company has expelled *Thomas Adams*, printer of the [only Republican paper in Boston, the *Independent] Chronicle* from their company: as no reason is assigned for it, we must suppose it was for some such reason as that for which the republicans of this city have been threatened with loss of their licenses—not subscribing to the good *royal doctrine* of *passive obedience* and *non-resistance*.

Today, the *Time Piece* of New York City announces its demise as a Republican newspaper:

> The Subscribers to the Time Piece are . . . to take notice that no libelous or inflammatory matter shall be inserted in [this] paper in [the] future . . . and that [I] will not be answerable for any debts contracted by Mr. [John Daly] Burk on account of the *Time Piece* from the date hereof.
>
> JAMES SMITH

SATURDAY, JULY 21, 1798

GENERAL ★ AURORA ★ ADVERTISER

There was a time, Citizens, when . . . we flattered ourselves that *the liberty of the press* was a right too dear to Americans to be resigned with tameness and too firmly secured to be violated with impunity. We will not say that time is past, but we will say that, under . . . an exaggerated and mischievous system of alarm and pretexts of order and submission to the Laws, we have seen a system maturing, openly hostile to the spirit of freedom, and measures carried *in the face of our Constitution;*—for what?—to screen from scrutiny the conduct of your own government . . . To the laws of our country we owe that profound submission which a Republican will never withhold. But to the *constitution* . . . we owe duties still more sacred, and these we will never violate . . .

Such are our sentiments with respect to the present unwarrantable system of legalized terror with which we are menaced. But this is not all; —personal violence is threatened and insolent suggestions held up to deter! . . . *[T]hey will come in vain* . . .

A number of boys a few evenings ago collected a band of HURDY *gur-dys, conch shells, pot lids* and *salt boxes* with a view to compliment an amiable young lady . . . but the musicians were prevailed upon to retire—to the great joy of the young lady and the neighborhood!

A few days ago, a French citizen, in passing Water street, was assaulted by four or five persons . . . From his hat they tore a [tri-colour] national cockade forcibly away . . . [T]his gentleman . . . served with distinction in our revolutionary war and was twice wounded. At the storming of an important redoubt [fortified emplacement] at Yorktown, he was the first who leapt into the entrenchment . . . Americans, be just . . . Reflect that those Frenchmen now among you have many claims on your humanity . . .

Federalist crowds pursue Republican leaders. Today, Vermont Republican Congressman Matthew Lyon encounters one crowd after another as he passes through New Jersey in his return to Vermont. The *Gazette of the United States* reports:

LYON, whose endeavors, like those of his associate and fellow-laborer [New York Republican Edward] Livingston, tended to excite mobs and riots for the overthrow of the government and constitution, has become himself the object of popular contempt. On his arrival at Trenton [New Jersey], an immense concourse of people attended him with their compliments, and the spirited sound of sundry rattling drums to the tune of the "Rogue's March" revived the grateful recollection of his *warlike* exploits at the *wooden sword* redoubt on Onion river. On resuming his seat on the stage, the admiring populace, with loud acclamations, still followed the redoubted knight, and the drums . . . fairly drummed him out of town. The hisses and hooting of the crowd were loud and universal. At Brunswick [New Jersey] the same honor awaited our renowned hero, this pink of chivalry, gentility, and knighthood.[551]

This evening, in the *Porcupine's Gazette,* Peter Porcupine suggests some Jeffersonian adultery:

It is said that JEFFERSON went to his friend Doctor Logan's farm and spent three days there soon after Dr. Logan's departure for France. *Quere:* What did he do there ? Was it to arrange the Doctor's *valuable manuscripts* ?

George Logan's wife, Deborah, explains the visit:

Soon after the departure of my husband, I received a visit from Thomas Jefferson who told me he had been greatly concerned for me . . . and advised me to evince my thorough consciousness of [my husband's] innocence and honour by showing myself in Philadelphia as one not afraid nor ashamed to meet the public eye. He said . . . [t]hat he was himself dogged and watched in the most extraordinary manner; and he apologized for the lateness of his visit (for we were at tea when he arrived) by saying that, in order to elude the curiosity of his spies, he had not taken the direct road, but had come by a circuitous route by the Falls of Schuylkill . . . He spoke of the temper of the times and of the late acts of the Legislature with a sort of despair, but said he thought even the shadows of our liberties must be gone if they attempted anything that would injure me . . .[552]

MONDAY, JULY 23, 1798

GENERAL ★ AURORA ★ ADVERTISER

"*Thou shalt not commit adultery,*" is one of the commandments of the Deity himself. Mr. Adams wishes us to believe that he is a true believer and very pious man . . . By their fruit ye shall know them, says the scripture: let us then test Mr. Adams' religion and morality by this rule. He has appointed Alexander Hamilton inspector general of the army; the same Hamilton who published a book to prove that he is AN ADUL-

TERER . . . Mr. Adams ought hereafter to be silent about *French* principles.

Tonight, in the *Gazette of the United States*:

> Bache has thought proper in several instances to make *Macpherson's Blues* the objects of his dull ridicule and [on Saturday] . . . affects to make merry with the serenade given by them in compliment to the young lady . . . Mr. B. must not consider the liberty of the press infringed or endangered if some of these boys resent a *personal insult* in a *personal way* and kick his breech.

We learn by the *Aurora* [on Saturday] that a Sansculotte Frenchman has recently had the audacity to walk the streets bearing the bloody emblem of French Fraternity. Some spirited citizen very meritoriously struck the *tri-color* from his *chapeau.*

TUESDAY, JULY 24, 1798

GENERAL ★ AURORA ★ ADVERTISER

> John Fenno has taken upon him to apply a joke . . . where Macpherson's blues had no concern whatever, to that corps. He then suggests that personal violence should follow. If such is a fit consequence, it ought to fall upon him . . .

Tonight, John Fenno in the *Gazette of the United States*:

> Bache's *pipes* on the subject of the serenade have been stopped, and *he knows how*—A poor sneak! he tells a falsehood in an ambiguous shape, and when called to account for it, evades the danger by another. But the best of the joke is that he would throw all the blame on Mr. Fenno's *malicious construction* . . .[553]

As Poor Richard observed,

> *He makes a Foe who makes a jest.*[554]

WEDNESDAY, JULY 25, 1798

GENERAL ★ AURORA ★ ADVERTISER

[T]he *United States* frigate, commodore Barry, and the *Delaware* sloop of war, capt. Decatur, went to sea on Friday last.

[New York.] We are informed that a number of people in and about Newburgh . . . assembled the other day to take down the liberty pole—This having excited the opposition of those who erected it, they assembled with arms . . .

Callender is gone. Jefferson is gone. Congress are gone. This morning, the Adamses secretly depart.[555] Benny and I remain. We face a rising tide of political violence and the season for yellow fever. Will we be strong enough? Poor Richard said,

> *The absent are never without fault,*
> *nor the present without excuse.*[556]

FRIDAY, JULY 27, 1798

GENERAL ★ AURORA ★ ADVERTISER

At a respectable meeting of the citizens of Kent and Queen Anne's counties [Maryland], on the banks of the river Chester on the 21st of July, after partaking of a fish-feast, the following [toast was] drank . . . By Peregrine Letherbery. *Benjamin Franklin Bache who remains firm at his post and supports with magnanimity the rights of his countrymen.*

Today, as President and Mrs. Adams pass through Newark, New Jersey, on their journey home, a local resident violates the Sedition Act. From reports:

[T]he approach of the President of the United States was announced— Great preparations were made for his reception by the true Federalists . . . The honorable exclusive friends of their country, with [black] cockades in their hats, paraded . . . The "very respectable part of the young men," (who had informed the President that they were surrounded by enemies of the government who were endeavoring to blast the buds of their patriotism) . . . procured a piece of cannon of the Company of Artillery, distinguished themselves in their new livery consisting of a blue jacket, not forgetting the emblems of all emblems, the adorable [Black] Cockade . . . and displayed flags from three conspicuous places in town.

[A]bout 11 o'clock A.M. the President's carriage was seen at the lower end of the town. The discharge of cannon commenced, a general peal from the bells joined . . . when to the astonishment and mortification of the self-constituted federalists, the President pushed his horses into full speed, kept the curtains of his carriages down, and passed the assembled friends to good order in a second, without even deigning to drop a nod of approbation . . .[557]

Luther Baldwin happening to be coming toward John Burner's dram [of liquor] shop, a person that was there says to Luther, "there goes the President and they are firing at his a--." Luther, a little merry, replies that he did not care if they fired through his a--. Then exclaims the dram seller, "that is sedition"—a considerable collection gathered—and the pretended federalists, being much disappointed that the president had not stopped that they might have the honor of kissing his hand, bent their malice on poor Luther, and the cry was that he must be punished . . .[558]

Luther Baldwin will be punished. The U.S. Federal Circuit Court of New Jersey will find Luther Baldwin guilty, under the new federal Sedition Act, of *"seditious words tending to defame the President and Government of the United States"* and order him to pay a fine of $400; $250 for speaking those words and $150 for costs and expenses.[559]

This evening, after President Adams arrives in New York City, a more violent incident occurs. *Porcupine* reports:

[A]bout half past ten in the evening, 5 young men were walking on the battery. Animated by the presence of our illustrious President who had . . . entered the city under the display of flags and the thunder of cannon, amidst the glitter of swords, a forest of bristling bayonets, and the shouts and acclamations of assembled thousands—they were singing, as is very common throughout the town, the Federal song, "Hail Columbia." A much larger number of boatmen and low fellows from the wharves and docks immediately collected, and, instigated by the deluding demon of French jacobinism . . . approached our young men, singing in opposition . . . the infamous French song "Ça Ira." . . . Both parties quickly met, and it was not long before the *alien* crew . . . began the dastardly attack and first insulted, and then beat and bruised them in a most shameful manner . . . Meantime, several watchmen and a number of people assembled, and the ruffians desisted from their purpose.[560]

Tonight, in the *Gazette of the United States*:

A wag, practicing on Benny's gullibility and self-love, has sent him a list of toasts, said to have been drank at a democratic dinner in Maryland which the zealous editor of the *Aurora* has published in this paper of this morning without adverting to the ridiculous names of the persons by whom they are said to have been given—Among others . . . Benjamin Franklin Bache [is toasted] by *Peregrine Letherbelly. Risum teneatis amici? [May you bear the laughter of your friends?]*

Tonight, in the *Porcupine's Gazette*:

General WASHINGTON Commands !!
HARK ! the DRUM beats to arms !! . . .
Nothing need be advanced to induce the young men . . . to re-enter the service when they learn they will be commanded by the great, illustrious, magnanimous General WASHINGTON . . . Your country, my boys, is threatened with invasion! Your houses and farms with fire, plunder and pillage! and your wives and daughters with ravishment and assassination by horrid outlandish sans-culotte Frenchmen !!! . . . To arms then, my dear brave boys! . . .   *JAMES HAMILTON, Recruiting . . .*

GENERAL ★ AURORA ★ ADVERTISER

Some of the [black] cockade gentry, we understand, have amused themselves by midnight howlings round the doors of the republicans. Some imitated with great *nicety* the mewing of cats, others the *barking* of dogs. The *braying* was so close a copy from nature that it was at one time believed that they had actually enlisted some of the *long eared aristocrats* into their serenade.

Tonight, in the *Gazette of the United States*:

Jeff[erson] is gone away. He is unquestionably the very soul of the party. His connexion with Bache, Logan, and others . . . leaves no doubt . . . The day after the last dispatches were communicated to Congress, Bache . . . &c, &c . . . were closeted with Jeff[erso]n.

It is no wonder that Bache snarls at our young serenading "cockade gentry" who, by a sympathy natural to musical minds, struck on the Rogue's March at passing the door of a Jacobin.

GENERAL ★ AURORA ★ ADVERTISER

The next night the aristocrats insult their betters by *infamous* serenades, we advise them to keep at a *respectable distance* and to hold themselves in readiness to *run* at the *first alarm*.

John Fenno has profited so little by the tuition of his *schoolmaster* to forget even his *spelling;* in his Gazette of Friday, he mistook the name of a respectable man, Mr. *Letherbery,* for a *Leatherbelly;* no wonder that a *Leatherhead* should take a Letherbery for a leatherbelly!

War . . . Today, Secretary of the Navy Benjamin Stoddert asks John Adams to approve a naval expedition against France in the West Indies:

At this season of the Year, and during the Months of August & September & part of October, the British armed-Ships are less alert in the West Indies . . . Our own force, on our own Coast . . . is well known to the French—And . . . it is not to be apprehended that our Coasts will be much molested by their Cruisers . . . unless, indeed, they could send a Force from Europe which is far from being probable.—The French islands, having no authorized intercourse with the United States, must depend in a great degree upon Captures for supplies of Bread & Salt meat . . .

Under such circumstances, and impressed . . . that our Force should be employed, while the French have but little force, in destroy-

ing what they have and in producing a scarcity of Provisions and the consequent discontent flowing from such a source in their islands, I have the honor, Sir, to submit . . . to send a cruise among the islands . . .[561]

President Adams will approve this expedition against the very French islands America had promised to defend.[562]

WEDNESDAY, AUGUST 1, 1798

GENERAL ★ AURORA ★ ADVERTISER

Letters were received in town from New York yesterday, about two o'clock, containing . . . details of a vast, universal, and decisive revolt of the Irish People against the English Government. The rising is stated to have been on the same day and form throughout the whole Island; that a fierce action had been fought between a numerous body of the English & Hessian [German mercenary] troops and the revolters, in which great obstinacy was manifested on both sides and the slaughter dreadful.

A man must sing "Hail Columbia" and wear a black cockade or he is called by [the governmental party] a disorganizer, a Jacobin, a pensioned tool of the French . . . It would seem really the view of some of the loudest vociferators for union to excite a civil war in our country; they cannot expect that, by their denunciations, their insults & their abuse, they can bully the republicans into silence or an acquiescence in their sentiments or measures.

Tonight, in the *Porcupine's Gazette*:

Last evening marched into town the guard from Macpherson's Blues who escorted the French prisoners [from the French privateer *CROYABLE*] to Lancaster . . .

THE proposed law for the punishment of libels will have an excellent effect, and I hope its first operation will be upon the *infamous Bache and his associates* who have been long in the habit of abusing the worthiest characters in the country . . . [I]f we are to suffer war, they may in the end retire . . . to the territory of the power whose interests they traitorously prefer to those of the United States. A JERSEYMAN

THURSDAY, AUGUST 2, 1798

GENERAL ★ AURORA ★ ADVERTISER

We may judge of *federal* ideas of respect . . . by their behavior towards [Republican Congressman Matthew Lyon] . . . Were a posse of people to meet President Adams on the public highway and insult him for his

203

public opinions and in a manner that would disgrace *even an English mob*, we should never hear the end of it . . .

On Friday evening last, a number of young friends of order assembled [in New York City] . . . It was conjectured . . . they intended offering an insult to [New York Republican Congressman] Edward Livingston . . . [A] *fracas* ensued . . .

Fenno attempts to make it believed that, in the affray in New York, the Republicans were the aggressors. This does not appear . . . We do not remember that a citizen was ever attacked from behind and in a situation to endanger his life without provocation, with premeditation, without warning, and merely on account of his politics except the editor of this paper, and this assault was surely not committed by a Republican. What house belonging to a tory has been attacked by stones and clubs ? We all know that that of the Editor of this paper was. Have any of the tory members of Congress been insulted by playing the Rogue's march before their doors? This feat was also reserved for the friends of order . . .

Today, George Washington observes:

[T]he French . . . have been deceived in their calculations on the division of the People, and the powerful support they expected from their [Republican] party is reduced to uncertainty; though it is somewhat equivocal still whether that party who have been the curse of this country and the source of the expenses we have to encounter may not be able to continue their delusion.[563]

Tonight, near Leesburg, Virginia, Jimmy Callender is arrested. He records:

I was returning from Leesburg . . . when about three miles from that village, I was overtaken by a man at full gallop. He enquired my name and said that he had orders to apprehend me. Leesburg is a little mole-hill of aristocracy and the junto had declared that if I came there they would find some means or other of using me ill. I returned with the courier. It was by this time dark . . .[564]

FRIDAY, AUGUST 3, 1798

GENERAL ★ AURORA ★ ADVERTISER

From the late lawless proceedings of the young men who wear the [black] American cockade, a doubt can no longer exist that it is the intention of the federalists to introduce into this country the system of [terror] . . . Anonymous letters—midnight insults and riots—and the sanguinary and abominable publications which daily issue from the press of Porcupine and other ministerial prints evince their diabolical design.

[T]he republicans should not lose a moment in concerting a plan for their mutual defense . . .

We understand the chief magistrate of this city has given such reproof to the noisy brawlers who nightly infest our streets that our citizens have some prospect of reposing henceforth in quiet . . . The wearing of a [black] cockade is not sufficient to justify continual insolence, impertinence, and outrage.

Today, Moreau de St. Méry gets a passport to return to France.[565]

Today, Jimmy Callender goes to court in Leesburg, Virginia. He reports,

> *I went to Leesburg before breakfast to confront this awful tribunal . . . I entered the hall of audience with a crowd at my heels . . . I answered all their questions with a ready indifference and asked in my turn for the . . . warrant against me . . . The warrant was made out in consequence of a complaint from Jonas Pott, overseer of the poor, and undoubtedly a worthy yoke mate to the rest of the gang. He represented that I was a vagrant . . . They told me I must either give some security for not becoming cumbersome or go to jail . . . They asked me what I meant to do? I told them that, as they would not let me send for bail, I could do nothing . . .*
> *An acquaintance of mine went to town . . . but not to give bail. He enquired how the court came to maltreat any person living under the protection of General [and Republican U.S. Senator from Virginia Stevens T.] Mason . . . [T]here the matter stuck [and I was freed] . . .*[566]

Tonight, in the *Gazette of the United States*:

MR. FENNO . . . The debate in the Senate upon annulling the Treaties with France was published by Bache.—The speeches of the Jacobinic members were dressed in their best robes while those of the Federalists were grossly misrepresented . . . [T]wenty and thirty of [the *Aurora*] . . . came in one mail by S. T. Mason to different characters here [in Virginia]. Mr. Mason, I must not withhold . . . [has] taken to his bosom . . . the notorious CALLENDER who is now with him at his house.   N.

SATURDAY, AUGUST 4, 1798

GENERAL ★ AURORA ★ ADVERTISER

It must prove consolatory to poor Callender, in his retirement, to learn that persons meriting the contempt of all mankind for their baseness and servility—*continue to hate and remember the severe and penetrating lash of his talents.*

Today, Maryland Republican Congressman Samuel Smith sends last Saturday's *Gazette of the United States*—with its report of Jefferson's meetings with Benny Bache —to Thomas Jefferson.[567]

Tonight, in the *Porcupine's Gazette*:

SEDITIOUS VIRGINIANS

Fredericksburgh [Virginia], July 21. Serious Information. It is said that the legislative body of this state will be called together immediately . . . for the purpose of taking into consideration the sundry acts of the second session of the fifth Congress . . . [T]hey will readily declare the acts alluded to unconstitutional and oppressive, which, [it] is to be feared, will be the cause of Virginia, the Southern and Western States . . . *(How pretty these indolent, factious, despicable wretches will look if the French should, one of these days, set the negroes to cut their throats! . . .)*

CARLISLE [Pennsylvania, July 4] . . . [T]he following toasts were drunk . . . 8. *Peter Porcupine;* may his quills gain keenness and strength by their exercise. 9. Confusion or conversion to all the whelps of the spitting *Lyon.* 10. May the harbours of America be ever shut against *United Irishmen* and other traitors. 11. May the *American* Eagle strangle the *French* cock . . . *(I would not have inserted a list of toasts containing one in favour of myself, had not the circumstance been misrepresented by that abominable miscreant BACHE. In his dirty poverty-struck Aurora of the other day, he made his stupid readers believe that "ADAMS, WASHINGTON, and PORCUPINE were the only persons toasted" on this occasion . . .)*

SUNDAY, AUGUST 5, 1798

Today, George Washington writes:

It is too difficult, I conceive, to pronounce with certainty on the strength of the French Party in the United States . . . for now, the Gazettes of the Bachites come forward with more boldness than ever . . . [I]t is certain that the Agents and Partizans of France leave nothing unessayed to bring all the Acts and Actors of Government into disrepute; to promote divisions among us; and to enfeeble all of opposition to the views of the Directory of that Country on the Rights, freedom and independence of the U. States.[568]

CHAPTER FIVE

THE PESTILENCE

*Benjamin [Bache] . . . in his Aurora . . . became of course one of the
most malicious Libellers of me. But the Yellow Fever arrested him in
his detestable Career . . .*

JOHN ADAMS,
PRESIDENT OF THE UNITED STATES, 1797–1801[569]

MONDAY, AUGUST 6, 1798

GENERAL   ★ AURORA ★   ADVERTISER

It is evident that as soon as [New York Republican Congressman] Mr.
[Edward] Livingston returned to that city from his duties in congress,
the tories . . . conceived, [that] . . . in New York, Livingston should be
the object of their envenomed malice. Night after night they paraded
before his doors, playing insulting tunes . . . merely as a prelude . . . Mr.
Livingston's house was to be pulled down and perhaps he sacrificed in
the disorder. The republicans fortunately took the alarm in time . . .

These outrages of the tories have had an admirable effect . . . The republicans, convinced of the lengths to which the tories would go, are
forming an armed association—convinced that there is at least as much
danger from domestic as from foreign foes. This prudent and proper step
of the republicans has struck the tories with dismay; they know that if
the arm of republicanism is once nerved to resistance, all their plans for
the overthrow of the constitution, for affiliating our government to that
of Britain, and for dragging us into a connection with that country must
vanish.

Today, Philadelphia's College of Physicians meets to discuss the twenty-six
reported cases of the malignant yellow fever. After conferring, they unanimously adopt a resolution

*"That the College inform the Board of Health that a malignant contageous
fever has made its appearance in Water-street between Walnut and
Spruce-streets . . ."*[570]

Tonight, in the *Porcupine's Gazette,* William Cobbett admits:

> I am not . . . an advocate for playing *God save the King* or for hoisting the *British flag* in the streets of America . . . All I wish to see is a sincere and efficient alliance between the two countries for their mutual interest and for their security against the power and intrigues of the infernal [French] republic.

Tonight, in the *Gazette of the United States*:

> MR. FENNO, HAVING seen in the *Aurora* of the 27th of July a set of Toasts that were drank at a fish-feast near Chester-Town . . . I have thought it proper to [state] . . . [t]here is . . . a violent opposition to the measures of the federal government . . . kept up by that *worthy patriot, enlightened statesman* and *toaster* of *Bache,*— Letherbury. Mr. L. was a lawyer of some note at the time the federal constitution was adopted and was strongly opposed to it—he was opposed to President Washington's proclamation of neutrality and has been ever since a reviler of him and the present President . . .   A CITIZEN OF KENT

One Bache, printer of the *Aurora*, not long since held forth in vehement terms against *adultery*. Is this the same villain . . . who is also the grandson of old *Ben Franklin* ?

TUESDAY, AUGUST 7, 1798

GENERAL   ★ AURORA ★   ADVERTISER

The memory of Dr. Franklin must be odious to the adherents of England, as he was hated and envied by them when living. A great man of the present days [Mr. Adams] peevishly complained a few years ago in Europe, "we are no more than satellites revolving round the old Doctor."

On Friday night departed this city the soul of the *Federal* party by name JOSEPH THOMAS . . . We understand that the recent[ly] discovered scheme of *swindling* and *forgery* has but barely budded . . . —For these few days past, the town has rung with nothing but JOSEPH THOMAS . . . [H]is bawling at election meetings, at which he was the leading man among the Federalists, his exertions at elections, his impudence at the bar, his vociferations against the democrats,——all together would never have rendered him as *famous* as he has become by his *swindling* and *forgeries* . . . Not deeming the numerous evidences of his zeal in the cause of Toryism; by spouting in favor of the administration on all occasions; by intrigue overturning the election of the people, and by heading an armed mob to intimidate republicans . . . a sufficient recommendation with the banks, he made it a practice, it is now discovered, . . . to deposit for collection forged notes to a large amount . . . Forged checks, in great numbers he had deposited with different persons . . .

—The sudden departure of the great leader of the faction has put that mercenary scoundrel Fenno into a terrible humour. It is not uncharitable to suppose that Thomas, who could make thousands by the dash of the pen, must have spared his friend Fenno a few hundred; who then can wonder that he should be out of humour to have this source dried up . . .

Joseph Thomas' flight from Philadelphia is a significant moment for Benny Bache. Thomas is the leader of Philadelphia's Federalists, a friend of two cabinet secretaries and of the President himself.[571] In April, Thomas led the meetings at Dunwoody's and Cameron's which prepared addresses to the President and enlisted Philadelphia's "young men" into Federalist militias.[572] On May 7th, brandishing a naked sword above his head, Thomas led the Federalist gang that attempted to burn Benny's house.[573]

Tonight, John Fenno's twenty-year-old son, Jack Ward Fenno (Irishman Mat Carey calls him *"a rash, thoughtless, and impudent young man"*),[574] bursts into the *Aurora*'s offices, ready for violence. "Newgate" Lloyd and I are present. Benny Bache:

> [John Fenno's] Son chose to take notice [of the article in the Aurora] and called on the Editor to require the author. He was told to send his father who was certainly able to take his own part and who could not expect that we should allow of a proxy in settling any difference between us. He then handed a piece for publication which he was told could not then be perused, as we were particularly busy preparing our packages for the Post, the time of closing being within a few minutes arrived. Upon this, he declared that if it was not published, he would treat the Editor as a scoundrel . . .[575]

Another eyewitness:

> When the lad came into the room, Mr. Bache was sitting; the young man was in extreme perturbation and spoke so inarticulately as to be perfectly unintelligible. He talked of his father being stiled a mercenary scoundrel . . . and of Joseph Thomas, and twirld in his trembling fingers a piece of paper which seems to have been what he called an apology. During the whole time of this trifling, Mr. Bache continued writing and urged in easy and temperate language that he was too busy to be troubled, that if he would either call again or send his father, he would talk to him but at that time had not leisure and begged that the lad would go about his business. He continued to write as before.[576]

Jack Ward Fenno:

> In consequence of a paragraph in the Aurora wherein my father was spoken of in villainous terms during his absence from the city, I waited on Mr. Bache to demand the author. He refused to give him up

when, dropping the point, I handed him a paper containing a recanta-
tion which I was willing to have substituted for personal satisfaction.
His behavior was that of a mean and contemptible coward—he stood
trembling and quaking before the "lad" of the person he had abused
but using at the same time as much insolence of deportment as his
fear would allow him, which appeared almost to deprive him of his
speech. I told him, if he neglected to recant the obnoxious terms,—that
I should treat him as a scoundrel—and that he was a lying, cowardly
rascal. Upon this he rose from his seat and made toward me—Lloyd of
Newgate and Duane (the calumniator of Washington, under the signa-
ture of Jasper Dwight) who appeared to be in his employ also bristled
up at the same time. Bache doubled his fist and made some show of
striking a blow at me but evidently appeared to want spirit to do it.
My friend, by this time, seized me by the arm and, having effectuated
the purpose for which I went, we withdrew.[577]

Joseph Thomas has brought matters between Benny and the Fennos to a head.
Whoever Thomas was, he certainly merits Poor Richard's admonition,

> *There is much difference between imitating a good man,*
> *and counterfeiting him.*[578]

Poor Richard also warned,

> *Men & Melons are hard to know.*[579]

Tonight, news is everywhere that the malignant yellow fever is in Philadelphia.
Tonight, in the *Porcupine's Gazette:*

THE YELLOW FEVER

Is in this city. It is now come out that it made its appearance about a
week ago. Several persons are dead with it, and according to all the accounts I have heard, it spreads with greater rapidity than it did last year.
A number of stories, with regard to its origin, are, as usual, on foot; but,
I believe, the best way would be to lay aside all vain disputes on this
subject and prepare, as quick as possible, to make provision for removing
those who have not the means of removing themselves to situations more
healthy.

Tonight, in the *Gazette of the United States:*

The rapid dissemination of reports respecting the appearance of that
mortal enemy of our city, the Yellow Fever, have within these few days,
excited the most alarming apprehensions.

The *Republicans* of New York, it seems, are arming and embodying a
military force against the *Tories,* in the terms of Mr. Bache: and this prospect of inter[ne]cine commotion, broil and bloodshed, he calls *"admirable," "prudent"* and *"proper"* . . .

Bache must be conscious of meriting what he unquestionably holds: the hatred of all mankind . . . Bache needs only to behold his own character in its naked colours to detest himself.

> *For he's a monster of such horrid mien,*
> *As to be hated, needs but to be seen.*

WEDNESDAY, AUGUST 8, 1798

GENERAL   ★ AURORA ★   ADVERTISER

The man in *English pay* who scribbles under the wing of John Fenno has nothing to lose by the late swindling but his own *sweet temper!*— Fenno's young sprig plucked up courage enough to go as far as the office of the *Aurora* yesterday evening in order to deny his *pappy* was the friend of *Jozey Thomas*—the lad was accompanied by a gentleman who acknowledged that he had reason to be ashamed of the youth's behavior.— Fenno's young lady in breeches came to require the name of the writer who called his papa a *mercenary scoundrel* and to demand *satisfaction* for his being stiled Jozey Thomas's friend—but when the person he was offended with rose from his seat, behold the "poor little foolish, fluttering thing"—literally ran away with its mouth full of froth and its knees trembling

This afternoon, as Benny walks along Philadelphia's Fourth-street with John Beckley (a good friend and former clerk of the U.S. House of Representatives), Jack Ward Fenno assaults Benny Bache.[580] Benny:

> [W]hile walking along Fourth street with a friend, I observed him coming towards me, but from his pusillanimous behavior the preceding day, had no expectation of an attack from him. As he approached, I observed indeed that he gave [me] much of the pavement, as desirous of avoiding me. But when he came abreast, he suddenly rushed on, closed in, and made a stroke which scratched a bit of skin off my nose. My cane for a moment became of little use, but soon, grasping it in the middle, made the side of his head or face feel the point of the serril and the top of his skull, its weight, having previously taken the impression of his teeth upon the knuckles of my left hand. I completely pinned him in the scuffle against the wall, whilst inflicting the merited chastisement. A crowd soon assembled and separated us. He made a great show of renewing the attack by the time 30 or 40 people were assembled. I stood ready to defend myself should he renew the assault for which he showed no inclination when set at liberty by the bystanders. Missing my comb, I deliberately passed by him in search of it, when he drew back and gave me the whole pavement.[581]

Jack Fenno:

> I am indebted to my younger brother who, observing Bache walking in Fourth street, with his bludgeon, accompanied by John Beckley, ran to communicate the intelligence. Upon which I immediately proceeded towards him and, after advancing full in his view for about one third of the square, came up with him. He drew back and brandished the CLUB—I advanced and, seizing him by the collar, struck him at the same instant in the face and repeated my blows as fast as possible. He repeatedly attempted to put his stick in my face; but having closed in with him, his arms were so cramped that his attempts proved very feeble. The scuffle issued in my driving him against the wall when I should have soon wrested the club from his hand—had not his companion very improperly seized my left hand and, disengaging it from round his body, held it fast. Bache instantly drew off. My attempts to get at him again were rendered ineffectual by those around; one of whom seized me round the body and held me fast, while Bache sneaked home, his nose barked and his sconce covered with blood,—conspicuous marks of Jacobin valour. I had no weapon but my fist and received no hurt in the transaction.[582]

As Poor Richard said,

> There's small Revenge in Words,
> but Words may be greatly revenged.[583]

Today, Philadelphia's City Hospital is open for fever victims. Four sick people are admitted. Today, Philadelphia's Academy of Medicine recommends to the Philadelphia Board of Health *"the appointment of a sufficient number of physicians to take care of such of the poor as may be affected with the fever . . ."*[584]

Tonight, in the *Gazette of the United States*, John Ward Fenno:

> The assertion of Bache, respecting my friend's declaring himself "ashamed of my conduct" is a falsehood, as he is ready to testify, as well as the correctness of the rest of what is here stated.

THURSDAY, AUGUST 9, 1798

GENERAL   ★ AURORA ★   ADVERTISER

Young Fenno in the way of preferment.
The lad yesterday afternoon made an attack in the street on the Editor of the *Aurora* with *tooth* and *nail*. He deserves a reward for the exploit better than his worthy predecessor Humphreys, as he was not a little mauled in the combat. He scratched the nose of his antagonist, and his teeth took off the skin of the editor's knuckles; for which he got in return a sound rap or two across the head and face.—Young Fenno mustered up courage enough last evening to attack unawares the editor of the

Aurora in the street and strike him—the poor boy carried back *some occupation for a plaister* [cast maker]—The son of *honest John* has qualified himself for a federal appointment by an assault on the editor of the *Aurora* : possibly he may be thought a fit follower of *Humphreys*.—

The little miss who misconducts the Presidential gazette was under the necessity of changing her apparel immediately after her *precipitate retreat* from the *Aurora* office—this accounts for the strong sensation which affected the olfactories of those who were present at the *fright*!—

Today, Philadelphia's newly opened City Hospital admits nine sick people.[585]

Tonight, in the *Porcupine's Gazette*:

[T]he "young lady in breeches," as Bache affected to call him [Jack Fenno], gave the hireling sufficient proof of *her* masculine powers, if black eyes, bloody nose, and a battered head may be considered as sufficient . . . Bache was . . . *armed with an enormous bludgeon.* Mr. Fenno was alone and unarmed; he nevertheless proved by many trials against the wall that Bache's skull was even more penetrable than could have been supposed. It was remarked by the by-standers that his countenance, naturally diabolical, exhibited at the moment Fenno gripped him a shocking picture of agony and dismay . . .

The Yellow Fever appears to be spreading very rapidly;—people are moving out of the city in every direction, and if the hot weather continues another week, there is no doubt that two thirds of the inhabitants will leave their homes.

Tonight, in the *Gazette of the United States*:

IT was observed by an old Almanack-maker who called himself *Poor Richard* that "co-existent with the Liberty of the Press is the Liberty of the Club" . . . Without assenting to this doctrine of Poor Richard, it might justly be expected that citizen Bache, who holds the old fellow to be infallible, should abide by him in his creed. Strange it may seem that he loudly complains of the practical operation of it.— Bache is advised to lay aside that great Herculean club he has heretofore carried; its weight must be fatiguing to the poor wretch; and unless he can make it more serviceable to him than it was yesterday afternoon, it certainly must be considered as a useless encumbrance.— Bache speaks of the "sound raps he gave young Fenno across the head and face." Will he "muster up courage enough" to come and take a peep at those "occupations for a plaister"?

MR. FENNO, On the second of August, a little dirty toper with shaved head and greasy jacket, nankeen pantaloons and woolen stockings, was arrested at a whiskey distillery near Leesburgh, Virginia under the vagrant act . . . To place [Republican U.S. Senator from Virginia] Mr. Mason's character in a true point of light, it must be observed that this Callender

. . . has found an asylum in his house [and] is the notorious Scotch fugitive, the calumniator of Washington, Adams, law, order, government, God . . . *A VIRGINIAN*

FRIDAY, AUGUST 10, 1798

GENERAL ★ AURORA ★ ADVERTISER

John Fenno informs [his readers] that J. T. Callender has found safe refuge in Virginia—as John's friends appear to use uncommon vigilance concerning Callender, perhaps he can also tell the name of the pious *tory* that threatened to *assassinate him* !

We shall trouble our readers a moment with a statement of the assault committed on the editor on Wednesday evening and of the causes which led to it.

Those who read the *Gazette of the United States* must have witnessed for a long time back a studied and uninterrupted course of calumny against the editor of the *Aurora*, consisting of unfounded assertions and the vilest billingsgate. In all this we considered Fenno as a faithful tool in his avocation—he labored in one of the branches of the system, which has been pursued in every shape, to put down the *Aurora* by persecution.

One of the points most labored by this faithful tool of the most profligate faction has been to represent the editor of the *Aurora* as in the pay of France. Till lately all that could be produced under this head was assertion and abuse, when Kidder was pushed forward to certify something [the Talleyrand letter] on which a specific charge could plausibly rest . . .

In retaliation for the above mentioned ground of detraction we accused him of being sold to the British and stated on the best authority his having received as a benefaction . . . the sum of $500 . . . Fenno has never ventured to even deny publicly having received this donation; he has observed the most profound silence on the subject, probably lest it should provoke to a production of the proofs. He shall yet hear from us on this subject before long.

Today is very hot, *"the mercury at 93 and upward."*[586] Eleven sick people are admitted to City Hospital. One report:

> *The deaths and new cases daily became more numerous; the alarm increased, and [as of today] the flight of the inhabitants [is] now general.*[587]

Today, the New York *Time Piece* announces the end of a partnership:

NOTICE

The Subscribers to the *Time Piece* are requested to pay Mr. [John Daly] Burk his accounts up to the 13th of June. Any debts since that period belong to the firm and are requested to remain until the books are settled between the proprietors, as a division must take place as soon as arrangements can be made between the parties.[588]   [WILLIAM SMITH]

MONDAY, AUGUST 13, 1798

GENERAL   ★ AURORA ★   ADVERTISER

FRIEND BACHE [a Quaker writes], I have long heard that thou art a bad man . . . I frequently suggested my opinions to Joseph Thomas . . . [I]n conversation one day, he declared that all democrats were rogues and thieves and that they ought all to be exterminated . . . [M]any good Federalists [he said] were of the same mind . . . Shocked at such barbarous declarations, I determined no longer to be a federalist . . . Now friend Bache, I cannot help believing that Providence . . . made the felon expose himself to prevent the horrid scene of citizens murdering each other . . .   I am now thy friend. OBADIAH

In the five days since Philadelphia's City Hospital has been open to receive yellow fever patients, thirty-one have been admitted; ten of the thirty-one have died, and not one of the thirty-one has been cured.[589]

Today, Federalists attempt once again to imprison Jimmy Callender. Two magistrates (Patrick Cavan and Joseph Smith) from Loudoun County, Virginia, attest:

> *[we were] called on by one of the constables of said county to examine a person by him apprehended, on suspicion of having eloped from the wheel-barrow, on the Baltimore roads, who on his examination, denied being a runaway—said his name was James T. Callender, lately from Philadelphia, printer of a paper published in that city; that he came from thence into this state (Virginia) at the particular request of general Mason at whose house he then resided; that his papers were at general Mason's—and that he (gen. Mason) would give any satisfaction that might be required respecting his character . . .*
>
> *Time being allowed Callender to procure his papers, at 5 o'clock (the time appointed for him to appear before the magistrates), Gen. S. T. Mason appeared in his behalf: produced a certificate of naturalization and said he was a man of good character.*[590]

Today, the President of the United States writes:

> *I believe, however, that the distinction of aristocrat and democrat, however odious and pernicious it may be rendered by political artifice as particular conjectures, will never be done away with . . . The distinction is grounded on unalterable nature, and human wisdom can*

do no more than reconcile the parties by equitable establishments and equal laws, securing as far as possible to every one his own.[591]

TUESDAY, AUGUST 14, 1798

GENERAL ★ AURORA ★ ADVERTISER

It is to be regretted that in this liberal country the accursed spirit of religious hatred should be secretly nourished against any sect but . . . [a] man of known intimacy with the recent motives and measures of the Administration has not scrupled to declare that the Alien bill was intended to operate against the unfortunate Irish Catholics who have been flying from oppression to the U.S. . . .

Tonight, in the *Gazette of the United States*:

A solicitude on the part of the people to preserve their civil privileges from the deathly embraces of French fraternity is strongly reprobated in the *Aurora* . . . and because the religious principles of the intrepid founders of our independence are professed to be precious to their posterity . . . the philosophical fanatics mean to raise a cry of religious hatred and persecution.

THURSDAY, AUGUST 16, 1798

GENERAL ★ AURORA ★ ADVERTISER

The news from Ireland and the local inquietude about the yellow fever so much arrest the public attention that the *great staunch Federal defaulter* is now scarcely talked of except among his particular friends, the tories . . .

Tonight, in the *Gazette of the United States*:

The present *Doers* of the *Aurora* are *["Newgate"] Lloyd* and *[William] Duane; the other member of the trio, Bache,* is or was absent since Saturday last.— It is an undoubted truth that some of the Jacobin papers are under the direction of as GREAT LIARS as ever escaped the hands of Justice in England, Ireland, or Scotland— . . . Since the passage of the Sedition Law, the scum, filth and foam of the *Aurora* Cauldron has flowed more than ever.

The two editors of the Gazettes printed in Portsmouth, (N.H.) have published their determination to exclude from their papers all incendiary, factious and anti-governmental speculations—Several others have done the same.

Gagging, though it be really an act of violence in itself, is more to be dreaded as being a prelude to greater and more atrocious villainy—after the victim is gagged appears the *stiletto* and *bow-string*.

Today, Secretary of State Timothy Pickering informs John Adams that he is ready to enforce the Alien Act.[592]

Today, from Loundon County, Virginia, Jimmy Callender writes,

The sedition bill will never extend its claws over this state. It is regarded not merely as a breach of the constitution but also of the special terms on which Virginia professed her acceptance of it. The legislature is expected to take up this business as soon as it meets.[593]

Those who can leave Philadelphia are doing so. Municipal employees have abandoned their posts. Today, by government report,

some of the prisoners in the east wing [of the Walnut-street prison] attempted to escape. Perhaps they were instigated from a consideration of the unguarded state of the city—the absence of the jailor—and the wish to escape from the fever. They seized upon the key of their apartment— forced their way out, knocked down Mr. Evans, a constable, then one of the assistant-keepers, and called to the convicts in the yard to come to their assistance. Mr. [Robert] Wharton, who was in a different part of the jail, on hearing the alarm, went immediately to the assistance of the keepers. Miller, the ring-leader, had an axe lifted to dispatch Mr. Evans, which Mr. R Wharton and Mr. Gass, an assistant-keeper, observing, prevented by well directed balls from their muskets which broke the bone of his right arm and entered his body—Mr. Wharton and Mr. Gass fired at the same time: the ball from the latter, it was generally supposed, proved fatal. Another of the assailants of the name of Vaughan struck Mr. Evans with a bar of iron. He then retreated to his apartment. Evans pursued him and lodged a ball in his lungs. He survived it about twenty-four hours.[594]

The *panders* of corruption and monarchy are railing against the Irish for accepting aid from the French . . .

This morning, Frenchman Moreau de St. Méry leaves Philadelphia for France. From his diary:

I tried to sell everything that could be turned into money of which I was very short, since my business was no longer going on. My passage aboard the cartel ship Adriastes was gratis, but the expense of moving the quarters for the four of us . . . from the lower deck to berths opening into the Great Cabin was seventy-two dollars a head . . . We also had to buy provisions for the entire crossing . . .

Early in the morning I said a number of good-byes; and at 9 o'clock my wife, my daughter and I boarded the packet schooner La Mouche for Newcastle, where the Adrastes had already gone . . . [M]y son had boarded her the night before . . .[595]

Would-be citizens flee John Adams. The rest flee the yellow fever. Unable to collect taxes from its departed population, today the city council of Philadelphia authorizes the mayor to borrow ten thousand dollars for *"lighting, cleaning and watching the city."*[596]

Tonight, in the *Gazette of the United States*:

The people of the United States are hourly contradicting the vile and abominable slanders on the government and its administration which are published in the *Aurora* and its miserable imitators. However—

They will lie on, till justice stops their breath.
For traitors, ne'er were conquered but by death.

TUESDAY, AUGUST 21, 1798

GENERAL ★ AURORA ★ ADVERTISER

Morris-town [New Jersey]. On Monday last, a party to the number of between 20 and 30 villains slyly made their appearance at Mendham— cut down the liberty pole erected there and bore away the cap with the greatest expedition and triumph.

Tonight, Claudius Chat, a jeweler and goldsmith, a ten-year resident of Philadelphia, and an advertiser in the *Aurora*, dies of malignant yellow fever. He took ill only last evening, went directly to his physician, returned home, and, despite cold baths, spent today in convulsive agony, ending in death.[597]

Tonight, in the *Gazette of the United States*:

From [Noah Webster's] Commercial Advertiser. In Mr. Jefferson's notes on Virginia . . . [he] is very pointed against all establishments in favor of religion. "The legitimate powers of government extend to such acts only as are injurious to others," says Mr. Jefferson; "but it does me no injury for my neighbor to say there are twenty gods or no god. It neither picks my pocket nor breaks my leg." With great deference to this philosopher . . . if my property or my limbs are less safe among atheists than among theists, the act of destroying that belief in God is a proper subject for legal cognizance.

[Noah] Webster's notices of the chapter on Religion in Jefferson's Notes are unfortunate . . . He asserts that this article is very pointed against all establishments in favor of religion . . . dependent on the government . . . [T]his obnoxious article happens to have been recognized by the constitution of the United States . . .

Today, Thomas Jefferson writes Republican Congressman Samuel Smith of Baltimore,

> *Your favor of Aug 4 came to hand by our last post, together with the "extract" . . . cut from a newspaper*[598] *stating some facts which respect me. I shall notice these facts. The writer says that "the day after the last dispatches were communicated to Congress, Bache . . . [was] closeted with me" . . .*
>
> *I sometimes received visits from Mr. Bache . . . I received them always with pleasure, because [he is a man] . . . of abilities and of principles the most friendly to liberty & our present form of government. Mr. Bache has another claim on my respect, as being the grandson of Dr. Franklin, the greatest man & ornament of the age and country in which he lived. Whether I was visited by Mr. Bache the day after the communication referred to, I do not remember.*
>
> *I know that all my motions at Philadelphia, here, and everywhere, are watched & recorded. Some of these spies, therefore, may remember better than I do the dates of these visits . . . I know my own principles to be pure . . . They are the same I have acted on from the year 1775 to this day . . . I only wish the principles of those who censure mine were also known . . . I am quite at a loss on what ground the letter writer can question the opinion that France had no intention of making war on us & was willing to treat [negotiate] . . . when we have this from [Bache's publication of] Taleyrand's letter . . .*
>
> *These observations . . . are not intended for a newspaper. At a very early period of my life, I determined never to put a sentence into any newspaper . . . I have thought it better to trust to the justice of my countrymen, that they would judge me by what they see . . . Though I have made up my mind not to suffer calumny to disturb my tranquillity, yet I retain all my sensibilities for the approbation of the good & just. That is, indeed, the chief consolation for the hatred of so many who, without the least personal knowledge & on the sacred evidence of Porcupine & Fenno alone, cover me with their implacable hatred.*[599]

GENERAL ★ AURORA ★ ADVERTISER

The Real FRIENDS *to the union are those,*

Who are friends to the authority of the people, the sole foundation on which the union rests.

Who are friends to liberty, the great end for which the union was formed.

Who are friends to the limited and republican system of government, the means provided by that authority for the attainment of that end . . .

War . . . Today, three large ships-of-war of the Republic of France, the *Concorde* (forty-four guns), *Medée* (forty guns), and the *Franchise* (thirty-eight guns), disembark approximately 1,100 French soldiers near the town of Killala in County Mayo, Ireland, to assist Irish rebels achieve independence from the British monarch. French General Joseph Amable Humbert commands French forces in Ireland.[600]

War . . . Today, in the waters of the French West Indies off Martinique, two large ships-of-war of the United States, the forty-four-gun, 400-man U.S. Navy frigate *United States* and the twenty-gun, 180-man U.S. Navy ship *Delaware,* open fire on and capture an armed schooner, the *Sans Pareil,* of the Republic of France. Navy Lieutenant John Mullowny, who commands the *United States*, records in his journal:

> *Between Martinico & Domini. All sail set in chace. A[t] 8 P.M. fired a bow-gun at the schoo[ner]. at 1/2 8 fired another which brought the chace too. She proved to be the Sans Pariel of Guadeloupe, Cap[tain] Touin. Eighty seven men 10 Guns 6 of which were thrown overboard . . . At 11 P.M. the Delaware came up. At 3 squally with rain . . . Tacked to the N.*[601]

GENERAL ★ AURORA ★ ADVERTISER

As the friends of order in this city were the first to attack and batter in the nighttime a citizen's [Benjamin Bache's] house; first in New York to injure the representative of that city [Edward Livingston]; so in New Jersey they have maintained their character for insolence, outrage and disorder . . . It is not the fault of the friends of order that it has not already produced bloodshed . . .

The public are desired to be on their guard against the depredations of a gang who . . . to the number of twenty-three, with *black cockades,* armed with pistols, swords, and clubs, made a sudden and lawless irruption into [Menham, New Jersey], and while the men of the place were in the field and meadows, with violent oaths and imprecations terrified the women and children, and in an heroic manner surrounded the liberty pole [symbol of the French and American Revolutions] in this place which had been raised the 4th of July last and ornamented with the cap of liberty and the American colors, and proceeded to cut it down . . .

Today, Pennsylvania Federal District Court Judge Richard Peters writes Secretary of State Timothy Pickering that Philadelphia still contains *"some rascals . . . both Aliens and infamous Citizens"* whom the law should pursue.[602]

Today, a tent city for the poor is ready along the Schuylkill River. One account:

After most of the citizens whose circumstances would permit had fled to the country, the poor began generally to suffer . . . The Board of Health, in conjunction with the Guardians of the Poor, concerted measures for the construction of temporary tents. They were soon afterwards erected on the banks of Schuylkill, between Spruce and Chestnut-streets. They were ready by the 24th of August where fugitives crowded . . . The tents were made of canvas and floored with boards. Here nineteen hundred and fifty persons were fed and some of them clothed . . . Guards were stationed with arms to preserve order and prevent any individuals from trespassing the rules. Schools for the instruction of children were instituted, at which 137 male and 143 female children attended . . .[603]

MONDAY, AUGUST 27, 1798

GENERAL ★ AURORA ★ ADVERTISER

The system of terror that has been countenanced by our administration and its understrappers: the animosity that has been stirred up in all parts of the union under that influence: and the *threats* and *acts of violence* which have been for some time put in practice in order to drive men into servility and dereliction of those principles for which America bled, are objects that republicans cannot too seriously consider nor too soon be prepared against.

The editor of the *Aurora* was educated in the lap of Republicanism; ever since he has thought and acted for himself, his thoughts and actions have been those of a democratic republican; he was taught to wish France a republic [rather than a monarchy] before the revolution was thought of. He rejoiced when the dawn of that revolution was witnessed. He grieved at the excesses which its masked enemies had the address to excite and falsely lay to the account of republicanism. He rejoiced at the victories of the French not because they were French but because they opened the bright prospect of universal enfranchisement, a prospect which has since with rapidity been realizing. He has uniformly opposed the measures of the late and present administration of the Federal government and always will oppose measures tending to . . . infringe the constitution and sap the liberty of the citizen. He was a member of the democratic society and continued to be one until its meetings were suspended. He then opposed excise laws as he now does alien, sedition and libel acts. If the editor has erred, the uniformity of his conduct proves at least that he erred from principle; this would not have been the conduct of a time-serving "hireling."

Poor Richard wrote,

Observe all men; thy self most.[604]

Tonight, in the *Gazette of the United States*:

Buried in the several Church burying grounds, exclusive of those at the Hospital, for the 48 hours ending at 8 o'clock last evening—48 adults—17 children.

One hundred and eleven new cases for the last 48 hours, reported by 23 Physicians.

TUESDAY, AUGUST 28, 1798

GENERAL   ★ AURORA ★   ADVERTISER

The encrease in the circulation of this paper has been beyond the editor's most sanguine expectations; and since persecution has assumed against him a "form and pressure," it has been rapid beyond parallel. Thus the daring hand of persecution already counteracts its own designs; disappointment and despair may prompt to more audacious stretches of illegal power—but under whatever form it may appear, of private assassination or public contempt of the established principles of the constitution and laws, or the more congenial instruments of oppressors, prisons, chains, gibbets, the axe or bowstring, it shall never shake the firm determination of the editor to discharge his duty conscientiously; he may be made a victim to the dark rage of the worst enemies of our government and liberties; but it shall not be said of him that he abandoned an important right guaranteed by the constitution because men, entrusted for a time with the authority of the people, dared to forget their duty, to trample on that right, and violate that constitution. It would be doubly criminal in him to shrink before the frowns of ambition or the malice of little men dazzled by the glory of power, at a time when the liberal support he received from various parts of the United States evince not only the stubborn consistency of freedom and the love of truth but a marked approbation of his past conduct as well as a determination to aid him in the arduous and expensive undertaking in which he is engaged.

[BENJAMIN FRANKLIN BACHE]

It appears certain that a [French] *squadron* sailed from Toulon up the Mediterranean . . . There can be no object . . . except the coast of England or Ireland; we have most repeatedly hinted at the latter as the most probable point of attack . . .

The silly Advertiser of New York exults at the provision of arms, &c. by the Virginians—but he forgets that the *despotic* spirit manifested in some of the Eastern [New England] states and also in *Jersey* towards men who adhere to *republican* principles and *detest monarchy* rendered it peculiarly necessary for the Virginians to be *doubly guarded*!

Today, Secretary of State Timothy Pickering writes the U.S. district attorney for Pennsylvania:

Judge Peters thinks there are some dangerous aliens in the neighborhood of Philadelphia who require his & your attention. I shall be happy to do anything to aid the measures you shall think proper respecting them.[605]

Tonight, in the *Gazette of the United States*:

A correspondent of the *Aurora* from the true cut-throat principles which animate the writers of our foreign Gazettes proposed yesterday that the whole faction should arm.—This day, a correspondent in the same paper of the same cut insinuates that the State of Virginia is arming against the other states. There has been a fracas at New York at the Old Coffee House in which a number of persons, said to be foreigners, fell upon a citizen, supposed with a design to destroy him. Burk, the *"Time Piece"* man, says that 900 United Irishmen can be produced if necessary. *Quere,* whether persons of such description are those the *Aurora* proposes to arm? As to the state of Virginia, the foreign gang will find themselves mistaken in counting upon her cooperation in their villainous designs.

Who are the characters that are intended to be stigmatized [by the Republicans] as Old Tories? They are Adams, Washington, Jay . . . Was the firm and virtuous Adams who signed the Declaration of Independence and managed affairs of the highest importance to foreign courts, was he an enemy and traitor to this country? Was the great and illustrious Washington, who led our armies in the field and whose fame as a guardian genius hovers over this land, was he opposed to the principles of our revolution and to our national independence?

GENERAL   ★ AURORA ★   ADVERTISER

Tyrants (or . . . men who are aiming to subjugate the people to their arbitrary control) always pursue a *preparatory system* to answer their purposes. They begin by employing a number of hirelings to extol their patriotism, to represent them but little short of deities. Songs are composed in praise of their political virtues by sycophant poet laureats. Baccanalians sing them over the bottle, and a tribe of courtiers introduce them in their festivals. They pursue measures to irritate those governments who are friendly to freedom, and seek an alliance by treaty with those who favor despotism. They employ venal presses . . . They deceive the people by publications which they stile official . . . [A]fter alarming the fears of the people on the invasion of their enemies, they acquire means to borrow money, raise a standing army, equip a navy, impose innumerable taxes . . .

Tonight, in the *Gazette of the United States*:

NEW YORK Aug. 25. The *Time Piece* . . . having as usual abused one of our citizens, a Mr. M'Dougal, he called at the office . . . The foreman of the press . . . told him he was willing to be considered as Mr. [John Daly] Burk himself and . . . would meet him . . . and give him satisfaction. The Old Coffee House was agreed . . . Mr. M'Dougal went at the time appointed . . . After a few words M'Dougal struck him, but before a second of time could pass, the door was burst in by a gang . . . Enquiry was instantly set on foot to identify the names and persons of some of the villains . . . [T]hey appeared to be a band of Irish . . . It will be useless, however, for any person of curiosity to go to his shop to look at him, for . . . they could [not] discover the hole where the envenomed Irish spider had retreated from the light and spins his daily web of slander for the *Time Piece* . . .

GENERAL   ★ AURORA ★   ADVERTISER

It behooves every republican who values the liberties of his country, his own security and that of his family to provide himself with arms and to habituate himself to the constant use of them—for the *tenets* preached up by the wretches who follow in the train of our administration are calculated to convert the people of these free states into two classes— *Janisaries [Indians] and Mutes !*

Cornwallis is appointed lord lieutenant of Ireland with full powers to coerce or conciliate as circumstances may require.

In 1781, when France was helping American rebels gain independence from the British monarch, Britain's Lord Charles Cornwallis commanded Britain's army at the final battle at Yorktown, Virginia. Now, in 1798, when France is helping Irish rebels gain independence from the British monarch, Britain's Lord Charles Cornwallis commands Britain's army in Ireland.

Today, the New York *Time Piece* closes. No final "good-bye." Just a final regular edition. John Daly Burk, its former co-editor, remains under indictment for sedition.[606] That sedition action and the threat of violence have closed the paper.

Benny Bache's sedition trial is more than a month away. Others have offered to pay any fine. Tonight, in the *Gazette of the United States*:

> It appears that all the honor of persecution for violating the Sedition Law will not accumulate on citizen *Aurora* . . . It has been stated that some of the printers who have incurred the penalty of the law against seditious publications are to be indemnified from a purse raised among the faction . . .

The encrease of subscribers to Bache's publications is a circumstance that merits attention . . . Bache says the encrease is beyond his most sanguine expectations, and since he has been persecuted, "has been rapid beyond parallel." However false or true this may be, there is no doubt that the more recent and outrageous attacks on the government and its administration have been made in the spirit of enterprize and experiment in order to try the strength of the laws and to excite the lukewarm partizans of the faction to come forward with their patronage.

SATURDAY, SEPTEMBER 1, 1798

GENERAL　　★ AURORA ★　　ADVERTISER

I do solemnly declare that . . . the majority of the legislature of the United States who voted for the [Sedition] act . . . have violated the clause in the constitution of the United States which declares that "*Congress shall make no law . . . abridging the freedom of speech or of the liberty of the press . . .*" And I do further solemnly declare, and I verily believe, if the president of the United States hath approved the said act; and if any of the judges have, by any official transaction endeavored to enforce it, that they have also violated that part of the constitution.

GEORGE NICHOLAS [*Lexington, Kentucky*]

Today, this notice:

THE HEALTH OFFICE.

Fellow Citizens,

September 1, 1798

Impelled by the awful progress and unparalleled malignity of the prevailing fever, we are constrained to address your feelings, as well as your reason, in order to avert the fatal destruction which, with rapid strides, is pervading our ill-fated city and suburbs.

The best skill of our physicians, and all the powers of medicine, it must be acknowledged, have proven unequal in the contest with this devouring poison . . .

We call your attention to the actual and undisguised state of our city. Consider the mortality and rapid increase of the sick at so early a period.—View the list of your physicians, and *mark how few are at their posts*; and we believe you will think, with us, that the preservation of health is only to be attained by flight . . .

WILLIAM JONES, President[607]

As Poor Richard wrote,

> *He's the best physician that knows the worthlessness*
> *of most medicines.*[608]

Benjamin Bache will not leave. If Federalist attacks and sedition prosecutions can't intimidate him, neither will the yellow fever!

MONDAY, SEPTEMBER 3, 1798

GENERAL   ★ AURORA ★   ADVERTISER

In consequence of a number of families removing from this city and leaving casks in their yards containing water which, from the late warm weather, has become putrid, thereby contaminating the air and breeding innumerable mosquitoes, would it not be prudent in the health committee to cause all tubs, casks, &c. to be turned bottom upwards to prevent a collection of stagnant water until the return of their owners?

THE DEMOCRATIC REPUBLICANS of the City are invited to meet at Fouquet's Hotel in Tenth, between Arch and Race streets, on Friday next, September 7, at two o'clock in the afternoon,—in order to determine upon candidates to be supported at the ensuing election for representatives in the Federal, State, and City Legislatures.

Today, Benny's fourth child is born. It's a boy. Benny and Peggy name the child Hartman to honor Peggy's deceased mother (whose maiden name was Hartman).

Today, the following notice:

MEDICAL ADVICE
To The Citizens of Philadelphia.

The following directions for the prevention and treatment of the prevailing fever are affectionately recommended to those citizens who are unable to procure the regular attendance of physicians by

BENJAMIN RUSH
SAMUEL P. GRIFFITTS
September 3d, 1798.

[Yellow fever] comes on like a cold . . . In the forming state of the fever, when the patient feels slightly indisposed, and before he is confined to bed, the following remedies generally check the disease:

A purge [to empty the bowels] of salts, castor oil, or a dose of jalap [a yellowish powder from morning glory plant roots] and calomel [a white tasteless powder]. If these fail of giving relief, a gentle sweat should be excited in the usual way. If there be much pain in the head or back, and the pulse be full or tense, ten or twelve ounces of blood should be lost before the use of the sweat and either before or after taking the purge . . .

After the disease is formed and appears with more or less of the following symptoms, viz. chills, great heat, head-ache, a redness in the eyes, sickness in the stomach, vomiting, pain in the back, limbs and bowels, &c. the following remedies are proper.

1. The loss of ten or twelve ounces of blood, two or three times a-day . . .

2. The bowels should be purged at the same time with calomel mixed with jalap and rhubarb, in powder or in pills—The operation of the purging medicine should be aided, when practicable, by clysters [enemas], composed of half an ounce of glauber salts [colorless sulfate crystals] dissolved in half a pint of warm water or a half a pint of warm water with sweet oil [olive oil], molasses, and common salt, of each a tablespoonful, in it . . .

3. If the stomach should be sick and oppressed with bile, a vomit of ipecacuanha [the dried root from a shrubby South American plant], or tartar emetic [a poisonous, white, metallic-tasting powder] may be given at any time on the 3rd or 4th day . . .

5. After the pulse is reduced by bleeding and purging, if the disease has not yielded, a profuse sweat should be excited by wrapping the patient up in blankets, with five or six hot bricks wetted with vinegar applied to different parts of his body, and giving him at the same time large and repeated draughts of hot camomile or sage tea, hot lemonade or weak punch, or any other hot liquor that is agreeable to him to drink . . .

6. Blisters should be applied to the wrists and ankles in common cases about the third or fourth day of the fever . . .

7. In case of delirious with a languid pulse, poultices [hot, moist coverings] of raw garlic, with a little mustard, should be applied to the feet . . .

It will be improper to depend exclusively upon any one of the above remedies. The combined force of them all is barely sufficient, in many cases, to overcome this formidable disease.[609]

Tonight, in the *Porcupine's Gazette*:

ELECTION NEWS. *From the Albany Centinel.* Poor *Bache,* the *Aurora* man, at Philadelphia, has calculated that . . . the *"republican"* interest will receive an accession of fourteen *props* when the election of members of Congress is completed in the several states . . . [I]n this state . . . *Bache & Co.* will find little other support . . . than to give effect to the "sedition bill" as a check on the libelous and government defaming conduct of himself and his coadjutors . . .

TUESDAY, SEPTEMBER 4, 1798

GENERAL ★ AURORA ★ ADVERTISER

A PRESSMAN WANTED
AT the OFFICE of the AURORA.
The situation is airy and healthful.

The malignant yellow fever is conquering the *Aurora*. Eight who work at the paper will die. Sixty-two who work for printers throughout the city will die.[610] Today, the fever takes Mary Fenno, John Fenno's wife of more than twenty years.[611]

WEDNESDAY, SEPTEMBER 5, 1798

GENERAL ★ AURORA ★ ADVERTISER

HEALTH OFFICE
WANTED immediately—A number of sober men who can be well recommended as drivers for the carriages employed by the Health-Officer— Good encouragement will be given to persons of good character if application is immediately made.

EIGHTY-SEVEN new cases of the prevailing fever, reported by 17 physicians, for the last 24 hours.

The Bank of North America and Bank of Pennsylvania were yesterday morning removed to the School-House in Germantown.

Today, John Fenno's *Gazette of the United States* fails to appear.

War . . . Today, off Puerto Rico, the United States Navy's forty-four-gun, four-hundred-man frigate *United States* fires upon and captures the French Republic's eight-gun sloop-of-war, the *Jaloux*. From the journal of Navy Lieutenant John Mullowny who commands the *United States*:

> *Pleasant, all sail set in chace of a sloop. at 4 P.M. fired a shot to bring the chace to. fired several in the course of the afternoon and evening. at 11 She bro't to all standing. She is a sloop from Guadeloupe on a cruise commanded by Citoyen Joseph Renne, called the Jealous of 8 Guns. had thrown 6 overboard . . .*[612]

Today, traveling from Philadelphia to his home in Western Pennsylvania, Republican House leader Al Gallatin passes through Reading, Pennsylvania, recently described as follows:

> Reading, the chief town of the county of Berks . . . consists at present of about five hundred houses . . . [T]hey are log-houses and the interstices between the trunks of the trees are filled up with stone or plaster . . . The town has little or no trade, and scarcely any manufactures . . . The population of Reading is estimated at about two thousand five hundred souls, consisting chiefly of lawyers and inn-keepers . . . [N]o increase of the number of inhabitants has been observed for several years . . . The sentiments of the inhabitants of this town and the neighboring country are very good and breathe a warm attachment to the federal government. There is no democratic society.[613]

A Reading newspaper reports Al Gallatin's arrival:

> [A]bout 6 o'Clock in the Evening, arrived in this Town, Albert Gallatin, Esq. a Member of Congress, from the Western Counties in the State of Pennsylvania, with his lady, &c. on his journey . . . for his Home, and lodged at the Federal Inn, the Sign of PRESIDENT WASHINGTON, which is kept by Mr. Jacob Baer. About or rather before 8 o'clock, all at once all the Bells of this Place (of the two churches and Courthouse) began ringing—Numbers of People were alarmed . . . [T]he Cannon (a little Swivel) was fired . . . Soon after, a Number of the Enemies of Gallatin collected, and among them a number of Reading Volunteer Blues, with a Drum and Fife, playing the Rogue's March, and marching before the Federal Inn. As some of Gallatin's friends expressed dreads of personal Abuse against him, Mr. Baer, the Innkeeper, (a very stout and resolute Man) posted himself on the inner stairs to guard his guest. Soon after the swivel was silenced; and it was agreed on to silence the Bells likewise, a number went to the Churches, finding the Ringers had locked themselves in to prevent coming to them, that unless they would cease ringing, all the windows would be broke, and they stormed, put an immediate Stop to the Ringing—after having lasted for nearly half an Hour in which the swivel was four or five times discharged . . . The evening was spent with very much virulent Talk and Exclamations, yet without any Blows.[614]

THURSDAY, SEPTEMBER 6, 1798

GENERAL   ★ AURORA ★   ADVERTISER

The Irish rebels, according to the Philadelphia Gazette and the New York Gazette, have been *subdued* and *completely put under* . . .

It is a subject of much regret that so great a dread of going to the City Hospital reigns among the indigent class of our fellow-citizens. Many of them have been known to conceal their illness until they could do so no longer for fear of being carried there.

A report for the city of Philadelphia describes the suffering:

> The scenes of distress which the Hospital exhibited were truly dismal: —there we could hear groans—the moanings—and the heavy sighs of "the hundreds sick." No connexions were near to view their distress or to soothe, with the tear of friendship, their "little hour." When the coachees which brought out the sick arrived, often might be seen an affrightened patient enter, supported by strange Nurses and bedewing his or her cheeks with tears. The nurses were often obliged to hold the patient in bed by force when struggling with delirium, and others seemed to sleep out their life without any feeling while the screams of many were heard at a distance. Some bled from the mouth and nose, and the black vomit issued in streams from others. Two and frequently three were placed in one coffin.[615]

This morning, the crowd in Reading, Pennsylvania, is waiting for Al Gallatin. As the local newspaper reports,

> [This] morning, before Mr. Gallatin set out on his Journey, a number of the Reading Blues collected at the Courthouse, marched regularly up and down past the Federal Inn, playing the Rogue's March, and before and while he helped his lady in the Carriage, they burned his effigy within a few yards of the carriage, on exclaiming: *"Stop de Wheels of de Gouvernement"* and others: *"Let them go on."* The Carriage drove off without Mr. Gallatin in, for he traveled on horseback, He preferred mounting back at the Stable and taking the Alley to get out of Town to join his Carriage at the lower end of it, and by this means to avoid being escorted by the Reading Blues.[616]

Today, Benny Bache feels feverish and suffers from aches in his muscles.[617]

FRIDAY, SEPTEMBER 7, 1798

GENERAL ★ AURORA ★ ADVERTISER

The prevailing disease which afflicts this city has already caused the suspension of three of our public newspapers, viz. *Carey's Recorder*, the *Gazette of the United States* and the *True American* . . . The *Aurora* office has hitherto escaped the affliction, how long it continues so remains in the hands of providence; should the office escape, our subscribers will continue to be served as usual, should the untoward fortune of our city also extend to us, our friends will make due allowance for what may be inevitable, a temporary suspension of our labors.

DEATHS

It is with singular regret we announce the death . . .

On Tuesday last, in the 43d year of her age Mrs. Mary Fenno, comfort of Mr. John Fenno, editor of the Gazette of the United States . . .

Benny continues feverish and sick. We are all worried. Today, if only as a precaution, Benny makes out his will, naming his father ("R. Bache of Settle"), his father-in-law, Adam Kuhn ("my respected father"), and Joseph Clay ("my friend") as executors. James Robinson and I witness his signature. If Benny does not survive the fever, he wants all of his property to go to Peggy,

to be by her used according to her own good sense, firmly confident from the tenderness and love which I have in every shape experienced from her uniformly, that she will bestow on our dear children a suitable and enlightened education such as will be worthy of us and advantageous to themselves and render them virtuous, generous, and attached to the immutable principles of civil Liberty.[618]

In a separate document, Benny names me to succeed him as editor of the *Aurora*.[619]

Tonight, in the *Porcupine's Gazette*:

ALLIANCE WITH GREAT BRITAIN

Assailed by evils as we are and beset with a nest of scoundrel Jacobins in the very bosom of the country, it is a pleasing circumstance to see that, amongst the friends of government, the destructive prejudice against Great Britain is daily and hourly wearing away . . . [T]he treaty will, and must, take place . . .

SATURDAY, SEPTEMBER 8, 1798

GENERAL ★ AURORA ★ ADVERTISER

ONE HUNDRED and TWENTY SEVEN new cases of the prevailing fever were reported for the last 24 hours by eighteen physicians.

Today, though news of the event will not reach Philadelphia until November, Britain's Lord Charles Cornwallis overpowers the French force which has come, under General Humbert, to help Irish rebels gain their independence from the British monarch. Theobald Wolfe Tone, Ireland's would-be George Washington, will be sentenced to hang.[620]

COMMUNICATION

Philadelphia at this time is nearly desolated, & though but few inhabitants left, we behold hearses continually carrying corpses to their graves.—What a havock would death have made had all continued in the city? . . .

[O]n the appearance of frost, all will flock in again, and some probably may exult on their cheating death once again, forget the past, and rush into their former wickedness, vices and mockery of Heaven. But take care, sinners, or next time you may be arrested and cut down.—Repent! Repent in time, and mend your ways.   ADMONITION

Today, George Washington writes the Managers of Philadelphia's City Hospitals,

> *Gentlemen: Among those who commiserate the afflicted Citizens of Philadelphia, I beg you to be persuaded that none do it with more sincerity or with more feeling than I do. And the poignancy is very much increased by the declaration of the malignancy of the fever and difficulty of cure.*[621]

Today, one month before he is to stand trial and face imprisonment for criticizing the President of the United States, publisher Benjamin Franklin Bache of the *Philadelphia Aurora* dies of malignant yellow fever at the age of twenty-nine.[622] His wife, Peggy, is faithful to the end. Though Peggy just gave birth to their fourth son, Hartman, she nurses Benny till the moment of his death. Liz Hewson observes:

> *A french doctor attended him who ordered frequent bathings. The tub leaked and there was that poor woman Margaret Bache just out of her bed continually in a room covered with water. It is a wonder she escaped with her life. She behaved with the greatest fortitude during his illness and after his death.*[623]

TUESDAY, SEPTEMBER 11, 1798

Today, the *Philadelphia Aurora* ceases publication. At one in the morning, the *Aurora*'s pressmen run off, in lieu of a newspaper, a handbill which reads as follows:

> In these times, men who see and think and feel for their country and posterity can alone appreciate the loss; the loss of a man inflexible in virtue, unappalled by power or persecution, and who in dying knew no anxieties but what were excited by his apprehensions for his country—and for his young family.[624]

In his *Poor Richard's Almanack* for 1757, Benjamin Franklin included the following:

> *GOD sees with equal Eye, as Lord of all,*
> *A Hero perish, or a Sparrow fall,*
> *Atoms, or systems, into Ruin hurl'd*
> *And now a bubble burst,—and now a World!* [625]

Years later, he wrote a special ten-year-old grandson,

> *I shall always love you very much if*
> *you continue to be a good Boy . . .*[626]

Ben Franklin loves that special grandson, this very day.

EPILOGUE TO BOOK ONE

THURSDAY, SEPTEMBER 13, 1798

Today, Secretary of State Timothy Pickering, enforcer of John Adams' Sedition Act, writes,

> *Bache the printer is dead and his principal clerk, an able man, is also finished, as, I am informed, is much of the matter his mischievous paper contained.*[627]

FRIDAY, SEPTEMBER 14, 1798

Today, only four days after the death of his nemesis, Benny Bache, and only ten days after the death of his beloved wife, Polly, publisher John Fenno of the *Gazette of the United States* dies of the malignant yellow fever.[628] John Fenno's twenty-year-old son, John ("Jack") Ward Fenno, will succeed to his father's post as publisher of the *Gazette of the United States.*

WEDNESDAY, SEPTEMBER 19, 1798

Tonight, in the *Porcupine's Gazette,* William Cobbett writes,

> *"AN ELEGY ON BACHE" cannot appear in my paper. A Briton scorns to mangle the carcass which he himself has slain, and much more, one that has been slain by the ALMIGHTY.*

SUNDAY, SEPTEMBER 30, 1798

Today, George Washington writes U.S. Secretary of War James McHenry:

> *I have lately received information . . . that the brawlers against Governmental measures . . . have, all of a sudden become silent; and, it is added, are very desirous of obtaining Commissions in the Army, about to be raised . . . [A]s there will be characters enough of an opposite description, who are ready to receive appointments, circumspection is necessary; for my opinion is of the first that you could as soon scrub the blackamore [Negro] white as to change the principles of a profest Democrat and that he will leave nothing unattempted to overturn the Government of this Country.*[629]

THURSDAY, OCTOBER 11, 1798

Today, Vice President Thomas Jefferson writes U.S. Senator Stevens Thomson Mason (Republican, Virginia),

[The Alien and Sedition Acts are] merely an experiment on the American mind to see how far it will bear an avowed violation of the constitution. If this goes down, we shall immediately see attempted another act of Congress, declaring that the President shall continue in office during life, reserving to another occasion the transfer of the succession to his heirs, and the establishment of the Senate for life. [630]

TUESDAY, OCTOBER 23, 1798

Tonight, in the *Gazette of the United States*, twenty-year-old Jack Fenno writes:

Notwithstanding a few local triumphs of the French faction, their cause may with truth be pronounced in the wane. The star of jacobinism must soon cease to shed its malign influence; for shadows, clouds, and darkness rest upon it.

Benjamin [Bache] . . . in his Aurora . . . became of course one of the most malicious Libellers of me. But the Yellow Fever arrested him in his detestable Career and sent him to his grandfather from whom he inherited a dirty, envious, jealous, and revengefull Spight against me for no other cause under heaven than because I was too honest a Man to favour or connive at his selfish schemes of ambition and Avarice.

**JOHN ADAMS,
PRESIDENT OF THE UNITED STATES, 1797–1801.** [631]

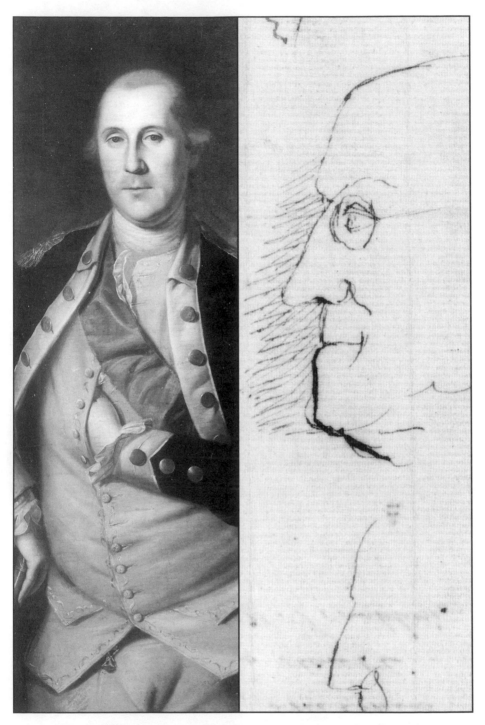

Gen. George Washington (1776)
by Charles Willson Peale
(oil painting).[632]

Dr. Benjamin Franklin (1790)
by Benjamin Franklin Bache
(notebook sketch).[633]

BOOK TWO

FATHER OF HIS COUNTRY

[JOHN ADAMS] is always an Honest Man, often a wise one, but

sometimes, and in some things, absolutely out of his senses.

DR. BENJAMIN FRANKLIN[634]

JOHN ADAMS [is] the advocate of a kingly government and of a titled

nobility to form an upper house and to keep down the swinish

multitude . . . JOHN ADAMS . . . would deprive you of a voice in

chusing your president and senate, and make both hereditary—This

champion for kings, ranks, and titles is to be your president . . .

BENJAMIN F. BACHE, EDITOR,
AURORA GENERAL ADVERTISER, 1790–1798[635]

Your Great Grandfather [BENJAMIN FRANKLIN] is properly thought

the father of American liberty—he it was who formed the American

mind and character for more than fifty years to become what America

now is, one of the greatest and the only free nation in the world . . .

WILLIAM DUANE, EDITOR,
AURORA GENERAL ADVERTISER, 1798–1822
(IN A LETTER TO BENJAMIN BACHE'S FIRST-BORN SON)[636]

I expect soon to see a proposition to name the 18th Century the

Franklinian Age, le Siècle Franklinnien . . . The title of "Founder of the

American Empire," which . . . the English newspapers give [to Dr.

FRANKLIN,] does not most certainly belong to him . . . [T]here is such
a prostitution of all Justice . . . to accomplish the Apotheosis of Dr.
F[RANKLIN] as ought to excite the indignation of every honest man.

JOHN ADAMS,
PRESIDENT OF THE UNITED STATES, 1797–1801[637]

As long . . . as everyone was unanimous about the politics of America,
it was not worth dividing the public opinion about a man. But as Mr.
Washington has at length become treacherous even to his own fame,
what was lent to him as a harmless general must be withdrawn from
him as a dangerous politician . . . It was his country and France
which gave him fame in defiance of England; and it will be his
country and France which, in defiance of England, will
take it away again.

BENJAMIN F. BACHE, EDITOR,
AURORA GENERAL ADVERTISER, 1790–1798[638]

Any Man who has lived long enough to be able to recollect or has read
enough of the History of France . . . must be astonished at their claims
of Gratitude; and can hear the arrogant Pretensions that we owe our
Independence to them only with a Mixture of Indignation and
Contempt.

JOHN ADAMS,
PRESIDENT OF THE UNITED STATES, 1797–1801[639]

[H]ad it not been for the aid received from France in men, money and
ships, your cold and unmilitary conduct, as I shall show in the course
of this letter, would in all probability have lost America; at least she
would not have been the independent nation she now is. You slept
away your time in the field till the finances of the country were

completely exhausted, and you have little share in the glory of the

final event. It is time, sir, to speak the undisguised language

of historical truth.

THOMAS PAINE,
U.S. SECRETARY FOR FOREIGN AFFAIRS, 1777–1779,
IN *A LETTER TO GEORGE WASHINGTON . . . ON AFFAIRS PUBLIC
AND PRIVATE* (PHILADELPHIA: BENJAMIN FRANKLIN BACHE,
112 MARKET ST., 1796)[640]

Franklin, whose fame had already opened him a free correspondence

with the literati of the European continent, was with perfect wisdom

dispatched to France . . . The father of the American liberties became

the general object of respect and love . . . [French Foreign Affairs

Minister] Vergennes, whose principles united the arbitrary policy of

the French court with the refined knowledge of a country peculiarly

distinguished by literature, became the social friend of Franklin . . .

Under such fortunate auspices, the principal difficulties to the

negociation were easily removed . . .

WILLIAM DUANE, EDITOR,
AURORA GENERAL ADVERTISER, 1798–1822[641]

The great character [GEORGE WASHINGTON] was a Character of

Convention . . . [N]orthern, middle, and southern statesmen and

northern, middle, and southern officers of the army expressly agreed

. . . to cover and dissemble all faults and errors, to represent every

defeat as a victory and every retreat as an advancement, to make

that Character popular and fashionable with all parties . . . as

the central stone in the geometrical arch. There you have the

revelation of the whole mystery . . .

JOHN ADAMS,
PRESIDENT OF THE UNITED STATES, 1797–1801[642]

[Favorable] ideas of Washington are probably entertained by the world at large; for few men were acquainted with his real character, and of those few, a very small number . . . will venture, except perhaps in whispers, to speak what they thought or think of his talents . . . [I]t was important to maintain, during the revolution, the popular opinion in his favour. Accordingly, there was no public disclosure . . . But is it proper that the truth should forever be concealed?

TIMOTHY PICKERING,
U.S. SECRETARY OF STATE, 1795–1800[643]

SEC. 3. And be it further enacted. That if any person shall be prosecuted under this act for the writing or publishing any libel aforesaid, it shall be lawful for the defendant . . . to give in evidence the truth of the matter contained in the publication . . .

SECTION THREE (TRUTH DEFENSE)
OF THE SEDITION ACT OF 1798[644]

[I]t will be some consolation to me to . . . do justice to them with posterity, since a gang of greater scoundrels never lived. We are to dance on [WASHINGTON'S] birth night, forsooth, and say they are great & good men, when we know they are little people.

JAMES MONROE,
PRESIDENT OF THE UNITED STATES, 1817–1825[645]

PROLOGUE TO BOOK TWO

George Washington wasn't winning the American Revolution. He was losing it. So, under cover of darkness on the evening of October 26, 1776, seventy-year-old Benjamin Franklin boarded his seven-year-old[646] namesake grandson, Benjamin Franklin Bache, into a carriage and headed south from Philadelphia beside the Delaware River to Chester, Pennsylvania, where a 130–man, sixteen-gun American warship the Reprisal waited, under orders of the Continental Congress, to carry them on a secret mission to Europe.

On that fateful night, little Benny Bache could not have known that he would not see his parents, Richard and Sarah Bache, again for nine long years, not until he was old enough to enter college. Little Benny Bache could not have known that from childhood till manhood, he would be in the care of the world-famous grandfather he had met only a year and a half before.

Instructions to Lambert Wickes, the Reprisal's thirty-four-year-old captain, from the Committee of Secret Correspondence of the American Continental Congress were to be opened only after the committee's chairman, Benjamin Franklin, was safely on board. They ordered Captain Wickes to transport Franklin and his party with all possible speed to France and not to stop, not even for British prizes, along the way. Thus began the historic mission which prompts these writings and which decided the independence of the United States of America.

(To illuminate certain details of this history, I have chosen to quote the weekly newspaper The Pennsylvania Gazette, *which Benjamin Franklin co-owned and edited from 1729 until 1748. I do so as a tribute to Franklin's newspaper career and as a further reminder that the roots of American democracy lie deep in the freedom of the press.)*

CHAPTER SIX

FABIUS

We shall have all the Sages and Heroes of France here
before long . . .
Our Fabius will be slow, but sure.

JOHN ADAMS,
JUNE 18, 1777[647]

The real Fabius was never despised by Hannibal; but his imitator, Mr.
Washington, was always despised by his enemy . . . For a long period
indeed the British succeeded in every considerable expedition purely
military which was attempted by them, so that, in this defensive war
as it was called, many months elapsed before one point actually and
seriously attacked was really defended on the part of Mr. Washington.

BENJAMIN F. BACHE, EDITOR,
AURORA GENERAL ADVERTISER, 1790–1798[648]

Early on the morning of May 28, 1754 (more than two decades before the American Revolution began and five years before I, William Duane, was born), a handsome twenty-two-year-old lieutenant colonel of Virginia militia committed an act of atrocity—the murder of a peaceable French diplomat, Lieutenant Joseph Coulon de Villiers de Jumonville—that started America's French and Indian War.[649] It was a war, however, he could not finish.

Captured at Fort Necessity by French soldiers under Jumonville's half brother (Captain Louis Coulon de Villiers) and released after confessing in writing to the "assassination," George Washington returned to Williamsburg, the capital of Virginia, a defeated soldier. He demonstrated clear military incompetence in constructing Fort Necessity (and deploying his militiamen) within musket range of a nearby forest and surrounded by higher ground,[650] and he would unquestionably need British forces not only to avenge his humiliation at Fort Necessity but also to push the French off frontier lands that Washington and fellow land speculators coveted in the Ohio Valley. Despite Washington's promise (as a condition of his release by Jumonville's brother) never to return to the region of Fort Necessity, George Washington would break that promise at the first opportunity.[651]

That opportunity came a year later, in the spring of 1755, when Great Britain supported Washington with a substantial force under British General Edward Braddock. Perhaps unaware that Washington lost Fort Necessity through an injudicious deployment of troops, Braddock relied on George Washington's advice[652] rather than on Ben Franklin's[653] in leading 1,300 British soldiers and Virginia militiamen to the frontier where Jumonville was killed. Franklin warned Braddock to avoid the trackless path through Virginia's uncleared woods: *"The only danger I apprehend of obstruction to your march is from ambuscades of Indians . . . and the slender line, near four miles long, which your army must make, may expose it to be attack'd by surprise in its flanks and to be cut like a thread into several pieces . . ."*[654] Washington urged, on the other hand, *"in the warmest terms I was Master of, to push on . . . leav'g the baggage and other Convoys with the Remainder of the Army to follow by slow and regular marches . . ."*[655]

In this march to the frontier, Braddock's and Washington's forces were injudiciously scattered, so that, on July 9th, a much smaller force of French and Indians surprised and destroyed, piece by piece, the entire British force. Braddock was killed, his troops were massacred, and Virginia's militiamen, despite Washington's entreaties, fled in a panic.[656] As one historian has observed, *"Rarely in history has an army suffered such destruction, never perhaps from an enemy of only half its numbers."*[657]

By the following year (1756), Britain and France were fully at war in America and abroad. As Horace Walpole, a member of the British Parliament, explained, *"the volley fired by a young Virginian in the backwoods of America set the world on fire."*[658]

To free America's frontiers from French encroachment, Britain dispatched hundreds of ships and ten thousand soldiers, driving the French off the frontier and defeating them in Canada. During the first three years of the war, Washington continued to lead Virginia's militiamen, but failed to undertake a single major engagement, constantly complaining of gunpowder and food shortages, the worthlessness of Virginia's paper money, and the cowardliness, perversity, niggardliness, and private preoccupation of his troops. Virginia's press chastised Washington for this failure to take the initiative,[659] but when Washington finally engaged the French in November of 1758 near the site of Braddock's massacre, his troops mistakenly fired on each other (killing fourteen and wounding twenty-six). As one historian has written, *"His first armed engagement (the ambush of Jumonville) had been called a murder; his second [at Fort Necessity] and third [with Braddock] had been bloody and humiliating defeats; now his fourth had been fratricidal."*[660] It is not surprising, therefore, that, one month later, Washington removed his colonel's uniform to preside over the fortune he acquired by inheritance (from father Augustine and brother James) and by a marriage of convenience[661] (in January of the following year) to Martha Dandridge Custis, a dowdy Virginia widow, somewhat older, awkwardly shorter, but possessed of seventeen thousand valuable acres.[662]

With the British victorious and the French at their mercy, Britain negotiated the Treaty of Paris in 1763 which ended not only the French and Indian War but also French rule throughout Canada and the rest of North America (except for New Orleans and environs). In a remarkable twist of fate, however, and to quell an uprising of Indians who feared westward expansion of land-hungry colonists (now that the French were gone), Britain issued a royal proclamation in 1763 which promised Chief Pontiac and warned George Washington (and fellow land speculators) that colonial settlement west of the Alleghenies would thenceforth be prohibited.[663]

Washington faced a real dilemma. He had killed Lieutenant Jumonville and made war against France to access those frontier lands. Now that Britain was becoming an obstacle to the very same lands, what might George Washington do?[664]

The French and Indian War had been costly for Britain, and, when the war ended, Britain wanted to recoup some of those costs. Taxpayers back in Britain were unhappy paying stamp and other taxes to support *inter alia* the American war, and they resented the much lighter tax burden that Americans had to bear.[665] Furthermore, with the war over, that ten-thousand-man British army would remain in America to defend against frontier Indians, so it seemed doubly fair for Americans to contribute to the cost of their own protection.

Britain based its American policies not only on the expectation of American gratitude but also on a theory that a British economist Adam Smith would later call "mercantilism."[666] Mercantilism viewed Britain and her colonies as inter-locking pieces in a puzzle of national self-sufficiency. For that self-sufficiency, it encouraged home-based manufacturing and agriculture, assured home markets for home-grown products (through the import/export restrictions of Britain's Navigation Acts), and sought favorable trade surpluses (exports over imports) to generate national wealth ("gold and silver") and a powerful military to defend mother country and colonies alike. As mercantilists viewed the matter, Britain and her colonies were "in it together." Each contributed what it could.

To obtain an American contribution toward the cost of American defence, Britain passed a Sugar Act in 1764 and a Stamp Act in 1765. The Sugar Act imposed an import duty (an "external tax") on molasses that New Englanders imported from non-British islands in the West Indies to manufacture rum, which they could trade for West African slaves, whom they then sold in the American South (or perhaps traded triangularly in the West Indies for more molasses). The Sugar Act was a mercantilist measure, protecting Britain's sugar growers in the British West Indies from non-British price competition in the North American home market.

The Stamp Act, on the other hand, was an "internal tax," a simple revenue-raising measure, lacking mercantilist trade protection as a justification. It required government stamps for many printed materials but most expensively for legal documents (e.g., deeds, customs clearances, licenses, and wills) which real estate developers like George Washington, merchant-traders like John Hancock, and their lawyers like John Adams had to file with (or obtain from) the government.

Whatever the British expectation of American gratitude, many Americans were bound to disappoint. Even before the war, John Hancock and other merchant-traders violated British import/export restrictions with smuggling operations to and from countries outside the protected British home market.[667] Important lawyers like John Adams defended such smugglers and shared their principal concern that Britain not use tougher warehouse inspections, stronger admiralty courts, etc., to turn paper regulations into enforceable ones. During the French and Indian War, colonial assemblies declined to authorize supplies or funds for arriving British troops (until Britain guaranteed reimbursement), and, when Britain legislated (by its Quartering Act in 1765) that Americans house re-maining British troops if barracks were unavailable, Americans were angry and even aghast at the idea. Finally, as soon as the war was over, George Washington and other land speculators trespassed the 1763 Proclamation line to the very lands whose trespass had cost Britain seven years of war. In 1767, the man who "can't tell a lie" instructed his real estate partner to mark lands in Western Pennsylvania beyond the proclamation line, suggesting the activity be *"snugly carried on by you under the pretence of hunting other Game."*[668]

News of the Stamp Act incensed America. On May 30th, 1765, Patrick Henry led the Virginia House of Burgesses to denounce the act. No taxation, he said, without representation in the British Parliament. Other colonies quickly fol-lowed.[669] Wealthy taxpayers, including George Washington, were quick to agree. In August, merchants, lawyers, and plantation owners organized "Sons of Liberty" gangs to terrorize stamp masters and burn stamped paper.[670] In September, John Adams issued his famous "Braintree Instructions" against the taxes (and against strengthened admiralty courts),[671] and, in October, a "Stamp Act Congress" in New York rejected taxation without representation as well as any proposal to seek such representation.[672] On November 1st, the day the Stamp Act was to become effective, tax protesters rioted in New York city.[673]

Why were Americans so ungrateful? That's what Britain wanted to know. After all, people back in England were themselves paying a stamp tax to support *inter alia* George Washington's war. Weren't Americans going to contribute *anything* to Britain's cost for *their* defense? Why hadn't the principle of rep-resentation come up before? Britain had regulated the American economy for over a hundred years (Britain's first Navigation Act passed in 1651), and the colonies never demanded parliamentary representation. Americans knew full well that having a few representatives in the British Parliament would not have prevented passage of the Stamp Act, and they knew full well that, even in Brit-ain, fewer than one in thirty had the right to vote for members of Parliament. So why were Americans complaining?

The American complaint, as Jimmy Callender would later recall, was that *"[t]he arbitrary proceedings of the king and parliament, in assuming a power to make laws for the colonies, without their concurrence, filled up the measure of American wrongs . . . This kind of reasoning cuts short all claims of grat-itude on the part of America towards England."*[674]

The King had promised, when chartering the colonies, that they were to be self-governing, meaning that they were to be left alone. The Stamp Act and other measures violated this promise and further violated the fundamental liberty of British subjects to be secure in their property until they or their representatives agreed to relinquish it. The British constitution was to protect such liberty, with the British monarch (largest property owner), the House of Lords (the landed nobility and their heirs), and the House of Commons (representing the rest) checking and balancing each other's interests to assure the enactment of virtuous law, but the British constitution had failed. Parliament was taxing Americans (taking their property) without their consent and without an American representative in Parliament to grant such consent. Parliament had been corrupted. That's why America complained.[675]

Taken aback by the American reaction, Britain repealed the Stamp Act in March of 1766; however, in 1767 a new British Chancellor of the Exchequer, Charles Townshend, decided to replace the Stamp Act's "internal taxes" with presumably more acceptable "external taxes," meaning import/export duties to protect British industries and agriculture. (The Townshend Act also created a new board of colonial customs officers to enforce Britain's Navigation Acts.) Again, the colonies said no.

In February of 1768, the Massachusetts provincial assembly charged that the Townshend duties also constituted taxation without representation and, in a circular letter, urged other colonies not to pay. Britain demanded a retraction of that letter, and when the Massachusetts and other assemblies refused to back down, Britain went about dissolving colonial assemblies. By autumn, extralegal colonial assemblies were refusing to import British goods, America was increasing its smuggling to and from countries outside the British trading group, and the Sons of Liberty were beating up British customs officials and any colonial wearing British cloth.[676]

Charles Townshend's death allowed Britain to take another backstep, so, on March 5th of 1770, Britain rescinded all the Townshend duties, except the duty on tea. With this tergiversation and despite an unpleasant incident the same day in Boston (frightened British sentries fired on a nighttime crowd of snowball-throwing colonists—killing five—in what outraged colonists called a "Boston Massacre"), the colonies resumed importation of British goods in May and restored relative calm to relations with Britain for the next three years.[677] Then came 1773 . . .

In 1773, Britain adopted measures which threatened America's real estate speculators and merchant-traders. In 1773, Britain prohibited her royal governors from making further grants of Crown land in America, causing land speculators like George Washington to fear they might never profit from the lands they coveted (and illegally marked) beyond the 1763 royal proclamation line.[678] (Britain enhanced those fears in June of the following year by passing the Quebec Act, extending the boundaries of Quebec south to the Ohio River and west to the Mississippi.)[679]

In May of 1773, Britain upset America's merchant-traders, ostensibly by renewing the remaining Townshend Act duty on tea (about to expire) but perhaps more so by allowing the British East India Tea Company to sell direct to the American public without any middlemen (and without any middleman markup). The elimination of middlemen lowered America's tea prices (even with the tea tax) to less than what tea drinkers in England had been paying, but lower tea prices came at the expense of American middleman profits. They even cut into tea smugglers' sales.[680] Thus, Boston's merchants (and smugglers) reawakened the public to the principle of the tea's taxation, encouraged Sons of Liberty to attack East India Tea Company agents, and finally, on the evening of December 16th, inspired some thirty stalwarts disguised as Mohawk Indians (one claims to have exchanged Indian grunts with John Hancock)[681] to dump 342 chests of British tea into Boston Harbor. It was a Boston Tea Party to be long remembered.

Having backed down on the Stamp Act, having rescinded all but one of the Townshend duties, and having defanged the remaining tea duty by eliminating the middleman markup, the British were livid that Massachusetts should countenance such law-breaking (under the apparent pretext of a tax protest) to advance the interests of John Hancock and other Boston merchants, and, on March 25, 1774, the British Parliament retaliated by ordering that, in the absense of just compensation, the Port of Boston be closed (as of June 1st) and Massachusetts be governed by martial law under British General Thomas Gage. All public gatherings, whether in simple town meeting or in Mohawk disguise, would henceforth be prohibited.[682]

The imposition of martial law and the outlawing of town meetings angered all Massachusetts citizens. Shifting Massachusetts' entry port from Boston north to Salem would (and did) cost thousands of Bostonian jobs. When news that the port would be closed reached Boston in May, Bostonians met at Fanueil Hall and resolved to end trade with Britain until the port reopened. They resolved to create a Solemn League and Covenant by which other colonies could join the Massachusetts boycott, and they urged other colonies to meet in congress to consider the crisis. Boston silversmith Paul Revere carried the news. Other colonies agreed to attend.

During that summer of 1774, extralegal colonial committees chose delegates for a First Continental Congress of the American colonies, which was held in Philadelphia at the end of the summer (starting September 5th) to consider the Boston Harbor closing and the Massachusetts hope for a unified response. While the Continental Congress was meeting, Massachusetts adopted additional "Suffolk Resolves" (which were sent to the Congress via messenger Paul Revere), urging no obedience be paid to British acts, no taxes be paid to the royal government, military preparations (like the stockpiling of arms) be made in case British troops in Boston moved against protesters, and, if the British were to seize any patriot leaders, a plan to respond in kind.

Fifty-five delegates from twelve colonies attended Philadelphia's First Continental Congress. Boston's prominent lawyer John Adams and powerful merchant/smuggler John Hancock were among the Massachusetts delegates. Handsome land developer and erstwhile colonel in Virginia's militia George

Washington adorned the Virginia delegation. Ben Franklin, America's foremost representative in Europe, remained in London as colonial agent for Massachusetts, Pennsylvania, New Jersey, and Georgia.

At the First Continental Congress, the colonies agreed (as a "Continental Association") not to import or consume British goods and, should Britain not repeal the "coercive" acts within the next year, no longer to export American products to Britain. The delegates approved Massachusetts' "Suffolk Resolves" with the caveat that colonists refrain from violence, and Congress compiled a list of grievances to be presented to King George III.

In asserting their rights and petitioning the British King, Americans were not objecting to living under a monarchy. To the contrary, they sought a stronger monarchy, not a weaker monarchy, to reverse the intolerable and coercive acts of Britain's most democratic institution, the British House of Commons. It was Parliament, after all, that was infringing on the king's prerogative to grant colonial self-government (a prerogative the king had exercised, the colonists argued, in chartering the colonies).[683] How ironic for King George's American subjects—and how little appreciated—that the same evolution of British liberties that allowed them to petition their British king now precluded their British king from reversing the acts of the British Parliament!

On October 26, 1774, America's First Continental Congress adjourned, recommending that the thirteen colonies quickly choose delegates for a Second Continental Congress (to convene next May 10th if Britain did not redress colonial grievances). Until May 10th, Philadelphia and the rest of America would await the king's response.

Although the following period of American history finds me, William Duane, taking up my pen against the British monarch in Ireland, India, and England,[684] I will, nevertheless, journalize this important time for you, dear reader, on the same day-to-day basis as I used in Book One.

WEDNESDAY, NOVEMBER 30, 1774 [685]

⇥ The Pennsylvania Gazette ⇤

[British] General [Thomas] Gage [in Boston] hath absolute orders from the Court to prevent the meetings of the Congress and to seize all such people as attempt to assemble . . .

The idea of sending another cargo of tea to Boston, with a military force, is most contemptibly ridiculous . . .

It is not the people of Boston only who are resolved not to pay the tax upon tea, but the common cause of all the American colonies . . .

Today, a thirty-seven-year-old Englishman whom Benjamin Franklin will describe as "my adopted political son"[686] disembarks at Philadelphia from the *London Packet*. He bears a letter of introduction from Ben Franklin (now ten years in London) to Benny Bache's father, Richard Bache:

The bearer, Mr. Thomas Paine, is very well recommended . . . He goes to Pennsylvania with a view of settling there. I request you to give him your best advice and countenance, as he is quite a stranger there. If you can put him in a way of obtaining employment . . . you will do well . . . My love to Sally and the boys.[687]

Tom Paine:

The favor of Dr. Franklin's friendship I possessed in England, and my introduction to this part of the world was through his patronage.[688]

Saturday, March 4, 1775. Today, settled on Philadelphia's Front-street across from the London Coffee House, Tom Paine writes a letter to Benjamin Franklin:

I am just now informed by Mr. [Richard] Bache of a vessel preparing to sail for London tomorrow, and lest I should not have an other opportunity as soon as I might wish, to acquaint you, I have taken this to acquaint you as laconically as I can of the services your good favors have been to me . . .

Your countenancing me has obtained me many friends and much reputation, for which, please accept my sincere thanks . . . [A] Printer and Bookseller here . . . has lately attempted a magazine, but having little or no turn that way himself, has applied to me for assistance. He had not above 600 subscribers when I first assisted him. We have now upwards of 1500 and daily increasing . . .[689]

Tuesday, April 18, 1775. Tonight, toward midnight, eight hundred British soldiers prepare to cross Boston's Charles River for an early-morning surprise raid on a stockpile of ammunition that colonists have illegally accumulated in Concord, Massachusetts. As the British soldiers prepare to depart, Boston silversmith Paul Revere and other messengers get ready to set off on horseback to forewarn Concord (and nearby Lexington, along the route). Fearing British soldiers might capture him before he gets clear of the city, Paul Revere sends a signal to comrades across the river in Charlestown. Paul Revere:

I agreed with a Colonel Conant and some other gentlemen [in Charlestown across the river] that if the British went out by water, we would shew two lanthorns in the North Church steeple, and if by land, one . . . for we were apprehensive it would be difficult [for us] to cross the Charles River or git over Boston neck.[690]

WEDNESDAY, APRIL 19, 1775

❖ The Pennsylvania Gazette ❖

Extract of a letter from London . . .
The determination of the ensuing [American] Congress [to meet May 10th] will be final and decisive . . . I am of the opinion that nothing will

move the King and his Ministers, but absolute submission or a successful resistance. But an offer from you of such a contribution to the relief of this country from its debt would disarm them of their only popular argument . . . [O]ur forefathers purchased their undoubted rights in Magna Carta by the gift of a sum of money to the King, and I think we need not blush to follow so great an example . . .

The S P E E C H of the LORD M A Y O R . . .
But, Sir, it will be said, is America then to enjoy the protection of Great-Britain and to contribute nothing toward the support of that very state which has so long given it protection and security, which has nursed it up to its present greatness? . . .

A number of families are moving themselves and their most valuable effects from the town of Boston into the country in consequence of the late advices from England . . .

[London] Orders are sent to Woolrich for a train of artillery to be got ready with all expedition to be shipped with the troops destined for Boston.

Early this morning, an event occurs in Lexington, Massachusetts that will relieve John Adams' "painful drudgery" in appearing daily before Boston's Admiralty Court to defend John Hancock against smuggling charges.[691] The eight-hundred-man British force which left Boston last night to seize an arms depot in Concord encounters about one hundred farmer-soldiers ("ready in a minute" militia) exercising on the Lexington village green, and when these country folk refuse to disarm and stand aside, the British brigade fires on, charges, and disperses the crowd, and continues their march toward Concord. By this action, America's war with Britain will begin.

Once the British soldiers arrive in Concord, find the stockpile of arms vanished, and prepare to return to Boston, "the shot heard 'round the world" sounds at Concord's Old North Bridge, and a withering barrage of gunfire arrests the British force. Only reinforcements of one thousand soldiers allow the British to retreat through the clanging of church bells and a corridor of musket fire to Charlestown, whence they recross the water to Boston.[692]

WEDNESDAY, APRIL 26, 1775

→ The Pennsylvania Gazette ←

Watertown [Massachusetts], Wednesday Morning [April 19], near 10 of the Clock.
To all Friends of American Liberty, be it known that this Morning before Break of Day, a Brigade of about 1000 or 1200 Men landed at Phipps's Farm at Cambridge, and marched to Lexington, where they found a Company of our Colony Militia in Arms upon whom they fired without any Provocation, and killed 6 Men and wounded 4 more.

Since the above-written we have received the following by a Second Express. Thursday [April 20], 3 o'Clock Afternoon . . .

I am this Moment informed by An Express from Woodstock, then two of the Clock Afternoon—That the Contest between the first Brigade that marched to Concord was still continuing this Morning at the Town of Lexington, to which said Brigade had retreated, that another Brigade had . . . landed with a quantity of Artillery . . . The Regulars, when in Concord, burnt the Court-House, took two Pieces of Cannon which they rendered useless, and began to take up Concord Bridge, on which Capt.—— (who, with many on both sides, were killed) made an Attack upon the King's Troops, on which they retreated to Lexington . . .

A letter has . . . been received from Newport dated last Friday Evening [April 22] at 7 o'clock, which mentions the latest advices received there, in substance, is "That the Brigade [of British troops] left Boston in Boats on Tuesday Night, landed at Watertown in the Morning, where they fired on the Minute Men; then proceeded to Concord, destroyed about fifty barrels of flour, and spiked up four Cannon; that on their Return they were fired upon by 3 or 400 Men; 40 of the King's Troops fell, and about 40 more Prisoners; that the Troops retreated; and were fired upon by a large number at Cambridge; and lost about 40 more; . . . that the Troops got into Boston; that Col. [of the Militia Artemis] Ward had 17,000 of the Colony Troops collected near the Place; that it was proposed to attack the General in Boston. Col. Putnam with a very large Number from Connecticut were on their March, and others from all Parts of the Massachusetts Colony . . ."

L O N D O N. We are assured from undoubted authority that the three Major Generals and the troops, both horse and foot, that are destined for America, are to embark with all possible expedition . . .

The Troops destined for America are now on their March for the Sea-Ports, where the Transport Vessels are ready prepared to receive them . . .

I find in Messiers Bradford's Journal, No. 1687, "A Plan of an union of the several colonies, &c. proposed by Benjamin Franklin, Esq., and unanimously agreed on by all the commissioners of the several colonies, met, by order of the Crown, at Albany in July, 1754." . . .

A word about "Albany in July, 1754" . . . In July of 1754 (while George Washington was unsuccessfully engaging Lieutenant Jumonville's half brother at Fort Necessity), Ben Franklin attended a colonial meeting in Albany, New York, to organize a common defense against frontier Indians. At this meeting, Ben Franklin proposed his "Albany Plan" of colonial union which *"framed that form of combination for the whole of the colonies by their delegates which properly assumed the name of Congress—a name and a system which was the basis of all the subsequent assemblies of the United States."*[693] Though the colonial governments refused, in 1754, to accept Franklin's plan, the colonies can now reconsider Franklin's plan in coordinating a military response to the British threat.

Today, not knowing that Benjamin Franklin is en route to Philadelphia aboard the *Pennsylvania Packet*, a Massachusetts provincial assembly at Watertown addresses a letter to him as Massachusetts' colonial agent in London:

> *From the entire confidence we repose in your faithfulness and abilities, we consider it the happiness of this Colony that the important trust of Agency for it, in this day of unequalled distress, is devolved on your hands . . .*
>
> *Our enemies, we are told, have dispatched to G[reat] Britain a Fallacious Account of the Tragedy they have begun; to prevent the operation of which . . . we most ardently wish, that the Several papers herewith Inclosed, may be immediately printed, and Disperced thro' every Town in England . . .   JOSEPH WARREN, President, P. T.*[694]

WEDNESDAY, MAY 3, 1775

→ The Pennsylvania Gazette ←

> *Extract of a letter from Boston. [Massachusetts] . . . We have been closely besieged, and no provision brought to market for several days which has reduced us to an allowance . . . The town was besieged by 20,000 men who it was expected would attack the fortifications.*
>
> *The wounded officers and soldiers were treated with great humanity by the inhabitants of Charlestown on their return . . .*

> *Extract of a Letter from New York . . . [W]e learn that General Gage had dispatched a frigate to England a few hours after the defeat of his troops. That the British Officers and Soldiers have done ample justice to the bravery and conduct of the Massachusetts Militia—they say that no troops ever behaved with more resolution . . .*

Today, the Massachusetts provincial assembly petitions the Second Continental Congress which is to convene in a week (on May 10th):

> *The Congress of this colony . . . request the direction and assistance of your respectable Assembly . . .*
>
> *We have . . . passed an unanimous Resolve for thirteen thousand six hundred Men, to be forthwith raised by this Colony; and proposals are made by us to the Congress of New Hampshire, and Governments of Rhode Island and Connecticut Colonies, for furnishing men in the same proportion . . . Reinforcement from Great Britain is daily ex-*

pected in this Colony, and we are now reduced to the sad alternative of defending ourselves by arms, or submitting to be slaughtered . . .

JOSEPH WARREN, President, P.T.[695]

WEDNESDAY, MAY 10, 1775

⤳ The Pennsylvania Gazette ⬳

P H I L A D E L P H I A. On Friday evening arrived here Capt. Osborne, from London, in whom came passenger the worthy Dr. BENJAMIN FRANKLIN, Agent for Massachusetts government and this province . . .

Yesterday arrived . . . George Washington, Patrick Henry . . . Delegates from Virginia . . .

And this Day the Hon. John Hancock . . . Samuel Adams, John Adams, and Robert Treate Paine, Esquires, Delegates for the Province of Massachusetts-Bay . . .

Today, the Second Continental Congress of the thirteen provinces opens in Philadelphia. Delegates are aware that, following hostilities at Concord and Lexington, twenty thousand militiamen from the four New England colonies have descended on Boston and surround the city.

After ten years in London as colonial agent and spokesman for Pennsylvania and, since 1770, for Massachusetts, Ben Franklin is now back in Philadelphia, having returned on Friday aboard the *Pennsylvania Packet* and having been chosen Saturday to join Pennsylvania's delegation to the Continental Congress. Deborah Read Franklin, Ben Franklin's wife of over forty-four years,[696] died before Christmas while Franklin was still in London, but their daughter, Sarah, and her husband, Richard Bache, welcome him back to Franklin Court. There he meets for the first time his five-year-old[697] namesake grandson, Benjamin Franklin Bache.

Today, as the Congress meets, a detachment of eighty-three militiamen, sponsored by Massachusetts and Connecticut and led by Ethan Allen and Benedict Arnold, surprise a small garrison of British soldiers and their wives and children at the British fort at Ticonderoga and Crown Point which guards the approaches to Lake Champlain in upper New York. Fearing that British reinforcements, entering from Canada, might use the fort's large store of cannon and artillery against the colonists, the colonists' plan is to seize these armaments. There is no fight. The British families surrender, and the Americans take possession of the cannon and other artillery.[698]

Monday, May 29, 1775. Today, John Adams writes Abigail:

Coll. Washington appears at Congress in his Uniform, and by his great Experience and Abilities in military Matters, is of much service to Us.[699]

George Washington is wearing the Virginia militiaman's uniform he hasn't worn for sixteen years. He is the only member of Congress in any type of military attire, and his tall, broad physique gives him an impressive military appearance.

Thursday, June 15, 1775. Today, in the Continental Congress, the Journals report:

> The report of the committee being read and debated,
> *Resolved,* That a General be appointed to command all the continental forces, raised, or to be raised, for the defence of American liberty . . .[700]

John Adams writes:

> *[W]e were embarrassed with more than one Difficulty . . . a Southern Party against a Northern, and a Jealousy against a New England Army under the Command of a New England General . . . I found too that even among the Delegates of Virginia there were difficulties . . . In several Conversations I found more than one very cool about the Appointment of Washington . . . Full of Anxieties . . . I walked with [my cousin] Mr. Samuel Adams in the State House Yard for a little exercise and fresh Air before the hour of Congress, and there represented to him the various dangers that surrounded Us. He agreed to them all, but said "What shall We do?" I answered him . . . I was determined to take a Step which should compell them and all the other Members of Congress to declare themselves for or against something. "I am determined this Morning to make a direct Motion that Congress should adopt the Army before Boston, and appoint Colonel Washington Commander of it." . . .*
>
> *Accordingly, when congress had assembled, I rose in my place, and . . . concluded . . . that though this was not the proper time to nominate a General, yet . . . I had no hesitation to declare that I had but one Gentleman in my mind for that important command, and that was a gentleman from Virginia who was among Us . . . Mr. Hancock . . . Mortification and resentment were expressed as forcibly as his Face could exhibit them.*
>
> *Mr. Samuel Adams Seconded the Motion . . . The Subject came under debate, and several Gentlemen declared themselves against the Appointment of Mr. Washington . . . [P]ains were taken out of doors to obtain a Unanimity, and . . . the dissentient Members were pursuaded to withdraw their Opposition . . .*[701]

The Journals continue:

> The Congress then proceeded to the choice of a general, by ballot, when George Washington, Esq. was unanimously elected.[702]

Friday, June 16, 1775. Today, in the Continental Congress, the Journals report:

The president from the chair informed Geo: Washington, Esq. that he had the order of the Congress to acq[uaint] him that the Congress had by a unanimous vote made choice of him to be general and com[mander] in chief to take the supreme command of the forces raised . . . Whereupon Colonel Washington, standing in his place spoke as follows:

"MR. PRESIDENT,

"Tho' I am truly sensible of the high Honour done me in this Appointment, yet I feel great distress, from a consciousness that my abilities and military experience may not be equal to the extensive and important Trust . . .

"[L]est some unlucky event should happen, unfavourable to my reputation, I beg it be remembered, by every Gentleman in the room, that I, this day, declare with the utmost sincerity, I do not think myself equal to the Command I am honored with . . . ."[703]

John Adams writes:

> We owe no thanks to Virginia for Washington. Virginia is indebted to Massachusetts for Washington, not Massachusetts to Virginia. Massachusetts made him a general against the inclination of Virginia. Virginia never made him more than a colonel . . . I was subjected to almost as bitter exprobrations for creating Washington commander-in-chief . . . [704]

Benny Bache (as an adult) will observe:

> A Virginia planter by no means the most eminent, a militia-officer ignorant of war both in theory and useful practice (We do not forget the virgin public act of Mr. Washington . . .), and a politician certainly not of the first magnitude; such was the outset of this gentleman in the American revolution. He was therefore paid in advance when he was suddenly made commander in chief.[705]

Tonight, in Boston, hearing that British troops plan to reoccupy the Charlestown isthmus, Israel Putnam of Connecticut leads patriot forces to occupy and fortify Breed's Hill, closer to Boston and more exposed than Bunker Hill but still in command of the harbor and city.[706]

Saturday, June 17, 1775. Today, in the Continental Congress, the Journals report:

IN CONGRESS
The delegates of the United Colonies . . . To George Washington Esq. WE . . . do, by these presents, constitute and appoint you to be General and Commander in chief . . .

The Congress then proceeded to the choice of officers in the army by ballot: . . . Horatio Gates, Esq . . . Charles Lee, Esq.[707]

Today, in Boston, in an effort to reoccupy the Charlestown isthmus, British General Sir William Howe leads 1,500 British soldiers across the bay (by barge) to make an assault on Breed's Hill, which the patriots, under Massachusetts Major General Joseph Warren, now occupy. General Howe's troops land on the beach a half mile from Charlestown, plunder and burn the town, and then foolishly attempt a frontal attack on the hill without protection from the British men-of-war (whose guns cannot be raised sufficiently to bear upon the summit). The result is that the patriots pick off the clearly identifiable British officers and proceed to slaughter the oncoming troops.

When the British are reinforced with five hundred additional soldiers, they finally take the hill, kill General Warren, but pay a tremendous price in dead and wounded. This "Battle of Bunker Hill" (erroneously so called) shows the capabilities of the American militiamen, who inflict twice as many casualties as the British. Why did the militiamen lose the hill? They simply ran out of ammunition.[708] Farmers don't have enough gunpowder to fight a European army.[709]

Tuesday, June 20, 1775. Today, James Warren, president of the Massachusetts provincial assembly, reports to John Adams on the Battle of Bunker Hill:

> *They Landed about 2000 . . . [They w]ere more than once repulsed by the Bravery of our men . . . who, had they been supplied with Ammunition and a Small reinforcement of Fresh men, would . . . have in all probability beat them to pieces . . .[710]*

Today, in the Continental Congress, the Journals report:

> GEORGE WASHINGTON, ESQ. . . . —you are to repair with all expedition to the colony of Massachusets Bay, and take charge of the army of the United Colonies.[711]

Wednesday, June 21, 1775. Today, in the Continental Congress, the Journals report:

> Mr. Thomas Jefferson appeared as a delegate for the Colony of Virginia, and produced his credentials, which were read and approved . . .[712]

WEDNESDAY, JUNE 28, 1775

→ The Pennsylvania Gazette ←

Watertown, June 20. We just received an Account by a Man, who is said to have swam out of Boston, that we killed and wounded 1000 of the Ministerial troops . . . The whole of the troops landed at Charlestown were 5000.

On Friday morning, the Generals WASHINGTON and [Charles] LEE set off from [Philadelphia] to take command of the American army at Massachusetts-Bay. They were accompanied from town by the troop of light horse, and by all the officers of the city militia on horseback, who at-

tended them about five miles, when they returned, but the former continued with them.

Monday, July 3, 1775. Today, George Washington finally arrives in Cambridge, Massachusetts (just outside Boston), and makes his headquarters on the Harvard College campus at the Harvard president's house. (Harvard's president, Samuel Langdon, compacts his living into a single room.) George Washington writes Congress:

> *I arrived safe at this Place on the 3d Instant; after a Journey attended with a good deal of Fatigue, & retarded by necessary Attentions to the successive Civilities which accompanied me in my whole Rout.*[713]

Gen. Washington was *"retarded by . . . civilities."* Benny Bache will, as an adult, observe:

> *Mr. Washington as appears took ten days to go from New-York to the camp before Boston, to assume his new command at a critical moment. Had he sent an aide-de-camp or a servant to engage relays of horses and avoided these civilities, he might have arrived in half the time.*[714]

Saturday, July 8, 1775. Today, Ben Franklin writes his London landlady and dear friend, Polly Hewson, about his five-year-old grandson, Ben Bache, and about Polly's infant daughter, Elizabeth:

> *I have much Delight in my Grandsons. Mr. and Mrs. Bache join in Love to you and yours. Ben, when I delivered him your Blessing, enquired the Age of Elizabeth, and thought her yet too young for him; but as he made no other Objection, and that will lessen every day, I have only to wish being alive to dance with your Mother at the Wedding.*[715]

Friday, July 21, 1775. The colonies must have some plan of confederation to manage the war. Today, Benjamin Franklin circulates, in the Continental Congress, his plan for a confederated national government. The Journals report:

Franklin's Articles of Confederation

ART I. The Name of this Confederacy shall henceforth be *The United Colonies of North America* . . .

ART IV . . . Delegates shall be annually elected in each Colony to meet in General Congress . . .

ART. VI. All Charges of Wars . . . shall be defray'd . . . by each Colony in proportion to its Number of Male Polls [voters] between 16 and 60 Years of Age . . .

ART. VII. The Number of Delegates to be elected and sent to the Congress by each Colony shall be . . . one Delegate . . . for every [5000 voters] Polls . . .

ART. IX. An executive Council shall be appointed by the Congress out of their own Body, consisting of [12] Persons . . . Appointments for Three Years, whereby One Third of the Members will be changed annually. And each Person who has served the said Term of three Years as Counsellor shall have a Respite of three Years before he can be elected again . . .[716]

Ben Franklin believes that a federal (confederated) government should consist simply of a single-chamber legislature with delegates annually elected from small voting districts of equal population throughout the country. Small districts mean that the national legislature will be large (Franklin's would have 125 members)[717] and, therefore, can't be bribed. Equally important, small districts mean candidates don't have to be wealthy or have wealthy connections to run for office. They can be ordinary people who know and are known to the neighbors who must elect them.[718] Each of Franklin's voting districts has an equal number of voters, so citizens are represented equally and states strictly in proportion to their populations. For Franklin, annual elections are the final guarantee that delegates won't stray from their constituents' wishes.

In Franklin's federal government, a majority of the legislature makes law. There is no veto. There is no second or upper chamber to represent individual colonies or the wealthy class. There is no separate executive branch or chief executive. Because the purpose of an executive branch is to carry out the legislature's laws, the legislature chooses its own executive, and to assure that no individual has too much authority (as a king), the executive is to be a council rather than an individual. Finally, so the council doesn't act too homogeneously (as an individual), one third of the council departs office each year.

Sunday, July 23, 1775. With the radical shortage of arms and ammunition, the War of Independence may have to be fought with spears! Today, George Washington gives the following order:

> *The people employed to make spears are desired by the General to make four dozen of them immediately, thirteen feet in length, and the wood part a good deal more substantial than those already made[. P]articularly in the New Hampshire Lines, [they] are ridiculously short and light . . .[719]*

Today, John Adams writes his wife, Abigail, of the importance Europe attaches to Ben Franklin:

> *Dr. Franklin has been very constant in his attendance on Congress from the beginning . . . The people of England have thought that the opposition in America was wholly owing to Dr. Franklin; and I suppose their scribblers will attribute the temper and proceedings to him . . .[720]*

WEDNESDAY, JULY 26, 1775

> ⇾ The Pennsylvania Gazette ⇽

Extract of a letter from the Camp at Cambridge, July 11 . . . Our people are situated from Charles River about 200 rods below [Harvard] College, where we have a redoubt [fortified emplacement] . . . [W]e have a complete line of circumvallation [around Boston] from Charles River [in Cambridge] to Mistick River [in Charlestown] . . . nor do I expect it will be many days before the contest begins which will probably bring on a general engagement . . . [O]ur people . . . are strongly fortified . . . so strong that I believe every man [the British!] in Boston . . . must fall before they could force a passage that way into the country . . .

Friday, August 4, 1775. The Continental army has no gunpowder. Today, George Washington writes the Continental Congress:

> *Our Situation in the Article of Powder is much more alarming than I had the most distant Idea of. But on ordering a new Supply of Cartridges yesterday, I was informed to my very great Astonishment that there was no more than 36 Bbbls. in the Massachusetts Store, which with the Stock of Rhode Island, New Hampshire & Connecticut makes 9937 lb. not more than 9 Rounds a Man . . . I immediately went to confer with the Speaker of the [Massachusetts] House of Representatives upon some Measures to obtain a Supply from the neighbouring Townships, in such a manner as might prevent our Poverty being known as it is a Secret of too great consequence to be divulged in the General Court, some Individual of which might perhaps indiscreetly suffer it to escape him, so as to find its way to the Enemy the Consequences of which are terrible, even in Idea. I shall also write to the Governours of Rhode island, Connecticut & the Committee of Safety in New Hampshire on this Subject, urging in the most forcible Terms the Necessity of an immediate Supply if in their Power. I need not enlarge on our melancholy Situation; it is sufficient that the Existence of the Army & the Salvation of the Country depends upon some thing being done for our relief both speedy and effectual & that our Situation be kept a profound Secret.* [721]

Thursday, August 10, 1775. The other colonies have no gunpowder either. Today, Benjamin Franklin writes General Philip Schuyler:

> *[I]t occurr'd to me to endeavour obtaining from our Committee of Safety a Permission to send you what powder remain'd in our Hands, which tho' it was thought scarcely safe for our selves to part with it, they, upon my Application, . . . chearfully agreed to. Accordingly I this Day dispatch a Waggon with 2400 lb. weight which actually empties our Magazine . . .* [722]

Saturday, August 12, 1775. Today, Benny Bache turns six years old. Benny's home at the rear of Franklin Court is now an important place to meet for America's revolutionary war leaders who are constantly conferring with Benny's grandfather.

Saturday, August 26, 1775. Pennsylvania will use spears! Today, Benjamin Franklin writes the Pennsylvania Committee of Safety:

> *It has been regretted by some great Soldiers . . . that the use of Pikes [spears] was ever laid aside, and many experienc'd Officers of the present Times agree . . . [I]ts length reaching beyond the Bayonet, and the compound Force of the Files (every Man laying hold of the presented Pike) rendring a Charge made with them insupportable by any Battalion arm'd only in the common Manner. At this time therefore, when the Spirit of our People supplies more Men than we can furnish with Fire Arms, a Deficiency which all the industry of ours ingenious Gunsmiths cannot suddenly supply; and our Enemies, having at the same time they were about to send regular Armies against undisciplin'd and half-arm'd Farmers and Tradesmen, with the most dastardly Malice endeavour'd to prevail on the other Powers of Europe not to sell us any Arms or Ammunition; the Use of Pikes in one or two Rear Ranks is recommended to the Attention and Consideration of our Battalions.*[723]

Today, George Washington attributes his lack of action to gunpowder shortages:

> *[I]t would not be prudent in me to attempt a measure which would necessarily bring on a consumption of all the Ammunition we have, thereby leaving the Army at the Mercy of the Enemy, or to disperse; and the Country to be ravaged and laid waste at discretion . . . I know by not doing it, that I shall stand in a very unfavourable light in the opinion of those who expect much & will find little done . . . [S]uch however is the fate of all those who are obliged to act the part I do . . .*[724]

Benjamin Rush will recall to John Adams:

> *In the summer of 1775 or thereabouts I dined in company with General, then Colonel, [Adam] Stephen on his way from Virginia to the camp [in Cambridge]. I sat next to him. In a low tone of voice he asked me who constituted General Washington's military party . . . "Are they men of talents?" said he. "Yes, I said." "I am glad to hear it," said the General, "for General Washington will require such men about him. He is a weak man. I know him well. I served with him during the last French war."*[725]

Wednesday, August 30, 1775. Today, for the first time, the Pennsylvania Committee of Safety issues spears to Pennsylvania's militia.[726]

Tuesday, September 19, 1775. Today, George Washington writes the Continental Congress:

> *The State of Inactivity in which this Army has lain for some Time by no Means corresponds with my Wishes by some decisive Stroke to*

relieve my Country from the heavy Expence its Subsistence must cre-ate . . .

It gives me great Pain to be obliged to sollicit the Attention of the Honorable Congress to the State of this Army, in Terms which imply the slightest Apprehension of being neglected: But my Situation is inexpressibly distressing to see the Winter fast approaching upon a naked Army . . . [T]he Military Chest is totally exhausted . . . [T]he greater part of the Troops are in a State not far from Mutiny . . . [I]f the Evil is not immediately remedied and more punctuality observed in [the] future, the Army must absolutely break up . . .[727]

Friday, September 29, 1775. Today, in the Continental Congress, the Journals report:

> *Resolved,* That a Committee of three members be appointed to repair immediately to the camp at Cambridge, to confer with George Washington . . .[728]

Saturday, September 30, 1775. Today, in the Continental Congress, the Journals report:

> *Resolved,* That . . . Doctr. Franklin [and two others] . . . be the Committee for the purpose expressed in the resolution of yesterday [to meet with George Washington] . . .[729]

Monday, October 2, 1775. Today, in the Continental Congress, the Journals report:

> Instructions to the Committee . . .
> 2. That in the conference with the General, the Committee declare to him the Sense of the Congress respecting an Attack on the Ministerial Troops at Boston and on Bunkers Hill, viz. That . . . it will be adviseable to make the Attack upon the first favourable occasion and before the Arrival of [British] Reinforcement which the Congress apprehend may be soon expected . . . But that the attack should nonetheless be made . . . as soon as a favourable Opportunity shall offer . . .[730]

Tuesday, October 3, 1775. Today, in the Continental Congress, the Journals report:

> *Resolved,* That General Washington may, if he thinks proper, for the encouragement of an attack on Boston, promise, in case of success, a month's pay to the army . . .[731]

Friday, October 6, 1775. Today, in the Continental Congress, the Journals report:

> *Sherman.* I think we must have powder . . .
> *[James] Duane.* We must have powder; I would send for powder to London or anywhere. We are undone if we have not powder . . .[732]

Sunday, October 29, 1775. Today, in a letter to his wife, John Adams articulates his love for New England:

> *New England has, in many respects, the advantage [over] every other colony in America, and, indeed, of every other part of the world that I know anything of . . . The people are purer English blood; less mixed with Scotch, Irish, Dutch, French, Danish, Swedish etc., than any other; and descended from Englishmen, too, who left Europe in purer times than the present, and less tainted with corruption than those they left behind.*[733]

Saturday, November 11, 1775. Today, George Washington writes the Continental Congress:

> *Our Powder is wasteing fast, notwithstanding the strictest care, economy, and attention is paid to it; the Long Series of wet weather we have had renders the greater part of what has been Served out to the men of no use . . .*[734]

Monday, November 27, 1775. Today, Abigail Adams writes her husband, John, of her anxiety over the idea of independence:

> *[I]f we separate from Britain, what Code of Laws will be established? How shall we be governed so as to retain our Liberties? Can any goverment be free which is not administered by general stated Laws? Who shall frame these Laws? Who will give them force and energy? . . . I feel anxious for the fate of our Monarchy or Democracy or what ever is to take place . . .*[735]

John Adams has decided not to consider any plan for state or national government this year. John Adams:

> *[I]t would have been most natural to have made a motion that Congress appoint a Committee to prepare a Plan of Government . . . but I dared not make such a Motion . . . I knew that every one of my friends, and all those who were most zealous for assuming Government, had at that time no Idea of any other Government but a Contemptible Legislature in one assembly, with Committees for Executive Magistrates and Judges . . .*[736]

Tuesday, November 28, 1775. Today, from his camp at Cambridge, George Washington writes the Continental Congress:

> *I am very Sorry to be necessitated to mention to you the egregious want of publick Spirit, which reigns here. Instead of pressing to be engaged in the Cause of their Country, which I vainly flattered myself would be the case, I find we are likely to be deserted . . .*
>
> *[T]here has been Nothing wanting on my part to infuse a proper Spirit amongst the Officers that they may exert their influence with the soldiery . . .*[737]

Today, George Washington writes his aide-de-camp, Joseph Reed:

> *The Connecticut Troops will not be prevail'd upon to stay longer . . .*
> *and such a dirty, mercenary Spirit pervades the whole, that I should*
> *not be at all surprised at any disaster that may happen . . . Could I*
> *have foreseen what I have & am likely to experience, no consideration*
> *upon Earth should have induced me to accept this Command . . .*
> *Powder is also so much wanted that nothing without it can be*
> *done . . .*[738]

Wednesday, November 29, 1775. Today, in the Continental Congress, the Journals report:

> *Resolved,* That a committee of five be appointed for the sole purpose of corresponding with our friends in Great Britain, Ireland, and other parts of the world . . .
> The members chosen, . . . [Five including] Dr. [Benjamin] Franklin, Mr. [John] Jay . . .[739]

This committee will be known as the Committee of Secret Correspondence!

Saturday, December 2, 1775. Today, in the Continental Congress, the Journals report:

> *Resolved,* That what artillery of different kinds can be spared from New York and Crown Point, be procured and forwarded to the army before Boston . . .[740]

Monday, December 4, 1775. Today, George Washington writes the Continental Congress:

> *The great want of powder is what the Attention of Congress Should*
> *be particularly applied to. I dare not attempt any thing Offensive, let*
> *the temptation or advantage be ever So great, as I have not more of*
> *that most essential article than will be absolutely necessary to defend*
> *our Lines Should the enemy Attempt to attack them . . .*[741]

Ben Franklin:

> *When I was at the Camp before Boston, the Army had not 5 rounds*
> *of Powder a Man. This was kept a Secret even from our People. The*
> *World wonder'd that we so seldom fir'd a Cannon. We could not afford*
> *it.*[742]

Saturday, December 9, 1775. Today, Ben Franklin is writing friends in Europe to inquire about foreign assistance.[743] Excerpts from his letter to Charles Dumas in The Hague, Netherlands:

> *[W]e wish to know whether, if as it seems likely to happen, we*
> *should be obliged to break off all connection with Britain, and declare*

ourselves an independent people, there is any state or power in Europe, who would be willing to enter into an alliance with us . . .

[T]he committee of congress, appointed for the purpose of establishing and conducting a correspondence with our friends in Europe, of which committee I have the honour to be a member, have directed me to request of you, that as you are situated at the Hague, where ambassadors from all the courts reside, you would make use of the opportunity that situation affords you, of discovering, if possible, the disposition of the several courts with respect to such assistance or alliance . . .

We have hitherto applied to no foreign power . . .

[B]oth arms and ammunition are much wanted . . .[744]

Thursday, December 14, 1775. Pierre Penet and Emanuel Pliarne, two private arms merchants from France, are visiting George Washington's camp on the Harvard campus with a proposal to sell arms and ammunition. Regrettably, they cannot, as private merchants, provide the quantity of arms and ammunition that America needs to fight a war with a major European power.[745] Today, George Washington writes the Continental Congress of their arrival:

The Two french Gentlemen who will appear before you with this, brought recommendations to me from Governor Cooke of Providence, their names are, Messieurs Pennet and De Pliarne.

They propose a plan for supplying this Continent with Arms and Ammunition . . . I have declined entering into any engagements with them, but have prevailed with them . . . to lay their proposals before Congress or a Committee of Congress . . .[746]

Today, Richard Smith, a Massachusetts delegate, writes in his diary:

[American General Benedict] Arnold is near Quebec but has not Men enough to surround it & his Powder so damaged that he has only 5 Rounds apiece . . . Gen. Washn in great Want of Powder & most of the Connectt. Troops have left his Army.[747]

Friday, December 22, 1775. Today, the Continental Congress tries to prod George Washington into action. The Journals report:

Resolved, That if General Washington and his council of war should be of opinion, that a successful attack may be made on the troops in Boston, he do it in any manner he may think expedient, notwithstanding the town and the property in it may be destroyed.[748]

Saturday, December 23, 1775. Today, in the Continental Congress, the Journals report:

Report of the Committee [of the Continental Congress] directed to repair to Ticonderoga . . .

Your Committee have directed the immediate Transportation of the

Cannon from St. Johns and Ticonderoga, which are not wanted for the defence of those places, and the boats on lake George are now employed in bringing over those that lay at the landing. it being impracticable to move the rest til there is enough snow to admitt of their being Carried on Slays. Mr. Knox is gone to Ticonderoga to Chuse such Cannon as will be wanted at Cambridge.[749]

Monday, December 25, 1775. Today, George Washington writes,

Nothing new has happened in this Quarter . . . except the setting in of a severe spell of cold Weather & considerable fall of Snow . . .
Our want of Powder is inconceivable. A daily waste & no Supply administers a gloomy prospect . . .[750]

Thursday, December 28, 1775. While French arms dealers Penet and Pliarne were visiting George Washington, yet another Frenchman—this one a secret agent of the French government—has been meeting clandestinely with Benjamin Franklin. Today, Achard de Bonvouloir, that secret French government agent, prepares his report to the French Ministry of Foreign Affairs:

I am going to tell you word for word . . . conversations I had with Mr. Franklin and 3 other good men who compose the Privy Council. I entered into their intimacy as a private individual through the channel of an honest Frenchman . . . He is city Librarian [for Mr. Franklin's Library Company of Philadelphia] . . .
I made no offer to them . . . They asked whether France would aid them and at what cost . . . Each comes by dusk by different routes to a marked place . . .
1st. Their affairs are in good state and of this I am sure, having emissaries in more than one place and whom I pay for information . . .
They are persuaded that they cannot maintain themselves without a nation to protect them from the sea, that only two powers are in a position to help them: France and Spain . . .
Everyone here is a soldier. The troops are well clothed, well paid, and well commanded. They have about 50,000 men hired and a greater number of volunteers who do not wish to be paid. Judge how men of this character fight . . .
I know everything of the greatest secrecy that takes place . . . I can reveal to you all their deliberations, as I know them all, but actually they consist of the means of procuring munitions . . .
They have all said they are fighting to become free, that they are linked by oath and that they will cut each other up rather than yield, that they know well that they cannot maintain themselves at sea and that only France is in condition to protect their commerce without which their country cannot flourish, that they are ignorant whether . . . France would be willing to have for awhile exclusive trade with them to pay back the costs that their cause will occasion . . .

The news is that two French officers arrived at camp with proposals to make. They asked me what I thought about it. I replied I knew nothing about it . . .

[They asked could they] have directly from France arms and other provisions of war in exchange for produce from their country and . . . be given free entrance and exit through the French ports? . . .

I replied I do not know whether you would be given free entrance and egress in the French ports. That would mean declaring openly for you and war would follow. Perhaps they could close their eyes, that's what you need. I repeat Gentlemen I can say nothing. I amount to nothing; I have good friends, that's all . . .[751]

Fifty thousand men hired? Well clothed?

Saturday, December 30, 1775. Penet and Pliarne, the two private French arms merchants who visited Washington's camp, have come to Philadelphia with an introduction from Washington. Today, in the Continental Congress, the Journals report:

A letter from general Washington, dated 14th December, being delivered by two strangers was read.

Resolved, That the same be referred to the Secret Committee who are directed to confer with the bearers, and pursue such measures as they may think proper for the interest of the United Colonies.[752]

Today, in Paris, French Naval Minister Antoine Sartine writes French Foreign Minister, the Comte de (i.e., the Count of) Vergennes:

I hasten to inform you that I have just renewed in Marseille the most precise orders as to forbid the loading of arms and war ammunition destined for Northern America either on English vessels or on vessels of any other nation in accordance with his Majesty's decision which you have conveyed to me, Sir [Etc.][753]

Sunday, December 31, 1775. Today, in the first battle since George Washington became commander in chief, an American army that Washington ordered into Canada[754] suffers an agonizing defeat at Quebec. Colonel Benedict Arnold reports to Washington:

I have no Doubt you will soon hear of Our Misfortune on the 31. Ulto . . . Our loss and repulse [at Quebec] struck an Amaseing Panick into both Officers & Men, and had the Enemy improved their Advantage, our affairs here must have been Intirely ruined. It was not in my power to Prevail on the Officers to Attempt saveing Our Mortars . . . [T]hey fell into the hands of the Enemy.—Upwards of One Hundred Officers and Soldiers Instantly set off for Montreal, and it was with the greatest difficulty I persuade the rest to make a stand . . . Inclosed is a List of the killed and Wounded . . . and had the Genl [Montgomery] not been basely deserted by his Troops, we should doubtless have carried the Town . . .[755]

WEDNESDAY, JANUARY 3, 1776

⇨ The Pennsylvania Gazette ⇦

Published by order of the
[PENNSYLVANIA] COMMITTEE OF SAFETY. The Committee [of Safety] need not remark to any intelligent and sensible man in the province the indispensable necessity there is of instantly providing ourselves with large quantities of Gun-powder—when the quarrel between the Mother Country and the Colonies is drawing to a hasty decision by arms, when the ministry threatens to overwhelm us the ensuing year with numerous mercenary soldiers brought even from the most distant and barbarous nation in Europe—at a time too when, from the wicked vigilance and industry of this ministry, every court in Europe has been solicited and prevailed on so far to aid their designs against our liberties as to refuse selling us either arms or ammunition . . .

Thursday, January 4, 1776. Today, George Washington responds to congressional exhortations that he attack Boston:

The resolution relative to the Troops in Boston, I beg the favour of you, Sir, to assure Congress, shall be attempted to be put in execution the first moment I see a probability of success . . . but if this should not happen as soon as you may expect or my wishes prompt to, I request that Congress . . . do me the justice to believe that circumstances & not want of inclination are the cause of delay.[756]

WEDNESDAY, JANUARY 10, 1776

⇨ The Pennsylvania Gazette ⇦

THIS DAY IS PUBLISHED, and now selling, by ROBERT BELL, in Third-street, PRICE TWO SHILLINGS, COMMON SENSE, addressed to the Inhabitants of AMERICA, on the following interesting Subjects. I. Of the Origin and Design of Government in general. 2. Of Monarchy and Hereditary Succession. 3. Thoughts on the present State of American Affairs. On the present Ability of America, with some miscellaneous Reflections.

> *Man knows no Master save creating HEAVEN,*
> *Or those whom choice and common good ordain.*
>
> *THOMSON.*

Today, under the pseudonym "Common Sense," Tom Paine publishes what will be the best-selling pamphlet ever written in the English language.[757] Tom Paine:

In October, 1775, Dr. Franklin proposed giving me such materials as were in his hands towards completing a history of the present transactions [with the British] and seemed desirous of having the first volume out the next Spring. I had then formed the outlines of "Common Sense" and finished nearly the first part; and as I supposed the doctor's design in getting out a history was to open the new year with a new system, I expected to surprise him with a production on that subject, much earlier than he thought of; and without informing him what I was doing, [I] got it ready for the press as fast as I conveniently could and sent him the first pamphlet that was printed off.[758]

This pamphlet will persuade the American colonies to choose independence. Three years from now, Tom Paine will recall:

I think the importance of that pamphlet was such that if it had not appeared, and at the exact time it did, the Congress would not now be sitting where they are [representing independent states]. The light with which that performance threw upon the subject gave a turn to the politics of America which enabled her to stand her ground. Independence followed in six months after it, although, before it was published, it was a dangerous doctrine to speak of . . .

In order to accommodate that pamphlet to every man's purchase and to do honor to the cause, I gave up the profits I was justly entitled to . . . I gave permission to the printers in other parts of this State [Pennsylvania] to print it on their own account. I believe the number of copies printed and sold in America was not short of 150,000—and is the greatest sale that any performance ever had since the use of letters . . .[759]

Tom Paine's *Common Sense* refocuses the American complaint with Great Britain and sets America's sights on a new ideal. It does not protest Britain's import/export restrictions, "external" or "internal" taxes, customs inspections, admiralty courts, land grants, settlement restrictions, or other impositions on propertied men like Adams, Hancock, and Washington. It does not argue for the well-ordered liberty of the British subject (within a hierarchy of king, lords, and commoners) or for the greater exercise of monarchical authority to curb the abuses of the British Parliament.

Common Sense attacks the fundamental structure of British governance, the British constitution itself, condemning monarchy, nobility, hereditary succession, class privilege, royal prerogative, and feudal servitude. It urges freedom from Britain (independence) not to obtain the "ordered liberty" of English subjects under a king and titled aristocracy, nor to obtain freedom from mercantilist restrictions, freedom of property, freedom of trade, or freedom of enterprise (which America's affluent particularly desire). Tom Paine urges freedom from Britain to secure an American democracy, to achieve political freedom and equality for every citizen. Freedom from Britain (independence), freedom of trade or property (free enterprise), the freedom of English subjects ("ordered liberty"), and the freedom of democracy (equality) are different "freedoms," and *Common Sense* urges democratic freedom as the basis for an American Revolution.

As Tom Paine turns America's discussion from property rights to democratic rights, from British rights to equal rights, every American—not especially the merchant, propertied, or upper class—becomes a stakeholder.[760] From *Common Sense*:

> *I know it is difficult to get over local or long standing prejudices, yet if we will suffer ourselves to examine the component parts of the English Constitution, we shall find them to be the base remains of two ancient tyrannies, compounded with some new Republican [popular] materials.*
>
> *First.—The remains of monarchical tyranny in the person of the king.*
>
> *Secondly.—The remains of aristocratical tyranny in the persons of the peers [House of Lords].*
>
> *Thirdly.—The new Republican [popular] materials, in the persons of the [House of] Commons, on whose virtue depends the freedom of England.*
>
> *The two first, by being hereditary, are independent of the people; wherefore in a constitutional sense they contribute nothing toward the freedom of the state . . .*
>
> *Mankind being originally equals in the order of creation, the equality could only be destroyed by some subsequent [improper] circumstance.*
>
> *To say that the Constitution of England is a union of three powers, reciprocally checking each other is farcical . . .*
>
> *As the exalting one man [the king] so greatly above the rest cannot be justified on the equal rights of nature, so neither can it be defended on the authority of scripture; for the will of the Almighty, as declared by Gideon and the prophet Samuel, expressly disapproves of government by kings . . .*
>
> *To the evil of monarchy we have added that of hereditary succession; and, as the first is a degradation and lessening of ourselves, so the second claimed as a matter of right is an insult and imposition on posterity. For all men being originally equals, no one by birth could have a right to set up his own family in perpetual preference to all others for ever . . .*
>
> *For 'tis the republican and not the monarchical part of the Constitution of England which Englishmen glory in, viz. the liberty of choosing an House of Commons from out of their body . . .*
>
> *Where there are no distinctions, there can be no superiority; perfect equality affords no temptation . . .*[761]

If America is to choose democracy (as opposed to monarchy or aristocracy), how should America structure its state and national governments? Tom Paine's idea of government is simple and very democratic:

> If there is any true cause of fear respecting independence, it is because no plan [of government] is yet laid out. Men do not see their way out. Wherefore, as an opening into that business, I offer the following . . .
>
> Let the assemblies [in each colony] be annual, with a president [of the assembly] only. The representation more equal, wholly domestic, and subject to the authority of a [Federal] Continental Congress.
>
> Let each colony be divided into six, eight, or ten convenient districts, each district to send a proper number of delegates to [a Continental] Congress, so that each colony send at least thirty. The whole number of Congress will be at least 390. Each Congress to sit and choose a President by the following method. When the delegates are met, let a colony be taken from the whole thirteen colonies by lot, after which let the Congress choose (by ballot) a President from out of the delegates of that province. In the next Congress, let a colony be taken by lot from twelve only [&c.] . . .
>
> Always remembering, that our strength is continental, not provincial. Securing freedom and property to all men, and above all things the free exercise of religion, according to the dictates of conscience . . .
>
> But where, say some, is the king of America? I'll tell you, friend, he reigns above and doth not make havoc of mankind like the royal brute of Great Britain . . . For as in absolute governments the king is law, so in free countries, the law is king; and there ought to be no other . . .
>
> A government of our own is our natural right . . .[762]

Ben Franklin had a considerable share in *Common Sense*—in motivating Tom Paine to write it and in furnishing materials.[763] He received the first copy.[764] *Common Sense* advocates the same structure of democratic government that Ben Franklin favors, i.e., a single-chamber legislature tied to the broadest possible suffrage, an executive chosen from and completely dependent upon that legislature, equal representation of citizens regardless of property ownership, representation of states in direct proportion to their populations, small congressional districts and yearly elections to keep delegates known by and constantly accountable to their local constituencies.

John Adams objects:

> In the course of this winter appeared a Phenomenon in Philadelphia a Star of Disaster, [a] Disastrous Meteor, I mean Thomas Paine. He came from England, and got into such company as would converse with him, and ran about picking up what Information he could concerning our affairs, and finding the great question was concerning Independence, he gleaned from those he saw the common-place arguments, such as the necessity of independence at some time or

other; the peculiar fitness at this time; the justice of it; the provocation to it, our ability to maintain it, &c. &c . . . In the latter part of the winter . . . he came out with his pamphlet . . .

The arguments in favor of independence I liked very well; but one third part of the Book was filled with Arguments from the old Testament to prove the Unlawfulness of Monarchy, and another third in planning a form of government for the separate states in one assembly and [a similar form of government] for the United States in a Congress. His Arguments [against monarchy] from the old Testament were ridiculous . . . The other third part relative to a form of Government I considered as flowing from simply Ignorance and a mere desire to please the democratic Party . . . I regretted to see so foolish a plan recommended to the People of the United States, who were all waiting only for the countenance of Congress to institute their State governments. I dreaded the effect so popular a pamphlet might have among the people and determined to do all in my power to counteract the effect of it. My continual Occupations in Congress allowed me no time to write any thing of any Length; but I found moments to write a small pamphlet . . . under the title of "Thoughts on Government, in a letter from a gentleman to his friend."[765]

Sunday, January 14, 1776. Today, George Washington writes the president of the Continental Congress:

I am exceedingly sorry that I am under the necessity of applying to you & calling the attention of Congress to the State of our Arms which is truly alarming . . . I gave it in orders that the Arms of such men as did not reinlist should be (or such of them as were good) retained . . . But Sir I find with much concern that from the badness of the Arms & the disobedience of too many in bearing them off without a previous inspection that very few were collected . . . I hope It is in the power of Congress to afford us relief; If it is not, what must, what can be done?[766]

Today, from Cambridge, Washington also writes his military secretary, Lieutenant Colonel Joseph Reed, who is in Philadelphia:

We are now without any Money in our treasury, Powder in our Magazines, Arms in Our Stores . . .

Our Inlistments are at a stand [still] . . .

[S]o many [arms] have been carried off, partly by stealth, but chiefly as condemn'd, that we have not at this time 100 Guns in the Stores . . .

How to get furnish'd I know not. I have applied to this and the Neighboring Colonies, but with what success time only can tell . . .

Few People know the Predicament we are In, on a thousand Accts;

fewer still will believe, if any disaster happens to these Lines, from what causes it flows . . .

Could I have forseen the difficulties which have come upon us— could I have known that such a backwardness would have been discoverd in the old Soldiers to the Service, all the Generals upon Earth should not have convinced me of the propriety of delaying an attack upon Boston till this time. When it can now be attempted I will not undertake to say . . .[767]

Monday, January 22, 1776. Since Ben Franklin left London for America, his former deputy, Arthur Lee, has been meeting with another French secret agent, Caron de Beaumarchais, who is also a famous playwright (*The Barber of Seville* and *The Marriage of Figaro*). Today, Beaumarchais submits a very personal and very secret proposal to the King of France:

To the King Only.

Sire.—When considerations of State impel you to extend a helping hand to the Americans, Policy requires that your Majesty proceed with such caution that aid secretly conveyed to America may not become in Europe a brand to kindle strife between France and England . . . Moreover, since the present state of finances does not at once permit of as great an expenditure as events seem to require, it is my duty, Sire, to submit to your judgment the following plan, having for its principal object, under the semblance of a purely commercial affair, to remove all suspicion that your Majesty or your Council are at all interested in the matter . . .

The unvarying impression . . . should be the delusion that your majesty has nothing to do with it, but that a Company is about to entrust a certain sum to the prudence of a trusted agent to furnish continuous aid to the Americans . . . in exchange for returns in the shape of tobacco. Secrecy is the essence of the rest . . .

Your Majesty will begin by placing one million at the disposal of your agent, who will style himself Roderique Hortalez and Company, this being the signature and title of the firm under which I have agreed to conduct the entire business . . .

[I]n procuring powder and in conveying it without delay to the Americans . . . the real device of the operation consist[s], as Roderique Hortalez hopes, in secretly procuring, with the sanction of your majesty, all necessary powder and saltpetre of your Registrars, on a basis of from four to six sols a pound . . .

[I]f the assets in tobacco and the sale of this return proceed as I have indicated, your Majesty can soon recommence, by the hand of Hortalez, the redistribution of the three millions arising from the sale and profit of these returns, and begin the operation anew on a larger scale . . .

Such is the scheme that I submit to your Majesty . . . In case your Majesty does not adopt it, I shall, at least, be credited with having

*again shown in your service a zeal as extended as my experience and
as active and pure as it is unalterable.*[768]

Today, American General Horatio Gates writes George Washington's second in
command, General Charles Lee:

> *There is a Pamphlet come by Irwin [General William Irvine] from
> Philadelphia, entitled "Common Sense"—it is an excellent perfor-
> mance—I think our friend Franklin has been principally concern'd in
> the Composition.*[769]

Thursday, January 25, 1776. At the direction of Congress, Colonel Henry
Knox has heroically hauled cannon and other artillery from Ticonderoga (captured well before George Washington became commander in chief) across the
winter wilderness to the outskirts of Boston. Today, John Adams writes,

> *[W]e rode to Framingham, where we dined. Colonel Buckminster,
> after Dinner, shewed us the Train of Artillery brought down from Ti-
> conderoga by Colonel Knox. It consists of Iron, 9 Eighteen Pounders,
> 10 Twelve, 6 Six, 4 Nine Pounders; three 13 inch mortars, Two Ten
> Inch Mortars; one Eight Inch and one six and an half howitz; and one
> eight inch and a half, and one eight. Brass Cannon. eight Three Pound-
> ers, one four pounder; 2 six pounders, one Eighteen Pounder, and one
> Twenty-four Pounder. One eight Inch and an half Mortar, one Seven
> Inch and a half dtto, and five Cohorns.*[770]

Friday, February 9, 1776. Today, George Washington writes the Continental
Congress:

> *I have tried every Method I could think of to procure Arms for our
> men. They realy are not to be had . . . [T]here are near 2000 men now
> in Camp without firelocks . . .*[771]

Saturday, February 10, 1776. Today, George Washington observes to his military secretary, Colonel Joseph Reed:

> *I know the unhappy predicament I stand in. I know that much is
> expected of me; I know that without Men, without Arms, without Am-
> munition, without any thing fit for the accommodation of a Soldier
> that little is to be done; and which is mortifying, I know, that I cannot
> stand justified to the World without exposing my own Weakness & in-
> juring the cause by declaring my wants . . . In short my Situation has
> been such that I have been oblig'd to use art to conceal it from my own
> Officers. The Congress, as you observe, expect, I believe, that I should
> do more . . .*[772]

Sunday, February 11, 1776. The lack of arms and ammunition remains critical. Spears are in limited use. Should bows and arrows be added? Today, Benjamin Franklin writes George Washington's second in command, General
Charles Lee:

We have got in a large Quantity of Saltpetre [to make gun powder] 120 Ton, and 30 more expected. Powdermills are now wanting. I believe we must set to work and make it by hand. But I still wish with you that Pikes could be introduc'd; and I would add Bows and Arrows. Those were good weapons, not wisely laid aside. 1. Because a Man may shoot as truly with a Bow as with a common Musket. 2. He can discharge 4 arrows in the time of charging and discharging one Bullet. 3. His Object is not taken from his View by the Smoke of his own Side. 4. A Flight of Arrows, seen coming upon them, terrifies and disturbs the Enemy's Attention to his Business. 5. An Arrow sticking in any Part of a Man puts him hors du Combat 'till 'tis extracted. 6. Bows and Arrows are more easily provided every where than Muskets and Ammunition.[773]

Sunday, February 18, 1776. Today, George Washington writes the Continental Congress:

The late freezing Weather having formed some pretty strong Ice . . . and consequently a less dangerous Approach to the Town, I could not help thinking, notwithstanding the Militia were not all come in, and we had little or no Powder to begin our Operation by a regular Cannonade and Bombardment, that a bold & resolute assault upon the Troops in Boston . . . might be crown'd with success; and therefore, seeing no certain prospect of a Supply of Powder . . . I called the General Officers together for their opinion . . .[774]

George Washington agrees with his generals not to attack Boston. Benny Bache will (as an adult) write:

As to holding the lines before Boston, Mr. Washington found his countrymen posted in them; and he has not much to boast in having suffered the enemy to continue in that city for eight months and an half, after he had the command in that quarter.[775]

Monday, February 26, 1776. Today, George Washington writes the Continental Congress:

We are making every necessary preparation for taking possession of Dorchester Heights as soon as possible with a view of drawing the Enemy out . . . I should think, If any thing will Induce them to hazard an engagement, It will be our attempting to fortifye these heights; as on that event's taking place, we shall be able to command a great part of the Town, and almost the whole harbour . . .

Within three or four days I have received sundry accounts from Boston of such [British] movements there, such as taking the Mortars from Bunker Hill, the putting them with several Pieces of Heavy Ordinance on board of Ship, with a quantity of Bedding, the Ships all taking in Water, the baking a large quantity of Biscuit, &c, as to Indicate an embarkation of the Troops from thence . . . [T]he Inhabitants of the Town generally believe that they are about to remove . . .[776]

Tuesday, February 27, 1776. Today, the French royal court at Versailles receives French spy Achard de Bonvouloir's report of his conversations with Benjamin Franklin at the end of December.[777]

Friday, March 8, 1776. Today, four Select Men of Boston memorialize discussions they've had with the British concerning the anticipated British evacuation of Boston:

> *As his Excellency [British] General Howe is determined to leave the Town with the Troops under his Command, a Number of the Respectable Inhabitants being very anxious for its preservation & Safety have Applyed to [British] General Robertson for this purpose, who at their request has communicated the same to his Excellency Genl. Howe, who has assured him that he has no intention of destroying the Town Unless the troops under his Command are molested during their Embarkation or at their departure by the Armed force without . . . If such an Opposition should take place, we have the greatest reason to expect the Town will be exposed to Intire destruction . . .*
>
> John Scollay, Timo. Newell,
> Thos Marshall, Samuel Austin[778]

George Washington will tacitly honor this agreement. The British army will depart Boston with all their arms and without a fight.

Tuesday, March 12, 1776. Today, in France, the French Minister for Foreign Affairs, the Comte de Vergennes, presents to King Louis XVI his thoughts on how to deal with Britain and the rebellious American colonies:

> *[I]t is problematic whether [France] should desire the subjection or the independence of the English colonies . . . [France is] threatened in either hypothesis with dangers it is not perhaps in the power of human foresight to anticipate or to avert . . .*
> *[T]he lively preference which the King . . . [has] for the preservation of peace seems to prescribe measured steps . . .*
> *1st. We must avoid compromising ourselves . . . 2nd. We must not flatter ourselves, nevertheless, that the most absolute and vigorous inaction will guarantee us from all suspicion . . . The English . . . will always believe that we are not allowing such a good opportunity of injuring them to escape . . . 3rd. the continuation of the war, at least for a year, appears desirable . . . because the English army, weakened by her victories or her defeats, will not be in a condition to undertake a vigorous enterprise [elsewhere, as against France] . . . 4th. the most assured means of attaining this end would be, on the one hand, to keep the English Ministry persuaded that the intentions of France . . . are pacific . . . whilst on the other hand, we should sustain the courage*

*of the Americans by some secret favours and by vague hopes that
would prevent the steps which it is sought to induce them to take for a
reconciliation and that would contribute to cause those ideas of independence to burst forth, which as yet are only secretly budding among
them . . .*

*[I]t would not accord with the King's dignity nor with his interests
to enter into a compact with the insurgents. That compact, indeed,
could only be of value if they became independent . . .*[779]

Sunday, March 17, 1776. Today, the British evacuate Boston, and George
Washington writes the Governor of Rhode Island:

*I have the pleasure to Inform you that this morning the Ministerial
Troops evacuated the Town of Boston without destroying It . . .*

*Where their destination is or what plans they have in view is alto-
gether unknown; most probably the next attempt will be against New
York or some more Southern Colony.*[780]

Tom Paine:

*[Washington] commenced his command in June, 1775, during the
time the Massachusetts army lay before Boston, and after the affair of
Bunker Hill. The commencement of his command was the commencement of inactivity. Nothing was afterwards done, or attempted to be
done, during the nine months before Boston.*

*If we may judge from the resistance at Concord and afterwards at
Bunker Hill, there was a spirit of enterprise at that time, which the
presence of Mr. Washington chilled into cold defense. By the advantage
of a good exterior he attracts respect, which his habitual silence tends
to preserve; but he has not the talent of inspiring ardor in an army.
The enemy removed from Boston in March, 1776, to wait for reinforcements and to take a more advantageous position at New York.*[781]

Tuesday, March 19, 1776. Today, John Adams writes his wife, Abigail, about
Tom Paine's plan for a government:

*You ask what is thought of "Common Sense." . . . All agree there is a
great deal of good sense delivered in clear, simple, concise, and nervous style . . . But his notions and plans of continental government are
not much applauded. Indeed, this writer has a better hand in pulling
down than building . . . I should have made a more respectable figure
as an architect if I had undertaken such a work. The writer seems to
have very inadequate ideas of what is proper and necessary to be
done in order to form constitutions for single colonies, as well as a
great model of union for the whole . . .*[782]

Monday, April 1, 1776. Today, George Washington writes his aide, Lieutenant
Colonel Joseph Reed,

My Countrymen I know, from their form of Government & steady Attachment heretofore to Royalty, will come reluctantly into the Idea of Independancy, but time and persecution bring many wonderful things to pass; & by private Letters which I have lately received from Virginia, I find Common Sense is working a powerful change there in the Minds of many Men.[783]

Saturday, April 6, 1776. Today, in a chilling premonition of the French Revolution, the French Comptroller General of Finance, Anne-Robert-Jacques Turgot, warns King Louis XVI that any protracted French involvement in a war to help America could preclude "relief of our people" and thereby threaten the state:

The state of our finances is not so desperate that if it were absolutely necessary to support a war, we could not find resources—if it were with a probability of such decisive successes as would shorten its duration. But, nevertheless, it must be admitted that we ought to avoid it as the greatest of misfortunes, because it would render impossible, for a long time, and perhaps forever, a reformation that is absolutely necessary for the prosperity of the state and the relief of our people. In making a premature use of our strength, we should run the risk of making permanent our weakness.[784]

Friday, April 12, 1776. Today, John Adams writes his former law clerk William Tudor:

You talk about Common Sense, and Say it has been attributed to me. But I am as innocent of it as a Babe . . .

I could never reach the Strength and Brevity of his style, nor his elegant Symplicity, nor his piercing Pathos. But I really think in other Respects, the Pamphlet would do no Honour even to me. The old Testament Reasoning against Monarchy would have never come from me. The Attempt to frame a Continental Constitution is feeble indeed. It is poor, and despicable . . .[785]

Monday, April 22, 1776. Today, in Philadelphia, an advertisement appears for John Adams' pamphlet *Thoughts on Government Applicable to the Present State of the American Colonies*. Adams' pamphlet directly responds to Tom Paine's *Common Sense*.[786] Adams warns:

I think a people cannot be long free, nor ever happy, whose government is in one Assembly. My reasons for this opinion are as follow. 1. A SINGLE Assembly is [s]ubject to fits of humour, starts of passion, flights of enthusiasm, partialities of prejudice . . . and all these errors ought to be corrected and defects supplied by some controuling power. 2. A SINGLE Assembly is apt to be avaricious . . . 3. A SINGLE Assembly is apt to grow ambitious . . . 4. A REPRESENTATIVE Assembly . . . is unfit to exercise the executive power for want of . . . secrecy and dispatch. 5. A REPRE-

SENTATIVE Assembly is still less qualified for the judicial power; because it is . . . too little skilled in the laws. 6. BECAUSE a single Assembly possessed of all the powers of government, would make arbitrary laws for their own interest, execute all laws arbitrarily for their own interest, and adjudge all controversies in their own favour . . .

[S]hall the whole power of legislation rest in one Assembly? Most of the foregoing reasons . . . prove that the legislative power ought to be more complex . . .

And this shews the necessity too, of giving the executive power a negative upon the legislative . . .[787]

John Adams' pamphlet, *Thoughts on Government . . .*, will powerfully influence the deliberations of various states on how to fashion state government. It will prove paramount in the decisions of five.[788] John Adams:

I was the first member of Congress who ventured to come out in public, as I did in my "Thoughts on Government, in a Letter from a Gentleman to his Friend" . . . in favor of a government in three branches . . . This pamphlet, you know, was very unpopular. No man appeared in public to support it but [Dr. Benjamin Rush] . . .

Franklin leaned against it . . . Mr. Thomas Paine was so highly offended with it that he came to visit me . . .[789]

Paine, soon after the Appearance of my Pamphlet, hurried away to my Lodgings and spent an Evening with me. His Business was to reprehend me for publishing my Pamphlet. Said he was afraid it would do hurt, and that it was repugnant to the plan he had proposed in his Common Sense. I told him it was true it was repugnant, and for that reason I had written it and consented to the publication of it; for I was afraid of his Work [as] he was of mine. His plan [for government by a single-chamber, popularly elected, proportionately representative legislature] was so democratical, without any restraints or even an Attempt at any Equilibrium or Counterpoise, that it must produce confusion and every Evil Work. I told him further that his Reasoning [against monarchy] from the Old Testament was ridiculous . . . I perceived in him a conceit of himself and a daring Impudence which have developed more and more to this day.

The . . . part of Common Sense which relates wholly to the question of independence, was clearly written . . . Phrases . . . such as "The Royal Brute of England," "The Blood upon his Soul," and a few others . . . had as much Weight with the People as his Arguments. It has been a general Opinion that this pamphlet was of great Importance in the Revolution.[790]

Tom Paine:

I have had doubts of John Adams ever since the year 1776. In a conversation with me at that time, concerning the pamphlet "Common

Sense," he censured it because it attacked the English form of govern-ment. John was for independence, because he expected to be made great by it; but it was not difficult to perceive, for the surliness of his temper makes him an awkward hypocrite, that his head was as full of kings, queens, and knaves as a pack of cards.[791]

Saturday, May 4, 1776. Today, an abridged edition of Tom Paine's *Common Sense* is published in France.[792] Ironically, Edmé Jacques Genêt, editor of the French periodical *Affaires de L'Angleterre et de L'Amérique*, will associate the name Adams with *Common Sense* by attributing the pamphlet's authorship to Massachusetts legislator Samuel Adams (John Adams' cousin).[793] John Adams:

> *What a poor ignorant, Malicious, short-sighted, Crapulous Mass, is Tom Pains Common Sense . . .*[794]

Thursday, May 9, 1776. Today, a report from the Massachusetts General Court (legislature) to the Massachusetts delegates at the Continental Congress:

> Inclosed you have an Account of Powder . . . we not having at present in our Colonial Magazine so much as a single Barrel: 'tis true Salt petre is manufacturing in most of our Towns with good Success but we have only one of our Powder Mills yet at work. [T]he others we hope will be ready soon . . .[795]

Friday, May 10, 1776. Today, in the Continental Congress, the Journals report:

> The Congress then resumed the consideration of the report from the committee of the whole, which being read, was agreed to as follows:
> *Resolved,* That it be recommended to the respective assemblies and conventions of the United Colonies, where no government sufficient to the exigencies of their affairs have been hitherto established, to adopt such government as shall, in the opinion of the representatives of the people, best conduce to the happiness and safety of their constituents in particular, and America in general.[796]

Sunday, May 12, 1776. Today, John Adams writes his friend Massachusetts political leader James Warren:

> *Common Sense [Tom Paine], by his crude, ignorant Notions of a Government by one Assembly, will do more Mischief in dividing the Friends of Liberty than all the Tory Writings together. He is a keen Writer but very ignorant of the Science of Government.*[797]

Today, in France, King Louis XVI dismisses Comptroller General of Finance Anne-Robert-Jacques Turgot, who has warned that France cannot afford a pro-tracted involvement in America's War of Independence. The king won't support Turgot's financial reforms and won't heed his warnings about America.[798] In leaving his post, Turgot writes the King of France:

All I wish, Sire, is that you may always believe my vision was wrong and the dangers I pointed out to you were chimerical.[799]

Wednesday, May 15, 1776. Today, in the Continental Congress, the Journals report:

> The Congress took into consideration the draft of the preamble [by Mr. Adams] brought in by the committee, which was agreed to . . .
> *Ordered.* That the said preamble, with the resolution passed the 10th instant, be published.[800]

John Adams:

> *In the beginning of May, I procured the appointment of a committee to prepare a resolution recommending to the people of the States to institute governments . . . [I]t passed the 15th inst. It was indeed, on all hands, considered by men of understanding as equivalent to a declaration of independence . . .*[801]

WEDNESDAY, MAY 22, 1776

→ 𝕿𝖍𝖊 𝕻𝖊𝖓𝖓𝖘𝖞𝖑𝖛𝖆𝖓𝖎𝖆 𝕲𝖆𝖟𝖊𝖙𝖙𝖊 ←

> *The PROTEST of divers of the inhabitants of this province,*
> *in behalf of themselves and others.*
> *To the Honourable the REPRESENTATIVES*
> *of the province of PENNSYLVANIA.*
> GENTLEMAN, WE, the inhabitants of the City and Liberties of Philadelphia, in behalf of ourselves and others, the inhabitants of Pennsylvania, conceive it our duty to represent unto this House as followeth:
> That whereas the Hon. Continental Congress hath by a resolve, bearing the date the 15th instant, recommended the taking up and establishing new governments throughout all the United Colonies, under the "AUTHORITY of the PEOPLE," and as the chartered power of this House is derived from our mortal enemy the King of Great-Britain . . . — We therefore, in this solemn manner, in behalf of ourselves and others, do hereby renounce and protest against the authority and qualification of the House for framing a new government.

The royal charters of colonial government no longer hold legitimacy. Pennsylvania, Massachusetts, and other newly independent American nation-states have to create their own constitutions to express their various conceptions of self-government.

Monday, June 10, 1776. Today, in the Continental Congress, the Journals report:

> *Resolved,* . . . that no time be lost . . . that a committee be appointed to prepare a declaration to the effect of the said first resolution, "That

these United Colonies are, and of right ought to be, free and independent states" . . .[802]

Tuesday, June 11, 1776. Today, in the Continental Congress, the Journals report:

> *Resolved,* That the Committee to prepare the declaration consist of five members:
>
> The members chosen, Mr. [Thomas] Jefferson, Mr.[John] Adams, Mr. [Benjamin] Franklin, Mr. [Roger] Sherman, and Mr. [Robert] Livingston.
>
> *Resolved,* That a committee be appointed to prepare a plan of treaties to be proposed to foreign powers.[803]

John Adams:

> *Not long after [my resolution for the states to institute their own governments], three greatest measures of all were carried. Three committees were appointed, one for preparing a declaration of independence, another for reporting a plan of a treaty to be proposed to France, and a third to digest a system of articles of confederation to be proposed to the States . . . The committee of independence were Thomas Jefferson, John Adams, Benjamin Franklin, Roger Sherman, and Robert R. Livingston. Mr. Jefferson had been now about a year a member of Congress, but had attended his duty in the house a very small part of the time, and when there, had never spoken in public. During the whole time I sat with him in Congress, I never heard him utter three sentences together. It will naturally be inquired how it happened that he was appointed on a committee of such importance . . . Mr. Jefferson had the reputation of a masterly pen; he had been chosen a delegate in Virginia in consequence of a very handsome public paper which he had written in the House of Burgesses, which had given him the character of a fine writer . . .*[804]

Wednesday, June 12, 1776. Today, in the Continental Congress, the Journals report:

> *Resolved,* That the committee to prepare a plan of treaties to be proposed to foreign powers consist of five members.
>
> The members chosen, . . . Mr. [Benjamin] Franklin . . . Mr. [John] Adams [and three others] . . . [805]

Wednesday, June 19, 1776. Today, congressional delegate Thomas Jefferson of Virginia delivers his first draft (with his own edits) of the Declaration of Independence for John Adams to review, including:

> *We hold these truths to be* ~~sacred & undeniable~~ *self evident; that all men are created equal & independent, that from that equal creation they derive rights inherent and inalienable . . .*[806]

Jefferson's draft appears to reject Divine Right (which has historically been used to justify monarchy) as the determinant of human rights and to use the laws of natural creation as the basis for equal rights.

Friday, June 21, 1776. Today, after incorporating John Adams' suggestions, Thomas Jefferson delivers a revised draft of the Declaration of Independence for Benjamin Franklin to review, including:

> *We hold these truths to be ~~sacred & undeniable~~ self-evident, that all men are created equal & independent, that ~~from that equal creation they derive rights~~ they are endowed by their creator with inherent & inalienable rights . . .*[807]

This draft, which follows Adams' review, restores Divine Right as the source of human rights!

Thursday, July 4, 1776. Today, the Continental Congress of the United States issues a Declaration of Independence, including,

> *We hold these truths to be self evident; that all men are created equal; that they are endowed by their Creator with certain inalienable rights . . . that to secure these rights, governments are instituted among men, deriving their just powers from the consent of the governed, that whenever any form of government becomes destructive of these ends, it is the right of the people to alter or abolish it, and to institute new government . . .*
>
> *We therefore the Representatives of the United States of America, in Congress assembled . . . publish and declare that these United colonies are & of right ought to be free and independent states . . .*[808]

John Adams will recollect to Benjamin Rush (a congressional delegate from Pennsylvania):

> *Do you recollect the pensive and awful silence which pervaded the house when we were called up, one after the other, to the table of the President of Congress to subscribe what was believed by many at that time to be our own death warrants? The silence and the gloom of the morning were interrupted, I well recollect, only for a moment by Colonel Harrison of Virginia, who said to Mr. Gerry [of Massachusetts] at the table: "I shall have a great advantage over you, Mr. Gerry, when we are all hung for what we are now doing. From the size and weight of my body I shall die in a few minutes, but from the lightness of your body, you will dance in the air for an hour or two before you are dead." The speech procured a transient smile, but it was soon succeeded by the solemnity with which the whole business was conducted.*[809]

Monday, July 15, 1776. Today, in the West Room of the Pennsylvania State-house at Philadelphia, a constitutional convention begins work on a Pennsylvania state constitution.[810]

Tuesday, July 16, 1776. Today, the Pennsylvania constitutional convention chooses Ben Franklin to preside as President. Tom Paine:

> *They had the wisest and ablest man in the State, Dr. Franklin, for their President, whose judgment alone was sufficient to form a constitution, and whose benevolence of heart would never concur in a bad one.*[811]

Ben Franklin supports Tom Paine's vision of democratic government, that is, government by a single-chamber legislature, elected annually by the widest possible suffrage.[812]

Tuesday, July 30, 1776. Today, in the Continental Congress, Ben Franklin speaks on proposals to create a confederation of America's new nation-states. The issue is whether a confederated congress should distribute voting power to each state equally, to each state according to wealth, or to each state according to population. John Adams took notes:

> Article 17. "In determining questions, each Colony shall have one vote." . . .
> *Dr. Franklin* moves that votes should be in proportion to [population] numbers. *Mr. Middleton* moves that the vote should be according to what they pay.[813]

As president of the convention that is currently designing a very democratic constitution for the state of Pennsylvania, Ben Franklin asks the American Continental Congress that its proposed Articles of Confederation reflect the sovereignty and equality of the people:

> *[T]he XVIIth Article, which gives one Vote to the smallest State and no more to the largest when the Difference between them may be as 10 to 1 or greater is unjust and injurious to the larger States . . .*
> *[T]he Practice hitherto in Congress of allowing only one Vote to each Colony was originally taken up under a Conviction of its Impropriety and Injustice, was intended to be in some future time corrected, and was then and since submitted to only as a temporary expedient . . . This clearly appears by the Resolve of Congress dated Sept. 6, 1774, . . . "That in determining Questions in this Congress, each colony or Province shall have one vote: the Congress not being possessed of or at present able to procure proper Materials for ascertaining the importance of each Colony."*
> *That importance has since been suppos'd to be best found in the Numbers of People . . .*[814]

Franklin believes that each American, not each state, should have equal representation in a national congress. Allowing one vote for each state (without adjusting for differences in population) gives the citizen of a less populous state greater representation (and political power!) than the citizen of a more populous state. That's not "equality," at least not as Tom Paine and Ben Franklin use the term.

Wednesday, July 31, 1776. Today, the British Minister to France David Murray (Lord Stormont) reports to British Secretary of State Lord Weymouth that France won't be sending arms to America:

> *Besides the desire that this Court [of France] naturally have to protract the American War till it waste our Strength and Treasure, which desire must make them averse to anything that tends to damp the Hopes of the Rebels, they think My Lord that France is a Gainer by the Trade she is beginning to carry on with America . . . Opinion in the French Cabinet is that they should give us friendly Professions, but should avoid any step that can tend to discourage the Rebels . . . I have been informed too . . . that they would not suffer the Rebels to be supplied with Ammunition . . .*[815]

Friday, August 2, 1776. Today, under the presidency of Benjamin Franklin, the Pennsylvania constitutional convention decides that *"the future legislature of the state shall consist of one branch only . . . ,"* meaning a state assembly but no state senate.[816]

Saturday, August 3, 1776. Today, in France, private French arms supplier Pierre Penet writes Benjamin Franklin of his difficulties in shipping arms to the colonies:

> *We are forced Sir to acquaint you that all the Houses you have in Spain and Portugal . . . make no remittances to [our company in] Nantes, we have now in our stores Goods ready to send you to the amount of Forty thousand Guineas, but two of your Ships have arrived here from Cadiz in Ballast [with nothing on board to trade] one is Hancock and the other the Adams . . . [W]e shall immediately dispatch this Vessell with a Cargo of Ammunition provided however we can obtain from Manufacturers the credit we require, and we beg you will send us remittances by the first opportunity . . .*[817]

Monday, August 12, 1776. Today, at his home in Franklin Court, where America's war leaders continue to visit with his grandfather, Benny Bache turns seven years old.

Wednesday, August 14, 1776. Today, Abigail Adams warns her husband that Massachusetts has delayed the creation of a new state government and that some prefer government by a one-chamber legislature:

> *Mr. Smith [from South Carolina] call'd upon me today and . . . gave us [an account] of the universal joy of his province upon the Establishment of their New Government . . . This State [Massachusetts]*

seems to be behind hand of their Neighbors. We want some Master workmen here. Those who are capable seem backward in this work and some who are so tenacious of their perticuliar plan as to be loathe to give it up. Some who are for abolishing both House and Counsel, affirming Business was never so well done as in provincial Congress . . .[818]

Thursday, August 15, 1776. Tom Paine's vision of democratic government is enjoying great readership in France. Today, in Paris, congressional emissary Silas Deane writes:

The pamphlet called Common Sense has been translated, and has a greater run, if possible, here than in America. A person of distinction writing to a noble friend in office has these words; [transl.] "I think as you, my dear Count, that Common Sense is an excellent work, and that its author is, of the millions of writers that we know, one of the greatest legislators; isn't it marvellous that, if the Americans follow the beautiful plan their compatriot has laid out for them, they will become the most flourishing and happiest people who ever existed."

Thus freely do men think and write in a country long deprived of the essentials of liberty; as I was favored with a sight of the letter and permitted to take this extract, I thought it worth sending you as a key to the sentiments of some of the leading men.[819]

Friday, August 16, 1776. Today, John Adams laments:

The Convention of Pennsilvania has voted for a single Assembly . . . [W]hat surprises me not a little is that the American Philosopher [Benjam′ · ′ranklin] should . . . be a zealous Advocate for it.[820]

Sunday, August 18, 1776. Today, congressional emissary Silas Deane writes from Paris:

I went to Versailles, and [French Foreign Minister Count de Vergennes] . . . gave us immediate admission . . . I pursued nearly the line marked out by my instructions . . .

To which he replied . . . That . . . the court had ordered their ports to be kept open and equally free to America as to Britain. That, considering the good understanding between the two courts of Versailles and London, they could not openly encourage the shipping of warlike supplies . . .

I went to Versailles [again yesterday] . . . and waited on M. Gerard, first secretary of foreign affairs . . . from whom I had . . . assurances . . . that, in one word, I might rely on whatever Mons. Beaumarchais should engage in the commercial way of supplies . . .[821]

Today, in the name of the company he has formed to conceal the French government's arms shipments to America, French secret agent Caron de Beaumarchais writes the Continental Congress:

The respectful esteem I bear . . . has induced me to form . . . an extensive commercial house solely for the purpose of serving you in Europe, there to supply you with the necessaries of every sort, to furnish you expeditiously and certainly with . . . powder, ammunition, muskets, cannon, or even gold for the payment of your troops . . .

RODERIQUE HORTALEZ & CO.[822]

WEDNESDAY, AUGUST 21, 1776

✦ The Pennsylvania Gazette ✦

We hear that the following is a Copy of the Declaration of Rights passed by the Convention of this State.
A DECLARATION OF THE RIGHTS OF THE INHABITANTS OF THE STATE OF PENNSYLVANIA.
1. THAT all men are born equally free and independent, and have certain natural inherent and unalienable rights, amongst which are the enjoying and defending life and property . . .
2. That all men have a natural and unalienable right to worship Almighty God according to the dictates of their own consciences . . .
7. That all elections ought to be free, and all freemen having a sufficient evident common interest with, and attachment to the community, have a right to elect officers or be elected into office . . .
12. That the people have a right to freedom of speech and of writing and publishing their sentiments . . .
16. That the people have a right to assemble together . . .

With Ben Franklin as its president, the constitutional convention of Pennsylvania is writing America's most democratic state constitution.

Tuesday, August 27, 1776. At eight o'clock tonight, under instructions from George Washington, his secretary, Robert Harrison, makes a report to the Continental Congress on the battle for Long Island:

> *I this minute returned from our Lines on Long Island where . . .*
> *from the Enemy's having landed a considerable part of their Forces and many of their Movements, there was reason to apprehend they would make in a little time a Genl Attack. As they would have a Wood to pass through before they could approach the Lines, It was thought expedient to place a number of Men there on the different Roads leading from whence they were stationed . . . This being done, early this Morning a Smart engagement ensued between the Enemy and our Detachments, which being unequal to the force they had to contend with, have sustained a pretty considerable loss. At least many of our Men are missing, among those who have not returned, are Genls Sullivan and Lord Stirling . . .*
> *While These Detachments were engaged, a Column of the Enemy de-*

*scended from the Woods and marched towards the Center of our Lines
. . . Today Five Ships of the Line came up towards the Town . . .*[823]

Thursday, August 29, 1776. This afternoon, at half past four, George Washington writes the Continental Congress of his disastrous defeat on Long Island:

> *I am sorry to inform Congress that . . . I [cannot] ascertain our Loss, I am hopefull part of our Men will yet get in . . .*
> *The Weather of late has been extremely wet . . . which has occasioned much sickness and the Men to be almost broke down . . .*[824]

Today, John Adams writes his former law clerk William Tudor:

> *[C]oncerning the late Skirmishes, upon Long Island . . . I think We have Suffered in our Reputation for Generalship, in permitting the Enemy to Steal a March upon Us . . . Our Officers don't seem Sufficiently Sensible . . . that Stratagem, Ambuscade, and Ambush are the Sublimest Chapter in the Art of War . . .*
> *Have We not put too much to the Hazard in sending the greatest Part of the Army over to Long island from whence there is no Retreat?*[825]

Saturday, August 31, 1776. Today, George Washington issues General Orders for a retreat from Long Island to New York City:

> *Both officers and soldiers are informed that the Retreat from Long Island was made by the unanimous advice of all the General Officers . . . [I]t was thought unsafe to transport the whole of [the] Army on[to] an Island, or to engage [the enemy] with a part and therefore unequal numbers; whereas now [our] whole Army is collected together without Water intervening, while the enemy can receive little assistance from their ships; their Army is and must be divided into many bodies . . . whereas ours is connected and can act together. They must affect a landing under so many disadvantages that, if officers and soldiers are vigilant and alert to prevent surprise and add spirit when they approach, there is no doubt of our success.*[826]

George Washington also writes the Continental Congress:

> *Inclination as well as duty would have induced me to give Congress the earliest Information of my removal [retreat] and that of the Troops from Long Island and Its dependencies to this [New York] City the night before last; but the extreme fatigue . . . rendered me . . . entirely unfit to take pen in hand . . .*
> *In the Engagement on the 27th Generals Sullivan and Stirling were made prisoners . . . I [have not] been yet able to obtain an exact account of our Loss; we suppose it from 700 to a Thousand killed and taken. Genl Sullivan says [British Admiral] Lord Howe is extremely desirous of seeing some of the Members of Congress . . .*[827]

Monday, September 2, 1776. It is not going well. Today, George Washington writes the Continental Congress:

> *Our situation is truly distressing . . . The Militia . . . are dismayed, Intractable, and Impatient to return. Great numbers of them have gone off; in some Instances, almost by whole Regiments, by half Ones & by Companies at a time . . . [W]hen their example has Infected another part of the Army, When their want of discipline & refusal of almost every kind of restraint & Government, have produced a like conduct, but too common to the whole, and an entire disregard of that order and subordination necessary to the well doing of an Army . . . our condition is more alarming and, with the deepest concern I am obliged to confess my want of confidence in the Generality of the Troops . . .*
>
> *All these circumstances fully confirm the opinion I ever entertained, and which I more than once in my Letters took the liberty of mentioning to Congress, that no dependence could be put in a Militia . . .*[828]

Wednesday, September 4, 1776. Today, John Adams writes:

> *Our Generals, I fear have made a Mistake in Retreating from Long Island. I fear they will retreat from the City of New York next . . . I don't like these Measures. I wish there was more firmness . . . The Panick, which is Spread upon this occasion is weak and unmanly. It excites my shame, and Indignation . . .*[829]

Sunday, September 8, 1776. Before attacking New York City, British Admiral Richard Howe has suggested a meeting with delegates of the Continental Congress on New York Harbor's Staten Island. Today, Ben Franklin writes George Washington:

> *The Congress having appointed Mr. Adams, Mr. Rutledge, and my self to meet [British Admiral] Lord Howe and hear what Propositions he may have to make, we purpose setting out to-morrow and to be at Perth Amboy on Wednesday morning . . . What we have heard of the Badness of the Roads between that Place and New York makes us wish to be spar'd that part of the Journey.*[830]

Monday, September 9, 1776. Today, Ben Franklin, John Adams, and Edward Rutledge (a South Carolina congressional delegate) set out from Philadelphia by carriage and on horseback for their meeting with British Admiral Richard Howe on Staten Island. John Adams describes the journey:

> *[T]he first night we lodged at an Inn in New Brunswick [New Jersey]. On the Road, and at all the public Houses, We saw such Numbers of Officers and Soldiers, straggling and loytering, as gave me, at least, but a poor Opinion of the Discipline of our forces, and excited as much indignation as anxiety . . .*
>
> *The Taverns were so full we could with difficulty obtain Entertain-*

ment. *At Brunswick, but one bed could be procured for Dr. Franklin and me in a chamber little larger than the bed, without a Chimney, and with only one small Window. The Window was open, and I, who was an invalid and afraid of the Air in the night, shut it close. "Oh!" says Franklin, "don't shut the window. We shall be suffocated." I answered I was afraid of the Evening Air. Dr. Franklin replied, "the Air within this Chamber will soon be, and indeed is now, worse than that without Doors. Come, open the Window and come to bed, and I will convince you. I believe you are not acquainted with my Theory of Colds." Opening the Window, and leaping into Bed, I said I had read his Letters to Dr. Cooper, in which he had advanced that Nobody ever got cold by going into a cold Church or any other cold air; but the Theory was so little consistent with my experience that I thought it a Paradox . . . The Doctor then began an harrangue upon Air and Cold and Respiration and Perspiration, with which I was so much amused that I soon fell asleep and left him and his philosophy together . . .*[831]

Wednesday, September 11, 1776. Today, British Admiral Richard Howe meets with Ben Franklin, John Adams, and Edward Rutledge. The issue of American independence isn't negotiable for either side, so the meeting goes nowhere. The battle for New York City will begin.[832]

Monday, September 16, 1776. Today, George Washington reports his loss of New York City:

> *On Saturday about Sunset, Six more of the Enemy's Ships . . . went up the East River . . . In half an Hour, I received Two Expresses . . . that the Enemy, to the amount of Three or Four thousand, had marched to the River & were embarked . . . However, Nothing remarkable happened that night; but in the morning they began their Operations. Three Ships of War came up the North [Hudson] River . . . and about Eleven O'Clock those in the East River began a most severe and Heavy Cannonade . . .*
>
> *As soon as I heard the Firing, I rode with all possible dispatch towards the place of landing, when to my great surprise and Mortification, I found the Troops that had been posted in the Lines retreating with the utmost precipitation and those ordered to support them . . . flying in every direction and in the greatest confusion, notwithstanding the exertions of their Generals to form them. I used every means in my power to rally and get them into some order but my attempts were fruitless and ineffectual and on an appearance of a small party of the Enemy, not more than sixty or seventy, their disorder increased and they ran away in the greatest confusion without firing a Single Shot . . .*
>
> *Finding that no confidence was to be placed in these Brigades, and apprehending that another part of the Enemy might pass over to Harlem plains and cut off the retreat to this place, I sent orders to secure*

the Heights . . . which being done, the retreat was effected with but lit-
tle or no loss of Men, tho of a considerable part of our Baggage . . .
Most of our Heavy Cannon, and a part of our Stores and provisions,
which we were about removing, was unavoidably left in the City . . .
We are now encamped with the main body of the army on the Heights
of Harlem . . .[833]

Benny Bache will (as an adult) observe:

[Washington] attempted against a naval enemy, possessed of a su-
perior land-force, to defend Long Island and other situations capable
of being taken in the rear by water. He consented to have depots of the
most important stores left in New-York or its vicinity; a place exposed
to attack by water; instead of having them placed in strong positions
in the country behind him; so when deprived of many of these by the
enemy, he could no longer keep together his troops, or prevent great
sickness, or execute various military projects.[834]

Tuesday, September 17, 1776. Today, in the Continental Congress, the Journals report:

Congress took into consideration the plan of treaties to be proposed to
foreign nations . . .
Resolved, That the following plan of a treaty be proposed to His Most
Christian Majesty [of France].
PLAN OF TREATIES . . .
ART. XXVI. It shall be lawful for all and Singular the Subjects of the Most
Christian king, and the Citizens, People, and inhabitants of the said
States, to Sail with their Ships with all manner of Liberty and Security
. . . [even] to the Places of those who are now are or hereafter shall be at
Enmity with the Most Christian King or the United States . . . And it is
hereby Stipulated that free Ships [ships under the flag of neutral nations]
shall also give a Freedom to Goods, and that every Thing shall be deemed
free and exempt which shall be found on board the Ships . . . Contraband
goods being always excepted.
ART. XXVII. [U]nder the Name of Contraband, or prohibited Goods, shall
be comprehended arms, great guns, bombs with their fuzees [&c.] . . .[835]

This commercial treaty to be proposed to France comprises the "Plan of 1776,"
an American offer to replace British mercantilism with freedom of the seas and
freer American trade. Freedom of the seas even includes the right to trade with
a friend's enemies during wartime (except for arms shipments, of course).[836]
John Adams:

[I argued t]hat . . . in preparing Treaties to be proposed to foreign
Powers and in the Instructions to be given to our Ministers, we ought
to confine ourselves strictly to a Treaty of Commerce. That such a

Treaty would be an ample Compensation to France for all the Aid We should want from her . . .[837]

When we met [in committee] to deliberate on the subject, I contended for the same Principles which I had before avowed and defended in Congress, namely that we should avoid all alliance . . . that a treaty of commerce . . . which would opperate as a Repeal of the British Acts of Navigation . . . and admit France into an equal participation of the benefits of our commerce . . . would be an ample Compensation to France for Acknowledging our Independence and for furnishing Us . . . Supplies of Necessaries . . . Franklin . . . ventured so far as to intimate his concurrence with me in these Sentiments; though, as will be seen hereafter, he shifted them as easily as the Wind ever shifted, and assumed a dogmatical Tone in favor of the Opposite System . . . When it came before Congress . . . [m]any motions were made to insert in [the Treaty of commerce] Articles of entangling Alliance . . . It was chiefly left for me to defend . . . We did defend it with so much Success that the [model] Treaty passed without one Particle of Alliance . . .[838]

WEDNESDAY, SEPTEMBER 18, 1776

⇢ The Pennsylvania Gazette ⇠

The proposed PLAN or FRAME of GOVERNMENT for the Commonwealth or STATE of PENNSYLVANIA . . . (Printed for Consideration.)

Sect. 1. THE Commonwealth of State of Pennsylvania shall be governed hereafter by an Assembly of Representatives . . . and a President and Council . . .

Sect. 6. Every freeman, of the full age of twenty-one years, having resided in this State or Commonwealth for the space of one whole year . . . and paid public taxes during that time, shall enjoy the rights of an elector [voter] . . .

Sect. 9. The Members of the House of Representatives shall be chosen annually by ballot . . .

Sect. 13. The doors of the House . . . shall be and remain open . . .

Sect. 14. The votes and proceedings of the House of Representatives shall be printed weekly . . .

Sect. 18. The Supreme Executive Council shall consist of nine members to be chosen . . . by the House of Representatives . . . to serve for three years . . . elections . . . of one third annually for ever . . .

The President and Vice President shall be chosen annually by the joint ballot of the House of Representatives and the Council out of the members of the Council. No person shall be President for a longer space of time than three years together . . .

Sect. 36. The printing presses shall be free to every person who under-

291

takes to examine the proceedings of the legislature or any part of the government; and the House of Representatives shall not pass any act to restrain it . . .

The Pennsylvania constitutional convention will adjourn in ten days. William Temple Franklin (Benny Bache's cousin) will recall:

[A] convention was assembled at Philadelphia in July, 1776, for the purpose of settling a new form of government for the then State of Pennsylvania. Dr. Franklin was chosen president of this convention. The constitution formed and established at that period for Pennsylvania was the result of the deliberations of that assembly and may be considered as a digest of Dr. Franklin's principles of government. The single legislature and the plural executive appear to have been his favorite tenets.[839]

Under the leadership of Benjamin Franklin, Pennsylvania has followed Tom Paine's prescription for truly democratic government, i.e., universal manhood suffrage, a single legislative chamber which is popularly and proportionately elected every year, and a plural executive chosen by and serving at the pleasure of that legislature. Convention member Timothy Matlock:

When the debate was nearly closed, Doctor Franklin was requested by the Convention to give his opinion . . . and he declared it to be clearly and fully in favour of a legislature to consist of a single branch, as being much the safest and best.[840]

Another observer:

[The convention] concluded justly that the power of government really resided in the body of the people and, considering we have no hereditary King nor Lords, whose prerogatives entitle them to negatives [vetoes] in their own right, a negative or power of controuling the united will of the whole community is not only absurd and ridiculous, but highly dangerous.[841]

Tom Paine:

The Constitution formed by the Convention of 1776, of which Benjamin Franklin (the greatest and most useful man America has yet produced) was President, had many good points in it . . .

The sage Franklin has said, "Where annual election ends, tyranny begins"; and no man was a better judge of human nature than Franklin . . . When a man ceases to be accountable to those who elected him . . . he ceases to be their representative . . . "I am elected," says he, "for four years; you cannot turn me out, neither am I responsible to you in the meantime. All that you have to do with me is to pay me." . . .

[A] Senate is an imitation of what is called the House of Lords in England . . . This is aristocracy. This is one of the pillars of John

Adams's *"stupendous fabric of human invention"* . . . *John Adams knew but little of the origin and practice of the Government of England. As to constitution, it has none.*

The Pennsylvania Convention of 1776 copied nothing from the English Government . . . All the members of the Legislature established by that Constitution sat in one chamber and debated in one body . . .[842]

To those, like John Adams, who argue for a second legislative chamber (a senate) to represent propertied interests, Ben Franklin answers:

The Division of the Legislature into two or three branches in England, was it the product of Wisdom or the effect of Necessity arising from the preexisting Prevalence of an odious Feudal System? which government, notwithstanding this Division, is now become in Fact an absolute Monarchy . . .[843]

If this [wealthy] minority is to chuse a Body expressly to controul that which is to be chosen by the great Majority of the Freemen, what have this great Majority done to forfeit so great a Portion of their Right in Elections? Why is this power of Controul, contrary to the spirit of all Democracies, to be vested in a Minority instead of a Majority? . . . [T]he accumulation . . . of Property . . . and its Security to Individuals in every Society must be an Effect of the Protection afforded to it by the joint strength of the Society in the Execution of its Laws. Private Property is therefore a Creature of Society, and is subject to the Calls of that Society, even to its last farthing; its Contributions therefore to the public Exigencies are not to be considered as conferring a Benefit on the Publick, entitling the Contributors to the Distinctions of Honour and Power, but as the Return of an Obligation . . .

[T]he important ends of Civil Society, and the personal Securities of Life and Liberty, these remain the same in every Member of the society; and the poorest continues to have an equal Claim to them with the most Opulent . . .[844]

To those, like John Adams, who say *"a plural executive is a great evil . . . ,"*[845] Ben Franklin answers:

[Will] its errors or Failures . . . [be] more or greater than . . . expected from a single Person?[846]

To those, like John Adams, who prefer the executive to have a longer term of office *"beyond the Reach of every annual Gust of Folly and of Faction,"* Ben Franklin answers:

On this it may be asked, ought it not also to be out beyond the reach of every triennial, quinquennial, or septennial Gust of Folly and of Faction, and, in short, beyond the Reach of Folly and of Faction at any period whatever? Does not this reasoning aim at establishing a Mon-

archy at least for life . . . or, to prevent the Inconveniences . . . , does it not point to an hereditary succession?[847]

The Pennsylvania Constitution of 1776 applies Ben Franklin's philosophy of democratic government. Before this new constitution, an English Quaker and wealthy merchant aristocracy ruled Pennsylvania. Ninety percent of Philadelphians (including virtually all the artisans and ordinary working people) couldn't vote because they couldn't meet heavy property qualifications. Those who lived outside Philadelphia, like German and Scotch-Irish farmers, met property qualifications but were underrepresented by voting apportionment which discounted the outlying districts.[848] Under this new constitution, all this will change. Universal manhood suffrage (without property qualification and with enlarged representation for outlying districts) will work a social revolution, shifting political control from the old wealthy English aristocracy to the more recently immigrated Germans and Scotch-Irish. In the words of one historian, *"In no state were the leveling principles of democracy so thoroughly carried out as in Pennsylvania."*[849]

What might this democratization do to Pennsylvania's war effort? Will Pennsylvania's aristocrats fear the newly enfranchised democrats more than they fear British rule? Might the newly enfranchised immigrant groups decide their enemy has been their homegrown aristocracy rather than the British king? John Adams:

> *[Pennsylvania will be] rendered much less vigorous in the cause by the wretched ideas of government which prevail in the minds of many people in it.*[850]

Wednesday, September 25, 1776. Today, George Washington writes:

> *We are now, as it were, upon the eve of another dissolution of our Army . . . [U]nless some speedy and effectual measures are adopted by Congress, our cause will be lost . . . [A] good Bounty [should] be immediately offered . . . To place any dependance upon Militia is assuredly resting upon a broken staff . . .*[851]

Thursday, September 26, 1776. Today, John Adams writes:

> *The late Events at New York have almost overcome my Utmost Patience . . . The Cowardice of New England men is an unexpected discovery to me . . . I conclude that such detestable Behaviour of whole Brigades could not have happened without the worst Examples in some Officers of Rank . . .*
>
> *I pity the Situation of the General . . . I make it my Rule to cover all Imperfections in the Generals . . .*
>
> *I recollect that Polybius . . . never imputed any defeat to the fault of the men but universally to the folly and incapacity of their Commanders. Our Generals and other Officers must learn the same Justice and Policy. General imputations of Cowardice . . . are false, or, if true, it is*

the fault of the Officers . . . The frequent Surprizes by which our Offi-
cers and Men are taken, in the most palpable trapps, convince me that
there is a dearth of Genius among them . . .[852]

Today, in the Continental Congress, the Journals report:

Agreeable to the order of the day, Congress proceeded to the appointment of commissioners to the court of France:
Resolved, That three be appointed.
The ballots being taken, Mr. [Benjamin] Franklin, Mr. [Silas] Deane,
and Mr. [Thomas] Jefferson, were elected . . .
Resolved, That secrecy shall be observed until the further Order of
Congress; and that until permission be obtained from Congress to disclose
the particulars of this business, no member be permitted to say any thing
more upon this subject than that Congress have taken such steps as they
judged necessary for the purpose of obtaining foreign Alliance.[853]

John Adams declines to be nominated.[854]

Friday, September 27, 1776. Today, congressional delegate Richard Henry Lee
of Virginia writes Thomas Jefferson:

The plan of foreign treaty is now finished . . . In my judgment, the
most eminent services that the greatest of sons can do America will
not more essentially serve her and honor themselves than a successful
negotiation with France. With this country, everything depends on it
. . . We find ourselves greatly endangered by the Armament at present
here . . . I fear the power of America will fail in the mighty struggle . . .
The idea of Congress is that yourself and Dr. Franklin should go on
different ships– The Doctor, I suppose, will sail from hence.[855]

Seventy-year-old Benjamin Franklin will travel to France. Today, he observes
to fellow congressional delegate Benjamin Rush,

I am old and good for nothing; but, as the store-keepers say of their
remnants of cloth, I am but a fag end, and you may have me for what
you please to give.[856]

Thomas Jefferson will not travel. Thomas Jefferson:

[S]uch was the state of my family that I could not leave it, nor could
I expose it to the dangers of the sea, and of capture by British ships,
then covering the ocean . . . I declined therefore, and Dr. [Arthur] Lee
was appointed in my place.[857]

Arthur Lee, Ben Franklin's former deputy, who is already in London, will replace Jefferson as the third American commissioner.

Sunday, September 29, 1776. Today, John Adams writes Colonel Henry Knox
about Washington's defeats in New York:

I agree with you that there is nothing of the vast in the Characters of the Ennemy's General or Admiral . . . But I differ in Opinion from you when you think that, if there had been, they would have Annihilated your Army . . . It is very true that a silly Panick has been spread in your Army and from thence even to Philadelphia. But Hannibal spread as great a Panick, once at Rome, without daring to take Advantage of it . . .

The Rumours, Reports, and Letters . . . represent the New England Troops as Cowards, running away perpetually . . . I must say that your Amiable General [Washington] gives too much Occasion for these reports by his Letters . . .[858]

Tuesday, October 1, 1776. Caron de Beaumarchais' shipments of French government arms have yet to arrive. Today, Ben Franklin's Committee of Secret Correspondence writes commercial agent William Bingham in the French West Indies to learn whether Beaumarchais' "fronting" company, Roderique Hortalez & Cie., has delivered the arms there:

We are now at the 1st of October . . . [W]e desire you to enquire of the General and Governor [of Martinique] whether they have received any Arms or ammunition from Monsr. Hortalez with directions to deliver the same to any person properly authorized by Congress to receive them . . . If none such are arrived, enquire if they have any advice of such and request that they make known to you when they do arrive.

We desire you to make the like application to the Governor of st. Eustatia . . .[859]

Today, fearing that news of Washington's defeats will discourage France from sending arms, Ben Franklin writes Congressional agent Silas Deane in Paris:

[W]e suppose the [British] Generals Military opperations will be ushered into the World with an eclat beyond their true merits or at least the conduct of our people and their present Situation will be misrepresented as ten times worse than the reality. We shall therefore State these things to you as they really are. The Fleet under Ld. Howe . . . remained several Weeks at Staten island without making any attempt. The first they did make was on Long Island when they landed 20,000 men or upwards. [A]t this time we had our Army consisting of not more than 20,000 [e]ffective men stationed at Kings bridge, New York, and on Long Island. 6 to 7000 was the whole of our Force on the latter and about 3000 of them . . . took possession of some heights and intended to annoy the Enemy in their approaches.

They however out General'd us, and got a body of 5000 Men between our people and the Lines, so that we were surrounded and of course came off second best . . . Genl. Howe . . . expected to have

*caught every man we had on that Island, but Genl. Washington saw
and frustrated his design by an unexpected and well conducted retreat across the Sound . . .*

*The Enemy immediately marched up a large Body of Men opposite
to Hell Gate. Our people threw up entrenchments on York island to oppose their landing, but Shame to say, on the day of Tryal, two Brigades
behaved infamously and cou'd not be stopped by the intreatys or
Threats of the General [Washington] who came up in the midst of their
flight . . .*

*The Enemy took possess[ion] of [New York] city and incamped on
the plains of Harlem. Our side occupy the Heights of Harlem . . . [T]he
City of New York has been on Fire and its said one fifth or one sixth of
it is reduced to ashes . . .*[860]

American defeats on Long Island and at New York sound like Washington's loss
at Fort Necessity in 1754 and Braddock's massacre in 1755. Washington's
troops were *"injudiciously deployed," "out general'd,"* and in flight despite
"intreatys or Threats of the General."

Wednesday, October 2, 1776. Today, John Adams writes Brigadier General
Samuel Holden Parsons of Connecticut that the army could have won the battles of Long Island and New York City:

*I think, Sir, that the Enemy, by landing upon [Long] Island, put it
compleatly in our Power to have broke their plans for this Campaign
and to have defended New York. But there are strong Marks of Negli-
gence, Indolence, Presumption, and Incapacity on our Side, by which
scandalous Attributes We lost the Island wholly and Manhattan Island
nearly . . . Sir, it is manifest that our Officers were not acquainted
with the Ground; that they had never reconnoitered the Enemy; that
they had neither Spies, Sentries, nor Guards placed as they ought to
have been; and that they had been shamefully remiss in Obtaining Intelligence of the Numbers and Motions of the Enemy as well as of the
nature of the Ground . . .*

*[F]or a General to be surprized by an Enemy, just under his nose,
in open day and caught in a State of wanton Security, from an over-
weening presumption in his own Strength, is a crime of so capital a
nature as to admit of neither Alleviation nor Pardon . . .*

*Be this as it may, I think the Enemy have reached their Ne plus for
this Year. I have drawn this Conclusion from the Example of Hannibal . . .*[861]

Thursday, October 3, 1776. Today, American General Anthony Wayne writes
Benjamin Franklin that Washington mishandled the defense of New York:

*We are not a little Surprized at the Avacuation of Long Island, the
Surrender of that was Opening the door to the Island of New York.
Our people can't possibly hold that place, when the North [Hudson]*

*and East Rivers are free for the Enemies fleet, as by that means they
can at any time land troops on the back of our Posts, a Circumstance
which I fear has not been sufficiently guarded against . . .*[862]

Friday, October 4, 1776. Today, John Adams writes Abigail of his unhappiness
with Ben Franklin's new Pennsylvania Constitution:

> *I am seated in a large Library Room with Eight Gentlemen round
> about me, all engaged in Conversation . . . The proceedings of the late
> [Pennsylvania] Convention are not well liked . . . Their Constitution is
> reprobated . . .*
>
> *We live in the Age of political Experiments. Among many that will
> fail, some, I hope, will succeed—But Pensilvania will be divided and
> weakend and rendered much less vigorous in the Cause, by the
> wretched Ideas of Government which prevail in the Minds of many
> People in it.*[863]

Friday, October 11, 1776. Today, from London, the French chargé d'affaires
in London, M. Garnier, writes to French Foreign Minister the Comte de Vergennes at the court of Versailles in France:

> *The [British] royal army in America is in possession of Long Island.
> The enclosed letters from General Howe detail his operations . . .*
>
> *[Y]ou will be undoubtedly astonished, Sir, that [Howe] has carried
> it out at so small a cost, since he computes only about 400 [British]
> men, as many dead as injured, or taken in his army, while one sees
> the loss of the Americans at 3,300 men, including 1,000 prisoners,
> among whom are three generals. They have also lost 32 pieces of artil-
> lery.*
>
> *You should very much believe that they speak with the greatest con-
> tempt of the defence of these last items. They claim that the American
> retreats were poorly executed, and that they allowed the British to sur-
> prise the fortified emplacement they could have defended to their best
> advantage . . .*
>
> *To hear the consequences that [British] Government supporters
> draw from this, it may appear that everything is done and that the en-
> tire of America is enclosed on Long Island. The Americans can no
> longer hold any part, and it is inevitable that they will surrender . . .*[864]

Tuesday, October 22, 1776. Today, the Continental Congress gives Ben Franklin his instructions for the mission to France:

> *You will solicit the Court of France for an immediate supply of
> twenty or thirty thousand Muskets and bayonets, and a large supply of
> Ammunition, and Brass Field Pieces to be sent under convoy by
> France. The United States engage for the Payment of the Arms, Artillery
> and Ammunition and to indemnify France for the Expence of the Con-
> voy . . .*[865]

Thursday, October 24, 1776. Today, the Committee of Secret Correspondence of the Continental Congress writes a secret letter to Charles W. F. Dumas, Ben Franklin's friend and correspondent in The Hague (Netherlands):

> *Our Worthy Friend Doctor Franklin being indefatigueable in the Service of his Country and few Men so qualify'd to be useful to the Community of which he is a Member, You will not be surprized that the Unanimous Voice of the Congress of Delegates from the United States of America has called upon him to Visit the Court of France in the Character of one of their Commissioners for Negociating a Treaty of Alliance &c with that Nation . . . We request to hear from you frequently, . . . make use of the Cypher [secret code]. The Doctor has communicated the knowledge of it to one of our Members.*[866]

Today, the committee prepares Secret Orders for Captain Lambert Wickes of the Continental warship *Reprisal*, which will carry Franklin to France:

> *The Honourable Congress having thought proper to Submit the Ship Reprisal under your command to our direction for the present voyage or Cruize. You are to be governed by the following orders.*
>
> *The Honble Doctor Franklin being appointed by Congress one of their Commissioners for negociating some publick business at the Court of France. You are to receive him and his Suite aboard the Reprisal . . .*
>
> *When they are on board you are to proceed with the utmost diligence for the port of Nantes in France where they will land . . . It is of more important that you get Safe and Soon to France than any prizes that you cou'd take, therefore you are not to delay time on this outward passage for the Sake of Cruizing, but if . . . Doctor Franklin may approve of your Speaking any Vessels you see, do therein as he shall direct . . .*[867]

Today, the Committee of Secret Correspondence writes U.S. commissioner Silas Deane in Paris that Benjamin Franklin is coming:

> *The Congress having committed to our charge and management their ship-of-war called the Reprisal, commanded by Lambert Wickes, esq., carrying sixteen six-pounders and about one hundred and twenty men, we have allotted her to carry Doctor Franklin to France and directed Captain Wickes to proceed to the Port of Nantes where the doctor will land and from thence proceed to Paris . . .*[868]

Saturday, October 26, 1776. Tonight, under cover of darkness, seventy-year-old Benjamin Franklin and his seven-year-old grandson, Benjamin Franklin Bache, slip out of Philadelphia by carriage, heading south along the Delaware River to Chester, Pennsylvania, where they spend the night.[869]

Sunday, October 27, 1776. This morning, Dr. Franklin and Benny Bache travel three miles south of Chester, along the Pennsylvania coast to Marcus Hook, where the sixteen-gun, 130–man United States Sloop-of-War *Reprisal* waits, under orders from the Continental Congress, to transport them on a secret mission to France. Captain Lambert Wickes, the *Reprisal*'s commander, sets sail today for France.[870]

Wednesday, November 6, 1776. Today, in Paris, Silas Deane writes the Continental Congress,

> Two hundred pieces of brass cannon, and arms, tents and accoutrements for thirty thousand men, with ammunition in proportion, and between twenty and thirty brass mortars, have been granted to my request, but the unaccountable silence on your part has delayed the embarkation some weeks already. I yesterday got them in motion . . . but I am hourly trembling for fear of counter orders . . .[871]

News of Washington's defeats will cause France to retreat. Orders will soon come to prevent those arms from departing.

Saturday, November 16, 1776. To bar passage of British men-of-war up the North (Hudson) River, George Washington relies on Fort Washington (which faces the river on the northernmost end of New York Island) and Fort Lee (on the opposite New Jersey shore). Today, Washington loses Fort Washington. George Washington:

> [T]he Attack began about Ten O'Clock which our Troops stood and returned the Fire in such a Manner as gave me great Hopes the enemy was intirely repulsed. But at this Time a Body of [British] Troops cross'd the Harlem River in boats and landed inside of the second Lines, our Troops being then engaged in the first . . . Colo. Cadwallader ordered his Troops to retreat in order to gain the Fort. It was done with much Confusion; and the Enemy crossing over came in upon them in such a Manner that a number of them surrendered.
> At this time the Hessians advanced on the North Side of the Fort in very large Bodies . . . At this time I sent a Billet to Col Magaw, directing him to hold out . . . But before this reached him, he had entered too far into a Treaty to retract. After which Colo. Cadwallader told another messenger, who went over, that they had been able to obtain no other Terms than to surrender as Prisoners of War [giving up their arms, ammunition, and stores of every kind] . . .[872]

Sunday, November 17, 1776. Today, General Nathanael Greene, who commands Forts Washington and Lee, writes Colonel Henry Knox:

> The misfortune of losing Fort Washington, with between two and three thousand men, will reach you before this, if it has not already. His Excellency General Washington has been with me for several days. The evacuation or reinforcement of Fort Washington was under consideration, but finally nothing concluded on . . .
> General Washington, General Putnam, General Mercer, and myself went to the island to determine what was best to be done, but just at the instant we stepped on board the boat, the enemy made their ap-

pearance on the hill . . . This was done while we were crossing the river . . . There we all stood in a very awkward situation. As the disposition was made, and the enemy advancing, we durst not attempt to make any new disposition . . .[873]

Tuesday, November 19, 1776. Today, George Washington laments the loss of Fort Washington:

This is a most unfortunate affair and has given me great Mortification as we have lost not only two thousand Men that were there, but a good deal of artillery, and some of the best Arms we had. And what adds to my Mortification is that this Post, after the last Ships went past it, was held contrary to my Wishes and Opinion as I conceived it was to be a dangerous one; but being determined on by a full Council of General Officers . . . I did not care to give an absolute order for withdrawing the Garrison till I could get round and see the Situation of things and then it became too late as the Fort was Invested. I had given it, upon the passing of the last Ships, as my opinion to Genl. Greene, under whose care it was, that it would be best to evacuate the place; but, as the order was discretionary, and his opinion differed from mine, it unhappily was delayed too long . . .

It is a matter of great grief and surprize to me to find the different States so slow and inattentive to . . . levying their quotas of Men. In ten days from this date, there will not be above 2000 men . . .

I am wearied almost to death with the retrograde Motions of things, and I solemnly protest that a pecuniary reward of 20,000£ a year would not induce me to undergo what I do . . .[874]

In his defeat at Fort Washington, George Washington has lost more than 2,900 troops (most captured), which is one third to one half of his army.[875]

Thursday, November 21, 1776. Today, Washington's former aide-de-camp Joseph Reed writes Washington's second in command, Major General Charles Lee, concerning Washington's indecisiveness:

I do not mean to flatter, nor praise you at the Expence of any other, but I confess I do think that it is entirely owing to you that this Army & the Liberties of America (so far as they are dependent on it) are not totally cut off. You have Decision, a Quality often wanting in Minds otherwise valuable & I ascribe to this our escape from York Island . . . & I have no Doubt [that,] had you been here, the Garrison at Mount Washington would now have composed a Part of this Army . . .

Col. Cadwallader . . . informs that the Enemy have a Southern Expedition in View—that they hold us very cheap in Consequence of the late Affair at Mount Washington where both the plan of Defence & Execution were contemptible . . .

George Washington's own judgment . . . would, I believe, have saved the men and their arms, but, unluckily, General Greene's judgment was contrary. This kept the General's [Washington's] mind in a state of suspense till the stroke was struck. Oh! General—an indecisive Mind is one of the greatest Misfortunes that can befall an Army—how often I lamented it this Campaign.[876]

The news continues bad. Today, George Washington loses Fort Lee on the New Jersey side of the Hudson River. He must now abandon New Jersey. George Washington reports:

The unhappy affair of the 16th has been succeeded by further Misfortunes. Yesterday Morning a large body of the Enemy landed between Dobb's Ferry and Fort Lee . . . [O]ur men were ordered to meet them, but finding their numbers greatly superior and that they were extending themselves to seize on the passes over the River, it was thought proper to withdraw . . . We lost the whole of the Cannon that was at the Fort, except two twelve pounders . . .[877]

[W]e have not an Intrenching Tool and not above 3000 Men, and they much broken and dispirited, not only with our ill success but the Loss of their Tents and Baggage, I have resolved to avoid any Attack, tho' by so doing I must leave a very fine Country [New Jersey] open to their Ravages or a plentiful Store House from which they will draw voluntary Supplies . . .[878]

Tom Paine, serving at Fort Lee as an aide-de-camp to General Nathanael Greene, flees with the rest of the troops.[879] Tom Paine:

[T]he injudicious choice of positions taken by [General Washington] in the campaign of 1776 . . . necessarily produced the losses and misfortunes that marked that gloomy campaign. The positions taken were either islands or necks of land. In the former, the enemy, by the aid of their ships, could bring the whole force against a part of General Washington's, as in the affair of Long Island; and, in the latter, he might be shut up as in the bottom of a bag.

This had nearly been the case at New York, and it was so in part; it was actually the case at Fort Washington; and it would have been the case at Fort Lee, if General Greene had not moved precipitately off, leaving everything behind, and by gaining Hackensack bridge, got out of the bag of Bergen Neck.[880]

Adjutant General Timothy Pickering will recall:

Some who have been taught to believe [George Washington] to have been a great commander . . . think it scarcely possible that it was left to [a] late period . . . to make the discovery of his military deficiencies. In truth it was not. They had become perfectly apparent . . . at a very early period of our revolution. The second campaign had not passed away before they were manifest . . . to the few officers nearest to him

. . . who were witnesses of his conduct on occasions calling for prompt discernment and decision . . .[881]

Sunday, November 24, 1776. Today, General Charles Lee responds to Adjutant General Joseph Reed's letter of November 21st:

I receiv'd your most obliging flattering letter—lament with you that fatal indecision of mind which in war is a much greater disqualification than stupidity or even want of personal courage—but eternal defeat and miscarriage must attend the man of the best parts if curs'd with indecision.[882]

Wednesday, November 27, 1776. Today, George Washington writes from Newark, New Jersey:

The force here . . . is weak and it has been more owing to the badness of the weather that the Enemy's progress has been checked than any resistance we could make . . . Their plan is not entirely unfolded, but I shall not be surprized, if Philadelphia should turn out the object of their Movement . . .[883]

Today, off the coast of France and despite congressional instructions not to delay his mission by taking prizes, Dr. Franklin allows Captain Lambert Wickes of the sloop *Reprisal* to engage and capture two British prizes. Benny's cousin, William Temple Franklin, writes:

The sloop [Reprisal] was frequently chased during the voyage by British cruisers and several times prepared for action; but being a good sailer and the captain having received orders not unnecessarily to risk an engagement, she as often escaped her pursuers . . . [O]n the 27th of November, being near the coast of France though out of soundings . . . [s]everal sail were seen about noon, and the sloop brought to and took a brig from Bordeaux bound to Cork (being Irish property), loaded with lumber and some wine . . . In the afternoon of the same day, he came up with and took another brig, from Rochfort, belonging to Hull, bound to Hamburgh, with brandy and flax-seed . . .[884]

The day after tomorrow, Benjamin Franklin will arrive in Quiberon Bay (France) with these prizes, an Irish-owned brigantine, the *George,* and another vessel, *La Vigne,* from Hull.[885]

Tuesday, December 3, 1776. Today, from Paris, American commissioner Silas Deane writes the Committee of Secret Correspondence:

The late affairs at Long Island, of which we had intelligence in October, and the burning of New York, the report of Carleton's having crossed the lakes [from Canada], and that you were negotiating has absolutely ruined our credit with the greater part of individuals . . . I have attended the closer to dispatch the supplies of the army . . .[886]

Wednesday, December 4, 1776. Today, with his ship resting at Auray on the French coast of Brittany, Benjamin Franklin writes Silas Deane in Paris:

> *I have just arrived on board the Reprisal, Captain Wickes, a small vessel of war belonging to Congress. We are at Quiberon Bay, awaiting a favorable wind to go on to Nantes . . . Congress in September named you, Mr. Jefferson, and myself to negociate a treaty of commerce and friendship with the court of France. Mr. Jefferson, then in Virginia, declined. Thereupon, [my former deputy in London] Mr. Arthur Lee, at present in London, was named in his place . . .*
>
> *We fell in with two brigantines at sea, one Irish and the other English, which we captured and brought into Nantes. I do not know that the captain can get permission to sell them there, as that would be in contradiction of the treaties between the two crowns [of Britain and France] . . .*
>
> *If you could find some means to notify Mr Lee of his nomination it would be well to do so.*[887]

Thursday, December 5, 1776. Today, George Washington writes:

> *As nothing but necessity obliged me to retire before the Enemy and leave so much of the Jerseys unprotected, I conceive it to be my duty . . . to make head against them so soon as there be the least probability of doing it with propriety . . . [S]orry I am to observe, however, that the frequent calls upon the Militia of this State, the want of exertion in the principal Gentlemen of the Country, or a fatal supiness and insensibility of danger . . . have been the causes of our late disgraces . . . My first wish is that Congress may be convinced of the propriety of relying as little as possible upon Militia . . .*[888]

Saturday, December 7, 1776. New Jersey is at the mercy of the British. Today, George Washington retreats from New Jersey across the Delaware River into Pennsylvania. His army camps along the western shore of the Delaware, facing Trenton, New Jersey.[889]

Sunday, December 8, 1776. Today, the British seize Newport and the rest of Rhode Island. With George Washington in full retreat across New Jersey, British General Sir Henry Clinton withdrew some British troops from pursuing Washington in order for them to conquer Rhode Island. There is no resistance.[890]

Today, having arrived at the port of Nantes in France, Benjamin Franklin writes the president of the Continental Congress:

> *Our Friends in France have been a good deal dejected with the Gazette Accounts of Advantages obtain'd against us by the British Troops. I have help'd them here to recover their Spirits a little . . .*
>
> *Our Voyage tho' not long was rough, and I feel myself weakened by*

it: But I now recover Strength daily, and in a few days shall be able to undertake the Journey to Paris . . .

I find it is generally suppos'd here that I am sent to negociate, and that Opinion appears to give great Pleasure, if I can judge by the extream Civilities I meet with from Numbers of the principal People, who have done me the Honour to visit me . . .[891]

Tuesday, December 10, 1776. Today, George Washington writes:

Our numbers . . . being reduced by sickness, desertion, and political deaths (on or before the first instant, and having no assistance from the militia), were obliged to retire before the enemy . . . I tremble for Philadelphia. Nothing, in my opinion, but Gen. Lee's speedy arrival . . . can save it . . .[892]

Today, in Paris, the French Foreign Ministry orders the police to arrest "with great publicity and severity" any French soldier who claims to have government support for service in America![893]

Wednesday, December 11, 1776. Congress can't believe that Washington won't defend Philadelphia. Today, in the Continental Congress, the Journals report:

Whereas a false and malicious report has been spread . . . that the Congress was about to disperse;

Resolved, that General Washington be desired to contradict the said scandalous report, this Congress having a better opinion of the spirit and vigor of the army . . . than to suppose it can be necessary to disperse . . .[894]

Thursday, December 12, 1776. Reassurance from Washington isn't forthcoming. Today, fearing the British will seize Philadelphia, the Continental Congress flees to Baltimore, where it will remain until March. Masses of Philadelphia's citizenry also flee.[895] The *Pennsylvania Gazette* will not appear again till February.

Today, in Paris, congressional emissary Silas Deane (whose arms shipments and volunteers to America have been embargoed by the French government) writes the Committee of Secret Correspondence:

Just as I closed my despatches . . . I was agreeably surprised with a letter from Dr. Franklin, at Nantes [France], where he arrived after thirty days passage, with two prizes . . . Nothing has for a long time occasioned greater speculation than this event, and our friends here are elated beyond measure . . . [F]or me, I will not attempt to express the pleasure I feel on this occasion, as it removes at once difficulties under which I have been constantly in danger of sinking.[896]

George Washington's second in command, General Charles Lee, doesn't appreciate Washington's generalship and doesn't want to leave New Jersey to join him in Pennsylvania. Today, Lee writes General Horatio Gates:

The ingenious manoeuvre of Fort Washington has unhing'd the goodly fabrick We had been building—there never was so damn'd a stroke—entre nous, a certain great man is most damnably deficient. He has thrown me in a situation where I have a choice of difficulties—if I stay in this Province, I risk myself and Army, and if I do not stay, the Province is lost forever.[897]

Saturday, December 14, 1776. Ships of Roderique Hortalez et Cie., loaded with arms and ammunitions that Caron de Beaumarchais has acquired from French government arsenals, remain in French ports. Today, as Silas Deane feared, the ships are restrained by new French government orders. Caron de Beaumarchais reports:

At the beginning of the present business, that is to say, in 1775 and 76, all that transpired of the designs of the King of France . . . was that this sovereign intended to observe the most strict neutrality . . .

M. de Beaumarchais' company, trading under the title of Roderique Hortalez & Cie . . . had bought for the Americans sufficient goods to form immense cargoes and had freighted for its American correspondents eight or ten vessels in various French ports . . . The [French] Ministry [was] distracted with the complaints of [the British Minister to France] Viscount Stormont . . .

At last, having heard the English Ambassador say that there were munitions of war in the Company's vessels, the administration sent to Havre, on the 14 December 1776, an order to stop all these vessels and to examine them minutely.

This caused such a stir that the Company, not being able, by any submission or offer, to obtain permission for these vessels to leave port, was obliged to disarm them entirely . . .[898]

Sunday, December 15, 1776. Today, General Washington writes the Council of Safety of Pennsylvania:

The Spirit of disaffection that appears in this Country, I think, deserves your serious attention. Instead of giving any Assistance in repelling the Enemy, the Militia have not only refused to obey your General Summons and that of their Commanding Officers, but, I am told, exult at the approach of the Enemy and our late misfortunes . . .[899]

Tuesday, December 17, 1776. Charles Lee won't come to Washington's rescue. He has been captured by a party of British dragoons at Mrs. White's Tavern in Basking Ridge, New Jersey. Today, George Washington laments the event:

Gen Lee. Unhappy man! Taken by his own imprudence, going three or four miles from his own camp and within twenty of the enemy . . . [A] party of light horse seized him in the morning . . . and carried him off in high triumph and with every mark of indignity, not even suffering him to get his hat or surtout coat.[900]

Wednesday, December 18, 1776. Today, General Washington writes:

> [I]*f every nerve is not strain'd to recruit the New Army with all possible expedition, I think the game is pretty near up, owing, in a great measure, to the insidious Arts of the Enemy, and disaffection of the Colonies . . . and placing too great a dependence on the Militia . . .*
> *You can form no Idea of the perplexity of my Situation. No Man, I believe, ever had a greater choice of difficulties and less means to extricate himself . . .*[901]

Thursday, December 19, 1776. Today, the first of Tom Paine's sixteen *"Crisis"* essays appears.[902] With the power of expression that persuaded America to choose independence, Tom Paine tries to raise America's morale. George Washington will order Paine's words to be read to every regiment camped along the Delaware:

> *These are the times that try men's souls. The summer soldier and the sunshine patriot will, in this crisis, shrink from the service of their country; but he that stands [for] it now, deserves the love and thanks of man and woman. Tyranny, like hell, is not easily conquered; yet we have this consolation with us, that the harder the conflict, the more glorious the triumph . . .*[903]

Friday, December 20, 1776. The British have decided not to attempt a Delaware crossing for an attack on Philadelphia but rather to return to New York for the winter. Washington is clearly at their mercy. Today, Washington writes the president of Congress:

> *We find Sir that the Enemy are daily gathering strength from the disaffected. This Strength like a Snow ball by rolling, will Increase unless some means can be devised to check effectually the progress of the Enemy's Arms . . . [T]he militia of those States which have been frequently called upon will not turn out at all or with so much reluctance and sloth as to amount to the same thing. Instance New Jersey! Witness Pennsylvania! Could any thing but the River Delaware have sav'd Philadelphia? . . .*
> *Every exertion should be used to procure Tents . . . [A]bove all, a Store of Small Arms should be provided, or Men will be of little use . . . Militia . . . coming in without were obliged to be furnished, or become useless. Many of these threw their Arms away; some lost them, whilst others deserted and took them along . . .*[904]

Today, in Paris, Britain's Minister Plenipotentiary to France David Murray (Lord Stormont) prepares another report on Ben Franklin's arrival in France:

*If reports are true, [Franklin] has already abused their ignorance
. . . concerning the Americans as far as to proclaim roundly . . . that
the affairs of the rebels are in a flourishing condition, while ours are
desperate . . .*[905]

Saturday, December 21, 1776. Today, from Philadelphia, Committee of Secret Correspondence member Robert Morris writes Benjamin Franklin and the other American commissioners in Paris:

*I am the only member of Congress in this city . . . [T]hese unfortu-
nate events commenced with the loss of Fort Washington, by the reduction of which the enemy made about two thousand seven hundred
prisoners . . . [B]efore General Washington had time to make any new
arrangements at Fort Lee, on the west side of the North [Hudson]
River, to which he had crossed with about eight thousand men, a large
body of [British] troops landed above and another below him, so that
he was near being inclosed with a force vastly superior. In this situation he had nothing left for him but to retire . . . leaving behind him . . .
most of our large cannon and mortars. He retreated to Hackensack
[New Jersey], and was there in hopes of making a stand . . . but the
vigilance of the enemy did not give him time for this. They pursued,
and he retreated all the way through the Jerseys to Trenton, and
thence they forced him across the Delaware, where he remains . . .
General Howe issued a proclamation on the 30th of November, offering pardon to all who should submit . . . and all Jersey, or far the
greater part of it, is supposed to have made their submission . . .
In this perplexing situation of things the Congress were informed
this day [last] week that an advanced party of Hessians and High-
landers . . . were pushing for Cooper's Ferry, opposite the city [of Phil-
adelphia] . . . There were no troops to oppose them . . . [I]t was
therefore deemed unsafe for Congress . . . This city was for ten days the
greatest scene of distress that you can conceive; everybody but Quakers were removing their families and effects, and now it looks pretty
dismal and melancholy . . .
[Britain's] General Clinton, with from three to four thousand
men, has invaded Rhode Island, and, it is said, has taken possession
of it . . .
For my part I see but two chances for relief; one is from you. If the
court of France open their eyes . . . they may . . . afford us succors that
will change the fate of affairs; but they must do it soon; our situation is
critical and does not admit of delay . . . If they join us generously in
the day of our distress, without attempting undue advantages because
we are so, they will find a grateful people to promote their future glory
and interest with unabating zeal . . .*[906]

Physician General Benjamin Rush will recall:

> *After the retreats and retreats of our army in the year 1776, I went out as a volunteer physician to General Cadwalader's corps of Philadelphia militia. During this excursion I rode with Colonel J. Reed from Bristol to headquarters on the Delaware nearly opposite to Trenton. On the way he mentioned many instances of General Washington's want of military skill and ascribed most of the calamities of the campaign to it. He concluded by saying "he was only fit to command a regiment." General Gates informed me . . . that Patrick Henry of Virginia had said the same thing of him when [Washington] was appointed commander in chief.*
>
> *A little time later than this time, General Mifflin told me "he was totally unfit for his situation, that he was fit only to be the head clerk of a London countinghouse."*[907]

This afternoon, at two (Paris time), Ben Franklin and his seven-year-old grandson, Benjamin Franklin Bache, arrive in Paris, France.[908]

Wednesday, December 25, 1776. Today, Christmas Day, George Washington begins the first of two victories he can claim in the American War of Independence. Benny Bache (as an adult) will write:

> *The small microscopic exploits of Trenton and Princeton (which succeeded one another) were like the efforts of despair and the acts of a partizan rather than of a great commander in chief . . .*[909]

Tonight, using the presumed sanctity of Christmas as a cover for his actions, George Washington leads two thousand troops across the icy Delaware River to surprise a Hessian detachment of about half his number who are sleeping off the effects of Christmas grog and homesickness at their outpost in Trenton, New Jersey.[910] George Washington reports:

> *The evening of the 25th I ordered the Troops intended for this service to parade back of McKonkey's Ferry . . . that we might easily arrive at Trenton by five in the Morning . . . But the quantity of Ice made that Night impeded the passage . . . This made me despair of surprising the Town . . . before the day was fairly broke, but as I was certain there was no making a Retreat without being discovered and harassed on repassing the River, I determined to press on . . . The upper Division arrived at the Enemys advanced post exactly at Eight O'Clock . . . The out Guards made but small opposition . . . We presently saw their main body formed, but from their Motions, they seemed undetermined how to act . . . Finding from our disposition that they were surrounded and that they must inevitably be cut to pieces if they made any further resistance, they agreed to lay down their arms . . . Our loss is very trifling indeed, only two Officers and one or two privates wounded.*[911]

Monday, December 30, 1776. Today, from Baltimore (where Congress has fled from fear of a British attack on Philadelphia), the Continental Congress issues revised instructions to its Paris commissioners:

> *Upon mature deliberation of all circumstances, Congress deem the speedy declaration of France and European Assistance so indispensably necessary to secure the Independence of the these States, that they have authorized you to make fresh tenders to France . . . Your wisdom, we know will direct you to make such use of these powers as will procure the thing desired . . .*[912]

These broad instructions allow the commissioners to offer France an alliance! John Adams:

> *I had myself the honour to be the first . . . on the subject of foreign alliances . . . to contend . . . that we ought not to give France any exclusive Privileges . . . That diminishing the Power of the natural Enemy of France . . . was quite enough to make it her interest to support us . . . They put me upon the Committee to draw up the Treaty, and the Committee appointed me to draw it, which I did . . . It was in perfect conformity to these Principles, and accepted by Congress . . . After the Treaty was finished and Dr. Franklin sent off with it, who sailed in October, I went home for a visit to my Constituents. [W]hile I was gone in the month of December, [t]he terms of enlistment of the Army expired, General Washington was obliged to retreat across the Jersies, and some gentlemen Saw the Necessity of Foreign alliances in a Stronger Light, and moved for Instructions to the Commissioners to offer some Additional Motives to engage.—These Propositions had been made before, and I had always combated them with success, but now they prevailed . . . I never was more mortified in my life than upon finding, at my Return to Congress, what they had done.*[913]

Friday, January 3, 1777. Today, in his second, equally small victory, Washington engages and defeats a group of British stragglers at Princeton, New Jersey. Though Washington's force is small, it outnumbers the enemy twenty-five to one. Washington describes the engagement:

> *Our Situation was most critical and our strength [force] small . . . On the Second, according to my expectation, the Enemy began to advance . . . and after some skirmishing, the head of their Column reach'd Trenton . . . We were drawn up on the other Side of the Creek. In this Situation we remain till dark . . . [A]t twelve O'Clock after renewing our Fires and leaving Guards at the Bridge in Trenton . . . [we] March'd by a round about road to Princeton where I knew they could not have much force left . . . We found Princeton about Sunrise [on the 3d] with only three Regiments of Infantry and three Troops of Light-Horse in it, two of which were upon their March for Trenton. These*

three Regiments made a gallant resistance . . . upwards of one hundred of them were left dead in the Field . . .[914]

British General Sir William Howe reports, *"The loss upon this occasion to his majesty's troops is 17 killed . . ."*[915] Timothy Pickering observes:

> *The most brilliant military exploits ascribed to Washington are the capture of the Hessians at Trenton, and the maneuvers by which he . . . fell victoriously upon some of [Cornwallis'] regiments left at Princeton . . . In themselves, these were small affairs . . .*[916]

CHAPTER SEVEN

LIGHTENING-SNATCHER

Mr. Bache has another claim on my respect, as being the grandson of Dr. Franklin, the greatest man & ornament of the age and country in which he lived.

THOMAS JEFFERSON,
PRESIDENT OF THE UNITED STATES, 1801–1809[917]

Before the visible dawn of American freedom, the colonies were known to Europe but as the magazines from which England drew materials for her fabrics, her manufactures and her commerce . . . An obscure man, a native of America, penetrating the gloom in which this vast continent was obscured, by the force of natural genius and the strength of his mind, placed himself, without effort, among the first philosophers of the age . . . [T]he moral apothegms of Franklin soon became as celebrated as his philosophical experiments were new and successful, and Europe learned to consider the American people as a society whose wisdom and virtue rivaled if not surpassed the classical Arcadians . . . The Father of American liberties became the object of general respect and love.

WILLIAM DUANE, EDITOR,
AURORA GENERAL ADVERTISER, 1798–1822[918]

By now, dear reader, you may be wondering how I, William Duane, can be both a newspaperman and an historian. I might answer that in 1796 (after I arrived in America but before I began work at the *Philadelphia Aurora*), I was engaged by Tom Paine's old friend[919] book publisher John "Walking" Stewart to write the fourth and final volume, *The Revolutionary Part*, of John Gifford's *History of France from the Earliest Time Till the Death of Louis Sixteenth . . . And Continued from the Above Period until the Conclusion of the Present War, by a Citizen of the United States*, 4 vols. (Philadelphia: Stewart & Rowson, 1796–98).[920] My volume, *The Revolutionary Part*, appeared, as you may have guessed, in 1798. So I've had some practice.

My volume (IV) tracks the French Revolution from its very roots, including, of course, its American roots. Henceforth, I will refer to that volume as "my history." In my history, I write,

> Franklin, whose fame had already opened him a free correspondence with the literati of the European continent, was with perfect wisdom dispatched to France, where he found the public mind greatly influenced by men of letters peculiarly prepared to give him the most flattering reception. The father of American liberties became the general object of respect and love . . .
>
> [French Foreign Minister] Vergennes, whose principles united the arbitrary policy of the French court with the refined knowledge of a country peculiarly distinguished by literature, became the social friend of Franklin. His unaffected manners, his sensible gracefulness, had obtained a sort of influence over the French minister, that he acted as if he were ashamed to pursue with the American the wily insincerity practiced with courtiers . . . Franklin by plain manners and an utter contempt for affectation . . . instead of being considered as ambassadors usually deserve to be . . . was esteemed as a new and different character, and his circle of society became as extensive as he could desire and circumscribed only by his avocations and by want of adequate leisure.—
>
> Under such fortunate auspices, the principal difficulties to the negociation were easily removed . . .[921]

The French upper classes know Franklin for his writings on electricity, first published in France in 1752. The lower classes know Franklin for the ideas of *Poor Richard's Almanacks* (translated into French as the *"science"* of *"Bonhomme Richard"*). The French royal court honored Franklin as early as 1767. France's Academy of Sciences elected him to membership in 1772. Everyone in France loves Franklin! Even John Adams admits it:

> His reputation was more universal than that of Leibnitz or [Sir Isaac] Newton, Frederick [The Great] or Voltaire, and his character more beloved and esteemed than any or all of them. Newton had astonished perhaps forty or fifty men in Europe . . . But this fame was confined to men of letters. The common people know little and cared nothing about such a recluse philosopher. Leibnitz's name was more confined still . . . Frederick was hated by more than half of Europe . . . Voltaire whose name was more universal . . . was considered as a vain and profligate wit, and not much esteemed or beloved by anybody, though admired by all who knew his works. But Franklin's fame was universal. His fame was familiar to government and people, to kings, courtiers, nobility, clergy and philosophers, as well as plebeians, to such a degree that there was scarcely a peasant or a citizen, a valet de chambre, coachman or footman, a lady's chambermaid or a scullion in a kitchen, who was not familiar with it, and who did not consider him a friend to mankind.[922]

Saturday, January 4, 1777. Today, from Paris, Ben Franklin writes his Committee of Secret Correspondence:

> *I arrived here about two Weeks since, where I found Mr. Deane. Mr. Lee has since join'd us from London . . .*
> *The Cry of this Nation is for us, but the Court, it is thought, views an approaching War with Reluctance . . . As soon as we can receive a positive Answer from these Courts, we shall dispatch an Express with it.*[923]

Jacques-Donatien Le Ray de Chaumont, an important supplier to the French military, has taken charge of settling Franklin and Benny Bache in Paris. He has written Franklin,

> *This morning, Monsieur, your grandson and I have seen a boarding school which is convenient for Benjamin. If his account of it to you allows you to choose it, depend on my complete supervision.*[924]

Ben Franklin will live at Chaumont's residence in the Paris suburb of Passy, two miles along the road from Paris to the royal court at Versailles. Today, Benny Bache settles into Chaumont's home to begin attending a nearby school.[925]

Sunday, January 5, 1777. The French government has embargoed America's long-awaited arms shipments. Today, Franklin writes French Foreign Minister Vergennes:

> *We are . . . instructed to solicit the Court of France for an immediate Supply of twenty or thirty Thousand Muskets and Bayonets, and a large Quantity of Ammunition and brass Field Pieces, to be sent under Convoy . . . This Application is now become the more necessary, as the private Purchase made by Mr. Deane of those Articles is render'd ineffectual by an Order forbidding their exportation . . .*
> *[W]e may possibly, unless some powerful Aid is given us or some strong Diversion made in our favor, be so harass'd and be put to such immense Expence, as that finally our People will find themselves reduc'd to the necessity of Ending the War by an Accommodation [with Britain].*[926]

Wednesday, January 8, 1777 (circa). Today, Benjamin Franklin prepares a memorandum for French Foreign Minister Vergennes:

> *The situation of the United-states requires an immediate supply of Stores of various sorts, of which a proportion of Military for the opening and supporting the coming Campaign . . .*
> *Difficulties have arose at the different ports, where Military Stores have been collected and Objections made to their being shipp'd for the United-states in French ships though Charter'd on Account of the States, in the name of private Persons, by which great Delay has been*

already occasioned, and the Damages in consequence will be irreparable unless speedily relieved . . .

To Remedy these Difficulties it is with submission requested that Warlike stores already purchased or that may hereafter be purchased for the United States may be shipped in French ships for the said United States, directly . . .

[W]ithout this or some Measure effecting the same Design, the United States will be disappointed of the Stores they expected . . .

NB. The Stores in the Amphitrite, those ready to be Shipp'd from the other Ports [Le Havre and Nantes], are now detain'd by the above Obstacles.[927]

Through Franklin's diplomacy, the French government arms shipments will be immediately released.

Sunday, January 12, 1777. Today, Ben Franklin writes his good friend (and former London landlady) Mary Hewson:

My dear Polley

Figure to yourself an old Man with grey Hair appearing under a Martin Fur Cap, among the Powder'd Heads of Paris. It is this odd Figure that salutes you . . .

I have with me here my young Grandson Benja Franklin Bache, a special good Boy. I give him a little French Language and Address, and then send him over to pay his Respects to Miss Hewson . . .[928]

"Miss Hewson" is Elizabeth Hewson, Mary's two- or three-year-old daughter.

Wednesday, January 15, 1977. Franklin is being watched by everyone! Today's entry in a Paris police journal includes a surveillance report of his activities:

DOCTOR FRANKLIN, who lately arrived in this country from the English colonies, is very much run after and fêted, not only by the savants, his confreres, but by all people who can get hold of him, for he is difficult to be approached, and lives in a reserve which is supposed to be directed by the Government. This Quaker wears the full costume of his sect. He has an agreeable physiognomy, spectacles always on his eyes but little hair, a fur cap always on his head. He wears no powder but neat and linen very white, a brown coat makes his dress. His only defence is a stick in his hand . . .

There has been no lack of prints of Franklin, whose portrait has become the fashionable New Year's gift of the year. People keep it on the mantel as they formerly kept a statuette, and the singular costume of this grave personage leads our fops and women to turn his likeness into . . . those futile knick-knacks . . .

If he sees our ministers, it is at night (that is, in Paris, not at court) and with the greatest secrecy, but he has frequent conferences with the

Sieurs de Beaumarchais and le Rez de Chaumont [the French military supplier]. The first of these is the tou tou [confidant] of Madame de Maurepas [wife of the French Prime Minister], and probably bears some messages . . .[929]

Friday, January 17, 1777. Today, from Paris, Franklin writes the Continental Congress:

> *[W]e are endeavouring to expedite several Vessels laden with Artillery, Arms, Ammunition, and Cloathing which we hope will reach you in time for the campaign . . .*
>
> *The Hearts of the French are universally for us, and the Cry is strong for immediate War with Britain. Indeed every thing tends that way, but the Court has its reasons for postponing . . .*[930]

Wednesday, January 22, 1777. Today, from his headquarters at Morristown (New Jersey) about halfway from Philadelphia to New York City, George Washington writes the Continental Congress:

> *I shall be glad to know what Stock of small Arms you at present have, and what are your Expectations shortly. The Necessity that we have been and are now under, of calling in and arming the Militia Scatters our Armoury all over the World in a Manner . . . The new raised Regiments will call for a great Number of Arms; and I do not at present see how they are to be Supplied.*[931]

Thursday, January 23, 1777. Franklin's negotiations with France have released the arms shipments from their embargo. Today, from the port of Nantes, Ben Franklin's nephew, Jonathan Williams, reports to his uncle,

> *I have the pleasure to inform you that the last Lighter went to the Ship [Mercure] yesterday . . . I am impatient to hear that the [A]mphitrite is gone . . .*[932]

The *Amphitrite* leaves tomorrow.[933]

Saturday, January 25, 1777. Today, from the French port of Nantes, Ben Franklin's nephew writes him again, including,

> *I am treated here with as much Respect as if I were the Nephew of a prince. So much is your name respected that I hear the Ladies of Nantes are about making an addition to their heads in imitation of your Hair Cap, which they intend to call "à la Franklin."*[934]

Sunday, January 26, 1777. Today, George Washington writes the Continental Congress:

> *By a Resolve of Congress passed some time ago, General Schuyler [of the Northern Army] is directed to apply to me for 94 Tons of powder, a Quantity which it is impossible I should have by me and for which I do not know where to direct him to apply. I could wish that*

Returns were made to me of the Quantity of Powder on hand and where it is to be found that I may not be at a loss at any time of Emergency.[935]

Monday, January 27, 1777. If America's Northern Army is to defend against a British army entering from Canada, it needs arms and ammunition. Today, George Washington writes Major General Philip Schuyler, who commands the Northern Army:

> *I know your difficulties will be great in procuring a proper Quantity of Ordnance and Ordnance Stores against next Campaign, but . . . if our adventures are lucky, we shall be well supplied with Field Artillery from France . . . The Enemy have given out that they have taken a ship from France with Artillery on board, but I never heard of her being brought in, so I hope it is not true.*[936]

Today, Ben Franklin writes a friend:

> *I suppose you would want to know something of the State of Affairs in America. In all probability we shall be much stronger in the next Campaign than we were in the last; better arm'd; better disciplin'd, and with more Ammunition. When I was at the Camp before Boston, the Army had not 5 rounds of Powder a Man. This was kept a Secret even from our People. The World wonder'd that we so seldom fir'd a Cannon. We could not afford it. But we now [shall have] Powder in Plenty.*[937]

Friday, January 31, 1777. Today, George Washington writes the Continental Congress:

> *Our army is shamefully reduced by desertion, and except [unless] the people in the Country can be forced to give Information when Deserters return to their old Neighborhoods, we shall be obliged to detach one half of the army to bring back the other.*[938]

Wednesday, February 5, 1777. Today, from Philadelphia, Benny Bache's father, Richard Bache, writes Benjamin Franklin:

> *On the approach of the Enemy towards this City [last autumn] I had your Library packed up and sent to Bethlehem [Pennsylvania], where I intend it shall remain 'till our public affairs wear a better aspect. I removed my Family . . . to a place called Goshen in Chester County, having procured in a good farm house two comfortable rooms for them. They yet remain there . . . The Enemy may determine to pay us a visit in the spring . . .*
>
> *I suppose you have been informed from the Congress of their appointing me Post Master General [I think because] . . . your Services may be required in France for a much longer time than you or I perhaps had any Idea of when you left home . . .*

*With most anxious expectation of hearing from you, and with un-
feigned Love to yourself . . . and Benny I subscribe myself . . . [&c.]*[939]

Friday, February 14, 1777. Shortly after his arrival in France, Ben Franklin
ordered Lambert Wickes, the *Reprisal*'s captain, to cruise against British shipping. Today, Captain Wickes reports:

> *This will inform you of my Safe arrival after a tolerable Successfull
> Cruize, having Captured 3 Sail of Brig's, one Snow and One Ship.
> [T]he Snow is the Falmouth [England] Packet bound from thence to
> Lisbon. [S]he is mounted with 16 guns and had Near 50 Men on
> board. She Engaged Near an hour before she struck . . . Three of our
> prizes is Arrived and I expect the other two in to Morrow . . .*[940]

Sunday, February 23, 1777. Today, from Philadelphia, Benny Bache's mother,
Sarah Bache, writes Ben Franklin:

> *We have been patiently awaiting to hear of your Arrival for some
> time . . . I have refused dinning at Mr. Climers to day that I might have
> the pleasure of writing to you and my dear Boy who I hope behaves so
> as to make you love him. We used to think he gave little trouble at
> home, but that was perhaps a Mothers partiality . . .*[941]

Monday, February 24, 1777. Today, in Paris, the French periodical *Affaires
de l'Angleterre et de l'Amérique* publishes the Pennsylvania Constitution of
1776, which the Duc de La Rochefoucauld has translated with the help of Benjamin Franklin.[942] John Adams:

> *In 1775 and 1776 there had been great disputes, in Congress and in
> the several States, concerning a proper constitution for the several
> States to adopt for their government. A Convention in Pennsylvania
> had adopted a government in one representative assembly, and Dr.
> Franklin was the President of that Convention. The Doctor, when he
> went to France in 1776, carried with him the printed copy of that Con-
> stitution, and it was immediately propagated through France that this
> was the plan of government of Mr. Franklin . . . Mr. Turgot, the Duke
> de la Rochefoucauld, Mr. Condorcet, and many others, became enam-
> ored with the Constitution of Mr. Franklin.*[943]

Saturday, March 1, 1777. Today, George Washington writes the legislature of
New York:

> *[I]n opposition to all my Orders and notwithstanding my utmost
> Vigilance, most of the Regiments . . . took off with them many [public
> arms] that were put into their hands. These . . . may, I should Sup-
> pose, . . . aided by the Supreme Civil Power in each State, be regained
> to the Public. Unless some such Step as this is adopted and attended
> with Success, I fear we shall not be able to furnish a Sufficient Num-
> ber for our Soldiers.*[944]

Monday, March 3, 1777. Today, George Washington writes the Governor of Connecticut:

> *As I have, in many of my late Letters, mentioned the distress that the Continent in general is under for the want of Arms; I need only repeat to you the Necessity that there is for making a Collection . . .*[945]

WEDNESDAY, MARCH 26, 1777

⊹ The Pennsylvania Gazette ⊰

P H I L A D E L P H I A. Tuesday last arrived here the Brig Sally, Capt. Stocker, in 11 weeks from Nantz in France, with 6,800 stand of small arms, a large number of gun-locks, &c.

Those are French arms!

Saturday, March 29, 1777. Today, George Washington writes the Continental Congress,

> *The arrival [from France] of the Arms, Locks and Flints, you have been pleased to mention, is a most fortunate and happy event. I join you most sincerely, in congratulations upon the occasion . . .*
>
> *I am happy to say the Arrival of the [French] Ship [Mercure] at Portsmouth . . . is confirmed by other Letters . . . Some of the letters say that a French general, Colo[nel] and Maj[o]r came passengers in the Ship who are highly recommended by Doctr. Franklin.*[946]

Today, Washington also writes the Governor of Connecticut,

> *I have the pleasure to inform you that a Vessel arrived at Philadelphia a few days ago from France, with Eleven thousand stands of Arms and some other Military Stores. The Accounts of the Intentions of France were most favorable.*
>
> *The late arrival of [French] Arms at Portsmouth is so ample that we shall have no future complaint for the want of them . . .*[947]

Thursday, April 3, 1777. Large quantities of French arms are arriving. Today, George Washington writes the Governor of Rhode Island:

> *The late ample arrivals of [French] Arms at Philadelphia and at Portsmouth . . . puts me out of all further uneasiness on account of that necessary Article. The Eleven hundred and Seventy Six stand which you received from the Continental Agent at Boston will be very near the Number wanted for your two Continental Battalions when Compleat . . .*[948]

In March, ten vessels of Beaumarchais' Hortalez et Cie. sailed for America. The *Amphitrite* and the *Mercure* arrived in Portsmouth, New Hampshire, with fifty-eight Brass Cannon, 16,700 stands of arms, 110 barrels of gunpowder, tents for ten thousand, clothing for twelve thousand, &c. A procession of French government arms is now begun, employing such French ships as the *Amphitrite, Mercure, Comte de Vergennes, Flammand, Mère Bobie, Seine, Thérèse, Amélia,* and *Marie Catherine*. This year, eighty ships will clear Bordeaux alone for the U.S. Many others will set sail to Santo Domingo or other French West Indies ports where their cargoes will be transshipped to the U.S. This year, America will import thirty thousand guns from France.[949]

Sunday, April 6, 1777. There is much speculation as to why Washington is so inactive. Today, John Adams evades the question:

> You have had many rumors propagated among you which I suppose you know not how to account for. One was that Congress, the last summer, had tied the hands of General Washington, and would not let him fight, particularly on the White Plains. This report was totally groundless. Another was that at last Congress untied the General, and then he instantly fought and conquered at Trenton. This also was without foundation for his hands were never tied, so they were not untied. Indeed . . . a question has been asked Congress . . . whether the General was bound by the advice of a council of war? No member of Congress, that I know of, ever harbored or conceived such a thought . . . [T]he General, like all other commanders of armies, was to pursue his own judgment after all.[950]

Wednesday, April 9, 1777. Today, from France, Benjamin Franklin writes the Continental Congress:

> The Desire that military Officers here of all Ranks have of going into the Service of the United States is so general and so strong as to be quite amazing. We are hourly fatigu'd with their Applications and Offers, which we are obliged to refuse; and with hundreds of Letters which we cannot possibly answer to Satisfaction . . .
> We have purchased 80,000 Fusils, a Number of Pistols, &c . . . They were King's arms and second-hand, but so many of them are unus'd and [so] good that we Esteem it a great Bargain if only half of them should arrive. We applied for the large brass Cannon to be borrow'd out of the King's Stores . . . You will soon have the Arms and Accoutrements for the Horse except Saddles, if not intercepted by the Enemy . . .
> The separate Constitutions of the several [American] States are also translating and publishing here, which afford abundance of Speculation to the Politicians of Europe. And it is a very general Opinion that if we succeed in establishing our Liberties, we shall . . . receive an immense Addition of . . . Families who will come over to participate [in] our Privileges . . . Tyranny is so generally established in the rest of the World that the Prospect of an Asylum in America for those who love Liberty gives general Joy, and our Cause is esteem'd the Cause of all Mankind.[951]

Monday, April 14, 1777. Today, a French noblewoman, the Countess Conway (whose husband Thomas Conway is en route to America) writes Benjamin Franklin:

> *I Commence to read and write a litle the english but I Know not Speak yet that language . . . I pray you to Signify to me a day and a hour where I can render homage to you; I am the wiffe of thomas Conway departed by l'amphitrite for to aid his Brother americains end to Share the glory with them.*[952]

Sunday, April 20, 1777. Many other idealistic Frenchmen are volunteering to serve in the American Revolution, joining a parade of supply ships. Today, the French nobleman the Marquis de Lafayette, who is only nineteen years old, sets sail for America aboard his own specially commissioned frigate, *Victoire.*[953] With him are other titled French soldiers, including the Baron Johann de Kalb bearing an offer from French Count Charles-François de Broglie (a marshal in the French army) to lead America's army.[954]

A British pamphlet, published this year at the behest of the British government, warns French King Louis XVI against allowing French officers to fight in America:

> *You are arming, imprudent monarch. Do you forget in what century, in what circumstances, and over what nation you reign? . . . The legislators of America are proclaiming themselves disciples of the French philosophers. They are executing what these [philosophers] have dreamed. Will not the French philosophers aspire to be legislators in their own country? . . . How dangerous to place the flower of your officers in communication with men enthusiastic for liberty! You will take alarm, but too late, when you hear repeated in your court vague and specious axioms which they have meditated in the forests of America . . .*[955]

Louis XVI will not heed such advice!

Today, from Braintree, Massachusetts, Abigail Adams writes her husband, John, that political wrangling is preventing adoption of a new Massachusetts state constitution:

> *I believe we shall be the last State to assume Government. Whilst we Harbour such a number of designing Tories amongst us, we shall find government disregarded and every measure brought into contempt . . . We abound with designing Tories and Ignorant avaricious Whigs.*[956]

Thursday, April 24, 1777. Today, George Washington writes Virginia congressional delegate Richard Henry Lee:

> *I profess myself to be of that class, who never built sanguinely upon the assistance of France, further than her winking at our supplies from thence for the benefits derived from our trade . . .*

The great delay in appointing the general officers, the resignation of some of them, the non-acceptance of others, and I might add the unfitness of a few, joined to the amazing delay in assembling the troops, and the abuses which I am satisfied have been committed by the recruiting officers . . . have distressed me . . .[957]

Friday, April 25, 1777. Today, Robert Gordon, British Commissary of Provisions, writes British Treasury Secretary John Robinson:

Captain [James] Grayson learned . . . that a ship from France had landed at Boston 15,000 stands of arms and some ammunition and dry goods on the 23rd March last; she mounted 20 guns.[958]

Sunday, April 27, 1777. Today, John Adams writes his friend Massachusetts political leader James Warren:

I must confess that I am at a Loss to determine whether it is good Policy in Us to wish for a War between France and Britain . . . I dont wish to be under obligations to [France] . . . , and I am very unwilling they should rob Us of the Glory of vindicating our own Liberties . . .

It is a Cowardly Spirit in our Countrymen which makes them pant with so much longing Expectation after a French War. I have very often been ashamed to hear so many Whigs groaning and Sighing with Despondency, and whining out their Fears that We must be Subdued unless France should step in. Are We to be beholden to France for our Liberties? . . . France has done So much already . . . She has received our Ambassadors, protected our Merchant Men, Privateers, Men-of-War, and Prizes, admitted Us freely to trade, lent Us Money, and Supplied Us with Arms, Ammunition, and Warlike stores of every Kind.[959]

Friday, May 9, 1777. Today, from Philadelphia, the Committee of Secret Correspondence of the Continental Congress writes the American commissioners in Paris:

This letter is intended to be delivered to you by John Paul Jones Esquire, an Active and brave Commander in our Navy . . . [W]e have directed him to go on board the Amphitrite, a French Ship of 20 guns, that brought in a valuable cargo of stores from Monsr. Hortalez & Co., and with her repair to France . . .

Capt. Jones is instructed to Obey your Orders . . . You see by this Step how much dependance Congress place in your advices . . .[960]

Monday, May 12, 1777. Today, in Paris, Ben Franklin records news from Boston about the arrival of French arms:

That a ship was arrived from Europe with 364 Cases of Arms containing 11,987 Stands; 1,000 Barrels of Gunpowder; 48 Bales of Cloth for Soldiers Cloathing; and other valuable Articles, which came very seasonably; and they had just received News at Boston that two other

Ships were arrived at a distant Port, with the same kind of Cargo's . . .[961]

Thursday, May 22, 1777. Today, from Paris, Ben Franklin writes Benny Bache's father, Richard Bache:

> *I have just received yours of March 10 . . . I rejoice to hear that the Family are all well. I did not hear before that they were out of Town . . . Ben's Letter is enclos'd. He dines with me every Sunday and some Holidays. He begins to speak French readily, and reads it pretty well, for the time . . .*
>
> *I thank you for the News you send me of the Skirmish &c. As our Troops will be much better arm'd and cloth'd this Year than they were the last, and the Enemy with all the Recruits they can muster no stronger; I hope for a continual Amendment of our Affairs. War is not yet commenc'd in Europe, but all are preparing for it . . .*
>
> *Our Privateers and Cruisers in the Channel have rais'd the Insurance in London. [American] Capt. Conyngham imprudently returning into Dunkirk with two Prizes, was . . . put into Prison . . .*
>
> *I wish to know some Particulars from you . . . Did you remove my Library and Instruments and where are they?*[962]

Sunday, May 25, 1777. Today, Franklin writes Congress how his naval activities may force France into the war with England:

> *The want of such a free Port appears in the late Instance of [American] Capt. Connyngham's Arrest at Dunkirk, [France], with the Prizes he brought in. For tho' the fitting out may be cover'd and conceal'd by various Pretences, so as at least to be wink'd at by the Government here . . . yet the bringing in of Prizes by a Vessell so fitted out is so notorious an Act, and so contrary to Treaties, that if suffered must occasion an immediate War . . .*
>
> *The Marquis de Fayette, a young Nobleman of great Family Connections here, and great Wealth, is gone to America in a Ship of his own, accompanied by some Officers of Distinction, in order to serve in our Armies. He is exceedingly beloved, and every bodys good wishes attend him . . . He has left a beautifull young Wife big with Child . . .*[963]

Wednesday, May 28, 1777. Today, Abigail Adams writes her husband that she shares his objections to a single-chamber legislature:

> *I recollect a remark of a writer upon Goverment [you] who says that a single assembly is subject to all the starts of passion and to the caprices of an individual.*
>
> *We have lately experienced the Truth of the observation. A French vessel came into Boston laiden with a large Quantity of dry goods . . . [S]ome things were offerd for sale by the captain at a higher rate than the Regulated price . . . Upon this a certain B[osto]n . . . Whig [demo-*

crat] Blustered about and insisted upon it, if he [the captain] would not comply, he ought to be orderd out of the Harbour, and [the demo-crat] procured a very unanimous vote for it in the House, but, upon its being sent up to the Counsel, there was but one vote in favour of it . . . [964]

The propertied class can afford the price!

Friday, May 30, 1777. Arms, ammunition, and money are now flowing from France to the United States. Today from Philadelphia, the Committee of Secret Correspondence (renamed the Committee of Foreign Affairs) writes the American commissioners in Paris:

> *The Amphitrite safely arrived Portsmouth, New Hampshire. The Seine at Martinique . . . We request you to expedite the Loan of Two Millions . . .* [965]

Wednesday, June 18, 1777. French volunteers are arriving. Today, John Adams writes Abigail:

> *We shall have all the Sages and Heroes of France here before long . . .*
> *Our Fabius will be slow, but sure.* [966]

Thursday, June 19, 1777. Today, George Washington writes:

> *An immediate declaration of War [by France] against Britain in all probability could not fail to extricate us from all our difficulties and to cement the Bond of Friendship so firmly between France and America as to produce the most permanent advantages to both . . .* [967]

Friday, June 20, 1777. Today, from Philadelphia, Tom Paine writes Benjamin Franklin:

> *I have . . . the pleasure of acquainting you of my being appointed Secretary to the Committee of Foreign Affairs [of the Continental Congress].* [968]

Wednesday, June 25, 1777. Today, William Carmichael, a deputy to the American commissioners in Paris, explains Franklin's plan to get France into the war against Britain:

> *[T]he [French] court shuns everything in Europe which might appear a glaring violation of their treaties with England. This line of conduct has delayed the stores so long promised . . . As such is their miserable policy, it is our business to force on a war in spite of their inclinations to the contrary, for which I seek nothing so likely as fitting out privateers from the ports and Islands of France . . . The natural antipathy of the nations is such that their passions being once fully excited, they will proceed to such atrocious acts of reprisal and mutual*

*violence, as will occasion clamor and altercations, which no soft word
can palliate . . .*

> *As the English ministry seemed convinced of the pacific, or rather
> undecided, state of the rulers here, they hasten . . . to end the war . . .
> Could they be provoked to unequivocal proofs of violence and breach
> of treaty, it would be a great point gained . . .*[969]

Saturday, June 28, 1777. Today, from the French port of St. Malo, American
Captain Lambert Wickes reports to his commander, Benjamin Franklin, on the
success of naval operations out of French ports (which Franklin has expanded
in the hope of provoking war between England and France):

> *We sail'd in Company with Captains Johnston and Nicholson from
> St. Nazair May 28th, 1777, fell in with the Fudrion about 40 leagues to
> the West of Bell Isle who chased us, fired Several Guns at the Lexing-
> ton . . . Nothing more happen'd till we Arrived of the No. end of Ireland
> June 19th when we took two Brigs and two Sloops one of which we
> sunk . . . took the Sloop Jassan from White Haven . . . took Scotch sloop
> from Prussia bound to Dublin . . . the Brig. Jenny and Sally from
> Glasgo bound to Norway . . . took a brig from Dublin bound to Irwain,
> Sunk her, took three large Brigs loaded with Coals from Whitehaven
> bound for Dublin, sunk them in Sight of that Port . . . took the Brig
> Crawford from Glasco bound to St. Ubes. 23d took the ship Grace
> from Jamaica bound to Liverpool . . . We stood down the Irish Channel
> 25th. took the sloop John and Peter from Haver de grass . . . 26th. At 4
> PM took a Snow from Gibraltar bound to London loaded with cork . . .
> Saw a large Ship off Ushant, Stood for her at 10 AM discovered her to
> be a large Ship of War standing for us, Bore away and made Sail from
> her. She chased us till 9PM and Continued firing at us from 4 till 8 at
> Night . . . We escaped by heaving our Guns overboard and lightning
> the Ship . . . The Prizes is sent into L'Orient, Nantz . . .*[970]

Wednesday, July 1, 1777. Today, from Philadelphia, Benny Bache's father,
Richard Bache, writes Ben Franklin:

> *I purpose in a few days to bring my Family to Town. Sally [Benny's
> mother] expects to lay in about the middle of August. [S]he cannot be
> accommodated . . . where she now is; some people are of opinion that
> the Enemy will still push at this City. I cannot think they will ever get
> here . . .*
>
> *My Love to Ben, tell him I want to know how his Head is, we flatter
> ourselves it is quite well by this time . . .*[971]

Benny Bache will have a new sister, Eliza, very soon!

Friday, July 4, 1777. Today, in London, the British instruct their minister at
Paris, David Murray (Lord Stormont) to give France an ultimatum on Franklin's
naval operations:

> *[P]eace, however earnestly wished, cannot be maintained unless effectual stop is put to our just causes of complaint . . . The views of the Rebels are evident[. T]hey know that the honour of this Country . . . will not submit to such open violation of solemn Treaties and established Laws . . . The necessary consequence must be a war, which is the object they have in view, and they are not delicate in the choice of means that may bring about an end so much desired by them.*[972]

Monday, July 7, 1777. Today, from New York, British Commander in Chief for North America Sir William Howe writes British Colonial Secretary Lord George Germain that French military officers and French artillery may make a big difference in the war's conduct:

> *[T]he war is now upon a far different scale with respect to the increased powers and strength of the [American] army . . . their officers being much better and the addition of several from the French service and a very respectable train of field-artillery. An officer of the 71st regiment lately arrived from Boston declares he saw fifty pieces of brass cannon landed there . . .*[973]

Tuesday, July 15, 1777. Britain knows that Ben Franklin's naval operations seek to instigate war between France and Britain. Today, the British Minister to France David Murray (Lord Stormont) meets with French Foreign Minister the Comte de Vergennes and then with Prime Minister the Comte de Maurepas. From Stormont's report:

> *I likewise told [Vergennes] that I knew the Rebels had a Design of Purchasing more Vessels at Nantes to Cruize against us, that two Americans who had lately escaped out of an English sail . . . were sent to Nantz by Franklin with that view, and were amply supplied by Him with Money, as this was a Design He greatly encouraged, well knowing the direct and necessary tendency it had to a Rupture between the two Courts . . .*
>
> *I spoke to [Maurepas] of the two Americans gone to [secure] ships at Nantes—of the constant Encouragement Franklin gave to all such Designs, and of the aim that Franklin had in view; he admitted this, said it was clear that all this was done in Hopes of forcing a Rupture, that these insults on our Coast, and cruizing against us in Europe, could have no other Aim . . . He ended with saying that this Project should be prevented . . .*[974]

Wednesday, July 16, 1777. Today, French Foreign Minister Vergennes submits a protest to the American commissioners at Paris:

> *You cannot forget that, at the first conversation I had with both of you, I assured you that . . . as to your commerce and navigation, we would grant every facility compatible with the exact observation of our treaties with England . . . I must point out to you the article of the*

treaty which forbids the power of allowing privateers free access to our ports, unless through pressing necessity, as also with respect to the deposit and sale of their prizes. You promised, gentlemen, to conform thereto.

After so particular an explanation, we did not press the departure of the Ship Reprisal, which brought Mr. Franklin to France, because we were assured that it was destined to return with merchandise. We had quite lost sight of this vessel . . . when, with great surprise, we understood that she had entered L'Orient, after taking several prizes . . .

[W]e had no reason to expect that the same Sieur Wickes would prosecute his cruising in the European seas, and we could not be otherwise than greatly surprised that, after having associated with the privateers the Lexington and the Dolphin to infest the English coast, they should all three of them come for refuge into our ports. You are too well informed, gentlemen, and too penetrating not to see how this conduct affects the dignity of the king, my master, at the same time it offends the neutrality, which his majesty professes . . . The king cannot dissemble it, and it is by his express order, gentlemen, that I acquaint you that orders have been sent to then ports on which the said privateers have entered, to sequester and detain them . . .[975]

Today, the British Minister to France writes London:

A little Time will show the real Intentions of France, if after her strong Professions, the succors to the Rebels should be continued and the American Privateers suffered to take Shelter and refit in her ports, the Consequence is clear. She must be resolved to [have] a War.[976]

Sunday, July 20, 1777. Today, from the French port of St. Malo, American Captain Lambert Wickes writes his fellow American Captain Henry Johnson:

[I] beg you would not leave that port untill you receive orders to do from the Hon[orable] Commissioners at Paris, but hold yourself in readiness to depart on Receipt of their orders from Paris . . . I think the reason the Gentlemen has not wrote you is owing to the hurry of Business now on hand, as our late Cruize has made a great deal of Noise & will probably bring on a War between France and England which is my sincere wish . . .[977]

Thursday, July 31, 1777. In the United States, British Commander in Chief for North America Sir William Howe has sailed from New York to attack Philadelphia. Today, George Washington learns this and writes:

Genl. Howe's Object and Operations no longer remain a Secret. At half after nine O'Clock this Morning, I received an Express from Congress advising that the Enemy's Fleet, consisting of 228 Sail, were at the Capes of Delaware yesterday in the forenoon. This being the case there can be no doubt but he will make a vigorous push to possess

Philadelphia, and we should collect all the force we can to oppose
him . . .

As the Troops are on their March from hence, I shall not add
more . . .[978]

Monday, August 4, 1777. Today, as Washington prepares to bring his army back from New Jersey to Pennsylvania, the Continental Congress takes charge of the Northern Army. The Journals report:

Congress took into consideration the letter from General Washington, wherein "he wishes to be excused from making the appointment of an officer to command the northern army"; and thereupon

Congress proceed to the election of an officer; and the ballots being taken, Major General Gates was elected to the command [of the Northern Army] . . .[979]

Congress has replaced General Schuyler as head of the Northern Army. John Adams:

[T]he New England Officers, Soldiers and Inhabitants, knew Gates
in the Camp at Cambridge . . . The New England Soldiers would not
enlist to serve under [New Yorker Schuyler] and the Militia would not
turn out . . . I was therefore under a Necessity of supporting
Gates . . .[980]

Tuesday, August 5, 1777. Today, George Washington writes:

I have, from the first, been among those few who never built much
upon a French war. I ever did, and still do think, they never meant
more than to give us a kind of underhand assistance; that is, to supply
us with Arms, &c. for our Money and trade.[981]

Tuesday, August 12, 1777. Today, in Paris, Benny Bache turns eight years old. Benny attends Le Coeur's boarding school, about a half day's ride from his grandfather, whom he visits each weekend and on holidays.[982]

Saturday, August 16, 1777. Today, at Bennington, Vermont, General John Stark, who refuses to be part of the Continental army and is the object of congressional hearings to censure him for this refusal,[983] leads an independent force of about 1,800 Hampshire Grants men to overpower five hundred Hessian mercenaries who have been detached, under Hessian Lieutenant Colonel Baum, from the British Northern Army, under General John Burgoyne, that is marching south from Canada.[984]

Tuesday, August 19, 1777. Today, Horatio Gates takes command of America's Northern Army, which is being reinforced with New England militiamen and equipped with massive quantities of French arms and ammunition which have arrived this spring and summer. The Northern Department does not report to Washington, and Washington declined even to recommend a commander for it. Washington:

The Northern department in a great measure has been considered as separate, and more peculiarly under [Congress'] direction, and the officers commanding there always of their nomination. I have never interfered further than merely to advise, and to give such aids as were in my power, on the requisitions of those Officers.[985]

Wednesday, August 20, 1777. Today, near Saratoga, New York, British Lieutenant General John Burgoyne, leading Britain's Northern Army, writes British Colonial Secretary Lord George Germain:

No operation, my lord, has yet been undertaken in my favour . . . Mr. [Horatio] Gates . . . is now strongly posted near the mouth of the Mohawk River, with an army superior to mine . . . He is likewise far from being deficient in artillery, having received all the pieces which were landed from the French ship which got into Boston.[986]

Friday, August 22, 1777. Today, Washington reports to Congress his reaction to news that the British are threatening Philadelphia:

I am honored with your favor containing the intelligence of the Enemy's arrival in Chesapeak Bay . . . I have issued orders for all the Troops here to be in motion tomorrow morning very early with intention to march them towards Philadelphia.[987]

Today, as George Washington sets off for Philadelphia, he orders Major General Sullivan to raid Staten Island but with so few soldiers that they are quickly put to flight. Washington:

It is unfortunate that an affair, which had so prosperous a beginning, should have terminated so disagreeably as in a great measure to defeat the good consequences that might have attended it . . . I am not sufficiently acquainted with circumstances to form a certain judgment of what might have been expected from this expedition . . .[988]

Sir Henry Clinton:

With respect to my own Post, it was threatened & once attacked with 7000 22.augt—had it been with 14,000, as would have been the Case if Washington had not been a Blockhead, I should have lost Staten and Long Island—even as it was, the good Conduct alone of the officers commanding at those stations saved them.[989]

Saturday, August 23, 1777. However unsuccessful George Washington's military operations may be, Ben Franklin is directing a naval operation that may force France into the war against Britain. Today, Silas Deane reports to the Committee of Foreign Affairs (formerly the Committee of Secret Correspondence) of the Continental Congress on Franklin's naval operations, starting with Franklin's decision to disregard congressional instructions and seize British prizes on his voyage to France:

The first that arrived was the Reprisal with two prizes; this caused much speculation, and at our first audience [with the French Foreign Ministry] after, we were told that, by the treaties subsisting between France and England, ships of war belonging to any foreign power at war with either could not be entered into their ports . . . and, as you will see in the treaty of commerce of 1713, confirmed by all subsequent treaties . . .

[T]he Reprisal [was] repaired and fitted for another cruise; which she made on the coast of Spain, taking, among other English prizes, the packet [mail] boat from Lisbon; with which Captain Wickes returned to [France's] port d'Orient. On this the English Ambassador complained loudly, and the English merchants were alarmed. Insurance rose in London, and it was generally supposed there would be a restitution of the prizes and detention of Captain Wickes, or a declaration of war. This Court then ordered the prizes as well as Capt. Wickes to leave the port in twenty four hours. The former were sent out but sold to French merchants, and Captain Wickes, his ship being leaky was permitted to stay. Soon after this, Captain Johnson arrived in the Lexington, and we, having bought a cutter, . . . sent her and the Lexington, under the command of Captain Wickes as commodore, with the design of intercepting the Irish linen ships . . . [A]s they sailed quite round Ireland and took or destroyed seventeen or eighteen sail of vessels, they most effectually alarmed England, prevented the great fair at Chester, occasioned insurance to rise, and even deterred the English merchants from shipping goods in English bottoms at any rate, so that in a few weeks forty sail of French ships were loading in the Thames on freight; an instance never before known.

But upon this the English Ambassador complained in a higher tone . . . [O]rders were sent from the Court [of France] to detain [Captain Wickes'] vessel and the Lexington until further orders. This was owing partly to Captain Wickes having repeatedly come into the ports of France with prizes and refitted his ship for fresh cruises, it being contrary to the treaty which they pretend to hold sacred . . . and the consequent threatenings of the British ministry. In this situation [we] remain at present . . .

[W]e bought a luggger at Dover and . . . sent Captain Cunningham in her, and ordered him to intercept the packet between England and Holland . . . Cunningham took her. As she had a prodigious number of letters on board, he imagined it was proper he should return to Dunkirk instead of continuing his course; in his return he also took a brig of some value and brought both prizes into port. This spread the alarm far and wide, and gave much real ground of complaint . . . The Ministry, therefore, to appease England ordered the prizes to be returned, and Cunningham and his crew to be imprisoned . . . But not discouraged thereby, another cutter was bought and equipped completely in the port of Dunkirk. Cunningham and his crew were set at *liberty, and with some address and intrigue got again to sea . . . His first adventure greatly raised insurance on the northern trade, even the packet boats from Dover to Calais were for some time insured. On his leaving the port of Dunkirk the second time, he had orders to proceed directly for America, but he . . . attacked the first vessels they met with, and plundered and burnt as they went on. Our last accounts are that they had taken or destroyed about twenty sail . . . [T]o appease the British ministry, [our naval purchasing agent] Mr Hodge has been arrested and confined . . . [T]he politics of this Court are intricate and embarrassed with connexions and alliances . . . Some other prizes have arrived in different ports, particularly two valuable Jamaicamen sent to Nantes a few days since . . . [T]he owners . . . lodged claims, showing that they . . . were English property captured by American privateers, and consequently by treaty could not be sold in France. This obliged the government to arrest the prizes or openly violate the treaty . . .* [990]

Today, French Foreign Minister Vergennes advises French King Louis XVI on how to deal with the ultimatum that Britain's ambassador, Lord Stormont, has delivered on Franklin's naval operations:

If the King consents to compel the surrender . . . of the prizes that American privateers may bring into his ports . . . it will have the effect of declaring them and their countrymen to be pirates . . . in order to avoid, perhaps for the moment, compromising ourselves with the English. It will have the effect of facilitating the reconciliation of the latter with the others . . .

The need and desire for peace must doubtless induce some sacrifices . . . Peace being preferable to war, although such peace as we could conclude with England would be but precarious, it might be proposed from this aspect to renew, and that in the most explicit manner, the orders that the American privateers and their prizes be not admitted within the ports of France except under absolutely urgent circumstances . . .

These orders issued, the tenor and the copies of them might, if the king shall permit, be officially communicated to the English Ministry . . . [991]

Vergennes' plan is adopted.

Today, George Washington writes the Continental Congress:

I beg leave to inform you that the [American] Army marched early this morning and will encamp this Evening, I expect, within Five or Six Miles of Philadelphia. Tomorrow Morning, it will move again, and I think to march it thro' the City . . . that it may have some influence on the minds of the disaffected there and those who are Dupes to their artifices and opinions. The March will be down Front and up Chestnut Street, and I presume about Seven O'Clock.[992]

Tonight, George Washington, twenty staff officers, and their servants stay at George Logan's home, Stenton, outside Philadelphia in Germantown.[993]

Tuesday, September 2, 1777. Today, from Philadelphia, John Adams writes to his wife, Abigail, about Washington's Fabian tactics:

> *Washington has a great Body of Militia assembled and assembling, in Addition to a grand Continental Army. Whether he will strike or not, I cant say. He is very prudent, you know, and will not unnecessarily hazard his Army. By my own inward Feelings, I judge, I should put more to risque if I were in his shoes . . .*
>
> *I wish the Continental Army would prove that any Thing can be done. But this is sedition at least. I am weary however, I own, with so much Insipidity.*[994]

Thursday, September 11, 1777. Today, George Washington confronts the British army on its march from the Chesapeake Bay toward Philadelphia. In the Battle of Brandywine Creek, Washington allows his army to be outflanked (as in New York), to suffer the loss of a thousand men, and to avoid complete destruction only through British forbearance in its pursuit.[995] Tonight, at midnight, Washington prepares his report to the Continental Congress:

> *I am sorry to inform you that, in this day's engagement, we have been obliged to leave the enemy masters of the field. Unfortunately the intelligence received of the enemy's advancing up the Brandywine and crossing at a ford about six miles above us, was uncertain . . . This prevented my making a disposition adequate to the force with which the Enemy attacked us on the right; in consequence of which the troops first engaged were obliged to retire before they could be reinforced. In the midst of the attack on the right, that body of the Enemy which remained on the other side . . . attacked the division there . . . and the light troops . . . who, after a severe conflict, also retired. The Militia . . . being post at a ford, about two miles [away], had no opportunity of engaging . . .*[996]

Adjutant General Timothy Pickering will much later write:

> *I had been in the army hardly three months when the Battle of Brandywine took place. While going with an order from the General [Washington] . . . , the action began . . . But before our arrival the troops had been defeated and retired. I joined the General. The British were advancing in line. There was no adequate force to oppose them . . . [T]he body of the enemy, left at Chad's Ford, crossed and defeated our troops posted there to receive them. Thus the day closed. In the course of it, I had observed nothing which indicated commanding talents in the General . . .*[997]

The nineteen-year-old French nobleman volunteer, the Marquis de Lafayette, now a major general in the American army, is wounded at Brandywine. Another French volunteer on the scene, the engineer and future American general Du Portail, observes:

> If the English had followed their advantage that day, Washington's army would have been spoken of no more. [998]

Tuesday, September 16, 1777. Today, Washington loses another battle, this time the "Battle of the Clouds." Washington reports:

> When I left Germantown with the Army, I hoped I should have had an opportunity of attacking them either in Front or on their Flank, with a prospect of Success; But . . . [o]ur March . . . was greatly impeded thro' want of Provisions which delayed us so long that the Enemy were apprized of our Motions and gained the Grounds near the White Horse Tavern, with a part of their Army turning our right flank, whilst another part, composing the Main Body, were more advanced towards our left. We should have disappointed them . . . But the Heavy rain which fell that evening and in the course of the night, totally unfitted our Guns for Service and nearly the whole of the Ammunition with which the Army had been compleated . . . In this Situation it was judged necessary that we should proceed [retreat] as far as Reading Furnace for the security of the army. Owing to these accidents . . . the Enemy have had an opportunity of making their advances without being attacked. [999]

A comment by Adjutant General Timothy Pickering:

> [W]e expected another general attack. Fortunately for the American army (so I have always thought) after some smart skirmishing, it began to rain; and [British] General Howe halted . . .
>
> It was during this skirmishing . . . I found the General [Washington] surrounded by officers, and everything in suspense . . . [Y]ou will imagine how urgent was the occasion when I could address [Washington] in this language; "Sir, the advancing of the British is manifest . . . If we are to take the high grounds on the other side of the valley, we ought to march immediately . . . Pray, Sir decide." . . .
>
> [T]he emphatic words ["Pray, Sir, decide"] . . . so strongly marked the General's want of decision.
>
> Having been under arms nearly all day during an incessant rain, the ammunition in the cartridge boxes (which were badly made) was spoiled. This obliged us to keep out of striking distance . . . until the army could safely encamp and make up musket cartridges. This caution occasioned two or three night marches. In one of them, General [Nathanael] Greene and I fell together in the rear of the army. In that situation, I thus accosted him. "General Greene, I had once conceived an exalted opinion of General Washington's military talents; but since

*I have been in the army, I have seen nothing to enhance that opinion."
In fact, it was lowered, and so Greene must have understood me; for
he answered promptly and precisely in these words—"Why the General does want decision: for my part, I decide in a moment."*[1000]

Thursday, September 18, 1777. Today, news that Washington won't prevent
an attack on Philadelphia reaches the city. This autumn, like last, Philadelphians must flee. *The Pennsylvania Gazette* does not appear.[1001]

Friday, September 19, 1777. Tom Paine writes of this morning:

> *[A]bout one in the morning the first alarm of [the British] crossing
> was given, and the confusion, as you may suppose was very great. It
> was a beautiful still moonlight morning and the streets as full of men,
> women and children as on a market day . . . I was fully persuaded
> that unless something was done the city [Philadelphia] would be
> lost . . .*[1002]

Today, John Adams writes in his diary,

> *At 3 this Morning, was waked . . . and told that the Members of Con-
> gress were gone, some of them, a little after Midnight. That there was a
> Letter from Mr. Hamilton, Aid de Camp to the General, informing that
> the Enemy . . . had it in their Power to be in Philadelphia before Morn-
> ing, and that if Congress was not removed, they had not a moment to
> lose. [We] arose, sent for our Horses, and after collecting our Things,
> rode off after the others . . . We rode to Trenton . . .*[1003]

Saturday, September 20, 1777. This morning, Tom Paine visits the commander in chief and later writes:

> *I breakfasted . . . at General Washington's quarters, who was at the
> same loss with every other to account for the accidents of the day. I
> remember his expressing his surprise, by saying, that at the time he
> supposed everything secure and was about giving orders for the army
> to proceed down to Philadelphia, that he most unexpectedly saw a
> part [of his army] . . . hastily retreating . . . A new army once disor-
> dered is difficult to manage . . .*[1004]

There's more bad news. Late tonight, the British surprise and massacre American soldiers outside Philadelphia at the Battle of Paoli. A British account:

> *Upon intelligence that [American] General [Anthony] Wayne was
> lying in the Woods with a Corps of 1500 men and four Pieces of Can-
> non, . . . [British] Major Grey was detached late at night with the 2d.
> Battalion of Light Infantry, a Troop of Light Dragoons, 42d and 44th.
> Regiments to surprize this Corps . . . Without the least noise our Party,
> by the Bayonet only, forced and killed all their out sentries and Pic-
> quets, and rushed in upon their Encampment, directed by the lights of
> their fires, killed and wounded not less than 300 in their Huts and*

about the fires, the 42d. sat fire to them, as many of the Enemy would not come out, chusing rather to suffer in the Flames than be killed by the Bayonet. The Party took between 70 and 80 prisoners, including several officers . . . We had one Officer and 3 men killed, and four wounded. The Party returned to their Camp that morning.[1005]

Sunday, September 21, 1777. Today, John Adams writes in his diary:

It was a false alarm which occasioned our Flight from Philadelphia. Not a Soldier of Howe's has crossed the Schuylkill. Washington has again crossed it, which I think is a very injudicious Maneuvre . . . If he had sent one Brigade of his regular Troops to have [headed] the Militia, it would have been enough. With such a Disposition, he might have cutt to Pieces Howe's army in attempting to cross any of the Fords . . .

I fear . . . the same timorous, defensive Part which has involved us so many Disasters. oh, Heaven! grant us one great Soul! One leading Mind would extricate the best Cause from that Ruin which seems to await it for the Want of it . . . One active, masterly Capacity would bring order out of this Confusion and save this Country.[1006]

Tuesday, September 23, 1777. Today, George Washington writes the Continental Congress, now situated in Lancaster, Pennsylvania:

I have not had the honor of addressing you since your adjournment to Lancaster and I sincerely wish that my first letter was upon a more agreeable subject. The Enemy, by a variety of perplexing Manoevres thro' a Country from which I could not derive the least intelligence (Being to a man Disaffected), contrived to pass the Schuylkill last night . . . They marched immediately towards Philadelphia, and I imagine their advanced parties will be near that City to Night. They had so far got the Start before I recd. certain intelligence that any considerable Number had crossed that I found it in vain to think of overtaking their Rear . . .

[T]he strongest Reason against being able to make a forced March is the want of Shoes . . . At least one thousand Men are barefooted and have performed the late marches in that condition . . .[1007]

Today, Elias Boudinot of New Jersey, America's Commissary General of Prisoners, writes his brother, Elisha:

After marching and countermarching and forced marching, we have lain still at this place and peaceably suffered about 7,500 men of the Enemy to cross the Schuylkill and enter the City of Philadelphia and never fired a Gun at them. Many are the reasons given for this Conduct . . . but I confess it is all arabic to me and by no means satisfactory.[1008]

Wednesday, September 24, 1777. Today, from Lancaster, French volunteer Baron Johann de Kalb writes Comte Charles-François de Broglie (the marshal in France's army who offered to lead America's army):

> [H]aving left Philadelphia on the 15th, the Congress sent after me to tell me that I was appointed Major General . . . however, I am very undecided what to do. I should certainly have some reasons for remaining; I have still more to return home . . .
>
> I have not yet told you anything of the character of General Washington. He is the most amiable, obliging, and civil man but as a General he is too slow, even indolent, much too weak and is not without his portion of vanity and presumption. My opinion is that if he gains any brilliant action, he will always owe it more to fortune or to the faults of his adversary than to his own capacity. I will even say that he does not know how to profit by the clumsiest mistakes of the enemy. He has not yet been able to get rid of his old prejudice against the French. I therefore think that in a short time, there will not be one of our officers in their service . . . If I return to Europe it will be in a great measure because it is impossible to succeed in the great project which I took up with so much pleasure.[1009]

Friday, September 26, 1777. Today, at ten in the morning, about 1,500 British troops, led by British General Charles, Lord Cornwallis, occupy Philadelphia. There is no resistance. A large part of the British army remains encamped in Germantown, about ten miles outside the city.[1010]

Saturday, October 4, 1777. Early this morning, George Washington surprises the British army camp at Germantown, but, when Washington's soldiers become preoccupied with dislodging a British detachment from a large stone house (Cliveden) belonging to Pennsylvania's Colonial Chief Justice Benjamin Chew, the British army has time to regroup and turn the tide. In this battle, Washington loses one thousand men, twice as many as the British. Washington reports his defeat to the Continental Congress:

> We marched about Seven O'Clock the preceding Evening [the 3d], and . . . attacked their Picket . . . about Sun rise the next Morning [and] . . . the Light Infantry and other Troops encamped near the picket which [were] forced from the Ground, leaving their baggage. They retreated a considerable distance, having previously thrown a party into Mr. Chew's house, who were in a situation not to be easily forced and had it in their power from the Windows to give us no small annoyance and in a great measure to obstruct our advance . . .
>
> The Morning was extremely foggy which . . . obliged us to act with more caution and . . . gave the Enemy time to recover . . . and what was still more unfortunate, it served to keep our different parties in ignorance of each Other's movements and . . . occasioned them to mistake one another for the Enemy, which I believe more than any thing

else contributed to the misfortune which ensued. In the midst of the most promising appearances, when every thing gave the most flattering hopes of victory, the Troops began suddenly to retreat and intirely left the Field in spite of every effort that could have been made to rally them.[1011]

Benny Bache will (as an adult) write:

[I]t is here and there the complaint of an unsuccessful general that his troops want courage; yet when his troops can march barefooted in the snow and suffer many other hardships with constancy, it is but too certain a proof that what they most want is confidence. Hence the militia which fought so well at Lexington and Bunker's hill in New England . . . too often fled when under the more immediate direction of General Washington; other troops commonly keeping them company. The bravest have some regard to their personal safety; and when they suspect that their lives are likely to be thrown away uselessly, they are prompt in noticing defects in their position in the day of battle.[1012]

Wednesday, October 15, 1777. Today, at Saratoga, New York, militiamen of New England—who have swelled America's Northern Army, under General Horatio Gates, to fourteen thousand and have inflicted three weeks of artillery shelling and small arms fire on the British Northern Army which has entered from Canada—have a tremendous American victory in sight. Today, Britain's Lieutenant General John Burgoyne, who commands this British Northern Army, holds a war council with fellow officers which he memorializes:

The lieutenant-general states to the council the present situation of affairs.

The enemy in force, . . . upwards of fourteen thousand men and a considerable quantity of artillery are on this side of the Fish Kill and threaten an attack. On the other side the Hudson's River . . . is another army of the enemy . . . They have likewise [French] cannon on the other side of the Hudson's River . . .

The first question he desired them to decide was, Whether an army of 3500 fighting men, and well provided with artillery, were justifiable . . . in capitulating in any possible situation? . . .

Resolved . . . that the present situation justifies a capitulation . . .[1013]

Thursday, October 16, 1777. Today, President of the Continental Congress Henry Laurens informs his son, John, that there's much criticism of Washington in the Congress:

I am writing in Congress and in the midst of much talk (not regular Congress) buz!

Says one "I would, if I had been Comm' of that Army with such powers, have procured all the necessaries which are said to be wanted without such whining Complaints."

"I would," says 2d., "have prevented the amazing desertions which have happened . . ." 3d "It is very easy too prevent intercourses between the Army and the Enemy . . . but we never mind who comes in and who goes out of our Camp."

"In short," 4th. "our Army is under no regulations or discipline" etc etc etc.[1014]

Friday, October 17, 1777. Today, an extraordinary event! At Saratoga, New York, British Lieutenant General John Burgoyne surrenders his five-thousand-man British Northern Army to American General Horatio Gates and America's Northern Army of fourteen thousand militiamen. It's a credit to General Gates, a credit to America's militiamen, and—perhaps most of all—a credit to Benjamin Franklin's diplomacy and to the generous assistance of France.

The French arms and ammunition that arrived this spring and summer equipped Horatio Gates' fourteen-thousand-man army. As one historian has observed, *"the arms and ammunition that stopped Burgoyne at Saratoga originally came from French arsenals."*[1015] As another observed, *"if it had not been for the great quantities of powder by importation from France before the Saratoga campaign, the Revolution would have broken down long before that time."*[1016] Of the 2,250,000 pounds of gunpowder that Americans have used to this time, 90 percent has come from France.[1017]

Meanwhile, some in the Continental Congress want to wrest control of the war from George Washington and place it in a new war board to which they would promote certain military figures. Today, Washington urges that the Continental Congress not promote a French officer Thomas Conway to be a major general:

[I]f there is any truth in a report . . . that Congress hath appointed, or as others say are about to appoint, Brigadier Conway a Major-General in this Army, it will be as unfortunate a measure as ever was adopted. I may add (and I think with truth) that it will give a fatal blow to the existence of the Army . . . General Conway's merit, then, as an Officer, and his importance in this Army, exists more in his own imagination than in reality . . . I am very well assured . . . that [the brigadiers] will not serve under him . . .

To Sum up the whole, I have been a slave to the service. I have undergone more than most Men are aware of to harmonize so many discordant parts; but it will be impossible for me to be of any further service, if such insuperable difficulties are thrown in my way.[1018]

Saturday, October 18, 1777. Today, George Washington learns of the Saratoga victory,[1019] though not from General Gates. Tom Paine:

The campaign of 1777 became famous, not by anything on the part of General Washington, but [rather] by the capture of [British] General Burgoyne and the army under his command by the Northern Army at Saratoga under General Gates. So totally distinct and unconnected was the latter of the authority of the nominal Commander-in-Chief that the two generals did not so much as correspond, and it was only by a letter of [American] General [George] Clinton that George Washington was informed of the event.[1020]

Wednesday, October 22, 1777. Today, Britain's commander in chief in North America, General Sir William Howe, submits his resignation. Britain's General Sir Henry Clinton will succeed him.[1021]

Monday, October 27, 1777. Today, George Washington reflects on his military failures and on General Gates' victory:

[The Northern Army] exhibits a striking proof of the advantages which result from unanimity and a spirited conduct in the Militias. [T]he Northern Army . . . was reenforced by upwards of 12,000 Militia who shut the only door by which Burgoyne could Retreat and cut off all of his supplies. How different our case !—the disaffection of great part of the Inhabitants of this State—the languor of others and internal distraction of the whole, have been among the great and insuperable difficulties I have met with, and have contributed not a little to my embarrassment this Campaign,—but enough! I do not mean to complain . . .[1022]

Thursday, October 30, 1777. Feelings against Washington continue to develop. Today, from Washington's headquarters, Tom Paine writes congressional delegate Richard Henry Lee of Virginia:

I wish the Northern Army was down here. I am apt to think that nothing materially will take place on our part at present. Some means must be taken to fill up the Army this winter. I look upon the recruiting service at an end . . .[1023]

The outpouring of New England militias for Horatio Gates' Northern Army has created an embarrassment for George Washington, whose defeats have lost him the power to recruit an army.

Tuesday, November 11, 1777. Today, John Adams leaves the Continental Congress for his home in Braintree, Massachusetts.[1024]

Thursday, November 20, 1777. Today, Pennsylvania's attorney general writes Massachusetts congressional delegate James Lovell:

Thousands of Lives and millions of Property are yearly sacrificed to the insufficiency of our Commander-in-Chief. Two battles he has lost for us by two such blunders as might have disgraced a Soldier of three months standing.[1025]

Thursday, November 27, 1777. Today, in the Continental Congress, the Journals report:

> *Resolved,* That Major-general Gates be appointed president of the Board of War;
>
> *Resolved,* That Mr. President inform Major-general Gates of his being appointed president of the new Board of War, expressing the high sense Congress entertain of the General's abilities and peculiar fitness to discharge the duties of that important office, upon the right execution of which the success of the American cause does eminently depend . . .[1026]

Today, Massachusetts congressional delegate James Lovell writes the victorious General Horatio Gates:

> *We want you in different places . . . We want you most near Germantown. Good God! what a situation are we in! How different from what might have been justly expected! You will be astonished when you come to know accurately what numbers have at one time and another been collected near Philadelphia to wear out stockings, shoes, and breeches. Depend on it for every ten soldiers placed under the command of our Fabius, five recruits will be wanted annually during the war. The brave fellows at Fort Mifflin and Red Bank have despaired of succor and been obliged to quit. The naval department has fallen into circumstances of seeming disgrace. Come to the Board of War if only for a short season . . .*
>
> *[I]f it was not for the defeat of Burgoyne and the strong appearances of a European war, our affairs are Fabiused into a very disagreeable posture . . .*[1027]

Thomas Conway, the French officer whose promotion George Washington opposes, also sends congratulations to Horatio Gates:

> *Heaven has been determined to save your Country, or a weak General and bad Councellors would have ruind it.*[1028]

Friday, November 28, 1777. Today, the Continental Congress chooses someone to replace Silas Deane as a commissioner in Paris. The Journals of the Continental Congress report:

> Congress proceeded to the election of a commissioner to the Court of France in the room of S. Deane, Esq. and the ballots being taken,
>
> John Adams, a delegate in Congress from Massachusetts bay, was elected.[1029]

John Adams:

> *Mr. Langdon came in from Philadelphia and leaning over the Bar whispered to me that Mr. Deane was recalled, and I was appointed to France . . . I could scarcely believe the news to be true . . .*[1030]

Wednesday, December 10, 1777. Today, in the Continental Congress, the Journals report criticism of George Washington's "forbearance":

Resolved, That General Washington be informed that Congress have observed, with deep concern, that . . . since the loss of Philadelphia . . . the army has been irregularly and scantily supplied . . . while large quantities of stock . . . are still remaining in the counties of Philadelphia [&c.] . . . which, by fortune of war, may soon be subjected to the power of the enemy;

That Congress . . . can only impute [General Washington's] forbearance . . . to a delicacy in exerting military authority on the citizens of these states; a delicacy which . . . may . . . prove destructive to the army and prejudicial to the general liberties of America;

That . . . General Washington should, for the future, endeavor as much as possible to subsist his army from such parts of the country as are in his vicinity . . . and that he issue orders for such purpose . . .[1031]

While the British army enjoys Philadelphia, George Washington settles his motley army at Valley Forge, a hilly campground about twenty miles north of the city. Physician General Benjamin Rush:

> *On my way to Yorktown [Pennsylvania], where the Congress then sat, I passed through the army at Valley Forge, where I saw similar marks of filth, waste of public property, and want of discipline which I had recently witnessed in the hospitals. General Sullivan (at whose house I breakfasted) said to me, "Sir, this is not an army—it is a mob." Here a new source of distress was awakened in my mind. I felt for the safety and independence of my country as well as for the sufferings of the sick under my care. All that I had heard from General Stephen, Colonel Reed, Mr. Mifflin, and some others was now revived in my mind. I found alarm and discontent among many members of Congress. While there, I wrote a short account of the state of our hospitals and of the army to Patrick Henry and concluded my letter by quoting a speech of General Conway's unfriendly to the talents of the Commander in Chief.*[1032]

Saturday, December 13, 1777. Today, in the Continental Congress, the Journals report:

Resolved, That two inspectors general be now appointed:
Congress proceeded to the election, and, the ballots being taken, Brigadier General [Thomas] Conway was elected . . .
Resolved, That another major general be appointed in the army of the United States.
The ballots being taken, Brigadier General [Thomas] Conway was elected.[1033]

Thursday, December 18, 1777. In Paris, the news is good! The French arms and ammunition that Benjamin Franklin released in January and that allowed Horatio Gates his victory at Saratoga may be followed by French fleets and armies. Today, Benjamin Franklin writes the Continental Congress:

[W]e received your Dispatches . . . by a Packet from Boston, which brought the great News of Burgoyne's Defeat and Surrender, News that apparently occasion'd as much general Joy in France as if it had been a Victory of their own Troops over their own Enemies; such is the universal, warm and sincere Goodwill and Attachment to us and our Cause in this Nation.

We took the Opportunity of pressing the Ministry by a short Memorial to the Conclusion of our propos'd treaty . . .

M. Gerard, one of the Secretaries, came Yesterday to inform us, by order of the King, that . . . in council it was decided and his Majesty was determined to acknowledge our Independence and make a Treaty with us of Amity and Commerce; that in this Treaty no Advantage would be taken of our present Situation to obtain terms from us which otherwise would not be convenient for us to agree to; his Majesty desiring that the Treaty, once made, should be durable, and our Amity subsist forever . . . that, in doing this, he might probably soon be engag'd in war, with all the Expences, Risque and Damage usually attending it, yet he should not expect any Compensation from us on that Account, nor pretend that he acted wholly for our sakes; since, besides his real Goodwill to us and our Cause, it was manifestly the Interest of France that the power of England should be diminish'd by our Separation from it . . .[1034]

Friday, December 19, 1777. Today, the Continental Congress hears complaints from Pennsylvania and New Jersey about George Washington's Fabian tactics. The Journals report:

Congress resumed the consideration of . . . the remonstrance from the executive council and assembly of Pennsylvania; Whereupon,

Resolved, That a copy of the remonstrance be transmitted by express to General Washington, and that he be desired to inform Congress . . . what measures are agreed upon for the protection of . . . Pennsylvania . . . :

That General Washington be further informed that, in the opinion of Congress, the State of New Jersey demands . . . the protection of the armies of the United States . . .[1035]

Pennsylvania's executive council and general assembly have remonstrated against Washington's retreat to Valley Forge:

1st. That by the Army's removal . . . [a] great part of this state . . . must be left in the Power of the Enemy, subject to their Ravages . . .

2d. . . . [T]oo many of our People are so disaffected already . . . [T]hose who have taken the most active Part in support of our Cause will be discouraged & give up all as lost.

3d. [B]y the removal of our Army, it will be impossible to recruit . . .

4th. The Army removing . . . must give a fatal Stab to the Credit of the Continental Currency . . . [I]t is very difficult to purchase from many of our most able Farmers the necessary Provisions of our Army, owing to their fear of the money . . .[1036]

Tuesday, December 23, 1777. Today, George Washington writes the president of the Continental Congress:

> [U]nless some great and capital change suddenly takes place in that line, this Army must inevitably be reduced to one or other of these three things. Starve, dissolve, or disperse in order to obtain subsistence . . .
>
> Yesterday afternoon . . . to my great mortification, I was not only informed, but convinced, that the men were unable to stir on Acct of Provision, and that a dangerous Mutiny, begun the Night before and [which] with difficulty was suppressed . . . was still much to be apprehended . . .
>
> All I could do under these circumstances was to send out a few light Parties to watch and harass the Enemy . . . [W]ith truth, then, I can declare that no Man in my opinion ever had his measures more impeded than I have by every department of the Army.[1037]

Tuesday, December 30, 1777. Today, the Marquis de Lafayette writes George Washington of dissatisfaction in the Continental Congress:

> There are open dissensions in Congress, . . . stupid men who without knowing a single word about war undertake to judge you, to make ridiculous comparisons; they are infatuated with Gates without thinking of the different circumstances, and believe that attaking is the only thing necessary to conquer . . .
>
> I have been surprised at first to see the new establishment of this board of war, to see the difference between the northern and southern departements, to see resolves from Congress about military operations—but the promotion of Conway is beyond all my expectations . . . I found that he was an ambitious and dangerous man . . . I wish your excellency could let them know how necessary you are to them . . .[1038]

Thursday, January 1, 1778. Today, French Foreign Minister Vergennes' first secretary, Gérard de Rayneval, reports to Vergennes that Franklin appears to be negotiating with the British:

> Mr. Hutton . . . who left London on Friday, arrived yesterday afternoon . . . He told us that he came on purpose to see his old friend Dr. Franklin who called there during the evening. Their interview was cordial and affectionate . . .
>
> This man sees the King and Queen [of England] a good deal . . . If he is a fresh emissary, I regard him as more dangerous than any other, because of his merit, of the confidence he inspires, and of his old ties. He told me plainly during the conversation that he had a tête-à-

tête conference of one hour with the King; that that prince, whom he adores, breathes nothing but peace, that . . . he was disposed to grant to the Americans everything they might ask, except the word independence.[1039]

Tuesday, January 6, 1778. Today, from Maryland, an admirer writes George Washington:

The morning I left camp, I was informed . . . that a strong faction was forming against you in the new Board of War and in the Congress . . . At my arrival at Bethlehem, I was told of it there, and was told that I should hear more of it on my way down. I did so, for at Lancaster I was still assured of it. All the way down, I heard of it, and I believe it is pretty general over the country . . .

The method they are taking is by holding General Gates up to the people, and making them believe that you have had a number three or four times greater than the enemy, and have done nothing; that Philadelphia was given up by your management; and that you had many opportunities of defeating the enemy . . .[1040]

Thursday, January 8, 1778. Today, in Paris, the King of France informs Ben Franklin that France will sign an alliance with the United States. As one historian will write, *"Franklin's greatest work for the salvation of American independence was accomplished."*[1041]

Today, the King of France writes the King of Spain:

SIR, MY BROTHER AND UNCLE:

England, our common and inveterate enemy, has been engaged for three years in a war with her American Colonies. We had agreed not to meddle [and] . . . made our free trade to the one that found most advantage . . . In this manner America provided herself with arms and ammunition, of which she was destitute. I do not speak of the succors of money and other kinds which we have given her, the whole ostensibly, on the score of trade. England has taken umbrage at these succors and has not concealed from us that she would be revenged sooner or later. She has already, indeed, seized several of our merchant vessels and refused restoration . . .

Such was the posture of affairs in November last. The destruction of the army of Burgoyne and the straitened condition [thereby] of Howe have totally changed the face of things . . . I have thought . . . having consulted upon the propositions which the insurgents make, that it was just and necessary to treat with them to prevent their reunion with the mother country.[1042]

Tonight, at six o'clock, the Comte de Vergennes' secretary, Conrad-Alexandre Gérard de Rayvenal, meets with Ben Franklin and the other American commissioners. From Gérard's report of the meeting:

I declared that, being now able to speak to them without reserve, I would announce to them that the King, being henceforth persuaded that the United States were resolved to maintain their independence, had decided to co-operate efficaciously to uphold it and cause it to be firmly established; that the deliberation . . . guaranteed the sincerity of his disposition and the firmness . . . that they were exempt from all views of ambition and aggrandizement; that he only desired to bring about irrevocably and completely the independence of the United States; that he would find therein his essential interest in the weakening of his natural enemy . . .

The Doctor . . . observed that this was what they had proposed and solicited vainly for a year past . . .

I showed myself eager to satisfy him, and explained to him that two treaties might be concluded, the first, of peace, and the second, of eventual alliance . . . that the general basis of the treaty would be equality and reciprocity; that the King was too great, too just, and too generous to profit by the circumstances, to snatch from them any advantage . . . that His Majesty was eager to give to Europe as well as America on this occasion an example of disinterestedness, by asking of the United States only such things as it might suit them to grant equally to any other Power whatsoever . . . [1043]

Monday, January 12, 1778. Today, from Pennsylvania, Physician General Benjamin Rush writes anonymously to Governor Patrick Henry of Virginia:

[Our] army, what is it? A major-general belonging to it called it a few days ago, in my hearing, a mob. Discipline unknown or wholly neglected . . . The northern army has shown us what Americans are capable of doing with a General at their head. The spirit of the southern army is in no way inferior to the spirit of the northern. A Gates, a Lee, or a Conway would in a few weeks render them an irresistible body of men. [1044]

This month, George Washington's Commissary General of Prisoners, Elias Boudinot, visits American General Charles Lee, formerly Washington's second in command, who is still being held prisoner by the British. Elias Boudinot:

In January 1778, I was sent by Genl Washington over to New York (with consent of Genl Howe) to examine into the actual Situation of our Prisoners and had orders to pay particular attention to Genl Lee and accomplish his exchange if possible. The Morning after my Arrival, I waited on Genl Lee . . . When Breakfast was over, Genl Lee asked me up into his Room . . . [He] began to urge the impossibility of our troops, under such an Ignorant Commander in Chief [as Genl Washington], ever withstanding British Grenadiers & Light Infantry . . . [1045]

Saturday, January 31, 1778. Today, Benny Bache's father, Richard Bache, writes Ben Franklin:

> *I acquainted you before how soon after Sally's lying in (when she
> . . . produc[ed] a fine Girl) we were obliged to quit the city [of Phila-
> delphia] . . . [W]e moved to a place near Trenton where we staid till
> the latter end of last Month, when our Army going into Winter Quar-
> ters . . . we were oblig'd to leave most of the furniture behind . . .*
> *We are happy to hear that Ben likes his School and that he improves
> fast. We esteem it a happy circumstance his going with you, for as
> things have turned out, had he remained here, he would have lost a
> deal of precious time, which is now usefully, I hope, employed . . .*
> *[T]he little Stranger sends Ben and you a kiss apiece . . .*[1046]

Friday, February 6, 1778. Today, in Paris, Benjamin Franklin and his fellow American commissioners sign the Franco-American Treaty of Amity and Commerce, and, knowing that this treaty's recognition of the United States as an independent sovereignty will inevitably put France and Britain at war, they also sign a Franco-American Treaty of Alliance. From the Treaty of Alliance:

THE FRANCO-AMERICAN TREATY OF ALLIANCE
The Most Christian King and The United States of North America . . .
having this day concluded a Treaty of Amity & Commerce . . . [and] in
case Great Britain in resentment of that connection . . . should break the
peace with France . . . concluded and determined on the following articles:
Article 1. If war should break out between France & Great Britain . . .
his Majesty and the said United States shall make it a common cause . . .
as becomes good and faithful allies . . .
Article 6th. The most Christian King renounces forever . . . any part of
the Continent of North America which before the Treaty of Paris in 1763
or [as in the case of Canada] in virtue of that Treaty were acknowledged
to belong to the Crown of Great Britain . . .
Article 8th. Neither of the two parties shall conclude either truce or
peace with Great Britain without the formal consent of the other first
obtained, and they mutually engage not to lay down their arms until the
independence of the United States shall have been formally or tacitly
assured by the Treaty or Treaties that shall terminate the war . . .
Article 11. The two parties guarantee mutually from the present time
and forever against all other powers, to wit, the United States to his most
Christian Majesty the present possessions of the Crown of France in
America [including those in the West Indies] . . .[1047]

From the Treaty of Amity and Commerce:

THE FRANCO-AMERICAN TREATY OF AMITY AND COMMERCE

The Most Christian King and the thirteen United States of North America . . . agreed upon the following articles: . . .

ARTICLE I. There shall be . . . perpetual peace between his most Christian King, his heirs, and successors, and the said United States.

ART. II. The most Christian king and the United States engage, mutually, not to grant any particular favour to other nations in respect to commerce and navigation which shall not immediately become common to the other party . . .

ART. XIX. It shall be lawful for the ships of war of either party, and privateers, freely to carry . . . ships and goods taken from their enemies . . . to and [to] enter the ports of the other party . . . On the contrary, no shelter or refuge shall be given in their ports to such as shall have been made prize . . . of either of the parties . . .

ART. XXIV. It shall not be lawful for any foreign privateers not belonging to the subjects of the most Christian King, nor citizens of the said United States . . . to fit their ships in the ports of either the one or the other . . . or to sell what they have taken . . .

ART. XXV. It shall be lawful for all and singular the subjects of the most christian king and the citizens, people and inhabitants of the said United States to sail with their ships with all manner of liberty and security . . . from any port to the places of those who are . . . at enmity with the most Christian King or the United States. It shall likewise be lawful . . . to sail . . . from the places . . . of those who are enemies . . . And it is hereby stipulated that *free ships shall also give a freedom to goods,* and that every thing shall be deemed to be free and exempt which is found on board . . . contraband goods being always excepted . . .

ART. XXVI. [U]nder this name of contraband . . . shall be comprehended arms, great guns, bombs with their fusees . . . cannon ball, gunpowder [&c.]

ART. XXX. It is also agreed that all goods, when once put on board the ships and vessels of the contracting parties, shall be subject to no further visitation . . . [n]or . . . be put under any arrest or molested . . .[1048]

As I write in my history,

> *The examination of these treaties, and of all the other circumstances under which they were formed, presents an example of generosity in political transactions that is at once as extraordinary as it is rare and honourable to the negotiators and the nations concluded in it. They exhibit the first evidence of philosophy in modern times, blending true liberality with diplomatic proceedings.*[1049]

In the Treaty of Amity and Commerce, France neither demands nor receives any trade preference, just the promise of being treated as favorably as America treats any other nation. Similarly, France does not demand or receive any limitation upon those with whom the United States may trade. Freedom of the seas, the freedom of neutral nations to trade anywhere, even to the ports of a friend's enemies during war (unless bringing instruments of war), is honored. In my history, I write,

> *It is, however, clear that France in forming these treaties had neither taken advantage of the circumstances in which she herself stood, [nor] of the exigency under which the soliciting party [America] was placed, nor of any provision for a contingency either in point of expenditure or future remuneration of any kind.*
>
> *The whole appears rather as the sacrifices of an affectionate friendship than the cold stipulations of a selfish diplomacy; it was the emanation of the characters and circumstances that produced it. To America there was a direct, immediate, and stupendous good, in return for which France was to be entitled for a remote and circumscribed advantage; a privilege which could not be considered as an equivalent [even] exclusive of the remoteness. This privilege was . . . to be in fact mutual . . . of passing ships of war into the ports of the United States during a future possible war, without the officers of the United States taking cognizance of the validity or invalidity of the capture . . . and at the same time excluding the enemies of France from a similar privilege . . .* [1050]

Tuesday, February 10, 1778. Today, as if to celebrate France's commitment to America's democratic revolution, the Enlightenment philosopher of tolerance and rationality François Marie Arouet, known everywhere as Voltaire, appears in Paris for the first time in twenty-eight years. He is ill and has but a few months to live.[1051] The Marquis de Condorcet:

> *A crowd of men and women of every rank and condition, from whom his verses had drawn the tears of humanity . . . were eager to behold him . . . Ministers, and proud prelates, were obliged to respect the idol of the nation . . . His carriage, which could scarcely proceed along the streets, was surrounded by a numerous multitude, who blessed him and celebrated his work.* [1052]

Saturday, February 14, 1778. Today, America's newest commissioner to the court of France, John Adams of Massachusetts, sets sail from Boston to France aboard the Continental frigate *Boston,* Captain Samuel Tucker. Like Ben Franklin, John Adams brings with him a very young child, his ten-year-old son, John Quincy Adams.[1053]

Thursday, February 22, 1778. Today, in France, Benjamin Franklin takes Benny Bache out of school to meet the great Voltaire at his private apartment. The Marquis de Condorcet:

> *Franklin was eager to see a man whose reputation had long been spread over both worlds; Voltaire, although he had lost the habit of*

speaking English, endeavored to support the conversation in that language; and afterwards, reassuming the French, he said: "I could not resist the desire of speaking the language of Mr. Franklin for a moment."

The American philosopher presented his grandson to Voltaire, with a request that he give him a benediction. "God and liberty!" said Voltaire: "it is the only benediction which can be given to the grandson of Franklin."[1054]

Friday, February 27, 1778. Today, the Marquis de Lafayette writes George Washington of the growing opposition to America's commander in chief:

I understood that John Adams spoke very disrespectfully of your Excellency in Boston . . . [E]nemy's of yours are so low, so far under your feet, that it is not of your dignity to take notice of 'em. I don't speak however of the honorable, the Continental Congress, for, if I was General Washington, I schould write very plain to them.[1055]

John Adams:

The News of my Appointment [on the mission to France] was whispered about, and General Knox came up to dine with me, at Braintree. The design of his Visit was As I soon perceived to sound me in relation to General Washington. He asked me what my Opinion of him was. I answered with the Utmost Frankness, that I thought him a perfectly honest Man, with an amiable and excellent heart, and the most important Character at that time among Us, for he was the Center of our Union. He asked the question, he said, because, as I was going to Europe it was of importance that the Generals Character should be supported in other Countries. I replied that he might be perfectly at his ease on the Subject for he might depend upon it, that both from principle and Affection, public and private I should do my Utmost to support his Character at all times and in all places, unless something should happen very greatly to alter my Opinion of him . . . I mention this incident, because that insolent Blasphemer of things sacred and transcendent Libeller of all that is good Tom Paine has more than once asserted in Print, the scandalous Lye, that I was one of a Faction in the fall of the Year 1777, against General Washington. It is indeed a disgrace to the moral Character and the Understanding of this Age, that this worthless fellow should be believed in any thing. But Impudence and Malice will always find Admirers.[1056]

Jimmy Callender:

During the revolution, [Mr. Adams] was one of the party discontented with Mr. Washington, and favoured the projects for turning him out.[1057]

Tom Paine:

> *John Adams was one of the chiefs of a party at York-town in Penn-sylvania, in the latter end of the year 1777 and beginning of '78, for dismissing Washington from the command of the army, because, they said, he was not capable of it and did nothing.* [1058]

Saturday, March 21, 1778. The alliance between France and America will yield many victories for America. Today, in London, British Colonial Secretary Lord George Germain writes a highly confidential communication to the Lords of Admiralty:

> *My Lords, the French King . . . having signed a treaty of amity and commerce with the agents of His Majesty's rebellious subjects in North America and there being reason to suppose that a squadron of French ships of war . . . is sailed for North America . . . I have received the King's commands to signify to your lordships that His Majesty's plea-sure that you do instruct the commander of His Majesty's ships in North America . . . that he do collect as great a force as he immediately can and do his utmost to attack, defeat, and utterly destroy the said squadron in preference to all other services which he may have re-ceived instructions to perform.* [1059]

Today, the King's instructions are sent to British General Sir Henry Clinton, the new commander in chief for British forces in North America:

> *[I]t is our will and pleasure that you do evacuate Philadelphia, and having embarked all the troops, as also the ordinance, stores, provi-sions and everything belonging to us or necessary for our troops, you are to proceed with the whole to New York . . .*
>
> *If . . . you shall find yourself in danger of being overpowered and forced by the superior numbers of the enemy, or your retreat likely to be cut off, in either of these cases, it is our will and pleasure that you withdraw our troops from New York . . .* [1060]

Friday, March 27, 1778. Today, on the orders of the King of France, orders are issued to French Admiral Charles-Hector, Comte d'Estaing:

> *1st.—Departure from Toulon . . . Landing by the Delaware River . . . [&c.]* [1061]

A French fleet of twelve ships-of-the-line and five frigates, under Admiral d'Estaing, will soon be leaving for America! [1062]

Saturday, March 28, 1778. Today, the King of France writes to the United States Continental Congress:

> *VERY DEAR AND GREAT FRIENDS AND ALLIES:*
> *The Treaties we have signed with you . . . are a certain guaranty to you of our affection . . . as well as of the interest which we take . . . in*

your happiness and prosperity . . . [W]e have appointed Mr. Gerard, sec-retary of our council of state, to reside near you in quality of our minister plenipotentiary . . .

You will learn, undoubtedly with gratitude, the measure which the conduct of the King Of Great Britain has induced us to take, of sending a fleet to endeavor to destroy the English forces upon the shores of North America . . .

The Count d'Estaing, vice-admiral of France, is charged to concert with you the operations . . .

Moreover, we pray God that he will have you, very dear and great friends and allies, under his holy protection.

Written at Versailles, the 28th of March, 1778.
Your good friend and ally, LOUIS.[1063]

Tuesday, March 31, 1778. Today, Ben Franklin writes Benny Bache's parents, Richard and Sarah Bache, that France's first Minister Plenipotentiary to the United States, Conrad-Alexandre Gérard de Rayvenal, will soon be leaving for Philadelphia:

His Excellency, M. Gérard . . . is a Friend to your Country and to your Father which gives him a double Claim to your Civilities . . . It is so long since I have heard from you, and there have been such Burn-ings and Devastations made by the Enemy, that I know not whether, even if Philadelphia is recover'd, you have a House left to entertain him in . . .

Benny continues well, and minds his Learning . . .[1064]

CHAPTER EIGHT

THE DUKE OF BRAINTREE

I ought not to conceal from you, that one of my colleagues [Mr. Adams]
is of a very different Opinion from me in these matters. He thinks . . .
Gratitude to France is the greatest of Follies, and that to be influenc'd
by it would ruin us. He makes no secret of having these Opinions . . .
I am persuaded . . . that he means well for his Country, is always an
Honest Man, often a wise one, but sometimes, and in some things,
absolutely out of his senses.

DR. BENJAMIN FRANKLIN [1065]

Dr. Franklin's behavior had been so excessively complaisant to the
French ministry . . . I had been frequently obliged to differ from him
and sometimes to withstand him to his face; so that I knew he had
conceived an irreconcilable hatred of me and that he had propagated
and would continue to propagate prejudices, if nothing worse, against
me in America from one end of it to the other.

JOHN ADAMS,
PRESIDENT OF THE UNITED STATES, 1797–1801 [1066]

Wednesday, April 1, 1778. Today, after a long journey from America, John
Adams arrives at Bordeaux, France. He is too late to participate in treaty negotiations. The Franco-American Treaty of Amity and Commerce of 1778 and
the Franco-American Treaty of Alliance of 1778 are on their way to Philadelphia for ratification. John Adams writes:

> When I arrived in France, the French nation had a great many
> questions to settle. The first was, Whether I was the famous Adams? Le
> fameux Adams? Ah, le fameux Adams. In order to speculate a little on
> this subject, the pamphlet entitled "Common Sense" had been printed
> in the "Affaires de Angleterre et de l'Amérique," and expressly [and
> wrongly] ascribed to Mr. Adams, the celebrated member of Congress—
> le célèbre member du congres. It must be further known that, although
> the pamphlet, Common Sense, was received in France and in all Eu-
> rope with rapture, yet there are certain parts of it that they did not
> choose to publish in France. The reasons of this any man may guess.
> Common Sense undertakes to prove that monarchy is unlawful by the

Old Testament. They, therefore, gave the substance of it, as they said; and, paying many compliments to Mr. Adams, his sense and rich imagination, they were obliged to ascribe some parts to republican zeal. When I arrived at Bordeaux, all that I could say or do could not convince anybody but that I was the fameux Adams.[1067]

Thursday, April 2, 1778. Tonight at dinner in Bordeaux, a French woman flirts with New Englander John Adams. John Adams writes in his diary:

> *One of the most elegant Ladies at Table, young and handsome, tho married to a Gentleman in the Company, was pleased to Address her discourse to me . . . "Mr. Adams, by your Name I conclude you are descended from the first Man and Woman, and probably in your family may be preserved the tradition which may resolve a difficulty which I could never explain. I never could understand how the first Couple found out the Art of lying together?" To me . . . this question was surprizing and shocking: but although I believe at first I blushed, I was determined not to be disconcerted . . . I answered her "Madame . . . I rather thought it was by Instinct . . . resembling the Power of Electricity . . ." When this Answer was explained to her, she replied "Well I know not how it was, but this I know it is a very happy shock." . . . The decided Advances made by married Women, which I heard related, gave rise to many reflections in my mind . . . The first was if such a[re] the manners of Women of Rank, Fashion and Reputation [in] France, they can never support a Republican Government nor be reconciled with it. We must therefore take great care not to import them into America.*[1068]

Thursday, April 9, 1778. Having arrived in Paris last night from Bordeaux and having stayed overnight at a downtown hotel, today John Adams visits Benjamin Franklin at Franklin's residence in the suburb of Passy. Adams writes in his diary:

> *Went in a Coach to Passy with . . . my son. [We visited] Dr. Franklin with whom I had served the best part of two Years in Congress . . . [H]e received me accordingly with great apparent Cordiality. Mr. Dean [whom I am replacing] was gone to Marseilles to embark with [the French fleet under Admiral] D'Estaing for America. Franklin undertook the care of Jesse Deane [Mr. Deane's son] . . . [a]nd he was soon sent, with my son [John Quincy Adams] and Dr. Franklin's Grandson Benjamin Franklin Bache . . . to the Pension [boarding school] of Mr. Le Coeur at Passy . . .*
>
> *Dr. Franklin presented to me the Compliments of Mr. Turgot, the late [French] Controuler of the Finances and a very pressing Invitation to dine with him . . . I went with Dr. Franklin . . . and dined with*

this Ex-Minister . . . [T]wenty others of the Great People of France were there . . .

Dr. Franklin had shewn me the Apartements and Furniture left by Mr. Deane . . . I determined to put my Country to no further expence on my Account but to take my Lodgings under the same Roof with Dr. Franklin . . .[1069]

Friday, April 10, 1778. Today, John Adams writes in his diary:

When I arrived in Paris, I found a different style. I found great pains taken, much more than the question was worth, to settle the point that I was not the famous Adams. There was a dread of sensation . . . Nobody went so far in France . . . that I was the infamous Adams . . . I certainly joined both sides in this, in declaring that I was not the famous Adams, because this was the truth.

It being settled that he was not the famous Adams, the consequence was plain; he was some man that nobody had ever heard of before, and therefore a man of no consequence—a cipher . . . I was not the famous Adams.

Seeing this and saying nothing,—for what could a man say? . . . I behaved with as much prudence and civility and industry as I could; but still it was settled, absolutely and unalterably, that I was a man of whom nobody had ever heard before—a perfect cipher; a man who did not understand a word of French, awkward in his figure, awkward in his dress; no abilities, a perfect bigot and fanatic.[1070]

Saturday, April 11, 1778. Today, at the Royal Court of France at Versailles, John Adams meets the French Foreign Minister, the Comte de Vergennes. John Adams:

Went to Versailles with Dr. Franklin . . . visited the Secretary of State for foreign Affairs, the Count de Vergennes and was politely received. He hoped I should stay long enough in France to acquire the French Language perfectly . . . Hoped the Treaty would be agreable, and the Alliance lasting. Although the Treaty had gone somewhat farther than the System I had always advocated in Congress and further than my Judgment could yet perfectly approve, it was now too late to make any Objections . . .

I was then shewn the Pallace . . .

Although my Ignorance of the Language was very inconvenient and humiliating to me, yet I thought the Attentions which had been shewn me . . . manifested . . . in what estimation the new Alliance with America was held.[1071]

Sunday, April 12, 1778. Today, in Paris, John Adams writes:

It is the universal Opinion of the People here, of all Ranks, that a Friendship between France and America is the Interest of both Countries, and the late Alliance, so happily formed, is universally popular; so much so that I have been told by Persons of good Judgment that the Government here would have been under a Sort of Necessity of agreeing to it even if it had not been agreable to themselves. [1072]

Franklin's work is revealed: *"[T]he Government here would have been under a Sort of Necessity of agreeing to it even if it had not been agreable to themselves."*

Monday, April 13, 1778. Today, acting in pursuance of the new Franco-American alliance, a French war fleet of twelve ships of the line and five frigates, under the command of French Admiral Comte d'Estaing, sets sail from Toulon, France for Philadelphia's Delaware River. Their mission is to surprise the British army and fleet at Philadelphia. Traveling aboard the fleet's flagship, the *Languedoc,* is France's first Minister Plenipotentiary to the United States, Conrad-Alexandre Gérard de Rayvenal, formerly first secretary to the Comte de Vergennes. Also aboard the *Languedoc* is one of the American commissioners at Paris, Silas Deane, who's been recalled by Congress. [1073]

Thursday, April 16, 1778. Today, from Paris, a British spy reports:

J. Adams is arrived very disappointed to find everything concluded. [T]alks of returning. [1074]

Today, John Adams writes in his diary,

Doctor Franklin is reported to speak French very well, but I find, upon attending to him, that he does not speak it grammatically, and, indeed, upon enquiring, he confesses that he is wholly inattentive to the Grammar. His Pronunciation too upon which the French Gentlemen and Ladies compliment him, and which he seems to think is pretty well, I am sure is very far from being exact. [1075]

Tuesday, April 21, 1778. Of today, John Adams writes,

Dr. Franklin, one of my Colleagues, is so generally known that I shall not attempt a Sketch of his Character at present. That He was a great Genius, a great Wit, a great Humourist, and a great Satyrist, and a great Politician is certain. That he was a great Phylosopher, a great Moralist, and a great Statesman is more questionable. [1076]

Wednesday, April 22, 1778. Today, in America, American Commissary General of Prisoners Elias Boudinot meets with George Washington's former second in command General Charles Lee, just released from captivity. Boudinot records:

When [Genl Lee] came out [from being a prisoner] . . . Genl Washington gave him command of the Right Wing of the Army, but before he took charge of it, he requested leave to go to Congress at York town; which was readily granted.

Before he went, I had an interview with him.— . . . He said he was going to Congress . . . That he found the Army in a worse situation than he expected and that General Washington was not fit to command a Sergeant's Guard . . .

He went to Congress . . . He returned to the army and took command of the right wing—He immediately began to rebel ag[ains]t Genl Washington . . . He assured himself that Genl Wushington was ruining the whole cause . . .[1077]

Thursday, April 23, 1778. Word is out in Philadelphia that France has signed an alliance with the United States.[1078]

Wednesday, April 29, 1778. Tonight, in Paris, John Adams writes in his diary:

Dined with the Marshall de Maillebois . . .

It is proper in this place to insert an Anecdote. Mr. Lee and I waited on the [French Foreign Minister] Count de Vergennes one day . . . [H]e said he would take a Walk with us . . . As We walked across the Court of the Castle of Versailles, We met the Marshall Maillebois. Mutual Bows were exchanged, as We passed, and Mr. Lee said to the Count de Vergennes, "That is a great general, sir." "Ah!" said the Count de Vergennes, "I wish he had the Command with you!" . . .

My feelings, on this Occasion, were kept to myself, but my reflection was. "I will be buried in the Ocean, or in any other manner sacrificed, before I will voluntarily put on the Chains of France" . . .

After dinner We went to the [French] Academy of Sciences, and heard Mr. D'Alembert as Secretary perpetual, pronounce Eulogies on several of their Members lately deceased. Voltaire and Franklin were both present, and there presently arose a general Cry that Monsieur Voltaire and Monsieur Franklin should be introduced to each other. This was done and they bowed and spoke to each other. This was no Satisfaction. There must be something more. Neither of our Philosophers seemed to divine what was wished or expected. They however took each other by the hand . . . But this was not enough. The Clamour continued, untill the explanation came out "Il faut s'embrasser, a la françoise." The two Aged-Actors upon this great Theatre of Philosophy and frivolity then embraced each other by hugging one another in their Arms and kissing each others cheeks, and then the tumult subsided. And the Cry immediately spread through the whole Kingdom and I suppose over all Europe Qu'il etoit charmant. Oh! il etoit enchantant, de voir Salon et Sophocle embrassans. How charming it was! Oh! it was enchanting to see Solon and Sophocles embracing![1079]

→ The Pennsylvania Gazette ←

POSTSCRIPT TO THE PENNSYLVANIA GAZETTE OF MAY 2, 1778.

Y O R K- T O W N [Pennsylvania], May 4.

On Saturday last Simeon Dean, Esq. arrived at Congress, express from the American Plenipotentiaries at the Court of France, and delivered his Dispatches to his Honour, the President.— The Important Contents are, by a Correspondent, thus communicated . . .

[S]igned at Paris on the 6th of February, a Treaty of Alliance and Commerce between the Crown of France and the United States of America. almost in the very terms on which the American Plenipotentiaries had been instructed by Congress . . . [Terms set forth.] . . .

These important advices were brought over in Le Sensible, Mons. Marignie, Commander, a Royal Frigate of France, of all twelve-pounders and 300 men.

Sunday, May 3, 1778. Today, from Philadelphia, Virginia's delegates to the Continental Congress write Virginia Governor Patrick Henry:

> *Having heard these Treaties [with France] read but once in Congress . . . we find that his most Christian Majesty has been governed by principles of Magnanimity and true generosity, taking no advantage of our circumstances, but acting as if we were in these plenitude of power and in the greatest security . . . We are shortly to receive considerable Stores from France . . .* [1080]

Monday, May 4, 1778. This afternoon, in the Continental Congress, the Journals report:

> Congress resumed the consideration of the treaty of amity and commerce concluded at Paris on the 6th of February . . .
>
> *Resolved unanimously,* That the same be and is hereby ratified.
>
> Congress also took into consideration the treaty of Alliance, concluded at Paris on the 6th day of February . . .
>
> *Resolved unanimously,* That the same be and is hereby ratified . . .
>
> *Resolved,* That this Congress entertain the highest sense of the magnanimity and wisdom of his most Christian Majesty . . . and the commissioners, or any of them, representing these states at the court of France, are directed to present the grateful acknowledgment of this Congress to his most Christian Majesty for his truly magnanimous conduct . . . and to assure his Majesty, on the part of this Congress, it is sincerely wished that the friendship so happily commenced between France and these United States may be perpetual. [1081]

Tuesday, May 5, 1778. Today, George Washington orders a celebration of the French alliance:

It having pleased the Almighty Ruler of the Universe propitiously to defend the cause of the United American States, and finally by raising up a powerful friend among the princes of the Earth, to establish our Liberty and Independence upon a lasting foundation; it becomes us to set apart a day for gratefully acknowledging the Divine Goodness, and celebrating the event, which we owe to His benign interposition. The several Brigades are to be assembled at 9 o'clock tomorrow morning, when their Chaplains will communicate the intelligence contained in the Postscript of the [Pennsylvania] Gazette of 2nd inst . . . and offer up a thanksgiving, and deliver a discourse suitable to the occasion.[1082]

Wednesday, May 6, 1778. Today, Washington's troops celebrate the French alliance. One eyewitness account:

The wine circulated in the most genial manner—to the King of France—the friendly European powers—the American States—the Honorable Congress, and other toasts of a similar nature, descriptive of the spirit of freemen.

The general [Washington] himself wore a countenance of uncommon delight and complacence . . . The [army], in particular never looked so well, nor in such good order, since the beginning of the war.[1083]

George Washington has good reason to celebrate. Tom Paine:

The capture of Burgoyne [at Saratoga] gave an éclat in Europe to the American arms, and facilitated the alliance with France. The éclat, however, was not kept up by anything on the part of General Washington. The same unfortunate languor that marked his entrance into the field, continued always. Discontent began to prevail strongly against him, and a party formed in Congress, while sitting at York Town, in Pennsylvania, for removing him from the command of the army. The hope, however, of better times, the news of the alliance with France, and the unwillingness of showing discontent dissipated the matter.[1084]

Franklin's negotiations and the French alliance may have saved George Washington his command!

Friday, May 8, 1778. Today, in Paris, John Adams meets the King of France, Louis XVI. John Adams:

Dr. Franklin . . . went with me to Versailles to attend my Presentation to the King. We visited the [French Foreign Minister] Count de Vergennes at his Office, and at the hour of eleven, the Count conducted Us into the Kings Bed Chamber where his Majesty was dressing. One Officer putting on his Coat, another his Sword &c. The Count went up to the King and informed him that Mr. Adams was present to be presented to his Majesty, the King turned round and looked upon me and smiled. "Is that Mr. Adams," said his Majesty? Being answered in the affirmative by the Count, he began to talk to me, and with such rapidity that I could not distinguish one Syllable nor understand one Word . . . The Count de Vergennes observing his Majestys Zeal . . . said, Mr. Adams will not answer your Majesty, for he neither speaks nor understands our Language as yet . . . "Pas un mot" [not a word?] said the King . . . The Count de Vergennes then conducted me to the Door of another Room, and desired me to stand there, which I did untill the King passed. After the usual Compliments of the King to the Ambassadors, his Majesty was preparing to retire when the Count de Vergennes again repeated to the King that I did not take upon me to speak french and the King repeated his question, does he not speak it at all? and passing by all the others in the Row made a full Stop before me, and evidently intended to observe and remember my Countenance and Person . . .[1085]

Saturday, May 16, 1778. Today, from the town of York, Pennsylvania (where the Continental Congress now meets), Tom Paine writes Ben Franklin:

I live in hopes of seeing and advising with you respecting the History of the American Revolution, as soon as a turn of affairs make it safe to take a passage for Europe . . . Mr. and Mrs. Bache are at Manheim near Lancaster; I heard they were well a few days ago . . . Miss Nancy Clifton . . . said the enemy had destroyed or sold a great part of your furniture . . .[1086]

Wednesday, May 27, 1778. Today, in Paris, John Adams writes in his diary:

I must now, in order to explain and justify my own Conduct give an Account of that of my Colleague Dr. Franklin . . . I found that the Business of our Commission would never be done unless I did it. My two Colleagues would agree in nothing. The Life of Dr. Franklin was a Scene of continual discipation. I could never obtain the favour of his Company in a Morning before Breakfast which would have been the most convenient time to read over the Letters and papers, deliberate on their contents, and decide upon the Substance of the Answers. It was late when he breakfasted, and as soon as Breakfast was over, a crowd of Carriages came to his Levee or, if you like the term better, to his Lodgings, with all Sorts of People; some Phylosophers, Academicians and Economists; some of his small tribe of humble friends in the litterary Way whom he employed to translate some of his ancient Compositions, such as his Bonhomme Richard [Poor Richard] and for what I know his Polly Baker &c.; but by far the greater part were Women and Children, come to have the honour to see the great Franklin, and to have the pleasure of telling Stories about his Simplicity, his bald head and scattering strait hairs, among their Acquaintances. These visitors occupied all the time, commonly, till it was time to dress to go to Dinner. He was invited to dine abroad every day and never declined unless when we had invited Company to dine with Us. I was always invited with him, till I found it necessary to send Apologies, that I might have some time to study the french Language and do the Business of the mission . . . It was the Custom in France to dine between one and two O Clock: so that when the time came to dress, it was time for the Voiture [carriage] to be ready to carry him to dinner . . . [W]e could rarely obtain the Company of Dr. Franklin for a few minutes, and often when I had drawn the Papers and had them fairly copied for Signature . . . I was frequently obliged to wait several days, before I could procure the Signature of Dr. Franklin to them. He went according to his Invitation to his Dinner and after that went sometimes to the Play, sometimes to the Philosophers but most commonly to visit those Ladies who were complaisant enough to depart from the custom of France so far as to procure Setts of Tea Geer as it is called and make Tea for him . . . After Tea the Evening was spent, in hearing the Ladies sing and play upon their Piano Fortes and other instruments of Musick, and in various Games as Cards, Chess, Backgammon, &c. &c. Mr. Franklin I believe however never play'd at any Thing but Chess or Checquers. In these Agreable and important Occupations and Amusements, the Afternoon and Evening was spent, and he came home at all hours from Nine to twelve O Clock at night . . . I should have been happy to have done all the Business or rather all the Drudgery if I could have been favoured with a few moments in a day to receive his Advice concerning the manner in which it ought to be done. But this condescention was not attainable . . . [1087]

Friday, May 29, 1778. Tonight, in Paris, John Adams writes in his diary:

The Disposition of the People of this Country for Amusements, and the Apparatus for them, was remarkable in this House, as indeed it was in every genteel House that I had seen in France. Every fashionable House had compleat Setts of Accommodations for Play, a Billiard Table, a Bacgammon Table, a Chesboard, a Chequer Board, Cards, and twenty other Sorts of Games, that I have forgotten. I often asked myself how this rage for Amusements of every kind, and this disinclination to serious Business, would answer in our republican Governments in America. It seemed to me that every Thing must run to ruin. [1088]

Saturday, May 30, 1778. John Adams is resentful. Of today, he writes:

Dr. Franklin, who had no Business to do or who at least would do none, and who had [a relative] . . . for his private Secretary without consulting his Colleagues and indeed without saying a Word to me who lived in the same house with him and had no private Secretary, though I had all the Business to do, thought fit to take into the Family a French private Secretary . . . For what reason or for what Purpose he was introduced I never knew. Whether it was to be a Spy upon me . . . I gave myself no trouble to enquire.[1089]

Tuesday, June 2, 1778. Of today, John Adams writes:

> *On the Road from Paris and from Passi to Versailles . . . stood a pallace . . . [T]his pallace had been built [by King Louis XV] . . . for Madame Pompadour, [his mistress] whom he visited here almost every night for twenty Years, leaving a worthy Woman his virtuous Queen alone at Versailles, with whom he had sworn never to sleep again . . . Here were made Judges and Councillors, Magistrates of all Sorts . . .*
>
> *What havock, said I to myself, would these manners make in America? Our Governors, our Judges, our Senators, our Representatives and even our Ministers would be appointed by Harlots for Money, and their Judgments, Decrees and decisions be sold to repay themselves or perhaps to procure the smiles (and Embraces) of profligate Females.*
>
> *The foundations of national Morality must be laid in private Families.*[1090]

Thursday, June 18, 1778. Today, Virginia Governor Patrick Henry writes Virginia congressional delegate Richard Henry Lee:

> *Let not Congress rely on Virginia for soldiers. I tell you my opinion [that] they will not be got here until a different spirit prevails. I look at the past condition of America as at a dreadful precipice from which we have escaped by means of the generous French, to whom I will be everlastingly bound by most heartfelt gratitude . . . Surely, Congress will never recede from our French friends. Salvation depends upon our holding fast to our attachment to them . . .*[1091]

Today, France liberates Philadelphia, as Britain withdraws its army to New York for fear of the coming French fleet. Just before noon, George Washington makes a report to the Continental Congress:

> *I have the pleasure to inform Congress that I was this minute advised . . . that the Enemy evacuated the City early this morning . . . [A]bout Three Thousand of the Troops embarked aboard Transports . . . I have put Six Brigades in motion, and the rest of the Army are preparing to follow with all possible dispatch. We shall proceed towards Jersey and govern ourselves according to circumstances . . .*[1092]

British Commander in Chief for North America Sir Henry Clinton reports to British Colonial Secretary Lord George Germain:

> *My Lord, I have the honor to inform your lordship that pursuant to His Majesty's instructions I evacuated Philadelphia on the 18th of June at 3 o'clock in the morning . . .*[1093]

Sunday, June 28, 1778. As the British retreat from Philadelphia across New Jersey toward New York, George Washington attempts a pursuit, which he must abandon today following the Battle of Monmouth Courthouse. George Washington:

> [H]aving received intelligence that the Enemy were prosecuting their Rout towards Monmouth Court House [in New Jersey], I dispatched a thousand select men under Brigadier General [Anthony] Wayne and sent the Marquis de la Fayette to take command of the whole advanced Corps . . .
>
> The Enemy . . . had changed their disposition and placed their best troops in the Rear . . . in consequence of which I detached Major General [Charles] Lee with two brigades to join the Marquis at English Town . . .
>
> I determined to attack their Rear . . . and sent orders by one of my Aids to General [Charles] Lee to move on and attack them . . .
>
> After marching about five Miles, to my great surprise and mortification, I met the whole advanced Corps retreating, and, as I was told, by General Lee's orders, without having made any opposition, except one fire . . . I proceeded immediately to the Rear of the Corps . . . and gave directions . . .
>
> [T]he Enemy had both their Flanks secured by thick Woods and Morasses, while their front could only be approached thro a narrow pass . . . [The Continental Troops advanced . . . b]ut the impediments in their way prevented their getting within reach before it was dark. They remained upon the Ground . . . during the Night . . . In the meantime the Enemy . . . about 12 OClock at Night marched away in such silence . . .
>
> The peculiar Situation of General Lee at this time requires that I should say nothing of his Conduct. He is now in arrest.[1094]

Tuesday, June 30, 1778. Today, in a letter to George Washington, General Charles Lee expresses outrage at the tongue-lashing Washington delivered during the Battle of Monmouth Courthouse:

> [N]othing but misinformation of some very stupid, or misrepresentation of some very wicked, persons could have occasioned your making use of such very singular expressions as you did on my coming up to the ground where you had taken post: they imply'd that I was guilty of either disobedience of orders, of want of conduct, or want of courage . . .
>
> I can boldly say that, had we remained on the first ground, or had we advanc'd, or had the retreat been conducted in a manner different from what it was, this whole army and the interest of America would have risk'd being sacrificed.[1095]

Historians (and a court-martial) will vindicate General Lee.[1096]

FOR THE NEXT THREE YEARS (UNTIL THE FRENCH COMPEL HIM TO FIGHT AT YORKTOWN, VIRGINIA), GEORGE WASHINGTON WILL REFUSE TO FIGHT ANOTHER BATTLE WITH THE BRITISH ARMY!

Wednesday, August 12, 1778. Today, in Paris, Benny Bache turns nine years old. During weekend visits with his grandfather, Benny shares the household with John Adams, who now has living quarters there. Benny Bache sees John Quincy Adams even more frequently, as John Adams has enrolled his son at Le Coeur's pension, where Benny boards and studies weekdays.[1097]

Monday, September 14, 1778. Now that France has fully recognized the independence of the United States of America, Congress decides to appoint a single Minister Plenipotentiary (ambassador) to France, thereby terminating the present arrangement of three commissioners. Today, in the Continental Congress, the Journals report:

> Congress proceeded to the election of a minister plenipotentiary to the court of France, and the ballots being taken,
> Dr. Benjamin Franklin was elected.
> *Resolved,* that a committee of five be appointed to present a letter of credence to his Most Christian Majesty, notifying the appointment of Dr. Franklin, minister plenipotentiary of these States at the court of France.[1098]

By deciding to have Ben Franklin as its sole minister to France, Congress deprives John Adams of all diplomatic credentials!

Wednesday, October 21, 1778. Today, the Continental Congress grants leave to Major General Marquis de Lafayette, who was wounded at the Battle of Brandywine Creek. The Journals report:

> *Resolved,* That the Marquis de la Fayette, major-general in the service of the United States, have leave to go to France . . .
> *Resolved,* That the President write a letter to the Marquis de la Fayette, returning him the thanks of Congress for that disinterested zeal which has led him to America, and for the services he hath rendered to the United States by the exertion of his courage and abilities on many signal occasions.
> *Resolved,* That the minister plenipotentiary of the United States of America at the court of Versailles, be directed to cause an elegant sword, with proper devices, to be made and presented, in the name of the United States, to the Marquis de la Fayette.[1099]

Saturday, December 4, 1778. Today, commissioners John Adams, Arthur Lee, and Benjamin Franklin discuss French aid. Arthur Lee records:

> *In a conference of the commissioners on the subject of a memorial to Count Vergennes, drawn up by Dr. Franklin, to obtain funds to enable them to pay interest of the [French] loan, Mr. Adams observed*

"that he thought we ought to state the interest France had in support-
ing us, how little the expense was in proportion to that interest, and
not make it a matter of mere grace." It was his opinion, he said, "that
this court did not treat us with any confidence, nor give us any effec-
tual assistance." Dr. Franklin took it up with some warmth, and said
"he did not see how they were defective; they had sent a fleet and given
us money." Mr. Adams replied, "that the monied assistance was piti-
ful, and that the fleet had done us no service." Dr. Franklin answered,
"that was not their fault, as they took the wisest method of making it
useful."[1100]

Saturday, December 5, 1778. Today, from Paris, John Adams writes his good
friend James Warren of Massachusetts,

There is another thing which I am obliged to mention. There are so
many private Families Ladies and Gentlemen that [Dr. Franklin] vis-
its so often . . . and so much intercourse with Academicians that all
these things together keep his mind in such a constant state of Dissipa-
tion that if he is left alone here, the Public Business will suffer in a de-
gree beyond description . . .[1101]

Friday, December 18, 1778. Today, John Adams writes the wife of a Massachusetts colleague,

What shall I say, Madam, to your Question whether I am as much
in the good graces of the Ladies as my venerable Colleague [Dr. Frank-
lin]. Ah No! Alas, Alas No!
The Ladies of this Country have an unaccountable passion for old
Age, whereas our Country women you know, Madam, have rather a
Complaisance for youth if I remember right. This is rather unlucky for
me, for I have nothing to do but to wish myself back again to 25.
I will take the Liberty to mention an anecdote or two amongst a
multitude to shew you how unfortunate I am in being so young. A
Gentleman introduced me the other day to a Lady. Voila, Madame,
says he, Monsieur Adams, notre Ami, Le Colleague de Monsieur Frank-
lin! Embrassez le . . . [Kiss him.] . . . Ah No, Monsieur, says the Lady, il
est trop jeune. [He is too young.]
So that you see. I must wait patiently, full 30 years longer before I
can be so great a favorite.[1102]

Wednesday, January 6, 1779. Tonight, at a ball in Philadelphia to celebrate
Ben Franklin's birthday, George Washington pays special attention to Ben
Franklin's daughter (Benny's mother!), Sarah Bache, who writes Ben Franklin:

I have lately been several times invited abroad with the General
and Mrs. Washington. He always inquires after you in the most affec-
tionate manner and speaks of you highly. We danced at Mrs. Powell's
your birthday or night . . .[1103]

Thursday, January 14, 1779. Today, in the Continental Congress, the Journals report:

> Whereas it hath been represented to this House by the . . . minister plenipotentiary of France that "it is pretended the United States have preserved the liberty of treating with Great Britain separately from their ally . . ."
>
> *Resolved, unanimously,* That as neither France or these United States may of right, so these United States will not, conclude either truce or peace with the common enemy without the formal consent of their ally first obtained, and that any matters or things which may be insinuated or asserted to the contrary thereof tend to the injury and dishonor of the said states . . .[1104]

Tuesday, February 9, 1779. Today, John Adams writes in his diary,

> *Any Thing to divert Melancholly and to sooth an aching Heart. The Uncandor, the Prejudices, the Rage, among several Persons here, make me Sick as Death.*
>
> *Virtue is not always amiable. Integrity is sometimes ruined by Prejudices and by Passions. There are two Men in the World who are Men of Honour and Integrity, I believe, but whose Prejudices and violent Tempers would raise Quarrells in the Elysian fields, if not in Heaven. On the other Hand, there is another [Franklin], whose Love of Ease and Dissipation will prevent any thorough Reformation of any Thing, and his Silence and Reserve render it very difficult to do any Thing with him . . .[1105]*

Sunday, February 14, 1779. Today, John Adams writes his cousin, Samuel Adams:

> *The Marquis de la Fayette did me the Honour of a Visit, yesterday, and delivered me your favour of 25 of Oct . . .*
>
> *How Congress will dispose of me, I don't know. If it is intended that I shall return, that will be very agreable to me, and I think that this is the most probable opinion . . .*
>
> *I confess I expected the most dismal consequences from [the possible removal of the commissioners] . . . But the arrival of Franklin's commission [as sole commissioner] has relieved me from many of these Fears—This Court have Confidence in him alone . . .[1106]*

Saturday, February 20, 1779. Today, from Paris, John Adams writes his complaints to Abigail:

> *A new commission has arrived by which the Dr. [Franklin] is sole minister . . . I am reduced to the condition of a private citizen. The Congress have not taken the least notice of me. On the 11th of September they resolved to have one minister only in France. On the 14th they chose the Dr. In October they made out his commission, the Alliance*

sailed on the 14th January, and in all that interval they never so much as bid me come home, bid me stay, or told me I had done well or done ill . . . I should not be at all surprised if I should see an accusation against me for something or other, I know not what, but I see that all things are possible . . .[1107]

Sunday, February 28, 1779. Today, John Adams writes Abigail:

I suppose I must write every day in order to keep or rather to restore good Humour, whether I have any thing to say or not.

The Scaffold is cutt away, and I am left kicking and sprawling in the Mire. It is hardly a state of Disgrace that I am in but rather of Neglect and Contempt . . . If I had deserved such Treatment, I should have deserved to be told so at least . . .

I have given Notice here and written to Congress of my Intentions to return . . .

If I ever had any Wit it is all evaporated—if I ever had any Imagination it is all quenched . . .

I believe I am grown more austere, severe, rigid, and miserable than ever I was.—I have seen more occasion perhaps.[1108]

His diplomatic credentials withdrawn, John Adams will now begin his return journey to the United States, setting off from Paris for the port city of Nantes.[1109]

WEDNESDAY, MARCH 3, 1779

⇒ 𝕿𝖍𝖊 𝕻𝖊𝖓𝖓𝖘𝖞𝖑𝖛𝖆𝖓𝖎𝖆 𝕲𝖆𝖟𝖊𝖙𝖙𝖊 ⇐

The British Court leave no stone unturned to break the present connections between France and America; and they have secretly offered to restore to France all their acquisitions in the last war [the French and Indian War], and to allow her many special advantages in trade, provided she will relinquish her alliance with these States: But his Most Christian Majesty, though his disposition is pacific as it is generous, is determined to be as faithful to his new allies as Congress has been to him: and to make no settlement but with their consent and upon the surest basis of their Independence and Liberty.

Monday, March 8, 1779. Today, from Philadelphia, retiring French Minister Plenipotentiary Gérard de Rayvenal writes two dispatches to French Foreign Minister Vergennes in Paris:

[R]elative to the probable views of the Opposition Leaders . . . Their object is to add an alliance [with Britain] to any peace with Britain . . .

Congress has only some vague Lamentations of Mr. John Adams who guarantees that France will not aid the States with anything . . .[1110]

Another idea of the [pro-British] Faction here . . . is to alter the re-

quirements of making peace so as to negotiate it separately with England and to accept any kind of alliance with that Power, for which the credit will inure to the benefit of the faction . . .

It is probably in pursuit of this that Messrs. Adams and Lee are exerting all their efforts to render our actual negotiations impossible so that new English commissioners, whose confidence they feel sure to enjoy and with whom they flatter themselves they can negotiate, will have time to arrive.[1111]

Thursday, April 22, 1779. Today, Benjamin Franklin writes his sister, Jane Mecum:

I live about two Miles out of the City, in a great Garden, that has pleasant Walks in which I can take Exercise in a good Air . . . I have last Week sent Benny to Geneva where there are as good Schools as here, & where he will be educated a Republican . . .[1112]

Monday, May 3, 1779. Today, from Paris, Ben Franklin writes his grandson, Benny Bache:

Dear Benny . . . [I]t gave me great Pleasure to hear of your safe Arrival at Geneva . . . You now have a fine Opportunity of learning those things that will be reputable and useful to you when you come to be a Man . . . You ought to be very respectful to Mr Cramer . . .

Love . . .

YOUR AFFECTIONATE GRANDFATHER[1113]

Tuesday, May 4, 1779. Today, Ben Franklin informs the British that he will not negotiate a truce independently of the French:

[T]his Proposition of a Truce, if made at all, should be made to France at the same time it is made to America . . . America has no desire of being free from her engagements to France. The chief is . . . not making a separate Peace; and this is an obligation not in the power of America to dissolve, being an obligation of Gratitude and Justice towards a nation which is engaged in a War on her Account and for her protection; and Would be forever binding, whether Such an article existed or not in the Treaty; and tho' it did not exist, an honest American would cut off his right hand rather than Sign an Agreement with England contrary to the spirit of it.[1114]

Wednesday, May 12, 1779. During the two months since John Adams left Paris to return to the United States, he has been stalled in the French ports of Nantes, Brest, and St. Nazaire. Today, he writes in his diary:

Conjectures. Jealousies, Suspicions—I shall grow as jealous as any Body.

I am jealous [suspicious] that my Disappointment [in leaving for America] is owing to an Intrigue . . . that this Device was hit upon by

*Franklin . . . to prevent me from going home, lest I should tell some
dangerous Truths . . .*

*Does the old Conjurer dread my Voice in Congress? He has some
Reason for he has often heard it there, a Terror to evil doers.*[1115]

Sunday, May 30, 1779. Today, from Geneva, Benny Bache writes his grandfather, Benjamin Franklin:

> *Dear grand papa, I take the liberte to wright to you for to tell you
> that I am in good health. [My supervisor] M. Marignac Gives his com-
> pliments to you and says that I am a good boy. I will do all that can
> for to be the first of the class. M. Cramer is in good health . . . I have
> notings mor for to tell you for the presente.*
>
>

*I am your affectionaite Son
B. Franklin B.*[1116]

Wednesday, June 2, 1779. Today, Ben Franklin writes Benny Bache's father,
Richard Bache:

> *I have had a great deal of pleasure in Ben . . . 'Tis a good honest lad,
> and will make, I think, a valuable man. He had made as much profi-
> ciency in his learning as the boarding school he was at could well af-
> ford him; and, after some consideration where to find a better for him,
> I at length fixed on sending him to Geneva. I had a good opportunity
> by a gentleman of that city who had a place for him in his chaise, and
> has a son of about the same age at the same school. He promised to
> take care of him . . . He went very cheerfully, and I understand is very
> happy. I miss his company on Sundays at dinner. But, if I live and I
> can find a little leisure, I shall make the journey next spring to see him
> and to see at the same time the old 13 United States of Switzer-
> land . . .*[1117]

Thursday, June 3, 1779. Today, Ben Franklin writes his daughter, Sarah Bache
(Benny's mother):

> *The clay medallion of me you say you gave to Mr. Hopkinson was
> the first of the kind made in France. A variety of others have been
> made since of different sizes; some to be set in lids of snuffboxes, and
> some so small as to be worn in rings; and the numbers sold are in-
> credible. These, with the pictures, busts, and prints (of which copies
> upon copies are spread every where) have made your father's face as
> well known as that of the moon . . .*
>
> *Ben, if I should live long enough to want it, is like to be another
> comfort to me. As I intend him . . . as a Republican [not a monarchist],
> I have sent him to finish his education at Geneva. He is much grown,
> in very good health, draws a little, as you will see by the inclosed,
> learns Latin, writing, arithmetic, and dancing, and speaks French bet-*

ter than English . . . He has not been long from me. I send the accounts I have of him, and I shall put him in mind of writing to you . . .[1118]

Tuesday, June 8, 1779. Today, John Adams writes Edmund Jenings, an American friend living in Europe:

Dont misunderstand this. It was not Versailles, Paris, France— French Dress, Cookery, or Gallantry that made me unhappy . . . but my own Countrymen.[1119]

Friday, June 18, 1779. Today, after an exasperating wait for more than three and a half months, John Adams sets sail for Boston aboard the French frigate *Le Sensible.* Traveling with him is the new French Minister to the United States, Anne-César de La Luzerne, and a secretary to the French legation, the Marquis de Barbé-Marbois. As La Luzerne departs, French Foreign Minister Vergennes writes him a warning:

We clearly perceive that an opposition party exists in Congress, which, if not sold to England, nevertheless favors the views of that power and which seeks to establish and to bring into credit principles diametrically opposed to those which form the basis and spirit of our treaties with the United States . . . [I]t is indubitable that, among them, may be counted Mr. John Adams who has been a Deputy to France and who has just returned to America. The party in question is principally engaged in effecting a reconciliation between the United States and England, in negotiating with and forming an alliance with the court of London. As you know the existing engagements between the King [of France] and the Americans, you can judge yourself that the system of . . . Adams is directly opposed to these engagements and that if Congress should adopt it, it would destroy the alliance it has contracted with His Majesty.[1120]

Wednesday, June 23, 1779. Today, on the open ocean of the North Atlantic en route to America, John Adams records in his diary:

This Forenoon, fell strangely, yet very easily into Conversation with [the secretary to the French legation] M. M.[arbois].
Is there not one Catholic [church in Philadelphia], said M.M.? . . . [S]aid I, There is a Roman catholic Church . . . consisting partly of Germans, partly of French, and partly of Irish.—All Religions are tolerated in America, said M.M . . . But Mr. Franklin never had any.—No said I, laughing, because Mr. F. had no—I was going to say what I did not say and will not say here. I stopped short and laughed.—No, said Mr. M., Mr. F. adores only great Nature, which has interested a great many People of both Sexes in his favour.—Yes, said I, laughing, all the Atheists, Deists, and Libertines, as well as the Philosophers and Ladies are in his Train—another Voltaire . . . —Yes, said, Mr. M., he is celebrated as the great Philosopher and the great Legislator of America.—

He is, said I, a great Philosopher, but as a Legislator of America, he has done very little.

It is universally believed in France, England and all Europe, that [Dr. Franklin's] Electric Wand has accomplished all this revolution but nothing is more groundless. He has [done] very little. It is believed that he made all the [state] Constitutions and their Confederation but he made neither . . . I am sure it cannot be my Duty, nor the Interest of my Country, that I should conceal any of my sentiments of this man . . . It would be worse than Folly to conceal my Opinion of his great Faults.[1121]

Thursday, July 15, 1779. Tonight, Brigadier General Anthony Wayne seizes the incomplete British fortifications at Stony Point, New York. George Washington, who will make his headquarters at White Plains, reports this event to Congress:

I had the honor to inform Congress of a successful attack upon the enemy's post at Stony Point . . . by Brigadier-General [Anthony] Wayne and the corps of light infantry under his command . . . He improved upon the plan recommended by me, and executed it in a manner that does signal honor to his judgment and to his bravery. In a critical moment of the assault, he received a fleshwound in the head with a musket-ball, but continued leading on his men with unshaken firmness . . .

The necessity of doing something to satisfy the expectations of the people, and reconcile them to the defensive plan we are obliged to pursue, and to the apparent inactivity which our situation imposes upon us . . . concurred to determine me to the undertaking . . .[1122]

George Washington has not seen a battle in more than a year!

Thursday, July 29, 1779. Today, George Washington complains to Joseph Reed, the president of Pennsylvania's executive council, that a disparaging article in the *Maryland Journal* is unwarranted:

[W]hen it is well known that the command was in a manner forced upon me, that I accepted it with the utmost diffidence, from a consciousness that it required greater abilities and more experience than I possessed, to conduct a great Military machine . . . it is rather grating to pass over in silence charges which may impress the uninformed . . .[1123]

General Charles Lee, formerly George Washington's second in command, wrote the disparaging remarks in the form of twenty-five queries, including,

Query 9th. "Whether it is salutary or dangerous . . . to inculcate and encourage in the people an idea that their welfare, safety and glory depend on one man?

10th. "Whether amongst the late warm or rather loyal addresses of this city [Philadelphia] to his Excellency General Washington, there was

370

*a single mortal . . . who could possibly be acquainted with his mer-
its? . . .*

"Whether the armies under Gates . . . and the detachment under
Stark to the northward . . . gave the decisive turn to the fortune of
war? . . ."[1124]

Monday, August 2, 1779. Today, after a forty-five-day crossing aboard the
French frigate *Le Sensible*, John Adams arrives at Boston's harbor.[1125]

Thursday, August 12, 1779. Today, in Geneva, Benny Bache turns ten years
old. To obtain a republican education, Benny lives under the watchful eye of
Philibert Cramer, who is the brother of Voltaire's publisher and a friend of Jean-
Jacques Rousseau. Is there any question that Benny will be a child of the Enlightenment? Philibert's wife, Catherine, has practically adopted Benny Bache,
and the Cramers' son, Gabriel, is Benny's best friend.[1126]

Thursday, August 19, 1779. Today, from Paris, Ben Franklin writes Benny
Bache in Geneva:

> *My Dear Child,*
>
> *Do not think I have forgotten you, because I have been so long with-
> out writing to you. I think of you every day, and there is nothing I de-
> sire more than to see you furnish'd with good Learning, that I may
> return you to your Father and Mother so accomplish'd, with such
> Knowledge & Virtue as to give them Pleasure, and enable you to be-
> come an honourable Man in your own Country. I am therefore very
> willing you should have a Dictionary, and all such other Books as M.
> du Marignac or M. Cramer shall judge proper for you . . .*
>
> *I continue very well, Thanks to God; and I shall always love you
> very much if you continue to be a good Boy; being ever*
>
> > *Your Affectionate Grandfather   B. Franklin*
>
> *Let me know what you are learning, & whether you begin to
> draw.*[1127]

Wednesday, September 1, 1779. Today, in Boston, a constitutional convention
begins work on a new Massachusetts state constitution.[1128] John Adams, now
back in Boston, is to be its principal author. Just as Pennsylvania's constitution
is seen to be Ben Franklin's, the new Massachusetts constitution will be seen
to be John Adams'. John Adams:

> *Upon my return from France in 1779, I found myself elected by my
> native town of Braintree a member of the convention for forming a
> constitution for the state of Massachusetts. Here I found a chaos of ab-
> surd sentiments concerning government . . . Lieutenant-Governor
> Cushing was avowedly for a single assembly like [Dr. Franklin's con-
> stitution in] Pennsylvania. Samuel Adams was of the same mind . . .*
> *In short, I had at first no support but from the [radically conservative]
> Essex Junto who had adopted my ideas in the "Letter to Mr. Wythe."*

They supported me timorously and at last would not go with me to so high a mark as I aimed at, which was a complete negative [veto] in the governor upon all laws. They made me draw up the constitution, and it was finally adopted with some amendments very much for the worse . . . A foundation was here laid of much jealousy and unpopularity among the democratical people . . .[1129]

Sunday, September 19, 1779. Today, from his home in Braintree, John Adams writes his friend Benjamin Rush, who has resigned from the army to practice medicine in Philadelphia:

I have little to Say about the Time and manner of my being Superceeded [by Benjamin Franklin]. Let those reflect upon them selves who are disgraced by it, not I. Those who did it are alone disgraced by it. The Man who can shew a long Series of disinterested Services to his Country cannot be disgraced even by his Country.[1130]

Thursday, September 23, 1779. Tonight, the American naval operations in Europe, operating under the auspices of Benjamin Franklin, enjoy a heroic victory. Off Flamborough Head on the east coast of England, a small American vessel, named the *Bon Homme Richard ("Poor Richard")* to honor Franklin, overcomes a much larger British vessel, the fifty-gun ship-of-war *Serapis,* in a fiery encounter. In the midst of the battle, as *Bon Homme Richard* fills with flames and water, Captain John Paul Jones boldly declares—in words that will live for centuries—*"I have not yet begun to fight."*[1131]

Monday, September 27, 1779. Today, the Continental Congress grants John Adams new diplomatic credentials. The Journals report:

Resolved, That Congress proceed to the election of a minister plenipotentiary for negotiating a treaty of peace and a treaty of commerce with Great Britain.
Congress accordingly proceeded, and the ballots being taken,
Mr. John Adams was elected.[1132]

Wednesday, September 29, 1779. Today, John Adams receives his commissions from Congress to negotiate treaties with Great Britain:

1. For peace.
The Delegates of the United States,
To all who see these Presents, send Greeting
It being probable that a Negotiation shall soon be commenced for putting an End to the Hostilities . . . Know Ye, therefore, that We . . . Have nominated and constituted . . . John Adams our Minister Plenipotentiary . . . to confer, treat, agree, and conclude with . . . his Britannic Majesty . . . the great Work of Pacification . . .

Samuel Huntington, President
2. The Commission for making a Treaty of Commerce with Great Britain . . .

> *The Delegates of the United States,*
> *To all who see these Presents, send Greeting*
> *It being the desire of the United States that the Peace which may be*
> *established between them and his Britannic Majesty may be permanent*
> *and accompanied with the mutual Benefits derived from commerce,*
> *Know Ye, therefore, that We . . . have nominated and constituted . . .*
> *John Adams our Minister Plenipotentiary . . . to sign, and thereupon*
> *make a Treaty of Commerce.*
>
>

Samuel Huntington, President[1133]

John Adams sees these commissions as a victory over Franklin. John Adams:

> *The first insinuation of the Propriety, Expediency, and necessity of*
> *appointing a Minister Plenipotentiary to reside in Europe ready to ne-*
> *gotiate a Peace . . . was made to Congress a year before this time . . .*
> *[I]t was the Expectation of the French Ministry that Dr. Franklin*
> *would be elected. In this respect Congress disappointed them . . .*[1134]

Thursday, September 30, 1779. France has now liberated Rhode Island! The British have withdrawn their forces to New York as a precaution against the French fleet, under Admiral d'Estaing, which has returned from the West Indies and is reportedly off the coast of Georgia. Today, British Commander in Chief Sir Henry Clinton reports to London:

> *The Admiral . . . imagined he had every reason to believe that*
> *d'Estaing's fleet was on the coast of Georgia and to suppose he might*
> *probably visit some part of this continent . . . In these opinions . . . the*
> *fleet assembled in New York . . .*
> *I was induced by the Admiral's suggestion to . . . evacuate Rhode is-*
> *land and to avail myself of the force left inactive there.*
> *[F]resh advices concerning [the French fleet under] d'Estaing ar-*
> *rived . . . [T]he Admiral . . . could not spare a ship to protect Rhode Is-*
> *land. Such forcible arguments then appear for quitting [Rhode Island],*
> *as the rescuing the garrison, stores etc. from the most unprotected*
> *state and the giving full security to the harbour of New York.*[1135]

Friday, October 8, 1779. Today, from Philadelphia, the new French Minister to the U.S., Anne-César de La Luzerne, reports to French Foreign Minister Vergennes that John Adams' feelings toward Franklin may have prejudiced his view of France:

> *Nearly two months of living with Mr. Adams have let me get to*
> *know him . . .*
> *[Mr. Adams said] "I have not been able to forget entirely where I*
> *was left in the nomination of M Franklin to be Minister Plenipotentiary*
> *to France; No one even deigned to tell me whether to remain in France*
> *or return, and I took the latter choice because I refused to debase my-*
> *self or compel myself to play a meaningless role which I was con-*

demned to do and which appeared undignified for a gentleman."
Furthermore, Mr. Adams did not enjoy watching the attention that
Parisians heaped on Mr. Franklin, while hardly anyone recognized
him. I could believe that this painful situation, painful for a man
whose purpose is public admiration, has caused him some bias
against France.[1136]

Saturday, October 9, 1779. Today, French Admiral Comte d'Estaing who has returned from the West Indies with an enlarged fleet of twenty-two ships of the line and eleven frigates, disembarks a French army of 3,600 for an assault on the British at Savannah, Georgia. Joining a much smaller American army of only six hundred men, under General Benjamin Lincoln, the French carry Savannah's outposts, plant French and American flags on the ramparts, but are repulsed by British forces, who were forewarned of the attack. One hundred eighty-three French officers and soldiers are killed; 454 French soldiers are wounded. French Admiral d'Estaing himself receives two wounds.

Though the French do not, by today's attack, liberate Savannah, their appearance off the coast of Georgia arrests the British campaign in the South and causes the British to withdraw their forces from Rhode Island to concentrate them in New York.[1137] With winter ahead, d'Estaing will now return his fleet to France.

Thursday, October 28, 1779. Today, in New York, British Commander in Chief Sir Henry Clinton finishes a report to London:

My Lord, I inform your lordship that the troops from Rhode Island
arrived here yesterday, the evacuation of the place having been com-
pleted . . .
The troops arrived here in perfect health. I hope from the attention
the Admiral gives to procuring information of [French Admiral]
D'Estaing's movements that we shall soon have such accounts as will
admit of my employing them to very useful purposes.[1138]

Today, in Boston, John Adams' new constitution for the state of Massachusetts goes before the Massachusetts constitutional convention.[1139] From John Adams' draft:

In the government of the Commonwealth of Massachusetts, the leg-
islative, executive, and judicial power shall be placed in separate de-
partments, to the end that it might be a government of laws, and not of
men.
CHAPTER II.
THE FRAME OF GOVERNMENT
Section I.
ART. I. THE department of legislation shall be formed by two branches,
A SENATE and HOUSE OF REPRESENTATIVES; each of which shall
have a negative [veto] on the other . . .

And the first magistrate [the governor] shall have a negative [veto] upon all the laws [of the legislature] . . .

Section II. Senate

I. *There shall be . . . forty persons [in a senate] . . . to be chosen . . . by the respective districts . . . by the proportion of the public taxes paid by the said districts . . . provided that the number of such districts shall be never more than sixteen . . .*

II. *The senate shall be the first branch of the legislature . . . [E]very male person . . . having a freehold estate within the commonwealth of three pounds, or other real or personal estate of the value of sixty pounds, shall have a right to give in his vote for the senators . . .*

V. . . . *[N]o person shall be capable of being elected as a senator who is not of the Christian religion and seised in his own right of a freehold within this commonwealth of the value of three hundred pounds and who has not been an inhabitant . . . seven years . . .*

Section III. House of Representatives

I. *THERE shall be in the legislature of this commonwealth a representation of the people annually elected and founded in equality.*

II. . . . *[E]very corporate town, containing one hundred and fifty ratable polls [voters], may elect one representative . . .*

III. . . . *[N]o person shall be qualified or eligible to be a member of the said house, unless he be of the Christian religion, and for one year . . . an inhabitant of, and have been seised in his own right of a freehold in the value of one hundred pounds . . .*

IV. *Every male person . . . having a freehold estate . . . of the annual income of three pounds, or other estate real or personal or mixt of the value of sixty pounds, shall have a right to vote in the choice of a representative . . .*

CHAPTER III. EXECUTIVE POWER.
SECTION I. Governor.

ART. I. *THERE shall be a supreme executive magistrate, who shall be styled, THE GOVERNOR . . .*

ART. II. *The governor shall be chosen annually; and no person shall be eligible to this office unless . . . seised in his own right of a freehold . . . of the value of one thousand pounds; and unless he shall be of the Christian religion.*

III. *Those persons who shall be qualified to vote for senators and representatives . . . shall . . . give in their votes for a governor . . .*[1140]

The Massachusetts constitutional convention will adopt, with only minor changes, John Adams' plan for government. It will submit the constitution to Massachusetts towns with an explanatory text, "ADDRESS OF THE CONVENTION . . . TO THEIR CONSTITUENTS," including:

The House of Representatives is intended as the Representative of the Persons, and the Senate [as a Representative] of the property of the Com-

*monwealth . . . each having a Negative [veto] upon the Acts of [the] other
. . . Your Delegates considered that Persons who . . . have no Property
are either those who live upon a part of a Paternal estate, expecting the
fee [title] thereof, who are but just entering into business, or those whose
idleness of Life and profligacy of manners will forever bar them from
acquiring and possessing Property. And we will submit it to the former
class, whether they would not think it safer . . . than . . . to have their
Privileges liable to the control of Men, who will pay less regard to the
Rights of Property because they have nothing to lose.*

*The Power of Revising, and stating objections to any Bill or Resolve
that shall be passed by the two Houses, we were of opinion ought to be
lodged in the hands of some one person . . . We have thought it safest to
rest this Power in [the Governor's] hands . . .*[1141]

As one historian will observe, *"The Senate of Massachusetts was created in
order to protect property against democracy."*[1142] John Adams:

*Is it not . . . true that Men in general, in every Society, who are
wholly destitute of property, are also too little acquainted with public
Affairs to form a Right Judgment and too dependent on other Men to
have a Will of their own? . . . Such is the Frailty of the human Heart
that very few Men who have no Property have any Judgment of their
own.*[1143]

Ben Franklin, Tom Paine, and other supporters of the Pennsylvania Constitution of 1776 will disapprove of John Adams' new Massachusetts constitution.
John Adams:

*Paine's wrath was excited because my plan of government was essentially different from the silly projects that he had published in his
Common Sense. By this means I became suspected and unpopular
with the leading demagogues and the whole Constitutional Party in
Pennsylvania.*[1144]

Tuesday, November 2, 1779. Today, in Philadelphia, the most democratic of
all state institutions, the Pennsylvania Assembly, chooses Tom Paine to be its
Clerk.[1145]

Saturday, November 13, 1779. Today, with his new congressional commissions to negotiate peace and commerce with Great Britain and with his draft
of the new Massachusetts constitution in hand, John Adams begins his return
to France:

*On the Thirteenth day of November 1779, I had again the melancholly Tryal of taking Leave of my Family, with the Dangers of the
Seas and the Terrors of British Men of War before my Eyes . . . We went
to Boston and embarked on Board the Frigate* [Sensible] . . .[1146]

Wednesday, December 15, 1779. Today, George Washington writes the Continental Congress:

> *I beg leave to add that, from a particular consultation of the Commissaries, I find our prospects are infinitely worse than they have been at any period of the War, and that unless some expedient can be instantly adopted, a dissolution of the Army for want of Subsistence is unavoidable. A part of it has been again several days without Bread . . . [T]his deficiency proceed[s] . . . from the absolute emptiness of our magazines every where and the total want of money or credit to replenish them. I look forward to the consequences with an anxiety not to be described.*
>
> *The only temporary resource we seem to have left . . . is this—To solicit a loan of four or five thousand barrels [of gunpowder] out of the quantity provided for the use of the French fleet and army . . . I know the measure recommended is a disagreeable one, but motives of delicacy must often yield to those of necessity.*[1147]

George Washington hasn't fought a battle in a year and a half!

Wednesday, January 5, 1780. Today, from the army's headquarters which he has reestablished at Morristown, New Jersey, George Washington writes the Continental Congress:

> *Many of the [men] have been four or five days without meat entirely and short of bread, and none but on very scanty supplies. Some for their preservation have been compelled to maraud and rob from the Inhabitants, and I have it not in my power to punish or to repress the practice. If our condition should not undergo a very speedy and considerable change for the better, it will be difficult to point out all the consequences that may ensue.*[1148]

Wednesday, February 9, 1780. Today, John Adams arrives in Paris with his new commissions to negotiate peace and commerce treaties with Britain.[1149] John Adams:

> *In 1780, when I arrived [back] in France, I carried a printed copy of the report of the Grand Committee of the Massachusetts Convention, which I had drawn up; and this became an object of speculation. Mr. Turgot, the Duke de la Rochefoucauld, and Mr. Condorcet, and others admired Mr. Franklin's Constitution and reprobated mine.*[1150]

Thursday, February 10, 1780. Today, John Adams visits the French court at Versailles. John Adams:

> *I never heard the French Ministry so frank, explicit, and decided . . . in their declarations to pursue the War with vigour and afford effectual Aid to the United States. I learned with great Satisfaction that they are sending, under Convoy, Cloathing and Arms for fifteen thousand*

Men to America; that seventeen Ships of the Line are already gone . . .
and that five or six more at least are to follow in Addition to ten or
twelve they have already there.[1151]

This year, France will send more than thirty warships (plus a huge fleet of
support ships) to fight America's war!

Saturday, February 12, 1780. Today, in Paris, John Adams writes French Foreign Minister Vergennes:

> I have now the honor to acquaint you that, on the twenty ninth day
> of September last, the Congress of the United States of America did me
> the honour to elect me their Minister Plenipotentiary to negotiate a
> peace with Great Britain and also to negotiate a Treaty of Commerce
> with that Kingdom . . .
> I am persuaded it is the Intention of my Constituents, and of all
> America, and I am sure it is my own determination, to take no Steps
> of Consequence in pursuance of my commissions, without consulting
> his Majestys Ministers . . .
> I beg the favor of your Excellency's opinion . . .[1152]

Sunday, February 13, 1780. Today, the French Foreign Minister surprises
John Adams with his response:

> I have received the letter which you did me the honor to write me on
> the 12th of this month . . . I am of the opinion that it will be prudent to
> conceal your eventual character and above all to take the necessary
> precautions that the object of your commission may remain unknown
> to the Court of London . . .[1153]

John Adams immediately answers the Comte de Vergennes:

> I have received the Letter which your Excellency did me the honour
> to write me . . . I have now the Honour to inclose, attested Copies of
> both [my commissions].
> With regard to my Instructions . . . they contain nothing inconsistent
> with the Letter or Spirit of the Treaties between his Majesty and The
> United States . . .[1154]

Thursday, February 24, 1780. Today, the French Foreign Minister is insistent
with John Adams:

> As to the Full Power which authorizes you to negotiate a Treaty of
> Commerce with the Court of London, I think it will be prudent to make
> no comment of it to any Person whatsoever and to take all possible
> Precautions that the English Ministry may not have any Knowledge of
> it prematurely.[1155]

John Adams:

> *[The Comte de Vergennes'] anxiety to have my Commission . . . concealed excited some Surprize and some perplexity. I was not clear that I suspected his true Motives . . . However Time brought to light what I but imperfectly suspected. The Count . . . meditated . . . to get my Commission to negotiate a Treaty of Commerce annulled . . .*[1156]

Friday, February 25, 1780. Today, John Adams gives in to the French Foreign Minister:

> *I . . . shall conform myself to your advice . . . I shall not think myself at liberty to make any publication of my Powers to treat of Peace . . . My other Powers shall be concealed, according to your advice . . .*[1157]

Saturday, March 4, 1780. With the French government imposing demands of silence on him, John Adams can do nothing and suspects that Franklin is responsible. Today, he writes his friend, Massachusetts congressional delegate James Lovell:

> *My Situation here will naturally make all the Dr.'s Friends jealous of me, lest I should be Set up as his Successor—and this will make my Situation delicate and disagreeable.—I assure you . . . I have no Ambitions to be the Dr.'s Successor.—it is a Plan of too much Envy, and too much difficulty for any body to be happy in.*
>
> *What the Congress will think proper to do with me, I know not.— To keep me here will cost them a great deal of Money . . .*[1158]

Sunday, March 5, 1780. France has decided to send America a six-thousand-man army, under General Rochambeau, and a substantial fleet, under Admiral de Ternay. Today, French Foreign Minister Vergennes issues instructions to the Marquis de Lafayette, who is returning to the United States:

> *Monsieur the Marquis de La Fayette may return to America in eagerness to join General Washington, whom he will alert, on the condition of secrecy, that the King of France, wishing to give United States a new sign of his affection and his interest for their security, has decided to despatch, at the beginning of the spring, the relief of six ships of the line and of six thousand regular infantry troops.*
>
> *The convoy is ordered, if there is no obstacle to confront, to Rhode island in order to be at closer range to assist the main American army and to join it if General Washington judges it necessary . . .*[1159]

Today, Ben Franklin writes George Washington some words which should warm Washington's welcome for arriving French officers:

> *Some day you will come to France. On this side of the water you would enjoy the great reputation that you have acquired. It would be free from the reproaches made by the jealousy and envy of fellow citizens, the contemporaries of a great man who strive to cast a slur upon him while he is living . . .*[1160]

Saturday, March 18, 1780. To pay for the war, the Continental Congress has printed so much paper money that the Continental dollar has only one fortieth of its original face (nominal) value in the marketplace. Adjusting for this inflation, the Continental Congress today reduces its obligation to redeem paper dollars in gold or silver (specie), officially devaluing its currency so that a holder of Continental dollars must pay forty paper dollars to receive one milled silver or gold dollar. The Journals report:

> [I]nsomuch that [Continental bills] are now passed, by common consent, in most parts of the United States, at least 39–40ths below their nominal value, and still remain in a state of depreciation . . .
> *Resolved,* That . . . silver and gold be receivable [by holders of Continental bills] . . . at the rate of one Spanish milled dollar in lieu of 40 dollars of the bills now in circulation . . .[1161]

Sunday, March 19, 1780. Today, Ben Franklin writes the president of Pennsylvania's executive council, Joseph Reed:

> *I am glad to see that you continue to preside in our new State [of Pennsylvania] . . . The disputes about the [Pennsylvania state] Constitution seem to have subsided. It is much admired here and all over Europe and will draw many families of fortune to settle under it as soon as there is peace.*[1162]

Wednesday, May 3, 1780. Today, in France, a French army of 5,500 soldiers, commanded by French General Comte de Rochambeau, departs the French port of Brest for the United States. Transporting and accompanying this army is a French fleet commanded by French Admiral Le Chevalier de Ternay, consisting of six French ships of the line, five frigates, thirty-two transports, and a hospital ship. The French force is destined for Newport, Rhode Island, which another French fleet, under Admiral Comte d'Estaing, liberated last October by threatening British forces along the coast.[1163]

Friday, May 12, 1780. Today, after three days of naval bombardment, Charleston, South Carolina falls to the British Southern Army, led by General Charles Cornwallis. American Major General Benjamin Lincoln surrenders his American army of two thousand Continentals, four hundred cannon, and three of the United States' seven frigates. With South Carolina and Georgia now securely in British hands, only American General Horatio Gates' army remains to challenge Charles Cornwallis in the south.[1164]

Tuesday, May 16, 1780. Today, George Washington writes the Marquis de Lafayette, who informed Washington less than a week ago[1165] that France is sending him a large army and a fleet of several ships-of-the-line:

> *Since you left me I have more fully reflected on the plan which it will be proper for the French fleet and army to pursue on their arrival upon the Coast; and it appears to me, in the present situation of the enemy at New York, that it ought to be our first object to reduce that*

post . . . I would therefore advise you to write to the [General] Count
De Rochembeau and [Admiral] Monsr. De Ternay . . .[1166]

Sunday, May 28, 1780. Today, George Washington writes the president of
Pennsylvania's Executive Council:

> I assure you, every Idea you can form of our distresses, will fall
> short of the reality. There is such a combination of circumstances to
> exhaust the patience of the soldiery that it begins at length to be worn
> out, and we see in every line of the army, the most serious features of
> mutiny and sedition. All our departments, all our operations are at a
> stand, and unless a system very different . . . be immediately adopted
> throughout the states, our affairs must soon become desperate beyond
> the possibility of recovery . . . Indeed I have almost ceased to hope. The
> country in general is in such a state of insensibility and indifference to
> its interests, that I dare not flatter myself with any change for the
> better . . .
>
> This is a decisive moment; one of the most—I will go further and
> say the most—important America has seen. The Court of France has
> made a glorious effort for our deliverance, and if we disappoint its in-
> tentions by our supineness, we must be contemptible in the eyes of all
> humankind . . .
>
> We should consider what was done by France [in sending its fleet]
> as a violent and unnatural effort of the government, which for want of
> sufficient [financial] foundation, cannot continue . . . In modern wars,
> the longest purse must chiefly determine the event . . . France is in a
> very different position [from Britain] . . . [I]f the war continues an-
> other campaign, [the French Minister of Finance] will be obliged to
> have recourses to the taxes usual in time of war which are very heavy
> and which the people of France are not in a condition to endure for
> any duration. When this necessity commences, France makes war on
> ruinous terms [for its society] . . .
>
> I mention these things to show that . . . we must make one great ef-
> fort for this campaign . . .
>
> The matter is reduced to a point. Either Pennsylvania must give us
> all the aid we ask of her, or we can undertake nothing. We must re-
> nounce every idea of cooperation, and must confess to our allies that
> we look wholly to them for our safety. This will be a state of humilia-
> tion and littleness . . . I have [not] the least doubt that you will employ
> all your influence to animate the legislature and the people at large.
> The fate of these states hangs upon it.[1167]

Friday, June 16, 1780. Today, French military supplier Jacques-Donatien Le
Ray de Chaumont (at whose residence Ben Franklin and John Adams are stay-
ing in Passy) makes a report to the French Foreign Ministry of a conversation
he has had with John Adams:

I have had a conversation with Mr. Adams so interesting that I think His Excellency the Count de Vergennes should be informed of it . . . Mr. Adams . . . persists in thinking . . . that it is France which is under obligations to America. These principles, on becoming one of the Peace Congress, he will carry with him into it, and he is a man to publicly support them, which, in my opinion, would be very scandalous . . .

I called on M. Adams to give him news . . . adverse to the American Congress, because [Congress] had fixed the [convertible] value of paper [money] at forty per cent in specie [gold]. I observed to M. Adams that the commercial world had reason to complain, and especially French merchants . . . I added that many merchants would be unable to fulfill their obligations . . .

Mr. Adams replied that . . . the French had less reason to complain than anybody else, since France derived the greatest advantages, because, without America, to which France would not be under too great an obligation, England would be too powerful . . . that the merchants in danger of bankruptcy would be delighted to have the pretext of the fixed valuation (fixation) . . .[1168]

John Adams:

After the arrival of the news from America of the resolution of congress of the 18th of March 1780, for the redemption of the paper money at forty for one . . . M. Leray de Chaumont, Dr. Franklin's landlord and intimate friend and companion, and M. Monthieu, another of his intimate friends, came to visit me in my apartment at the Hotel de Valois, Rue de Richelieu in Paris . . . concerning that resolution of Congress which they said had excited a sensation in France and an alarm at court . . . I endeavored to show them the equity, the policy, and the necessity of the measure . . .[1169]

Tuesday, June 20, 1780. In America, the failure to enlist soldiers in George Washington's army has created a crisis. Today, George Washington writes the Continental Congress:

The period is come when we have every reason to expect the [French] Fleet will arrive, and yet . . . it is impossible for me to form and fix on a system of cooperation. I have no basis to act upon and of course were this generous succour of our [French] Ally now to arrive, I should find myself in the most awkward, embarrassing, and painful situation. The General [Rochambeau] and the Admiral [de Ternay] . . . will require of me a plan of the measures to be persued . . . but circumstanced as I am, I cannot even give them conjectures . . .

[F]or want of knowing our prospects, I am altogether at a loss what to do. For fear of involving the Fleet and Army of our Allies in circum-

stances, which, if not seconded by us, would expose them to material inconvenience and hazard, I shall be compelled to suspend it . . .[1170]

Wednesday, June 21, 1780. The Continental Congress' devaluation of America's paper currency to demand forty paper dollars (rather than one paper dollar) for a milled silver or gold dollar (specie) has created a crisis for French suppliers who have accepted American paper dollars on their one-to-one promise of silver or gold. Today, in Paris, French Foreign Minister Vergennes writes John Adams:

> *[T]he assembly of Massachusetts has determined to adopt the resolution of Congress, fixing the value of the paper money at forty for one in specie . . .*
>
> *I have no right to analyze or comment upon the internal arrangements which congress may consider just and useful . . . But . . . I am far from agreeing that it is just and agreeable . . . to extend the effects to strangers as well as to citizens of the United States . . . I shall content myself to remark to you that the French, if they should be obliged to submit . . . would find themselves victims of the zeal, and I may say the rashness, with which they have exposed themselves in furnishing the Americans with arms, ammunition, and clothing; in a word, with all the things of the first necessity of which the Americans stood in the most urgent need . . . [T]he subjects of the king . . . have counted on the thanks of congress . . . It was with this persuasion, and in a reliance on the public faith, that they received paper money . . . The unexpected reduction of this same paper overturns their calculations, at the same time as it ruins their fortunes . . .*
>
> *I shall not conceal from you that [our Minister in the United States] the Chevalier de la Luzerne has already received orders to make the strongest representations on the subject in question . . .*[1171]

Thursday, June 22, 1780. Today, despite the fact that he no longer holds a commission to negotiate with France (his commission is now to negotiate with Britain), John Adams addresses French Foreign Minister Vergennes on the question of America's currency devaluation, including:

> *No man is more ready than I am to acknowledge the obligations we are under to France; but the flourishing state of her marine and commerce and the decisive influence of her councils and negotiations in Europe, which all the world will allow be owing in great measure to the separation of America from her inveterate enemy and to her new connexions with the United States, show that the obligations are mutual. And no foreign merchant ought to be treated in America better than her native merchants . . .*[1172]

At the same time, John Adams tries, by a separate letter, to prevent the French Foreign Minister from making an appeal to Congress:

When your Excellency says that his Majesty's minister at Philadelphia has already received orders . . . I would submit it to your Excellency's consideration whether those orders may not be stopped and delayed a little time, until his Excellency Mr. Franklin may have opportunity to make his representations to his Majesty's Minister to the end that, if it should appear that those orders were issued in consequence of misinformation, they may be revoked . . .[1173]

Friday, June 23, 1780. Today, John Adams writes Benjamin Franklin:

Count de Vergennes . . . informs me that the Chevalier de la Luzerne has orders to make the strongest representations [to Congress on the devaluation question]. I am not sure whether his Excellency means that such orders were sent . . . I submit to your Excellency, whether it would not be expedient to request that those orders may be stopped until proper representations can be made at court . . .[1174]

Saturday, June 24, 1780. Today, in a letter to the Comte de Vergennes, Ben Franklin tries to prevent the French protest to Congress:

In consequence of the enclosed letter, which I have received from Mr. Adams, I beg leave to request of your excellency that the orders [to the French Minister at Philadelphia] therein mentioned, if not already sent, may be delayed till [Mr. Adams] has prepared the representations he proposed to lay before you on that subject, by which it will appear that these orders have been obtained by misinformation.[1175]

Friday, June 30, 1780. Today, the French Foreign Minister writes John Adams:

I have received the letter which you did me the honor to write me on the 22d inst . . . I had . . . thought . . . to convince you that the French ought not to be confounded with the Americans and that there would be a manifest injustice in making them sustain the loss with which they are threatened.

The details into which you have thought proper to enter have not changed my sentiments; but I think all further discussion on this subject will be needless . . .

His Majesty is the more persuaded that Congress . . . will assuredly perceive that the French deserve a preference before other nations who have no treaty with America and who even have not, as yet, acknowledged her Independence.[1176]

John Adams will recall:

I thought it my indispensable duty to my country, to congress, to France and the Count himself, to be explicit . . . I could see no practicability of any distinction . . . I thought if any was equitable, it would be in favor of American soldiers and early creditors . . . and not in favor of foreigners . . . However, upon the receipt of my letter the Count fell into a passion, and wrote me a passionate and ungentlemanly reply.[1177]

Today, French Foreign Minister Vergennes also writes Ben Franklin:

You ask me, in accordance with Mr. Adams request, that the orders given to [our Minister Plenipotentiary to the U.S.] M. le Chevalier de Luzerne, in relation to the [devaluation] resolution of Congress . . . be revoked . . . because [Mr. Adams] is able to prove these orders to have been based on misinformation.

Mr. Adams, on the 22d instant, addressed to me a very long discussion on the matters in question; but his letter contains nothing but abstract arguments, hypotheses, and calculations which . . . are anything but analogous to those of the alliance which subsists between his Majesty and the United States . . .

The King is so persuaded, Monsieur, that your personal opinion . . . differs from that of Mr. Adams, that he does not apprehend giving you any embarrassment in soliciting you to support before Congress the representations which his minister is charged to lay before that body . . . The King expects that you will lay the whole before Congress, and His Majesty flatters himself that this senate, imbued with other principles than those developed by Mr. Adams, will satisfy His Majesty that it judges the French worthy of some consideration on its part, and that it knows how to appreciate the marks of interest which His Majesty does not cease to manifest towards the United States.[1178]

John Adams:

The Count, and he says the King, was persuaded that the Doctor was fully of opinion with him; that is to say, in favor of the orders. How did he know this? . . . There is no way of accounting for this strange phenomenon, but by supposing that the whole business was previously concerted between the minister and the ambassador to crush Mr. Adams and get possession of his commission for peace. No expression can be too vulgar for so low an intrigue, for so base a trick . . .[1179]

Saturday, July 1, 1780. Today, in another letter to the French Foreign Minister, John Adams stands firm:

I had this morning the honor of your letter of the 30th of June.

It is very certain that the representations from his Majesty . . . will be attended to by Congress . . . As in my letter of the 22d of last month, I urged such reasons as appeared to me incontestable . . .

I have the honor to agree with your Excellency in opinion that any further discussions of these questions is unnecessary.[1180]

John Adams will recall:

> *I was piqued a little, and wrote him, as I thought, a decent, though, in a few expressions, a gently tingling rejoinder. This was insufferable; and now both the Count and the Doctor, I suppose, thought they had got enough to demolish me and get my commission.* [1181]

Thursday, July 6, 1780. Today, from New Jersey, George Washington writes his brother-in-law, Fielding Lewis:

> *I may lament in the bitterness of my soul, that the fatal policy which has pervaded all our measures from the beginning of the War, and from which no experience however dear bought can change, should have reduced our army to . . . removing our Stores from place to place to keep them out of the way of the enemy instead of driving that enemy from our country—*
>
> *It may be asked how these things have come to pass? the answer is plain-and may be ascribed to . . . a fatal jealousy [fear] (under our circumstances) of a Standing Army—by which means we neglected to obtain Soldiers for the War when zeal and patriotism run high, and men were eager to engage for a trifle or for nothing; the consequence of which has been that we have protracted the War—expended Millions and tens of Millions of pounds which might have been saved, and have a new Army to raise and discipline once or trice a year, and with which we can undertake nothing because we have nothing to build upon, as the men are slipping from us every day by means of their expiring enlistments. To these fundamental errors, may be added another which I expect will prove our ruin, and that is the relinquishment of Congressional powers to the States individually, all the business is now attempted, for it is not done, by a timid kind of recommendation from Congress to the States . . .*
>
> *[W]e are attempting an impossibility and very soon shall become (if it is not already the case) a many headed Monster—a heterogenious mass—that never will or can steer to the same point. The contest among the different States now is not which shall do the most for the common cause—but which shall do least.* [1182]

Benny Bache will later write:

> *Whoever reads the correspondence of Mr. Washington will in truth find that, during a part of the war, his troops were commonly as his friends have intimated, "few and bad;" and they will equally find that the proximate causes of the fact which such as he describes, namely, the employment of a fluctuating militia instead of troops inlisted for suitable periods; the want of arms, the want of clothing; &c.—But Mr. Washington forgot to speak of the ulterior causes, most of which rested principally with himself. A man of spirit and address, for example, would have brought things to a short issue [to a head] . . . But Mr.*

Washington was too timid and frigid and too tenacious of his post. Perhaps he was afraid of hearing it retorted that his own bad generalship had caused the loss of many and various stores, and that an army was not likely to be kept steadily together which was dispirited by distress, defeat, and inactivity. A great man . . . like Hannibal . . . knows how to provide resources, even when neglected by his Legislature and his nation.[1183]

Monday, July 10, 1780. Today, Ben Franklin writes French Foreign Minister the Comte de Vergennes:

I received the letter your Excellency did me the honor of writing to me, dated June 30th, together with the papers accompanying it, containing the correspondence of Mr Adams . . . [I]n this I am clear, that if the operation [of the dollar devaluation] directed by Congress . . . occasions, from the necessity of the case, some inequality of justice, that inconvenience ought to fall wholly on the inhabitants of the United States who reap with it the advantages obtained by the measure; and that the greatest care should be taken that foreign merchants, particularly the French, who are our creditors, do not suffer by it. This I am so confident the Congress will do . . .[1184]

Today, the large French fleet under Admiral de Ternay (carrying the 5,500-man French army under General Rochambeau) arrives at Newport, Rhode Island.[1185]

Thursday, July 13, 1780. Today, George Washington writes,

It cannot be too much lamented that our preparations are still so greatly behind-hand. Not a thousand Men that I have heard of have yet joined the army . . .[1186]

Today, in Paris, unaware that France has sent a fleet of warships (which arrived in Newport on Monday), John Adams urges French Foreign Minister Vergennes to provide more naval assistance:

Most people in Europe have wondered at the inactivity of the American army for these two years past . . . The true cause of it is, the English have confined themselves to their strong holds in seaport towns, and have been sheltered from all attacks and insults by the guns of their men-of-war, and forever will be so, while they have superiority at sea . . .

The English, ever since the alliance, have been fearfully apprehensive of an attack upon their strong hold upon the coast by the French. This is what induced them to retreat from Philadelphia to New York . . .

I beg leave to entreat in the most earnest manner that a powerful fleet may be ordered to winter somewhere in North America . . .

[T]he state of things in North America has really become alarming,

and this merely for the want of a few French men-of-war upon that coast. [1187]

Monday, July 17, 1780. Today, John Adams resumes discussion with the French Foreign Minister about his commissions to negotiate peace and commercial treaties with Britain:

> *In your Excellency's letter to me of the 24th of February last, I was honored with your opinion . . . "With regard to the full powers which authorize you to negotiate a treaty of commerce with the Court of London, I think it will be prudent not to communicate them to . . . the British Ministry . . ."*
>
> *I should have been very happy if your Excellency had hinted at the reasons, which were then in your mind, because . . . I am not able to collect any reasons . . .* [1188]

Tuesday, July 18, 1780. Furious that Vergennes won't allow him to deal with Britain, today John Adams writes his American confidant Edmund Jenings:

> *I had myself the honour to be the first who ventured to break the Tie in Congress on the subject of foreign alliances—and to contend against very great Men, whom I will not name at present, that it was the interest and Policy of France to Support our Independency . . . that we ought not to give France any exclusive Priviledges . . . That diminshing the Power of the natural Enemy of France . . . was quite enough to make it her interest to support us . . . and if my Life should be Spared I am determined Posterity shall know which was my Treaty and which was other Peoples Treaty.* [1189]

Thursday, July 20, 1780. Today, in Paris, French Foreign Minister Vergennes informs John Adams that France has already sent to America the fleet Adams requested:

> *I have received the letter which you did me the honor to write me on the 13th of this month . . . The [Admiral] Chevalier de Ternay and the [General] Count de Rochambeau are sent [to America] with the express design which is the subject of your letter. They will concert their operations with Congress and with General Washington . . .*
>
> *You will perceive, Sir, by this detail that the King is far from abandoning the cause of America and that his Majesty, without having been solicited by Congress, has taken effectual measures to support the cause of America.* [1190]

Saturday, July 22, 1780. Today, in the United States, George Washington writes the Continental Congress:

> *I have sent on definitive proposals of co-operation to the French General and Admiral . . . The die is cast, and it remains with the*

States either to fulfil their engagements, preserve their credit, and support their independence, or to involve us in disgrace and defeat.[1191]

Tuesday, July 25, 1780. Today, in Paris, the French Foreign Minister answers John Adams' letter of the 17th:

> I have received the letter, which you have done me the honor to write on the 17th of this month. I have read it with the most serious attention . . . I persist in thinking that the time to communicate your Plenipotentiary power to [British Colonial Secretary] Lord [George] Germain is not yet come, and you will find [with this letter] the reasons on which I ground my opinion. I have no doubt you will feel the force of them, and that they will determine you to think with me. But if that should not be the case, I pray you, and even require you, in the name of the King, to communicate your letter and my answer to the United States and to suspend until you shall receive orders from them, all measures with regard to the English Ministry.[1192]

Wednesday, July 26, 1780. Today, John Adams writes a stiff reply to the Comte de Vergennes on the issue of Adams' peace commission:

> I have received the letter which your excellency did me the honour to write on the 25th of this month . . .
> I shall transmit [my letter and your excellency's answer] to Congress . . .
> There is a great body of people in America as determined as any to support their independence and their alliances, who, notwithstanding, wish that no measure may be left unattempted by Congress or their servants to manifest their readiness for peace . . .
> I can not . . . agree in the sentiment that proposing a treaty of peace and commerce [to Britain] is discovering a great deal of weakness . . .
> Your excellency's letter will convince [Congress] that my apprehensions were wrong, and your advice will undoubtedly be followed, as it ought to be; for they cannot promise themselves any advantages from the communication [with the British] equivalent to the inconveniency of taking a measure of this kind—which ought not to be done but in concert—against the opinion of the ministry of France.[1193]

Thursday, July 27, 1780. Today, John Adams responds unappreciatively to French Foreign Minister Vergennes' disclosure that a fleet and army have been dispatched to America:

> Since my letter of the 21st, and upon reading over again your Excellency's letter to me of the 20th, I observed one expression, . . . "that the king, without having been solicited by the Congress, had taken measures . . ."
> Upon this part of your letter, I must entreat your Excellency to recollect that Congress did as long ago as 1776, before Mr. Franklin was

sent off to France, instruct him . . . to solicit the King for six ships of the line . . . But if it was only suspected by Congress that a direct application from them to the king was expected, I am assured that they would not hesitate a moment to make it . . .

I certainly will not disguise my sentiments from your Excellency . . .[1194]

Saturday, July 29, 1780. Today, obviously upset, the French Foreign Minister writes John Adams:

I have received the letter, which you did me the honor to write on the 27th of this month. When I took upon myself to give you a mark of my confidence by informing you of the destination of Messrs de Ternay and Rochambeau, I did not expect the animadversion which you have thought it your duty to make on a passage of my letter of the 20th of this month. To avoid any further discussions of that sort, I think it my duty to inform you that Mr. Franklin being the sole person who has letters of credence to the King from the United States, it is with him only that I ought and can treat of matters which concern them . . .[1195]

Monday, July 31, 1780. Today, French Foreign Minister Vergennes writes Ben Franklin:

The character with which you are invested . . . induce me to communicate to you a correspondence which I have had with Mr Adams.

You will find, I think, in the letters of that Plenipotentiary, opinions and a turn which do not correspond either with the manner in which I explained myself to him or with the intimate connexion which subsists between the King and the United States . . . I desire, that you will transmit them to Congress that they may know the line of conduct which Mr. Adams pursues with regard to us, and that they may judge whether he is endowed, as Congress no doubt desires, with that conciliating spirit which is necessary for the important and delicate business with which he is intrusted.[1196]

John Adams will write:

I know of no right that any government has to require of an ambassador from a foreign power to transmit to his constituents any complaints against his colleagues, much less to write libels against them . . . [Franklin] proved himself, however, a willing auxiliary, but it was at the expense of his duty and his character . . .

It seems that the Count was not perfectly satisfied that his first letter, of the 30th of June, and the Doctor's representations to Congress in obedience to it, would be sufficient to accomplish all his purposes. This thunderbolt, flaming and deadly as it was, must be followed by another still more loud and terrible, to bellow throughout America, and consequently, over all the world. On the 31st of July, 1780, he writes another letter to Dr. Franklin, in which he more distinctly explains his design and desire to get Mr. Adams removed from his commission for peace . . .

The expressions "that congress may judge . . ." brought the matter home to the business and bosoms of congress. The design could no longer be concealed. I had no other business at that time confided to me but my commissions for peace and a treaty of commerce with Great Britain. The latter he intended to destroy, and in this he succeeded.[1197]

With the French government refusing to deal any longer with John Adams, Mr. Adams leaves France for the Netherlands, where he will spend two frustrating years (until the American Revolution is won!) before obtaining Dutch recognition and a commercial treaty.[1198] Benjamin Franklin:

He is gone to Holland to try, as he told me, whether something might not be done to render us a little less dependent on France.[1199]

John Adams:

[I] was pursued into Holland by the Intrigues of Vergennes and Franklin at least as much as I ever had been in France, and was embarrassed and thwarted, both in my negotiations for a loan and in those of a political nature, by their Friends, Agents, and Spies, as much at least as I ever had been in France.[1200]

Monday, August 7, 1780. Today, French Foreign Minister Vergennes transmits his correspondence with John Adams to the new French minister, the Chevalier de La Luzerne, in the United States. He also instructs his new minister:

I give you these details, Monsieur, in order that you confer confidentially with the President [of Congress] and principal members of the Congress, and thus enable them to judge whether the character of Mr. Adams is such as to qualify him for the important task confided to him by Congress. As far as I am concerned, I foresee that this plenipotentiary will do nothing but raise difficulties and cause vexation on account of a stubbornness, a pedantry, a self-sufficiency and a self-conceit which render him incapable of handling political questions, and especially of treating with the representatives of the great powers who, assuredly, will not accommodate themselves either to the tone or logic of Mr. Adams. These reflections seem to me to deserve all the more attention because this plenipotentiary . . . seems to me to be only very feebly attached to the alliance; so that it would cost him nothing to take steps which would imply the ingratitude of the United States, whilst the opposite sentiment forms the basis of his instructions. Is such an agent suitable for us, can he be suitable for the United States?[1201]

Wednesday, August 9, 1780. Today, Ben Franklin writes the Continental Congress:

> *Mr. Adams has given offence to the Court here, by some sentiments and expressions contained in several of his letters written to the Count de Vergennes. I mention this with reluctance . . . I send them herewith. Mr. Adams did not show me his letters before he sent them . . . Mr. Adams . . . seems to have endeavored supplying what he may suppose my negotiations defective in. He thinks, as he tells me himself, that America has been too free in expressions of gratitude to France; for that she is more obliged to us than we to her; and that we should show spirit in our applications. I apprehend that he mistakes his ground, and that this Court is to be treated with decency and delicacy. The King, a young and virtuous Prince, has I am persuaded, a pleasure in reflecting on the generous benevolence of the action in assisting an oppressed people, and proposes it as part of the glory of his reign. I think it right to increase his pleasure by our thankful acknowledgments, and that such an expression of gratitude is not only our duty, but our interest . . . Mr. Adams, on the other hand . . . seems to think . . . a greater air of independence and boldness in our demands will procure us more ample assistance. It is for the Congress to judge and regulate their affairs accordingly.*
>
> *M. de Vergennes, who appears very much offended, told me yesterday that he would enter into no further discussions with Mr. Adams, nor answer any more of his letters . . . [Mr. Adams] says the ideas of this Court and those of the people in America are so totally different that it is impossible for any Minister to please both . . . But . . . I cannot imagine that he mistakes the sentiments of a few for a general opinion . . .*[1202]

John Adams will write:

> *Dr. Franklin's "reluctance" upon this occasion, I believe, was not implicitly believed by congress, if it was by any individual member of that sagacious body. Sure I am that I have never given the smallest credit to it. The majority . . . saw, as I have always seen, that it was Dr. Franklin's heart's desire to avail himself of these means and this opportunity to strike Mr. Adams out of existence as a public minister, and get himself into his place . . .*
>
> *I now leave your readers to judge whether the Doctor had sufficient reason to complain to congress against me for officially intermeddling in his department and this from ennui and idleness . . . This affair of the currency was no more in his department than it was in mine . . . I had as good a right to answer [the Count] as the Doctor had. It is true I did not show my letters to the Doctor. I was not desired by the Count to consult with him. I had no doubt upon the subject. From a year's residence with him, in 1778 and 1779, in the same family, I knew his*

extreme indolence and dissipation, and consequently, that I might call upon him half a dozen times and not find him at home; and if I found him, it might be a week before I could get his opinion, and perhaps never . . .

"He thinks that America has been too free in expressions of gratitude to France; for that she is more obliged to us than we to her." I cannot, or at least will not deny this accusation, for it was my opinion at that time, has been ever since, and is so now . . .[1203]

Saturday, August 12, 1780. Today, in Geneva, Switzerland, Benny Bache turns eleven years old. Living under the tutelage of Gabriel Louis Galissard de Marignac (a regent of the college and academy of Geneva), Benny attends school from half past seven in the morning to seven in the evening, six days a week. As a New Year's greeting to his grandfather at the beginning of this year, Benny wrote,

I am aware of all the kindness that you have for me. I promise you, my dear papa, that I will always hold the memory of it in my heart . . . I feel how I am responsible to you and how I must do things on my part to make me worthy of all the attentions that you have given me.[1204]

CHAPTER NINE

VICTORY

[B]elieve me, it was not to the exertions of America that we owe the Reduction of this modern Hannibal. Nor shall we always have it in our power to Command the aid of 37 [French] sail of the Line and 8,000 [French] Auxillary veterans—Our Allies have learned that, on this Occasion, our regular troops were not more equal to one half their Land force . . . [O]ur means & numbers were far inadequate . . .

AMERICAN MAJOR GENERAL ANTHONY WAYNE,
YORKTOWN, VIRGINIA[1205]

Wednesday, August 16, 1780. At two this morning at Camden, South Carolina, Britain's two-thousand-man Southern Army, led by British General Charles Cornwallis, surprises and completely demolishes America's four-thousand-man Southern Army, led by American General Horatio Gates ("the hero of Saratoga"). In this disastrous encounter, the American army suffers two thousand casualties, and Gates abandons his reputation, his military career, and America's Southern Army by ignominiously fleeing in the midst of battle, on the army's fastest horse and with a personal guard of six, to Hillsborough, North Carolina. As Alexander Hamilton asked,

> *Was there ever an instance of a General running away, as Gates has done, from his whole army? and was there ever so precipitous a flight? One hundred and eighty miles in three days and a half. It does admirable credit to the activity of a man at his time of life. But it disgraces the General and the soldiers . . .*[1206]

At this Battle of Camden, Baron Johann de Kalb of the French army, who accompanied the Marquis de Lafayette to America and volunteered without pay for the American cause, dies of multiple musket balls and a sabre wound to his head.[1207]

Thursday, August 17, 1780. The failure in recruitment for the Continental army has jeopardized the possibility of a Franco-American operation this year. Today, George Washington writes the Committee of Co-operation:

> *We are now arrived at the middle of August . . . [O]ur operations must commence in less than a month from this, or it will absolutely be too late . . .*
>
> *I am sorry to add that we have every reason to apprehend we shall*

*not be in a condition at all to undertake any thing decisive. The com-
pletion of our Continental batalions . . . has been uniformly and justly
held up as the basis of offensive operations. How far we have fallen
short of this . . .*[1208]

There will be no Franco-American operation until next year.

Sunday, August 20, 1780. Today, George Washington writes the Continental Congress:

> *To me it will appear miraculous if our affairs can maintain them-
> selves much longer in their present train. If either the temper or the
> resources of the Country will not admit of an alteration, we may ex-
> pect soon to be reduced to the humiliating condition of seeing the
> cause of America, in America, upheld by foreign Arms. The generosity
> of our Allies has a claim to all our confidence and all our gratitude,
> but it is neither for the honor of America, nor for the interest of the
> common cause, to leave the work entirely to them.*[1209]

Tuesday, September 12, 1780. Today, George Washington writes the commander of France's fleet in the West Indies:

> *The situation of America at this time is critical. The Government
> without finances; its paper credit sunk, and no expedients it can
> adopt [are] capable of retrieving it . . . [British General Sir Henry]
> Clinton, with an army of ten thousand regular troops . . . [is] in pos-
> session of [New York] one of our capital towns, and a large part of the
> State to which it belongs . . . [and] a fleet, superior to that of our allies,
> not only to protect him against any attempts of ours, but to facilitate
> those he may project against us. [British General] Lord Cornwallis,
> with seven or eight thousand men, [is] in complete possession of two
> States, Georgia and South Carolina; a third, North Carolina, by recent
> misfortunes at his mercy . . .*
>
> *By a Letter lately received from General [Horatio] Gates, we learn
> that, on the 16th of last month, attempting to penetrate and regain the
> State of South Carolina, he met with a total defeat near Camden
> [South Carolina], and the remainder dispersed, with the loss of all
> their cannon and baggage . . .*
>
> *I write to you with that confidence and candor which ought to sub-
> sist between allies and between military men . . . To propose at this
> time a plan of precise cooperation would be fruitless . . .*[1210]

Friday, September 15, 1780. Today, George Washington writes the Continental Congress:

> *I have the honor to inform Congress that to-morrow I set out for
> Hartford to have an interview on the 20th with the [French General]
> Count De Rochambeau and the [French Admiral] Chevalier De Ter-
> nay.*[1211]

Friday, September 22, 1780. Today, George Washington concludes two days of talks at Hartford, Connecticut, with French General Rochambeau and French Admiral de Ternay. The Marquis de Lafayette has acted as interpreter. Washington memorializes his position, including:

> *1st. That there can be no decisive enterprise . . . without a constant naval superiority.*
> *2d. That of all the enterprises which may be undertaken, the most important and decisive is the reduction of New York . . .*[1212]

Tuesday, September 26, 1780. Another of Washington's generals has failed him. Today, George Washington reports the bad news from his headquarters, across the North (Hudson) River from West Point:

> *I arrived here yesterday, on my return from an interview with the French General and Admiral and have been witness to a scene of treason as shocking as it was unexpected. General [Benedict] Arnold, from every circumstance, had entered into a plot for sacrificing West Point. He had an interview with Major André, the British Adjutant-General, last Week . . . By an extraordinary concurrence of incidents, André was taken on his return with several papers in Arnolds handwriting that proved the treason. The latter unluckily got notice of it before I did, went immediately down the river . . . and proceeded to [British headquarters in] New York.*[1213]

Monday, October 2, 1780. Today, from Paris, Benjamin Franklin writes the U.S. Minister to Spain, John Jay:

> *At length I got over a Reluctance that was almost invincible and made another Application to the [French] Government here for more Money . . . I have now the Pleasure to acquaint you that my Memorial was received in the kindest and most friendly Manner, & tho' the Court here is not without its Embarrassments on Account of Money, I was told to make myself easy, for that I should be assisted with what was necessary . . .*
> *I being much pleased with the generous behavior just experienced, I presented another Paper, proposing . . . that the Congress might furnish their Army in America with Provisions in Part of Payment for the Sum lent us. This Proposition I was told was well taken; but, it being considered that the States having the Enemy in their Country and obliged to make great expenses for the Present Campaign, the furnishing so much Provisions as the French Army might need might straiten and be inconvenient to the Congress, his Majesty did not at this time think it right to accept the offer. You will not wonder at my loving this good prince. He will win the Hearts of all America.*[1214]

Sunday, October 8, 1780. Today, Benjamin Franklin belatedly breaks the bad news to John Adams:

I ought to acquaint you, a governo, as the merchants say, that M. le Comte de Vergennes, having taken much amiss some passages in your letters to him, sent the whole correspondence to me, requesting that I would transmit it to Congress. I was myself sorry to see those passages. If they were the effects merely of inadvertence and you did not on reflection approve of them, perhaps you may think it proper to write something for effacing the impressions made by them. I do not presume to advise you, but mention it only for your consideration.[1215]

Monday, October 30, 1780. Today, George Washington and the Marquis de Lafayette (now commanding six battalions of light infantry in advance of the main army) exchange letters. The Marquis de Lafayette writes Washington:

Any enterprise will please the people of this Country, [and] show them that . . . we have men who do not Lay still . . . The French Court have often Complain'd to me of the inactivity of that American Army who Before the Alliance had distinquish'd themselves [at Saratoga] By theyr spirit of enterprise. They have often told me, your friends Leave us now to fight theyr Battles and do no more Risk themselves. It is moreover of the greatest political importance to let them know that on our side we were Ready to Cooperate . . . [I]f any thing may engage the ministry to give us the ask'd for support, it will be our proving to the nation on our side we had been Ready . . . I well know the Court of Versailles, and was I to go to them, I would think it very impolitical to go there unless we had done something.[1216]

George Washington answers:

It is impossible, my Dear Marquis, to desire, more ardently than I do to terminate the campaign by some happy stroke; but we must consult our means rather than our wishes and not endeavour to better our affairs by attempting things, which for want of success may make them worse. We are to lament that there has been a misapprehension of our circumstances in Europe; but, to endeavour to recover our reputation, we should take care that we do not injure it more . . .[1217]

George Washington hasn't fought a battle in two and a half years.

Wednesday, November 22, 1780. Today, in the Continental Congress, the Journals report:

On the report of a committee, Congress agreed to the following letter and representation to his most Christian Majesty [of France] . . .

GREAT, FAITHFUL, AND MOST BELOVED
FRIEND AND ALLY,

[W]e ought not to conceal from your Majesty the embarrassments which have attended our national affairs . . .

A naval superiority in the American seas having enabled the enemy *in the midst of last winter to divide their army and extend the war to the southern states, Charles Town [South Carolina] was subdued . . .*

The acquisition of Charles Town, with the advantages gained in Georgia . . . encouraged the British commander in that quarter to penetrate through South Carolina into the interiour parts of North Carolina . . .

To divert the reinforcements destined for those states, they are now executing an enterprise against the seacoast of Virginia . . .

At a time when we feel ourselves strongly impressed by the weight of past obligations, it is with the utmost reluctance that we yield to the emergency of our affairs in requesting additional favors . . . From a full investigation of our circumstances, it is manifest that, in aid of our utmost exertions, a foreign loan . . . will be indispensably necessary . . .[1218]

Monday, December 4, 1780. Today, on reports of a complaint lodged against Franklin in Congress, Foreign Minister Vergennes writes French Minister Luzerne in Philadelphia:

I have too good an opinion of the intelligence and wisdom of the members of Congress and of all true patriots to suppose that they will allow themselves to be led astray . . . As to Dr. Franklin, his conduct leaves nothing for Congress to desire. It is as zealous and patriotic as it is wise and circumspect, and you may affirm with assurance . . . that the method he pursues is much more efficacious than it would be if he were to assume a tone of importunity in multiplying his demands, and above all in supporting them by menaces, to which we should neither give credence nor value, and which would only tend to render him personally disagreeable . . .

Furthermore, . . . upon the first request of their minister, we have promised him a million of livres to put him in a condition to meet the demands made on him from this time till the end of the year . . .[1219]

Friday, December 8, 1780. Washington is desperate. Someone must detail his needs to France. Today, in the Continental Congress, the Journals report:

Resolved, That a minister be appointed to proceed to the Court of Versailles for the special purpose of soliciting the aids requested by Congress, and forwarding them to America without loss of time.

Ordered, That Monday next be assigned for electing the said minister.[1220]

Sunday, December 10, 1780. Today, from his camp at New Windsor, New York (north of West Point along the North [Hudson] River), George Washington writes New York political leader Gouverneur Morris:

[R]elative to an enterprize against the enemy in New York . . . Where are the men? Where are the provisions? Where the cloaths, the everything necessary to warrant the attempt . . . ? Our numbers . . . were diminished in the Field so soon as the weather set in cold; near 2000

Men on account of cloaths which I had not to give . . . [W]e have nei-
ther money nor credit adequate to the purchase of a few boards for
Doors to our Log huts . . . [W]e cannot dispatch an Officer or common
Express upon the most urgent occasion for want of the means of sup-
port . . . I have not been able to obtain a farthing of public money for
the support of my Table for near two Months . . .[1221]

Monday, December 11, 1780. Today, in the Continental Congress, the Journals report:

Congress proceeded to the election of a minister agreeably to the order of the 8th, and the ballots being taken, Colonel John Laurens was unanimously elected.[1222]

Lieutenant Colonel John Laurens, an aide-de-camp of General Washington and son of Henry Laurens, the former president of the Continental Congress, will leave for Paris to request additional funds.

Monday, January 1, 1781. New Year's Day. Today, about 2,400 men (approximately one fourth) of the Continental army turn a New Year's celebration into a mutiny.[1223] From his camp at New Windsor, New York, George Washington reports:

On the night of the 1st instant, a mutiny was excited by the Non-
Commissioned Officers and Privates of the Pennsylvania Line which
soon became so universal as to defy all opposition. In attempting to
quell this tumult in the first instance, some Officers were killed, others
wounded, and the lives of several common Soldiers lost. Deaf to the
arguments, entreaties, and utmost efforts of all their Officers to stop
them, the Men moved off from Morris Town, the place of their Canton-
ment, with their Arms and six pieces of Artillery: and from Accounts
just received by Genl. Wayne's Aid De Camp, they were still in a body
on their March to Philadelphia to demand a redress of their griev-
ances. At what point this defection will stop, or how extensive it may
prove, God only knows; at present the Troops at the important Posts
in this vicinity remain quiet, not being acquainted with this unhappy
and alarming affair; but how long they will continue so cannot be as-
certained . . .

The aggravated calamities and distresses that have resulted from
the total want of pay for nearly twelve Months, the want of cloathin . . .
and not unfrequently the want of provisions, are beyond descrip-
tion . . .[1224]

Wednesday, January 10, 1781. Congress does not want John Adams to alienate America's French ally. Today, President of the Continental Congress Samuel Huntington writes a warning to John Adams:

Congress consider your correspondence with the Count de Vergen-
nes on the subject of communicating your plenipotentiary powers to

the ministry of Great Britain as flowing from your zeal and assiduity in the service of your country; but I am directed to inform you that the opinion given to you by that minister [Vergennes], relative to the time and circumstances proper for communicating your powers and entering upon the execution of them, is well founded.[1225]

The British have burned Richmond! Today, Thomas Jefferson, now Governor of Virginia, writes George Washington:

On the 31st. of December, a Letter . . . came to my hands notifying that in the morning of the preceding day, 27 Sail of vessels had entered the capes . . . [T]he 2d inst . . . it was ascertained they were enemies and had advanced up James river . . . They marched from Westover at 2 o Clock in the afternoon of the 4th. and entered Richmond at 1 o Clock in the afternoon of the 5th. A regiment of infantry and about 30 horse continued on without halting at the Foundery. They burnt that, the boring mill, the magazine, and two other houses . . . The next morning they burnt some buildings of public and some of private property, with what stores remained in them, destroyed a great quantity of private stores and about 12 o Clock retired to Westover where they encamped within the neck the next day. The loss sustained is not yet accurately known . . . Their numbers from the best intelligence I have had are about 1500 infantry and as to their cavalry accounts vary from 20 to 120, the whole commanded by the parricide [Benedict] Arnold. Our militia . . . can be called in slowly. On the day the enemy advanced to this place, 200 only were called in . . . The whole country in the tide waters and some distance from them is equally open to similar insult.[1226]

Monday, January 15, 1781. Today, George Washington summarizes the nation's needs to Lieutenant Colonel John Laurens, who is preparing to leave for France:

To me it appears evident:

That the efforts we have been compelled to make for carrying on the war have exceeded the natural abilities of this country, and by degrees brought it to a crisis, which renders immediate and efficacious succours from abroad indispensable to its safety . . . The depreciation of our currency was, in the main, a necessary effect of the want of . . . funds; and its restoration is impossible for the same reason . . .

That the patience of the army, from an almost uninterrupted series of complicated distress, is now nearly exhausted, and their discontents matured to an extremity . . .

That, the people being dissatisfied with the mode of supporting the war . . . may weaken those sentiments which begun it . . .

That, from all the foregoing considerations result: 1st, The absolute necessity of an immediate, ample, and efficacious succour of money.

2dly, The vast importance of a decided effort of the allied arms on this
Continent [for] the ensuing campaign . . . Without the first, we may
make . . . the period [end] to our opposition. With it, we should be in a
condition to continue the war . . .

That, next to a loan of money, a constant naval superiority on these
coasts is the object most interesting . . . This superiority, (with an aid
in money), would enable us to convert the war into a vigorous offen-
sive . . .

That an additional succour of troops would be extremely desirable.
Besides a reinforcement of numbers, the excellence of the French
troops, that perfect discipline and order in the corps already sent,
which have so happily tended to improve the respect and confidence of
the people for our allies . . . all these considerations evince the im-
mense utility of an accession of force to the corps now here.[1227]

Today, Washington also writes a letter to Benjamin Franklin, explaining Laurens' mission:

The present infinitely critical posture of our affairs made it essen-
tial, in the opinion of Congress, to send from hence a person who had
been eye-witness to their progress and who was capable of placing
them before the Court of France in a more full and striking point of
light than was proper or even practicable by any written communica-
tions . . .

What I have said to him, I beg leave to repeat to you, that to me
nothing appears more evident than that the period [termination] of
our opposition will very shortly arrive if our allies cannot afford us
that effectual aid, particularly in money and in a naval superiority
which are now solicited . . .[1228]

Today, Washington also writes a letter of thanks to Benny Bache's mother, Sarah Bache, for organizing Philadelphia's women to sew 2,500 shirts for the army:

Although the friendship of your Father may oblige him to see some
things through too partial a Medium, Yet the indulgent manner in
which he is pleased to express himself respecting me is indeed very
pleasing . . . Mrs. Washington requests me to present her Compliments
to Mr. Bache and yourself . . .[1229]

Sunday, January 21, 1781. Today, another mutiny in the Continental army. George Washington reports:

I have received the disagreeable intelligence that a part of the [New]
Jersey Line had followed the example of that of Pennsylvania; and
when the advices came away, it was expected the revolt would be gen-
eral. The precise intentions of the Mutineers was not known, but their
complaints and demands were similar to those of the Pennsylvanians

. . . I have ordered as large a Detachment as we could spare from these Posts to march under Major General Howe . . . to compel the Mutineers to unconditional submission . . .[1230]

Tuesday, February 6, 1781. Today, George Washington writes his representative at the Continental Congress on matters of army reorganization:

You will have heard of the defections of the Pennsylvania line . . . It has ended in a temporary dissolution of the line. One half has been absolutely discharged and the remainder have been furloughed to reassemble in the beginning of April . . . [A] part of the Jersey line since followed their example and gave us an opportunity, after compelling all the mutineers to an unconditional surrender, to make examples of two of the most active leaders . . .[1231]

Twelve mutineers were forced to compose the firing squad that executed two of their leaders.

Sunday, February 11, 1781. Today, Lieutenant Colonel John Laurens, accompanied by Thomas Paine, sets sail from Boston for France aboard the frigate *Alliance*, Captain John Barry.[1232] Tom Paine:

Nothing was done in the campaigns of 1778, 1779, 1780 in the part where George Washington commanded, except the taking of Stony Point by General Wayne. The Southern States in the meantime were overrun by the enemy. They were afterwards recovered . . .

In all this General Washington had no share. The Fabian system of war, followed by him, began now to unfold itself with all its evils; but what is Fabian war without Fabian means to support it? The finances of Congress, depending wholly on emissions of paper money, were exhausted. Its credit was gone. The Continental Treasury was not able to pay the expense of a brigade of wagons to transport the necessary stores to the army, and yet the sole object, the establishment of the Revolution, was a thing of remote distance. The time I am now speaking of is in the latter end of the year 1780.

In this situation of things, it was found not only expedient, but absolutely necessary for Congress to state the whole case to its ally . . . Colonel John Laurens was sent to France as an envoy extraordinary on this occasion, and by private agreement between him and me I accompanied him. We sailed from Boston in the Alliance frigate, February 11, 1781.[1233]

Tuesday, February 13, 1781. Today, in France, Ben Franklin petitions French Foreign Minister Vergennes for additional aid:

[T]he following is a paragraph of a letter from General Washington, which I ought not to keep back from your Excellency, viz. "[O]ur present situation makes one of two things essential to us; a peace or the most vigorous aid of our allies . . ." [F]or effectual friendship and for

the aid so necessary in the present conjuncture, we can rely on France alone and in the continuance of the King's goodness towards us.

I am grown old. I feel myself much enfeebled by my late long illness, and it is probable I shall not long have any more concern in these affairs. I therefore take this occasion to express my opinion to your Excellency that the present juncture is critical . . .[1234]

Monday, February 19, 1781. Today, French Foreign Minister Vergennes writes French Minister Luzerne in Philadelphia:

I have no doubt that . . . [John Adams] is a zealous patriot . . . but his character and turn of mind are essentially opposed to what is proper in political intercourse; he is, and will be, a negotiator as embarrassing for his superiors as for those who have affairs to negotiate with him. I am so convinced of this as to foresee with a certain pain Mr. Adams taking a part in the negotiations for peace. I have already observed this to you in previous dispatches and repeat it now, so that you may see, if you are not able to have him replaced, have him at least given a colleague capable of restraining him.[1235]

Thursday, March 1, 1781. Today, the United States have finally ratified Articles of Confederation. By the terms of the Articles, the Continental Congress will continue to make national decisions:

Article V . . . [D]elegates shall be annually appointed in such manner as the legislature of each state shall direct . . .

In determining questions in the United States in Congress assembled, each state shall have one vote . . .

Articles IX . . . The United States in Congress assembled shall never engage in a war . . . nor enter into any treaties or alliances, nor coin money, nor regulate the value thereof . . . nor borrow money . . . nor appoint a commander in chief of the army or navy unless nine [of the thirteen] states assent to the same . . .[1236]

These Articles of Confederation do not reflect Ben Franklin's plan. They do not provide for direct popular election of delegates by small voting districts of equal population size. They don't provide for state representation in proportion to population. Delegates "appointed . . . as the legislature of each state shall direct" are those that state senates (the "interests of property") will allow.

Under these Articles, the national government will continue ineffective, lacking the ability to tax, draft soldiers, or compel state compliance with its legislation. Continental currency is worthless. The Continental Congress will stop printing money this month.[1237]

Friday, March 9, 1781. Today, from France, French Foreign Minister Vergennes writes the French minister in Philadelphia:

I confess to you that, whatever good opinion I may entertain of the patriotism of John Adams, I see him, with regret, entrusted with so dif-

ficult and so delicate a duty as that of pacification, on account of his pedantry, stubbornness and self-importance, which will give rise to a thousand vexations to the despair of his co-negotiators. [1238]

Today, on his mission to get more French aid, Lieutenant Colonel John Laurens, accompanied by Thomas Paine, arrives at the French port of L'Orient. [1239]

Monday, March 12, 1781. John Laurens will not reach Versailles until later in the month. [1240] In the meantime, Ben Franklin has acted on his own and today reports the results to the president of Congress:

> *I had the honor or receiving . . . your Excellency's letter, together with . . . a copy of [the instructions] to Colonel Laurens . . . I immediately drew a memorial, enforcing as strongly as I could the requests that are contained in that letter . . . Mr. Laurens not arriving, I wrote again and pressed strongly for a decision on the subject . . .*
>
> *Upon this, I received a note, appointing [last] Saturday for a meeting with the [French Foreign] minister which I attended punctually. He assured me of the King's good will to the United States; remarking, however, that, being on the spot, I must be sensible of the great expense France was actually engaged in and the difficulty of providing for it . . . but that . . . his Majesty had resolved to grant them the sum of six millions not as a loan but as a free gift . . .* [1241]

Thursday, March 15, 1781. Today, at the Battle of Guilford Courthouse at Guilford, North Carolina, British General Charles Cornwallis prevails over America's Southern Army, which General Nathanael Greene has rebuilt, primarily from state militias, following Horatio Gates' ignominious defeat last August at the battle of Camden, South Carolina. Although, in today's battle, North Carolina militiamen occupy the front lines only briefly and abandon the field after firing just two volleys, Greene's men inflict many casualties on the British. [1242] After this battle, Nathanael Greene will lead his army south into South Carolina, and General Cornwallis will lead his British army deeper into North Carolina and then back to Virginia.

Tuesday, March 20, 1781. Today, from Paris, Lieutenant Colonel John Laurens writes the Continental Congress:

> *Upon my arrival here I found that the letter of Congress to his Most Christian Majesty of the 22nd of November, 1780, had been delivered by our Minister Plenipotentiary [Dr. Franklin]; that he had proceeded to negotiate the succors solicited by Congress . . .* [1243]

Lieutenant Colonel Laurens will, nonetheless, explain America's plight to the Count de Vergennes. John Laurens:

> *I endeavored to represent . . . [t]hat . . . the immense pecuniary resources of Great Britain and her constant naval superiority were advantages too decisive to be counterbalanced by any interior exertions*

on the part of the United States . . . that [America's] aggravated calamities . . . began now to produce dangerous uneasinesses and discontents . . . that . . . the succor solicited was . . . indispensable. [1244]

Tuesday, March 27, 1781. Today, George Washington writes Virginia that he has no troops to spare:

> *By the expiration of the times of service of the old troops, by the discharge of the Levies engaged for the Campaign only, and by the unfortunate dissolution of the Pennsylvania line, I was left . . . with a Garrison barely sufficient for the security of West Point . . .*
>
> *In my late tour to the Eastward, I found the accounts I had received of the progress of recruiting . . . much exaggerated . . .*
>
> *You will readily perceive, from the foregoing state, that there is little probability of adding to the force already ordered to the southward . . .* [1245]

Monday, April 9, 1781. Today, from his camp at New Windsor, George Washington writes his emissary, Lieutenant Colonel John Laurens, in Paris:

> *[B]e assured, my dear Laurens, that day does not follow night more certainly than it brings with it some additional proof of the impracticability of carrying on the war without the Aids you were directed to sollicit. As an honest and candid man, as a man whose all depends on the final and happy termination of the present contest, I assert this. While I give it decisively as my opinion, that, without a foreign loan, our present force (which is but the remnant of an Army) cannot be kept together this campaign, much less will it be encreased and in readiness for another . . .*
>
> *We are at this hour suspended . . . [W]e cannot transport the provisions from the States in which they are Assessed to the Army, because we cannot pay the Teamsters who will no longer work for Certificates. It is equally certain that our Troops are approaching fast to nakedness, and that we having nothing to cloath them with. That our Hospitals are without medicines . . . That all our public works are at a stand . . . [B]ut why need I run into the detail, when it may be declared in a word, that we are at the end of our tether, and that now or never our deliverance must come.* [1246]

Thursday, April 12, 1781. Today, Benjamin Franklin answers William Carmichael's report that John Adams and others have disparaged Franklin in Congress:

> *I thank you very much for your friendly hints of the Operations of my Enemies, and of the means I might use to defeat them. Having in view at present no other Point to gain but that of Rest, I do not take their Malice so much amiss . . . [Certain enemies] are open, and so far, honourable Enemies; the Adams, if Enemies, are more covered. I never*

*did any of them the least injury and can conceive no other Source of
the Malice but Envy . . . Those who feel Pain at seeing others enjoy
Pleasure and unhappy because others are happy, must daily meet
with so many Causes of Torment, that I conceive them to be already in
a State of Damnation . . .* [1247]

Thursday, April 19, 1781. Today, from Paris, French Foreign Minister Vergennes writes his minister in Philadelphia:

*The letter that Congress wrote Mr. Adams concerning his correspondence with me only dealt with the issue of when this minister should
communicate his commission to the court at London . . . I would have
preferred Congress . . . to establish a rule for him not to permit himself
the smallest departure from the advice of the King; this is the only way
to contain Mr. Adams and to make us the masters of his conduct. I beg
you to make this point to the president of Congress, to do everything
you can to make him see the justice of it, and to have him engage the
Congress to send supplementary instructions to Mr. Adams . . .* [1248]

Monday, April 23, 1781. Today, the Marquis de Lafayette writes George Washington that the slaves at Mount Vernon are volunteering to fight with the British:

*When the enemy came to your house, many negroes were ready to
join him . . . [Y]ou cannot conceive how unhappy I was to learn that
M. Lund Washington went on board the enemy battleships and consented to give them provisions.* [1249]

Monday, April 30, 1781. Today, from his camp at New Windsor, New York, George Washington writes his estate manager Lund Washington (a distant cousin) at Mount Vernon:

*[T]hat which gives me the most concern is that you should go on
board the enemys Vessels and furnish them with refreshments . . . You
ought to have considered yourself as my representative and should
have reflected on the bad example of communicating with the enemy . . .*

*I . . . believe that your desire to preserve my property and rescue the
buildings from impending danger were your governing motives. But to
go on board their Vessels; carry them refreshments; commune with a
parcel of plundering Scoundrels, and request a favor by asking the
surrender of my Negroes, was exceedingly ill judged . . .* [1250]

British General Charles Cornwallis will have two thousand American Negro
slaves on the British side at Yorktown. Many of George Washington's slaves will
join the British to fight George Washington. [1251]

Friday, May 11, 1781. Today, French Foreign Minister Vergennes writes the French minister in Philadelphia that Lieutenant Colonel John Laurens is tactless and offensive:

> *We flatter ourselves especially, Monsieur, that Congress will not only not share but will condemn high-handedly the discontent that distinguishes M. Laurens, and that it will seek to inspire in this officer a few of the facts of our customs and some of the considerations which are due to the ministers of a great power; he has made several demands, not only with unfit importunity, but even employing threats.*[1252]

Fortunately, Franklin is on the scene to deflect Laurens' provocations.

Monday, May 14, 1781. Today, from Paris, Ben Franklin writes the Marquis de Lafayette:

> *I hope that by this time, the ship which has the honor of bearing your name, is safely arrived. She carries clothing for nearly twenty thousand men, with arms, ammunition, &c. which will supply some of your wants, and Colonel Laurens will bring a considerable addition . . .*
>
> *This Court continues firm and steady in its friendship, and does everything it can for us. Can we not do a little more for ourselves?*[1253]

Tuesday, May 22, 1781. Today, George Washington and French General Rochambeau meet at Wethersfield, Connecticut, to plan the coming campaign. George Washington still favors an attack on New York City. From notes of the meeting:

> *ROCHAMBEAU—Should the squadron from the West Indies arrive in these seas . . . what operations will General Washington have in view, after a union of the French army with his own?*
>
> *WASHINGTON—The Enemy, by several detachments from New York, have reduced their force at that post . . . [I]t is thought advisable to form a junction of the French and American Armies down to the vicinity of New York to be ready to take advantage of any opportunity which the weakness of the enemy may afford. Should the West Indies Fleet [under Admiral de Grasse] arrive upon the Coast, the force thus combined may either proceed in the operation against New Y[or]k, or may be directed against the enemy in some other quarter . . .*[1254]

Monday, May 28, 1781. Today, George Washington writes the French Minister in Philadelphia, the Chevalier de La Luzerne:

> *[O]ur object is New York. The Season, the difficulty and expense of Land transportation, and the continual waste of men in every attempt to reinforce the Southern States, are almost insuperable objections . . . ; nor do I see how it is possible to give effectual support to those States*

and avert the evils which threaten them while we are inferior in naval force in these Seas.[1255]

Friday, June 1, 1781. Today, Lieutenant Colonel John Laurens, still accompanied by Thomas Paine, departs the French port of Brest for the United States aboard the frigate *Résolu.* Tom Paine:

> *The event of Colonel Laurens's mission, with the aid of the venerable Minister, Franklin, was that France gave in money, as a present, six millions of livres, and ten millions more as a loan, and agreed to send a fleet of not less than thirty sail of the line, at her own expense, as an aid to America. Colonel Laurens and myself returned from Brest the first of June following, taking with us two millions and a half of livres (upwards of one hundred thousand pounds sterling) of the money given, and convoying two ships with stores.*[1256]

Monday, June 11, 1781. Today, from Rhode Island, French General Rochambeau writes French Admiral de Grasse in the West Indies,

> *I will not deceive you, Sir; these people are at the end of their resources; Washington will not have half the troops that he counted upon having, and I believe, although he is silent on the subject, that he has not 6,000 men; that Lafayette has not 1,000 men of the regular troops with the militia to defend Virginia; about as many are marching to join him; that General Greene has made an attack upon Camden and has been repulsed; and I am ignorant as to when and how he will rejoin Lafayette . . . The arrival of M. Le Comte de Grasse can save [this country]; all the means we have at hand avail nothing without his help and the naval superiority that he can secure.*[1257]

Today, from New York, British Commander in Chief Sir Henry Clinton writes British General Charles Cornwallis in Virginia:

> *I am threatened with a siege at this post . . . With respect to . . . the enemy . . . it is probable they may amount to at least 20,000, besides reinforcement to the French . . . Thus circumstanced, I am persuaded . . . the sooner I concentrate my force the better. Therefore . . . I beg leave to recommend it to you . . . to take a defensive station in any healthy situation you choose (be it at Williamburg or York Town). And I would wish . . . the following corps may be sent to me . . . Two battalions of Light infantry, 43rd regiment . . . [&c.]*[1258]

Tuesday, June 12, 1781. Today, from Virginia, former congressional delegate Richard Henry Lee writes the Continental Congress that cavalry from the British Southern Army, under Charles Cornwallis, have attacked Charlottesville Virginia (seat of government since the fall of Richmond), and that Virginia Governor Thomas Jefferson has resigned and fled:

I suppose you have been informed of the junction of the enemies forces on James river and many of their subsequent movements . . . [T]he enemy halted their main body in the forks of Pomunkey, and detached 500 Cavalry with an Infantryman behind each to Charlottsville where our uniformed Assembly was collected by adjournment from Richmond. The two houses were not compleated, and Mr. Jefferson had resigned his office and retired, as some of our dispersed Delegates report, when the enemy entered Charlottsville this day [and] night and dispersed the whole, taking Mr. Digges the Lieutenant Governor prisoner and some Delegates, Mr. Lyons the Judge and many others . . . You will then judge of the situation of this country, without either executive or Legislative authority, every thing in the greatest possible confusion . . . Let the Congress send [Washington] immediately to Virginia . . .[1259]

Jefferson "resigned" (Jefferson also used this word)[1260] and fled eight days ago (June 4th) when the British cavalry attacked Charlottesville, ending plans for a gubernatorial election (Jefferson's term expired June 1st). Jefferson fled to one of his plantations, Poplar Forest, in Bedford County, where he will remain in hiding six weeks or more. Virginia's legislature will hold hearings on this conduct.[1261]

Wednesday, June 13, 1781. Today, George Washington writes French General Rochambeau:

It is to be regretted that the Count [de Grasse]'s stay upon this coast will be limited . . .

[Y]ou have in your communication to him confined our views to New York alone . . . [W]ill it not be best to leave him to judge . . . which will be the most advantageous quarter for him to make his appearance in . . . Should the British fleet not be there, he could follow them to the Chesapeak which is always accessible to a superior force.[1262]

France (in the person of French Admiral de Grasse), not Washington, will choose to engage the British at Yorktown, Virginia.

Friday, June 15, 1781. Today, the Continental Congress withdraws John Adams' credentials as America's sole minister to make peace with Great Britain. The Journals report:

The committee reported the draft of a commission . . . for negotiating a peace, which being amended, was agreed to as follows: . . .

That we . . . have thought proper to renew the powers formerly given to the said John Adams and to join four other persons in commission with him; and . . . by these presents do nominate, constitute, and appoint . . . Benjamin Franklin, John Jay, Henry Laurens, and Thomas Jefferson in addition to the said John Adams, giving and granting to them . . . full power and authority . . . relating to the establishment of peace.

Having reduced John Adams to one of five peace commissioners, Congress gives Adams and his fellow commissioners clear instructions:

> For this purpose [of negotiating peace with Britain] you are to make the most candid and confidential communications upon all subjects to the ministers of our most generous ally, the King of France; to undertake nothing in the negotiations for peace or truce without their knowledge and concurrence; and ultimately to govern your selves by their advice and opinion, endeavoring in your whole conduct to make them sensible how much we rely upon his majesty's influence for effectual aid in everything that may be necessary to the peace, security, and future prosperity of the United States of America.[1263]

Saturday, June 16, 1781. Today, French General Rochambeau writes French Admiral de Grasse:

> General Washington has but a handful of men, which could possibly reach to about 7,000 or 8,000. The army of Cornwallis is in the heart of Virginia, between Richmond and Fredericksburg . . . You can well understand that under these conditions how urgent it is that you bring some troops with you; this country is at bay, all its resources are failing at the same time: the continental paper is worth absolutely nothing.[1264]

Monday, June 18, 1781. Today, a French army of 4,400 soldiers, under General Rochambeau, starts its march south from Rhode Island to join George Washington's two-thousand-man Continental army near New York City.[1265]

Wednesday, June 20, 1781. Today, France liberates Richmond and the rest of Virginia, as British General Charles Cornwallis withdraws Britain's Southern Army to a point of possible embarkation for New York (accommodating Sir Henry Clinton's fear that French reinforcements of Washington may imperil New York). Cornwallis repositions the British army at Yorktown, Virginia, where the York River opens to the Chesapeake and the Atlantic.[1266]

Thursday, June 21, 1781. Today, Massachusetts congressional delegate James Lovell writes John Adams why Adams is no longer the only peace commissioner:

> France . . . presses us for an Arrangement . . . Franklin, Jay, H. Laurens, and Jefferson are added to you [as peace commissioners] . . . [Y]our other parchments are untouched . . . I presume you will be at very little Loss to come at the Clue of this Labyrinth. [Vergennes] persuaded [Congress] of the absolute Necessity of the most cordial Intercourse between him . . . and Suppleness [Franklin] . . . I must officially convey to you some Papers.[1267]

Adams' "other parchments" will, however, also be touched.

Thursday, July 12, 1781. Today, the Continental Congress withdraws John Adams' credentials to negotiate a commercial treaty with Britain. The Journals report:

A motion was made by Mr. Madison, seconded by Mr. Mathews, That the [commerce] commission and instructions for negotiating a treaty of commerce between these United States and Great Britain given to the honourable John Adams on the 29 day of September, 1779, be and they are hereby revoked.

On the question to agree to this, the yeas and nays being required . . . So it was resolved in the affirmative [20 yeas to 6 nays].[1268]

Friday, July 13, 1781. Today, Massachusetts congressional delegate James Lovell writes John Adams' wife, Abigail:

[Y]our all [Mr. Adams] is not servile enough to gain the unbounded affection of the foreign Court at which he resided when he had the Correspondence which produced the two Resolves of Congress . . . [Y]ou would have found that [the Count de Vergennes] wrote two Letters in a pet against Mr. A[dams] to old F[ran]k-l[i]n and that the latter had also written a most unkind and stabbing one hither which he was under no necessity of doing, as he needed only to have transmitted the Papers given to him for the Purpose by the former.[1269]

Sunday, July 15, 1781. Today, George Washington writes Richard Henry Lee of Virginia:

The fatal policy of short enlistmts . . . is now shedding its baneful influence . . . [N]ot half the Men which were required to be with the Army as recruits for the Continental Batt[alio]ns by the first day of Jan[uar]y last are yet arrived—and of those asked by me from the Militia, not one is come.[1270]

As an adult, Benny Bache will write:

It may be insisted here that Mr. Washington had under him a few and bad troops, and that his situation was always destitute. But were all this true, is it not part of a general to create everything; resources, skill, courage, ardor, and numbers. This was the talent of Henry IV of France . . .[1271]

Saturday, July 21, 1781. Today, from Philadelphia, Massachusetts congressional delegate James Lovell writes another letter to John Adams, this time about the loss of Adams' commerce commission:

The whole of the Proceedings here in regard to y[ou]r two commissions are, I think, ill judged, but I persuade myself no dishonour intended. [T]he business greatly in every View chagrins me. [T]his you will have learnt from my former Letters written in an half-light.[1272]

Today, George Washington writes French Admiral the Comte de Grasse:

> *I have the honor to inform you that the allied Armies have formed a junction and taken a position about Ten miles above the enemy's posts on the North end of [New] York Island . . . The French Force consists of 4400 Men. The American is at this time very small . . .*[1273]

George Washington has but two thousand men![1274]

Monday, July 30, 1781. George Washington doesn't want to move south. Today, he writes the Marquis de Lafayette:

> *[F]rom the change of circumstances with which the removal of part of the Enemy's force from Virginia to New York will be attended, it is more than probable that we shall intirely change our plan of operations. I think we have already effected . . . substantial relief to the southern States by obliging the enemy to recall a considerable part of their force from thence. Our views must now be turned towards endeavouring to expel them totally from those States if we find ourselves incompetent to the siege of New York . . .*
> *I approve your resolution to reinforce General Greene . . .*[1275]

It is not George Washington's army but rather Rochambeau's that caused the withdrawal of British troops from the south. Likewise, it is not George Washington's army but General Nathanael Greene's that has been clearing the British from the Carolinas.[1276] Tom Paine:

> *Mr. Washington had the nominal rank of Commander in Chief, but he was not so in fact. He had, in reality, only a separate command. He had no controul over, or direction of, the army to the northward under Gates that captured Burgoyne [at Saratoga], nor of that to the South, under Green, that recovered the southern States. The nominal rank, however, . . . makes him appear as the soul and center of all military operations in America.*[1277]

Thursday, August 2, 1781. Today, George Washington writes the Continental Congress:

> *Congress will readily conceive the disagreeable situation in which I find myself, when they are informed that I am not stronger at this advanced period of the Campaign than when the Army first moved out of their Winter Quarters . . . [N]ot a single Man had come in from Massachusetts . . . [O]nly 176 from Connecticut had arrived at that post yesterday. In short, not a single Militia Man from any State has joined the Army, except the few just mentioned, about 80 Levies of New York, and about 200 State Troops of Connecticut, both of which were upon the Lines previous to my leaving our Winter Cantonments . . .*
> *The General Return for June, which I have lately sent by Capt. Roberts to the Board of War . . . exhibits an Army upon paper rather than*

an operating Force . . . [T]he Civil departments having been totally destitute of Money, have been unable to hire or pay the Men necessary for their uses . . .[1278]

Benny Bache will (as an adult) write:

A commander in chief . . . should be able to choose decisive positions; he should shine in the arts of subsisting and recruiting an army . . . in a talent for obtaining information; in the invention of stratagems; in the supply of expedients for the cases (and many are the cases) untouched by the general rules; in inspiring a soul into an army; and in the provoking an enemy to disadvantageous action.

What are the talents however which Mr. Washington has displayed . . . ? Let us read . . . his diligent correspondence for three long years and a half, and doubtless omitting nothing calculated (according to his maturer judgment) for advancing his reputation.—Did he ever anticipate that experience of which we have been speaking; did he even always keep pace with it; did he detect the impropriety of many professional measures which were imposed on him by Congress and others; does he animate us? What still life for three years and a half! We find that the time passes, but we scarcely perceive that he is at war; and if he ever seems a general, it is because he has to contend with those who were not. He relates, he argues, and sometimes he even projects; but how seldom does he act with success.[1279]

Wednesday, August 8, 1781. Today, a French fleet of twenty-eight ships of the line, under French Admiral the Comte de Grasse, bearing a French army of 4,600, under French Major General the Marquis de St. Simon, heads north from the West Indies to join another French fleet of eight ships of the line, under French Admiral the Comte de Barras, which will head south from Newport, Rhode Island. Another French army of four thousand, under French General the Comte de Rochambeau, has already left Newport, Rhode Island, for the march south. These French fleets and French armies all follow orders from France to support George Washington.[1280]

Sunday, August 12, 1781. Today, in Geneva, Switzerland, Benny Bache turns twelve years old. He is a bit homesick. This week, he will write his grandfather,

[I] know that it is impossible for you to write me because of your busy schedule, but I would very much like to have news from you, and I beg you to write me some as soon as it will be possible for you and if you have the time . . .[1281]

Tuesday, August 14, 1781. Today, George Washington writes in his diary:

Matters having now come to a crisis and a decisive plan to be determined on, I was obliged, from the shortness of Count de Grasse's promised stay on this coast, the apparent disinclination in their Naval Officers to force the harbour of New York and the feeble compliance of

the States to my requisitions for Men, hitherto, and little prospect of greater exertion in the future, to give up all idea of attacking New York; and instead thereof to remove the French Troops and a detachment from the American Army to the Head of Elk [at the head of the Chesapeake Bay, Maryland] to be transported to Virginia for the purpose of co-operating with the [French] force from the West Indies against the [British] Troops in that State.[1282]

Thursday, August 16, 1781. Today, from Paris, Ben Franklin writes John Adams in the Netherlands that Adams is no longer sole commissioner to negotiate peace with Great Britain:

> *I have the honor to inform your excellency that I yesterday received despatches . . . ordering me upon an additional service, that of being joined with yourself and Messrs. Jay, H[enry]. Laurens and T. Jefferson in negotiations for peace . . . I shall be glad to learn from your excellency what steps have already been taken in this important business.*[1283]

Sunday, August 19, 1781. Today, French General the Comte de Rochambeau leads his French army south from New York toward Virginia.[1284]

Friday, August 24, 1781. Today, the French fleet at Newport, Rhode Island, now commanded by French Admiral the Comte de Barras (French Admiral de Ternay died in December), sets sail for the Chesapeake Bay and Virginia with eight ships of the line, four frigates, and eighteen transports. This fleet carries critical siege artillery and other provisions for the armies of General Rochambeau and Washington which are now marching from New York to Virginia.[1285]

Today, in Amsterdam, John Adams receives letters from Massachusetts congressional delegate James Lovell (June 21st) and Ben Franklin (August 16th), informing him that the French Foreign Minister and Ben Franklin have deprived him of his position as sole commissioner to make peace with Great Britain.[1286]

Saturday, August 25, 1781. Today, in Amsterdam, in composing an answer to Ben Franklin's letter of August 16th, John Adams suffers a nervous collapse.[1287] John Adams:

> *I found myself attacked by a fever, of which at first I made light, but which increased very gradually and slowly until it was found to be nervous fever of a very malignant kind, and so violent as to deprive me of almost all sensibility for four or five days and all those who cared anything about me of the hopes of my life . . .*[1288]
> *I was seized with . . . a nervous Fever, of a dangerous kind, bordering upon putrid. It seized upon my head, in such a manner that for five or six days I was lost, and so insensible to the Operations of the Physicians and surgeons, as to have lost the memory of them . . .*[1289]

For the next six weeks, John Adams will be incommunicado.[1290]

Today, Tom Paine and John Laurens arrive in Boston Harbor aboard the frigate *Résolu*, bringing money and supplies from France. Tom Paine:

> *We arrived at Boston the twenty-fifth of August . . . De Grasse arrived with the French fleet in the Chesapeake at the same time, and was afterward joined by that of Barras, making thirty-one sail of the line. The money was transported in wagons from Boston to the bank at Philadelphia . . .*[1291]

Monday, August 27, 1781. Today, not knowing that Lieutenant Colonel John Laurens and Tom Paine have arrived in Boston with money from France to pay Washington's soldiers, George Washington writes Robert Morris, Superintendent of Finance for the Continental Congress:

> *I must entreat you, if possible, to procure one month's pay in specie for the detachment which I have under my command. Part of those troops have . . . upon several occasions shown marks of great discontent. The service [down south in Virginia] they are going upon is disagreeable to the Northern Regiments; but I make no doubt that a douceur [bribe] of a little hard money would put them in proper temper. If the whole sum cannot be obtained, a part of it will be better than none, as it may be distributed in proportion to the respective wants and claims of the Men. The American detachment will assemble in this neighbour-hood today; the French Army to-morrow.*[1292]

Monday, September 3, 1781. Today, on their march to Yorktown, Virginia, the French army parades, in dress-white uniforms, through the streets of Philadelphia to the sounds of a military band, the cheers of Americans, and the salutes of General Washington, their commander General Rochambeau, and the American Continental Congress. A French clergyman records the scene:

> *The arrival of the French army at Philadelphia was more like a triumph than simply a passing through the place; the troops made a halt about a quarter of a league from the city, and in an instant were dressed as elegantly as ever the soldiers of a garrison were on a day of review; they then marched through town, with military music playing before them, which is always particularly pleasing to the Americans; the streets were crowded with people, and the ladies appeared at the windows in their most brilliant attire. All Philadelphia was astonished to see people who had endured the fatigues of a long journey so ruddy and handsome, and even wondered that there could possibly be Frenchmen of so genteel an appearance.*
>
> *The troops next marched in single file before the Congress and [before] M. Le Chevalier de la Luzerne, minister from the court of France . . .*
>
> *The maneuvers of our troops raised the most flattering expectations in the minds of the spectators; and they did not hesitate to declare that such soldiers were invincible.*[1293]

Frenchman Comte Guillaume de Deux-Ponts observes:

> *Congress was on the route, and we showed it the respect the King had ordered us to show, the thirteen members of the Congress taking off their thirteen hats at each salute of the flag . . .* [1294]

American Brigadier General Anthony Wayne:

> *The french troops are the finest & best body of men I ever beheld— their Officers and Gen'l & I will be answerable for their being soldiers; we have the highest Opinion of their Discipline & can not doubt their prowess.* [1295]

WEDNESDAY, SEPTEMBER 5, 1781

⇨ The Pennsylvania Gazette ⇦

On Thursday last arrived in this city, their Excellencies GENERAL WASHINGTON and the COUNT DE ROCHAMBEAU, with their respective Suites. They were met and accompanied to town by his Excellency the President of the State [of Pennsylvania], the Financier-general, and many other Gentlemen of distinction. Every class of citizens seemed to vie with each other in shewing marks of respect to this ILLUSTRIOUS PAIR of Defenders of the Rights of Mankind.

Today, Superintendent of Finance for the Continental Congress Robert Morris writes in his diary:

> *The Commander in Chief having repeatedly urged, both by letter and in conversation, the necessity of advancing a month's pay to the detachment of troops marching to the southward . . . and my funds and resources being at the time totally inadequate to make that advance, . . . I made application to the Count de Rochambeau . . .*
>
> *General Washington was extremely desirous that the troops should receive their month's pay, as great symptoms of discontent had appeared on their passing through this city without it . . .*
>
> *Count de Rochambeau very readily agreed to supply at the head of the Elk twenty thousand hard dollars . . .* [1296]

The French will pay George Washington's army to fight at Yorktown!

Today, September 5th, at the entrance to the Chesapeake Bay off Yorktown, Virginia, the largest and most significant naval battle of the American Revolution begins, as twenty-eight French ships-of-the-line from the West Indies, under French Admiral de Grasse, challenge nineteen British ships-of-the-line (and a fifty-gun British ship) from New York, commanded by British Rear Admiral Thomas Graves. A five-day engagement (the Battle of the Virginia Capes) ensues, in which the French navy is victorious, inflicting 336 casualties on the British force (at the cost of 220 French killed and wounded), damaging a seventy-four-gun British ship so badly that it has to be burned and abandoned, and causing British Rear Admiral Graves to retreat with his fleet to New York. This French victory means that the British will not be able to reinforce Cornwallis in Virginia and, even more important, that Cornwallis cannot escape by water from the Yorktown embankment on which the French and American armies now have him trapped.[1297]

Friday, September 7, 1781. British Commander in Chief Sir Henry Clinton knows he faces a calamity. Today, he writes British Colonial Secretary Lord George Germain:

> *The force of the enemy opposed to his lordship [Lord Cornwallis] will consist of the French troops arrived [from the West Indies] with De Grasse which are reported to be between three and four thousand; those [French troops under General Rochambeau] with Washington 4000; the rebel continentals about 4000; and in all probability a very numerous militia if they can arm them.*
>
> *This my lord, is a very alarming report . . . Things appear to be coming fast to a crisis . . .*[1298]

WEDNESDAY, SEPTEMBER 12, 1781

✦ The Pennsylvania Gazette ✦

NEW YORK, Sept 5. By accounts from the Chesapeake, dating the 31st ult. the arrival of the French fleet or squadrons, consisting of 28 sail, including frigates and inferior vessels, were arrived at Lyn-Haven Bay, in Virginia, from whence a 64–[gun ship of the line] and two frigates were dispatched up York River, and had taken a position off York-Town.

PHILADELPHIA, September 12. By an express which arrived here last Wednesday evening . . .

Extract of letter from his Excellency General Washington to the President of Congress . . .

"With great pleasure to transmit to your Excellency . . . [an announcement of] the late arrival in the Chesapeake of Admiral de Grasse with 28 [French] ships of the line . . ." . . .

Note, the above fleet is exclusive of that [French fleet] under the command of Count Barras [which is arrived from Newport].

Upon the above news arriving in the city, the bells of Christ Church were rung, and joy appeared in every countenance. About seven o'clock a large body of citizens waited on the Minister of France to congratulate him upon this important intelligence. They gave him three cheers, and concluded with crying out "Long Live the King of France."

Today, September 12th, British Commander in Chief Sir Henry Clinton writes British Colonial Secretary Lord George Germain:

*Other matters of most serious moment now attract our attention—a
French army of at least eight thousand men, a powerful fleet of the
same nation cooperating with them—the continental army . . . —to
these may be added a numerous and warlike militia. Your lordship
knows that France . . . [has] made considerable loans and sent them
supplies of all sorts. Nothing therefore is wanting but to prevail on
those already enlisted to remain.*

*[I]n this situation of affairs your lordship must be sensible that . . . I
may perhaps be unable to preserve our present possessions. For (as I
have often had the honour of suggesting to your lordship) if the enemy
retain only a few weeks superiority at sea, we shall certainly be
beat . . .*

*Lord Cornwallis has good 6000 men with him . . . I had some inten-
tion of moving into Jersey . . . But the instant I knew of the French actually being there and that Washington had moved decidedly to meet
them, I saw no way of relieving his lordship [Lord Cornwallis] but by
joining him . . .*[1299]

There are approximately 32,000 French soldiers and sailors at Yorktown,[1300]
four to six times the number of George Washington's army, and more than
twice, if not three times, the number of all Americans at Yorktown, including
militia. Indeed, there are many more French soldiers on the ground than American Continentals. The entire blockading force at sea is French.[1301]

Sunday, September 16, 1781. Today, from Yorktown, British General Lord
Cornwallis writes British Commander in Chief Sir Henry Clinton:

*The enemy's [French] fleet has returned. Two line of battleships and
one frigate lie at the mouth of this river, and three or four line of battleships, several frigates, and transports went up the bay . . .*

*PS . . . [T]hey have thirty-six sail of the line. This place is in no state
of defence. If you cannot relieve me very soon, you must be prepared to
hear the worst.*[1302]

By engaging British Admiral Thomas Graves' fleet in the Battle of the Virginia
Capes, the French fleet from the West Indies (under French Admiral de Grasse)
has allowed the French fleet from Newport (under Count de Barras) to slip into
the Delaware River with vital siege artillery and provisions for the allied armies.[1303]

Wednesday, September 26, 1781. Today, British Commander in Chief Sir
Henry Clinton writes British Colonial Secretary Lord George Germain:

*I have received a letter from the [British] Admiral [Graves in the
Chesapeake] . . . to inform me that the enemy, being absolute masters
of the navigation of the Chesapeake, there was little probability of getting into York River but by night and an infinite risk to any supplies
sent by water, at the same time acquainting me that he had on the 5th*

*a partial action with the French fleet of 24 sail of the line and that the
two fleets had been in sight of each other ever since . . .*

*On the 17th I received another letter from the Admiral [Graves] . . .
saying . . . that . . . he determined to shelter in New York . . .*[1304]

Of French and American forces which encircle Charles Cornwallis at Yorktown, the naval part of this circle consists strictly of French warships (more than thirty) and sailors (nineteen thousand!).[1305] America has no warships in this naval blockade.

Friday, October 12, 1781. The siege of Yorktown is begun. Today, George Washington writes the Continental Congress on its progress:

*We . . . established our first parallel within 600 Yards of the enemy's
Works with the loss of only one Officer of the French artillery wounded
and 16 privates killed and wounded, the greater part of which were of
the French line . . .*

*The 9th at 3 O'Clock in the Afternoon, the French Battery on the left
. . . opened—and at 5 O'Clock the American Battery on the right . . .
opened also . . .*

*We were informed that our shells did considerable execution in the
Town, and we could perceive that our shot . . . injured them much.
The 10th, two French Batteries . . . opened, as did two more American
Batteries . . . The fire now became so excessively heavy that the enemy
withdrew their Cannon from their embrazures . . . In the evening, the
Charon Frigate of 44 Guns was set on fire by a hot Ball from the
French Battery on the left . . .*

*We last night advanced our second parallel within 300 yards of the
enemy's Works . . .*

*I cannot but acknowledge the infinite obligations I am under to His
Excellency, the Count de Rochambeau . . . and indeed the Officers of
every denomination in the French Army for the assistance which they
afford me. The experience of many of those Gentlemen, in the business
[of siege warfare] before us, is of the utmost advantage . . . [T]he
greatest harmony prevails between the two Armies . . .*[1306]

Orchestrating the siege at Yorktown is strictly a matter for the French. Washington has no experience in siege warfare. The French perfected the art.[1307] Rochambeau has taken part in fourteen sieges.[1308] General Lebigne, the Chevalier Du Portail, and other French officers and engineers take charge of siege operations.[1309]

Monday, October 15, 1781. Today, finally recovered from his nervous collapse, John Adams writes the Continental Congress:

*I have received the new commission for peace [as part of a five-
man commission] and the revocation of my [sole peace] commission
and instructions of the 29th of September, 1779. To both of these mea-*

sures of Congress, as to the commands of my sovereign, I shall pay the most exact attention . . .

[A]ccording to the best judgment I can form, it will not be worth while for Congress to be at the expense of continuing me in Europe with a view to my assistance at any conferences for peace, especially as Dr. Franklin has given me intimations that I can not depend upon him for my subsistence in the future . . .

In short, my prospects both for the public and for myself are so dull and the life I am likely to lead in Europe is likely to be so gloomy and melancholy and of so little use to the public, that I can not but wish it may suit with the view of Congress to recall me.[1310]

Tuesday, October 16, 1781. Today, George Washington reports to Congress on Yorktown fighting:

[H]aving deemed the two Redoubts [fortified emplacements] on the left of the enemy's line sufficiently injured by our shot and shells to make them practicable, it was determined to carry them by assault on the evening of the 14th. The following disposition was accordingly made. The Work on the enemy's extreme left to be attacked by the American Light Infantry under the command of the Marquis de La Fayette; the other by a detachment of the French Grenadiers and Chasseurs, commanded by Major-General, the Baron Vioménil . . . [W]e succeeded in both . . . Nothing could exceed the firmness and bravery of the Troops. They advanced under the fire of the Enemy without returning a shot, and effected the business with the Bayonet only . . . [A]ttacks on the part of the French and American Columns were Conducted . . .

The enemy last night made a sortie for the first time. They entered one of the French and one of the American Batteries . . . They were repulsed . . . The French had four officers and twelve privates killed and wounded, and we had one serjeant mortally wounded . . .[1311]

Two French soldiers die for each American death at Yorktown. Two French soldiers are wounded for each American wound at Yorktown. French casualties exceed 250.[1312]

A word about Lieutenant Colonel Alexander Hamilton at Yorktown . . . John Adams writes:

You inquire what passed between W.[ashington] and Hamilton at Yorktown? Washington had ordered, or was about to order, another officer to take command of the attack upon the redoubt. Hamilton flew into a violent passion and demanded the command of the party for himself and declared if he had it not, he would expose General Washington's conduct in a pamphlet.[1313]

Hamilton's scorn of Washington is no surprise to me. Those who trumpeted Washington in the highest strains at some times spoke of him at others in the strongest terms of contempt . . . Hamilton, Pickering, and many others have been known to indulge themselves in very contemptuous expressions . . . The history with which Hamilton threatened to destroy the character of Washington might diminish some of that enthusiastic exaggeration which represents him as the greatest general, the greatest legislator, and the most perfect character that ever lived . . .

I lose all patience when I think of a bastard brat of a Scotch pedlar [Hamilton] daring to threaten to undeceive the world in their judgment of Washington by writing an history of his battles and campaigns.[1314]

Friday, October 19, 1781. Today, the British army of Lord Cornwallis surrenders, signaling the end of the American Revolution. The British army files out of the village of York between two lines of French and American soldiers, though the British clearly attribute their loss to the French rather than to the Americans. A French observer:

[T]hey would not raise their eyes to look upon their conquerors . . . The English officers, in coming out, had the honesty to salute even the lowest French officer, something that they would not do to Americans even of the first grade . . . In all the time that the British remained at York, one did not see them have any communication with the Americans, while they lived constantly with the French and sought constantly to give them proof of their esteem . . .[1315]

British General Charles O'Hara, acting on behalf of General Charles Cornwallis (who has pleaded illness), attempts to surrender Cornwallis' sword to French Commander in Chief General the Comte de Rochambeau, but Rochambeau magnanimously refuses to accept the surrender weapon and directs the British general to George Washington.[1316]

Today, George Washington writes the Continental Congress:

I have the Honor to inform Congress that a Reduction of the British army, under the Command of Lord Cornwallis, is most happily effected . . .

On the 17th instant, a Letter was received from Lord Cornwallis . . . [T]hat Correspondence was followed by the Definitive Capitulation, which was agreed to and Signed on the 19th . . .[1317]

Tom Paine:

We arrived at Boston the twenty-fifth of August . . . DeGrasse arrived with the French fleet in the Chesapeake at the same time, and was afterwards joined by that of Barras, making thirty-one sail of the line.

The money was transported in wagons from Boston to the bank at
Philadelphia . . . And it was by the aid of this money, and this fleet,
and of Rochambeau's army, that Cornwallis was taken; the laurels of
which have been unjustly given to Mr. Washington . . .

I have had, and still have, as much pride in the American Revolution as any man, or as Mr. Washington has a right to have; but that
pride has never made me forgetful whence the great aid came that
completed the business. Foreign aid (that of France) was calculated
upon at the commencement of the Revolution. It is one of the subjects
treated of in the pamphlet "Common Sense," but as a matter that
could not be hoped for unless independence was declared. The aid,
however, was greater than could have been expected.[1318]

Saturday, October 20, 1781. Today, General Charles Cornwallis writes his
commander in chief, Sir Henry Clinton:

I have the mortification to inform your Excellency that I have been
forced to give up the posts of York and Gloucester and to surrender . . .

[O]n the morning of the 16th, I ordered a sortie of about 350 men
. . . killing or wounding about 100 of the French troops who had the
guard of that part of the trenches and with little loss on our side. This
action . . . proved of little public advantage . . . I had therefore only to
choose between preparing to surrender next day or endeavoring to get
off with the greatest part of the troops . . . [A] diversion by the French
ships of war that lay at the mouth of the York River was to be expected
. . . I therefore proposed to capitulate . . .[1319]

Friday, October 26, 1781. Today, from Yorktown, American Brigadier General
Anthony Wayne writes Robert Morris:

The surrender of Lord Cornwallis with his Fleet & Army . . . is an
event of the utmost consequence & if properly improved may be productive of a Glorious & happy peace; but if we suffer that unworthy
torpor & supineness to seize us which but too much pervaded the
Councils of America after the Surrender of Gen'l Burgoyne [at Sara-
toga], we may yet experience great Difficulties,—for believe me, it was
not to the exertions of America that we owe the Reduction of this modern Hannibal. Nor shall we always have it in our power to Command
the aid of 37 [French] sail of the Line and 8,000 [French] Auxiliary
veterans.—Our Allies have learned that, on this Occasion, our regular
troops were not more equal to one half their Land force . . . [O]ur
means & numbers were far inadequate . . . [1320]

As one historian will recall, "At Saratoga, France furnished the guns and ammunition that led to Burgoyne's surrender; at Yorktown, it was French money,
troops, and ships that brought Cornwallis to a like fate."[1321]

Monday, October 29, 1781. Today, on his return voyage to England,[1322] British Commander in Chief Sir Henry Clinton writes British Colonial Secretary for North America Lord George Germain:

> *Your lordship will therefore of course suppose my surprise was great when I heard [the French Admiral] de Grasse had brought with him 28 sail of the line and that [our British Admiral] Sir Samuel Hood had only 14 . . . To this inferiority, then, I may with confidence assert, and to this alone, is our present misfortune to be imputed.*[1323]

Friday, December 14, 1781. Today, in Amsterdam, John Adams writes former Massachusetts congressional delegate Francis Dana:

> *I have recd a new Commission for Peace in which [five of us] are the ministers. I have recd also a Revocation of my Commission to make a Treaty of Commerce with [Britain].—These last novelties, I suppose, would nettle Some Men's Feelings; but I am glad of them. They have removed the cause of Envy, I had like to have said, but I fear I must retract that, since 18 [cypher for Adams] still stands before 17 [cypher for Franklin] in the Commissioners.*[1324]

Friday, January 25, 1782. Today, Benjamin Franklin writes Benny Bache:

> *Dear Benny,*
>
> *I received your letter . . . together with the drawings which please me . . . But I expect you will improve; and that you will send some to me every half Year that I may see how you improve . . .*
>
> *Let me know whether you learn Arithmetick in your School . . . I am ever, my dear Child,*
>
> *Your Affectionate Grandfather, B. Franklin*[1325]

Saturday, February 16, 1782. Peace negotiations will soon begin. Today, Ben Franklin writes an English friend, David Hartley:

> *[T]here has been mixed in some of your conversations and letters various reasonings to show that, if France should require something of us that was unreasonable, we should then not be obliged by our treaty to join with her in continuing the war. As there had never been such requisition, what could I think of such discourses . . . [K]nowing your dislike of France, and your strong desire of recovering America to England, I was impressed with the idea that such an infidelity on our part would not be disagreeable to you; and that you were therefore aiming to lessen in my mind the horror I conceived at the idea of it. But we will finish here by mutually agreeing that neither you were capable of proposing, nor I of acting on, such principles.*[1326]

Wednesday, February 27, 1782. Today, the British Parliament votes to end the war with America and to negotiate peace.[1327]

Friday, March 22, 1782. Today, Benjamin Franklin opens peace negotiations with Britain by writing his old friend, the British Secretary of State for the Colonies, the Earl of Shelburne:

> *I embrace the opportunity of assuring the Continuance of my ancient Respect for your Talents and Virtues, and of congratulating you on the returning good Disposition of your Country in favour of America, which appears in the late Resolutions of the Commons . . . I hope it will tend to produce a General peace . . . to which I shall, with infinite Pleasure, contribute every thing in my Power.*[1328]

Saturday, April 6, 1782. Today, British Secretary of State Lord Shelburne responds to Benjamin Franklin's letter:

> *I have been favoured with your Letter and am much oblig'd by your remembrance . . . Your letter, discovering the same disposition, has made me send you Mr. Oswald . . . I have thought him fittest for the purpose. He is a pacifical man, and conversant in those negotiations which are most interesting to mankind . . .*[1329]

Tuesday, May 28, 1782. Today, in the Continental Congress, a committee reports a meeting with the French minister in Philadelphia. The Secret Journals of the Continental Congress report:

> [T]he minister [from France] communicated some parts of a despatch which he had received from the Count de Vergennes, dated the 9th of March, 1781 . . . respecting the conduct of Mr. Adams; and . . . gave notice to the committee of several circumstances which proved it necessary that Congress should draw a line of conduct to that minister of which he might not be allowed to lose sight . . .
>
> The minister concluded on this subject that if Congress put any confidence in the king's friendship . . . they would be impressed with the necessity of prescribing to their plenipotentiary . . . a thorough reliance on the king and would direct him to take no step without the approbation of his majesty . . .[1330]

Wednesday, July 10, 1782. Today, British negotiator Richard Oswold reports to Lord Shelburne, now Britain's Prime Minister, that, after discussions with Franklin that started in early April, Franklin has set forth, at a meeting this morning, conditions of peace, some "necessary," some "advisable," that Great Britain should offer America:

> *1st. Of the first class necessary to be granted, Independence full and complete in every sense, to the Thirteen States, and all troops to be withdrawn from thence. 2d. A settlement of the boundaries . . . 3d. A confinement of the boundaries of Canada . . . on an ancient footing. 4th. A freedom of fishing on the Banks of Newfoundland and elsewhere, as well for fish as whales . . .*
>
> *Then, as to advisable articles . . . 1st. To indemnify many people . . .*

2d. Some sort of acknowledgment . . . of our error in distressing those countries so much as we have done . . . 3d. Colony ships and trade to be received . . . 4th. Giving up every part of Canada . . . [1331]

Since March, Ben Franklin has had to conduct British peace negotiations on his own. The four other American peace commissioners aren't available. Commissioner Henry Laurens was captured by the British while crossing the Atlantic. He won't join the negotiations till just before a treaty signing. Thomas Jefferson won't cross the Atlantic unless the British assure his safe-conduct. Thus, he won't come until after a final treaty is ratified and hostilities have ceased.[1332] John Jay arrived in Paris on June 23rd but has been incapacitated by influenza.[1333] John Adams won't return to Paris from the Netherlands, loathing to be near Franklin or to consult with Vergennes.[1334]

Saturday, July 20, 1782. Today, from the Netherlands, John Adams writes his American friend Edmund Jenings:

> *[Franklin's] base Jealousy of me and his Sordid Envy of my Commission for making Peace, and especially of my Commission for making a Treaty of Commerce with Great Britain, have stimulated him to attempt to commit an Assassination upon my Character at Philadelphia, of which the World has not yet heard, and of which it cannot hear untill the Time shall come when many voluminous State Papers may be laid before the Publick, which ought not to be untill we are all dead.—But this I swear, I will affirm when and where I please that he has been actuated and is still by a low Jealousy and a meaner Envy of me, let C.[ount] Vergennes or F.[ranklin] himself complain of it again to Congress if they please, it would be my day to answer there in Person or by Letter.—The anonymous Scribbler charged me with clandestinely hurting Franklin.—I have done nothing clandestine.—I have complained of Franklin's Behavior in Company with Americans. So have I in Company with the French & Spanish Ambassadors . . . This is an odd Sort of Clandestinity.—that I have no Friendship for Franklin I avow.—that I am incapable of having any with a Man of his Moral Sentiments, I avow. As Far as such State shall compel me to act with him in publick affairs, I shall treat him with decency & perfect Impartiality. Further than that I can feel for him no other sentiments than Contempt or Abhorrence . . .* [1335]

Saturday, July 27, 1782. Today, British Prime Minister Lord Shelburne writes his peace negotiator, Richard Oswald:

> *I am to acknowledge receipt of your [letter of the 10th] . . . [Y]ou are at liberty to communicate to Dr. Franklin . . . to satisfy his mind, that there never have been two opinions, since you were sent to Paris, upon the most unequivocal Acknowledgment of American Independency . . . But to put this matter out of all Possibility of Doubt, a Commission will be immediately forwarded to you containing Full Power*

. . . to make the Independency of the Colonies the Basis & Preliminary of the Treaty now depending & so far advanc'd that, hoping as I do with you that the Articles call'd <u>advisable</u> will be dropp'd & those call'd <u>necessary</u> alone retained as the ground of Discussion, it may be speedily concluded . . . I shall consider myself as pledg'd to the Contents of this Letter.[1336]

Monday, August 12, 1782. Today, in Paris, Benjamin Franklin sends U.S. Foreign Affairs Secretary Robert Livingston a tally of monies France has advanced to America:

All the accounts given us . . . made the debt [to France] to an even sum of eighteen millions, exclusive of the Holland loan [ten millions] for which the king [of France] is guarantee . . . [Y]ou will discover several fresh marks of the King's goodness toward us, amounting to the value of near two millions. These added to the free gifts made to us at different times, form an object of at least twelve millions, for which no returns but that of gratitude and friendship are expected. These, I hope may be everlasting.[1337]

Today, in Geneva, Switzerland, Benny Bache turns thirteen years old. For the past several months, he has been witnessing an unsuccessful democratic uprising in Geneva, and this week, he writes in his diary:

I prepared to go to the class for the first time for several months during which the Genevese had had some troubles, which had, so to speak, [shut] the town and which had not ceased until France, Switzerland, and Piedmont were engaged and had sent troops now occupying the town, . . . [T]he professors were obliged to teach their classes in their own houses, such was the state of Geneva.[1338]

Though Geneva has neither king nor formal nobility, an old aristocracy denies political rights to ordinary burghers and artisans. This year, inspired by the writings of Voltaire and Rousseau, the "natives" of Geneva have demonstrated for a more democratic government. As Benny can see, a standing army is a formidable response to such claims.[1339]

Sunday, August 18, 1782. Today, in The Hague, John Adams drafts (but decides not to send) a request that Congress replace him as a peace commissioner:

For my own Part, I will be very explicit with Congress. If I were now the sole Minister for treating of Peace, I should decidedly refuse to enter into any Conferences with any one whatsoever without full powers to treat with the United States of America. If I had been alone [as the sole negotiator], when the first messengers were sent over, I mean when . . . Mr. Oswald came over, my answer would have been clear, that I would never treat with such a Plenipotentiary—If my Opinion had been asked by Dr. Franklin, I should have given him the same . . .

But instead of this, Dr. Franklin . . . tells them that no express Acknowledgment of our Independence will be insisted on [except as part of a peace treaty]. Thus it is that all American Affairs are conducted by Dr. Franklin—I have not refused to act in the [peace] commission with him [only] because I thought it possible that I might . . . do some little good in it or prevent some evil. But I despair of doing much to such a degree that I beg Congress would release me from this Tye and appoint another Minister of that commission in my Room. [1340]

Sunday, September 1, 1782. Today, Britain's Secretary of State, Thomas Townshend, instructs his peace negotiator, Richard Oswold:

I am commanded to signify to You His Majesty's [King George III's] Approbation of Your conduct in communicating to the American Commissioners . . . that the Negotiation for Peace and the Cession of Independence of the Thirteen United Colonies were intended to be carried on and concluded . . . I am commanded to signify to you His Majesty's disposition to agree to the Plan of Pacification proposed by Doctor Franklin himself . . . The Articles specified by Doctor Franklin, and recited in your Letter to the Earl of Shelburne of the 10th of July last, are . . . stated by you as all that Doctor Franklin thought necessary; and His Majesty . . . has authorized You to go to the full extent of them . . . [1341]

Friday, September 6, 1782. Today, from the Netherlands, John Adams writes U.S. Secretary of Foreign Affairs Robert Livingston:

You require Sir to be furnished with the most minute Details of every Step that Britain may take towards a Negotiation for a General or partial Peace . . . Dr. Franklin wrote me that he should keep me informed of any thing that passed by. But I have had no advice from him since the Second of June.

[A]lthough it is proper to be open . . . and confidential with the French Ministers, yet we ought to have opinions, Principles, and Systems of our own . . . [O]ur Ministers should not be bound to follow their Advice, but when it is consonant with our own . . . Congress should firmly support their own ministers against all Secret Insinuations . . . Either Congress shall recall all their ministers from Europe and leave all Negotiations to the French Ministry or they must Support their Ministers against all Insinuations . . . To send Ministers to Europe who are supposed by the People of America to see for themselves, while in effect they see or pretend to see nothing but what appears thro' the eyes of a French Minister is to betray the just[Deputations] of that people. [1342]

Friday, September 20, 1782. Today, from Paris, American Matthew Ridley (a European business agent for Maryland) writes John Adams about a conversation with John Jay:

I have had one serious Conversation with J[ay]. He appears to me very desirous of seeing you—were it only for a few hours—he says he has some things to consult you upon that he cannot put to Paper . . . I find . . . J.[ay] firm—I wish he was supported . . . The English have come here for Peace . . .

I believe very little if any progress is made . . . I wish sincerely you knew all that is passing here . . .[1343]

Ben Franklin has been suffering with kidney stones since the third week in August,[1344] so John Jay has taken on a larger role in the British peace negotiations.[1345]

Wednesday, October 2, 1782. Today, alluding to French naval losses earlier in the year,[1346] French Foreign Minister Vergennes writes France's ambassador to Spain:

In a word, our great goal, the goal common to the two crowns [France and Spain] and to all the warring powers, being a prompt and honorable peace . . . it is by . . . more trenchant means that we must get there.

When I speak of a prompt peace, I speak from personal knowledge of the need and necessity. We no longer can entertain any disastrous illusions. Our means are no longer the same. Our respective navies, which ought to be stronger in number than at the outset of the war, are, for both of us, below what they were at the beginning. That of England is, however, more consistent today than it was then. As to financial means, I don't hesitate to say that ours, after six hundred millions in extraordinary expenses, are very weak . . .[1347]

Friday, October 5, 1782. Today, Ben Franklin, John Jay, and Richard Oswold agree to a draft of a preliminary peace agreement to be submitted to the British king.[1348] The treaty, based on Franklin's four *necessary* articles (plus freedom to navigate the Mississippi), acknowledges complete American independence, the Mississippi as America's western boundary, and rights to fish in the waters of Newfoundland.[1349]

Tuesday, October 15, 1782. Today, from Geneva, Benny Bache writes Ben Franklin,

Dear Grand Papa . . .

My life is uniform. I get up at half after 7, I breakfast to 8, from 8 to 11 I am in class, at 11 I have a Latin lesson to 12, from 12 to 1 I dine and learn by heart a lesson that our Regent gives us, from 1 to 3 I go to class, from 3 to 5 I do a task luncheon and do a theme, from 5 to 6 I do another Latin lesson, from 6 to 7 I translate Joseph Andrews and write my journal, from 7 I do my drawing lesson to 8, and then I sup and go to bed.

That is the work I do the Monday, the Tuesday and Friday; the

Wednesday and Saturday I have no drawing master. Almost every Thursday and Sunday I go to Mme. Cramer's . . .[1350]

Thursday, October 17, 1782. Today, three weeks after receiving news (from Matthew Ridley's September 20th letter) that John Jay needs support against Vergennes,[1351] John Adams leaves the Netherlands to join Franklin and Jay. As one historian has observed, *"Neither Adams's good reasons nor his bad ones sufficiently explained his remaining in the Netherlands in the face of British overtures and his misgivings about Franklin."*[1352]

Thursday, October 24, 1782. Today, John Jay notes in his diary:

I dined at Passy with Dr. Franklin, where I found [the secretary to the Count de Vergennes,] M. [Gérard de] Rayvenal . . . He desired to know the state of our negotiation with Mr. Oswold. We told him that difficulties had arisen about our boundaries . . . He asked us what boundaries we claimed. We told him . . . He contested out right to such an extent to the north . . . He inquired what we demanded as to the fisheries. We answered . . . He intimated that our views should not extend further than a coast fishery . . . Mr. Franklin explained very fully their importance to the Eastern states . . . He then softened . . .[1353]

Saturday, October 26, 1782. This afternoon, John Adams arrives in Paris, having toured Utrecht, Breda, and Antwerp en route from Amsterdam.[1354]

Sunday, October 27, 1782. Today, anticipating negotiations with the British, John Adams writes in his diary:

R.[idley] is still full of J.[ay]'s Firmness and Independance. [Jay h]as taken upon himself to act without asking Advice or even communicating with the C.[omte] de V[ergennes]—and this even in opposition to an Instruction [from Congress] . . . W. has . . . been very desirous of perswading F.[ranklin] to live in the same house with J.[ay].—Between two as subtle Spirits, as any in this World, the one malicious, the other I think honest, I shall have a delicate, a nice, a critical Part to Act. F.[ranklin]'s cunning will be to divide Us. To this End, he will provoke, he will insinuate, he will intrigue, he will maneuvre . . .[1355]

Tuesday, October 29, 1782. Today, Matthew Ridley visits John Adams and writes in his diary:

Called to see Mr. Adams. Dined with him. He is much pleased with Mr. Jay. [I w]ent in the morning to see D[r.] Franklin—[He] did not know of Mr. Adams Arrival. Spoke to Mr. A.[dams] about making a visit to Dr. F[ranklin]. He told me it was time enough—[I] represented to him the necessity of meeting. He replied there was no necessity— that after the usage he had received from [Franklin], he could not bear to go near him . . . He said the D[r.] might come to him. I told him it

*was not [his] place– the last comer always paid the first visit. He re-
plied the Dr. was to come to him [since] he was first [in appointment]
in the Comm[issio]n. I ask[ed] him how the D[r.] was to know he was
here unless he went to him. He replied that was true, he did not think
of that, and would go. Afterwards while pulling on his Coat, he said he
would not, he could not bear to go where the D[r.] was. With much
persuasion, I got him at length to go.* [1356]

Tonight, John Adams pays a visit to Franklin. [1357] Mr. Adams:

*I told him without reserve, my opinion of the policy of this Court,
and of the principles, wisdom, and firmness with which Mr. Jay had
conducted the negotiations in his sickness and my absence, and that I
was determined to support Mr. Jay to the utmost of my power in the
pursuit of the same system. The Doctor heard me patiently, but said
nothing.* [1358]

Thursday, October 31, 1782. Today, from Paris, John Adams writes U.S. Secretary for Foreign Affairs Robert Livingston:

*I set off for Paris, where I arrived on Saturday, the 26th of this
month . . .
I find a construction put upon . . . our instructions by some persons
which I confess I never put upon it myself . . . obliging us to agree to
whatever the French ministers shall advise us to do, and to do nothing
without their consent . . . I cannot think it possible to be the design of
congress . . .* [1359]

Tuesday, November 5, 1782. Today, John Adams writes in his diary:

*Mr. Jay likes Frenchmen as little as Mr. Lee . . . He says they are not
a Moral People. They know not what [morality] is. He dont like any
Frenchman.—The Marquis de la Fayette is clever, but he is a Frenchman.— Our Allies don't play fair, he told me . . . They want to place
the Western Lands, Mississippi, and whole Gulph of Mexico into the
Hands of [their ally] Spain.* [1360]

John Jay not only hates the French. He hates all Catholics. [1361]

Wednesday, November 6, 1782. Today, John Adams writes American Foreign
Affairs Secretary Robert Livingston:

*[Y]ou will, I am sure, not take it amiss if I say that it is indispensa-
bly necessary for the service of Congress and the honor of the office
that [our affairs] be kept impenetrably secret from the French minister
in many things . . .* [1362]

Friday, November 8, 1782. Today, John Adams writes Foreign Affairs Secretary Robert Livingston:

In one of your letters you suppose that I have an open, avowed contempt of all rank . . .

If Mr. Jay and I had . . . taken the advice of the Count de Vergennes and Dr. Franklin . . . we should have sunk in the minds of the English . . .

The injunctions upon us to communicate and to follow the advice that is given us seem to be too strong . . .[1363]

Today, John Adams also writes his wife, Abigail:

G.[reat] B.[ritain] has . . . acknowledged Us a Sovereign State & independent Nation . . . Jay & I peremptorily refused to Speak or hear before We were put upon an equal Foot [by their first recognizing our independence before a treaty was written]. Franklin as usual would have taken the Advice of the C.[ount] de V.[ergenne] and treated without [formal recognition in advance] but nobody would join him.

As to your coming to Europe . . . I know not what to say. I am obliged to differ in Opinion so often from Dr. Franklin and the C. de Vergennes . . . and these Personages are so little disposed to bear Contradiction, and Congress have gone so near enjoining upon me passive Obedience to them, that I do not expect to hold any Place in Europe longer than next Spring . . . The Artifices of the Devil will be used to get me out of the Commission for Peace. If they succeed, I abandon Europe for ever for the Blue Hills [of Massachusetts] without one Instants Loss of Time or even waiting for Leave to return.[1364]

Saturday, November 9, 1782. Today, John Adams receives a visit from the Marquis de Lafayette. John Adams:

M. de la Fayette came in and told me he had been at Versailles . . . After some time he told me, in a great air of confidence, that he was afraid the Count [de Vergennes] took it amiss that I had not been to Versailles to see him. The Count told him that he had not been officially informed of my arrival, he had only learned of it from the returns of the police . . . Franklin brought the same message to me from the Count, and said he believed it would be taken kindly if I went. I told both the Marquis and the Doctor I would go to-morrow morning.[1365]

Sunday, November 10, 1782. Today, John Adams visits the Comte de Vergennes, receiving compliments for obtaining Dutch recognition of the U.S. as well as a Dutch commercial treaty:

The Comte invited me to dine . . . We went to dinner . . . The Comte who sat opposite was constantly calling out to me, to know what I would eat and to offer me petits Gateaux, Claret and Madeira &c. &c . . . The Compliments that have been made since my Arrival in France upon my Success in Holland would be considered a Curiosity, if com-

mitted to Writing . . . Vous avez fait reconnoitre votre Independence
[You have won recognition for your Independence] . . . Another said
Monsieur vous etes le Washington de la Negotiation [You are the Wash-
ington of Negotiation] . . . Compliments are the Study of this People
and there is no other so ingenious at them.[1366]

Alexander Hamilton:

Stating this incident, [Adams] . . . might have added, they have also
a very dexterous knack of disguising a sarcasm.[1367]

As a historian will later observe, "*Adams never learned the true extent of*
French influence on his Dutch negotiation."[1368] Vergennes was pulling the
strings at every turn.[1369]

Tuesday, November 12, 1782. Today, Mr. Adams writes in his diary:

The Compliment of "Monsieur, vous etes le Washington de la Negoti-
ation" [Sir, you are the Washington of negotiations] was repeated to
me by more than one person . . . A few of these Compliments would kill
Franklin if they should come to his ears.[1370]

Wednesday, November 20, 1782. Today, John Adams records Franklin's attitude on New England fishing rights and on America's western boundary, two
important peace issues:

Franklin said . . . [t]hat the Fisheries and Mississippi could not be
given up. That nothing was clearer to him than that the Fisheries were
essential to the northern States, and the Mississippi to the Southern
and indeed both to all. I told him that [French Ambassador] Mr. Gér-
ard had certainly appeared to America to negotiate to these Ends, vizt.
to perswade Congress to give up both . . . I said . . . We must be firm
and steady and should do very well.—Yes he said he believed We
should do very well and carry the points.[1371]

Franklin, Adams, and Jay will carry these points, but, if France seems less than
fully supportive, it must be remembered that France only obligated herself, by
the Franco-American Alliance, to achieve America's Independence—not these
greater benefits.[1372]

Saturday, November 23, 1782. Today, French Foreign Minister Vergennes
writes his minister at Philadelphia:

There is nothing in our treaties [with the United States] which
obliges us to prolong the war to uphold the ambitious pretensions
which the United States may make either on fisheries or on bounda-
ries.[1373]

Saturday, November 30, 1782. Today, without first consulting the French Foreign Ministry, John Adams, John Jay, and Ben Franklin sign with Great Britain

a "Preliminary Peace Treaty" that grants full American independence, American fishing rights, and the Mississippi as America's western boundary.[1374]

Wednesday, December 4, 1782. Today, John Adams writes American Secretary of Foreign Affairs Robert Livingston:

> It is with much pleasure that I transmit [to] you the preliminary treaty between the King of Great Britain and the United States of America . . .
>
> As the objects for which I ever consented to leave my family and country are thus far accomplished, I now beg leave to resign all my employments in Europe . . . I should not choose to stay in Europe merely for the honor of affixing my signature to the definitive treaty . . .[1375]

Thursday, December 12, 1782. Today, John Jay writes Secretary of Foreign Affairs Robert Livingston:

> You will receive from us a joint letter with a copy of the preliminaries . . . It gives me great pleasure to inform you that perfect unanimity has hitherto prevailed among your Commissioners here; and I do not recollect that since we began to negotiate with Mr. Oswold there has been the least division or opposition between us . . .[1376]

Sunday, December 15, 1782. Today, the Comte de Vergennes writes Ben Franklin of his displeasure that the commissioners did not consult with France before signing:

> I am at a loss, Sir, to explain your conduct and that of your colleagues on this occasion. You have concluded your preliminary articles without any communication between us, although the instructions from Congress prescribes that nothing shall be done without the participation of the King . . .
>
> You are wise and discreet, Sir; you perfectly understand what is due to propriety; you have all your life performed your duties . . .[1377]

Tuesday, December 17, 1782. Today, Benjamin Franklin formally responds to the Comte de Vergennes:

> Nothing has been agreed in the preliminaries contrary to the interest of France . . . Your observation is, however, apparently just, that in not consulting you before they were signed, we have been guilty of neglecting a point of bienséance. But, as this was not from want of respect for the King whom we all love and honor, we hope it will be excused . . .
>
> It is not possible for any one to be more sensible than I am, of what I and every American owe to the King, for the many and great benefits and favors he has bestowed upon us . . . And I believe that no Prince

was ever more beloved and respected by his own subjects, than the King is by the people of the United States. [1378]

Thursday, December 19, 1782. Today, the Count de Vergennes writes his ambassador in Philadelphia:

> *I have the liberty to send you a translation of the preliminary articles which the American Plenipotentiaries have agreed to and signed with Great Britain, to be made into a treaty when the terms of peace between France and England shall be settled.*
>
> *You will surely be gratified, as well as myself, with the very extensive advantages which our allies, the Americans, are to receive from the peace; but you certainly will not be less surprised than I have been at the conduct of the Commissioners. According to the instructions of Congress, they ought to have done nothing without our participation. I have informed you that the King did not seek to influence the negotiation any further than his offices might be necessary to his friends. The American Commissioners will not say that I have interfered and much less that I have wearied them with my curiosity. They have cautiously kept themselves at a distance from me. Mr. Adams, one of them, coming from Holland . . . had been in Paris nearly three weeks without imagining that he owed me any mark of attention, and probably I should not have seen him till this time if I had not caused him to be reminded of it . . .*
>
> *I think it proper that the most influential members of Congress should be informed of the very irregular conduct of their Commissioners in regard to us. You may speak of it not in the tone of complaint. I accuse no person; I blame no one, not even Dr. Franklin. He has yielded too easily to the bias of his colleagues, who do not pretend to recognize the rules of courtesy in regard to us . . . If we may judge of the future from what has passed here under our eyes, we shall be but poorly paid for all that we have done for the United States and for securing to them a national existence.* [1379]

Thursday, December 26, 1782. Today, Ben Franklin writes the Rev. Samuel Cooper of Boston:

> *We have taken some good steps here toward peace. Our independence is acknowledged; our boundaries as good and extensive as we demanded; and our fishery more so than the Congress expected . . .*
>
> *I am extremely sorry to hear language from Americans on this side of the water, and to hear of such language from your side, as tends to hurt the good understanding that has so happily subsisted between this court and ours. There seems to be a party with you that wish to destroy it. If they could succeed, they would do us irreparable injury. It is our firm connection with France that gives us weight with England and respect throughout Europe. If we were to break our faith*

with this nation, on whatever pretense, England would again trample on us . . . We cannot, therefore, be too much on our guard how we permit private resentments of particular persons to enter into our public councils . . . In my opinion, the true political interest of America consists in observing and fulfilling, with the greatest exactitude, the engagements of our alliance with France and behaving at the same time towards England so as not to extinguish her hopes of a reconciliation.[1380]

Friday, January 3, 1783. Today, in the Continental Congress, the Journals report:

The minister plenipotentiary of France transmitted to the secretary for foreign affairs a note . . .

Philadelphia, December 31, 1782.
The minister plenipotentiary . . . received orders to express . . . the satisfaction which the King his master has felt for the conduct [the Congress] have held on the overtures that were made at different periods by the British commissioners commanding at New York to bring about a partial negotiation with the United States [independent of France] . . .

Resolved, That the [American] Secretary for foreign affairs inform the Minister of France that Congress learn with great pleasure that the steps taken by Congress . . . in opposition to the attempts of the British court to bring about a partial negotiation has been satisfactory to his Most Christian Majesty: that his Majesty's conduct . . . is sufficient to inspire a just abhorrence of every act derogatory to the principles of the alliance . . .[1381]

Monday, January 20, 1783. Today, France adds its signature to the Preliminary Peace Treaty between Britain and America. Hostilities will now cease. A "definitive" treaty between all warring parties will be signed in September when France's allies, Spain and the Netherlands, have agreed to the treaty.[1382]

Thursday, January 30, 1783. Today, from Geneva, Benny Bache writes his grandfather,

I have not received the parcel of Books you mentioned me in your letter that you had sent to me. I shall mention when I receive them. I heard yesterday with a great deal of pleasure that the peace was made Because that gives me hopes of seeing you soon if you have not changed your resolution of coming and Because that takes away a great part of your occupations.[1383]

Wednesday, February 5, 1783. John Adams wants to be the first Minister Plenipotentiary (ambassador) from the United States to Great Britain. Today, he writes the president of Congress:

The Resolution of Congress of the 12 July 1781 "that the Commission and the Instructions . . . given to the Honourable John Adams . . . be and they are hereby revoked" was duly received by me in Holland, but no Explanation of the Motives to it or the Reasons on which it was founded was ever transmitted to me . . .

[It is now time in] my own opinion . . . to send a Minister directly to St. James's with a Letter of Credence to the King as a Minister Plenipotentiary and a Commission to treat of a Treaty of Commerce . . .

[I]f I had to give my vote for a Minister to the Court of Great Britain . . . I should think of no other object of my Choice than [Mr. Jay] . . . provided that Injustice must finally be done to him who was the first object of his Country's choice.[1384]

Thursday, February 6, 1783. Today, John Adams pursues the subject of his appointment as Minister to Great Britain in a letter to Thomas McKean, a congressional delegate from Delaware:

The most important mission of all is now opened to the Court of Great Britain.—You know very well that I have been unfairly treated in that Matter, and you must be sensible that it is impossible for me to stay in Europe at any other Court . . . In the Name of Common Justice, then give me my [quietus] and let me return home, by accepting my Resignation immediately, that I may not be exposed to the further disgrace of waiting in Europe with the Air of a Candidate and an Expectant of that Mission, if foreign Finesse and domestic Faction have determined that I shall not have it . . .[1385]

Tuesday, February 11, 1783. Today, Virginia congressional delegate James Madison writes Thomas Jefferson:

Congress yesterday received from Mr. Adams several letters dated September not remarkable for any thing unless it be a display of his vanity, his prejudice against the French Court & his venom against Doctr. Franklin.[1386]

Tuesday, February 25, 1783. Today, the American commissioners in Paris sign an agreement with France on the funding of America's obligations. Article II of this agreement includes:

[I]t has been found proper to recapitulate here the amount of the preceding aids granted by the King [of France] to the United States, and to distinguish them according to their different classes . . .

In the third class are comprehended the aids and subsidies furnished to the Congress of the United States, under the title of gratuitous assistance, from the pure generosity of the King, three millions of which were granted before the treaty of February, 1778, and six millions in 1781; which aids and subsidies amount in the whole to nine million livres turnois. His Majesty here confirms, in case of the need, the gratuitous gift to the said Congress of the said thirteen United States.[1387]

This recapitulation of French aid may be one of the great understatements of the eighteenth century. France has bankrupted herself in aiding America, expending perhaps two billion livres to send 47,000 officers and men, 3,668 cannon, and sixty-three ships of the line across the Atlantic to wage the Americans' war.[1388] France had as many as 8,400 soldiers on American soil at one time. Six hundred thirty-seven Frenchmen lost their lives in the effort to liberate Savannah; 186 Frenchmen gave their lives at Yorktown.[1389]

Wednesday, March 12, 1783. Today, the Continental Congress receives the Preliminary Peace Treaty as well as a fifty-five-page "Peace Journal," prepared by John Adams and placed in the packet for Secretary of Foreign Affairs Robert Livingston. The journal includes Adams' personal diary entries on his success in the Netherlands, his steadfastness in dealing with Britain, and his independence from (contrasted with Franklin's subservience to) France.[1390] John Adams:

> *[C]onsidering that, in the Conferences for the Peace, I had been very free which I had Reason to expect would be misrepresented by Franklin, I suddenly determined to throw into the Packet for [Secretary for Foreign Affairs Robert] Livingston, what was intended for another.— Let them make the most and the worst of it.*[1391]

Tuesday, March 18, 1783. Today, James Madison writes fellow Virginian Edmund Randolph:

> *In this business [of negotiating without consulting the French court], Jay has taken the lead & proceeded to a length of which you can form little idea. Adams has followed with cordiality. Franklin has been dragged into it . . . The dilemma to which Congress are reduced is infinitely perplexing. If they abet the proceedings of their ministers, all confidence with France is at an end . . .*[1392]

Thursday, March 20, 1783. Today, Benjamin Franklin writes fellow peace commissioner Henry Laurens:

> *I hear frequently of [Mr. Adams'] Ravings against M. de Vergennes and me, whom he suspects of Plots against him which have no Existence but in his troubled Imagination. I take no Notice and we are civil when we meet . . .*[1393]

Friday, March 21, 1783. Despite all France has done, John Adams is deeply suspicious. Today, he writes a friend, Massachusetts political leader General James Warren:

> *[I]t is devoutly to be wished that . . . some other Minister may take the place of Vergennes . . . He has meant us too much Evil, is too conscious of it, and too sensible that we know it . . .*

It is not easy to assign the Reason for his long continual Rancour against the Rights to our Fisheries and the Western Lands, against our obtaining loans or subsidies from the King . . . He wished to keep us dependent . . .

His attack on me in his Letters to Dr. Franklin which the Dr. was left to transmit to Congress without informing me was an attack on the Fishery and Western Country. Franklin's motive was to get my Commission, and Vergennes' motive was to get it for him, not that he loved Franklin more than me but because he knew Franklin would be more obsequious—The Pretense that I had given offence was a mere Fiction. Such an invention they knew would be the most likely to intimidate Members of Congress and carry their Point. I repeat it, it was not true that I had given offence. To suppose that I had is to suppose him the most Senseless Despot that ever existed. The Secret was that I was known to be a Man who would neither be deceived, wheedled, flattered, or intimidated into a surrender of them. Franklin he knew would let him do as he pleased and assist him without an excuse for it . . .

I cannot account for his Enmity to us . . . He thought by crippling us, he could keep us dependent and oblige us to join France in a future War against England . . . But he has been vastly disappointed, and the truth is that the American Ministers made the Peace in Spite of him, let his hireling Trumpeters Say what they will.[1394]

Tuesday, March 25, 1783. Today, from Philadelphia, American Secretary of Foreign Affairs Robert Livingston writes the American peace commissioners in Paris:

I feel no little pain at the distrust manifested in the management of [the treaty negotiations]; particularly in signing the treaty without communicating it to the court of Versailles till after the signature . . . The concealment was, in my opinion, absolutely unnecessary . . .[1395]

Friday, March 28, 1783. Today, John Adams writes Abigail:

If I receive the Acceptance of my Resignation, I Shall embark in the first ship . . .

I am Sometimes half afraid that those Persons who procured the Revocation of my Commission to King George may be afraid I shall do them more harm in America than in England, and therefore of two Evils to choose the least and manoeuvrer to get me sent to London . . .

Nothing in Life ever cost me so much Sleep, or made me so many grey Hairs, as the Anxiety I have Suffered for these Three Years . . . No body knows of it. Nobody cares for it.[1396]

Wednesday, April 9, 1783. Today, John Adams writes his friend General James Warren:

I hope this will find you in Congress . . .
It is utterly inconceivable how Congress have been deceived into

such Instructions as they gave Us which, without all Controversy, would have ruined our Country, if they had been obeyed . . .

I am in expectation every hour of receiving your Acceptance of my Resignation, and indeed I stand in need of it. The Scenes of Gloom, Danger, and Perplexity I have gone thro' . . . have affected my Health to a great degree and, what is worse, my Spirits.—Firm as Some People have been complaisant enough to suppose my Temper is, I assure you it has been shaken to its foundations . . . When a Man sees entrusted to him the most essential interests of his Country—sees that they depend essentially upon him, and that he must defend them against the Malice of Enemies, the Finesse of Allies, the Treachery of a Colleague . . . you may well imagine a Man does not sleep on a Bed of Roses . . .

The Fever, which I had in Amsterdam, which held me for five days, exhausted me in such a Manner that I never have been able to recover from it entirely . . . But I am not yet however so weak as to stay in Europe with a Wound upon my Honour—And if I had the Health of Hercules, I would go home Leave or no Leave the Moment another Person is appointed to Great Britain—No fooling in such a Match—I will not be horse jockeyed—at least if I am, De Vergennes and Franklin shall not be the Jockies . . .

It is not that I am ambitious of the Honour of a Commission to St. James's . . . I could be happier I believe at the Hague. But my Enemies, because they are Enemies or Despisers of the Interests of my Country, shall never have such a Triumph over me . . . Decide my Fate therefore as soon as possible . . .[1397]

Thursday, April 10, 1783. Today, John Adams writes his former co-commissioner Arthur Lee, now a Virginia congressional delegate:

I expect soon to see a proposition to name the 18th Century, the Franklinian Age, le Siecle Franklinnien, & am willing to leave the Question, whether it shall have this epithet or that of Frederick, to the Dr. & the King: tho' the latter will stand a poor Chance with a certain French Writer who, within a few weeks, has said that the Dr. after a few ages, will be considered as a God, and I think the King has not eno' of the Caesar in him to dispute . . .

The title of "Founder of the American Empire" which . . . the English newspapers give [the Dr.] does not, most certainly belong to him . . . [T]here is such a prostitution of all Justice, such a Confusion of Right & Wrong, virtue and vice, to accomplish the Apotheosis of Dr. F.[ranklin] as ought to excite the indignation of every honest man.[1398]

Sunday, April 13, 1783. Today, John Adams writes his Massachusetts colleague James Warren:

I have in some late Letters opened to You in Confidence the Dangers which our most important Interests have been in . . . from the vain,

*ambitious and despotic Character of one Minister, I mean the C.[ount]
de Vergennes. But You will form but an imperfect idea after all of the
Difficulties We have had to encounter, without taking into Consideration another Character, equally selfish and interested, equally vain
and ambitious, more jealous and envious, and more false and deceit-
ful. I mean Dr. Franklin . . .*

*His whole Life has been one continued Insult to good Manners and
to Decency . . . [T]he Effrontery with which he has forced [his illegiti-
mate] Offspring up in the World, not less than his Speech of Polly
Baker [sympathizing with an unwed mother], are Outrages to Morality and Decorum which would never have been forgiven in any other
American. These things, however, are not the worst of his Faults. They
shew, however, the Character of the Man; in what Contempt he holds
the opinions of the World, and with what Haughtiness he is capable of
persevering through Life in a gross and odious System of Falsehood
and Imposture . . .*

*[S]trict and impartial Justice obliges me to say that, from five Years
of Experience of Dr. Franklin which I have now had in Europe, I can
have no Dependence on his Word. I never know when he speaks the
Truth and when not. If he talked as much as other Men and deviated
from the Truth as often in proportion as he does now, he would have
been the Scorn of the Universe long ago. But his perpetual Taciturnity
has saved him . . .*

*[H]is Philosophy and his Politicks have been infinitely exaggerated
. . . until his Reputation has become one of the grossest impostures that
has ever been practiced upon Mankind since the Days of Mohamet . . .*

*A Reputation so imposing . . . produces all the Servility . . . that is
produced by the imposing Pomp of a Court and of Imperial Splendour.
He had been very sensible of this and has taken Advantage of it.*

*As if he had been conscious of the Laziness, Inactivity and real In-
significance of his advanced Age, he has considered every American
Minister who has come to Europe as his natural enemy . . . From the
same detestable Source came the Insinuations and prejudices against
me, and the shameless abandoned Attack upon me . . . These are my
Opinions, tho' I cannot prove them otherwise than by what I have seen
and heard myself . . . The C.[ount de Vergennes] . . . has found him so
convenient a Minister, ready always to comply with every Desire,
never asking for any thing but when ordered and obliged to ask for
Money, never proposing any thing, that he has adopted all His Passions, Prejudices, and Jealousies, and has supported him as if his own
Office depended upon him. He and his office of interpreters have filled
all the Gazettes of Europe with the most senseless Flattery of him, and
by means of the Police, set every Spectacle, Society, and every private
Club and Circle to clapping him with such Applause as they give to
Opera girls. This being the unfortunate Situation of foreign Affairs,
what is to be done?*

Franklin has, as he gives out, asked Leave to resign . . . I wish with all my Soul he was out of public Service and in Retirement, repenting of his past Life and preparing, as he ought to be, for another World . . .

France has suffered as much as America by the unskillful and dishonest Conduct of our foreign affairs. They have no Confidence in any but him . . . They have not only not confided in any other, but have persecuted every other . . .

For my own part, I have been made a Sacrifice to such Intrigues in so gross a manner that unless I am restored and supported, I am unalterably determined to retire.[1399]

Tuesday, April 15, 1783. Today, at West Point in upstate New York, a new military order, the Society of the Cincinnati, holds its first meeting. George Washington will be its president. From a statement of the society's purpose:

[T]he officers of the American Army . . . combine themselves into one SOCIETY OF FRIENDS to endure as long as they shall endure, or any of their eldest male posterity, and, in failure thereof, the collateral branches, who may be judged worthy of becoming its supporters and members.[1400]

Are George Washington and his fellow officers creating a titled and hereditary order of nobility?

Wednesday, April 16, 1783. Today, John Adams writes Abigail:

I begin to suspect that French and Franklinian Politicks will now endeavor to get me sent to England for two Reasons, one that I may not go to America where I should do them more Mischief as they think than I could in London. 2. That the Mortifications which they and their Tools might give me there might disembarrass them of me sooner than any where.

Is it not Strange and Sad that Simple Integrity should have so many Ennemies? . . . If I would have given up the [firm positions I took], I might have had [like Franklin] Gold snuff Boxes, Clappings at the Opera, I don't mean from the Girls, millions of Paragraphs in the Newspapers in praise of me, Visits from the Great, Dinners, Wealth, Power, Splendor, Pictures, Busts, statues, and every Thing which a vain heart, and mine is much too vain, could desire . . . Liberty and Virtue! When! oh When will your Ennemies cease to exist or to persecute![1401]

Thursday, May 1, 1783. Today, in the Continental Congress, the Journals report:

Ordered, That a commission be prepared to Messrs. J. Adams, B. Franklin and J. Jay, authorising them, or either of them in the absence of the others, to enter into a treaty of commerce between the United States of America and Great Britain.[1402]

John Adams has recovered his commission to negotiate a commercial treaty with Britain but again must share the commission with Franklin.

Friday, May 2, 1783. Today, John Adams writes in his diary,

> I told Mr. Hartley [who replaced Richard Oswold as Britain's nego-
> tiator] the Story of my Negociations with the C. de Vergennes about
> communicating my [peace and commerce] Mission to [British Colonial
> Secretary] Ld. G. Germaine 3 Years ago and the subsequent Intrigues
> and Disputes, &c. It is necessary to let the English Ministers know
> where their danger lies, and the Arts used to damp the Ardour of re-
> turning friendship . . .
> In Truth Congress and their Ministers have been plaid upon like
> Children, trifled with, imposed upon, deceived. Franklin's Servility
> and insidious faithless Selfishness is the true and only Cause why this
> Game has succeeded. He has aided Vergennes with all his Weight, and
> his great Reputation, in both Worlds, has supported this ignominious
> System and blasted every Man and every Effort to shake it off. I only
> have had a little Success against him.[1403]

Sunday, May 25, 1783. Today, from Paris, John Adams drafts a letter to Foreign Affairs Secretary Robert Livingston:

> Any one who knows anything of my History may easily suppose that
> I have gone thro' many dangerous, anxious & disagreeable Scenes be-
> fore I ever saw Europe: But all I ever Suffered in public life has been
> little in Comparison of what I have suffered in Europe, the greatest &
> worst part of which has been caused by the Dispositions of the C. de
> Vergennes, aided by the Jealousy, Envy & selfish Servility of Dr. Frank-
> lin.[1404]

Adams will choose not to send this letter.

Monday, May 26, 1783. Today, the Continental Congress votes to disband the army . . . The Journals report:

> Resolved, That the Commander in Chief be instructed to grant fur-
> loughs to the non-commissioned officers and soldiers in the service of the
> United States, inlisted to serve during the war, who shall be discharged
> as soon as the definitive treaty of peace is concluded . . .[1405]

Monday, June 23, 1783. Today, Benjamin Franklin writes Benny Bache,

> My dear Child . . .
> I . . . am pleased to see that you improve in your writing . . .
> I write by this Post to Mr. Marignac, requesting that he would per-
> mit you to come and see me and stay with me during the Vacation of
> the Schools . . . I hear you have been sick, but . . . I hope you are . . .
> strong enough to undertake the Journey . . .[1406]

Wednesday, July 2, 1783. Today, from Geneva, Benny Bache responds to his grandfather,

> *I received your letter . . . I was very glad when I read that you desired me to come during the Vacation of the School to see you. I have been sick, but I am now recover'd and Strong enough to undertake the Jorney . . . I only expect an occasion to undertake the agreeable jorney to see you.* [1407]

Wednesday, July 9, 1783. Today, John Adams writes Secretary of Foreign Affairs Robert Livingston:

> *Since the dangerous fever I had in Amsterdam two years ago, I have never enjoyed my health. Through the whole of the last winter and spring, I have suffered under weaknesses and pains which have scarcely permitted me to do business. The excessive heats of the last week or two have brought on my fever again, which exhausts me in such a manner as to be very discouraging, and incapacitates one for everything. In short, nothing but a return to America will ever restore me to health . . .*
>
> *Your late despatches [of March 25], sir, are not well adapted to give spirits to a melancholy man or to cure one sick with a fever . . . [H]ow you could conceive it possible for us to treat at all with the English, upon supposition that we had communicated every the minutest thing to this court . . . I know not . . . The instructions were found to be absolutely impracticable.* [1408]

Saturday, July 19, 1783. Today, Benny Bache leaves Geneva to resume life with Ben Franklin in Paris.

Tuesday, July 22, 1783. Today, from Paris, Benjamin Franklin answers John Adams' charges in a letter to Foreign Affairs Secretary Robert Livingston:

> *[N]either [the evidence] handed us thro' the British Negotiators (a suspicious Channel) nor the Conversations [with the French] respecting the Fishery, the Boundaries . . . &c., recommending Moderation in our Demands, are of Weight Sufficient in my Mind to fix an opinion that this Court wished to restrain us in obtaining any Degree of Advantage we could . . . [T]hose Discourses are fairly resolvable by supposing a very natural [French] Apprehension that we, relying too much on the Ability of France to continue the War in our favour and supply us constantly with Money, might insist on more Advantages than the English would be willing to grant and thereby lose the Opportunity of making Peace, so necessary to our Friends . . .*
>
> *I ought not to conceal from you, that one of my colleagues [Mr. Adams] is of a very different Opinion from me in these matters. He thinks the French Minister one of the greatest Enemies of our Country, that he . . . afforded us, during the War, the assistance we receiv'd only to*

keep it alive, that we might be so much the more weaken'd by it; that to think of Gratitude to France is the greatest of Follies, and that to be influenc'd by it would ruin us. He makes no secret of having these Opinions, expresses them publicly, sometimes in presence of the English Ministers, and speaks of hundreds of Instances which he could produce in Proof of them. None of which however, have yet appear'd to me . . .

If I were not convinc'd of the real Inability of this Court to furnish the further Supplys we ask'd, I should suspect these Discourses of a person in his Station might have influenced the refusal; but I think they have gone no farther than to occasion a Suspicion that we have a considerable Party of Antigallicans in America, who are not Tories, and consequently to produce some doubts of the Continuance of our Friendship. As such Doubts may hereafter have a bad Effect, I think we cannot take too much care to remove them; and it is, therefore, I write this to put you on your guard, (believing it my duty tho' I know that I hazard by it a mortal Enmity) and to caution you respecting the Insinuations of this Gentleman against this Court, and the Instances he supposes of their ill will to us, which I take to be as imaginary as I know his Fancies to be that the Count de V. and myself are continually plotting against him, and employing the News-Writers of Europe to depreciate his Character &. But as Shakespear says, "Trifles light as Air," &c. I am persuaded, however, that he means well for his Country, is always an honest Man, often a wise one, but sometimes, and in some things, absolutely out of his senses.[1409]

Tuesday, August 12, 1783. Today, in Paris, Benny Bache turns fourteen years old. He arrived two weeks ago and wrote his mother,

I have left off my Latin and Gr[eek] to learn writing, fencing, dansing, and Drawing.[1410]

Benny Bache will also study printing in his grandfather's printshop in Passy, under the shop's master printer, Maurice Meyer.[1411]

Wednesday, September 3, 1783. Today, in Paris, American peace commissioners Benjamin Franklin, John Adams, John Jay, and Henry Laurens sign, on behalf of the United States, the Definitive Treaty of Peace with Britain. The American War of Independence has ended.

ARTICLE 1st. His Britannic Majesty acknowledges the [sovereign] United States . . .
ARTICLE 2d. [I]t is hereby agreed and declared that the following are and shall be their Boundaries, viz . . . from thence on a due west Course to the River Mississippi, Thence by a Line drawn along the Middle of the said River . . .[1412]

By this agreement, America's western boundaries extend to the center of the Mississippi River, far beyond the lands George Washington killed Jumonville to secure, far beyond the 58,000 acres Washington now owns on the "illegal" side of the 1763 proclamation line.[1413] The lands of Fort Necessity and Braddock's massacre are now open for American settlement.

Sunday, September 7, 1783. Today, John Adams writes in his diary:

> *This morning I went out to Passy, and Dr. Franklin put into my hands the following resolution of Congress, which he received last night . . .*
> *Ordered that a Commission be prepared to Mess[rs]. John Adams, Benjamin Franklin, and John Jay, authorizing them . . . to enter into a Treaty of Commerce between the United States and Great Britain . . .*[1414]

Shortly after learning that Franklin must be part of his reinstated commission to negotiate a commercial treaty with Great Britain, John Adams suffers another nervous collapse. John Adams:

> *I soon fell down in a fever, not much less violent than I had suffered two years before in Amsterdam . . . Not all the skill and kind assiduity of my physician, nor all the scrupulous care of my regimen . . . was found effectual for the restoration of my health. Still remaining feeble, emaciated, languid to a great degree, my physician and all my friends advised me to go to England to drink the waters and to bath[e] in them . . .*[1415]

Wednesday, September 10, 1783. Today, John Adams writes Massachusetts congressional delegate Elbridge Gerry:

> *I beg you would make a Point of putting Jay and me into the Commission for treating with Denmark, Portugal, [&c.] . . . Smuggling Treaties into Franklin's hands alone is continued by Vergennes on purpose to throw slights upon Jay and me . . .*
> *[Y]ou ought to have some sympathy for the Feelings of your Ministers and more for their Reputations . . . Our affairs will all [go] extremely well if we are supported.—But if Franklin is suffered to go on with that low Cunning and mean Craft with which he has always worked and by which he has done so much Mischief, the publick will suffer.*[1416]

John Adams' self-touting to Congress has had repercussions. Today, Ben Franklin writes John Adams:

> *I have received a letter from a very respectable person in America containing the following words, viz:*
> *"It is confidently reported . . . that the court of France was at the bottom against our obtaining the fishery and [western] territory . . . se-*

cured to us by the treaty; that our minister at that court [meaning Mr. Franklin] favored, or did not oppose this design against us, and that it was entirely owing to the firmness, sagacity and disinterestedness of Mr. Adams with whom Mr. Jay united, that we have obtained these important advantages."

I therefore think that I ought not to suffer an accusation which falls little short of treason to my country to pass without notice when the means of effectual vindication are at hand . . . I have no doubt of your readiness to do a brother commissioner justice by certificates that will entirely destroy the effect of that accusation.[1417]

Saturday, September 13, 1783. Today, John Adams responds to Ben Franklin's letter of the 10th:

I have received the letter . . . It is unnecessary for me to say anything upon this subject more than to quote the words which I wrote in [my diary on] the evening of the 30th of November, 1782, and which have been received and read in Congress, viz:

"I told [Dr. Franklin] my opinion without reserve of the policy of this court and of the principles, wisdom, and firmness with which Mr. Jay had conducted the negociations in his sickness and my absence, and that I was determined to support Mr. Jay to the utmost of my power in the pursuit of the same system. The Doctor heard me patiently, but said nothing.

"The first conference [with the British] we had afterwards . . . Dr. Franklin turned to Mr. Jay and said: 'I am of your opinion and will go on with these gentlemen without consulting this court.' "[1418]

Sunday, December 7, 1783. Today, Massachusetts congressional delegate Samuel Osgood writes John Adams:

I hope it will not be altogether useless to communicate . . . the Reasons . . . of several important Decisions of Congress respecting our foreign ministers. The first . . . respected your Commission for Peace . . . [W]hat suggested to Congress the Idea of an Alteration . . . [were] the several Letters that passed between you and the C.[ompte]] de V[ergenne]s respecting the [currency devaluation] Resolutions of Congress of March 1780; and also [your insistence on] the publication of your Commission for a commercial treaty with great Britain . . . [I]t was expedient that you should [be] pointedly instructed . . . New Instructions were made out for you alone . . . "you are ultimately to govern yourself by the advice of the minister of his most Christian Majesty," etc . . . But it was not sufficient to let it rest here. [T]here should be more than one Peace Commissioner . . . Congress having agreed upon five . . .

[T]he Reasons of the Measure . . . Doctor Witherspoon has been candid enough on the floor of Congress to hint . . . was your obstinate Dis-

pute with the C.[ount] de V.[ergenne]s. I have always suppos'd that the object was to clip your Wings . . .

After the Provisional Treaty arriv'd, some were heartily pleased, and others discovered a Degree of Mortification. It was evident that our Comm'rs acted for themselves . . . [I]t was said that they had grossly disobeyed their instructions . . . They had made and signed a Treaty without their Knowledge or Concurrence . . . It was a Matter of Surprize and Astonishment to the Franklinites that the God of Electricity consented to act with you secretly. However, if I might be allowed to form an opinion, it would be that the electrical Machine discharged itself invisibly . . . He does not consider his most C[hristian] M[ajesty] as an Ally, but as a Father to the United States . . . whenever he mentions him it is in this light.

The next act of Congress of Consequence was the recalling your Commission for entering into a commercial Treaty with G.[reat] B.[ritain] . . . I suppos'd then and am more confirmed in my Opinion now that it was a foreign Manoeuvre, not merely to mortify you . . .

You will pardon me in candidly mentioning to you the Effects of your long [Peace] Journal, forwarded after the signing of the provisional Treaty. It was read by the Secretary in Congress . . . Several Gentlemen . . . appeared overmuch disposed to make it appear as ridiculous as possible; several ungenerous Remarks were made upon it, as being unfit to be read in Congress, and not worth the Time expended in reading it . . .[1419]

Alexander Hamilton will observe:

The reading of this journal extremely embarrassed his friends, especially the delegates of Massachusetts, who more than once interrupted it and at last succeeded in putting a stop to it on the suggestion that it bore the marks of a private and confidential paper . . . The good humor of that body yielded to the suggestion.

The particulars of this Journal; . . . I recollect one . . . "Monsieur Adams, vous etes le WASHINGTON de negociation." Stating the incident, he makes this comment upon it: "These people have a very pretty knack of paying compliments." He might have added they have also a very dexterous knack of disguising a sarcasm.[1420]

Tuesday, December 23, 1783. Today, George Washington submits his resignation as commander in chief:

Happy in the confirmation of our Independence and Sovereignty, and pleased with the opportunity afforded the United States of becoming a respectable Nation, I resign with satisfaction the Appointment I accepted with diffidence.[1421]

George Washington has seen the war to its end. Tom Paine:

Mr. Washington's merit consisted in constancy. But constancy was the common virtue of the Revolution. Who was there that was inconstant? I know of but one military defection, that of [Benedict] Arnold; and I know of no political defection among those who made themselves eminent when the Revolution was formed by the Declaration of Independence.[1422]

Wednesday, January 14, 1784. Today, in the Continental Congress, the Journals report:

Resolved, unanimously, nine states being present, that the said definitive treaty [of peace between the United States of America and his Britannic Majesty signed on the 3d day of September, 1783] be, and the same is hereby ratified by the United States in Congress assembled . . .[1423]

Monday, January 26, 1784. Today, Benjamin Franklin writes Benny's mother, Sarah Bache, of Franklin's fear that, in the new Society of the Cincinnati, George Washington is creating a hereditary order of nobility for the United States:

Your Care in sending me the Newspapers is very agreeable to me. I received by Capt. Barney those relating to the Cincinnati. My Opinion of the Institution cannot be of much Importance; I only wonder that, when the united Wisdom of our Nation had, in the Articles of Confederation, manifested their Dislike of establishing Ranks of Nobility, . . . persons should think proper to distinguish themselves and their Posterity from their fellow Citizens and form an Order of Hereditary Knights in direct Opposition to the solemnly declared Sense of their Country! . . .

[T]he descending Honour to Posterity who could have no Share in obtaining it is not only groundless and absurd, but often hurtful to that Posterity, since it is apt to make them proud . . . and thence falling into . . . Meannesses, Servility, and Wretchedness . . . which is the present case with much of what is called the Noblesse in Europe . . .[1424]

Ben Franklin will show a copy of this letter to Honoré-Gabriel Riqueti, the Comte de Mirabeau, urging him to write an essay against the evils of hereditary succession. Mirabeau will do so this September, using material from Franklin's letter in his *Considerations on the Order of Cincinnati.*[1425] Many will mark Mirabeau's attack on hereditary succession as the beginning of the French Revolution![1426]

Tuesday, April 6, 1784. Today, back in the Netherlands, where he is still seeking a loan for the United States,[1427] John Adams writes Arthur Lee:

A friend of mine in Massachusetts, in a letter some months ago, gave me a confused hint that Franklin had written to somebody, at me, or towards me, or against me, or about me; but I could make nothing of it and did not know until I received your letter that he had written against me to Congress. What he can have said after allowing me to be sensible and honest, as you say he does, I am curious to know.[1428]

Friday, April 9, 1784. Today, John Adams lets anger distend his handwriting as he responds to Massachusetts congressional delegate Samuel Osgood's letter of December 8th:

> *It can be no Surprise to any one who knows the real Character of the Man [Franklin], that Mr. Jay and I were joined [in independent negotiations with Britain] by our Colleague.—He never joined nor would join until he found we were United and determined to go through without him. Then he joined, because he knew his Destruction would be the Consequence of his standing out. That he had leave [from France] to join I doubt not, and [that] he communicated all he could [to France] I doubt not. But the business was so constructed that he could not communicate any Thing & could not hurt Us, and the Signature of the Treaty without communicating he could not hinder, and this Secured us from Delays which would have lost Us the [Peace?] . . .*
>
> *The Instances for a Minister to Question do not surprise me. Nothing . . . can surprise me . . . [Franklin's] Success, in so many of his Selfish Plans and Hostilities against Others and the Ardor with which he is supported in all of them for his Obsequiousness by Politicians to whom all the Arts and Maxims of Aristotle, his Disciple Machiavelli, and their Disciples, the Jesuits, are familiar in Theory and Practice, have emboldened a mind enfeebled with Age, the Stone & the Gout, and eaten with all the Passions which may prey upon old Age unprincipled, until it is no longer under the restraint even of Hypocrisy. He told me that the United States ought to join France in two future wars against G.[reat] B.[ritain]—the first to pay the Debt we owe her for making war for us and the second to show ourselves as generous as she had been.—it is high time his Resignation was accepted. He has done Mischief enough. He has been possessed of the lowest Cunning and the deepest Hypocrisy I ever met. [T]he latter he every day lays aside more and more, it being now he thinks unnecessary. I am informed he has lately written against me to Congress. What he can have said after allowing me to be desirable and honest I know not. He has heretofore talked to Congress and misrepresented Expressions in private Conversation between him and me alone in anxious Consultation upon our dearest public Interests in the worst of times, without giving me the least hint that he disapproved what I said.*
>
> *I have been so sensible of danger from Foreigners that I was determined that no danger or fear of Prisons or Death, no Hardships of Voyages . . . or Perils of . . . Ministers or Assassins should deter me from attempting all in my power to ward it off.—But I was not aware of the*

Perils from false Brethren which have been worse than all the rest. Nevertheless, thro all Difficulties & Dangers, I have executed every Thing I have under taken, and all is secured. I am now indifferent about all the laughers, Weepers, Cursers & Flatterers. My first wish of my Soul is to go home. If the People of America have not now sense & spirit enough to put all to rights, they ought not in divine Justice to be free. [1429]

Friday, May 7, 1784. With the British peace treaty now ratified, peace commissioner John Jay has asked Congress for permission to return to the United States. Today, in the Continental Congress, the Journals report:

> [B]eing this day informed . . . that Mr. J. Jay proposed to embark for America in the month of April . . . Mr. Jay was put in nomination; and the ballots being taken,
> Mr. John Jay was elected Secretary for foreign affairs . . .
> *Resolved,* That a minister plenipotentiary be appointed in addition to Mr. John Adams and Mr. Benjamin Franklin, for the purpose of negotiating treaties of Commerce.
> Congress proceeded to the election, and the ballots being taken, Mr. Thomas Jefferson was elected . . . [1430]

Wednesday, May 12, 1784. Today, from Paris, Benjamin Franklin writes the Rev. Samuel Mather of Massachusetts (son of Cotton Mather):

> *This powerful monarch continues its friendship for the United States. It is a friendship of the utmost importance to our security, and should be carefully cultivated . . . A breach between us and France would infallibly bring the English again upon our backs; and yet we have some wild heads among our countrymen who are endeavoring to weaken that connexion! Let us preserve our reputation by performing our engagements; our credit by fulfilling our contracts; and friends by gratitude and kindness; for we know not how soon we may again have occasion for all of them.* [1431]

Friday, August 6, 1784. Today, Thomas Jefferson finally arrives in Paris, joining Ben Franklin and John Adams in their commission to negotiate commercial treaties with European powers. [1432]

Thursday, August 12, 1784. Today, in Paris, Benny Bache turns fifteen years old. This summer, Benny spends his time watching hot-air-balloon ascensions, flying kites, swimming in Paris' Seine River, and meeting the many famous people who visit his grandfather. [1433]

Thursday, August 19, 1784. Today, Benjamin Franklin writes his publisher in England, William Strahan,

[Y]ou do wrong to discourage the Emigration of Englishmen to America . . . Emigration does not diminish but multiplies a Nation . . . It is a Fact that the Irish emigrants and their children are now in Possession of the Government of Pennsylvania by their Majority in the Assembly, as well as of a great Part of the Territory; and I remember well the first Ship that brought any of them over.[1434]

Sunday, September 19, 1784. Benny Bache and his grandfather continue to enjoy hot-air-balloon ascensions. Today, Benny Bache writes in his diary,

I went with my grandpapa to the Abbé Armons' to see the balloon of the Messr. Roberts which was about to start; I pointed the telescope; at eleven o'clock everything was ready and the balloon should have been started. My grandfather was playing chess and told me to inform him as soon as I saw it start. Three minutes before 12, I heard a cannon fired and a minute afterwards, I saw the balloon rise. Everybody was looking. The wind was south, a little to the west. I leave the Abbés and come with a telescope to take my place upon the roof of our house . . . Every one looked through the telescope in turn . . .

It was in the shape of a cylinder terminated by two hemispheres . . . The aeronauts tried, with little oars which they had, to drive a little against the wind, but this did not succeed.[1435]

Friday, October 8, 1784. Benny Bache will learn the type foundry business. Today, he writes in his diary:

My grandfather has caused a master founder to come to Passy to teach me to cast types. He will come tomorrow to remain all the winter.[1436]

Thursday, November 11, 1784. Today, Benjamin Franklin writes Richard Bache, Benny's father:

Your Family having pass'd well thro' the Summer gives me great pleasure. I still hope to see them before I die. Benny continues well, and grows amazingly. He is a very sensible and a very good Lad, and I love him much. I had Thoughts of . . . fitting him for Public Business, thinking he might be of Service hereafter to his Country; but being now convinc'd that Service is no Inheritance, as the Proverb says, I have determin'd to give him a Trade [in printing and letter founding] that he may have something to depend on . . . He has already begun to learn the business from Masters who come to my House, and is very diligent in working and quick in learning . . .[1437]

A French onlooker, at about this time, writes:

With Franklin, there is a youth of sixteen years, bright and intelligent, who looks like him physically and who, having decided to become a printer, is working to that end. There is something very

imposing in the sight of the American Legislator's grandson taking part in so simple a task.[1438]

Sunday, December 12, 1784. Today, John Adams writes Massachusetts congressional delegate Elbridge Gerry:

I have never answered particularly your most friendly & instructive letters . . . I really could not do it without entering into Discussions which related to Gentlemen with whom I have acted. I have received one way or another extracts of two or three Letters of Dr. Franklin which relate to me—the most unprovoked, the most cruel, the most malicious misrepresentations which ever were put upon Paper. I scorned to put my Pen to Paper in my own Vindication—I was determined to rest my Cause upon what was known to Congress . . .[1439]

Thursday, February 24, 1785. This morning, in the Continental Congress, the Journals report:

Congress proceeded to the election of a Minister Plenipotentiary to represent the United States of America at the court of Great Britain; and the ballots being taken, the hon. John Adams was elected . . .[1440]

Later today, Massachusetts congressional delegate Elbridge Gerry writes John Adams:

Attempts have been made to determine the choice [of Minister plenipotentiary to the Court of London] & this Morning it was effected & devolves on yourself. I am happy to give You the Information . . .

[A]s what were urged by the states opposed to your Choice . . . One part of your Secret Journal, wherein mention is made of a Compliment paid you as being "the Washington of the Negotiations" and that a paragraph of one of your letters describing the proper Character of Minister for London, that he should be possessed of the "cardinal Virtues," compared with other letters of yours claiming the appointment, are urged as Traits of a weak passion to which a Minister ought never to be subject . . .[1441]

Thursday, March 10, 1785. Today, in the Continental Congress, the Journals report:

Congress proceeded to the election of a Minister plenipotentiary to represent the United States at the Court of Versailles; and the ballots being taken, the hon. Thomas Jefferson was unanimously elected . . .[1442]

Tuesday, April 5, 1785. Today, Benny Bache writes in his diary:

My grandfather has prevailed upon M. Didot, the best printer of this age and even the best that has ever been, to consent to take me into his house for some time in order to teach me his art. I take my meals at the house of Mrs. Le Roy, a friend of my grandpapa; I went thither to day with my cousin and made acquaintance with his family and something more; he combines in his house engraving, the forge, the foundry and the printing office; it is a very amiable family, it seems to me; the meals are frugal.[1443]

Friday, April 8, 1785. Today, John Adams writes Englishman Dr. Richard Price to thank him for his book on the American Revolution:

> Some time since I received from Dr. Franklin a copy of the first edition of your Observations on the Importance of the American Revolution, and lately a copy of the second. I am much obliged to you . . .[1444]

Dr. Price's book[1445] includes a letter, dated March 22, 1778, from former French Comptroller General Anne-Robert-Jacques Turgot to Dr. Price, in which Turgot states,

> Mr. Franklin by your desire has put into my hands the last edition of your "Observations on Civil Liberty," etc . . .
>
> The fate of America is already decided. Behold her independence beyond recovery. But will she be free and happy? . . .
>
> I am not satisfied . . . I observe that by most of the [state] constitutions the customs of England are imitated without any particular motive. Instead of collecting all authority into one [assembly], that of the nation, they have established different bodies, a body of representatives, a council, and a governor, because there is in England a House of Commons, a House of Lords, and a King. They endeavour to balance these different powers, as if this equilibrium, which in England may be a necessary check to the enormous influence of royalty, could be of any use in republics founded upon the equality of all the citizens . . .[1446]

On reading this letter, John Adams is upset. John Adams:

> Mr. Turgot, in a letter to Dr. Price, printed in London, censured the American Constitution[s] as adopting three branches, in imitation of the Constitution of Great Britain. The intention was to celebrate Franklin's Constitution and condemn mine.[1447]

Monday, May 2, 1785. Today, John Adams answers Elbridge Gerry's letter of February 24th, which reported that some in Congress viewed Adams' Peace Journal as displaying *"a weak passion,"* i.e., vanity:

> The Imputation of a weak Passion has made so much Impression on me that it may not be improper to say a little more about it . . .
>
> If I had given in to . . . sending Useless Arms to America at great Prices [and] . . . not disputed with France . . . I could have obtained a Confidence . . . infinitely more gratifying to a weak Passion than I shall ever enjoy during my Life . . .
>
> [I]f I had adopted [as Dr. Franklin] . . . that "The United States ought to join France in two Future Wars against England . . ." I could

. . . even now have all the Emissaries thro the World . . . employed to gratify my weak Passions . . .[1448]

Wednesday, May 4, 1785. Today, Benny Bache writes in his diary:

I have been to Passy. My grandfather has received permission from Congress to give up his office. Mr. Jefferson will fill his place. My grandpapa has fixed upon the month of June for his departure.[1449]

Friday, May 6, 1785. Ben Franklin will be moving his Passy printshop to Philadelphia. Today, Benny Bache writes in his diary:

I have taken a press of my grandfather's to pieces.[1450]

Saturday, May 7, 1785. Today, Benny Bache writes in his diary:

I had the box for packing up the press made at the carpenter's.[1451]

Tuesday, May 10, 1785. Today, eighty-year-old Ben Franklin writes Benny Bache's parents, Sarah and Richard Bache:

Having at length received from Congress Permission to return home, I am now preparing for my departure . . . [M]y Friends here are so apprehensive for me that they press me much to remain in France. They tell me I am among a People who universally esteem and love me; that my Friends at home are diminish'd by Death in my Absence; that I may there meet with Envy and its consequent Enmity . . . The Desire however of spending the little remainder of Life with my Family is so strong . . . Ben is very well, and growing amazingly. He promises to be a stout as well as a good Man . . .[1452]

Thursday, May 12, 1785. Today, John Adams' son, John Quincy Adams, leaves Paris for the United States. He will enter Harvard College as a junior.[1453] In a week, Adams himself will leave for London as U.S. Minister Plenipotentiary to Great Britain.

Tuesday, May 17, 1785. Today, Thomas Jefferson presents himself at Versailles as America's new Minister Plenipotentiary. Thomas Jefferson:

The succession to Dr. Franklin at the court of France was an excellent school of humility. On being presented to any one as the Minister of America, the common-place question used in such cases was "c'est vous, Monsieur, qui remplace le Docteur Franklin?" "It is you, Sir, who replace Doctor Franklin?" I generally answered "no one can replace him, Sir; I am only his successor."[1454]

Wednesday, June 1, 1785. Today, in London, John Adams is presented to Britain's King George III. John Adams:

The King . . . asked me whether I came last from France, and upon my answering in the affirmative, he put on an air of familiarity, and, smiling, said, "there is an opinion among some people that you are not the most attached of all your countrymen to the manners of France." I was surprised at this, because I thought it an indiscretion and a departure from the dignity. I was a little embarrassed, but determined not to deny the truth . . .[1455]

Wednesday, June 8, 1785. Today, Benny Bache writes in his diary:

To day I begin to have the packing done.[1456]

Tuesday, July 12, 1785. Today, Ben Franklin and Benny Bache leave their home in Passy to return to the United States. Today, Benny writes in his diary:

[A]fter having dined at Mr. de Chaumont's, my grandfather ascended his litter in the midst of a very great concourse of the people of Passy; a mournful silence reigned around him and was only interrupted by sobs.[1457]

Thomas Jefferson:

I can only . . . testify in general that there appeared to me more respect and veneration attached to the character of Doctor Franklin in France than to that of any other person in the same country, foreign or native . . . When he left Passy, it seemed as if the village had lost its Patriarch . . .[1458]

Friday, August 12, 1785. Today, in the middle of the Atlantic Ocean, en route to Philadelphia, Benny Bache turns sixteen years old.

Tuesday, September 13, 1785. Today, Benny Bache writes in his diary:

We are arrived at Philadelphia. The joy which I felt at the acclamations of the people, on seeing a father and mother, and many brothers and sisters may be felt and not described.[1459]

CHAPTER TEN

THE RIGHTS OF MAN

A Convention in Pennsylvania had adopted a government in one representative assembly, and Dr. Franklin was the President of that Convention. The Doctor, when he went to France in 1776, carried with him the printed copy of that Constitution, and it was immediately propagated through France that this was the plan of government of Mr. Franklin . . . Mr. Turgot, the Duke de la Rochefoucauld, Mr. Condorcet, and many others, became enamored with the Constitution of Mr. Franklin.

JOHN ADAMS,
PRESIDENT OF THE UNITED STATES, 1797–1801[1460]

Mr. John Adams, whose want of liberality to Dr. Franklin continued through life, survived his death and carried persecution against his grandson . . . betrayed a gross malevolence on the subject of this constitution of Pennsylvania . . .

WILLIAM DUANE, EDITOR,
AURORA GENERAL ADVERTISER, 1798–1822[1461]

One legislative assembly and an executive composed of many persons (possessing few powers and no splendor) will soon form the favorite articles of every enlightened politician's creed. To those who require the sanction of great names before they can adopt any opinion, I will observe that these were the favorite propositions of Rousseau and Franklin.

"CASCA,"
AURORA GENERAL ADVERTISER, OCTOBER 16, 1795[1462]

[Gen. Washington] is very jealous of Dr. Franklin & those who are governed by Republican Principles from which he is very averse.

PAUL WENTWORTH, BRITISH SPY[1463]

JOHN ADAMS [is] the advocate of a kingly government and of a titled nobility to form an upper house and to keep down the swinish

456

multitude . . . JOHN ADAMS . . . would deprive you of a voice in chusing your president and senate, and make both hereditary . . .

BENJAMIN F. BACHE, EDITOR,
AURORA GENERAL ADVERTISER, 1790–1798 [1464]

I only contend that the English Constitution is in theory the most stupendous fabric of human invention, both for the adjustment of its balance and the prevention of its vibrations, and that the Americans ought to be applauded instead of censured for imitating it so far as they have.

JOHN ADAMS,
PRESIDENT OF THE UNITED STATES, 1797–1801 [1465]

The American Revolution is now history. How is that history to be written? What freedom have American soldiers won? What freedom have French soldiers learned? George Washington retires to Mount Vernon. John Adams becomes Minister to Great Britain. Thomas Jefferson becomes Minister to France. Ben Franklin and Benny Bache return to Philadelphia. In my history (written much later, in 1798), I observe:

> *The negociations at Paris [which ended the American Revolution] in 1783, like the fall of the monarch [in France in 1793,] ten years after, gave the signal for party contest, and the annals of America exhibit the phenomenon in politics of her ministers at the close of their country's triumph, engaged in a clandestine correspondence and defaming their fellow minister, [Benjamin Franklin,] to secure to themselves the reputation of having accomplished what the character of Franklin only could have ever obtained. History, which disclaims all bias and which owes every tribute to the memory of the glorious dead, will not stoop to name those who were the defamers of Franklin. But it is connected with the present state of America [in 1798] to state the facts, for at that period was laid the foundation of those dangers which now threaten America . . .*
>
> *In the secret proceedings of party in America, since the period of 1783, little has been publicly displayed; but . . . in the convention of 1787 [which wrote the federal Constitution], and from thence to this day, . . . the same Machiavellian systems of political duplicity have been gradually sapping the foundations of American liberty . . .*
>
> *The efforts that were made to reduce the United States to a monarchy were barely unsuccessful. It was to public opinion only that the failure can be with justice attributed; for it has to be acknowledged on all hands that those who proposed a monarchical form were much more alert than the friends of an equal representative government.*

The French Revolution opened new objects of hope and of fear . . . [I]t was not . . . [that revolution's] horrors that alarmed men averse to free government; it was the dangers to which ambition was exposed by the prevalence of those equal principles which France had borrowed from America and enlarged and promulgated as the common right of all man-kind. [1466]

So let's resume . . .

WEDNESDAY, SEPTEMBER 21, 1785

⤐ The Pennsylvania Gazette ⤐

PHILADELPHIA, On Wednesday last arrived, in the ship London Packet, Captain Truxtun, His Excellency Doctor FRANKLIN, late Minister Plenipotentiary from the United States of America to the Court of France, after an absence of near nine years.

The important scenes in which this man has been a principal agent . . . furnish a striking example . . . how greatly a single individual may dignify a nation. The exalted names of WASHINGTON and FRANKLIN will be the boast of Americans in centuries to come.

The Doctor was received at the wharf by a number of citizens who attended him to his house with acclamations of joy. A discharge of cannon announced his arrival, and the bells rang a joyful peel to his welcome.

With the Doctor came his [grandson] . . . Master Benjamin Bache . . .

On Thursday, the Hon. the General Assembly [of Pennsylvania] . . . presented the following address, which was read by the Speaker . . .

We are confident, Sir . . . that your services in the public councils and negociations . . . will be recorded in history to your immortal honor . . .

On Friday . . . the Faculty of the University of Pennsylvania presented the following Address . . .

Among the many benevolent projections which have held so ample a foundation for the esteem and gratitude of your native country, permit this seminary to reckon her first establishment upon the solid principles of Equal Liberty . . . restored thro' the influence of our happy [state] Constitution . . .

Saturday last the following ADDRESS was presented by a Committee of fifteen members of the Constitutional Society . . .

In the course of a long and bloody war, we have been deeply indebted to your wisdom and vigilance for the frequent support we have received . . . from our great and good allies . . . You must not think yourself flattered when we add that your personal character as a philosopher and a citizen has given weight to your negociation . . .

It would be endless to enumerate the great variety of instances in which you have benefited the state of Pennsylvania . . . We cannot, how-

ever, omit to express the high veneration with which we view you as the father of our free and excellent constitution. In this great work, we persuade ourselves that you, in conjunction with the other patriots of the convention over which you presided, have erected a strong hold to the sacred cause of liberty which will long continue . . . to resist the assaults of all its enemies . . .

WILLIAM ADCOOK, Chairman . . .

To which the DOCTOR was pleased to present the following
ANSWER . . .

Gentlemen . . . I think myself happy in returning to live under the free constitution of this commonwealth and hope with you that we and our posterity may long enjoy it.

BENJAMIN FRANKLIN.

A Committee from a respectable Meeting of Citizens at Byrn's Tavern having waited on Doctor FRANKLIN to propose to him a Seat in the [state] Executive Council at the ensuing Election; it is with the greatest satisfaction, the Committee announce to the Public his accession to the Proposal, to which they do not apprehend there will be a dissenting voice in the city.

Another eyewitness reports:

Mr. Franklin arrived . . . in better health than when he left Paris. He has been received like a titulary god—it was a general holiday. The vessels in port were all in flags, even the British. [The French Sculptor] monsieur Houdon was with him.

Monsieur Franklin has returned his grandson, already full grown, to the lad's mother. This child was only a boy when he was taken to Paris in 1776.[1467]

Friday, September 23, 1785. Today, Tom Paine writes from New York:

To Honorable Benjamin Franklin, Esq . . .

It gives me exceeding great pleasure to have the opportunity of congratulating you on your return home . . .[1468]

He also sends congratulations to Benny Bache:

Master Bache was too young when he went away to remember me; but do me the service to make him a sharer of my congratulations.[1469]

Sunday, September 25, 1785. Today, Ben Franklin writes Tom Paine:

Your kind Congratulations on my safe Return give me a great deal of Pleasure; for I have always valued your friendship . . .

Be assured, my dear Friend, that instead of Repenting that I was your Introducer into America, I value myself on the Share I had in procuring for it the Acquisition of so useful and valuable a Citizen.

I shall be very glad to see you . . .[1470]

Between now and the time Tom Paine leaves for France, he will be a frequent visitor at the Franklin home.[1471]

Sunday, October 30, 1785. Today, eighty-year-old Benjamin Franklin writes his dear friend Mrs. Mary Hewson in London:

> *I am plung'd again into public Business, as deep as ever . . . Ben is at College to compleat his Studies . . .*[1472]

WEDNESDAY, NOVEMBER 2, 1785

→ The Pennsylvania Gazette ←

PHILADELPHIA, November 2. Saturday last, the Council and General Assembly of this state met in the Assembly room, for the purpose of choosing a President . . . for the ensuing year; when His Excellency BENJAMIN FRANKLIN, Esq; was chosen President . . . of this commonwealth. After which, proclamation of the election was made at the Court-House, amidst a great concourse of people who expressed their satisfaction by repeated shouts . . .

Saturday, May 6, 1786. Today, in a letter to his friend Mary Hewson, in London, Ben Franklin continues his long-standing pleasantry that Benny Bache will someday marry Mary's daughter, Elizabeth:

> *Ben is finishing his studies at college and continues to behave as well as when you knew him, so I think he will make you a good son.*[1473]

Saturday, August 12, 1786. Today, Benny Bache turns seventeen years old. He studies at the University of Pennsylvania.

Tuesday, August 22, 1786. Today, delegates from fifty towns in Hampshire County, Massachusetts, meet in Hatfield, Massachusetts, to discuss the plight of farmers whose inability to pay debts and taxes subjects them to imprisonment and their farms to foreclosure. From minutes of the meeting:

> *The convention . . . were of opinion that many grievances and unnecessary burdens now lying upon the people are the sources of . . . discontent . . . throughout this Commonwealth. Among which the following articles were voted as such, viz.*
> *1st. The existence of the Senate.*
> *2d. The present mode of representation.*
> *3d. The officers of the government not being annually dependent on the representatives of the people, in General Court [legislature] assembled for their salaries . . .*
> *4th. All the civil officers of government not being annually elected by the representatives of the people in General Court [legislature] assembled . . .*
> *19th. Voted, That whereas several of the above articles of grievances*

arise from defects in the constitution [of Massachusetts]; therefore a revision of the same ought to take place . . .[1474]

These Massachusetts citizens want to discard John Adams' Massachusetts constitution, to eliminate the Massachusetts senate (leaving a single-chamber legislature), to have that single-chamber legislature choose government officers annually, and to discard wealth qualifications for office-holders, etc. In short, they propose to replace John Adams' aristocratic government with Ben Franklin's democratic Pennsylvania Constitution of 1776!

Having served their country and been paid in worthless currency, having incurred debts to recultivate their farms, and now (in the face of a recession) lacking the cash to pay back those debts or even to pay their Massachusetts taxes, these debtor farmers can't obtain debt relief from the Massachusetts legislature (*"The House of Representatives is intended as the Representative of the Persons, and the Senate of the property of the Commonwealth . . ."*) because the Massachusetts senate, representing (and composed of) their wealthy creditors, won't agree.

Other Massachusetts counties will meet. Farmers must get debt relief (and constitutional change), or, once again, they'll take up arms!

WEDNESDAY, SEPTEMBER 20, 1786

✧ The Pennsylvania Gazette ✧

BOSTON, September 6. It is somewhat extraordinary, says a correspondent, that the existence of the [Massachusetts] senate should be complained of by the several county conventions as a grievance; . . . and can attribute it to no other cause than that body's keeping their doors always shut, and thereby debarring their constituents from a knowledge of their debates and proceedings.

A sensible writer in the Hampshire Herald, of last Tuesday, says, "County conventions have proved the occasion, and some of the members have been the fomenters of riots and tumultuous raising of the people . . ."

WEDNESDAY, SEPTEMBER 27, 1786

✧ The Pennsylvania Gazette ✧

BOSTON, September 14. Monday last about 1000 men, with arms of various sorts assembled at Concord . . . On Tuesday, they took possession of the grounds opposite the Court-house, and kept a number of guards marching backward and forward, from the line they formed in the Court-house, to prevent any persons, other than their own friends and comrades approaching it . . . About two o'clock in the afternoon, a man acting as a Sergeant, with two drums and fifes, went some distance and in about half an hour returned at the head of about 90 armed men from the countries of Hampshire and Worcester . . . A convention from about 26 towns, in consequence of a circular letter from Concord, were sitting in the meeting-house . . .

Those debtor farmers will no longer allow merchant creditors, fancy lawyers, or even the courts of Massachusetts to jail them or foreclose their farms!

WEDNESDAY, OCTOBER 18, 1786

✣ The Pennsylvania Gazette ✣

BOSTON . . . October 7. The General Court [the Massachusetts legislature] is now deeply engaged in devising measures for restoring peace to the deluded inhabitants of the several refractory counties, and for giving efficacy, permanency, and dignity to the laws and constitution of the Commonwealth [of Massachusetts].

WEDNESDAY, DECEMBER 27, 1786

✣ The Pennsylvania Gazette ✣

BOSTON . . . Extract of a letter from a Gentleman in Worcester, dated Tuesday evening, December 5, 9 o'clock.

We have been in an alarm for twelve days past. Last week the insurgents in this county and the county of Berkshire, were collected to join those from Middlesex and Bristol, to stop the Courts of Common Pleas and Sessions at Cambridge . . . They were headed by [Daniel Shays], who, it is said, had about 100 from Hampshire . . .

On Monday the militia in the town of Worcester was paraded, and 170 men appeared in support of government . . . I have just heard that the militia from Brookfield are on the march in support of government . . .

Wednesday morning, 11 o'clock. Insurgents still in town. The postrider, who brought the above letter, informs, That he was yesterday morning at Patch's Tavern in Worcester; That . . . the number of insurgents amounted to 1800 or 2000 men.

Monday, January 1, 1787. *New Year's Day.* Today, in London, John Adams completes Volume One of his three-volume response to Frenchmen, like Turgot, and Americans, like Tom Paine and Massachusetts rebel Daniel Shays, who prefer Ben Franklin's Pennsylvania Constitution of 1776 with its simple one-chamber legislative government over Adams' Massachusetts constitution with a wealthy chief executive and propertied state senate to veto the democratic house of representatives. John Adams:

> *The intention [of Turgot's letter] was to celebrate Franklin's Constitution and condemn mine. I understood it, and undertook to defend my constitution, and it cost me three volumes.*[1475]

In John Adams' *Defence of the Constitutions of Government of the United States of America Against the Attack of M. Turgot, in His Letter to Dr. Price, Dated the Twenty-second Day of March, 1778,* John Adams reviews ancient and modern governments to conclude that the English constitution, with its two-chamber legislature (including the House of Lords!) and strong executive (the king!), is, at least in theory, the best of all possible forms. John Adams:

> *M. Turgot had seen only the constitutions of New York, Massachu-*
> *setts, and Maryland, and the first constitution of Pennsylvania. His*
> *principal intention was to censure the three former. From these three,*
> *the [federal] constitution of the United States was afterwards almost*
> *entirely drawn.*
>
> *The drift of my whole work was to vindicate these three constitu-*
> *tions . . .* [1476]

In May, a Constitutional Convention in Philadelphia will decide a new federal Constitution for the United States of America. John Adams' *Defence* will be widely circulated and extremely influential at that convention.[1477] From Volume One of Adams' *Defence*:

> M. Turgot, in his letter to Dr. Price, confesses, "that he is not satisfied with the constitutions which have hitherto been formed for the different states of America." He observes, "that, by most of them, the customs of England are imitated without any particular motive. Instead of collecting all authority into one centre, that of the nation, they have established different bodies, a body of representatives, a council, and a governor, because there is in England a house of commons, a house of lords, and a king. They endeavor to balance these different powers, as if this equilibrium, which in England may be a necessary check to the enormous influence of royalty, could be of any use in republics founded upon the equality of all the citizens, and as if establishing different orders of men was not a source of divisions and disputes."
>
> There has been, from the beginning of the revolution in America, a party in every state who have entertained sentiments similar to those of M. Turgot. Two or three of them have established governments upon his principle . . . [I]t becomes necessary to examine it . . .[1478]
>
> I . . . contend that the English constitution is, in theory, . . . the most stupendous fabric of human invention; and that the Americans ought to be applauded instead of censured, for imitating it as far as they have done . . . The Americans have not indeed [adequately] imitated it in [failing to give] a negative [an absolute veto] upon their legislature to the executive power; in this respect their balances are incomplete, very much I confess to my mortification . . .[1479]
>
> M. Turgot intended to recommend to the Americans . . . a single assembly of representatives of the people, without a governor and without a senate . . .
>
> Shortly before the date of M. Turgot's letter, Dr. Franklin had arrived

in Paris with the American [state] constitutions, and, among the rest, that of Pennsylvania, in which there was but one assembly. It was reported, too, that the Doctor had presided in the convention when it was made, and there approved it . . .

M. Turgot . . . tells us our republics are "founded on the equality . . ." But, what are we to understand here by equality? . . . Was there, or will there ever be, a nation whose individuals were all equal, in natural and acquired qualities, in virtues, talents, and riches? The answer of all mankind must be in the negative. It must then be acknowledged that in every state, [as] in the Massachusetts, for example, there are inequalities which God and nature have planted there . . .

In this society of Massachusettensians then, there is, it is true, a moral and political equality . . . [T]here are, nevertheless, inequalities of great moment . . . 1. There is an inequality of wealth . . . 2. Birth . . . In the Massachusetts, then, there are persons descended from some of their ancient governors, counsellors, judges . . .[1480]

[T]his natural aristocracy . . . is a fact essential to be considered in the institution of a government . . .[1481]

The great question therefore is, What combination . . . ? The controversy between M. Turgot and me is whether a single assembly of representatives be this form? He maintains the affirmative. I am for the negative . . .[1482]

If there is, then, in society such a natural aristocracy . . . how shall the legislator avail himself of their influence for the equal benefit of the public? and how, on the other hand, shall he prevent them from disturbing the public happiness? I answer, by arranging them all, or at least the most conspicuous of them, together in one assembly, by the name of a senate; by separating them from all pretensions to the executive power, and by controlling their ambition and avarice by an assembly of representatives on one side and by the executive authority on the other.[1483]

In M. Turgot's single assembly, those who should think themselves most distinguished by blood and education, as well as fortune, would be most ambitious . . . It is from the natural aristocracy in a single assembly that the first danger is to be apprehended in the present state of manners in America; and with a balance of landed property in the hands of the people, so decided in their favor, the progress to degeneracy . . . would . . . grow faster or slower every year . . .

The only remedy is to throw the rich and the proud into one group, in a separate assembly, and there tie their hands; if you give them scope with the people at large or their representatives, they will destroy all equality and liberty with the consent and acclamations of the people themselves . . . But placing them alone by themselves, the society avails itself of all their abilities and virtues; they become a solid check to the representatives themselves, as well as to the executive power . . .[1484]

In [the constitution of Lacedæmonia], there were three orders, and a balance, not indeed equal to that of England, for want of a negative [veto] in each branch; but the nearest resembling it of any we have yet seen. The king, the nobles, the senate, and the people, in two assemblies, are surely more orders than a governor, senate, and house . . . The Lacedæmonian republic . . . had the three essential parts of the best possible government; it was a mixture of monarchy, aristocracy, and democracy.[1485]

Thomas Jefferson:

Can any one read Mr. Adams' defence of the American constitutions without seeing he was a monarchist?[1186]

Sunday, January 7, 1787. John Adams is not the only American with monarchical leanings. Today, New Yorker John Jay writes George Washington about the upcoming Federal Constitutional Convention:

What is to be done? . . .

Would the giving any further power to Congress do the business? I am much inclined to think it would not . . .

Large assemblies often misunderstand or neglect the obligations of character, honour, and dignity . . .

Shall we have a king? Not in my opinion while other experiments remain untried. Might we not have a governor-general limited in his prerogatives and duration? Might not Congress be divided into an upper and lower house—the former appointed for life, the latter annually—and let the governor-general . . . have a negative on their acts? Our government should in some degree be suited to our manners and circumstances, and they, you know, are not strictly democratical.[1487]

WEDNESDAY, JANUARY 31, 1787

✦ The Pennsylvania Gazette ✦

BOSTON. *January 16 . . . An A D D R E S S to the good people of the Commonwealth [of Massachusetts] . . .*

It is now become evident that the object of the insurgents is to annihilate our present happy constitution, or to force the General Court [Massachusetts legislature] into measures repugnant . . . If the constitution is to be destroyed, and insurrection stalk unopposed by authority, individuals . . . will . . . meet force with force . . . I must conjure the good people of Massachusetts . . . to cooperate with government in every necessary action . . .

Given at the Council-chamber in Boston, the twelfth day of January, 1787 . . .

JAMES BOWDOIN
[Governor of Massachusetts]

✣ The Pennsylvania Gazette ✤

WORCESTER, [Massachusetts], January 25. Last Monday, Major General Lincoln, with the troops under his command, arrived in town, in order to protect the court of common pleas . . . These courts have been violently obstructed in their business by bodies of armed men ever since September last . . . General Shepherd, with 1200 of the militia of the county of Hampshire, in support of government is posted at Springfield . . .

Friday, February 9, 1787. Today, in Philadelphia, as if anticipating John Adams' *Defence,* Benjamin Franklin, Tom Paine, and other republicans form the "Society for Political Enquiries" to counter monarchical influences.[1488] Society president Ben Franklin will host the biweekly meetings at Franklin Court. Tom Paine writes its statement of purpose, including:

> *Accustomed to look up to those nations from whom we have derived our origin, [we have] . . . grafted on an infant commonwealth the manner of ancient and corrupted monarchies. In having effected a separate government, we have as yet effected but a partial independence. The Revolution can only be said to be complete when we shall have freed ourselves no less from the influence of foreign prejudices than from the fetters of foreign power . . . From a desire of supplying this deficency . . . it is now proposed to establish a society for mutual improvement in the knowledge of government . . .*[1489]

✣ The Pennsylvania Gazette ✤

BOSTON. February 1. Copy of a letter from the Honorable General Shepherd to his Excellency the Governor [of Massachusetts], dated Springfield, [Massachusetts] January 26, 1787 . . .

The unhappy time has come in which we have been obliged to shed blood. [Daniel] Shays who was at the head of about 1200 men, marched yesterday afternoon about 4 o'clock towards the public buildings, in battle array . . .

I then ordered Major Stephens who commanded the artillery to fire upon them, he accordingly did . . . The fourth or fifth shot put the whole column into the utmost confusion. Shays made an attempt to display the column, but in vain . . . Had I disposed to destroy them, I might have charged upon their rear and flanks, with my infantry and two pieces, and could have killed the greater part of his whole army within twenty-five minutes . . .

John Adams' Massachusetts constitution is safe! John Adams:

*In justice to myself, I ought to say, that it was not the miserable vanity of justifying my own work [the Massachusetts constitution], or eclipsing the glory of Mr. Franklin's, that induced me to write [my De-*fence of the Constitutions of Government of the United States].

I never thought of writing till the Assembly of Notables in France had commenced a revolution, with the Duke de la Rochefoucauld and Mr. Condorcet at their head, who I knew would establish a government in one assembly . . .

At the same time, every western wind brought us news of town and county meetings in Massachusetts, adopting Mr. Turgot's ideas [of government by a single assembly], condemning my [Massachusetts] Constitution, reprobating the office of governor and the assembly of the Senate as expensive, useless, and pernicious, and not only proposing to toss them off, but rising in rebellion against them . . .

[I]n this view I wrote my defence of the American Constitutions. I had only the Massachusetts Constitution in view, and such others as agreed with it in the distribution of the legislative power into three branches, in separating the executive from the legislative power . . .[1490]

Thursday, February 22, 1787. Today, in Paris, the King of France convenes, for the first time since 1626, a meeting of an Assembly of Notables (144 members, including seven princes of the blood, the leading archbishops, seven dukes, eight marshals, nine marquis, nine counts, a baron, presidents of parliaments, etc.) to deal with the 3–4 billion livres of debt that has put France on the verge of bankruptcy. Former Finance Minister Turgot's warning, in April of 1775, that France could not afford a protracted war for the independence of the United States has proved to be correct. The 1.225-billion-livre debt incurred in preparing for and fighting the "national war" has created a crisis.[1491]

Thomas Jefferson:

The [French Finance] Minister (Calonne) stated to them that the annual excess of expences beyond the revenue, when Louis XVI. came to the throne, was 37. millions of livres; that 440. millns, had been borrowed to reestablish the navy; that the American war had cost them 14440. millns. (256. mils. of Dollars) and that the interest of these sums, with other increased expences, had added 40 mllns. more to the annual deficit . . .[1492]

Monday, March 19, 1787. Today, General Henry Knox writes George Washington concerning the upcoming Constitutional Convention:

As you have thought proper, my dear Sir, to request my opinion respecting your attendance at the [federal constitutional] convention, I shall give it . . . I take it for granted that . . . you will be constrained to accept of the president's chair. Hence the proceedings of the convention will more immediately be appropriated to you . . . Were the con-

vention to propose only amendments and patchwork to the present defective confederation, your reputation would in a degree suffer. But, were an energetic and judicious system to be proposed with your signature, it would . . . doubly entitle you to the glorious republican epithet, The Father of your Country.[1493]

George Washington will attend and preside.

Tuesday, March 20, 1787. Today, in London, Abigail Adams writes her son, John Quincy Adams:

Your papa enjoys better Health than he has for many years . . . Before this reaches you, his Book will have arrived. I should like to know its reception. I tell him they will think in America that he is for sitting up a King. He says no, but he is for giving the Governors of every state the same Authority which the British king has under the true British constitution, balancing his power by the two other Branches . . .[1494]

Sunday, April 15, 1787. Tom Paine will shortly leave for France. Today, Ben Franklin writes a letter of introduction to the Duc de La Rochefoucauld:

I am glad to see that you are named as one of the general assembly to be convened in France. I flatter myself that great good may accrue to that dear nation from the deliberations of such an assembly . . .

I send herewith a volume of the transactions of our Philosophical Society, another for M. de Condorcet, and a third for the Academy . . .

The bearer of this is Mr. Paine, the author of a famous piece entitled Common Sense, published here, with great effect. He is an ingenious honest man, and as such I beg leave to recommend him to your civilities.[1495]

Tuesday, April 17, 1787. Today, Ben Franklin writes the Marquis François-Jean de Chastellux (who served in the American Revolution with French General Rochambeau):

The newspapers tell us that you are about to have an assembly of Notables to consult on improvements of your government. It is somewhat singular that we should be engaged in the same project here at the same time, but so it is, and a convention for the purpose of revising and amending our constitution is to meet in this place next month. I hope both assemblies will be blessed with success, and that their deliberations and counsels may promote the happiness of both nations.

In the state of Pennsylvania, government, notwithstanding our parties, goes on at present very smoothly . . . Massachusetts has lately been disturbed by some disorderly people . . . Mr. Paine whom you know, and who undertakes to deliver this letter to you, can give you full information on our affairs.[1496]

Thursday, April 26, 1787. Today, one month before the Federal Constitutional Convention, Thomas Paine leaves for France.[1497] He will not participate in America's Constitutional Convention. For Paine, America's revolution is complete, and France's revolution is about to begin. He will arrive in France, just as he did in America, with letters of introduction from Benjamin Franklin.

Tuesday, May 8, 1787. Today, Ben Franklin writes a foundry customer, Francis Childs of New York, who has complained about the type fonts he has received from Franklin's foundry:

> *You are always complaining of imperfections in the Founts . . . They were all cast after the best Rules of the Foundries in England . . . However, to oblige you . . . you shall have the Sorts you want if you send a List of them in Numbers. My grandson [Ben Bache] will cast them as soon as he has taken his Degree and got clear of the College; for then he purposes to apply himself closely to the Business of Letter founding, and this is expected in July next.*[1498]

Sunday, May 12, 1787. Today, New Yorker John Jay writes John Adams with praise for Adams' *Defence of the Constitutions of Government of the United States of America Against the Attack of M. Turgot*:

> *Accept my thanks for the book you were so kind as to send me. I have read it with pleasure and with profit . . . A new edition of your book is printing in this city and will be published next week.*[1499]

Friday, May 25, 1787. Today, in France, the Assembly of Notables (i.e., high clergy and nobility) adjourns without deciding the taxes to resolve France's financial crisis. During its meeting, the French hero of the American Revolution the Marquis de Lafayette proposed that the common people (the "Third Estate") join the clergy (the "First Estate") and nobility (the "Second Estate") to decide on any taxes that might be required.[1500] The principle is new to France but not to America: no taxation without representation.

Because the Assembly of Notables has declined to act, the king will be forced to convoke the Estates-General (including the Third Estate), so representatives of the common people will come to Paris. They will also begin a democratic revolution.[1501]

Today, in Philadelphia, representatives of thirteen United States of America meet in convention to decide upon a new federal Constitution. Though the deliberations of the convention are in secret, James Madison of Virginia records the debates:

> Mr. ROBERT MORRIS . . . proposed George Washington Esq. late Commander in chief for president of the Convention . . .
> The nomination came with particular grace from Penna. as Doctor Franklin alone could have been thought of as a competitor . . . [T]he state of the weather and of [Dr. Franklin's] health confined him to his house.[1502]

Saturday, May 26, 1787. Today, Thomas Paine arrives at Havre-de-Grâce in France.[1503]

Monday, May 28, 1787. Today, in Philadelphia, four convicts from the Walnut-street prison carry the incapacitated eighty-two-year-old Benjamin Franklin to the Federal Constitutional Convention.[1504]

Thursday, May 31, 1787. Today, at the Federal Constitutional Convention in Philadelphia, James Madison records:

> The . . . Resolution *"that the national Legislature ought to consist of two branches"* was agreed to without debate or dissent, except that of Pennsylvania, given probably from complaisance to Doctor Franklin who was understood to be partial to a single House of Legislation.[1505]

Friday, June 1, 1787. Today, at the Federal Constitutional Convention in Philadelphia, James Madison records:

> The Committee of the whole proceeded to Resolution . . . "that a national executive be instituted, to be chosen by the national legislature . . ."
>
> Mr. WILSON moved that the Executive consist of a single person . . .
>
> A considerable pause ensuing and the Chairman asking if he should put the question, Doctor FRANKLIN observed that it was a point of great importance and wished that the gentlemen would deliver their sentiments on it before the question was put . . .
>
> Mr. RANDOLPH strenuously opposed a unity in the Executive magistracy. He regarded it as the foetus of monarchy. We had, he said, no motive to be governed by the British Government as our prototype . . .
>
> Mr. MADISON thought it would be proper, before a choice should be made between a unity and a plurality in the Executive, to fix the extent of the Executive authority . . .
>
> Mr. SHERMAN was for the appointment [of the Executive] by the Legislature and for making him absolutely dependent on that body, as it was the will of that which was to be executed . . .[1506]

Saturday, June 2, 1787. Today, Benjamin Rush, a Pennsylvania delegate to the Federal Constitutional convention, writes Englishman Richard Price:

> *Mr. Adams' book [Defence of the Constitutions . . .] has diffused such excellent principles among us that there is little doubt of our adopting a vigorous and compounded [two-chamber] federal legislature. Our illustrious minister in this gift to his country has done us more service than if he had obtained alliances for us with all the nations of Europe.*[1506a]

Today, at the Federal Constitutional Convention in Philadelphia, James Madison records:

> Doct. FRANKLIN moved [that] . . . the Executive . . . receive no salary . . . [T]there will always be a party for giving more to the rulers . . . Generally indeed the ruling party carries its point, the revenues of princes

always increasing . . . The more the people are discontented with the oppression of taxes; the greater the need the prince has of money to distribute among his partizans and pay the troops that are to suppress all resistance . . . I am apprehensive, therefore, perhaps too apprehensive, that the Government of these States may in future times end in a Monarchy. But this Catastrophe I think may be long delayed if, in our proposed System, we do not . . . [make] our posts of honor, places of profit. If we do, I fear that tho' we do employ at first [for the Executive] a number [of people], and not a single person, the number will in time be set aside [and] it will only nourish the foetus of a King . . . [S]hall we doubt finding three or four men in all the U. States with public spirit enough . . . to preside [without pay] over our civil concerns and see our laws are duly executed?[1507]

Monday, June 4, 1787. Today, at the Federal Constitutional Convention in Philadelphia, one hears John Adams in the voice of Alexander Hamilton. James Madison records:

Mr. HAMILTON move[s] . . . to give the Executive an absolute negative [veto] on the laws . . .

Doctor FRANKLIN said he was sorry to differ . . . He had had some experience of this check in the Executive on the Legislature, under the proprietary Government of Penn. The negative of the Governor was constantly made use of to extort money . . . When the indians were scalping the western people and notice of it arrived, the concurrence of the Governor in the means of self-defence could not be got till it was agreed that his Estate should be exempted from taxation . . . He was afraid; if a negative should be given as proposed, that more power and money would be demanded, till as last eno' would be gotten to influence & bribe the Legislature into a compleat subjection to the will of the Executive . . .

Col. MASON observed . . . The probable abuses of a negative [veto] had been well explained by Dr. F . . . The Executive may refuse its assent to necessary measures till new appointments shall be referred to him . . . We are not indeed constituting a British Government, but a more dangerous monarchy, an elective one . . .

Doctor FRANKLIN . . . [said] The first man put at the helm will be a good one. No body knows what sort may come afterwards. The Executive will always be increasing here, as elsewhere, till it ends in Monarchy.[1508]

WEDNESDAY, JUNE 6, 1787

⇨ The Pennsylvania Gazette ⇦

[Adv. front pg., top left]

Just published, and to be sold by
HALL and SELLERS; J. CRUKSHANK;
and YOUNG and M'CULLOCH
(Price 7ƒ6 bound, or 6ƒ in blue covers.)
A DEFENCE OF THE
CONSTITUTIONS OF GOVERNMENT

Monday, June 11, 1787. Today, at the Federal Constitutional Convention, Benjamin Franklin delivers a speech on proportional representation:

> I . . . think the Number of Representatives should bear some Proportion to the Number of the Represented, and that the Decisions should be by the Majority of members, not by the Majority of States . . .
>
> [T]he present method of voting by States was submitted to originally by Congress under a Conviction of its Impropriety, Inequality, and Injustice . . .[1509]

Monday, June 18, 1787. Today, at the Federal Constitutional Convention, Alexander Hamilton echoes the ideas of John Adams. James Madison records:

> Mr. HAMILTON had been hitherto silent on the business before the Convention . . . He was obliged therefore to declare himself . . . The members of Cong[res]s, being chosen by the States & subject to recall, represent all the local prejudices . . . It is ag[ain]st all the principles of a good Government to vest the requisite powers in such a body as Cong[res]s . . .
>
> In his private opinion, he had no scruple in declaring, supported as he was by the opinions of so many of the wise & good, that the British Government was the best in the world; and that he doubted whether any thing short of it would do in America . . . Their house of Lords is a most noble institution. Having nothing to hope for by a change and a sufficient interest by means of their property in being faithful to the national interest, they form a permanent barrier against every pernicious innovation . . . No temporary Senate will have firmness eno' to answer the purpose . . . Gentlemen . . . suppose seven years a sufficient period . . . from not duly considering the amazing violence & turbulence of the democratic spirit . . .
>
> As to the Executive, it seemed to be admitted that no good one could be established on Republican principles . . . The English model was the only good one on this subject. The Hereditary interest of the King was so interwoven with that of the Nation and his personal emoluments so great that he was placed above the danger of being corrupted . . . [O]ne of the weak sides of Republics was their being liable to foreign influence & corruption . . . Let one branch of the Legislature hold their places for life . . . Let the Executive also be for life . . . It will be objected probably that such an Executive will be an elective Monarch . . . He wd. reply that Monarch is an indefinite term . . .[1510]

Alexander Hamilton's notes for this speech reveal his preferences:

> *British constitution best form . . .*
> *[T]wo political divisions—the few and the many . . .*
> *[T]hey should be separated . . .*

[I]f separated, they will need a mutual check.
This check is a monarch . . .
There ought to be a principle in government capable of resisting the popular current . . .
The monarch . . . ought to be hereditary, and to have so much power that it will not be in his interest to risk much to acquire more. [1511]

Thomas Jefferson:

[A colleague] takes great pain to prove . . . that Hamilton was no monarchist . . . This may pass with uninformed readers, but not with those who have had it from Hamilton's own mouth. I am one of those, and but one of many. At my own table, in presence of Mr. Adams . . . and myself, in a dispute between Mr. Adams and himself, he avowed his preference of monarchy over every other government, and his opinion that the English was the most perfect model of government ever devised by the wit of man, Mr. Adams agreeing "if its corruptions were done away." [1512]

Mr. Adams observed "purge that constitution of its corruption and give to its popular branch equality of representation, and it would be the most perfect constitution ever devised by the wit of man." Hamilton paused and said "purge it of its corruption and give to its popular branch equality of representation, & it would become an impracticable government: as it stands at present, with all its supposed defects, it is the most perfect government which ever existed." And this was assuredly the exact line which separated the political creeds of these two gentlemen. The one was for two hereditary branches and an honest elective one: the other for a hereditary king with a house of lords & commons, corrupted to his will and standing between him and the people. [1513]

George Washington will choose monarchists Hamilton and Adams to preside at the highest posts in his administration. Alexander Hamilton will lead the Federalist party.

Friday, June 22, 1787. Today, in Paris, Tom Paine writes Benjamin Franklin:

I arrived at Paris on the 30th of May, and the next day began delivering the letters you were so kind as to honor me with. My reception here, in consequence of them, has been abundantly cordial and friendly. I have received visits and invitations from all who were in town. [1514]

Saturday, June 30, 1787. Today, at the Federal Constitutional Convention in Philadelphia, Benjamin Franklin argues the merits of a plural executive (an executive council) rather than a single president:

The steady Course of public Measures is most probably to be expected from a Number [in an executive council].
A single Person's Measures may be good. The Successor differs in

Opinion of those Measures, and adopts others; often is ambitious of distinguishing himself by opposing them, and offering new Projects. One is peaceably dispos'd; another may be fond of War, &c. Hence foreign States can never have that Confidence in the Treaties or Friendship of such a Government, as in that which is conducted by a Number.

The single Head may be Sick; who is to conduct the Public Affairs in that Case? When he dies, who are to conduct till a new election? If a Council, why not continue them?[1515]

Ten years from now, Benny Bache will argue:

In the independent times of the ancient republics, no one thought of giving to a general a supreme command close to the seat of government for four years certain. Yet this and many other high prerogatives, internal and external, are given for this term to the American President . . . [I]t is sufficient reason for changing the present institution of a solitary president—And what reason is there per contra; what evil in a plural directory, gradually renewed? . . . The person at present chosen as vice-president would, in this case, no longer as now be an inert person . . . The executive government would no longer exhibit the fluctuating character of an individual, but approach nearer to the fixed abstract of the American nation.[1516]

Wednesday, July 18, 1787. Today, in London, U.S. Minister to Great Britain John Adams sends the second volume of his *Defence of the Constitutions of Government of the United States* to the printer.[1517] Next Wednesday, John Jay will write him on the success of his first volume.

Your book circulates and does good. It conveys much information . . . when the defects of our national government are under consideration, and when the strongest arguments are necessary to remove prejudices . . .[1518]

Wednesday, August 1, 1787. Today, from New York, where he is trying, at his grandfather's behest, to collect an old foundry debt from Francis Childs (the dissatisfied foundry customer), Benny writes his grandfather:

My father's letter informs me also, to my great satisfaction, of the raising [up in Franklin Court] of the Printing Office & Foundry. In all probability we shall succeed . . . provided we make a few alterations in the several founts, so as to suit them a little better to the english taste . . . I'll try to procure a specimen of them that you may judge for yourself of their merit . . .

Childs still keeps out of the way. I suspect on purpose to avoid my making any demands on him. I'll use however my utmost activity to find him out and recover the debt . . .[1519]

Thursday, August 9, 1787. Today, at the Federal Constitutional Convention in Philadelphia, James Madison records:

> Mr. Govr. MORRIS moved to insert 14 instead of 4 years citizenship as a qualification for Senators: urging the danger of admitting strangers into our public Councils . . .
>
> Doct. FRANKLIN was not against a reasonable time, but should be very sorry to see any thing like illiberality inserted into the Constitution . . . We found in the course of the Revolution that many strangers served us faithfully and that many natives took part against their Country. When foreigners, after looking about for some other Country in which they can obtain more happiness, give a preference to ours, it is a proof of attachment which ought to excite our confidence & affection.[1520]

Friday, August 10, 1787. Today, at the Federal Constitutional Convention, property qualifications for elected officials are discussed. James Madison records:

> Mr. PINCKNEY. The Committee as he had conceived were instructed to report the proper qualifications of property for the members of the Nat. Legislature . . . He was opposed to the establishment of an undue aristocratic influence in the Constitution, but he thought it essential that the members of the Legislature, the Executive, and the Judges, should be possessed of competent property to make them independent & respectable . . .
>
> Doctr. FRANKLIN expressed his dislike of every thing that tended to debase the spirit of the common people . . . Some of the greatest rogues he was ever acquainted with were the richest rogues. We should remember the character which the Scripture requires in Rulers, that they should be men hating covetousness. This Constitution will be much read and attended to in Europe, and if it should betray a great partiality to the rich, will not only hurt us in the esteem of the most liberal and enlightened men there but discourage the common people from removing into this Country.[1521]

Sunday, August 12, 1787. Today, preparing for his final examination at the University of Pennsylvania,[1522] Benny Bache turns eighteen years old. Earlier this month, he wrote his grandfather,

> *The Convention I hear is adjourned. [I]t must be no small comfort for you to have a short resting spell. I really think your illness was in great measure owing to the fatigue you suffered while it was sitting, but I hope this respite from that business will fortify your health . . .*[1523]

Monday, September 17, 1787. Today, at the Federal Constitutional Convention in Philadelphia, Ben Franklin delivers a speech:

> I confess that I do not entirely approve of this Constitution . . .
>
> I agree to this Constitution, with all its Faults, if they are such, because

I think a General Government necessary for us, and there is no *Form* of Government but what may be a Blessing to the People if well administred . . .

The Opinions I have had of its Errors I sacrifice to the Public Good. I have never whisper'd a Syllable of them abroad. Within these Walls they were born, & here they shall die. If every one of us in returning to our Constituents were to report the Objections he has had to it . . . we might prevent its being generally received and thereby lose all . . .[1524]

As I wrote in my history, Franklin thought the new Constitution,

though it was not wholly entitled to his admiration, was yet preferable to any hereditary establishment.[1525]

Next, as James Madison records,

[Dr. Franklin] then moved that the Constitution be signed . . . ". . . by the unanimous consent of the States present the 17th of Sept. &c . . ."

This ambiguous form ["of the States"] had been drawn up . . . in order to gain the dissenting members and put into the hands of Doctor Franklin that it might have the better chance of success . . .

Mr. RANDOLPH then rose and, with an allusion to the observations of Doc. Franklin, apologized for his refusing to sign the Constitution . . .

The members then proceeded to sign the instrument.

Whilst the last members were signing it, Doct. FRANKLIN, looking towards the Presidents Chair at the back of which a rising sun happened to be painted, observed to a few members near him that Painters had found it difficult to distinguish in their art between a rising and a setting sun . . . I have, said he, often . . . looked at that [sun] behind the President without being able to tell whether it was rising or setting: But now at length I have the happiness to know that it is a rising sun . . .

The Constitution being signed by all the members except Mr. Randolph, Mr. Mason, and Mr. Gerry . . . the Convention dissolved itself by an Adjournment . . .[1526]

George Washington has said virtually nothing at the Federal Constitutional Convention. John Adams will observe,

Washington got the reputation of being a great man because he kept his mouth shut.[1527]

The convention has adopted John Adams' constitution, not Ben Franklin's. Ben Franklin, it is said, shed a tear when he gave his acquiescence.[1528]

John Adams has, in the United States Senate, an aristocratic branch of government resembling the British House of Lords. The United States Senate admits very few members (only two from each state), who won't have to answer for their actions very frequently (facing reelection only once each six years) and who are chosen, under the new federal constitution, not by the people but by state legislatures, where propertied state senates and wealthy state governors can generally control the choice. (Even should U.S. senators be elected directly by the people, the U.S. Senate would remain the handmaiden of aristocracy, because statewide elections require great wealth and reputation to reach an electorate whose size and dispersion won't allow the voters to know the candidates personally.[1528a]) Finally, a majority of U.S. senators do not necessarily represent a majority of the people. Like England's "rotten boroughs," less populous states have a disproportionate and undemocratic role. John Adams:

> *Now, sir, let me ask you, whether you can discover no "resemblance of aristocracy in our form of government"? Are not great, and very great, important and essential powers entrusted to a few, a very few?*
>
> *[The very small number of] senators, composed of two senators from each state, are an integral part of the legislature . . . These [few men] possess an absolute negative on all the laws of the nation. Nor is this all. These few, these very few . . . have an absolute negative upon the executive authority in the appointment of all officers . . . They, moreover, have an absolute negative on all treaties . . . They are also an absolute judicature in all impeachments . . .*
>
> *How are these . . . senators appointed? Are they appointed by the people? Is the constitution of them democratical? They are chosen by the legislatures of the several states. And who are the legislatures of these separate states? Are they the people? No. They are a selection of the best men among the people, made by the people themselves . . . Yet there is something more. These legislatures are composed of two bodies, a senate and a house of representatives, each assembly differently constituted, the senate more nearly "resembling aristocracy" than the house. Senators of the United States are chosen, in some states, by a convention of both houses; in others, by separate, independent, but concurrent votes. The senates in the former have great influence, and often turn the vote; in the latter, they have an absolute negative in the choice.[1529]*

With each state possessing the same Senate vote as every other state, a citizen of one state may have ten times more representation in the United States Senate than the citizen of another state. This is not what Ben Franklin and Tom Paine mean by political "equality."

The U.S. President has nearly monarchical power. In fact, the President can veto the decisions of a majority in the Congress. This is not the executive power that French democrats prefer. John Adams:

> *The Prince of Orange, William V., in a conversation with which he honored me . . . was pleased to say . . . "Sir, you have given yourselves a king under the title of president."*
>
> *Turgot, Rochefoucauld, and Condorcet, Brissot . . . and Mazzei were all offended that we have given too much eclat to our governors and presidents. It is true, and I rejoice in it, that our presidents, limited as they are, have more power, that is, executive power, than the stadt-*

*holders, the doges . . . or the kings of Lacedæmon or of Poland . . .
[O]ur president's office has "some resemblance of monarchy," and
God forbid that it should ever be diminished.*

*All these monarchical powers . . . are "deduced" from morality and
liberty; but if they had been more deliberately considered and better digested, the morality and liberty would have been better secured, and of
longer duration, if the senatorial limitation of them had been omitted.*[1530]

The President is also to be elected not by the people but by presidential electors
who are to be chosen as state legislatures decide. Propertied state senates,
wealthy governors, and aristocratic caucuses can determine, therefore, the
presidential selection, much as they can determine the choice of U.S. Senators.
John Adams explains:

*[T]he electors are balanced against the people in the choice of the
president. And here is a complication and refinement of balances,
which, for any thing I recollect, is an invention of our own, and peculiar to us.*

*The state legislatures can direct the choice of electors by the people
at large, or by the people in what districts they please, or by themselves, without consulting the people at all. However, all this complication of machinery . . . [has] not been sufficient to satisfy the people.
They have invented a balance to all balances in their caucuses. We
have congressional caucuses, county caucuses, city caucuses, district
caucuses . . . and in these aristocratical caucuses, elections are decided.*[1531]

The President and Senate are not hereditary, though some might find this preferable. They need not be, as John Adams writes John Taylor, Virginia's farmer-
philosopher:

*You appear to me, in all your writings to consider hereditary
descent as essential to monarchy and aristocracy . . . But is this
correct . . . ? It may be hereditary, or it may be for life, or it may be for
years or only for one year . . . Monarchy, in this view of it, resembles
property. A landed estate may be for years, a year . . . or any number
of years . . .*[1532]

The President and U.S. senators will have terms of office twice and thrice as
long as members of the House of Representatives (and, "during good behavior,"
can be reelected for life).

Friday, October 5, 1787. Today, an anonymous correspondent writes in a Philadelphia newspaper,

I am fearful that the principles of government inculcated in Mr. Adams's
treatise *[Defence of the Constitutions of Government of the United
States]*, and enforced in the numerous essays and paragraphs in the news-

papers, have misled some well designing members of the late Convention . . .

Mr. Adams's *sine qua non* of a good government is three balancing powers . . . Mr. Adams . . . has not been able to adduce a single instance of such a government; he indeed says that the British constitution is such in theory [only] . . . The state of society in England is much more favorable to such a scheme of government than that of America. There they have a powerful hereditary nobility, and real distinctions of rank and interests . . .

I shall now examine the construction of the proposed general government . . .

[W]e see the house of representatives are on the part of the people to balance the senate who I suppose will be composed of the better sort, the well born, &c . . . The senate . . . is constituted on the most unequal principles . . . The term and mode of its appointment will lead to permanency . . . The President, who would be a mere pageant of state unless he coincides with the views of the Senate, would either become the head of the aristocratic junto in that body or its minion; besides, their influence being the most predominant, could the best secure his reelection to office . . .

[T]he organization of this government . . . would be in practice a permanent ARISTOCRACY.[1533]

Tom Paine:

At the time I left America (April, 1787), the Continental Convention that formed the Federal Constitution was on the point of meeting . . .

It was only to the absolute necessity of establishing some Federal authority . . . that an instrument so inconsistent . . . obtained a suffrage . . .

I declare myself opposed to several matters in the Constitution, particularly to the manner in which what is called the Executive is formed, and to the long duration of the Senate; and if I live to return to America [from France], I will use all my endeavors to have them altered. I have always been opposed to . . . what is called a single executive . . . A plurality [a council] is far better . . . [I]t is necessary to the manly mind of a republic that it loses the debasing idea of obeying an individual . . .

As the Federal Constitution is a copy, though not quite so base as the original, of the form of the British Government, an imitation of its vices was naturally to be expected . . .[1534]

Had that Convention, or the law members thereof, known the origin of the negativing power used by kings of England, from whence they copied it, they must have seen the inconsistency of introducing it into an American Constitution . . .

At the time this Constitution was formed, there was a great departure from the principles of the Revolution among those who then as-

sumed the lead, and the country was grossly imposed upon . . .

The [Pennsylvania] Constitution of 1776 was conformable to the Declaration of Independence and the Declaration of Rights, which the present [U.S.] Constitution is not; for it makes artificial distinctions among men in the right of suffrage, which the principles of equity know nothing of . . .[1535]

Saturday, October 27, 1787. Today, the first of eighty-five articles titled "Federalist" and anonymously signed "Publius" appears in New York newspapers. These anonymous articles urge ratification of the new federal Constitution to resolve interstate issues of commerce and currency, international affairs, national defense, disputes between states, etc. Alexander Hamilton, the New York lawyer and Federalist leader who prefers a hereditary monarch and senators for life, wrote today's Publius article, as he will write a majority of these so-called Federalist papers. John Jay (who, Tom Paine says, prefers *"that the Senate should have been appointed for life"*[1536]) will also write some, though, for the next decade, Hamilton will be thought to be their exclusive author.[1537] Despite Hamilton's preference for monarchy, he accepts the new Constitution for its promise of a strong central authority and for its checks and balances against Franklinian democracy. The Publius articles will run through next April, be copied by newspapers throughout the country (including the *Pennsylvania Gazette*), and be collected in two volumes under the title *The Federalist*.

Thursday, November 6, 1787. Today, a letter from "An Officer of the Late Continental Army" appears in a Philadelphia newspaper:

[T]he very men who advocate so strongly the new plan of government and support it with the infallibility of Doctor Franklin affect to despise the present constitution of Pennsylvania which was dictated and avowed by that venerable patriot. They are conscious that he does not entirely approve of the new plan, whose principles are so different from those he established in our ever-glorious constitution, and there is no doubt that it is the reason that has induced them to leave his respected name out of the ticket for the approaching election.[1538]

Thursday, November 22, 1787. Today, Benny Bache graduates from the University of Pennsylvania and receives his Bachelor of Arts degree.[1539]

Thursday, December 6, 1787. Today, a letter from "Z" appears in a Boston newspaper:

When I read Dr. FRANKLIN'S address to the President of the late Convention, in the last Monday's Gazette, I was at a loss . . .

[S]ays the Doctor, "In these sentiments I agree to this Constitution, with all its faults, if they are such, because I think a general government necessary for us, and there is no FORM of government but what may be a blessing to the people, if well administered." But are we to accept a form of government which we do not entirely approve of, merely in the hopes that it will be administered well? . . .

He evidently, I think, builds his hopes that the Constitution proposed will be a blessing to the people,—not on the principles of the government itself, but on the possibility that, with all its faults, it may be well administered . . . No wonder he shed a tear, as it is said he did, when he gave his sanction to the New Constitution.[1540]

Saturday, December 29, 1787. Today, from Paris, Thomas Paine reports the reaction abroad to America's new Constitution:

It seems a wish with all the Americans on this side of the water, except Mr. John Adams, that the President-General has not been perpetually eligible. Mr. Adams, who has some strange ideas, finds fault because the President is not for life, and because the Presidency does not devolve by hereditary succession.[1541]

Saturday, February 2, 1788. Today, from Paris, the Marquis de Lafayette writes his American comrade-in-arms Henry Knox:

We are Anxiously Waiting for the [ratifying] results of the State Conventions. The new [American] Constitution is an Admirable Work—, although I take the liberty to wish for some Amendments—[but] the point is to have it first adopted by Nine States—and then you may get the dissention by means of some improvements which Mr. Jefferson, Common Sense [Tom Paine], and myself are debating in a Convention of our own as honestly as if as if we were to decide upon it . . .[1542]

Saturday, April 19, 1788. Today, Ben Franklin writes an old friend in Paris,

I live in a good House which I built 25 Years ago . . . A dutiful and affectionate Daughter, with her Husband and Six Children compose my Family. The Children are all promising . . . The eldest, Benjamin, you may remember. He has finish'd his Studies at our University, and is preparing to enter into Business as a Printer, the original occupation of his Grandfather . . . I do not expect to continue much longer a Sojourner in this World, and begin to promise myself much Gratification of my Curiosity in soon visiting some other.[1543]

Sunday, April 20, 1788. Today, John Adams departs England for New York aboard the *Lucretia*, Captain Callahan.[1544]

WEDNESDAY, JUNE 11, 1788

✢ The Pennsylvania Gazette ✢

At a meeting of the friends of the Federal Government at Epple's Tavern on Saturday evening, it was unanimously agreed that a Procession [parade] ought to take place in Philadelphia in the event of the Adoption of the proposed [Federal] Constitution by a ninth state . . .

In consequence of the ratification of the federal government by Pennsylvania (says a corespondent), a convention will be absolutely necessary to alter our state constitution . . .

If Pennsylvania's Federalists can get their state to ratify the proposed British-style federal Constitution, they should also be able to get Pennsylvania to abandon Ben Franklin's Pennsylvania Constitution of 1776, with its single-chamber legislature, and adopt John Adams' more aristocratic British model.

Saturday, July 12, 1788. Today, from Paris, the Duc de La Rochefoucauld writes Benjamin Franklin:

> *While you are busy in these great matters, France, whom you left talking zealously of liberty for other nations, begins to think that a small portion of this same liberty would be a good thing for herself. Good works for the last thirty years, and your good example for the last fourteen, have enlightened us much* . . .[1545]

Thursday, July 31, 1788. Today, George Washington answers a letter from *American Magazine* publisher Noah Webster on the planning for Yorktown:

> *I . . . can only answer very briefly, and generally from memory: that a combined operation of the land and naval forces of France in America, for the year 1781, was preconcerted the year before . . . that it was determined by me (nearly twelve months beforehand) at all hazards to give out and cause it to be believed by the highest military as well as civil Officers that New York was the destined place of attack, for the important purpose of inducing the Eastern & Middle States to make greater exertions in furnishing specific supplies than they otherwise would have done, as well as for the interesting purpose of rendering the enemy less prepared elsewhere . . . I can add that it never was in contemplation to attack New York* . . .[1546]

Is this the man who can't tell a lie? John Adams:

> *Colonel [Timothy] Pickering made me a visit [on one occasion], and, finding me alone, spent a long evening with me. We had a multitude of conversation. I had then lately purchased [a book] . . . and there was a letter in it that he was extremely unhappy to see there. I asked what letter is that? Col. Pickering answered, "It is a letter from General Washington [of July 31, 1788]"* . . .
>
> *Colonel Pickering said he was extremely sorry to see that letter in print. I asked him why? What do you see amiss in it? What harm will it do? Col. Pickering said, "It will injure General Washington's character." How will it injure him? Stratagems are lawful in war. Colonel Pickering answered me, "It will hurt his moral character. He has been generally thought to be honest . . . [T]hat letter is false, and I know it to be so. I knew him to be vain and weak and ignorant, but I thought he was well-meaning; but that letter is a lie, and I know it to be so." I objected and queried.*
>
> *Pickering explained and descended to particulars. He said it was false in Washington to pretend that he had meditated beforehand to de-*

ceive the enemy and to that end to deceive the officers and soldiers of his own army; that he had seriously meditated an attack upon New York for near a twelve month and had made preparations at an immense expense for that purpose. Washington never had a thought of marching to the southward, till the Count de Grasse's fleet appeared upon the coast. He knew it, and Washington knew it; consequently that letter was a great disgrace . . .

[H]e dwelt . . . on Washington's ignorance, weakness, and vanity. He was so ignorant that he had never read anything, not even on military affairs; he could not write a sentence of grammar, nor spell his words, &c., &c., &c. To this I objected. I had been in Congress with Washington in 1774 and in May and part of June 1775 and read all his letters to Congress in 1775, 1776, 1777 and had formed a quite different opinion of his literary talent. His letters were well written and well spelled. Pickering replied, "He did not write them, he only copied them." Who did write them? "His secretaries and aides . . ."[1547]

Friday, August 8, 1788. Today, in France, prompted by cries for popular participation in a decision to impose new taxes, the King of France calls for representatives of the three French estates (including the Third Estate, meaning the common people) to meet next May at the court at Versailles.[1548]

Saturday, August 9, 1788. Today, from Paris, U.S. Minister to France Thomas Jefferson writes Virginia Governor James Monroe:

This nation is at present under great internal agitation. The authority of the crown on one part and that of the parliaments on the other . . . The moderation of government has . . . [yielded] daily one right after another to the nation. They have given them provincial assemblies which . . . stand somewhat in the place of our state assemblies. They have . . . acknowledged the king cannot lay a new tax without the consent of the states general, and they will call the states general the next year. The object of this body when met will be a bill of rights, . . . a national assembly . . . and some other matters of that kind. So that I think it probable this country will within two or three years be in enjoiment of a tolerably free constitution . . .

I heartily rejoice that 9 states have accepted the new [U.S.] constitution . . . This constitution forms a basis which is good, but not perfect. I hope the states will annex to it a bill of rights, securing those which are essential against the federal government; particularly freedom of religion, freedom of the press . . .[1549]

Tuesday, August 12, 1788. Today, in Philadelphia, Benny Bache turns nineteen years old. Under the watchful eye of his grandfather, he manages the printing house and foundry his grandfather built.

Friday, October 24, 1788. Today, from Philadelphia, Benjamin Franklin writes his friend M. le Veillard, now the Mayor of Passy:[1550]

Never was any measure so thoroughly discussed as our proposed new [federal] Constitution . . . You seem to me to be so apprehensive about our President's being perpetual. Neither he nor we have any such intention. What danger there may be of such an event we are all aware of . . . As to the two chambers [of the legislature], I am of your opinion that one alone would be better . . .[1551]

Saturday, January 24, 1789. Today, in France, the French government announces rules by which delegates to the Estates General will be elected and provides that each body of electors may send a *cahier de doléances* (list of grievances) with its delegates for the government to consider.[1552]

Wednesday, February 4, 1789. Today, in the United States, presidential electors, chosen by state legislatures, cast their votes for President and Vice President of the United States.

Monday, March 2, 1789. Today, Benjamin Franklin writes,

I am too old to follow printing again myself, but, loving the business, I have brought up my grandson Benjamin to it, and have built and furnished a printing-house for him, which he now manages under my eye.[1553]

Friday, March 13, 1789. Today, in Paris, Thomas Jefferson writes Francis Hopkinson with his concerns about the newly ratified Constitution of the United States:

I disapproved from the first moment . . . the want of a bill of rights to guard liberty against the legislative as well as executive branches of the [federal] government, that is to say, to secure freedom in religion, freedom of the press, freedom from monopolies, freedom from unlawful imprisonment, freedom from a permanent military, and a trial by jury in all cases determinable by the laws of the land. I disapproved also the perpetual reeligibility of the President . . . With respect to the declaration of rights, I suppose the majority of the United states are of my opinion . . . These my opinions I wrote within a few hours after I had read the constitution . . .

P. S. Affectionate respects to Dr. Franklin . . .[1554]

Monday, April 6, 1789. Today, in New York, the electoral votes for President and Vice President of the United States are counted. Sixty-nine electors (chosen by the states) have unanimously cast one of their two electoral votes to make George Washington the first President of the United States. They have cast less than half (thirty-four) of their remaining votes for John Adams, yet that number is the second highest and so makes him Vice President. The Federalists assume power. Benny Bache will write:

Tall and imposing in his person, silent and reserved in his manners, opulent in his fortune, and attached by a high post to a success-

ful cause: Mr. Washington . . . found indeed no rival to his reputation in his own particular army; for he had condemned his own army to such complete inaction or had allowed so little opportunity to those who commanded under him to become signalized (unless by misfortunes occasioned chiefly by his own bad arrangements) that he had become the sole remarkable person in it.[1555]

Benjamin Rush will recall to his friend, John Adams,

Feeling no unkindness to G. Washington during the years of the war after 1777 and after the peace, I cordially joined in all the marks of gratitude and respect showed to him . . . At no time after the year 1777, however, did I believe him to be the "first in war" in our country. In addition to the testimonies of Stephen, Reed, and Mifflin, I had directly or indirectly the testimonies of [General Nathanael] Greene, [Alexander] Hamilton, Colonel [Tench], your son-in-law, and of many of the most intelligent officers who served under him to the contrary. Nor have I ever dared to join in the profane and impious incense which has been ever offered to his patriotism and moral qualities by many of our citizens. Were I to mention all that I have heard of his "heart," and from some of his friends too, it would appear that he was not possessed of all the divine attributes that have been ascribed to him. But enough of this hateful subject! . . . I earnestly request that you destroy this letter as soon as you read it. I do not wish it to be known that General W.[ashington] was deficient . . .[1556]

Except for Timothy Pickering's indiscretions, Washington's former army officers won't tarnish his image. John Adams:

That Washington was not a schollar is certain. That he was too illiterate, unlearned, unread for his station and reputation is equally beyond dispute. He had derived little Knowledge from Reading, none from Travel . . .

The most experienced and scientific Officers about him, Lee, Gates, Steuben, Conway, etc. thought little of him: some of them despised him too much. Green, Knox, Clinton, without thinking highly of him . . . were his sworn and invariable Friends. Mifflin, one of his Generals, Hamilton, Burr have been very discreet, Pickering, his Quarter Master, has at times been outrageous . . .[1557]

WEDNESDAY, APRIL 8, 1789

✦ The Pennsylvania Gazette ✦

AN ADDRESS from the Subscribers, [certain] Members of the Legislature of the Commonwealth of Pennsylvania . . .

Friends and Fellow-Citizens!

[A] majority of your present legislators have entered into a number

*of resolutions calculated to induce you to call a convention for the pur-
pose of altering the constitution of this commonwealth . . . You can easily
remember that this is the fourth attempt of the same aristocratic party
to betray you into a voluntary surrender of your liberties by the alteration
of your frame of government . . . [Y]ou can all see that the establishment
of a second house of the legislature, in which the better born may be
separated from the common countrymen in their deliberations, which is
the avowed object of the opposers of your simple constitution . . . will
greatly increase the expences and burdens of your government . . .
[C]alling a convention to alter your form of government [because] . . .
" . . . it is in many cases contradictory to the federal constitution of the
United States;" is equally frivolous . . .*

THOMAS KENNEDY, THOMAS BEALE [&c.]

Like Benjamin Franklin, the Pennsylvania Constitution of 1776 will soon be
gone.

Wednesday, April 15, 1789. Today, in New York City, John Fenno publishes
his first issue of his Federalist newspaper, the *Gazette of the United States.*[1558]

Tuesday, April 21, 1789. Today, at the opening session of the new United
States Senate, Vice President John Adams addresses the members, including:

> *It is with satisfaction that I congratulate the people of America on
> the formation of a National Constitution . . . on the acquisition of a
> House of Representatives chosen by themselves, of a Senate thus com-
> posed by their own State Legislatures, and on the prospect of an exec-
> utive authority in the hands of one whose portrait I shall not presume
> to draw.*[1559]

Friday, May 1, 1789. Today, in the U.S. Senate, Pennsylvania Senator William
Maclay objects to the way John Adams refers to the President as *"His most
gracious . . ."* William Maclay:

> *I must speak or nobody would. "Mr. President [of the Senate, John
> Adams], we have lately had a hard struggle for our liberty against
> kingly authority . . . The words [you have] prefixed to the President's
> speech ["His most gracious speech"] are the same that are usually
> placed before the speech of his Britannic Majesty. I know they will give
> offence . . . I therefore move that they be struck out . . ."*
>
> *Mr. Adams rose in his chair and expressed the greatest surprise
> that anything should be objected to on account of its being taken from
> the practice of that [British] Government under which we had lived so
> long and happily formerly . . . that, for his part he was one of the first
> in the late contest [the American Revolution] and, if he could have
> thought of this, he never would have drawn his sword . . .*
>
> *The unequivocal declaration that he would never have drawn his
> sword, etc. has drawn my mind to the following remarks: That the*

motives of the actors in the late Revolution were various can not be doubted. The abolishing of royalty, the extinguishment of patronage and dependencies attached to that form of government, were the exalted motives of many . . . Yet there were not wanting a party whose motives were different. They wished for the . . . creation of a new monarchy in America, and to form niches for themselves in the temple of royalty.

This spirit manifested itself strongly among the officers at the close of the war . . . This spirit they developed in the Order of the Cincinnati, where I trust it will spend itself in a harmless flame and soon become extinguished. That Mr. Adams should, however, so unequivocally avow this motive . . . [1560]

Tuesday, May 5, 1789. Today, outside Paris, a French monarch addresses representatives of the common people (the Third Estate) for the first time in nearly three centuries. Twelve hundred deputies of the three Estates General of France (the clergy, nobility, and common people) are assembled for the opening ceremony at the Hall of Menus in the Versailles Palace. France's middle class, through its representatives, must face the national debt which, as King Louis XVI explains, was accumulated "in an honorable cause."[1561]

WEDNESDAY, MAY 6, 1789

❧ The Pennsylvania Gazette ❧

NEW-YORK, May 1 . . .
Yesterday [April 30] at two o'clock was solemnly Inaugurated into office, our ILLUSTRIOUS PRESIDENT.
The ceremony was begun by the following procession from the Federal State-House to the President's house, viz.
Troop of Horse.
Assistants.
Committee of Representatives.
Committee of Senate.
Gentlemen to be admitted in the Senate Chamber.
Gentlemen in coaches.
Citizens on foot.
On their arrival, the President joined the procession in his carriage and four, and the whole moved through the principal streets to the State-House . . .

When the van reached the State-House, the troops opening their ranks formed an avenue, through which, after alighting, the President advancing to the door, was conducted to the Senate Chamber, where he was received by both branches of Congress, and by them accompanied to the balcony or outer gallery in front of the State-House, which was decorated with a canopy and curtains of red interstreaked with white for the formal occasion. In this manner the oath of office required by the constitution was administered by the Chancellor of this state, and the illustrious WASHINGTON thereupon declared by the said Chancellor PRESIDENT OF THE UNITED STATES.

Today, May 6th, in Paris, Thomas Jefferson advises the Marquis de Lafayette, who is participating in the meeting of the Estates General, to disregard fellow noblemen and to serve the common people (the Third Estate):

> *Your principles are decidedly with the tiers etat [third estate], and your instructions against them . . . You will in the end go over wholly to the tiers etat, because it will be impossible for you to live in a constant sacrifice of your own sentiments to the prejudices of the Noblesse [nobility] . . .* [1562]

Saturday, May 9, 1789. Today, in the United States Senate, Pennsylvania Senator William Maclay records debate concerning a title for America's chief executive:

> At length the committee came in and reported a title—*His Highness, the President of the United States of America and Protector of the Rights of the Same.*
>
> Mr. Few had spoke a word . . . I got up and expressed my opinion . . . Mr. Reed got up . . . Mr. Strong spoke . . . Mr. Dalton, after some time, spoke . . . Mr. Izard . . . was for a postponement. I could see that the President [of the Senate, John Adams] kindled at him . . .
>
> Up now got the President [of the Senate, John Adams], and for forty minutes did he harangue us from the chair . . . On he got on his favorite topic of titles, and over the old ground of the immense advantage, of the absolute necessity of them.
>
> Gentlemen [he said], I must tell you that it is you and the President that have the making of titles . . . [1563]

John Adams will lead the Senate (the "aristocratic chamber") to seek titles, but the House of Representatives (the "democratical chamber") will oppose them. Following a deadlock of the two houses,[1564] no legislation for special titles will be adopted.

Monday, May 11, 1789. Today, in the United States Senate, John Adams suffers some embarrassment from the harangue he delivered Saturday on titles. Pennsylvania Senator William Maclay:

> *[S]undry gentlemen of the Senate [were] dissatisfied with our Vice-President . . . His grasping after titles has been observed by everybody. Mr. Izard, after describing his air, manner, deportment, and personal figure in the chair, concluded by applying the title of [His] Rotundity to him.* [1565]

Saturday, May 23, 1789. Today, U.S. Congressman James Madison of Virginia writes his friend, Thomas Jefferson, in Paris:

J. Adams espoused the cause of titles with great earnestness . . . The projected title was—His Highness the President of the U.S. and protector of their liberties. Had the project succeeded it would have . . . given a deep wound to our infant government.[1566]

Thursday, June 4, 1789. Today, Dr. Benjamin Rush writes his friend John Adams:

I find you and I must agree not to disagree, or we must cease to discuss political questions . . .

Why should we accelerate the progress of our government towards monarchy? Every part of the conduct of the Americans tends to it. We shall have but one deliverer, one great, or one good man in our country. For my part, I cannot help ascribing the independence and new government to thousands . . .

I shall add . . . that I am as much a republican as I was in 1775 and 6, that I consider hereditary monarchy and aristocracy as rebellion against nature, that I abhor titles and everything that belongs to the pageantry of government . . .[1567]

Tuesday, June 9, 1789. Today, John Adams writes Benjamin Rush,

No! you and I will not cease to discuss political questions . . .

That every Part of the Conduct and Feelings of the Americans tends to that species of Republick called a limited Monarchy I agree. They were born and brought up in it . . .

I also am as much a Republican as I was in 1775. I do not "consider hereditary Monarchy or Aristocracy as Rebellion against Nature." On the contrary, I esteem them both as Institutions of admirable wisdom and exemplary Virtue in a certain stage of Society in a great nation. The only Institutions that can possibly preserve the laws and Liberties of the People, and I am clear that America must resort to them as an asylum during discord, Seditions and Civil War, and that at no very distant period of time. I shall not live to see it—but you may. I think it therefore impolitick to cherish prejudices against Institutions which must be kept in view as the hope of our Posterity. I am by no means for attempting any such thing at present. Our country is not ripe for it in many respects, and it is not yet necessary, but our ship must ultimately land on that shore or be cast away.

I do not abhor Titles, nor the Pageantry of Government. If I did I should abhor Government itself, for there never was, and never will be, because there never can be, any government without Titles and Pageantry.[1568]

Wednesday, June 17, 1789. Today, in France, representatives of the Third Estate (the common people) refuse to recognize a second "upper chamber" of nobility and clergy to veto their decisions. They declare that they constitute the sole National Assembly, that they fully represent the general will of the nation, that existing taxes are null and void until ratified by their assembly, and that the nobility and clergy must join them. As I write in my history,

> From the moment of this event . . . may justly be dated the commencement of the revolution—when privileged orders and feudal distinctions—the stupendous fabric of ecclesiastical authority and the magnificence and power of the hoary monarchy of France, crumbled into ruin beneath the breath of a nation awakened into action . . .[1569]

Friday, June 19, 1789. Today, John Adams writes Benjamin Rush,

> What do you mean . . . by Republican systems? . . . You seem determined not to allow a limited monarchy to be a republican system, which it certainly is, and the best that has ever been tryed . . .
>
> How can you say that Factions have been few in America? Have they not rendered Property insecure? . . . have not Majorities voted property out of the pocketts of others into their own with the most decided Tyranny?[1570]

Today, John Adams also writes Major General Benjamin Lincoln:

> Tho I cannot say that there is no Colour for the objection against the Constitution that it has too large a proportion of Aristocracy in it, yet there are two checks to the Senate evidently designed and prepared, The House of Representatives on one side and the President on the other. Now the only feasible remedy against this danger [of too much Aristocracy] is to compleat the Equilibrium by making . . . the President [with a full veto] as independent of the other Branches as they are of him. But the Cry of Monarchy is kept up in order to deter the People from succoring to the true Remedy and to force them into . . . an entire reliance on the popular branch and a rejection of the other two.[1571]

Friday, June 26, 1789. Today, John Adams writes that government leaders must have titles:

> Why will you afflict the modesty of any gentlemen by expecting that they will give themselves titles[?] They expect that you their creators will do them honor. They . . . will not be offended if you assert your own majesty by giving your own representatives in the executive authority the title of majesty. Many . . . think Highness not high enough, among whom I am one . . .[1572]

Sunday, July 5, 1789. Today, Vice President John Adams writes Benjamin Rush,

> You say you "abhor all titles." . . . There is no person and no Society to whom Forms and Titles are indifferent . . . [W]e shall find national Titles essential to national Government . . . It is to make offices and laws respected; and not so much by the virtuous parts of the Commu-

nity, as by the *Profligate, the criminal and abandoned, who have little reverence for Reason, Right or Law, divine or human. They are over-awed by Titles frequently, when Laws and Punishments cannot restrain them . . .*[1573]

Saturday, July 11, 1789. Today, from Paris, U.S. Minister to France Thomas Jefferson sends Tom Paine news of the French Revolution:

> *A conciliatory proposition from the king having been accepted by the Nobles . . . the Commons [Third Estate] voted it to be a refusal and proceeded to give a last invitation to the clergy and nobles to join them . . . This done, they declared themselves a National Assembly, resolved that all the subsisting taxes were illegally imposed . . . The aristocratical party made a furious effort . . . The Common chamber (that is the Tiers [Third Estate] and the majority of clergy who joined them) bound themselves together by a solemn oath never to separate till they had accomplished the work for which they met. Paris and Versailles were thrown into tumult and riot . . . 48 of the Nobles left their body and joined the common chamber . . . [T]he next day the king wrote a letter with his own hand to the Chamber of Nobles and the minority of the Clergy, desiring them to join immediately the common chamber. They did so, and thus the victory of the Tiers [Third Estate] became complete . . . The National Assembly then (for this is the name they take) . . . are now in complete and undisputed possession of the sovereignty. The executive and aristocracy are now at their feet: the mass of the nation, the mass of the clergy, and the army are with them. They have prostrated the old government and are now beginning to build a new one from the foundation.*[1574]

Tuesday, July 14, 1789. Today, in an act of violence that will come to symbolize the French Revolution, a throng of ordinary French citizens seize Paris' old arsenal and prison (the Bastille), kill its guards, and release its prisoners. Henceforth, the French Revolution will be celebrated annually on July 14th ("Bastille Day").[1575]

Thursday, July 16, 1789. Today, Paris delegates to the French Assembly proclaim the hero of the American Revolution the Marquis de Lafayette as "commander of the militia" (now the National Guard).[1576] Lafayette has designed a new emblem of democracy for his militiamen, the king, and everyone else to wear. It's a tricolored cockade. Colors are red, white, and blue.[1577]

Friday, July 17, 1789. Today, Thomas Jefferson writes Tom Paine:

> *The people of Paris forced the prisons of St. Lazare, where they got some arms. On the 14th, they took the Invalids, and Bastille . . . The city committee is determined to embody 48,000 Bourgeois and named the Marquis de la Fayette commander in chief.*[1578]

Friday, July 24, 1789. Today, in the United States, John Adams writes Benjamin Rush:

> *I deny that there is or ever was in Europe a more free Republic than England or that any liberty on earth ever equalled English liberty . . . I agree with you that hereditary Monarchy and hereditary Aristocracy ought not yet to be attempted in this Country—and that three balanced Branches ought to be at stated Periods elected by the People. This must and will and ought to continue till intrigue and Corruption, Faction and Sedition shall appear in those elections to such a degree as to render hereditary Institutions a Remedy against a greater evil . . .*
>
> *The Nation ought not to degrade its conductor by too low a Title . . . I totally deny that there is any Thing in Reason or religion against Titles proportioned to Rank and Truth, and I affirm that they are indispensably necessary to give Dignity and Energy to Government . . .*
>
> *The most modest Title you can give [your national Conductor] in any reasonable Proportion to the wealth, Power, and population of this Country and to the constitutional authority and Dignity of his office is "His Majesty, the President." This is my opinion, and I scorn to be hypocrite enough to disguise it.*[1579]

Wednesday, July 29, 1789. Today, from Paris, Thomas Jefferson answers James Madison's letter of May 23rd:

> *The [American] President's title as proposed by the senate was the most superlatively ridiculous thing I ever heard of. It is a proof the more of the justice of the character given by Doctr. Franklin of my friend [John Adams]: "Always an honest man, often a great one, but sometimes absolutely mad." I wish [John Adams] could have been here [in Paris] during the late scenes. If he could then have had one fibre of aristocracy left in his frame, he would have been a proper subject for bedlam.*[1580]

Tuesday, August 4, 1789. Tonight, two noblemen, the Viscount Louis-Marie-Antoine de Noailles (Lafayette's brother-in-law, who volunteered with him in the American Revolution) and the Duc de La Rochefoucauld (president of the Constituent Assembly, who first translated and published Ben Franklin's Pennsylvania Constitution of 1776 in France), both admirers of Franklin and America, lead the French Constituent Assembly to end feudalism and attendant seignorial privilege in France. Property will no longer create special rights or personal servitudes.[1581] As I write in my history,

> *several of the nobility . . . offered, as a sacrifice on the altar of liberty, those privileges the late declaration had left them; declaring that they considered the title of a citizen of France as the most honourable dignity they could possess.*[1582]

Sunday, August 9, 1789. Today, in Paris, Thomas Jefferson passes on to William Carmichael, former assistant to the American commissioners, some news Jefferson received from America:

> *The Senate and Representatives differed [and deadlocked] about the title of the President . . . I hope the terms of Excellency, Honor, Worship, Esquire forever disappear from among us from that moment. I wish that "Mr." would follow . . .*
>
> *Congress were to proceed . . . to propose amendments to the new [U.S. federal] constitution. The principal would be the annexing a Declaration of Rights to satisfy the minds of all on the subject of their liberties . . .*
>
> *To detail you the events of this country . . . The [French] legislature will certainly have no hereditary branch, probably not even a select one (like our Senate) . . . [V]ery many are for a single house, and particularly the Turgoists . . . Their representation will be an equal one, in which every man will elect . . .*[1583]

Wednesday, August 12, 1789. Today, in Philadelphia, Benjamin Franklin Bache turns twenty years old. He spends much time at the bedside of his eighty-four-year-old grandfather, transcribing the last chapter of Ben Franklin's autobiography.[1584]

Sunday, August 23, 1789. Today, in France, the French Constituent Assembly sets forth principles to guide a new French constitution. As I write in my history,

> *It was on the twenty-third that the majority completed the decrees which were to form the foundation of a constitution for France and condensed them for general information in the following important nineteen resolutions—1st. That all power originally was derived from the people, and would continue to flow from that source alone . . . 4th. That the national assembly shall be permanent. 5th. That the national assembly shall be composed of only one chamber. 6th. That the return [term] of the deputies to the national assemblies shall be for two years . . . 10th. The king can refuse his assent to any act of the legislative body. 11th. In that case where the king shall interpose his negative, that negative shall be considered only as suspensive. 12th. The negative of the king shall cease to exist on the election of the national assembly which next follows that in which the law was proposed. 5th. No tax or contribution in kind, or in money, can be levied . . . by any other means than by an express decree of the assembly . . .*[1585]

Thursday, August 27, 1789. Today, in Paris, a majority of the new French Constituent Assembly adopts a "Declaration of the Rights of Man" which the Marquis de Lafayette drafted with the help of U.S. Minister to France Thomas Jefferson.[1586] From the "Rights of Man" (as I report in my history):

1st. Men are born and always continue free and equal in respect of their rights; civil [i.e., any] distinctions, therefore, can only be founded on public utility . . .

3dly. That the people composing the nation are essentially the source of all sovereignty . . .

6thly. The law is an expression of the will of the community; all citizens have a right to concur, either personally or by their representatives in its formation . . .

10thly. No man ought to be molested on account of his opinions, not even of his religious opinions . . .

11thly. The unrestrained communication of thought and opinions being one of the most precious rights of man, every citizen may speak, write, and publish freely . . .[1587]

The Constitution of the United States of America has yet to have such a Declaration or Bill of Rights to limit the power of government.

Friday, August 28, 1789. Today, in Paris, U.S. Minister to France Thomas Jefferson writes Congressman James Madison:

Their declaration of rights is finished . . . I think they will . . . take up [the plan] of the constitution . . . [O]urs has been professedly their model . . .

It is impossible to desire better dispositions toward [the United States] than prevail in this [French] assembly. Our proceedings have been viewed as a model for them on every occasion . . . and treated like that of the bible, open to explanation but not to question. I am sorry . . . anything should come from us to check it.

The placing them on a mere [equal] footing with the English will have this effect. When, of two nations, one has spent her blood and money to save us . . . while the other has moved heaven, earth, and hell to exterminate us in war . . . to place these two nations on a[n equal] footing is to give a great deal more to one than to the other, if the maxim be true that to make unequal quantities equal, you must add more to the one than the other. To say, in excuse, that gratitude is never to enter into the motives of national conduct is to revive a principle which has been buried . . . with its kindred principles of the lawfulness of assassination, poison, perjury, &c . . . I know but one code of morality for man whether acting singly or collectively . . .[1588]

Thursday, September 10, 1789. Today, the French Constituent Assembly votes 849 to 89 to have a single-chamber legislature (simply to represent the people) à la Franklin and refuses to have a second, "upper" chamber (like the British House of Lords) to represent nobility or property.[1589]

Friday, September 11, 1789. Today, the French Constituent Assembly votes (673 to 325) to subordinate the wishes of the King of France to the wishes of the single-chamber national legislature, making his veto of legislation subject to override by a simple majority vote in two succeeding legislatures.[1590]

Wednesday, September 16, 1789. Today, from New York, unaware that France has already decided on a single-chamber legislature, John Adams writes a French nobleman, Count Sarsfield:

> *We are very anxious about the state of Europe and that of France in particular. Will the States general claim authority to controul the Crown, or will they be contented to advise it? Mixed in one assembly with the commons, will not the nobles be lost? Out numbered and out acted on all occasions? If in earnest a constitution is to be established, you must separate the Nobles by themselves, and the Commons must be placed in another assembly . . . In short, your government must have three branches and your Executive and Legislative must be ballanced against each other, or you will have confusions. Let my acquaintance, the Marquis of Condorcet, say what he will . . .*[1591]

Friday, September 18, 1789. Today, in New York, U.S. Senator William Maclay writes in his journal:

> *By this and yesterday's papers France seems traveling to the birth of freedom. Her throes and pangs of labor are violent. God give her a happy delivery! Royalty, nobility, and vile pageantry, by which a few of the human race lord it over and tread on the necks of their fellow-mortals, seem likely to be demolished with their kindred Bastille, which is said to be laid in ashes. Ye gods, with what indignation do I review the late attempt of some creatures among us to revive the vile machinery! O Adams, Adams, what a wretch art thou!*[1592]

Saturday, September 26, 1789. Today, with lower-class mob violence (against bread shortages, salt prices, unsafe mining conditions, vestiges of aristocracy, etc.) continuing to increase in Paris and the rest of France, Thomas Jefferson leaves for the United States. He will receive and accept President Washington's invitation to become the first U.S. Secretary of State.[1593]

Thursday, November 5, 1789. Today, in Philadelphia, an aged and ill Benjamin Franklin writes an English correspondent,

> *I hope the fire of liberty, which you mention as spreading itself over Europe, will act upon the inestimable rights of man, as common fire does upon gold; purify without destroying them; so that a lover of liberty may find a country in any part of Christendom.*[1594]

WEDNESDAY, NOVEMBER 11, 1789

⇨ The Pennsylvania Gazette ⇦

HINTS for the Members of [the upcoming PENNSYLVANIA CONSTITUTIONAL] CONVENTION . . .

Of the Executive Branch. I. Your Executive should consist of a single person . . . But the value of this quality (unity) depends on II. The Duration of the appointment . . . putting [it] beyond the reach of every annual gust of folly and of faction . . .

Of the Legislative Branch . . . [E]stablish a legislature of two houses. The upper should represent the property, the lower the population of this State . . .

A F A R M E R

Saturday, November 21, 1789. Today, Pennsylvania opens a state constitutional convention to revise Ben Franklin's Pennsylvania Constitution of 1776. With the new federal Constitution as their model, influential Pennsylvanians want to divide the Pennsylvania state legislature between an upper house to represent property and a lower house to represent the people. Despite illness, Ben Franklin publishes a pamphlet this month that argues for retaining his Pennsylvania Constitution of 1776:

> *I am sorry to see the Signs . . . of a Disposition among some of our People to commence an Aristocracy by giving the Rich a predominancy in Government, a Choice peculiar to themselves in one half of the Legislature to be proudly called the UPPER House, and the other Branch, chosen by the Majority of the People, degraded by the Denomination of the LOWER; and giving this upper House a Permanency of four Years and but two to the lower . . .*[1595]

As Pennsylvanians prepare to abandon Franklinian democracy, Ben Franklin suffers gastrointestinal distress and takes to bed. During his remaining months, his grandson, Benny Bache, will remain at his bedside to transcribe his autobiographical recollections.[1596]

Friday, December 4, 1789. Today, from his bed, Ben Franklin writes his British friend David Hartley,

> *The Convulsions in France are attended with some disagreeable Circumstances; but if by the Struggle she obtains and secures for the Nation its future Liberty, and a good Constitution, a few Years' Enjoyment of those Blessings will amply repair all the Damages their Acquisition may have occasioned. God grant that not only the love of liberty, but a thorough knowledge of the rights of man, may pervade all Nations of the Earth, so that a Philosopher may set his Foot anywhere on its Surface, and say, "This is my Country."*[1597]

Sunday, December 6, 1789. Today, Benny Bache writes his future wife, Peggy Markoe:

> *You may remember that, from the first of our more intimate Acquaintance with one another, I promised to make known . . . every Circumstance that might in the least tend to throw some light on my Character, disposition, Circumstances, Expectations, &c . . .*

In conversing with a Friend of yours . . . [she] betrayed an idea that I was or was to be a Man of Fortune . . . By my conversation, I found my excellent Grand Father the Source of this ideal . . . on supposition of my being a Favorite with him . . .

The trouble [my Grand Father] took in my Education, the circumstance of my being under his care since seven years of age, etc. were undoubtedly Grounds for the supposition to people in General, but to those who are acquainted with Dr. F—— would rather give Rise to an opinion directly contrary; the true one that ought to be entertained by those who wish not to be disappointed. The profession [of printing] I have been brought up in and am intended for might have convinced many that I was never intended to be made a Man of Fortune, but rather to endeavor at becoming one . . .

The Position of the Building erected for containing my Printing Materials . . . might have also had an improper influence [in creating the false impression] . . .[1598]

Thursday, December 24, 1789. Today, the French Constituent Assembly takes a giant step toward religious freedom by decreeing non-Catholics (except Jews) the same civil rights (to vote, to hold office, to become a military officer, etc.) as Catholics.[1599]

Tuesday, February 2, 1790. Today, Vice President John Adams writes a Pennsylvania friend,

I congratulate you on the prospect of a new Constitution for Pensilvania. Poor France I fear will bleed for too exactly copying your old one.

When I see such miserable crudities approved [in France] by such Men as Rochefoucauld and Condorcet, I am disposed to think very humbly of human understanding.[1600]

Monday, February 15, 1790. Today, as President of the Society for the Abolition of Slavery, Benjamin Franklin submits a memorial against slavery to the United States Senate.[1601] A Pennsylvania Senator records,

Attended in Senate. Our Vice-President [Mr. Adams] produced the petitions and memorials of the Abolition Society [against Slavery]. He did it rather with a sneer . . . Izard, in particular, railed at the society; called them fanatics, etc. Butler made a personal attack on Dr. Franklin, and charged the whole proceeding to anti-Federal motives; that the Doctor, when member of the [constitutional] convention, had consented to the Federal compact. Here he was acting in direct violation of it. The whole business was designed to overturn the Constitution . . .[1602]

Saturday, February 27, 1790. Today, Vice President John Adams writes Francis Adrian Vanderkemp, his Mennonist pastor friend from the Netherlands who translated Adams' *Defence of the Constitutions* . . . into Dutch:

I can say for myself, and I believe for most others who have been called "Leading Men" in the late revolution, that we were compelled against our inclinations to cut off the hands which united us to England and that we should have been very happy to have had our grievances resolved, and our dependence continued . . .

I will candidly confess that an hereditary Senate without an hereditary Executive would diminish the Prerogatives of the president and the liberties of the people. But I contend that hereditary descent in both when controlled by an independent representation of the people is better than corrupted, turbulent and bloody elections; and the knowledge you have of the human heart will concur with your knowledge of the history of nations to convince you that elections of Presidents and Senators cannot be long conducted in a populous, oppulent, and commercial nation without corruption, sedition, and civil war.[1603]

WEDNESDAY, MARCH 3, 1790

→ 𝕮𝖍𝖊 𝕻𝖊𝖓𝖓𝖘𝖞𝖑𝖛𝖆𝖓𝖎𝖆 𝕲𝖆𝖟𝖊𝖙𝖙𝖊 ←

The CONSTITUTION of the Commonwealth of PENNSYLVANIA, as altered and amended by the CONVENTION . . . and by them proposed for the consideration of their constituents.

ARTICLE I.

Sect. I. The legislative power of this commonwealth shall be vested in a General Assembly which shall consist of a Senate and House of Representatives.

Sect. 2. The Representatives shall be chosen annually . . .

Sect. 5. The Senators shall be chosen for four years . . . and shall never be . . . more than one third the number of Representatives . . .

Sect. 22. Every bill which shall have passed the House of Representatives and the Senate shall, before it becomes a law, be presented to the Governor . . . [I]f he shall not approve it, he shall return it . . . If two thirds of that House shall agree to pass the bill . . . [a]nd if approved by two-thirds of [the Senate] . . . it shall be a law . . .

ARTICLE II.

Sect. I. The Supreme Executive Power of the commonwealth shall be vested in a Governor . . . Sect. 3. The Governor shall hold his office during three years . . .

Sect. 7. He shall be Commander in Chief of the Army and Navy of this commonwealth . . .

Sect. 8. He shall appoint all officers . . .

By this new Pennsylvania Constitution of 1790, Pennsylvania's government will now resemble the British model that Vice President John Adams so favors. Though Pennsylvania will not institute property qualifications for voters or for office holders, the larger constituencies and longer terms of office for Pennsylvania state senators and for the Pennsylvania governor (as for U.S. senators and for the U.S. President) will have the same effect. The larger a candidate's constituency, the more wealth, reputation, and influence he must have to become known to his constituents. The longer an officeholder's term of office, the less is he immediately accountable to the people and the more he becomes susceptible to wealthy interest groups. Though Pennsylvania continues to have a lower ("people's") house of representatives, with small voting districts and annual elections, this assembly will be subject to veto by an independent governor and by the state senate. Franklin's vision of democratic government has died in Pennsylvania. Soon too will Franklin. Tom Paine:

> The [Pennsylvania] Constitution formed by the [Pennsylvania] Convention of 1776, of which Benjamin Franklin (the greatest and most useful man America has yet produced) was president, had many good points in it which were overthrown by the [Pennsylvania] Convention of 1790 under the pretense of making the Constitution conformable to that of the United States . . .
>
> Investing any individual, by whatever name or official title he may be called, with a negative over the formation of the laws is copied from the English Government, without ever perceiving the inconsistency and absurdity of it when applied to the representative system . . .
>
> The complaint respecting the Senate is the length of its duration, being four years. The sage Franklin has said, "Where annual election ends, tyranny begins" . . .[1604]

Tuesday, March 16, 1790. Today, from Paris, Tom Paine writes:

> With respect to the French revolution, be assured that every thing is going on right. Little inconveniences, the necessary consequences of pulling down and building up, may arise; but even these are much less than ought to have been expected. Our friend, the Marquis [de Lafayette] is . . . acting a great part. I take over with me to London the key to the Bastile, which the Marquis entrusts to my care as his present to General Washington and which I shall send by the first American vessel to New York. It will be yet some months before the new Constitution will be completed, at which time there is to be a procession, and I am engaged to return to Paris to carry the American flag.[1605]

Saturday, March 27, 1790. Today, Vice President Adams writes Francis Adrian Vanderkemp, his friend from the Netherlands:

> With all your compliments and elogiums of my "Defence [of the Constitutions of Government of the United States]," would you believe that neither the whole nor any part of it has been translated into French? . . . No! The popular leaders have views that one assembly may favor but three branches would obstruct. Such is the lot of humanity. A Demagogue may hope to overawe a majority in a single elective assembly, but may dispair of overawing a majority of independent

*hereditary Senators, especially if they can be reinforced in case of ne-
cessity by an independent executive . . .*

*Our experience in America corresponds . . . The last year, a writer
in Boston under the signature of Laro attacked the Governor, Mr. Hancock in a course of Newspapers . . . [A]n accident might have blown
up these coals to a flame, and produced broken heads . . .*

*In the national election this last year, there was a very subtle but a
very daring intrigue . . . Letters were written to the southern states
representing that the Northern States would not vote for Washington
and . . . that Adams was likely to have a unanimous vote, and Washington not; the effect was that [the southern states did not vote for Adams and that] Adams had not even a majority for fear of his having
unanimity. The tendency of these things to confusion is obvious . . .*

*I confess Sir I can think of no remedy, but another [Constitutional]
Convention. When bribery, corruption, intrigue, maneuver, violence,
force, shall render elections too troublesome and too dangerous, another Convention must be called, who may prolong the period of Senators from six years to twelve or twenty or thirty or forty or for life; or if
necessary propose the establishment of hereditary Senators . . . Let the
people of [a state] elect their number of Senators or authorize the President to appoint them to hold their places for life descendible to their
Eldest male heirs . . . And if the election of President should become
terrible, I can conceive of no other method to preserve liberty, but to
have a national convention called for the express purpose of electing
an hereditary President. These appear to me the only hopes of our posterity . . .[1606]*

Sunday, April 4, 1790. Today, Vice President Adams writes his friend Benjamin Rush:

*The History of our [American] Revolution will be one continued Lye
from one end to the other. The essence of the whole will be that Dr.
Franklin's electrical Rod smote the Earth and out sprung General
Washington. That Franklin electrified him with his rod—and thence
forward these two conducted all the Policy, Negotiations, Legislatures
and War . . . If this Letter should be preserved, and read in an hundred years hence, the Reader will say "the envy of this J. A. could not
bear to think of the Truth . . ." . . .*

*Limited Monarchy is founded in Nature. No Nation can adore more
than one Man at a time. It is a happy Circumstance that the object of
our Devotion [George Washington] is so well deserving of it . . .*

*If I said in 1777 that "we should never be qualified for Republican
Government till we were ambitious to be poor" I meant to . . . say that
No Nation under Heaven ever was, now is, or ever will be qualified for
a Republican Government, unless you mean . . . resulting from a Bal-
lance of three powers, the Monarchical, Aristocratical, and Democrati-*

cal. I meant more, and I repeat more explicitly, that Americans are particularly unfit for any Republic but the Aristo-Democratical-Monarchy . . .[1607]

Tuesday, April 13, 1790. Today, Benjamin Rush writes John Adams:

> In my notebook, I have recorded a conversation that passed between Mr. Jefferson and myself on the 17th of March, of which you were the principal subject. We both deplored your attachment to monarchy and both agreed that you had changed your principles since the year 1776 . . .[1608]

Saturday, April 17, 1790. Today, at his home in Franklin Court, Dr. Benjamin Franklin dies at the age of eighty-five. His twenty-year-old grandson, Benjamin Franklin Bache, is at his side.[1609] Benny Bache:

> He has left us, I hope, to live in a happier Country. If he only sleeps, he has forgotten his pain & sleeps quietly.—After an illness of about two Weeks added to his old Complaint he expired . . . [H]e could not resist; he struggled with death, however, longer than his Friends could wish.
>
> Ten Days before his Death, when the Disorder was near its Height, he called me to his Bedside . . . From that day he grew worse & worse, and took but little Food.—In the morning of the 17th of April he refused all sustenance by shaking his head, for the Day before he spoke for the last time.—Whenever I approached his Bed, he held out his hand & having given him mine, he would take & hold it for some time . . . He did not change his Position that Day. And at a quarter before eleven at Night, his breathing was quicker & more feeble . . . This alarmed me and occasioned my calling my Father . . . but he came too late. My Grand Father gave a Sigh, breathed a few seconds & died without Pain.[1610]

WEDNESDAY, APRIL 21, 1790

⇒ The Pennsylvania Gazette ⇐

> On Saturday night last departed this life, in the 85th year of his age, Dr. BENJAMIN FRANKLIN, of this City. His remains will be interred THIS AFTERNOON, at four o'clock, on Christ-Church burial-ground.

Many years ago, Ben Franklin wrote his own epitaph:

The body of
B. Franklin Printer
(Like the Cover of an Old Book

Its Contents torn out
And stript of its Lettering & Gilding)
Lies here, Food for Worms
But the Work shall not be lost;
For it will, (as he believ'd) appear once more,
In a new and more elegant Edition
Revised and corrected
By the Author.[1611]

Thursday, April 22, 1790. Today, in the U.S. House of Representatives, the Annals of Congress report:

BENJAMIN FRANKLIN

Mr. MADISON rose and addressed the House as follows;

Mr. Speaker: As we have been informed, not only through the channel of the newspapers but by a more direct communication, of the decease of an illustrious character whose . . . patriotic exertions have contributed in a high degree to the independence and prosperity of this country . . . I therefore move . . .

"The House being informed of the decease of BENJAMIN FRANKLIN . . . that the members wear the customary badge of mourning for one month."

Which was agreed to.[1612]

Tuesday, April 27, 1790. Today, Thomas Jefferson writes William Short, American chargé d'affaires in Paris:

You will see, in the newspapers which accompany this, the details of Dr. Franklin's death. The house of representatives resolved to wear mourning and do it. The Senate neither resolved it nor do it.[1613]

Under the leadership of Vice President John Adams (who presides as Senate president), the U.S. Senate (the aristocratic branch of government that Benjamin Franklin opposed) refuses to mourn Franklin's death. President Washington also refuses to let the executive branch mourn.[1614] Only the "People's House" (the House of Representatives) and the people themselves will mourn the loss of their champion.

WEDNESDAY, APRIL 28, 1790

☞ The Pennsylvania Gazette ☜

[O]n Wednesday last, at the funeral of our late learned and illustrious citizen Dr. FRANKLIN . . .

The concourse of spectators was greater than ever was known on a like occasion, it is computed that not less than 20,000 persons attended and witnessed the funeral. The order and silence which prevailed, during the procession, deeply evinced the heartfelt sense entertained by all classes of citizens, of the unparalleled virtues, talents and services of the deceased.

Today, April 28th, the *Gazette of the United States* publishes the first of thirty-two articles to appear through next April under the title "Discourses on Davila."[1615] In these articles, Vice President of the United States John Adams resumes his attack on Franklinian democracy which the Marquis de Condorcet (who is an honorary citizen of New Haven, Connecticut) has championed in his recently published *Letters from a Common Citizen of New Haven to a Citizen of Virginia on the Uselessness of Dividing Legislative Power between Several Bodies.*[1616] In this work, Condorcet urges France to adopt a single-chamber legislature with a plural executive chosen by and accountable to that legislature. In today's "Discourse on Davila," Vice President Adams answers Condorcet:

> *[I]f the common people are advised to aim at collecting the whole sovereignty in single national assemblies, as they are by the Duke de la Rochefoucauld and the Marquis of Condorcet; or at the abolition of the regal executive authority; or at a division of the executive power, as they are by a posthumous publication of the Abbé de Mably, they will fail of their desired liberty . . . [I]t is a sacred truth, and as demonstrable as any proposition whatsoever, that a sovereignty in a single assembly must necessarily, and will certainly be exercised by a majority, as tyrannically as any sovereignty was ever exercised by kings or nobles.*[1617]
>
> *If the people have not the understanding and public virtue enough, and will not be persuaded of the necessity of supporting an independent executive authority, an independent senate, and an independent judiciary power, as well as an independent house of representatives, all pretensions to a balance are lost, and with them all hopes of security to our dearest interests, all hopes of liberty.*[1618]

Saturday, May 1, 1790. Today, from London, Tom Paine writes President George Washington:

> *Our very good friend, the Marquis de Lafayette, has intrusted to my care the key of the Bastille, and a drawing handsomely framed, representing the demolition of that detestable prison, as a present to your Excellency . . . I feel myself happy in being the person through whom the Marquis has conveyed this early trophy of the spoils of despotism, and the first ripe fruits of American principles transplanted into Europe . . .*
>
> *I returned from France to London about five weeks ago; and I am engaged to return to Paris, when the Constitution shall be proclaimed, and to carry the American flag in the procession. I have not the least doubt of the final and complete success of the French Revolution. Little ebbings and flowings, for and against, the natural companions of rev-*

olutions, sometimes appear, but the full current of it is, in my opinion, as fixed as the Gulf Stream . . .[1619]

Saturday, May 22, 1790. Today, in the French Constituent Assembly, as I write in my history,

it was decreed that the right of peace and war belonged to the nation, and that war could not be declared but by a decree of the national assembly . . .[1620]

Friday, June 11, 1790. Today, Vice President John Adams writes,

The great and perpetual distinction in civilized societies has been between the rich who are few and the poor who are many . . . The inference of wisdom is that neither poor nor the rich should ever be suffered to be masters. They should have equal power . . . The French must finally become my disciples . . .

In this country the pendulum had vibrated too far to the popular side, driven by men without experience or judgment, and horrid ravages have been made upon property by arbitrary multitudes or majorities of multitudes. France has severe trials to endure from the same cause. Both have found, or will find, that to place property at the mercy of a majority who have no property is "committere agnum lupo." My fundamental maxim of government is never to trust the lamb to the wolf.[1621]

Today, in Paris, on the floor of the French Constituent Assembly, the Comte de Mirabeau announces Franklin's death:

Franklin is dead. He has returned to the bosom of the Divinity, the genius who freed America and shed torrents of light upon Europe . . .

The sciences owe Franklin their tears, but it is Liberty—it is the French people who should mourn him most deeply; the liberty that we enjoy he aided us to attain, and the sparks of his genius glow in the Constitution that is our boast . . .

Congress has ordered in the fourteen confederated states a mourning period of two months . . .

Would it not be worthy of you, gentlemen, to . . . participate in this homage rendered before the entire world to the rights of man and to the philosopher who has contributed most to spreading them throughout the world . . . Free and enlightened Europe owes at least a token of remembrance and regret to one of the greatest men who have ever served philosophy and liberty.

I propose that it be decreed that the National Assembly for three days wear mourning for Benjamin Franklin.[1622]

The Duc de La Rochefoucauld seconds Mirabeau's motion. The French Constituent Assembly will notify the U.S. Congress of its decision to mourn Franklin's death.[1623] Thomas Jefferson:

No greater proof of his estimation in France can be given than the late letters of condoleance on his death from the National assembly of that country and the community of Paris, to the President of the U.S. and to Congress, and their public mourning on that event. It is I believe the first instance of that homage having been paid by a public body of one nation to a private citizen of another.[1624]

This year, the Marquis de Luchet publishes a list of those responsible for the French Revolution. He writes:

FRANKLIN. It is impossible to give the tableau of a revolution without including this immortal name. This philosophical republican enlightened the heroes of liberty. Before him, the majority of publicists had reasoned like educated slaves of their masters; like Montesquieu [who argued for checks and balances in government] they used all their wit to justify the status quo and to coat our institutions with deceptive poison; he alone, studying the natural rights of man, sweeping away the dust and sand, that is, the external circumstances of weakness and poverty, of inequality, of all kinds of aristocracy, discovered the foundations of society; he demonstrated that the edifice was unsound wherever it was not based on the common accord of men and reciprocal agreements. No, one may never speak of liberty without paying a tribute of homage to this immortal defender of human nature.[1625]

Sunday, June 13, 1790. Today, in France, in an address before the Society of 1789, the Duc de La Rochefoucauld pays tribute to Benjamin Franklin:

[T]he world has not [adequately] reflected on Franklin's bold legislative effort. Having declared their independence and placing themselves in rank of nations, each of the different colonies, today the United States of America, chose a new structure of government. Maintaining their old admiration for the British constitution, nearly all of these new states composed their governments with the same British elements, variously modified. FRANKLIN alone, ridding the political machine of its numerous wheels, of the admired counterweights which complicated it, proposed to reduce it to the simplicity of a single legislative body. This grand idea frightened the Pennsylvania legislators, but the philosopher reassured half and caused the adoption of this principle, which THE FRENCH NATIONAL ASSEMBLY has made the basis for the French constitution.[1626]

Saturday, June 19, 1790. Today, in France, the *Journal de la Société de 1789* publishes the Duc de La Rochefoucauld's explanation of why he prefers a single-chamber legislature:

Franklin was the first to propose to put the idea into practice: the respect the Pennsylvanians bore him made them adopt it, but it alarmed the other states and even the constitution of Pennsylvania has since been changed. In Europe this opinion has had more success . . . I dare admit that I was one of the small number of those who was struck by the beauty of the simple plan which he had delineated and that I did not need to change my opinion when the judgment of the profound thinkers and eloquent orators who have treated the subject before the National Assembly led that body to establish as a principle of the French constitution that the legislation shall be entrusted to a single body of representatives . . . France will not retrogress toward a more complicated system, and doubtless she will have the glory of maintaining the one she has established.[1627]

Other leaders of the French Revolution testify to their admiration for Franklin's Pennsylvania Constitution of 1776. Ben Franklin's friend,[1628] Jacques-Pierre Brissot de Warville:[1629]

> *I regard the Constitution of Pennsylvania as the model of an excellent government . . .*
> *The code of Pennsylvania will prove that America had philosophers and statesmen when she threw off the yoke of Great Britain . . .*
> *There they exclude forever the authority of a single person. There they confine the power to make laws to a general assembly of the representatives of the state and give the right to enforce the laws to a removable council . . .*[1630]

Today, the French Constituent Assembly abolishes all titles and coats of arms in France.[1631] As I write in my history,

> *While titles and distinctions remained . . . the constitution and its preamble appeared but an unsubstantial theory . . . M. Foucault opposed the motion, as tending to destroy the most powerful motives to emulation—"What he asked would you do with the man whose brevet recited— that he was created a count for saving the state?" M. La Fayette instantly replied, "I would omit the word 'created a count' and insert only that he had saved the state." . . . [T]he viscount of Noaille concurred . . . "We do not speak of . . . the marquis Franklin, but of Benjamin Franklin . . ." . . . Thus in one moment were three hundred thousand persons torn from those proud titles inherited or acquired which had monopolized into their hands all the places of trust and honor of a great nation . . .*[1632]

Saturday, July 24, 1790. Today, in France, the *Journal de la Société de 1789* attacks the idea of a hereditary hierarchy in France by publishing Ben Franklin's letter against George Washington's "Order of the Cincinnati." In the coming years of the French Revolution, other French journals will also cite and translate Franklin's letter.[1633]

Thursday, August 12, 1790. Today, Benny Bache turns twenty-one years old. He is now of age. He will preside over the printing house his grandfather built. He has already announced plans to publish a newspaper.[1634]

Saturday, October 2, 1790. Today, Benny Bache publishes the first issue of the *Philadelphia Aurora.*[1635]

GENERAL ★ AURORA ★ ADVERTISER

PUBLISHED DAILY, BY BENJ. FRANKLIN BACHE . . .

It has been the wish of a number of the Editor's friends to see a Paper established on a plan differing in some respects from those now in circulation . . .

These wishes, coinciding with the advice which the publisher has received from his late Grand Father, suggested the idea of the present work . . .

The Freedom of the Press is the Bulwark of Liberty . . . [T]he Publisher can safely promise that no consideration whatever shall induce him blindly to submit to the influence of any man or set of men: His PRESS SHALL BE FREE.

Friday, December 10, 1790. Today, U.S. Senator William Maclay of Pennsylvania writes in his journal:

> *This day was unimportant in the Senate . . .*
> *A packet arrived a few days ago from France, directed to the President and members of Congress . . . It contained a number of copies of the eulogiums delivered on Dr. Franklin by order of the [French] National Assembly. Our Vice-President [John Adams] looked over the letter some time and then began reading the additions that followed the President [of the French National Assembly]'s name. These appellations of office he chose to call "titles" and then said some sarcastic things against the [French] National Assembly for abolishing titles. I could not help remarking that this whole matter was received and transacted with a coldness and apathy that astonished me; and the letter and all the pamphlets were sent down to the [House of] Representatives as if unworthy of our body [the Senate].*[1636]

Wednesday, January 26, 1791. Today, the U.S. Senate receives a message from the president of the French National Assembly. The Annals report:

> A message was received from . . . the President of the National Assembly of France . . .
> Mr. President,
> *The National Assembly has worn, during three days, mourning for Benjamin Franklin . . .*

The name of Benjamin Franklin will be immortal in the records of Freedom and Philosophy . . .

It will be remembered that every success which he obtained in his important negociations [in France] was applauded and celebrated . . . all over France as so many crowns conferred on genius and virtue.

Even then the sentiment of our rights existed in the bottom of our souls . . .

At last the hour of the French has arrived;—we love to think that the citizens of the United States have not regarded with indifference our first steps towards liberty . . .

We hope they will learn with interest the funeral homage which we have rendered to the Nestor of America.

SIEYES, *President.* [1637]

The U.S. Senate responds coldly to the message! U.S. Senator from Pennsylvania William Maclay writes today in his journal:

A letter from the National Assembly of France, on the death of Franklin, was communicated from them and received [by the Senate] with coldness that was truly amazing. I can not help painting to myself the disappointment that awaits the French patriots . . . anticipating the complimentary echoes of our answers, when we, cold as clay, care not a fig for them, Franklin or freedom. We deserve—what do we deserve ? To be d——d! [1638]

Thomas Jefferson:

On the death of Dr. Franklin, the King & Convention of France went into mourning. So did the House of Reps. of the U.S.: the Senate refused. I proposed to General Washington that the executive department should wear mourning; he declined it . . . [1639]

Wednesday, March 16, 1791. Today, Tom Paine's extraordinary book *The Rights of Man* (Part One) appears in the bookstalls of England. [1640] Excerpts:

As it was impossible to separate the military events which took place in America from the principles of the American Revolution, the publication of those events in France necessarily connected themselves with the principles which produced them. Many of the facts were in themselves principles; such as the declaration of American independence and the treaty of alliance between France and America which recognized the natural right of man and justified resistance to oppression. The then Minister of France, Count Vergennes was not the friend of America . . . Count Vergennes was the personal and social friend of Dr. Franklin; and the Doctor had obtained, by his sensible gracefulness, a sort of influence over him . . .

The situation of Dr. Franklin as Minister from America to France should be taken into the chain of circumstances . . . He was not the diplomatist of a court, but of a MAN. His character as a philosopher had been long established, and his circle of society in France was universal.

Count Vergennes resisted for a considerable time the publication in France of the American [state] Constitutions, translated into the French language; but even in this he was obliged to give way to public opinion and a sort of propriety in admitting to appear what he had undertaken to defend. The American [state] Constitutions were to liberty what a grammar is to language: they define its parts of speech and practically construct them into syntax . . .

When the war closed a vast reinforcement to the cause of liberty spread itself over France by the return of the French officers and soldiers [from America] . . .

[French Finance Minister] M. Necker was displaced in May, 1781 . . . [T]he revenue of France . . . was become unequal to the expenditure . . . because the expenses [with the cost of helping the Americans] had increased; and this was the circumstance which the nation laid hold of to bring forward a revolution.[1641]

[O]ne of the first works of the [French] National Assembly . . . published a Declaration of the Rights of Man . . .

I. Men are born, and always continue, free and equal . . .

II. The end of all political associations is the preservation of the natural and imprescriptible rights of man . . .

III. The nation is essentially the source of all sovereignty . . .[1642]

The two modes of government which prevail in the world are first, government by election and representation: Secondly, government by hereditary succession. The former is generally known by the name of republic; the latter by that of monarchy and aristocracy.

Those two distinct and opposite forms erect themselves on the two distinct and opposite bases of Reason and Ignorance . . .

[W]e have next to consider . . . that species of government which is called mixed government . . . A mixed government is an imperfect everything, cementing and soldering the discordant parts together . . . In mixed governments there is no responsibility· the parts cover each other till responsibility is lost . . . In this rotary motion, responsibility if thrown off from the parts, and from the whole . . .

But in a well constituted republic . . . [t]he parts are not foreigners to each other, like democracy, aristocracy, and monarchy . . .[1643]

Tuesday, April 26, 1791. Today, in Philadelphia, Thomas Jefferson sends a copy of Tom Paine's *Rights of Man* to Jonathan Smith of Philadelphia, whose brother plans to publish an American edition of Paine's work. Jefferson also sends Smith an accompanying note:

> *Th: Jefferson presents his compliments . . . [H]e sends him Mr. Paine's pamphlet. He is extremely pleased to find it will be reprinted here,*

and that something is at length to be publicly said against the political heresies which have sprung up among us. He has no doubt our citizens will rally a second time round the standard of Common Sense.[1644]

In the end, Benny Bache will publish the first American edition of Tom Paine's *Rights of Man* in the *Aurora's* printshop.[1645] To Thomas Jefferson's surprise, however, Benny will choose to include Jefferson's note. Thomas Jefferson:

> *I thought no more of this . . . till the pamphlet appeared, to my astonishment with my note at the head of it . . . [By "political heresies"] I had in view certainly the doctrines of Davila. I tell the writer [John Adams] freely that he is a heretic, but certainly never meant to step into a public newspaper with that in my mouth . . .*[1646]

George Washington's secretary, Tobias Lear, reports John Adams' reaction to Tom Paine's book:

> *After a little hesitation, [Mr. Adams] laid his hand upon his breast, and said in a very solemn manner, "I detest that book and its tendency from the bottom of my heart."*[1647]

Wednesday, April 27, 1791. Today, the *Gazette of the United States* publishes the last of Vice President Adams' "Discourses on Davila":

> Mankind had tried all possible experiment of elections of governors and senates . . . but they had almost unanimously been convinced that hereditary succession was attended with fewer evils than frequent elections. This is the true answer, and the only one, as I believe . . .

Many are outraged at Adams' monarchical and aristocratical preaching. John Adams:

> *The rage and fury of the Jacobinical journals against these discourses [on Davila] increased as they proceeded, intimidated the printer, John Fenno, and convinced me that to proceed would do more hurt than good.*[1648]

No more "Discourses on Davila" will appear. Thomas Jefferson:

> *Mr. Adams had originally been a republican. The glare of royalty and nobility, during his mission to England, had made him believe their fascination a necessary ingredient in government, and Shays' rebellion, not sufficiently understood where he then was, seemed to prove that the absence of want and oppression was not a sufficient guarantee of order. His book on the American constitutions, having made known his political bias, he was taken up by the monarchical federalists in his absence, and, on his return to the U.S., he was by them made to believe that the general disposition of our citizens was favorable to monarchy. He here wrote his Davila, as a supplement to the former work . . .*[1649]

June, 1791. In Paris, Tom Paine writes the Marquis de Condorcet, Paris' leading representative in the Constituent Assembly:

> *Being the citizen of a land that recognizes no majesty but that of the people, no government except that of its own representatives, and no sovereignty except that of the laws, I tender you my services in helping forward the success of those principles which honor a nation and contribute to the advancement of the entire world; and I tend them not only because my country is bound to yours by the ties of friendship and gratitude, but because I venerate the moral and political character of those who have taken part in the present enterprise . . .* [1650]

Wednesday, July 20, 1791. Today, in Philadelphia, the eighth of eleven newspaper articles anonymously signed "Publicola" appears in the *Gazette of the United States* (as well as other newspapers throughout the United States). These articles challenge Tom Paine's *Rights of Man* and depreciate Paine's vision of democracy. Everyone assumes "Publicola" is John Adams (resuming the heresies of his "Discourses on Davila"), but his son, John Quincy Adams, has been writing the "Publicola" articles (presumably with his father's help). From today's "Publicola":

> *VIII . . . Mr. Paine has undertaken to compare the English and French constitutions, upon the article of representation. He has of course admired the latter, and censured the former . . . To attempt to govern a nation like this, under the form of democracy, to pretend to establish over such beings a government which according to Rousseau is calculated only for a republic of Gods, and which requires the continual exercise of virtues beyond the reach of human infirmity, even in its best state; it may possibly be among the dreams of Mr. PAINE, but is what even the [French] National Assembly have not ventured to do . . .* [1651]

Saturday, September 27, 1791. Today, in proof of the inviolability of France's new religious freedom, the Constituent Assembly removes all reservations upon Jews becoming citizens. [1652]

Tuesday, September 30, 1791. Today, in Paris, the French Constituent Assembly adjourns. The French Constitution of 1791 is now operative and calls for a single-chamber French Legislative Assembly with the power to override any royal veto. [1653]

Friday, October 7, 1791. Today, La Rochefoucauld addresses the new French Legislative Assembly on its single-chamber structure:

> *Your most important debt perhaps is to justify your predecessors in the bold resolution they have taken for the nation in confiding the law-making authority to a single body. Franklin is the first to have proposed it and the citizens of Pennsylvania listened to his voice—but since that time . . . the powerful influences of ancient habits—have made them return to the complications of the British system of government. The Na-*

tional Constituent Assembly has seized upon this great idea; it has seen, moreover, in its adoption the inestimable advantage of cementing the principles of equality . . .[1654]

Thursday, December 15, 1791. Today, almost three years after America adopted its new U.S. Constitution, more than two years after America inaugurated its first president, and a year and a half after France adopted Thomas Jefferson and the Marquis de Lafayette's "Declaration of the Rights of Man and the Citizen," America finally ratifies ten amendments to its new Constitution. These we call the "Bill of Rights." From the first five:

FIRST ARTICLE: Congress shall make no law respecting an establishment of religion, or prohibiting the free exercise thereof; or abridging the freedom of speech, or of the press; or the right of the people peaceably to assemble, and to petition the Government for a redress of grievances.

SECOND ARTICLE: A well regulated Militia being necessary to the security of a free State, the right of the people to keep and bear Arms, shall not be infringed.

THIRD ARTICLE: No soldier shall, in time of peace be quartered in any house without the consent of the Owner, nor in time of war, but in a manner to be prescribed by law.

FOURTH ARTICLE: The right of the people to be secure in their persons, houses, papers, and effects, against unreasonable searches and seizures, shall not be violated, and no Warrants shall issue, but upon probable cause . . .

FIFTH ARTICLE: No person . . . shall be . . . deprived of life, liberty, or property, without due process of law . . .

Thomas Jefferson:

[M]y objection to the constitution was that it wanted a bill of rights, securing freedom of religion, freedom of the press, freedom from standing armies, trial by jury and a constant Habeas corpus act. Colo[nel] Hamilton's was that it wanted a king and house of lords. The sense of America has approved my objection and added the bill of rights, not the king and lords.[1655]

The Bill of Rights responds to many Americans, like Thomas Jefferson and Benjamin Franklin, who fear the federal government's drift toward monarchy. The First Article prohibits the government from establishing a state church or restricting the free expression of ideas. The Second Article discourages the government from replacing citizen militias with a government army to hold the people in fear. The Third, Fourth, and Fifth Articles prohibit the government from wrongly intruding, through an army or otherwise, on the lives and property of the people.

Thursday, February 9, 1792. Today, in London, Thomas Paine finishes Part Two of his *Rights of Man*, inscribing it to the Marquis de Lafayette *"in Gratitude for your services to my beloved America."* Excerpts:

With respect to the organization of the legislative power, . . . [i]n America, it is generally composed of two houses. In France it consists of but one . . .

The objections against two houses are . . . [t]hat two houses arbitrarily checking or controlling each other is inconsistent; because it cannot be proved, on principles of just representation, that either should be wiser or better than the other. They may check in the wrong as well as in the right . . .[1656]

I proceed in the next place to aristocracy.

What is called the [British] House of Peers [Lords] . . . amounts to a combination of persons in one common interest. No reason can be given why a house of legislation should be composed entirely of men whose occupation consists in letting landed property than why it should be composed of those who hire, or of brewers, or bakers, or any other separate class of men . . .

The only use to be made of this power (and which it has always made) is to ward off taxes from itself and throw the burden upon such articles of consumption by which itself would be least affected . . .

Men of small or moderate estates are more injured by the taxes being thrown on articles of consumption than they are eased by warding it from landed property . . . They consume more of the productive taxable articles in proportion to their property than those of large estates . . .[1657]

It has been customary to call the Crown the executive power, and the custom has continued, though the reason has ceased . . .

[I]t is the laws that govern, and not the man.[1658]

Saturday, June 16, 1792. Today, from the United States, Thomas Jefferson, now U.S. Secretary of State, writes the Marquis de Lafayette:

Behold you then, my dear friend, at the head of a great army, establishing the liberties of your country against a foreign enemy . . . While you are exterminating the monster aristocracy, and pulling out the teeth and fangs of its associate, monarchy, a contrary tendency is discovered in some here. A sect has shewn itself among us who declare they espoused our new constitution . . . only as a step to an English constitution, the only thing good and sufficient in itself in their eye . . .[1659]

Tuesday, June 19, 1792. Today, from the United States, U.S. Secretary of State Thomas Jefferson writes Tom Paine:

I received with great pleasure the present of your pamphlets [six copies of Part Two of The Rights of Man] . . . Would you believe it possible that in this country there should be high and important characters who need your lessons in republicanism, and who do not heed them? It is but too true that we have a sect preaching up and panting after an English constitution of King, lords, and commons and whose heads are itching for crowns, coronets and mitres . . .[1660]

Wednesday, September 19, 1792. Today, no longer safe from the British monarch in his native England, Tom Paine returns to Paris.[1661] He is a popular figure in France. The Marquis de Condorcet has published Tom Paine's views on a well-constituted government in the June–July issue of *Chronique du Mois,*[1662] and, though Paine is not a French citizen, he has been chosen by four departments (districts) of France to represent them at the French National Convention (which opens in two days). As I write in my history,

> *Thomas Paine, whose illustrious writings so much promoted the cause of freedom in the American revolution, and in his development of the deformity of the English government, had been elected by four departments, L'Aisne, L'Oise, Puy de Domme, and Pays de Calais; he chose the latter.*[1663]

Thursday, September 20, 1792. Today, at Valmy in France, the French army—singing "Ça Ira" (the song of the French Revolution which honors Benjamin Franklin and the American Revolution)—marches to a great victory over the Austrian and Prussian armies, which have entered France at the invitation of the French king. By inviting foreign armies to subdue his own people and to crush their democratic revolution, French King Louis XVI has sealed his fate.[1664]

Saturday, September 22, 1792. Today, the French National Convention unanimously votes to end the monarchy in France, and today Tom Paine writes,

> *You have before this time heard that the National Convention met punctual to the day appointed. The Members verified their powers on the 20th and met in Convention the 21st ult. The first business done was to abolish the bagatelle of Royalty which was decreed unanimously. This day, the Convention will appoint a Committee of Constitution to consist of nine Members who are to bring in a plan of the new Constitution. Affairs are turning round fast . . .*[1665]

Today, as I write in my history,

> *A committee was appointed to revise and new model the constitution, consisting of . . . [nine including] Thomas Paine, Brissot, . . . and Condorcet.*[1666]

France is no longer a monarchy. France is a republic. France needs and will have her first republican constitution!

Tuesday, September 25, 1792. Today, Tom Paine issues an Address to France:

> *I receive with affectionate gratitude the honor which the late National Assembly has conferred upon me by adopting me a citizen of France: and the additional honor of being elected by my fellow citizens a member of the National Convention . . .*

It has been my fate to have borne a share in the commencement and complete establishment of one revolution (I mean the Revolution of America). The success and events of that revolution are encouraging to us . . .

The principles on which that Revolution began have extended themselves to Europe; and an overruling Providence is regenerating the old world by the principles of the new. The distance of America from all the other parts of the globe did not admit of her carrying those principles beyond her own situation. It is to the peculiar honor of France that she now raises the standard of liberty for all nations; and in fighting her own battles, contends for the rights of all mankind . . .

[W]hen . . . the Constitution is made conformable to the Declaration of Rights; when the bagatelles of monarchy, royalty, regency, and hereditary succession, shall be exposed with all their absurdities, a new ray of light will be thrown over the world . . .[1667]

Monday, October 22, 1792. Today, in Paris, Jacques-Pierre Brissot de Warville's journal, *Le Patriote François*, publishes Tom Paine's "Essay for the Use of New Republicans in Their Opposition to Monarchy." Tom Paine writes:

From one point of view, we should not perhaps censure kings for their savage cruelty, their brutality and their oppressions; it is not they who are in fault; it is hereditary succession; a swamp breeds serpents; hereditary succession breeds oppressors . . .

Let the Rights of Man be established, Equality enthroned, a sound Constitution drafted, with its powers clearly defined; let all privileges, distinctions of birth, and monopolies be annulled . . .

[T]he presence of a king entails the presence of an aristocracy and of taxation reaching thirty millions. This is doubtless why Franklin styled Royalism "a crime as bad as poisoning."[1668]

John Adams:

I have the honor and consolation to be a republican on principle . . . I am not, however, an enthusiast who wishes to overturn empires and monarchies for the sake of introducing republican forms of government, and therefore, I am no king-killer, king-hater, or king-despiser . . .[1669]

My opinion of the French Revolution has never varied from the first assembly of the notables to this hour. I always dreaded it, and never had any faith in its success or utility . . . My friend Brissot has recorded a conversation with me at my house in Grosvenor Square [in London], which I esteem as a trophy. He says, and says truly, that I told him that the French nation were not capable of a free government, and that they had no right or cause to engage in a revolution.[1670]

Friday, November 2, 1792. Today, in Paris, Thomas Paine writes William Short, former private secretary to Thomas Jefferson:

I received your favor conveying a letter from Mr. Jefferson and the answers to Publicola for which I thank you. I had John Adams in my mind when I wrote the pamphlet [The Rights of Man] *and it has hit as I expected.*[1671]

Saturday, December 15, 1792. Today, the French National Convention proclaims that France will end aristocracy and feudalism in any country the French army occupies.[1672]

Tuesday, December 18, 1792. Today, in London's Guildhall, the British Crown tries Tom Paine *in absentia* for his "seditious" writings against the monarchy.[1673] From a trial account:

The Attorney General read the contents of a third letter, which he received from THE SECOND PERSON in America (Mr. [John] Adams). "Having the honour of his acquaintance," the Attorney General said, "I wrote to him relative to the prosecution and in answer I was informed that it is the wish of Thomas Paine to convene the people of Great Britain . . . to adopt a constitution similar to that of France and to establish a government proceeding directly from the sovereignty of the people . . . "[1674]

Partly on the basis of U.S. Vice President John Adams' testimony, Britain convicts Tom Paine of seditious libel, permanently exiles him, orders his *Rights of Man* suppressed for all time, and threatens to imprison any British bookseller who sells *Rights of Man*.[1675]

Monday, January 21, 1793. Today, to the cries of *Vive la nation!* and by the swift descent of the guillotine's blade, the King of France pays with his life for the independence he gave America.[1676] Had the French king not entered America's war against the British monarch, he would not have bankrupted his kingdom, he would not have had to call the Third Estate to Paris, and he would not have inspired so many Frenchmen (more than forty thousand came to America!) with the idea of democratic revolution. Had Louis XVI not chosen to help America, the British monarch would still rule America, and the French monarch would still rule France. Perhaps it was emotion, not reason, that put Louis XVI on the path to his own destruction. Perhaps, under the spell of a balding American in the garb of Jean-Jacques Rousseau, the king and his people succumbed to the highest ideals of a changing age. John Adams:

[F]our of the finest writers that Great Britain produced, Shaftesbury, Bolingbroke, Hume, and Gibbon . . . and three of the most eloquent writers that ever lived in France . . . Voltaire, Rousseau, and Raynal, seem to have made . . . strenuous exertions to render mankind in Europe discontented with their situation in life and with the state of society, both in religion and government. Princes and courtiers as well as citizens and countrymen, clergy as well as laity, became infected.

The King of Prussia, the Empress Catherine, were open and undisguised. The Emperor Joseph the Second was suspected, and even the excellent King of France grew impatient and uneasy under the fatiguing ceremonies of the Catholic Church. All these and many more were professed admirers of Mr. Franklin. He was considered as a citizen of the world, a friend to all men and an enemy to none . . .

When the association of Encyclopedists [Enlightenment philosophers] was formed, Mr. Franklin was considered as a friend and zealous promoter of that great enterprise which engaged all their praises. When the society of economists was commencing, he became one of them, and was solemnly ordained a knight of the order by the laying on the hands of Dr. Quesnay, the father and founder of that sect . . . Throughout his life he courted and was courted by the printers, editors, and correspondents of reviews, magazines, journals, and pamphleteers and those little busy meddling scribblers that are always buzzing about the press in America, England, France, and Holland. These, together with some of the clerks in the Count of Vergennes's office of interpreters (bureau des interprètes) filled all the gazettes of Europe with incessant praises of Monsieur Franklin. If a collection could be made of all the Gazettes of Europe for the latter half of the eighteenth century, a greater number of panegyrical paragraphs upon "le grand Franklin" would appear, it is believed, than upon any other man that ever lived . . .

"Eripuit cœlo fulmen;
mox sceptra tyrannis."

By the first line, the rulers of Great Britain and their arbitrary oppressions of the Colonies were alone understood. By the second was intimated that Mr. Franklin was soon to destroy or at least to dethrone all kings and abolish all monarchical governments. This, it cannot be disguised, flattered at that time the ruling passion of all Europe . . .

Hence the popularity of all the insurrections against the ordinary authority of government during the last century . . . When, where, and in what manner all this will end, God only knows. To this cause Mr. Franklin owed much of his popularity. He was considered to be in his heart no friend to kings, nobles or prelates. He was thought a profound legislator, and a friend of democracy. He was thought to be the magician who had excited the ignorant Americans to resistance. His mysterious wand had separated the Colonies from Great Britain. He had framed and established all the American constitutions of government, especially all the best of them, i.e., the most democratical. His plans and his example were to abolish monarchy, aristocracy and hierarchy throughout the world. Such opinions as these were entertained by the Duke de La Rochefoucauld, M. Turgot, M. Condorcet, and a thousand other men of learning and eminence in France, England, Holland, and all the rest of Europe . . .

Such was the real character, and so much more formidable was the

*artificial character, of Dr. Franklin when he entered into partnership
with the Count de Vergennes, the most powerful minister of State in
Europe, to destroy the character and power of [John Adams,] a poor
man almost without a name, unknown in the European world, born
and educated in the American wilderness, out of which he had never
set foot til 1778 . . .*[1677]

Friday, February 1, 1793. Today, the War of the French Revolution between
Britain and France begins. Britain will attempt, through another war, this time
with France, to end the democratic revolution that began in America almost
twenty years ago. The British monarch will fight to end democracy and restore
monarchy in France and will lead Europe's other monarchies against Europe's
only democracy and against America's only ally.

Friday, February 15, 1793. Today, as France faces a war crisis that will, for a
time, radicalize French politics, a nine-man drafting committee, chaired by the
Marquis de Condorcet and composed of Condorcet, Tom Paine, Brissot de Warville, and other admirers of Benjamin Franklin, submits The French Constitution of 1793 to the entire French National Convention.[1678]

Saturday, March 2, 1793. Today, from New York, John Adams writes Abigail:

Smith says my Books [Defence of the Constitutions of Government of
the United States] *are upon the Table of every Member of the Committee for framing a Constitution of Government for France except Tom
Paine . . .*[1679]

This may be true, but the committee's chairman, Condorcet, has agreed with
Tom Paine to model the constitution of the French Republic after Ben Franklin's Pennsylvania Constitution of 1776.[1680] John Adams:

*The political and literary world are much indebted for the invention
of the new word IDEOLOGY . . . It was taught in the school of folly; but
alas! Franklin, Turgot, Rochefoucauld, and Condorcet, under Tom
Paine, were the great masters of that academy.*[1681]

Monday, April 22, 1793. Today, despite America's treaty of alliance with
France (promising to defend the French West Indies, etc.), the onetime Fabius
who is President of the United States issues a Proclamation of Neutrality
(drafted by U.S. Supreme Court Justice John Jay) which declines to support
France's war for democracy against the British monarch. As I write in my history

*[T]he disposition that dictated it and the latent principle upon which it
was predicated were in direct opposition to the obligations of treaties
and contrary to the common principles of liberality which entitle men
to a return for good offices conferred in critical circumstances.*[1682]

Thomas Jefferson, who opposes the proclamation, respects the French alliance, but will not endure the heat of political wrangling,[1683] will soon offer his resignation as Washington's Secretary of State.

Wednesday, April 24, 1793. Today, in the largest typeface the *Philadelphia Aurora* has used to date, Benjamin Franklin Bache publishes the French Constitution of 1793. His grandfather would be very pleased. Excerpts from the French Constitution of 1793, as translated in the *Aurora*:

Primary Assemblies.

In the primary assemblies, every man aged 21 years has a right to vote, provided that his name is inscribed on the civic table and that he shall have resided one year in France.

The primary assemblies shall be so distributed in each department [state] that none shall consist of less than 400 [representatives], or more than 900, members . . .

Administrative Bodies.

There shall be in each department an administrative council of 18 members . . . to correspond with the executive government . . .

The administrators are to be elected in the private assemblies, and the half renewed every two years.

Executive Council.

I. The executive council of the Republic shall be composed of seven general agents or ministers . . .

III. Each of the ministers shall alternatively preside in the executive council, and the president shall be changed every fifteen days. To this council it belongs to execute all the laws and all the decrees passed by the legislative body . . .

The ministers are to be chosen in the primary assemblies . . .

The ministers are to be chosen for two years. The half shall be renewed every year . . . The executive council are accountable to . . . the legislative body.

Legislative Body.

The [national] legislative body is to consist of one chamber, and to be renewed annually by elections . . .

The number of deputies . . . is to be newly fixed every ten years according to the increase or decrease in population . . .[1684]

Federalists may claim their Fabius as the "Father of His Country" and applaud the Duke of Braintree for America's British-style constitution, but France honors America's true "Papa"[1685] and adopts his vision of democracy at the founding of the French Republic. The Pennsylvania Constitution of 1776 is alive today in France.[1686] So, too, is Franklinian democracy.

Armed cavalry on Philadelphia's High-street during
America's Reign of Terror.[1687]

BOOK THREE

AMERICAN REVOLUTION

I do not "consider hereditary Monarchy or Aristocracy as Rebellion
against Nature." On the contrary, I esteem them both as Institutions of
admirable wisdom and exemplary Virtue . . . and I am clear that
America must resort to them as an asylum during discord, Seditions
and Civil War . . . Our country is not ripe for it in many respects . . .
but our ship must ultimately land on that shore or be cast away.

JOHN ADAMS,
PRESIDENT OF THE UNITED STATES, 1797–1801 [1688]

[T]he energy of [William Duane's Aurora], when our cause was
laboring and all but lost under the overwhelming weight of its
powerful adversaries, its unquestionable effect in the revolution [it]
produced in the public mind . . . arrested the rapid march of our
government towards monarchy . . .

THOMAS JEFFERSON,
PRESIDENT OF THE UNITED STATES, 1801–1809 [1689]

Dr. Franklin's behavior had been so excessively complaisant to the
French ministry . . . I had been frequently obliged to differ from him
and sometimes to withstand him to his face; so that I knew he had
conceived an irreconcilable hatred of me and that he had propagated
and would continue to propagate prejudices, if nothing worse, against
me in America from one end of it to the other. Look into Bache's

Aurora and Duane's Aurora for twenty years and see whether my expectations have not been verified.

JOHN ADAMS,
PRESIDENT OF THE UNITED STATES, 1797–1801 [1690]

[B]y a singular fortune, your Great Grandfather [Benjamin Franklin] has been for more than thirty years of my life the constant idol of my affections as a politician—he has been my hero—and it is a felicity to me that I am so nearly connected with his posterity . . .

WILLIAM DUANE, EDITOR,
AURORA GENERAL ADVERTISER, 1798–1822
(IN LETTER TO BENJAMIN BACHE'S FIRSTBORN SON) [1691]

I have always regarded Duane, and still regard him, as a sincere friend of liberty, and as ready to make every sacrifice to its cause but that of his passions.

JAMES MADISON,
PRESIDENT OF THE UNITED STATES, 1809–1817 [1692]

PROLOGUE TO BOOK THREE

We return to Philadelphia in 1798 . . . President Adams has abrogated Ben Franklin's Franco-American Alliance of 1778. He has leagued America with her foremost enemy, the British monarch, against her only ally, the democratic Republic of France. He has made the French Revolution and Franklinian democracy our nation's enemies. He has armed the country, taxed the people, dispatched the navy, and brought back Fabius to fight a war—though undeclared—with the French Republic. He has ended America's freedoms of speech and of the press.

Adams predicted, "America must resort to [hereditary monarchy or aristocracy] as an asylum during discord, Seditions and Civil War." Could this be the time? Could John Adams see himself as an American monarch whose family occupies important government posts, whose son will succeed to the presidency, who will wage war with or without the people's assent, who will use a mercenary standing army (officered by political loyalists) to suppress his opposition, who will support a religious establishment to honor his prayer and fast days, preach his political sermons, and define his enemies as infidels, who will imprison his critics or exile them without trial, who will control the press, devalue the Constitution, and define democracy as a threat to his rule?

Will America be fighting another revolution against another monarch? Virginia is reportedly arming against the federal government. Republican militias face government partisans on the streets of the capital. The message of the mob replaces the message of the Constitution. Would-be citizens leave America by the boatload. Immigrants to America are no longer welcome.

John Adams fears the ghost of Franklin at the Philadelphia Aurora. He's tried to silence that ghost with a gag bill. He's indicted and arrested Young Lightening-Rod for sedition. He's encouraged and rewarded attacks upon that editor.

Ben Franklin is dead. Young Lightening-Rod is dead. Thomas Jefferson has fled. Is the Aurora dead? The rest of us must answer that question.

We resume this history in mid-October. I, William Duane, want to collect some old debts, revive the paper, and involve a wealthy Philadelphia Republican and Aurora contributor, Tench Coxe . . .

CHAPTER ELEVEN

SURGO UT PROSIM

The Freedom of the Press is the Bulwark of Liberty . . .

B. F. BACHE, EDITOR,
AURORA GENERAL ADVERTISER, 1790–1798[1693]

Philadelphia, October 13, 1798.

Caesar Rodney
Sir, Mrs. Bache, having lain in [with her new child] only a few days before her husband's decease and having nonetheless attended him day and night, has been obliged to retire to her father-in law's [the farm called "Settle"] . . . The heavy calamity that afflicts this city would alone be a Sufficient cause for troubling you on the present occasion for the Small arrear due to this office; but the death of the late Editor & the State of his Family, with the general Stagnation of Circulation, are doubly pressing motives for paying the discharge of the following bill . . .

I promise that my effort shall be directed to emulate the former excellence of the Aurora, and to render it as it has hitherto been—the only authentic Source of genuine public information. Educated in the principles & admiration of Franklin and firmly attached to the true interests of my country, I venture to presume that the character of the paper will not Suffer under my guidance.

Wm Duane[1694]

October 15th, 1798

Tench Coxe, Esq. Philadelphia,
Sir, A report having been spread in town on Saturday that Mrs. [Margaret] Bache was dead, I thought it expedient to go to Settle and ascertain the course I had to pursue in the event of the report being true. I was happy, however, to find her, all children, and all the family in perfect health.

Your Queries to me (which I had forwarded to her as you desired) she returned . . .

1. About 700 Subscribers in Philadelphia.

2. About 5 to 600 [additional] in the country . . .

13. [F]rom some conversations which I had with Mr. B. I suppose that there is due south of the Delaware between 15 & 20,000 Dollars! Mark this plain observation from experience: Newspaper Debts are the worst of all others! . . .

15. Since the 1st of July there has been near 200 additional sub-scribers . . .

I am very anxious to see you and Mr. Clay [executor of Mr. B's estate], if possible together, in order to mention some matters of the utmost interest to the Aurora.

Your faithful and grateful servant
Wm Duane[1695]

Peggy Bache and I will reopen the *Aurora*. Her name will appear on the masthead. I will edit and manage the paper. We each lost a spouse this year. Benny's four children need a man to take charge of their inheritance. My children need the *Aurora*, too. My son, William John, now eighteen, has a job at the paper.[1696] Besides, I find Peggy Bache a very attractive woman.[1697]

THURSDAY, NOVEMBER 1, 1798

GENERAL ★ AURORA ★ ADVERTISER

PUBLISHED *(DAILY)* FOR MARGARET H. BACHE . . .

Under the guidance of *BENJAMIN FRANKLIN BACHE*, this paper has for eight years maintained a character of freedom and intelligence, un-rivaled . . . until calamity for a while arrested its career and deprived society of the Editor.

Of him and his paper—the principles were the same as those . . . which cherished the imperishable love of liberty in the hour of oppression and which . . . terminated in the humiliation of our tyrant and the establishment of our national independence. Upon those principles it was that the *Aurora* was established; upon those alone has it been, with tried constancy, hitherto conducted.

But he whose love of truth and of science, whose zeal to promote the true interest and happiness of his country and the common good of man-kind—whose integrity and firmness gave birth and body to the *Aurora*, is no more . . .

After such a man . . . the most earnest efforts of subordinate talents must require a liberal consideration—Upon the principles of the Aurora, upon an undeviating adherence to the principles of our constitution, and an unwearied watchfulness against those eternal foes of republics, ava-rice, ambition, and corruption—the successor of *Benjamin Franklin Bache* in the editorial duty confidently relies for public candor and re-gard.

Efforts have not been wanting to destroy . . . the credit and interests of this paper—and either to suppress it forever or convert it into a vehicle of atrocious delusion.

Little did the enemies of republican freedom know that among the last and most solemn injunctions made by *Benjamin Franklin Bache* was that his paper should be continued with inflexible fidelity to the principles upon which it was founded and reared up—an injunction manifesting at once his integrity and the firmness of his mind at the hour of death—it was an injunction which love and honour must cherish and from which virtue could not depart—but such sentiments enter not into the bosoms of the enemies of equal freedom.

[The] moment when calamity had depopulated our city . . . was chosen by the publisher of a paper . . . to heap the most malignant aspersions upon the morals and reputation of *Benjamin Franklin Bache*—at a moment too when he no longer lived to expose the atrocity of the calumny . . . An apprentice belonging to this office had, soon after the death of the Editor, broke into a store in Market Street and stolen a considerable quantity of goods . . . Upon these facts, that person who, under the name of Peter Porcupine, confers so much ignominy on the American morals and literature, asserted that the apprentice above mentioned had been trained up to this nefarious mode of life by the late Editor, that the watch which had been stolen was found in this office or house, and that no person was employed in this office who did not carry pistols for such purposes . . .

[T]he late Editor's reputation is too much above the reach of [such] detraction . . .

Matthew Lyon of Vermont has had the honour of being the first victim of a law framed directly in the teeth of the Constitution of this federal republic—the ancients were wont to bestow particular honour on the first citizen who suffered in resisting tyranny.

"Surgo ut prosim." Today, almost two months after Benny's death, the *Philadelphia Aurora* resumes publication. As our masthead motto proclaims, *"I rise so that I may be useful."*

While the *Aurora* was closed, Republican Congressman Matthew Lyon (whose congressional "spitting" incident prompted Federalist House Speaker Jonathan Dayton to regulate congressional reporting and to expel Benny from the House floor when he refused to cooperate) was in his home state of Vermont, campaigning for reelection to the House of Representatives. In the midst of this campaign, the federal government indicted Matthew Lyon for sedition (October 5), arrested him (October 6), tried him without legal representation (October 8), fined him $1,000, and sentenced him to four months in prison (starting October 9). His "seditious libel" was the claim that President John Adams has demonstrated *"a continual grasp for power"* and an *"unbounded thirst for ridiculous pomp, foolish adulation, or selfish avarice,"* &c.[1698] Today, Vermont Republican Congressman Matthew Lyon is in jail.

Tonight, in the *Gazette of the United States*:

The Fever is Gone !
NO NEW CASES have occurred for the last 24 hours. We most heartily congratulate our Readers and the Public, upon this state of things, so long anxiously looked for.

Our lately exiled fellow-citizens are returning in crowds; and the Roads in the vicinity of the city, on every quarter, present an aspect resembling the rear of a retreating army [with its baggage and families].

SATURDAY, NOVEMBER 3, 1798

GENERAL ★ AURORA ★ ADVERTISER

One of the counts in the indictment against MATTHEW LYON is that he had insinuated that the President of the United States was devoted to fondness for "ridicule, pomp, idle parade, and selfish avarice." (What was that Roman's name that said Heliogabalus was not a plain man, and died for it?)

Should the French land a large army in Ireland, will they be more to blame in assisting the Irish to establish an elective government, like ours, than the English were in assisting . . . to restore the old absolute military despotism of France . . . ? . . . If the Irish wish for an elective government and freedom for other religious societies besides the church of England . . . will they be more to blame in asking for and using foreign assistance than we were? Will the French who sent us a fleet, an army, clothing, arms, ammunition, and money be more blamable for giving the Irish such assistance? If Washington, Rochambeau and [La]Fayette took Cornwallis at York Town, why may not an Irish general and one or two French generals take Cornwallis in Dublin? If taxation and representation in 1775 were held to be inseparable for two millions of Americans who made many of their own provincial laws, why ought they not to be held inseparable for three millions of Catholics in Ireland who have not had (Great God of Liberty) a single vote ?

Thomas Adams, editor of the [Republican] Independent Chronicle at Boston, was arrested by Colonel Bradford, Marshal of that district, and brought before the Circuit Court to answer to an indictment found against him by the grand jury, for sundry libellous and seditious publications in his paper tending to defame the government of the United States . . .

While the *Aurora* was closed, the Adams administration moved to disable the nation's next-largest[1699] republican newspaper, the *Independent Chronicle* of Boston, Massachusetts, indicting *Chronicle* publisher Thomas Adams under the new federal Sedition Law for *"sundry libellous and seditious publications."* The government arraigned Thomas Adams about a week ago (October 23) before Judges William Paterson and John Lowell at the Federal Circuit Court in Boston, where bail was set and Thomas Adams ordered to stand trial in June.[1700]

Tonight, in the *Porcupine's Gazette*:

COMMUNICATION.

On Thursday, the AURORA again made its appearance to disgrace the city and heap indignities on our Government. The *Aurora*, I am informed, is conducted by one DUANE, a wretch, who not long since emigrated to this country, was some months ago turned out of the House of Representatives by the Speaker for his insolence . . . at a time when Duane [was] a short-hand writer;—this Duane is also said to be the miscreant who wrote, under the assumed name of *[Jasper] Dwight*, the infamous letter to our immortal WASHINGTON—and such a character as this, by Mrs. Bache and her friends, has been thought worthy of conducting the *Aurora.*

The first paper published for Mrs. Bache by this reptile contains the following observation —

"Matthew Lyon of Vermont has had the honour of being the first victim of a law framed *directly in the teeth of the Constitution of this Federal Republic*—the ancients were wont to bestow particular honour on the first citizen who suffered in *resisting tyranny.*"

We would have believed that Americans had submitted to indignities *enough* from the conduct of the French government . . . but it appears that our degradation was not complete, and the American people are to be obliged to Mr. Duane for coming to this country to inform them that a LAW made by *their* government, and declared to be a *constitutional law* by the Judiciary (the only constitutional judges) is a law . . ."directly in the teeth of the constitution." . . . On the abandoned profligacy and unbounded insolence of this miscreant, I make no comment . . . Our government protects our property from the plunder of *United Irishmen,* our lives from the knife of the assassin; therefore, our government should be dear to us . . . [T]hose creatures coming into this country in a state of extreme wretchedness and, having acquired in their country a talent of defaming government, immediately begin here their trade in order to gain a subsistence, and this they call *"the sacred liberty of the press."* . . . But alas! do we find every good American manfully stepping forward to crush this abandoned faction, formed of a few profligate Americans, late tenants of [N]ewgate [prison] and our own gaols; of United Irishmen, and fugitives from Scotland, of Frenchmen, and other restless foreigners, who have everything to gain and nothing to lose . . .

The friends of our government, believing its conduct to be just, wise, and upright, too much despise and disregard the vile slanders of a Duane, a Bache, and a ["Newgate"] Lloyd, while those creatures by our supineness are daily gaining ground . . . AN AMERICAN

(I myself have read this first paper published in the name of MRS. BACHE . . . I by no means look upon DUANE or any other vagabond journalist newsmonger as the proper object of attack. The proprietor of the paper, the person whose name it bears, who causes it to be published, is the only one who is responsible for its contents either in the eye of reason or the eye of the law. That person, therefore, whether bearded or unbearded, whether dressed in breeches or petticoats, whether a male or female sans-culotte, shall receive no quarter from me . . . [William Cobbett])

SUNDAY, NOVEMBER 4, 1798

War . . . Today, in the Atlantic, north of the French West Indies, a French privateer captures an armed American schooner. A report:

Thomas M'Connell, who was captured in the schooner Highlander, of Baltimore, mounting 12 guns and carrying 22 men . . . informed Captain Willis that, . . . in lat. 19, 10, long 59,00, he fell in with a French privateer, from Guadaloupe, mounting 12 guns, 9 and 6 pounders, with 96 men and 80 muskets, whom he engaged for three glasses. In the beginning of the action, M'Connell's first mate was shot thro' the right shoulder and his second killed; and owing to the superior number of men and musquetry on board the enemy, was obliged to strike. M'Connell had three seamen and one officer killed, first officer and one seaman wounded—The enemy had 8 killed, and 3 wounded and received much damage in the hull and rigging which obliged them to put into Bassaterre to repair, where they carried M'Connell and crew whom they immediately put into jail . . . Capt. M'Connell received the worst of treatment and bad language from the French during his confinement. The only name they called him and the rest of the prisoners was "John Adams's Jack Asses."[1701]

MONDAY, NOVEMBER 5, 1798

GENERAL ★ AURORA ★ ADVERTISER

While the late editor of this paper lived, all the sluices of *English vulgarity* . . . were constantly pouring forth in torrents against him from the pen of the *noted English corporal Porcupine*, but with no other effect than . . . a sense of shame for the society that tolerated . . . it . . .

[T]he upholders of the present English government will never cease to hate the memory of Dr. Franklin, and they would carry their hatred into a curse on all his posterity, if possible, for his having torn, by the force of his genius, this new empire from the baneful bondage of Britain . . . [A]spersions o[n] that venerable man were resorted to with the varied view of pleasing the *envious* rivals of his former celebrity . . . and wounding the repose of his grandson; but with the like effect;—*Franklin's* fame was no longer under the conservation of filial duty or family reverence; it belonged to his country and to history—upon the American nation every aspersion cast on Franklin must rest; when he ceases to be revered by his country, his country will cease to be respected . . .

[T]he English jackal [Porcupine] . . . pursued his grandson likewise to the grave—and endeavored to heap calumny on *his* memory whom he had not the courage to face while yet he lived. That calumny was exposed . . . in our paper last Thursday . . . [T]he assassin of the dead being exposed to public execration . . . comes forth with a *threat*, and against whom—a *woman, and a widow*—and for what? For defending the reputation of her husband . . .

One word more, and then let public shame perform the rest—Whenever the writer of the articles in Porcupine's paper of Saturday thinks fit to call at this office, he shall see the person who wrote the defence of the late Editor published in last Thursday's *Aurora*, who also is the writer of this; and who, whether in petticoats or breeches, will be ready to give him *suitable satisfaction!*

Porcupine and Fenno will find me a tireless defender of Ben Franklin and the Baches. If we don't take Peggy's name off the masthead, however, Peggy will become the principal focus for Fenno's and Porcupine's attacks.

TUESDAY, NOVEMBER 6, 1798

GENERAL ★ AURORA ★ ADVERTISER

It is either true or false that Mr. Adams has advocated the doctrine of hereditary rank and permanent office. If he has advocated such doctrines, it is high time the fact should be known and established . . . [T]he leaders of what is called the federal or government party have advocated the political conduct and principles of Mr. Adams . . . To decide, therefore, whether this approbation be given to acts founded on sound republican virtue or to those which may emanate from a principle destructive of the present form of our constitution, and unfriendly to the habits and feelings of the people, is an enquiry of infinite importance . . .

This afternoon, Jack Fenno in the *Gazette of the United States*:

Two young Widows have just commenced their Editorial careers . . . [O]ne cannot too much admire at the bungling stupidity of the logger-headed boobies . . . under the sanction of those ladies' names . . .

The other "young Widow" who "commenced her Editorial career" is Ann Greenleaf, who is trying to continue the nation's third-largest[1702] Republican paper, the New York *Argus,* after the death of her husband, Thomas Greenleaf, on September 14th from yellow fever.[1703]

Tonight, William Cobbett in the *Porcupine's Gazette*:

MOTHER BACHE.

Has published a second number of her infamous Gazette, with her name at the head of it. I now look upon her as having declared herself. Her friends (if she yet has any) can no longer plead her ignorance of her name being made use of, and I shall, therefore, treat her as the profligate Authoress of the *Aurora.*—Adieu, PEG, 'till I have a moment's leisure.

THURSDAY, NOVEMBER 8, 1798

GENERAL ★ AURORA ★ ADVERTISER

Philadelphia presents the novel case of a *ruffian* . . . standing forth before the public the avowed assailant of a feeble woman, when the wretch *dares not* meet the man who alone is responsible for what appears in this paper.

The proprietors of the Argus and Aurora have the misfortune to be left *widows,* and behold the *age of chivalry* is not past, neither their sex nor their misfortunes can shield them from the attacks of two *military heroes,* two corporals—*corporal Fenno and corporal Porcupine.*

Two blackguards at a time attacking even a man is at least *too* much— What must the condition of their morals and education be who attack a *woman* !

We are not surprized that corporal Cobbett should be particularly scurrilous against women, since he *beats* the woman who is unfortunately linked to the *beast* : we are only astonished that he shews any affection for *children,* particularly for Fenno, as it is well known that at Bustletown, [Cobbett] subjected his own infant to the knot.

It must not be thought that we in any way desire to derogate from the *character* of William Cobbett[. W]e only couple him with his co-corporal Fenno to elucidate the *pretensions* of the latter.

It would have been imagined, considering the youth of editor Fenno, that the late calamities of his own family would have made some impression upon *his* mind, and at least have taught *him* to respect the feelings of *others.* But he seems to have been so thoroughly bred in the school of vice, that even female grief cannot be respected by him.

In page 70, vol. Ist. [of Mr. Adams' *Defence of the Constitutions of Government of the United States*] we find another testimony . . . to the excellence of the British constitution (of king, lords, and commons) . . . "I only contend (says the Doctor) that the English constitution is in theory the most stupendous fabric of human invention . . . and that the Americans ought to be applauded instead of censured for imitating it as far as they have . . ."

Tonight, in the *Porcupine's Gazette*:

Luther Baldwin, of Newark, was arrested on Saturday last, by the marshal of the state of New-Jersey, under the late Sedition Act, for expressing a wish *that the President of the United States was dead.*

(Yes; the great wish, the longing desire of the French faction. THE PRESIDENT is almost the only bar in their way to general pillage.—God preserve his life!)

FRIDAY, NOVEMBER 9, 1798

GENERAL ★ AURORA ★ ADVERTISER

(The following is taken from a letter written by Col. [Matthew] LYON [of Vermont], since he was committed to gaol [prison], and directed to Gen. STEVENS THOMPSON MASON, of Virginia, Senator of the United States.

In Gaol in VERGENNES [Vermont]. October 14

DEAR GENERAL . . . I mourn with you the death of our good friend BACHE—he was too good a man to be tortured with the Sedition Law— God saw it in that light and took him to himself.

I shall trouble you no longer at this time than to request you to give my respects to my friends in Virginia . . . and to let them know the operation of the Sedition Law in Vermont . . .   [MATTHEW LYON]

Under the British government, you could talk as you pleased, write as you pleased, censure *King George the Third,* if you pleased. But *John Adams* is not to be censured; he is *immaculate* ! Did you, or did you not, fight for LIBERTY? The *causes* of our revolutionary war appear in the present day as a dream . . . *Unanimity in Judge, lawyer, and Jury* ! *A Judge* appointed by *John Adams,* an *Attorney* appointed by *John Adams,* a *Jury* summoned, *selected* by a *Marshall* appointed by *John Adams* !!! It is time—But, as Benedict Arnold says—HUSH !

A clerk in a particular office is specially appointed to search the *obnoxious papers* for suitable matter to cut them up at law—a *wag,* referring to the fact, observed that the clerk seldom searched the scriptures.

Tonight, in the *Porcupine's Gazette*:

> There is a vagabond *Irishman* or *Scotchman*, in the third parish of *Dedham* [Massachusetts], who has stirred up a few ignorant people to erect a liberty pole, with a painted board, and the words *Liberty, Equality, no stamp act, no sedition or Alien bill, downfall to tyranny in America, peace and retirement to the President* . . .
>
> Many of the justices of the peace, on their way to the Sessions, had opportunity to behold this standard of insurrection against the laws and magistracy of the country.

Porcupine does not have to worry! Massachusetts Federalists have already brought charges under the new federal Sedition Act against David Brown, the middle-aged "vagabond" who stirred up the people to erect a liberty pole. Boston's Federal Marshal Samuel Bradford is searching for David Brown with a warrant for his arrest.[1704]

SATURDAY, NOVEMBER 10, 1798

GENERAL ★ AURORA ★ ADVERTISER

Extract of a letter from Doctor Logan, dated Bordeaux [France], September 9, 1798, to his Wife.

"I have the pleasure to inform you that I embark this day on board the ship *Perseverance* for Philadelphia and shall bring with me dispatches to restore that harmony, the loss of which has been so sensibly felt by both countries. All American vessels in the harbours of France have been released—all American prisoners have been set at liberty; and the most positive assurances have been made that France is ready to enter into a treaty for the amicable accommodation of all matters in dispute . . .

GEORGE LOGAN."

The warhawks will be now more than ever distracted. The publication of a letter from Dr. Logan is a cruel blow . . . to the candidates for [military] contracts, commissions, and commissaryships !

The man who *dares* even to hint that the President of the United States is proud or avaricious is locked up in solitary confinement—Oh Liberty !!! . . . The place of *victim Lyon's* confinement is without shelter from a freezing northern climate or fire-place to dispel the chilling damps—if he should be frozen to death, *could an honest jury bring in a verdict ?*—MURDER !

The *[news]paper-searching* clerk in a certain office may be appropriately compared with a *familiar* of the *Inquisition*—with this odd feature of resemblance; that as the latter is employed to support *religion*, so the other is employed to support *liberty !*

Tonight, in the *Porcupine's Gazette*:

> Now is the crisis advancing. The abandoned faction, devoted to France
> . . . have fifty thousand men, provided with arms, in Pennsylvania. If vig-
> orous measures are not taken; if the provisional army is not raised without
> delay, A CIVIL WAR, OR A SURRENDER OF INDEPENDENCE, IS NOT
> AT MORE THAN A TWELVE MONTH'S DISTANCE . . .
>
> The partizans of France are linked together in one chain, from Georgia
> to N. Hampshire. The seditious impudence of the *Democratic Societies*
> has given place to the dark and silent system of organized treason and
> massacre, imported by the UNITED IRISHMEN . . . And yet the pretended
> friends of America are asleep . . .

Tonight, in the *Gazette of the United States*:

> We are happy in perceiving the growing *jealousy of foreigners*. The
> inundation of suspicious characters, particularly from Ireland and France,
> should awaken the most serious concern . . .
>
> ---
>
> We have now before us a file of "The Redacteur," the French official ga-
> zette, almost every page of which contains some insult to our beloved
> President. In one we read . . . "John Adams has ordered a day of general
> fasting. This is truly laughable."
>
> ---
>
> Today about eleven o'clock, our beloved General [Washington] arrived in
> town. Detachments from the different troops of horse met him on the
> road, at and from Chester, and escorted him to the city . . . McPherson's
> Blues [the Federalist volunteer corps of "young men,"] and Captain
> Hozey's company were drawn up in the centre square, and, as he ap-
> proached, he alighted from his carriage, and with his secretary Mr. Lear,
> passed the line uncovered to the usual salute of presented arms . . . Having
> got into his carriage again, he was escorted to Mrs. White's in Eighth-
> street, where a guard from McPherson's Blues was immediately
> mounted . . .
>
> Major General Alexander HAMILTON and the Hon. James McHenry,
> Secretary at War, also arrived this day, and accompanied the Lieutenant
> General to his lodgings in Eighth street.

Tonight, after dark, George Logan arrives back at his farm in Germantown from
his private peace mission to France. He has messages to deliver to the U.S.
Secretary of State from the French Directory (France's plural executive), and
he will set out in the morning to find Timothy Pickering who has yet to return
from Trenton, New Jersey, the temporary seat of the federal government while
the yellow fever beset Philadelphia.[1705]

The *blues* . . . have the honor of first testifying their loyalty and attachment to the hoary *general;* may they never encounter a worse duty . . .

It is hoped that the guard of state has been selected from those who are not subject to *growing pains!*

Why shouldst thou rail O Fenno! at thine enemies for laughing at the *fastings* of the federalists, ordained by thy *beloved President,* when the citizens of Philadelphia know that the day, *"so holy,"* was celebrated by thy fellow FEDS in riot, drunkenness, and assault. Only ask capt. Josey Thomas now—who at length returned to the bosom of his fond friends and the seat of his former federal and literary glories!

Though we may not think it *quite safe* to sum up the follies of the present day, still it may possibly be permitted a *freeman born* to amuse himself with recalling past scenes . . .

ANECDOTES.

[1.] AT a theatrical representation given at Versailles and to which the three American envoys were invited (not the late unsuccessful ones, reader) . . . a resemblance of the late Dr. Franklin, the *selected commissioner* of the three and with whom the court then had communication, was introduced . . . with a civic wreath. Whether the spectacle excited any disagreeable movements in the mind of a *certain personage* [Mr. Adams] . . . we cannot say. [W]e know, however, that it operated . . . to excite the animal power of *locomotion [for his departure]* . . .

[2.] Lieutenant General Washington, *once General in Chief of Republic America,* has in his possession a profile of himself . . . with a wreath and crown. This, together, with a profile of the late doctor Franklin, were presented to the doctor whilst in France. A certain personage [Mr. Adams] . . . was in Paris at the same time. It would be *highly dangerous* to accuse him even of envy, but . . . the *complimentary crown* offended his highness so much (perhaps because it was over the head of another) that he took great pains to dismantle the frame and cut off the offending object with his penknife. The deficiency is now observable in the portrait which is still in the possession of the late President.

Quere.—What may we think of a Person whose *republicanism* cannot even suffer the semblance of a crown to remain upon another's image, but who at the same time may be *hereafter* shrewdly suspected of craving a real crown for his own *knapper.*

Today, George Logan visits Secretary of State Timothy Pickering in Trenton, New Jersey. George Logan:

After a conversation of considerable length with Mr. Pickering, during which at times he manifested a great degree of irritation against

535

the French, I took my leave; he waited on me to the door, on the threshold of which, with a voice altered by the agitation of his mind, he stammered out these words, too singular not to be related:

"Sir, it is my duty to inform you that the government does not thank you for what you have done."

Considering Mr. Pickering as Secretary of State and the Public organ of the executive, I was astonished at his folly. In this the most important transaction of my life, I had the approbation of my conscience. I never experienced a more perfect satisfaction than what arose from the reflection of having done my country so considerable a service.[1706]

Tonight, in the *Gazette of the United States*:

If we do not speedily close our doors upon the hordes of ruffians yearly disgorging upon us, America will erelong be converted into one vast house of assassins.

If the revolutionary vermin of foreign countries should continue to encrease and fatten as they have heretofore done on the sufferings and distress of the community, it is not difficult to foresee the speedy dissolution of this . . . most enlightened republic. Then we should see committees of public safety and revolutionary tribunals composed of Callenders, Reynolds, Burks, and Duanes. The heads of rich men would roll down the kennels . . .

Tonight, in the *Porcupine's Gazette*:

The President of the United States is expected at Trenton, on his way back to Philadelphia, in a few days. It must give pain to every one, Mother Bache and her gang excepted, to hear that Mrs. Adams will, from indisposition, be unable to accompany him.

ALARMING!

At a meeting of Herodsburg (Kentucky), present 200 citizens, resolves . . . were agreed to, censuring the late measures of the general government. Similar resolves have been entered into by the inhabitants of Montgomery county (K.), Madison county, and Lincoln county (K.)

We can *account* for these discontents and clamours. No papers circulate in Kentucky except the *Aurora*, that herald of Sedition . . .

(This article is taken from a New York newspaper . . . It seems to me that [the writer] has mistaken an effect for a cause. The preference given to the Aurora is proof of previous discontent . . .)

TUESDAY, NOVEMBER 13, 1798

GENERAL ★ AURORA ★ ADVERTISER

The New York Gazette has long been afflicted with the incurable malady of dreaming about the *Aurora* . . . [A] story is now brought forth that "no paper circulates to *Kentucky but the Aurora.*" . . . [T]he plain truth is that three papers in this city have double or triple the number of subscribers in that state . . . [W]e have the pleasure to learn however that a large subscription to the *Aurora* has lately been made . . .

Today, in Lexington, Kentucky, the Kentucky senate concurs in resolutions passed three days ago by Kentucky's house of representatives, including:

> III. *Resolved,* That . . . [by] abridging the freedom of speech or of the press . . . the act of the Congress of the United States passed on the 14th of July 1798 [the Sedition Law] . . . is not law, but is altogether void and of no effect . . .
> VI. *Resolved,* That . . . "An act concerning aliens" . . . to authorize the President to remove a person . . . on his own suspicion, without accusation, without jury, without public trial, without confrontation of the witnesses against him, without having witnesses in his favor, without defence, without counsel, is contrary to . . . the Constitution, . . . not law . . . void and of no force.[1707]

Kentucky's attorney general, John Breckinridge, submitted these proposals, but Thomas Jefferson secretly composed them. Thomas Jefferson:

> *At the time when the Republicans of our country were so much alarmed at the proceedings of the federal ascendancy . . . it became a matter of serious consideration how head could be made against their enterprises on the Constitution. The leading republicans in Congress found themselves of no use there . . . They concluded to retire from that field, take a stand in their state legislatures, and endeavor there to arrest their progress . . .*[1708]

Today, having returned to Philadelphia from Trenton, New Jersey, George Logan locates George Washington at Rosanna White's Eighth-street boarding-house. George Washington:

> *Mr. Lear, My Secretary, being from our lodgings on business, one of my servants . . . informed me that a Gentleman in the Parlor below desired to see me . . . In a few minutes I went down and found the Rev. Doctr. Blackwell and Doctr. Logan there. I . . . gave my hand to the former; the latter did the same towards me . . . I was backward in giving mine . . . Finally, in a very cool manner and with an air of indiffe[re]nce, I gave him my hand . . . I addressed all my conversation to Doctor Blackwell; the other [Dr. Logan] all his to me, to which I only gave negative or affirmative answers, as laconically as I could . . .*
> *He observed that the situation . . . with respect to France has induced him to make the Voyage . . . This . . . induced me to remark that there was something very singular in this. That he who could be viewed as a private character, unarmed with powers and presumptively unknown in France, should suppose he could effect what these gentlemen of the first respectability in our Country, specially charged*

under the authority of the Government, were unable to do. With this observation he seemed a little confounded; but recovering . . . said that the Directory was apprehensive that this Country, viz. the Government of it or Our Envoys . . . was not well disposed towards France . . . To this I finally . . . asked him if the Directory looked upon us as worms; and not even allowed to turn when tread upon? . . . and I hoped the spirit of this Country would never suffer itself to be injured with impunity by any nation under the Sun. To this he s[ai]d he told Citizen Merlin [president of the French Directory] that if the U.S. were Invaded by France, they w[oul]d unite to a man to oppose the Invaders.[1709]

George Logan's wife, Deborah, reports:

[A]t this interview, the general asked him what was the reason the Directors had treated him so well, when the government of France has assumed so different a tone to our commissioners? Doctor Logan replied that his own conduct, and not theirs, was all he could account for.[1710]

Tonight, in the *Gazette of the United States*:

THE jacobins have taken up the trick of late, which they have borrowed from their friends, the French, of employing ladies in their wicked maneuvers . . . [T]he amiable daughters of America will lose greatly by mingling in the stormy element of politics . . . [T]his ill-chosen business, if you pursue it, will spoil your beauty, as well as mar your happiness; it will plant your bosoms with thorns, and deform your lovely faces with wrinkles before their proper time. *Be warned; retreat,* before it is too late.

A Friend of the Fair.

Tonight, windows are broken at the offices of the *Philadelphia Aurora*.

WEDNESDAY, NOVEMBER 14, 1798

GENERAL ★ AURORA ★ ADVERTISER

PUBLISHED *(DAILY)* FOR THE HEIRS OF BENJ. FRANKLIN BACHE

Starting this morning, Peggy's name no longer appears on the *Aurora*'s masthead.

THURSDAY, NOVEMBER 15, 1798

GENERAL ★ AURORA ★ ADVERTISER

Put out the light, and then put out the light. Shakespeare. That the *Aurora* office is still under the particular patronage of the tory federalists appears from their demolitions Tuesday night. It is no new thing that the

aristocratic junto should admit the propriety of *breaking windows*, since they are not *yet* taxed.

Tonight, in the *Gazette of the United States*:

DOCTOR LOGAN . . . had the unpardonable effrontery to wait upon General Washington. Upon his introduction, he offered his polluted hand to the General who declined returning his fraternal salutation.

Tonight, in the *Porcupine's Gazette*:

THE *gentle* and *impartial* Mr. Claypoole, in his Gazette . . . says "the raising of a *provisional army* . . . may be very justly called into question." . . . [T]he attempt to spread abroad such an opinion is a most wicked Jacobin trick. The gentle Claypoole is, in fact, no more than the *avant courier,* the *go-before,* the *entering wedge,* of PEG BACHE.

MONDAY, NOVEMBER 19, 1798

GENERAL ★ AURORA ★ ADVERTISER

Official accounts from Constantinople . . . [bring] advice that [British] Admiral Nelson attacked the French fleet [of Napoleon] before Alexandria [Egypt], and partly burned and sunk almost the whole of it.

Tonight, in the *Gazette of the United States*:

Our belief in the intelligence of the ruin of the French "Army of Egypt" . . . has since been completely justified by more recent intelligence . . . French cruizers will now be everywhere chased from the Mediterranean . . .

Here, let us not omit to enumerate the immense consequence of this victory to the trade of the United States . . . [H[ow great a load of reproach and ignominy we have escaped through the wisdom of one man [John Adams] who may with justice be styled (to copy the old Roman solecism) THE SECOND FOUNDER OF THE REPUBLIC . . . when the firmness of administration, as was foreseen and foretold, results in security and prosperity.

TUESDAY, NOVEMBER 20, 1798

GENERAL ★ AURORA ★ ADVERTISER

A MEETING of the UNITED IRISHMEN in Philadelphia will be held at 7 o'clock on FRIDAY EVENING, 23d instant. Brethren will please to apply for cards of admission to citizen   D. CLARKE

Tonight, in the *Gazette of the United States*:

IT has often been the lot of this Gazette to warn the people of the United States against those underhanded conspiracies which we had reason to know were forming . . . The following . . . justifies all our apprehensions . . .

A Meeting of the United Irishmen in Philadelphia will be held at 7 o'clock on Friday evening, 23d instant . . .

N.B. This "Notice" is copied from an obscure publication, called the *Aurora,* the same that was formerly carried on by a Mr. Bache.

The people of America have long been abused by a detestable banditti of foreign invaders who, through the medium of the press, have found constant means of libeling truth and honesty . . . Let them be brought to the bar of public justice and made to answer its demands . . .

Who but remembers the torpid state in which we slumbering lay, when the warning voice of Mr. Adams first roused us to behold the gigantic danger which threatened and surrounded us? Who but remembers the consternation produced by the *war speech,* and the howlings of the jacobins at that timely alarm ? They had till then succeeded in stifling the spirit of the country . . .

The Federalists, abandoning all tame and half-way measures, should act with a zeal worthy their cause and their country. Let us no longer "peep our swords half-out their scabbards," but draw them forth and brandish them to vengeance.

WEDNESDAY, NOVEMBER 21, 1798

GENERAL ★ AURORA ★ ADVERTISER

Heretofore General Washington was wont to be called the *second founder of the republic,* as *Franklin* was the first. [W]e are now told, and it is confessedly a solecism, that our modest and unassuming President merits that *title*!

Let us no longer "peep our swords out of the scabbards" says young *Fenno*—"*Twenty more, kill them,*" says *Bobadil.*

Fenno *deigns* to think the *Aurora "obscure,"* perhaps through envy. Pity 'tis, the *compliment* cannot be returned, but like the *gallows maker* in the play, he is *eminently* NOTORIOUS.

Tonight, in the *Gazette of the United States:*

THE man who doubts the organization of a party in this country to overthrow its constitution and government and to model both with the assistance of France must be a creature of doubtful gender . . .

Look at the Jacobins . . . take a lesson from them . . .

Let, therefore, ASSOCIATIONS be formed in every considerable City

and Town of the United States (the example may be set in Philadelphia
. . .) let committees be appointed; funds raised, presses employed; let
information be disseminated at cheap rates everywhere; let the ignorant
be instructed; the wavering confirmed; the banditti watched in their *up-
risings and downyings*; and I will offer my neck to the guillotine if, in
twelve months after the scheme is brought into operation, they are not
completely crushed.

The *President* left his seat in Quincy for Philadelphia on Monday week.

THURSDAY, NOVEMBER 22, 1798

GENERAL ★ AURORA ★ ADVERTISER

Much clamour is raised against Doctor Logan, by our Federal Aristocrats, for being the bearer of dispatches; and he was threatened with
being arrested for treason . . . These *consistent* Federalists have been
continually thundering out their anathemas against the French for capturing our vessels . . . but no sooner do [the French] stop the taking of
our vessels and offer us restitution for those already taken than [George
Logan,] the man whom [the Federalists] suppose has been instrumental
in effecting this change of conduct in the French government, is charged
of being a traitor to his country . . . A proof, this, that they are displeased
with this manifestation of an amiable disposition on the part of France;
that they wish for war; and that nothing short of war with France will
satisfy them.

The Editor of the Boston Centinal exultantly mentions that lately a
Liberty Pole (termed by him a *Jacobin Pole)* which had been erected at
Dedham [Massachusetts], had been prostrated with the dirt; and that
one FAIRBANKS, a *deluded ringleader,* charged with being an *accessory*
in erecting this rallying point of *insurrection* and *civil war,* was apprehended by the marshal of the district, accompanied by several *good citizens* of a neighboring town, and carried to Boston for examination, part
of which he underwent the same evening with Judge Lowell.

What! is it to be deemed seditious and considered an act of insurrection in our citizens to erect a liberty pole, reared in the commemoration
of our dear-bought FREEDOM and INDEPENDENCE, purchased with
their treasure and *their* blood ? . . . But so it is—*"Hail Columbia, happy
Land !"*

Federal Marshal Samuel Bradford of Boston has yet to apprehend David Brown,
the middle-aged "vagabond" who "stirred up" people to express their discontent
by erecting a liberty pole in Dedham, Massachusetts, but Bradford has arrested,
under the Sedition Law, Dedham farmer Benjamin Fairbanks, who was present
during its erection. Mr. Fairbanks faces a June sedition trial at the Federal
Circuit Court in Boston.[1711]

Today, George Washington writes Alexander Spotswood:

> *You ask my opinion of these [alien laws] . . .*
> *Consider to what lengths a Certain description of men in our Coun-*
> *try have already driven . . . matters and then ask if it is not time and*
> *expedient to resort to protecting Laws against Aliens (for Citizens you*
> *certainly know are not affected by that law) who acknowledge no alle-*
> *giance to this Country and in many cases are sent among us . . . for*
> *the express purpose of poisoning the minds of our people and to sow*
> *dissentions among them, in order to alienate their affections from the*
> *Government of their Choice, thereby endeavoring to dissolve the*
> *Union . . .*[1712]

Tonight, in the *Gazette of the United States*:

> CITIZENS OF PHILADELPHIA, A Meeting of the United Irishmen has
> been announced yesterday through the medium of Mrs. Bache's newspa-
> per—it is therefore asked what can be the intention of a meeting so des-
> ignated? . . .
> Americans beware! Look upon these United Irishmen, whatever ap-
> pearances they may put on, even with cockades in their hats, as so many
> serpents within your bosom . . . [K]eep a strict watch over United Irish-
> men—be persuaded that they are your enemies . . .

FRIDAY, NOVEMBER 23, 1798

GENERAL ★ AURORA ★ ADVERTISER

[Adv]

To be had at this office . . .
GIFFORD'S HISTORY OF FRANCE . . .
IN THREE VOLUMES ROYAL QUARTO
With a continuation, containing the
HISTORY OF THE REVOLUTION
to the close of 1796.
By WILLIAM DUANE.
The four volumes bound . . . PRICE 20 Dollars
The Revolutionary history may be had separately . . .

Tonight, in the *Gazette of the United States*:

> The *United Irishmen* in Philadelphia who are to assemble tonight, we
> are credibly informed, are composed of disaffected, illiterate Irish, Scotch,
> Dutch, and even—Americans!—Hence it would be no bull to say citizen
> Logan is an United *Irishman*.

GENERAL   ★ AURORA ★   ADVERTISER

In 1776 you fought against Britain and for liberty; and now you are unwilling to fight for Britain and John Adams. In 1776 you fought for the right of raising your money as you pleased, and now you are against John Adams raising it for you. In 1776, you fought in principle against parliament imposing sedition bills upon you, and now that your own representatives have done it, you murmur . . . In 1776, you fought for the right of speaking and publishing your sentiments as you pleased, and now that the Congress has determined that it is expedient of you to give up this right or to suspend the exercise of it, instead of submitting like good citizens, you seem determined to make greater use of your tongues than ever. These alone, independent of many other proofs which might have been adduced, manifestly shew . . . depravity . . .

Tonight, in the *Porcupine's Gazette*:

The PRESIDENT arrived in the city last evening about eight o'clock. The vessels of war, the troops of horse, artillery, &c. were prepared to receive him with due honors. The horse went on to meet him but returned with the news that he would not arrive 'till to day. In the meanwhile, he came in as privately as possible.

This day, at twelve o'clock, CAPTAIN DECATUR, from the *Delaware* sloop of war fired a federal salute on the occasion, which was accompanied by a salute fired by the 9th artillery, and by a peal from the bells of Christ Church.

MONDAY, NOVEMBER 26, 1798

GENERAL   ★ AURORA ★   ADVERTISER

The President of the United States arrived in town Friday evening . . . The Bells were not rung for the president on his arrival on Friday owing to his well known dislike of parade and empty adulation.

The address of the *United Irishmen* shall have a place about the close the week. [I]t was received too late on Saturday for this day's paper.

This morning, George Logan visits John Adams at the President's House in Philadelphia. President Adams:

I knew [Mr. Logan] had been . . . a zealous disciple of that democratical school which has propagated many errors in America and perhaps many tragical catastrophes in Europe . . . After his return [from France], he called upon me and, in a polite and respectful manner, . . . to express the desire of the Directory as well as his own to accommodate all disputes with America . . .

But the testimonies of . . . Mr. Logan . . . would have had no influence to dispose me to nominate a minister [to France], if I had not received authentic, regular, official, diplomatic assurances . . .[1713]

George Logan's wife, Deborah:

The President asked him many questions, all of which he answered with his usual candour. Nor did the President show to him any of that irritability of temper . . . [O]nly a little sally escaped him when the assurances of the Directory that they would receive a minister were repeated to him. He arose from his chair, and, with a characteristic action used when in earnest, "Yes," said he, "I suppose if I were to send Mr. Madison . . . or Dr. Logan, they would receive either of them. But I'll do no such thing; I'll send whom I please."[1714]

Today, Thomas Jefferson writes Virginian John Taylor:

I owe you a political letter. Yet the infidelities of the post office and the circumstances of the times are against my writing fully & freely, whilst my own dispositions are as much against mysteries, innuendoes & half-confidences. I know not which mortifies me most, that I should fear to write what I think, or my country bear such a state of things. Yet Lyon's judges and a jury of all nations are objects of rational fear . . .[1715]

Tonight, in the *Gazette of the United States*:

The public attention has been called during the past week to the flagrant and atrocious fact of the existence of a society of *United Irishmen* in this City . . . Every United Irishman ought to be hunted from the country, as much as a wolf or a tyger.—For a more bloody and remorseless band of organized assassins never polluted the fountains of society . . .

TUESDAY, NOVEMBER 27, 1798

GENERAL ★ AURORA ★ ADVERTISER

Dr. LOGAN we understand took the earliest opportunity of paying his respects to the President of the United States with whom he had a long conference yesterday morning.

The important information which we presume has been communicated by Dr. LOGAN to the Executive will, we doubt not, tend to secure us from the evils of a calamitous and fruitless war with which we were so imminently menaced.

Those who remember how much America is indebted to the patriotism and disinterested services of La Fayette . . . during our revolutionary war against the tyranny of Britain . . . will hear with pleasure that he has . . . written to General Washington . . . to prevent hostilities from taking place between the two Republics . . .

We shall not wonder if now that La Fayette has endeavored to secure the peace of America, the tory presses should teem with scurrility and abuse against him.

War is the Federal Cry, and behold the *presidential* and *ambassadorial* solecism—we are told we must go to war in order to prevent war—That is something like the man who cut his own throat in order that he should not *die before his time.*

Tonight, in the *Porcupine's Gazette*:

ADMIRAL NELSON'S VICTORY [over Napoleon's fleet at the Battle of the Nile in Egypt is] a bone too big for the Democrats to swallow . . . MOTHER BACHE swears bloodily it is *all a lie.* PEG knows better; but she . . . is letting the weight down upon her gang little by little . . . They now behold the power of France cut off, and with it all *their hopes of plunder.*

Tonight, in the *Gazette of the United States*:

THE *United Irishmen of Philadelphia* . . . have, it seems, AN ADDRESS on the anvil . . . What have Americans to do with the *Addresses of Irishmen* ?

Poor Logan and his dreams of peace seem both alike to have vanished.— Sunk, quite sunk in oblivion. It is cruel after a man has traveled so many thousands of miles for the *public good,* to meet no other salutation than *"How foolish you look!"*

WEDNESDAY, NOVEMBER 28, 1798

GENERAL ★ AURORA ★ ADVERTISER

Fenno asks what have Americans to do with the addresses of Irishmen? . . . A question might be asked better founded, however, what had *Irishmen* to do with the addresses of *Americans,* with the addresses of the American Congress, in 1776 ?

The tories will never forgive Dr. Logan for his endeavors to prevent a war: any more than for being a *republican* !

Tonight, in the *Porcupine's Gazette*:

The Officers of M'Pherson's Blues yesterday waited on the PRESIDENT to pay their respect to him on his return to the city.

The [French] Directory, in releasing the American ships and cargoes, have at least manifested such a disposition to peace with America they have never condescended to shew towards their *most sacred and excellent Majest[ies]* of Europe.

If a party or faction, whoever small, whether designated by the epithet of *federalists* or *tories*, uniformly oppose measures calculated to produce peace . . . and strenuously advocate the expediency of an alliance with Great Britain, the happy effects of a war with France, the propriety of abolishing the liberty of the press, to destroy the use of *free* speech, and deprecate the idea of an individual's saving his country from the horrors of an impending war, such a faction cannot have the real interests of their country at heart: *This is Treason against the People;* and the authors of it should be immediately ousted from the confidence of their supporters, and driven from their strongholds, with the punishment due to their evil machinations.

The object of the journey of our illustrious General Washington to Philadelphia, we learn, is to hold a Council of Officers on the military arrangements of the United States;—and he has already had communications on the subject with Major-Generals HAMILTON, and the *Secretary at War.* The General, it is said, will not leave Philadelphia until he has paid his respect to the PRESIDENT of the *United States,* and taken his *commands,* on the object of his journey.

The *grand council* which has been assembled in this city for some days, consisting of a *selection* of military officers, it is reported, have manifested a disposition to advise the organization of a large STANDING ARMY. If this should prove to be the fact . . . the people of America must look to their LIBERTIES . . .

Standing armies once established, a great and despotic body is created in the state, with interests hostile to the public liberties and, living under despotic laws, inconsistent with the spirit of a free government in any other circumstance than that of actual war.

Tonight, in the *Gazette of the United States:*

Public expectation waits on tip toe for the results of that august assemblage which now graces the city by its presence. It seems to be a thing of general expectation, however, that the Provisional Army will be raised and appointed . . .

Standing mercenary armies were first established in France in the fourteenth century—In America they were first attempted to be permanently established near the close of the eighteenth.

An enormous and unnecessary army—an equally unnecessary navy—and the institution of heavy *taxes* . . . has no doubt produced a species of influence where offices and appointments have been held out . . . and this influence . . . has given birth to a volume of adulation that will be, to future times, a painful monument [to] our rapid debasement from the sincerity of *republican* citizens to the humiliating manners and idiom of *monarchical subjects* . . .

The Presidential speech for the opening of Congress is said to be already on the *Federal anvil*—it is likely to undergo many severe strokes before it is *fit* for the public ear.

Tonight, in the *Porcupine's Gazette*:

PEG BACHE, I hear, begins to cry, "peace in Europe!" She is like all the *Poissarde* crew [lower-class market women] . . . when they once feel the point of your shoe or the lash of your horsewhip, they instantly call out for a cessation of hostilities. MOTHER BACHE and her gang have tried what *threats of war can do* . . . [T]hey now wish to persuade people that *Great Britain is going to make peace* and that poor America will be left in the lurch . . .

PEG lies like her husband . . . However, if Great Britain is about to make peace, don't you think, PEG, that *we had better make peace along with her?* And in order to be entitled to do that, don't you think *we had better join her in the war now?* Lay the *Poissarde* aside a bit; leave talking bawdry, and give me a civil, modest answer.

A very staunch *Federalist*, and who in our revolution displayed the strength of his *British attachments*, being asked his opinion of a standing army, said it was absolutely necessary to frighten *the Virginians and Kentuckians* !

At a very numerous meeting of the people of Orange, State of Virginia; at their court house . . . to take into account the alarming situation of the United States . . . Whereupon, the following address was presented . . .

TO THE GENERAL ASSEMBLY OF . . . VIRGINIA . . .

Shall we act, or shall we perish ? Shall usurpation threaten us by war into its measures? Is it necessary to submit to one of these evils as the very means of escaping the other ?

Tonight, William Cobbett in the *Porcupine's Gazette*:

There is no making any good of them . . . Once a Jew, a Jew always, and once a Jacobin, a Jacobin forever.

TUESDAY, DECEMBER 4, 1798

GENERAL ★ AURORA ★ ADVERTISER

The *echoes* of our ministerial *oracles* assert that the army of mercenaries contemplated to be raised are intended entirely for *home service*—this declaration is *as surprisingly candid* as important.

Yesterday an armed brig in our harbor, in discharging her guns, sent a cannon ball thro' the roof of Mr. Elgar's store in Greenwich street . . . The ball entered the south side of the roof, went clear throughout the opposite side, and lodged at the door of the house No 74, opposite the circus. It is next to a miracle that no further injury was done.

Tonight, in the *Gazette of the United States*:

The people of the United States will cease to wonder at the increased vilification heaped on Great Britain from the press of the *Aurora* when they learn that the present "doer" of that infamous paper is a miscreant whose conduct as a Printer in the East-Indies had been such as to call for the most rigorous interposition of the government—

Lord Cornwallis found it necessary to put the *forger* "Jasper Dwight" in Irons with an intention of sending him to his account in England—from this situation the culprit contrived to escape to this country—

Quere. Does not the treaty with Great Britain provide for surrendering Fugitives from justice ? Or did the vagabond arrive in America anterior to this salutary provision ?

The Cornwallis who placed me in irons in India is the same Cornwallis whom America defeated, with French help, at Yorktown, Virginia, in 1781 and the same Cornwallis whom Ireland failed to defeat, despite French help, two months ago on the Heights of Ballinamuck. Cornwallis was Governor-General of India when I published my newspaper in Bengal Province (1791–1794) before coming to America. My paper, the *Bengal World,* endorsed the French Revolution, criticized British slavery practices in Africa, disclosed abuses in the British East India Army, and, for such seditious writings, got me imprisoned at Fort Williams (site of Calcutta's Black Hole) and, in January of 1795, deported in irons.[1716] Whether Governor General of India, Viceroy of Ireland, or commander of the British army in Virginia, Charles Cornwallis is a soldier of the British monarch and an enemy to America, to Ireland, to France, and to me!

WEDNESDAY, DECEMBER 5, 1798

GENERAL ★ AURORA ★ ADVERTISER

Only one reporter was suffered to take the debates in the House of Representatives last session; it appears that there are to be two in the present . . . Be it remembered that the most important debate which took place in the House of Representatives last session, *has not yet been published*,— to wit, the debate on the execrated *Sedition Bill*.

By the management of affairs in the House of Representatives with regard to reporters, the party that puts the Speaker in the chair can always manage to have debates on odious measures suppressed by prohibiting any but a favored reporter who, though he may be the most able and honest man in the world, is liable to be influenced by the apprehension of a loss of bread for *disobedience !*

Tonight, in the *Gazette of the United States*:

The Dagger-Men, it seems, had prepared something which was called, "the address of the United Irishmen." This was put into the hands of *Jasper [Dwight]* in order to be pruned of its barbarities. He promised at the beginning of last week to give it place in the course of that week. But the keen indignation of the public, excited by the daring designs of these villains, has deprived them of their wonted assurance. The piece has not appeared.

THURSDAY, DECEMBER 6, 1798

GENERAL ★ AURORA ★ ADVERTISER

Where are the soldiers for a mercenary army [of the federal government] to be had? . . . [S]ay the good federalists, we can raise an army of Irish emigrants—and these to a man are *United Irishmen;* there are dilemmas on all sides, but one thing is certain, we can find *officers enough*, so that an army of 20,000 *officers* may be a handsome military establishment—*if the people will consent to pay them !*

FRIDAY, DECEMBER 7, 1798

GENERAL ★ AURORA ★ ADVERTISER

Matthew Lyon, it appears, has been with astonishing generosity allowed to purchase a stove and fire wood, and most condescendingly permitted to have them in prison with him.

Tonight, in the *Porcupine's Gazette*:

> *A Hint to the Federal Government on the subject of the ALIEN BILL ... [Y]esterday, the ... legacy of the molten Lightening Rod tells us that* America cannot look ... for a STANDING FORCE ... to Ireland—for "ALL THE IRISH EMIGRANTS IN AMERICA ARE UNITED IRISHMEN."— *Nota Bene !*

SATURDAY, DECEMBER 8, 1798

GENERAL   ★ AURORA ★   ADVERTISER

KENTUCKY LEGISLATURE ...

The [Kentucky] House ... moved the following RESOLUTIONS ...
I. *Resolved,* That the several states composing the United States of America are not united on the principle of unlimited submission to their general government ... that whensoever the general government assumes undelegated powers, its acts are unauthoritative, void, and of no force ...

Today, President Adams delivers his Second Annual Address at the opening of the Third Session of the Fifth Congress of the United States:[1717]

> *Gentlemen of the Senate and Gentlemen of the House of Representatives ...*
>
> *[N]othing is discoverable in the conduct of France which ought to change or relax our measures of defense. On the contrary, to extend and invigorate them is our true policy. We have no reason to regret that these measures have been thus far adopted ...*
>
> *[T]o send another minister [to France] without more determinate assurances that he would be received would be an act of humiliation to which the United States ought not to submit ... [W]hether we negotiate with her or not, vigorous preparations for war will be alike indispensable ...*
>
> *We ought without loss of time to lay the foundation for an increase of our Navy ...*[1718]

MONDAY, DECEMBER 10, 1798

GENERAL   ★ AURORA ★   ADVERTISER

OF THE SPEECH ...

[T]he speech says "nothing is discoverable in the conduct of France which ought to change or relax our measures of defence." The plain English of this is that France is not desirous of peace with us ... [W]e must unquestionably discredit the speech, for the *free relinquishment of our property* [American ships] *to the amount of half a million of dollars,* was a something in which a man not short-sighted or blind, must discern a disposition to peace . . .

Tonight, in the *Gazette of the United States*:

The *Dagger-Men* shall hear from me again, anon.

N. B. If Jasper is determined to suppress the promised "Address of the United Irishmen," bring it to me, and I will give it place.

TUESDAY, DECEMBER 11, 1798

GENERAL ★ AURORA ★ ADVERTISER

The arrangements for the [President's] speech on Saturday, whether by accident or otherwise, were remarkable; on the President's right were the British minister [to the U.S. Robert Liston] . . . and, on the British minister's left, General Washington; on the President's left were . . . the general officers [of the new federal army], and, in their rear . . . the political and civil functionaries . . . [T]he poor devils of short-hand writers were, by order of Mr. Speaker, shoved still further in the rear merely to prove the strength of their *oracular* and *intuitive* faculties.

[PHILADELPHIA.] On Saturday evening, Lankford Heron, Brick-maker, a native of Virginia, was taken out of his house in Hickory Lane, sign of the Liberty cap and pole, and brought before alderman Jennings who committed him to the city gaol for damning the President, all that took his part, and that wore the Black Cockade, &c.

Today, in the U.S. House of Representatives, the Annals of Congress report:

ALIEN AND SEDITION LAWS.

MR. HARPER [Federalist, S. Carolina] said no member of this House could be ignorant of the use made of [the alien and sedition laws] . . . No one could be ignorant of the ferment which had been raised and sedulously kept up on account of those laws. I do know, said he, of a certainty that this ferment has been raised and is kept up by a misrepresentation of the content of those laws . . . In order, therefore, to enable the people to judge for themselves . . . he offered a resolution . . .

"*Resolved, by the Senate and House of Representatives,* That the Secretary of State be, and he is hereby authorized, to cause to be printed and distributed throughout the United States ——copies of two acts [the Alien and Sedition Acts] . . ."[1719]

Tonight, in the *Gazette of the United States*:

When General Washington came into Congress Hall to hear the President's Speech, the members of both houses rose to him—an honor never paid to any but the President himself.

551

We are happy to learn that measures are pursuing to bring to justice the hardened villain who charged one of the most illustrious characters of our city with the horrid crime of MURDER. Indeed it is high time this infamous *Jasper* had resumed that *iron* situation which he fled from.

WEDNESDAY, DECEMBER 12, 1798

GENERAL ★ AURORA ★ ADVERTISER

The French vessels *Jaloux* [captured September 5th] and *Le Sanspareil* [captured August 23rd], having been condemned as lawful prizes, are to be sold by the Marshal at the Coffee house on Saturday next.

A letter received by way of New York . . . dated the 11th of October, says that the whole of [Ireland] was at that time in a general convulsion . . . The letter further adds that [British] General Lake had been defeated in several actions, and that the Irish rebels were carrying everything before them . . .

Today, with a gibe at George Logan, President Adams issues a public reply to a message from the United States Senate, including:

I have seen no real evidence of any change of system or disposition in the French Republic toward the United States. Although the officious interference of individuals without public character or authority is not entitled to any credit, yet it deserves to be considered whether that temerity and impertinence of individuals affecting to interfere in public affairs between France and the United States, whether by their secret correspondence or otherwise, and intended to impose upon the people and separate them from their Government, ought not to be inquired into and corrected.[1720]

THURSDAY, DECEMBER 13, 1798

GENERAL ★ AURORA ★ ADVERTISER

Mr. Harper having moved without success for the printing of several thousands of the Sedition Bill in order to have them dispersed through the United States, as the *Aurora* has at this time the most *extensive circulation* of any *Daily American Paper*, we are solicitous to shew our readiness on any occasion, where the member [of Congress] is in a reasonable disposition, to agree with him—We, therefore, republish the Sedition Bill, commonly called

THE GAG BILL
[Complete text of the Sedition Act follows.]

Today, George Washington writes the Secretary of War:

Nothing has been communicated to me respecting our foreign relations to induce the opinion that there has been any change in the situation of the country as to external danger which dictates an abandonment of the policy of the law in question . . . [N]o decisive indications have been given by France of a disposition to redress our past wrongs and do us future justice . . .[1721]

FRIDAY, DECEMBER 14, 1798

GENERAL ★ AURORA ★ ADVERTISER

It was observed that the President's reply to the Senate was "*confoundedly confused*"—upon which it was neatly remarked that it was *hastily written*. No praise could be more decisive than what DR. LOGAN has received in the form of an implied censure—*for having rescued his country from a wanton and fruitless war.*

Today, in the U.S. House of Representatives, the Annals of Congress report:

ALIEN AND SEDITION LAWS.

The House having again taken up Mr. HARPER'S proposition for printing 20,000 copies of the above laws . . .

Mr. DAWSON [Republican, Virginia] would move [an amendment] to have printed with these laws all parts of the Constitution which appeared to him to relate to the subject . . .

Mr. HARPER [Federalist, S. Carolina] desired to pass by the extreme futility of publishing to the people, at this day, parts of a Constitution which had been in force ten years . . .

Mr. GALLATIN [Republican, Pennsylvania] . . . was convinced that there was as much necessity for the proposed amendment [to publish the Constitution] as for the original resolution [to publish the Sedition Act]; and that, therefore, if the resolution was adopted, the amendment ought to be adopted also . . .

The question on the original resolution was then taken and decided in the negative—yeas 34, nays 45 . . .[1722]

SATURDAY, DECEMBER 15, 1798

GENERAL ★ AURORA ★ ADVERTISER

The reply of the President to the Senate . . . merits a serious regard . . . The interference of an unauthorized person [Dr. Logan] to save his country from the horrible evils of a war is not only censurable but also ought to be corrected, says the public servant of the people.

It is wondered how [Mr. Adams] will reconcile his own conduct whilst in Europe in 1778, during our revolutionary war, when trying to impress into our service a state to which he was not sent. In that case, was he not also an *unauthorized* individual endeavoring to bring an *uncon-nected nation* into the situation which all abhor?

A majority of the house of representatives, having refused to circulate copies of the constitution with the unconstitutional [alien and sedition] bills, a subscription was opened yesterday evening for the circulation of a suitable number [of constitutions]—One hundred and eleven dollars were directly subscribed. Subscriptions received by the editor of the *Aurora*.

Tonight, in the *Gazette of the United States*:

Yesterday morning, Lieut. Gen. WASHINGTON left this city on his journey to Mount Vernon, Virginia.

TUESDAY, DECEMBER 18, 1798

GENERAL ★ AURORA ★ ADVERTISER

The Legislature of Virginia it appears have granted leave for the *introduction* of a Bill for "securing the members of the Legislature from prosecutions under the Sedition Bill in case they should think proper, in the course of their proceedings, to charge the Congress with an infraction of the constitution in the passage of it."

Tonight, in the *Porcupine's Gazette*:

FABRICATING.

The other day *Mother Bache's* paper . . . contained a letter fabricated by some United Irishmen of New York. This letter stated that the French had made a successful landing in Ireland, that they were joined by numerous friends, that they had . . . beaten General Lake in three separate engagements.

Those who first fabricated and published this knew well that nobody but rabble would believe it . . .

Tonight, in the *Gazette of the United States*:

What is a United Irishman? May not Irishmen unite as well as we ? Look to Ireland for his character, and behold it is written in blood . . . An Irish *gentleman* is one of the finest characters in nature. The rest of the nation is represented by the bulk of those who came to this country— such men as Burke, Lyon, Reynolds . . . and Duane, the bare mention of whom is sufficient without the trouble of elucidation . . .

By carnage and plunder they subsisted there: in massacre and ravage they can be happy here . . . The scheme, in its rude outline, is to bring on a revolutionary state in America . . . They coalesced with the Jacobins (most of the leaders of whom have actually been admitted within the pale of the society) . . . Do I hear some one cry, "Name them! Name them!"

Lend me your patience and I will . . . They should have a dissemination as wide as the extent of the evil . . .

List of UNITED IRISHMEN . . .

Samuel Wiley, *Teacher in the College;* John Black, *Ditto* Thomas M'Adams, *Schoolmaster;* John O'Reilley, *Ditto* —— Moffat, Zachary's Court —— Reynolds, Robert Bronston —— Duane, *alias Jasper Dwight;* Matthew Lyon *of Vermont,* . . . Andrew Magill; James T. Callender, Lloyd *of Newgate;* J[ohn] D[aly] Burke, *late delegate from N. York* . . .

Teachers and journalists are on the *Gazette of the United States'* list of America's enemies. I am on it. Other *Aurora* people are on it. Jimmy Callender, Jimmy Reynolds, and my most important friend and assistant Newgate Lloyd[1723] all contribute to the *Aurora.*

WEDNESDAY, DECEMBER 19, 1798

GENERAL ★ AURORA ★ ADVERTISER

The Tories, when they find a man's public conduct so steadfast in the cause of the Constitution and civil liberty as to wound their feelings,— resort to the stale trick of calling him an *Alien* or a *Frenchman* or an *Irishman*—the nature of these aspersions, it must be confessed, is rather flattering, considering whence they come and what is the cause of the assertion.

Tonight, in the *Gazette of the United States*:

Our government is under a moral obligation to DECLARE WAR against France . . .

THURSDAY, DECEMBER 20, 1798

GENERAL ★ AURORA ★ ADVERTISER

There is not an advocate for monarchy in this country who does not mingle professions of veneration for republican principles with the incessant efforts to subvert the constitution and to destroy liberty.

Today, from her home in Quincy, Abigail Adams writes her nephew, William Shaw, the President's new private secretary:

I receive the papers regularly which will now become more interesting as Congress proceed in business . . . The Aurora shows that tho Bache is dead, he yet speaketh, or rather that the party which supported him are determined to have a press devoted to them. Whether the influence is foreign or domestick, or both together, it is of

consequence that it should be made to keep within the bounds of deco-
rum and . . . yeald to the laws. I expect we shall have to use some of
the tribute [money] due to Talleyrand before the daring Spirit of Ken-
tucky and its mother State will be quiet . . .[1724]

Tonight, in the *Gazette of the United States*:

Newspaper Jacobinism is in a hectic in the United States—The saffron-
coloured *Aurora,* enveloped in murkey clouds and deceptive fogs, is now
the only harbinger of delusive *mock-suns.* Old [New York] *Argus,* who
once had pretensions to an hundred eyes, is now a *cyclop* with one and
that blurry:—and the [Boston] *Chronique*—alas!—*"sans wit—sans
sense—sans sous."*

It's true. The nation's two other leading republican newspapers, the New York
Argus (now managed by Thomas Greenleaf's widow) and Boston's *Independent
Chronicle* (whose publisher, Thomas Adams, has been ill since his indictment
under the Sedition Act) are fragile!

FRIDAY, DECEMBER 21, 1798

GENERAL ★ AURORA ★ ADVERTISER

TO THE FREEMEN . . . OF PHILADELPHIA
[Today] will be an election for a Representative in the [Pennsylvania]
General Assembly. It is of importance that you should appear and give
your suffrages,—and these should be given to a man who is a friend to
your Liberties, to your Constitution, and to your peace . . . GEORGE
LOGAN . . . Convince the world that you still love liberty, and that those
who would rob you of it have your contempt and execration,—*Peace !
Peace ! Peace !*

Today, at noon, the majority of Pennsylvania's Federalist-controlled House of
Representatives delivers an *"ADDRESS to John Adams, President of the United
States:"*

*Sir, . . . We have seen . . . the unlimited ambition of the rulers of the
French people—that the Atlantic itself gives no bounds to their projects
of subjugation; and that the United States of America are threatened
. . . not so much with open hostility . . . as with a division, by means of
a dark and insidious policy, of the people from the government of their
choice . . . That you, Sir, have been constantly aware of the effects of
this policy . . . must be highly gratifying to the patriotic pride of every
independent mind . . .*[1725]

John Adams answers:

*The insidious and malevolent policy [of France] of dividing people
and nation from their government is not original; the French have not
the credit even of the invention of it . . .*

Candor must own that our country lies under a reproach . . . of pro-ducing individuals who are capable not only of dark interferences by usurpation in our external concerns, but also capable of forgetting or renouncing their principles, feelings and habits in a foreign country and becoming enemies to their own . . . Whether this is owing to a want of national character or a want of criminal law, a remedy ought to be sought.

The solemn pledge you give to co-operate with the general govern-ment in averting all foreign influence and detecting domestic intrigue is very important to the common welfare of our country and will give great satisfaction to the Union . . .[1726]

Tonight, Jack Ward Fenno in the *Gazette of the United States*:

UNITED IRISHMEN.

There came last night to my House two ruffians, one of whom lurked about the porch, while the other, as I stood at my own door, struck me on the head with a bludgeon. Amazed at such baseness, I turned into my office to seize a stick, instead of pressing on the assailant, whereby I might have promptly punished his audacity . . . I went after the nocturnal assassin this morning to return his domiciliary visit. A woman came forward to say he was not at home. He will not, however, pass unpunished . . . and if these Dagger-Men choose to push things to extremities, they will find me better prepared.   JOHN WARD FENNO.

SUNDAY, DECEMBER 23, 1798

Today, Abigail Adams writes her nephew, Presidential Secretary William Shaw:

You sent me two Auroras one of which containd a most insolent comment upon the president's speech. A Friend also sent me the [Boston Independent] Chronicle. It certainly has not taken its lesson . . .[1727]

MONDAY, DECEMBER 24, 1798

GENERAL   ★ AURORA ★   ADVERTISER

Friday evening the election of a member to the seat . . . in the Pennsylvania Legislature closed, when upon counting up the votes in the several districts . . . the numbers appeared to be

Total for George Logan	1,256
For F. A. Muhlenberg	769
Majority for Logan	487

The election of *Dr. Logan* is the best reply which could have been given by the *people* to the *President*.

Franklin declares all power to be in the people when the servants violate their duties or when they violate the constitution.

Today, in Richmond, Virginia, the Virginia state senate concurs in resolutions passed three days ago by the Virginia House of Delegates, including:

> *First.* *Resolved,* That the General Assembly of Virginia doth unequivocally express a firm resolution to maintain and defend the Constitution of the United States . . .
>
> *Fourth.* That the General Assembly doth also express its deep regret that a spirit has in sundry instances been manifested by the Federal Government to enlarge its powers . . . the obvious tendency and inevitable result of which would be *to transform the present republican system of the United States into an absolute, or, at best, a mixed monarchy.*
>
> *Fifth.* That the General Assembly doth particularly protest against the palpable and alarming infraction of the Constitution in the two late cases of the "Alien and Sedition Acts," passed at the last session of Congress . . .
>
> *Sixth.* That this State . . . by its convention which ratified the Federal Constitution expressly declared, among other essential rights, "the liberty of conscience and of the press cannot be canceled, abridged, restrained, or modified by any authority of the United States" . . .
>
> *Seventh.* That the good people of this Commonwealth . . . doth hereby declare that the acts aforesaid are unconstitutional . . .[1728]

James Madison drafted these resolutions for Virginia, just as Thomas Jefferson drafted similar resolutions for Kentucky. Together, they'll be known as the "Virginia and Kentucky Resolutions."

Tonight, William Cobbett in the *Porcupine's Gazette*:

> Madame Bache is constantly congratulating her jacobinic horde on the inestimable blessings resulting from the late embassy of the notorious Logan: to him she says they may look as their saviour . . . They say this Logan has effected the raising of the embargo; that he has induced the Directory to cause a momentary suspension of depredations on our commerce, &c . . . I do believe he was the envoy of Jefferson and Co . . . but it is not to Doctor Logan nor Thomas Jefferson that we are indebted; it is to the energetic measures of our government—which they opposed and would have prevented had it been in their power . . .
>
> UNITED IRISHMEN . . .
> I did regret that Mr. Fenno brought his list of disaffected Irish forward so soon; but it seems to have produced a most excellent effect. It has

558

awakened the attention of every body in the city, and there is good reason to believe that it will have the same effect in distant places. All that is wanted to crush the enemies of government is *to make them well known* . . .

Every discovery, every fact . . . is an eulogium on the wisdom of Congress in passing the Alien and Sedition Laws . . .

To return to the *United Irishmen* . . . [T]heir views in both countries were and are the same; *to excite a rebellion to be supported by France.*

TUESDAY, DECEMBER 25, 1798
[CHRISTMAS DAY]

Today, from Mount Vernon, George Washington answers a letter from the French hero of the American Revolution the Marquis de Lafayette:

> *It is equally unnecessary for me to apologize to you for my long silence* . . .
>
> *To give you a . . . view of the politics and situation . . . a party exists in the United States, formed by a Combination of Causes, which oppose the Government and are determined (as all their Conduct evinces), by Clogging its Wheels, indirectly to change the nature of it and to subvert the Constitution . . . The friends of Government, who are anxious to maintain its neutrality and to preserve the country in peace and adopt measures to produce these, are charged by them as being Monarchists, Aristocrats, and infractors of the Constitution . . . [T]hey arrogated to themselves . . . the sole merit of being the friends of France . . . denouncing those who differed in opinion, whose principles are purely American* . . .
>
> *You have expressed a wish . . . that I would exert all my endeavors to avert the Calamitous effects of a rupture between our Countries . . . But France . . . whilst it was crying peace, Peace and pretending that they did not wish us to be embroiled in their quarrel with great Britain, they were pursuing measures in this Country so repugnant to its sovereignty and so incompatible with every principle of neutrality, as must inevitably have produced a war with the latter. And when they found the Government here was resolved to adhere steadily to its plan of neutrality, their next step was to destroy the confidence of the people in and to separate them from it; for which purpose their diplomatic agents were specially instructed; and in the attempt were aided by inimical characters among ourselves, not . . . because they loved France . . . but because it was an instrument to Facilitate the destruction of their own Government* . . .
>
> *After my valedictory address to the people of the United States, you would no doubt be surprised to hear that I had again consented to Gird on the Sword . . . I could not remain an unconcerned spectator* . . .[1729]

Even were it true that France's *"diplomatic agents"* (such as its first Minister to the U.S., Edmond Genêt) were *"pursuing measures in this Country so repugnant to its sovereignty and so incompatible with every principle of neutrality,"* how would this have been different from what Ben Franklin did in France in 1777 to end France's declared neutrality and to force her into America's war with Britain? And Franklin had no alliance to justify his behavior! Has Washington forgotten ?

Today, George Washington also writes U.S. Minister in The Hague William Vans Murray:

> The Alien and Sedition Laws are not the desiderata in the opposi-
> [t]ion . . . [S]omething there will always be for them to torture and to
> disturb the public mind with their unfounded and ill favored forebod-
> ings.[1730]

THURSDAY, DECEMBER 27, 1798

GENERAL ★ AURORA ★ ADVERTISER

The people of France, after centuries of slavery, altered their form of government from a monarchy to a republic. This certainly was not a new project, for we had only eleven years before . . . done the very same things but with the difference of *six or seven centuries* less of provocation.

On Tuesday evening arrived in town the author of the Declaration of American Independence—Thomas Jefferson, Vice President of the United States.

The results of the election in the country is galling to the tories . . . notwithstanding every artifice and calumny which could be devised to render Dr. Logan odious to the eyes of the people . . .

Matthew Lyon [of Vermont] we understand has obtained a majority of 664 votes in the recent election for member of the next Congress. The good man *Roger* [Griswold, Federalist Congressman from Connecticut] has undertaken to wipe the *saliva* off the face of the odious Sedition Bill–it is the misfortune of some folks to be always employed upon *dirty* work.

George Washington refuses to shake hands with George Logan, yet Pennsylvanians elect George Logan to their state assembly! John Adams jails Matthew Lyon for sedition, but Vermonters reelect Matthew Lyon to Congress! Flickers of hope!

Tonight, in the *Gazette of the United States*:

> Mr. FENNO, The very judicious observations of a writer in your paper
> on the tenor of the *Aurora* advertisements also accounts for an odd cir-

cumstance which occurred a few days ago. Upon an order for the publication of a Bankrupt's notice, application was made to the court to point out some medium for publication. "Extremely well thought of," said his honor: "it is highly proper that the court should direct in such as case; suppose we say Claypoole's, Bradford's or—or—or—The *Aurora*." . . .

[I]t must on all hands be allowed "highly proper" that those who find themselves already bankrupted by jacobinism can no where else so appropriately figure as in a Gazette the principles of which tend to bankrupt the whole community.

SATURDAY, DECEMBER 29, 1798

GENERAL   ★ AURORA ★   ADVERTISER

AN ADMONITION TO YOUNG FENNO

It ought to be remembered that Fenno deceas'd was an insolvent in Boston before he became printer . . .

Before the young gentleman consigns to infamy all the unfortunate, he should wipe away the stain which equally belongs to his own family . . .

[H]ow just must the President's observation be that we have persons among us of no character—but is it the nation or administration to whom this best applies ?

The United Irishmen stand precisely in the same *odious circumstances* with relation to England that John Adams stood 20 years ago—they consider George III an intolerable tyrant *now*, as he did *then*.

Tonight, in the *Gazette of the United States*:

Extract of a letter from Northampton County, state of Pennsylvania, dated December 17th, 1798.

"As to politics, they run very high here; and there is much disturbances among the people of Northampton county in particular in regard to the taxation. They have plainly told the assessors, on the peril of their lives, not to pretend to execute the orders of assessment, in consequence of which the assessors have returned their warrants to the commissioners . . . How far this matter will be carried God only knows."

MONDAY, DECEMBER 31, 1798

GENERAL   ★ AURORA ★   ADVERTISER

The farmers of Pennsylvania have generally become alarmed by the attempt made by the federal assessor to feel the depth of their pockets . . . for war money !

> The farmers suspect that the executive administration is somewhat extravagant when it asks for a house tax . . . at a time when their apprehensions of a war with the French Republic have ceased . . .

Before the designs . . . to do away [with] the concern of every individual in the *freedom* and *peace* of his country can be accomplished, there must be a gag bill to stop the press and voice and a standing army to dragoon us to obedience . . . [W]e must be as destitute of *virtue, the love of liberty,* of republican government, and of everything that gives us a national character;—but we are told we have not a character,—there is some consistency at least in the *projects* of some people.

Today, John Adams writes Abigail:

> *Logan's election to the legislature will give the Jacobins a triumph . . . Logan seems more fool than knave. It is thought the V. P. stays away from very bad motives. I am told he is considered here as the Head of the opposition to Government both in the old Dominion [Virginia] and Kentucky. He is certainly acting a part that he will find hard to justify . . .* [1731]

Today, an Episcopal Minister, John Cosens Ogden, presents John Adams with a petition from three or four thousand Vermonters who beg a presidential reprieve for their reelected congressman, Matthew Lyon.[1732] John Adams responds to the Rev. Ogden that, *"penitence must precede pardon"* and warns, *"as for you, sir, your interference in this business will prevent your receiving any favours from me."*[1733]

As the year draws to a close, Alexander Hamilton, who is now second in command of America's new federal army, warns Brigadier General Jonathan Dayton:

> *The late attempt of Virginia and Kentucky to unite the State legislatures in a direct resistance to certain laws of the Union can be considered in no other light than as an attempt to change the government. It is stated, in addition, that the opposition party in Virginia . . . have followed up the hostile declarations . . . by an actual preparation of the means of supporting them by force; that they have taken measures to put their militia on a more efficient footing—are preparing considerable arsenals and magazines . . . Amidst such serious indications of hostility, the safety and the duty of supporters of the government call upon them to adopt vigorous measures of counteraction. It will be wise in them to act upon the hypothesis that the opposers of the government are resolved, if it shall be practical, to make its existence a question of force . . .*
>
> *To preserve confidence in the officers of the general government by preserving their reputations from malicious and unfounded slanders*

is essential to enable them to fulfill the ends of their appointment . . . Renegade aliens conduct more than one of the most incendiary presses in the United States—yet, in open contempt and defiance of the laws, they are permitted to continue their destructive labors. Why are they not sent away? [1734]

Tonight, in the *Gazette of the United States:*

THE AURORA

MR. FENNO, . . . *Citizen Jasper* is not the man I took him for . . . I am told the *Aurora* is so hampered with debt and disgrace that it must soon sink . . .

CHARITY

Tonight, in the *Porcupine's Gazette*:

Fellow Citizens, New Year's eve is approaching when it is feared that the idle practice which has for some time prevailed in the City and Liberties of *Shooting out the Old Year and Shooting in a New One,* as it is absurdly called, will be repeated which has often been attended with dangerous and alarming consequences . . . [T]he constables and watchmen are particularly enjoined to be vigilant and active in arresting such daring violators of the public peace . . .

ROBERT WHARTON,
Mayor [of Philadelphia]

TUESDAY, JANUARY 1, 1799

GENERAL ★ AURORA ★ ADVERTISER

The little old man who got his two sons [Thomas and John Quincy Adams] established at Berlin and who has his nephew [William Shaw] fixed in his Secretaryship, wanted his son-in-law, Col. S.[mith] appointed adjutant-general . . . *Timotheus* has been canvassing for "the Chief," and it is understood that son-in-law will get a regiment . . .

Today, Secretary of State Timothy Pickering writes the U.S. district attorney for New York that President Adams wants the editor of the New York *Time Piece* to leave the country:

I have laid before the President of the U. States your letter of the 28th relative to the prosecution against J.[ohn] D.[aly] Burke for a libel. All circumstances considered, the President thinks it may be expedient to let him off, on the condition . . . that he Burke forthwith quit the United States. The vessel in which he embarks should be known, with her destination. Such a turbulent, mischievous person ought not to remain on this side of the Atlantic . . . [1735]

GENERAL   ★ AURORA ★   ADVERTISER

The close of the old and the opening of the new year were celebrated by a chearful party of republicans who, having spent the last hours of 1798 in rational conversation, proceeded to the lodgings of Thomas Jefferson with a band of instrumental music. On their way, they were met with another party of republicans engaged in the same festive purpose.

A letter from Vergennes in Vermont says—Colonel [Matthew] Lyon continues under as strict a state of confinement as before. At his own expence, he has provided a stove with firing and put four squares of glass to the window. Nevertheless he is reelected by a majority of between eight and nine hundred votes. His conduct on any occasion has not been more praiseworthy than in preventing, by his entreaties and arguments, the violence which the people were about to commit upon his confinement. He opposed several proposals for liberating him by force . . .

Tonight, in the *Porcupine's Gazette*:

From Mother Bache . . . and such people, it is natural to expect to hear the government of Great Britain continually stigmatized as a tyranny and the rebels of Ireland applauded as combatants in the glorious cause of [freeing] their country from oppression . . .

To defend the conduct of Great Britain with respect to . . . Catholic Emancipation . . . I will tell you a real and true impediment . . . to the admission of Romanists into either house of [the Irish] parliament or into the executive offices of the state . . . is that Romanists refuse to take the oath of supremacy . . . The kings and queens of this realm, and their successors, are declared to be supreme heads, that is, governors of the church of Ireland . . . It is very notorious that all Irish Romanists acknowledge the authority, pre-eminence, and jurisdiction of the bishop of Rome . . .

Tonight, in the *Gazette of the United States*:

It is said the French have a Frigate in their Navy called *Le Bache*.

On Monday was presented to the President of the United States, by a citizen of Vermont, a petition from Matthew Lyon, one of the representatives in Congress for that state, (now confined in prison in consequence of a conviction of seditious practices), praying for a remission of the punishment to which he has been sentenced.

GENERAL ★ AURORA ★ ADVERTISER

TO THE CITIZENS OF THE UNITED STATES . . .

I embarked for Europe; on my arrival at Hamburg, I met with the distinguished friend to our country, General La Fayette. He procured for me
the means of pursuing my journey to Paris. Regarding himself equally
the citizen of the United States and of France, he views with particular
anxiety the existing difficulties . . . and has written to general Washington . . . [C]itizen Merlin [chief of the Directory] . . . informed me that
France had not the least intention to interfere in the public affairs of the
United States; that his country had acquired great reputation in having
assisted the United States to become a free Republic; they would not
disgrace their own Revolution by attempting its destruction. He observed
that with respect to the violation of our flag, it was common to all Neutrals and was provoked by the example of England and intended to place
France on an equal ground with her . . .   GEORGE LOGAN

Today, Abigail Adams writes her nephew, William Shaw:

> *I would have you continue to send me the papers as you have done,*
> *and Mother Bache's . . . The re-election of Lyon and the choice of Logan*
> *are mortifying proofs that "there is something rotten in the State of*
> *Denmark," that a low groveling faction still exists amongst us . . . I*
> *was much diverted with your account of Logan's visit—*[1736]

GENERAL ★ AURORA ★ ADVERTISER

Mr. *Adams* says the American character is equivocal—the following
toasts, given by a *party* of his *warmest* admirers, are not of the *equivocal*
character,—

"*Confusion to emigrant patriots*" . . .

the first example among mankind in which *patriotism* is made an object
of reproach . . .

Tonight, Jack Ward Fenno in the *Gazette of the United States*:

> The measure of raising a subscription from the friends of government
> to prolong the existence of the dying *Aurora* is too *selfish* for men of honor
> to promote. The writhings of the *nate dea* [risen goddess] are, to be sure,
> diverting enough to make us wish for a continuation of the amusement—
> but in charity we should remember that the Goddess will, after all, have
> to say, "this may be sport to you; but it is death to me."

Democracy howls with a louder and more piteous cry as it advances toward its trials.

MONDAY, JANUARY 7, 1799

GENERAL ★ AURORA ★ ADVERTISER

War or peace with France is the important, the awful question which now agitates the public mind . . .

Tonight, William Cobbett in the *Porcupine's Gazette*:

Among the circumstances of the glorious [British] Victory of the Nile, two have tickled my risible faculties. The one is the capture of [the French ship] *Le Franklin*, the old lightening-catcher; and the other is the clatter that there must have been among the mathematical, chemical and philosophical instruments while the British Tars were pouring their thunderbolts . . . If Raynal, Voltaire, Rousseau, and the rest of the tribe has met with such a fate as soon as they began to vomit forth their poison, how happy would it have been for the world!

TUESDAY, JANUARY 8, 1799

GENERAL ★ AURORA ★ ADVERTISER

During the recess of Congress, the *Secretary* [of Congress] made a bargain with a printer who had married the sister of Mr. *Senator Goodhue* of Massachusetts to print the business of the Senate. *Fenno* executed this work *before* . . . Some senators, finding this out, spoke to the Secretary and threatened if the printing was not given to Fenno, the matter should be brought before the house . . . and the Yankee printer lost his job to the great profit of master Fenno . . .

SATURDAY, JANUARY 12, 1799

GENERAL ★ AURORA ★ ADVERTISER

TO THE CITIZENS OF THE UNITED STATES . . .
Whilst I was in Paris, Mr. Skipwith, the Consul General of the United States, received officially from the government in France an Arrette by which the embargo was removed from all American vessels in French ports, accompanied by another directing the release and kind treatment of all our seamen . . . On my arrival in Philadelphia, I embraced the earliest opportunity of waiting on the Secretary of State, with the public dispatches entrusted to my care . . . I also waited on the President of the United States. GEORGE LOGAN

This morning, the *Aurora*'s compositors and pressmen write Peggy Bache:

> *Madam, In Saturday last, we learned from Mr. Duane, with regret and surprise, of your intention to lower the wages of your Compositors to seven dollars per week . . . also refusing another hand at Press.— Our astonishment is certainly justifiable when we look to the daily increase of the Paper in popularity, its circulation more than usually extensive, and its friends so respectable and numerous;—it must truly be allowed that the Aurora has, for esteem and merit, in a few short weeks established itself unrivaled . . .*
>
> *Madam, the Compositors . . . say that if they were by the piece . . . the charge for the matter daily composed would actually amount to the same . . . allowed by every office in the city . . . However we except [Fenno] and Cobbett (but God forbid they should be precedent to you in any case), even these execrable furnaces of abuse allow their Compositors to be worth seven dollars, although their composition is not so great as ours by a third and they seldom, if ever, light candles . . .*
>
> *The pressmen . . . the toil we bear at night will scarcely admit of us to renew the next day's labour.—We must, therefore, in consideration of our health, repeat to you our former request, that is,—"another hand at press, and the present salary."*

—Compositors—	—Pressmen—
John H. Robertson	Jacob Franck
Samuel Starr	Bartholomew Graves
George White	John Alexander
Jos. Robinson	
Robert Crombie[1737]	

Peggy answers the compositors and pressmen:

> *M. H. Bache has given every consideration . . . Hitherto the Aurora has certainly not done more than support itself . . . [S]he would rather increase than lessen the establishment of every person employed in the Office, but she fears she cannot give more than what is given to compositors in the Printing Offices whose papers are more profitable from advertisements. She does not wish or expect that the pressmen should exert themselves beyond their abilities. The Editor must, however, determine, for she is inadequate to the task, how many Pressmen are absolutely necessary . . .*[1738]

TUESDAY, JANUARY 15, 1799

GENERAL   ★ AURORA ★   ADVERTISER

☞ *The Pressmen and Compositors of this office, having unwarrantably and without cause, neglected to perform their duty, the paper is unavoidably published in this form [half-size without advertisements].*

PRINTERS.
FOUR COMPOSITORS and TWO STEADY AND
WILLING PRESSMEN WANTED, at the *Aurora* office.
And TWO SMART LADS as APPRENTICES.

This morning, the *Aurora*'s compositors and pressmen write Peggy Bache:

> Madam, . . . A fact we will submit to your consideration.—Mr.
> Graves, one of your pressman, with due respect to the Official Capac-
> ity of your Editor, informed him, agreeable to his promise of a fourth
> pressman, that there was one out of employ and conjured him . . . to
> employ this person. At this, he got passionate for an alleged assump-
> tion of power and discharged him . . .
> We have concluded, in our minds, that if your goodness had been
> consulted, his discharge would not have taken place;—at the same
> time, we must say—that we have pledged ourselves to each other that
> if a reasonable cause was not assigned . . . we all would be obliged to
> quit our employ . . .
> The late Compositors and Pressmen <u>of the Aurora</u>.[1739]

Peggy immediately answers:

> M. H. Bache informs the late Pressmen & Compositors of the Au-
> rora that the conduct of the Aurora Office is entirely under the di-
> rection of Mr. Duane & and that she cannot interfere in any shape
> whatever.[1740]

Today, George Washington expresses his displeasure with opposition to the
Sedition Act:

> Unfortunately, and extremely do I regret it, the State of Virginia has
> taken the lead in this opposition . . . though in no State except Ken-
> tucky (that I have heard of) has Legislative countenance been ob-
> tained, beyond Virginia . . .
> But at a crisis as this, when every thing dear and valuable to us is
> assailed; when this [Republican] party hangs upon the Wheels of Gov-
> ernment . . . when every Act of their own Government is tortured by
> constructions . . . into attempts to infringe and trample upon the Con-
> stitution with a view to introduce monarchy . . . ought characters who
> are best able to rescue their Country from the pending evil to remain
> at home? . . .
> [I]f their conduct is viewed with indifference . . . their numbers, ac-
> cumulated by Intriguing and discontented foreigners under proscrip-
> tion, who were at war with their own governments; and the greater
> part of them with all Government, their numbers will encrease, and
> nothing short of Omniscience can foretell the consequences . . .[1741]

Tonight, in the *Gazette of the United States*:

> *Duane* was at Pole's auction on *Saturday evening last*. On the *same* evening at the *same* place, a gentleman *lost* his pocket-book containing about 40 dollars.

WEDNESDAY, JANUARY 16, 1799

GENERAL ★ AURORA ★ ADVERTISER

A list of names was some time ago published in the *Gazette of the United States* whereto was prefixed a variety of heinous charges against the society of United Irishmen . . . [S]everal . . . who were not members of that body . . . stept forward to demand a justification from the editor of that paper . . . Mr. Brobston . . . in consequence of justice not being done him as he wished, took upon himself to take satisfaction. An altercation ensued, and Mr. Fenno received a blow which felled him to the ground. A prosecution was commenced by Fenno . . . The Defendant pleaded guilty . . . The Court in consideration that the defendant had taken the law into his own hands, declared that he should be fined, but in consideration of the atrocity of the provocation, made the fine only 15 dollars.

☞ *This is the case about which Fenno . . . made so much noise and roared about assassination and "to arms"!*

This morning, Benny's doctor brother, William Bache, delivers to Jack Fenno, at the *Gazette of the United States,* the following note:

> *SIR, I have seen your paper . . . —In what were termed "A List of United Irishmen," recourse was had (to evade the laws) to the pitiful artifice of printing my surname with a blank prefixed . . . I, Sir, feel it no insult to be called an United Irishman. I glory in the illustrious epithet; but the above calumnies on me . . . gave me the right to demand the satisfaction due for any personal insult . . .*
>
> *My friend who bears this is in possession of my further sentiments.*
>
> JAMES REYNOLDS. [1742]

Tonight, in the *Gazette of the United States*:

> What ought we to think of the honorable provision made for the heirs of Benjamin Franklin Bache, when the Compositors and Pressmen refuse to be concerned in the dirty business?
>
> It is reported that a dispute took place some few days since, among the writers in the *Aurora,* on the subject of the merits of their respective essays; and that, upon their appealing to the proprietor, she very modestly decided in favor of the Irishman's *performances.*

Jack Fenno is on dangerous ground when he puns about Peggy's being pleased with my "performances."

On Tuesday Fenno took some liberties with the name of a gentleman [Dr. James Reynolds, who] on this occasion . . . condescended to bring himself down to the level of Mr. *Fenno's* gentility and to demand *reparation* or *satisfaction*—but this *military non-commissioned hero* declared with great *trepidation and obviously with truth* that he really was not in the habit of acting like a *gentleman*. He must be a *coward* indeed who can suffer himself to be called to his beard a *coward*—Contempt is the *cheap* protection of such infamy . . .

Forty-one days have elapsed since the President promised a communication to Congress relative to our situation with France . . . In the meanwhile, a considerable loan with a heavy interest is saddled on our backs, a tax is to be collected . . . with all the dangers arising from an augmentation of a *standing army* . . .

Tonight, in the *Gazette of the United States*:

A splendid Ball was given last evening at the Theatre in honor of the President of the United States . . . [A] flooring had been thrown over the Pit, forming a very handsome area for dancing . . .

At about 8 o'clock, the President entered, music playing the march. The dancing then commenced and continued 'till about 11, when the painted Cloth was rolled up and displayed the supper tables on the stage, elegantly arranged and decorated. General Macpherson presided—on his right sat the President . . . After supper, the company returned to dancing and about one separated without an occurrence to mar the pleasure of the entertainment.

The following is a copy of a paper posted up in the public Coffee-room of this city, yesterday at two o'clock, in the presence of Robert Moore, esq. and several of the gentlemen who usually assemble there.

Philadelphia, January 17, 1798.
In Consequence of the unprovoked calumnies continually issued against me by John Ward Fenno, editor of the Gazette of the United States, I was induced to waive the consideration of my place in society and to put him on the footing of a gentleman. Upon Tuesday evening I sent a letter and message to him by a friend, demanding a proper apology or a meeting. He refused to give either. I am now therefore reduced to the necessity of suing him at law—(but my views are not merce-

nary)—or of again putting myself on a level with him—(by attacking him like a ruffian in the streets) or of thus posting him as a LIAR, a SCOUNDREL, and a COWARD. JAMES REYNOLDS

Tonight, in the *Gazette of the United States,* Jack Fenno writes:

The . . . note was handed me by Dr. William Bache on Wednesday morning . . . I told the messenger that I was resolved to hold no terms with such a man as his friend. On which he replied that he then must have recourse to personal satisfaction. To which I rejoined that I was prepared to meet him on any ground. He said he would bear my answer to his friend.

I have not since heard from him. I am informed that he stole into the Coffee-house last evening and attempted to post up a hand-bill, containing a number of opprobrious epithets. This piece, conveying the false implication that he had challenged me, proves him to be a Liar. The pitiful trick he has practiced shews him to be a most filthy coward: To elucidate his character further on this score, he has been publicly horse-whipped. He is, moreover, a traitor and an outlaw.

The Gallows, it thus appears, is at issue with him: to place one's self in a situation to take his life would therefore be partaking his crime in cheating the vengeful monster of what ought to be its undisputed claim.

I thank my God that the tongue of a perjured villain, a proven coward, a traitor and an outlaw, slit as it is by the undeviating hand of public justice, can make no impression to my prejudice.

JOHN WARD FENNO.
Philadelphia, Jan. 18

Tonight, in the *Porcupine's Gazette,* Peter Porcupine writes:

CONSOLATION
For Reynolds . . . Lloyd, and Mother Bache . . .
Wolfe Tone, who was to head the French troops destined for Ireland, had been taken and was to have been tried as a rebel but gave the government the slip by *cutting his own throat . . .*

SATURDAY, JANUARY 19, 1799

GENERAL ★ AURORA ★ ADVERTISER

Dear Sir . . . I send you the following statement of my interviews with J. W. Fenno . . . W[ILLIAM]. BACHE

I called upon John Ward Fenno . . . and when he read the letter which I presented, he asked me what Dr. Reynolds expected—this question however strange I replied to, "that he must retract what had been asserted in his paper or Give the Dr. that satisfaction

which every gentleman had the right to respect." He replied that
he would not give the Dr. the satisfaction . . .

This morning, Jack Fenno has his associate, Richard Oswold, deliver the following note to Benny's brother, William Bache:

> FOR the shameful and studied falshoods with which you have as-
> sailed my character, in a publication under your signature, I demand
> satisfaction. My friend, Mr. Oswold, who bears this note, is authorized
> to take any necessary stepts on my behalf.   JOHN WARD FENNO[1743]

This afternoon at three, Jack Fenno posts two announcements at Philadelphia's
Merchants' Coffee House:

> Dr. William Bache, having traduced my character by the most
> shameful and studied falsehoods, and having refused me satisfaction
> when called upon, I hereby publish him as a Liar, a Coward, and a
> True Democrat.   JOHN WARD FENNO

> James Reynolds, commonly called Doctor Reynolds, having asserted
> that I refused to fight him, when I had not received a challenge, and
> having neglected to answer a defiance which I sent him, I do hereby
> publish him for an infamous Liar and Coward . . .
> JOHN WARD FENNO[1744]

SUNDAY, JANUARY 20, 1799

Today, from Mount Vernon, George Washington writes the Rev. Mr. Bryan, Lord
Fairfax:

> [T]hat [Republican] party . . . have been uniform in their opposition
> to all measures of Government . . . torturing every act, by unnatural
> construction into a design to violate the Constitution, introduce mon-
> archy, and to establish aristocracy . . . [W]hat is more to be regretted,
> the same Spirit seems to have laid hold of the major part of the Legis-
> lature of this State, while all the other States in the Union (Kentucky,
> the child of Virginia, excepted) are coming foreword with the most un-
> equivocal evidence of their approbation . . .[1745]

MONDAY, JANUARY 21, 1799

GENERAL ★ AURORA ★ ADVERTISER

TO THE EDITOR.

John Ward Fenno, having refused to give Dr. Reynolds the satisfaction
of a *gentleman*, having suffered his real conduct to be exposed . . . , I

have refused to meet with him . . . It is sufficient for me that John Ward Fenno is now sufficiently notorious.   WILL. BACHE

Tonight, in the *Gazette of the United States*:

B.[ache] told Mr. Oswold, "that until I had answered the challenge from his friend Dr. Reynolds, he should have nothing to say to me,—after which he was at my service." As it was utterly impossible that I ever could meet Reynolds, I considered this reply as a dastardly evasion and proceeded to post him . . . in the Merchants' Coffee-House at 3 o'clock, P.M. [on Saturday] . . . At about 11 o'clock at night, two men rushed into the Coffee House and awakened the bar keeper who, being ordered to set up alone for a club, had fallen asleep. On examination, he found, after they had ran out, that they had removed the . . . papers.

Nothing changes! Last June, William Bache opposed Irishman Jimmy Reynolds' dismissal from the Philadelphia Infirmary and, for this, got himself dismissed as well. Now William intercedes to defend Jimmy Reynolds against the Fennos. Can you understand how I feel about the Baches?

TUESDAY, JANUARY 22, 1799

GENERAL   ★ AURORA ★   ADVERTISER

TO THE READERS OF THE AURORA

The compositors and pressmen who lately took themselves out from this office have appealed to our readers. The tribunal before which they have arraigned themselves demands respect . . .

They have stated their case—hear the other side.

This paper for several years has yielded a very slender revenue from a variety of causes. A large sum has been sunk in its establishment by the late editor. The expence of the office since its establishment has been greater than that of any other office in the United States . . . The paper having nearly doubled in number and circulation since its revival, the labor became greater on the pressmen . . . It was agreed that an advance of wages should be made where the labor had increased, but that a reduction should be made to the standard of other offices where the labor was equal . . .

On the 14th instant, they were called upon (as they have been every Saturday since the paper has recommenced and duly paid) to make their bills according to the new regulations . . . [B]oth pressmen and compositors left the office without any notification of their purpose . . .

The paper was thus left unfinished—and the copy that had been given out by the editor was either accidentally or purposely mislaid, so that the business could not be accomplished by any other persons at that time. Under a representation of these circumstances, the editor

was authorized to accede to any terms they should dictate—and they were on Sunday expressly informed . . .

On Monday they came to business as usual . . . One of the pressmen . . . received notice to provide himself at the end of the week with another situation.

Soon after, the compositors and pressmen, one by one, took themselves off, without even the usual notification of a week, or even saying whether they would return or not. At two o'clock on Monday, nothing had been done at press or case for Tuesday's paper . . . and the paper appeared without any advertisements on Tuesday . . .

The editor informed them that not one man of them should return on any terms.

And now those men are angry! . . .

The readers will now judge . . .   THE EDITOR

As there is no tax laid upon *windows* by the *house* and *land* tax and as there is an admeasurement of windows carrying forward throughout the states, it is to be presumed we shall soon have a *tax upon day light* . . .

WEDNESDAY, JANUARY 23, 1799

GENERAL ★ AURORA ★ ADVERTISER

FOREIGN INFLUENCE

THE public attention has been employed for some time on the danger of foreign influence . . . From what foreign quarter [is] the greatest danger of influence . . . to be apprehended? . . . The conclusion with me is . . . Great Britain . . .

[T]he most powerful, perhaps, of all her motives is her *hatred and fear* of the *republican example* of our governments . . . The same acute and predominant feeling . . . has displayed itself, with all its force, in its instant alarm at the propagation of republican principles into France . . .

The truth is Great Britain, as a monarchy . . . must view with a malignant eye the United States as the real source of the present revolutionary state of the world . . . It will consequently spare no effort to defeat [our] success by drawing our Republic into foreign wars, by dividing the people among themselves, by separating the government from the people, by establishing a faction of its own in the country, by magnifying the importance of characters among us known to think more highly of the British government than of their own . . . The MEANS of this influence are as obvious as the motives . . .

[T]he great flood-gate of British influence—*British Commerce.* The capital in the American trade . . . [t]hree fourths of this is British . . .

As a vehicle of influence, the press . . . must be allowed all its importance . . . The inland papers, it is well known, copy from the city papers;

this city more particularly, as the centre of politics and news. The city papers are supported by advertisements. The advertisements for the most part relate to articles of trade and are furnished by merchants and traders. In this manner, British influence steals into our newspapers and circulates under their passport . . .

ENEMY TO FOREIGN INFLUENCE

James Madison wrote[1746] and Thomas Jefferson submitted[1747] this morning's article on "Foreign Influence." Republicans must persuade America that British influence, not French influence, jeopardizes the country.[1748]

Tonight, in the *Porcupine's Gazette*:

Lieutenant General Washington, having contemplated every martial arrangement necessary at this crisis, has returned to Mount Vernon. The permanent army will be forthwith organized and, though the French should not advance, may have the opportunity to avenge their country if the sedition of . . . Kentucky should rise to overt rebellion. The late resolutions of the motley banditti of that state are of unexampled audacity . . . At this eventful period, Virginia is like [the volcano] Hecla of Vesuvius, exploding the most fiery particles. Angry remonstrances, seditious speeches, and rash resolutions abound . . .

SATURDAY, JANUARY 26, 1799

GENERAL ★ AURORA ★ ADVERTISER

DISSENT of the Minority of the Senate of this State [of Pennsylvania] from the Address . . . to the President of the United States . . .
   WE Dissent from this address . . . We hear from different parts of the union, and we know that even in the very neighborhood where we are assembled, numbers of people are discontented; that the Acts of the last Session of Congress have agitated the public mind to a violent degree..

Today, Thomas Jefferson writes a friend,

I shall make to you a profession of my political faith . . . in confidence . . .
   I do then, with sincere zeal, wish an inviolable preservation of our current constitution . . . and I am opposed to monarchising it[s] features by the forms of its administration with a view to conciliate a first transition to a President & Senate for life, & from that to a hereditary tenure of these offices, & thus to worm out the elective principle . . . I am not for transferring all the powers of the States to the general government, & those of that government to the Executive branch. I am for a government rigorously frugal & simple . . . and not for a multiplication of officers & salaries merely to make partisans, &

*for increasing, by every device, the public debt on the principle of it[s]
being a public blessing. I am for relying, for internal defence, on our
militia solely, until actual invasion . . . and not for a standing army in
time of peace which may overawe the public sentiment . . . I am for
free commerce with all nations . . . I am for freedom of religion &
against all maneuvers to bring about a legal ascendancy of one sect
over another; for freedom of the press & against all violations of the
Constitution to silence by force & not by reason the complaints or criti-
cisms, just or unjust, of our citizens against the conduct of their
agents. And I am for encouraging the progress of science . . . To these I
will add that I was a sincere well-wisher to the success of the French
revolution and still wish it may end in the establishment of a free &
well-ordered republic . . . [T]hough feeling deeply the injuries of
France, I did not think war the surest means of redressing them..*

*These, my friend, are my principles; they are unquestionably the
principles of the great body of our fellow citizens . . .*[1749]

MONDAY, JANUARY 28, 1799

GENERAL   ★ AURORA ★   ADVERTISER

It is frequently asked, what are we raising an army for? Various are
the answers. Some say the people are so corrupt and vicious that we
must have this rod held *in terrorem* over them . . . However, few can see
the necessity of it . . . [A] judicious writer observes, ". . . When the people are easy and satisfied, the whole country is an army."

Tonight, in the *Gazette of the United States*:

A Gentleman called a few days since at the office of the *Aurora* where
he found *[Jasper] Dwight* administering the honors of the shop—While
he was detained, one or two of your rank Irishmen came in and enquired
for the vulgar and impudent Dissent of the minority of the Pennsylvania
Legislature to the address to the President. They were informed that there
were none then to be had; that *Mr. Jefferson had sent for and taken them
all*, but that a number more would be struck off in a few days.

To the Inhabitants of Chester County [Pennsylvania]
I noticed that a number of persons had convened at the house of Mr.
Richard Robinson at Paoli for the purpose of taking into consideration
the propriety of addressing the legislature of the union to repeal the alien
and sedition laws.—[I]t appears from an advertisement of these persons
in the *"Aurora"* that an adjourned meeting is to be held at the house of
major Bones on the 28th inst . . . Fellow citizens, do not be duped by
having any thing to do with these people, their meetings, or their petitions

or remonstrances . . . It cannot be the wish of an honest man that this country be an asylum for alien enemies, felons, and convicts . . .

A Chester County Man

[DUBLIN, IRELAND] COURT MARTIAL. The Court sat about 11 o'clock, when Mr. [WOLFE] TONE was introduced . . . splendidly dressed in the French uniform . . .

The charge was then read to him . . . of adhering to the King [of Britain]'s enemies—attempting to levy war within the Kingdom, &c., &c . . . [H]e . . . at length pleaded guilty, and immediately after, producing a paper, he spoke nearly to the following effect:

"The influence and connection of Great Britain I have ever considered the bane of the prosperity and happiness of Ireland—These it has been the first wish of my heart to destroy, and the moment I found the *proper resources* of the country inadequate to the conflict, I applied to [the French] nation who had the will and the power to assist her . . .

"But in life, success is omnipotent—I have made an attempt in which *Washington succeeded*—and *Kosciusko failed*—the deliverance of my country . . .

"The Court must be sensible I have given no unnecessary trouble . . . [I]n return, it is my wish that the sentence may, if possible, be executed within an hour." . . .

Mr. TONE is about two and thirty, and has left an amiable wife . . . and three children in Paris.

The victory of French forces in America gave America her independence and gave George Washington his presidency. The defeat of French forces in Ireland has left Ireland in British servitude and has cost Ireland's would-be George Washington his life!

Tonight, in the *Porcupine's Gazette*:

CIVIL WAR !

ALEXANDRIA [VIRGINIA], January 14 . . . *Extract of a letter* . . . "Times are alarming, civil dissensions, if not actual civil war, may be expected. A bill is ordered to be brought into the [Virginia] house arraying the state's judges against those of the United States in cases that may occur under the sedition act . . . The government of the United States must protect itself or yield to the force of Virginia . . ."

(I apprehend nothing from the arms of Virginia alone; but she will call to her all the malcontents, all the villains, all the robbers, all the United

Irishmen, from every part of the continent . . . But, take care, Virginia! Take care! Pause and reflect before you rise *en masse.*

[WILLIAM COBBETT])

Tonight, in the *Gazette of the United States:*

I was called upon to make an excursion a few days ago through the county of Montgomery [Pennsylvania] . . . observing . . . the alarming extent and increasing virulence of the United Irishmen . . . [A] great disproportion of outcasts from the French and Irish nations, but particularly of the latter, have unguardedly been admitted as settlers. These . . . have combined with certain Americans who have sold their birthright . . . [D]emocrats . . . have been advanced to the office of magistrats . . . A very full meeting of these discontented gentry was held . . .

The most notorious character in the above group is said to be an Irishman who, for a length of time, commanded a company of United Irishmen in his native country . . . Since the promulgation of the Alien bill . . . this captain John [Fries], if you please, has been assiduously riding about the country for the purpose of misleading the people as to the true intent of this bill, the house tax, the stamp tax, and the sedition bill . . .

That France had it in contemplation to reduce these states under her dominion so early as the year 1756—that she at that time had agents in Philadelphia in pursuance of that plan—that she commenced the war of 1778 against Great Britain and sent armies to America with this express view are well established by facts of general notoriety . . .

In the assiduous flatteries heaped on our *great* men by public acts of the Revolutionizers, in their statues of Franklin and Jefferson, and the apotheosis of the former in the Heathenish Pantheon—in their affected humility of conceding to America the honor of setting them an illustrious example by her revolution, we discover ramifications of the same system . . .

WEDNESDAY, JANUARY 30, 1799

GENERAL ★ AURORA ★ ADVERTISER

On Friday, the 25th inst. Mr. Havens presented to the [U.S.] House of Representatives the following MEMORIAL from the Inhabitants of the county of Suffolk in the state of New York . . .

The laws . . . commonly known by the name of Sedition Law . . . commonly called the Alien law . . . your memorialists conceive to be unconstitutional . . .

These measures appear to be founded on the alarm which has been excited and industriously circulated throughout the United States about the danger of a French invasion; but your memorialists see no good reason to believe that this alarm can be well founded . . .

No policy can be worse for a nation than to introduce great and certain evils in order to guard against imaginary dangers . . .

Today, President John Adams approves and signs into law,

AN ACT
*For the Punishment of certain
crimes therein specified.*

Be it enacted, &c. That if any person, being a citizen of the United States . . . shall, without the permission or authority of the government of the United States, directly or indirectly commence or carry on any verbal or written correspondence with any foreign government . . . with an intent to influence the measures or conduct of any foreign government . . . in relation to disputes or controversies with the United States . . . he or she shall . . . be punished by a fine not exceeding five thousand dollars and by imprisonment during a term not less than six months nor exceeding three years . . . [1750]

John Adams' response to George Logan's peace effort will always be known as the "Logan Act"!

THURSDAY, JANUARY 31, 1799

GENERAL ★ AURORA ★ ADVERTISER

The committee of vigor . . . are now preparing and will bring forward in a few days a bill for a *provisional declaration of War against France*—In other words—a bill authorizing *the President of* the United States to declare war *when he thinks fit !* Was it for this the British treaty was entered into? Was it for this the bravest hearts and wisest heads of America sustained a seven years barbarous war?—Was it for this that the citizens of America chose representatives ?

Tonight, Jack Fenno in the *Gazette of the United States*:

[PENNSYLVANIA] Certain disaffected persons in the township of Blockley near this city a few days ago erected a liberty-pole bearing an inflammatory label against the government of the United States. Two or three orderly citizens, justly offended by this daring outrage on the laws and honor of their country, immediately leveled it . . .

TWO HUNDRED DOLLARS REWARD.

WHEREAS, two Irishmen came last night, drunk, to [my] house . . . one of whom held his club over the head of a young man in the office, suspended for an answer to the question if his name was Fenno; the other of whom held in his right hand a naked cutlass; and whereas the aforesaid cowardly ruffians, after bullying the clerk for some time and threatening vengeance and destruction against me, departed without leaving their names or their business, I hereby offer the above award to be paid on conviction. They are both described to me as raw Irishmen, and filthy, dungeon'd looking villains . . . JOHN WARD FENNO

N.B. A third stood sentry out-side the door.

FRIDAY, FEBRUARY 1, 1799

GENERAL ★ AURORA ★ ADVERTISER

It seems poor Fenno is again frighted, and valiantly advertised 200 dollars reward—payable on the *conviction* of men who can be *convicted* of nothing—but scaring him.

Tonight, in the *Porcupine's Gazette,* Peter Porcupine writes:

MR. FENNO is certainly right in pursuing these assassins [who came to his house] by every means in his power and will be fully justified, in the eye of God and man, if he blows their brains (if they have any) about his room, should they attempt to attack him.—The same villains, on the same evening, armed in the same way, *came to my house also.* My clerk did not call me down. If he had, and if they had struck me, they would now be in hell.

Tonight, in the *Gazette of the United States*:

The law of Congress, imposing a tax on houses, being now about to be put in force, the democrats have commenced their usual opposition and have stirred up many honest but illiteral people . . . [T]here is at this moment on the ridge road, about 9 miles from this city, a very lofty Liberty Pole, with a red and white pennant flying at its head and a board nailed to it, exhibiting the following inscription HEED YOUR LIBERTY, 1799 . . . I have left my address with the Printer of this paper and will be happy to accompany any of you to the above described spot for the purpose of demolishing this detested sign of anarchy and jacobinism.

A FEDERALIST

SATURDAY, FEBRUARY 2, 1799

GENERAL ★ AURORA ★ ADVERTISER

Colonel [Matthew] Lyon is returned [to Congress] for the Western district of Vermont . . . [T]he votes for Col. Lyon are 4676, being 96 more than on the last trial . . .

Today, Alexander Hamilton writes U.S. Senator Theodore Sedgwick (Federalist, Massachusetts):

What, my dear sir, are you going to do with Virginia? This is a very serious business . . . [T]he proceedings of Virginia and Kentucky, with the two laws [the Alien and Sedition Acts] complained of, should be referred to a special committee . . .

The government must not merely defend itself, it must attack and arraign its enemies . . . [T]he measures for raising the military force should proceed with activity . . . When a clever force has been collected, let them be drawn toward Virginia, for which there is an obvious pretext—& then let measures be taken to act upon the laws [the Alien and Sedition Acts] & put Virginia to the Test of resistance.[1751]

Tonight, in the *Porcupine's Gazette*:

SEDITION POLES.

READING [PENNSYLVANIA]. *Sir,* YOU have undoubtedly heard that an association was formed . . . to go under my command and destroy the sedition poles at this time standing within the county of Berks [Pennsylvania] . . . I set off on the day appointed from Hamburgh to the house of Isaac Wetzstein's . . . I then ordered my men to hang their swords to their wrists and pistols in hand, rode full gallop to the house and immediately surrounded the pole . . . [A]s soon as the seventeenth stoke of the axe was applied to this emblem of sedition, down it fell . . . We then . . . proceeded against a pole at the house of John Weaver . . . I ordered my axeman to the pole . . . [&c.]   PHILIP STRUBING

(And when the people of the country found that the time was elapsing to have the Sedition Bill . . . and Assessed Taxes repealed, they gathered themselves together to their leaders and said unto them: Up, make us poles . . . And lo! they erected poles . . . But o Israel ! the joy will be of short duration, the poles will be turned into firewood, the laws which you endeavor to oppose will stand . . . and ye who oppose the execution of these laws will bring the strong arm of the government of the Union upon them . . .)

MONDAY, FEBRUARY 4, 1799

GENERAL   ★ AURORA ★   ADVERTISER

Mr. EDITOR . . . An increase of heavy taxes to support a standing army in time of peace are the seeds of ruin to a republican government like ours . . .   *A CITIZEN OF MONTGOMERY COUNTY*

TUESDAY, FEBRUARY 5, 1799

GENERAL   ★ AURORA ★   ADVERTISER

SIGNS of the TIMES.
The *Religion* of *Peace* employed to promote *war!*
A *Republic* rushing into a war in support of *Monarchy!*

Today, without risking disclosure (to Federalist postal spies) that James Madison is the author, Thomas Jefferson writes Madison that his January 23rd *Aurora* piece ("Foreign Influence") is a great success:

> *A piece published in Bache's paper on* Foreign Influence *has had the greatest currency and effect. To an extraordinary first impression [printing] they have been obliged to make a second, and of an extraordinary number. It is such things as these the public want. They say so from all quarters, and that they wish to hear reason instead of* disgusting blackguardism *. . . [W]e are sensible that this summer is the season for systematic energies and sacrifices. The engine is the press. Every man must lay his purse and his pen under contribution . . . [L]et me pray and beseech you to set apart a certain portion of every post day to write what may be proper for the public . . . I will let you know to whom you may send so that your name shall be sacredly secret . . .*[1752]

FRIDAY, FEBRUARY 8, 1799

GENERAL ★ AURORA ★ ADVERTISER

TO THE FREEMEN OF THE WESTERN
DISTRICT OF VERMONT.
Vergennes Gaol [Jail], January 13.

FELLOW CITIZENS,

WITH a heart truly overflowing with gratitude have I, in this dismal prison, received the intelligence that you have again considered me entitled to your confidence . . . as your Representative in the Congress of the United States . . . This undissembled conduct . . . corroborates with the truly noble and generous efforts of the patriots of Virginia and Kentucky in holding up to abhorrence tyranny and unconstitutional laws . . . The story has already been told, in every country where representative government is known, that one of the national representatives of the United States of America has been imprisoned for writing and publishing; that when the Executive are doing right, they shall have his support but whenever they should do wrong, he would not be their humble advocate . . . M.[ATTHEW] LYON

Today, in the U.S. House of Representatives, the Annals of Congress report:

ALIEN AND SEDITION ACTS

Mr. HARTLEY [Republican, Pennsylvania] said that, since presenting the petition . . . from York county, praying for repeal [of the Alien and Sedition Acts] . . . he had been written to on the subject. He gave notice, therefore, that he should call up the petition for consideration on Monday . . .[1753]

Starting Monday, Congress takes up petitions to repeal the Alien and Sedition Acts. As Fenno's recent attacks on Jimmy Reynolds demonstrate, Federalists seem ready to act against the Irish. Tonight, I attend a meeting of Irishmen who want to petition against the Alien Act. Jimmy Reynolds (head of Philadelphia's Society of United Irishmen) and I will gather signatures.[1754]

SATURDAY, FEBRUARY 9, 1799

GENERAL   ★ AURORA ★   ADVERTISER

The French arrest our commerce as the British had done, and continue to do. But they never impressed our seamen [into service].

War . . . This afternoon, off the island of St. Kitts in the French West Indies, the thirty-eight-gun, 340–man United States Navy frigate *Constellation* attacks and captures the French Republic's forty-gun ship-of-war *L'Insurgente*, out of Guadeloupe. U.S. Navy Captain Thomas Truxton writes the U.S. Secretary of the Navy:

> *I stretched under Montserrat and towards Guadaloupe . . . [A]t Noon, that Island bearing W.S.W five leagues Distance, discovered a large Ship to the Southward on which I bore down . . . [S]he hoisted the french national Colours and fired a gun to Windward (which is a Signal of an Enemy). I continued bearing down on her, and at 1/4 past 3 P.M . . . as soon as I got in a Position for every Shot to do Execution, I answered by commencing a close and successful Engagement, which lasted untill about half after 4 PM, when she struck her Colours to the United States Ship Constellation . . . She proves to be the celebrated french national Frigate, Insurgente of 40 Guns and 400 Men, lately out from France . . . I have been much shattered in my Rigging and Sails, and my fore top Mast rendered from Wounds useless . . . I hope the President and my country will for the present be content with a very fine Frigate being added to our infant Navy, and that too with the loss of only one Man killed and three wounded, while the Enemy had (the french Surgeon reports) Seventy killed and wounded; several were found dead in Tops &c. and thrown overboard . . .* [1755]

The French Governor-General of Guadeloupe, Edmé Etienne-Borne Desfourneaux, will respond to this attack by declaring war on all American shipping.[1756]

Tonight, in the *Gazette of the United States*:

TO DOCTOR LOGAN . . .
SO, Doctor, you have been in France!
Not (as of old) to learn to dance . . .
The all-important joyful news
To Fame was handed by your spouse.

(Not *Virgil's Fame*—an ugly witch—
Her modern shape's like Madame Bache.) . . .

With only two days before Congress takes up the Alien and Sedition Acts, we plan to solicit worshippers at St. Mary's Catholic Church on Fourth-street to sign our petition to repeal the Alien Act. Many non-citizen Irish worship at St. Mary's,[1757] and we will wait for them after tomorrow morning's church service.

SUNDAY, FEBRUARY 10, 1799

Today, four of us—Samuel Cumings (a printer at the *Aurora*), Dr. Jimmy Reynolds (Benny's friend and mine), Robert Moore (a recent arrival from Ireland), and I—post notices on the front gates and at both sides of the front door of St. Mary's Church on Fourth-street. Before the mass begins, a church member rips down two of these notices, but we wait with the petition amidst the tombstones of the church cemetery for the congregation to emerge. When the church service ends, violence begins.[1758]

MONDAY, FEBRUARY 11, 1799

GENERAL ★ AURORA ★ ADVERTISER

We are told we shall have a standing army of 50,000 men without enquiring *for what* purpose—it may be useful to enquire whence are the men to come? The major part of the soldiers on the present establishment are aliens—principally *Irish*—the marines are of the same complexion . . .

Tonight, the *Gazette of the United States* reports yesterday's violence at St. Mary's:

SHOCKING OUTRAGE

The repose of the city was yesterday (Sunday) disturbed by a more daring and flagitious riot than we remember to have outraged the civil law and the decorum of society for more than forty years . . . The selection of the Lord's Day for exciting a general scene of confusion and disorder, whilst it sufficiently characterizes the principles of the actors, is also a very strong collateral evidence that their intentions were of the most atrocious nature.

Four men (two of whom are United Irishmen, and the other two of a similar description of character) had the unparalleled effrontery and profanity to assault the members of the Catholic Church during divine service with a most seditious and inflammatory petition against the Alien and Sedition Laws . . .

[T]hey had affixed a placard to the door of the Church in the following terms,

"The natives of *Ireland* who worship at this Church are requested to remain in the yard after Divine service until they have affixed their names to a memorial for the *repeal* of the *Alien Bill.*"

After having disturbed and broken up the ceremonies of the Church, several of them were detected by the wardens . . . reading this inflammatory paper from the eminence of a tombstone to a considerable crowd surrounding them . . .

"You lie, you rascal," was the spirited reply of a young man, "you are *no Irishman;* you are a traitor." [One] fellow immediately drew a pistol and presented it at the young man . . . The other instantly knocked him down and trampled on him. The rioters were pursued, overtaken, and carried before the mayor for examination. One of them was committed to prison—the other three found bail. A fifth, who was apprehended in committing an assault on the house of one of the evidences, is also in jail.

RIOT

By the exertions of the peace officers and the spirited cooperation of several active citizens, the five following persons were yesterday apprehended and brought before Robert Wharton, esq., Mayor of the city . . . :

James Reynolds, —— Moore, —— Rice, Wm. Duane, —— Cummens . . .

Duane prints a Democratic newspaper in Philadelphia . . . The whole five call themselves Irishmen.

MR. FENNO,

. . . That there is such a banditti, organized for the subversion of government and the establishment of a system of terror and anarchy, can no longer be doubted by the most incredulous. *"The United Irishmen"* have at length broken out into acts which render them no longer the objects of uncertain suspicion . . . [T]hey bid defiance to our laws, they threaten our fellow citizens with assassination, and even the temples of the most High God *whom we worship* are made the theatres of their violence and foul abomination.

Fellow citizens, guard yourselves ere it is too late against these cut-throats . . . Your persons, your religion, your government, are threatened . . .   Sunday Evening.   M.

Tonight, in the *Porcupine's Gazette*:

Yesterday this city witnessed a scene the most outrageous and the most scandalous that was ever beheld or heard of in a state of society . . .

The daring riot of yesterday ought to excite universal attention . . . The times are serious. All that we are able to perceive, we may rest assured, is more than the outward *signs,* the mere indication, of a deep, secret, systematized, and extensive plan of violence.—"Again, therefore, I say unto you, *watch.*"

The following petition has been presented to the [U.S.] House of Representatives, signed by upwards of 1200 citizens . . .

The petition of the subscribers, inhabitants of Northampton County, Pennsylvania . . .

The authority given to the president to raise troops in any number and to borrow money without any limitation . . . are, in our opinion, transfers of powers . . . [T]he increase of the regular military force, and the authorizing of the executive to accept the services of volunteer corps in any number, these corps probably influenced by party spirit, and certainly to be officers at presidential discretion, are measures of far more dangerous tendency . . .

We think we can discover, in many of the public acts, which have latterly taken place, a regular and systematic plan to aggrandize and strengthen the executive at the expence of the other departments of the state . . . The Alien Law gives to the President a judicial authority which . . . forms . . . the very essence of despotism. The sedition law is calculated to throw around his person and character an inviolability only to be recognized in the corrupted monarchies of Europe . . . To avert this is the object which your petitioners have in view. They, therefore, solicit the repeal of the laws above referred to . . .

Today, in the U.S. House of Representatives, the Annals of Congress report:

ALIEN AND SEDITION ACTS

Mr. LIVINGSTON presented a petition from a number of aliens, natives of Ireland, resident within the United States, praying for a repeal of the alien law . . .[1759]

Tonight, in the *Gazette of the United States*:

The impudent, seditious, and inflammatory memorial, which we had occasion yesterday to notice, purports to be . . . to obtain "a repeal of *the law concerning Aliens.*" [T]he real design, without doubt, [is] to obtain the most extensive enrollment possible of existing United Irishmen and . . . to make new converts . . .

Where is the American that would own Duane or Reynolds or any other United Irishman for a fellow-citizen? If there is one, he is a fit tenant only for Hell or for France . . .

Tonight, in the *Porcupine's Gazette*:

UNITED IRISH RIOT . . .

Last Sunday four men; to wit; *Reynolds* (commonly called *Doctor*

Reynolds), *Duane,* Mother Bache's Editor, one *Moore,* lately from Ireland, *Rice,* a clerk, and Cummens a Journeyman printer, were apprehended and taken before Robert Wharton, Esq. Mayor of the city, for RIOT, the scene of which was at the Roman Catholic Church in *Fourth street.*

During divine service, some of them went and stuck up placards on the walls to the following purport:

> *"The natives of Ireland who worship at this Church are requested to remain in the yard after Divine service until they have affixed their names to a memorial for the repeal of the Alien Bill."*

The trustees and some of the congregation pulled down these placards; they were stuck up again, and again pulled down . . . When the church broke up . . . *Reynolds,* who was placed at the east end of the church and who had been ordered out, drew a pistol . . .

When the prisoners were taken before the Mayor, a scene took place . . . [I]n rushed *[Thomas] McKean* the *Democratic Judge,* violently agitated with passion. The Mayor began to explain . . . When the Judge had listened to him for a time, he replied, *that the men might take their hats and go home . . .*

A word of explanation . . . For Sunday afternoon, we were held incommunicado. Near dark, when papers to commit us had been completed, we were handcuffed and paraded through the streets of Philadelphia (which had filled with people) to the house of the Federalist mayor, Robert C. Wharton, who proceeded to question us for another half hour.[1760] Pennsylvania's Supreme Court Judge Thomas McKean finally intervened. An eyewitness report:

> *Whilst Robert Wharton, Esq. Mayor of the city was engaged in taking the recognizances of . . . persons accused as authors of the riot, some person knocked vehemently at the door and demanded admission; the constables refusing to open it, Mr. M'Kean called out "I am Chief Justice of the state." The mayor, on hearing that the Chief Justice was there, opened the door and gave Mr. M'Kean admittance. No sooner had he entered than he called out with a loud voice, accompanied by a menacing air, "What is the reason, Mr. Mayor, of all this fuss, that you keep the city in an uproar with a mob marching these gentlemen up one street and down another, hand-cuffed and tied, for half the day together."*
>
> *The Mayor attempted to state the nature of their offence, the evidence of their having insulted the congregation of the Church, and that one of them had presented a loaded pistol to the breast of one of the members . . . but Mr. M'Kean would hearken to nothing from the Mayor or Gentlemen present, and charged the members of the Congregation with having committed an assault on the prisoners and said "that they and not the prisoners were the aggressors, that he would have dismissed the matter in quarter of an hour, for the prisoners had the right*

to take up their hats and go about their business." The Mayor pro-
ceeded to take the recognizances and Mr. M'Kean afterwards left the
room apparently in great passion.[1761]

Judge Thomas McKean will be our Republican candidate for Governor of Penn-
sylvania in next autumn's election. Needless to say, Philadelphia Mayor Robert
Wharton will support the Federalist choice, Pennsylvania's ultra-Federalist U.S.
Senator, James Ross.

McKean hasn't put an end to the matter. My Irish friends and I will stand trial
for "seditious riot" on the 21st of the month!

WEDNESDAY, FEBRUARY 13, 1799

GENERAL ★ AURORA ★ ADVERTISER

**The Petition of the Irish exiles to Congress was presented to the House
of Representatives yesterday . . .**

Today, in the U.S. House of Representatives, the Annals of Congress report:

ALIEN AND SEDITION ACTS
Mr. GREGG [Republican, Pennsylvania] presented a remonstrance
against the alien and sedition laws signed by two hundred and seventy of
the inhabitants of that part of Mifflin county which lies north of Tuffey's
mountain . . .
Mr. G. said he had also two petitions and remonstrances on the subject
signed by 320 of the inhabitants of Cumberland county in this State . . .
Mr. HAVENS [Republican, New York] also presented a memorial from
Queen's county in the State of New York, praying for repeal of the alien
and sedition laws . . .[1762]

Today, from Philadelphia, Thomas Jefferson writes Archibald Stewart in Virginia:

I avoid writing to my friends because the fidelity of the post office is
very much doubted . . . A wonderful & rapid change is taking place in
Pennsylvania, Jersey, & N York. Congress is daily plied with petitions
against the alien and sedition laws & standing armies. Several parts
of this State are so violent that we fear an insurrection. This will be
brought about by some if they can. It is the only thing we have to fear.
The materials now bearing on the public mind will infallibly restore it
to its republican soundness . . . if the knowledge of facts can only be
disseminated . . .[1763]

Eighteen thousand Pennsylvanians have signed petitions against John Adams'
Alien and Sedition Acts, his federal army, and his war taxes. That's 90 percent
of Pennsylvanians who voted in the 1796 Presidential election.[1764]

Tonight, in the *Porcupine's Gazette,* Peter Porcupine writes:

JUDGE M'KEAN

"His Honor," the "Doctor of Laws, &c., &c., &c., &c., &c.," does certainly feel somewhat alarmed on account of his conduct on Sunday last . . . Interfering with the chief magistrate of the city; interrupting him in the actual execution of his office; telling him he was actuated by *party motives;* and asserting that the rioters who stood prisoners under his warrant might take their hats and go home; all this is indeed most scandalous and criminal . . .

The prisoners had been guilty of a most daring breach of the laws of God and Man; yet, notwithstanding this, they saw their conduct justified by the *Chief Justice* of the State, *by the very man whom they well knew was to preside at their trial !*

THURSDAY, FEBRUARY 14, 1799

GENERAL ★ AURORA ★ ADVERTISER

Those folks who make so much noise about receiving subscriptions to a petition on Sunday, after divine service, are very little scrupulous about *lying* all the rest of the week . . . It is very remarkable that among the most vociferous against the signing a name to a liberal memorial and elegant composition—are the most ardent admirers of *political sermons!*

Tonight, in the *Gazette of the United States*:

THE DEMOCRATIC JUDGE [M'KEAN] . . .

CALLENDER, this little reptile, . . . was never *discountenanced* by . . . the Chief Justice . . . BACHE, the Chief Judge's companion at Civic Festivals . . . neither . . . No one among all the libellers was ever prosecuted or bound over. Their *politics were perfectly French* . . . I could mention oné civic festival at which he assisted, where a *"revolution in Great Britain"* was toasted; and another, where a toast was *"success to the United Irishmen"* . . .

FRIDAY, FEBRUARY 15, 1799

GENERAL ★ AURORA ★ ADVERTISER

In the English print of Tuesday and Wednesday last, . . . the Chief Justice of this State . . . is openly and expressly charged with committing acts deserving of *punishment—insulting* a magistrate in the discharge of his duty—of attempting to destroy the independence of the magistracy—insulting the mayor in the execution of his office—and of acting partially toward men guilty of a daring breach of the laws of God and man, men who knew he was to preside at their trial . . .

But let us ask what is the foundation for this calumny? Four persons engaged in soliciting subscriptions to a petition to Congress were attacked and one of them struck. The assailants, having committed the assault, fly for constables, and the insulted persons are brought before the mayor.—Some *friends* of *good order* make a riot, a large concourse of people assemble, and for five hours they fill the street from the house of the mayor to that of the Chief Justice; the latter, anxious to learn the cause of such unusual disquietude, proceeds to the mayor's house and expresses the wish that the persons had been committed, if deserving of commitment, or dismissed if not . . .

It will be observed that the crime against the laws of God and man was the taking subscriptions to a petition against the *Alien Bill* !

But what is the most malicious and daring is the assertion that the Chief Justice was to preside at the trial of those violators . . . The fact is that the parties have been bound over to appear at the court of *Oyer* and *Terminer* which sits next Monday and over which Judge *Coxe* presides . . .

The *clue* to all this calumny is simply this—the republicans mean to propose Judge *M'Kean* for *Governor* of this State . . . and the people of Pennsylvania are attempted to be deceived into the views of the English party by heaping calumnies on the man who fought in our revolution against Britain—who held the presidency of Congress in days of peril, and who has administered our laws . . .

SATURDAY, FEBRUARY 16, 1799

GENERAL ★ AURORA ★ ADVERTISER

The Rev. J. C. Ogden, who some time ago, presented a petition from *Matthew Lyon's* constituents to the President of the United States, upon his return to Litchfield in Connecticut, has been arrested by a Mr. Wolcott and put into prison for a demand of 200 dollars!

Mr. Ogden on his return home to his wife, who lives with her aged mother in Connecticut, was seized under some pretext at the suit of [Treasury Secretary] Oliver Wolcott and thrown into prison.[1765] *The Rev. Mr. Ogden is now serving a four-month prison sentence!*[1766]

MONDAY, FEBRUARY 18, 1799

GENERAL ★ AURORA ★ ADVERTISER

A bill was read in the senate on Saturday for authorizing the president of the United States to raise an army of 30,000 mercenaries and to embody 75,000 volunteers for three years . . .

Since we are not menaced by external danger, for what end can a standing army, with all its concomitant taxes and *curses*, be attempted thus to be set up ?

Word from overseas is that France wants to negotiate.[1767] Does Adams want to negotiate? Today, the President delivers a message to a closed-door meeting of the Senate:

> *I nominate William Vans Murray, our minister resident at The Hague [Netherlands], to be minister plenipotentiary of the United States to the French Republic.*
>
> *If the Senate shall advise and consent to his appointment, effectual care shall be taken, in his instructions, that he shall not go to France without direct and unequivocal assurances from the French Government, signified by their minister of foreign relations, that he shall be received in character . . .*
>
> JOHN ADAMS[1768]

Time will tell whether Adams is serious. Meanwhile, the war continues!

Today, the Court of Oyer and Terminer opens at the State-house in Philadelphia. Our trial for seditious riot at St. Mary's is scheduled for Wednesday.

TUESDAY, FEBRUARY 19, 1799

GENERAL   ★ AURORA ★   ADVERTISER

[T]he war shall be the *war of a party* . . . The following extract of a letter from the Secretary of War . . . is too plain to be misapprehended . . .

> *[A] Company of Volunteer Cavalry, Artillery, or Infantry, desirous of serving in the Provisional Army should associate to the numbers required . . .*
>
> *[I]t being deemed important not to accept of companies composed of disaffected persons . . . it will be proper [that] proper certificates from prominent and known characters . . . be also presented.*
>
> *A company prepared to present the aforesaid exhibits should make a formal offer of their services to the President . . .*[1769]

What, may it please your honor, is meant by "disaffected persons," are they all such persons as have dared to express disapprobation of any public measure; who have had the presumption at any time to suppose that Mr. Jefferson would make a better president than Mr. Adams, or who do not on all occasions declare the most holy reverence for the sacred person of the chief magistrate?

Today, Federalist leaders from all parts of Pennsylvania gather at Dunwoody's Tavern on High-street (launching point for last year's attacks on the *Aurora*) to decide "unanimously" that Pennsylvania's ultra-Federalist U.S. senator, James Ross, will oppose Republican Judge Thomas McKean in the statewide gubernatorial election next October 8th.[1770]

WEDNESDAY, FEBRUARY 20, 1799

GENERAL ★ AURORA ★ ADVERTISER

Numerous surmises were in circulation yesterday concerning the new mission to France. Some would have it that it was but a foil to divert public attention from the enormous army measures . . .

Today, Abigail Adams writes the President's secretary, William Shaw:

> It appears to me . . . from the conduct of Reynolds as well as of the Chief Justice that a crisis is working up which will call for all the energy of the Government to suppress . . . As to the conduct of McKean, he should never sit upon the Bench as Judge again . . .[1771]

Today, my trial for "seditious riot" at St. Mary's Church opens at Philadelphia's Court of Oyer and Terminer. Joseph Hopkinson (composer of the patriotic song "Hail Columbia" and deputy attorney general for the county of Philadelphia)[1772] is the government prosecutor. Alex Dallas, who represented Benny before Judge Richard Peters last June, is now my lawyer. From the transcript of today's proceedings:

> At a court of Oyer and Terminer, held at the State House in Philadelphia . . . before J. D. Coxe, Esq., presiding judge; R. Keen, Jonathan B. Smith, and A. Robinson, Esqrs., assistant judges, two indictments were laid against William Duane, editor of the Aurora, James Reynolds, M.D., Robert Moore, Esq., and Samuel Cuming, printer for an alleged riot, &c . . .
>
> [A twelve man jury is impaneled] . . .
>
> JOHN CONNOR sworn.
>
> Mr. Hopkinson. Relate what you saw . . .
>
> Ans.— . . . During the service, Mr. Gallagher, jr . . . was going round the church to different gentleman of the congregation, to their pews. He came to the pew where I sat; [and] . . . intimated to me that . . . there was to be a seditious meeting after prayers were over . . .
>
> Mr. Dallas . . . did you see or hear anything to disturb divine worship ?
>
> Ans.—No . . .
>
> JAMES GALLAGHER, jr., sworn . . .
>
> The Court. What was the observation?
>
> Ans.—[Defendant Samuel] Cuming said I was an impertinent scoundrel for tearing down [a petition notice before the church service began]. I told him no Jacobin paper had a right to a place on the walls of that church. He was immediately after joined by several others.

Ques.—Was Mr. Moore, Mr. Duane, or Dr. Reynolds among them?

Ans.—No: I did not see them; I saw Mr. Duane for the first time that day at the Mayor's office . . . I waited till service was over . . . I went down the alley at the south side of the church, and I saw a crowd . . . I heard a person declaring he would not be forced or pushed out of the [church] yard, and the cry of "turn him out;" I got into the crowd, when I saw Dr. R[eynolds] keeping four or five persons at bay; I went forward . . . Before I had time to catch hold of Dr. R.[eynolds], he presented a pistol to my breast . . . I had my hands raised with a view to put him out; he declared he would shoot any man that would lay hold of him; I struck at him, he wheeled . . . and the pistol fell by his groin . . . Mr. Lewis Ryan took hold of him, threw him down . . . I kicked him twice or three times while he was down . . .

THADDEUS M'CARNEY sworn.

Ques.—Do your recollect being in church on Sunday week?

Ans.—Yes; I am a member of that congregation . . .

Ques.—Are you a citizen of the United States?

Ans.—No; I have been in the country only two years . . .

Ques.—Do you know whether it was or was not the desire of a number of the members of the congregation for the petition to be brought that day to obtain signatures?

Ans. I believe it was, because I for one would put my name to it . . .

The evidence on both sides being closed, Mr. Dallas rose on behalf of the accused, and addressed the court and jury.

May it please your Honours, Gentlemen of the Jury: . . .

[H]ow much astonished must you be to hear the evidence that has been produced . . . ! Who has not heard that a dark conspiracy has been formed to overthrow not alone the Constitution, but to subvert the very principles of our form of government? . . . [Y]ou have heard them called Jacobins! . . .

Is it possible that it should be said to be criminal to solicit signatures to a decent and dignified memorial for a redress of grievances? . . . Is this a ground for a charge of riotous proceedings? . . .

Mr. *James Gallagher, jr.* [i]ntoxicated with the phantasy of Jacobinism, his heart is struck upon seeing the walls contaminated with this Jacobinical notice and he valorously resolves to pull it down . . . [A]fter coming from the altar, his boiling zeal leads him to the most influential characters in the church who are successively alarmed . . . [F]orth he issues, foaming with political fury . . . These are the words of this young hero, "when he was down I kicked him three times." This act . . . was perfectly consistent with the heroism of our temporary politics, for by kicking Dr. Reynolds three times while he was down, he became qualified to carry dispatches to France . . .

The jury retired, and in about half an hour entered in a letter, and sealed it, their verdict . . .[1773]

On Saturday, the 9th instant, expired the time for which Col. Matthew Lyon was sentenced to imprisonment . . . The reelection of Col. Lyon is a good comment of the people of Vermont on the Alien and Sedition Acts.

Today, in the U.S. House of Representatives, the Annals of Congress report:

ALIEN AND SEDITION LAWS

Mr. GALLATIN presented a petition from seven hundred and fifty-five inhabitants from the county of Chester [Pennsylvania] and another of seventy-eight inhabitants of Washington county . . . praying for a repeal of the alien and sedition laws.

Mr. BROWN presented petitions and remonstrances of the same nature from one thousand nine hundred and forty inhabitants of Montgomery county and from one thousand, one hundred inhabitants of Northampton county, both in the state of Pennsylvania.

Mr. McCLENACHAN presented a petition of the same kind from five hundred and eighty-seven inhabitants of the Northern Liberties of Philadelphia . . .[1774]

This morning, the jury's verdict is unsealed. Tonight, in the *Gazette of the United States*:

THE SUNDAY RIOT

IT is not improbable but that our readers may be desirous to be acquainted with what legal proceedings have been taken in consequence of the riot that took place at *St. Mary's Chapel, on the Sunday* before last . . . [T]he defendants were bound over . . . Mr. Thackery, engraver, was security for the appearance of William Duane . . . The Court proceeded to the trial of the defendants. The jury . . . brought in a verdict of *not guilty.*

This city has been kept in a state of agitation during the whole of last and part of the present week by a transaction which, had it not undergone the form of a violent prosecution and a solemn, deliberate, fair, and open trial, could scarcely believed to have taken place in a society not utterly degenerated . . .

The persons implicated were Dr. *James Reynolds, Robert Moore*, Esq., *William Duane*, editor of the *Aurora*, and *Samuel Cumming*, printer. Two of them American citizens, all of them Irishmen or sons of Irishmen. They had been appointed a committee to receive the subscriptions of such natives of Ireland as might chuse to pray for a repeal of the Alien Bill. The memorial is already before the public, and in the peaceable and orderly act of receiving subscriptions, they were set upon by a number of persons and assaulted . . .

The four were each bound in 4000 dollars recognizances to stand trial. The trial took place on Wednesday, and the defendants were by the verdict of a jury found NOT GUILTY . . .

During the pendency of the trial, the papers called *federal*, including the *English* paper, let loose all the flood-gates of falsehood and malevolence . . . [H]ad the *Aurora* dared to repel this injustice, there would have been found some hungry minion to *move* the court.

But the verdict of an honest jury is the best reply to such unprincipled measures . . . To the honor of that jury, composed principally of frank Germans or their descendants, they gave a verdict of *not Guilty* to the utter confusion and shame of the authors of such a prosecution.

Tonight, in the *Porcupine's Gazette*:

Lyon yesterday resumed his seat . . .

SATURDAY, FEBRUARY 23, 1799

GENERAL ★ AURORA ★ ADVERTISER

The Connecticut members [of Congress] are horribly alarmed by the encreasing number of the *Aurora* that passes into that State . . .

POLITICAL REFLECTIONS . . .

The French Republic has been, and still is, in a state of war and danger, and this state of war and danger have given to the [French] Executive an immense army to command, innumerable offices to bestow, a mighty mass of money to deal out, a control over the freedom of speech and of the press . . .

The usurped sway ascribed [by detractors] to the [French] Directory . . . cannot then be too much pondered and contemplated by Americans . . . They ought most generously to reflect on the evils of a state of war . . . to destroy the equilibrium of the departments of power by throwing improper weights into the Executive scale and to betray the people into snares which ambition may lay for their liberties . . .

It deserves to be well considered also that actual war is not the only state which may supply the means of usurpation. The real or pretended apprehensions of it are sometimes of equal avail to the projects of ambition . . .

[T]he fetters imposed on liberty at home have ever been forged out of the weapons provided for defence against real, pretended, or imaginary dangers from abroad.

A CITIZEN OF THE UNITED STATES

James Madison contributed this morning's "Political Reflections."[1775]

MONDAY, FEBRUARY 25, 1799

GENERAL ★ AURORA ★ ADVERTISER

[LONDON.] "In consequence of the remonstrance of the American Minister" (says a late London paper . . .) "the state prisoners in the several gaols in Dublin received official notice . . . that they could not go to any part of the United States as had been proposed." . . .

This is the first *direct* exercise of the powers given to the President by the unconstitutional, inhuman, *Turkish* law respecting aliens . . .

Recollect, fellow-citizens, that our ancestors emigrated to this country with the view of escaping from the fangs of power . . . [A]sk yourselves whether . . . the oppressed of all nations have not the same right and title to migrate to this country and enjoy liberty as ourselves . . .

Today, in the U.S. House of Representatives, the Annals of Congress report:

Mr. GREGG [Republican, Pennsylvania] presented two petitions praying for a repeal of the alien and sedition laws . . .

Mr. GALLATIN [Republican, Pennsylvania] presented another petition . . .

Mr. LIVINGSTON [Republican, New York]: one of a similar nature, signed by 2,500 citizens of New York.

Mr. HEISTER [Republican, Pennsylvania]: one of the same kind, from 1,400 inhabitants of Berks county.

Mr. BAYARD [Federalist, Delaware]: one from the inhabitants of Newcastle county, State of Delaware, signed by between 700 and 800 persons . . .

On motion of Mr. GOODRICH [Federalist, Connecticut], the House went into a Committee of the Whole on the report of a select committee on the petitions praying for a repeal of the alien and sedition laws . . . [T]he committee beg leave to report the following resolutions:

Resolved, That it is inexpedient to repeal the act passed the last session, entitled "An act concerning aliens."

Resolved, That it is inexpedient to repeal the [sedition] act . . .

Mr. GALLATIN rose and spoke . . .

When Mr. GALLATIN had concluded, the question was taken and carried—yeas 52, nays 48.[1776]

Al Gallatin "rose and spoke," yet no one heard him. The Federalists drowned out his words!

Today, President Adams names two additional peace envoys (neither of them in Europe) for the mission to France and preconditions their departure on his receiving assurances from French Foreign Minister Talleyrand that they will be well received.[1777]

Today, President Adams approves and signs into law:

AN ACT
For the augmentation of the Navy.
BE it enacted &c., That . . . in addition to the naval armament already authorized by law, there shall be built within the United States, six ships of war, of a size to carry, and which shall be armed with not less than, seventy-four guns each; and there shall be built or purchased with the United States, six sloops of war, of a size to carry, and each shall be armed with, eighteen guns each . . . ; and a sum not exceeding one million of dollars shall be and is hereby appropriated . . .[1778]

TUESDAY, FEBRUARY 26, 1799

GENERAL   ★ AURORA ★   ADVERTISER

The committee appointed to report upon the petitions from various parts of the Union against the *Alien* and *Sedition Bill*, brought up their report yesterday, which caused a very animated debate. After which, on the question implicating the repeal of those laws, the vote for repeal were 48, noes 52. So that the laws remain unrepealed !

Today, Thomas Jefferson writes James Madison:

Yesterday [the President] . . . sent in the nomination of [two additional] . . . Envoys . . . but declaring the two . . . should not leave this country till they should receive from the French Directory assurance that they should be received with the respect due . . . etc. This, if not impossible, must at least put off the day . . . of reconciliation and leave more time for new projects of provocation. Yesterday witnessed a scandalous scene in the House of Representatives. It was the day for taking up the report of their committee against the Alien and Sedition laws, &c . . . Gallatin took up the Alien, & Nicholas the Sedition Law; but after a little while of common silence, [the Federalists] began to enter into loud conversations, laugh, cough, &c., so that for the last hour of these gentlemen's speaking, they must have had the lungs of a vendue master [auctioneer] to have been heard . . . It was impossible to proceed. The question was taken & carried in favor of [retaining these laws] . . . 52 to 48 . . .[1779]

[T]he gentlemen now nominated [as envoys to France] are not to proceed until the president shall have received from the government of France assurances that they shall be received . . . [T]ime is lost . . . sending to France and receiving the replies . . . The matter must be done circuitously . . . And after the most satisfactory answers shall have been received, we shall be then precisely at the point from which we may now directly set out. Our ministers will then have to sail from hence to France. So that there is a super-addition of delay . . . procrastination . . .

Tonight, William Cobbett in the *Porcupine's Gazette*:

For several days past, there has been a good deal of grumbling . . . respecting my comments on the report which *Duane* and *Mother Bache* had circulated on the subject of the *nomination* . . . I denied that Mr. Murray was *to go to Paris alone to make a treaty.* I most positively denied that any Envoy or Envoys were to go . . . *'till* THE PRESIDENT HIMSELF *had assurances of their being honorably received;* and, if we are to credit the new report . . . I was perfectly correct, for, they now tell us, that the President has nominated THREE ENVOYS and that they are not to go to France till the assurances are received BY HIMSELF.

Why all the war measures . . . when there exists a conviction that peace is at our will ? Are standing armies such an amusement to the people that they are willing to be drained of their hard earnings to enjoy the spectacle ?

Today, President Adams approves and signs into law:

AN ACT
Concerning French citizens that have been or may be captured and brought into the United States.
BE it enacted . . . , That the President of the United States be and is hereby authorized to exchange or to send away from the United States to the dominions of France . . . all French citizens that have been or may be captured . . .[1780]

Today, Federalists in President Adams' home state of Massachusetts undertake another effort to disable America's second-largest Republican newspaper, the *Independent Chronicle* of Boston, whose publisher, Thomas Adams, has been ill since his federal indictment in October under the Sedition Act (his trial is set for June). This time, Federalists use the Massachusetts common law of criminal libel to indict not only Thomas Adams but also his younger brother and business manager, Abijah Adams, for a February 18th article that criticizes Massachusetts for failing to adopt the Virginia and Kentucky Resolutions. Use of state law means that defendants can't claim truth as a defense and that prosecutors don't have to wait for a federal court to reconvene. There will be an immediate trial. It's a serious threat. Thomas Adams is too sick to attend. The jailing of his younger brother threatens the paper's very existence.[1781]

FRIDAY, MARCH 1, 1799

GENERAL ★ AURORA ★ ADVERTISER

Yesterday in the Senate, Mr. Jefferson gave notice that, inasmuch as the law *seemed* to require the retirement of the Vice President of the United States from the duties of President of the Senate before the close of the Session, in order that the Senate might elect a President pro tem; he gave notice that he should on the next day retire in order that a President of the Senate, pro tem. might be chosen.

The Federalist majority in the U.S. Senate will choose Pennsylvania gubernatorial candidate and ultra-Federalist U.S. Senator James Ross to be the President *pro tempore* of the U.S. Senate.

Today, in Boston, *Independent Chronicle* business manager Abijah Adams goes on trial for seditious libel. (The publisher of the *Chronicle,* Thomas Adams, is too ill to stand trial.) Judge Francis Dana presides. The verdict: guilty. The sentence: imprisonment of the *Chronicle*'s manager for thirty days, payment of all prosecution costs, and a $500 one-year surety bond. What will become of the *Chronicle?*[1782]

SATURDAY, MARCH 2, 1799

GENERAL ★ AURORA ★ ADVERTISER

(COPY.) . . . *[French] Minister of Foreign Relations [Talleyrand] to Citizen Pichon, Secretary of Legation of the French Republic [in The Hague]* . . .

I HAVE received successively, Citizen, your letters . . . to detail to me your conversation with Mr. Murray [U.S. Minister at The Hague, Netherlands] . . .

[W]hatever plenipotentiary the government of the United States might send to France to put an end to our differences would be undoubtedly received with the respect due to the representative of a free, powerful and independent nation . . . CH. MAU. TALLEYRAND

Adams has a copy of this letter but insists Talleyrand's assurances be given directly to him. Is Adams stalling?

Tonight, in the *Gazette of the United States*:

A gentleman with a horse-whip in his hand observed, the other day, a filthy, squalid and villainous looking wretch, muffled up in a great cloak, fleeing before him like a thief from the hands of justice. From the description, it was very probably *[Jasper] Dwight,* one of the editors of the *Lucifer.* Conscience frequently knocks thus at the hearts of villains and even visits them inwardly with those terrors which a sense of guilt infallibly produces.

FRIDAY, MARCH 4, 1799

GENERAL ★ AURORA ★ ADVERTISER

"The common practice of all nations" is resorted to by the committee who reported on the petitions for a repeal of the Alien and Sedition Laws as an argument why the Alien Law is right . . .

If the common practice of all nations is to legitimate the same practice here, we may next expect to hear that John Adams is a King; for it is the *common* tho' not universal practice of nations to have a *King;* and therefore HE must be a King !

Today, from Quincy, Abigail Adams writes the President's secretary, William Shaw, in Philadelphia:

If you see Fenno and are acquainted with him, tell him I say that I see the Death of his Father in many of his papers. I regret his loss and that of the public . . .[1783]

Tonight, in the *Gazette of the United States*, Jack Fenno makes an amazing announcement:

I have always looked upon this [federal] government in the light in which it appears to have been viewed by General Washington and the Convention who framed it—a mere substitute for a better . . . [T]he reins of government are too lax . . . [The tendency of *every* amendment [each amendment being part of the Bill of Rights] has been to contract its means and impair its wholesome energies . . .

In the right of inserting a paltry piece of paper into the ballot boxes once or twice a year . . . I behold but a despicable substitute for that security and repose which I shall in vain look for . . . [L]iberty, nominal liberty . . . exists [as] a magnificent nothing in the stead of security and peace. At this moment indeed, it has given way to a more absurd and unmeaning substitute, *Republicanism* . . .

In no Christian country but our own . . . are moral institutions wholly disregarded . . . Where the sacred [place] of the church is guarded by national provisions from the inroads of infidelity . . . it reciprocates that protection . . .

This vacuum might . . . be supplied by the powerful influence of the press; but here too all is hopeless; a more potent engine to the destruction of this government and country does not exist . . .

If the independence of America is not to pass away . . . it may perhaps one day be made a question whether every ignorant impostor who comes along is to be allowed unadvisedly . . . to utter the most venomous slanders and lies, unchecked by any supervision or restraint . . .

I no longer behold, when I look around, any thing much to struggle for! A country overrun by turbulence and faction . . . the people split into two deadly parties whose impending collision must as surely produce bloodshed and misery as that of flint and steel emits the spark . . .

The government, though feeble, might have had energy imparted to it for self-preservation . . . A war with France, "a long obstinate and bloody war" could alone affect this. Peace, peace; let us have peace is now the cry, and peace we are to have. It is a peace of which I will never partake . . .

The sun of federalism is fast retiring behind the clouds of turbulence and treason . . . In a little while, it may be seen no more . . .

It is an high satisfaction to me that, in the step I have thought fit to take, I leave at his [Presidential] post a man whose firmness (to renew the prostituted term) has stood a thousand times greater trials than mine and whom not all the hell of democracy in arms could divert from his duty . . .

Though I wish to be considered as relinquishing all interest or concern in the Gazette from this day, I shall nevertheless give directions to have it continued until the papers which are paid for in advance shall be supplied . . .   JOHN WARD FENNO

SATURDAY, MARCH 5, 1799

GENERAL   ★ AURORA ★   ADVERTISER

MIGHTY MARVELOUS

[A] very singular production appeared yesterday in the GAZETTE OF THE UNITED STATES—[T]he strange mixture of the incomprehensible *and the* ridiculous—*of* vapidity *and* bombast—*egregious vanity & naked hypocrisy—pitiful whining and outrageous rant—which it displays, surpass any thing perhaps that has ever appeared in a newspaper notorious for all that turpitude which it condemns as well as for the defects which it laments.*

Tonight, in the *Porcupine's Gazette,* William Cobbett writes:

For the information of my readers at a distance, I here observe that, last evening, *Mr. John Ward Fenno, Editor* and *Proprietor* of the *"Gazette of the United States"* (that Gazette to which mine has been so frequently and so largely indebted) notified his readers of his resolution to discontinue its publication . . .

This notification is accompanied with a *political view* of the United States . . . I have seen few things more excellent than this view . . .

Tonight, in the *Gazette of the United States:*

APPROACHING ELECTION . . .

It is now ascertained who are to be the candidates for the office of governor at the ensuing election. It is announced that the enemies of our administration have fixed upon Thomas M'Kean, and it is well understood that its friends have determined to support JAMES ROSS, of Washington [county] . . .

Pennsylvania, seated in the centre of the United States, wealthy, populous, commercial, and extensive as it is, must, while the present division of sentiment subsists between . . . parts of our country, direct and govern its policy . . . [T]he influence of Pennsylvania in the scale of American consequence would be immense . . . The effects then of the election of governor will be incalculable . . .

Fenno is right! Pennsylvania could prove the *"keystone in the democratic arch"* for next year's presidential election. If the five New England states (Massachusetts, New Hampshire, Rhode Island, Vermont, Connecticut) give their thirty-nine presidential electoral votes to John Adams and seven southern states (Virginia, Delaware, North Carolina, South Carolina, Kentucky, Georgia, Tennessee) give their fifty-two electoral votes to Thomas Jefferson, the choice of President of the United States could depend on three middle Atlantic states (Pennsylvania with fifteen electors, New York with twelve, and New Jersey with seven), and the coming Pennsylvania gubernatorial election in October could set the stage for a Jeffersonian victory.

FRIDAY, MARCH 6, 1799

GENERAL ★ AURORA ★ ADVERTISER

"Poor Fenno!" "Poor Lad!" are now the common theme of charitable conversation—the young ladies lament that a young fellow should be so ingenious as [to] form an object *with his own hands* so hideous as to *skeer* him out of his wits !

Today, in the *Gazette of the United States,* Jack Fenno announces:

The publication of the *Gazette of the United States* will not be discontinued. It will be conducted by the present proprietor until it can be devolved upon a successor who can do justice to the principles and cause which it has furthered.

Today, President John Adams issues a proclamation:

BY THE PRESIDENT
Of The United States of America.
A PROCLAMATION.

AS . . . the most precious interests of the people of the United States are still held in jeopardy by the hostile designs and insidious arts of a foreign nation, as well as by the dissemination among them of those principles subversive of the foundations of all religious, moral and social obligations . . . I do hereby recommend accordingly that Thursday, the 25th of April next, be observed throughout the United States of America as a day of solemn humiliation, fasting, and prayer—That citizens . . . call to mind our numerous offences against the most high God . . . That he would withhold us from unreasonable discontent—from disunion, faction, sedition, and insurrection . . . That he would succeed our preparations for defence and bless our armaments by land and by sea . . .

By the President JOHN ADAMS
TIMOTHY PICKERING *Secretary of State.*[1784]

Tonight, in the *Porcupine's Gazette*:

THIS WINTER

Seems to have no end. The Snow covers the ground; the Delaware is filled with ice and nearly frozen over, and the water freezes in the house. We have had four months and ten days dead winter. Since the 18th of October, there has not been above *six days* fit for *ploughing.*

THURSDAY, MARCH 7, 1799
GENERAL ★ AURORA ★ ADVERTISER

Fenno has not been put into a *strait waistcoat;* nor has he been even at the hospital as was reported—his disorder was of the *Phobia* species, under the paroxysms of which the maniac is prone to utter "words full of sound and fury meaning nothing."

Tonight, in the *Porcupine's Gazette*:

The publication of the *Gazette of the United States* will not be discontinued.

GENERAL ★ AURORA ★ ADVERTISER

The Federal party do not think the Federal Government strong enough—the powers of the executive are by them deemed too much restrained . . . It will be a recollection of every person who has considered the intrigues of the monarchical party in the convention that established the constitution how ardent and active such persons were who supported such principles . . .

The party which espoused monarchical principles on that occasion . . . succeeded in obtaining something *like* the rotten fabric of British institution . . . [T]hey sat down relying on their activity to produce by future corruption, according to the British system, the same effects . . .

In Fenno's paper of the 4th inst, the secrets of that faction to which he was but the foul-mouth piece were exposed to public view. [T]he *Federal box* was opened by a boy who knew not how to manage the cumbrous machinery . . . We have . . . the confession of *Fenno* and his declared detestation of our present form of government . . .

Tonight, in the *Porcupine's Gazette*:

A letter from a gentleman in Northampton county in this state, dated the 5th instant, mentioned that the marshal of the United States had arrived there with twenty eight writs against persons who had opposed the assessors of the direct tax in the execution of their duties. The citizens were to assemble at Bethlehem yesterday to enter into recognizances before Judge Henry.

SATURDAY, MARCH 9, 1799

GENERAL ★ AURORA ★ ADVERTISER

EXPIRED
On the 4th Day of March, 1799
At 5 o'clock in the Evening
Of a Malignant Distemper
After a miserable existence of 14 years,
3 months, and 9 days,
THE GAZETTE OF THE UNITED STATES . . .
Incapable of perceiving the dignity of Republicanism,
over the abasement of Monarchy and Aristocracy . . .

Tonight, in the *Porcupine's Gazette:*

MR. FENNO'S VIEW . . .
This spirited production, to which . . . I gave my most unqualified ap-

probation I am glad to hear approved of by every man of sense and candor . . .

His opinions are all correct . . . But why do not those who disapprove of this performance *reply to it?*

MONDAY, MARCH 11, 1799

GENERAL ★ AURORA ★ ADVERTISER

In *[Porcupine's] Gazette,* we are told that all of Fenno's ideas are correct concerning our constitution and forms of government . . . [T]he friends of Republican government are called upon to defend by argument the constitution which we have all sworn to support. Republican government is attacked by monarchists in the very bosom of the Republic . . .

The citizens of this land have achieved their liberty against all the force of the British monarchy . . .

The people have said that a government of equal laws, without empty titles or wicked distinctions, shall be our government.

We are asked for arguments—we have already given them, the world has applauded our choice, and are following our example. But further arguments are called for—they are ready—THE PEOPLE OF THESE FREE UNITED STATES ARE READY—WE WILL DEFEND OUR REPUBLICAN FORM OF GOVERNMENT WITH OUR BAYONETS.

Tonight, in the *Gazette of the United States:*

ANOTHER INSURRECTION

Has broken out in the Western part of this state . . .

Col. William Nichols, Marshal of the District of Pennsylvania, returned yesterday to the city from a journey to Northampton [county, Pennsylvania] and immediately laid before the President [of the United States] a detail of recent transactions there . . .

He [had] . . . proceeded to the scene of insurrection and arrested twenty-three persons for sundry acts of resistance to the operation of the law imposing a tax on houses . . .

On Friday evening, the Marshal, with nineteen of the arrested persons, being at the tavern of Abraham Levering in Bethlehem [Pennsylvania], a body of horse to the number of sixty, well armed and part of them in uniform, beset the house and rescued the prisoners. The party was composed of militia from the [Pennsylvania] counties of Bucks, Montgomery and Northampton and were commanded by a fellow who bears a captain's commission in the militia of Montgomery county; he is a German, of the name of [John] Fries . . .

These disturbances all refer directly to the political posture of affairs between this country and France . . .

One pleasant circumstance has grown out of this alarming intelligence—an immediate stir among the [federal army] volunteers who are, we learn, to be immediately paraded for review in order to be perfectly prepared for the defence of their government and country at a moment's warning.

CHAPTER TWELVE

KINGLY GOVERNMENT

*[T]he army [of 1798] was raised on principles precisely monarchical
. . . Let us explain it by the following supposition. The present
Congress will cease to exist on the 3d of March, 1799. On the 4th
Mr. Adams may get a certificate from some confidential judge that
Virginia or Tennessee is in a state of rebellion. Whether the story be
true or false rests entirely within his breast. He directly calls
out the militia . . . [H]e and his militia are absolute masters of
America . . . [A] royal interregnum might readily put an end
to the government.*

**JAMES THOMSON CALLENDER,
SKETCHES OF THE HISTORY OF AMERICA (1798)** [1785]

*In the independent times of the ancient republics, no one thought of
giving to a general a supreme command close to the seat of
government for four years certain. Yet this and many other high
prerogatives, internal and external, are given for this term to
the American President . . . [I]t is sufficient reason for changing
the present institution of a solitary president—And what reason
is there per contra; what evil in a plural directory, gradually
renewed . . .* [1786]
*[The constitution of the United States] evidently
had its formation before the United States had sufficiently
un-monarchized their ideas and habits. They dismissed the
name of king, but they retained a prejudice for his authority.
Instead of keeping as little, they kept as much of it
as possible for their president . . .* [1787]

**B. F. BACHE, EDITOR,
AURORA GENERAL ADVERTISER, 1790–1798**

*The more the People are discontented with the Oppression of Taxes,
the greater Need the Prince has of Money to . . . pay the Troops that are
to suppress all Resistance . . . It will be said that we do not propose to
establish Kings. I know it. But there is a natural Inclination in
Mankind to kingly Government . . . I am apprehensive, therefore,—*

perhaps too apprehensive,—that the Government of these States may in future times end in a Monarchy . . .

DR. BENJAMIN FRANKLIN
AT THE FEDERAL CONSTITUTIONAL CONVENTION,
JUNE 2, 1787[1788]

A Highwayman is as much a Robber when he plunders in a Gang as when single; and a Nation that makes an unjust War is only a great Gang.

DR. BENJAMIN FRANKLIN[1789]

SECOND ARTICLE: A well regulated Militia being necessary to the security of a free State, the right of the people to keep and bear Arms, shall not be infringed.
THIRD ARTICLE: No soldier shall, in time of peace be quartered in any house without the consent of the Owner, nor in time of war, but in a manner to be prescribed by law.
FOURTH ARTICLE: The right of the people to be secure in their persons, houses, papers, and effects, against unreasonable searches and seizures, shall not be violated, and no Warrants shall issue, but upon probable cause . . .

ARTICLES FROM THE BILL OF RIGHTS
OF THE U.S. CONSTITUTION

TUESDAY, MARCH 12, 1799

GENERAL ★ AURORA ★ ADVERTISER

The public attention has been engaged for two or three days by some occurrences that have taken place in Northampton county in this state. Efforts are making to magnify these occurrences into a terrible and bloody conspiracy against the government &c . . .

It is a well known circumstance that in the schedule made out for . . . the House Tax, passed at the session of Congress before the last, there was a column set apart for registering the number of windows in every house, although no tax has been laid on windows . . .

In Northampton County, while a [tax assessor] person was in the act of measuring the windows of a house, a woman poured a shower of hot water over his head; in other places they were hooted at . . . but no other violence done than the *hot water war* carried on by the female . . .

We are informed that a body of Volunteers are to be called out and marched into Northampton County, but we cannot believe that such a measure can be deemed either necessary or wise. The discontents in Northampton county were directed against the window admeasurements

608

. . . No tumult has arisen or violence been done to any person but what was done with the *hot water* . . . [P]ossibly there may be found some unfledged Alexander, desirous of burning up some of the flourishing towns in the course of such an expedition . . .

Today, the President of the United States issues a proclamation:

BY THE PRESIDENT
Of The United States of America.
A PROCLAMATION.

WHEREAS combinations to defeat the execution of the laws for the valuation of Lands and Dwelling-Houses within the United States have existed in the counties of Northampton, Montgomery and Bucks in the state of Pennsylvania and have proceeded in a manner subversive of the just authority of the government by misrepresentations to render the law odius, by deterring the public officers of the United States to forbear the execution of their functions, and by openly threatening their lives . . .

WHEREFORE, I JOHN ADAMS, President of the United States do hereby command all persons being insurgents . . . on or before Monday next . . . to disperse and retire peaceably . . . and I do require all officers and others . . . according to their respective duties and the laws . . . to prevent and suppress such dangerous and unlawful proceedings.

JOHN ADAMS, *By the President,*
TIMOTHY PICKERING, *Secretary of State.*[1790]

Tonight, William Cobbett in the *Porcupine's Gazette*:

NEW INSURRECTION!

"If the provisional army is not raised without delay, a *civil war* or a *surrender of Independence* is not at more than a twelve month's distance."   *Porcupine,* 10th Nov. 1798.

I most certainly hope that events may not justify the burning of me for a Wizard! . . .

FRIDAY, MARCH 15, 1799

GENERAL   ★ AURORA ★   ADVERTISER

The terrible hot water insurrection in Northampton county is cooled down to an ordinary process at law, to which all the parties have voluntarily submitted.

Today, having promoted the Macpherson's Blues commandant,[1791] William Macpherson, to be brigadier general in the new federal army and ordered him to lead the army against Pennsylvania's war-tax protesters, John Adams leaves Philadelphia for his home in Quincy, Massachusetts.[1792] He will not return till mid-October.

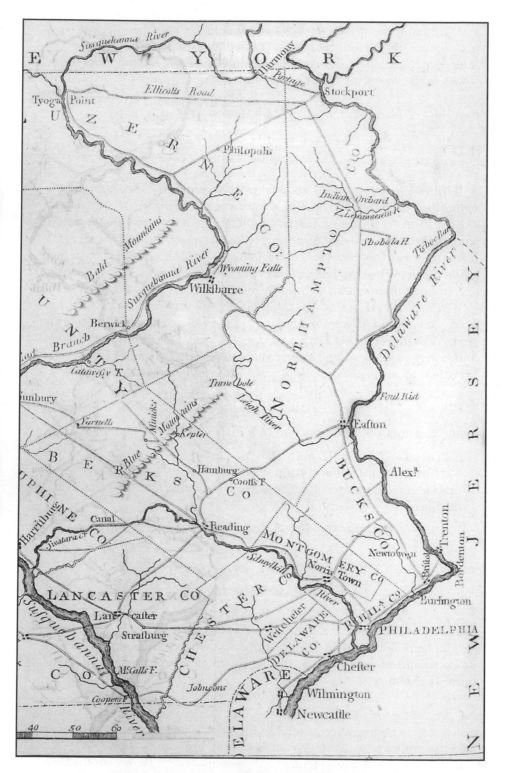

The eastern counties of Pennsylvania in 1799.[1793]

SATURDAY, MARCH 16, 1799

GENERAL ★ AURORA ★ ADVERTISER

Appointment. William Macpherson, esq. to be a Brigadier General in the army of the United States.

The black-cockaded Federalist militia, the Macpherson's Blues, now hold the authority of the new federal army. Their commandant, William Macpherson, will lead that army in Pennsylvania. A Blues cavalry lieutenant will be his aide-de-camp.[1794]

Today, off Guadeloupe in the French West Indies, the U.S. Navy's thirty-six-gun, 340–man frigate *Constellation,* under U.S. Navy Captain Thomas Truxton, makes another French capture. Captain Truxton reports to the Secretary of the Navy:

> *I have captured off the Road of Bassateeer Guadaloupe a [French] Letter of Marque Schooner called the Union, mounting 6 Carriage Guns and navigated with Thirty two Men (Lading Provisions and Dry Goods) and have brought her into this Road . . .*[1795]

Tonight, in the *Porcupine's Gazette*:

THE INSURRECTION.

The roads have been so very bad for several days past that it is not surprizing we have no news from the scene of insurrection. General Macpherson is, it is said, to command the troops which are to march on Tuesday next against the Insurgents . . .

TUESDAY, MARCH 19, 1799

GENERAL ★ AURORA ★ ADVERTISER

FROM THE VIRGINIA GAZETTE.

"[I have said] I considered disunion as a deplorable event—but less deplorable than a perpetuity of expensive armies—perpetuity of expensive navies—perpetuity of excessive debts—perpetuity of excessive taxes—and all the oppressive consequences resulting therefrom . . ."

[Virginia Congressman] WM. B. GILES

Tonight, in the *Gazette of the United States*:

It is a fact that the FRENCH faction in Northampton have assumed and do now wear the *French cockade.*

No orders have yet been published relative to the marching a military force against the insurgents in Northampton County in this state; but we are informed that different volunteer companies are directed to hold themselves in readiness . . .

WEDNESDAY, MARCH 20, 1799

The sons of *St. Patrick* kept their anniversary festival on Monday last . . . VOLUNTEERS [toasts] . . . *The immortal Franklin—"Where liberty is, there is my country."*

Today, U.S. Secretary at War James McHenry writes Pennsylvania Governor Thomas Mifflin:

TO suppress the insurrection in the counties of Northampton, Bucks, and Montgomery in the state of Pennsylvania in opposition to the laws of the United States, the President has thought it necessary to employ a Military Force . . . The corps of militia first desired on this occasion are the troops of cavalry belonging to this city and one troop from each of the counties of Philadelphia, Bucks, Chester, Montgomery and Lancaster. These troops, I have the honor to request, your Excellency will order to hold themselves in readiness to march on or before the 28th instant under the command of Brigadier General WILLIAM MACPHERSON.[1796]

Tonight, in the *Gazette of the United States*:

A gentlemen who arrived in town hall last evening from Haerlahey's, where a meeting of a number of dissatisfied persons from Bucks, Northampton, and Montgomery [Counties] was held on Monday informs us that, at that meeting (which consisted of about 200 persons), a disposition of unconditional submission to the laws of the United States was uniformly adopted!

If the insurrection in Northampton is in reality subsiding, and its agents retiring to their shells, what is to follow? Are the perpetrators of so daring an outrage on the laws, honor, and dignity of the government to escape with impunity?

THURSDAY, MARCH 21, 1799

Some pains have been taken by some enemies of the peace and happiness of these States to spread abroad an idea that the late obstructions to the assessments in Northampton and Bucks [counties] had grown to the height of rebellion . . . Every indication of tumult has ceased there . . . and citizens . . . have displayed every disposition to submit with decency to the laws.

GENERAL   ★ AURORA ★   ADVERTISER

Whence this precipitation on the part of the government of the United States to march troops against the people of Northampton and Bucks? Are those people *in arms* against the government? No one will dare say they are. Whence then, it may be again asked, such precipitation?

Even [John] FRIES has declared his readiness to submit and to take his trial when summoned thereto; and yet we hear nothing but military movements !!

GENERAL   ★ AURORA ★   ADVERTISER

The President in his proclamation directs the citizens of Northampton and Bucks, who are said to be in arms against the law, to disperse . . . Have the people who have been in arms dispersed or not? No doubt whatever that they have . . . If this be the fact . . . what is the pretense for marching troops into that country? . . . If the *civil* authority is competent to all objects in the accused counties, and of this there is abundant proof, why is a military force resorted to . . . ?

Tonight, in the *Porcupine's Gazette,* Peter Porcupine writes:

I am astonished to see so little indignation expressed at the conduct of the NO-TAX insurgents in Pennsylvania . . . Are men weak enough to believe that the government can long live under the annual visitation of an unpunished revolt? . . .

There is in these states a faction, a numerous and desperate faction, resolved on the overthrow of the Federal government, and the man who will not allow that there is a *danger* to be apprehended, is either too great a fool to perceive it or too great a coward to encounter it.

GENERAL   ★ AURORA ★   ADVERTISER

Is it not very extraordinary that the Executive should persist in the determination to march troops into the county of Northampton, notwithstanding there is not the smallest appearance of disturbance? What can influence such a determination? Is it that certain favorite *contractors, commissioners,* and *quarter-masters* may have grist supplied for their mills? . . . Or is it that the system of alarm may be perpetuated to furnish arguments for standing armies and *against the government of the people?*

FRIDAY, MARCH 29, 1799

GENERAL ★ AURORA ★ ADVERTISER

Yesterday the remainder of the persons who were implicated in opposing the laws in Northampton county arrived in town and surrendered themselves before Judge Peters ... Several aged people who were implicated in the opposition to the assessment but who were unable to travel from the severity of the weather and the depth of the roads have sent certificates of magistrates to the proper offices in this city and are excused from present attendance, bail being given ...

SATURDAY, MARCH 30, 1799

GENERAL ★ AURORA ★ ADVERTISER

All the [implicated] ... citizens of Northampton ... have surrendered themselves and have given bail for their appearance at court—Does this look as if there was an insurrection ?

Tonight, in the *Gazette of the United States*:

A citizen proposes that, in the event of the volunteer corps being ordered to quell the insurrection in Northampton, an armed association should be immediately formed to protect the city against the United Irishmen and other freebooters who are still tolerated among us.

Tonight, in the *Porcupine's Gazette,* Peter Porcupine writes:

INSURRECTION.

[I]t is probable the march of the troops from this city for Northampton will take place about Wednesday next.—Various detachments of regular troops are already on their march thither; these, it is supposed, will form a body of 500 men ...

Merely to quell such an insurrection as this will answer but little purpose. It is a weed that has poisoned the soil; to crop off the stalk will only enable it to spring up again and to send out a hundred shoots instead of one. It must be torn up by the root; the *principles of insurrection must be eradicated,* or anarchy must ensue.

WEDNESDAY, APRIL 3, 1799

GENERAL ★ AURORA ★ ADVERTISER

A CAUTION

The Inhabitants of Montgomery, Bucks, and Northampton Counties, who may be proprietors of windmills or watermills, are hereby notified that they should keep them still the ensuing week, so as to give no provocation ...

Today, in Reading, Pennsylvania (northwest of Philadelphia in the county of Berks), members of the new federal army pass through town. From *sworn* declarations of Berks County citizens:

JACOB GOSSIN, *Reading [Pennsylvania] . . . Wednesday the 3rd of April, about 15 of the Lancaster troop of Horse, commanded by Captain Montgomery, came to my house, and having secured my workmen to prevent their assisting me, observed to them that if I was desirous to keep or preserve my house, I should fell the [liberty] pole . . . Like highwaymen, with a pistol in one hand and a sword in the other, they approached me, threatening to dispatch me instantly . . . My wife met with similar treatment, who . . . in consequence of her fright . . . fell sick . . . Another one of my children was kicked and spurned to the ground—Then they took my ax and cut down the [liberty] pole, departed carrying with them the ax, my property . . .*

JOHN STROHECKER. *On the 3d of April 1799, at noon while I was dining, about thirteen of the Lancaster troop of horse came to my house. Two or three of whom, entering the door, went into an adjoining room, and took several setting poles belonging to my boats . . . I rose from table, went out, and asked them what authority they had to take those poles? one of them answered that they intended to cross Schuykill [River], upon which I observed . . . you must call to the ferry man—who lives on the opposite side . . . [U]pon my taking hold of the pole, he held it firmly with one hand and with the other hand drew a pistol, saying, God damn your soul! . . . In the interim, they spied a pole which my children, in their puerile amusement, had erected for a liberty-pole, with a small strip of canvas attached to it for a flag. But fearful the horsemen might carry them off, the children took down this pole and placed it in the said room where it was discovered by the horsemen who thereupon took it out of the house and cut it to pieces to the great terror of the children. After this, they returned and the greater part entered the house with their swords drawn, cursing and swearing most profanely and violently, taking the poles with several rudders . . . And my wife, who having just recovered from a severe indisposition of two years, was brought into a relapse . . .*

RANDOLPH SAMPLE. *On the 3rd of April 1799 . . . I perceived a party of the Lancaster troop of horse, about 16 or 17 in number . . . who . . . surrounded me with their swords drawn . . . I was forced to go out and cut at the [liberty] pole . . .*

ISAAC FETHER. *On the 3d of April 1799, 16 or 17 of the Lancaster troop of Horse came to my house, and forming themselves into military order, drew their swords—one of them rode up to the house and knocked on the window with such violence that the fragments of a pane of glass flew into the room. I went out to enquire their wishes; upon my arrival at the door, I observed several stationed near it who . . . demanded my axe; when I asked what they intended to do with it;*

*they replied to cut down this damned liberty pole . . . I procured the
axe and offered it to them, they however did not take it, but peremptorily commanded me . . . to cut down the pole myself . . . threatening
that if I made the least resistance or manifested the smallest reluctance, they would run their swords through my body.—In the meantime, my wife came out of the house . . . was discovered by them and
instantly beset by several who hastily ran up to her with their swords
drawn, notwithstanding her advanced state of pregnancy, commanding her to return immediately within doors.*[1797]

FRIDAY, APRIL 5, 1799

GENERAL   ★ AURORA ★   ADVERTISER

Four troops of volunteer cavalry, attached to the militia of this state,
and two troops of volunteer cavalry attached to the Presidential army,
marched from this city yesterday for Northampton, under the brigadier
general Macpherson.

The corps of Engineers, under captain Elliot, took the same route on
Wednesday.

War . . . Today, off Antigua in the French West Indies, the fourteen-gun United
States Navy brig *Eagle,* Captain Hugh G. Campbell in command, captures the
French privateer sloop *Bon Père* with ten guns and fifty-five men on board. The
Eagle dispatches the *Bon Père* to Savannah, Georgia.[1798]

SATURDAY, APRIL 6, 1799

GENERAL   ★ AURORA ★   ADVERTISER

The force marched into Northampton appears perfectly well calculated to produce rather than prevent discontent—It is perfectly well
known to every man that has marched thither from this city that there
is no force to oppose them, no body in arms, not even a riot to quell—
There are many gone thither, however, very desirous of exciting commotion . . . Some young heroes were heard to declare that if some of the
insurgents were not hanged or shot before their return, they would never
march a foot on public service again.

MONDAY, APRIL 8, 1799

GENERAL   ★ AURORA ★   ADVERTISER

MANIFESTO

*The following is translated for this paper from the Manifesto in the
German language, issued to the inhabitants of Northampton, &c. &c.*
Wm. MACPHERSON, Brigadier General of the armies of the U. States,

commander of the troops ordered to act against the insurgents of North-ampton, Montgomery, and Bucks in the State of Pennsylvania.

FELLOW CITIZENS,

Being ordered by the President of the United States . . . to suppress and disperse all unlawful combinations . . . I therefore have thought it proper to inform the people . . . of the danger to which they expose them selves by combining . . .

The act against which the present treasonable opposition is made is that for laying and collecting a tax for the common defence . . .

All agreed that we should not submit to the conditions which France proposed but prepare for our defence . . . This manner of proceeding required money, and, in order to obtain that, a tax became necessary . . .

Therefore I again forewarn you not to aid or abet those violators of the laws . . .

WM. MACPHERSON. By order of the general.

Tonight, in the *Porcupine's Gazette:*

[T]hose who look upon these insurgents as sinning from ignorance are themselves extremely ignorant of their character and motives. Can any man for one moment suppose that there can be the majority of a county in Pennsylvania *who do not understand the true intent and meaning of the house tax?* Go and talk to these insurgents, and you will find that they know all that is going forward in Philadelphia as well as you do. It is the greatest nonsense in the world to presume that they do not understand a law *merely because they oppose its operation;* as well as we may presume that *Reynolds, Mother Bache,* &c., &c., did not understand the alien & sedition bills.—

Tonight, in the *Gazette of the United States:*

On Saturday evening last, a detachment of the cavalry of this city arrived in town from the camp near Seller's on the Bethlehem road, 31 miles from Philadelphia, having in custody the noted [insurgent, John] Fries . . .

Fries was taken on Friday afternoon, about five miles from the camp, by a detachment of cavalry dispatched for the purpose. He was holding a sale at vendue [auction], when the troops approached; and made no attempt to escape until they appeared in sight, when he ran through some fields into a wood, and was taken after a pursuit of near two miles . . .

Judge Peters arrived at head quarters on Saturday morning at eleven o'clock.

TUESDAY, APRIL 9, 1799

GENERAL ★ AURORA ★ ADVERTISER

SALEM [MASSACHUSETTS], March 29 . . . [David] Brown, who was committed to the jail in this town last week by John Lovejoy, esq. of

Andover, was yesterday examined before Thomas Bancroft, esq. for uttering seditious pieces . . . and being present, assisting, aiding, and abetting the erection of a [Liberty] Pole and Label at Dedham, with the following inscription, *"Liberty and Equality, The Vice President and the Minority, A Speedy Retirement to the President, No Sedition bill, No Alien bill, Downfall to the Tyrants of America."* . . . He is recognized in the sum of 4000 dollars to appear at the Circuit Court to be held in Boston next June.

[NEW LONDON, CONN. *Bee*] The respectable clergyman [J. C. Ogden] who, *from no political motive*, interceded in behalf of col. Lyon during his imprisonment, was on his return from Philadelphia arrested on the suit of Oliver Wolcott, esq. Secretary of the Treasury of the U. States (can we here say "from no political motives"?) and thrown into prison . . .

THURSDAY, APRIL 11, 1799

GENERAL ★ AURORA ★ ADVERTISER

[BUCKS COUNTY, PENNSYLVANIA.] Extract of a letter dated Quakertown, April 8, 1799 . . . *"The system of terror here, I am sorry to say, is carried far beyond what, in my opinion, the public good requires. Detachments are out every day or night apprehending one or other individuals . . . The scenes of distress which I have witnessed among these poor people, I cannot describe when we have entered their houses. Conceive your house entered at dead of night by a body of armed men and yourself dragged from your wife and screaming children. These poor people are extremely ignorant but they have feelings, and they always consider that death awaits any one who is seized, be he culpable or not. I am sorry to say that there have been many instances of an inhuman disposition exhibited . . ."*

SATURDAY, APRIL 13, 1799

GENERAL ★ AURORA ★ ADVERTISER

Extract of a letter dated Miller's-town (50 miles from Philadelphia), April 10, 1799 . . . *"We are now quartered in a Whig town where the people have always been true republicans . . . The inhabitants are principally Germans. Nearly all the male inhabitants on the approach of our army fled from their homes, and their wives and children exhibit a very unhappy scene of distress. Had I conceived that some things which I have witnessed here could have taken place, I should never have given my assent to march a mile on the expedition. One effect produced by the distresses here is that every individual whom I meet is disgusted, and a sentiment generally prevails which, contrary to ex-*

*pectation, will, I apprehend, completely destroy the federal influence
in the next election . . ."*

TUESDAY, APRIL 16, 1799

GENERAL ★ AURORA ★ ADVERTISER

Extract of a letter from an officer of the Northern Army, dated Miller's Town April 11th, 1799. *"With respect to military operations, they still continue; and the number of persons confined in heavy irons encreases . . . [A] number of troops who derive their authority from the federal government live at free quarters [in private homes] on the people . . . I cannot believe, however, that these troops are authorized to proceed thus; I rather conclude that it is the effect of that licentiousness into which ignorant men, or indeed enlightened men, will run, when possessed of an unnatural power over their fellow citizens . . ."*

Extract of another letter of the same date. *"The stationing of a body of troops here until the next election may induce the people to emigrate to some of the southern states, but it will not influence the vote of a single man who remains . . ."*

A Gentleman now on the expedition against the insurgents writes, *"that the only paper read in those parts of the country, where treason has raised her head, is the Aurora. This accounts in part for the defection of these ignorant and deluded wretches."* . . .

FRIDAY, APRIL 19, 1799

GENERAL ★ AURORA ★ ADVERTISER

FOREIGN INTERFERENCE AT ELECTIONS . . .

Cobbett, the British printer *Cobbett,* who . . . reviles representative government, impudently insinuates that the Chief Justice [of Pennsylvania, Thomas McKean] is acting basely and the people stupidly . . . Mr. JAMES ROSS'S election is openly supported and advanced by this British agent . . .

Cobbett's insidious propping of the British constitution at the expence of the constitutions of the United States is, to be sure, *a most audacious foreign interference in our elections* and attempt to sap our political principles . . .

Let him look at the judiciary of Ireland—a kingdom of three or four millions of people . . . [T]he Parliament of England is chosen for that *great* and *injured* people by fewer persons than are entitled to vote in a single American county.

Tonight, in the *Porcupine's Gazette,* Peter Porcupine answers:

[T]his day's paper . . . may serve as an answer to . . . Mother Bache's filthy dishclout [dishcloth] of this morning—A propos: this *delicate* dame began her Editorial career by rejoicing at the abolition of *"castration in Italy."* I quote her very words, and I will, one of these days, give the modest essay at length . . .

I hereby give notice that on Monday next, I shall publish an extract from WIDOW BACHE's first paper which will render my Gazette of that day *unfit for any decent woman to read.* I have heard a good deal about the *delicacy* of this woman, and I therefore think it necessary to undeceive the duped publick.

Tonight, in the *Gazette of the United States*:

From Northampton . . . It is probable the army will return through Reading and visit some disturbed parts of Bucks and Montgomery [counties] in their march home . . . We are informed by a gentleman who has been continually with the troops that their conduct has not only been irreproachable but remarkable for discipline and good order . . .

SATURDAY, APRIL 20, 1799

GENERAL ★ AURORA ★ ADVERTISER

[Adv.]	JUST PUBLISHED At No. 118 Market Street (Price A Quarter Of A Dollar) *THE PORCUPINIAD.* A HUDIBRASTIC POEM, Addressed to WILLIAM COBBETT . . . "Thank Heaven I am No citizen of America" . . .

Today, in Reading, Pennsylvania, troops of John Adams' new federal army visit the newspaper office of Jacob Schnyder, editor and publisher of the *Reading Eagle,* which has published anonymous reports of military abuses. From Jacob Schnyder's *sworn* declaration:

On the 20th of April 1799, John Fry, [Sergeant] Reichard, and three other of the Lancaster troop of horse came to my printing-office, while I was closely engaged at work. One . . . demanded the author of a piece published some time previous in the Reading Eagle.

I observed to him that it was not customary with printers to give their authors names . . . I did not think myself at liberty to comply with this request . . . [T]hey desired to go with them to the Captain . . . I was forc'd to Michael Wood's Inn, where the captain lodged . . . I was accosted thus politely, Is this the damn'd rascal? Is this the damn'd son of a bitch? &c. His throat should be cut . . . [T]he captain ordered his praise worthy troops to take me to the market-house and ordered

the trumpeter, the common whipper, to give me twenty-five lashes . . .
[T]he troops . . . forced me to the market-house . . . I then pull'd off my
vest, and the trumpeter gave me, to the best of my recollection, six
strokes with a cowhide, when one observed it was sufficient.[1799]

MONDAY, APRIL 22, 1799

GENERAL ★ AURORA ★ ADVERTISER

The presses of the United States which favor British politics and connexions are constantly libelling the talents, character, &c. of America. They abuse Doctor Franklin, whose services in the revolution . . . entitle him to the esteem of every patriot . . .

Any man can see by whom and for what Mr. Cobbett has been sent to America. The service required a monstrous stock of confidence, if the British expected him to go the lengths he has done in meddling in our internal affairs, in our elections, in our intercourse with foreign nations . . .

Not long before the arrival of Mr. Cobbett in America, a formal and official report of the *Lords of the British Council* was made to the *King of Great Britain*, concerning the United States, in which it was stated to his Britannic Majesty that *"a party was formed in favor of Great Britain."* They naturally wanted a printer or two, and the British government was so obliging as to send them Mr. Cobbett . . .

Tonight, in the *Porcupine's Gazette*, William Cobbett writes:

MOTHER BACHE

Must hang bye 'till to-morrow. I have no room for her today. The foreign intelligence is of importance, and were I to omit it, my readers would find themselves but badly compensated by the prose of Mrs. Bache, though it is excessively *luscious.*

Next Thursday is the day appointed by the President to be observed as a *General Fast.* —I hope the people of all religions will join us in a hearty prayer for the destruction of the French and their traitorous partizans.

TUESDAY, APRIL 23, 1799

GENERAL ★ AURORA ★ ADVERTISER

The trial of prisoners charged with treasonable practices we are informed will come up in the course of this week before the [U.S.] district court . . . sitting in this city.

Tonight, in the *Gazette of the United States*:

The Grand Jury of the Circuit Court of the United States, now sitting in this city, have found Bills against three of the Northampton Insurgents for High Treason, of this number, *[John] Fries* is one . . . Yesterday afternoon several troops of this city arrived here from Reading . . .

Tonight, Peter Porcupine in the *Porcupine's Gazette*:

MOTHER BACHE
Must hang bye for another day or two.

WEDNESDAY, APRIL 24, 1799

GENERAL   ★ AURORA ★   ADVERTISER

ORDER and GOOD GOVERNMENT

A transaction that has taken place during the recent extraordinary military expedition merits the earnest and dispassionate consideration of every man who feels the least respect for the laws or holds the least pretension of regard for our free constitution and equal rights.

A troop of horse belonging to Lancaster, in this state, was ordered on the public service as a part of the body of volunteers that had proffered their services to the President of the United states.

On their march to join the army, they were guilty of some excesses in Reading . . . A statement of the transaction was . . . published in a German newspaper at Reading, the printer of which is a Mr. *Schnyder.*

Upon the breaking up of the army a few days ago, the Lancaster troop, under the command of *Captain Montgomery*, retraced its march through the same town where they halted. A sergeant and several troopers were dispatched to Mr. *Schnyder's* house from which they took him by force.

He was brought before the captain, and after a series of interrogatories, this self-appointed Dictator ordered Mr. Schnyder to be taken to the market-house, stripped naked, and there punished by the infliction of 25 lashes! . . .

This, among numerous others, is a striking evidence of the danger which a free state is exposed to from an army . . . The army, placed without that controul [that the people have over the militia,] requires but a very small accession of numbers to destroy the public liberties and to exalt some wicked villain over the national ruin of a despotic throne.

Tonight, William Cobbett in the *Porcupine's Gazette*:

Pennsylvanians, recollect that the only press in this city which has had the audacity to espouse the cause of [Chief Justice Thomas] McKean is [the *Aurora,*] that prostituted, that infamous, that blasphemous press from which have issued *Paine's Age of Reason, Paine's Letter to General Washington* and from which the *Atheistical Calendar [of the French Republic]* is annually issued . . . This, Pennsylvanians, is the press, the *only press,* through which McKEAN is recommended to you as a proper person to be your Governor.

Tonight, in the *Gazette of the United States:*

> Yesterday afternoon, returned to the city, Brigadier General MAC-PHERSON, Commander in chief of the forces lately employed against the Northampton rebels . . . A large concourse of people, whom the occasion had assembled, . . . received him with reiterated shouts. The General having passed the line of Infantry, they filed off by sections, joined the cavalry, and escorted him to his quarters in Eighth-street, where he retired amidst the customary honors of the Military and the again-repeated shouts of the multitude.

THURSDAY, APRIL 25, 1799

GENERAL ★ AURORA ★ ADVERTISER

> [T]he deliberate and savage violation of the law—committed by men in military uniform and who had *pledged themselves to the President to maintain law and order* . . . marks the danger [to] the public liberties from men placed beyond the reach of civil institutions . . .
>
> Application was made to General Macpherson upon the subject . . . he promised to enquire into it—but the men were marched off . . . !

By presidential proclamation, today is a national day for prayer and fasting. Life is relatively quiet. William Cobbett's friend the Rev. James Abercrombie doesn't preach! In Philadelphia's Second Presbyterian Church, however, the Rev. Ashbel Green delivers his Fast Day sermon:

> *My brethren— . . . [T]he profanation of the name of God, the disregard of the public worship, the contempt of gospel institutions, the neglect of family government and family religion, the dissoluteness of youth, the wanton and wicked reviling of magistrates . . . the cherishing of seditious practices, the opposition to the laws of the country, the prevalence of dueling, the open practice of adultery and fornication, the multiplied instances of fraud and swindling . . . the devotedness of thousands to a covetous pursuit of wealth . . . have encreased upon us, with a rapid accumulation, within a short space . . . And shall I lay open the source . . . ? . . . an enthusiastic attachment, in multitudes of people in this country to the revolution and cause of the French. This attachment has given an easy introduction to the atheistical, infidel, and immoral principles of that people . . .*
>
> *I am now to remark we have not been . . . free from the judgments of God . . . For six years past, the pestilence has been sent into our land in a manner that never was before known to us . . . With our prayers, let us resolve to join our endeavors for the suppression of vice . . .* [1800]

FRIDAY, APRIL 26, 1799

GENERAL ★ AURORA ★ ADVERTISER

Let it be known that JAMES ROSS is nominated and approved [for Governor of Pennsylvania] by PETER PORCUPINE, that Porcupine is a *foreign emissary*, that HE has *reviled* our revolution, *despised* our civil institutions, and has *laboured assiduously* to render our country subservient to Great Britain . . .

MONDAY, APRIL 29, 1799

GENERAL ★ AURORA ★ ADVERTISER

[The Rev. J. C. Ogden] has been confined in the cell of Litchfield [Connecticut] by the Secretary [of the Treasury, Oliver Wolcott] of the United States for delivering the petitions of the western district of Vermont in behalf of col. Lyon . . . It was supposed that the parson had the sum with him which was raised in Philadelphia to pay col. Lyon's fine . . .

This confinement was undoubtedly preconcerted in Philadelphia on the part of Mr. Secretary [of the Treasury, Oliver Wolcott], and our Members of Congress. The time of the messenger's departure [from Philadelphia] was known to Mr. Pickering and others. He left the stage house at twelve o'clock, came in the mail stage, halted two days in New York, and one in New-Milford [Connecticut]. It was universally known that this business led him by way of Litchfield . . .

All this malevolence arises solely from the wishes of col. Lyon's foes to have detained him in the cell in Vergennes . . .

Who will be astonished if hereby we gain a LYON in Connecticut more formidable than him in Vermont? Do not such proceedings multiply Lyons ?

Tonight, in the *Porcupine's Gazette,* Peter Porcupine writes:

I *know* [Democratick Judge] M'Kean . . . *I will never live six months under his sovereign sway* . . . I look upon it as my duty to the publick to assist in opposing M'Kean's election . . .

This was day fixed on for *Mother Bache,* &c., &c. but, as I forgot to inform the ladies of it on Saturday, I must put it off till to-morrow.—If, after this warning, they should be incautious enough to look at Peg's bawdry, it will be no fault of mine . . .

TUESDAY, APRIL 30, 1799

GENERAL ★ AURORA ★ ADVERTISER

THE FAST DAY.
Unlike the political festival of 1798, that of the 25th of April, 1799,

passed over with a composed and impressive *silence*—our streets were not thronged with boisterous ruffians, *"mad with the Tuscan grape and ripe for blood"*—the pomp of military parade was not seen in our peaceful streets—the windows of our citizens were not assailed with stones—and the President did not send back the *Aurora* unread—because it has never been served him since the *fast day* of 1798 . . .

Joe Thomas who, with a sword drawn, led a phalanx of *Bacchanals* through our streets on the fast day of 1798—has since fled from the uplifted hand of justice . . .

It is a very striking evidence of the growing moderation of politicians that the Rev. Mr. Abercrombie did not preach . . .

Today, in Philadelphia, the U.S. Circuit Court for Pennsylvania, with Judge James Iredell presiding, opens a nine-day trial for high treason of John Fries, the German-speaking auctioneer who, on March 7th, led a throng of Northampton residents to release seventeen or eighteen fellow war tax protesters who were in the custody of U.S. Marshal John Nichols at Reiter's Tavern House near Bethlehem, Pennsylvania. Prosecution testimony includes:

COLONEL NICHOLS, the marshal: . . . *The prisoner at the bar was at the head of the infantry, with his sword drawn; the horse marched into the yard and formed in front of the house; the infantry marched round the house . . . I had a good deal of conversation with . . . Captain Fries . . . His reason was that he was opposed to those laws—the alien law, the stamp act, and the house-act; and said they were unconstitutional . . . I then begged him to use his influence in persuading the people to disperse . . . His answer was that he had no influence; that he could do nothing. After this, I consulted with Judge Henry and others, what was best to be done; it seemed to be their opinion that I had better submit and give up the prisoners.*[1801]

JACOB EVERLY: . . . *I was out with the marshal . . . I looked out of the window and saw a company of rifleman, all with three-coloured cockades, marching Indian file around the house. I counted them; there were forty-two in that company . . .*[1802]

JOSEPH HORSEFIELD: . . . *The marshal still continued to hesitate. By this time, a number of persons got into the house, adorned with three-coloured French cockades . . . I then worked my way downstairs again, in order to be ready for a jump. By this time, I understand that the prisoners were delivered.*[1803]

WEDNESDAY, MAY 1, 1799

GENERAL ★ AURORA ★ ADVERTISER

BOSTON, April 25. yesterday, Mr. ABIJAH ADAMS [of Boston's *Independent Chronicle*] was discharged from his imprisonment . . . Mr. ADAMS returns his thanks to his numerous friends . . .

625

Tonight, in the *Porcupine's Gazette,* Peter Porcupine writes:

MOTHER BACHE.

This impudent woman, in the first number of her paper, published a most infamous libel against me in which my wife was in some sort mentioned. I was preparing to render her famous at that time; but, upon consideration, I desisted . . .

It is said by some silly wretches that the woman is not to blame; for it is not she *who writes in the paper.* I have been informed to the contrary; and I have every reason to believe that she wrote, with her own hand, the paragraphs I am about to quote. Besides, if the paper be *published by her,* every one but a soft-brained sot must know that she is answerable for its contents, both in the eye of reason and of the law.

In order to avoid the lash of satire and, perhaps, the penalty of the law also, she has lately taken her name from the head of the paper and put *"the heirs of Benjamin F. Bache"* in its stead. This is a miserable trick. Every one knows that she is one of the heirs and that the paper is the joint property of her and her children..

[T]he notice of *her resolution* to continue the paper [proves incontestably that the publication was a voluntary deliberate act on her part]. Poor Ben expired about midnight, and, as appears by the date, "HIS WIDOW" had this notice (which appears in a handbill) struck off before his corpse was cold! It was actually hawked about the city before daylight had scarcely made its appearance, and long before the husband's dead body was put under ground. There's *"delicacy",* there's *"sensibility"* for you! This noble act alone would, I think entitle the "WIDOW'" to the honourable rank of *Citoyenne Française* . . .

Now for the "WIDOW'S" first essay. She begins her career with an enumeration of the *benefits* which the French *sans culottes* have conferred on the world. After reciting their praise-worthy efforts to restore the *Rights of Man,* she comes to their efforts, no less praise-worthy, for restoring the *Rights of Woman.*

EXTRACTS
From Mother Bache's Paper of November 1st.

"One of the first acts of the Roman legislature [under French rule] was the prohibition of the use of the . . . horrible practice of castration . . ."

M[rs]. Bache's Comments

"Before the revolution, this *shocking* practice was carried on to such an extent that the barber's sign boards in the streets of Rome were inscribed with . . . *Here boys are* CASTRATED *with wonderful dexterity!!* Thus we see how the vile Jacobins abolish without mercy the ancient customs of ancient States . . ."

There's *"delicacy"!* There's *"female modesty"!* Is the American reader willing that foreigners look upon this as a specimen of the language of *republican* women? If he be, I can have no manner of objection to it.—

The compassion of this "lady" is of a curious kind. She can hear of murders and massacres in France . . . and yet, behold, how *tender-hearted* she becomes toward *the poor little Italian boys!* with what maternal zeal, with what courageous resentment, with what savage fury, she falls upon the *remorseless barbers! . . .*

N.B. I learn with pleasure that this woman is neither of *English* nor *American* birth.

THURSDAY, MAY 2, 1799

GENERAL ★ AURORA ★ ADVERTISER

During the late wonderful expedition, a body of our *federal* infantry . . . exhibited . . . military sagacity and valor . . . [W]hen one of the wagons was attacked, a sentinel gave the alarm; the drums beat to arms . . . The enemy was seen at the rear of the baggage in great force; the corps of heroes . . . marched up in Hessian time to the point of action; two horrid weapons were discovered protruding their muzzles from behind the wagon; a platoon was ordered to fire; a hefty groan was heard, and a violent concussion of the earth . . . Be it remembered, these were regular troops that *killed the bull !*

Today, in Massachusetts, publisher Thomas Adams of Boston's *Independent Chronicle* sells the nation's second-largest Republican newspaper to his Federalist landlord, Bostonian James White. Thomas Adams sacrificed his health for the *Chronicle*'s republicanism, and his federal sedition trial is but a month away. Now that Thomas Adams' paper has been *bought up for prostitution,*[1804] Thomas Adams will himself die within a week.[1805]

FRIDAY, MAY 3, 1799

GENERAL ★ AURORA ★ ADVERTISER

LIBERTY POLES ! ! ! . . .

Is it possible . . . the erection of a pole, decorated with the classical and long established emblem of Liberty, the LIBERTY CAP, can possibly be . . . incompatible with the good order of society ? No, the enemies of the Liberty Cap are only to be found in that class of beings who *maintain monarchy to be the* ne plus ultra *of human excellence, and a republic a non-entity* . . . I hope the citizens of America will never, through improper deference to those in power, concede the wholesome practice of erecting Liberty Poles, and whenever one shall fall by the ax of aristocracy, may ten thousand be reared in its stead. These are the undisguised sentiments

AN OLD FASHIONED REPUBLICAN.

Tonight, in the *Porcupine's Gazette,* Peter Porcupine writes:

MOTHER BACHE.

A correspondent observes that the fury of this citizen against the *Italian Barbers* appears very natural, when we recollect the *loss* [of cohabitation] she had recently experienced.

MONDAY, MAY 6, 1799

GENERAL ★ AURORA ★ ADVERTISER

When SCHNYDER the printer in Reading was dragged out of his house by captain Montgomery's *brave* troop, and punished like a felon, complaint was made to GENERAL MACPHERSON . . . The General listened to the complaint . . . *and did nothing !* . . .

Let the people look at the case of SCHNYDER—it is a serious [one] and truly alarming—every individual obnoxious to a troop may be treated in the same manner and, in the ebbs and flows of party, no man can say that his turn may not come to be tied up to a post and whipped at the discretion of a banditti—If the laws are no longer to protect the citizen, let it be publicly announced that each citizen may arm himself and prepare for his defence.

TUESDAY, MAY 7, 1799

GENERAL ★ AURORA ★ ADVERTISER

TO THE REV. ASHBEL GREEN . . .

To you it appears [in your April 25th Fast Day sermon] that our sins and sufferings are *"principally to be attributed to an enthusiastic attachment in multitudes of the people to the revolution and cause of France"* and that this has brought down on us *"the judgment of God"* and sent into *"our land the pestilence in a manner that never was known before."* . . .

You ought to have known that the pestilence has been a frequent visitor to these states. That so long ago as 1699, as 1702, and so late as 1736, this city was previously afflicted by the pestilence. The French revolution had not then commenced, nor even our own revolution which is becoming equally odious with that of the French in the eyes of your party . . . GUATIMOZIN

Tonight, in the *Porcupine's Gazette,* Peter Porcupine writes:

[A] statute of [Vermont], authorizing the selectmen of each town to take possession of all church lands . . . [was] adjudged . . . *unconstitutional* . . .

(Mother Bache, give us your pious opinion on this.—You dare not. You

628

. . . must not allow that the Federal Government is the guardian of the people's rights . . .)

N.B. Not a word about the *poor dear little Italian boys.*

GENERAL ★ AURORA ★ ADVERTISER

GENERAL MACPHERSON AND THE LANCASTER COUNTY TROOP

The General has taken *"an affectionate adieu"* of the *Lancaster County troop* . . . The General publicly thanks Capt. Montgomery and his troop for dragging an *unaccused and an unconvicted citizen from his dwelling, tearing his cloaths from his back, and whipping him in a public market place !!* . . . After such an avowal, it would not be surprising if every citizen of Philadelphia, who was obnoxious to Macpherson's Blues, should in turn be dragged out of his house and treated as Mr. Schnyder was . . .

Tonight, in the *Porcupine's Gazette*:

FRIES.

The trial of this man closed last night about six o'clock when the jury retired, and the court adjourned. At ten o'clock, the Court met again, and the jury came in with their verdict—GUILTY.

GENERAL ★ AURORA ★ ADVERTISER

ST. TAMMANY.

The Anniversary of the American tutelary Saint, falling on Saturday, the brotherhood of St. Tammany held their customary festival at the Wigwam, near the upper Ferry . . . After partaking of the feast . . . the following [16] toasts were given, accompanied by music and the discharge of cannon . . . 4. The Grand Sachem of one of our councils, Thomas Jefferson . . . one gun . . . 6. Our departed brother Benjamin Franklin Bache—Patriotic and good, great and virtuous—may the glorious inheritance of a well spent life animate every brother to an imitation of his example . . . 9. Our brother Thomas M'Kean—may his enemies be punished for their abuse and persecution of him by beholding him the next Chief of the tribe of Pennsylvania—2 guns . . . 16. The Great old Sachem of the tribe of Pennsylvania, Benjamin Franklin, who directed the thunder and humbled the oppressor of the thirteen tribes, one gun.

It is a good time to toast Benny Bache and his grandfather. It is the anniversary (to the week) of the Macpherson's Blues attack on the office of the *Aurora*.

TUESDAY, MAY 14, 1799

GENERAL ★ AURORA ★ ADVERTISER

[Concerning the late expedition of the Federal troops to Northampton, t]he fact concerning the living of a certain troop at free quarters is well known . . .

[T[ ]he brutal proceeding [of the Federal troops] at Lancaster . . . deserves particular notice . . .

Sedition poles are what were called in 1776 *Liberty poles*. These lovers of order . . . the Lancaster troops, on their march to join the generals, took upon themselves to cut down some of those poles. In what manner were they justified in the attempt?

Not by any law—No law forbids the erection of liberty poles . . . In trespassing upon the ground where the pole was erected, they acted illegally . . .

Today, Thomas Jefferson writes his friend Archibald Stuart:

The cause of republicanism, triumphing in Europe, can never fail to do so here in the long run. Our citizens may be deceived for a while & have been deceived; but as long as the presses can be protected, we may trust to them for light . . .[1806]

Tonight, in the *Porcupine's Gazette*:

THE TRUE CHRISTIAN HERO

In Brown's paper a few days back, I saw a communication defending the Sermon of . . . *Doctor Green* against the attacks of Mother Bache and her gang . . . But I had one particular objection, . . . that the *Philadelphia Gazette* had been chosen as a vehicle for the defence . . .

Brown's is the only paper in which I saw an eulogium on the Constitution *merely because it admitted JEWS to the Magistracy*. In fact, I am sure Brown's paper had done more mischief than Bache's in this way, because it has been read with a less suspicious eye . . .

Tonight, in the *Gazette of the United States*:

TO THE EDITOR OF THE AURORA . . .

On the return of the troops who performed the expedition to Northampton, we observed that, during their absence, several publications had appeared in the *Aurora* under the form of "extracts of letters" whereby the most unfounded imputations were attempted to be fixed on the troops themselves and on their commander. In one of these extracts it is alleged that "a number of the troops who derived their authority from the Federal

government lived *at free quarters on the people."* . . . These slanders were
so notoriously false . . .

BATTALION ORDERS

The Artillery, Grenadiers, and Infantry are ordered to parade at
the Menage in Chestnut-street on Thursday the 16th inst. precisely
at 4 o'clock completely equipped for the purpose of going through
their firings . . .   *By order of the Commandant* JOHN M'CAULEY

WEDNESDAY, MAY 15, 1799

GENERAL   ★ AURORA ★   ADVERTISER

If the ruffian who assaulted the late editor of the *Aurora* received a
confidential charge to a minister at a foreign court, Montgomery, the
chosen commander of a select corps of volunteers who dragged Mr.
Schnyder to the whipping post where he was scourged, merits the high
consideration of our executive. Perhaps he will succeed Macpherson
who, for the merit of overlooking the offence in the ruffian, will be promoted . . .

At a time when standing armies seem to be rising on the depression
of the militia, we ought to be watchful and jealous of our rights . . . Let
us . . . take the constitution in one hand and the sword in the other . . .
[L]ethargy and blind implicit faith . . . will, if not corrected, produce
Montgomerys and Schnyders in every part of the Union . . . *! !*

Today, about noon, officers from the Macpherson's Blues and other units of the
new federal army pay a visit to the *Philadelphia Aurora*.[1807] Peter Miercken,
an organizer of the infamous Federalist dinners at Cameron's Tavern in Southwark a year ago,[1808] takes the lead. From the testimony of witnesses (including
my own):

JOHN MASSEY . . . *A meeting was held at Hardy's, composed generally of the officers of the five troops of cavalry that had been on duty in
Northampton county. Some publications, said to be written by some
one on the expedition, had been published in the Aurora, which attributed irregularities to the troops.—It was agreed by the meeting to go in
a body to demand of Mr. Duane to designate the troop to have acted
irregularly . . .*[1809]

BERNARD M'MAHON . . . *[S]ometime before 12 o'clock, eight or ten
persons called at the front office, or accounting office, and asked for
Mr. Duane; they asked where he was, and as I did not know, I told
them so. They went away as I supposed, but in a few moments afterwards, I heard something of a noise and saw a few people running in*

the street towards Franklin court; and it struck me it was those people, and I accordingly went to the printing office . . .[1810]

FROM MY TESTIMONY: *They planted centinels above and below the stairs, at the entrance of the court towards the street; they chose that hour of the day when the market is cleared and the butchers at dinner.*[1811]

ROBERT OLIPHANT . . . *Mr. Duane was busily employed in writing; the appearance of the officers did not appear to have any effect on him, for he continued writing and speaking while questioned . . . Duane told them he could not at that time, with propriety, make known what they required; he alleged several reasons, among others that . . . he did not want to prejudice the prisoners to be tried . . . Mr. Miercken then rushed forward and seized Duane by the shirt collar . . .*[1812]

BERNARD M'MAHON . . . *[I] went to the printing office, and was making my way up as fast as practicable, when I found those and some-other gentlemen dragging Mr. Duane downstairs . . . I was forced down with the crowd and saw Mr. Duane knocked down before I could well recover my position on my legs . . . He was struck down so often, and so severely, that I thought his life in danger . . . I saw the big man they call Peter Miercken knock him down . . . After he knocked him down the first time, they formed a ring around him while he was lying senseless on the ground, and when he recovered and sprung upon his legs, they knocked him down again, repeatedly . . . From their violence and cruelty, I had no reason to expect any other effect than his being beaten to death . . .*[1813]

FROM MY OWN TESTIMONY: *I knew nothing of boxing, and Miercken had studied under Mendoza . . . [T]he first recollection I had on recovering sense was some of the gang lashing at me as I lay, with a cowskin or some instrument of that kind . . . My whole body, head, and limbs were beaten, bruised, and lacerated—both my temples were swelled . . . my head, back, breast, and thighs were black and blue . . .*[1814]

THOMAS BRADLEY . . . *Duane hallooed out murder, but to no effect . . . [T]hey beat him most unmercifully up and down the court—he was covered with blood, his clothes torn off, and so cruelly treated that I thought they would have certainly killed him . . . I saw Duane's son make his way through the ring in the early part, after his father had been knocked down a few times—he made his way to his father—I felt exceedingly concerned at the sight of the boy, he was crying, and pushing his way between the legs of the assailants—his father was lying on the ground, and he threw himself on his father's body to protect him from the blows—I saw the boy receive a violent blow from one of them, and some of the others were so cowardly as to kick the boy.*[1815]

WILLIAM JOHN DUANE (my son) . . . *I saw Miercken, with some others, hold my father by the neck and dragging him along down the* stairs. I attempted to force my way after him, but they apparently stationed persons over us, they would not let me move . . . [A] great bustle took place below in the passage; and some of the persons who had been stationed above then went down; I slipped downstairs with them; 6 or 8 of them only remained in the office to prevent the workmen from interfering or going down—Two or three had been posted at the office door; some went to the press and obliged the workmen to quit work . . . When I got below, I endeavored to get forward in search of my father, whom I found prostrate on the ground lying on his face. One of them stopped me, and asked why I rushed forward so? I told him I wished to get to my father. He said it was a great pity he was my father, for he was a damned rascal. I reached him where he was and found he was alive. A kind of ring had been formed round him, which kept constantly agitating, and one person in the ring struck me in the head and knocked me down. I fell at the west side of the alley. I don't know how or who took me up. [1816]

MY OWN ACCOUNT: *Nearly strangled on the way downstairs, the editor by his struggles extricated his throat from the hands of the two ruffians . . . while the general exclamation of the friends of order and regular government were "Knock him down"—"Drag him to the market-house and flog him"—"Kick the rascal"—"Knock him down Miercken." . . . [T]he editor finding there was nothing to be done but to die hard—or fight it out—made as much use of his hands as one man could do, attacked by above ten different persons nearly all of whom were nearly ten years younger and some of them double the weight of the editor. This extraordinary conflict continued above half an hour, during which the editor was knocked down above twelve times . . . one lifted him up, while the other knocked him down—and this repeatedly. After recovering a few moments from this violence, the editor was called upon for the author repeatedly, and he was so obstinate as not to be beaten out of his honor or integrity . . . An immense crowd had gathered . . . [T]he Editor, while making a blow at the bully of the gang, Miercken, was knocked down from behind . . . In this state of insensibility, the heroes walked round the body, like mourners at a funeral, and while the editor lay senseless, beat him over the head, the face, and sides with the whip. Each of the heroic commanders declaring that the blows were inflicted for their several troops . . . [T]he people who stood around looking with dumb astonishment, were heard to murmur loud . . . Among other of the exploits of the heroes was the knocking down of a son of the Editor who had flown to his father's defence . . .* [1817]

Tonight, the *Gazette of the United States* reports the attack on me:

This morning about 12 o'clock, the Officers of the first and second Troop of Volunteer Cavalry, and the officers of the first, second, and third

City Troops, called upon the Editor of the *Aurora* to know . . . what Troop was meant in yesterday's *Aurora* as living in "free quarters" on the late expedition to Northampton.—The editor answered that he would not designate the troop at present . . . He was then told he must . . . The Editor then said he would fight any man with Pistols; on which it was generally observed, don't fight him with Pistols—whip the rascal . . . [T]he Editor was forced downstairs. When, in the courtyard, the Editor was asked repeatedly to give up the author, which he absolutely refused to do, and was then whipped as he deserved. He was asked how did you come by your information? He answered it was anonymous; after which he again and repeatedly refused to give up the author, and was again whipped.

THURSDAY, MAY 16, 1799

GENERAL   ★ AURORA ★   ADVERTISER

The late editor of the *Aurora* was publicly unprovokedly assaulted, and the violator of public law was as publicly honored by an appointment on a public mission. The present editor, without the advantage of being a descendant of [Benjamin Franklin,] the memorable founder of the American republic, could not hope to escape . . .

Yesterday a *band* of those *friends of good order and regular government* to the amount of near THIRTY entered the Office of the *Aurora*—and while the editor was pursuing his business, assaulted him . . . *Peter Miercken* who was the principal of those dastards with several others seized the Editor by violence, struck him several times on the head, while others held his hands. By force they dragged him down stairs into Franklin court, and there repeated their violence by reiterated blows from above TEN different persons . . .

After having satiated their malice . . . they sought to add what they conceived to be dishonour on the Editor by several blows with a whip . . .

If any circumstance could more deeply impress on his mind . . . to guard, with the vigilance of republican jealousy, against the artifices, the intrigues and the injustice of arbitrary men;—this conduct would only more and more attach him to his principles—but he has never slackened since he has had the honor to hold his present situation—and while he holds it, his hand must perish or his vital principles must be suspended by the hand of some of those assassins before he will shrink from exposing villains and crimes to public obloquy.

Wm. DUANE, Editor of the *Aurora*.

The above statement was drawn up by the editor in the few moments after the lovers of good order and regular government had departed . . .

Today, the federal army officers reassemble for an assault on me and the *Aurora*'s printing office:

ISRAEL ISRAEL: *I heard the alarm had increased, that further violence and barbarity was intended, and as an old citizen, I thought it was my duty, as far as in me lay, to interfere and prevent it if possible. I was told a number of these gentlemen were at Hardy's . . . I went alone and sent in for Mr. Miercken and told him I understood they were assembled to act the second part of the tragedy of the preceding day by attacking Duane again and destroying his press . . . I told him that this conduct of theirs would rouse the people and probably lead to civil war; that although they might build very much on the troop of officers, the strength of the community was not with them. He said you have a right to do as you please, but by God, we will have satisfaction.*[1818]

VICE PRESIDENT THOMAS JEFFERSON: *[T]hese friends of order, these enemies of disorganization, assemble a second time to pull down the printing office of the young and amiable widow of the grandson of Benjamin Franklin. On the other hand, a body of real republicans, of men who are real friends of order, assemble in arms, and . . . mounted guard to protect the office of this widow, the person of her Editor, of his journeymen, his apprentices, and his son.*[1819]

Yes, dear reader, a large crowd of republicans gathers at the *Aurora*'s offices and stands firm against the reassembled federal army officers. As darkness approaches, a federal officer seizes a bayonet from one of my new Republican guard.[1820]

Tonight, Jack Fenno in the *Gazette of the United States*:

MURDER ! MURDER ! MURDER !
Citizen Dwight in his *candid* account of the magnanimous manner in which he received his flagellation has forgotten to mention that he bellowed MURDER! from the time he was taken hold of 'till the discipline was completely gone through—I dare say this omission has arisen from the haste in which he drew up his statement, and he will no doubt correct the error in his next edition.

Jasper Dwight told his customers on Saturday last that in Monday's *Aurora* he would publish a *laboured* vindication of the troops employed in the Northampton Insurrection; and he has this morning exhibited himself as a *belaboured* vindication of the same subject. We would advise this gentlemen to change his climate—the cowskin of America cuts as keenly as the lash of India.

We published, yesterday, a statement which was communicated by an eye-witness of the flagellation inflicted upon one of the United Irishmen concerned in propagating that *Diablerie* of slanders and lies, called the *Aurora,* and who it since appears, is the fellow who calls himself "the Editor of the *Aurora.*"

Although the punishment of this caitiff is of no more consequence than that of any other vagabond, yet as he has the impudence to make a parade of his sufferings and his *republicanism,* we shall bestow a remark or two which the insignificance of the object would not otherwise require.

A body of men, as respectable in character as any in the United States . . . make a further sacrifice . . . in defence of their country and its constitution. In their absence on this expedition, they are maligned with every slander that the foul malice of an incendiary can invent, and after their return, are insulted . . .

When the officers reflected on these things . . . and more especially when they reflected that . . . the same villain and the same paper had called the great and good Washington a hypocrite, a fool, a liar, and a *coward,* a tyrant and a murderer—the present illustrious Chief Magistrate, who cooperated so powerfully in council with his immortal compeer in the field, in obtaining our Independence, "a blind, bald, toothless, crippled, dotard"— . . . when they reflected on these things, and reflected that the author of them was not an American but a foreigner, and not merely a foreigner, but a United Irishman, and not merely a United Irishman, but a public convict and fugitive from justice; they might have determined that nothing from so vile a source could stain their well-established credit, and they might have let him go . . . But then must they have stifled every distinctive attribute of a soldier and a man of honor, and sunk to the level of the Democratic crew . . .

SATURDAY, MAY 18, 1799

GENERAL ★ AURORA ★ ADVERTISER

TO THE PUBLIC . . .

In that calamitous moment—which my country and virtue herself must daily deplore—that snatched *Benjamin Franklin Bache* from this post of honor, it is my felicity that he named me in his Will as the man who ought to succeed him as the Editor of the *Aurora.*

When I undertook the trust, I foresaw its dangers and hazards. Honored with the most affectionate and unrestrained confidence of that incomparable man, I believe I knew better than any other person the sacrifices he had made to the service of his country and the preservation of its liberties, and the hideous persecution which he suffered in supporting these principles for which so much American blood had been shed.

I could not be insensible that when the descendant of Dr. Franklin— the heir of his principles and his virtues—suffered so much—that, unsurrounded by the reverend honors which belong to that great man and his posterity, I must be at least as much exposed as he was to the assaults of the common enemies of *this republic* and of liberty itself . . .

Solicitous of respect and regard only in proportion as I should be found to really merit it, I sought not to be conspicuous [in the execution of my honorable trust], nor did I deign to more than smile at the pointless malignity with which I have been so often assailed.

The present is an occasion in which I am bound to stand forward—and to challenge the industrious satellites of party to name *the vice* much less the crime of which I have, in the course of between 36 and 37 years, been guilty . . .

Three insinuations have been promulgated concerning me—

1. That I am a foreigner.
2. That I have been a convict and a fugitive from justice, whose republicanism has been derived from gaols, dungeons, and pillories.
3. That I am an United Irishman,

To the first and last of these insinuations, I simply reply—that I drew my first breath in America, have loved my country from my first reasoning hour—that I spent my early years a part in New York and at a later period in this city . . .

I am proud to say both my parents were Irish. The death of my father and the natural partiality of my mother for her own country carried me, before I was yet a youth, to Europe, and to Ireland I am indebted for my education . . .

As to the insinuation that I am an United Irishman . . . —If to have studied the history of the British empire attentively . . . [if] to have learned to detest the stupendous perpetuity of oppression which Britain has heaped for 600 years on that otherwise blessed country be an error or a crime, then I am decidedly an United Irishman as any man in that or this country . . .

It only remains to notice the second insinuation . . .

It has been more than once asserted that during my residence in India (where I lived for eight years) I had been imprisoned. It is true I was there twice a state prisoner . . .

[I]t will serve to shew the tyranny of the British government . . . I learned my crime was the issuing of proposals for publishing a work of two volumes, entitled, *"The Policy of Asia."* Under despotic governments it is not unusual to see the press attacked, authors imprisoned, and printers tortured for works already printed—it was left with the English government in Asia to anticipate the contents of a work only half written at the time, and not yet printed . . .

Since my return to my native country, I have found but few of my old friends—but I have been blessed with many that are new and dear to me—my personal dealings and domestic character will speak for themselves—I, in perfect charity, most sincerely wish those who attempted my life could say as much.

WILLIAM DUANE

This is a portrait of me, William Duane, engraved by a French refugee, Charles Balthazar Julien Févret de St. Mémin, who lives in Philadelphia on Third-street, engraves about eighty-five such profiles per year, and advertises his services in the *Aurora*.[1821]

On Friday, the 10th inst. departed this life, after a lingering illness, at Boston, THOMAS ADAMS, late Editor of the *Independent Chronicle*, in the 42d year of his age.

The Circuit Court of the United States yesterday afternoon decided in favour of Mr. Lewis's motion for granting John Fries a new trial.

Jury misconduct will allow tax protester John Fries a new trial next year.

Tonight, Jack Fenno in the *Gazette of the United States*:

To complete the character of the vagrant who calumniated the great and good Washington, under the signature of Jasper Dwight, he has avowed himself an United Irishman.

[Adv.]   A BAYONET,
WRESTED from the musquet of a fellow in uniform, at the front of the *Aurora* office, by one of the Officers of the United States, on the night of the 16th inst. at the time they were assaulted in passing the street by the mob there assembled may be had, by proving property, at the Marine barracks.

MONDAY, MAY 20, 1799

GENERAL ★ AURORA ★ ADVERTISER

The *Gang* are quite dolorous at their ineffectual efforts to pull down the *Aurora* or murder its Editor;—they have learned some things useful by their last exploit—

1. That the public indignation is roused.
2. That the republicans are the only respecters of the law.
3. That a reiteration of violence would carry public vengeance to their firesides.

A young federal lawyer . . . was heard to declare a few days ago—that altho' he did not think the life of the Editor of the *Aurora* worth 100 dollars, yet he should consider his death worth 200.
"Hail Columbia, happy land,
"Hail ye heroes, heaven-born band."

Tonight, in the *Porcupine's Gazette*:

Adams, the printer and publisher of the infamous *Chronicle* at Boston, is DEAD.

Tonight, Jack Fenno in the *Gazette of the United States*:

In the last *Aurora* is the most singular gallimaufry [hodgepodge] of falsehood, Democratic, and jailbird impudence, terrified apprehension, and guilty cowardice, signed Wm. Duane. What I have to notice, however, is a gross and palpable lie. He says he had the felicity to be named in Franklin Bache's will as the man who "ought to succeed him." Now, although such a nomination were enough of itself to draw any man to everlasting infamy, and, although it be of no consequence whether if Tom, Dick, or the D—l, happened to be named, yet as the Gentleman took the pains to come and inform me of the state of the facts, in complaisance to him, I can do no less than say that it is an utter falsehood and that Wm. Duane is not named nor alluded to.

There can scarcely be a more laughable object than a fellow making pretensions to character, whom every circumstance indicated to have been born and bred in a brothel . . .

It is equally curious to hear a wretch pretend to have written a Book . . . under whose hands the least distinguished offspring of literature, a news-paper, has become, by the gross vulgarity and ignorance it has displayed . . . the reproach and scandal of the age and nation.

Nor is it less ludicrous to hear a fellow boast of debauching the king's guards with his wine, who could never in his life 'till very lately, muster money enough without difficulty to purchase his diurnal half-pint of Gin.

It is a serious reflection that the stupidity and dullness of such Gazettes as those of Duane . . . have the deleterious operation on society from their peculiar aptitude to the minds of those on whom they are designed to take operation.

I set about forming a new Democratic Dictionary . . .

A *Republican.* The scape-gallows, Duane . . .

A *Tory.* General Washington.

The *friends and supporters of American Liberty and Independence.* United Irishmen.

The *enemies* of d[itt]o. The Government, the officers, soldiers and sailors . . .

TUESDAY, MAY 21, 1799

GENERAL ★ AURORA ★ ADVERTISER

Several citizens having intimated that a full and particular statement of the transactions which took place in this office last week was looked for by the public, the Editor . . . gives the following detail . . .

In the height of their rage, a menace was thrown out that they would tear down the *Aurora* Printing-Office, in consequence of which a number of Republican citizens collected with arms and ammunition to mount guard in the Printing-Office. The banditti have assembled several times since and have raised a purse of 1500 dollars to defray the expences of the prosecution against them! . . .

Several occurrences have arisen which strongly manifest the public indignation at these outrages . . . [T]he most important is the spirit of association among the republicans who have joined the militia volunteer companies in considerable numbers.

[WILLIAM DUANE.]

TO THE REPUBLICAN CITIZENS OF PENNSYLVANIA . . .

My fellow citizens, the moment is arrived when it has become essential to your safety that you should be *soldiers* as well as citizens . . . After the outrages which were committed both here and in Reading, which of you will say that it may not be his turn next . . . [M]en intent upon hostility have associated themselves in military corps. [I]t becomes your duty to associate likewise . . . MENTOR

The federal army officers' attack on the *Aurora* has prompted guardians of the press to start a Republican militia for its protection![1822] *[W]ithout any agency or knowledge of mine, a body of young men presented themselves to me and offered to uniform if I would command them; a young man . . . in the United States army, was their lieutenant, and I accepted the command.*[1823]

Tonight, in the *Gazette of the United States*:

If a daring banditti had declared that none of their brotherhood should be punished by law and that civil process dare not touch them, what should we think of the energy of the municipality that was terrified by the threat. This is precisely the cry of the jacobins with regard to their partizans and accomplices.

THURSDAY, MAY 23, 1799

GENERAL ★ AURORA ★ ADVERTISER

The *Mamelukes* have contrived to get the Editor of the *Aurora* bound over to keep the peace—*thirty more, kill them says Bobadil!* . . . The hero who presented a pistol to the breast of a person in the *Aurora* Office on Wednesday, the 15th inst. is said to be *George Way*—some one observed he wished to be in the *way* of promotion.

Crowds of armed citizenry, Federalist and Republican, fill the city streets every day. If someone were to discharge a musket, this city and perhaps the country could erupt in civil war.[1824]

Tonight, in the *Gazette of the United States*, Jack Fenno writes:

IN the *Aurora* of [the day before] yesterday, the faction of which that paper is the organ are expressly called upon to associate themselves in the military corps, not for the purpose of defending their country from foreign invasion; not with a view to support their government against the machinations of domestic traitors, but avowedly to act against the *Friends of Government.*

Under the authority of Duane himself, it is stated that to accomplish this object, considerable accessions of military strength have already been made to the Militia Companies; and that a band of Jacobins mount guard every evening at his office . . .

Duane says that during the horse-whipping he received t'other day, the people who stood looking with *dumb* astonishment were heard to *murmur aloud!!* Will this blundering bull maker again tell us he is an *American?*

SATURDAY, MAY 25, 1799

GENERAL ★ AURORA ★ ADVERTISER

PRINTING TYPES

ANY PERSON, having a small fount of SMALL PICA, new or in good condition, to dispose of, may hear of a purchaser on application to the editor of the *Aurora.*

☞ *AGAIN—The subscribers to the* AURORA, *who are in arrears, are requested to remit them to the* heirs of B. F. Bache, *or they may certainly expect their papers to be discontinued as soon after this date as there is time to receive the answers from their respective residences.*

THE *Price of the* DAILY AURORA *is Eight Dollars per Annum, Subscribers at a distance from the City to pay Five Dollars in advance* . . .

FOR SALE
A QUANTITY OF *WASTE PAPER*
FIT FOR GROCERS OR TRUNKMAKERS
ENQUIRE AT THIS OFFICE.
AN APPRENTICE
WANTED TO THE PRINTING BUSINESS
AT THE OFFICE OF THE AURORA

TO PAPER-MAKERS

PROPOSALS for supplying this office with Super-royal paper of good quality will be received in writing addressed to the Editor, post paid. The quantity required for a regular supply will be about TWENTY-FIVE RHEAMS a week. The terms per Rheam, or per 100 Rheams for Cash must be mentioned, and a specimen enclosed if convenient . . .

THE REPUBLICAN BLUES

Will meet at 7 o'clock on Saturday Evening, the 24th instant, at the house of citizen Morrow, in Chestnut-street, for the purpose of receiving the signatures of such friends of good order as are inclined to attach themselves to said company . . .

☞ *The militia legion will assemble at 2 o'clock, on Monday afternoon the 27th, provided as before with blunt cartridge.*

The *Aurora*'s advertisements tell much about Republican newsprinting in 1799!

TUESDAY, MAY 28, 1799

GENERAL   ★ AURORA ★   ADVERTISER

General Macpherson approved the conduct of the troops under his command on the Quixote expedition—he told them that they behaved well—The general was present at Reading when the base and lawless attack was made upon the printer, and yet he tells them that they behaved well! . . . It now remains to be seen whether the government authorized such proceedings—If they did authorize them, no notice will be taken of General Macpherson's misconduct; if they did not, he will be called to immediate account . . .

TUESDAY, JUNE 4, 1799

GENERAL   ★ AURORA ★   ADVERTISER

The late Mr. [Thomas] Adams was spirited to the last moment and conducted the *Chronicle* in Boston with honour to himself and to the Republicans of that town . . .

The only paper that dares to publish the truth [in Connecticut] . . . is the [New London] *BEE* whose spirited Editor braves the malice and enmity of the surrounding foe . . .

Tonight, in the *Gazette of the United States*:

The important rank which Pennsylvania holds in the Union renders her conduct with regard to the General Government extremely interesting; and there is reason to dread that if we should raise up characters in the administration of the state who are opposed to the General Administration for the avowed purpose of "stopping the wheels of government," the whole fabric may eventually be shaken . . .

With this view, therefore . . . we do most earnestly recommend to our Fellow-citizens of the county of Lancaster, JAMES ROSS, of ALLEGANY, as a proper person to be chosen Governor at the next Election . . .

[THE GRAND JURY OF LANCASTER COUNTY]

GENERAL ★ AURORA ★ ADVERTISER

Peter Miercken is off—like his predecessor *Joe Thomas. Peter* was seen on Wednesday on his way to the Southward—this was expected, his house has been *shut some days* . . .

Mierckin the *bruizer* it is expected will have to pay a visit to his old master *Mendoza*—where he will have the satisfaction of enjoying the *sweets* of that country he so *bully-like defends.*

GENERAL ★ AURORA ★ ADVERTISER

It is said that Peter Miercken is only gone southward to *collect his debts*—we have not heard but we understand he means to *come back* . . .

Tonight, in the *Gazette of the United States:*

Mr. Peter Mierckin, to whom the citizens of Philadelphia, are so greatly indebted for his humane exertions during the calamity of last summer, is charged in the *Aurora* of yesterday *"with treading in the footsteps of Joseph Thomas."* [I]t is there stated that he has *gone off;* and *that his House has been shut this week.*

A paragraph so false, so base, and infamous, will disgrace even the *Aurora* . . .

Mr. Miercken left home on Tuesday last to collect some debts due to him in the Delaware State; his House has never been shut, and his friends hourly expect him with as much Exultation as the Author of the paragraph must apprehend it with Fear and Horror . . .

GENERAL ★ AURORA ★ ADVERTISER

The operation of the *military* dependants on the *federal* government appears not to be confined . . . [I]n the same month, we hear of outrages committed in Virginia and Connecticut, as well as Pennsylvania . . . [A]t Alexandria, the printer of a newspaper is assailed by men armed with daggers and in his own house—in Reading in this state, a printer is dragged from his own house . . . —in the capital of this state, the same nefarious plan is pursued—and in Connecticut . . . a clergymen [is] confined for a small debt upon the precaution of the secretary of the federal treasury, *Oliver Wolcott* . . . We hear that last week fifteen or twenty of those recruits . . . forced themselves into the cell of the Clergyman in Litchfield prison for the honorable purpose of tarring and feathering him . . .

Humphries, with his ship carpenters, assaulted the former editor of the *Aurora*, for which he was brought to the bar of *justice* and *fined* 50 dollars. When he went to pay it, he was informed that it had been *already done*—Afterwards he was sent on public business to France! It is probable that the *gentlemen* volunteer officers had *an eye on Humphries* when they attacked the present editor. *Ep. Times.*

It was Benny's turn a year ago. Now, it is mine.

TUESDAY, JUNE 11, 1799

GENERAL ★ AURORA ★ ADVERTISER

MR. EDITOR . . . When I first heard of a French conspiracy for the subversion of our government published in the English paper *[Porcupine's Gazette]* . . . I greedily ran over the contents of each paper . . . and at last, out came the story of the *famous* packet directed to Benjamin Franklin Bache . . . I could scarcely sit a moment still, ran around to my acquaintances . . . and freely consigned Bache to punishment and infamy; but judge, Mr. Editor, my confusion when Bache, with so much manliness, called upon them for his packet . . . [M]y neighbors laughed at me. What's come of your prophecy now, said one ?—You foresee truly, said another; what death must Bache die, said a third—ask Porcupine; he is in the secret, replied a fifth; whilst I stood, in the middle, as still as a mouse, and as sheepish as Hamilton when he wrote the story about Reynold's wife . . .   ROBERT SLENDER.

Tonight, in the *Gazette of the United States*:

They tell us La Fayette is coming to coax and wheedle us . . . The Directory cannot send armies; but they can send La Fayette . . .

The great effort of the *Faction*, both *in* and *out* of Congress, has been directed against the *army* and *navy*. Keep these down, has been the cry from Gallatin in Congress to Duane in the drain shop . . . Is it not evident that had the country remained without either, France would have made no advances to a negotiation . . . ?

WEDNESDAY, JUNE 12, 1799

GENERAL ★ AURORA ★ ADVERTISER

From the RICHMOND EXAMINER . . . [T]he once peaceful streets of Philadelphia, are, perhaps, by this time, transformed into a field of battle. A body of armed men conceive themselves injured by the printer of the *Aurora*. Instead of asking for legal redress, they knock him down, kick him when lying senseless at their feet, and, as the climax of barbarity and beastliness, they knock down his son, a youth of sixteen years of age, who, on the impulse of filial sensibility, was attempting to rescue his father. Next day, these *friends of order*, these enemies of *disorganization*, assemble a second time to pull down the printing office of the young and amiable widow of the grandson of Benjamin Franklin. On the other hand, a body of *real* republicans, of men who are *real* friends of order, assemble in arms, and according to our best private advices, they have for sixteen successive days, mounted guard to protect the office of this widow, the person of her Editor, of his journeymen, his apprentices, and his son. This miserable work arises from the effect of those printed falsehoods that have been so industriously disseminated throughout the United States by pensioner Fenno . . .

(Signed) THOS. JEFFERSON

If any of the republican news printers shall think fit to copy these extracts from *The Examiner*, they are further desired to mention that the publication was made without the privacy and contrary to the desire of the Vice-President . . . [O]f Thomas Jefferson . . . [i]t is to be desired that he would write and publish more frequently than he hitherto has done . . .

Has Thomas Jefferson finally written for a newspaper? Jimmy Callender, the *Aurora* writer who fled Philadelphia, now edits the *Richmond Examiner*!

THURSDAY, JUNE 13, 1799

GENERAL ★ AURORA ★ ADVERTISER

Extract of a Letter. Hartford [Connecticut] . . . The *Aurora* is looked upon by many here as an important check on federal ambition and extravagance that has been the salvation of millions of the country; and many would patronize it, would not such a measure point them out as objects of *persecution*—The republicans here who are able *are marked* and the others are *not able* to afford the expence or endure the oppression and malice of its enemies. You, perhaps, have not any just idea of the state of politics here . . . [that] the commission of an aged and respectable justice of the peace should be refused him for suffering a man . . . to plough his land on the President's *fast;* and that of another withheld for taking the *[New London] Bee*, a little weekly newspaper . . . It is also said . . . that the publication of that paper in New London is the only reason why a *navy yard* is not established at that port . . .

The Post-Office in this state, like every other public institution, is subjected to all the abuses of party—neither private letters nor newspapers escape, the former are broken open and sometimes withheld . . . and particularly the newspapers—yet no one dares to complain—lest, like Paul, he should be ruined by prosecution.

Had our situation in point of distance been the same with regard to England in which Ireland stands at this time, instead of retiring to their farms in peace and security . . . our citizens would be sold into the service of Prussia for life . . .

SATURDAY, JUNE 15, 1799

GENERAL   ★ AURORA ★   ADVERTISER

☞ *The Members of the new Republican Company of Infantry are requested to attend at their parade on Saturday Evening next at 8 o'clock to elect officers and on other business. Known republicans desirous of joining the company may learn particulars on application to WILLIAM J. DUANE, junr. Sec'ry pro. tem.*

My son, William John, helps me with the Republican guard.

Tonight, in the *Gazette of the United States*:

The Editor of the *Aurora* has stated with tears in his eyes that 300 of the Irish emigrants have been shipped to Russia to serve as soldiers. He would have preferred, so much does he love liberty, that these *United Irishmen* had been permitted to encrease the *corps of Patriots* in the United States for which he is now *actually beating up recruits.* It happens that the sober, industrious, and well attached to government . . . do not think with this Editor . . .

SUNDAY, JUNE 16, 1799

War . . . Today, in the Atlantic, northeast of Puerto Rico, the U.S. Navy's twenty-four-gun ship *Ganges* fires on and captures a French privateer, the *Vainqueur.* Captain Thomas Tingey reports to the Navy Secretary:

As the day open'd we knew or believ'd her to be a French privateer Sloop of 10 Guns . . . and she was scarce more than 3 or 4 guns shot distance. She led us however with every sail in the Ship sett 'til 3 in the Afternoon, having ran near 90 miles & discharg'd upward of 40 Guns at him, some of the last of which were charg'd with canister shott which went round him like hail . . . During the chace he had cast overboard (in order to lighten his vessel & facilitate her sailing) his boat, some of his provision, all his Guns except two, and much other heavy materials but to no effect. After—or about 1 PM finding we approach'd him & that he must fall—he hoisted French colours & fir'd a Gun to the windward to give him opportunity of striking in form, which he at length did, but so near that a broad-side from the Ship would probably have totally destroy'd him—It proved to be the Privateer Sloop Vainqueure of Guadeloupe of 8 Guns & 85 men . . .[1825]

The *electrical conductor* of BENJAMIN FRANKLIN . . . has touched the immediate connection between our planet and the universe. The great American who invented it stands . . . blasphemed in himself, in his memory, and in his posterity by our *Gothic British Printer* [Peter Porcupine].—The reason is plain. The image of the illustrious FRANKLIN, grasping in his right hand his own electrical conductor and in his left the American fragment of the British sceptre, destroys his peace . . .

Today, Thomas Jefferson writes a college student,

To preserve the freedom of the human mind then & freedom of the press, every spirit should be ready to devote itself to martyrdom, for as long as we may think as we will & speak as we think, the condition of man will proceed in improvement.[1826]

[T]he Irish are treated more inhumanly by the British than [the British king] dared to treat us during our glorious struggle for independence . . . What he dare not do in 1779 he does with impunity in 1799! *Fenno likes this.*

Tonight, in the *Gazette of the United States*, Jack Fenno writes:

The *Aurora* a few days since gave circulation to . . . notorious falsehoods and calumnies taken from the *Richmond Examiner* . . .

What ought to be the punishment of the inventor (Callender) and the propagator (Duane) of such libels upon government? Ought grand juries to sleep and justice shut her eyes? Of what events are such a torpid state of things and inattention to such flagrant offenders the harbingers?

From THE VIRGINIA EXAMINER . . . The ringleader of the riot and assault in the *Aurora* office was Peter Mierckin. This man is tall, muscular and capable of great animal exertion. He went to London . . . to study under Mendoza, the Jewish boxer, . . .

Mr. Duane himself, though not bulky, is active, well made, and, before this affair, he was known to be a man of great personal intrepidity. In fair fighting, the chance is he would successively have knocked down half a dozen of such figures . . .

For more than fortnight after the 16th of May, the streets of Philadelphia were filled with crowds of people who wanted nothing but *the firing of the first musket* to precipitate Pennsylvania, and perhaps the continent, into the horrors of a civil war. *Blood will have blood*, says Shakespeare. The mischief only wants a small beginning. We are happy to say that, within the last fortnight, the appearances of an immediate contest have become less alarming. By our last advices, however, the *Aurora* Office continued under the protection of a party of armed citizens . . .

Tonight, in the *Gazette of the United States*:

The following curious printed circular having been received by a young Irishman . . . [and] as every thing relating to so dignified a personage as the *Aurora*-man must be interesting, it would be wrong [that] the public should not know of his establishing . . . a body guard for his sublime person.

Citizen,

[T]he New Republican Company . . . [will have] another meeting on Saturday evening next at 7 o'clock . . . The uniform agreed upon at two meetings was as follows: White hat, with green under, and cock's neck feather; green coatee, with yellow collar, edging, and buttons gilt, cloth superfine; dimity waistcoat and pantaloons; half boots; black collar; cartridge box in front; cockade, a large silver eagle on a very small black ground. The meeting on Saturday will be held in the private room under the *Aurora* printing-office; where if you really mean to belong to the corps you are requested to attend. Health and esteem,

WILLIAM DUANE   June 19, 1799.

CHARLESTON [South Carolina] . . . *[E]xtract from a letter* . . . I strongly suspect that all this history of the Lancaster troop [in Reading] will turn out to be a falsehood . . . [A]t Philadelphia, it was published in the *Aurora* and in that paper only.

The editors of the *Aurora* being by many suspected . . . to be in the pay of France, it was not to be expected that they would . . . applaud the patriotism of that portion of our fellow citizens in Pennsylvania . . . enforcing its laws . . . [T]hose who are acquainted with the jacobinic and exotic temper of the *Aurora* must have expected to see in that paper every shaft of calumny against our citizen soldiers . . .

Tonight, in the *Porcupine's Gazette*:

[BOSTON, MASSACHUSETTS.] On Monday, the 10th inst. David Brown who had pleaded *guilty* to an indictment for seditious writings and practices was sentenced by the court to pay a fine of 400 dollars and to eighteen months in prison . . .

The last count in the indictment was for procuring a label to be painted and affixed to a pole erected in Dedham [Massachusetts] . . . *"No stamp act; no sedition, no alien bill; no land tax. Downfall to the tyrants of America; peace and retirement to the President; long live the vice president and the minority."* . . .

David Brown appears to be between 40 and 50 years of age . . . and audaciously predicts that the people will "finally break out like the burning mountains of Etna."

TUESDAY, JUNE 25, 1799

GENERAL ★ AURORA ★ ADVERTISER

MARTIAL LAW

[I]f the people cannot see, in the outrages committed on all occasions in various parts of these States by persons holding military authority under the United States, the danger to which the public liberties are exposed, they deserve to be dragooned into military subjection— . . .

Last Saturday night about 11 o'clock, a number of officers of the *United States* Frigate . . . were walking down South street, committing every act of outrage upon the citizens they met with—they began with upsetting a cart, then to upset a chair before James Carr, the coachmaker's door—from thence they proceeded on a little farther where they attacked *Three Women*, who were sitting before their doors, by pulling up their clothes and laying hold of them—(decency forbids any further remarks here) They took with them a chair and went a little further, when one of them cried out—*"a sail ! a sail !"* and immediately crossed the street to two women and committed like indecencies . . . Mr. Durnell, a constable, who lives in the neighborhood, hearing a noise came out . . . [H]e was immediately attacked in a furious manner and stabbed with a dirk . . .

Today, George Washington writes the Governor of Connecticut:

No well informed and unprejudiced man, who has viewed with attention the conduct of the French Government since the Revolution in that Country, can mistake its objects or the tendency of the ambitious plans it is pursuing. Yet strange as it may seem, a party, and a powerful one too . . . affect to believe that the measures of it are dictated by a principle of self-preservation . . . War with France they say is the wish of this Government; that on the Militia we should rest our Security . . .

With these and such like ideas attempted to be inculcated upon the public mind (and prejudices not yet eradicated) with all the arts of sophistry and no regard to truth, decency, or respect to characters, public or private, who happen to differ from themselves in Politics, I leave you to decide on the probability of carrying . . . an extensive plan of defence . . . into operation . . .[1827]

Tonight, in the *Gazette of the United States*:

THE *Aurora* thinks it *right,* and to be *desired,* that the French should . . . *subvert the independence of other nations* . . . [H]e is now raising *cock-necked* troops . . .

WEDNESDAY, JUNE 26, 1799

GENERAL ★ AURORA ★ ADVERTISER

[Adv.]   *CENTRE HOUSE TAVERN AND GARDENS* . . .
            FOURTH OF JULY
    A full CONCERT will be presented to the public gratis . . .

Tonight, in the *Gazette of the United States*:

There is a boldness of sinning . . . in the editor of the *Aurora* which surpasses, in bare faced devotion to the French cause, almost any thing that has yet appeared. In the capital of one of the most important states in the union, this man has the *unparalleled effrontery* to attempt to organize *a company of armed men* and to proscribe *insignia* for them, altogether *Gallick.* As the American soldiers wear *black hats,* he directs his company to wear *white hats;* as a *Cock* is an emblem of the French, he orders them to wear *cocks neck feathers;* as a *small* triangle on a *large black ground* is the American cockade, he requires a *large silver eagle* to be mounted on a *very small black ground,* to shew as much as possible, by his regulations, a contempt for the *national military insignia.*

THURSDAY, JUNE 27, 1799

GENERAL ★ AURORA ★ ADVERTISER

The present struggle on the subject of government, between the hereditary despotic kings and the people, is waged no less with *the pen* and *with the press* than with *the sword.* This country has not taken any part in the contest with the sword . . . We cannot however say that we have taken no part with *the pen nor with the press.*

The American newspapers, sermons, magazines, and pamphlets [published by the Federalists] have

1. Held republicanism in contempt. 2. Ridiculed democracy. 3. Violently counterargued equal liberty. 4. Roundly condemned resistance to the unlawful and unconstitutional acts of power. 5. Openly advocated an established church. 6. Offered extenuations for even the doctrine of the divine right of kings. 7. Persuaded to a chief magistracy to be constitutionally unimpeachable . . .

In short, the far greater part of the American presses have entered into an alliance, offensive and defensive, with the monarchical and despotic combined powers against the republican states.

FRIDAY, JUNE 28, 1799

GENERAL ★ AURORA ★ ADVERTISER

REPUBLICAN GREENS.

YOU are requested to attend at your Parade on Saturday Evening at Six o'Clock—to form arrangements for the celebration of the Anniversary of American Independence—and transact other business.
WM. DUANE, Commanding Officer.

Poor *corporal Fenno* raves grievously about the new republican company—when he hears that there is another republican company besides the greens nearly completed—the *bile* must discolour the delicate crimson of his *smock visage* . . .

Tonight, in the *Gazette of the United States*:

MR. FENNO, Duane . . . publish[es] the following account [from the *Richmond Examiner*] of himself:
"Duane prints every day paragraphs an hundred times more obnoxious than those for which Abidjah Adams [of Boston's Independent Chronicle] *was dressed in a stone jacket . . ."* . . .
How long are we to be insulted by wretches who can thus boast of their obnoxious qualities . . . ?

SATURDAY, JUNE 29, 1799

GENERAL ★ AURORA ★ ADVERTISER

MILITARY RESENTMENT . . .

[BALTIMORE, MARYLAND, June 7.] To oppose with all the little energy I possess the establishment of a mercenary *Standing Army* is one of the many pledges I have made to the public . . . Exercising only that independent spirit which . . . should actuate the conduct of the Editor of an American newspaper, I discharged that duty incumbent on my situation by decrying an establishment more to be dreaded . . . than the exertions of . . . the "FIVE HEADED MONSTER" [the French Directory] . . . [s]ince which I have received all the *private persecution, calumny,* and *back-biting* in the power of the most inveterate malice to invent . . .

[Y]esterday, finding the danger of attempting to shew their superiority over the people by *open* violence, these *brave* and *spirited* officers—after whipping a poor, unfortunate devil . . . marched him with more than savage triumph from Fort M'HENRY to my office, where they gave orders to their *Jannissaries* to play the *officers march* before my door . . .

After the *mercenaries* had left my office, I waited on the sergeant, and asked him why, with fixed bayonets, he drew up his men and ordered his musicians to play that insulting air, *the Officer's march*, at my office door. He declared it was by the order of his superior officers!! . . .

ALEX MARTIN,
Editor of the *Baltimore American*.

Tonight, in the *Gazette of the United States*:

The *Aurora*, a paper which is not only *free* to but *invites* every calumny against the government of the United States and whatever else is calculated to incite the people to oppose the laws has recently (see the *Aurora* of the 27th instant) enumerated . . . cases in which, it is asserted, the American news-papers (or far *the greater part of them*), sermons, magazines and pamphlets have directly attacked or waged war, with the pen, upon republican states . . . that the American news-papers . . . have *held republicanism in contempt* . . . They *have ridiculed Democracy.*

It is answered that sound American patriots consider *pure Democracy* as one of those *Plagues* which have been suffered occasionally to *afflict mankind*. It is everything that can be dictated by the most *turbulent, wicked*, and *ambitious men*, carried into *effect* by an *inflamed* and *ignorant* multitude. It is a *mob-government; a government* without *branches*, where *every individual* has a right to oppose *every individual; where* laws are made in the same way . . . as *Town resolves* in public *squares* or *State-house yards* . . . The existing government of the United States is a well poised and balanced machine. It is equally distant from a *democratic, aristocratic,* or *monarchical* government, while it partakes of the principles of each. It will be the endeavor of the Federalists to perpetuate this government, and they will take up arms to prevent mad Democrats, at the nod of their demagogues, from changing it for a *pure Democracy* . . . Americans of *sound principles* have argued against every kind of liberty which would disturb the *social order* . . .

When it pleases Heaven to deprive a banditti of their leader, the devil not uncommonly infuses a greater portion than ordinary of his infernal spirit into some menial villain of the gang by the assistance of which he is soon enabled to usurp the command . . .

Thus has it been with the ex-shoe black of the late *Aurora*-man; but his progress has been rarely paralleled in rapidity or its constant tendency towards the highest point of baseness.

He began by calling General Washington a fool, a coward, and a murderer—he called Mr. Adams a blind, bald, toothless, crippled old dotard—he justified and defended the Northampton insurgents—and maligned the general and the army who quelled them . . .

That a fellow thus lost to every sense of shame, thus brazen and bold in his opposition at and ridicule of the friends and defenders of the government and country in which he lives and fattens, should devote himself to the interests of the enemies of America is by no means extraordinary.

MONDAY, JULY 1, 1799

GENERAL ★ AURORA ★ ADVERTISER

More military discipline.—Last Tuesday, at Reading, three officers of the standing army, one of whom was disguised in coloured clothes, went to the house of *Mr. Schnyder* printer (who was so barbarously treated by Montgomery's horse of Lancaster) and seized a young man who acts as translator of English and German to Mr. Schnyder. They were in the act of beating him, when Mr. Heister the younger rushed from the adjoining house to the aid of the injured man. Mr. Heister had suddenly snatched up a gun barrel with which he struck the officer in disguise and obliged the others to decamp precipitately—though the whole three were armed.

Tonight, in the *Gazette of the United States*:

The *Aurora* says that the safety of all *republican* governments *depends* on the success and *exertions* of the French. This same lying vehicle is daily sounding the *alarm* of danger to *this* republic; and this assertion is only an additional proof (which indeed was not wanting) of the *traitorous* views of the Irish and native rebels amongst ourselves !

Tonight, in the *Porcupine's Gazette*:

[NEW YORK] John D.[aly] Burke has left the United States. It is hardly necessary to say that this is the same Burke who printed the *Time-Piece* in our city in connexion with the learned doctor Smith. Having a number of prosecutions on him for libels against the United States, he made application to the President who, on Burke's promising immediately to depart from the United States, ordered the suspension of said prosecutions.

I have ever been of the opinion that Infidelity is generally the fruit of ignorance . . . [T]here is no more blasphemy in [Thomas Paine's] *Age of Reason* than in *Common Sense* and the *Rights of Man* . . . [T]he same holy scripture which enjoins us to *fear God* also enjoins us to *honour the king* . . . [I]t was such works as *Common Sense* and the *Rights of Man* which prepared the minds of the ignorant in this country for the reception of that blasphemous publication . . .

THURSDAY, JULY 4, 1799

GENERAL ★ AURORA ★ ADVERTISER

This day being the Anniversary of American Independence, the citizens engaged in the publication of the *Aurora*, will have to suspend their labours for the day and join in the general festival—the next number of this paper therefore will appear on Saturday morning next.

REPUBLICAN GREENS.

The impossibility of obtaining uniforms and equipment for more than *one fourth* of the corps (between the 15th of June and 4th of July) renders it necessary . . . that you should not exercise with the legion in this imperfect state. The whole corps in and out of uniform will assemble in their own parade at 6 o'clock in the morning of the 4th of July . . . It is expected that all members will dine together, along with the Republican Blues, where the declaration of Independence will be read & an oration delivered, &c.

WILLIAM DUANE, *Captain.*

FRIDAY, JULY 5, 1799

[As announced, there is no edition of the *Aurora* today.]

Tonight, in the *Gazette of the United States:*

The Anniversary of Independence was yesterday celebrated in this city with the usual demonstrations of joy and festivity. The First and Second troops of Volunteer Cavalry . . . the Volunteer Grenadiers and Macpherson's Blues paraded at 10 o'clock in the morning in High-street, when a salute was fired by the Artillery . . . At two o'clock, they repaired to Mr. Weed's ferry on Schuylkill [River] to dinner, where they were honored with the presence of Brigadier General Macpherson . . . At six, they again took up their line of march . . .

In the course of the day, a thief-looking vagabond, with a white hat and feather, was observed strutting about the streets like a turkey-cock in a barnyard: This was Jasper Dwight, captain of the cock-necked troops.

SATURDAY, JULY 6, 1799

GENERAL ★ AURORA ★ ADVERTISER

ANNIVERSARY FESTIVAL

THURSDAY was kept in this city as a day of general Jubilee . . .

The Republican volunteer militia legion under Col. *[John] Shee* paraded in the morning on the north side of the centre square, and the legion of Federal Volunteers, under General Macpherson, on the south side of Market-street . . .

After the military exercises were concluded, the corps marched severally to their places of entertainment . . .

The Republican Blues, commanded by Captain Summers, and the Republican Greens, by Capt. Duane, at their meeting, after reading the Declaration of Independence, drank the following [16] Toasts: 1. *The day we celebrate,* that gave birth to a nation and the great example now followed by mankind.—Yankee Doodle, a volley. 2. *The sovereign people of the United States* . . . 3. Dr. Franklin, the great patriarch of American liberty—may republicanism like the electric principle pervade the universe. 9 cheers. He's gone to the blessed abodes. 4. The Republics of Europe.—More of them.—*Ça ira.* 5. The freedom of the Press—devoted to truth, fear[ful] only of falsehood . . . 8. The author of the Declaration of Independence—who prefers the activity of republicanism to the calm of despotism.—3 volleys . . . 14. Thomas M'Kean . . .

VOLUNTEERS . . .

B. F. Bache—the man who preferred honorable competency and domestic virtue to public distinction & fortune at the expence of principle.—How sweet's the love that meets return.

The female democrat that *would not marry a coach* . . .

General Washington—May the glories of his youth never be obliterated by the mistakes of his age.

TUESDAY, JULY 9, 1799

GENERAL ★ AURORA ★ ADVERTISER

There will be a vast deal of tautology in the names of our naval vessels. We had an *Adams* [a U.S. frigate] lately launched in the east river [of New York]—another U.S. ship of war, the *[John] Adams* is mentioned in the Charleston papers to have been a few days ago brought forth near that city; and report states that another of that blessed name is now on the stocks in this city. The name will be certainly a host of strength in itself and completely protect our commerce. Is this flattery or not? Surely, we outstrip the British in this instance. In the navy of England, there is only one Royal George . . . The name of *Washington honours but one small vessel* . . .

Tonight, in the *Porcupine's Gazette*:

Jasper, the Gallic Irish *Aurora* man, is about establishing a life guard for his own carcass. It is said the French republic are to pay for the uniform which is to be *green,* with the French Cock feather in their cap. They have called themselves the *French Irish Blues,* or the *Aurora* Life Guard; it is added that three recruits have already inlisted!!

WEDNESDAY, JULY 10, 1799

GENERAL ★ AURORA ★ ADVERTISER

[E]very day [we] experience the benefit of a navy and army. Our citizens can no longer walk the streets in safety . . . A government cannot long remain popular when its hirelings tyrannize with impunity over the people and are despised by them. Military establishments are fruitful sources of despotism, and we fear that the public have seen only a small part of the many evils which we are yet to feel.

Tonight, in the *Porcupine's Gazette,* Peter Porcupine writes:

COMMUNICATION . . .

In an Oration delivered by Mr. How, at Trenton, on the 4th of July, . . . [s]peaking of the revolutionary war [and] . . . the conduct of France during the negociations in 1783 . . . [h]e fairly states the *Claims of Gratitude* which have been lately urged by the partizans of France from Jefferson to Duane . . . Mr. H., by reference to authentic documents contained in the appendix to Mr. Morse's sermon of 29 Nov. 1798, will find, 1st, "that one of the negociators (viz. Doctor Franklin) joined the Count de Vergennes and his secretary [Rayvenal] in opinion that the independence of America *should be . . . not acknowledged as a preliminary to negociation.*" 2d, That "Mr. Adams had not yet arrived from Holland, and *Dr. Franklin was so much in the French interest,* THAT HE WAS NOT CONSULTED [by Mr. Jay] . . ." 3d, That "Dr. Franklin was with the French generally in opinion . . ." . . . 4thly, That *"French influence* procured Dr. Franklin to be appointed sole minister at the court of France." . . .

And to conclude, it was "the virtue and firmness of Messrs. *Adams and Jay* that defeated the views of the French, and though *fettered with one colleague* (Franklin) . . . THEY, notwithstanding all these embarrassments, gained by the treaty every important point for America . . ." . . .

How unjust, is it not then, in an American to encircle the brow of Franklin with any part of the laurels gained by Adams and Jay in opposing him . . . To these two men, and to the candor and honesty of the British court and their envoys, are we indebted for our Independence . . . Ever honored and respected be their names, and may the searing iron of infamy ever brand the name of the cowardly Frenchified hypocrite, the prototype of Gallo-Americans !

It is reported that *Duane* expects to be brigadier general of militia, if M'Kean is chosen governor, and that the company of Americans who have at present the honour to be under the command of this United Irishman are looked upon as so many men in paste-board by the maneuvering of whom the general is to learn the art military.—*Quere.*—if Duane should be the commander of a considerable corps, may it not be expected that he will employ one of his present employers for a Surgeon to it ! One good turn deserves another.

Curious Toast.

On the 4th of July, one of the Democratic clubs toasted *"The Female Democrat who refused to marry A COACH"* ! If the female to whom I suppose they alluded had refused to marry *one of the horses,* though her refusal would have surprized me much, it would have given more sense to the toast.

Porcupine's speculation on my appointment of a surgeon refers to Peggy's step-father, Dr. Adam Kuhn. His speculation about Peggy's willingness to marry me is just that, though I agree with his repeated description of Peggy Bache as "luscious"![1828]

THURSDAY, JULY 11, 1799

GENERAL ★ AURORA ★ ADVERTISER

BLOOMFIELD, *FOURTH OF JULY, 1799* . . . [T]he citizens of Bloom-field . . . assembled at the Tree of Liberty . . . After the exercises . . . the citizens retired to Mr. Jacob Ward's tavern when . . . the following toasts . . . 9. The celebrated Patron of Liberty, Benjamin Franklin . . .
VOLUNTEERS
The Vice President, Thomas Jefferson—3 cheers
May the presence of the Marquis de La Fayette in America destroy the influence of the British federal faction.
May the whole tribe of British Printers, Porcupine . . . Fenno, &c. in America meet with their deserts, *the American altar* . . .

Tonight, in the *Porcupine's Gazette*:

LA FAYETTE . . .
It is said and, I believe, not without good foundation, that this revolutionary war hero is about to re-visit America . . .
Those who hire and who pay the *Aurora* have certainly informed their agents of their intention to send him . . . On the 4th of July, *success to this intended mission* was toasted by a gang of democrats in Maryland . . . They never toast at random.—This "hero" was sunk into merited obscurity, but, as he is, it seems, to be dragged out of it for the purpose of wheedling America, I shall, now-and-then, honour him with a notice which the contemptibleness of his character would not otherwise entitle him to.

The *Aurora* of yesterday; the paper in which General Washington has been styled "a coward, a traitor, and a murderer," Mr. Adams, "a blind, bald, crippled, toothless, dotard," . . . and the French Republic, "the liberator of oppressed nations, the friend and defender of liberty, and the asserter of natural and unalienable rights of mankind," this same paper yesterday contained this sentiment—not ironically—but in a manner which must arouse every feeling of the President's heart to blast the insolent caitiff: "THANKS TO OUR BETTER FORTUNE, WE ARE BLESSED WITH A WISE AND VIRTUOUS ADMINISTRATION" !!! If the President should not feel this as the deepest insult, well may we exclaim "Sic transit gloria mundi."

MR. [THOMAS] COOPER's [FAREWELL] ADDRESS.
To the Readers of the Sunbury and
Northumberland [Penn.] Gazette, June 29, 1799.

[A]s this is the last opportunity I shall have to intrude on the patience of the public in the capacity of editor, I shall dedicate the space that is left to a subject of some importance . . .

[M]easures have been adopted . . . to stretch to the utmost the constitutional authority of our executive . . . I can best illustrate my meaning by supposing a case. Let me place myself in the President's chair at the head of a party in this country aiming to . . . reduce by degrees to a mere name the influence of the people. How should I set about it? what system should I pursue?

Ist . . . [M]y first business would be to undermine [the] Constitution and render it useless . . .

2. My next object would be to restrict by every means in my power the liberty of speech and of the press . . . For the free discussion of public characters is too dangerous for despotism to tolerate . . . Hence too I would express the idea that all who opposed my measures were enemies of the Government, that is (in my construction) of their country . . .

3. In conformity to this plan, I would treat with derision and abhorrence the doctrines of the Rights of Man and the sovereignty of the people. I would seize upon every folly of the French in particular to bring those principles into contempt . . .

4. The more completely to enlist the ambitious, the needy, and the fashionable under my banners, I would take care it should be known that no place, no job, no countenance might be expected by any but those whose opinions and language were implicitly and actively coincident with my own.

5. . . . By strict attention to the forms of religion . . . by a declared preference of religious characters—by loud exclamations against infidels and atheists—by frequent appointment of days of humiliation and prayer, I would gain over the interest of the clergy and acquire the popular reputation of sanctity . . .

6. It would be my evident interest to cultivate the monied interest of the country . . .

7. But the grand engine, the most useful instrument of despotic ambition would be a standing army. The system of volunteer corps among the fashionable and would-be-fashionable young men . . .

It would therefore be my business to invent, to forge, to create reason for appointing a standing force, if no real motive existed. If there were no fears, I would manufacture subjects to alarm . . .

THOMAS COOPER

Forty-year-old lawyer Thomas Cooper, who served as stand-in editor (April 19–June 29) for the *Sunbury and Northumberland Gazette,* grew up well-to-do in Westminster, England, attended Oxford (which made him a barrister-at-law), moved to Manchester (where he helped found the Manchester *Herald*), and used his considerable intellect (in and out of corresponding societies) to criticize Britain's slave trade, defend Tom Paine's *Rights of Man,* oppose Britain's war with France, and run afoul of the king's 1792 Proclamation Against Seditious Writings. Rather than muzzle his political beliefs, Tom Cooper quit the British monarch in 1794, taking his wife, Alice, and the Cooper children (she bore him five) to seek democracy, write politics, and practice law in Pennsylvania's rural Northumberland County, where, despite the disfigurements of a minuscule (under five foot), tapered body and a gigantic head (he looks like a wedge), Tom Cooper gains heroic stature in opposing the President of the United States and allying himself with the *Philadelphia Aurora.*[1829]

Tonight, in the *Porcupine's Gazette*:

MOTHER BACHE

With that satan-like malignity which her very name seems now to imply, endeavours to excite a jealousy against the *President,* by observing that several of the vessels of war bear HIS NAME while "the name of WASHINGTON honours only one small vessel." . . . [D]oes the impudent editress recollect what she and her soon-forgotten spouse have called this man whose name, it seems, now "honours" a vessel ? does she recollect that they have called him a LEGALIZER OF CORRUPTION, an IMPOSTOR, or an APOSTATE? nay, does she recollect that the name which now *"honours"* a vessel has been branded, in the *Aurora,* with THE CHARGE OF MURDER? . . . And the shameless woman who owns this paper has now the assurance to complain that "the name of Washington HONOURS but one small vessel." . . .

The *Aurora* does not, as some people imagine, give the cure; on the contrary, *it takes its cure from them.* Their ideas are very clear and precise. *Another revolution that will lay the property of the rich at their mercy is their sole object* . . .

In *Pennsylvania,* in particular, things are fast approaching to a crisis. The good men must come forth, or the bad will rule over them with more than despotick sway. *Property must be defended by those who hold it, or it will certainly change hands!*

GENERAL ★ AURORA ★ ADVERTISER

Extract of a letter from Bucks County, dated July 11th 1799. "The letters from [British Minister to the United States] Robert Liston to [Canadian] President Russell are enclosed.—it is of importance they should be promptly communicated to the American people . . ."

(COPY.)   (No. III)   *Philadelphia, 23d May, 1799.*

SIR . . . On public affairs I have scarcely any thing to add—ONE STEP FURTHER ON THE ROAD TO A FORMAL WAR BETWEEN FRANCE AND THE UNITED STATES *has been taken by the Governor of Guadeloupe [in the French West Indies]*, WHO IN CONSEQUENCE OF THE CAPTURE OF THE INSURGENTE FRIGATE, has authorized French ships of war to capture all American vessels, whether belonging to the government or to individuals. But the resolution of the Directory [of France] on the great question of peace or war is not yet known . . .

In the interior of this country, the declamations of the *democratic faction* on the constitutionality and nullity of certain acts of the Legislature have misled a number of poor ignorant wretches into a resistance to the laws and a formal insurrection—*This frivolous rebellion* has been quelled by a *spirited effort of certain volunteer corps lately embodied,* WHO DESERVE EVERY DEGREE OF PRAISE. But the conduct of these gentlemen having been *shamefully calumniated by SOME of the POPULAR newspapers,* they have *ventured to take the law into their own hands and to punish one or two of the printers (by a smart flogging), a circumstance which has given rise to much animosity,* to threats, and to a commencement of armed associations *(particularly the United Irishmen),* and *some apprehend that the affair may lead to a partial civil war!* The portion of the jacobinic party who could carry matters to this extremity is *but small: the government is on its guard* AND DETERMINED TO ACT WITH VIGOUR . . .

ROBT LISTON

OBSERVATIONS OF THE EDITOR

The originals of the foregoing documents have been transmitted officially to the [President] . . . The public, however, are entitled to an examination . . . They were seized on a horse stealer of the name of Sweezy in Bucks County of this state. Sweezy had been one of [a] gang . . . [which] was outlawed and fled to Nova Scotia and Canada . . . [He] was sent to this city with dispatches, and, on his return with the above documents, was pursued under the former outlawry . . . [and] left behind . . . these documents . . .

Tonight, in the *Porcupine's Gazette:*

MR. LISTON'S LETTERS . . .

The letters . . . seized and broken open were sent down and *lodged in the hands of McKEAN,* from the press of whose friend and intimate acquaintance, DUANE, they have this day been published . . . with a set of the most stupid attempts at perversion that were ever conceived by Democratick ignorance.

While the *United Irishman* was throwing out his *threats* to publish these letters, I was afraid he did not mean to do it . . . The letters breathe a desire of seeing America maintain her honour in a war with France . . . As to the *Democrats,* the *partizans of France and M'Kean,* the MEN WITHOUT A GOD, they are too wicked to be reformed and too despicable to be reasoned with.

Tonight, in the *Gazette of the United States*:

[N]othing can save these *United States* from the . . . *cursed effects of a holy French brotherhood* but the intervention of a *Washington* and a well appointed *army.* The *jacobins* know this well; and hence their opposition to the army; thence the Editor of the *Aurora,* on the 29th of June inst. copied from a Baltimore paper, established to propagate French principles, the following paragraph. "I (the Baltimore printer) discharged the *duty incumbent on my situation* by *decrying* an establishment (the American *army,* raised expressly *to prevent or meet French hostilities)* more to be dreaded . . . than the exertions of *[the French Directory] . . .*"

TUESDAY, JULY 16, 1799

GENERAL ★ AURORA ★ ADVERTISER

[British Minister Robert Liston's] letter, marked (No. 3) . . . displays . . . the minute concern and interests which the British minister takes in our most minute transactions . . . and it displays something still more important for the public consideration, that when the band of ruffians who *took the law . . . into their own hands* in attacking Mr. Schnyder of Reading and the *Editor of this Paper,* Mr. Liston informs his colleagues in British employment that the [American] government was *determined to act with vigor . . .* [W]hen with vigor?—If the Printer had beat the thirty federal officers or when the violation of law and order on the part of these federalists had produced resistance on the part of the people, then the government would act with determined vigor !

Tonight, in the *Gazette of the United States*:

[The] Duane's of the *Aurora* think it would "serve the *cause of virtue* and promote the *freedom of mankind*" were the *French* to be *conquerors* in the *four quarters of the world* ! These men may call themselves *real republicans,* it is most certain they are not *real Americans.*

SUNDAY, JULY 21, 1799

Today, George Washington replies to a suggestion that he become a candidate for president:

> [With] the line between Parties . . . so clearly drawn and the views of the opposition to clearly developed as they are at present . . . [my] personal influence would be of no avail . . .
>
> [This is] a time when I am thoroughly convinced I should not draw a single vote from the Anti-Federal side and, of course, should stand upon no stronger ground than any other [Federal] character well supported; and when I should become a mark for the shafts of envenomed malice and the basest calumny to fire at, when I should be charged not only with irresolution but with concealed ambition, which waits only an occasion to blaze out; and, in short, with dotage and imbecility . . .
>
> [N]o problem is better defined in my mind than that principle, not men, is now and will be the object of contention; and that I could not obtain a solitary vote from that [Republican] Party . . . Prudence on my part must arrest any attempt . . . to introduce me again into the chair of Government.[1830]

MONDAY, JULY 22, 1799

GENERAL **★ AURORA ★** ADVERTISER

REPUBLICAN GREENS.
☞ BE particular to attend in uniform this evening at your usual parade—at half past five . . . W. DUANE, Captain.

Tonight, Peter Porcupine in the *Porcupine's Gazette*:

What is said in Mother Bache's paper I think worth no attention. Her base misrepresentations are intended to urge on the democrats to open rebellion . . .

WEDNESDAY, JULY 24, 1799

GENERAL **★ AURORA ★** ADVERTISER

BRITISH INFLUENCE.
[T]he dispatches of Robert Liston are objects of too great public concern to be suffered to pass into oblivion . . . [I]t is high time that we should look back and around us—and enquire how . . . British influence has been practicing . . . [W]e have evidence . . . 1. We have it in the records of the British Privy Council, in the most authentic form, that Britain had formed a party devoted to her interests in the U. States. 2. We have it in the hand-writing of John Adams, now President of the United States, that British influence has been employed, and with

663

effect, in securing the appointment of an officer of the most confidential and important trust under the government . . . 4. We have it under the hand writing of Robert Liston, the British ambassador, residing among us, that the American government has embarked in concert with the British, in measures of aggression . . . calculated for the dismember- ment of France . . . [I]n America, during the year 1798, Great Britain has expended Secret Service money to the amount of one hundred and eighty thousand pounds sterling—or 800,000 dollars.

Today, Secretary of State Timothy Pickering writes the President of the United States:

> *There is in the Aurora of the city an uninterrupted stream of slander on the American government. I inclose the paper of this morning. It is not the first time that the editor has suggested that you had asserted the influence of the British government in affairs of our own and insin- uated that it was obtained by bribery. The general readers of the Au- rora will believe both. I shall give the paper to Mr. Rawle, and, if he thinks it libellous, desire him to prosecute the editor . . .*
>
> *The Editor of the Aurora, William Duane, pretends he is an Ameri- can citizen, saying that he was born in Vermont, but was when a child, taken back with his parents to Ireland, where he was educated. But I understand the facts to be, that he went from America prior to our revolution, remained in the British dominions till after the peace, went to the British East Indies, where he committed or was charged with some crime, and returned to Great Britain, from whence, within three or four years past, he came to this country to stir up sedition and work other mischief. I presume, therefore, that he is really a British subject and, as an alien, liable to be banished from the United States. He has lately set himself up to be the captain of a company of volun- teers, whose distinguished badges are a plume of cock-neck feathers and a small black cockade and a large eagle. He is doubtless a United Irishman, and the company is probably formed to oppose the authority of the government; and, in case of war and invasion by the French, to join them.* [1831]

Today, Timothy Pickering also writes William Rawle, the federal district attor- ney for Pennsylvania:

> *I inclose the Aurora of this morning and beg you to examine it. If the slander on the American government will justify a prosecution against the Editor or Author, be pleased to have it commenced.* [1832]

Extract of a letter dated Hartford, July 21 . . . "You may be well sur-prised at this state of things in Connecticut . . . when you learn what lengths this domineering party proceeds . . . We have only the one print [the *New London Bee*] which dares even to take a glimpse of the worst practices or the wicked measures. Several attempts have been made in the post-office to obstruct its circulation and in many cases with success . . . The federal party . . . took another step, they interfered with the stage drivers, and every paper sent by that medium was destroyed . . ."

Today, Secretary of State Pickering again writes the U.S. district attorney for Pennsylvania, William Rawle:

Since I saw you this morning on the subject of the letters of the Brit-ish minister, seized & broken open in Bucks County in Pennsylvania, proposing that the offenders should be inquired for and prosecuted, I have received a letter from the President of the United States, directing such an investigation & prosecution.

For this purpose, I inclose [the Aurora] . . . published on Saturday (not Friday), July 19th in which Mr. Liston's letters are published. This suggests a further question, Whether the publisher *ought not to be prosecuted? I beg you to consider whether he is liable . . .* [1833]

Tonight, in the *Gazette of the United States*:

It is well observed, by an elegant writer, "that the *Grecians,* while the *Romans* were in the *course* of their *conquests, ceased not to praise* their *disinterestedness* and *regard* them as the *defenders of Liberty . . ."Rome,* however, *swallowed* up *Greece . . .*

France is *treading* in the *steps* and pursuing the *policy* of *ancient Rome.* The *Democrats* of the *United States,* like the *Democrats* of *Greece,* are lavish in their praise of *France . . .*

The *Aurora* expects to find the *American people stupid* enough to be-lieve that the French . . . are not *ambitious . . .*

Fenno amuses his readers with dry allusions to the lessons that he lately learned at school—these things are new in the lad's memory . . . *Fenno* tells us that Rome swallowed up all the free states of Greece—but he either did not know or had not honesty enough to tell that they did not fall until they had grown *corrupt* . . . Liston could unravel volumes more extraordinary than history, Grecian or Roman, is acquainted with.

To asperse the memory of Dr. Franklin seems to have become part of the duty enjoined by their employers on the editors of our "federal" presses; the reasons are obvious . . . [T]hese men envy the spotless fame of the *founder of American liberty* . . .

It is unnecessary for us to enter into a refutation of the calumnies lately received . . . and industriously propagated respecting the conduct of Dr. Franklin in the negociations at Paris . . . The journals of the old Congress bear ample testimony to his fidelity and solicitude to promote the interests of his country; and it is from such unquestionable authority as these journals that the misrepresentation of his conduct . . . with a view of enhancing the merits of John Adams . . . have long since received a complete refutation.

Tonight, in the *Gazette of the United States*:

The best *guarantees* of the *security* and *honor* of the United States . . . are a good *army* and *navy* . . . [H]ow then does it happen that an *army* and *navy* . . . still are *opposed* by the *different tribes* of *Democrats?*

These *partizans* of *France* do not relax, although their *object* has become *visible* . . . Some write *common place Philippics* against the *army* and *navy* . . . while *Duane* openly in his *writings* and *orations* encourages the *brigands* to *prepare* for a *trial* of *strength*, and *embodies* a *corps of men, uniformed a la Francois.*

TUESDAY, JULY 30, 1799

GENERAL ★ AURORA ★ ADVERTISER

AN ADDRESS TO THE GERMANS
OF CUMBERLAND COUNTY [PENNSYLVANIA] . . .

Is it possible that you would give your votes at the next election for James Ross to be your next governor..? . . .

Do you not know that the majority of your German fellow-citizens in our county, in Berks, Northampton, Bucks, Northumberland, and Montgomery, are almost unanimously against Ross and the sedition bill, and for M'Kean? . . .

[T]he time fast approaches when your eyes will be opened . . . The soldiery will be billeted at your dwellings; if they plunder you . . . , you must speak kindly of them; for if you say, write, or print any thing against it, you will be served according to the examples you have seen in Reading and Philadelphia. The heavy taxes that will necessarily follow to support these banditti will make you think . . .
"LET M'KEAN BE OUR GOVERNOR."

Today, at midmorning, the U.S. marshal for the District of Pennsylvania once more enters the offices of the *Philadelphia Aurora* and arrests its editor for

666

seditious libel against the government of the United States. He takes me before Judge Richard Peters, who gives me until Friday to obtain sureties for my appearance at trial.

WEDNESDAY, JULY 31, 1799

GENERAL   ★ AURORA ★   ADVERTISER

Several anxious enquiries having been made concerning the Editor yesterday—and as he could not attend to them all and perform his duty at the same time—he is induced to satisfy them and inform the readers of the *Aurora* generally in this manner—that the Editor was yesterday between nine and ten o'clock arrested by John Nichols, esq., marshal of this district, upon a warrant from Judge Peters, and on behalf of the administration, for publishing in the *Aurora* of the 24th instant, certain matters alleged to be defamatory or untrue concerning the administration.

By the marshal he was treated in a gentlemanly manner—and by Judge Peters, he was politely allowed until Friday morning to bring forward securities. To those who are personally acquainted with the Editor, no declarations concerning his past or future conduct are necessary—to those who know him only as the organ of public sentiment—a trustee for the public to detect and expose public errors, and to promote the public good—he can give only these brief and steadfast assurances, that he has not published a fact that he cannot prove, and that neither persecution nor any other peril to which bad men may expose him, can make him swerve from the cause of republicanism—or prove himself unworthy to be the successor of the descendant of Franklin in whose steps it is pride and pleasure to tread, with the same confidence in his country and the laws . . .

BRITISH INFLUENCE . . .

During our own revolution, we had authorized our ministers in Europe, as Dr. Franklin and John Adams, to use their efforts to draw some of the European nations into the war against Great Britain. They succeeded in drawing in France & Holland . . . But before [these nations] had taken a share in the war, while they were neutrals, our agents distributed commissions under the authority of Congress to citizens of . . . France to cruize against the enemies of America.

When the French minister [Edmond] Genet came here [at the beginning of the war between Britain and France] and distributed a few commissions to American citizens to cruize against the common enemy of republicanism, the British minister blustered and threatened and [Washington] had the French minister very meekly recalled.

Tonight, in the *Gazette of the United States*:

We are informed that the people concerned in publishing the *Aurora* were yesterday morning arrested for a gross and virulent libel upon the government of the United States, wherein they asserted that Great Britain distributed, in one year, 800,000 dollars secret service money amongst the officers of the federal Government.

Great wits jump, Bache, in the *Aurora* of the 29th, *attempts* to *treat* with *ridicule* . . . the *Roman History* which [has] been lately introduced into this Gazette to *illustrate* the *designs* of the French and shew that they, *like the Romans*, aim at nothing short of *universal domination.* "Fenno, (he says) *amuses* his readers with *dry allusions* to the lessons which he lately learned at school; these things are new in the Lad's memory . . ." *Bache,* for this, and a *thousand* such *strokes,* deserves at least the credit of being *true to the cause.*

Tonight, in the *Porcupine's Gazette*:

From the Connecticut Courant. HARTFORD, July 20 . . . [W]e . . . notice . . . an express or an implied approbation of the Alien and Sedition Laws . . . [T]here is, in many places, a direct and cordial approbation of them . . .

The only thing that is wanting to establish their complete popularity is a prompt and faithful execution of them. If several hundred intriguing, mischief making foreigners had been sent out of the country twelve months ago, and a few more Matthew Lyons had been shut up in prison for their seditious libels, we should not have had so many *Duanes, Burkes, [New London] Bees,* and a host of other villains filling the country with falsehoods, slanders, and factions . . .

THURSDAY, AUGUST 1, 1799

GENERAL ★ AURORA ★ ADVERTISER

BRITISH INFLUENCE . . .

We have received from a person in Wilmington, Delaware, the following letters. Both the originals were seen there while COBBETT was waiting to know whether the British . . . bait for Secretary Jefferson would take him in.

[To THOMAS JEFFERSON, U.S Secretary of State]

Hague, August 6, 1792.

Dear Sir, Mr. Cobbett, who will deliver you this letter, is an English gentleman . . . A gentleman in *the family of the English Ambassador* here . . . asks [me] to give him a letter of introduction to some person in Philadelphia which may, *from his first arrival there,* shew him to be a man of worth and merit . . .

[U.S. Minister to The Hague] W. SHORT

[To THOMAS JEFFERSON, U.S. Secretary of State]
Wilmington, (Delaware State) November 2d, 1792
SIR . . . Ambitious to become the CITIZEN of a FREE state, I have
left my *native* country, *England,* for *America.* I bring with me,
youth, a small family, a few useful literary talents, and that is all.
Should you have *an opportunity of serving me,* my conduct shall
not shew me ungrateful . . .   WM. COBBETT . . .

Upon these letters of the British printer we offer no other present comment than his subsequent declarations that he *would not accept the
citizenship of the United States . . .*

Federal Electioneering Diplomacy

A country storekeeper not many miles from this city has had a letter
sent to him containing a threat to burn his store unless he *deposits a
sum of money* in a certain place by such a time. The writer tells him
that he understands he is no *friend* to *French* principles, but that
he (the letter writer) is . . . The storekeeper of course shews the letter
to all his customers, and the honest people accordingly execrate the
French . . .

It is remarkable that this circumstance has taken place in the neighborhood of *Bustletown . . .* Our remote readers should be acquainted
also that *Bustletown* is the summer residence of [William] Cobbett, the
printer to the British government, and who is so active in his canvass for
Mr. Ross—!

The forgery of letters is no new *British trick*—a letter intimating a
design on the part of some supposed French incendiaries that they meant
to burn Philadelphia about two years ago—the letter was laid before the
late *Hillary Baker,* then mayor of this city, the hand writing was known
to be that of *Porcupine*—the matter was declared to be only a joke, the
city remained unburnt, but such tricks as that of Bustletown occasion
this being called out of oblivion.

Today, the President of the United States writes U.S. Secretary of State Timothy
Pickering:

> *I have received your favor of the 24th of July, inclosing an Aurora of
> July 24th, imbued with rather more impudence than is common to
> that paper. Is there anything evil in the regions of actuality or possibil-
> ity that the Aurora had not suggested of me? You may depend upon it,
> I disdain to attempt a vindication of myself against the lies of the Au-
> rora, as much as any man concerned in the administration of the af-
> fairs of the United States. If Mr. Rawle does not think this newspaper
> libellous, he is not fit for his office and if does not prosecute it, he will
> not do his duty . . .*
>
> *The matchless effrontery of this Duane merits the execution of the
> alien law. I am very willing to try its strength upon him.*[1834]

Today, Timothy Pickering writes President John Adams:

> *The day before yesterday, I received . . . a letter concerning a publication by Thomas Cooper, an Englishman . . . addressed to the readers of the Sunbury and Northumberland Gazette on the 29th of June. This address has been republished in the Aurora of July 12th, which I now inclose . . .*
>
> *Cooper was a barrister in England . . . and a warm opposition man . . . Cooper has taken care to get himself admitted to citizenship. I am sorry for it; for those who are desirous of maintaining our internal tranquillity must wish [him] . . . removed from the United States . . .*
>
> *[W]aiting the expression of your will, I remain . . .*
>
> TIMOTHY PICKERING
>
> *P.S. A prosecution against Duane, editor of the Aurora, has been instituted on the charge of English secret-service money distributed in the United States; and I have desired Mr. Rawle to examine his newspaper and to institute new prosecutions as often as he offends. This, I hope, will meet with your approval.*[1835]

FRIDAY, AUGUST 2, 1799

GENERAL ★ AURORA ★ ADVERTISER

Fifty-one applications were made at this office since Tuesday morning to become security for the Editor of the *Aurora* in the prosecution lately set on foot by the men who are vexed about . . . *British Influence* ! Republicans of America, if you were all but as firm, the *Boston Chronicle* would not be *bought up* for prostitution, and American republican sentiments would triumph over British influence and monarchical doctrines.

Extract of a letter dated Easton [Northhampton County, Pennsylvania], July 30. A Captain Peter Falkner [of the federal army] who has been recruiting up this way . . . manifested the tyrannical disposition of the military . . . These military officers seem to consider themselves above all law but that of their own will. The people are generally discontented and an opinion prevails that it is intended to excite the people to resistance and violence in order to create a pretext for quartering troops in different places and finding employment for this detestable and useless army.

The Germans of Philadelphia who have so steadily and uniformly supported the cause of freedom must view with pleasure the change which has taken place among their countrymen in York county . . . and we have no doubt that their exertions will ensure the victory to the Republican cause.

Today, I appear with two sureties before Judge Richard Peters, who releases me pending trial in October (when the federal court reconvenes). It seems the trial John Adams planned for Benny Bache last October will be held for me a year later.

Tonight, in the *Gazette of the United States* Jack Fenno announces:

> The Editor of this Gazette, having received several letters expressing a desire to be ascertained of his intention to continue in his present occupation, takes this opportunity to mention that he has relinquished his design of declining it, and that the Gazette of the United States will still be continued as heretofore by JOHN WARD FENNO

SATURDAY, AUGUST 3, 1799

GENERAL ★ AURORA ★ ADVERTISER

BRITISH INFLUENCE . . .

That British influence should be employed in America or British money is not so surprising . . . Would they scruple to corrupt abroad who are so abandoned to corruption at home?

Queries to be debated by the next meeting of the philosophical society of Philadelphia.

1st. Whether it is most commendable to knock down an independent honest news printer or to knock down his son?

2d. When thirty-six men have surrounded one, and when this one offers to fight the whole posse in succession, whether it is the greatest proof of bravery to accept of the one man's challenge or to turn upon him, all in a body, beat him down, and kick him when lying senseless? . . .

4th. Whether does it shew the highest sense of honour, of delicacy, and of manhood, to menace the widow Bache or to employ the infamous printer of the British ambassador's Gazette to write bawdry paragraphs against her?

Extract of a letter dated Richmond, [Virginia] July 24 . . . Mr. Meriwether Jones, a zealous republican, and who is otherwise a gentleman of a very popular character . . . set up a newspaper, viz. The *[Richmond] Examiner*, and, as his own health is a little impaired, he some months ago engaged Callender . . . to come down here and assist him . . .

In order to silence the *Examiner's* battery, some desperadoes formed a plan for attacking the printing-office and seizing upon Callender. The report is that they were to drive him out of the city; but the most probable issue is that they would have murdered him. The scheme seemed so black that a person to whom it had been entrusted came and told it to one of the friends of Captain Jones on Monday afternoon, some hours before it was to have been put into execution . . .

A party of armed men remained upon guard before the office of the *Examiner* till twelve at night . . . The conspirators had actually subscribed [to] a written agreement respecting this business. Undoubtedly they looked up to the government for protection and promotion, having before their eyes the impunity with which Duane was flogged . . . [W]hat kind of government must that be whose favour is courted by the collection of mobs and the perpetration of riots? . . .

Tonight, in the *Porcupine's Gazette,* William Cobbett writes:

MOTHER BACHE.

This loving wife, who could pen a masculine address to the publick before her husband's carcass was stiff; this modern matron who, in the first paper (which bore her own name at the head of it), rejoiced that the practice of *"castrating boys"* was abolished in Italy *for the good of woman kind,* published in her bawdy and prostituted Gazette of [Thursday] . . . barefaced and ridiculous lies . . .

Hillary Baker [the mayor of Philadelphia] not only never saw a letter of my forging, but he never saw a line of my writing, to my knowledge, in his whole lifetime. As to the *threatening letter* alluded to . . . such a letter has been received by a very respectable man about two miles from *Bustleton;* but Mother Bache is deceived if she imagines that people are to be persuaded that the letter was not actually sent by the Democratic faction with a view to alarming the Federalists of property and preventing them from exerting their influence, against *the Scourge, M'KEAN.* It is true *I live at Bustleton,* but, one *Miles,* M'Kean's relation and one of his *patrons,* lives much nearer the person to whom the letter was sent than I do! . . .

JEFFERSON.

This philosopher seems to have been so stung by certain reflections which I published . . . that all his philosophy could not restrain him from an act of spite . . . I did not see his communications to *Duane* 'till about an hour ago. It is, therefore, out of my power to comment on them 'til Monday which I shall then do in a letter addressed to myself. I will prove clearly that he communicated Mr. Short's and my letter to Duane, and after that, I think that no one will blame me for condescending to return him my thanks for his kindness . . .

Mother Bache and good man, Duane, have published some parts of the late European News; but they are devilishly sparing of their *comments.* They used to comment a good deal; but, as the Sans-culottes are nearly driven out of Italy, I suppose the sympathetick Widow is in tears, lest *"the horrible practice of castration"* should be revived . . .

Tonight, in the *Gazette of the United States*:

William Duane, who has been hired for some time past to conduct Bache's *Aurora,* was brought up before Judge [Richard] Peters, on Friday morning, and bound, himself in 2000 dollars, and two sureties in 1000 dollars each.

His trial is expected to come on before Judge Paterson, in October next.

SUNDAY, AUGUST 4, 1799.

Today, Elijah Griffiths writes Thomas Jefferson:

> [T]he republican interest has gain'd rapidly the last 6 months in this State [of Pennsylvania] . . . If the Aurora finds its way into your neighborhood, the whiping business which follow'd the Northampton expedition . . . must be known to you. Those things must have taken place through want of policy . . . (They) very sensibly lessen'd the popularity of the party in Pennsylvania & New Jersey . . . (and) may probably have that effect elsewhere . . . (so there is) no doubt of Mr. Thomas McKean being Elected to the Governor's chair [in Pennsylvania] by a very respectable majority. [1836]

Today, from Mount Vernon, George Washington writes Secretary of State Timothy Pickering:

> [A] question which I intended to propound . . . I find solved in the Aurora which came to hand last night.
>
> The question I allude to is whether the officers of Government intended to be acquiescent under the direct charge of bribery, exhibited in the most aggrivated terms by the Editor of the above paper? The most dangerous consequences would in my opinion have flowed from such silence and therefore could not be overlooked, and yet I am persuaded that if a rope a little longer had been given him, he would have hung himself up something worse, if possible, for there seems to be no bounds to his attempts to destroy all confidence that the people might and (without sufficient proof of its demerits) ought to have in their government; thereby dissolving it and producing a disunion of the States. That this is the object of such Publications as the Aurora . . . those who "run may read." . . .
>
> They dare not, at present, act less under cover, but they unfold very fast and, like untimely fruit or flowers forced in a hot bed, will, I hope . . . , soon wither and in principle die away . . .
>
> All of the Administration or some of the members are now to look for it, for Mr. Duane, I perceive, in his address to the public on the occasion of his arrest, has assured it "that he has not published a fact which he cannot prove, and that neither persecution nor any other peril to which bad men may expose him can make him swerve from the cause of republicanism." [1837]

Secretary of State Pickering has instituted proceedings against me for claiming John Adams wrote of British influence in the Washington administration. For the article in yesterday's *Aurora*, a federal indictment will include:

THE Grand Inquest of the United States of America for the Pennsylvania District . . . do present that William Duane . . . being an ill-disposed person designing and intending to defame the government of the United States . . . and to cause it to be believed that the President and principal executive officers of the said United States were bribed and corrupted . . . on the third day of August . . . wickedly and maliciously did print . . . in a certain newspaper called the Aurora . . . "That British influence should be employed in the America . . . or British money is not so surprising . . ."[1838]

I will answer all these indictments in the sedition trial that is scheduled to occur in October (when the Pennsylvania federal court reconvenes).

CHAPTER THIRTEEN

KEYSTONE OF DEMOCRACY

Pennsylvania, seated in the centre of the United States, wealthy, populous, commercial, and extensive as it is, must, while the present division of sentiment subsists between . . . [the northern and southern] parts of our country, direct and govern its policy . . . [T]he influence of Pennsylvania in the scale of American consequence would be immense . . . The effects then of the election of governor will be incalculable . . .

JOHN WARD FENNO, EDITOR,
GAZETTE OF THE UNITED STATES, 1798–1800[1839]

MONDAY, AUGUST 5, 1799

GENERAL ★ AURORA ★ ADVERTISER

BRITISH INFLUENCE! . . .

The declaration of American independence was the proud national instrument which first declared to nations that *All Men are EQUAL*. This illustrious and immortal memorial of American wisdom and American virtue . . . has scintillated over the whole Universe:—this grand and indelible register of Man's Right and of the wrongs of a nation at the hands of a tyrant gave at once a deadly blow to every class of meretricious distinctions and absurd titles—It established the right of men . . . to govern themselves . . .

Notwithstanding the efforts made, and the plan of monarchical government presented by [Federalist leader] *Alexander Hamilton* to the [constitutional] convention, the whole stupendous efforts of British intrigues and corruption were not sufficient to smother the primitive principles of our revolution.

A circumstance transpired on Friday night last which must eminently tend to convince the citizens of the danger in which they will be exposed as soon as a mercenary *standing army* is quartered among them . . . About eleven o'clock, two . . . soldiers went into the tavern of Mr. Davis near Fell's Point market-house; they appeared to be intoxicated, and pressed a man in the house to play at cards for money—Mr. Davis assured them that he would not allow gambling in his house; the soldiers insisted, and on Mr. D. ordering them out of the his house, one of them drew his bayonet from the belt and stabbed Mr. D. in the left side; another person interfered, and the second soldier made a lunge with his bayonet which, by the man's dodging, took him on the left temple and laid the flesh open to the extremity of the back of his head.

These men, with a number of others, we understand, were detached from the fort *to support the dignity of government* . . .

Tonight, in the *Gazette of the United States*:

Whatever declension has been witnessed by the *Aurora*, Darby the conductor or Editor if you will, is certainly in better case. It is said of him that he gets his daily allowance of gin "which was not so before," as will also be seen by an old soliloquy handed us by one of his ci-devant associates:

DARBY DWIGHT'S SOLILOQUY OVER A GIN CASK.
Is this a gin cask that I see before me,
The bung-hole toward my mouth ? Come let me suck thro'— . . .
I smell thee yet as pungent, and as strong,
As that I PLEDGED MY WATCH FOR . . .

How did Darby come by this watch? for certain a watch was pledged for gin, and that by Darby.

Tonight, in the *Porcupine's Gazette:*

I intended to have saluted my good friend Jefferson this day; but there is a fact or two with respect to which I wanted to be very clear, and which I cannot come at without examining certain pamphlets and papers. This I shall be able to do to-morrow, and the philosopher may expect to hear from me the next day.

TUESDAY, AUGUST 6, 1799

GENERAL ★ AURORA ★ ADVERTISER

The proceedings in York County have [so] shocked the weak nerved of the British faction, they rely now on the exertions of the *army!* It has been asserted, and with confidence, that the officers of the standing army are to be brought forward to vote at the election—and that their commissions are to be insisted on as their qualifications!

An *Officer* of the standing army now on the recruiting service at a town not a hundred miles from Montgomery County, a few days ago in the presence of a number of respectable citizens, declared that it was his intention to put the Editor of the *Aurora* to death . . . The Editor feels as perfectly tranquil on this as on the real attempts of *Peter Mierckin*

... and it is very probable that this military enragé is looking out for *promotion,* the Editor will not publish his name to disappoint him—but he will inform any one who enquires of him personally, or the gallant hero himself if he should think it eligible to call !

THURSDAY, AUGUST 8, 1799

GENERAL ★ AURORA ★ ADVERTISER

Mr. EDITOR ... At a tavern in Market-street a few days ago, a person who calls himself a Major was blustering very loudly on peace and moderation—among a variety of meek ejaculations, he did not forget to curse the *Vice President* and Mr. *[Alexander James] Dallas* and Mr. *[Albert] Gallatin* and the Editor of the *Aurora*—he wished heartily to have a guillotine erected for the four and very honorably declared that he would give an hundred dollars to be your Executioner.   A CITIZEN

REPUBLICAN GREENS
Parade for exercise out of uniform on THURSDAY evening next, precisely at 6— and every Thursday and Saturday evening till further orders.
WM. DUANE, Captain.

Tonight, in the *Gazette of the United States*:

The editor of the *Aurora* (see that paper of the 6th July), while *he acknowledges Mr. Jefferson* to be the *author* of the *letter* to *Mazzei,* paraphrases the *highly obnoxious* and *rebellious sentiment* it contains in the following toast: *"The author of the declaration of independence, who prefers the activity of republicanism to the calm of despotism."* Two *insurrections subdued* [the rebellion in western Pennsylvania against the Whiskey Tax in 1794 and now the so-called Fries Rebellion of 1799] have not yet *taught* this man that the *lovers of their country* know how to *sail* with *safety* on Mr. Jefferson's *"tempestuous sea of liberty."* ...

[T]he *Aurora* ... *prays devoutly* that the *French* may *annihilate the British fleet. Such* are your *lovers* of *"the tempestuous sea of liberty,"* and *haters* of the *present state of order* and *good government* which they denominate, *"the calm of despotism."*

FRIDAY, AUGUST 9, 1799

GENERAL ★ AURORA ★ ADVERTISER

TO THE INDEPENDENT ELECTORS OF PENNSYLVANIA.
FRIENDS & FELLOW CITIZENS ...
[I]t is not on British Authority alone, my friends, that we rest our assertions of a pernicious foreign British influence here. In the year 1792,

Mr. John Adams, at this time our president and then our vice president, was so confident of the matter that he suggested it *in writing* to an officer of the general government and incited that officer *keenly* to watch the operation and effects of it . . .   A PENNSYLVANIAN.

The assertion that John Adams witnessed British influence in George Washington's administration will certainly be part of my federal sedition trial in October.

SATURDAY, AUGUST 10, 1799

GENERAL   ★ AURORA ★   ADVERTISER

[Federalists] talk of the *passions, prejudices and fears* . . . [T]heir adherents . . . accused *Judge M'Kean* . . . of being a friend to *France* when they knew he was only the enemy of *tyranny and monarchy;* of being desirous of a war with Great Britain when he was only solicitous of avoiding a war; . . . [o]f being an United Irishman, only because he thought the people of Ireland barbarously oppressed . . .

Today, George Washington writes Major General Charles Cotesworth Pinckney (much is illegible but subject to reasonable surmise):

> *Recruiting in the . . . has progressed tolerably well, . . . others it is at a stand; and indeed . . . tion that can be . . . the enemies to our government . . . In a word, the Aurora, . . . which emanate from it, . . . which supports the same . . . are subordination in . . . In short, to prostrate . . . introduce anarchy in the military . . . have attempted to do in the Civil government of this Country.*
> *When, where, and how such things are to terminate is beyond the reach of human Ken; but . . . they cannot progress much further without an explosion. indeed . . . the Aurora (if one . . . publications) seem desirous . . . Crisis. His innuendos and charges . . . longer to be borne, and . . . to his account (and I have no doubt . . .) there is a contest in Philadelphia for the honor of becoming his Bail . . . other things, in language, and . . . impossible to be misunderstood, the Government is not only accused of being under . . . [British] influence but of bribery to a considerable amount . . . [I]f it shall be found that it is all calumny . . . to poison the minds of the People . . . punishment ought to be inflicted . . .*[1840]

SUNDAY, AUGUST 11, 1799

Today, from Mount Vernon, George Washington writes Secretary of War James McHenry:

There can be no medium between the reward and punishment of an Editor who shall publish such things as Duane has been doing for sometime past. On what ground then does he pretend to stand in his exhibition of the charges or the insinuations which he has handed to the Public? . . . I hope and expect that the Prosecutors will probe this matter to the bottom. It will have an unhappy effect on the public mind if it be not so . . . [1841]

MONDAY, AUGUST 12, 1799

GENERAL ★ AURORA ★ ADVERTISER

AN APPRENTICE
WANTED TO THE PRINTING BUSINESS.
Enquire at this office.

Today, Benny Bache would have been thirty years old.

Today, Secretary of State Timothy Pickering writes the U.S. district attorney for New York:

> *The audacious calumnies against the Government, with which many of the presses devoted to promote the views of France and of opposition to our own Government have lately teemed in a more than usual degree, have suggested the necessity of efficient measures to correct them by legal process. In particular, a paper is published in New York, under the title of the "Argus," which possesses the character of extreme virulence. It is not received at my office, but, from the passages which are studiously copied from it into the Aurora, I am satisfied that that character is not improperly ascribed to it. I request that you procure it daily at the public expense and to prosecute the publisher for every libel upon the Government.* [1842]

Secretary Pickering also writes the U.S. district attorney for Maryland:

> *[A] paper is published in Baltimore, under the title of the "American," which possesses the character of extreme virulence . . . [F]rom the passages which are studiously copied from it into the Aurora . . . I request that you procure it daily at the public expense and prosecute the publisher for every libel upon the Government.* [1843]

Tonight, in the *Porcupine's Gazette*, Peter Porcupine writes:

TO THOMAS JEFFERSON . . .

SIR, In the *Aurora* of the 1st instant, there appeared two letters . . . [T]he story told by your friend *Duane*, respecting the channel through which he came by the letters, is a LIE.

Your friend *Duane* (who formerly inhabited the jails of Calcutta) states

that the copies were received from a person who saw them at Wilmington
. . . *You* and *Duane* may endeavor to persuade people that this is the truth;
but the most stupid, even your stupid partizans, will never believe you
. . . What share *you* had in this falsehood I cannot pretend to say; but as
it is *certain* that you, and *you alone,* could furnish copies of the letters
and as they came forth accompanied with a lie *intended to persuade the
public that you did not furnish them,* it is by no means unfair to presume
that if you were not the inventor of the falsehood yourself, you gave your
consent . . . to the making use *a falsehood of some kind or another . . .*

[Duane claims] that *I was sent out by the British government* to carry
on the business of corruption . . . But, Sir, was it not strange that the British Government should choose such an instrument as I was ? Their diplomatic corps must be very weak if they were compelled to beat up for
recruits amongst the non-commissioned officers of a regiment of foot . . .
Besides, there is another consideration in which you, my dear Jefferson,
were deeply involved; if the British Government did really send me out
to prosecute the work of *corruption,* how came they to send me to YOU
in particular? Your reputation was, by them, as well known then as
now . . .

What must the statesmen of other countries . . . think of a VICE PRES-
IDENT OF THE UNITED STATES entering into a literary warfare with a
PRINTER and taking, for an *auxiliary,* a man who confesses he was driven
from the British dominion, after having inhabited its jail ?

These questions, Sir, are asked by the *people,* and, therefore, you who
are "the man of the people" ought to answer them . . .

Wm. COBBETT

TUESDAY, AUGUST 13, 1799

GENERAL	★ AURORA ★	ADVERTISER

BRITISH INFLUENCE !

From the moment that Britain failed to subject us by arms—she resolved to pursue our humiliation by perfidy—the peace of 1783 was
scarcely concluded, when laws calculated to cramp and obstruct our
commerce were introduced into the British parliament . . .

Today, John Adams responds to Secretary of State Timothy Pickering's letter
of August 1st (which enclosed Thomas Cooper's farewell address, as it appeared
in the July 12th *Aurora*):

*And now, Sir, what shall I say to you on the subject of "libels and
satires? Lawless things, indeed." I have received your private letter of
the 1st of this month . . .*

*At the time when we were inquiring for an agent to conduct the af-
fairs of the United States before the [British] commissioners at Philadelphia, Mr. Cooper wrote to me a solicitation for that appointment . . .*

*Mr. Read was appointed, and the disappointed candidate is now, it
seems, indulging his revenge. A meaner, a more artful, or a more malicious libel has not appeared. As far as it alludes to me, I despise it; but
I have no doubt it is a libel against the whole government; and as
such, ought to be prosecuted . . .*[1844]

Tonight, in Philadelphia, a rousing Federalist meeting at Dunwoody's Tavern
supports James Ross, U.S. senator from Pennsylvania, to be the next Governor
of Pennsylvania.[1845]

WEDNESDAY, AUGUST 14, 1799

GENERAL ★ AURORA ★ ADVERTISER

A RARE ONE—A GOOD PUN.

A gentleman of open and avowed Republican principles . . . was on a
late occasion in company where the glass was briskly moving and Toasts
were given from all parts of the table (as is the order of the day) highly
complimentary to the French Republic, to Democrats, Jacobins, &c.;
being called on to give a toast . . . filled a bumper, and gave *"The inside
of a leg of mutton"* for his toast; an explanation from all parts of the table
was called for—the inside of the leg of mutton, said the gentleman, is a
BONYPART.

Today, Timothy Pickering writes the U.S. district attorney for Virginia:

*[A] paper is published in Richmond, under the title of the "Exam-
iner" which possesses the character of extreme virulence . . . from the
passages which are studiously copied from it into the Aurora . . . It is
my request, therefore, that it may be examined as often as it abuses . . .
that its Editor or Editors be prosecuted . . .*[1846]

Tonight, in the *Gazette of the United States*:

It is not a little curious that while the tabernacles of Democracy are
filled with cries against standing armies as contrary to the constitution,
the Democrats themselves are raising the only illegal forces that appear.
Cock-necked troops and cabalistic corps are formed in express violation
of the laws which forbid private armed applications for any purpose whatever. It is of little import that these motley bands consist of some barren
half-dozens altogether—If they consisted of but two men each, they
should be Disarmed.

ELECTION.

At a numerous and respectable meeting of the citizens of Philadelphia
and the Liberties, held at Dunwoody's in the city of Philadelphia, on Tuesday the 13th inst. for the purpose of fixing upon a suitable person to fill
the important office of Governor of the state . . .

Resolved, as the sense of this meeting, That JAMES ROSS of Pittsburg unites, in an eminent degree, the requisites . . .

ROBERT WHARTON, Chairman
[Mayor of Philadelphia]

THURSDAY, AUGUST 15, 1799

GENERAL ★ AURORA ★ ADVERTISER

[From the Virginia *Argus*.] On Friday last, a complaint was heard . . . at the instance of Mr. Callender of the office of the *Examiner* against . . . the committee of brother associators [for harassing Mr. Callender] . . .

Mr. Call, for the defendants . . . blamed the *Examiner* for copying the abominations of the AURORA . . . [The lawyer for the *Examiner* answered] . . . we consider the *Aurora* the most valuable newspaper in America.

Tonight, in the *Porcupine's Gazette*:

The enemies of government have long been in the habit of saying that the men who support it are the old tories . . . It was first propagated by the memorable editor of the *Aurora* and has been retailed by his satellites through all parts of the union . . .

Is the President an old tory? Is General Washington an old tory? Is Mr. Hamilton, the inspector general of the army, an old tory? Are the secretary of state and the secretary of war old tory? . . . I am much mistaken if there is a solitary one among them . . .   CIVIS

FRIDAY, AUGUST 16, 1799

GENERAL ★ AURORA ★ ADVERTISER

MR. EDITOR . . . Suppose . . . Schnyder the printer had gotten a number of men and flogged Captain Montgomery, would the fault have been as trivial as Montgomery's flogging the printer—Or had Mr. Duane and ten or thirty of his friends went and kick'd, cuff'd, and rib-roasted any of the *valiant* officers who maltreated him, would the fault be only equal to theirs? . . .   ROBERT SLENDER

It would be an act of public injustice to withhold from public reprobation the proceedings of a meeting held at Dunwoody's on the 13th inst . . . [P]arty violence has seldom assumed a more indecent or insolent tone . . .

Beware who you appoint to the office of governor . . . *exclude from the important station a man who is not only unfit to govern* the state

but who is brought forward as the mere machine and tool of a party . . .
Let Thomas M'Kean be the man of your choice . . .

Today, President John Adams writes Secretary of State Pickering concerning the address to Pennsylvania's independent voters, which appeared in the August 9th *Aurora* and which repeated the claim that John Adams wrote of British influence in the Washington administration.

> *I have read the address to the independent electors of Pennsylvania, and am very anxious to know where all this will end. The trial [of Duane] will bring out some whimsical things. At present, I will say nothing. I have no apprehension for myself or the public from the consequences.* [1847]

Tonight, in the *Porcupine's Gazette*:

> Will not Judge M'Kean arrest and bind over the Irish Jail-bird editor of the *Aurora* for the following libellous recommendation in the *Aurora* of this morning?

> *"exclude from the important station"* (of Governor) *"a man who is not only unfit to govern . . ."* [&c.]

> A truer picture could not be drawn, and the Judge knows that *"The greater the truth, the greater the libel."*

SATURDAY, AUGUST 17, 1799

GENERAL ★ AURORA ★ ADVERTISER

A design is on foot among the ministerialists to postpone the operation of the New Census until after the election of the next president in the fall of 1800. Thus the four [north]eastern states will retain an ascendancy in that election to which their present share of population does not entitle them. Since 1790, the middle and southern states have encreased vastly in population. The eastern states are in that respect stationary . . .

We have already observed that Kentucky, Tennessee, and Georgia should send at least *sixteen* or *twenty* representatives to congress; and that these three great and growing states send, at present, no more than *five*. If they had been fairly represented, no alien or sedition acts, no standing armies, or endless navies would have hung, at this day, like a millstone around the neck of American liberty.

SIR, If one may judge from what has taken place on former occasions, we shall see at the approaching election certain *disciplined corps*, headed by proper leaders, come up to the place of voting to give in tickets put into their hands by the said leaders who are to stand by and see that each *does his duty* in the manner required. It strikes me, Sir, that this is a most flagrant violation of the constitution and laws which were

meant to secure to the elector a free and uncontrouled choice be enabling
him to give his vote in *Secret* . . .   AN ELECTOR

The committee of *slander* lately encouraged in business by resolutions
at Dunwoody's begins to feel that there is such a thing as retaliation—in
pity to them we will spare them while they behave discreetly.

Tonight, in the *Gazette of the United States*:

MODERN CHARACTERS,
By Shakespeare and others.
CAPTAIN DUANE
The *Captain* of the Rabble issued out
With a black, shirtless train; each was an host;
A million strong of *vermin*, every villain—
No part of Government, but lords of anarchy,
Chaos of power; and privileg'd destruction;
OUT LAWS OF NATURE, *yet they may be used*
As tools of tumult, in the hands of knaves.

For two or three days past, the alarm of the [Yellow] Fever has been
received in this city . . . We have the fullest reliance on the vigilance and
attention of the Board of Health . . .

Tonight, in the *Gazette of the United States*:

We quote the following *strange* paragraph from Callender's *[Rich-
mond] Examiner* of Friday last . . .

"*The treatment which Mr. Duane has received from the ministerial myrmidons in Philadelphia surpasses all description and
credibility. In the course of last winter, he was knocked down upon
a Sunday when at a Roman Catholic Chapel. He was then dragged
before that little contemptible duodecimo despot, KEARNY WHAR-
TON, the present mayor of Philadelphia. He was bound over . . . to
stand trial for having committed a riot . . .*

"*Upon that trial, not one witness could be adduced whose evidence went to incriminate him even circumstantially, so that, as
his counsellor Mr. Dallas observed to the court, it was absolutely
useless to make any defence . . .*

"This is the present state of public justice in the city of Philadelphia."

(To shew how much at random the author of the above has written, it might only be necessary to say that the Mayor of Philadelphia bears the name ROBERT WHARTON . . . That Robert Wharton is a tyrant to the wicked, to the licentious, and to the worthless and indolent is a fact . . .

[J. W. FENNO])

Interesting Information.

I DO hereby certify that I heard Thomas M'Kean, Chief Justice of Pennsylvania, declare *"That he wished Twenty Thousand United Irishmen would come into this Country, that they were a people who understood true Liberty and the Rights of Man,"* which I am willing to attest upon oath, if it should be necessary.   DAVID WATTS

N. B. A dozen affidavits can be produced to the above fact, if necessary.

THURSDAY, AUGUST 22, 1799

GENERAL ★ AURORA ★ ADVERTISER

The Committees who support the pretensions of Mr. Ross . . . profess an entire attachment to Mr. Adams, who has declared in one of his answers to an address, "THAT REPUBLICAN GOVERNMENT MAY BE INTERPRETED TO MEAN ANY THING." . . . (see Fenno's paper July 3d, 1798) . . . The Electors of Pennsylvania will remember that the federal constitution pledges the government to secure their liberties in these very words: "The United States (says the constitution) *guarantees* to every state in the union a *republican* form of government."

Tonight, in the *Gazette of the United States*:

MR. FENNO, . . . We have long heard of the falsehoods of the *Aurora;* we have long been persuaded that the Editor has been in the pay of the French, either immediately from their Ambassador or Consuls, or now through their friends. We have to the shame of our laws heard him abuse and traduce the best characters of the nation . . . That such printers ought to be considered as enemies, no one can doubt who knows any thing of the spirit of party in our state . . .

There are numbers who, from the time that Mr. Jefferson was disappointed of the President's chair, have never ceased to infuse evil reports of the President and officers of Government into the minds of their friends and dependents, many of whom never had any other information than from the polluted fountain of the *Aurora* . . . [I]t is not consistent with common sense that infidel printers should be permitted to keep up enmity against the government by false suggestions and among people as ignorant as [they are] . . . willing to do right, if not misled by the friends of Mr. Jefferson and the French, made up of the enemies of the Government and of Christianity . . . I hope the Congress will, at their next meeting, take some order with the licentious and Frenchified printers through the United States.

Yours, VERITAS

SATURDAY, AUGUST 24, 1799

GENERAL   ★ AURORA ★   ADVERTISER

EQUAL RIGHTS

THE civil rights of the citizens of this country are too valuable to be destroyed by ignorance or design; they form . . . a commodious shelter from the storms of party rage, the overflowings of aristocracy, or a corrupt Monarchical interest . . .

In the days of seventy-six, those days of genuine republicanism, the . . . principle of equal rights was then the fundamental principle which was recognized by the people of this country . . . [T]he voice of tyranny or the interests of aristocracy . . . gave it all the false colouring of a state of anarchy . . .

Equal rights . . . can be maintained only by the establishment of equal laws, that is, by laws which secure to every individual citizen the full enjoyment of the fruits or effects of his strength and his faculties. If nature has established a difference in the possession of this strength and these faculties, it is not the business of civil law to increase this difference or inequality . . . On the contrary, it is the duty of the community to furnish instruction where it is most requisite and to give strength where it is most wanted . . . It has been either an error or a crime in almost all the governments of the earth to favor that part of the community which least required their assistance: and the principle of equal rights was abandoned to encrease the spendour or augment the extravagant or vicious enjoyments of those whose fortunate condition in life already sufficiently secured them against the sufferings and the miseries to which another portion of the community was constantly exposed. Civil laws should be founded on the strictest moral principle . . . [T]his can be affected only by the establishment of rules of reciprocal justice which shall exclude every idea of aristocratic inequality . . . [and] abandon every idea of imitating the corrupt laws and baneful establishments of the Old World . . .

FRANKLIN

Tonight, in the *Gazette of the United States*:

HEALTH-OFFICE

8th MO, 22d, 1799.

THE Board of Health, desirous of giving to their fellow citizens all the information they are possessed of relative to the prevalent disease [of yellow fever] in our city, think it their duty to state . . . that during the last 6 days, there have been a number of persons taken ill, principally in the lower part of the city and Southwark, many of whom have died after a few days sickness and that, at present, there is still a considerable number sick . . .

By order of the Board,   EDWARD GARRIGUES, Pres.

At a respectable meeting of a number of the Citizens in the southern part of the County of Philadelphia, agreeable to public notice at the house of Cadwallader Evans in Southwark, for the purpose of promoting the election of JAMES ROSS, esq. of Pittsburg . . .

Resolved, That in the opinion of this meeting . . . [James Ross] should be a man . . . perfectly free from the influence of those perfidious and sacrilegious principles of Jacobinism . . .

Resolved . . . we are determined individually to use all honourable means to our power to promote the election of said James Ross to the office of Governor of this Commonwealth.

Resolved, that the following persons be a committee to exert themselves in their respective wards and furnish tickets for the election.

FOR SOUTHWARK.

Joshua Humphreys . . .

Peter Miercken . . . [and about fifty others]

Joshua Humphreys' son, Clement, assaulted Benny Bache in the Southwark shipyard. Peter Miercken led the troops that assaulted me at the *Aurora* office.

SUNDAY, AUGUST 25, 1799

This morning, from his pulpit in Christ Church (across Second-street from the *Porcupine's Gazette* offices), the Rev. James Abercrombie delivers a sermon:

. . . The mantle of death, brethren, is at length again unfolded and spread over our once happy city, literally fulfilling the declaration of the apostle: for while we were saying "peace and safety, sudden destruction hath come upon us."[1848]

MONDAY, AUGUST 26, 1799

GENERAL   ★ AURORA ★   ADVERTISER

AURORA OFFICE, AUGUST 26.

The necessity of guarding against similar calamities [as] those which so heavily and particularly afflicted this Office last year, renders it prudent to remove the Office to Bristol in this state within this week— It is proposed to publish tomorrow's newspaper in this city; the removal will necessarily occasion a suspension of one day at least.

There is mass evacuation of Philadelphia to avoid the malignant yellow fever. The federal government is moving, as it did last autumn, about twenty miles northeast along the Delaware to Trenton on the New Jersey side of the river. The *Aurora* also moves upriver but settles south of Trenton (and closer to Philadelphia) in the town of Bristol in Pennsylvania's Bucks County. The *Aurora* will remain in Bristol until October 19th.

Tonight, in the *Gazette of the United States*:

☞ *The Office of the GAZETTE OF THE UNITED STATES will be removed tomorrow to the first brick House in Eleventh, above Arch street. In consequence of this removal the Paper will not be published on Tuesday.*

Starting in September and until the fever subsides, the *Gazette of the United States* will be printed on a half-sheet.[1849] The *Aurora* and the *Gazette* have not forgotten what happened when they failed to leave last autumn. Porcupine hasn't forgotten either. On Thursday, the offices of the *Porcupine's Gazette* will move to Bustleton, Pennsylvania, where Cobbett has his summer home and where he will publish the paper weekly rather than daily.

FRIDAY, AUGUST 30, 1799

BACHE'S PHILADELPHIA AURORA

BRISTOL [PENNSYLVANIA] . . . A calamity, which appears to afflict our maritime cities as if it were a mark of the indignation of Heaven for the degeneracy of our nation from the magnanimity and virtue which obtained us our liberties, has caused the removal of *The Aurora Press* to this town—and a suspension of the publication from *Tuesday* to this *Morning* . . .

[O]ur friends stated some objections [to Bristol]—[S]ome . . . thought that the neighborhood of a[n army] camp was a very injurious one for a republican press—others (who appear not to have known the people) objected because they conceived Bristol to be a nest of tories—and a few because there were so many of the amiable and exemplary [Quaker] society of friends here.

With the Editor, all these reasons for avoiding Bristol would be the most powerful for choosing the situation—bred among Quakers, loving their domestic virtues and simplicity of manners, a class of men who never offend and whose system of religious discipline is the most democratic that was ever instituted . . . from such men, open always to truth, the Editor would have nothing to expect but good will.

As to Bristol being overrun with Tories, the Editor has not been so unfortunate as to find but one . . . [T]he Editor and all the numerous establishment have experienced the most impressive civilities and untired attention . . .

Tonight, in the *Gazette of the United States*:

Preparations for the electioneering campaign in Pennsylvania are making, with great spirit and activity. Alarm posts are established: the armies are marshaled, officered and equipped, and the recruiting service is prosecuting with ardour and perseverance . . . A general and decisive battle is expected in October. If talents, integrity and patriotism can influence the fate of the day, victory will crown the banners of General Ross.

WEDNESDAY, SEPTEMBER 4, 1799

GENERAL ★ AURORA ★ ADVERTISER

BRITISH PRINCIPLES . . .

The British constitution preposterously affects to maintain *"that the king can do no wrong"*—So Fenno openly advocates putting the American chief magistrate on the same footing by a dangerous and impolitic alteration of our federal constitution . . .

The British constitution sacrilegiously establishes *one set* of Christians (the Church of England) over the whole Christian church; so Fenno wishes an established church to be maintained no doubt out of the federal treasury . . .

[L]et the electors of Pennsylvania remember that Fenno is the printer of the Journals of the Senate and that Mr. Ross is a member of the majority of that Senate . . . Is he not a vigilant friend of our *constitution*, our *political principles*—and our *administration* when he never took a single measure to withdraw the printing from this young man *(Fenno)* who has abused them all? What sort of officers are we to expect Mr. Ross would appoint, were he governor of Pennsylvania—men who, like Fenno, abuse our civil and religious constitutions.

Today, in New York City, the federal government indicts widow Ann Greenleaf, publisher of the New York *Argus,* for the paper's claim that *"the federal government was corrupt and inimical to the preservation of liberty."* The New York *Argus* is the nation's second largest Republican newspaper (now that Federalist sedition prosecutions have defeated Boston's *Independent Chronicle*) and the only remaining Republican newspaper in New York City (now that John Adams has suppressed the New York *Time Piece* and exiled its Irish editor, John Daly Burk). Ann Greenleaf's trial is scheduled to occur just before New York's May 4th election of a new state assembly (whose members will decide the state's presidential electors!).[1850]

Today, the same grand jury indicts, under the Sedition Act, a member of the New York state assembly, Jedidiah Peck, for having circulated a petition against the Alien and Sedition Acts. Peck's petition claimed: *"The former is directed at Foreigners; the latter is levelled at ourselves. The former tyrannizes over Men, who in general have been born and bred under oppression. But it is the superlative wickedness of the latter to convert Freemen into Slaves."* The New York state assemblyman will stand trial next spring, just before he faces re-election to the New York state assembly.[1851]

Lastly today, the same New York grand jury indicts, under the Sedition Act, William Durell, publisher of the weekly *Mount Pleasant Register* (Mount Pleasant is thirty miles north of New York City) for *"false scandalous malicious and defamatory Libel of and concerning John Adams."*[1852]

John Adams' message to New Yorkers is clear. Looking to next spring's elections in New York, all public voices must support the Federalist vision.

FRIDAY, SEPTEMBER 6, 1799

GENERAL ★ AURORA ★ ADVERTISER

SUBSCRIBERS TO THE AURORA,
May have their papers in Philadelphia at No. 12 Market-street— those who remain in town are requested to give orders at that house, and the papers will be delivered daily at their residence. Papers will be delivered in Germantown at Oeller's Hotel. In Frankfurt, at Major Sullivan's at the Cross Keys. Letters for the Editor will be likewise received at those places. Subscribers in other parts of the Country are requested to send written directions how their papers are to be forwarded.

Today, in the *Gazette of the United States*:

HARRISBURG, [PENNSYLVANIA] *August 28.* On Saturday morning last, Wm. Nichols, Esq., Marshal of Pennsylvania, arrested Benjamin Moyer and Conrad Fahnestock, printers and proprietors of a Dutch *Aurora* of this borough, for publishing a *"false, scandalous, and malicious"* libel against the laws and government of the United States. They have given bail . . .

Today,[1853] in the *Porcupine's Gazette*:

Much has been said and written on the utility of newspapers—but . . . [w]as there ever such a damnable proposition as . . . *Read News-papers in schools !* I would as soon give my children *"the pickpockets vade mecum."* A news-paper, generally speaking is the manual of ignorance and rascality. For instance, Mother Bache's Atheistical paper would "supply the want of *preaching"* . . . MOTHER BACHE'S *for seditiousness, falsehood, bawdry, and blasphemy* . . .

ELECTION.

This business grows hotter and hotter. The Federal Battery at Dunwoody's was pretty loud some time ago and promised to continue so; but, whether by desertion or otherwise, it has since grown slack, and the enemy, profiting therefrom, have recommenced offensive operations with great fury and with not less skill than fury.

MONDAY, SEPTEMBER 9, 1799

GENERAL ★ AURORA ★ ADVERTISER

A Newspaper has been commenced at Easton, on the Eastern Shore of [Maryland] by a Citizen of the name of T. P. SMITH—it is entitled, "THE REPUBLICAN STAR," and from the talents and spirit of the Editor, excites expectations of benefiting the good cause. (Balt. Am.)

Another Republican paper has been lately established at Winchester, Virginia, by a Mr. *G. Trissler*, late of Fredericktown, a gentleman of very handsome abilities. The cause of virtue cannot have too many nor too able supporters.

Tonight, in the *Gazette of the United States*:

[W]hen the infamous Bache called [General Washington] a perjured peculator and a wilful assassin and [Mr. Adams] "an old, bald, blind, toothless and decrepid president," the vigilant Chief Justice of Pennsylvania was not so "fully impressed with the duties of his station" as to bind over [for trial] the abandoned calumniator. Nay, he has since, in some degree, even sanctioned "the magnitude and virulence of the lies" of the *Aurora* . . . by making it necessary that the advertisements of insolvent debtors, relative to their discharge, should be published in that vehicle of slander . . .

While the proposition for repealing the Alien and Sedition Bills were under consideration in Congress, four United Irishmen assembled a mob in one of the church yards . . . After a violent scuffle, the rioters were made prisoners and carried before the Mayor. During the examination, the Chief Justice . . . forced himself into the mayor's house, grossly insulted that magistrate while in the execution of the duties of his office, and declared that the prisoners *ought to take up their hats and go away* . . . With the unlimited power of pardon vested in such a man, what outrage will not escape punishment ? . . .

WEDNESDAY, SEPTEMBER 11, 1799

GENERAL ★ AURORA ★ ADVERTISER

TO THE ELECTORS OF NORTHUMBERLAND COUNTY.

Friends and Fellow-Citizens,

The time is fast approaching when you will have to decide upon . . . the [Governor] of the Republic of Pennsylvania . . .

It is well known that the *Republican* party are attached to a representative Constitution; to a Constitution of equal rights; free from all hereditary honours and exclusive privileges; where the officials of Government are responsible for their conduct . . . By this party the nomination of *Thomas M'Kean* is supported.

The *Federalists* on the other hand . . . think the government should have *more* and the people *less* power. To this party, and their Candidate, *Mr. Ross*, we owe the *Sedition Law* . . . To them we are indebted for the *British [Jay] Treaty*, that parent of our present dispute with France . . . To them we owe the *Alien Law* which has set aside trial by jury; has stopped the useful influx of Republican Men and Industry and Money. The leaders of this party are professed admirers of the British constitution . . . They are no friends to universal suffrage . . . To this party we are indebted for all our late taxes . . . for a Standing Army, an extensive Navy, and a strong tendency to premature hostility with the earliest friend of Republican America . . . Of this party, *James Ross* is the favoured Candidate . . .   C.

Our lawyer and friend Thomas Cooper wrote this morning's address "To the Electors of Northumberland County."[1854]

TUESDAY, SEPTEMBER 17, 1799

GENERAL   ★ AURORA ★   ADVERTISER

BRITISH INFLUENCE. (DISSIPATING).

While the despots of Europe are openly and declaredly engaging in a war . . . to destroy every vestige of *republican government*, it is satisfactory to a republican American to witness the revival of the national principles and spirit, and the dissipation of the most astonishing delusion that ever blinded a free and virtuous people.—From one end of the continent to the other, a reviving spirit of freedom and love of self government is visible—few can possess more certain or more general evidences of the fact than the editor of a public newspaper.

On no occasion perhaps since the bold animation which blazed forth in 1775 and which continued to pervade America to the close of 1783 has this generous, this necessary passion to save the national liberties and honor been more strongly manifested than they are now every day . . .

In our particular state . . . the exclamation from one end of Pennsylvania to the other is—*"Our eyes are opened"*—

Pursuant to public notice, about 350 Republican Citizens, chiefly from the upper part of Bucks County, met . . . *Resolved,* That . . . we will . . .

promote [Thomas M'Kean] . . . to the office of Governor of this Commonwealth . . .

Something very important is happening in Pennsylvania!

FRIDAY, SEPTEMBER 20, 1799

GENERAL   ★ AURORA ★   ADVERTISER

[T]he cause of France is the cause of liberty and man . . .

Today, U.S. Secretary of State Timothy Pickering instructs the U.S. district attorney for Pennsylvania to pursue the *Aurora*:

> *Besides the newspapers on which the prosecution of the Aurora has been commenced, I have [handed] you several others . . . If you find anything . . . which you think it proper . . . [illegible] on which he [can be] prosecuted . . .* [1855]

SATURDAY, SEPTEMBER 21, 1799

GENERAL   ★ AURORA ★   ADVERTISER

THE RETURNING SENSE OF THE COUNTRY . . .

Two years—nay eighteen months ago—so extravagant was the change that had taken place in public sentiment that it became almost dangerous for a *republican citizen* to acknowledge himself a *republican*, much less to maintain the principles of *equal liberty* and the *rights of mankind* upon which the governments we live under are established ! . . .

This national infatuation is broken—the satellites of Britain see it with mingled dismay and despair—their countenances and their conduct betray them—and the free American countenance once more wears the softened lineaments of the independent and benevolent republican . . .

This change of public sentiment now so powerfully operating throughout the union has been produced by a variety of causes. But there is one cause which we shall place above all others, and therefore first—This change has been effected.

1. By a *press* retaining its constitutional freedom, in spite of open threats, of frequent danger, of the persecutions of power, unconstitutional laws, and the efforts of private intrigue and corruption . . .

It is now but a few days more than a year since public calamity deprived his country and the cause of virtue of *Benjamin Franklin Bache*,—that inflexible man, that man worthy of his *name*—who, when nearly a majority of our fellows citizens, influenced by the error of great names, laid the national honor at the foot of that nation we had defeated in arms, stood steadfast at the post of danger and public trust.

To that man's labours and virtue do the people of America in a vast

693

measure owe their present rescue from ruin—it was he who stood almost alone—assailed by every species of slander and calumny—aspersed by the hired agents of Britain—and persecuted by the government of his native land—the government of that land which his immortal grandfather, *more than any other man*, had contributed to render glorious, independent, and free. It was he that dared brave all the menaces of assassination—the assaults of faction—and the oppression of irritated but perverted authority . . .

It requires not argument to prove that the *Aurora*, in the hands of *Benjamin Franklin Bache*, was the most formidable check upon ambition and false policy which this nation has possessed for five years past . . .

When we attribute this degree of honorable consequence to the memory of him, the memory of whose virtues and whose worth must long survive him; let it not be presumed that we wish to confer a stigma on *the few* prints which laudably stood true to those principles; or which are now returning back with credit to them; and when the pre-eminence is claimed for *the Aurora* as a tribute due to the superior talents of the late editor, the integrity of a *Greenleaf* [of the New York *Argus*] and an *Adams* [of Boston's republican *Independent Chronicle*], are not meant to be depreciated—to them all the honor that is due to the steadfast virtue, industry, and love of freedom belongs.

At a period not very remote, the United States could scarcely boast of *six* public papers out of nearly two hundred, which maintained the principles of 1776.

The *Argus* at New-York, edited by a citizen of the most determined zeal, was certainly the second in the union; though weakly supported by patronage and much harassed by foreign faction—and in the hands of its present editor holds a high character.

The *Chronicle* of Boston, conducted by a man of genuine virtue, was more conspicuous for the able productions of correspondents than for any proceeding from its own sources . . .

The *Farmer's Weekly Museum*, a weekly paper, conducted with genius and classical elegance at Walpole, Connecticut.

With a few more *plagiary papers* to the Southward, these were all the papers which dared to maintain the principles of *equal liberty* and the *sovereignty of the people* for a considerable length of time, in conjunction with the *Aurora*.

Efforts were made during the lifetime of the late editor to crush the *Aurora*, and efforts have been more recently made which shall be exposed in due time—both have proved fruitless.

The present editor of the *Aurora* knows that had the *Aurora* fallen, the *Argus* must have followed it. The effort to destroy the republican character of the *Chronicle* succeeded; the feeble old man of virtue was imprisoned and his poor heart broke . . . The *Farmer's Weekly Museum* has been changed from its republican character to the most violent advocation of monarchy . . .

The *Aurora*, amidst all changes and vicissitudes of politics and power, has remained unchanged—and has seen from the dreary prospect which surrounded it since arise a galaxy of republican prints, which, unawed by power and devoted to the republican constitutions of these states, diffuse knowledge and truth into all corners of the Union. Among these stand in pre-eminence—The *Albany Register;* the *Examiner* at Richmond, Virginia, the *American* at Baltimore; the *Bee* at New London, Connecticut; the *Herald of Liberty* at Washington, Pennsylvania; the *Epitome of the Times* at Norfolk, Virginia; the *Farmer's Register* at Greensburg, Pennsylvania; and about thirty others whose principles are known but whose rank for original writings is not yet established.

Such is the encreasing state of the republican presses in the Union. And to the constancy of the late Editor, and the force of the truths which he has published, do we attribute the salvation of the Press, the destruction of which we are decidedly of opinion was intended by the late odious law—a law for the repeal of which the public voice is prepared to cry aloud in the ears of their mistaken and deluded servants . . .

Today, at New London, Connecticut, a federal marshal arrests Charles Holt, publisher of Connecticut's only Republican newspaper, the New London *Bee.* The federal indictment charges the *Bee* with defaming the President of the United States and with impeding army recruitment by criticism of the new standing army. Charles Holt is brought before the U.S. Circuit Court at Hartford. Trial is set for April.[1856]

MONDAY, SEPTEMBER 23, 1799

GENERAL ★ AURORA ★ ADVERTISER

NOTICE IS HEREBY GIVEN TO THE FREEMEN
Of the City and County of Philadelphia..
That on Tuesday, the 8th day of October next, being the day of the General Election, are to be elected, viz . . .
Six representatives of the said City in the House of Representatives of . . . Pennsylvania.
One Governor of the State of Pennsylvania . . .
The Freemen . . . of Philadelphia are to hold their election at the State House in the said city. The election is to be opened between the hours of ten o'clock in the forenoon and one in the afternoon . . .
JONATHAN PENROSE, *Sheriff.*

Tonight, in the *Gazette of the United States:*

APPROACHING ELECTION . . .
To The Electors of Pennsylvania.
SINCE my last number, I have observed in the *Aurora* some further charges against Mr. Ross . . . Mr. Ross is charged with acting under a

695

foreign influence . . . [I]f to have sanctioned the plans of Mr. Washington, Mr. Adams and the most illustrious patriots in America . . . be a proof of his exclusive attachment to his country, no man less deserves the stigma attempted to be affixed by this abominable slander . . .

FEDERALISTS, You now stand behind the last dyke of your happiness, constitution, and laws . . . Victory finally completes your triumph, defeat plunges you into endless and irretrievable ruin. Let each individual then act as tho' the success of the election depended on his individual exertion; let him unite all the alacrity of hope, with all the energy of despair . . . [T]hen the glorious reward of victory certainly will be yours. MILO

FRIDAY, SEPTEMBER 27, 1799

GENERAL ★ AURORA ★ ADVERTISER

ALIEN. I don't trouble myself much about [the election]—

CITIZEN . . . ha'nt you been here fourteen years?

ALIEN. Yes, I have, but what of that ?

CITIZEN. What of that, . . . don't you live among us?—You have a family, and you know what is good . . .

AL[IEN]. Yes, I know that, but as I am an alien, I have no right to speak of what I think good—If I do, you know, I may be suspected—and so informed against, and next sent out of the country to the ruin of my little family.

CIT[IZEN]. You need not be a morsel afraid—Our President (God bless him) is a *very good* and a *very merciful man*—You are safe enough.

ALIEN. I expect I am—for let me tell you, I wish so to act as never to put myself in the power of a man who could sign any law that abolishes the trial by jury.

CIT[IZEN]. Aye, aye, I see how the land lies, you are a democrat.

ALIEN . . . I don't well understand the term.

CIT[IZEN]. A democrat is a leveller, a destroyer of all order, a lover of the French, who wish to overthrow all order sacred and human—A democrat delights in blood, murder, and rapine—& denies the being of both God and the devil.

ALIEN. God bless me—then I am no democrat; but in the name of common sense, who told you that a democrat is such a being?

CIT[IZEN]. Why Peter Porcupine—Fenno . . . [T]hese are men whom you will not find often mistaken. They are good federalists.

ALIEN. Yes, so I suppose—for you I think should know that Porcupine vilifies your constitution . . . and glories in being a British subject. Fenno says a republican government is the highest note in the gamut of nonsense . . .

CIT[IZEN]. Hoite-toite—what have I got here—I protest if any body should have told me—I would not have believed it—I find, by your way of talking, that Duane is your favourite and—you are a M'Keanite.

ALIEN. I told you before I don't trouble myself about such matters . . .

CIT[IZEN] . . . James Ross is a good man . . .

ALIEN. No never—remember he advocated the British treaty . . . the Alien and Sedition laws which he also supported, call loudly on every foreigner to oppose his election . . . His warmness on the bill for a standing army . . .

Tonight, in the *Gazette of the United States*:

"THE AURORA," a few days past, presented to its readers a calculation of the approaching election, rendering a majority of between 4000 and 5000 votes in favor of its patron *M'Kean* . . . Only change the state of the votes . . . from what Duane predicts to what it is well known . . . and the majority declares for *Mr. Ross.*

Tonight, in the *Porcupine's Gazette*:

[E]very under-working engine is put in motion to prepossess the people of the United States against the . . . [British] government . . . [T]hey are employed by the Democratic faction, they come forth from the *Aurora* and other French presses; from the same vile, slanderous, and infamous presses which have frequently proposed to make Mr. Adams . . . vacate his seat as President and go home about his business.

It is said that the New Envoys to France are not to depart, as yet. Probably the late news from Europe has induced the President to give up the idea of sending them. It is very certain that he will do what he looks upon as most conducive to the interests of his country, and I think he must, by this time, be fully persuaded that interest is not to be advanced by sending these Envoys to France.

FRIDAY, OCTOBER 4, 1799

GENERAL ★ AURORA ★ ADVERTISER

Mr. Holt, Editor and proprietor of the [New London] *Bee*, a republican paper in Connecticut, is summoned before the district court to answer for a publication upon the recruiting service. Sympathy for the unexperienced youths who were adventuring into war contrary to the inclination of parents and friends . . . dictated that production . . .

In a state where an aristocracy and clergy are confederated . . . Mr. Holt has held a post of danger and maintained it with honour . . . [M]odest, sensible, and unassuming, he has hitherto escaped the vengeance of advocates for war, for a limited monarchy, a separation of the State into two governments, a religious establishment, an army to subjugate Virginians and Kentuckyans and destroy republicans . . . [T]he Editor of the *Bee* has stood alone in the defence of his countrymen and neighbors . . .

Tonight, in the *Porcupine's Gazette*:

Mr. M'Kean's committee say . . . that in truth there does not exist a firmer advocate, a more successful supporter of law, of public tranquillity, of private property, and public credit. How far his conduct respecting the disturbance that took place on Sunday the tenth of February last, in the yard of St. Mary's Church in Philadelphia, corresponds with these assertions of his committee we submit to the public . . . Mr. M'Kean would hearken to nothing from the Mayor . . . and charged the members of the Congregation with having committed an assault on the prisoners and said "that they and not the prisoners were the aggressors, that he would have dismissed the matter in quarter of an hour, for the prisoners had the right to take up their hats and go about their business." . . .

SATURDAY, OCTOBER 5, 1799

GENERAL ★ AURORA ★ ADVERTISER

GENERAL ELECTION.

WHEREAS the Governor of the Commonwealth has . . . deemed it expedient, on the representation of the College of Physicians of Philadelphia, to change the place . . . for holding the election . . . [to] the Centre House Tavern, situated on the south side of High street, commonly called Market street . . . Public notice is therefore hereby given . . .

Tonight, in the *Gazette of the United States*:

FEDERALISTS! *Attend to the disposal of your Tickets !* The Editor of the *Aurora,* being lately in company with a gentleman whom he supposed coincided with him in politics, began to boast of their success in electioneering and, clapping his hand on the gentleman's knee, exultingly exclaimed *"Damme we are tricking them."* The gentlemen enquired in what manner. Why, replied he, one of their committee had just sent me two quires of their tickets sealed up, which he informed me were at my disposal . . .

BOSTON [MASSACHUSETTS]—*Russel's Gazette.* The electioneering business for Governor in Pennsylvania continues to be the principal subject of newspaper discussion. On the 8th of [this] month, the trial will be held whether the state [of Pennsylvania] is to be blessed with the solid talents and abilities of a rational Federalist or be cursed with the visionary and absurd politics of a Jacobin.

Massachusetts and the rest of the nation are watching the Pennsylvania gubernatorial election. Republicans view Pennsylvania as *the keystone in the democratic arch.*[1857]

SUNDAY, OCTOBER 6, 1799

Today, U.S. Attorney General Charles Lee offers some advice to John Adams:

> *Hoping it will not be deemed improper in me to give my opinion,
> before it is asked, relative to the suspension of the mission to France
> . . . Such a measure would exceedingly disappoint the general expecta-
> tion of America, and, exciting the jealousy and suspicion of many con-
> cerning your sincerity in makng the nomination, would afford your
> enemies an opportunity of indulging their evil dispositions . . .*[1858]

MONDAY, OCTOBER 7, 1799

GENERAL ★ AURORA ★ ADVERTISER

Some complaints have been made that the Editor has not published
enough of the later news from Europe . . .

The Pennsylvania Election has excited the liveliest interest in every
part of the Union and in truth must decide materially on the sentiments
of the people—whether they are willing to be a republic or become monarchists. We have therefore given a preference to what concerned the
election . . .

Today, at the U.S. Circuit Court in Rutland, Vermont, a Sedition Act indictment
is handed down against Anthony Haswell, publisher of Vermont's leading Republican newspaper, the *Vermont Gazette* in Bennington, for reprinting part of
a *Philadelphia Aurora* article on "British Influence" that charged President
Adams with choosing government workers on the basis of their political ideology. The indictment also cites the *Vermont Gazette* for carrying a lottery
advertisement in January to pay Vermont Republican Congressman Matthew
Lyon's fine. Anthony Haswell's trial will likewise be held in April.[1859]

TUESDAY, OCTOBER 8, 1799

GENERAL ★ AURORA ★ ADVERTISER

ELECTION.
TO THE ELECTORS OF PENNSYLVANIA . . .
Take Advice!

1. LOOK WELL TO YOUR
TICKETS.

2. LOOK WELL TO YOUR
BOXES.

3. LOOK WELL TO YOUR
TALLIES.

4. LOOK WELL TO YOUR
RETURNS.

Now or Never.

Tonight, in the *Gazette of the United States*:

Mr. M'Kean's committee endeavor to palliate his conduct at the Mayor's after the disturbance in St. Mary's church yard, by asserting "1st. That the city and its neighborhood has been much disturbed with the feuds and riots of intemperate party men. 2d. That the streets were crowded with people, and that the report was officially made to the chief justice that the prisoners were paraded hand-cuffed through the city." . . .

Mr. M'Kean did not take the time fairly "to understand the facts," for the moment he entered the Mayor's house . . . he most violently attacked and insultingly abused that magistrate . . .

WEDNESDAY, OCTOBER 9, 1799

GENERAL ★ AURORA ★ ADVERTISER

RETURN OF THE VOTES . . .	GOVERNOR . . .	
	M'KEAN	ROSS
Philadelphia City	1277	1708
Northern Liberties	999	292
Southwark	595	217
Germantown	518	278
Chester	153	216
Darby	155	229
Concord	69	315
Newtown	57	350
Oxford, &c.	259	304
	4082	3910

The federal party are so much alarmed at the idea of M'Kean being chosen Governor that they are apprehensive of success . . . next year . . . It is meditated, in the event of any splitting of the *eastern* and *southern* federal interests on the candidate for the next presidency, to seduce General Washington to offer himself again—

What will John Adams think of this? He arrives at Trenton today.[1860] The results are ominous for the Federalists, and the votes from the outlying counties (which protested Adams' war-taxes and suffered his army's retaliation) aren't in yet!

Tonight, in the *Gazette of the United States*:

Jedediah Peck, of Burlington, Otsego co[unty], State of New York, an influential Jacobin has been arrested under the sedition law.

GENERAL ★ AURORA ★ ADVERTISER

The Editor being under legal obligation to attend the federal district court to be held by adjournment at Norristown, Montgomery county, THIS DAY—it is hoped that a liberal indulgence will be made for any want that may possibly attend the usual quantity and quality of original matter, through the necessary *engagements of the Editor with the Lawyers.*

Since the passage of the sedition bill, a representative in congress has been fined and imprisoned in jail, where he was treated with the utmost indignity and tyranny, for animadverting on the conduct of the President . . . A number of prosecutions have also instituted against the republican printers . . . Another printer, in order to obtain presidential pardon, was obliged to transport himself from America . . .

Is the President the *ne plus ultra* of perfection ? can he never err, and will that office be always filled by infallible men ? Every person must answer no !

Today, I appear at the Pennsylvania Federal District Court which has convened at Norristown, Pennsylvania, to avoid Philadelphia's yellow fever. Judge Richard Peters is present, but Justice Bushrod Washington (George Washington's nephew) has yet to arrive. I must return on Monday.

Today, in the *Porcupine's Gazette*:

Nothing certain can be said as to the result of the election for Governor, but, as far as I can guess, from what I have heard, "THE DEMOCRATICK JUDGE" is destined to make Pennsylvanians feel all the abundant blessings resulting from the "Glorious Revolution" of 1775.

"OUR ENVOYS" . . . we have the pleasure to know . . . are still in this country.

SATURDAY, OCTOBER 12, 1799

GENERAL ★ AURORA ★ ADVERTISER

Summary of returns for Governor.
PHILADELPHIA CITY AND COUNTY.

	Ross.	M'Kean.
City District	1708	1277
N. Liberties do.	292	999
Southwark do.	217	397
Germantown do.	278	513
Busseltown do.	305	259
	2800	3649

Maj. in Philadelphia City and County for M'Kean 849.

DELAWARE COUNTY.

	Ross.	M'Kean.
Chester District.	261	150
Darby do.	229	155
Concord do.	315	69
Newton do.	350	57
	1155	431

Maj. in Delaware County for Mr. Ross, 734
Maj. in the City and the above 3 counties for Mr. M'Kean 125.

We are informed that Mr. M'Kean has a majority in the county of Berks of 3436 and in Montgomery County of 435. It is said that Mr. Ross has a majority in the county of Bucks of 117, and that in every other case, the Republican ticket has succeeded.

The *disconsolate* appearance of the Rossites on Wednesday induced a republican barber at a village in Bucks to set up a sign immediately on the close of the pole for Governor, with the following inscription:
Whigs shaved as usual for three cents.
Tories, owing to the encreased length of their faces, *double price*.

Men MAY be conquered—But Principles CANNOT.
BE it remembered that Luther Baldwin has been prosecuted and fined 150 dollars costs and expences, 250 for speaking seditious words, in the whole 400 dols . . .
Sometime in June 1798, President Adams was passing through this town . . . Luther, a little merry, [said] he did not care if they fired [a shot] through his a— . . . For this he has fallen a sacrifice . . .

In the election which has elevated Thomas McKean to the governorship of Pennsylvania, twice as many Pennsylvanians voted as in any previous Pennsylvania gubernatorial election. Republicans won 38,036 of 70,706 votes cast, a margin of 5,393. Majorities of 2,602 in Northampton County (where John Fries led the war tax protest) and of 3,363 in Berks County (where the federal army abused Reading's citizens and whipped *Reading Eagle* publisher Jacob Schnyder) gave Thomas McKean his winning margin.[1861] It is clear to everyone that John Adams' French war has put his political future at risk.[1862]

MONDAY, OCTOBER 14, 1799

GENERAL ★ AURORA ★ ADVERTISER

The Federal District Court held by adjournment at Norristown was opened on Friday by *Judge Peters;* the absence of *Judge Washington* prevented the Court from proceeding to business . . .

Today, the Federal District Court at Norristown doesn't open until three and then adjourns till tomorrow morning. I must come back again tomorrow.[1863]

TUESDAY, OCTOBER 15, 1799

GENERAL   ★ AURORA ★   ADVERTISER

The Establishment of the *Aurora* will be removed to Philadelphia on Saturday evening next, and the paper published there on the Monday following as usual.

[I]t is a general complaint now with the friends of *high* and *harsh* measures that the contest [for governor] has been decided by a coalition of the *German* and *Irish* interests . . . Those who applaud the acts by which hatred and disaffection have been fomented by the *religion of Christ* in Ireland for 200 years past, do not disagree with themselves in deploring that two numerous descriptions of the American population [the Germans and the Irish] should . . . discard prejudices which have been fostered to their common injury and common discredit.

Today, I return to Norristown, Pennsylvania, where Alexander James Dallas (my lawyer) and I face Judge Richard Peters and U.S. Supreme Court Justice Bushrod Washington (who has finally arrived) in a crowded courtroom. Though I won't publish the story for more than a year, I record (for future publication) what occurs:

[T]he Editor was compelled, at an heavy expence, to travel back and forward to attend the federal court at Norristown on an indictment laid and found for asserting [he had proof in the form of a letter] that Mr. Adams had asserted that British influence had been employed. [T]he Court expressed doubts as to the existence of such a letter. The Editor offered to go instantly to trial upon that issue, and an authenticated copy of the letter was at hand. The Court and the District Attorney were, for a moment, struck with astonishment, and a large concourse of people, assembled to see the Editor of the Aurora hauled over the coals of the sedition ordeal, expressed their feelings by a sudden but impressive emotion of surprize and conviction. Judge Washington relieved the District Attorney from his embarrassment by stating a legal difficulty in the form of a doubt whether Mr. Adams's letter, though produced, would be legal evidence; that if it were procured in evidence against Mr. Adams himself, it might possibly be admitted. Mr. Dallas, on the part of the Editor, [observed] that, as the sedition law admitted truth as a justification, the letter could not be refused. That all the Editor had asserted was that "Mr. Adams had asserted that British influence had been exercised," and the authentication of the letter and the expression in it was the proof of the truth. Some of that strange finesse which derogates so much from the

703

dignity of the bench of justice was then played off, and the trial was postponed as a matter of great favor to the Editor. Judge Peters who sat with Judge Washington on that occasion, learning from a person in court that the Editor meant to publish the indictment and proceedings, called upon the Editor in open court and recommended to him not to publish it, or he should be obliged to take notice of it. This proceeding, unprecedented in the annals of jurisprudence, impressed the Editor more deeply with the seriousness of the case. Soon afterwards he learnt that the indictment was withdrawn altogether.[1864]

My letter proving that John Adams saw British influence in the Washington administration would embarrass not only Adams but also Washington. The threat to release the letter produces a stand-off![1865]

Tonight, in the *Gazette of the United States*:

The PRESIDENT of the United States arrived at Trenton from Quincy on Wednesday last. It is expected he will remain there until the meeting of Congress.

Same day arrived at Trenton, Major General Hamilton, from New York . . .

Chief Justice Ellsworth and Governor Davie [two of the three proposed envoys to France] are also at Trenton.

FRIDAY, OCTOBER 18, 1799

GENERAL ★ AURORA ★ ADVERTISER

The republicans of Pennsylvania in general may consider the present election as a very fortunate opportunity to test their principles . . . At a moment when the enemies of republicanism counted high on the prospect of destroying it in Europe *(only as a prelude to destroying it here)*, the citizens of Pennsylvania have stood up like men, and by chusing a man of '76, declared that—a *republic means something* . . . [T]his state has declared its principles, and the Sister States have always respected the opinion of the Pennsylvanians.

It is said that matters of great pith and moment are shortly to engage the heads of the nation now in Trenton;—the most important of which [is] probably the question respecting the sailing of the ministers to the French republic . . .

On Saturday evening the 31st ult., the editor [of the New London, Connecticut *Bee*] was arrested by major Simon Clark, deputy marshal of the United States for the county of Hartford on an indictment for printing and publishing the *Bee* on May 8th last, which is said to contain sedition against the government of the United States. On the day following (Sunday), he was taken to Hartford and lodged in common prison; but on Monday, on his appearance before the Circuit Court, bail was taken . . . [T]rial postponed until . . . the 13th of April next . . .

War . . . Today, off Guadeloupe in the French West Indies, the U.S. Navy's brig *Pickering* does battle with a French privateer. From a report:

> [A] battle was fought between the United States brig Pickering, of 14 guns, four pounders and 70 men, and the French privateer schooner L'Egypte Conquise, of 18 guns, 14 nines, and 4 sixes, and 250 men; in which after an engagement which lasted nine hours, the Frenchman struck and was carried into St. Kitts . . . [N]ot being able to stand the fire of American cannon, she was obliged to strike to a force not much more than one third her equal in number.[1866]

SATURDAY, OCTOBER 19, 1799

GENERAL　　★ AURORA ★　　ADVERTISER

Reports have been circulated . . . that the President of the United States had proposed to resign . . .

We did not believe he had resigned or meant to resign, because . . . he is morally and politically bound to . . . oppose those *measures of war* which . . . men under *British influence* would provoke him, if possible to enter upon . . .

The mission [to France] has been temporarily suspended. *Alexander Hamilton* wishes it to be suspended for ever . . . [W]e believe the President will be obstinate on this occasion to save his country from war and his own *reputation* . . .

Tonight, in the *Porcupine's Gazette,* Peter Porcupine has some election talk that is sure to upset the President:

> The president of the United States is arrived at Trenton in New Jersey, where are at this time assembled all the principal officers of the federal government, civil and military. It has been whispered about that the president has signaled his intention of *resigning* as soon as congress meets; but, from what I have been able to learn, the report seems to be unfounded . . .
>
> The election of my *Democratick Judge* as Governor of Pennsylvania, undeniably the most influential state in the union, has, in my opinion *decided* the fate of what has been called *Federalism* . . . It has uniformly been my opinion that M'Kean would succeed, and I have as uniformly asserted that his success would be a sort of onset in a struggle which will terminate in the complete triumph of Democracy. I mean a *pure* (perhaps it should be *impure)* Democracy; not a Democracy that allows a man to make his underlings put *"honourable"* before his name and *"Esquire"*

after it; but a real Democracy, an *equality* Democracy, where sans-culotte slovens shall be "citizen each other" 'till the very walls blush at the obscenity . . . I look forward with great confidence to the time when *Duane* and *Callender* shall occupy the space now filled by *Dallas* and *M'Kean* . . .

The Yellow Fever, at Philadelphia, is nearly at an end for this year; people are fast returning into town.

Tonight, in the *Gazette of the United States*:

NORRISTOWN, October 15. In the Circuit Court of the United States, now holding at this place, by the honorable Judge Washington and Peters, two bills of the indictment, under the sedition law, have been presented by the grand inquest against Duane, editor of the *Aurora*.

Mr. Dallas moved a postponement until the next term. Some of the evidences for his client he said were absent . . . besides a number of documents . . . to which he could not have access with safety during the existence of the prevailing fever in Philadelphia . . .

Duane was sworn in proof of the necessity of the evidence alluded to and that he was not ready to proceed to trial.

The decision on this point was not made when the Court adjourned this day.

It being the first day, the Court proceeded to business. Mr. Dallas stated his reasons in support of the motion . . . Mr. Rawle answered; after which Judge Washington declared the opinion of the court that the [other] trials should proceed . . .

The public mind has for a length of time . . . been in an anxious and awful suspence respecting the third mission [to France] which it was contemplated in the beginning of the present year to dispatch to that Republic. Of late, the town has been filled with jarring rumors on this all-important topic . . .

It was hoped that before the final nomination could reach Paris, the [American] capture of the *Insurgent* and other acts of resistance on our part would have so wounded the pride of the Directory as to have produced a declaration of war or at least have effected an irreparable breach; or that, in the interim, his Most Christian Majesty [of Britain] might have trampled his rebellious subject [France] beneath the foot of his throne . . .

The effect of the nomination upon the Federal party . . . was like that of some tremendous tornado . . . Its cause has since undergone a regular declension, the future steps of which daily grow more certain. The election of M'Kean we owe to this sole cause—that of Monroe in Virginia is its most natural offspring—and the success of Jefferson to the Presidential Chair will become an event which no longer can or indeed ought to be opposed.

In the nine months since John Adams nominated new peace commissioners for a mission to France, he has done nothing to cause those commissioners to depart.[1867] Could the election in Pennsylvania make him reconsider? Porcupine's announcement that McKean's election has *"decided the fate of . . . Federalism"* might give pause. Should the mid-Atlantic states (meaning Pennsylvania, New York, and New Jersey) swing Republican next year, the Duke of Braintree will be gone!

TUESDAY, OCTOBER 22, 1799

GENERAL ★ AURORA ★ ADVERTISER

FEDERAL CIRCUIT COURT.

At the federal court held at Norristown on Tuesday last, present *Bushrod Washington* and *Richard Peters,* Esqrs. Judges, an indictment upon an information against the editor of this paper was presented and found by the grand jury, upon a charge at the suit of the United States under the Sedition Law, for publishing certain matters alleged not to be true in the *Aurora* of the 24th of July, and upon which the editor had been held to bail, himself in 2000 dollars and two other citizens in 1000 dollars each.

A second indictment was also presented and found by the grand jury, upon certain matters contained in the *Aurora* of the 3d of August last.

Some very interesting arguments and doctrines of law were given in discussing the question whether a trial should or should not be adjourned to next term . . . The court . . . decided that, in consideration of the mass of business to be transacted at this term, the trial be postponed to the 11th of June next.

Fresh bail was given . . .

The Editor restrains himself, out of respect to the recommendation of the constituted authorities, from giving copies of the indictments or a report of the arguments of the court and counsel—and is satisfied to remain silent on the subject of those charges until they shall be decided upon by due course of law . . .

Tonight, in the *Gazette of the United States*:

We learn from undoubted authority that the envoys to France are to sail on the 5th of November in the frigate *United States,* which now lies at Newport, ready to receive them.

WEDNESDAY, OCTOBER 23, 1799

GENERAL ★ AURORA ★ ADVERTISER

REPUBLICANS OF PENNSYLVANIA
ON THURSDAY NEXT . . .
A FAT OX WILL BE ROASTED
On Zeigler's plains, Spring Garden
in honor of our well beloved Governor,
ELECT, THOMAS M'KEAN . . .

James Monroe, it is supposed, will be the next governor of Virginia.

It is said at Trenton that the President of the United States has passed the *Rubicon*—he has directed the departure of the Envoys for Europe— and removed [from Trenton, New Jersey] to the Pennsylvania side of the Delaware to reside.

Today, U.S. District Court Court Judge Richard Peters, who presided with Judge Bushrod Washington at my trial at Norristown, writes Secretary of State Timothy Pickering:

> We returned from Norristown yesterday after the blowing up of the Court. We are all too much chagrined to say much about the Circumstances or the Consequences . . . We do not say anything about the true Reason of our breaking up. We assigned as a Reason that we had discovered, since the last adjournment, an Error in the Proceedings . . . I bound over the Defendants—Duane & 2 or 3 more . . . We think it will be absolutely necessary to hold a special Court sometime in January. But we dared not order it . . . [1868]

Neither John Adams nor George Washington wants Adams' admission of British influence in the Washington administration to become public. There will be no further court proceedings on that issue![1869] Peter Porcupine knows:

> [T]he culprit appeared before the Court at Norristown. There Mr. A[dams]'s letter was not produced, but Dallas mentioned it as part of the evidence in favour of his client, and he even showed the letter to several persons.—The trial was postponed, and there is, I think, every reason to believe that it will never come on . . . [I]t was not, therefore, necessary to say the worst at once. Duane, Coxe, Dallas &c. have kept back the rest of the letter as a rod over the old man's back. [1870]

Tonight, in the *Gazette of the United States*:

> The District Court, lately sitting at Norristown, is adjourned, all its proceedings having been nullified by the discovery of a flaw in the notification of the removal of the court [from Philadelphia to Norristown].

THURSDAY, OCTOBER 24, 1799

GENERAL ★ AURORA ★ ADVERTISER

By a Gentleman from Vermont, we learn that Col. *Matthew Lyon*, *Anthony Haswell*, Editor of the Vermont Gazette, and *Judah P. Spooner*, Printer at Fairhaven, have been indicted for Sedition before the Circuit Court for the District of Vermont.—(*Northern Budget.*).

Tonight, in the *Gazette of the United States*:

> [T]he present is an awful and pressing hour . . . An ancient and dangerous sedition, suppressed for a season . . . is about to revive, stronger from its temporary depression. An event has just occurred to consummate its highest temporary aims; and the ground is laid out on which it is again to advance with erect and towering head.

The Departments of [the federal] Government now at Trenton are occupied in preparations for returning to the City [of Philadelphia].

FRIDAY, OCTOBER 25, 1799

GENERAL ★ AURORA ★ ADVERTISER

The federal Circuit Court recently held at Norristown by adjournment is, we understand, dissolved. An evening paper of yesterday says in consequence of a *flaw* in the proceeding of adjournment ! We cannot believe this to be true because we heard Mr. Dallas argue that the holding of the court was not conformable to law, and he was overruled. We rather suspect that the recent *jarrings* in a certain town in *Jersey* have indicated the wisdom of postponing discussions which might operate politically on an approaching election—*look out in time republicans !*

Yesterday was displayed in this city a *Jubilee* recently very rare in its object—It was the triumph of the principles of republicanism . . . [R]epublicans assembled in Zeigler's plain in the Northern Liberties part of this city on Wednesday evening . . . A fine fat steer was, in ancient order, immolated on the altar of American liberty beneath the flag of America surmounted by the classical emblems of liberty and peace—the cap and wreath of laurel and palm . . .

Libations of red and white wines were poured out on the altar . . . At noon two *British twelve pounders* whose muzzles had ere muttered destruction in the ears of the free sons of America were heard to bellow forth triumph . . . Guns were fired in honor of each of the several counties which have displayed republican majorities in the recent election . . . The evening exhibited indeed a Jubilee . . . the citizens without arms but with colours, music, and wands, paraded the ground of festivity, and the night ushered in the morning with songs of 1776 and joy.

SATURDAY, OCTOBER 26, 1799

GENERAL ★ AURORA ★ ADVERTISER

The festivity and rejoicings held in consequence of the election of THOMAS M'KEAN had not ceased on Friday morning. Processions of citizens with lighted tapers accompanied by music continued through the streets the whole night. Several parties with instrumental music serenaded popular characters.

It was asked how it came that a concourse of at least ten thousand democrats should assemble and be merry and that all should return home peaceably and cheerfully—without a single shot, quarrel, or dispute?—It was answered *"Because there were no TORIES there to stir up dissention."*

The serenading parties visited among other places on Thursday night the house of the chief justice (he is at present on public duty in Bucks County)—the houses of the several members of the republican committee—The *Aurora* office—and [outgoing] Governor Mifflin's.

The Republicans did not, in their serenades, pay a single visit to Mr. Wharton, the Mayor . . .

It appears that the friends of Mr. *Ross* were so confident of his election that, after the close of the poll at Pittsburg, they carried him in triumph through that town . . . Five hundred soldiers of the standing army, we are told, were introduced at Pittsburg and voted for Mr. *Ross*—by *divine right* for they had no other.

Poor Fenno ! Alas *Poor Fenno !* . . . what a reproof !

Fenno in a fit of raving a few days ago—very solemnly declared that the people should now resolve to think of *Thomas Jefferson* for President at the next election—what a precious confession !

Today, at Mount Vernon, George Washington writes William Vans Murray:

A severe Electioneering contest has just closed in the state of Pennsylvania; adverse to the fortunes of the Federal Party by a considerable majority in favour of Chief Justice McKean ag[ains]t Mr. Ross, Senator for that state. Great pains was taken on both sides, and considerable abuse of character on one . . .

I most devoutly wish that the cogent, indeed unanswerable arguments you urged to dissuade our friend [the Marquis de Lafayette] from visiting the United States . . . may have prevailed. The measure would be injudicious . . . Embarrassing to himself; Embarrassing to his friends, and possibly embarrassing to the Government . . .[1871]

Extract of a letter . . . I understand that the trial of Mr. Duane on two indictments will commence at Norristown . . . They cannot *imprison his intellects,* tho' they may imprison his body.   [New York] *Argus.*

MR. EDITOR, I send you the following particulars of the proceedings of a court of the United States held lately at Norristown . . .

On Friday the 18th, after doing little business, the court adjourned till Monday, when it did not meet till three in the afternoon, and met but instantly to adjourn to the next morning ! [John] Fries' trial was announced and expected then to proceed, but then the court met only to bind over the witnesses and prisoners . . . to appear at the next circuit court in Philadelphia.

Thus, sir, an anxious multitude of jurors, witnesses, and citizens, waited a session of twelve days to see, to hear, and to do nothing more. The reasons for this extraordinary adjournment remains an impenetrable secret, excepting with the judges &c . . .   SPECTATOR

Today, Abigail Adams writes the President's secretary, William Shaw:

> *The State of Pennsylvania is a strange medly. I regret that any*
> *of my family should have a prevailing attachment to it. [T]heir*
> *late Election has withered all the laurels they ever had to boast of . . .*
> *Send me some newspapers—even tho it be peter's [Cobbett's] impu-*
> *dence . . .*[1872]

TUESDAY, OCTOBER 29, 1799

GENERAL ★ AURORA ★ ADVERTISER

We are informed . . . [t]hat one Beelems, a storekeeper in Pittsburg, who acts as Jackal to the Junto of Rossites at that place, went to the barracks on the day of their election for inspectors and brought a number of soldiers therefrom whom he caused to poll on said occasion.

Today, Thomas Jefferson writes a friend,

> *The success of McKean's election is a subject of real congratulation*
> *& hope . . .*[1873]

Tonight, in the *Gazette of the United States*:

Mr. M'Kean's election has been announced in a very apt, emblematic stile, by a Bloody Feast and terrific Fire-Works; for, if I am not mistaken, such a fire has been lighted up in Pennsylvania as will consume the Federal Union . . .

GENERAL ★ AURORA ★ ADVERTISER

This day, commencing the Second Year of the present Editor's responsibility;—in the publication of this Paper, the only assurance he will make of his future exertions is that they shall not at *least* be inferior to the past—

Tonight, in the *Gazette of the United States*:

A sagacious newsmonger to the Eastward says "the Election for Governor of Pennsylvania seems to excite very general *sympathy.*"

TUESDAY, NOVEMBER 5, 1799

GENERAL ★ AURORA ★ ADVERTISER

It is a painful and *impressive* truth . . . that those gazettes which the English here have established and many officers of the general government have contributed to support and employ even now perseveringly continue their "offensive alliance" against the *Governor elect.* Can Britain ever expect a favorable temper in this state, while printers, connected as *Cobbett* and *Fenno* are *known* to be, pursue, as a daily occupation, the vilest abuse of the man of our choice . . . If rash Englishmen will suffer a *mad youth* and *un-principled emissary (like Fenno and Cobbett)* to ruin their concerns, let their public agents here answer for the consequences beyond the Atlantic . . . Pennsylvania will . . . not suffer our elective constitutions to be wounded, through the sides of her Chief Magistrate, by the hired or emissary printers of a foreign monarchy.

Tonight, in the *Gazette of the United States*:

One of the public papers by the last mail says that the whispers which have been circulated of the president's intention to resign at the next meeting of congress are unfounded.

WEDNESDAY, NOVEMBER 6, 1799

GENERAL ★ AURORA ★ ADVERTISER

The *Gazette of the United States* wantonly attacks the Pennsylvania government of our choice by publishing that Mr. M'Kean's administration had commenced with a *bloody feast* and *fiery acts* because a number of citizens had roasted an ox, and others had displayed an elegant fire-work . . . In a paper of Cobbett's since the election, he attempts to ridicule the man whom Pennsylvania has chosen . . . He treats the election of Mr. M'Kean as a great step towards anarchy, bloodshed and ruin . . .

Today, in New York, Federalist leader Alexander Hamilton writes the state's attorney general, Josiah O. Hoffman:

> SIR, [The New York Argus's country edition] "Greenleaf's New Daily Advertiser" of this morning contains a publication entitled "Extract of a letter from Philadelphia, dated September 20th," which charges me with being at the "bottom" of an "Effort recently made to suppress the Aurora" (a newspaper of that city) by pecuniary means . . .
>
> A bolder calumny; one more absolutely destitute of foundation was never propagated . . .
>
> I therefore request that you will take immediate measures towards the prosecution of the persons who conduct the enclosed paper . . .
>
> A. HAMILTON[1874]

Tonight, in the *Gazette of the United States*:

> *From the Albany Centinel.* The Philadelphia *Aurora* trumpets forth paeans on the election of M'Kean to the office of Chief Magistrate of Pennsylvania . . . [T]he electors of Pennsylvania will probably give again their suffrages for *Jefferson* . . . to mount the Presidential Chair.
>
> ---
>
> The Circuit Court of the United States commenced their session in [Rutland, Vermont] on the Third inst. *Tony* [Haswell], the editor of the Bennington petty vehicle of sedition, and Judah P. Spooner, ci-devant printer to Lyon, were arrested on indictment found against them . . . [Haswell] appeared to contemplate a justification . . . by proving that he was paid for printing the libellous matter. That the seditious clause complained of was in fact no more than an advertisement for Lyon's lottery [to pay Lyon's sedition fine]. If receiving pay for printing sedition could be pleaded in justification, we fancy that not only little Tony but the *Aurora* man and many others, coadjutors and fellow labourers in the Gallic vineyard, might escape the pains and penalties of the law . . . I hope the time is fast approaching in which . . . the din of democracy no longer be heard in our land.

FRIDAY, NOVEMBER 8, 1799

GENERAL ★ AURORA ★ ADVERTISER

REPUBLICAN FESTIVITY.

Friday last was kept as a day of jollity at Pottsgrove, Montgomery County, [Pennsylvania] to celebrate the election of THOMAS M'KEAN . . . The republicans had a feast on the occasion at *George Phieger's* tavern, and after dinner several toasts were drank . . . After these toasts the following volunteers were given.

By Col. J. Heister. The liberty of the press . . . and the freedom of speech . . . [M]ay neither be abridged by despotism or unconstitutional laws . . .

By John Heister, Jr.—The memory of Dr. Franklin—the political Messiah of the western world.

By Major Hartman—The memory of Benjamin Franklin Bache, the man worthy of his name and his country, the modest man with a vast mind.

By Captain Townsend—The editor of the *Aurora*, the man found worthy to be the successor of Franklin and of Bache . . .

At a time [when] a whole people . . . had recognized and proclaimed as the basis and essence of all legislation a moral equality and [when] a democratic republic had been erected on the ruins of the aristocracy and the throne . . . a citizen . . . attempts . . . to revive the dying spark of royalty and bring into fashion the *Gothic order* . . .

The main drift of this work of Mr. Adams, entitled a defence, &c. &c *[of the Constitutions of Government of the United States]* . . . is to establish the superior beauty of a government of three branches affording a mutual balance and which should have an hereditary king and nobility . . . [T]he ruin of ancient commonwealths and Italian republics of the dark ages he boldly ascribes to the want of this balance . . .

It ought to be shewn that the tumults, seditions, insurrections, and wars which agitated and finally subverted all republics had their source in the ignorance of the great mass of mankind; in the insolence, intrigues, power, and tyranny of the Nobles; in the efforts of the people to acquire and share in the government, and in the absence of equality and adequate representation rather than in the want of Mr. Adams' impracticable and visionary balance.   AN AUTHOR

Tonight, in the *Gazette of the United States*:

M'Kean's election to chief magistrate may . . . convince the vain, indolent federalists of this state that they are not equal to their adversaries . . . [I]f they neglect the event . . . it will not be long before they and their country will be oppressed by a brutal democracy. The same votes that lifted M'Kean to the chair of first magistrate may raise a Duane . . . or any other vulgar demagogue to be inferior scourges. We may depend on it . . .

THE REPUBLICAN TRIUMPH,
A NEW SONG
Tune—"*BALLINAMONA*"

1.

Ye true sons of freedom, ye rude swinish throng,
Attend for a while, and I'll give you a song,
It's the triumph of freedom, we now celebrate,
A Republican Governor gain'd for the State.

> Sing Ballinamona, &c.
> *No Governing Tories for me* . . .

12.

Friends of Freedom now since we have gained our cause,
Let's be firm in supporting our country and laws,
But not that curst law of *Sedition* so ill,
If I do then curse me with an *Alien Bill.*

> Sing Ballinamona, &c.
> *No laws of Sedition for me.*

13.

The day of election the Tories regret,
Five Thousand and odds a majority great,
So here's to the health of *Republicans Green,*
And *Republican Blues* and old *Thomas M'Kean.*

> Sing Ballinamona, &c.
> *A Republican Governor for me.*

Today, in the city of New York and by order of the New York state attorney general, widow Greenleaf's foreman at the New York *Argus*, David Frothingham, is arrested for publishing the claim that Alexander Hamilton tried to buy the *Philadelphia Aurora*. Under New York's law of libel, the truth of the claim does not matter. The only issue is whether the claim injures Mr. Hamilton's reputation. David Frothingham is released on bail. His trial will take place on the 21st.[1875]

Tonight, in the *Gazette of the United States*:

> The President of the United States arrived in town last evening from New Jersey. The 2d troop of Volunteer Cavalry met him a few miles from the city and escorted him to his house in Market street.

Where is the *Porcupine's Gazette*? We hear that Cobbett has discontinued his paper![1876]

GENERAL ★ AURORA ★ ADVERTISER

ALEXANDER HAMILTON . . .

This distinguished man of *gallantry* . . . is once more before the public . . .

It is in the public recollection what villainy and slander—what violence and artifices have been set on foot to destroy *"The Aurora,"* before and since the death of the late editor.

It is a fact that, during last spring and summer, repeated efforts were made by several persons, some of whom are known to be *hangers-on* or *dependants*, or *sycophants* of certain political characters, to *"alter the politics"* or to suppress the *Aurora* altogether.

These efforts were treated exactly as they merited . . .

In an eastern paper, there lately appeared a letter, stating that a sum of 6000 dollars had been offered for part purchase of this paper, that it was probable that Alexander Hamilton was at "the bottom of it."

That the sum was offered is a fact which cannot be denied . . . And . . . there is the strongest reason to believe that he did take an active part in certain transactions calculated to destroy this paper . . .

Alexander Hamilton has now commenced a prosecution against Mrs. Greenleaf [of the New York *Argus*] for publishing a suggestion [of this matter]—the heart of this man must be formed of peculiar *stuff.*

GENERAL ★ AURORA ★ ADVERTISER

A number of the Republicans of Lancaster, having subscribed toward an entertainment on the happy event of our late election . . . the entertainment was accordingly provided in front of Mr. Boyd's house on Thursday, the 7th instant . . . An Orchestra was erected . . . The fare consisted of 780 lb of the best beef, two roasters weighing 35 lb, 4 hams weighing 63 lb . . . 125 loaves of bread . . . Two hogheads of excellent beer brewed in the borough, 12 gallons of the best French brandy and 24 gallons of excellent Madeira wine . . . The provisions were put on the table 300 feet in length at half after one o'clock . . . There were seated at the table, at one time, 412 persons . . . The following [17] toasts were drank . . . 1—The Republicans of Pennsylvania and their day of triumph—October 8, '99. 2—The sovereignty of the people . . . 3—Thomas M'Kean . . . 9 cheers . . . 9—Our envoys to the French Republic . . . VOLUNTEERS . . . By Captain Lefevre. The *Aurora*—And the Memory of its founder, Benjamin Franklin Bache.

The snarling Porcupine, it has been reported, intends making New-York the future scene of his venomous scurrility, in consequence of his ill-timed declaration that he would leave Pennsylvania should M'Kean be chosen governor. That assurance, and the hope that he would for once keep his word, very probably had an effect upon the election. To get rid of the monster was the wish of many who were in favor of Mr. Ross. But they considered the election of M'Kean a less[er] evil than the incumbrance with Porcupine. To these may be added those voters who read the papers to learn to estimate the candidates. Porcupine's abuse benefited M'Kean more than Duane's praise. And if this raving beast removes to New-York, busies himself equally at the next election for governor, and repeats there his wonderful "threat," we may expect to find a Livingston in the chair of that state. *MERCURY.*

Our information respecting the Envoys has been perfectly correct. They embarked [for France] on Sunday last from Newport in the frigate *United States,* of 44 guns, commodore Barry.

Alex. Hamilton has been much irritated at the very idea of his being at the bottom of an effort to purchase "The *Aurora*"—as if he never had any dealing with *newspapers!* . . .

Alexander Hamilton's prosecution against the *Argus* . . . The *gallant* inspector possibly supposed that he could *lug in* the *Argus* by terror, as "money could not make the mare go."

To judge Alexander Hamilton . . . it would seem as if he thought the public could forget his *defence* [of his *wenching*]—or . . . That he was the proposer of a monarchical form of government in the federal convention . . .

Tonight, in the *Gazette of the United States*:

A few evenings since, as Mr. Abel Humphreys was returning to his house in Second near Spruce-street, he was overtaken by certain ruffians at a short distance from his door. They called out to him *"who are you for ?"* and not receiving an answer, cried, *"we are for M'Kean:"* Mr. H. then said, *"I am for Ross;"* whereupon he was instantly beset by them all . . .

One of the M'Keanites who attacked Mr. Humphreys proves to be a member of Capt. William Duane's cock necked troops, and the whole three are said to be United Irishmen . . .

GENERAL ⋆ AURORA ⋆ ADVERTISER

"A feather shews how the wind blows," said Doctor Franklin. Fenno, whose foreign friends are jealous of every *American homespun thread,* is very resentful that the Republican Greens use *American game cocks feathers,* dressed and wired here; instead of importing Ostrich feathers from Great Britain brought thither from the British West Indies and dyed, dressed, and wired in London. He seems to have a violent antipathy to the American Game Cock, merely because the Cock is also an emblem in France of the high spirit which that wonderful people exhibit.

War . . . Today, south of Martinique in the French West Indies, the U.S. Navy's 220–man, twenty-eight-gun ship *Adams,* under Captain Richard V. Morris, captures the French privateer schooner *Le Onze Vendémiaire,* with four guns and sixty-seven men..[1877]

Tonight, in the *Gazette of the United States*:

In the paper, published by the *tender* and *infant* heirs of Benjamin Franklin Bache, we find offered for sale at the *Aurora* office "A quantity of *waste* paper, fit for grocers and trunk-makers." . . . [W]ith how much such graceful modesty the *Aurora* man, that "son of the morning," impresses us with his consciousness of the destiny which awaits his diurnal pages. No one will deny that the paper of the *Aurora* is waste . . . and that, from the necessities of a *young* family and the wants of an editor, it is always *for sale* for any purpose and for any price.

SUNDAY, NOVEMBER 17, 1799

George Washington worries that I can document British influence in his administration. Today, from Mount Vernon, he writes Secretary of War James McHenry:

The charge of British influence . . . is a perfect enigma; my curiosity leads me to enquire on what ground it is built, and you would oblige in giving me an explanation . . . because I shall think myself b[oun]d to answer any interrogatories which may be dictated by insidious impertinence.[1878]

TUESDAY, NOVEMBER 19, 1799

GENERAL ⋆ AURORA ⋆ ADVERTISER

Poor Fenno is much elated at the sale of the waste paper of "The *Aurora*" office—if exultation can console him on the occasion—we cannot envy or deny him all that solace which the mere efforts of imagination give him . . . and would not disturb him with a hint at the respective condition of our *subscription lists.*

THURSDAY, NOVEMBER 21, 1799

GENERAL ★ AURORA ★ ADVERTISER

To those who call themselves the friends of good order—it will be allowed "The *Aurora*," its late, or its present Editor, are under no species of obligation . . . after the attempts made upon the life and liberty of the late and present editor and after the attempt to SUPPRESS BY PURCHASE *this Press* . . .

Today, in New York City, at the Court of Oyer and Terminer, New York Attorney General Josiah O. Hoffman begins the trial of David Frothingham, widow Greenleaf's foreman at the New York *Argus*. From a trial report:

> The substance of the indictment was that, with a design to injure the name and reputation of General Hamilton, . . . [t]o cause it to be believed that he was hostile and opposed to the Republican Government of the United States, the defendant had published a libel in which it was alleged that General Hamilton was at the bottom of the efforts to purchase the *Aurora;* that Mrs. Bache had refused to sell her paper in consequence of the said efforts because, in the hands of General Hamilton or his agents, it would be used to injure republicanism . . . and lastly that Mr. Liston, the British minister, and General Hamilton were united in an effort to purchase the *Aurora*—that for the execution of this design, General Hamilton received of the British minister secret service money of the king of Great Britain . . .
>
> To prove the publishing of the paper charged as a libel, the assistant attorney-general was examined. He said that, in consequence of a letter he had received from General Hamilton and from a desire to avoid the prosecution against a woman, and a widow, he called on Mrs. Greenleaf . . . That Mrs. Greenleaf denied she was at all concerned in the management or direction of her press. That she introduced the defendant as the person who was accountable for whatever was printed under her name . . .
>
> The court admitted Gen. Hamilton to explain the innuendoes, but declared that, the law not allowing the truth or falsehood of a libel to be controverted in a trial for that offence, they would exclude all testimony as to those points on either side . . . He was . . . asked if he considered the *Aurora* as hostile to the government of the United States ? And he replied in the affirmative ! This closed the testimony.
>
> The defendant's counsel took the ground that Mrs. Greenleaf ought to have been the person prosecuted for the libel, if it was one, and not the defendant who was only her journeyman . . . Upon the second point also, the court was explicit that the defendant, even as a journeyman, was liable to the prosecution . . .

The jury, after being out about two hours, returned with a verdict of guilty.[1879]

Justice Radcliff will pronounce sentence on December 3rd. The jury has recommended clemency.[1880]

SATURDAY, NOVEMBER 23, 1799

GENERAL ★ AURORA ★ ADVERTISER

Alexander Hamilton's partiality for the liberty of the press cannot but be excessively gratified in the encrease of Republican newspapers and the decline of those who have advocated *crimes, monarchy,* and *public extravagance.* Within the last sixteen months, more than *twenty* newspapers have been established upon the avowed basis of *democratical republican* principles—in the same period those papers which advocate adverse principles have uniformly declined in public consideration and profit.

MONDAY, NOVEMBER 25, 1799

GENERAL ★ AURORA ★ ADVERTISER

Extract of a letter to the Editor, dated New-York, November 22. Yesterday I attended the Mayor's court in this city as a spectator—the trial of Mr. Frothingham as conductor of the *Argus* came on . . .

Major Gen. Hamilton was sworn and called upon . . . to prove that he was innocent of the charges . . . The *amorous general* was then called upon to explain certain innuendoes in the indictment . . . He was then asked whether he considered the *Aurora* as *hostile* to the government of the United States ? And he replied in the *affirmative* ! . . .

Tonight, in the *Gazette of the United States,* Jack Fenno writes:

As the Irish Editor of the *Aurora* seems to be as ignorant of the true construction of my Latin motto . . . I have resolved to rectify one of his mistakes at least . . .

> *The Caitiff whose object is plunder and blood,*
> *Has for Libels been cropt or in pillory stood,*
> *The law above all things will hate.*
> *In Europe or India, his mind will ne'er alter;*
> *There's no cure for his vice but the noose of a halter,*
> *And this will at last be his fate.*

GENERAL ★ AURORA ★ ADVERTISER

On Tuesday the 11th of Nov. inst. a respectable number of citizens of Mifflin County met in the borough of Lewistown to celebrate the happy success of the Republican cause in the State of Pennsylvania at the last election . . . In full persuasion of these sentiments, attended by the rifle corps of the borough, they marched to the public square and, accompanied with a discharge of their guns, drank the following [17] patriotic toasts . . . 7th. The *Aurora*, and other republican papers in this state and the United States—*May they never be awed by the threats of power from freely and decently investigating the conduct of men in office* . . .

Today, The President's Lady, Abigail Adams, writes her sister:

> *Cooper has lately appeard in the Aurora and, in his former Mad democratic Stile, abused the President, and I presume subjected himself to the penalty of the Sedition act. The greater part of the abuse leveld at the Government is from foreigners. Every Jacobin paper in the United States is Edited by a Foreigner . . . What a disgrace to our Country . . .*[1881]

GENERAL ★ AURORA ★ ADVERTISER

☞ *Subscribers whose files of "the Aurora" became defective owing to removals, stoppages in the Post office, and other accidents during the late sickness, may be supplied without any additional expence on application at the office, 112 Market-street.*

Tonight, in the *Gazette of the United States*:

> It is amusing (so far as any thing of so deep interest can be said to amuse) to see the method and deliberation with which the democrats proceed in their attacks upon the Constitution and Government of America . . . In Maryland, they have proposed to do away with all qualification, by property, for office—in New Jersey to effect a reform in the mode of election . . . These attempts have failed . . .

GENERAL ★ AURORA ★ ADVERTISER

The Philadelphia Gazette feels and groans under the encreasing popularity of *"the Aurora"* . . . and if the Editor of the *Aurora* does not laugh at them . . . they must attribute it to the superiority of his *Irish Education* . . .

Tonight, in the *Gazette of the United States*:

[O]ur system of Education . . . is no system at all; for the docile minds of the rising hope of the Commonwealth are left to fall indiscriminately a prey to United Irishmen, German Illuminati, and native Democrats from whom they acquire, about learning, enough to read the Infernal *Aurora* and to imbibe from it the admonitions of the Devil. Total ignorance is far better than such Education . . .

SATURDAY, NOVEMBER 30, 1799

GENERAL ★ AURORA ★ ADVERTISER

On Friday evening, an elegant supper and splendid ball was given by the republican ladies at the house of Jacob Crever, Esq.—Upwards of 60 ladies attended and congratulated each other on the recent success of *Thomas M'Kean* . . .

Tonight, in the *Gazette of the United States*:

I would recommend to the next stated *meeting* of the *Lyceum* that is *held* at Mr. Coleman's *school-room* the following question:
Whether it is probable, upon a fair calculation, that M'Kean will consume more Gin per annum than [departing Governor] Mifflin has done, or they both as much as Duane; also, whether they Gin, or Gin them, will most consume.

The Session of Congress commences on Monday next. As it is the last time they are to have the honor of sitting in Philadelphia, it is sincerely to be hoped they may "put on their best airs."

MONDAY, DECEMBER 2, 1799

GENERAL ★ AURORA ★ ADVERTISER

WANTED
A CAREFUL DRIVER who is sober and honest may hear of employment by applying at the Office of the *Aurora*.

Tonight, in the *Gazette of the United States*:

The gin-drinking pauper who is said to conduct Bache's paper boasts of having been highly complimented by a respectable English merchant of this city. The aspersion is undoubtedly a lie, as there is no man . . . who would not be ashamed and afraid to perpetrate such an act of humiliation and disgrace. The exultation with which the vagabond mentions it shews, however, that the compliments of a gentlemen are not "renewed upon him every day."

ADDRESS TO *A PIPE OF GIN*
By Jasper Dwight,
Occasioned by seeing a Quantity rolling into a Store.
O ! thou delicious-flavor'd, wholesome juice,
Not less for pleasure purpos'd than for use !
Source of Democracy and source of joy—
Come let me taste thee—Gin can never cloy.
(Puts his mouth to the Bung and sucks up a
draught thro' a straw—the owner of the gin
kicks him into the gutter—but new inspired—
he thus sings on) . . .
Thro' all the details of the rights of man,
Even when in dungeons by the vile tyrants chain'd
Thy powerful aid my sunken soul sustain'd;
And tho' a convict, devoid of every means,
I dream't of liberty and guillotines—
Whether in dram shop or in dungeon drear
Celestial Nectar by thou ever near—
(The operation of the draught occasions him to
fall down drunk in the street, where the Muse
of course left him.)

It is not surprising to hear the voice of jacobinism raised against the excellent *"Discourses on Davila"* [of John Adams]. The learned author, instead of attempting to mislead the public mind . . . has taken infinite pains . . . [in] convincing them that all men are under the influence of certain passions which will war with each other and produce discord unless regulated by a proper balance of powers in government and a vigorous execution of its laws.

WEDNESDAY, DECEMBER 4, 1799

GENERAL ★ AURORA ★ ADVERTISER

Yesterday at 12 o'clock, the President of the United States met both
houses of Congress in the Representatives' Chamber, where he ad-
dressed them as follows: . . .
[T]he commissioners . . . have made a report of the state of the buildings . . . in the city of Washington . . . [T]he removal of the seat of government [from Philadelphia] to that place, at the time required, will be practicable and the accommodations satisfactory . . .

JOHN ADAMS.

GENERAL ★ AURORA ★ ADVERTISER

At a meeting of a number of the republican citizens of Montgomery County on the evening of the 28th of November at the house of Michael Blank . . . the following [16] toasts were drank——1. The 8th of October, 1799. The Day on which . . . Republicanism defeated Aristocracy . . . 9. The German and Irish union that gave us a governor . . . 11. The heroes who fought and bled in the cause of freedom . . . 12. The memory of Dr. Franklin—a man whose talents shed lustre upon his country—may a blush crimson the American cheek for suffering so long his ashes to be violated by a British Hedge Hog. 13. The *Aurora*—the memory of the late, and success to the present, Editor. 14. Buonaparte, the intrepid hero in the cause of freedom . . . 16. May Asses' ears and black cockades become synonymous terms . . .

Tonight, in the *Gazette of the United States*:

NEW YORK, December 4. The [New York] Supreme Court yesterday delivered their sentence in the case of David Frothingham, previously convicted on a charge of aspersing the character of General Hamilton, by publishing that he had been at the "bottom of an attempt at suppressing by pecuniary means the *Aurora*." He was fined in the sum of one hundred dollars—ordered to be imprisoned for four months and to give security for his good behaviour for two years; himself in one thousand dollars and two sureties each in five hundred.

GENERAL ★ AURORA ★ ADVERTISER

Frothingham, foreman in the office of the *Argus* was sentenced to pay a fine of 100 dollars and to be confined for *four months* in Bridewell [prison] for copying a publication . . . reflecting on the *amorous* Gen. Hamilton. Be it remembered that the jury recommended Frothingham to the clemency of the court.—How kindly has it complied!

Tonight, in the *Gazette of the United States*:

It might afford not a little curious speculation to philosophize on the different substances of which the *Aurora* is at different times composed, and, by analyzing them, to assign every effect to its legitimate cause. Now, the lucubrations of this republican luminary are for the most part to be assigned to one or other of these different *moods,* viz. Either an horrible malice at want of money to pay for a glass of gin; or a state of idiocy for having procured it. In all the diversifications of the *Aurora,* the influence of these causes on Duane's mind may be distinctly discerned.

Though Jasper certainly stands among the most deserved candidates for the gallows, yet the jacobins, true to their cause, have resolved not to let his long services pass unrewarded and have serious thoughts of setting him up as a candidate for Congress at the next election. But the daily and increasing quantity of gin which this fellow exhausts will probably ere-that-time present a formidable obstacle in the way of preferment; and he may be thought a disgrace even to the republican cause.

TUESDAY, DECEMBER 10, 1799

GENERAL ★ AURORA ★ ADVERTISER

Fenno, whose enmity to talents is proverbial and . . . the natural effect of his stupidity and consequent expulsion at College . . . rails incessantly . . . *Porcupine* is extinguished by the odor of his own excrementations, but his pupil remains and inherits all his *vulgar honors*—his proverbial falsehood—and is approaching by rapid strides to the same goal.

The hope of subverting republicanism in Europe is certainly the main object and encouragement of the combined [European] emperors and kings. The British ministry has openly avowed this subject. It was not the superior power, the superior ambition, nor even the superior crim-inality of France—No; It was openly avowed in terms that it was a *re-publican government.* That was the *sin,* that was the *evil.*

SATURDAY, DECEMBER 14, 1799

GENERAL ★ AURORA ★ ADVERTISER

General Hamilton arrived in town yesterday and, it is said, means to *keep watch* in Philadelphia for the winter. He despairs doing any thing with the "*Aurora*" . . . but still considers it as the most cruel opposer of his views in the United States.

Mrs. Reynolds, alias *Maria,* the sentimental heroine of the memorable *vindication* [of Mr. Hamilton], is said to be in Philadelphia once more; in the early part of last year, she was in town and had the imprudence to intrude herself on women of virtue with a relation of her story—"that she was the Maria." She escaped on one occasion through the difficulty of finding a constable before she disappeared.

The prospects of the republicans have greatly brightened of late and are getting better and better; in our own state Governor M'Kean has been elected in a manner so decisive that the effect cannot but be useful to the republicans throughout the Union and a lesson to their adversaries: in Virginia, governor [James] Monroe has been chosen in a manner equally honourable and admonitory . . .

Tonight, in the *Gazette of the United States*:

[Adv.]   WILLIAM COBBETT
HAVING (in order to avoid the disgrace of living under the Government of M'Kean) REMOVED from Philadelphia to the City of NEW-YORK, requests any one in Pennsylvania, who may have a demand against him, to deliver an account thereof to Mr. JOHN MORGAN, No. 3, South Front Street . . .

[Adv.]   *To be Sold, at Auction,*
AT PORCUPINE'S HOUSE
On Thursday next at 9 o'clock,
A QUANTITY OF HOUSEHOLD FURNITURE
CONSISTING OF Chairs, Mahogany Tables, Bureaus, Stoves, and Stove-pipe, an excellent Roasting Jack, &c. &c. &c.
ALSO A COMPLETE PRINTING PRESS
With a variety of Books &c. &c. &c. The sale will begin at 9 o'clock precisely and will continue till all is sold off.

Tonight, at Mount Vernon, shortly before midnight, General George Washington, commander in chief of America's army during the American Revolution and during America's undeclared war with France, founder of the hereditary Society of the Cincinnati, and first President of the United States of America, dies of what is called "crupe" or "quinsey" or "cynanche." George Washington's wife, Martha, immediately burns certain of his papers, and his nephew, U.S. Supreme Court Justice Bushrod Washington, will discard some, remove signatures from others, and license their publication to Jared Sparks, a Harvard historian and future Harvard president, who will control, withhold, and even reword them (for the sake of Washington's reputation) and will be their only publisher for the next hundred years.[1882]

THURSDAY, DECEMBER 19, 1799

GENERAL   ★ AURORA ★   ADVERTISER

DIED,
AT Mount Vernon, on Saturday evening, December the 14th, at 11 o'clock, of an illness of 24 hours;
GEORGE WASHINGTON

Wednesday, December 18. Immediately after reading the journal, General Marshall came into the House of Representatives, apparently much agitated, and addressed the Speaker in the following words:

Information, sir, has just been received that our illustrious fellow citizen, the Commander in Chief of the American army, and the late President of the United States, is no more . . . The House immediately adjourned . . .

Tonight, in the *Gazette of the United States*:

☞ In consequence of the afflicting intelligence of the death of General Washington, MRS. ADAMS' Drawing room is deferred to Friday the 27th, when the Ladies are respectfully requested to wear white, trimmed with black ribbon, black gloves and fans, as a token of respect to the memory of the late President of the United States.

FRIDAY, DECEMBER 20, 1799

GENERAL ★ AURORA ★ ADVERTISER

Extract of a letter from Alexandria [Virginia] . . .
GEN. GEORGE WASHINGTON . . .

The disorder of which he died is by some called Crupe, by others inflammatory Quinsey, a disorder lately so mortal among children in this place . . .

The bells are to toll daily until he is buried which will not be until Wednesday or Thursday. He died perfectly in his senses, and from [physician] Mr. Dick's account, perfectly resigned.—He informed them he had no fear of death, that his affairs were in good order, that he made his will, and that his public business was two days behind hand.

SATURDAY, DECEMBER 21, 1799

GENERAL ★ AURORA ★ ADVERTISER

THE TRIUMPH OF DEMOCRACY

On Tuesday last THOMAS M'KEAN, the successful candidate for the office of Governor of Pennsylvania, was inducted into office to the great joy of the Republicans . . .

On Thursday the 28th ult. agreeable to notice given in the newspapers, about two hundred and thirty respectable inhabitants of Harrisburgh and its vicinity assembled at the court house, where they dined with cheerful hearts on a plentiful preparation . . . [T]hey then proceeded to the public ground . . . with music, where the following [26[toasts were drank, under as many discharges of capt. Connelly's artillery . . . 14. The memory of Benjamin Franklin—*"where liberty dwells, there is my country."* 15. The Memory of Benjamin Franklin Bache, the late Editor of the Aurora, the friend of his country, who withstood temptations, disregarded persecutions, and was faithful to the cause of republicanism, even unto death. 16. William Duane, Editor of the Aurora; the detector of falsehood and promoter of truth; he deserves well of his country . . .

TUESDAY, DECEMBER 24, 1799

GENERAL ★ AURORA ★ ADVERTISER

General Washington has died in the 69th year of his life . . . The general has left a very large fortune which, is supposed, will principally descend to the Custis family.

The important command of the army devolves on General Hamilton who is at present in Philadelphia . . .

The Senate of the United States have come to an order that members wear black during the session . . .

To-Morrow being CHRISTMAS DAY, and Thursday being appointed a day of solemn mourning in honor of the immortal leader of the American armies to independence,

GEORGE WASHINGTON,

lately deceased—the publication of this paper will be suspended for those two days.

Tonight, in the *Gazette of the United States*;

Brigadier General Macpherson is charged to superintend the ceremonial in the city of Philadelphia.

☞ THE friends of the Federal Government, in the city of Philadelphia, are requested to meet at Dunwoody's Tavern at six o'clock this evening for the purpose of consulting on the subject of the election of Electors of President and Vice President.

THURSDAY, DECEMBER 26, 1799.

George Washington's memorial procession, crossing
High-street on Philadelphia's Fourth-street, viewed
from within the covered country market.[1883]

GENERAL   ★ AURORA ★   ADVERTISER

Yesterday presented a scene of public mourning, of solemnity and respect, which this city has never before on any occasion witnessed in an
equal degree . . .

At eleven o'clock, conformable to orders, the United States corps under Brigadier General Macpherson paraded in the center of Chestnut
street, opposite Congress Hall.

The Militia corps, composing the Republican legion, commanded by
Colonel Shee . . . paraded in Fifth Street . . .

The procession commenced at twelve o'clock, with a troop of horse
leading down Walnut to Fourth Street, where they turned to the left, and
crossed, Chestnut, Market, and Arch Street, until they arrived at the
German Lutheran Church, in the following order.

Capt M'Kean's troop of Federal Horse.

Capt Price's Light	Infantry,	Republican
Captain Rush's	d[itt]o	d[itt]o
Capt. Kefsler's	d[itt]o	d[itt]o
Capt. Duane's	d[itt]o	d[itt]o . . .

THE BIER

Carried by six sergeants. Paul supported by six veterans . . .

The President of the United States and his lady were present . . .

TUESDAY, DECEMBER 31, 1799

GENERAL   ★ AURORA ★   ADVERTISER

FOR THE AURORA.

With pearly drop in city's eye,
Columbia's sons incessant cry;
O WASHINGTON !—in virtue try'd
Would thou had never liv'd—or never died.

CHAPTER FOURTEEN

UPPER CHAMBER

The Division of the Legislature into two or three Branches in England, was it the Product of Wisdom or the Effect of Necessity arising from the preexisting Prevalence of an odious Feudal System? . . . I am sorry to see . . . one half the Legislature [the Senate] . . . proudly called the UPPER HOUSE, and the other Branch, chosen by the majority of the People, degraded by the denomination of the LOWER; and giving to this upper House a Permanency of . . . [several] Years, and but two to the lower . . .

DR. BENJAMIN FRANKLIN[1884]

I now think the Number of Representatives should bear some proportion to the Number of the Represented, and that the Decisions should be by the Majority of Members, not by the Majority of States.

DR. BENJAMIN FRANKLIN,
AT THE FEDERAL CONSTITUTIONAL CONVENTION,
JUNE 11, 1787[1885]

Never was any measure so thoroughly discussed as our proposed new [federal] Constitution . . . As to the two chambers [of the legislature], I am of your opinion that one alone would be better . . .

DR. BENJAMIN FRANKLIN[1886]

WEDNESDAY, JANUARY 1, 1800

GENERAL ★ AURORA ★ ADVERTISER

AN ODE ON *THE COMMENCEMENT OF THE NEW YEAR*
MAID, Liberty, for ever dear,
The simple gift our Simple Parents gave !
Hail the sweet pow'r to shed the lonely tear !
And moralize upon the Patriot's grave;
To open Mem'ry's precious roll,

731

And from its stores refresh the soul;
To view the height where philosophic bards,
Thro' pain and toil, have bought rewards
Explor'd their way to Truth's secluded dome;
And bade her forth, with gentle hand,
To bless some free and peaceful land
And be their arbitress for days to come . . .

1800 ! A Presidential election year! A year to depose His Rotundity and end America's "Reign of Witches"!

Tonight, in the *Gazette of the United States*:

> At a meeting of a number of the citizens of the city of Philadelphia, pursuant to public notice on Tuesday the 24th December at the house of John Dunwoody, for the purpose of considering the propriety of addressing the Legislature in favor of an election of Electors for a President and Vice President of the United States by Districts, it was resolved that . . . [an] address be circulated for the signatures of the inhabitants of the city of Philadelphia . . .

If Federalists played by the rules they established in the last presidential election, Pennsylvania would award its fifteen presidential electoral votes to the candidate who wins a statewide popular election. Fearing, however, that last October's statewide majority for Thomas McKean will become next October's majority for Thomas Jefferson and knowing that, despite McKean's majority last October, a majority of counties voted for James Ross,[1887] the Federalist majority in the Pennsylvania state senate is obstructing renewal of the old election law and proposes instead to divide the electoral votes between the candidates on the basis of district elections (thereby giving John Adams nine of the state's fifteen presidential electors).[1888]

SATURDAY, JANUARY 4, 1800

GENERAL ★ AURORA ★ ADVERTISER

The Citizens are cautioned against a petition insidiously circulating . . . This petition is a party maneuver . . . and calculated to destroy all the happy effects of the late success of republicanism in this state.

Today, James Monroe, now Governor of Virginia, writes Thomas Jefferson:

> *I am strongly impressed with a belief that if A[dams] puts himself in the hands of the B[ritis]h faction, an attempt will be made to carry [enforce] the Sedition Act here [in Virginia] as an electioneering trick in the course of the summer. They must be deprived of a plausible pretext in w[hi]ch case an attempt will dishonor them . . .*[1889]

GENERAL ★ AURORA ★ ADVERTISER

We learn . . . that the bill . . . for election districts . . . has been thrown out of the [Pennsylvania] lower house. A bill has been passed by the house of representatives of this state for choosing electors . . . in the old form by a general ticket. This has been sent up to the senate but is not expected to pass.

GENERAL ★ AURORA ★ ADVERTISER

Among the parcels sold at Cobbett's auction were several marked thus on the outside . . .

Caricatures of the Vice President

Tonight, in the *Gazette of the United States*:

Extract of a Sermon . . . preached December 29, 1799, in Christ Church and St. Peter's, by the Rev. Mr. ABERCROMBIE, *one of the assistant Ministers of said Churches.* "BRETHREN . . . O WASHINGTON, LIVE FOR EVER ! . . ."

[To the President of the United States]
SIR . . . With grateful acknowledgment and unfeigned thanks for the personal respect and evidences of condolence expressed by Congress and yourself . . .   MARTHA WASHINGTON

MR. FENNO, A Correspondent wishes to be informed who is the Editor of the *Aurora*, a newspaper published lately in this city by B. F. Bache—It has been said the Editor is one Duane—who published a pamphlet with the signature of *"Jasper Dwight of Vermont,"* insulting the late General Washington . . .   A. B.

GENERAL ★ AURORA ★ ADVERTISER

While this country, by the recommendation of its Government, is paying its last honors to one of the most distinguished revolutionary Characters . . . it will be a pleasure to the sincere republicans to recollect similar homage to a genius, equally conspicuous in science and in politics; and the friend of WASHINGTON. When the eulogium of FRANKLIN was pronounced in the National Assembly of France, there was a profound and perfect silence . . . MIRABEAU EXCLAIMED . . . "Were it not worthy of us, gentlemen . . . to pay our share of that homage now rendered in sight of the universe, at once to the rights of man and to the philosopher who most contributed to extend the conquests of liberty over the face of the whole earth? . . ."

Today, in New York City, William Cobbett, alias Peter Porcupine, publishes a farewell issue of the *Porcupine's Gazette,* including:

TO THE SUBSCRIBERS TO THIS GAZETTE . . .

I now address to you the *farewell number* of PORCUPINE'S GAZETTE.

Remembering, as you must, my solemn promise to quit Pennsylvania in case my old democratic Judge, MACK KEAN, should be elected Governor; and, knowing as you now do, that he is elected to that office, there are, I trust, very few of you who will be surprized to find that I am no longer in that degraded and degrading State.

My removal from Philadelphia to New-York would certainly be a sufficient apology for the suspension of my paper from the 26th of October to this time . . . but the renewal of this intercourse between us . . . cannot take place, whether now or at any future time . . .

I began my editorial career with the *presidency of Mr. Adams* and my principal object was to render to his administration all the assistance in my power. I looked upon him as a stately well-armed vessel, sailing on an expedition to combat and destroy the fatal influence of French intrigue and French principles . . . but he suddenly tacked about [dispatching this mission to France], and I could follow him no longer . . .

I congratulate myself on never having, in a single instance, been the sycophant of the Sovereign People and on having persisted . . . in openly and unequivocally avowing my attachment to my native country and my allegiance to my King . . .

And now, *"my dear Philadelphians"* . . . I will, for the present, take my leave of you . . . I wish you joy of your new Governor . . . I wish you joy of your House of Assembly . . . and your Captain Duane and his company of volunteers . . . And, though last not least, I wish you joy . . . of your DOCTORS.   [WM. COBBETT]

WEDNESDAY, JANUARY 17, 1800

GENERAL   ★ AURORA ★   ADVERTISER

It is reported that the Legislature of New Jersey have risen without being able to pass a law directing the choice of Electors of President and Vice President of the United States . . . The House of representatives insisted upon the electors being chosen immediately by the people . . . while the council [the upper chamber] contended for the old practice . . . of their being chosen by the Legislature.

As in Pennsylvania, Federalists in New Jersey's state legislature won't allow a statewide popular vote to decide who gets the state's presidential electoral vote.[1890]

TUESDAY, JANUARY 21, 1800

GENERAL ★ AURORA ★ ADVERTISER

AN APPRENTICE WANTED
TO THE PRINTING BUSINESS. Enquire at this office.

Tonight, Jack Fenno in the *Gazette of the United States*:

IN most countries it would be found that the great mass of the people are incompetent to judge of public affairs of an extensive and complex nature, and, when so deceived, incompetent to select proper officers for the management of such concerns.

This is no imputation on their understanding; for their attention is occupied with other objects. An excellent sailor may know nothing of the mechanism of a watch—nor a watchmaker of the working of a ship. The choice of a majority is therefore no test of the qualifications of a candidate.

THURSDAY, JANUARY 23, 1800

GENERAL ★ AURORA ★ ADVERTISER

At a meeting of a number of the citizens of Montgomery county [Pennsylvania], held at the house of Nicholas Sweyer . . .
Resolved, That a Committee . . . draught a memorial to the Legislature of this State, soliciting that a law (directing the manner of choosing the electors of a President and Vice President) may be passed similar to those which have been heretofore on the same subject . . .

Today, in the Senate of the United States, Pennsylvania's Federalist Senator James Ross (who lost to Thomas McKean in the race for Governor of Pennsylvania) proposes that the Senate consider legislation to deal with the coming presidential election. The Annals of Congress report:

On motion of Mr. Ross [Federalist, Pennsylvania], that it be, *Resolved,* That a committee be appointed to consider whether any, and what, provisions, ought to be made by law for deciding disputed elections of President and Vice President of the United States, and for determining the legality or illegality of the votes given for those officers in the different states . . .

Suppose, said he, persons should claim to be Electors who had never been *properly* appointed, should their vote be received? . . .[1891]

Tonight, in the *Gazette of the United States*:

735

There has been much talk of late respecting a defection of the sub-scribers to the *Aurora,* said to have been occasioned by four testimonials of disrespect exhibited by the people who manage that paper towards the memory of the late General Washington.

MONDAY, JANUARY 27, 1800

GENERAL ★ AURORA ★ ADVERTISER

The proceedings in the Senate of the United States of last week indi-cate measures of particular interest on the tapis there. Accustomed to hear little either to instruct or inform in that house, we were not pre-pared to take notes there during the last week; however, . . . we expect to be able to attend to them in subsequent stages more at large.

Our state election for electors of President and Vice President has already caused some agitation in the Pennsylvania Legislature . . . The party hostile to the popular interests has obtained in our state Senate a majority, and they are determined that we shall be deprived of a law . . . rather than have the law which the people of the state approve and call for . . . [A Pennsylvania member of the Senate of the United States] Mr. *Ross* . . . has brought forward in the Senate of the United States a mea-sure expressly calculated to defeat the wishes of the people of this com-monwealth . . . We shall attend to this alarming attempt upon the freedom of this state . . .

It is understood that the legislature of New-Jersey has risen without enacting a law for choosing the electors of the next President of the United States. Appearances countenance the apprehension that the leg-islature of Pennsylvania also may rise under like circumstances.

SATURDAY, FEBRUARY 1, 1800

GENERAL ★ AURORA ★ ADVERTISER

The United States frigate which conveyed our Commissioners to the French Republic was spoken with on the 24th of Nov. within two days sail of Cadiz, all well.

War . . . Today, off Guadeloupe in the French West Indies, the U.S. Navy's 340–man, thirty-six-gun frigate *Constellation* pursues and fires upon the fifty-eight-gun French national ship-of-war *Le Vengeance.* In this engagement, thirty-eight Americans are killed or wounded. Captain Thomas Truxton reports:

Throughout these twenty-four hours, very unsettled weather, kept on our tracks beating up under Guadeloupe and at half past 7 A.M . . . saw a sail in the S. E . . . [D]iscovered she was a heavy French frigate, mounting at least 54 guns. I immediately gave orders for the yards to be slung with the chains, topsail sheet, &c. stoppered, and the ship cleared and everything prepared for action . . . [G]ot within hail of him at 8 P.M., hoisted our ensign, and had the candles in the battle lanterns all lighted and the large trumpet in the lee gangway ready to speak to him to demand the surrender of his ship to the U.S. of America, but he at that inst. commenced a fire from his stern and quarter guns directed at our rigging and spars. No parley being necessary, I . . . [gave my orders] to take good aim and fire directly into the hull of the enemy; and load principally with two round shot and now and then a stand of grape, &c . . . [T]hus a close and sharp action . . . continued until within a few minutes of 1 A. M. when the enemy's fire was completely silenced . . .[1892]

Today, former *Aurora* writer Jimmy Callender distributes a powerful piece of campaign literature, the first volume (184 pages) of his new work *The Prospect Before Us*:[1893]

In the fall of 1796, when the French began their depredations, the country fell into a more dangerous juncture than almost any the old confederation ever endured. The tardiness and timidity of Mr. Washington were succeeded by the rancour and insolence of Mr. Adams. The Parisian preference of Dr. Franklin was to be revenged. The British constitution was to be defended, not only by three volumes, but by the sixteen United States . . .

Every feature in the conduct of Mr. Adams forms a distinct and additional evidence that he was determined, at all events, to embroil this country with France . . .

Think what you have been, what you are, and what, under the monarch of Massachusetts, you are likely to become. Look at Schneider flogged by the federal troops in the marketplace of Reading . . . Think of Duane dragged from the office of the Aurora, and of Philadelphia driven to the verge of tumult and massacre . . .[1894]

For *The Prospect Before Us*, Jimmy Callender will suffer the penalties of the Sedition Act.

TUESDAY, FEBRUARY 4, 1800

GENERAL ★ AURORA ★ ADVERTISER

A Salem paper (Massachusetts) calls the proposition for renewing the laws for a popular election in Pennsylvania an effort of *Jacobinism*— these people sometimes speak very plainly—tho' cunning as they are no one can mistake them.

GENERAL ★ AURORA ★ ADVERTISER

[I]nteresting events have recently taken place in France . . . A counter-revolutionary plot appears to have been deeply laid . . . The ark of the republic appears to have been tossed about . . . [T]he Constitution of the 3rd year was annihilated, . . . [Napoleon's] Consulate established on its ruins . . .

The advocates of Representative Government admired the distinction of legislative power and the control of the popular over the Executive authority. They admired the plurality of the Executive, as it gave *five* men responsible for executive acts instead of *One* . . .

[F]eatures in the Constitution were objects of dislike, but freemen were indulgent to a system . . . which in its spirit and arrangement carried all the grand principles of social and human happiness into operation and laid down as its basis the immutable and eternal rights of man . . .

Time may yet develop new facts upon which the recent changes may be more accurately weighed . . .

Napoleon Bonaparte, who commands the armies of France, has seized dictatorial control of France!

GENERAL ★ AURORA ★ ADVERTISER

PARIS . . . *Letter from the minister for foreign affairs [of France] to the foreign ministers [of other states].*
    SIR, I HAVE the honour to inform you that the consuls of the French republic have taken into their hands the reins of government . . .   REINARD

Tonight, in the *Gazette of the United States*:

Tom Paine, awake only *at every new revolution,* lately sent a bundle of constitutions to Buonaparte . . .

Since the French Republic is overthrown, we shall probably hear so many alarms sounded respecting the danger [to] Republican Liberty from despotic conspiracies . . .

After denying during many days the authenticity of the late news, the *Aurora* people at length believed it, because Mr. Jefferson believed it . . .

GENERAL ★ AURORA ★ ADVERTISER

PARIS . . . Every one is endeavouring to recollect all the circumstances by which persons might have predicted the revolution which has just taken place.

Tonight, in the *Gazette of the United States,* Jack Fenno writes;

The late [counter]revolution in France appears to us an unequivocal decision of the popular sentiment in favor of *Royalty.* The *sovereign people* sacrificed the old government and zealously cooperated in seating the new into power under the hopes of thereby approximating the conclusion of a *peace.* As peace cannot be concluded or hoped for with the dominant moonshine usurpers, there can be little doubt that a consciousness of this will lead them to reinstate their lawful monarch; or that the people, finding peace not attainable through their means, will . . . *themselves* restore their exiled King.

GENERAL ★ AURORA ★ ADVERTISER

Mr. Hamilton's late defence of *"kiss* and *tell"* is said to be bought up by the friends of that gentleman. Should any friend to liberty have been so fortunate as to have saved one copy, the loan of it is requested . . .

Today, in the Senate of the United States, the Annals of Congress report:

Mr. Ross [Federalist, Pennsylvania], from the committee appointed the 28th of January last, reported a bill prescribing the mode of deciding elections of President and Vice President of the United States, which was read and ordered to a second reading.[1895]

GENERAL ★ AURORA ★ ADVERTISER

Several enquiries have been made at the Aurora office to know what is the nature and purpose of the *Caucuses* or secret meetings which have been held a few evenings past in the [United States] Senate Chamber, as if "the Aurora" must of necessity be in the secret . . . We candidly confess we are not in the secret on this occasion, but we *shrewdly suspect* what is going on . . .

I. Measures of intrigue, influence, and reconciliation concerning the Election for President.

II. Plans for encreasing the influence of the federal and diminishing that of the state legislatures . . .

The Pennsylvania state senate is preventing Pennsylvania from expressing its popular preference for Thomas Jefferson. Will the United States Senate prevent the nation from doing the same?

MONDAY, FEBRUARY 17, 1800

GENERAL ★ AURORA ★ ADVERTISER

JUST PUBLISHED AND TO BE HAD
AT THE OFFICE OF THE AURORA . . .
portrait of the Hon. THOMAS JEFFERSON, engraved by AKIN and HARRISON, jun. from the picture now in the Museum painted by C. W. Peale

Tonight, in the *Gazette of the United States*:

The civil dissensions in Pennsylvania threaten the complete disenfranchisement of the citizens at the ensuing election for President and Vice president.

TUESDAY, FEBRUARY 18, 1800

GENERAL ★ AURORA ★ ADVERTISER

MR. EDITOR,   I HAVE often doubted of the necessity . . . of two houses of Legislature . . . [T]here is some reason to doubt whether we (the people) have not lost. upon the whole, by the change that took place [in the Pennsylvania constitution] about the year 1790 . . .

Dr. Franklin (a name no longer popular among the well-born, the well-bred, and the fashionable adherents of our present rulers) was decidedly averse to the modern doctrine of checks and balances, nor could I ever understand the theory . . . [A] few considerations . . . lead me to doubt whether we ought not to abolish or to modify the Senate of the State of Pennsylvania . . .

[H]ow can we justify the absurdity of appointing our [Pennsylvania] Senate for four years and our immediate representatives [in the Pennsylvania House] for one year only?

Let us look to fact. [H]as there or has there not been a considerable change in public sentiment within the last four years? and do we not see that our house of assembly does, and our senate does not, represent that change ? . . .

[I]t appears that a government of 2 houses has been carried on at double the expence, on the average, which the government of one branch formerly cost us . . .

The only argument remaining . . . in favour of two houses is the alleged party spirit and precipitancy of one house . . . But this precipitancy has never been an evil of equal magnitude with the frequency of opposition of opinion between the Senate and the public . . . and the obstinate adherence that has sometimes occurred [among senators] to principles and practices directly opposed to those which the majority of their constituents are known to approve. The projects of the present dispute on the election law respecting electors . . . are not the only proofs . . .

C.

WEDNESDAY, FEBRUARY 19, 1800

GENERAL ★ AURORA ★ ADVERTISER

In our paper of the 27th ult. we noticed the introduction of a measure into the Senate of the United States by Mr. James Ross calculated to influence and affect the approaching presidential election . . .

We this day lay before the public a copy of that bill as it has passed the Senate. We noticed a few days ago the *Caucuses* (or secret consultations) held in the Senate Chamber . . . We stated that intrigues for the presidential election were among the objects. We now state it as a fact . . . that the bill we this day present was discussed at the *Caucus* on *Wednesday* evening last . . .

A BILL..

SECT. I. *Be it enacted* . . . That . . . the Senate and House [shall] choose by ballot, in each house, six members thereof, and the twelve persons thus chosen, together with the Chief Judge of the Supreme Court of the United States . . . shall form a Grand Committee and shall have the power to examine and finally decide all disputes relating to the election of President and Vice President of the United States . . .

SECT. 5. *And be it further enacted,* That . . . [the Committee] shall sit with closed doors . . .

SECT. 8. *And be it further enacted,* That the Grand Committee shall have power to enquire, examine, decide . . . upon the constitutional qualifications of the Electors appointed by the different states . . . upon all petitions and exception against . . . improper means used to influence their votes or against the truth of their returns [&c.] . . .

SECT. 10. *And be it further enacted,* That on the first day of March . . . the grand Committee shall make their final report . . . stating the legal number of [electoral] votes for each person [for President and Vice President] and the number of votes which have been rejected: the report shall be a final and conclusive determination . . .

SECT. 11. *And be it further enacted,* That when the grand committee shall have been duly formed . . . it shall not be in the power of either house [of Congress] to dissolve the committee or to withdraw its members . . .

With one member of this committee (the Chief Justice) appointed by the President (subject to U.S. Senate approval) and six members of this committee appointed by the senate itself, this committee's majority will have a monarchical and aristocratical veto on whether Thomas Jefferson becomes president!

FRIDAY, FEBRUARY 21, 1800

GENERAL ★ AURORA ★ ADVERTISER

Fenno says, "the *civil dissentions* in Pennsylvania threaten to complete the disenfranchisement of the citizens at the ensuing election." This is a more candid declaration than we could have expected from that quarter—it remains, however, untold by him that his *friends* are the authors of these *dissentions*—that they are caused by a contempt of the public will . . . That the member of the [U.S.] Senate who that faction sought to force upon the people as governor has been the mover and author of a bill in the federal senate of the most dangerous tendency to the constitution and liberties of this state and calculated in a particular case to bring in a *judge appointed* by the president of the United States to be an umpire in the legislative rights of this state and on the elective rights of the people. It is candid therefore in Fenno to acknowledge that the people of Pennsylvania are in danger of being disfranchised.

Today, in the Senate of the United States, the Annals of Congress report:

The Senate resumed consideration of the bill prescribing the mode of deciding disputed elections of President and Vice President of the United States.

On motion to strike out . . . It passed in the negative, yeas 11, nays 19 . . .[1896]

SATURDAY, FEBRUARY 22, 1800

GENERAL ★ AURORA ★ ADVERTISER

It appears that the Bill which we published a few days ago, concerning a kind of *Venetian Council* of 12, proposed to be instituted to determine upon our state elections, has not yet passed the Senate of the U.S.

The republican interest in New York state are endeavoring to obtain a general election ticket as Virginia has done and as Pennsylvania has hitherto had with universal satisfaction. The people of New York, by a vast majority, are in favour of a general ticket, but by an artful course of measures steadily pursued in that as in other states, the election of legislators and other public servants is in fact carried on in a great measure by an aristocratical *junto.*

Federalists in the New York, New Jersey, and Pennsylvania state legislatures refuse to allow statewide popular elections to decide who gets these states' presidential electors. They know that Thomas Jefferson could win such a state-

742

wide popular vote and have, therefore, retained the electoral choice to themselves. To alter the predictable outcome, Republicans will have to win control of the state legislatures, and the first opportunity to do so comes at the end of April, when New York holds its election for the state legislature.

MONDAY, FEBRUARY 24, 1800

GENERAL ★ AURORA ★ ADVERTISER

A transaction in our [Pennsylvania] state legislature took place on Thursday last which exceeds even the memorable transaction in Congress upon which the Speaker Dayton forgot the dignity of his station . . . In the morning sitting, the [Pennsylvania] house had under consideration . . . the election law . . . Mr. Fisher . . . met with Dr. Logan and began to insult him . . . Fisher called him a damn'd puppy—Logan called him a rascal on which he received a blow in the face from Fisher. The Doctor struck at him . . . [S]everal blows were given by different persons . . .

Tonight, in the *Gazette of the United States*:

The *Aurora* tells us that the dissentions in the Legislature have terminated in *blows;* and That Doctor Logan has been beaten up and laid up by Mr. Fisher.

HARRISBURG . . . We are credibly informed that his Excellency Thomas M'Kean was knocked down with a brick-bat while walking the streets of Lancaster by one Moses Simons who is said to be insane. It is said his Excellency was taken up almost lifeless.

Occurrences on board the United States ship *Constellation* of 28 guns, under my command, Feb 1, 1800 . . .
[A]t half past 7, A. M. . . . saw a sail . . . I discovered . . . she was a heavy French frigate . . . I was determined to continue the pursuit . . . I gained a position on his weather port . . . [T]hus a close and as sharp an action as ever was fought commenced . . .

[CAPT.] THOMAS TRUXTON

TUESDAY, FEBRUARY 25, 1800

GENERAL ★ AURORA ★ ADVERTISER

[I]t appears by the letter which we extract from *Fenno's* paper from Captain Truxton that he resolved to challenge the French frigate to action . . .

The people of the United States have unequivocally expressed their unwillingness for offensive war. A negociation has been set on foot to procure . . . a fair understanding with the French nation. How comes it then that an officer, deriving his authority from the executive, from the

743

first public servant of the people should commit such acts as violate the express will of the people . . . ?

Today, in the Senate of the United States, the Annals of Congress report:

A motion was made by MR. DAYTON [Federalist, New Jersey] that it be resolved

Resolved, That a Committee of Privileges, consisting of—members, be appointed to continue during the present session.

Ordered, That it lie for consideration until tomorrow.[1897]

WEDNESDAY, FEBRUARY 26, 1800

GENERAL   ★ AURORA ★   ADVERTISER

A prosecution has been commenced on an Eastern Printer [Anthony Haswell of the *Vermont Gazette*] for publishing an extract from [U.S. War Secretary] *Mr. M'Henry's* letter . . . recommending Tories as fit persons to hold commissions in the army under a government the principles of which they hate.

Today, in the Senate of the United States, the Annals of Congress report:

The Senate took into consideration the motion made yesterday that a standing Committee of Privileges . . . be appointed . . .

Resolved, That a Committee of Privileges, consisting of five members, be appointed to continue during the present session.

And, on motion to agree to the motion as amended, it passed in the affirmative—yeas 22, nays 7 . . .

A motion was made by Mr. TRACY [Federalist, Connecticut], that it be,

Resolved, That the Committee of Privileges be, and they are hereby, directed to enquire who is the editor of the newspaper printed in the city of Philadelphia, called the General Advertiser, or Aurora, and by what means the editor became possessed of the copy of the bill . . . which was printed in the aforesaid newspaper, published Wednesday morning, the 19th inst . . . And generally to enquire the origin of sundry assertions in the same paper, respecting the Senate of the United States, and the members thereof, in their official capacity, and why the same were published . . .

Ordered, That this motion lie for consideration.

The Senate resumed the second reading of the bill prescribing the mode of deciding disputed elections of the president and Vice President of the United States; and after progress, adjourned.[1898]

Today, Thomas Jefferson writes Samuel Adams of Boston,

A letter from you, my respectable friend, after three & twenty years of separation, has given me a pleasure that I cannot express . . . Your

*principles have been tested in the crucible of time & have come out.
You have proved that it was monarchy & not merely British monarchy
you opposed. A government by representatives, elected by the people at
short periods, was our object; and our maxim at that day was, "where
annual election ends, tyranny begins." Nor have our departures from
it been sanctioned by the happiness of their effects . . .*[1899]

Tonight, in the *Gazette of the United States,* Jack Fenno writes:

It ought to be remembered that the great object with the antifederalists
now is the election of Mr. Jefferson as President of the United States in
opposition to Mr. Adams. As to the cause of France, they care nothing
about it any farther than they can make it subservient to their own views,
more especially since the late change in that government which they confessedly do not understand . . .

The antifederalists may preach up the virtues of their candidate, but
the writer of this will consider the day on which they succeed in their
election as the commencement of a revolution . . .

THURSDAY, FEBRUARY 27, 1800

GENERAL ★ AURORA ★ ADVERTISER

A lawyer, whose federalism is of the highest tone, but who seldom
speaks upon politics unless when he expresses the sentiments of his
party, said a few evenings ago that it was *in vain for the federalists to
go against popular opinion while "The Aurora" was suffered to exist—
to proceed in the next election or in any other measure,* it was necessary
first to begin with pulling down that paper—or its present Editor!!

SATURDAY, MARCH 1, 1800

GENERAL ★ AURORA ★ ADVERTISER

We learn by a citizen who remained in the gallery of the Senate after
we had left it on Tuesday that a resolution was laid on the table, tending
to authorize the *committee of privileges* to make enquiries who is the
Editor of "the Aurora," and how he came to the publication of the Bill
which we gave in the paper a few days ago, concerning a committee of
both houses for deciding on disputed elections and other matters which
our friend could not recollect.

A free press is an alarming eye-sore to men whose actions cannot bear
the test of enquiry nor admit of defense by the same medium.

Tonight, in the *Gazette of the United States:*

THE AMERICAN ENVOYS have arrived at Lisbon.

GENERAL ★ AURORA ★ ADVERTISER

IN THE SENATE OF THE UNITED STATES . . .

A Motion was made that it be *Resolved*, That the committee of privileges be, and they are hereby, directed to enquire who is the Editor of the news-paper printed in the city of Philadelphia, called the General Advertiser, or Aurora, and by what means the Editor became possessed of the copy of a bill [&c.] . . .

It is curious to see wise men searching with a lantern at noon day for a man whom they commonly see before them without the aid of spectacles.

THE CAUCUS

On Saturday Evening last, these gentlemen who heretofore met at the Senate Chamber held a meeting or *Caucus* at a private lodging house of one of the members of the party. We had not time to go in search of their *subject*, but it was suspected to have been held to consider what was best to be done with that *dangerously active fellow* the Editor of the Aurora and to advise certain persons thereof accordingly.

Tonight, in the *Gazette of the United States*:

"REPUBLICANISM"

The following . . . is extracted from the Kentucky Gazette . . .

"On Wednesday last, a considerable number of republican citizens assembled at Thomas Stephensen's spring . . . [T]he following toasts were drank . . . 9. The memory of Gen. Washington, may his illustrious actions and services be faithfully recorded down to the year 1787, but no further . . ."

(Here may be seen . . . the confession of faith of those devoted to the principles of Jacobinism . . .)

A poor Maniac at Lancaster knocked Excellence [McKean] down with a brick . . . [T]he people who conduct the *Aurora* actually insinuated . . . a design of assassination. These things come from the same audacious miscreants who proclaim assassination to be no crime in ridding the earth of one whom they choose to call a tyrant.

GENERAL ★ AURORA ★ ADVERTISER

WHAT GOOD HAVE THE REPUBLICANS DONE?

This is a question often asked by their enemies. The answer is they have saved our country from war . . . in the face of the most constant and foul calumny, abuse, and reproach from the great Porcupines and the little Porcupines, the British spies and hirelings, and all their Tory party in this country . . .

TO THE EDITOR OF THE AURORA.

SIR . . . [A] committee of privileges is appointed to arraign an Editor for even publishing facts which relate to a branch of the Legislature . . . acting in their legislative capacity . . .

[T]he object of the leaders of the federal party is to trample under foot those who . . . are advocates for representative government . . . Scarcely a day passes over our head without some sarcasm upon the Sovereign people, some innuendo against republican government . . .

LOOK OUT.

The *Caucus* of Saturday evening was not as numerously attended as might have been expected; nor did they sit as long as usual. [T]here was some *thundering* for a moment or two . . .

Today, in the Senate of the United States, the Annals of Congress report:

The Senate resumed the second reading of the bill prescribing the mode of deciding disputed elections of President and Vice President of the United States.[1900]

WEDNESDAY, MARCH 5, 1800

GENERAL ★ AURORA ★ ADVERTISER

Some time ago *Fenno* exulted much at the supposed effect of the wit of that paper . . . [and] declared that the *Democrats* were *skeered* by it. Surely this pack of wits forgot to remember the *poetical beads* of the *Aurora* in 1796 . . .

Today, in the Senate of the United States, the Annals of Congress report:

BREACH OF PRIVILEGE

The Senate took into consideration the motion made on the 26th of February last, that an inquiry be had relative to a publication in a newspaper called the "Aurora" on the 19th of the said month . . .

Mr. COCKE [Republican, Tennessee] said he would not suffer a measure of this kind . . . What did the gentleman [Mr. TRACY] mean . . . ? [D]id he mean to get the consent of the Senate, acting in the character of an inquest, to an acknowledgment that the editor of the Aurora had been guilty of a crime, without any inquiry whether the publication in itself was criminal, or whether, if it was criminal, the Senate, as an independent and a single branch of the Legislature, had of itself the power to define the crime and inflict the punishment? . . .

Mr. TRACY [Federalist, Connecticut] . . . The committee are desired to inquire who is the editor of the Aurora; this will appear to be a proper inquiry, for the person is not publicly known: the imprint declares the paper to be published for the heirs of Benjamin Franklin Bache, but we do not know who are the heirs. The gentleman has told us that it is no crime to publish the doings of this body; but is it nothing to publish untruths respecting the official conduct of the members of this body? is it no crime to publish a bill while before this House? But are printers at liberty to tell lies about our transactions? The Aurora says that the bill which it published had passed the Senate; this every member knows to be contrary to the fact . . .

Mr. COCKE [Republican, Tennessee] . . . supposed the resolutions considered the publications in the Aurora as criminal, otherwise they would not make this stir about them. Gentlemen have asked, are the newspapers to be permitted to go on and villify the members of the Legislature without punishment? He answered [that] the printers of papers published on their own responsibility, and if they had no authority for any scandalous assertions respecting the Senate, they could be punished in the way pointed out by law. But would the members wish to draw the printers before the House and assume the judiciary power of the courts of justice ? . . .[1901]

Today, Peggy Bache and I enter an agreement whereby I become owner and publisher of the *Philadelphia Aurora*. By the transaction, *I have been put into conditional possession of the printing presses, types, utensils, &c. employed in conducting the newspaper . . . [U]ntil the purchase money . . . be fully paid, the presses, types, utensils, &c. are mortgaged to . . . Margaret . . .*[1902] This transaction assures that I, not Peggy, will be held responsible for the paper's operation in any of the Federalist legal actions. More important, Peggy's mortgage lien on the paper's assets will assure that Peggy, not the Federalists, will end up with the paper's assets (should the Federalists win a lawsuit and try to foreclose on the paper in satisfaction of their claim).

Today, the President's Lady, Abigail Adams, writes her sister:

> *At a late festival in Kentucky, amongst a number of Jacobin toasts is one to the memory of Genll. Washington to the year 17[8]9 and no longer, by which they mean to cast a slur upon the whole of his administration of the government. But Hence, wretches, to your native dens—the bogs of Ireland, the dens of Scotland, and the outcasts of Britain.*[1903]

Tonight, in the *Gazette of the United States*:

> Forlorn and destitute indeed must be the condition of a party which can look with idiot admiration on the drunken blackguardisms of a Callender, the brazen impositions of a Duane . . . There is a difficulty in deciding which of these two classes is sunk the lowest in moral and mental degradation—the seditious Herd who worship these uncouth idols or the

self-conceited nothings who court with so much avidity the foul incense of their praise.

THURSDAY, MARCH 6, 1800

GENERAL ★ AURORA ★ ADVERTISER

In the Senate yesterday, the resolution concerning the editor of the *Aurora* was called up and underwent some warm investigation. We were not aware of the Intention or should have attended, but we have been promised minutes of the debates and motions.

Some extraordinary doctrines were broached in the senate yesterday . . . on the privileges of the Senate, amounting in fact to a more arbitrary extent than any thing ever attempted in the British house of lords.

QUERIES TO A SENATOR.

1. Does the unbounded privilege of a Legislator extend to protect his public conduct from public investigation? . . .

The public appears anxious to learn the result of the late disgraceful violence in our state legislature—We have refrained from communication on this subject, because it is under the scrutiny of a committee . . .

Today, in the United States Senate, the Annals of Congress report:

The Senate resumed the consideration of the motion made on the 26th of February last, that an inquiry be had relative to a publication in a newspaper called the *Aurora* . . .

And after debate, the Senate adjourned.[1904]

FRIDAY, MARCH 7, 1800

GENERAL ★ AURORA ★ ADVERTISER

IN SENATE

Yesterday, the consideration of the resolution respecting the Editor of the *Aurora* being called for, Mr. Pinckney read in his place two or three resolutions . . . on the independence of the press . . .

Mr. Tracy of the senate declares that in his opinion *"the Aurora"* is the very worst paper in the United States—"O righteous Judge !—a second Daniel !"

Today, in the Senate of the United States, the Annals of Congress report:

The Senate took into consideration the motion made yesterday for amending the motion . . . that an inquiry be had relative to a publication . . . in a newspaper called the Aurora . . . And, after debate, the Senate adjourned.[1905]

Today, Republican U.S. Senator Stevens Thomson Mason of Virginia writes James Madison:

> *Ross's Bill for deciding on the Election of Pres[iden]dt & V P[residen]t is still before the Senate . . . still retaining the obnoxious principles of it . . .*
>
> *We have been three days upon and are now discussing a resolution ag[ains]t the Editor of the Aurora for a publication of the 19th of Feby. An amendment to connect with it an equally or more offensive publication of Fenno of the 13th was rejected by the usual Vote . . .* [1906]

Thomas Jefferson notes:

> *Heretical doctrines maintained in Senate. On the motion against the Aurora. That there is, in every legal body of men, a right of self-preservation . . . That the common law authorizes the proceeding proposed ag[ains]t the Aurora . . . That the privileges of Congress are and ought to be indefinite . . .* [1907]

SATURDAY, MARCH 8, 1800

GENERAL ★ AURORA ★ ADVERTISER

Published *(DAILY)* By WILLIAM DUANE, *Successor of* BENJAMIN FRANKLIN BACHE, at No. 112 Market Street, Philadelphia. EIGHT DOLLARS *per ann.*

TO SUBSCRIBERS

Those who are in arrear to this office for subscriptions and whose periods are near a close are requested to make immediate payment— as no paper will be forwarded to those who do not pay regularly, a rule necessary to the support of the liberal expenditures of a paper whose circulation is greater and more feared by the enemies of republicanism than any other in the nation.

The change in today's masthead proclaims my new position as the paper's publisher. Does "successor" suggest something more ?

Today, in the Senate of the United States, the Annals of Congress report:

> The Senate resumed the consideration of the motion . . . that an inquiry be had relative to a publication on the 19th of said month, in a newspaper called the Aurora . . .
>
> And, on the motion to agree to the original motion as amended, it was passed in the affirmative—yeas 19, nays 8 . . .
>
> So it was
>
> *Resolved,* That the Committee of Privileges be and are hereby directed to consider and report what measures it will be proper for the Senate to adopt in relation to the newspaper, printed in the city of Philadelphia, on

Wednesday morning the 19th of February, 1800, called the General Advertiser, or Aurora; in which it is asserted that the bill prescribing the mode of deciding disputed elections of President and Vice President of the United States had passed the Senate, when, in fact, it had not passed . . . and generally to report what measures ought to be adopted in relation to sundry expressions contained in said paper, respecting the Senate of the United States, and the members thereof, in their official capacity.[1908]

Today, Thomas Jefferson writes James Madison,

We have this day also decided in Senate on the motion for overhauling the editor of the Aurora. It was carried, as usual, by about 2 to 1 . . .

The feds begin to be very seriously alarmed about their election next fall. Their speeches in private, as well as their public and private demeanor to me, indicate it strongly. This seems to be the prospect. Keep out Pennsylv[ania], Jersey & N. York, & the rest of the states are about equally divided . . . [T]he event depends on the 3. middle states above men[tioned]. As to them, Pennsylvania passes no law for an election at present . . .

In N. York, all depends on the success of the city election which is of 12 members . . . which is sufficient to make the two houses joined together republican in their vote [for presidential electors] . . . If Pennsylvania votes, then either Jersey or New York giving a republican vote decides the election. If Pennsylv[ania] does not vote, then New York determines the election. In any event, we may say that if the city election of N. York is in favor of the Republican ticket, the issue will be republican . . . The election of New York being in April it becomes an early & interesting object . . .[1909]

If New York's Republicans elect a majority to New York's state legislature, that majority can award New York's presidential electors to Thomas Jefferson. Because New York City has so many seats in the state legislature, New York City is critical to that majority.

MONDAY, MARCH 10, 1800

GENERAL ★ AURORA ★ ADVERTISER

A certain federal Senator was heard to say some days ago *"If the Aurora is not blown up soon, Jefferson will be elected in defiance of every thing!"*

Today, in the Senate of the United States, the Annals of Congress report:

The Senate resumed the second reading of the bill prescribing the mode of deciding disputed elections of President and Vice President of the United States and, after debate,

Ordered, That it be recommitted to the original committee, further to consider and report thereon to the Senate . . .[1910]

TUESDAY, MARCH 11, 1800

GENERAL ★ AURORA ★ ADVERTISER

The bill for instituting a kind of tribunal to decide upon elections for President and Vice President, and about the publication of which by the Editor of this paper so much alarm has been excited in the Senate of the United States . . . was taken up in the Senate yesterday . . .

If there was nothing dangerous or hostile to the liberties of the people in this Bill, why has its publication given those who support it so much and such extraordinary alarm?

WEDNESDAY, MARCH 12, 1800

GENERAL ★ AURORA ★ ADVERTISER

TO SUBSCRIBERS.

THE Editor respectfully requests the attention of the Patrons of "The Aurora" to the following considerations. He enters on the proprietorship of this paper without any other capital than public confidence, and personal credit, and his industry. The funds for the maintenance of this paper must, therefore, be derived wholly from itself—and as the expenditures are considerable and necessarily regular, the income must be equally punctual to secure the editor from pecuniary embarrassment . . .

It is for these reasons determined that no paper shall be furnished from this office to any subscriber who shall not pay up all arrears due to this office . . .

Four years further continuance of such measures as we have seen for four years back would . . . not only bring this republic closer in its resemblance to the British monarchy; but the public liberties . . . would be all destroyed. [T]o save us from these multiplied evils . . . unite all hearts in placing at the head of government the author of the declaration of independence [Thomas Jefferson].

The *Argus*, a republican paper published for several years in New-York by the late worthy citizen *Thomas Greenleaf*, has been transferred to a new proprietor and its title changed . . .

Bad news for Republicans! Beleaguered by Federalist sedition prosecutions, Anne Greenleaf has closed the New York *Argus* and sold its equipment. Without the *Argus* and without the New York *Time Piece,* New York City has no established Republican paper[1911] to influence the upcoming election of state legislators (who will choose the state's presidential electors). What role will the

Aurora play? Will we distribute the *Aurora* free?[1912] New York's sedition trials are coming up just before the New York election. John Adams' methods of intimidation are clear.

THURSDAY, MARCH 13, 1800

GENERAL ★ AURORA ★ ADVERTISER

On Monday, we propose commencing a report of the recent extraordinary proceedings in the Senate concerning the Editor of this paper . . .

We consider the security of the *press* of at least equal moment with the *privileges*, real or assumed, of the Senate and hold ourselves bound to maintain that freedom established by the Constitution, and in the spirit of the Constitution, against every effort of an illegal or unconstitutional nature which may be made to destroy it.

We have waited in silence . . . the proceedings of the [United States] Senate . . . It remains to be seen whether the arbitrary and undefined powers of an English hereditary house of lords are to be adopted by men whose privileges the constitution has expressly defined and limited—and whether our Senate has the power to assert in their own body the various functions of *accusers, judges, jurors,* and *executioners,* in a case where they are also *parties.*

When the federal constitution was under consideration in 1787, the late venerable ROGER SHERMAN of Connecticut . . . prophetically said, "That the Senate of the United States, possessing both legislative and executive powers, was such a monster that it would swallow up and absorb every other body of the general government if it was not restrained . . ."

Friday the 11th of April next, the trial of CHARLES HOLT, Editor of the BEE, comes on at *New Haven* . . .

FRIDAY, MARCH 14, 1800

GENERAL ★ AURORA ★ ADVERTISER

The *federalists* begin to feel the imprudence . . . They now perceive the people awakened . . . Men who have been ruined for being *democrats* under a *democratic* government can now hold up their heads . . . But while the people are returning so rapidly in all parts of the union to . . . the principles of 1776 in opposition to the monarchical innovations and doctrines which have been imposed on this nation, the innovators redouble their activity for mischief . . .

GENERAL ★ AURORA ★ ADVERTISER

Witness the prosecution of Mr. [Thomas] Adams, printer of the Boston *Chronicle*, the only paper in that town which was dedicated to liberty! . . . [T]he consequence of this verdict was that Mr. Adams was sentenced to a long imprisonment which so injured his health that he died soon after the term of his captivity expired . . . Mr. Frothingham of New-York . . . was only an assistant in the printing office of Mrs. Greenleaf, proprietess of the *Argus*, one of the numbers of which paper contained a paragraph stating that Alexander Hamilton was at the bottom of a plan that was on foot for purchasing the *Aurora*—this could not be considered a libel in any country in the world but in the eyes of a *federal jury* . . . [T]he court sentenced him to a fine and imprisonment . . . the happy consequence of introducing the practice of English [common] law [where truth is no defence to a libel action] amongst a free people ! . . . I may be found a libeller if I publish that I saw the president of the United States riding pell-mell down Market street . . .

Today, in the Senate of the United States, the Committee on Privileges makes its report:

REPORT . . .

WHEREAS, on the 19th day of February now last past, the Senate of the United States being in session in the city of Philadelphia . . . publication was made in the newspaper printed in the city of Philadelphia, called the General Advertiser or Aurora . . .

Resolved, That the said publication contains assertions and pretended information, respecting the Senate, and the committee of the Senate and their proceedings, which are false, defamatory, scandalous and malicious, tending to defame the Senate of the United States, and to bring them into contempt and disrepute, and to excite against them the hatred of the good people of the United States; and that the said publication is a daring and high-handed breach of privileges of this house.

Resolved, That William Duane, now residing in the city of Philadelphia, the editor of the said newspaper, called the General-Advertiser, or Aurora be, and he is ordered to attend at the bar of this house . . . to make any proper defence for his conduct . . .[1913]

GENERAL ★ AURORA ★ ADVERTISER

We this day commence the debates on the extraordinary and unconstitutional measures which have been attempted in the Senate of the

United States to implicate and coerce the editor of this paper. We also give the report of the committee of privileges . . .

At present we shall restrain the sentiments which we feel and must utter on this monstrous attempt; an attempt which no act of the Editor shall ever sanction or countenance—no apprehensions of a personal kind shall ever induce him to betray the liberties of his country, the constitutional right of free discussion, or to submit to any authority which is not authorized by the Constitution or the laws.

The people of the United States are called upon to consider this question . . .

Today, in the Senate of the United States, the Annals of Congress report:

Mr. Ross, from the committee to whom was recommitted the bill prescribing the mode of deciding disputed elections of President and Vice President of the United States, reported amendments, which were read. *Ordered,* That they lie on the table.[1914]

TUESDAY, MARCH 18, 1800

GENERAL ★ AURORA ★ ADVERTISER

[W]hat can the public think of a party whose impotent vengeance is directed against such men as *Jefferson* . . . and who deign to employ such wretched tools for their calumny as *Fenno* and *Porcupine* ?

Suppose the Legislature of the state of Pennsylvania do not chuse to direct the mode in which Electors for the office of President shall be chosen. What then ?

Today, in the Senate of the United States, the Annals of Congress report:

The Senate took into consideration the report of the Committee of Privileges on the measures . . . to adopt in relation to . . . the General Advertiser, or Aurora; and,

On motion to adopt the first resolution reported, it was agreed . . . that the question should be taken on the following words:

Resolved, That the said publication contains assertions and pretended information, respecting the Senate . . . which are false, defamatory, scandalous, and malicious; tending to defame the Senate of the United States, and to bring them into contempt and disrepute, and to excite against them the hatred of the good people of the United States.

And on the question to adopt this part of the resolution, reported by the committee, it passed in the affirmative—yeas 20, nays 8 . . .[1915]

Tonight, in the *Gazette of the United States*:

THE AMERICAN ENVOYS have arrived at Lisbon and are proceeding to Paris.

GENERAL ★ AURORA ★ ADVERTISER

Monday being the Anniversary of the *Hibernian* Tutelary patron, libations were poured forth . . . [T]he Editor, proud of the Irish blood that flows in his veins and the Irish virtues which he imbibed in that happy but politically oppressed nation . . . hopes that there will be comparatively few of his American fellow countrymen and citizens who will not enter into the spirit . . . 1. The Anniversary of St. Patrick: May it ever inspire us . . . 2. The Fraternity of United Irishmen . . . 8. The Rights of Man . . . 11. The Liberty of the Press; May it flourish in spite of Sedition Laws and surmount the attacks of Committees of Privilege. VOLUNTEER TOASTS . . . May the *Aurora* rise never to set . . . The Memory of Benjamin Franklin, and B. Franklin Bache, and the spirit of emulation in his successor . . .

Today, in the Senate of the United States, the Annals of Congress report:

> The Senate resumed . . . in relation to a publication in the newspaper called the Aurora . . . and it was agreed . . . "that the said publication is a high breach of the privileges of this House;" and, on the question to agree thereto, as amended, it was determined in the affirmative—yeas 17, nays 11 . . .[1916]

GENERAL ★ AURORA ★ ADVERTISER

The legislature of this state adjourned *sine die* on Monday evening last.

Pennsylvania's legislature has adjourned without enacting a law to allow Pennsylvania to choose presidential electors and without setting a date for the state legislature to reconvene. Now what ?

Today, in the Senate of the United States, the Annals of Congress report:

> The Senate resumed consideration of the report of the Committee of Privileges . . . On motion to adopt this part of the report, as follows:
> *Resolved,* That William Duane, now residing in the city of Philadelphia, the editor of the said newspaper called the General Advertiser, or Aurora, be and he is hereby ordered to attend the bar of this House on Monday, the 24th day of March inst. at 12 o'clock and which time he will have the opportunity to make any proper defence for his conduct in publishing the aforesaid false, defamatory, and malicious assertions and pretended information: and the Senate will the proceed to take further order on the subject . . .
> It passed in the affirmative—yeas 18, nays 10 . . .[1917]

We published on Monday last the Report of the committee of privileges concerning the Editor of this paper. The Senate has been occupied several days during this week in debating two resolutions annexed thereto; in the first of which they *condemn* the Editor, and by the second propose to give him a *trial ! ! !*

On Tuesday the Senate agreed to part of the first resolution; on Wednesday to the remainder, they passed a vote that William Duane, Editor of the Aurora, be ordered to appear at their bar on Monday the 24th inst.

Upon the measures which the Senate have thus pursued, we forbear present comment. As a part of the government of his country, the Editor is under an obligation to respect them and to pay all the deference that is due to their constitutional and legal acts.

The Editor, however, owes a duty superior to that sense of respect and deference; he owes a duty to the constitution itself, to the public rights involved in him, and to his personal rights and honor.

From these superior duties no power on earth shall make him swerve; no terror—no force—no menace—no fear shall make him betray by any act of his those rights which are involved in these measures of the Senate.

By the constitution he will stand . . .

Some letters were published in the *Aurora* lately, stating the circumstances of the outrage committed . . . upon Dr. Logan at Lancaster in the house of assembly, for which publication an action has been instituted against the editor . . .

NEW YORK LEGISLATURE. March 12. In a committee of the whole on the bill directing the appointment of Electors of a President and Vice President of the United States by a general vote of the people of this state . . . After a pretty lengthy debate, a motion to reject the bill was carried, 59 to 54.

Today, in the Senate of the United States, the Annals of Congress report:

Ordered, That the Committee of Privileges prepare and lay before the Senate a form of proceedings in the case of William Duane.

The Senate took into consideration the amendments reported by the committee to the bill prescribing the mode of deciding disputed elections of President and Vice President . . . and having agreed thereto, the bill was ordered to the third reading as amended.[1918]

Tonight, in the *Gazette of the United States*:

The establishment of the last new *Constitution* in France [giving Napoleon complete power], which appears to have been completely effected, may be justly regarded as the final extinguishment of the last glimmering spark of *republicanism* in Europe . . .

The Sovereignty of the People is an useless and impracticable delusion which almost once in every age shoots like a baleful meteor athwart the earth—leaving in its track wretchedness and ruin . . .

A democrat heated with the gin-fumes of an Irish feast raves about the *Irish blood* in his veins. One would think these wretches must have very little blood, Irish or French, in their veins when their *minds* are so full of it.

SATURDAY, MARCH 22, 1800

GENERAL ★ AURORA ★ ADVERTISER

The legislatures of some of the states have availed themselves of the letter of the federal constitution to deprive the people of their votes in the choice of the electors of the president. They have retained the power to themselves, and by deriving the *Presidential* and the *Senatorial* power from the same source (the state legislatures), they have affirmed the cast, complexion, and the character of the executive magistrate and of a branch of the federal legislature . . . abandoning the constitutional principle of the sovereignty of the people . . .

ADVERTISEMENT

WHEREAS by virtue of certain articles of agreement, dated the 5th of March, 1800, between me and Margaret H. Bache, I have been put into conditional possession of the printing presses, types, utensils, &c. employed in conducting the newspaper, The AURORA, I think it right to notify the public that, until the purchase money which I have agreed to pay for the same be fully paid, the presses, types, utensils, &c. are mortgaged to and subject to a lien of said Margaret H. Bache under the articles of agreement aforesaid—And that the conveyance for carrying the said agreement into effect are or speedily will be duly recorded according to law. WILLIAM DUANE

Today, in the Senate of the United States, the Annals of Congress report:

MR. DAYTON [Federalist, New Jersey] from the Committee of Privileges, to whom it was referred to prepare and lay before the Senate a form of proceedings in the case of William Duane, reported in part; which report was read, amended and agreed to as follows:

When William Duane shall present himself at the bar of the House in obedience to the order of the 20th inst, the President of the Senate is to address him as follows:

1st. William Duane: You stand charged by the Senate of the United States, as editor of the newspaper called the General Advertiser, or Aurora, of having published in the same, on the 19th of February, now last past, false, scandalous, defamatory, and malicious assertions, and pretended information, respecting the said Senate . . .

Then the Secretary shall read the resolutions of the Senate . . . after which the President is to proceed as follows, viz:

1st. Have you anything to say in excuse . . .

2dly. If he shall make no answer, the Sergeant-at-Arms shall take him into custody . . .

3dly. If he shall answer, he is to continue at the bar of the House until the testimony (if any be adduced) shall be closed, and he shall retire while the Senate are deliberating . . .[1919]

SUNDAY, MARCH 23, 1800

Today, I meet with two lawyer friends, Thomas Cooper of Northumberland and Alexander James Dallas, to discuss my appearance tomorrow before the United States Senate. By subjecting me to a trial and the threat of arrest, the Senate has usurped the judicial authority of the courts and has refused to allow a challenge to its jurisdiction. It's not clear that the Senate will allow me to be represented by counsel.

Today, following the meeting, Thomas Cooper writes Thomas Jefferson:

> *Mr. Dallas, Mr. Duane and myself met to day, and after analyzing the most expedient method of proceeding on our side, we determined at length on the following. That Mr. Duane wld. write you [as President of the Senate] . . . That Mr. Duane shd be in . . . the Senate without formally presenting himself till it become necessary. That if the request to be heard by Counsel should be refused . . . he shall not obey the call [to appear] . . . That on the appearance of Counsel at the bar of the house, they shall state in the outset that they mean to object to the Jurisdiction of the Senate in the present case. That if they are estopped in this, they shall expressly decline entering into any further or other defence . . . That Duane shall be absent [from the Senate] and kept out of the way of the Sergeant at Arms . . . [I]f after these proceedings, the Sergeant, whether acting by order of the house or in consequence of any proclamation . . . should find him [and arrest him], that he fights the question [of his arrest] by application for an habeas corpus.[1920]*

MONDAY, MARCH 24, 1800

GENERAL ★ AURORA ★ ADVERTISER

The notification directed to be made by the Senate [of the United States] to the Editor of "The Aurora" was delivered at this office on Friday last and twelve o'clock this day appointed for further proceedings.

Unwilling to enter into discussion pending this new and unprecedented business, we can only say to the anxious public that the Editor continues determined to maintain his constitutional and legal rights . . .

We hear that the bill which was committed (respecting the election of the president and vice president of the United States) will probably come on in the [U.S.] Senate this week . . . It is this bill that has given rise to all the questions of *privilege* which have lately occurred . . .

Today, I appear before the Senate of the United States. The Annals of Congress report:

William Duane appeared at the bar of the House, agreeably to the summons of the 22d instant . . .

And the charge against the said William Duane having been read, he repeated his request to be heard by counsel.

On which he was ordered to withdraw and a motion was made as follows: . . .

Resolved, That William Duane having appeared at the bar of the Senate and requested to be heard by counsel . . . he be allowed the assistance of counsel . . . in denial of any facts . . . or in excuse and extenuation of his offence . . .

Resolved, That . . . William Duane be ordered to attend at the bar of this House at 12 o'clock on Wednesday next.[1921]

TUESDAY, MARCH 25, 1800

GENERAL ★ AURORA ★ ADVERTISER

The question concerning the Editor of the Aurora which has excited so much alarm in the public mind, was [yesterday] before the Senate . . . [A]t 12 o'clock, the Editor appeared before the Senate, when the president of the senate said as follows,

WILLIAM DUANE. You stand charged by the Senate of the United States, as Editor of the General Advertiser, or Aurora, of having published . . . false, scandalous, and malicious assertions and pretended information regarding the said senate . . . and therein to have been guilty of a high breach of the privileges of this house.

Then the secretary read the resolutions of the senate passed the 20th ult. with the preamble, after which the president proceeded as follows:

Have you anything to say in excuse or extenuation for said publication ?

To which the Editor replied as follows:

Mr. President:—Unpracticed in legal forms and dubious in this case—but willing to do everything that is consistent with propriety . . . I conceive it prudent to advise with men conversant in legal forms . . . My personal considerations in this case are nothing, but the rights of my country and fellow citizens are everything. I cannot surrender or betray them. I am willing to answer through my counsel . . .

The Editor was then directed to retire . . . After debating till four o'clock, the senate resolved . . . That William Duane . . . be allowed the assistance of counsel . . . who may be heard in denial of any facts charged against said Duane or in excuse and extenuation of his offence.

The Senate has allowed me to have counsel but tied my counsel's hands. It won't allow my lawyers to use the truth of my publications as a defense (as would be the case under the Sedition Act), and it won't allow them to challenge the Senate's claim of judicial authority over an ordinary citizen.

Tonight, in the *Gazette of the United States*:

> *D[uane], 'tis said, your honor, means to leave you*
> *Sure D[uane] could not wish so much to grieve you . . .*

WEDNESDAY, MARCH 26, 1800

GENERAL ★ AURORA ★ ADVERTISER

The exterminating Senator asks—"Has the senate infringed the legal and constitutional rights of the Editor of the Aurora," and he goes on to intimate that the Senate had a right to confine at their discretion in the *cells* or to levy a *fine*—To this question, we shall answer that the Senate have no power by the constitution or the law to deprive any man of his *liberty* or *property* . . .

A Federalist on coming out of the Senate on Monday was very solicitous to learn if *Duane* was committed—"No" replied a wag, "but the Senate are *committed*."

The matter at issue in the Senate of the United States concerning the Editor of this paper will be agitated in the Senate this day at 12 o'clock. The Editor, having taken advice of counsel in this case will this morning present that advice to the Senate and govern his conduct rigidly thereby. The opinions of counsel will appear in The Aurora to-morrow.

This morning, I deliver the following letter to the Senate of the United States:

To the President of the Senate.

SIR, . . . [H]aving received an authenticated copy of [the senate's] resolutions on Monday last in my case . . . I transmitted [them] to Messrs. Dallas and Cooper, my intended counsel, soliciting their professional aid . . . Their answers I have also the pleasure to inclose . . .

I find myself in consequence of these answers deprived of all professional assistance . . . I therefore . . . decline any further voluntary

761

attendance upon that body and leave them to pursue such measures
in this case as in their wisdom they may deem meet [suitable] . . .

WILLIAM DUANE[1922]

This afternoon, in the Senate of the United States, the Annals of Congress report:

> The VICE PRESIDENT communicated a letter signed William Duane . . . enclosing certain papers said to be a correspondence between him and his intended counsel . . .
>
> On motion that the papers referred to in the letter be read, it passed in the negative . . .
>
> The order of the day was called for.
>
> *Ordered,* That the Sergeant-at-Arms, at the bar of the House, do call William Duane. And the said William Duane did not appear. Whereupon,
>
> *Resolved,* That as William Duane has not appeared . . . and has addressed a letter to the President of the Senate . . . his letter be referred to the Committee of Privileges to consider and report upon.[1923]

THURSDAY, MARCH 27, 1800

GENERAL   ★ AURORA ★   ADVERTISER

A meeting was some time ago held in this city of persons principally belonging to this city and State, wherein an opinion was given that the destruction of "the Aurora" or removal of its editor was necessary for the success of the federal party at the presidential election.

This opinion was adopted, and it was determined to employ every means to break down the paper and dismay or ruin the editor. Every step taken hitherto has only tended to thwart the views of that party. But it may not be improper to apprize the public that, among other means, suits at law have been instituted which now amount to no less than NINE! some of them upon facts which the Editor is willing to perish if he does not prove.

Some of those who devised the Sedition Bill looked forward to the present period. It was hoped by that measure the danger of enquiry into the merits of public characters would be so great as to deter any man from discussion. Suits have been instituted in various parts of the union to terrify printers into silence or servility. Juries have been packed to condemn individuals where the truth was not allowed to be proved. But men are still found who dare speak the truth.

The first pretext for this persecution was the publication of a bill which had passed the senate two readings, involving the elective rights of this State. It was soon found that this was not tenable ground. Advantage was then taken of an error which the editor himself discovered and voluntarily rectified. The exposition of certain secret meetings of a party

762

(which was the most important ground because it was provable by the evidence of several members of congress) was next seized upon.

The rest is before the public. We have now but to add the correspondence of the editor with two gentlemen of the bar, to whom he has been compelled to resort for advice.

(copy)

TO A. J. DALLAS, Esq.

SIR, I enclose you a copy of the resolution of the senate passed yesterday, and must request you would favor me by appearing with Mr. [Thomas] Cooper as my counsel to-morrow at twelve o'clock . . .

WILLIAM DUANE

(Mr. Dallas's Answer)

SIR, . . . The Senate, having I understand charged you . . . proceeded without hearing you or notifying you of the charge . . . Before, however, any punishment shall be inflicted or any sentence pronounced, the Senate has been pleased to . . . allow you the assistance of counsel who may be heard in denial of any facts charged against you . . .

I cannot consent to act as counsel under so limited an authority. For you will at once perceive that it excludes any enquiry into the jurisdiction of the Senate . . . as well as any justification of the obnoxious publication by proving the truth of the facts which it contains. As to the rest, I cannot suppose that either you or your counsel would find it practicable to deny the existence of any fact which the Senate has already . . . examined and established.

A. J. DALLAS

(Mr. Cooper's Answer.)

SIR, . . . I heard sufficient of the debate yesterday (before I saw your letter) that the intent and meaning of the resolution is to preclude all argument on the jurisdiction and all the proof that might be offered in justification . . .

[T]o appear before a tribunal which, in a new and most important case, has prejudged you . . . would certainly tend to disgrace your cause and my character.

I cannot think you will be able to procure any professional assistance on such strange and unusual terms . . .

Where rights are undefined, and power is unlimited—where the freedom of the press is actually attacked, under whatever intention of curbing its licentiousness, the melancholy period cannot be far distant when the citizen will be converted into a SUBJECT.

THOMAS COOPER

Today, in the Senate of the United States, the Annals of Congress report:

MR. [JONATHAN] DAYTON [Federalist, New Jersey], from the Committee of Privileges . . . made report as follows:

Resolved, That William Duane, editor of the General Advertiser, or Aurora, having neglected and refused to appear at the bar of this

House at 12 o'clock on the 26th day of March instant . . . is guilty of contempt of said order and of this House, and that, for said contempt, he, the said William Duane, be taken into custody of the Sergeant-at-Arms attending this House, to be kept subject to the further orders of the Senate.

On Motion to agree to this first resolution reported, it passed in the affirmative—yeas 16, nays 12 . . .

The Senate resumed the third reading of the bill prescribing the mode of deciding disputed elections of President and Vice President . . . And after debate, the further consideration of this bill was postponed.[1924]

Tonight, in the *Gazette of the United States*:

A foreigner by education, if not by birth, acknowledging himself to have remained in the service of a foreign power until expelled from its dominions, attached to our country neither by the ties of patriotism, connection, nor interest, with a character known only by the infamy with which it is blackened, has long been suffered to calumniate the measures of our government, to traduce the individuals of whom it is composed, and to be one of the great engines . . . to surrender our independence to France. When at last a feeble attempt is made to curb and punish him, he boldly bids defiance to the highest court of judicature in the country . . . [T]he advice to resist the authority of the Senate is as plainly to be perceived as it is cautiously expressed; the resistance actually takes place, and that body, as though awed by the boldness of such a reptile as Duane, finds it necessary to take time to collect their scattered senses, to reanimate their drooping courage, before they can resolve to enforce their *constitutional right*.

FRIDAY, MARCH 28, 1800

GENERAL ★ AURORA ★ ADVERTISER

Mr. Dayton from the committee of privileges yesterday reported that the Editor should be taken into the custody of the Sergeant at Arms on a warrant to be signed by the President of the Senate; this report was agreed to . . .

The warrant for his apprehension stated that, for the Editor's *contempt* in not obeying the order of the house which required his attendance at the bar last Wednesday, he be taken into custody of the Sergeant at Arms, and then proceeded, "These are therefore to require you James Mathers, Sergeant at Arms to the Senate of the United States, forthwith to take into your custody the body of Wm. Duane and him safely keep until further orders of the Senate; and *all* MARSHALS, *Deputy Marshals, and all other civil officers of the United States,* and every other person, are hereby required to be aiding and assisting to you in the execution thereof . . ."

The great question of the Constitutionality and on the passage of the bill on the Election of the President of the United States comes on THIS DAY IN SENATE.

THE EDITOR *requests his friends who may wish to communicate with him to commit to writing what they wish to say under seal, and deliver at the office as usual, and they will be sure to reach him in less than 48 hours.*

Today—hard as it may be to believe—I, William Duane, publisher of America's largest newspaper, am in hiding from the Senate of the United States!

Today, in the United States Senate, the Annals of Congress report:

DISPUTED PRESIDENTIAL ELECTIONS
The Senate resumed consideration of the bill prescribing the mode of deciding disputed elections of President and Vice President of the United States . . .
Mr. [C.] PINCKNEY [Republican, South Carolina] addressed the chair . . . When Mr. P. had concluded, the question was taken on the passage of the bill, and it was determined in the affirmative—yeas 16, nays 12 . . .[1925]

Tonight, in the *Gazette of the United States*:

IN THE SENATE . . . Mr. Mason moved to strike out the latter part of the resolution which commands all Marshals, Constables, &c. to be aiding and assisting the said sergeant at arms in the execution of his duty [to take into custody William Duane].
The question upon this motion was taken by ayes and nays, and negatived—ayes 10—noes 19.

SATURDAY, MARCH 29, 1800

GENERAL ★ AURORA ★ ADVERTISER

[T]he period approaches when the people will have to chuse between the destruction of their liberties as a nation and the rejection of all those from public stations who have been aiding or abetting in those measures which have brought the nation and constitution into their present jeopardy . . .
Let the people compare the conduct of Mr. Adams . . . [L]et them examine the . . . addresses and answers during the *season of terror* in 1798 . . . These are serious considerations . . . [T]he people must act upon them at the approaching election or prepare themselves for the *calm of despotism* . . .
My countrymen! if you have not virtue enough to stem the torrent, determine to be slaves at once . . . Let not the persecution of an individual dismay you—better the Editor of the Aurora should perish than this

tyranny should be established—William Duane will never desert the liberties of his country—Let the people all declare they will stand by the constitution or perish with it, "and the *osiers* will tremble at the breath of their creator !"

Tonight, in the *Gazette of the United States*:

It was an error fatal to themselves . . . when the French, in their revolution, determined to imitate the republic of Rome rather than the British constitution . . . If they had followed Montesquieu [with his checks and balances] rather than Tom Paine, how glorious, instead of disreputable, would have been the result! . . . How did this country improve its condition and its fame, when under the auspices of George Washington and other leading men, the people formed a constitution similar to that of England . . . If the federal constitution had not been adopted, the Sabbath might have been abolished, and the guillotine erected in all its horrors.

It is disgraceful to mankind that such a man as Tom Paine, an ignoramus, a drunkard, and a blasphemer, should have had so much influence among them . . . The restoration of the white cockade in France, the emblem of lawful authority, would still the waves of anarchy . . . The restoration of the king, with limited powers, in France might be highly beneficial to the United States of America as well as to other countries.

[M]en will wonder that Paine's pamphlets were ever read, and that the pitiful proverbs of Franklin were ever popular.

The Letters of Messrs. Cooper and Dallas [concerning Duane] . . . were not . . . *read in Senate;* being too indecent, it was voted that they should not be read.

SUNDAY, MARCH 30, 1800

Today, Virginia Congressman John Dawson writes James Madison:

You have seen the proceedings in the case of Duane & altho you & <u>all</u> *persons in the U.S. (including no doubt, army & navy) are called on to assist in apprehending him, he is not yet taken . . .*[1926]

TUESDAY, APRIL 1, 1800

GENERAL ★ AURORA ★ ADVERTISER

Many citizens appear surprised that Mr. *Jefferson* should affix his name to the extraordinary warrant issued by the majority of the Senate against the Editor of this paper. But these people do not recollect that the Constitution declares the [Senate] President shall have no vote in any case unless the Senate is equally divided. The famous *Committee of Privileges* reported that he ought to sign it, and a majority decided in favour of the report. The Vice President could therefore have no choice left but to sign their act, leaving upon its authors the responsibility and the odium of the act for which Mr. Jefferson is no more accountable than for the *Sedition Law*, or Mr. Ross's law for regulating *elections* &c., a measure expressly designed to prevent Mr. Jefferson being elected President . . .

Tonight, in the *Gazette of the United States*:

HOUSE OF REPRESENTATIVES. Monday, March 31. The bill sent from the Senate this morning, prescribing the mode of deciding disputed elections of President and Vice President was read a first time, and upon the question shall the bill have a second reading, it was carried, ayes 53 . . .

WEDNESDAY, APRIL 2, 1800

GENERAL ★ AURORA ★ ADVERTISER

By oppressive acts towards the Editor of this paper, the authors and supporters of certain measures obtain one end at least—they defeat that activity and industry with which he personally watched over daring and dangerous measures. It was of some importance to those folks that no report could be given of several of their recent debates . . .

The Bill for deciding disputed elections of President, which passed the Senate on Friday, 16 to 12, demands public regard; it . . . goes to create a new branch in the government which can put whom they please at the head of our government. By our absence from the Senate Gallery, we are not able to report the debates . . .

Today, Virginia's Senator Stevens Thomson Mason writes James Madison:

You will have seen the high handed proceedings of the Senate ag[ains]t Duane. He is not yet taken & I believe those who ordered him to be arrested wish he may not . . .[1927]

THURSDAY, APRIL 3, 1800

GENERAL ★ AURORA ★ ADVERTISER

To URIAH TRACEY, Senator in Congress for the State of Connecticut, SIR, I have read with singular satisfaction your speech of the 5th [of March] . . . on the *free* presses of free America . . . [I]t would seem that, according to the Connecticut scale of morality, *falsehood* and *abuse* issuing from the English press of [Porcupine,] an Englishman in Philadelphia, is *meritorious*, whilst truth from the American press established by the Grand Children of Dr. Franklin and continued by a native American is detestable. REPUBLICAN

The new electoral council or college of Mr. Ross's invention, by being left at liberty to act without *rule* and in *secret*, may be very fitly compared with the secret council of Ten at Venice of old.

Today, from Philadelphia, Thomas Jefferson writes James Madison:

The Senate . . . have this day rejected a bill . . . for removing military troops from the place of election on the day of an election. You will have seen their warrant to commit Duane. They have not yet taken him . . .[1928]

Today, the United States Circuit Court for New York finds that William Durell of the upstate New York *Mount Pleasant Register* published a *"false, scandalous, malicious and defamatory Libel of and concerning John Adams."* The court will sentence Durell to serve four months in jail, to pay a $50 fine, and, upon release, to post a $2,000 security. The *Mount Pleasant Register* has ceased operation.[1929]

Tonight, in the *Gazette of the United States*:

It is certainly a most interesting spectacle for the people of America to behold their rights and privileges guarded and defended by Messrs. Duane, Dallas, and Cooper against the encroachment of about thirty eminent characters [senators] chosen from various quarters of the union and associated together for constitutional purposes . . . [T]he above respectable triumvirate are deeply versed in all the arcana of revolutionary schemes, both foreign and domestic . . .

FROM THE ALBANY REGISTER. [New York.] The late proceedings of the Senate of the United States, in relation to that zealous and undaunted advocate of the liberties of his country, the editor of the *Aurora*, are viewed by all unbiased men as an arbitrary stretch of power . . .

[T]he privileges of the Senate of the United States are derived from a written constitution or supreme law of this land, and that, it will be found, bestows no such privilege as they contend for in the case of Mr. Duane. If he has violated the law, let him be convicted and punished according to law—but let us have no unconstitutional court of inquisition.

FROM THE N[EW] L[ONDON] BEE [Connecticut.] The present number of this paper probably closes the editorial career of the Printer of the *Bee* in this state. On the 18th instant he is bound to appear at the bar of the Circuit Court of the United States for the District of Connecticut, then to sit at New-Haven, and to stand trial upon an indictment under the sedition law for publishing a piece in May last mitigating against the recruiting service. Situated in this predicament, he has heretofore forborne to detail the outrages of a set of men whose situation in society has protected their infamy . . .

Charles Holt will shortly have to close Connecticut's only Republican newspaper, the *Bee* of New London.[1930]

THURSDAY, APRIL 10, 1800

GENERAL   ★ AURORA ★   ADVERTISER

To-morrow will be the memorable festival so long celebrated in the Christian Church, commemorating the expiation of sinners offered by the founder of the Christian faith on the Cross—the pious people of Connecticut have also appointed that day for a solemn *fast* and *prayer*—and on the same day, a political *Auto da-fé* [sentence of Spanish Inquisition] is to be solemnized on the person of Mr. *Charles Holt*, a printer [of the New London *Bee*], who has been accused of the barbarous and heinous act of discouraging the recruiting of a standing army, for which he is that day (that is, on *Good Friday*, the day of solemn fast and prayer) he is to be tried under the Sedition law!—Else wherefore breathe we in a Christian land ?

Today, from Philadelphia, Thomas Jefferson writes a friend,

> *The bill for the election of President & V. P. passed the Senate in a much worse form than that in which Duane published it, for they struck out the clause limiting the powers of the electoral committee and [accorded] it to all subjects of enquiry. What its fate will be in the lower house we know not . . .*
>
> *You have heard of the proceedings against Duane. The marshal has not yet been able to get hold of him. Mr. Cooper . . . is indicted here . . .*[1931]

FRIDAY, APRIL 11, 1800

GENERAL   ★ AURORA ★   ADVERTISER

Franklin, a printer from the obscure colony of Pennsylvania, excited the admiration of the old world by the boldness of his ideas and the success of his grand experiments and discoveries . . . [I]n 1754, he framed that form of combination for the whole of the colonies by their Delegates which . . . properly assumed the name of Congress—a name and a system which was the basis of all the subsequent assemblies of the

United States . . . but you will find not one in one hundred of our youth who know anything about him . . . This is a lamentable description of national degeneracy!

Today, the Adams administration brings a Sedition Act indictment against Thomas Cooper of Northumberland for a handbill Tom Cooper wrote in November (blaming John Adams for high interest rates, &c).[1932] *[H]aving offended the senate by the active part he took in the case of the editor of the Aurora persecuted by the senate . . . it was determined to crush him. He had been all the winter in Philadelphia, and every day seen in public, yet no process was taken against him until three days before the meeting of the court on the 11th . . . He was indicted for a pretended libel on the president in a publication of the 2d of November which was an answer to a very virulent attack made upon him by Fenno . . .*[1933] Tom Cooper's trial begins on the 19th.

Today, the federal sedition trial of Charles Holt, publisher of the New London, Connecticut, *Bee,* begins at the Circuit Court in New Haven. His crime: describing John Adams' new army as a *"standing"* rather than a *"provisional"* army. George Washington's nephew, Judge Bushrod Washington, upholds the Sedition Act and demonstrates to the jury that Holt's publication is, in the words of an observer, *"libellous beyond even the possibility of a doubt."*[1934]

MONDAY, APRIL 14, 1800

GENERAL   ★ AURORA ★   ADVERTISER

Much pains are taken in the federal papers, openly and covertly with the curious and malicious view of prepossessing the public mind against the proposed *"History of General Washington by Mr. Scott."* The only objection to this work, as gathered from the railings of these candid men, is that the author is a *republican.*

Tonight, in the *Gazette of the United States*:

The condition of Church and State in America is such as to fill every considerate mind with the most unhappy sensations. In spite of that vanity and fastidiousness which led the Federal Convention, in founding their government, to preclude any connection . . . a strict and indissoluble alliance of religion to government has been ordained in the nature of things. Though formally sundered by Constitution and Laws; together they decline and together (it would seem) they are likely to perish . . . But here, Sir, Jacobinism is triumphant, and unless a different temper shall soon shew itself, it will soon trample underfoot all order, law, property, as it has done religion . . .

GENERAL ★ AURORA ★ ADVERTISER

[T]he important trial of John Fries for treason is now commencing . . .

[U.S.] CIRCUIT COURT

The Grand Jury returned yesterday morning the following bills [of indictment] as TRUE . . .

Thomas Cooper, of Northumberl. co.	libel
William Duane,	d[itt]o . . .
William Duane,	Misdemeanor
in opening and publishing letters of a foreign minister	

Though John Adams will have some difficulty in serving me with the papers (I am still in hiding from the Senate), he has ordered Timothy Pickering to reindict me under the Sedition Act (eliminating the "British influence" count which threatened to embarrass him at Norristown last October!).[1935] He also has had me indicted for opening (and revealing) the dispatches of British Minister Robert Liston.

GENERAL ★ AURORA ★ ADVERTISER

In the cause of liberty and the general promotion of republican sentiment . . . it is . . . in the power of every citizen to contribute . . . and he who does not do it, has abandoned duty . . .

Today, I write Jimmy Callender at the Richmond *Examiner*:

> *You will be surprised to learn that an indictment has been found against me for publishing the celebrated letters of [British Ambassador] Liston found on Sweezey . . . I am told they have withdrawn the indictment found against me at Norris Town last fall, predicated on an assertion concerning British influence as declared by Mr. Adams. It seems they found I had the actual letter of Mr. Adams in my possession.*
>
> *Mr. Cooper, late of Manchester (you know him personally & well), is to be tried for sedition on Saturday. He pleads his own cause. He applied for a subpoena for the president yesterday. The court refused . . . so that we have ONE MAN above the law . . .*
>
> *I have not been out of town, have lived in my own house, and have been several times on parade with the Legion. I keep retired only because there is no magistrate to be found who has . . . virtue or courage to act upon the habeas corpus right. If there was, I should take care to be arrested immediately. In the present circumstances, my only course is to defeat their malice and give a good example to others.[1936]*

GENERAL ★ AURORA ★ ADVERTISER

REPUBLICAN GREENS. ATTENTION.
ATTEND a meeting of the corp, TOMORROW, (Saturday 19th inst.)
at your usual parade . . .   JOHN RONEY, *Lieutenant*

I can't captain my militia corps while I am hiding. Tonight, the *Gazette of the United States* poetically suggests I am at George Logan's:

> From the Senate D——[uan]e flying,
> As advised by Mr. D——[allas];
> Out at St[e]nt[o]n snugly lying,
> Bids defiance to the gallows.
> There with L——[ogan], hatching treason,
> *Sowing seed* on his plantation,
> Brooding o'er Paine's Age of Reason,
> D——[uan]e seeks for consolation.
> Owl-like skulking, during day-light,
> In a dark and gloomy garret,
> Where with L——[ogan], does he rail at,
> Bingham's caucus, like a parrot . . .

SATURDAY, APRIL 19, 1800

GENERAL ★ AURORA ★ ADVERTISER

NEW HAVEN [Conn.] April 15. The Circuit Court of the United States commenced its session in this town yesterday. Mr. Holt, Editor of the (New London) *Bee*, we understand, is to receive his trial on Thursday.

Today, Thomas Jefferson writes Edmund Pendleton:

> *Duane's and Cooper's trials come on to-day. Such a selection of jurors has been made by the [Federalist] marshal as insures the event. The same may be said as to Fries &c . . . We have not yet heard the fate of Holt, editor of the Bee in Connecticut. A printer in Vermont is prosecuted for reprinting Mr. McHenry's letter to Gen. Darke . . .* [1937]

Today, at the U.S. Circuit Court in Philadelphia, Thomas Cooper goes on trial for seditious libel of the President of the United States.[1938] U.S. District Court Judge Richard Peters and U.S. Supreme Court Justice Samuel Chase preside. The Adams administration attend in force! Secretary of State Timothy Pickering, Secretary of War James McHenry, Secretary of the Navy Benjamin Stoddert, John Adams' private secretary (William Shaw), and Senators Uriah Tracy (Federalist, Connecticut) and Jacob Read (Federalist, South Carolina) of the Senate Committee on Privileges all attend. Tom Cooper acts as his own lawyer, though assisted by Alexander James Dallas who represented Benny and, with Tom Cooper, helped me in my appearance before the Senate. From the trial record:

Mr. COOPER then addressed the jury as follows: . . .

Directly or indirectly, the public if not the private character of the President of the United States is involved in the present trial. Who nominates the judges who are to preside? the juries who are to judge of the evidence? the marshal who has the summoning of the jury? The President . . .

Gentlemen of the Jury, I acknowledge, as freely as any of you can, the necessity of a certain degree of confidence in the executive government of the country. But this confidence ought not to be unlimited . . .

But in the present state of affairs, the press is open to those who will praise, while the threats of the law hang over those who blame the conduct of the men in power . . .

Judge CHASE then charged the jury as follows: Gentlemen of the jury— . . .

It appears from the evidence that the traverser went to the house of a justice of the peace with this [seditious] paper . . . It was indecent to deliver such a paper to the justice of the peace . . . This conduct showed that he intended to dare and defy the government and to provoke them . . .

You will find the traverser speaking of the President in the following words: "Even those who doubted his capacity, thought well of his intentions." This the traverser might suppose would be considered as a compliment . . . but I have no doubt that it was meant to carry a sting . . . [I]t was in substance saying of the President, "you may have good intentions, but I doubt your capacity." . . .

The traverser states that, under the auspices of the President, "our credit is so low, that we are obliged to borrow money at eight per cent in time of peace." I cannot suppress my feelings at this gross attack upon the President . . .

Taking this publication in all its parts, it is the boldest attempt I have known to poison the minds of the people . . .

This publication is evidently intended to mislead the ignorant and inflame their minds against the President and to influence their votes in the next election . . .

After the jury had returned with a verdict of Guilty:—

Judge CHASE. Mr. Cooper, as the jury have found you guilty . . . you will attend the court some time the latter end of the week—(the court appointed Wednesday).[1939]

GENERAL ★ AURORA ★ ADVERTISER

The People of North Carolina have commenced the choice of their Electors of President and Vice President of the United States. The republican ticket, it is said, will succeed.

Today, in the United States House of Representatives, the Annals of Congress report:

ELECTION OF PRESIDENT, &c.

Mr. HARPER [Federalist, South Carolina] moved that the Committee of the Whole should be discharged from further consideration of the bill from the Senate, respecting the election of President and Vice President . . . He thought some essential alterations were wanting, which could not be incorporated in the present bill in the House; he particularly referred to the powers of the Committee . . .

The motion was carried—yeas 54 . . .[1940]

The House of Representatives can't accept the Ross Bill as it came down from the Senate. The bright light of the *Aurora* won't allow that to happen.

Tonight, in the *Gazette of the United States*:

THE seat of Government being about to be transferred to the City of Washington [by June 15th] . . . , the Subscriber . . . offers for sale his Printing Establishment in Philadelphia, with all the stock of materials, &c. including the right and title to the GAZETTE OF THE UNITED STATES . . .

I need not say how much I should prefer to devolve the paper upon any other character than a Jacobin . . . It is not without a degree of regret that I resolve to cease my labors . . . J. W. FENNO

GENERAL ★ AURORA ★ ADVERTISER

Poor Fenno is really selling off! . . . The actual state of Fenno's Gazette for two years past is really a curious political subject to discuss— we can approach it upon grounds that few can conceive. The *Aurora*, during the first seven years of its existence, had double the circulation of Fenno's gazette and, taken altogether, was conducted at an expence about 25 per cent less than Fenno's paper—*Benjamin Franklin Bache* actually sunk *fourteen thousand seven hundred dollars* of his private fortune in supporting his paper.—The question thence arises . . . how many dollars must have been sunk in a paper of half its circulation in ten years? . . . [W]ho can tell whence the funds proceeded, for Fenno had no more private fortune than principle . . . [D]id it come out of the contingencies of our treasury or the secret service money of Great Britain ?

Tonight, in the *Gazette of the United States*:

In the year 1774, when the infamous David Williams of Deistical memory resided at Chelsea in the vicinity of London, Dr. Franklin, with whom he was *intimate,* took refuge in his house . . . Here the Philosopher of Pennsylvania concocted with his *pious* friend the plan of a *deistical* and *philosophical* lecture . . . a school of vice and irreligion . . .

WEDNESDAY, APRIL 23, 1800

GENERAL ★ AURORA ★ ADVERTISER

[A] faction devoted to a foreign king and a monarchical system exists within our country . . .

Today, U.S. Senator Stevens Thomson Mason of Virginia writes James Madison:

The most vigorous and undisguised efforts are making to crush the republican presses and stifle enquiry as it may respect the ensuing election of P[resident] & V[ice] P[residen]t. Holt the Editor of the Bee at New London in Con[necticu]t is condemned to imprisonment for 3 months & a fine of $200. [A] Printer in N York has been fined & imprisoned I know not for what. Hazewell a printer in Vermont is indicted & will no doubt be convicted for reprinting from another paper a copy of McHenry's letter to Genl Darke, which letter was actually published by [Secretary at War] McHenry himself in Fenno's paper.

Thos. Cooper of Northumberland was tried and convicted on last Saturday for a libel on the Pres[i]d[en]t. A more oppressive and disgusting proceeding I never saw. Chase in his charge to the jury (in a speech of an hour) shewed all the zeal of a well fee'd Lawyer . . . Cooper is to receive his sentence this day . . .[1941]

Today, at the U.S. Circuit Court sitting in Philadelphia, Judge Samuel Chase addresses Thomas Cooper. From the record:

Judge CHASE. Mr. Cooper, have you anything to offer to the court previous to passing sentence?

Mr. COOPER . . . I have been accustomed to make sacrifices to opinion, and I can make this. As to circumstances in extenuation, not being conscious that I have set down aught in malice, I have nothing to extenuate . . .

Judge CHASE . . . Mr. Cooper, you may attend here again.

Tomorrow is set for sentencing.[1942]

Today, John Adams proposes to his cabinet that the government start its own newspaper:

> *The President of the United States proposes to the heads of depart-ment a subject . . . of great importance to the honor, dignity and con-sistency of the government.*
>
> *In every service of Europe, I believe, there is a gazette in the service of the government, and a printer acknowledged and avowed by it—in every regular government at least. The Gazette of France before the Revolution answered the same purpose with the London Gazette in England . . . This Gazette is said by lawyers and judges to be prima fa-cie evidence in courts of justice in matters of state and of public acts of the government . . . It is a high misdemeanor to publish any thing as from royal authority which is not so . . . Addresses of the subjects, in bodies or otherwise, to the King and his answers, are considered as matters of State when published in the Gazette . . .*[1943]

THURSDAY, APRIL 24, 1800

GENERAL ★ AURORA ★ ADVERTISER

THE FOURTH BRANCH OF GOVERNMENT

The new anomalous body conjured up by the genius of Mr. *Ross* in his famous bill has not obtained all the notice which it requires. The attempt to destroy the Editor of this paper for giving the alarm on the subject might have shewn the public what its authors and supporters contem-plated . . . The truth is that this bill was calculated in its birth to set aside the public voice and to place in the hands of a few men—and we know what a few men in the Senate are capable of—the nomination of the chief magistrate . . .

Ross's men attempted to be invested with an *arbitrary power of de-cision* by which they could, of their own uncontrouled and unaccount-able will, set aside the suffrages of the people . . .

War . . . Today, off Guadeloupe in the French West Indies, the fourteen-gun, ninety-man U.S. Navy cutter *Pickering* captures a French privateer, *l'Active*, of twelve guns and sixty-two men.[1944]

Today, at the U.S. Circuit Court sitting in Philadelphia, a record of Thomas Cooper's trial includes:

> Mr. [Thomas] Cooper attended, and the court sentenced him to pay a fine of four hundred dollars; to be imprisoned for six months, and, at the end of that period, to find surety for his good behavior, himself in a thousand, and two sureties in five hundred dollars each.[1945]

GENERAL ★ AURORA ★ ADVERTISER

Mr. Cooper has been tried and by the verdict of a jury declared *guilty* under the *Sedition Law* on Saturday last. Yesterday morning he appeared at court and was sentenced to six months imprisonment and a fine of 400 dollars . . .

Republicans may rest compleatly assured that they will have every reason to be satisfied . . . with the whole tenor of Mr. Cooper's conduct on the occasion. He defended his own cause throughout, without the aid of counsel.

On the 11th instant Mr. *Charles Holt*, Editor of the *Bee* of New-London, was tried at the Circuit Court New Haven under a charge under the *Sedition Law* for discountenancing the recruiting for a *standing army*. This prosecution, which in any other times would excite astonishment, was supported by the attorney general upon the extraordinary point that Mr. Holt called the *provisional* army a standing army! He was sentenced to be confined *three months* and fined 200 dollars.

Tonight, in the *Gazette of the United States*:

The jury this morning found a verdict of GUILTY against John Fries for high treason . . .

GENERAL ★ AURORA ★ ADVERTISER

Some of the human species display tempers like the brute species; *Fenno* in irascibility approaches to that of a *cat*. In the struggles of political dissolution, as the last effort of hatred and despair, the animal *spits* its ruthless venom at the memory of Dr. *Franklin*. Through the whole course of British influence and dependence, the name of this sage is the uniform object of their toothless rage . . . It is *"working in his vocation"* to attack *Franklin*. [T]he British government are said to have expended a large sum of money, and a most nefarious artifice and stretch of power to *suppress* the publication of Dr. *Franklin's* life, for which he left materials to one of his descendants now in London.

Tonight, in the *Gazette of the United States*:

IN advertising the Establishment of the *Gazette of the United States* for sale . . . [i]t is my desire that propositions for the purchase (if any there may be) should be made immediately.

The paper will be sold with or without the Printing Office, and the most liberal terms given. A small sum only, in cash, will be required; and the remainder of the purchase money will be left to such arrangements that it may be paid out of the income of the Paper.   J. W. FENNO.

SUNDAY, APRIL 27, 1800

Tonight, the Macpherson's Blues are active. A report:

> *About ten o'clock at night, several bodies of armed men were seen parading the principal streets and bustling in every direction . . . The armed bodies . . . were the federal corps called Macpherson's Blues . . . About eleven o'clock . . . this military host was declared to be called out to search for the incorrigible fellow, the Editor of the Aurora . . . [T]he democrats were on the alert, and things soon after became quiet . . .*[1946]

MONDAY, APRIL 28, 1800

GENERAL ★ AURORA ★ ADVERTISER

The public now have an additional and striking evidence of the value of a free . . . press in the total rejection of that *odious Bill* which was introduced . . . by Mr. Ross of this state in the Senate of the U. States. The public will judge . . . the conduct of the Senate towards the Editor of this paper . . . who dared to publish a Bill . . . too abominable to be countenanced by the House of Representatives. Had this Bill been suffered to be stolen through the Senate unexamined, unpublished, and unexposed, it might have escaped the attention of the public until it would have been too late, and perhaps the country would have been saddled with a *secret tribunal* which, by possessing one enormous power, that of actually appointing the President of the United States, could command the fortunes and the liberties of the people.

TUESDAY, APRIL 29, 1800

GENERAL ★ AURORA ★ ADVERTISER

MORE FEDERAL RIOTS

Sunday evening last was selected above all others for throwing this city into a state of alarm. About ten o'clock at night, several bodies of armed men were seen parading the principal streets and bustling in every direction. The peaceable citizens could obtain no information . . .

The armed bodies it appeared were the federal corps called *Macpherson's Blues* . . .

[C]are was taken to produce incidents in abundance; it was said that a body of Insurgents from Northampton were coming into town with their pitchforks . . .

About eleven o'clock a new incident was turned up, and this military

778

host was declared to be called out to search for the incorrigible fellow, the Editor of the Aurora. [T]he effect was of course such as was expected. [T]he democrats were on the alert, and things soon after became quiet . . . [T]he federal Marshal assumed the power of calling out the military . . .

It has been asserted in the House of Assembly of this state that the people are not as capable of choosing electors for President and Vice President as the Legislature on account of their want of knowledge . . . If the people be not capacitated to perform the business of election, what political purpose are they competent to? none at all; there is an end to republican government.

Mr. *Holt*, editor of [the Republican paper,] the Bee, of New London, has been sentenced to two months imprisonment and 200 dollars fine, and for what, truly the whole of the *criminality* was predicated upon the assertion that the President had countenanced a *standing* army—The Lawyers for the prosecution maintained that it was not a Standing Army but a Provisional Army; and herein lay the CRIME ! From the *Bench* in the case of Mr. *Cooper* a few days ago, Judge *Chase* held the same *sophistry* . . .

Today, in the U.S. House of Representatives, the Annals of Congress report:

DISPUTED ELECTIONS.

The House resolved itself into a Committee on the bill prescribing the mode of deciding disputed elections of President and Vice President of the United States.

The bill, as amended by the select committee, provided for the appointment of a joint committee, with certain defined, but no decisive, powers.[1947]

The House has modified James Ross' Senate bill to say that a joint committee may review, but cannot decide, any matters of dispute concerning the election of President and Vice President! The House will send back this enfeebled version to the Senate.

Today, in the U.S. Circuit Court at Philadelphia, Judge Samuel Chase's trial of John Fries and other Pennsylvania war-tax protesters proceeds toward its inevitable conclusion. Alexander James Dallas (John Fries' lawyer) comments:

They [the defendants] had not the ordinary access to information, since our laws are published in English, and most of them only understood German . . . The assessors were sometimes interrupted in their journeys and sometimes jostled in the crowd; and the unmeaning epithets of Stamplers and Tories were rudely applied to the friends of the Government. But however censurable, where is the treason in such proceedings? A rioter and a traitor are not synonymous . . . Is there

any actual force resorted to? No! I find the bridle of one assessor
seized, and his leg laid hold of; but the man is not pulled off his horse,
nor is he the least injured in his person . . .[1948]

From the trial record:

The prisoner was arraigned and pleaded not guilty . . . Mr. Lewis and
Mr. [Alexander James] Dallas, before engaged to act for the prisoner, on
account of the conduct directed by the court . . . withdrew their assistance; so the prisoner was left without counsel . . .[1949]

Mr. Dallas:

Judge Chase had declared that the court had made up their minds
to the law relative to treason . . . [I]t became the subject of altercation
whether we had a right to address the jury upon the law . . .

[Fries' other lawyer and I] stated to the court that we were no
longer his counsel . . .

On the first trial of Fries, we were allowed to address the jury both
on the law and on the fact . . . We also read the statutes of Congress,
particularly the first section of the act called the Sedition Law, in or-
der to show that the legislature of the United States had declared the
offence of which Fries was charged to have committed to have been
only a riot . . .[1950]

From the record:

COURT. John Fries, you are at liberty to say anything you please to
the jury.

PRISONER. It was mentioned that I collected a parcel of people to
follow up the assessors; but I did not collect them. They came and fetched
me from my house to go with them.

I have nothing to say, but leave it to the court.

JUDGE CHASE then addressed the jury as follows: . . .

[T]he court are of the opinion that any insurrection or rising to resist
. . . the execution of any statute of the United States for levying or collecting taxes . . . under any pretence, as that the statute was unjust, bur-
thensome, oppressive or unconstitutional, is a levying of war against the
United States . . .

The Court are of opinion that military weapons . . . are not necessary
to make such an insurrection or rising amount to a levying of war . . .

The jury retired, for the space of two hours, and brought in their verdict, GUILTY. [Sentencing will be May 2d.][1951]

Today, New York begins three days of voting for state legislators who will choose
the state's presidential electors. New York's twelve presidential electors could
make Thomas Jefferson the next President of the United States.[1952] The nation
is watching!

GENERAL ★ AURORA ★ ADVERTISER

On the trial of Mr. Holt at New-London, the federal district attorney, a northern paper says, conceded the truth of the adultery of General *Hamilton* which was part of the libel charged !

Tonight, in the *Gazette of the United States*:

The Democrat hates the British government . . . because it has been the champion of religion and social order . . . It will require centuries to establish . . . a national spirit in the United States of America. The mixture is too heterogeneous; it is compounded of too many foul ingredients to permit any part to be proud of the whole . . .

GENERAL ★ AURORA ★ ADVERTISER

FROM THE N. Y. CITIZEN . . . Wm. DURRELL, late Editor of the *Mount Pleasant Register* . . . at the federal circuit court for the eastern district, held in New York, . . . was tried for reprinting a . . . *Libel* . . . [S]entence was pronounced on Wednesday the 9th inst . . . That he be imprisoned four months, pay a fine of 50 dollars and stand committed till the fine was paid and good security given for two years, himself in 1000 dollars and two sureties in 500 dollars each.

Today, at the U.S. Circuit Court in Philadelphia, Judge Samuel Chase imposes sentence on John Fries. From the record:

The prisoner being set at the bar, Judge CHASE, after observing to the other defendants what he had to say to Fries, would apply generally to them, proceeded:—you have already been informed that you stood convicted of the treason charged upon you . . .

It cannot escape observation that the ignorant and uninformed are taught to complain of taxes . . . and yet they permit themselves to be seduced into insurrections . . .

[I]t becomes you to reflect that the time you chose to rise up in arms to oppose the laws of your country was when it stood in a very critical situation with regard to France and on the eve of a rupture with that country . . .

What remains for me is a very painful but a very necessary part of my duty . . . The judgment of the law is, and this Court doth award "that you be hanged by the neck *until dead.*"[1953]

Tonight, in the *Gazette of the United States*:

Sentence of death has been passed on Fries, Hainey, and Getman, to be executed 23d May.

SATURDAY, MAY 3, 1800

GENERAL ★ AURORA ★ ADVERTISER

At the election in New York, the British faction there have used all their arts . . .

Extract of a letter from Chester County (Penn.), April 29th, to the Editor.

"The public in this part of the country is very much agitated in consequence of that famous Bill commonly called ROSS's BILL—

"We hope the oppression of the Editor will not prevent the *Aurora* from giving us the debates . . ."

Tonight, in the *Gazette of the United States*:

NEW YORK, May 1. *ELECTION* . . . It has been strongly declared that Thomas Jefferson, the object of the present election with the jacobins in this city, is an enemy to all religious establishments. That so very important an assertion should not rest in doubt, I quote the proof from his book . . . *"The legitimate powers of government extend to such acts only as are injurious to others. But it does me no injury for my neighbor to say there are twenty Gods or NO GOD. It neither picks my pocket nor breaks my leg."* And who will now dare to give his vote for this audacious howling Atheist ?

May 2. *ELECTION.* The poll of the election of the Senators and assemblymen in the legislature of the State . . . closed yesterday . . . The votes were not all canvassed at a late hour last evening . . .

Tonight, having learned that New York has elected a majority for Jefferson in the new state legislature, a caucus of New York Federalists decides to have their leader, Alexander Hamilton, urge Federalist governor John Jay to reconvene the old (holdover) state legislature (with its Federalist majority) to change the rules and award presidential electors now on the basis of district elections (each district to choose to certain number) rather than by the state legislature.[1954] Dirty!

SUNDAY, MAY 4, 1800

Today, Aaron Burr and other New York Republican leaders send a letter to me at the *Aurora*, warning that Federalists plan to overturn Jefferson's victory in New York.[1955]

By an authentic account of the Pole for members of Congress and members of the State Legislature of New York, the following appears to be the aggregate of the majorities in the several wards of the republican ticket and the federal—It will be understood that the whole of the republican ticket has been carried.

Maj . . . for the fedral Ticket		*Maj . . . for the Republican.*	
1st Ward	72	4th Ward	37
2nd Ward	234	5th Ward	82
3rd Ward	187	6th Ward	468
	439	7th Ward	301
			933

Clear majority for the whole
republican list. for the state Legislature, 440

Today, upset over the New York election result, John Adams fires his Secretary of War, James McHenry.[1956]

Today, the President's Lady, Abigail Adams, writes her sister:

You need not write to me after the present week. It is my present intention to leave here some time next week . . .

I shall have a very buisy week the next. It is the last time that I shall reside in this city, and, as present appearences indicate, the last time I shall visit it; The people are led blind fold by those who will ride them without saddle but well curbed and bitted.

It is generally supposed that N[ew] York would be the balance in the . . . scale . . . N[ew] York, by an effort to bring into their assembly antifederal Men, will make also an antifederal ticket for President; and this will give all the power sought by that Party . . . To this purpose was . . . Coopers libels—with all the host of Callenders lies . . . A whole year we shall hear nothing else but abuse and scandel, enough to ruin & corrupt the minds and morals of the best people in the world. Out of all this will arise something which tho we may be no more, our Children may live to Rue—I hope we may be preserved from confusion, but it is much to be dreaded.[1957]

Today, in Windsor, Vermont, the U.S. Circuit Court opens the federal sedition trial of Anthony Haswell, publisher of Vermont's and northern New England's leading Republican newspaper, the *Vermont Gazette* at Bennington.[1958] From the record of the trial:

The case being called, the District Attorney opened the case of the part of the United States. Evidence was produced to show that the passages of the indictment had been published in a newspaper called the *Vermont Gazette*, edited by the defendant; the first being part of an advertisement issued by a committee of Colonel [Matthew] Lyon's friends [for a lottery to raise money for his sedition fine], the second being an extract from the *Aurora* . . .

Judge Paterson charged the jury that . . . it [was not] necessary that the defendant should have written the defamatory matter. It was issued in his paper, it is enough.

The jury, after a short deliberation, returned a verdict of guilty, and the court sentenced the defendant to a fine of two hundred dollars and an imprisonment of two months.[1959]

Tonight, in the *Gazette of the United States*:

The Republican faction have carried every point at New York . . . Republican Senators are also elected for the District, of which the city is a component part, notwithstanding there was a small majority against them in the City. Thirteen Republican members for the Districts are also elected to the lower House of Assembly by a majority of 445. The result gives a dead majority to the election of Mr. Jefferson to the Presidency, even tho' M'Kean should not carry his point [in Pennsylvania].

TUESDAY, MAY 6, 1800

GENERAL ★ AURORA ★ ADVERTISER

The result of the New York election must speak to the federal administration in a very emphatical manner how general and decisive the public opinion is against their measures and the baleful policy they have pursued . . .

[T]here is a class . . . of people who always adore the *rising sun* . . .

The character of Mr. *Jefferson* is attacked . . . in the federal prints of New York, and what has been the effect? . . . Good Mr. *Secretary* Hamilton . . . did not frighten the *Democrats* out of their votes. Mr. *Secretary Hamilton* is about to sell the copyright of his [adultery] defence (secured according to law) to *John Ward Fenno*, who is soon to favour the world with a new edition . . . By this bargain, it is probable the immaculate *General*, the assailant of Jefferson, will make the *eleven hundred dollars* which he confesses Mrs. Reynolds cost him!

The state of our country in its domestic and foreign relations has not exhibited so promising a prospect, since the establishment of the federal constitution . . .

Mr. *Adams* in his extraordinary book [the *Defence of the Constitutions of Government of the United States*] . . . bestowed great pains on the principle of the *balance* . . .

The *balance* of public opinion appears, however, to be the most effectual . . . It is by *public opinion*, addressing itself freely to the actions of men entrusted with power, that freedom can be maintained . . .

While writing this article, the Editor has received a letter from New York . . . [with] a new and extraordinary instance of the confirmed depravity of a faction . . .

    Extract of a letter to the Editor, dated New-York, May 4th, 1800 . . . "Their despondency approaches to the melancholy of despair; at a party meeting held last night, it was suggested that Mr. Jay [the Governor] should immediately call the old legislature of this state together and that they should invest him with the power of chusing the Electors of President and Vice President in order to prevent the effects of the recent change in the people's minds from taking effect. Whether this will be attempted by Mr. Jay or not is uncertain. But when it was urged that it might lead to a civil war . . . a person present observed that a civil war would be preferable to having Jefferson . . . It might suit the abandoned politics of Hamilton and Pickering . . ."

Today, unaware that this morning's *Aurora* has revealed his plan to overturn the New York election results, Federalist party leader Alexander Hamilton writes New York Governor John Jay:

You have been informed of the loss of our Election in this City . . . *The moral certainty* . . . *is that there will be an Anti-Federal Majority in the ensuing Legislature; and the very high probability is that this will bring Jefferson into the Chief Magistracy, unless it can be prevented by* . . . *the immediate calling together of the existing Legislature* . . . *[I]n times like these in which we live, it will not do to be over scrupulous* . . . *The calling of the Legislature will have for object the choosing of Electors by the people in Districts. This (as Pennsylvania will do nothing) will ensure a majority of votes in the United States for Federal candidates* . . .

In weighing this suggestion, you will doubtless bear in mind that Popular Governments must certainly be overturned & while they endure prove engines of mischief . . .[1960]

Tonight, in the *Gazette of the United States*:

MR. FENNO,   IN your paper of the 5th of this month I have read a paragraph which reads that "the result of the election in New York ascertains the election of Mr. Jefferson to the Presidency." I do firmly believe this to be an erroneous prediction. I trust this country is not yet so abandoned of God.

FRIDAY, MAY 9, 1800

GENERAL   ★ AURORA ★   ADVERTISER

Extract of a letter from New York, May 7th. 1800 . . .
Thus you see, my friend, that the eyes of our yeomanry have been opened and in spite of all the threats of the *anglo-federalists*, republicanism has triumphed beyond our most sanguine expectations.—

New York Governor John Jay will not accept Alexander Hamilton's plan to overturn the New York elections. Popular opinion won't allow it. One the most active Republicans in the New York election, Mathew Davis, explains:

The result of the election was announced on the 2d of May. On the 3d of May, in the evening, a select and confidential Federal[ist] caucus was held. On the 4th a letter was written to William Duane, editor of the Aurora, stating that it was determined by the caucus to solicit Governor Jay to convene the existing [holdover] legislature forthwith for the purpose of changing the mode of choosing electors for president and placing it in the hands of the people by districts. The effects of such a measure would have been to neutralize the State of New-York, and . . . would have secured to the federal party their president and vice-president. The letter was published in the Aurora of the [7th] . . . of May and called forth the denunciations of those Federal papers whose conductors were not in [on] the secret . . . One of the New-York city papers reprinted the letter, and thus closes its commentary on it:— "Where is the American who will not detest the author of this infamous lie? If there is a man to be found who will sanction this publication, he is the worst of Jacobins!"[1961]

SATURDAY, MAY 10, 1800

GENERAL   ★ AURORA ★   ADVERTISER

Among other wise projects, lately brought forward in Congress, is the establishment of a national library at Washington . . . [B]ooks be purchased . . . Adams's *Defence of the American Constitutions*—Porcupine's edition . . . The *Cuckold's Chronicle* for the use of General Hamilton . . .

Today, still distraught over the New York election result, John Adams demands Timothy Pickering's resignation as Secretary of State and announces his decision to disband the federal army which Alexander Hamilton now commands.[1962]

Today, in the U.S. House of Representatives, the Annals of Congress report:

ELECTIONS OF PRESIDENT.

A message was received from the Senate informing that House that the Senate adhere to their disagreement to the amendments to the bill prescribing the mode of deciding elections of President and Vice President of the United States, made by this House and subsequently insisted on Whereupon

Mr. HARPER moved that this House do also adhere to their disagreement to recede; which was carried, and the bill, consequently, is lost.[1963]

The Ross bill is defeated. The *Aurora* has won. Peter Porcupine will confess,

This Bill was a sweeper. It would, had it passed into law, have in reality placed the election of the President in the hands of the Senate alone. That it would be much better for the country . . . is certain, but . . . [t]o lead the sovereign people through the farce of an election when the choice was finally to be made by thirteen men, seven of whom were to be nominated by the Senate, was a departure from frankness . . .[1964]

MONDAY, MAY 12, 1800

GENERAL ★ AURORA ★ ADVERTISER

ADDRESS

AT a moment when the national legislature is about to take its final departure from this city, the Editor is bound to offer . . . a few considerations which appear to be necessary on this occasion.

From the moment that the destinies of these states appeared to be committed on the issues of a fatal treaty [the Jay Treaty of 1795], "The Aurora," from circumstances unpremeditated but natural, became distinguished as the *national paper*—here it was that the genius and the virtue of the country rallied round the principles of the revolution and republicanism; here it was that the sparks of virtue . . . were cherished by the grandson of that sage to whom posterity will give the first claim to the glory of establishing the American nation and liberties.

It has been confessed by the enemies, and it will not be denied by the friends, of the publication that if this paper did not solely keep from total despair the staggering spirits of the persecuted and insulted friends of the republican form of government, it contributed more to sustain those liberties and to retrain the measures and designs of the enemies of free government than any other means.

It is not only discharging a duty of private affection but an act of public justice to call to remembrance and to make known under what efforts of disinterestedness and with what sacrifices *Benjamin Franklin Bache* persevered to assert the cause of virtue and his country.

This country should not forget, either for the country's honor, for the honor of republican justice, or for an example to others . . . how greatly the present auspicious return of the nation from delusion to a just consideration of its true happiness and interests is owing to the *free and manfully conducted Press* in the hands of *Benjamin Franklin Bache* . . .

In that last trying situation it was that, in a document attached to his will, specially designed to secure this paper to his country, he named the present Editor to be his successor—if in executing the trust so honorably confided to him—if in emulating the spirit and constancy of his predecessor, the present editor has obtained the same hatreds and the same friendships—if he has sustained with success and to the advantage of his country the character of the paper and justified the confidence reposed in him—even then a large share of that merit is due to him who made the choice and gave the example.

It is no longer criminal to read "The AURORA"—its subscription list is now so much encreased that with punctual payments and after employing *thirteen thousand* dollars annually in its unavoidable expences, it will afford a profit of 3,000 dollars a year to the proprietor and encreases daily in circulation and popularity . . .

The present editor undertook this arduous duty when the prospects of the country or of this establishment were not so flattering; and, under the voluntary assurances and proffers of support of the republican interest of a steady and effectual support, he also undertook the proprietorship of the paper . . .

Faithfully supported, the AURORA must continue to hold its accustomed rank & utility, notwithstanding the removal of the Legislature . . . It is the Editor's intention to be *near the Legislature* at their *future* sittings—and to persevere in the same vigilance and industry in the public service which has already obtained for "The Aurora" the unwilling praise of its enemies and the unqualified applause of its friends.

WILLIAM DUANE

Today, Secretary of State Timothy Pickering writes President Adams:

I had indeed contemplated a continuance in office until the 4th of March next; when, if Mr. Jefferson were elected President (an event which, in your conversation with me last week, you considered certain) I expected to go out, of course . . . I do not feel it my duty to resign . . .[1965]

John Adams responds immediately:

[Y]ou are hereby discharged from any further service as Secretary of State.[1966]

It's a day of celebration! Thomas Jefferson stops by the offices of the *Philadelphia Aurora,*[1967] and I attend this afternoon's anniversary banquet of the Republican Society of St. Tammany (guardian saint of the United States) at the great Wigwam near the Buck on the Passyunk road. When I finish my meal and depart the flower-strewn table, my fellow Republicans toast: *"Brother William Duane, three cheers."*[1968]

TUESDAY, MAY 13, 1800

GENERAL ★ AURORA ★ ADVERTISER

In the Senate of the United States on Saturday . . . Mr. Bingham presented the Remonstrance and Petition of the citizens of this city and county, &c. (lately published in the *Aurora*) praying the honorable Senate to reconsider the extraordinary proceedings in the case of William Duane.

We understand that Mr. Dayton was violently opposed to the permitting this remonstrance to be read—on account of the indecency of the language . . . complaining of the unconstitutional conduct of the servants of the people . . .

12 Members appeared against the reading . . . and 12 members in favor of it. But the President of the Senate [Mr. Jefferson] deciding in the affirmative, the remonstrance was read, to wit:

TO THE SENATE OF THE U. STATES,
THE REMONSTRANCE AND PETITION

Of the undersigned Citizens of the Republic of America, resident in . . . Philadelphia, respectfully Sheweth:

THAT WE . . . are fully persuaded that the surest safeguard of the rights and liberties of the people is the freedom of the Press . . .

[W]e had thought no law could be made by Congress abridging the freedom of the press. But we find by the proceedings of the Senate that the privileges of one house may effect what the constitution has forbidden . . .

[W]e observe in the proceedings of the senate another sedition law rising up to appall us; a sedition law that defies the counteraction of the laws of the land or the juries of our country . . .

We had thought that the plain and acknowledged principle of rational justice would have prevented the accusers from being also the judges, jury, and the punishers..

We . . . respectfully call upon the Senate to reconsider the resolutions by them adopted on the subject of privilege in the case of William Duane . . .

Mr. Dayton then moved the order of the day . . . We understand that upwards of a thousand signatures were presented on that day and as many more yesterday.

PARALLEL . . .

"By their works shall ye know them." . . . In the third year of the Presidency of John Adams, under the Sedition Law—alias the indemnity law. [Indictments:] 1. Abijah Adams, printer of a republican paper at Boston for an alleged libel . . . 2. Matthew Lyon, a member of Congress from Vermont under the sedition law . . . 3. Anthony Haswell, a printer in Vermont, for publishing an extract of a letter written by James M'Henry, Secretary of War . . . recommending Tories for [army] officers . . . 4. Charles Holt, printer at New-London, Connecticut, for publishing moral arguments against . . . military establishments . . . 5. *Thomas Frothingham*, a journeyman printer at New York, for . . . stating that Alexander Hamilton had endeavored to destroy the *Aurora* . . . 6. Luther Baldwin of N. Jersey for wishing the wadding of a cannon fired on a day of rejoicing were lodged in the president's posterior. 7. Benjamin Franklin Bache, Grandson of Benjamin Franklin, for publishing an article . . . 8. Thomas Cooper of Northumberland for publishing a number of truths about public men and measures . . . 9. William Duane of Philadelphia for asserting that Mr. Adams had asserted . . . British influence had been used under the federal Government with effect. [Also] Indicted for asserting that the British Government was a corrupt one. (N.B. These two indictments have been withdrawn, but they shall be published.) [Also] Indicted for publishing [British Minister] Liston's Letters found on Sweezy in which it was declared that the American Government was provoking France to a war. Two or three other suits which he does not know what they relate to.

The balance of this account is immense . . .

Tonight, in the *Gazette of the United States*:

As Congress are on the eve of concluding a session . . . it might be well, nay, it would certainly be *very* well if they should, previously to rising, declare war. I think the attempt at such a measure on the part of some spirited member would have good effect. The ties by which it is sought to bind us are truly Lilliputian; war would break them . . .

WEDNESDAY, MAY 14, 1800

GENERAL ★ AURORA ★ ADVERTISER

ST. TAMMANY

Monday, the Anniversary festival of the tutelary SAINT of the United States of America was observed by the social or Columbian order of St. Tammany. Agreeable to annual custom, they assembled in their great

Wigwam near the Buck on Passyunk road . . . Having lighted the great council fire and erected its standard of the orders & tribes & smoked the sacred calumet [and] . . . [a]fter partaking of the feast . . . the noise of hoarse canon was heard along with the songs, and shouts of joy, which were given with a number of toasts . . .

VOLUNTEERS.

By the Sachem THOMAS M'KEAN [Governor of Pennsylvania],— Peace and good government. By the Sachem Israel Israel—The Senate of the United States, may the ensuing election teach them to know and define their privileges . . . By other Brothers . . . Thomas Cooper, of Northumberland . . . suffering for truth under perversion of power . . . After Governor M'Kean, retired, his health with three guns. After he had retired—Brother William Duane, three cheers.

Today, John Adams approves and signs into law:

> *An Act supplementary to the act to suspend part of an act,*
> *entitled "An Act to augment the Army of the United States . . ."*
> *Be it enacted, &c.,* That it shall be lawful for the President of the United States to suspend any further military appointments . . .
> SEC. 2. *And be it further enacted.* That the President of the United States shall be, and hereby is, authorized to discharge on or before the fifteenth day of June next all such officers, non-commissioned officers, and privates as have heretofore been appointed, commissioned or raised . . .[1969]

Peter Porcupine:

> *This bill amounted to a disbanding of the army; because it was well known that Adams, who was now laying in a provision of popularity against the ensuing election for President, would issue orders for disbanding the moment the Congress adjourned . . .*[1970]

John Adams will reflect:

> *[T]he army was as unpopular as if it had been a ferocious wild beast let loose upon the nation to devour it. In newspapers, in pamphlets and in common conversation they were called cannibals. A thousand anecdotes, true or false, of their licentiousness were propagated and believed.*[1971]

Jimmy Callender:

> *It was as clear as evidence could make it that Mr. Adams himself was the prime mover of all those military outrages which had occurred in the annals of his inestimable army. Who flogged Schneider the German printer? Soldiers in the pay of the president . . . Of whom did the gang consist that attacked the printer of the Aurora? They were an attachment of the same corps.*[1972]

Today, in the Senate of the United States, the Annals of Congress report:

> MR. BINGHAM presented an additional remonstrance and petition of a number of citizens of . . . Philadelphia, "praying the Senate to reconsider the resolutions by them adopted on the subject of privilege in the case of William Duane."
>
> And on motion that the remonstrance be read, it passed in the negative—yeas 7, nays 12 . . .
>
> *Resolved,* That the Secretary of the Senate be and he is hereby, authorized to pay to James Mathers, acting as Sergeant-at-Arms to the Senate, out of the contingent fund the sum of one hundred and forty dollars, for extra services [in seeking the arrest of William Duane] . . .
>
> On motion that it be
>
> *Resolved,* That the President of the United States be requested to instruct the proper law officer to commence and carry on a prosecution against William Duane, editor of the newspaper called the Aurora, for certain false, defamatory, scandalous, and malicious publications in the said newspaper . . . tending to defame the Senate of the United States . . .
>
> It passed in the affirmative—yeas 13, nays 4 . . .
>
> *Ordered,* That the Secretary lay an attested copy of the foregoing resolution before the President of the United States . . .
>
> The PRESIDENT [of the Senate], agreeably to the joint resolution of the 12th instant, adjourned the Senate to meet again on the third Monday of November next, as the law provides.[1973]

Three to four thousand people have signed petitions to the United States Senate on my behalf.

Tonight, in the *Gazette of the United States*:

> That wretched vehicle of vulgar rage and ignorance, the *Aurora,* exults loudly in what is deemed, by the starveling scribblers in that Gazette, a scene of delicious confusion . . .

Duane says his *Aurora* is the Government paper and that he is going to the City of Washington. He might be employed at Washington, after a manner level to his *talents,* in carrying hods of bricks and mortar up a ladder, but, as to printing the government paper, it is impossible that a man of his modesty and independence of spirit could seriously think of such a thing.

THE Editor of this Gazette is happy to inform his Subscribers that he has made arrangements as to be able to continue the publication of the *Gazette of the United States* with encreased activity and exertion.

> Sensible of the important influence of Newspaper upon the public opinion, it will be studied to make this paper the vehicle of constant and steady opposition to the liberticidal designs of aspiring and restless demagogues . . .

The Editor and his associates will "intermit no watch against the wakeful foe" . . .

In pursuing their opposition to the vile faction which would place at the head of affairs an atheist and a traitor to his country, they hope to receive . . . the support and countenance generally of all true friends to the commonwealth as it stands . . .

THURSDAY, MAY 15, 1800

FENNO AGAIN

The *Gazette of the United States* is to live a little longer—the despair of its supporters has excited another effort, and Fenno who appears doomed to be the sport of an annual exhaustion and resuscitation, comes now forth with perfect gravity and tells his *twenty-six quires* [paper sets of twenty-four sheets each] of readers that he is "sensible of the importance of newspapers upon public opinion" . . . [&c.]

WHAT HAS THE AURORA SAID ? . . .

Timothy Pickering has been dismissed, *James M'Henry* has resigned— *Alexander Hamilton* has received a hint that his services will be no longer required . . . A motion was made by Mr. Harper in the house of representatives for the disbanding of the standing army . . .

Mr. [Samuel] Dexter has been nominated to the office of Secretary of the War Department . . . Mr. Dexter very candidly confesses that he is as well qualified for the office of feeder of the Chinese Emperor's crocodiles as for that of Secretary at War.

Today, John Adams issues orders to his departing Secretary of War:

> *I request you to transmit copies of the law for reducing the twelve regiments, which passed yesterday, to Major-Generals Hamilton and Pinckney, and also to the commandants of brigades, with orders to make immediate arrangements for reducing those regiments on the fourteenth of June . . .*[1974]

Tonight, in the *Gazette of the United States*:

> The Senate, previous to their adjournment yesterday afternoon, passed a resolution requesting the President of the United States to direct the Attorney General to institute a process against William Duane, Editor of the *Aurora*.

The Vice President of the United States left town yesterday morning.

GENERAL ★ AURORA ★ ADVERTISER

CAUCUSES

WERE held on Tuesday and Wednesday evenings . . . at which Timothy Pickering [attended] . . . One measure . . . appears to have been a necessary consequence of this meeting, the continuation of Fenno's paper . . . Fenno is again afloat, and after a simpering, sniveling course of farewell palavers about higher interests calling him to other purposes, he has come out again with the irascibility of a cat after castigation and spits forth malice with redoubled virulence and acrimony . . .

[Adv]   REPUBLICAN GREENS.

CONFORMABLE to the resolution of the 12th instant— the corps will parade out of uniform for exercise at 6 o'clock on Monday morning next and each succeeding Monday until further orders.

WILLIAM DUANE, *Captain.*

Today, John Adams writes identical letters to the United States Attorney General and to the U.S. District Attorney for Pennsylvania:

I transmit to you a copy of the resolution of the Senate of the United States, passed in Congress on the 14th of this month, by which I am requested to instruct the proper law officers to commence and carry on a prosecution against William Duane, editor of a newspaper called the Aurora for certain false, defamatory, scandalous, and malicious publications in the said newspaper of the 19th of February law past, tending to defame the Senate of the United States and to bring them into contempt and disrepute and to excite against them the hatred of the good people of the United States. In Compliance with this request, I now instruct you, Gentlemen, to commence and carry on the prosecution accordingly.

[JOHN ADAMS][1975]

Tonight, in the *Gazette of the United States*:

Duane gives us a pleasant list of Books . . . As he is to be the Government Printer, if we may believe himself . . . let there be procured for the use and behoof of said scapegrace;—*Meditations on a Prison-life by a Convict . . . Gallows in Pennsylvania; the Arts of Knocking off Fetters and Escaping Dungeons . . . ; an essay on the best means of eluding justice; an improved plan for a gin distillery; the Liar's vade mecum . . .*

Philadelphia Prison, May 16.

TO THE EDITOR.

Sir, I HEARD some days ago that my FEDERAL friends . . . are promoting a Petition to the President to procure a remission of my sentence . . .

I am not so attached to my present lodgings but I should be very glad to quit them . . . but I will not leave the place under the acceptance of a favor from the President Adams. Nor will I be the voluntary cats-paw of electioneering clemency. I know the late events have wonderfully changed the outward and visible signs of the politics of the [Federalist] party . . . But all sudden conversions are suspicious, and I hope the REPUBLICANS will be upon their guard . . .

THOS: COOPER.

WE understand that the President of the United States has signaled to the Executive offices that it will be necessary for them to be in the City of Washington by the 15th of June next. The President, we learn, will proceed to the City of Washington immediately.

CHAPTER FIFTEEN

RAT-CATCHER

Love of Power and the Love of Money . . . have in many minds the most violent effects. Place before the Eyes of such Men a Post of Honour that shall at the same time be a Place of Profit, and they shall move Heaven and Earth to obtain it . . . dividing the Nation, distracting its Councils, hurrying it sometimes into fruitless and mischievous Wars . . . But this Catastrophe, I think, may be long delay'd if, in our propos'd System, we do not sow the Seeds . . . by making our Posts of Honour Places of Profit . . .

DR. BENJAMIN FRANKLIN,
AT THE FEDERAL CONSTITUTIONAL CONVENTION,
PHILADELPHIA, JUNE 2, 1787[1976]

WEDNESDAY, MAY 21, 1800

GENERAL ★ AURORA ★ ADVERTISER

If Mr. *Pickering* has done anything which may have injured the country, as a public officer, he ought to be brought to an exemplary account . . .

The Editor pledges himself to the public that he is possessed of information of a *highly important nature* and that the present article is written expressly with a view to call the attention of the *President* and the *public* to the question; the President that he may discharge his duty by *scrutiny*, and the public that they may see whether justice is done.

If these things are done by the constituted authorities, then the editor will remain silent. If they are not done, then will the editor conceive himself bound to publish the facts—*the substantial and damning facts*—of which he is possessed.

The public will remember that no promise of this kind has ever been made in this paper which has not been duly fulfilled—that matters which no man unconcerned in public affairs could have conceived have been discovered by *the Aurora*—and many wicked measures frustrated by the timely interposition of *this free Press.*

Tonight, in the *Gazette of the United States*:

> The prospect of a French revolution gives new activity and virulence to those propagandists—*Duane* hisses from his retreat—*Cooper*, of Birmingham [England], howls a dismal threat from his den of Felons. In the opinion of Mr. *Cooper*, the PRESIDENT ought to ask his pardon!

THURSDAY, MAY 22, 1800

GENERAL   ★ AURORA ★   ADVERTISER

> A vote was taken in the Senate of the United States on the subject of a petition and remonstrance, presented by a very respectable number of citizens of Philadelphia, in the cause of the editor of the *Aurora*; and as it appeared that the members of the Senate were equally divided, Mr., Jefferson, president of that body, gave the casting vote in favor of the petition and remonstrance being read . . . [W]e are indebted to the patriotic firmness of Jefferson, author of the Declaration of American Independence, for this important decision . . . Americans, is it possible that you can hesitate for one single moment who shall be your President? Jefferson gives his casting vote in favour of the rights of the people to petition for redress of grievances, and Adams praises the British monarch.   *AMERICAN CITIZEN*

> The three citizens who were condemned under an extraordinary stretch of legal construction of the doctrines of *Treason*, [Pennsylvania tax protesters] Messrs. *[John] Fries, Hainey* and *Getman*, were yesterday reprieved by the President and immediately liberated . . .
>
> We cannot now refrain from expressing our abhorrence of the whole proceeding in the case of these unfortunate men, a case which . . . flowed from the extravagant measures which gave occasion to lay an unpopular tax . . . The acrimony of judge Chase . . . does no honor to our judiciary . . .

John Adams' decision to pardon John Fries and Pennsylvania's other war-tax protesters is one more concession to the popular feeling against his war measures.

Tonight, in the *Gazette of the United States*:

> The Government Offices, it is expected, will be removed in all next week . . .

Duane . . . has been so successful of late in discovering the intentions of the President . . . he has a strong title to credit.

No public event, during the administration of Mr. Adams, has excited such universal attention, or given birth to so many and various conjectures, as . . . the dismission of *Timothy Pickering* from the office of secretary of state and of *James M'Henry* as secretary at war . . .

Some suppose that altho' (as they say) *no suspicion* can attach to either of the displaced secretaries of improper dispositions of the immense public sums that have passed thro' their hands . . . their known, open, and manifest predilection for British interests . . . may have awakened the president's suspicions . . .

Others . . . say that the President's conduct is the stern effect of *peevish despair* on the result of the New York elections, fearing that he could not be again elected to office.

The following . . . copied from *Fenno's* gazette of yesterday evening . . . [has] a degree of candor in it which induces us to suspect that the *Moon* has already begun to operate on the young man and that before the end of the week, we shall again hear of his intending to *resign*.

"Duane . . . has been so successful of late in discovering the intentions of the President . . . he has a strong title to credit."

We wish to put a question to *Jonathan Dayton* [formerly Speaker of the U.S. House of Representatives and now] a member of the Senate . . . Jonathan Dayton of New Jersey, do you or do you not hold in your possession *thirty thousand* dollars, the property of the good people of the United States—which was advanced to you for public purposes but which you have never returned to the proper owners for more than two years ?

Messrs. *Fries, Hainey* and *Getman* were yesterday congratulated in the public streets by hundreds of humane citizens and . . . by many men who have been heretofore most violent against the *sinners of Democracy* . . .

Fenno asserts that Messrs. *Fries, Hainey* and *Getman* repented before they were reprieved. The fact, however, is otherwise, for they never were *guilty*, much less conceived themselves so to be.

Tonight, in the *Gazette of the United States*:

Duane in this morning's *Aurora* daringly asserts in the most explicit manner that Fries, Hainey and Getman NEVER WERE GUILTY and thereby charges the Judges, Jurors, and Witnesses with the intention of committing the horrid crime of MURDER!! The sentence which was this day to be executed on Fries, Hainey, and Getman is stiled in the *Aurora* a PUBLIC MURDER!!!!!!!

Dr. Benjamin Franklin asked, *"To put a man to Death for an offence which does not deserve Death, is it not Murder?"*[1977]

The war with Britain, which commenced in the year '75, had for its object, on the part of this country, the most pointed recriminations of monarchy. The declaration was made upon the most firm and republican ground; and its author, Mr. Jefferson, must stand in high estimation with the citizens of the United States, so long as they believe the power of the people to be superior to that of kings . . .

Can all this be said with truth of J. Adams? does he love liberty and genuine republicanism? does he hate monarchy and standing armies? No . . . in his book entitled "the Defence of the American Constitutions," he declares the British monarchy to be the most stupendous fabric of human invention . . . If Adams is a lover of monarchy, [as is] to be deduced from the principles of the book, he certainly ought not to be president of the United States. If, on the contrary, Jefferson is a republican, as appears by all his writings and by all his votes in public life, he certainly deserves the public suffrage . . .

Tonight, in the *Gazette of the United States*:

The close confinement of the culprits, Cooper and Duane, by affording them more leisure to scratch, has for some time past increased *if possible* the venom of that paper . . .

Mr. [James] Callender has announced, in a late number of the [Richmond, Virginia] *Examiner,* his intention to travel . . . [Probably] he designs paying a visit to the Philosopher of Monticello [Jefferson] in order to regale him . . . with the perusal of the second volume of the *"Prospect before us."* . . . The following precious *morceaux* are extracted from that work . . . *"The wretched timidity of Mr. Washington . . . had invited depredations on our shipping. His abject tameness to England, and his gross duplicity to France, had ensured the contempt of the one and the detestation of the other. It ought to have been the policy of Mr. Adams to retrace the mistakes of his predecessor . . ."*

Tonight, a warrant issues in Virginia for the arrest of Jimmy Callender under an indictment charging that *The Prospect Before Us* contains a seditious libel against the President of the United States.[1978]

SUNDAY, MAY 25, 1800

Today, Virginia Governor James Monroe writes Thomas Jefferson,

The G[rand] Jury, of w[hi]ch McClurg was for'man, presented Callender under the Sedition Law, & [Judge] Chase drew the warrant & dispatched the Marshal instantly in pursuit of him. This was yesterday at 12, since w[hi]ch we have not heard of either . . . Will it not be

proper for the Executive [Magistrate of Virginia] to employ counsel to defend him, and, supporting the law, give an éclat to a vindication of the principles of the State?[1979]

Mr. Anthony Haswell, in Vermont, is sentenced to two months' imprisonment and 200 dollars fine for publishing an advertisement for a lottery . . .

It was yesterday reported about town that [Treasury Secretary] *Oliver Wolcott* had resigned . . . Among the measures of the next session of Congress will of necessity be an enquiry into the transactions of the public departments for a few years past.

Today, Thomas Jefferson writes Virginia Governor James Monroe,

I think it essentially just and necessary that Callender should be substantially defended. Whether in the first stages, by publick interference, or private contributors may be a question. Perhaps it might be as well that it should be left to the legislature who will meet in time . . . It is become particularly their cause and may furnish them a fine opportunity . . . of doing justice in another way to those whom they cannot protect without committing the publick tranquillity . . .[1980]

Tonight, in the *Gazette of the United States*:

The vagrant editor of the *Aurora* has for several days past been *humbugging* his asinine followers and readers with tales of caucuses or private meetings of the Federalists in the last week . . . *What are you after doing Pat?* Why you'll surely lie yourself out of credit with the silly supporters of the *Aurora!* fie! fie! man, never leave your natural station, the vantage ground of general charges, scurrility and exclusive lying to descend into the plain field of facts . . .

Thomas Cooper, who has lately been sentenced and imprisoned for six months, under the *mild operations* of the sedition law, in a letter addressed to the editor of the *Aurora*, has exhibited the manly firmness of the philosophic republican . . . Among other things, Mr. Cooper says, "I will not be the voluntary catspaw of electioneering clemency." . . . The pardon of Mr. John Adams, if it should be offered to Cooper, Holt, Durell, and all the other Democrats that have been condemned under the Sedition act, would not ensure his election. It is too late—it is forever too late . . .

Mr. Humphreys, the father of the notorious Mr. Humphreys who, after being indicted and convicted for a most cowardly assault on the late Benjamin Franklin Bache, had his fine remitted and was commissioned by the President of the United States to carry dispatches to France—this Mr. Humphreys, the father, is a ship builder.

To him . . . was given the contract of building the *United States* frigate, a vessel that has certainly cost our country near a million dollars. This vessel of which captain Barry is the commander, has been twice out: once on a cruise and the second time with the late envoys to France.

She is returned. It is said an inquest has been held on her condition: and it is now said she has been condemned and found not seaworthy and is to be laid up. Such is the *federal gratitude,* and *federal economy !*

Today, Jimmy Callender is arrested in Virginia.[1981]

FRIDAY, MAY 28, 1800

GENERAL ★ AURORA ★ ADVERTISER

The President of the United States left town yesterday, drawn by four horses. But the federal blues did not parade to take leave. The President, we understand, will make a tour to the city of Washington before he returns to his seat in Braintree. His lady does not accompany him.

The *Pickeronians* are a little anxious to know what is the thing in reserve—and . . . expect to *provoke* an early discovery by flinging empty declarations at *"the Aurora."* They may shew their zeal but they cannot produce the intended effect.

Mr. Jefferson in his notes on Virginia has expressed himself strongly in favour of religious toleration; the bigots took occasion to call him a *deist,* and that hireling, Fenno, has been ordered to . . . call Mr. Jefferson an *atheist! . . .*

Is every man an Atheist who does not make a public parade of his religion or who does not abuse his fellow citizen for being of a very different persuasion ? I presume we shall not have so many FAST DAYS during his Presidency . . . [T]hey will leave this to such church-going sinners as Mr. Fenno and his gang . . . who laugh at religion in private, who cant about it in public, and accuse of Atheism all those who are content to take for their motto, "By their fruits shall ye know them." . . .

Fenno is finished! Tonight, in the *Gazette of the United States*:

HAVING become Proprietor of the *Gazette of the United States* by purchase from Mr. Fenno, I respectfully solicit the countenance and support of the present subscribers and of the Public generally . . .

CALEB BARRY WAYNE

From several years' acquaintance with Mr. Wayne . . . I can with confidence recommend him to the countenance and encouragement of the Public.

J. W. FENNO

THURSDAY, MAY 29, 1800

GENERAL ★ AURORA ★ ADVERTISER

FENNO, as we predicted a few days ago, has indeed sold out—and is succeeded by a young man of the name of *Caleb P. Wayne*—of whom as yet we know nothing; we shall hope to have something to say to his praise—because he must be very dull indeed if he does not profit by the errors of his predecessor.

We shall hope, among other things, to find less folly and more consistency—more love of country and less hatred of republicanism—because the contrary (with bad company) have ruined and blasted poor Fenno.

FRIDAY, MAY 30, 1800

GENERAL ★ AURORA ★ ADVERTISER

Porcupine, who was so warmly patronized in this city and who lately took refuge in New York, sailed for England on Tuesday last—*John Ward Fenno* succeeds Porcupine in the Bookselling business at New York.

A correspondent enquires whether the late apparent change in the disposition of our government towards the French republic—the dismissal of Pickering from office—the disbanding of the army, &c. are to be considered as the result of a conviction . . . or merely a palliative intended to operate on the minds of the people in the next election?—Also, whether the pardon of the insurgents is to be attributed to the pure lenity of the President? or to a sense of his declining popularity which he hoped to regain by this apparent lenity?—and whether it would be politic or safe to continue in office men whose conduct heretofore must excite at least a suspicion of duplicity in the present?

Mr. *Pickering*, after devoting so many years to the service of his country, has retired *so poor* . . . It would be worthy of the *subject* to enumerate the various services of Mr. *Pickering*—His services as a colonel of militia at Concord in 1774 and the consequences of his prudent *retreat*—his services in the quarter master's department during the revolution, with an account of the monies paid into his hands and yet what

remains unpaid of the public money on account of revolutionary services—whether interest is not fairly due to the public for monies in the
hands of public servants an unusual time (and at the same time as Mr.
Dayton is Timothy's friend, it might be useful to calculate the interest
on the public money in his hands since he was speaker).

Tonight, in the *Gazette of the United States*:

PARIS. April 5. The commissioners for carrying on the negotiations
between France and America held their first sitting [in Paris] on the third
and exchanged their powers.

SATURDAY, MAY 31, 1800

GENERAL ★ AURORA ★ ADVERTISER

It is worthy of remark that a number of remarkable characters have lately
gone or are going out of *Office*.
Mr. *Liston*, British Minister.
Mr. Porcupine, his printer.
Mr. Fenno d[itt]o
Mr. Pickering, their patron, protector, and friend . . .
Mr. M'Henry, Secretary at War.

MONDAY, JUNE 2, 1800

GENERAL ★ AURORA ★ ADVERTISER

Gordon in the 3d volume of his history of the American revolution
states that, on the 19th of October, 1781, the sum of two thousand one
hundred and thirteen pounds six shillings sterling was paid into the hands
of Timothy Pickering, Esq., the American quarter-master general at York
Town in Virginia. It was the amount of Lord Cornwallis' military chest
. . . Ist. Who is this same Timothy Pickering, Esq.? 2d. To whom has this
money been paid? 3d. When has it been paid?

Much surprize was expressed at the suddenness of the departure of
Judge Chase from this city . . . It now appears that he . . . set off for Richmond to wreak vengeance on Callender. A jury conveniently packed by
a federal *Marshal* has found a bill under the sedition law against *Callender*, *a*nd *Judge Chase* swears Callender must go to prison . . .

Tonight, in the *Gazette of the United States*:

Although the notorious and infamous Callender—who has been so constantly employed for several years past in framing lies to destroy the
confidence of the American people in their government—has at last been
taken hold of, Duane with his usual audacity charges the Marshal with

packing the jury in this case and plainly insinuates that Callender is not guilty of the crime alledged.

TUESDAY, JUNE 3, 1800

GENERAL ★ AURORA ★ ADVERTISER

Judge CHASE, the *pious* and *religious* Judge Chase, is going to Virginia where, he says, if a *virtuous* jury can only be collected, he'll punish CALLENDER with a vengeance.

Today, at the U.S. Circuit Court sitting in Richmond, Virginia, Judge Samuel Chase presides at the sedition trial of the *Aurora's* Jimmy Callender, who fled Philadelphia and now edits the *Richmond Examiner.* From the trial record:

The [libelous] matter set out in the indictment was as follows:
"The reign of Mr. Adams has been one continued tempest of malignant passions. As President, he has never opened his lips or lifted his pen without threatening and scolding . . ." . . .

Judge Chase stopped Mr. Nicholas and addressed the counsel for Mr. Callender, thus:—

. . . [Y]ou say that . . . the charges in the indictment are merely opinion, and not [expressions of] facts falsely asserted . . . Can any man of you say that the President is a detestable and criminal man? The traverser charges him with being a murderer and a thief, a despot and a tyrant! Will you . . . excuse yourself by saying it is but mere opinion . . . ?

Mr. WIRT [counsel for Mr. Callender].—Gentlemen of the Jury, . . . [I]f the law of Congress under which we are indicted be an infraction of the Constitution, it has not the force of law . . .

Here, Judge CHASE—Take your seat, sir, if you please. If I understand you rightly, you offer an argument to the petit jury to convince them . . . the Sedition Law is contrary to the Constitution . . . Now I tell you that this is irregular and inadmissible . . .

Mr. WIRT.—Since then the jury have the right to consider the law and since the constitution is the law, the conclusion is syllogistic that the jury have the right to consider the Constitution.

Judge CHASE. A *non sequitur,* sir.

Here Mr. Wirt sat down . . .

After two hours, the jury returned with a verdict of guilty, upon which the court sentenced the traverser to a fine of two hundred dollars, and an imprisonment of nine months.[1982]

The Federalists finally jail Jimmy Callender! Judge Chase spoke with John Mason in Baltimore before the trial. John Mason:

Judge Chase asked me if I had seen [Callender's pamphlet] the "Prospect before Us." I replied I had not . . . He observed that Mr. Martin, the attorney general of Maryland, had sent it to him, and that Mr. Martin had scored the passages that were libellous, and that he should carry it to Richmond with him; and that if the commonwealth of Virginia was not utterly depraved, or that if a jury of honest men could be found there, he would punish Callender. He said he would teach the lawyers of Virginia the difference between the liberty and the licentiousness of the press.[1983]

Virginia lawyer John Heath also saw Judge Chase before the trial. John Heath:

I was one of the counsel at the bar but was not concerned with Callender's case . . . I had occasion to apply to the court . . . While I was there, Mr. Randolph, the then marshal of Virginia, came in; he held a paper in his hand, and Judge Chase asked him what it was. Mr. Randolph replied that it was a pannel of the jury to try Callender. Judge Chase then asked him if he had any of those creatures or people called democrats on it. Mr. Randolph paused for a moment, and . . . replied that he made no discrimination. Judge Chase told him to look over the pannel; if there were any of that description, strike them off . . .[1984]

WEDNESDAY, JUNE 4, 1800

GENERAL ★ AURORA ★ ADVERTISER

In the primer composed for the use of American aristocrats, we shall find this Aphorism, "In Adams' fall, we sinned all."

[T]o what *purposes* [was it that] Mr. Pickering applied the 50,000 dollars drawn out of the public treasury on the 18*th of April* 1800 [?]

Mr. Anthony Haswell, the Editor of . . . the *Vermont Gazette* was arraigned before the circuit court of the United States, then sitting at Windsor for the District of Vermont . . . [T]he cause was called on, when the respondent brought forward evidence on the first count of the indictment to prove that col. Lyon was denied the privilege of pen, ink, and paper when he was first confined . . . On the second count, the respondent produced the certified correspondence [of] . . . James M'Henry, secretary of war of the United States . . . [which] says, in substance, there are many among those you denominate as old Tories . . . who, being men of probity and honor, I do not see why they should not be deemed eligible [as army officers] &c. . . . The attorney of the prosecution alleged that the publications were a libel against the government of the United States . . .

Today, U.S. Senator Gouverneur Morris of New York writes a former U.S. senator from New York, Rufus King:

[T]he thing which, in my opinion, has done the most mischief to the federal Party is the Ground given by some of them to believe that they wish to establish a monarchy.[1985]

THURSDAY, JUNE 5, 1800

GENERAL ★ AURORA ★ ADVERTISER

Charles Holt [of the New London *Bee*], a native citizen of the United States, has been tried under the Sedition Law and sentenced to pay two hundred dollars fine, and imprisoned three months. Notwithstanding the law has declared Mr. Holt a criminal, thousands of sober, prudent, industrious and respecting people in this country visit and aid him as a martyr for the righteous cause of liberty . . .

Tonight, in the *Gazette of the United States*:

Pat [at the Aurora], . . ."May the devil as of old take the swinish multitude to a sea bathing," is in truth the real wish of all your party, from the highest . . . to William Duane.

FRIDAY, JUNE 6, 1800

GENERAL ★ AURORA ★ ADVERTISER

We have repeatedly told the public that a person of the first credit in the family of the British minister in this city declared that *on a certain day Fenno's Gazette* was to be enlarged and to become their paper—it was enlarged—it is not yet two *months* since a lady of considerable understanding and information, in the presence of Mr. Adams, said that *Fenno's* was a British paper—in truth *Fenno* never denied the *fact* or contradicted our assertions—we publish the following from the Royal gazette of New-York without more than a single remark—Fenno continued to be patronized by the administration and by the Senate to the last hour that they continued in this city:

PORCUPINE'S FAREWELL
To The People Of The United States Of America

THIS is to inform all those of you, whom it may concern, that, being upon the point of returning to that "INSULAR BASTILE," Great Britain, I have fully and legally authorized Mr. John Ward Fenno (late of Philadelphia) who is my successor in business, to make a final adjustment of all my unsettled accounts. Those who may have any demands against me will, therefore, please to present them, duly authenticated, to Mr. Fenno at No. 141 Hanoversquare, New York . . .

You will, doubtless, be astonished that, after having had a smack of the sweets of liberty, I should think of rising from the feast; but . . . so it is with liberty, out of its infinite variety of sorts, it unfortunately happens that yours is perfectly the sort which I do not like . . .

With this I depart for that HOME where neither the moth of Democracy nor the rust of Federalism doth corrupt . . .

W. COBBETT. *New York, 29th May, 1800*

The friends of Mr. William Cobbett are informed that he sailed for England on Sunday last in the King's Packet, Lady Arabella. He leaves behind him the regret of all true friends to America for the loss of a champion so formidable once in her behalf . . .

Having succeeded to his business here, I shall, at all times, be happy in executing the orders of his friends and customers . . .

The Gazette of the United States having become the property of Mr. Wayne, all letters or concerns relating to that establishment are referred to him.

JOHN WARD FENNO
No. 141 Hanover-Square [New York], May 31.

Tonight, in the *Gazette of the United States,* Jack Fenno offers his own farewell to readers:

In relinquishing the profession of an editor—a profession which no consideration but the hope of being able one day to boast that "I have done the State some service" could have induced me, in a period like the past, so long to continue—I have to pay some ample acknowledgments to many excellent friends . . . All the conjoint persecutions or rancorous malice and cowardly stupidity which I have encountered . . . have still left far fainter traces on my mind that the demonstrations of personal attachment . . . JOHN WARD FENNO

SATURDAY, JUNE 7, 1800

GENERAL ★ AURORA ★ ADVERTISER

THE PRESIDENT

Is gone—what! gone? Yes!—dead?—mortally, *no;* politically, *aye?* But he has left town—How? In his coach and four with the blinds up— Ah! that's not a new thing, he has rode in the state coach with the blinds up for a long time . . . Did the blues parade?—No, what! not parade nor salute him whom the people delight to honor—the rock on which the storm beats—the chief who now commands? Did the republican militia parade?—no!

We have waited, hoping to hear something said about the *public money* which Brigadier General *Dayton* has held so long in his hands.

We have waited to hear what would be said concerning Mr. *Pickering*—and whether Mr. *Wolcott* or their friends would remain silent . . . The latter gentleman, as Secretary of the Treasury, ought to keep correct accounts . . .

The *Gazette of the United States*, it now appears, belongs to a kind of *underhand agency*, ostensively belonging to Mr. *Caleb Wayne*—we shall use the name of the publisher in the future to designate that paper, formerly called *Fenno's*, apparently with like propriety.

Tonight, in the *Gazette of the United States*:

The President of the United States arrived at Georgetown on Tuesday noon last where he was received with every demonstration of joy . . . He was said to have made his entry into the city of Washington, the future seat of government of the union, on Wednesday last.

The alternate abuse offered both to Mr. Adams and Mr. Pickering in the *Aurora* . . . serves to show the base disposition of the Jacobins to divide and to destroy the Federalists . . . United we stand—divided we fall a prey to all the horrors which France and Ireland have experienced from the bloody fangs of the Jacobins.

MONDAY, JUNE 9, 1800

GENERAL   ★ AURORA ★   ADVERTISER

LETTER OF JOHN FOWLER, MEMBER OF CONGRESS FROM . . .
KENTUCKY, TO HIS CONSTITUENTS

The election of a republican governor to the chair of Pennsylvania was the first intimation that the citizens of America still cherished the hope of preserving peace with France; yet notwithstanding this, the war party in Congress laboured incessantly, in conjunction with the executive administration, to force upon us the dreadful conflict. Our state [Kentucky] and Virginia remained firm: and the other southern states have joined us; and the accession of Pennsylvania would have given us a preponderance at the next election, had not a majority of six men, elected in the time of delusion to the [Pennsylvania] state senate, refused to concur in passing a law to prescribe the mode of electing the President and Vice President of the United States. The election of New York has now completely turned the beam . . .

Tonight, in the *Gazette of the United States*:

It is reported, but with what degree of truth we will not pretend to say, that the *Old Sorceress* in Race street and *Duane* are mutually concerned in the publication of the *Aurora*—and that all the *predictions* . . . in that paper are to be accounted for in this way.

GENERAL ★ AURORA ★ ADVERTISER

The senate requested Mr. Adams to institute a suit against the Editor of the *Aurora*; but it will not be expected that while he continues in his present critical situation, while the prospect of his re-election still exhibits the most gloomy aspect, he will gratify the resentments of the senate. However much he may participate in them, policy will dictate their concealment until they can be exercised with less hazard. Mr. Adams is not now "The ROCK on which the storm shall beat" in vain.

EPITOME OF THE TIMES.

(The Editor of the Epitome is mistaken; the suit is already instituted.)

Peter Porcupine will observe,

The Senate proceeded [against Duane]; but the Printer, by absconding till after the session was over, avoided the punishment intended for him . . . The Senate was never a very popular body; it was always regarded by the great mass of the people with a jealous eye. This attempt added to its unpopularity and cast on it an odium which it will not easily wipe off . . . [1986]

Tonight, in the *Gazette of the United States*:

[Adv.]   MACPHERSON'S BLUES
THE Members composing the Legion will assemble without uniform at the City Hall on Thursday next at 7 o'clock P.M. on Business of importance.   By Order of *Brig.Gen.Macpherson*

GENERAL ★ AURORA ★ ADVERTISER

Letters and newspapers must in future be directed to the respective officers of the Government at the City of Washington.

Tonight, at the City Hall in Philadelphia's State-house, the "young men of Philadelphia" who compose the Macpherson's Blues follow the President's direction for army units to disband. *At the time when the terror of faction was at the highest pitch in Philadelphia, this corps was the most active and willing to awe the people into silence and obscurity—The Theatre and every public place, even the churches, were crowded with this patriotic body—In fact the city of Philadelphia rather appeared under a military despotism than under a civil government . . .* [1987] This autumn, President Adams will pay for that despotism.

Tonight, in the *Gazette of the United States*:

Judge Chase, when about to pass sentence on Mr. Callender, observed that his offence against the laws was great . . . that Mr. Callender must have known that Mr. Adams was far from deserving the character he had given him . . . that the American people had repeatedly confided their most important concerns and dearest interests to Mr. Adams—that he was one of the principal characters in the revolution . . . That Congress . . . appointed him as a minister, in conjunction with two others, to make the treaty which terminated the war and established our independence, and that the best parts of that treaty of peace were to be ascribed to Mr. Adams . . . It was to be lamented . . . [t]hat Callender, avowedly for electioneering purpose, had ascribed to Mr. Adams a worse character . . .

FRIDAY, JUNE 13, 1800

GENERAL ★ AURORA ★ ADVERTISER

James Thomson Callender further declared . . . that he shall be able to prove by the evidence of Stevens Thomson Mason and William B. Giles that John Adams, president of the United States, has unequivocally avowed in conversation with them principles utterly incompatible with the principles of the present constitution of the United States . . . [Callender] was sentenced by Judge Chase to nine months imprisonment and to pay a fine of two hundred dollars.

Tonight, in the *Gazette of the United States*:

For the satisfaction of all true friends to America, the three most active and most notorious foreign emissaries, Cooper, Duane, and Callender, have all at last been punished for their audacious attempts to involve the United States in one scene of confusion and blood. This we hope will discourage those who sent them across the Atlantic from any further attempts to destroy the government and independence of the United States.

SATURDAY, JUNE 14, 1800

GENERAL ★ AURORA ★ ADVERTISER

MACPHERSON'S BLUES

We understand that the Military corps commonly called *Macpherson's Blues* had a meeting on Thursday evening and that it was resolved to dissolve the association on the 17th inst . . .

Their rise was at a season of alarm and political ferment, . . . [A]n advertisement calling upon the YOUTH of Philadelphia to meet at a public tavern . . . was couched in singular form, for the *youth* were explained to comprehend those between 16 and 23 years of age . . . [E]ffects not to be then foreseen arose from the example set by Philadelphia, for all the continent was taught, and the eulogy bestowed by the president on these youths of 23 gave our nether world, a high opinion of this *queer begotten association,* and the example was followed as we have seen . . .

Never was *l'esprit de corps* more strongly manifested than in the first months of its institution by this body . . . [M]en of sound republican principles but weak minds were seen enrolling themselves in ranks under the apprehension of their growing power and the consequent danger; and men . . . were seen disgracing the memories of their fathers and the independence of their country by the elevation of the black *British cockade! . . .*

This corps, sanctioned by the President . . . gave a species of law to the public of this city.—Weak men feared them . . . The theatre—the public streets—and even the domestic sanctuary was infested with their folly or their violence . . .

The republican part of the community . . . found it necessary to guard against the accumulating danger; and as a necessary *effect* of this danger, *the Republican militia legion was formed.*

From the moment the legion first appeared under arms, the city was released from the heavy weight of just apprehension. With the growth of the militia Legion, public confidence and public security have now been restored . . .

The blues are now no longer a military corps . . . and we shall not enumerate or particularize acts of theirs which we could point out for blame. The returning sense of the country . . . [has] rendered it prudent in them to take the steps they have done . . .

Tonight, in the *Gazette of the United States*:

The Gentlemen composing the Legion of Blues have been highly honoured in the *Aurora* of this morning by a torrent of abuse. They are accused of wearing the British cockade—of insolence—of alarming the peaceable inhabitants &c. &c. &c. They have only to reflect on the source from whence this abuse arises;—Washington, Adams, Pickering, Hamilton, Marshall & M'Henry, with innumerable other patriots and statesmen, have all received a share of abuse in that paper.

The Editor of the *Aurora* . . . asserts with his usual vulgarity "that History is but the record of the transactions and characters of men under three words, *crimes, fools, and villains."* Had he placed the word *Jacobin* before *"History,"* he had been right for once in his life, and, as it is, he has given us his character in three short words, as well as Judge Chase or any upright Judge will do it for him hereafter.

Today, the first standing army of the United States of America, established in 1798 under the signature of its second President, John Adams of Massachusetts, is officially disbanded! A report of celebration from North Farms, New Jersey:

> *The fifteenth of this instant being the day appointed by the Legisla-*
> *ture of the Union for Disbanding the Standing Army, [three hundred*
> *of] the citizens of this vicinity . . . in order to manifest that joy which*
> *every true American must feel on such a happy occasion, convened . . .*
> *at the house of capt. Thomas Baldwin at 4 o'clock P.M. where, after*
> *partaking of a genteel and wholesome collation under a shady bower,*
> *the following [sixteen] toasts were drank, each accompanied with the*
> *discharge of musketry . . . 8. May it never again be in the power of the*
> *Commander in Chief of the first division of New Jersey militia to say*
> *that a standing army is raised (to use his own polite language) to keep*
> *"the people under" . . . 15. The virtuous and persecuted DUANE, Editor*
> *of the Aurora—May his endeavors to unveil the secret plots of a crafty*
> *aristocracy, meet the approbation and reward of his grateful country.*
> *3 cheers . . .*[1988]

MONDAY, JUNE 16, 1800

GENERAL ★ AURORA ★ ADVERTISER

WAYNE [in his *Gazette of the United States*] calls the facts which we published (and published mildly compared with the *facts*) ABUSE of the BLUES—but he has not shewn us that the black cockade is not the *British cockade* . . .

Great stress is laid by weak men and by wicked men upon the *poverty* of Mr. Callender and his being born in a foreign country, as if his *poverty* or his *birth* could alter the *character* and *principles* of JUSTICE or as if these circumstances could deprive him of a RIGHT *established by* the law of the land for which his enemies profess such veneration . . .

Tonight, in the *Gazette of the United States,* Caleb Wayne writes:

MACPHERSON'S BLUES

THIS legion . . . has afforded to the Editor of the *Aurora* an opportunity of retailing, with his usual asperity, a string of falsehoods designed to injure its character . . .

That the [Republican] militia legion has recently increased in numbers we readily admit. And that the [Federalist Macpherson's] Blues, as part of the army of the United States, is about to be disbanded, will not be denied. It is, however, far from being honorable to the former that, during the period when the danger of foreign invasion was most imminent, their impoverished ranks displayed no more than ten or twelve to a company; or that, at a moment when the dawn of peace and security was most certain, their files should obviously augment . . . But even Jasper [Dwight], who thus speaks of their swelling ranks, has never been able to assemble in his forlorn corps more than 12 or fourteen soldiers . . .

The Blues [unlike the Republican militia legion] have never outraged the honor and dignity of their country, or bidden defiance to its laws, by marching exultantly through its streets to the war tunes of a declared and actual enemy . . . [W]hen on the mournful occasion of performing homage to the memory of their illustrious fellow-soldier, Washington, they *behaved with decorum and obeyed with implicitness the orders of the day* . . . Can this be observed of certain of the corps of that Legion whose respectability has been contrasted with the Blues ?

Duane calls the Black Cockade a British Cockade . . . [B]ut as we gained our Independence with *black cockades in our hats,* we shall not now give them give them up to please a wretch who was with the Enemy during the whole of our struggle for Independence and who is still a base foreign emissary.

TUESDAY, JUNE 17, 1800

GENERAL ★ AURORA ★ ADVERTISER

PUBLIC PLUNDER.

We have at length so far succeeded as to possess ourselves of a long and black series of *abuses* and *waste* of the public money . . .

We had some time ago stated that [former Secretary of State] *Timothy Pickering* had drawn on the 18th of April last the sum of 50,000 dollars from the public treasury. We now repeat the fact, and that at the time, he had in his hands unaccounted for the enormous sum of 300,000 dollars and more on the same account . . .

For this time we shall dismiss Mr. *Pickering,* because we have about FORTY *other friends of regular government* to bring in review . . .

Tomorrow we shall give *Jonathan Dayton's* account at large.

Timothy Pickering superintended the federal government's sedition actions against Benny and against me. Jonathan Dayton barred Benny and me from the House floor. It is time for them to be held to account![1989]

WEDNESDAY, JUNE 18, 1800

GENERAL ★ AURORA ★ ADVERTISER

A Secretary of the Treasury negligent, incompetent, or corrupt, may suffer or cause the public to be robbed to an immense account . . . If it shall appear that the public money has been withheld from the public

coffers while immense sums have been borrowed at enormous interest—
if it shall appear that those who have held those public monies have been
speculating in princely estates while they possessed those public monies,
then if they can say: these things ought to be so . . . we have mistaken
the true meaning of *oaths*, of *public obligations* . . .

Mr. *Dayton* was considerably indebted to the U.S. . . . Jonathan Dayton held in his hands a balance of Dols. 8,611 60 from the 3d March
1797, to the month of July following, and then he held in his hands the
small balance of Dols. 90,917 52 from the month of July, 1799, to the
22d January, 1800, and so far as his accounts are settled at the Treasury
Department, he appears still to hold in his hands the sum of Dols. 18,142
and 52 cents.

Tonight, in the *Gazette of the United States*:

The very affectionate reception and respectable addresses which have
everywhere met our venerable and vigilant President on his tour to and
from Washington has greatly encreased the malignity and chagrin of the
Jacobins, in consequence of which Duane has furnished a double stock of
lies from his chaldron of this morning.

THURSDAY, JUNE 19, 1800

GENERAL ★ AURORA ★ ADVERTISER

BALTIMORE, June 15. His excellency John Adams, president of the
United States, arrived in town yesterday . . . It is regretted that business
of an urgent nature required his departure so early as to induce him to
decline the civilities and honors intended him by our citizens.

Yesterday departed from their political existence, the military corps
called *M'Pherson's Blues*—wishing not to disturb the ashes of the de-
funct, we wish the regenerated citizens a more peaceful and useful, durable and happy, progress thro' the vale of life than they have experienced
as soldiers.

There are two public officers in Boston who hold the handsome sum of
300,000 dollars of the public money—and one of them is a *bankrupt! O
rare friends of regular government!*

Tonight, in the *Gazette of the United States*:

More Jacobin and United Irish Arithmetic.

Duane in accounting for his nine *unaccountable buckram millions,*
goes on thus: June 17. Timo[thy] Pickering to pocketing– 8,000,000.
[June] 18. Sharp Delaney, to d[itt]o 86,000 Jonathan Dayton 320,000
[June] 19. Another Collector, 117,000 Mr. Winder, a Clerk 2,500,000 Sun-

dry accounts in former papers 5,000,000 [Total] 16,023,000 . . . Query, for Jasper—how many times 16 in nine !

GENERAL ★ AURORA ★ ADVERTISER

The attempt in [Caleb] Wayne's paper to disguise a vast scene of wickedness is more truly characteristic of the *anglo faction* than any thing we have lately seen . . .

Queries addressed to . . . Oliver Wolcott, secretary of the treasury of the United States . . . Why, since the month of July 1799, when you settled Jonathan Dayton's account at the treasury, and he acknowledged a balance of 18,142 dollars and 52 cents, have you permitted that sum of the *public money* to remain in his hands until this day ? . . . [Mr. Dayton] has lately purchased 24,000 acres of land . . .

Tonight, in the *Gazette of the United States*:

By recent accounts from Virginia, the good people of that state begin to be alarmed at the late daring attempts of the Foreign Jacobins resident among us to destroy our Government; Callender is already punished by them, and they expect Pennsylvania will pay the same attention to his accomplice here . . .

Duane seems at last justly convicted, fully aware of his own base and contemptible situation in life, when he presumes that but one Federalist could be found to notice his innumerable absurd falsehoods, but true as this may be in general, the wretch has taken such high ground of late, in his charges against many of our most upright public officers for vast mal appropriations of the public monies, that we trust he will soon find to his cost that there will be sufficient notice taken of him *by all parties.* In any other country, such conduct would tend much to his *final elevation;* how it will end here will depend on the steps to be taken by those whom he has so basely attempted to injure . . .

GENERAL ★ AURORA ★ ADVERTISER

We have the satisfaction to state that the president has attended to the accounts which we have published and that he has thought it his duty to go in person to the office of the treasury and direct enquiries to be made and statements to be made out of various accounts. Among others we learn that Mr. Pickering's have been particularly attended to . . .

The President, we understand, arrived on *Thursday afternoon* at 4 o'clock P.M. at Mrs. White's [boarding house] without any *noise* or the *usual parade*, and on *Friday forenoon* walked several squares of the city.

We further understand that he *bowed* very condescendingly to certain *high flyers* who passed him during his promenade and stopped for near *ten* minutes with a *lady of RANK* to whom he told of his *"hair breadth escapes in the imminent deadly ruts"* . . . We are very sorry that he did not meet with *better* roads and . . . had any *harsh words* with the commissioners or bricklayers of the city of Washington . . .

Tonight, in the *Gazette of the United States*:

We are surprized to find the assertion in the *Aurora* that the late Secretary of State [Pickering] has drawn 300,000 dollars . . . should have made some impression on the public mind; after similar *falsehoods* respecting the late President Washington and Secretary Hamilton have been proved by official documents. So low is the credit of that paper in Philadelphia that assertions of this sort scarcely become subjects of conversation.   *COM. ADV.*

TUESDAY, JUNE 24, 1800

GENERAL   ★ AURORA ★   ADVERTISER

TO JOHN ADAMS,
PRESIDENT OF THE UNITED STATES.
Sir, The public feel a sensible interest in the part you have taken upon your return to this city in causing an enquiry to be made into certain public accounts. They are pleased to see the *bustle, assiduity,* and *early* attendance of Mr. Wolcott at five o'clock every morning at the old treasury office . . . At the same time, the public would like to know how it has happened . . .   A YORKER

Tonight, in the *Gazette of the United States*:

I am compelled by the considerations and justice . . . to declare the recent publications in the *Aurora* respecting pecuniary transactions . . . unfounded.

The *accounts of the [State] Department,* while it was conducted by Colonel Pickering, have been exhibited at the Treasury, and it is expected that they *will* be finally settled *soon after* the Offices are opened in Washington . . .

The balances to which the publications in the *Aurora* refer are the aggregate amounts of sums which have been remitted to public agents . . .

                    OLIVER WOLCOTT   Treasury . . .

The PRESIDENT of the United States left this city yesterday morning and proceeded on his journey to Massachusetts.

The public will be less surprized at the great increase of lies in the *Aurora* when they are told the following fact—are you not going too far ? said a more timid Jacobin to Duane.—too far, no,—replied Jasper, there are already so many prosecutions [against me] intended that I must be made a Bankrupt and take the benefit of the Act; therefore, all the new lies I publish for Electioneering or other party purposes *are clear gain.*

WEDNESDAY, JUNE 25, 1800

GENERAL ★ AURORA ★ ADVERTISER

Oliver Wolcott furnishes the *confession . . .* that "the balances to which *the Aurora* refer are the aggregate amounts of sums which have been remitted to ministers" &c. Then it appears that the *Aurora* has not asserted *unfounded facts*—but absolutely real and acknowledged transactions. But more, Mr. Wolcott . . . acknowledges that they have not been *yet settled . . .*

TO THE EDITOR . . . Mr. Wolcott assures that . . . they *will be* "finally settled *soon after* the offices are opened at Washington!" Whenever they shall be *finally* settled, the public will be in no small degree indebted for that event to the AURORA.   A   CITIZEN

DEATH
It is a cause of real joy to the sincere friends of our country that on THIS DAY, the Act of Congress "CONCERNING ALIENS" expires and ceases longer to disgrace the American code of laws. As a part of that system of terror which was artfully created for political purposes by a "WOULD BE" governing faction . . . [W]hile the remembrance of Mr. Adams' administration shall continue in the American mind, this act will contribute its full share to perpetuate a merited sentence of condemnation on the policy and justice of that administration.

By allowing the President to banish any would-be citizen—without a hearing—on the claim that the President "suspected" misbehavior, the "Alien Friends" Act gave the President a weapon of intimidation to silence many opposers of his administration. That law's two-year term has ended. It won't be renewed!

THURSDAY, JUNE 26, 1800

GENERAL ★ AURORA ★ ADVERTISER

[W]e must postpone . . . *Jonathan Dayton's* exposition of himself until Monday next.

Tonight, in the *Gazette of the United States*:

> Duane, defeated in his other calumnies, now charges the Public Officers with receiving commissions on the subordinate agencies under the auditorship or direction of the principal heads of departments. Although it is scarcely necessary to follow this villain any further, we once more assert from authority that nothing can be further from the truth.

If any thing . . . could enforce the necessity of an Alien Law, it would be the exultation of Duane at its death.

SATURDAY, JUNE 28, 1800

If the assertions by Mr. Wolcott are intended to exonerate Mr. Pickering from the charges that [were] produced against him in the *Aurora*, it was certainly necessary that something more than vague and unintelligible assertions should have been exhibited.

Tonight, in the *Gazette of the United States*:

ORIGINAL LETTER FROM DR. FRANKLIN

(The following is an original . . . [D]iscern at once the germ of deism, the embryo of rancour against church establishments, the feverish symptoms of a malcontent; and those daring doctrines "at which both the priest and philosopher may tremble.")

Philad. June 6th, 1753.

SIR, . . . *"The faith you mention has doubtless its use in the world . . . But I wish it were more productive of good works than I have generally seen it; I mean real good works; works of kindness, charity, mercy and public spirit; not holiday keeping, sermon reading or hearing, performing church ceremonies, or making long prayers, filled with flatteries and compliments, despised even by wise men and much less capable of pleasing the Deity . . ."*

B. FRANKLIN

Tonight, I emulate Dr. Franklin's liberality and Benny Bache's adoration. In a relatively private ceremony, I, a Roman Catholic, marry a courageous non-Catholic whom Jack Fenno calls "lusty"[1990] and "lovely,"[1991] Peter Porcupine calls "luscious,"[1992] and Benny's children call "mother." The former Peggy Bache becomes Peggy Duane, and I become husband to Benny's widow, stepfather to Benny's children, and so stepfather to Dr. Benjamin Franklin's great-grandchildren. I am now, as nearly as I will ever be, a Bache and a Franklin!

MARRIED—On Saturday evening 28th. inst. by the Rev. Bishop White, Mr. WILLIAM DUANE to MRS. MARGARET HARTMAN BACHE.

To the Editor of the Aurora.

[Y]ou have in your paper of the 18th inst. ventured to impose upon the public a false statement of facts in relation to my accounts as speaker of the house of representatives . . . [Y]ou can never forgive [me] for having firmly discharged my duty . . . against you personally . . .

The books of the Treasury will establish beyond all doubt the truth of . . . my assertion, and the falsehood of yours . . . I must be allowed to add that your paper has become so notorious and indeed proverbial for its slanders and its falsehoods that if it had been certain that those printers who might think proper to republish your misrepresentations would have at the same time quoted their authority, I should not have thought it necessary to . . . answer, convinced that . . . it would be sufficient only to make known that it originated in *"the Aurora."*   JONA: DAYTON

[NEWARK, NEW JERSEY.] We have not had it in our power to publish any information through the medium of the [Newark] *Centinel* which excited more General consternation and alarm than that copied from the *Aurora* this day and which tends to expose the abusive system practiced on our public funds . . .   *NEWARK CENTINEL.*

Tonight, in the *Gazette of the United States*:

A FACT
From the Aurora !
Married on Saturday evening the 28th inst. by the Right Rev. Doctor White, William Duane, to Mrs. Margaret Hartman Bache, of this city!!!!!!!!!!!

Some there are who affect to disbelieve Duane's statement of official peculation and fraud—to *such* the following queries are addressed: If the statements were false, would he have published them at a time when the President and Mr. Wolcott were both in the city and could detect, expose, and punish instantly any false accusation ? Would he have not waited till the President had gone to Quincy and the Secretary to Washington? . . .

If they were false, would he have dared in contempt and defiance of the Sedition law to give them to the public as facts? . . . *Mirror.*

[NEW YORK] The President of the United States has passed by this city, and no parade has been made upon the occasion . . . *N. Y. Paper.*

Tonight, in the *Gazette of the United States:*

Since the late auspicious nuptials of a happy Editor, his paper has been observed to be more than usually spiritless and vapid. A grave philosopher of my acquaintance supposes that those animal spirits which used to slash in petulance, aflame in anger, are now *flowing in a new channel!*

> *On the report of a marriage between lovely Peggy*
> *and a noted Jacobin.*
> Should B[ache] with Jasper clank the wedlock fetter,
> O let her not her stars too sorely curse.
> As there's no hope that he will ere be better,
> *So there's no fear he ever can be worse.*

WEDNESDAY, JULY 2, 1800

GENERAL ★ AURORA ★ ADVERTISER

A NEW POLITICAL CRISS-CROSS,
For children six feet high, and upwards.
The Treasury—This is the house that Jack built.
3,000,000—This is the malt that lay in the house that Jack built.
Tim. Pickering—This is the *rat* that eat the malt that laid
in the house that Jack built.
Billy Duane— This is the CAT that catch'd the *rat*, that eat the malt,
that laid in the house, that Jack built.
Sedition Law—This is the dog that snarl'd at the CAT, that catch'd the
rat . . .
Judge Chase—This is the cow with the crumpled horn, that CHASED
the dog that snarl'd at the cat, . . .
Mr. Adams— This is the maiden all forlorn, that FED the cow with the
crumpled horn, that chased the dog, that snarled at the
cat, that catch'd the rate, that eat the malt in the house
that Jack built . . .

Baltimore Am.

Tonight, in the *Gazette of the United States:*

Duane . . . is sketching a political print to be called "The Libeller Convicted, or an inside view of a Prison."

GENERAL ★ AURORA ★ ADVERTISER

Mr. Wolcott . . . says that *"tis expected Mr. Pickering's accounts WILL BE finally settled SOON AFTER the offices are opened at Washington."* . . . The question then will arise . . . of our *sweet scented* friend Brigadier General *Thunder* . . . Either the officers of the treasury must be right and Jonathan Dayton wrong. Or Jonathan Dayton right, and the treasury wrong . . . Did the Secretary of the Treasury know the transaction ?

Tonight, in the *Gazette of the United States*:

> To a Friend hurt by the notice of Duane.
> You seem surprised that Jasper fly,
>   On you his filthy slime has scatter'd;
> When a full mud cart passes by
>   Tis odds, my friend, that you're bespatter'd.

GENERAL ★ AURORA ★ ADVERTISER

THE DEVIL TO PAY AT WASHINGTON.

Oliver Wolcott has commenced a court of Inquisition at Washington, all the clerks in the treasury offices have been interrogated by the *Grand Inquisitor* of *Connecticut*, in order to discover the *men, women,* and *children* who let the Editor of the Aurora into the secrets of public delinquents—*trunks* have been broken open to seek for *letters*, &c. &c. but alas—all has ended in confusion worse confounded; *the game is up*, and there is no possibility of discovering who started it, but at the *Aurora* Office.

This day being the anniversary of American independence, the citizens engaged in the publication of the *Aurora* will have to suspend their labours for the day and join in the general festival—the next number of this paper, therefore, will appear on Monday morning next.

GENERAL ★ AURORA ★ ADVERTISER

FESTIVAL OF INDEPENDENCE . . .

The following are among the [16] toasts . . . By the Rifle company, commanded by Captain Huff, assembled at the House of Thomas Khrum . . . 11. The memory of Benjamin Franklin Bache, who devoted his abilities to the service of his country—May they in return bear him in grateful remembrance—9 cheers. 12. The successor of Benj. Franklin Bache,

Capt. Wm. Duane—6 cheers . . . TOASTS OF THE REPUBLICAN GREENS. At the middle Ferry, Schuylkill . . . 3. Franklin—The American patriarch of liberty and philosophy . . . 11. The memory of Benjamin Franklin Bache—a virtuous man in wicked times. VOLUNTEERS. The *cat* that caught the *rat*, that eat the malt that lay in the house that Jack built . . . On Friday the 4th inst., the officers of the 24th regiment of the Pennsylvania militia . . . assembled at Gray's Ferry and Gardens . . . VOLUNTEERS. "Billy Duane—the cat that catched the rat that eat the malt that lay in the house that Jack built. 1 gun, 3 cheers."

No news from France. Today, Treasury Secretary Oliver Wolcott writes Alexander Hamilton:

> *A great number of public men have heard the Pr. declare that he did not believe that the Fr. Govt. was sincere in making what he called the "overtures" upon which the last mission was founded. Nay more, the Pr. has declared that a Treaty was neither to be expected nor desired . . . at Trenton last Autumn & . . . that the Expulsion of the Envoys from France with circumstances of personal indignity would be favourable to the Interests of the UStates. I shall ever believe that the last mission to France was by the Pr. considered . . . to gain popularity at home by appearing to be desirous of peace . . .*[1993]

Tonight, in the *Gazette of the United States*:

> *To a* Captain [Duane] *on his hair breadth escapes*
> *from federal* hickory.
> How kind has Nature unto Jasper been,
> Who gave him frowning brows and dauntless mien.
> A tongue to swagger, eyes to flash dismay,
> And kinder still—gave *legs to run away!*

TUESDAY, JULY 8, 1800

GENERAL ★ AURORA ★ ADVERTISER

NATIONAL FESTIVITY . . .

Captain Potts infantry of Frankford and Kessler's of the Northern Liberties celebrated the Anniversary of the American Independence in a wood on the left of Germantown road . . . The following are the [15] toasts . . . 14. The Cat that catch'd the Rat that eat the Malt that lay in the house that Jack built—3 guns, 9 cheers . . . [A] number of Republicans . . . assembled on the verdant shores of the Schuylkill . . . [T]he following toasts . . . 10. The memory of Dr. Benjamin Franklin—the philosopher and disinterested patriot whose services contributed so greatly to the emancipation of our country and to the establishment of her liberty and independence, the purest gratitude for his services and the sincerest veneration for his memory. 11. The memory of Benjamin Franklin Bache, he who so firmly and inflexibly supported the cause of republicanism, defying the malignant and inveterate prosecution of his political enemies, may his early tomb be honored by the veneration of freemen, and respected and reverenced by our posterity . . .

VOLUNTEERS.

"Surgo ut Prosim"—May the victorious sheets of the Aurora continue in the disseminating of republican sentiments and in the detecting of public defaulters.

The Editor of the Aurora, William Duane—May his zeal and ardour in the Republican Cause ever merit the warmest acknowledgments of his fellow-citizens.

The persecuted of all nations—America their asylum from their cruel oppressors . . .

[From the New York *Royal Gazette*.] Impossible as it may seem, it is a fact that the calumnies which have lately appeared in the *Aurora* and copied with malignant avidity into the Argus and every Jacobin paper in the United States have obtained a temporary belief, even in our own [New York] Coffee-house. Duane, with unexampled impudence, has, by descending to a detail of falsehoods, put off the fabrications for truth with those who ought to have been above the reach of such infamous artifices.

WEDNESDAY, JULY 9, 1800

GENERAL ★ AURORA ★ ADVERTISER

OLIVER WOLCOTT VERSUS *OLIVER WOLCOTT*

At Washington, after a fruitless examination of all the trunks of the Clerks in the Treasury Offices, every Clerk suspected of Democracy was discharged a few days ago. The question therefore arises—*What have they been discharged for ?* Upon a suspicion of having communicated what has been published in the *Aurora.—a plain case.*

War . . . Today, in the French West Indies, the United States Navy captures another French ship. U.S. Navy Lieutenant John Shaw, in command of the twelve-gun, seventy-man schooner *Enterprize*, writes:

I fell in with the French privateer L'Aigle of 10 guns and 78 men—she engaged me with much spirit for 15 minutes when she lowered her colours . . . L'Aigle had [illegible] men killed, 3 wounded..[1994]

FRIDAY, JULY 11, 1800

GENERAL ★ AURORA ★ ADVERTISER

A number of the Republican citizens of Chester County met on the Banks of the Brandy-wine [Creek] to celebrate the ever memorable 4th of July '76 . . . [16] toasts . . . 4. The memory of the Patriarch of the American liberties, Dr. Franklin . . . 15. *William Duane*, Editor of the Aurora.—May his talents and industry in the cause of republicanism be amply rewarded by his fellow citizens—6 cheers, and 3 volleys.

Tonight, in the *Gazette of the United States*:

The Jacobins delight in toasting a poor devil of a fugitive, whom they call "The *Cat.*" Quere, to which of the feline tribe has this same *Cat* the honour to belong? Is it a *Wild Cat,* a *Bore Cat,* or only a *Puss in Boots ?*

> Jasper picks quarrels, when he's drunk at night,
> When sober in the morning, dares not fight;
> Jasper, to shun these ills that may ensue,
> Drink not at night, or drink at morning too.
>
> Duane, they say, has wit—for what ?
> For writing ?—No—for *writing not.*

MONDAY, JULY 14, 1800

GENERAL ★ AURORA ★ ADVERTISER

TOASTS. AT RHINE NECK (N.Y.) . . . By *Judge Hogeboom.* The Editor of the Aurora—May his types be a pillory to every rascal whose hands are soiled with public money.

Tonight, in the *Gazette of the United States*:

It is a fact obvious to all but Jacobinical eyes that of the immense multitude of toasts which of late have choaked up the columns of the *Aurora,* more than half are seditious and treasonable or flagrantly immoral and flagitious.

TUESDAY, JULY 15, 1800

GENERAL ★ AURORA ★ ADVERTISER

PUBLIC MONEY VERSUS PUBLIC LOANS . . .

Mr. Steele of the treasury declares that [Delaware Loan Commissioner] John Stockton's account was *adjusted* for the quarter ending the 21st of March 1800 and that *"there remained due to the United States a[n unpaid] balance of 2339 dollars and 29 cents for which he will be debited at a future settlement."* . . .

Tonight, in the *Gazette of the United States*:

Lost last night in a blind alley, a quatern of Gin, well *distilled.*—Whoever will return the precious liquor to Jasper Traitor, Esq. shall go snacks [share] in boozing!

WEDNESDAY, JULY 16, 1800

GENERAL ★ AURORA ★ ADVERTISER

TO WILLIAM DUANE: RAT CATCHER TO THEIR MAJESTIES THE PEOPLE OF THE UNITED STATES.

So! You have got a *title* and no doubt a patent for it!—You!—Who have been abusing nearly half the nation for partiality to the manners and Customs of *Great Britain* . . . I wish I could congratulate you on this occasion; but . . . the *King's rat catcher* never sets a trap for a *large one,* an *old one,* or a *fat one* . . .   AN OLD RAT-CATCHER

Tonight, in the *Gazette of the United States*:

Duane was once a Jew Cloathsman in London, from which corrupt place and from which occupation his *integrity* expelled him, somewhere about the year 1789, when he fled to India. He passed in London under the name of Jew AINE.

THURSDAY, JULY 17, 1800

GENERAL ★ AURORA ★ ADVERTISER

President Adams gave as toasts lately at Boston the following: *"The proscribed Patriots Hancock and [Samuel] Adams."* But he did not give the great orb round which he moved as a satellite—*Benjamin Franklin.*

Tonight, in the *Gazette of the United States*:

To The Editor of the Gazette of the United States.

SIR,   Being informed by a friend and countryman of mine (an Irish Gentleman) that there was an advertisement . . . a few days ago, offering a reward to any one who should return a noggin of Gin to Jasper Dwight Esq. Traytor; and conceiving . . . we were seen in company together late one evening at a *certain public house* which we are in the habit of frequenting, this is to inform you . . . the liquor was clubbed and fairly drunk between us.   THE LEARNED PIG

GENERAL ★ AURORA ★ ADVERTISER

TOASTS ON THE FOURTH OF JULY *AT NEW YORK* . . . The founders of American freedom—9 cheers . . . *William Duane* and all the republican editors of the United States . . . *AT STANFORD (NEW YORK)* . . . William Duane—May he continue to scrutinize the federal accounts— And may the *Aurora*, aided by the Sun of Liberty, illumine our political horizon and enable the people to discover how many millions constitute the modern balance of power . . . *AT CAROLINE (MARYLAND)* . . . *William Duane*—May his efforts in the cause of liberty be crowned with success, and may they meet with (as they merit) the gratitude of his country. 3 cheers . . . *HARRISBURGH (PENN.)* . . . The memory of Benjamin Franklin—where Liberty dwells, there is my country. 3 cheers . . . The *Aurora*—its former and present editors, prosperity will do justice to their exertions in the cause of Liberty.

GENERAL ★ AURORA ★ ADVERTISER

During the lethargy which had so long oppressed the public mind of America, it was almost treason to use the name of Dr. *Franklin*. The hatred which Mr. *Adams* has always manifested toward that great man and the hatred which the British have uniformly declared might well account for so extraordinary an event—people, however, again begin to dare and think and speak of Dr. *Franklin*, his name once more scintillates around the joyous horizon on the national festival—this is to be accounted for in the change of public opinion as it relates to Mr. Adams and the British . . .

War . . . Today, off Guadeloupe in the French West Indies, the United States Navy's twelve-gun, seventy-man ship *Enterprize*, under Navy Lieutenant John Shaw, fires on the French privateer *Le Flambeau*. A report:

> *She mounted 10 guns, had 110 men, fought 50 minutes, and had 37 men killed and wounded. The Enterprize had only 2 men slightly wounded. This prize is valuable from the quantity of plunder she had on board* . . . [1995]

GENERAL ★ AURORA ★ ADVERTISER

Cooper is in prison. Holt is in prison. Callender is in prison. Duane has ten or a dozen suits against him for speaking the truth. Certain proofs that these writers criticized too severely—in the opinion of their oppressors.

Tonight, in the *Gazette of the United States*:

An English gentleman, fatigued with the dark innuendo and involved *Irishism* of the *Aurora,* remarked that the title of that paper is a misnomer and that it ought to be called, The *Midnight.*

FRIDAY, JULY 25, 1800

GENERAL ★ AURORA ★ ADVERTISER

CUMBERLAND COUNTY, STATE OF NEW JERSEY . . . [20] toasts . . . *By James Lee.* The memory of the last, and success to the present Editor of that enlightening paper, the *Aurora . . .*

Tonight, in the *Gazette of the United States*:

WHEN your correspondent remarked on the title of the paper conducted by [William Duane] the foreign assassin of General Washington's fame, he was not apprized of the following fact in the life of the Gin-guzzling Jasper [Dwight]—a fact which gives considerable congruity to the title of *"Aurora"* as relative to its worthy Editor.

This *Gentleman,* it seems, was a *Peep-o'day Boy* [Protestant insurgent] in Ireland, and for some of his feats in that character was furnished with a passage at the King of Great-Britain's expence to a colony in the southern Ocean, whence, while under the care of a Jailer, he contrived an escape to the United States, where he struts a captain and shines a moralist. Such is the vagrant who, under the auspices of the Mammoth faction, has assumed the instruction of the people of the United States in politics and morality!

SATURDAY, JULY 26, 1800

GENERAL ★ AURORA ★ ADVERTISER

PARIS, JUNE 1. We are assured that the negociations with the ministers of the United States of America are advancing rapidly to an amicable conclusion. The *Publiciste* of the 27th April, announces, that "on the 30th precisely at 10 o'clock, was to be celebrated, in their temple of victory, A FETE in memory of one of the benefactors of humanity, BENJAMIN FRANKLIN."

GENERAL ★ AURORA ★ ADVERTISER

[W]e judge it fit to answer . . . what it is to which [Jonathan] Dayton alludes in his letter wherein he charges the Editor of being actuated by personal motives . . . At the period when Jonathan was carrying on . . . speculation . . . the Editor reported the Debates in Congress . . . Wm. Smith [Federalist] of S. Carolina . . . directed a mean and threatening letter to the Editor, desiring that the speech of Smith should be altered . . . The Editor peremptorily refused to alter it from what had been actually spoken . . . This letter Mr. Smith laid before Mr. Dayton [who] . . . took upon him to interdict the Editor from taking notes in short-hand thenceforward in Congress . . . Dayton, soon after having established the precedent, interdicted the late Editor of the *Aurora* also . . . It is not necessary to notice how Congressional proceedings have gone to the public ever since. The faction have derived this advantage from it: having none but men who are either afraid to publish what is done or who do not discern the importance . . . They write speeches which they never spoke . . .

War . . . Today, off the coast of Cuba, the twenty-four-gun, 220–man U.S. Navy ship *Ganges,* under Lieutenant John Mullowny, fires on and captures a French cruiser. Mullowny writes the Secretary of the Navy:

> *I mentioned having a French cruiser confined in the harbor of Mantanzes; he came out on the morning of the 27th inst. At 3 P.M. he was descried from the mast head, when I gave chace to him; at seven in the evening . . . I was about half a mile from him, I fired some shot . . . which did some damage to the vessel and wounded three men after which he hauled his wind and run ashore, where all the crew left her. I have the schooner with me, her name is the La Fortune, of six 6 pounders and seventy men . . .*[1996]

GENERAL ★ AURORA ★ ADVERTISER

TOASTS [ON THE 4TH OF JULY]. *MIFFLIN-TOWN [PENN.]* . . . [16] toasts . . . 10. The *Aurora* and its Editor—The terror of tories, traitors, and aristocrats; and the watchtower of our constitution . . . *NEW-TOWN, (PENN.)* . . . at James Thomas's Tavern . . . [16] Toasts . . . 13. The Memory of Benj. F. Bache, 3 guns. 5 cheers. 14. Capt. Duane, the Editor of the *Aurora.* "Who will neither be purchased, cajoled, intimidated, nor beat into compliance with the views of designing and despotic men." 7 guns. 7 cheers . . .

Tonight, I attend a dinner in my honor at the city of New York.

Tonight, in the *Gazette of the United States*:

> By a gentleman direct from Norfolk, we are told that the Yellow Fever is raging with considerable violence . . .

THURSDAY, JULY 31, 1800

GENERAL ★ AURORA ★ ADVERTISER

[U]nder the administration of so good and honest a man as Mr. Jefferson, men of every faith and clime will be happy. His whole life and all his writings prove that he is no bigot . . . He never canted about religion to gain popularity . . . He [is not] . . . proclaiming fasts in which the people have been excited to hate each other and an opportunity been employed to sound the alarm of war, and hue and cry against republicanism. He [is not] . . . playing with their credulity, superstition or fanaticism to exalt himself . . . Had President Adams attended less to fasting and more to the public accounts, religion and government would have been better obeyed and more respected. The paths of true piety want no political direction, and if any body of Christians revere their religion or respect their rights, they ought to guard against the insidious arts of bigotry and hypocrisy . . .

This afternoon, I return from New York to Philadelphia.

FRIDAY, AUGUST 1, 1800

GENERAL ★ AURORA ★ ADVERTISER

President Adams [was on July 4th] at the *Old South* meeting house in Boston, with the *school* committee, and an old tory Episcopal clergyman—hear Americans and be astonished! The Old South meeting house was made a *riding-school* by the British during the siege of Boston . . . An union of old Whig and old Tories, of church and state—of crowns and mitres . . .

Tonight, in the *Gazette of the United States*:

> Mr. Adams . . . has suffered more foul reproaches than the depraved inhabitants of Billingsgate [a London fish market] . . . As long as General Washington was at the head of government, he was the object . . . When he retired to humble life, on the very day on which that afflicting event took place, the audacious wretch who superintended the vilest newspaper that ever disgraced a free country—the *Aurora*, proclaimed the day as a *Jubilee*, a day of *thanksgiving* . . . The democrats know that they shall finally wear out the friends of government; that, one after another, they

will retire from the storm which beats upon every head, and leave the constitutional barque afloat in that *"tempestuous sea of liberty"* which Mr. Jefferson and his party so much admire.   BURLEIGH

The New York Gazette mentions that an entertainment had been given at Louvet's [H]otel to William Duane, Editor of the *Aurora!* It is concluded, with sufficient reason, that the party, originally composed of fools, subsequently consisted of drunkards; that treasonable sentiments were uttered, blasphemous toasts given, and smutty songs encored.

It is no bad specimen of the taste of a lusty young widow that she selected, for her *camarade,* the captain of cock-neck'd troop.

SATURDAY, AUGUST 2, 1800

GENERAL   ★ AURORA ★   ADVERTISER

[R]eligious and civil liberty is the inherent and inalienable right of all mankind, constituting the only basis and real foundation of human happiness . . .

Tonight, in the *Gazette of the United States*:

If we have the good luck to make a firm, lasting, and honorable peace with regicides, Duane will be appointed by apostate Talleyrand as chief cook and bottle-washer to the gang. Frenchmen will then overwhelm us . . .

NOVA-SCOTIA. HALIFAX. June 20. Mr. WILLIAM COBBETT has arrived here from New-York. This gentleman has disclosed such nefarious practices and horrid cruelties of the French Directory as will forever remain lasting testimonials of his resources and integrity; and his steady support of the Federal Government [in the United States] does him equal honor; and it is much to be regretted that the virulence of the Democratic Faction has constrained him to leave that *boasted Land of Liberty* which, if we judge from present appearances, will soon become a melancholy scene of anarchy, disorder, and civil dissentions.

NEW YORK, July 31. The public have been led to believe from the late change in the election of our State Representatives that the majority of the citizens approve of all the lies published in the *Aurora*. But, when we perceive how *little attention* is paid to the Editor of this paper, we need not be at a loss to know the sentiments of even the Democrats of this city with respect to this foreign renegado. Last evening, there was a supper given to the Aurora-man, and we learn that out of nearly 300 who were invited, not more than 25 attended on this occasion—and who were they?

Today, in New York, Federalist leader Alexander Hamilton writes Treasury Secretary Oliver Wolcott:

> *You have doubtless seen The Aurora publication of Treasury Documents in which my name is connected . . . I have thought of instituting an action of slander to be tried by a struck jury against the Editor . . . What do you think of this ? You see I am in a very belligerent humour.*[1997]

MONDAY, AUGUST 4, 1800

GENERAL ★ AURORA ★ ADVERTISER

In [Federalist] Noah Webster's *Commercial Advertiser* of New York, there appeared the following article: . . .

> ". . . Last evening, there was a supper given to the Aurora-man, and we learn that out of nearly 300 who were invited, not more than 25 attended on this occasion—and who were they?"

Having noticed the above, we shall notice the toasts . . . The Editor's duty here [at the paper] required a short absence—unable to accept one out of every hundred of the invitations he had from the most respectable and venerable characters of that city, it was suggested that an entertainment be given by a select party—it was accordingly given. The Editor left that city on Thursday afternoon; the following is copied from the *American Citizen*:

> "On Wednesday evening, a number of republican citizens gave an entertainment at Lovett's hotel to William Duane, Editor of the *Aurora*, when the following toasts (interspersed with patriotic and social songs) were drank:
>
> 1. The people of the United States . . . 2. The Constitution . . . 3. The President, a speedy and honorable retirement from the cares of office . . . 6. The memory of Benjamin Franklin . . . 7. The Press . . . 10. The comptroller and auditor of the federal accounts . . . 14. Public opinion—The terror of wicked magistrates and the high court of appeal among free nations. 15. The Sedition Law—May the American people never place men in office whose character and conduct may require such a shield. 16. The memory of the Alien Law—May we remember it as . . . a conspiracy . . . to exclude from our shores the persecuted friends of liberty. 17. May all peculators experience the disgrace of Timothy Pickering, Jonathan Dayton, and Co.

> VOLUNTEERS

> By William Duane—The state of New York—May the example which she has given . . . be emulated and imitated in her sister states.

AFTER MR. DUANE RETIRED

William Duane—The firm and enlightened Editor of the *Aurora;* virtuous and undaunted in the worst of times, the friend of his country, and the scourge of her enemies.

[Federalist] *Noah Webster* says that, in order to give republicanism a permanent existence, the poorer class of people should be excluded from elections . . . If excluding a portion of the people from elections constitute the only durable basis of republicanism, then we might truly say that republicanism may *mean any thing.*

Tonight, in the *Gazette of the United States*:

Many of the retainers of the *Aurora* Office have a very forlorn and disconsolate air. Of some the creditors are importunate, and, to others perhaps the churlish laundress has not returned the *only shirt* they have in the world. Alas, poor Devils, your lot is a hard one . . . [F]or your immediate employer, Cash must be a stranger to him, for democratic subscribers never pay and *Gin* is excised!

TUESDAY, AUGUST 5, 1800

GENERAL   ★ AURORA ★   ADVERTISER

The Philadelphians have commenced their election operations—the republicans have published their tickets for candidates . . .

Tonight, the *Gazette of the United States* mocks a Republican meeting and a Philadelphian Jew, Benjamin Nones:[1998]

SIR, Actuated by motives of curiosity, I attended the meeting of Jacobins on Wednesday evening last at the State-house . . . I will endeavor to recount . . .

Cit F——r. I move—hic—the *readings* of this here meeting be printed in the *Aurora*—hic—and that a suitable address be printed above it. (Carried.)

Several: adjourn, adjourn . . .

Cit. B——r. Citizens before we *sojourn,* I will remark that I know Republicans are always pretty much *harrassed* for the rhino [cash], but I must *detrude* upon your generosity tonight by *axing* you *launch* out some of the *ready* for the citizen who provides for the room. I know Democrats haven't many *English Guineas* amongst them but I hope they have some . . . and if they will *j[u]st* throw them into *my hat* as they go along, I shall be *definitely* obliged to them . . .

Citizen N[ones](the Jew.) I hopsh you will consider dat de monish ish

832

very scarch, and besides you know Ish just come out by de Insholvent Law.

Several. Oh yes, let N[ones] pass . . .   AN OBSERVER

WEDNESDAY, AUGUST 6, 1800

British influence and tory ascendancy were compared a few evenings since by a lady to,

"The closing watch of night,
Dying at the approach of light."

Today, U.S. Senator William Bingham (Federalist, Pennsylvania) writes America's Minister to Great Britain, Federalist Rufus King:

After many tedious preparatory Steps . . . [the Senate] at length issued their Warrant & Duane absconded. Very little Exertion was made to discover & arrest him. He appeared publicly immediately after the Session & and assumed great Consequence from his sufferings as a persecuted Patriot & Martyr to the Liberty of the Press. He elevated himself into such Notice as to be repeatedly toasted at the democratic Feasts on the 4th July. As the sedition Law contemplated this offense & attaches a Penalty to it, I thought it would have been more expedient to have sent him to the Courts . . .[1999]

Tonight, in the *Gazette of the United States*:

The *Aurora* has looked very *cloudy* for some days. It resembles a farthing candle more than a beautiful morning. It sheds no *light,* and its *heat,* like that of the season, is dull and malignant. Of this paper, the downfall is at hand.

THURSDAY, AUGUST 7, 1800

TO MR. WILLIAM DUANE . . . Like many other moderate men . . . I have been deterred by the cry of *"Jacobin,"* &c. from enquiring whether "THE AURORA" rested on the broad basis of truth, upon which I now perceive it to stand . . . and herewith transmit the amount of subscription for one year [eight dollars].   FERDINANDO FAIRFAX,
Shannon-hill, Berkley (Vir.)

The *Gazette of the United States* augurs the speedy downfall of "The *Aurora.*" The augury is but the echo of the wish . . . [So t]hat master *Wayne* should not want *data* to proceed, we shall give him a few of the symptoms of the approaching fall of the *Aurora. NEW SUBSCRIBERS.* In May 1800, 124. In June, 138. In July, 56. In August, up to the 8th, 15. [Total] 333. We only recommend to Mr. Wayne to compare this new accession with the *whole subscription* to the Gaz. of U.S. and let the public know the difference between the sums total.

The annexed letter was received thro' the Post-Office yesterday. The Editor has received many such for some time past . . . Things at the *Aurora* Office are not as they have been; visitors of the above description would be sure to meet a very warm reception . . .

"Mr. DUANE, *Be upon your guard—against the machinations of newly imported English agents, for I have heard three of them swear that your House would soon be burnt down, and yourself in it. Take this hint from one who gives it of humanity only.* AMERICANUS."

Tonight, in the *Gazette of the United States*:

A stupid Virginia Negro driver who dates from *Shannon Hill* (Berkley) has undertaken to write a letter to Duane, enclosing the price of a year's subscription for the Country *Aurora* and telling him that he has "been deterred by the cry of Jacobin &c. from enquiring whether 'the *Aurora*' rested on the *broad basis* of truth."

Anybody who reads this must burst into a *broad* laugh, and yet this Sir Ferdinando Fairfax—this knight of the woeful phiz [face]—no doubt concluded he was paying a very high compliment to the man he was addressing by insinuating that until lately he had supposed the newspaper published a pack of lies . . . Well, Duane takes it as a high compliment . . . and publishes the letter, forsooth.—This is the *very first instance* in which Duane ever undertook to *puff* himself off *his own* Newspaper— How so? Why he never published a single batch of 4th of July toasts, wherein "Billy Duane" was drank, for one—in the shape of himself, of a Cat or of a Rat Catcher, or some other useful beast—No ! No ! He was too modest—He never said a word about the New York feasting where he dined without about a dozen of *his peers*—whether Cats or Rats, no matter which, and where, "after Mr. Duane retired"—"William Duane" was toasted—No No—He was too modest!!!

[W]hen the constitution of the United States was formed, it was an object of the most particular care to keep the power of declaring war out of the hands of *one man* . . . [T]he people chose to keep the power of declaring war *from the President*, and they gave it *to the Congress alone*. The personal conduct of Mr. Adams, under these circumstances, merits the serious attention of the people. In a reply of his to the *young* men of Boston (who were full enough before, no doubt, of war and heat) Mr. Adams openly and ardently exhorts them to fly to arms.—*"To arms, my young friends, to arms, especially on the ocean"* are his words, as it is remembered. Congress had not then, nor have they since, declared war.

Tonight, in the *Gazette of the United States*:

> *A HONEY MOON PARODY,*
> *BY THE EDITOR OF THE AURORA*
> *"Friend and Pitcher."*
> The wealthy *Feds* with gold in store
>   Will still desire to grow richer:
> Give me but these, I ask no more,
>   My *Franklin Bride*, my *Lloyd*, and pitcher.
> My Lloyd so *bare*, my wife so fair
>   With such what Paddy can be richer,
> Give me but these, a fig for care,
>   With my sweet bride, my Lloyd and pitcher.
> In dirtiest job I'd never grieve
>   To toil, a Democratic ditcher,
> If, that when I return at eve,
>   I might *enjoy my bride* and pitcher . . .

Every schoolboy in politics knows that the maintenance of a free Republic . . . depends upon the proper and judicious distribution of power. It is a principle upon which our ancestors have practiced successfully for many countries, in this country and *England*. Mr. Jefferson, in the year 1781, was so far an American in his politics and had had so little converse with the Constitution mongers of *Paris* that he was wholly unadulterated on this subject . . . Such were the sound opinions of Mr. Jefferson before he went to France.

The early French philosophers Turgot and the Girondists thought differently, and, accordingly, Dr. Franklin and Mr. Jefferson, as soon as they came in contact with them, became wonderfully converted. Hence it was that Mr. Jefferson so openly and strenuously condemned the division of Congress into two branches and professed that liberty could not be secured except by a single legislative assembly—Hence also the loud and vehement denunciations of the Senate by all the tools of faction and in all the venal newspapers in the employment of that faction and of France. Here also Mr. Jefferson's denunciation of the Federal constitution in his letter to Mazzei where he maliciously and falsely asserts, "that Washington and the British faction . . . had wished to impose on them the form of the British constitution." . . .   DECIUS.

If, in 1787, Ben Franklin had been younger, healthier, and acknowledged as the "Father of His Country" and Thomas Jefferson and Tom Paine been available to join Franklin at the Federal Constitutional Convention (Jefferson and Paine were then in France), what structure of government would the nation's three best-known democrats have led the Convention to accept? Would Jefferson now be complaining, as he does in his letter to Philip Mazzei, that the Federalists try *"to draw over us the substance, as they have already done the forms, of the British government . . . ."*?[2000]

WEDNESDAY, AUGUST 13, 1800

GENERAL   ★ AURORA ★   ADVERTISER

MR. DUANE. I enclose for you an article which I deemed it but justice to my character to present for insertion in the *Gazette of the United States* in reply to some illiberalities . . . in that paper of the 5th inst. When I presented it to Mr. Wayne . . . he informed me he would not publish it . . . I need not say more . . .   B. NONES

To the Printer of the Gazette of the U.S.
SIR . . . I am accused of being a *Jew,* of being a *Republican:* and of being *poor.*

I *am* a *Jew.* I glory in belonging to that persuasion, which even its opponents, whether Christian or Mohammedan, allow to be of divine origin—of that persuasion of which Christianity itself was originally founded and must ultimately rest—which has preserved its faith secure and undefiled for near three thousand years—whose votaries have never murdered each other in religious wars or cherished the theological hatred so general, so inextinguishable, among those who revile them . . .

I am a Republican ! Thank God . . . I have not been so proud or prejudiced as to renounce the cause for which I fought as an American throughout the whole of the revolutionary war, in the militia of Charleston and in Polasky's legion, . . . in almost every action which took place in Carolina and in the disastrous affair of Savannah . . . On religious grounds I am a republican. Kingly government was first conceded to . . . the Jewish people as a punishment and a curse . . . Great Britain has a king, and her enemies need not wish her the sword, the pestilence, and the famine . . .

I am a *Jew* and, if for no other reason, for that reason I am a *republican* . . . In the *monarchies* of Europe, we are hunted from society—stigmatized as unworthy of common civility, thrust out as it were from the converse of men; objects of mockery and insult . . . Among the nations of Europe, we are . . . *citizens* nowhere *unless in Republics.* [I]n France and in the Batavian Republic [the new French-controlled Netherlands republic] alone are we treated as men. In republics we have *rights;* in monarchies we live but to experience *wrongs* . . .

How then can a *Jew* but be a *Republican?* in America particularly. Unfeeling and ungrateful would he be, if he were callous to the glorious and benevolent cause of the difference between his situation in this land of freedom and among the proud and privileged law givers of Europe.

But I am *poor,* I am so, my family also is large, but soberly and decently brought up. They have not been taught to revile a Christian, because his religion is not so *old* as theirs. They have not been taught to mock . . . I know that to purse-proud aristocracy, poverty is a crime, but it may sometimes be accompanied with honesty, even in a Jew . . .

I was discharged by the insolvent act because, having the amount of my debt owing me from the French Republic, the differences between France and America have prevented the recovery of what was due to me in time to discharge my creditors. Hitherto it has been the fault of the political situation of the two countries that my creditors have not been paid; when peace shall enable me to receive what I am entitled to, it will be my fault if they are not finally paid . . .

This is a long defence, Mr. Wayne . . . The Public will now judge who is the proper object of ridicule and contempt, your facetious reporter or
Your Humble Servant,
BENJAMIN NONES.

Tonight, in the *Gazette of the United States:*

Mr. Nones has sent a long essay to the Editor of the *Aurora* . . . He has chosen a proper vehicle for the insertion of his *defence,* as he calls it . . . [S]uch silly stuff . . .

A Decision for Duane.
Will's head and his purse had a quarrel of late;
He with both came to me to decide the debate
Not great was the diff'rence—Indeed this was it—
Has my purse the most cash or my head the most wit?
I know not, cry'd I, which at *present* is worst,
But surely your head had the *vacuum* first.

GENERAL ★ AURORA ★ ADVERTISER

The harvest calling for the timely attention of the farmer, the republican farmers and others of Chester county postponed the celebration of the 4th of July to the 1st of August, on which day the most numerous assembly of citizens that ever was seen in this county met . . . [D]inner being over, the following [sixteen] toasts were given . . . 16. The *Aurora*. May it never cease to shine, until the heat of its rays shall have scorched the roots of every aristocratic tree and twig in the United States. 6 cheers, 1 gun.

Today, Thomas Jefferson writes Jeremiah Moor,

[T]he right of electing & being elected . . . When the constitution of Virginia was formed, I was in attendance at Congress. Had I been here [in Virginia], I should probably have proposed a general suffrage . . . Still I find very honest men who, thinking the possession of some property necessary to give due independence of mind, are for restraining the elective franchise to property . . . I [however] believe we may lessen the danger of buying and selling votes by making the number of voters too great for any means of purchase. I may further say that I have not observed men's honesty to increase with their riches . . .[2001]

GENERAL ★ AURORA ★ ADVERTISER

TO THE REPUBLICANS OF THE COUNTY OF PHILADELPHIA.
Fellow-citizens . . . In this boasted land of liberty, we behold citizens immured in prisons . . . for exercising the faculties of their minds and questioning the measures of a public servant! We have seen citizens, fathers of families, treated like ruffians by the military under federal authority . . . [W]e have seen the people of Pennsylvania rob'd of an essential right, the right to vote in the college of electors . . . We have beheld the most daring attempts to plunge us into war for party purposes . . . [W]e have seen the principles of monarchy openly avowed . . . republican government and the sovereignty of the people derided, and liberty and equality held up to scorn . . . and to cap the climax of aggression, we have beheld an attempt made to supersede the Constitution by a law of the Legislature by which the most estimable right of the people was to be transferred to a . . . secret committee organized by intrigue and acting without responsibility . . . To your posts then on the day of election—encounter your enemy with constitutional weapons . . . unite in a common cause—

act as becomes freemen—and liberty and happiness will be your reward.

By order of the [Philadelphia Republican] Committee,

ISAAC WORRELL, Chairman

MONDAY, AUGUST 18, 1800

GENERAL   ★ AURORA ★   ADVERTISER

The following note was received on Saturday by the Editor from his lawyer, and is given merely to shew how things GO ON in the STATE COURTS . . .

TO Mr. WILLIAM DUANE.

SIR, The following actions are marked for trial.—For trial 28 *Aug.*— *Respublica vs. Duane,* . . . *Fisher vs. Duane, Keppele vs. Duane, Stevens vs. Duane.*—1 Sept. *Meirken vs. Duane*

There is in New England a last legal right in the ministers of the Congregational Church to which Mr. Adams . . . belong[s] to exact from the members of all other Religious Societies within their congregational limits a contribution or Church tax to support them. These ministers have it in their power to seize the milk cows, working oxen, horses, and other property of a *Baptist,* a *Mennonist,* a *Presbyterian,* a *Quaker,* an *Episcopalian,* a *Roman Catholic,* a *Lutheran,* a *Calvinist,* a *Methodist,* &c. to pay the Church Dues and to support them . . . President Adams . . . [has] not . . . come forward and exerted [his] abilities and influence to do away [with] so unwarrantable a law . . . The Congregational Church is spread over all five New England states . . .

It may be asked what Mr. Adams and the other New Englandmen in the general government have to do . . . The ready answer is, let them do as Mr. Jefferson did, in 1776, immediately on the commencement of the American revolution. Virginia then had an established church that had such exclusive rights. Mr. Jefferson (though of that established church) introduced and carried a bill in the legislature by which all religious societies were made equal to and independent of each other.

In 1792, republicans in France dethroned King Louis XVI and disestablished the Catholic Church (France's First Estate). In 1798, republicans in Ireland sought to expel Britain's King George III and disestablish the Church of England. In 1800, Republicans in the United States want to unseat "His Rotundity" and disestablish the Congregational Church!

Tonight, in the *Gazette of the United States*:

A great part of the abuse of the Administrators of the Federal Government issues from jail-birds—From *Cooper,* through the sewer of the *Aurora;* and from *Callender,* who dates his productions from "Richmond gaol." Such fellows, thus situated, it is true, have prescriptive right to rail at government:

"For all goes wrong in Church and State,
Seen through perspective of the grate."

THURSDAY, AUGUST 21, 1800

GENERAL ★ AURORA ★ ADVERTISER

NEW YORK, August 19. Capt. Gardiner, who arrived here on Saturday . . . informs that, at the time he left Paris, which was about the 12th of June, the negociations between our commissioners and those of the French republic were going on but somewhat retarded . . .

Tonight, in the *Gazette of the United States*:

THAT arch-politician and sapient news-monger Duane has favoured the public with . . . intelligence from France concerning the rupture of negociations between our Envoys and the French government . . . Everyone knows how extremely favorable to France and oppressive to America was the treaty of 1778 made by old Franklin, and nothing could be more likely than that the French commissioners should . . . insist upon the unqualified renewal of that fatal treaty . . . and nothing could be more likely than that the American envoys were instructed to consent or to agree to no such disgraceful condition . . .   PLUTARCH

SUNDAY, AUGUST 24, 1800

This morning, from his pulpit at Philadelphia's Christ Church (the "English" church on Second-street), Porcupine's friend the Episcopal minister James Abercrombie sermonizes about Thomas Jefferson:

Beware—Men, Brethren, and fellow Christians—Beware of ever placing at the Head of Civil Society a man who is not an avowed Christian and an exemplary believer in our Holy Religion which . . . will be dishonored by such a choice . . . Can a Blessing from [God] be expected upon the community under such circumstances?—No, verily ! but a curse may be justly expected . . .[2002]

THURSDAY, AUGUST 28, 1800

GENERAL ★ AURORA ★ ADVERTISER

An episcopal clergyman in this City who has injured not only his church but his family by his intimacy and connexion with PORCUPINE has, we understand, re-commenced his career of *pulpit politics* . . . This man . . . on Sunday last in his sermon several times exhorted his hearers to oppose Mr. Jefferson . . . Profligate men such as *Porcupine* and *Fenno* openly advocated a National Church . . . [H]ow superior is the toleration of our happy country over that of the established churches . . .

Long *John Allen* of Connecticut . . . attributed the change of public opinion on public affairs to the newspapers—Thus he speaketh—"If so much mischief can be produced by one *Aurora* and its underlings, what would happen provided publications of a similar tendency were scattered throughout the country?" There is much force in what Long *John Allen* saith, and it is hoped the republicans will attend to it.

A LETTER OF JOHN ADAMS (COPY)

Quincy, May, 1792.

DEAR SIR, . . . The legislature of Massachusetts last winter, upon a petition of the North Parish in Braintree, separated it from the rest of the town . . . and gave it the name of Quincy. By this measure, you see, they have deprived me of my title of "Duke of Braintree" . . . I should have been happy to see [our new British ambassador] Mr. [Thomas] Pinckney before his departure . . . [O]ur new ambassador has many old friends in England . . . [which] contributed to limit the duration of my commission [as ambassador to Britain] to three years in order to make way for themselves to succeed me . . . [K]nowing as I do the long intrigue and suspecting as I do much British influence in the appointment, were I in any executive department, I should take the liberty to keep a vigilant eye upon them . . .

JOHN ADAMS

This letter of Mr. *Adams* was written while the venerated general *Washington* was president and Mr. *Adams* vice-president . . . [I]t proves British influence . . .

SATURDAY, AUGUST 30, 1800

GENERAL ★ AURORA ★ ADVERTISER

The author of the following interesting document is known to the Editor; several other gentlemen of the first reputation also knows the author . . .

TO GEORGE WASHINGTON FROM AN OLD FELLOW SOLDIER. *New York, April 25, 1795 . . .*

SIR . . . Why is it that people already begin to express an uneasy solicitude for your honor? . . . Have you ever examined the characters by which you are surrounded? . . . a man . . . who in the Federal Convention proposed, avowed and advocated a system bearing all the strong marked features of a monarchy . . . who proposed early in your cabinet questions of doubt on the acknowledgment of the French republic . . . who invariably applied the influence of the government to shackle the freedom of the press . . .

Tonight, in the *Gazette of the United States*:

THE REV. MR. ABERCROMBIE'S *SERMON.*

TO THE PUBLIC . . . [T]he SERMON which I preached on Sunday last in Christ-Church and St. Peter's . . . has given rise to the calumnies . . . As a member of the community, I have a right to express my sentiments on subjects of a political nature, and I WILL express them. As a Christian minister, I not only have a right, but I conceive it my duty . . .

JAMES ABERCROMBIE

MODESTY OF AN UNITED IRISHMAN.

Duane has long been notorious for *modesty*. The following is the top of the climax: In this morning's *Aurora*, he prefaces a letter to Gen. Washington (which he, in his usual stile, calls a *Document*) in the following manner—"*The author is known to the* EDITOR; *Several* OTHER GENTLEMEN ! *(how long since you, citizen Equality, became a gentleman?) of the* FIRST REPUTATION!!!!! *(Good Luck!) also* KNOWS *the Author.* Quere. Would it not be well for a *Gentleman* to be a *Grammarian?*

MONDAY, SEPTEMBER 1, 1800

GENERAL ★ AURORA ★ ADVERTISER

TO THE REV. MR. ABERCROMBIE

In your discourse on the last Lord's Day, you took occasion to introduce *political opinions* with religious topics—you called Mr. *Jefferson* a deist and augured the destruction of the country should he be raised to the presidential chair.

I have ever been thought to believe that the duties of the ministry of God's holy church was to inculcate among other doctrines this sublime maxim, "Peace on earth, and good will among men." . . . yet you have endeavored *to arm brother against brother*, you have prostituted God's holy word to further the cause of a *faction*, and under the semblance of Religion, you have inculcated doctrines of which you ought to be ashamed . . .

[Y]ou are a free man, you are an independent citizen of a free country, you have therefore a privilege of opening your sentiments when and where you please, but, in the name of God, whose gospel you profess, never profane his temple with the mere temporal concerns of this world . . . [I]ntroduce not the religion of Jesus to further private ends . . .

VALERIUS

Tonight, in the *Gazette of the United States*:

POLITICAL . . .

It is a fact . . . that the most profligate and malicious and false public newspaper that ever existed in any country and under any government is now
. . . printed *in the city of Philadelphia* . . . This paper (since I have begun,
I may as well go through with its history) has existed now about ten years
altogether . . . A grandson of Benjamin Franklin (it is almost too notorious
to tell) was the Editor of this paper for the space of eight years. This
circumstance . . . will further explain (to such as are strangers to the influence Mr. Franklin possessed in the State of Pennsylvania) the reason
why this newspaper, under the superintendance of his grandson, has been
able to effect such mischief in opposing, from the beginning, the measures
and systems of the federal government—Benjamin Franklin Bache, received the greater part of his juvenile education, under the immediate
care and supervision of his Grandfather. He accompanied him to France
when Mr. Franklin went over to negotiate the treaty of Alliance between
the United States and the French Monarchy and was placed at Passy, near
Paris, where his grandfather chiefly resided—here it was that young Benjamin acquired a proficiency in the French language—here he formed that
invincible attachment for France and everything that was French, which
early habit, united and assisted with his Grandfather's notorious partiality
for and commendation of them, must naturally inspire—He saw his old—
fond and amorous Grand Sire in the habit of caressing and being caressed
by the seducing females of France, and his youthful blood was doubtless
often fired by scenes of tenderness and love, though his infant years were
an obstacle to his participation in the full delight they were calculated to
confer. After an absence of several years, young Benjamin returned to his
native country. He was yet a youth and not entitled to assume the *"Toga
virilis."* He therefore completed his education . . .

With these qualifications and little previous apprenticeship to the trade
did young Benjamin commence . . . A set of types and a printing press,
which had been bequeathed to him as a legacy by his Grandfather, composed the apparatus with which he began his professional career . . .

The French Revolution came and it operated like an electric shock
upon the Editor . . . A new day, in short had dawned. This was the proud
and natal day of "the Aurora." We shall mark the course he took, [ere] he
sunk into the still slumbers of the silent grave.   MUTIUS SCAEVOLA

WEDNESDAY, SEPTEMBER 3, 1800

GENERAL   ★ AURORA ★   ADVERTISER

We learn that a pretended pious christian who, on hearing that *B. F.
Bache* was dead, wished that his soul was in hell, burning at that instant—is now advocating Mr. Abercrombie's political sermon.

843

Today, from the new federal city of Washington, Treasury Secretary Oliver Wolcott responds to Alexander Hamilton's letter of August 3rd:

> *I have attended to the publications in the Aurora. We may regret but we cannot prevent the mischiefs which these falshoods produce . . . [W]e may as well attempt to arrest the progress of fire in a mess of gun powder as to suppress these calumnies; they must have their course and the vindication of official characters must be left to an enquiry by Congress . . . Colo. Pickerings conduct will be found correct; Mr. Dayton's incorrect . . .*[2003]

Tonight, in the *Gazette of the United States*:

POLITICAL . . .

Bache spoke and translated the French language . . . *He* always had the earliest intelligence of . . . the French Republic . . . to pass it through his newspaper to the enamored partisans of the Republic here. Civic festivals were continually advertized, and all the *Sans Culottes* were invited to attend the celebration. The Federal Government, but more especially President Washington, was held up to scorn and ridicule because resistance was made to the fitting out of French privateers in our ports and to the sale of French prizes . . .

"[T]he Aurora" continued faithful to the [French] republic in every change of her mutable condition. The federal government and all who had any share in the administration were themes of daily reproach, misrepresentation, and slander. The *form* no less than the manner in which the government was administered were condemned, because they approached to a resemblance of the British constitution, and because the French had adopted and were then practicing upon the model which *Monsieur Franklin* had always recommended and admired. It is well known that the present [two-chamber legislature, single executive] constitution of the State of Pennsylvania (which in good hands would be the most perfect system of State government in the Union) could never have been ratified *in the life time of Mr. Franklin*. A single democratic representative assembly was his darling theory. In no other form could the happiness of the people be promoted. Nor could the true dignity of man's nature be displayed where the doctrine of a chief or control over his passions was an ingredient in the constitution.

From all the preceding detail of facts, some of which are merely historical, I shall draw this inference—That the ghost of Benjamin Franklin still haunts and hovers over the destinies of the federal government, that his apparition will never be allayed . . . and lastly that the people of this country must make their election between the alternative of abandoning the haunted castle, commonly called the federal constitution, or submit to the impertinent daily visits of a troublesome spectre, commonly called "the Aurora."

By what strange fatality it has happened, I know not, but this is the fact, that the successor to Benjamin Franklin Bache, as Editor of the *Aurora, is a British subject.* Yes, Billy Duane, who was sort of an upper workman in the "Aurora office" at the time Benjamin Franklin Bache died, is a British refugee from Bengal or some other British possession in the East Indies, where he superintended and published a newspaper and whence he was suddenly compelled to depart for fear of a prosecution against him *for libelling the government.* Thus we see that his *present* occupation is no *new* thing to him—he was proficient in the trade when he came here . . .

That such a newspaper should be tolerated in the capital city of the United States is no proof that our laws are more favorable to the liberty of the press than those of other nations. On the contrary, it is proof that our laws are incompetent to restrain or suppress its daring licentiousness; and any one may venture to predict with the utmost certainty the speedy downfall of any government that tolerates such a sapping engine within its jurisdiction . . . To the shame of my country, be it confessed that the newspaper called "the Aurora" . . . enjoys more patronage both at home and abroad than any public newspaper in America . . .

MUTIUS SCAEVOLA

There is no question that "the ghost of Benjamin Franklin still haunts and hovers over the destinies of the federal government." That friendly ghost, spectacles and all, presides at the *Philadelphia Aurora.*

SATURDAY, SEPTEMBER 6, 1800

GENERAL   ★ AURORA ★   ADVERTISER

Parson *Abercrombie* and his adherents avow a love of *monarchy*—they wish for an established church. Monarchy and established churches have ever been favourable to servility and hypocrisy, because the whole influence and power of the *throne* and the *church* centered in *one*, or a few individuals . . . [T]his in substance comprehends the causes which have arisen from *kingly governments* and the interests of *churches* connected with those of *States.*

Tonight, in the *Gazette of the United States:*

POLITICAL

IT is no difficult thing to account for the celebrity of "the Aurora" when we take into view the following peculiarities which distinguish it from all other newspapers. First, its origin and operation for several years under the superintendence of a grand-son of Benjamin Franklin. Secondly, its publication at Philadelphia, the capital of the United States and hitherto the Seat of Government. Third, that it is the official governmental paper of the French Republic . . . Fourthly, that the writers of it are chiefly foreign desperados who came or were sent here to write down the government. Fifthly, and lastly, that its present Editor is a British subject. Each of these are powerful operative causes of the success of "the Aurora" at home and abroad . . .

In the course of this investigation, I have attributed much importance to "the Aurora" in supposing it capable of destroying the federal Government. It is extensively circulated; it is read by all who take it and by many more who do not pay for it. It is the model and the standard for all the underling Jacobin prints throughout the country. It is copied by them. It is the "people's paper" in the same sense that Mr. Jefferson is "the man of the people."

It is published in the capital of the State of Pennsylvania where the Governor of the state and almost every state officer are [now] its immediate influential patrons. It is conducted with a diabolical zeal and activity, and it has also this peculiar advantage, that, whether it publishes lies or truth, the assertions are equally credited at a distance and equally assist the democratic cause.

Such is the paper called "the Aurora."—By exposing it to the American public, "what it was in the beginning, is now, and ever shall be" so long as it endures, I have not been without a hope that it might be rendered odious in their sight and that some of its mischievous effects might be thereby counteracted . . . I shall still cherish the hope that there is yet left among us . . . enough attachment to the federal government and to those who administer it to secure federal majorities at the approaching election; and lastly, enough of religion to reject the creed of atheism and revolution which is daily preached as orthodox by their great High Priest William Duane, the editor of "the Aurora." MUTIUS SCAEVOLA.

TUESDAY, SEPTEMBER 9, 1800

GENERAL ★ AURORA ★ ADVERTISER

Toleration in religion, complete and perfect, was not known, except among the *Hindus*, in any part of the earth before our revolution. In Pennsylvania, a few years before the revolution . . . even here in this city of brotherhood . . . *Papist* was a term of reproach as constant as *Democrat* or *Jacobin* in the mouth of good federalists two years ago! . . . In the state of Virginia before the war, a Quaker on going into that state *a third time* was liable to the punishment of death ! A Roman Catholic clergyman dared not to go even once within its boundary to exercise even an office of charity !

Our revolution has obliterated these impious institutions. [T]he New England states alone support intolerance. In Virginia, Mr. *Jefferson* has been the author and mover of those laws which put down the national church there and abolished *tythes* [taxes on the general population to support the church]. This is a sin for which those who deal in tythes will never forgive him; this is Mr. *Jefferson's* crime in their eyes . . . [T]he Roman Catholics are now building a Church in Norfolk, Virginia . . . From this happy state of toleration, the furious zealots for the British government would bring us back to our former condition . . .

Tonight, in the *Gazette of the United States*:

> *Extract of a letter from New England.* "I understand from some of the newspapers that Mr. Abercrombie, one of your Episcopal Clergymen . . . has drawn down the vengeance of all the Jacobins and, among the rest, their redoubtable champion, Duane. Why Mr. Abercrombie should be attacked more than other Clergymen I cannot conceive . . ."

GENERAL ★ AURORA ★ ADVERTISER

FORGERY
A PROP FOR PARSON ABERCROMBIE

In the *Philadelphia Gazette* of Friday, there appeared a letter of which the following is an exact copy.

> *"Having heard that there were several objections to Mr. Jefferson for his disbelief in the importance of Christianity, I gave myself little trouble on a subject which, as a follower of Moses and the Old Testament, I had little to do. But since the abuse offered to Mr. Abercrombie, I have examined the merits and find that Mr. Jefferson . . . by making a belief of twenty Gods or even NO GOD unimportant, has struck at all religion! Therefore, Mr. Abercrombie will be considered in a COMMON CAUSE . . . [W]e all abhor the very name of an Atheist.* MOSES S. SOLOMONS,
> *Second Street, Philadelphia"*

Upon the first perusal of this article, we perceived its *imposture.* No person of the Jewish church could object to a man who was the avowed advocate of universal toleration! No Hebrew could be hostile consistently to a man who, in the very introduction to the Declaration of Independence, declared *all men equal* and implores a *Divine Providence.* Upon examination, no person of the name of *Moses S. Solomons* was found in Second Street. Recourse was then had to the Hebrew church in Cherry Alley ! No such person was known there! . . . The Editor then applied to one of the Hebrew congregation . . . [T]he following certificate was obtained . . .

> *I have been for several years a Parnass (or president) to the Hebrew congregation . . . [N]o such man as Moses S. Solomon has*

> *ever been or is now a member of a Hebrew congregation of this*
> *city.*   A MEMBER OF THE HEBREW CHURCH . . .

Such are the means employed by *Parson Abercrombie* and his *gang* to prop up their hypocritical profess[ion]s of religion!

Benjamin Nones (whose letter appeared in the August 13th *Aurora*) provided the certificate.[2004]

Tonight, in the *Gazette of the United States*:

> That *"Gentleman of the first reputation"* DUANE, who receives letters "admiring the *ability* with which *L'Aurora* is conducted" . . . has become seriously alarmed at the encreasing circulation of the *Gazette of the United States*. He attempts to impose a belief on his gaping readers that it has but five hundred subscribers!!! If the Advertisement for a thousand Rheams of paper per year gives him such qualms as lately discovered, we would publish a list of subscribers which should . . . *"shake his gall bladder."*

CHAPTER SIXTEEN

VICTORY

*Franklin declares all power to be in the people when the servants
violate their duties or when they violate the constitution.*

B. F. BACHE, EDITOR,
AURORA GENERAL ADVERTISER, 1790–1798[2005]

*[T]he American Revolution . . . attempted to overturn tyranny but
only half completed its design. The party who at present hold
the government . . . have now taken the ground and
doctrines of George the third.*

JAMES THOMSON CALLENDER,
SKETCHES OF THE HISTORY OF AMERICA (1798)[2006]

*In 1798 and 1799, monarchy openly exulted, and democracy was a
term of bitterest reproach. The execrable planners of this dangerous
and desperate system, thanks to the freedom of the press, are now
fallen; fallen, we sincerely hope, to rise no more.*

WILLIAM DUANE, EDITOR,
AURORA GENERAL ADVERTISER, 1798–1822[2007]

*[T]he energy of [William Duane's Aurora], . . . its unquestionable effect
in the revolution produced in the public mind . . . arrested the rapid
march of our government towards monarchy . . .*

THOMAS JEFFERSON,
PRESIDENT OF THE UNITED STATES, 1801–1809[2008]

*FIRST ARTICLE: Congress shall make no law respecting an
establishment of religion, or prohibiting the free exercise thereof;
or abridging the freedom of speech, or of the press; or the right
of the people peaceably to assemble, and to petition the
Government for a redress of grievances.*

FROM THE BILL OF RIGHTS
OF THE UNITED STATES CONSTITUTION

God grant that not only the love of liberty, but a thorough knowledge
of the rights of man, may pervade all Nations of the Earth, so that
a Philosopher may set his Foot anywhere on its Surface, and say,
"This is my Country."

DR. BENJAMIN FRANKLIN[2009]

THURSDAY, SEPTEMBER 11, 1800

GENERAL ★ AURORA ★ ADVERTISER

Did not a person holding a public office under the present administration say that if *Jefferson* should be elected president, the records of the department of state ought never to be suffered to go into his hands?

Tonight, in the *Gazette of the United States*:

MR. EDITOR . . . I was a Democrat and was fully intent upon voting for Tom Paine, pshaw, I mean Tom Jefferson at the next election; but by the salutary counsel of my Friends . . . I have now become (I hope) a good Federalist . . . I have been accustomed to read the *Aurora* (by the advice of Duane) every morning . . . but . . . Mr. Worthy, the schoolmaster . . . said, "what, have you also degraded yourself so far as to become a subscriber for that infamous and abandoned paper; a paper constantly teeming with the greatest scurrility against every good man; from whose shaft of Malice even Washington was not exempted and which, not content, now seeks to undermine the throne of God himself?" . . .

DICK VULCAN

FRIDAY, SEPTEMBER 12, 1800

GENERAL ★ AURORA ★ ADVERTISER

NEW JERSEY . . .

FELLOW CITIZENS . . . It is true, citizens of New Jersey, you cannot exercise a direct voice in the appointment of electors for president and vice president. You have respectfully petitioned for this privilege . . . [Y]our last two legislatures . . . declared that you are unworthy . . . and it remains for you to decide, at the approaching election, whether those who deprive you of an invaluable right . . . yet retain your confidence . . . Your united and decisive voice will remove the grievances . . . The powerful states of Virginia, Pennsylvania and New York have nobly led the way. You have witnessed the effects of those republican triumphs.—You have seen the confusion of the cabinet, the dissolution of any army which had cost you millions, and the whole system of terror staggering under the strokes. Arouse then . . .

Federalist-controlled state legislatures in the crucial mid-Atlantic states (Pennsylvania, New York, New Jersey) have denied their citizens the right to vote for presidential electors, retaining that right for the legislators to exercise themselves. But, in May, New Yorkers reconstituted their state legislature with a Republican majority, so the state's twelve presidential electoral votes will go to Jefferson. Might New Jersey do the same? Might Pennsylvania?

Tonight, in the *Gazette of the United States*:
> *Liberty, Equality, and the rights of Man*
> On the authority of several letters, we state that twenty unfortunate negroes were to be executed near Richmond for being concerned in the *holy right of Insurrection!!*

MONDAY, SEPTEMBER 15, 1800

GENERAL ★ AURORA ★ ADVERTISER

THE PUBLISHING OFFICE of the Aurora is removed from No. 112, Market street, to the apartment underneath the Printing Office in Franklin Court, between 106 and 108, Market street.

Tonight, in the *Gazette of the United States*:

> A FAVORITE BEER-HOUSE SONG . . .
> There came a saucy Irishman, from somewhere near Killarney,
> A scurvy cunning Jacobin, and very full of blarney . . .
> He kiss'd poor Benny Bache's wife; he lied for Coxe and Dallas
> 'Till by the rules of honesty, he well deserved the gallows;
> He feed our pliant lawyers to put off each fair trial;
> Thus tho' by fifty he was sued—yet still he did defy all;
> O! was not he an arch knave, this cunning Will Duane O,
> To dupe both law and justice too, as well as Tom M'Kean O
> George Washington he call'd a Knave, the President a Rogue, Sir
> And treated every honest man, as if he had the brogue, Sir . . .

Extract of a letter from New Jersey . . . "From the most accurate calculations . . . a large majority of our next legislature will be federal, consequently Mr. Jefferson will have no votes in New Jersey . . ."

New Jersey will be lost! Will Pennsylvania hold the key to the presidency?

WEDNESDAY, SEPTEMBER 17, 1800

GENERAL ★ AURORA ★ ADVERTISER

BUCKS COUNTY [PENN.]
At a large and respectable meeting of the REPUBLICAN CITIZENS of Bucks county, held (pursuant to public notice) at the house of Josiah

Addis in Buckingham Township, on Saturday, the 13th of September, the following resolutions were adopted, viz . . .

Whereas . . . the republican part of our Legislature have done their utmost to secure to Pennsylvania her constitutional voice in the election of the next President by proposing to renew the law under which we have hitherto acted and prospered, but were prevented by a majority of the Senators [who] . . . ought, as soon as possible to be replaced . . .

Resolved, That we will individually exert ourselves . . . to promote the election of the said [Republican] William Rodman [to the Pennsylvania state Senate] . . .

Resolved, That the thanks of this meeting be given to that distinguished, persecuted, yet still triumphant republican William Duane, for his attendance and valuable communications to this meeting, long may he continue in the advance guard of republicans, and the phalanx of aristocracy fall before the awakened spirit of American freedom.

THOMAS LONG, Chairman

Tonight, in the *Gazette of the United States*:

Duane has been attending the Jacobin meetings in different parts of the State. At one held in Bucks county, a Resolution of Thanks was passed for his attendance and *valuable communications,* &c. That *Duane* should be there is natural, and he will go wherever the whiskey circulates . . .

FRIDAY, SEPTEMBER 19, 1800

GENERAL ★ AURORA ★ ADVERTISER

John Adams is no Democrat. Doctor Franklin was one . . . And one of his political axioms was that all rights were derived from the people and in a democracy must revert to them at certain stated periods, agreeably to the terms of the constitutional compact.

Tonight, in the *Gazette of the United States*:

That *"Gentleman of the First Reputation," Duane,* is going about the country and stopping at every Jacobin Tavern keeper's, where he assembles two or three of the Ostlers [stablemen]. These, with two or three United Irishmen who accompany him, he calls a meeting; one of his companions then produces a string of resolutions written by *Duane* in which a number of the inhabitants who are 7, 8, and 10 miles off are named as a committee. Among these resolutions, there is always one expressing thanks for *his* attendance, *his* republican firmness, *his* patriotism, and regret at *his* persecution—he gets these agreed to by the drunken fellows present and then publishes them in the *French Gazette*. This is the way so many meetings are accounted for. He goes in the country with his pockets full of resolutions. He is a *modest* man!!!

SATURDAY, SEPTEMBER 20, 1800

GENERAL ★ AURORA ★ ADVERTISER

LEGIONARY ORDERS . . .

The militia legion will display in line in Monday the 22d inst. At 9 o'clock in the morning at Germantown. The corps from the City, Southwark, and the Northern Liberties will march from their respective parades at 6 o'clock . . . JOHN SHEE, Commandant

REPUBLICAN GREENS

YOU muster for an inspection of arms THIS row evening, at 5 o'clock, in Franklin Court—And on Monday morning, punctually at 6 o'clock, ready for march . . . WM. KANE, Secretary

TUESDAY, SEPTEMBER 23, 1800

GENERAL ★ AURORA ★ ADVERTISER

LETTER TO THE EDITOR, Dated Richmond [Virginia]. September 12, 1800. ". . . One Thomas Prosser, a young man who had fallen heir, some time ago, to a plantation within six miles of the city, had behaved with great barbarity to his slaves. One of them named Gabriel, a fellow of courage and intellect above his rank in life, laid a plan of vengeance. Immense numbers immediately entered into it . . . [R]ain made the passage impracticable . . . Five fellows were hung this day; and many more will share the same fate. Their plan was to massacre all the whites . . ."

Today, in the *Gazette of the United States*:

The Insurrection of the Negroes in the southern states, *which appears to be organized on the true French plan*, must be decisive with every reflecting man in those States of the election of Mr. Adams . . .

Today, Thomas Jefferson writes Dr. Benjamin Rush:

I promised you a letter on Christianity . . .
The delusion into which the X, Y, Z plot shewed it possible to push the people; the successful experiment made . . . on the clause of the constitution which, while it secured the freedom of the press, covered also the freedom of religion, had given to the clergy a very favorite hope of obtaining an establishment of a particular form of Christianity thro' the U.S.; and, as every sect believes its own form the true one, every one perhaps hoped for its own, but especially the Episcopalians & Congregationalists. The returning good sense of our country threatens abortion to their hopes, & they believe that any portion of power confided to me will be exerted in opposition to their schemes. And they

believe rightly; for I have sworn upon the altar of god eternal hostility against every form of tyranny over the mind of man.[2010]

WEDNESDAY, SEPTEMBER 24, 1800

GENERAL   ★ AURORA ★   ADVERTISER

It is well known that Mr. Jefferson, among the other matters of complaint, inserted . . . in his draft of the Declaration of Independence one article . . . [against] the British king . . . withholding his assent from laws passed in Virginia and other colonies prohibiting the importation of Africans as slaves. This clause in the Declaration of Independence was struck out of the draft on the motion of an *eastern* [New England] member of Congress . . .

In Wayne's *Gazette [of the United States]* of yesterday evening, the insurrection of the Negroes in Virginia and Carolina is thus treated— "The Insurrection of the Negroes in the southern states, *which appears to be organized on the French plan,* must be decisive with every reflecting man in those states of the election of Mr. Adams . . ." . . .

We augur better things from this unhappy but, thank God, partial revolt.—We augur from it the effectual stoppage of the African trade. We augur from it measures for a gradual emancipation of the offspring of those who now exist in slavery upon the same plan long since suggested by Dr. *Franklin* and which Mr. *Jefferson* endeavored without effect to accomplish. We augur from it, not bloodshed nor massacre by military execution or the gibbet, but the election of that man whose whole life has been marked by measures calculated to procure the emancipation of the blacks and to ameliorate the condition of those whom the fatal policy of the British has entailed us.

Benjamin Franklin was president of America's first antislavery society, the Pennsylvania Society for Promoting the Abolition of Slavery.[2011]

Tonight, in the *Gazette of the United States*:

Monday the *twenty-second day of September,* the *Shee [Republican] Legion* of this city paraded and marched to *Beggars* town—for what—to drink gin with *Duane*—eat a Bull at *Logan's*—or was it to *celebrate the coronation of King George the III ?*

THURSDAY, SEPTEMBER 25, 1800

GENERAL   ★ AURORA ★   ADVERTISER

The Republican legion of this City had a day of military exercise at Germantown, the 22d instant . . . on [what] was formerly a *British camp* where the myrmidons of George III assembled . . . ; there were more than *fifty* persons under arms in the Legion on Monday who had a share in the battle of Germantown. The honest German citizens cheered at the sight of the assemblage of a body of Republicans, whose military parades are conducted without breaking the peace of the city . . .

TO THE ELECTORS OF PENNSYLVANIA . . .

Our annual election is now at hand . . . [O]n the political complexion of the next Legislative Body of the State, very much indeed must depend . . .

The Constitution of the United States has provided that "Each state *shall* appoint, in such manner as the legislature thereof may direct, a number of electors . . ." Such electors have been three times chosen in Pennsylvania [so that] . . . the whole number of electors of President and Vice President was voted for by individuals duly qualified throughout the state, *in one ticket.*

The republican members of the present legislature, in their last session, proposed a similar law . . . But those inimical to the appointment of Republican candidates . . . insisted on an election by districts and those *so modified and arranged as totally to preclude a true manifestation of the will of the State.* This unfair, as well as unprecedented mode of appointing the electors of Pennsylvania, could not be conscientiously acceded to . . .

But, surely, Pennsylvania will not submit to a total disenfranchisement . . . The Constitution of the United States directs that "each state *shall* appoint," &c.—We have, therefore, *one* resource left . . . The LEGISLATURE may themselves appoint the electors . . . It is, fellow citizens, within the compass of a probability that upon the vote of a single member of the Senate of this State may rest the decision of the mighty contest which is now agitating the mind of every American citizen . . .

Tonight, in the *Gazette of the United States*:

Duane says that *fifty* persons who were under arms in the Legion on Monday had a share in the battle of Germantown—but he don't say a word about whose army they were in; we know that many of them are recently from *Britain* and *Ireland.*

[ALEXANDRIA, VIRGINIA.] [I]t is evident that the French principle of liberty & equality have been [in]fused into the minds of the Negroes; and that the incautious and intemperate use of these words by some whites amongst us have inspired them with hopes of success . . .

By whom is the *Aurora* and the rest of the Jacobin Newspapers . . . conducted and supported? By men hostile to our liberties . . . ; these are men who offer you an infidel for Chief Magistrate in preference to a virtuous and steadfast believer in God; these are the assassins who have assailed the character of our beloved Washington, accused him of the greatest of crimes; who have impiously attempted to blast his blushing honours and tarnish his immortal glory . . . VULCAN

FRIDAY, SEPTEMBER 26, 1800

GENERAL ★ AURORA ★ ADVERTISER

THE COMMITTEES of the City and county of Philadelphia appointed to devise a plan for concentrating the votes of the republicans . . . are requested to meet . . . on Wednesday eve . . .

THE REPUBLICAN COMMITTEE OF SELECTION
For the City of Philadelphia . . . at the house of John Miller, sign of the Green Tree . . . THIS NIGHT at 7 o'clock

REPUBLICAN MEETING
THE Republican Citizens of the District of Southwark . . . at Crosby's tavern . . . on business of importance

It is pleasing to see the old sentiments of America, after a deplorable eclipse, once more bursting from behind the clouds . . . [T]he address of the Republicans of Kent county [Pennsylvania] will exemplify these remarks—

"The old fashioned principles of '76—those principles which recognize the rights of man and the sovereignty of the people, principles on which the Declaration of Independence and our constitutions were predicated . . . have been outraged, ridiculed and attempted to be exploded . . . The memory of a FRANKLIN—of that Franklin who pleaded the cause of the new to the old world; whose transcendent genius gave popularity to American freedom in Europe; and whose philosophy, by disarming heaven of its terrors, lessens the chances of sudden death; has been assailed by a British caitiff [Porcupine] who, boasting the patronage of the clergy, tories and federalists, daily outraged decency . . . When death itself cannot shield from slander, and the malignant breath of envy blasts beyond the grave, the living cannot hope to escape; and the second magistrate of the United States, the incomparable Jefferson, has been the theme of incessant slander and abuse. The man who could pen the Declaration of Independence . . . has no Sedition Law to protect him. But like the waves that dash against the rock, the calumnies of his enemies serve only to [mark] his strength and recoil on their authors."

Tonight, in the *Gazette of the United States*:

Paddy Duane is eternally prating about the patriotism of '76. We should be glad to hear from this vile foreign outcast where he was in '76 ?

It appears *from the evidence given on the trials of the Negroes* . . . that the most intensive plans of murder and desolation have been organized in the Southern States. *That Frenchmen* have been the projectors of these infernal plans. That in the massacre of the whites, *Frenchmen* alone were to have been spared; and it appears, from Duane's publication of Wednesday, that the *Aurora,* a paper devoted to the furtherance of *French* measures, is already employed to palliate and to excuse these enormities . . . with auguries, drawn from the opinions heretofore delivered by Mr. Jefferson . . . to inspirit the Insurgents . . .

SATURDAY, SEPTEMBER 27, 1800

GENERAL ★ AURORA ★ ADVERTISER

ANGLO-FEDERAL *WISHES*
[FOR A PRESIDENTIAL ELECTORAL VOTE].

		Jefferson	*Adams*
1.	Massachusetts,	0	16
2.	N. Hampshire,	0	6
3.	Rhode-Island,	0	4
4.	Vermont,	0	4
5.	Connecticut,	0	9
6.	New-York ,	12	0
7.	New-Jersey,	0	7
8.	Pennsylvania,	0	0*
9.	Delaware,	0	3
10.	Maryland,	0	10
11.	Virginia,	21	0
12.	North-Carolina,	8	4
13.	South-Carolina,	8	0
14.	Kentucky,	4	0
15.	Georgia,	4	0
16.	Tennessee,	3	0
	* No vote.	60	63

It is easy to see why Federalists want to keep Pennsylvania's fifteen presidential electoral votes away from Thomas Jefferson, even if that means preventing Pennsylvania's participation in the presidential election!

TUESDAY, SEPTEMBER 30, 1800

GENERAL ★ AURORA ★ ADVERTISER

GENERAL REPUBLICAN MEETING . . .
The Republicans of the City of Philadelphia are requested to convene at the State House at 6 o'clock on Wednesday evening, the 1st of

October . . . The attempts which have been made by our adversaries to divide and deceive the republicans . . . must shew the necessity of decision and encrease rather than diminish the spirit of vigilance and union . . .

[PARIS.] The negociation was opened on the part of the French Commissioners on the supposition that the treaty of 1778 was still in force . . . But the American Envoys were not authorized to renew this treaty . . . *France waived this point* in consequence of the assurances of the American envoys that they *could not renew it . . .*

Today, in Paris (where Tom Paine has remained since Britain outlawed him for his *Rights of Man*), Tom Paine writes Thomas Jefferson:

> *The [American] commissioners, Ellsworth and company, have been here about eight months, and three more useless mortals never came upon public business . . . I went to see Mr. Ellsworth . . . because I had formerly known him in Congress.*
>
> *"I mean not," said I, "to press you with any questions, or to engage you in any conversation upon the business you are come upon, but I will nevertheless candidly say . . . [t]he [Jay] treaty with England lies at the threshold of all your business. The American Government never did two more foolish things than when it signed that treaty and recalled Mr. Monroe . . ."*
>
> *Mr. Ellsworth put on the dull gravity of a judge and was silent. I added, ". . . the principle that neutral ships make neutral property must be general or not at all." I then changed the subject . . . and inquired after Samuel Adams (I asked nothing about John), Mr. Jefferson, Mr. Monroe and others of my friends . . .*
>
> *I know that the faction of John Adams abuses me pretty heartily. They are welcome. It does not disturb me . . .*
>
> *I suppose you have seen or have heard of the Bishop of Llandaff's answer to my second part of "The Age of Reason." . . . [A]s soon as the clerical Society for Promoting Christian Knowledge knew of my intention to answer the Bishop, they prosecuted, as a society, the printer . . . to prevent that answer appearing . . .*
>
> *Remember me with much affection to my friends and accept the same to yourself.*
>
> *THOMAS PAINE*[2012]

War . . . Today, in the French West Indies, the twelve-gun, seventy-man U.S. Navy schooner *Experiment* seizes a French merchantman bound for France. U.S. Navy Lieutenant Charles Stewart reports:

We cruized to windward of St. Bartholomews till the 1st of October, which day we fell in with and captured the French armed (three masted) schr. Diana, out two days from Guadaloupe, laden with sugar, coffee, and cotton bound to France under convoy of a brig of 16 nine pounders and 150 men. This schr. mounted 8 nine pound canon-ades (6 of which they threw overboard in the chace) and 45 men . . .[2013]

Tonight, in the *Gazette of the United States*:

THE HAND-BILLS

DUANE pretends to disown the Hand Bills which have been circulating among his party . . . It is worthy of remark that the strictures in the *Aurora* upon this subject are headed by no less than four different notices to the *united* Republicans to convene in several places for as many different purposes;—There is the committee of *Concentration*, the committee of *Important Business*—the committee of *Selection,* and the committee for promoting the *Republican Interest.*

It is very well known that the whole squad . . . are striving hard to bring about a coalition . . . Duane undertakes to act the mediator . . .

Extract of a letter from Virginia. The slave holders in our county will no longer permit the *Aurora* and other *Jacobin* papers to come into their houses as they are convinced the late insurrection is to be attributed entirely to this source and to incendiary handbills and pamphlets from the same presses.

From the Charleston City [South Carolina] Gazette . . . [To the Editors]. A LETTER copied from the [August 28th] *Aurora* . . . signed JOHN AD-AMS . . . wherein are contained some comments on my appointment as minister-plenipotentiary to the court of Great-Britain . . . is a forgery . . . To my fellow-citizens of South Carolina . . . I should deem it unnecessary to urge a syllable of justification . . .   *THOMAS PINCKNEY*

FRIDAY, OCTOBER 3, 1800

GENERAL ★ AURORA ★ ADVERTISER

It will be remembered that the Editor of this paper was indicted at Norristown in this state, under the *Sedition Law,* for publishing a declaration of Mr. Adams that British influence had been used . . . Upon an offer of the editor by his counsel to produce that Letter in Court, some confusion was manifested and some legal *pantomime* was played off [so] the trial was postponed. But the *Indictment was withdrawn* by order of the President . . . We think it proper to republish Mr. Adams' letter . . .

Quincy, May, 1792.
DEAR SIR, . . . [O]ur new ambassador [Thomas Pinckney] has many old friends in England . . . [which] contributed to limit the

duration of my commission [as ambassador to Britain] to three years . . . [S]uspecting as I do much British influence in the appointment, were I in any executive department, I should take the liberty to keep a vigilant eye upon them . . .   JOHN ADAMS

During the last sitting of Congress in this city, many members had expressed doubts of such a letter written by Mr. Adams; and some of them [were] apprehensive that some imposition had been practiced to bring [the Editor] into the power of those who had manifested a disposition to destroy this paper and the editor.

After repeated representations of this kind, the Editor saw the necessity of satisfying them . . . The Editor was informed that Mr. Adams did not deny the authenticity of the letter; but that he endeavored to give it an explanation different from its apparent tenor by endeavoring to shew that it was not [South Carolinian Federalist] Mr. Thomas Pinckney who was alluded to but [South Carolinian Republican] Charles Pinckney, now of the senate . . . The election comes on in South Carolina, it is believed, the second Monday in October . . .

It is nearly eighteen months since the prosecution was commenced against the Editor for publishing Mr. Adams' letter . . . to prove that British Influence had been practiced . . . When the federal court at Norristown deferred the trial, the court contrary to right and to law enjoined the Editor not to publish the proceedings there. *Judge Peters* expressly told the editor if he published, he should be obliged to *take notice of it!* The Editor could not but smile at the *imprimatur*, but knowing the strong ground upon which he stood suffered the matter to go over. The indictments were withdrawn . . . To shew the public that no imposition was attempted, the editor published the letter of Mr. Adams; suspecting that the withdrawing of the suit was intended to produce the suppression of the letter altogether . . .

Fellow Citizens, . . . [C]ertain essays under the signature of *Publicola* . . . have been since republished in London . . . The title runs thus; "Answer to Paine's *Rights of Man* by *John Adams, esquire, originally* printed in *America.*" . . . This book was read by the Council for the King in Mr. [Thomas] Paine's trial . . . It is not stated or admitted by the writer that there are any defects inherent in the [British] constitution, though hereditary . . . with a christian hierarchy to aid them . . .

If one were to propose to change our [American Constitution, from a] single quadrennial executive chosen *by the board of electors*, into an executive *council of seven*, chosen *yearly* by the joint votes of the members of the federal Senate and House of Representatives—If the same person were to propose *annual* Senators instead of a senate for the present term . . . he would be . . . *an enemy of the federal constitution.* On the other hand, if, instead of an executive council chosen by the legislature, . . . an hereditary king be indicated, foretold, represented as inevitable, and *"insinuated,"* and if, instead of annual elections, the deviation from our present mode of appointing Senators be also in the *opposite* extreme, and a corps of *hereditary* nobles . . . are recommended . . . do not such persons *insensibly betray . . . hostility to the constitution of the United States & to our present tranquillity?* Let the books of Mr. Adams senior and junior be candidly and prudently explained with these reflections in our minds . . .

A CONSTITUTIONALIST

Are the Duke of Braintree and the bespectacled ghost at the *Philadelphia Aurora* both enemies to the American Constitution? John Adams wanted the monarchical and aristocratical constitution of Great Britain. Ben Franklin would have preferred the democratic constitution of Pennsylvania in 1776 or the constitution of the French Republic in 1793.[2014]

SATURDAY, OCTOBER 4, 1800

GENERAL ★ AURORA ★ ADVERTISER

[T]he friends of *peace will vote for Jefferson*—the friends of war will vote for *Adams* . . .

Tonight, in the *Gazette of the United States*:

DUANE takes new degrees every day in the School for Scandal. In bad English, nay in bad Irish, he calumniates the government and religion of this country. His acrimony is so excessive that it defeats its own purpose, and the sober and steadfast unite now in exclaiming, with DRYDEN,

> *Let him rail on—let his invective Muse,*
> *Have four and twenty letters to abuse—*
> *Which, if he jumble to one line of sense,*
> *Indict him of a capital offence.*

FEDERALISM. *WHEN THE RULERS ARE WISE,*
THE PEOPLE ARE HAPPY

ELECTORS are to vote in the last month of the present year for a President of the Union. The interest of America is deeply at stake . . .

America, in seventeen hundred and seventy six, stood tremulous in a perilous condition . . . Washington and Adams, with a band of worthies, appeared, repelled the foe, & founded the American empire. Characters who erected an empire are suitable to rule a nation . . . Washington and Adams made no treaty with France: for they knew she would have observed none . . .

POLYBIUS

The *Gazette of the United States* is fond of asking questions—one good turn deserves another, we solicit answers to the following questions: Why is not John Adams's letter [on British influence] published in that paper? . . . Why is Mr. Abercrombie about to remove to New York? Why did Fenno remove thither? Why did Porcupine remove thither? . . .

JOHN ADAMS's POLITICAL OPINIONS . . .

We now take up Mr. *Adams's* answers to the memorable addresses of the reign of terror in 1798 when Mr. *Adams* exposed himself to the condemnation of history by his *Fast Day* and the *furious denunciation* of his fellow citizens; when he exulted religion while he breathed *War*—and forgot the duty he owed to his country . . . The addresses form a phenomenon in politics . . . No. 1—"I cannot profess my attachment to the principles of the French Revolution . . . An anxiety for the establishment of a government in France on the basis of the equal rights of mankind, *as far as such a government is practicable,* I feel in common with you." *Fenno,* June 1, 1798. No. 2—"The words republican government . . . may be interpreted to mean anything . . ." *Fenno,* July 3, 1798 . . .

So what does "republican government" mean? Thomas Jefferson:

[I]nstead of saying, as has been said, "that it may mean anything or nothing," we may say with truth and meaning that republican governments are more or less republican as they have more or less of the element of popular election or control in their composition; and believing . . . that the evils flowing from the duperies of the people are less injurious than those from the egoism of their agents, I am a friend to that composition of government which has in it the most of this ingredient . . .[2015]

[A] pure republic is a state of society in which every member of mature and sound mind has an equal right of participation, personally, in the direction of the affairs of the society. Such a regimen is obviously impracticable beyond the limits of an encampment or of a small village. When numbers, distance, or force oblige them to act by deputy, then their government continues republican in proportion only as the functions they still exercise in person are more or fewer and, as in those exercised by deputy . . . for more or fewer purposes, or for shorter or longer terms.[2016]

In the General Government, the House of Representatives is mainly republican; the Senate scarcely so at all, as not elected by the people directly and so long secured [by six-year terms] against those who do elect them; the Executive more republican than the Senate from its shorter [four-year] term . . . If, then, the control of the people over the organs of their government be the measure of its republicanism . . . it must be agreed that our governments have much less of republicanism than ought to have been expected . . . And this I ascribe . . . to a submission of true principle to European authorities, . . . to . . . fears of the people . . .[2017]

Tonight, in the *Gazette of the United States*:

A Virginia paper says that some WHITE PEOPLE have been concerned in the late Negro insurrection . . . What say the United Irishmen ? Do they know any who were concerned? . . . We are fond of asking questions, Duane.

TUESDAY, OCTOBER 7, 1800

GENERAL ★ AURORA ★ ADVERTISER

Attempts were lately made to impress the public mind with a belief that the *republicans* of the United States had instigated the late conspiracy of the negroes in the neighborhood of Richmond, Virginia . . . The reports . . . [are] wholly false.

Tonight, in the *Gazette of the United States*:

DUANE, Dare you name the *villain* who called *Washington* a MURDERER ? We are fond of asking questions, Jasper.

WEDNESDAY, OCTOBER 8, 1800

GENERAL ★ AURORA ★ ADVERTISER

QUESTIONING!

There are some questions that answer themselves . . . Who was the villain that called Jefferson an Atheist? Who was the knave that said Alexander Hamilton was not an adulterer? Who was it that said John Adams was not a monarchist? . . . Who pays the expence of printing the *Gazette of the United States?* . . .

Tonight, in the *Gazette of the United States*:

Tommy Cooper . . . would make a much more capable Editor, we think, than Duane, having the advantage of being in *jail* already, for which the latter is only a pretty and fair candidate.—No punishment can reach Cooper at present; Duane is still at large and has less leisure by far than the former.

GENERAL ★ AURORA ★ ADVERTISER

MATTER OF FACT

The following letter was received by the Editor . . . "What will the Federalists now say of Mr. Adams' republicanism? What will they say of Alexander Hamilton's federalism?"—O ! Shame !

Lancaster, Pennsylvania, October 5, 1800.

SIR, . . . I affirm that Alexander Hamilton, esq. did declare to me, at a meeting on official business, that he was a monarchist: that I stated the fact in 1795, from a sense of duty, to Timothy Pickering, esq., then Secretary of State and War . . . in the presidency of General Washington, and that Mr. Hamilton was afterwards appointed, in effect, commander of the army by Mr. Adams and the senate . . . I assert also that an examination of Doctor Benjamin Rush . . . will prove Mr. Adams to be a monarchist. I assert also that an examination of col. John Taylor, of Caroline, in Virginia, and of col. John Langdon, [U.S. senator] of New Hampshire, will prove that Mr. Adams made, in their hearing before 1797, the declaration that he expected or hoped to see the time . . . that the people of the United States would not be happy without an hereditary chief magistrate and a senate that should be hereditary or for life . . .

[Former U.S. Commissioner of Revenue] TENCH COXE.

Tonight, in the *Gazette of the United States*:

THE GRAND QUESTION STATED

At the present solemn and momentous epoch, the only question to be asked by every American, laying his hand on his heart, is "shall I continue in allegiance to

GOD—AND A RELIGIOUS PRESIDENT;
Or impiously declare for
JEFFERSON—AND NO GOD!!!"

GENERAL ★ AURORA ★ ADVERTISER

JOHN ADAMS's POLITICAL OPINIONS . . .

No. 3—"I believe, however, that the difference of *aristocrat* and *democrat*, however odious and pernicious it may be rendered by political artifice at particular conjectures, *will never be done away*, as long as some men are taller and others shorter, some wiser and others sillier, some more virtuous and others more vicious, some richer and others poorer. The distinction is grounded on unalterable nature, and human wisdom can do no more than reconcile the parties . . . securing as far as possible to every one his own. The distinction was intended by nature, for the order of society and the benefit of mankind . . ."

Fellow-Citizens, . . . Mr. [Thomas] Paine's assertion is that he has the authority of one or two persons for saying that Mr. Adams had declared that *the presidency* should be made *hereditary*. It is true that the manner in which Mr. Paine has stated this matter is such as not to give all possible effect to the assertion . . . Such assertions as those concerning Mr. Adams have been in circulation for some years . . . The very serious report of what was said *to two senators* has occasioned an alarm which can never be allayed or suppressed without the obvious and natural satisfaction which so very important a matter requires * . . .

A CONSTITUTIONALIST

 * *It has been asserted upon information from two senators of the United States that Mr. Adams, when Vice President, declared to them in the Senate Chamber that "he expected or hoped to see the time when a conviction would exist that the people of the United States cannot be happy without an hereditary Chief Magistrate and a Senate hereditary for life."*

Tonight, in the *Gazette of the United States*:

SCENE, *"The AURORA OFFICE."* . . .

In one corner appears a face, with Spectacles, on which there is a perpetual and ghastly smile . . . Duane, sitting in a melancholy attitude by a table, on which lie Paine's *Age of Reason,* Volney's *Ruins* . . . and the accomplished letter writer [Jefferson]. His right hand rests on the table; his left hand grasps a will by which he was nominated the successor and appointed to perform the business of B.[enjamin] F.[ranklin] B.[ache]. On one side appears a door which opens into an entry. This entry leads to a parlour where the object of his adoration is at work. Duane throws his head back, strikes it violently with his left hand, and, in plaintive tone, sings!

> Whene're with love-struck eyes I view,
>> This room where Treason first drew breath,
> I think of thee, my widow true,
>> And him who left thee late for Plu-
>>> to's dark and dreary shades of death,
>>> to's dark and dreary shades of death . . .
>> *(Looks at the Wall.)*
> I'll bore a hole, like that one thro'
>> Which Pyramus felt Thisbe's breath,
> Thro' this, sweet Widow, I to you
>> Will sigh and sing, "Ah! love me do,
> 'Ere deep-despair sends me to Plu-
>> to's dark and dreary shades of death,

to's dark [and dreary shades of death.]
If you will listen to me thro'
This Hole, I'll waste my Irish breath,
In telling how I'll be true,
How pleas'd thy Benny's trade pursue,
Till time shall send me down to Plu-
to's dark and dreary shades of death,
to's dark [and dreary shades of death.]

Rises from the table and beckons to the figure with Spectacles who brings him a bottle, &c.

From the Boston Commercial Gazette. IT seems to be the lot of our Independence that the French never will let us alone to exercise and enjoy it. They tampered with old Doctor *Franklin* and coaxed him and wheedled him till they got him willing to accept a scrap of it for the country—a little dirty scrap, for the terms would have been such as to keep us poor and dependent on France . . . The true patriots *Jay* and *Adams*, whom neither flattery nor gold could buy, spurned at the idea and insisted on independence absolute and unlimited . . . Let the people mark the men who are tools to her, let none such be Elected.

SATURDAY, OCTOBER 11, 1800

GENERAL   ★ AURORA ★   ADVERTISER

Thursday last, completing the period of confinement adjudged by [Judge Samuel] CHASE under the sentence of a *packed jury*, on the estimable and intelligent THOMAS COOPER of Northumberland, he was received by the republicans of Philadelphia in a manner suitable to the dignity and constancy of his character . . .

Tom Cooper has completed his prison sentence for criticizing the President of the United States. His release, however, is hardly a joyous occasion. Alice Cooper—Tom's wife of more than twenty years and the mother of his five children—died a week ago, just days before Tom left prison.[2018]

SUNDAY, OCTOBER 12, 1800

War . . . Late today, in the Atlantic, the U.S. Navy's twenty-eight-gun, two-hundred-man ship *Boston* attacks the twenty-four-gun, 230-man ship-of-war *Le Berceau* of the French Republic. U.S. Navy Captain George Little reports:

At Meridian the Chase bore S. West distance about 3 Leagues. At 4 P.M. the ship was Clear for Action. At 1/2 past 4 P.M. hoisted our Collers and gave the chace a shot from the bow Gun. She hoisted french collers and Fired a Gun to Windward and began to Shorten Sail for Action . . .

*[T]his ship proved to be the French National Ship Le Berceau.
Mounting 24 Guns on one Deck, 22 long French Nines and 2 twelve
pounders, and 230 Men Commanded by Louis Andre Senes . . .*

*With regret I mention our loss on board the Boston—4 killed in the
action, 3 mortally wounded, since dead . . . Eight were wounded, but
are on the recovery . . . [T]he captain of le Berceau fought his ship gal-
lantly, so long as she was in a situation capable of being defended.
Soon after he had struck, his fore and main masts went over the side,
and his ship was otherwise in a very shattered condition . . .*[2019]

<hr>

MONDAY, OCTOBER 13, 1800

GENERAL ★ AURORA ★ ADVERTISER

<hr>

REPUBLICAN NOTIFICATIONS . . .

Information on the business of the election will be received and forwarded if left at the *Aurora* Office, Franklin court—the Editor's house,
No. 17 Filbert-street, [&c.]

<hr>

JOHN ADAMS's POLITICAL OPINIONS . . .

"If there are any who still plead the cause of France and attempt to
paralyze the efforts of your government, I agree with you, *they ought to
be esteemed our greatest enemies.*"   Folsome 239.

"Whatever pretexts the French people . . . had for their efforts in the
annihilation of the monarchy, we certainly, far from being under any
obligation had no right or excuse to interfere for their assistance . . . The
French revolution has ever been incomprehensible to me . . ."

Tonight, in the *Gazette of the United States*:

The American who recollects the important services, as well as the
eminent public and private virtues of George Washington [will remember
that] . . . wretches, with the cruelty of United Irishmen and the audacity
of foreign miscreants, attempted to brand our *American* hero with the
epithet MONOCRAT, MURDERER, and TRAITOR; and from the press of
the *Aurora* in 1797, they declare that "Mr. Washington has *at length* become TREACHEROUS even to his own fame." . . .

And now all you who prefer the present settled order of things to Mr.
Jefferson's "political convulsions" and *"tempestuous sea of liberty,"* AT-
TEND to the following extract from the *Aurora* press, for this declares the
designs of the faction, and you may profit by it on the election ground.

EXTRACT

"To prevent any other man from availing himself of a like dangerous
ascendancy, as Mr. Washington, to do mischief, it is necessary to revise
the federal and state constitutions *without delay* . . . The same experience which tells us that America ought not to place confidence in

individuals tells us nevertheless that she is too prone to do it . . . If evil once in fifty years results from having an exclusive President in a country, it is sufficient reason for changing the present institution of a solitary President [to] . . . a *plural Directory,* gradually renewed. The person at present chosen as Vice President would, in this case, no longer, as now, be an inert personage. The executive government would no longer exhibit the fluctuating character of an individual but approach nearer to the fixed abstract of the American nation. The French Directory, consisting of five persons, of which one is yearly replaced, has exhibited vigor, secrecy and celerity . . ."

TO THE PEOPLE OF PENNSYLVANIA . . .

At the ensuing election of a President and Vice President, the . . . importance of the vote of Pennsylvania in deciding this momentous question is known and acknowledged by both parties . . .

TUESDAY, OCTOBER 14, 1800

GENERAL ★ AURORA ★ ADVERTISER

ATTENTION
CITIZENS OF PHILADELPHIA
TAKE YOUR CHOICE
FEDERAL   REPUBLICAN

THE ELECTIVE FRANCHISE

THERE is no part of our Constitution more sacred than that which secures to the people the right of suffrage. This is the essential principle and characteristic of republican government; the means by which the general will prevails and the people are truly said to govern themselves . . . In the election of President, the people exercise the highest act of sovereignty . . . What think you then of a law *to subject the election of president, without appeal, to the decision of 13 men; sitting with closed doors; the votes of all the electors before them; with affidavits tending to invalidate them taken perhaps ex parte from* ANYBODY . . . ?

Fellow Citizens, NOW OR NEVER . . .   A WATCHMAN.

Tonight, in the *Gazette of the United States*:

FEDERALISTS TO YOUR POSTS.
Your enemies are this moment on the Election Ground . . .
DELAY NO LONGER.

If you have not voted, go instantly . . .

GENERAL ★ AURORA ★ ADVERTISER

A federal writer in the N.C. *Raleigh Register* . . . says, speaking of the Sedition Law, "not one native American has been prosecuted under it." . . . [T]his statement was untrue, as besides Bache, Greenleaf, Durell, Peck, Frothingham, Durell, Haswell, Spooner and Holt, some other names of native Americans might be added who have been prosecuted under this act; and out of the nine mentioned, only two (Peck and Spooner) have had the actions against them entirely withdrawn;—Bache and Greenleaf escaped by death—Duane is yet holden for trial; Durell was pardoned by the President after a short imprisonment; and Haswell, Frothingham & Holt suffered the full terms of confinement . . .

Tonight, in the *Gazette of the United States*:

[T]he *Monster* still lives who called *Washington*—a MURDERER!!!!

GENERAL ★ AURORA ★ ADVERTISER

Another Republican Newspaper has been published in *Pittsfield, Massachusetts*, under the title of *The Sun* . . .

Today, from Maryland, former Maryland Congressman Gabriel Duvall writes James Madison:

The result of our elections . . . has exceeded our most sanguine expectations . . . The consequence will be that Mr. Jefferson will get five, perhaps six [electoral] votes in Maryland . . . A good deal of the opposition which has been made to the re-election of Mr. Adams has proceeded from a belief in many that he is a Monarchist . . .[2020]

Today, at the U.S. Circuit Court sitting in Philadelphia (it has not adjourned to Norristown as it did last fall), I am indicted under the Sedition Act, by instruction of President Adams, for libeling the Senate of the United States.[2021]

GENERAL ★ AURORA ★ ADVERTISER

FEDERAL CIRCUIT COURT

This court is now sitting in Philadelphia, Judges PATERSON and PETERS preside. On Friday, a Bill was found by a Grand Jury against WILLIAM DUANE, Editor of this paper, for publishing certain matters alleged to be libelous against the *Senate of the United States* under the memorable Sedition law. This is the same subject which occupied the attention of the Senate in April last . . . Mr. *Dallas* on the part of the defendant stated that . . . it was sufficiently known that an attempt was made under the name of privilege to decide upon the case in the Senate itself. The refusal of the defendant to submit . . . prevented any further steps being taken; and it was not until after nearly all the persons whose testimony would be necessary . . . had left the city that the charge was, by the recommendation of the President, known to have been referred to this tribunal. The evidence of several members of the senate and others were deemed essential . . .

JUDGE PATERSON. If the evidence in question is indispensable, then it may be proper to afford time . . . Let the cause be postponed.

War . . . Today, in the French West Indies, the United States Navy's twenty-four-gun, 220–man ship *Merrimack,* Captain Moses Brown in command, captures the French Sloop *Phoenix* and takes it to St. Kitts.[2022]

From the STATE & FEDERAL CAROLINA GAZETTES . . . His [British influence] letter, it is understood, was written to Mr. Tench Coxe of Philadelphia who, at the time of its date, possessed an office under the government . . . [It was] the famous Duane, Editor of the *Aurora,* to whom the letter was given (as Candour observes) for him "to publish his remarks upon it." . . . Duane asserted in his paper that the American government has been influenced by British gold, and the attorney general, convinced that the charge was the opposite of truth, initiated a prosecution, and the letter was lodged with Mr. Dallas, the Lawyer, as a justification of Duane, who . . . was to have the use of it in case of need. The prosecution has been stopped, and with propriety, because although an honest jury would no doubt be of opinion that the assertion was untrue, yet they probably would acquit the defendant upon his exhibiting Mr. Adams's letter as a ground, or a pretended ground, for that assertion . . .

ALEXANDER HAMILTON has been some time occupied in writing another *Vindication* of himself, *contra* JOHN ADAMS. It is already printed at New York . . . We expect soon to be able to exhibit this secret *curiosity* . . .

Tonight, in the *Gazette of the United States*:

Congress are to hold their first session at the city of Washington on the third Monday in next month. The President is expected in town on his way thither this day or to-morrow.

GENERAL ★ AURORA ★ ADVERTISER

The arrival of the Cartel ship *Benjamin Franklin* in 47 days from Bordeaux. By this vessel there are dispatches for the president of the United States . . . Generals *La Fayette* and *Kosciusko* were both at Paris and attended at a public entertainment on the 4th July, commemorative of American Independence. There were present the American Envoys, four of the former French ministers to this country [&c.]

SATURDAY, OCTOBER 25, 1800

GENERAL ★ AURORA ★ ADVERTISER

[C]all to mind the *gloomy days of proscription* when the republican citizen was menaced in the streets of the city with assassination.—When houses were entered by armed men and the *solemnity of a fast day* converted into a night of *terror* and *burglary*, when the swords of a gang led by *Joe Thomas*, who has since absconded loaded with dishonor, gleamed in the affrighted eyes of women and penetrated to the fire sides of families . . .

Men of great experience at the time disbelieved what we had published . . .

It is well known that, at the period alluded to, the unfortunate French, who had no choice but to remain here, were daily assaulted in the public streets. The French government (in order that those . . . who adhered to the republic should be distinguished from those who were hostile) had ordered a badge or cockade to be worn. Those who obeyed the impulse of feeling and obligation were insulted in these streets and in maritime places and [had] the cockades torn out of their hats at the very moment when our own administration was setting up a similar badge to distinguish the adherents of Britain from the friends of peace and republicanism . . . As a part of this system, alarming letters were sent to President Adams, to the Mayor, and the Governor, denouncing a design of the French to burn the city. The answer of Mr. Adams to the [infuriated] addresses of that day aggravated the alarm. And it was openly announced in the paper of FENNO, then patronized by Mr. *Adams* and printer to the Senate, that a *Sicilian Vespers* ought to take place in the city.

ELECTORS OF PRESIDENT AND VICE PRESIDENT.
Pennsylvanians of all Parties are very deeply interested to avoid the hardship and evils of being deprived of Presidential Electors . . .

To the Senate and House of Representatives of the Commonwealth of Pennsylvania . . .

An extraordinary Meeting of the Legislature having been called by the Governor's proclamation to take place in November [on the 5th . . . w]e hope nothing will, by any means, occur to deprive Pennsylvania of her full share in electing the president . . .

The late elections for Congress have given a clear and certain indication of the Public Sentiment in this State . . .

This month's Pennsylvania elections delivered a *"clear and certain indication of the Public Sentiment"* in Pennsylvania, because Republicans received three out of every four votes cast, winning ten of thirteen congressional seats, fifty-five of seventy-eight Pennsylvania state assembly seats, and six of seven Pennsylvania state senate seats.[2023]

Tonight, in the *Gazette of the United States*:

> HAIL! to the day, which joyous now appears,
> To crown the toils of many, many years . . .
> The Joys of office, gratify desire:
> No more plain Mr. now! I strut Esquire.
> > Off, off gin twist; and brandy tody hence:
> > Draughts which are drank by men of "common sense" . . .
> What! What, what's the news! a wrong return?
> Have I a second time defeat to mourn?
> No, no dear sir, pray calm your raging mind,
> We've long since left all virtue, truth behind . . .
> Then hear me—all the gin send to Duane,
> The brandy to his Highness T—[om] Mc—[Kean] . . .

The President of the United States passed thro' N. York on Thursday on his way to the Seat of Government.

MONDAY, OCTOBER 27, 1800

GENERAL ★ AURORA ★ ADVERTISER

ALEXANDER HAMILTON VERSUS JOHN ADAMS . . . EXTRACTS *[from the New Vindication] . . .* No. 2. "The letter which has just appeared in the public prints, written by [Mr. Adams] when Vice-President to Tench Coxe, is of itself conclusive evidence . . . This letter avows the *suspicion* that the appointment of Mr. Pinckney has been procured or promoted by British Influence . . ." No. 3. "But a more serious question remains—How will Mr. Adams answer to the government and country for having thus wantonly given the assertions . . . [which] the enemies of the administration have impudently thrown upon it? Can we be surprised that such a torrent of slander has poured out against it when a man, the second in official rank, the second in the favor of the friends of the government, stooped to become one of the calumniators?"

Alexander Hamilton's public criticism of John Adams, published as a pamphlet, *Letter from Alexander Hamilton, Concerning the Public Conduct of John Adams, Esq. President of the United States*,[2024] demonstrates the chaotic condition of the Federalists.

WEDNESDAY, OCTOBER 29, 1800

GENERAL ★ AURORA ★ ADVERTISER

John Adams says these are *bad times;* perhaps he thinks the days of proscription, when Lyon languished in prison; when the black British cockade was mounted; when he sent back the *Aurora* because it was printed on a sabbath of his own making; when war and alarm echoed through every part of the continent; when the boys of 25 were extolling him into a demi-god—these were the good *times.* Yes ! "these were the times Mr. *Rigmarol*," but I hope we never shall see *such times* again.

Six years ago, Mr. Adams, being Vice President, declared . . . America could not be happy without an *hereditary magistrate* and an *hereditary senate. Alexander Hamilton,* holding an office . . . under President Washington, avowed his wish for a monarchy in the United States seven years ago. Mr. Adams and Mr. Hamilton . . . knew the monarchical opinions of the other. Hamilton, knowing the monarchical dispositions of Mr. Adams, yet supported him for the Presidency. *Adams,* knowing Hamilton's opinions, submitted to appoint him acting head of the army.

THURSDAY, OCTOBER 30, 1800

GENERAL ★ AURORA ★ ADVERTISER

TO THE PUBLIC . . .
In the month of April 1794, I, being then commissioner of revenue in the Department of the Treasury of the United States, was sitting in one of my office chambers in the Treasury at Philadelphia, treating on business with a person there. Mr. Langdon, then of the Senate of the United States, of New Hampshire and sometime Chief Magistrate of New Hampshire, came in. He was apparently very grave and in pain of mind . . . As soon as we were private, I asked Mr. Langdon what was the matter . . . He said he was conferring in the Senate Chamber with the Vice President Mr. Adams and Mr. Taylor of the Senate, and that Mr. Adams had said much about republican government and finally expressed himself in favor of an hereditary President of the United States . . .

TENCH COXE

Tonight, in the *Gazette of the United States*:

Never was there a greater mistake committed by Federalists than was evinced at the late [Pennsylvania] Election . . . [A] great number of men, *professedly* Federal, voted for the Democratic Candidate . . . What has been the consequence of this cowardly conduct ?—The answer will be found by observing something very like a *French Cockade* already exhibited in the hats of the exulting Jacobins . . .

SATURDAY, NOVEMBER 1, 1800

GENERAL   ★ AURORA ★   ADVERTISER

Let Mr. Adams remember the language in which he has opposed the living and reprobated the departed venerable Franklin . . .

TENCH COXE

Today, James Madison writes Thomas Jefferson,

> *What an important Denoument has lately been made! Hamilton's attack upon Mr. Adams [for complaining about British influence] is a perfect Confirmation of all that that arch and very clever Fellow Duane has been so long hinting at, or rather affirming. It will be a Thunderbolt to both. I rejoice with you that Republicanism is likely to be so completely triumphant . . .*[2025]

SUNDAY, NOVEMBER 2, 1800

Tonight, from the new President's House in Washington, John Adams writes Abigail,

> *We arrived here last night, or rather yesterday at one o'clock, and here we dined and slept. The building is in a State to be habitable. And now we wish for your Company . . .*
>
> *Before I end my Letter, I pray Heaven to bestow the best of Blessings on this House, and all that shall hereafter inhabit it. May none but honest and wise Men ever rule under this roof.*[2026]

A praiseworthy wish, except for the word "rule"!

TUESDAY, NOVEMBER 4, 1800

GENERAL   ★ AURORA ★   ADVERTISER

Fellow Citizens ! attend ! watch well the proceedings of your [Pennsylvania] Legislature! Set a mark on the men who may persist in the usurpation which goes to disenfranchise the state of the all important right of choice in the election of President and Vice President of the United States.

When the constitution of the United States was under discussion, every man who dared to doubt of its excellence . . . was stigmatized as a friend of disorder and anarchy. Yet behold . . . It is almost in the power of *two* or *three* abandoned individuals, by disenfranchising our state, to impose a President on the Union, contrary to the strongest wishes of the people . . .

It certainly would be much the best that the people should vote; but there is not time. It is impossible. The assembly did not make a law last session . . .

All New England has ordered Elections by the ballots of their Legislatures . . . They have 39 votes which they secure, in this manner, for Mr. Adams . . .

The Federal Constitution says, "each State SHALL appoint Electors of a president, &c." *Monarchy*, ill disguised under the assumed name of *Federalism*, says *Pennsylvania shall not!* . . .

In Pennsylvania's state elections this October, citizens had the chance to vote for their entire state assembly (elected annually à la Franklin) and thus awarded 70 percent of their state assembly's seats to Republicans. Because, however, Pennsylvania's state senators hold longer, four-year "aristocratical" terms of office (à la Adams), seventeen of twenty-four senators did not have to face this *"annual gust of folly."* For this reason alone, the Federalists retain a slim majority of two (13–11) in the Pennsylvania state senate. The people's preference is clear, yet *"it is almost in the power of two or three abandoned individuals, by disenfranchising our state, to impose a President on the Union, contrary to the strongest wishes of the people."*[2027]

Today, in a Richmond, Virginia prison cell where he is serving a nine-month prison sentence for criticizing the President of the United States, Jimmy Callender completes his second volume (152 pages) of *The Prospect Before Us*, including:

> The public officers have rushed to public plunder . . . [C]onsult the editor of the Aurora. Intelligent, intrepid, indefatigable, this gentleman, like his predecessor, Mr. Bache, deserves, if any man can deserve it, the perpetual gratitude of the United States. The faction did well understand their interest when they made an effort to murder him. Beside Mr. Duane, the majority of American newsprinters appear like petty figures around the pedestal of a statue.[2028]

WEDNESDAY, NOVEMBER 5, 1800

GENERAL ★ AURORA ★ ADVERTISER

NEW YORK, Nov. 3. At a select meeting of the citizens, at Lovett's Hotel, on Thursday evening . . . the following [13] toasts were drank, viz. 1. The triumph of Republicanism . . . 3. The speedy arrival of the republican millennium . . . 10. The republican printers . . . VOLUNTEERS . . . *William Duane*—the Cicero of Anglo-Federal conspiracies.

Today, in Lancaster, Pennsylvania, the Pennsylvania state legislature convenes in special session to decide whether and how Pennsylvania will appoint presidential electors. In less than a month, on December 3rd, the nation's presidential electors must cast their votes.[2029]

Tonight, in the *Gazette of the United States*:

> From the multitude of hints and allusions thrown out in the *Aurora* respecting our [Pennsylvania] state senate, it is easily seen that the Jacobins are extremely restless on the subject of [Pennsylvania's] appointing electors of President . . .
>
> This is the all important day for the meeting of the [Pennsylvania] Assembly. The senate is understood to have a majority of two on the Federal side . . . [T]heir conduct will confirm the good opinion of every friend to consistency, except *Billy Duane*.

THURSDAY, NOVEMBER 6, 1800

GENERAL ★ AURORA ★ ADVERTISER

SUBSCRIBERS

THE Subscribers to the AURORA, living in and near the City of Baltimore, will please to pay their subscriptions to BONSALL & NILES Booksellers of that City—Those of New-York to Mr. HENRY HERFORD No. 251, Water Street.—And those of Easton, Maryland, to Mr. THOMAS MOORE, Merchant of that town . . .

SATURDAY, NOVEMBER 8, 1800

GENERAL ★ AURORA ★ ADVERTISER

HALLOA Messmates! What's to pay in the *hold?* There's a devilish racket below! "Rats, rats, rats"—Is the ship among the breakers? Has she sprung a leak, or are we got on the lee shore? The *state-room* is all in an uproar—same of the lubbers jump out of the cabin . . .

"Rats, rats, rats"—curse such vermin, they now begin to take to the shore . . .

The old pilot, who drew up the articles for the frigate "Independence" is ready to step on board, and if we give him "the long pull, the strong pull, and the pull altogether," he will take his station, and, we hope . . . restore harmony and good humor among the whole crew.

Today, in Washington, Treasury Secretary Oliver Wolcott (one of the "rats") writes John Adams:

> Sir,—I have, after due reflection, considered it a duty which I owe to myself and family to retire from the office of Secretary of the Treasury . . . at the close of the present year.[2030]

Tonight, in Washington, the building which houses government accounting and war department records bursts into flame. Treasury Secretary Oliver Wolcott seems to be at the scene before anyone else. New Secretary of War Samuel Dexter (James McHenry's replacement) is also at the fire. All war department records are destroyed.[2031]

WEDNESDAY, NOVEMBER 12, 1800

GENERAL ★ AURORA ★ ADVERTISER

WAR OFFICE BURNT . . .
Extract of a letter from Washington City dated November 8.
About 7 o'clock this evening, I was alarmed by fire in this city. We all ran as usual, and behold it proved to be the War Office. Before I got there all was involved in uncontrollable flames . . . The accountant's department was in the same building, but he had the good fortune to save the greatest part of his papers—the books and papers in the war-office were entirely consumed. How it originated nobody knows . . . We had but two small engines, ill proved with water, and about 30 house-buckets.

Brown.

Tonight, in the *Gazette of the United States*:

BALTIMORE, Nov. 10. By a gentleman direct from the city of Washington . . . [O]n Saturday evening last, about 7 o'clock, P.M. a fire broke out in the building occupied by the war-office, supposed to have been commenced in the chamber of the secretary himself . . . Mr. Wolcott, with one of the clerks who first discovered the smoke issuing from the secretary's chamber, burst open the door, but they were instantly repelled, almost suffocated . . . Mr. Dexter himself arrived at the unhappy moment of conflagration, very much injured by a fall from his carriage, which overset in that city.

THURSDAY, NOVEMBER 13, 1800

GENERAL ★ AURORA ★ ADVERTISER

It appears from papers by the Southern mail of yesterday that the fire at Washington *originated* in the apartment of Mr. *Dexter*, secretary of war, which had been *locked up for the last two weeks*. This wants some explanation . . .

As all the inhabitants ran to assist in quenching the fire at the war-office, and as *Oliver* got there first—he certainly must know, if any body does know, how it commenced.

The President, since his residence at Washington, has been severely afflicted with fever and ague.

Tonight, in the *Gazette of the United States*:

Duane . . . is now at Lancaster [Pennsylvania] . . . to obtain . . . the proceedings of our Legislature . . .

FRIDAY, NOVEMBER 14, 1800

GENERAL ★ AURORA ★ ADVERTISER

Extract of a letter from John Langdon, Esq. Senator in Congress from New Hampshire to Samuel Ringgold, Esq . . .

"Portsmouth, October 19, 1800.
DEAR SIR . . . I am now packing my baggage, shall set out in a stage to-morrow morning for the city of Washington . . .

In the conversation held between Mr. Adams, Mr, Taylor, and myself, Mr. Adams certainly expressed himself (as far as my memory serves me) in the very words . . . That he hoped or expected to see the day when Mr. Taylor and his friend Mr. Giles would be convinced that, *the people of America would not be happy without an hereditary Chief Magistrate and Senate—or at least during life . . .*

[U.S. Senator] JOHN LANGDON . . ."

OMENS

Mr. Adams is sick at Washington.

Oliver Wolcott has been almost suffocated.

Mr. Dexter has been threwn out of his carriage and much bruised.

And *Parson Abercrombie* is so ill with a cold that it is with difficulty he can breathe.

The [first], we fear, has taken too great a dose of *Hamilton's Lozenges*.

The [last] has been ill since the account of the New York election was received . . .

Tonight, in the *Gazette of the United States*:

The fire caught in a room on the second floor and raged with such violence as to render it impracticable to extinguish it. The papers in the lower story only were saved.

GENERAL ★ AURORA ★ ADVERTISER

FROM LANCASTER . . . "The fire at Washington appears to have taken place exactly as was foretold in the *Aurora* some weeks ago, pray refer to the article and republish it with the most particular account of the fire that appears in the papers . . .

"It would be useful to enquire & discover, whether Mr. Pickering's papers, as Secretary of War, and Mr. Hamilton's correspondence, while Inspector General, with Mr. McHenry have been preserved in this accidental conflagration. I regret that I cannot go to the spot to peep into this scene of . . . desolation. I admire the ardor of Mr. Wolcott and commiserate his danger—O there are . . . such Villains !"

GENERAL ★ AURORA ★ ADVERTISER

The *federal fireworks* at Washington will be found to have made a very rueful chasm in our *war history.* Alexander Hamilton's projects and Timothy Pickering's transactions while secretary will have had a *partial sweep* to avoid the scrutinizing research of a Jeffersonian administration.

The War Office may be burnt, every body may know nothing about it; two men may deprive the state of Pennsylvania of its vote for President and stand excused to their own consciences . . . and Maria [may be] once more admitted into the bed chamber [of Hamilton]; yet believe me, my friend, inequity will work its own ruin—Republicanism will triumph . . .

In this afternoon's *Gazette of the United States*:

☞ What does this mean *"The fire at Washington appears to have taken place exactly as was foretold in the Aurora?!!"* Ha, what ? they *knew it* then! . . . "O there are Villains, such Villains!!!"

The conduct of the Federal[ist] Senators in the State Legislature has excited the indignation . . . of the inveterate Jacobins . . . [T]herefore, SEN-ATORS, *Beware ! !* . . . [M]ark well certain characters now in Lancaster . . . [R]emember that those who predicted the *burning of the War Office,* also predicted that *two Senators* were *"to be put out of the way! . . ."* . . . *SENATORS, Beware!!*—for "O there are such Villains." . . .

The second session of the Sixth Congress will commence at the City of Washington this day.

The *Lancaster Journal extra* of Wednesday has made some discoveries!—That the democratic party has circulated with great avidity the news of a treaty with France. It might have added that this is not the first time . . . In 1778, for instance, a treaty [of alliance] with France was celebrated by illuminations and bonfires, ringing of bells, and religious adoration of the almighty . . .

This paper goes on to say that "the only plea of consequence that they have been able to urge for the election of Mr. Jefferson is that he would PRODUCE a peace with France." Was this the only reason of consequence? . . . Was it of no consequence to put the executive authority into the hands of a republican and take it out of the hands of an avowed and long professed and proven monarchist? . . .

But it is said . . . "He [Mr. Adams] is a good and faithful servant," he who threatened to lay a state in dust and ashes for differing from him in political opinion. He who impiously declared the finger of heaven pointed at war with that same France with which he has concluded a peace! He is a good and faithful servant . . . who appointed young *Humphreys* to a considerable office for . . . assaulting the grandson of Franklin to whom and to whose family Mr. Adams has been always hostile! . . .

We are told that "everything the Democrats have asked is accomplished." But in this we are not told true. None of the above evils have been rectified by Mr. Adams. He can never cleanse himself from the foulness of his assent to the law calculated to secure his character and those of inferior officers from scrutiny, and the more because he had great exceptions to screen from public scrutiny, and others under him had crimes to account for.

"The alien law is at an end." So it is by its own limitation. "The operation of the sedition law has ceased."—This is not true. The family of Thomas Adams of Boston have to lament the death of that worthy man, one of its Victims. *Thomas Cooper,* the loss of his wife, another; what can compensate Anthony Haswell, printer of Vermont, for his imprisonment under that law, and his only crime the publication of a letter written by James M'Henry, secretary of War, recommending old Tories as officers in the standing army. [W]ho will compensate Matthew Lyon for his imprisonment for a letter written before the law had existence! When was Callender released from the sentence pronounced by the noted *[Judge Samuel] Chase?*

[L]etter dated Washington . . . "Whether the federal[ist] senators in your [Pennsylvania] legislature will continue to oppose the known wishes and sentiments of the great majority of their constituents in the state at large . . . will be for themselves to determine but . . . will only tend, by the attempt to deprive Pennsylvania of her right of suffrage in the election of the president, to encrease the personal responsibility of the senators and continue alive those feuds and animosities in your state which, for the sake of union, peace, and concord, it were to be wished . . .

This afternoon, in the *Gazette of the United States*:

DUANE
Storms and raves at the honest, dignified, and noble stand made by the Federal[ist] Senators of Pennsylvania . . .

If the present occasion is important, it is the more necessary the Senate should hold to their constitutional rights . . . as a safeguard in times like these . . . where a temporary popular frenzy might overturn the government . . .

SENATORS OF PENNSYLVANIA . . .
When the tumult of the hour shall pass . . . you will stand foremost . . . if you resolutely persist . . . in spite of . . . Duane . . .

Today, from the new city of Washington, the President's Lady, Abigail Adams, writes her sister:

I arrived in this city on Sunday the 16th ult. Having lost my way in the woods on Saturday in going from Baltimore, we took the road to Frederick and got nine miles out of our road. You find nothing but a Forest & woods on the way, for 16 and 18 miles not a village. Here and there a thatchd cottage without a single pane of glass, inhabited by Blacks . . . My intention was to have reachd Washington on Saturday . . .

I arrived about one o'clock at this place known by the name of the city, and the Name is all that you can call so . . . The Presidents House is in a beautifull situation in front of which is the Potomac with a view of Alexandr[i]a. The country around is romantic but a wild, a wilderness at present.

I have been to George Town . . . It is the very dirtyest Hole I ever saw for a place of any trade or respectability of inhabitants. It is only one mile from me but a quagmire after every rain. Here we are obliged to send daily for marketting . . . As to roads we shall make them by the frequent passing before winter . . .

The letter of Hamilton, which you have no doubt seen, can never be answerd properly but by the person to whom it is addrest, because no one else knows all the circumstances . . . many of which are as grose lies as Duane has told in the Aurora . . .[2032]

MONDAY, NOVEMBER 24, 1800

GENERAL ★ AURORA ★ ADVERTISER

It cannot be sufficiently deplored that the federal constitution should be so inexplicit as to lead to such a variety of modes of chusing Electors as have been adopted throughout the Union . . .   FRANKLIN

Today, in Virginia, Thomas Jefferson sets out from Monticello for the city of Washington. He will spend tonight with James Madison.[2033]

TUESDAY, NOVEMBER 25, 1800

GENERAL ★ AURORA ★ ADVERTISER

From the AMERICAN CITIZEN . . . Is not twenty-thousand dollars in the hands of the meek Jonathan Dayton valuable . . . ? Is not five hundred thousand dollars in the hands of Timothy Pickering valuable? . . . Is five thousand dollars per annum, annually paid to the *accurate* Oliver Wolcott, nothing . . . ? . . .

That the *Aurora* man (alias the cat that catched the rat) has been the primary cause of war-office burnings I sincerely believe—though I am certain that he did not wish such an event, as most surely it deprived him of several columns of very curious and well digested matter. Yet when we consider that Duane has for a long time been dealing with the Devil and that his sooty majesty has furnished him with an invisible coat under cover of which garb he has introduced himself into federal caucuses, public offices, and secret places and exposed in a most cruel manner federal peculations, what security have the exclusive friends of religion and good order against so subtle a disguise, aided by that two edged sword, his accursed pen, but by destroying the proofs of their own iniquity? No doubt there were several papers in the war office unfit for the public eye . . .   MARPLOT

WEDNESDAY, NOVEMBER 26, 1800

GENERAL ★ AURORA ★ ADVERTISER

The [Editor of the *Gazette of the United States*] . . . well knows that as Porcupine fell with the elevation of a republican governor, so must [he] by the elevation of a republican President . . .

Tonight, in the *Gazette of the United States*:

Duane.
The night I to pillory went,
Lloyd visited me in the prison;
All my money before I had spent.
Long ere I was sent th ere for treason.
Said Lloyd, "Duane, why don't you borrow!"
Quoth I, "dear Sir, they won't trust me,"
Here I must remain to my sorrow,
And no noggin of Gin for the thirsty.
To warm the back for the whip
To warm &c.
Callender.
With convicts 'tis true we were pent.
With Gov'nrs now we rank equal;
'Tis well to this country we're sent,
Where we rank as first men of the people.

MONDAY, DECEMBER 1, 1800

GENERAL   ★ AURORA ★   ADVERTISER

That the Federal Constitution is materially defective in its provisions respecting the election of President can no longer be doubted. If it be in the power of the Legislature of any state to . . . set at naught the opinion of a majority of their constituents . . . then is the government at the devotion of a faction . . . What is to be done in case the state of Pennsylvania shall be deprived of her vote in the ensuing election? . . .

The puerile and circuitous mode of chusing the President by Electors was unworthy . . . of the framers of the federal constitution . . . [They] have left the way open to such maneuvers and tricks as are only fit to be practiced by a petty British corporation . . . The only expedient that suggests itself is a CONVENTION OF THE PEOPLE . . . deciding upon the kind of amendment which it would be proper to propose . . . namely, *"That the Presidential Election be held on this same day throughout the Union and the choice be made immediately by the People without the intervention of Electors."* . . .   A PLAIN REPUBLICAN

Tonight, in the *Gazette of the United States*:

No other principle was better understood or more conclusively established by the state [of Pennsylvania's constitutional] convention than that the legislative power of the commonwealth should be divided into two equal component parts, *viz.* a Senate and House of Representatives . . .

The Senatorial branch of every government, judiciously constructed, are chosen for longer periods than the other branch in order that they may carry with them the temper and moderation of one period to qualify the violence and fury of another. They are composed of characters more mature and dignified as to age and situation and fewer in number in order that . . . a wholesome check be formed to democratic innovation and change, the bane of all free governments. [N]ow as these also are the principle reasons for the establishment of a Senate, they are also the *precise reasons why democracy would have it destroyed* . . .

We understand that the House of Representatives of Pennsylvania, on Saturday last, acceded to the proposition of the Senate for the appointment of fifteen Electors . . . seven to be chosen by the Senate and eight by the House of Representatives . . .

The thirteen Federalist senators (a majority of two) in Pennsylvania's state senate have allowed their state to participate in the nation's presidential election under an arrangement by which John Adams receives seven of the state's fifteen presidential electoral votes. Pennsylvania's participation in the presidential election is allowed but neutralized! Pennsylvania's democratic majority (the 75 percent who voted Republican in October's state election) have been thwarted! Thomas Paine, still in Paris, will explain:

> *The complaint respecting the [Pennsylvania] Senate is the length of its duration, being four years. The sage Franklin has said, "Where annual election ends, tyranny begins" . . . When a man ceases to be accountable to those who elected him and with whose public affairs he is intrusted, he ceases to be their representative and is put in a condition of being their despot. He becomes the representative of nobody but himself. "I am elected," says he, "for four years; you cannot turn me out, neither am I responsible to you in the meantime . . ." The conduct of the Pennsylvania Senate in 1800, respecting the choice of electors for the presidency of the United States, shows the impropriety and danger of such an establishment . . . By the conduct of the Senate at that time, the people were deprived of their right of suffrage, and the state lost its consequence in the Union. It had but one vote . . . If the people had chosen the electors . . . the State would have had fifteen votes which would have counted . . .*
>
> *The circumstance that occurred in the Pennsylvania Senate in the year 1800 . . . justifies Franklin's opinion, which he gave by request of the [Pennsylvania Constitutional] Convention of 1776, of which he was president, respecting the propriety or impropriety of two houses negativing each other. "It appears to me," said he, "like putting one horse before a cart, and the other behind it, and whipping them both . . ."*[2034]

A year before he died, Benny Bache wrote,

The office and the structure of the American Senates, by whatever name called (whether in the federal or state governments) seem to have been dictated under the influence of habit . . . [N]or is any class of men more advanced in political corruption . . . than the Senators. [2035]

WEDNESDAY, DECEMBER 3, 1800

GENERAL ★ AURORA ★ ADVERTISER

ELECTION DAY.

This being the first Wednesday in December, the day appointed by law for the Election of a President and Vice President of the United States, in all the States—time and circumstance, the suspense and anxiety of all parties, will perhaps render this occasion more favorable for a free examination of the political aspects of this country . . . free from the bias of party . . . whomever may be the favorite . . .

War . . . Early this morning (half past four) off Dominica in the French West Indies, the thirty-six-gun, 307-man U.S. Navy frigate *Philadelphia*, Captain Stephen Decatur (Senior), chases and captures the French privateer *La Levrette*, of six guns and fifty-one men. [2036]

Tonight, in the *Gazette of the United States*:

This day decides the grand, the important question respecting our Chief Magistrates. It is in fact already decided. Although some time must elapse ere the official returns can be known, we can in full confidence greet . . . on the election of . . .
The Hon. JOHN ADAMS Esq. and Gen. CHARLES C. PINCKNEY.

FRIDAY, DECEMBER 5, 1800

GENERAL ★ AURORA ★ ADVERTISER

The public will recall that among the papers left by DR. FRANKLIN . . . was his own life written by himself . . . Year after year has since elapsed without either the appearance of the work or an apology . . . Temple Franklin actually sold the copy right of Dr. Franklin's works to Mr. Dilly of London . . . Before, however, this publication was made, the British ministry . . . purchased from Mr. Dilly the right to the work . . . hoping by these means altogether to suppress the works . . . What motives could induce the British government to obtain the suppression of such a work but its containing a detail of facts injurious to itself? . . .

When we further consider that the name of Franklin has been treated with invariable contempt by men in this country high in political consideration and that no opportunity has passed unimproved of depreciating his moral character and impairing the value of his public services, can we help pausing to examine whether there does not exist some secret causes . . . ? . . . I hope the subject will receive . . . attention . . .

A FRIEND TO TRUTH

Tonight, in the *Gazette of the United States*:

Some of Jefferson's friends still hope—

SATURDAY, DECEMBER 6, 1800

GENERAL ★ AURORA ★ ADVERTISER

The Federalists augur much comfort because the *Aurora* says not much on the *state of things*—silence is sometimes very eloquent.

Puns, the wits say, are the excrement of wit—the *Gazette of the United States* has been in a *voiding* state several days!—and the creatures that *live upon it*—have been redigesting the *stuff*!

Havre [France], November 8. "The envoys of the American government, whose object is to perfect the work of reconciliation desired by all the friends of peace, are now in our city. All the civil and military authorities are eager to render their homage to the representatives of an allied nation, acknowledged since the year 1778 as the most sincere friends of the French nation. A guard of honor of 50 men has been sent to them; for which they have returned thanks according to custom. They would have already set sail if contrary winds had not retarded the departure of the American frigate *Portsmouth*. The calm will keep them here for 8 days."

In the [Pennsylvania] Senate on Wednesday . . . the old 13 threw a somerset and had the minority completely on their backs . . . so that the votes of this state are either to be neutralized or not given at all.

Tonight, in the *Gazette of the United States*:

(The following observations were written previous to the decision in the Pennsylvania Legislature.) . . .

[W]hen we read the insolent menaces promulgated in the *Aurora* . . . , we should be led to suppose that the Senate of Pennsylvania is some upstart, arrogant body, usurping powers which do not belong to them, and checking the progress of the other House . . . Does our constitution place the Senate in this disgraceful position? . . .

But it is pretended by . . . a host of petty scribblers in the *Aurora* that the late elections have evinced the wishes of the people, that a vast majority coincide with the wishes of the republican members of the House, and therefore the federal members of the Senate should yield . . . [I]t is said the minds of the people are greatly changed since the present senators were elected and, therefore, they are not the representatives of the present opinion of their constituents—

Granted. And here we see the vast importance, particularly in a republic, of a body constituted like the Senate—Here we see the wisdom and foresight of those who framed our constitution—Why was a certain degree of permanency given to this body? Most undoubtedly for times like the present . . . The Senate is our anchor which prevents us from being blown to and fro by every changing blast of popular delusion or caprice. It is known that a people, however honest or patriotic, cannot at all times withstand the falsehoods and lying intrigues of artful, designing demagogues . . . and if there were nothing to check their misguided fury, they would tear the state to atoms. This necessary, indispensable check is the Senate . . .

I hope, therefore that the people, before they join in the hue and cry against their Senate and *"consign to execration"* (as they are modestly desired by Duane) some of their most meritorious citizens, will seriously examine the difference between the two branches of the Legislature . . . [I]f the state is disenfranchised, the reproach must fall on those who have arrogantly endeavored to vest the whole legislative power in one branch of the Legislature . . .

WEDNESDAY, DECEMBER 10, 1800

GENERAL ⋆ AURORA ⋆ ADVERTISER

F E N N O in his supplementary catalog of imported books has the following parenthesis as a recommendation of Boecker's Sermons: (. . . *unfolds many facts and private anecdotes, tending to place the character of the arch hypocrite and impostor, Franklin, in a more detestable point of light, if possible, than that in which it stood before).* Thus it is that a shameless young man can dare to insult the whole country by attempting to rob the honoured dead of his fair fame. Where is the spirit which ought to protect the sacred memory of America's brightest ornament? . . . Too long did that British emissary *Porcupine* libel the same great and good man; being an *Englishman* and the tool of his government, *[Porcupine]* was more excusable than an American who has no pretext . . .

THURSDAY, DECEMBER 11, 1800

GENERAL ⋆ AURORA ⋆ ADVERTISER

The constitution of the United States gives to each state a share in the election of President . . . and trusts to the State legislatures to direct the best mode . . . What then must be thought of the men who . . . have defeated this right of the People . . . Citizens of Pennsylvania, as ye have the opportunity, watch well these thirteen Culprits . . .

This evening, in the *Gazette of the United States*:

> *From the Washington Federalist* . . . ". . . [T]hat a spirit has been manifested . . . to cover the authors of our independence with odium . . ." . . . the files of the *Aurora* exhibit the most incontestable evidence.
>
> IF there was one man among us who, more than any other, deserves to be considered as the "Author of Independence," the world will unite in saying that man was GENERAL WASHINGTON . . . [T]he people of America have for years witnessed the unremitting efforts of the *Aurora* to cover with odium even HIM whose name is the pride and boast of our country.
>
> Few among the living rendered more effectual service than General HAMILTON, and on none has more odium been cast . . .
>
> Colonel PICKERING was a valuable and faithful officer . . . Colonel Pickering has been treated as the vilest and most despicable of men.
>
> If, in the political line, any two men rendered to America, struggling for liberty, more distinguished service than others, those two men are JOHN ADAMS and JOHN JAY. In addition to their brilliant services in Congress, they negotiated that treaty which severed us forever from Great-Britain; and, in spite of the influence of a Gallic party, obtained for us those boundaries and those advantages which make it truly INDEPENDENT.
>
> These are the men on whom those, who during our contest for liberty were engaged against us, labor to heap up obloquy. With too much truth, therefore, does the *Aurora* say, "that a spirit has been manifested for some years back, even in America, to cover the authors of our independence with odium."

Neither the *Gazette of the United States*, nor the *Philadelphia Aurora*, nor any other journal can decide for you, dear reader, who is the "Author of Independence," the "Author of Democracy," or even the "Father of His Country." It is for you, dear reader, to decide.

SATURDAY, DECEMBER 13, 1800

GENERAL ★ AURORA ★ ADVERTISER

"It is said that several of the important records, to which William Duane had recourse last summer, have, with other highly interesting documents which would have been proper for Mr. Jefferson to have seen, been destroyed by the fire at the Federal city . . ." (Herald.)

The accounts published in "The Aurora" are not all from the war office, but from the *treasury department* over which *Oliver Wolcott* so unfortunately and so long presided—it is true the accounts of the ac-

countant of the war office were noticed among others; and Pickering's accounts of monies held since the revolution . . . may have been there; but the other accounts of *Dayton, Pickering* . . . and about a hundred others are all safe, unless, as was threatened in the event of Jefferson's election, another fire should purify the defaulters.

Tonight, in the *Gazette of the United States*:

RETURN OF VOTES
For President And Vice President of the United States

	Adams	Pinckney	Jefferson	Burr
New Hampshire	6	6		
Massachusetts,	16	16		
Rhode Island				
Connecticut	9	9		
Vermont,				
New-York,			12	12
New-Jersey	7	7		
Pennsylvania,	7	7	8	8
Delaware,	3	3		
Maryland,	5	5	5	5
Virginia,			21	21
Kentucky,				
Tennessee				
North-Carolina				
South-Carolina,				
	53	53	46	46 . . .

THIRTEEN *United States* saved themselves from a foreign yoke and THIRTEEN *Senators* of *Pennsylvania* have saved these States from anarchy and Jacobinism. The number *Thirteen* must be gratefull to Americans.

SUNDAY, DECEMBER 14, 1800

Today, in Washington, Thomas Jefferson writes Robert Livingston:

The constitution to which we are all attached was meant to be republican . . . Yet we have seen it so interpreted and administered as to be truly what the French have called "monarchie masquée." Yet so long has the vessel run on this way and been trimmed to it that to put her on her republican track will require all the skill . . . of her ablest and best friends . . .[2037]

GENERAL ★ AURORA ★ ADVERTISER

General Davie has arrived on the *Portsmouth* at Norfolk and brought the Treaty with France.

Letter to the Editor . . .
"Good news from South Carolina ! . . . Jefferson and Burr will have every vote in that state—ca ira."

One state's vote, that of South Carolina, changes everything!

GENERAL ★ AURORA ★ ADVERTISER

PEOPLE OF AMERICA.
*Our Country and our form of government are rescued
From the talons of Monarchists.*
In spite of intrigue,
In spite of terror,
In spite of unconstitutional laws,
In spite of British influence,
In spite of the Standing Army,
In spite of the Sedition Law . . .
The public voice of America and of virtue Prevails . . .
OFFICIAL RETURNS,
Of Votes for PRESIDENT and V. PRESIDENT.

	Jeffer.	Burr.	Adams.	Pinck..
Connecticut	0	0	9	9
Rhode Island	0	0	4	2
New-York,	12	12	0	0
New-Jersey	0	0	7	7
Pennsylvania,	8	8	7	7
Delaware,	0	0	3	3
Maryland,	5	5	5	5
Virginia,	21	21	0	0
Massachusetts,	0	0	16	16
New-Hamp.	0	0	6	6
S. Carolina,	8	7	0	0
Total	54	53	57	53

VOTES TO COME IN
Vermont, North-Carolina, Georgia, Kentucky, Tennessee.
THE [PROJECTED] WHOLE VOTE

Jeffer.	Burr.	Adams.	Pinck..
73	70	65	61

Huzza!—Huzza!—out neighbors! lend your eyes, spectacles and all! *From the [very Federalist] Philadelphia Gazette of last night,*

"Since Thursday last, the eight percent Stock of the United States has experienced a fall of 5 1–2 per cent, *in consequence of the election of Mr. Jefferson.*"

A good Federalist, who constantly hears the rev. Mr. Abercrombie, declared yesterday in the street that if "Jesus Christ were to come from Heaven, and say so, he would not believe Jefferson could ever be president."—This man no doubt is not an atheist—nor a deist—nor a jacobin—he is one of the true High Church Tory Christians.

Arrangements are making for a festive celebration—uniting the objects of national joy with benevolence . . . [L]et the whole meet on one joyous day for temperate recreation and congratulation.

What a contrast does the conduct of the republicans exhibit in the present triumph! with that of their adversaries. No insults passing the streets—no rioting or breaking windows—no savage orgies as the streets exhibited four years ago. Men turn around now and reflect that peace and concord is once more to bless our cities and our country, that the cries of war and spies of sedition no longer infest our firesides.

We hear, without being able to vouch for its authenticity, that a FRENCH MINISTER has arrived at Norfolk. *Nat. Intl.*

Tonight, in the *Gazette of the United States*:

From recent information, it appears highly likely that Mr. Jefferson will be the President of the United States for the four ensuing years, commencing on the fourth day of March next. This circumstance, so much regretted by the Editor of this Gazette and all real Americans, may be attributed to . . . certain Gentlemen whose non-attendance at the post of duty at the important hour will be remembered . . .

THURSDAY, DECEMBER 18, 1800

GENERAL ★ AURORA ★ ADVERTISER

The following is copied from [a Federalist paper] of last evening— *"There is nothing easier accounted for than the different effects which have been produced by the present and last election. At the last, the democrats were frustrated . . . Assaults, window breakings, &c. were the consequence.—In the present election, it appears that the Federalists have been disappointed.—What is the effect? We have no riotings, assaults, or commotions . . .*"

Upon this paragraph we shall ask, was *Joe Thomas* a republican? was young *Nichols,* the son of a federal marshal, a republican? Whose windows were broke? The windows of the *Aurora* Office. Who were insulted—Judge McKean, Mr. [Alexander James] Dallas, *Israel Israel,* Benjamin Franklin Bache! . . . We have indeed no riotings now—and for *sound* and *solid* reasons; that kind of work has gone too far—M'Pherson's blues could no longer impose upon this city, they who covered riot and disturbed the police under countenance of the magistrates and men in place. The marshal cannot now usurp the authority of the governor of the state to call out a train of military Janazaries, under pretence of keeping the peace, breaking it and spreading alarm. The functions of power are now restored to their legitimate organs and the violences of former days dare not now be acted again. The *thirty ruffians* who attacked this office, more than a year ago, are now some of them professing to be republicans, others of them *bankrupts,* and all of them *stink* in the *nose of society.*

Extract from a [letter to the editor from a Pennsylvania] Member of Congress at Washington . . .

"At length our wishes are accomplished, and I may venture to congratulate you, and indeed my country, on the success of the republican cause in the election of Mr. Jefferson.—auspicious event! would to Heaven I could be with you and our mutual friends in Philadelphia this moment to participate in the common joy! our exultations here [in Washington] are confined to too narrow a sphere—a wilderness is not the place to enjoy the incipient millennium.

"You have, ere this will reach you, heard the result of our twin sister South Carolina—I call her twin sister because if Pennsylvania had not been cursed with a Senate hostile to the public will . . . her voice would also have been undividedly in favour of Jefferson. South Carolina has snatched us from disgrace and ruin—no feelings in union with monarchy operated upon her Legislature!"

Today, in Washington, Thomas Jefferson writes John Breckenridge:

[T]he State of S. Carolina (the only one about which there was uncertainty) has given a republican vote and saved us from the consequences of the annihilation of Pennsylvania . . . General Davie has arrived here with the treaty formed (under the name of a convention) with France. It is now before the Senate for ratification . . . He believes firmly that a continental peace in Europe will take place and that England also may be comprehended.[2038]

GENERAL ★ AURORA ★ ADVERTISER

THE period which we have looked for so long and with so much anxiety has at length arrived . . . On Thursday arrived in Hampton Roads, the United States ship *Portsmouth*, Captain M'Neil, in 45 days from Havre [France]. General Davie, one of our envoys to the French Republic returned in the *Portsmouth* . . .

The accounts now in circulation are that all differences with the French Republic have been amicably adjusted; that a treaty, honorable to both nations, has been concluded; and that it now only remains for the President and Senate . . . to ratify a treaty concluded under their auspices and put an end to the contentions which have so long distracted the people of this country.

The news from Europe is not momentous. Negociation still continued the order of the day, and a general peace seemed probable.

Tonight, in the *Gazette of the United States*:

Extract of a letter from Washington . . . The Aurora-man has without doubt been let into the secret of the French Treaty. He will not be in a hurry to publish it. The Anti's here say it is a bitter pill . . .

GENERAL ★ AURORA ★ ADVERTISER

CONVENTION OF AMITY & COMMERCE
BETWEEN THE
UNITED STATES AND THE FRENCH REPUBLIC . . .

The first consul of the French republic [Napoleon Bonaparte], in the name of the French people, and the president of the United States of America . . . have agreed to the following articles:

Article I. There shall be a firm, inviolable, and universal peace, and a true and sincere friendship between the French Republic and the United States of America, as well as their countries, territories, cities, and places, as between their citizens and inhabitants, without exception of persons and places.

II. The Ministers Plenipotentiary of the two parties, not being empowered at present to agree relative to the treaty of alliance of the 6th of February, 1778 [or] to the treaty of commerce of the same date . . . said treaties . . . shall have no effect . . .

III. The ships belonging to the state taken on either side, or which may be taken before the exchange of ratifications . . . shall be mutually restored . . .

IV. The properties captured . . . shall be mutually restored . . .

America and France will be at peace. They will no longer, however, be allies!

The Fourth of March 1801 will become as celebrated in history as the 4th of July 1776 for the emancipation of the American states from British influence and tyranny. The election of a Republican President is a new declaration of independence, as important in its consequences as that of '76 and of much more difficult achievement.

Our former contest with England was merely a matter of strength. The contest which has just been closed was a war of interest, vice and corruption against principle, virtue, and patriotism. Our country became filled with foreign spies and domestic traitors who were on the eve of subverting our constitution and liberty—but the irresistible voice of a free people has banished them forever and declared that the fourth of March 1801 shall become the birthday of our regenerated independence and liberty.

The anglo-federalists are about to lose all their honorable distinctions: president, secretaries, senators &c. will be shortly mixed with the obscure swinish multitude;—what a sad reversal of good order !

(B. AM.)

Today, President John Adams writes a friend,

How mighty a power is the spirit of party! How decisive and unanimous it is! Seventy-three for Mr. Jefferson . . . In the case of Mr. Jefferson, there is nothing wonderful . . . What course is it we steer and to what harbor are we bound? . . . I am wholly at a loss. [2039]

In the legislative system of Pennsylvania, of *what use is the SENATE?* . . .

[W]e have for some time had reason to doubt whether the machine of government (to use the metaphor of the illustrious Franklin) can proceed efficaciously for having one horse [the House] to draw before and two [the Senate and Executive] to drag behind.

Nor can we see the consistency of having one set of representatives to *express* the public will and another to *oppose* it: one to build up, and another to pull down. Nor can we divine why the least numerous and least perfect class of representatives should have it in their power to controul or paralize the operation of the rest.

Nor why the partial representatives of public opinion *four years ago* shall counteract or controul the public sentiment of the *present* day. In the election of such a Senate, no room is allowed for those changes in the public mind which more recent facts and more accurate discussion have reasonably occasioned . . . Such has been, is, and such will be the case; and hence are the people of Pennsylvania *at this moment* deprived of their due share in the election of the most important Magistrate in the Union . . .

All these objections were foreseen at the adoption of the present constitution. Experience has confirmed them . . . *Power entrusted for too long a period will certainly be abused* . . .

We forebear . . . to strengthen our opinions by any reference to the Senate of the UNION, although (and with concern We speak it) the history of that Body and of the sessions for the last two years in particular would furnish facts and arguments in our favour . . .

Most Democratic-Republicans accept America's state and federal constitutions, while resisting the power of long office terms, wealth, and misplaced or misused authority to deny the will of the democratic majority. Others such as Benny Bache, Jimmy Callender, Tom Paine, and I would amend America's state and federal constitutions, replacing two-chamber legislatures and powerful chief executives with annually elected, single-chamber legislatures that would choose their own executive councils to execute their laws.[2040] We are, therefore, the "radicals"[2041] among Democratic-Republicans. We cling to Dr. Franklin's dream.[2042]

TUESDAY, JANUARY 6, 1801

GENERAL ★ AURORA ★ ADVERTISER

FESTIVAL

On Saturday the 3d last, a numerous and respectable assemblage of American, German, English, and Irish republicans, citizens of the United States of America, met at the house of Millar, the sign of the Green Tree in North Fourth street, to celebrate the favourable commencement of the 19th century and the success of republican exertion. Dr. [James] Reynolds was called to the chair . . . The toasts were as follows:—1. May the progress of the present century amply fulfil the auspicious promises of its commencement . . . 2. Peace on earth and good will towards man— May this be the ruling principle of every nation . . . 3. The world our

country—Man our fellow citizen—Benevolence our religion . . .
5. Thomas Jefferson . . . 6. Aaron Burr . . . 7. The Freedom of the Press—
May every public character be open to its examination; and virtue triumph over calumny without the despicable aid of a Sedition Law.
8. Universal Toleration—may republicans commiserate and forgive the
ignorance of those whose religion consists in abusing the religion of their
neighbors. 9. The Federal Constitution—May its errors (if it contains
any) be calmly discussed and peaceably amended . . .

VOLUNTEERS.

The memories of Dr. B. Franklin and of the grand-son who inherited
his virtues and followed his footsteps—B. F. Bache . . .

The Citizen Duane, whose courage, whose perseverance and abilities,
have contributed so essentially to the freedom of the American press . . .

WEDNESDAY, JANUARY 7, 1801

GENERAL   ★ AURORA ★   ADVERTISER

EASTON . . . [A] number of the citizens of Easton and its vacinity assembled at the house of Mr. Heckman to certify their pleasure at the late
glorious triumph of republicanism . . . TOASTS. 1. The third of December 1800—the legitimate offspring of the Fourth of July, 1776. *6 rounds.
6 cheers* . . . 2. Thomas Jefferson . . . *6 rounds. 6 cheers.* 3. Aaron Burr
. . . *6 rounds. 6 cheers* . . . 4. Thomas M'Kean . . . *6 cheers* . . . 6. William Duane—"Blessed be he that holdeth out to the end and fainteth
not." *3 rounds. 3 cheers.* 7. The Editors of the Democratic Presses
throughout the Union—May they never be shackled by gag-laws or corrupted by British gold. *1 round. 1 cheer* . . . 10. The Treaty with
France—May the quarrels of Republics, like those of lovers, terminate
in a renewal of former sentiments—*1 round. 1 cheer.* 11. The Sedition
Law—a speedy decease and no resurrection to the principles which originated it . . . 13. The year 1798– the reign of terrorism, British influence,
black cockades, and federal insolence.

"Prone to the dust oppression shall be hurl'd,
Her name, her nature wither'd from the world."

14. The memory of Benjamin Franklin—who snatch'd the lightening
from Heaven and the Scepter from tyrants. *1 round. 1 cheer.*

TUESDAY, JANUARY 20, 1801

GENERAL   ★ AURORA ★   ADVERTISER

The first consul [Napoleon Bonaparte] has pleased to appoint citizen
Pichon, late secretary of the French commission which treated with our

envoys, commissary general of the commercial relations of France with the United States and chargé d'affaires, till the appointment of a French minister. It is believed that this gentleman will sail very soon for Washington.

Tonight, at seven o'clock, a fire breaks out in the Washington building which houses the Treasury Department records. Though War Secretary Samuel Dexter is now acting also as Treasury Secretary, witnesses report seeing former Treasury Secretary Oliver Wolcott removing trunks of materials from the Treasury Department while the fire rages![2043]

SATURDAY, JANUARY 24, 1801

GENERAL ★ AURORA ★ ADVERTISER

MEMENTO !
THE TREASURY DEPARTMENT
BURNT DOWN;
SO WAS
THE WAR DEPARTMENT . . .

Whole Handkerchiefs of Papers were previously carried off by persons *well known.*—More of this hereafter.

The baseness and servility . . . of the men in power, cannot fail to bring to the minds of men . . . the days of Roman dishonor, under Tiberius, Nero, and those Caesars, the most despicable of the human race.

What do you think, dear reader? Is it Rome burning? Or Valhalla?

MONDAY, JANUARY 26, 1801

GENERAL ★ AURORA ★ ADVERTISER

From the BOSTON CHRONICLE..
"BUONAPARTE has been pleased to say that the Americans are indebted to the French nation for their independence. Agreed—provided she will acknowledge that their revolution was owing to the Americans . . . For if we could not have secured our independence but by the treaty of '78 . . . France, without it, would never have tho't of being a Republic and of diffusing the blessings of equal liberty among her citizens . . ."
(. . . It is a mistake that the idea of a Republic was borrowed from America by the French. The project of a Republic was started in France more than a century before our Revolution. We do not want the evidence . . . to prove that Louis XVI was sorry for the aid given to America; the despots of Europe and their adherents have discovered the true cause—it was philosophy *real* and *fashionable* that procured French aid for

American liberty.—It was the single influence and reputation of Dr. Franklin which obtained the aid of France—and to this cause we may attribute all the fulminations against philosophers—and the slanders against Franklin from British presses.)

[Washington, January 21.] Last evening about dusk a fire was discovered in the treasury department. When discovered, one of the rooms of the accountant was in a full blaze . . . *(National Intel.)*

Extract [of a letter] to the Editor dated Washington, January 21, 1801. "You were singularly fortunate in obtaining an inspection of the treasury books before their removal to this place, as I believe the copies you kept are the only traces that now remain of the books you had in your possession; you may recollect that I told you the books of one of the departments which you saw were committed to the care of Farrell, [so] it is remarkable that the fire commenced in that apartment, and all the books under his care are said to be consumed in the fire last night."

TUESDAY, JANUARY 27, 1801

GENERAL ★ AURORA ★ ADVERTISER

The denouement of the federal tragi-comedy has been a flaming one, two fire-works in one act and so close after the heels of each other . . .

Extract of a Letter, dated Washington, Jan. 22 . . . [A]ll the books containing the Auditor's reports and those which were in Duane's possession are destroyed . . .

THURSDAY, FEBRUARY 12, 1801

GENERAL ★ AURORA ★ ADVERTISER

Yesterday was the day . . . [electoral] votes for President and Vice President of the United States were to be counted . . . yet we cannot let pass an essay which appeared in the *Washington Federalist* . . . and which shews [a] design . . . to establish a perpetual President or Dictator . . . The piece in the *Federalist* which we allude to begins thus:

"It is now universally understood that Mr. Burr and Mr. Jefferson have received from the electors an equal number of votes . . . It is by no means impossible that they may also have an equal number of votes in the house of representatives . . . It is certainly of very great importance to decide what will be the result should neither of them have a constitutional majority . . .

"Congress . . . have the power to declare what officer shall act as President . . . without limitation of time, however long that period may be, before his successor shall be elected . . . [T]here is a great . . . propriety that the [current] President . . . should con-

tinue to act . . . until the next election in course: that is, for another four years."

Thomas Jefferson will speak to John Adams. Mr. Jefferson:

> *I called on Mr. Adams. We conversed on the state of things. I observed to him that a very dangerous experiment was then in contemplation to defeat the Presidential election by an act of Congress declaring the right to devolve on him the government during any interregnum; that such a measure would probably produce resistance by force and incalculable consequences which it would be in his power to resist by negativing such an act. He seemed to think such an act justifiable and observed that it was in my power to fix the election by a word in an instant, by declaring I would not turn out the federal [Federalist] officers . . . Finding his mind made up as to the usurpation of the government . . . I urged it no further . . .*[2044]

No such usurpation will occur. Five days from today, in the U.S. House of Representatives, Republican Matthew Lyon of Vermont, the Irish newspaper publisher who spit in the face of the Federalists and went to prison for criticizing the President, will have a final revenge. Congressman Lyon will cast the deciding vote to make Thomas Jefferson the new President of the United States.[2045] America's second revolution, this one clearly for democracy, is at its end.

WEDNESDAY, MARCH 4, 1801

GENERAL ★ AURORA ★ ADVERTISER

From the earliest period recorded in the page of history to the present time, mankind has been endeavouring to ascertain what form of civilized society would be most conducive to the happiness of the species. Incapable of leisure for political pursuits, the mass of people have found it expedient to commit the business of the community at large to a few persons who were rewarded for the attention thus paid to the affairs of the public. But in every age and in every nation, the possession of power has proved an almost irresistible temptation to extend and abuse it . . . Even at this day—at the commencement of the 19th century! the proud and infatuated monarch of Great Britain, which pretends to be the most civilized nation of the earth, has the insolence to term the people his *subjects*, and they have the stupidity to glory in the degrading titles and fawn upon their tyrants . . .

Occasionally the people (as at Athens) have attempted to take the power of governing themselves into their own hands. Occasionally republics have been formed with checks upon the persons appointed as temporary rulers. But like all new experiments upon subjects of great importance . . . experience alone can point out the practical difficulties . . . Hence the trials of a popular form of government . . .

The history of the monarchical forms of government have taught us, however, that the rights of the people have been successfully trampled upon chiefly by the means of standing armies . . . by means of too much power imprudently granted or boldly assumed by the rulers of a nation in the disposal of money, of place, and of contracts—and by shackling the freedom of the Press.

The remedies evidently indicated are *never to trust great power to any man or body of men: never to entrust it long: to preserve to the people the right of recalling at short periods every person placed by them in a political situation; and to preserve inviolate the freedom of the press.*

The importance of these political maxims were first felt and acted upon in AMERICA . . . In 1798 and 1799, monarchy openly exulted, and democracy was a term of bitterest reproach. The execrable planners of this dangerous and desperate system, thanks to the freedom of the press, are now fallen; fallen, we sincerely hope, to rise no more.

Today, in the new federal city of Washington, America inaugurates its third President, Thomas Jefferson of Virginia. Today, the Sedition Act expires. Those who face or suffer the Sedition Act's penalties will receive a presidential pardon from our new and very democratic President of the United States. From President Jefferson's Inaugural Address:

> *We are all republicans: we are all federalists. If there be any among us who would wish to dissolve this union or to change its republican form, let them stand undisturbed as monuments of the safety with which error of opinion may be tolerated where reason is left free to combat it. I know indeed that some honest men fear that a republican government cannot be strong . . . Sometimes it is said that man cannot be trusted with the government of himself. Can he then be trusted with the government of others? Or have we found angels in the form of kings to govern him? Let history answer this question.*[2046]

Philadelphia celebrates President Jefferson's inauguration with the most extensive and splendid procession the city has ever seen (excepting the pompous procession of 1787). Joining other units of the Republican Militia Legion, I lead my Republican Greens from Philadelphia's State-house, down Walnut-street to Second-street, thence up Second-street to Race-street, &c.[2047] As we cross High-street, only a block from the *Aurora*'s office, and pass the High-street covered country market, how could I not feel the warmth of home, the pride of country, and the thrill of freedom? I have won my final battle with monarchy.

EPILOGUE TO BOOK THREE

Tuesday, March 31, 1801. Today, former President John Adams writes his former Navy Secretary, Benjamin Stoddert, about their Federalist party:

> *No party that ever existed knew itself so little or so vainly overrated its own influence and popularity, as ours. None ever understood so ill the causes of its own power or so wantonly destroyed them. If we had been blessed with common sense, we should not have been over-thrown by . . . Duane, Callender, Cooper and Lyon, or their great patron and protector [Thomas Jefferson]. A group of foreign liars, encouraged by a few ambitious native gentlemen, have discomfited the education, the talents, the virtues, and the property of the country. The reason is, we have no Americans in America. The Federalists have been no more American than the Anties.*[2048]

Thursday, April 16, 1801. Today, former President John Adams writes South Carolinian Christopher Gadsden:

> *What is the reason that so many of our "old standbys" are infected with Jacobinism? The principles of this infernal tribe were surely no part of our ancient political creed.*
>
> *"Foreign meddlers," as you properly denominate them, have a strange and mysterious influence in this country. Is there no pride in American bosoms? Can their hearts endure that Callender, Duane, Cooper and Lyon should be the most influential men in the country, all foreigners and all degraded characters? It is astonishing to me that the "tribes of law-followers" should adopt principles subversive of all law, should unite with the ignorant and illiberal against men of understanding and property.*[2049]

Saturday, May 23, 1801. Today, President Jefferson writes me:

> *I asked if you could give me a list of the prosecutions of a public nature against you & over which I might have a controul; observing that whenever in the line of my functions I should be met by the Sedition law, I should treat it as a nullity. That therefore, even in the prosecution recommended by the Senate, if founded on that law, I would order a nolle prosequi [an order not to prosecute] . . . The trial on behalf of the Senate being postponed, you have time to explain your wishes to me, and if it be done on a consultation with Mr. Dallas, it may abridge the operations which shall be thought proper.*
>
> *I accept with acknowledgment Mrs. Bache's compliments & beg*

leave to tender her my sincere respect & to yourselves salutations & my best wishes . . .[2050]

President Jefferson will explain his policy to an outraged Abigail Adams:

I discharged every person under punishment or prosecution under the Sedition law, because I considered and now consider that law to be a nullity as absolute and as palpable as if Congress had ordered us to fall down and worship a golden image . . . [The discharge] was accordingly done in every instance without asking what the offenders had done or against whom they had offended but whether the pains they were suffering were inflicted under the pretended sedition law. It was certainly possible that my motives . . . might have been to protect, encourage and reward slander; but they may also have been . . . to protect the Constitution violated by an unauthorized act of Congress. Which of these were my motives must be decided by a regard to the general tenor of my life. On this I am not afraid to appeal to the nation at large, to posterity, and still less to that Being who sees himself our motives, who will judge us from his own knowlege of them, and not on the testimony of Porcupine or Fenno.[2051]

Tuesday, September 15, 1801. Today, John Adams writes his son, Thomas:

Have a care that you do not let Captain Duane know that I am reading Cicero de Senectute [Cicero concerning Old Age] again, because he will immediately insert in his Aurora Borealis that I recollected those words in the 17th Chapter . . . ["nothing seems so royal as to engage in the pursuit of land cultivation"]. He will say that there is nothing in building stone walls or in collecting heaps of compost but the tang of royalty and monarchy which . . . attracts my esteem and affection, and all the Germans and all the Irish and all the Quakers and Anabaptists will say they believe him, and the Presbyterians will shake their heads and say it is too true . . . I do not recollect to have seen an Aurora since I became a monarch of stony fields, Count of Gull Island, Earl of Mt. Ararat, Marquis of Candlewood Hill, and Baron of Rocky Run . . .[2052]

Monday, October 25, 1802. Today, President Jefferson instructs his U.S. Attorney General, Levi Lincoln:

I shall take no other revenge than, by the steady pursuit of economy and peace and by the establishment of republican principles in substance and in form, to sink federalism into an abyss from which there shall be no resurrection for it.[2053]

Tuesday, December 21, 1802. Today, in Washington, Federalist William Plumer writes:

Soon after my arrival, I thought it my duty from the high office Mr.
Jefferson holds, not from respect to him, to wait upon him . . . I was
with other members introduced into the levee chamber. In a few mo-
ments, his lank majesty entered in a brown coat, red waistcoat,
striped corduroy small clothes, injured by time & soiled with dirt, ger-
man hose & slippers without heels. I thought he was a servant, but a
voice soon announced it was the President . . . I have never prized hu-
mility . . . I was soon roused from these reflections by beholding over
the chimney piece an elegant portrait of the late illustrious Washington
& family & on one side of the Hall [an oil painting of] the Apotheosis of
that never to be forgotten man; but can you, if you can, believe me, at
the other side of the same room sat Thomas Payne, the calumniator of
the illustrious dead! Yes, he was there conversing & behaving with all
the airs & familiarity of an equal with the President. There is too much
truth to the adage, <u>a man is known by his company.</u>

It is said that Mr. Payne frequently dines with the President . . . The
federalists believe the President will have cause to rue the day in
which he invited this man to return to this country . . .

Duane is another of the Great man's associates. This man who a
few years since branded the Senate of the United States with the epi-
thet of <u>rascals</u> is now their official printer. In times like these, posts of
honour are private life . . .[2054]

Thursday, March 8, 1804. Today, I write twelve-year-old Franklin Bache (oldest of Benny's four sons and now one of mine):

I know very well that when you read your lessons, you will com-
pare the good and the bad actions of the Romans with those of men in
America—it is fit you should. Every American is bound to do it, and
you have a particular obligation in you to do so from your name in
every respect. Your Great Grandfather is properly thought the father of
American liberty—he it was who formed the American mind and char-
acter for more than fifty years to become what America now is, one of
the greatest and the only free nation in the world . . .

You have therefore not only to pursue the path which your ancestor
prepared for you but [also] that in which your own father walked with
equal virtue, taking into view the shortness of his life. It is my particu-
lar ambition, my dear boy, that you should be worthy of both—

By a singular fortune, your Great Grandfather has been for more
than thirty years of my life the constant idol of my affections as a poli-
tician—he has been my hero—and it is a felicity to me that I am so
nearly connected with his posterity as to stand in the relation of father
to you and to be loved by you and your brothers and mother, to see us
all so happy and fond of each other—and growing up in prosperity as
you grow up in years . . .

Love your brothers and sisters, and love and honor your parents and relatives, and you can in no manner more gratify me, unless in realizing the hope of seeing you one day distinguished as an ornament to your country, a true Franklin, and . . . I shall partake of the honor of being your guardian guide and to stand in the relation of father to you.[2055]

Sunday, July 7, 1805. Today, former President John Adams writes Dr. Benjamin Rush:

I have not seen an Aurora a long time, but last night I was told that, in the late papers of Mr. Duane, he or his writers are elaborately answering my Defence [of the Constitutions of Government of the United States] and recommending a government of one assembly . . . There is a body of people in every state in the union who are both in heart and head of this sect. This tribe will always be courted by the seekers of popularity and opposers of a good systematic government. They are properly the sans-culottes of this country.[2056]

Tuesday, March 10, 1807. Today, my wife, Peggy, writes her brother, Peter Markoe:

[M]y orphan children . . . are all fast approaching that Time of life that requires a little assistance to put them forward in the world. Now only conceive, my dear Brother, what I must feel when I reflect that I have four Boys who are educated and supported by Mr. Duane. There are very few fathers in law [stepfathers] that would have acted as Mr. D. has done. He has a large family & children of his own; however, he says he glories in protecting Benjamin's children.[2057]

Saturday, March 30, 1811. Today, former President Thomas Jefferson writes:

This paper [the Philadelphia Aurora] has unquestionably rendered incalculable services to republicanism through all its struggles with the federalists, and has been the rallying point for the orthodoxy of the whole Union. It was our comfort in the gloomiest days and is still performing the office of a watchful sentinel.[2058]

Wednesday, December 4, 1811. Today, former President John Adams writes Dr. Benjamin Rush:

We have seen advertised in the Aurora . . . Dr. Franklin's works and especially his journal in France . . .
I am told, too, that Colonel Duane has announced his intention to take me in hand for what I have published concerning Dr. Franklin. He is welcome. I have published my proofs as well as complaints. Let the world judge.[2059]

Sunday, October 19, 1823. Today, former President Jefferson writes President James Monroe:

[T]he energy of [William Duane's Aurora], when our cause was laboring and all but lost under the overwelming weight of its powerful adversaries, its unquestionable effect in the revolution produced in the public mind . . . arrested the rapid march of our government towards monarchy . . .[2060]

Thursday, July 29, 1824. Today, former Secretary of State Timothy Pickering writes:

[I]t was important to maintain, during the revolution, the popular opinion in [Washington's] favour. Accordingly, there was no public disclosure . . . These early impressions in favor of Washington remain on the minds, generally, of his surviving contemporary fellow-citizens, and have passed, naturally, into the minds of the succeeding generation. Hence to question the reality of those imputed excellencies is deemed little short of treason. But is it proper that the truth should forever be concealed?[2061]

1927. This year, yet another edition of the Rev. Mason Locke Weems' book *A History of the Life and Death, Virtues and Exploits of General George Washington*, first published in 1800, just a few months after Washington's death, appears in bookstores throughout the United States:

"George," said his father, "do you know who killed that beautiful little cherry tree in the garden?" This was a tough question; and George staggered under it for a moment; but quickly recovered himself: and looking at his father, with the sweet face of youth brightened with the inexpressible charm of all-conquering truth, he bravely cried out, "I can't tell a lie, Pa; you know I can't tell a lie . . ."[2062]

FINIS

AUTHOR'S FINAL NOTE

A Patriot is a dangerous post;
When wanted by his country most,
Perversely comes in evil times,
When virtues are imputed crimes.

SWIFT[2063]

Dear Reader,

The election of 1800 shifted power to the Republicans for the next quarter century. Thomas Jefferson served as president for two terms (1801–1809). His Secretary of State, James Madison, succeeded him to the presidency for two terms (1809–1817), and Madison's Secretary of State, James Monroe, succeeded him to the presidency for two terms (1817–1825). France and Britain remained important.

During Jefferson's presidency, James Monroe returned to France as Jefferson's special envoy, and, in 1803, just two years after Jefferson took office, France ceded to the United States, for less than three cents an acre, all the land between the Mississippi River and the Rocky Mountains.[2064] By this Louisiana Purchase, Jefferson and France doubled the size of the United States of America and reduced their common enemy, Federalist New England, to a small fraction of the country. During Madison's presidency, a Republican majority in Congress responded to continuing British naval provocations with a Declaration of War against Britain, and, during the ensuing War of 1812, a British army marched into Washington and set fire to all U.S. government buildings, including the presidential mansion (which was later rebuilt and repainted as the White House). During Madison's presidency, the British finally vanquished Napoleon at the Battle of Waterloo, thereby restoring France to a monarchy, under Louis XVI's brother, French King Louis XVIII.

During this time, William Duane remained at the *Aurora*'s helm, finally relinquishing the paper in 1822. His son, William John (who was beaten, with his father, by federal army officers in 1799), worked at the paper for several years, married one of Benjamin Bache's younger sisters, Deborah, entered Pennsylvania politics, and, in 1833, became Secretary of the Treasury under President Andrew Jackson.

William and Peggy Duane were married for thirty-five years. They had five children. When William Duane died, in 1835, at the age of seventy-five, Peggy followed him the very next year.

William Cobbett (Peter Porcupine) finally returned to America in 1817 but, two years later, announced plans to take Tom Paine's remains (then ten years in the grave) back to England, hired two gravediggers to exhume Paine's bones, and departed America, the bones in his baggage, never to return. What Porcupine did with those bones, no one—not even in England—knows.

On March 9, 1964, the U.S. Supreme Court held, in the landmark case of *The New York Times Co. v. Sullivan*, that the First Amendment of the United States Constitution protects a newspaper's honest criticism of government officials, even when that criticism is false and defamatory. In rendering the court's opinion, Mr. Justice Brennan wrote:

> *This is the lesson which is to be drawn from the great controversy over the Sedition Act of 1798 . . . which first crystallized a national awareness of the First Amendment . . .*
>
> *Although the Sedition Act was never tested in this Court (the act expired by its terms in 1801), the attack upon its validity has carried the day in the court of history . . . The invalidity of the Act has also been assumed by Justices of this Court . . .*[2065]

Obviously, *American Aurora* concurs.

I hope *American Aurora* will also add credence to the following propositions: *First,* that historians and publishers need not fear exposing the public to large quantities of history's source materials which comprise, after all, our safest vehicle for time travel. *Second,* that the public need not eschew footnotes or resort to historical fiction to find the past exciting. History's first-person / present-tense materials, properly presented, can be thrilling. *Third,* that those who value democracy and truth must always defend America's Bill of Rights, even against those boasting the credentials of our founding fathers. *Fourth,* that it is not by chance that America's Presidents and senators are, on average, wealthier than members of the House of Representatives; it is by design, &c. *Fifth,* that, as Poor Richard sagaciously, perhaps tautologically, and much too quietly observed,

> *Historians relate not so much what is done,*
> *as what they would have believed.*[2066]

The historian's testimony is, at best, only hearsay.

Those who view the past as prologue may recognize monarchy and aristocracy (enemies to the *American Aurora*) in the America of today, entrenched in our Constitution (as this work explains) and revealed in such contemporary issues as "the imperial presidency," "legislative deadlock," "vested interests," "term limits," "campaign financing," "lobbying," "the military-industrial complex," and "civil liberties." They will see "Democratic-Republicans" still championing the will of the majority against the wiles of the "establishment" and the freedoms of our Bill of Rights against them both. Not least of all, they will find ghosts of Poor Richard, Young Lightning Rod, and the Rat-Catcher still stalking our nation's pressrooms, reminding the sentinels of our freedoms that, at the aurora of this great nation, the true "Father of His Country" wanted "the republic for which it stands" to be a truly democratic republic.

I wish to thank Yale University's Sterling Professor of History Emeritus Edmund S. Morgan for his review of matters historical, novelist Leslie Epstein for his review of my presentation method, editor *extraordinaire* Robert Weil, writer Samia Serageldin, and research assistant Scott Hovey for their very helpful editing, my friend Laurel Cohen for a final proofing, and friends Anne-Marie Soullière, Jonathan Matson, Thomas Cottle, Michael Fenlon, David Emmons, Beverly Head, Ronald Sampson, David Levington, Steve Sohmer, Gaddis Smith, and John Roberts for special words of encouragement. I also thank historian Anna-Coxe Toogood of Philadelphia's Independence National Historic Park, the staffs at Boston College's O'Neil Library and Burns Library, the American Antiquarian Society, the Massachusetts Historical Society, the American Philosophical Society, and the Library of Congress. I gratefully acknowledge that my interest in America's political history was first excited by an extraordinary high school history teacher, the late Richard S. Wickenden at Tabor Academy, and that my passion for equality and human rights was first kindled by the moral teachings and courageous example of the Rev. William Sloane Coffin, Yale's chaplain when I was at Yale in the early 1960s. I thank my wife, Anne, whose love provides the safety net for all my endeavors, and our unique and wonderful gifts, Jill and Tadd. Finally, I thank and love my country for recognizing the right to publish a work such as this.

I take leave of you, dear reader, with a remembrance of Monday, September 17, 1787, the last day of the Federal Constitutional Convention in Philadelphia. James Madison records:

> *Whilst the last members were signing [the new U.S. Constitution], Doct^r FRANKLIN, looking towards the President's Chair at the back of which a rising sun happened to be painted, observed to a few members near him that painters found it difficult to distinguish in their art a rising from a setting sun. I have, said he, often . . . in the . . . vicissitudes of my hopes and fears . . . looked at that [sun] behind the President without being able to tell whether it was rising or setting; But now at length I have the happiness to know that it is a rising and not a setting Sun.*[2067]

May it always be so.

Appreciatively,
RICHARD N. ROSENFELD
Chestnut Hill, Massachusetts
Monday, August 26, 1996

NOTE ON THE ILLUSTRATIONS

The author gratefully acknowledges permission to reproduce photographs of Charles Willson Peale's painting, *George Washington, 1776* (34.1178, Dick S. Ramsay Fund) from the Brooklyn Museum; of Benjamin Franklin Bache's sketch of Benjamin Franklin from the American Philosophical Society; of the Birch Prints (BRP) from the American Antiquarian Society (BRP plates #2, 3, 8, 9, 11, 12, 18, and 29) and The Rare Book Department of the Free Library of Philadelphia (BRP plates #15, 19, 20, and 22); of the three newspapers and of the map of Pennsylvania from the American Antiquarian Society; and of the St. Mémin portrait of William Duane from the National Portrait Gallery, Smithsonian Institution.

ENDNOTES

This work's text is set in a modern-day version of Caslon, one of Dr. Franklin's favorite typefaces.[2068] Deviations from modern-day spelling and punctuation are either in the original documents or as reminders of typesetting by hand (and, in the case of newspapers, often by candlelight), spelling by phonetics (e.g., "Lightening-Rod"), and other factors in eighteenth-century orthography. The apparent compliance of historical writings with modern-day spelling and punctuation conventions may reflect editorial changes by the editors of certain source references, as well as by your author *qua* editor, to enhance readability.

KEY TO ACRONYMS

AALP   Phyllis Lee Levin, *Abigail Adams* (New York: Ballantine Books, 1988).

AANL   Stewart Mitchell, ed., *New Letters of Abigail Adams, 1788–1801* (Boston: Houghton Mifflin, 1947).

ABDM   Matthew L. Davis, *Memoirs of Aaron Burr with Miscellaneous Selections from His Correspondence* (New York: Harper & Brothers, 1836–37), 2 vols.

ADR   Robert R. Palmer, *The Age of the Democratic Revolution* (Princeton: Princeton Univ. Press, 1959–1964), 2 vols.

AFC   Herbert J. Storing, ed., *The Complete Anti-Federalist* (Chicago: Univ. of Chicago Press, 1981), 7 vols.

AGA   *Aurora General Advertiser* (Philadelphia).

AGBE   Edwin G. Burrows, *Albert Gallatin and the Political Economy of Republicanism 1761–1800* (New York: Garland Pub., 1986).

AGHA   Henry Adams, *The Life of Albert Gallatin* (Philadelphia: J. B. Lippincott, 1879).

AGW   Raymond Walters, Jr., *Albert Gallatin: Jeffersonian Financier and Diplomat* (New York: Macmillan, 1957).

AHFR   *Annales historiques de la révolution française* (Reims, Paris: Firmin-Didot, 1924–).

AHO   Alexander Hamilton, *Observations on Certain Documents Contained in No. V and VI of "The History of the United States for the Year 1796," in Which the Charge of Speculation Against Alexander Hamilton, Late Secretary of the Treasury Is Fully Refuted. Written by Himself* (Philadelphia: Printed for John Fenno, by John Bioren, 1797). REDX 32,222.

AHP   Harold C. Syrett et al., eds., *The Papers of Alexander Hamilton* (New York, 1961–1987), 27 vols.

AHR   *American Historical Review* (Washington: American Historical Association, 1895–), 70+ vols.

AHWL   Henry Cabot Lodge, ed., *Works of Alexander Hamilton* (New York, London: G. P. Putnam's Sons, 1904), 12 vols.

AHWO   John C. Hamilton, ed., *The Works of Alexander Hamilton* (New York: Charles S. Francis, 1851), 7 vols.

ALLR   Richard Henry Lee, *Life of Arthur Lee* (Boston: Wells and Lilly, 1829), 2 vols.

ANAM   *The Annals of America* (Chicago: Encyclopaedia Britannica, 1968), 20 vols.

ANC   *The Debates and Proceedings in the Congress of the United States . . . March 3, 1789 to May 27, 1824* (Washington: Gales and Seaton, 1834–56), 42 vols.

APS   American Philosophical Society.

A&R   John A. Schutz and Douglass Adair, eds., *The Spur of Fame: Dialogues of John Adams and Benjamin Rush, 1805–1813* (San Marino: Huntington Library, 1966).

AWSC   Charles J. Stillé, *Major-General Anthony Wayne and the Pennsylvania Line* (Philadelphia: J. B. Lippincott, 1893).

BARC   Henry B. Carrington, *Battles of the American Revolution, 1775–1781* (New York: A. S. Barnes, 1876).

BASN   Albert Hall Bowman, *The Struggle for Neutrality: Franco-American Diplomacy during the Federalist Era* (Knoxville: Univ. of Tennessee Press, 1974).

BBDC   Bernard Bailyn, ed., *The Debate on the Constitution* (New York: Literary Classics of the United States, 1993), 2 vols.

BBMM   Beverly W. Bond, Jr., *The Monroe Mission to France, 1794–1796* (Baltimore: Johns Hopkins Press, 1907).

BCAN   Clarence Saunders Brigham, *History and Bibliography of American Newspapers, 1690–1820, Including Additions and Corrections, 1961* (Hamden, Conn.: Archon Books, 1962).

BCMP   Catherine Drinker Bowen, *Miracle at Philadelphia* (Boston: Little, Brown, 1966, 1986).

BEJ   Elias Boudinot, *Journal of Historical Recollections of American Events During the Revolutionary War* (Trenton, 1899).

BFA   Henry Steele Commager, ed., *The Autobiography of Benjamin Franklin and Selections from His Other Writings* (New York: Modern Library, 1950).

BFAW   Carl Van Doren, ed., *Benjamin Franklin's Autobiographical Writings* (New York: Viking Press, 1945).

BFBB   Bernard Fay, *The Two Franklins: Fathers of American Democracy* (New York: AMS Press, 1969).

BFBC   *Bache Papers, Castle Collection,* American Philosophical Society. Microfilm.

BFBL   Lucien Cramer, *Les Cramer, une famille génévoise. Leur relations avec Voltaire, Rousseau, et Benjamin Franklin Bache* (Génève, 1952).

BFBP   John D. R. Platt, "*Independent National Historic Park: Home and Office of Benjamin Franklin Bache . . .*" (Washington, D.C.: Office of History and Historic Architecture, U.S. Dept. of the Interior National Park Service, 1970).

BFBR   B. F. Bache, *Remarks Occasioned by the Late Conduct of Mr. Washington, President of the United States* (Philadelphia: Printed for Benjamin Franklin Bache, 1797). REDX 31,759.

BFBS   Jeffery Alan Smith, *Franklin and Bache: Envisioning the Enlightened Republic* (New York: Oxford Univ. Press, 1990).

BFBT   James Tagg, *Benjamin Franklin Bache and the Philadelphia Aurora* (Philadelphia: Univ. of Pennsylvania Press, 1991).

BFBW   Benjamin Franklin Bache, *Truth Will Out! The Foul Charges of the Tories Against the Editor of the Aurora Repelled . . .* (Philadelphia, 1798). REDX 33,648.

BFCV   Carl Van Doren, *Benjamin Franklin* (New York: Viking Press, 1938).

BFFC   Alfred Owen Aldridge, *Franklin and His French Contemporaries* (New York: New York Univ. Press, 1957).

BFFS   Willis Steell, *Benjamin Franklin of Paris* (New York: Minton, Balch, 1928).

BFLC   Claude-Anne Lopez, *Mon Cher Papa. Franklin and the Ladies of Paris* (New Haven: Yale Univ. Press, 1990).

BFPL   Leonard W. Labaree et al., eds., *Papers of Benjamin Franklin* (New Haven: Yale Univ. Press, 1959–), 31 vols.

BFPO   John Clyde Oswald, *Benjamin Franklin Printer* (N.P., 1917).

BFPP   Luther Samuel Livingston, *Franklin and His Press at Passy* (New York: Grolier Club, 1914).

BFSG   Gerald Stourzh, *Benjamin Franklin and American Foreign Policy* (Chicago: Univ. of Chicago Press, 1954).

BFSM   Albert Henry Smyth, ed., *The Writings of Benjamin Franklin* (New York: Macmillan, 1905–07), 10 vols.

BFWE   Esmond Wright, *Franklin of Philadelphia* (Cambridge, Mass.: Belknap Press of Harvard Univ. Press, 1986).

BFWS   Jared Sparks, ed., *The Works of Benjamin Franklin* (Boston: Hilliard, Gray, 1836–40), 10 vols.

BFWT   William Temple Franklin, *Memoirs of the Life and Writings of Benjamin Franklin* (London: Henry Colburn, 1818), 2 vols.

BGH   George Bancroft, *Histoire de l'action commune de la France et de l'Amérique pour l'indépendance des États-Unis,* transl. by Comte Adolphe de Circourt (Paris: F. Vieweg, 1876), 3 vols.

BP   *Boston Patriot* (Boston, Mass.), newspaper.

BRL   L. H. Butterfield, ed., *Letters of Benjamin Rush* (Princeton, N.J.: Princeton Univ. Press, 1951), 2 vols.

BRP   William Russell Birch & Son, *The City of Philadelphia, in the State of Pennsylvania, North America; As It Appeared in the Year 1800* [consisting of 28 copperplate engravings executed during 1798 and 1799] (Philadelphia: W. Birch, 1800).

BSDR   Samuel Flagg Bemis, *Diplomacy of the American Revolution* (Westport, Conn.: Greenwood Press, 1983).

CEFP   Edward S. Corwin, *French Policy and the American Alliance of 1778* (New York: B. Franklin, 1916, 1970).

CFFR   Frances Sergeant Childs, *French Refugee Life in the United States, 1790–1800* (Baltimore: Johns Hopkins Press, 1940).

CFR   *Chronicle of the French Revolution* (London: Chronicle Publications, 1989).

CGD   John J. Meng, ed., *Despatches and Instructions of Conrad Alexandre Gérard, 1778–1780* (Baltimore: Johns Hopkins Press, 1939).

CLMS   Theodore Thayer, *The Making of a Scapegoat: Washington and Lee at Monmouth* (Port Washington, N.Y.: Kennikat Press, 1976).

CMLV   Marquis de Condorcet, *The Life of Voltaire, to Which Are Added Memoirs of Voltaire, Written by Himself* (Philadelphia: W. Spotswood, 1792), 2 vols.

CRIS   John C. Miller, *Crisis in Freedom: The Alien and Sedition Acts* (Boston: Little, Brown, 1952).

DAB   Allen Johnson et al., eds., *Dictionary of American Biography* (New York: Charles Scribner's Sons, 1928–44), 20 vols.+ Suppl.

DAQW   Alexander DeConde, *The Quasi-War: The Politics and Diplomacy of the Undeclared War with France, 1797–1801* (New York: Charles Scribner's Sons, 1966).

DERD   Elisha P. Douglass, *Rebels and Democrats: The Struggle for Equal Political Rights & Majority Rule During the Revolution* (Chapel Hill, N.C.: Univ. of North Carolina Press, 1955).

DFMC   Guillaume de Deux-Ponts, *My Campaigns in America: A Journal Kept by Count William de Deux-Ponts, 1780–81.* Transl. by Samuel Abbott Green (Boston: J. K. Wiggin & Wm. Parsons Lunt, 1868).

DGW   Donald Jackson and Dorothy Twohig, eds., *The Diaries of George Washington* (Charlottesville, Va.: Univ. Press of Virginia, 1976–79), 6 vols.

DIMJ   James Munves, *Thomas Jefferson and The Declaration of Independence: The Writing and Editing of the Document* . . . (New York: Charles Scribner's Sons, 1978).

DJDH   Jonathan R. Dull, *A Diplomatic History of the American Revolution* (New Haven: Yale Univ. Press, 1985).

DJFN   Jonathan R. Dull, *The French Navy and American Independence* (Princeton: Princeton Univ. Press, 1975).

DJNM   John Durand, ed., *New Materials for the History of the American Revolution* (New York: Henry Holt, 1889).

DMAF   Manning J. Dauer, *The Adams Federalists* (Baltimore: The Johns Hopkins Press, 1968).

DMSM   Kenneth and Anna M. Roberts, eds., *Moreau de St. Méry's American Journey, 1793–1798* (New York: Doubleday, 1947).

DNL   Henri Doniol, ed., *Histoire de la participation de la France à l'établissement des États-Unis d'Amérique* (Paris: Imprimerie Nationale, 1884–92), 6 vols.

DRDK   Kenneth Gordon Davies, ed., *Documents of the American Revolution 1770–1783,* Great Britain Colonial Office Series (Dublin: Irish Academic Press, 1972–76), 21 vols.

DSFR   John Hall Stewart, *A Documentary Survey of the French Revolution* (New York: Macmillan, 1951).

EHFJ   Jean Pierre Marie Flourens, *Éloge historique de Benjamin Delessert* (Paris: Didot Frères, 1850).

EMAF   Stanley Elkins and Eric McKitrick, *The Age of Federalism* (New York: Oxford Univ. Press, 1993).

FBRS   Bernard Fay, *The Revolutionary Spirit in France and America* (New York: Cooper Square Publishers, 1966).

FETT   James Morton Smith, *Freedom's Fetters: The Alien and Sedition Laws and American Civil Liberties* (Ithaca, N.Y.: Cornell Univ. Press, 1956).

FFKL   Lee Kennett, *The French Forces in America 1780–1783* (Westport, Conn.: Greenwood Press, 1977).

FNE   Allan Forbes and Paul F. Cadman, *France and New England,* (Boston: State Street Trust, 1925), 2 vols.

FUMR   Richard B. Morris, *The Forging of the Union, 1781–1789* (New York: Harper & Row, 1987).

GJAY   Jerome A. Greene, *The Allies at Yorktown: A Bicentennial History of the Siege of 1781* (Denver: U.S. National Park Service, 1976).

GLBE   Lawrence Henry Gipson, *The British Empire before the American Revolution* (New York: Knopf, 1936–70), 15 vols.

GLEF   Louis R. Gottschalk, *The Era of the French Revolution (1715–1815)* (Boston: Houghton Mifflin, 1929).

GLM   Deborah Norris Logan, *Memoir of Dr. George Logan of Stenton,* edited by Francis A. Logan (Philadelphia: Historical Society of Penn., 1899).

GLP   Frederick B. Tolles, *George Logan of Philadelphia* (New York: Oxford Univ. Press, 1953).

GUS   *Gazette of the United States* (Philadelphia).

GWCA   Charles H. Ambler, *George Washington and the West* (New York: Russell & Russell, 1971).

GWD   John C. Fitzpatrick, ed., *The Diaries of George Washington, 1748–1799* (Boston: Houghton Mifflin, 1925), 4 vols.

GWF   James Thomas Flexner, *George Washington . . .* (Boston: Little Brown, 1965–72), 4 vols.

GWFB   Bernard Fay, *George Washington: Republican Aristocrat.* (Boston: Houghton Mifflin, 1931).

GWFS   Douglas Southall Freeman, *George Washington: A Biography* (New York: Charles Scribner's Sons, 1948–1957), 7 vols.

GWKB   Bernhard Knollenberg, *Washington and the Revolution. A Reappraisal* (New York: Macmillan, 1940).

GWKC   Thomas A. Lewis, *For King and Country* (New York: HarperCollins, 1993).

GWMK   Marvin Kitman, *The Making of the President 1789* (New York: Harper & Row, 1989).

GWPA   Philander D. Chase, ed., *The Papers of George Washington: Revolutionary War Series* (Charlottesville: Univ. Press of Virginia, 1985–), 6 vols.

GWPB   Dorothy Twohig, ed., *The Papers of George Washington: Presidential Series* (Charlottesville: Univ. Press of Virginia, 1987–), 6 vols.

GWPD   W.W. Abbot, ed. *The Papers of George Washington: Colonial Series* (Charlottesville: Univ. Press of Virginia, 1983–1995), 10 vols.

GWRH   Rupert Hughes, *George Washington . . .* (New York: William Morrow, 1926–30), 3 vols.

GWW   John C. Fitzpatrick, ed., *The Writings of George Washington* (Washington, D.C.: U.S. Government Printing Office, 1931–44), 39 vols.

GWWF   Worthington Chauncey Ford, ed., *The Writings of George Washington* (New York, London: G. P. Putnam's Sons, 1889–[93]), 14 vols.

GWWS   Jared Sparks, ed., *The Writings of George Washington* (New York, 1848), 12 vols.

HMP   Mme. Du Hausset, *Mémoires de madame du Hausset, femme de chambre de madame de Pompadour, et extrait des mémoires historiques et littéraires de Bachaumont, de l'année 1762 à l'année 1782 avec avant-propos et notices, par Fs. Barrière* (Paris: Firmin-Didot, 1846).

HNYJ   Thomas Jones, *History of New York During the Revolutionary War: and of the Leading Events in the Other Colonies at That Period* (New York: New-York Historical Society, 1879), 2 vols.

HP   Hewson Family Papers, American Philosophical Society.

HSKD   Sanford W. Higginbotham, *The Keystone in the Democratic Arch: Pennsylvania Politics 1800–1816* (Harrisburg: Penn. Historical and Museum Commission, 1952).

IRPT   Thomas Pakenham, *The Year of Liberty: The History of the Great Irish Rebellion of 1798* (London: Phoenix, 1992).

ITHP   Isaiah Thomas, *The History of Printing in America* (New York: Weathervane Books, 1970).

JAAA   L. H. Butterfield, Marc Friedlaender, and Mary-Jo Kline, eds. *The Book of Abigail and John: Selected Letters of the Adams Family, 1762–1784* (Cambridge: Harvard Univ. Press, 1975).

JABW   Walt Brown, *John Adams and the American Press* (Jefferson, N.C.: McFarland, 1995).

JAC   Peter Shaw, *Character of John Adams* (Chapel Hill: Univ. of North Carolina Press, 1976).

JADA   Lyman H. Butterfield, ed., *The Adams Papers: Diary and Autobiography of John Adams* (Cambridge, Mass.: Belknap Press of Harvard Univ. Press, 1961–1962), 4 vols.

JADR   James H. Hutson, *John Adams and the Diplomacy of the American Revolution* (Lexington: Univ. of Kentucky, 1980).

JAFA   Charles Francis Adams, ed., *Familiar Letters of John Adams and His Wife Abigail Adams During the Revolution* (Boston: Houghton, Mifflin, 1875).

JAFC   L. H. Butterfield et al., eds., *The Adams Papers: Adams Family Correspondence* (Cambridge, Mass.: Belknap Press of Harvard Univ. Press, 1963–93), 6 vols.

JAFW   Charles Francis Adams, ed., *Letters of John Adams Addressed to His Wife* (Boston: Little, Brown, 1841), 2 vols.

JAGC   Gilbert Chinard, *Honest John Adams* (Gloucester, Mass.: Peter Smith, 1976).

JAOF   *Old Family Letters: Copied from the Originals for Alexander Biddle; Series A-B.* (Philadelphia: J. B. Lippincott, 1892).

JAPA   Robert J. Taylor, ed., *The Adams Papers: Papers of John Adams* (Cambridge, Mass.: Belknap Press of Harvard Univ. Press, 1977–), 8 vols.

JAPM   Adams Papers Microfilm, Massachusetts Historical Society.

JAPP   Zoltan Haraszti, *John Adams and the Prophets of Progress* (Cambridge: Harvard Univ. Press, 1952).

JAPS   Page Smith, *John Adams* (New York: Doubleday, 1962), 2 vols.

JAPW   George A. Peek, Jr., ed., *The Political Writings of John Adams* (New York: Liberal Arts Press, 1954).

JATJ   Lester J. Cappon, ed., *The Adams-Jefferson Letters . . .* (Chapel Hill: Univ. of North Carolina Press, 1959).

JAWJ   John Wood, *The Suppressed History of the Administration of John Adams (from 1797 to 1801) As Printed and Suppressed in 1802*, J. H. Shelburne, ed. (Philadelphia, 1846).

JAWL   *Warren-Adams Letters, Being Chiefly a Correspondence Among John Adams, Samuel Adams, and James Warren,* (Boston: The Mass. Historical Society, 1917–25), 2 vols.

JAWO   Charles Francis Adams, ed., *The Works of John Adams . . .* (Boston: C. C. Little, J. Brown, 1850–1856), 10 vols.

JBZP   Edmund Berkeley and Dorothy Smith Berkeley, *John Beckley: Zealous Partisan in a Nation Divided* (Philadelphia: American Philosophical Society, 1973).

JCC   Worthington C. Ford et al., eds., *Journals of the Continental Congress 1774–1789* (Washington, D.C., U.S. Govt. Print Off., 1904–37), 34 vols.

JCCS   *Secret Journals of the Acts and Proceedings of Congress, from the First Meeting thereof to the Dissolution of the Confederation by the Adoption of the Constitution of the United States.* (Boston: Thomas B. Wait, 1820–21), 4 vols.

JCHT   Michael Durey, *"With the Hammer of Truth": James Thomson Callender and America's Early National Heroes* (Charlottesville: Univ. Press of Virginia, 1990).

JCHU   James Thomson Callender, *The American Annual Register, or, Historical Memoirs of the United States, for the year 1796* (Philadelphia: Bioren & Madan, 1797). REDX 31,905.

JCPB   James Thomson Callender, *The Prospect Before Us* (Richmond: Jones, Pleasants, Lyon, 1800), 2 vols. REDX 37,083 & 37,084.

JCSH   James Thomson Callender, *Sketches of the History of America* (Philadelphia: Snowden & M'Corkle, 1798). REDX 33,485.

JCUS   James Thomson Callender, *The History of the United States for 1796 . . .* (Philadelphia: Snowden & McCorkle, 1797). REDX 31,906.

JDBM   Charles Campbell, ed., *Some Materials to Serve for a Brief Memoir of John Daly Burk, Author of a History of Virginia* (Albany, N. Y.: J. Munsell, 1868).

JHB   W. T. Baxter, *The House of Hancock* (Cambridge, Mass.: Harvard Univ. Press, 1945).

JHHA   Herbert S. Allan, *John Hancock, Patriot in Purple* (New York: Beechhurst Press, 1953).

JJPA   Henry P. Johnston, ed., *The Correspondence and Public Papers of John Jay, 1763–1826* (New York: G. P. Putnam's Sons, 1890–93), 4 vols.

JMAD   Gaillard Hunt and James Brown Scott, eds., *The Debates in the Federal Convention of 1787 Which Framed the Constitution . . . Reported by James Madison . . .* (Buffalo, N.Y.: Prometheus Books, 1987), 2 vols.

JMAP   William T. Hutchinson and William M. E. Rachal, eds., *The Papers of James Madison* (Chicago: Univ. of Chicago Press, 1962–), 17 vols.

JMAW   Gaillard Hunt, ed., *Writings of James Madison* (New York: G. P. Putnam's Sons, 1900–10), 9 vols.

JMOW   Stanislaus M. Hamilton, ed., *The Writings of James Monroe* (New York: G. P. Putnam's Sons, 1898–1903), 7 vols.

JPBL   Lance Banning, *The Jeffersonian Persuasion* (Ithaca, N.Y.: Cornell Univ. Press, 1978).

JPJ   Phillips Russell, *John Paul Jones: Man of Action* (New York: Blue Ribbon Books, 1927)

JWM   Edgar S. Maclay, A.M., ed., *Journal of William Maclay, United States Senator from Pennsylvania, 1789–1791* (New York: D. Appleton, 1890).

JWMA   William Maclay, *Sketches of Debate in the First Senate of the United States in 1789–90–91* (New York: Burt Franklin, 1880).

KGFJ   Sir John Fortescue, ed., *The Correspondence of King George the Third (1760–1783)* (London: Macmillan, 1927–28), 6 vols.

KMM   Monica Mary Gardner, *Kosciuszko: A Biography* (New York: C. Scribner's Sons, 1920).

KRW   Ethelbert Dudley Warfield, *The Kentucky Resolutions of 1798* (New York: G. P. Putnam's Sons, 1894).

LC   Library of Congress.

LCC   Edmund Cody Burnett, ed., *Letters of Members of the Continental Congress* (Washington, D.C.: Carnegie Institution of Washington, 1921–36), 8 vols.

LCCS   Paul A. Smith, ed., *Letters of the Members of the Continental Congress* (Washington, 1994–), 21 vols.

LFCA   Louis Gottschalk, *Lafayette Comes to America* (Chicago: Univ. of Chicago Press, 1935).

LFGB   Louis Gottschalk, *Lafayette Between the American and the French Revolutions, 1783–1789* (Chicago: Univ. of Chicago Press, 1950).

LFL   Louis Gottschalk, ed., *The Letters of Lafayette to Washington, 1777–1799* (Philadelphia: American Phil. Society, 1976).

LFM   George Washington Lafayette, ed., *Mémoires, correspondance, et manuscrits du General Lafayette, publiés par sa famille* (Bruxelles: Société Belge de Librairie, 1857), 2 vols.

LFSL   Stanley J. Idzerda, ed., *Lafayette in the Age of the American Revolution: Selected Letters and Papers, 1776–1790* (Ithaca, N.Y.: Cornell Univ. Press, 1977), 5 vols.

LJLC   Jean-Pierre-Louis de Luchet, *Les contemporains de 1789 et 1790, ou les opinions débattues pendant la première législature . . .* (Paris: Lejay fils, 1790), 3 vols.

LP   *The Lee Papers: Collections of the New-York Historical Society for the Year 1872* (New York: New York-Historical Society, 1872–75), 2 vols.

LTNA   François-Alexandre-Frédéric, duc de La Rochefoucauld-Liancourt, *Travels Through the United States of North America, the Country of the Iroquois, and Upper Canada, in the years 1795, 1796, and 1797 . . .* (London: R. Phillips, 1799), 2 vols.

LWSR   William Bell Clark, *Lambert Wickes, Sea Raider and Diplomat* (New Haven: Yale Univ. Press, 1932).

MCA   Mathew Carey, *Autobiography* (Brooklyn, N.Y.: Eugene L. Schwaab, 1942).

MFBS   Frank Luther Mott, *Golden Multitudes: The Story of Best Sellers in the United States* (New York: Macmillan, 1947).

MFDR   Frank Moore, *The Diary of The Revolution* [reprinted] (Hartford: J. B. Burr, 1876).

MHCC   Honore-Gabriel Mirabeau de Riquetti, *Considerations on the Order of Cincinnatus To Which Are Added Several Original Papers Relative to That Institution* (London, 1784).

MHS   Massachusetts Historical Society.

MJFE   John C. Miller, *The Federalist Era 1789–1801* (New York: Harper & Row, 1960).

MJOR   John C. Miller, *Origins of the American Revolution* (Boston: Little, Brown, 1943).

MJSS   Joachim Merlant, *Soldiers and Sailors of France in the American War for Independence (1776–1783),* transl. by Mary Bushnell Coleman (New York: Charles Scribner's Sons, 1920).

MJTF   John C. Miller, *Triumph of Freedom 1775–1783* (Boston: Little, Brown, 1948).

MLA   Aleine Austin, *Matthew Lyon, "New Man" of the Democratic Revolution, 1749–1822* (Univ. Park: Pennsylvania State Univ. Press, 1981).

MRFC   Richard G. Miller, *Philadelphia–The Federalist City: A Study of Urban Politics, 1789–1801* (Port Washington, N.Y.: Kennikat Press, 1976).

MRPM   Richard B. Morris, *The Peacemakers: The Great Powers and American Independence* (New York: Harper & Row, 1965).

MSOH   Samuel Eliot Morison, *The Oxford History of the American People* (New York: Oxford Univ. Press, 1965).

ND   Dudley W. Knox, ed., *Naval Documents Related to the Quasi-War between the United States and France* (Washington, D.C.: U.S. Government Printing Off., 1935–38), 7 vols.

NDR   William Bell Clark et al., eds., *Naval Documents of the American Revolution* (Washington: U.S. Government Printing Office, 1964–), 10 vols.

NGL   George Washington Greene, *The Life of Nathanael Greene* (New York: Hurd and Houghton, 1867), 3 vols.

NJUV   Julian Ursyn Niemcewicz, *Under Their Vine and Fig Tree: Travels Through America in 1797–1799, 1805 . . .* transl. and ed. by Metchie J. E. Budka (Elizabeth, N.J.: Grassmann Publishing, 1965).

ODF   *Our Debt to France* (New York: Washington Lafayette Institution, 1926).

PAAS   *Proceedings of the American Antiquarian Society* (Worcester, Mass.: American Antiquarian Society).

PAFC   John McMaster and Frederick Stone, eds., *Pennsylvania and the Federal Constitution 1787–1788* (New York: Da Capo Press, 1970), 2 vols.

PAPS   *Proceedings of the American Philosophical Society* (Philadelphia: American Philosophical Society, 1838–), 100+ vols.

PDS   Cornelius William Stafford, ed., *The Philadelphia Directory for 1798* (Philadelphia: William W. Woodward, 1798).

PG   *Porcupine's Gazette* (Philadelphia).

PGP   *Pennsylvania Gazette* (Philadelphia).

PHL   William Wirt Henry, *Patrick Henry: Life, Correspondence and Speeches* (New York: Charles Scribner's Sons, 1891), 3 vols.

PJFR   James Breck Perkins, *France in the American Revolution* (Williamstown, Mass.: Corner House Publishers, 1970).

PMHB   *Pennsylvania Magazine of History and Biography* (Philadelphia: Historical Society of Penn., 1877–), 96+ vols.

PRA   *The Complete Poor Richard's Almanacks Published by Benjamin Franklin,* reproduced in facsimile by Whitfield J. Bell, Jr. (Barre, Mass.: Imprint Society, 1970), 2 vols.

RARW   Gordon S. Wood, *The Radicalism of the American Revolution* (New York: Vintage Books, 1993).

RANV   M. L'Abbé Robin, *Nouveau voyage dans l'Amérique septentrionale en l'année 1781, et campagne de l'armée de M. Le Comte de Rochambeau* (Philadelphia, 1782).

RDCS   Jared Sparks, ed., *The Diplomatic Correspondence of the American Revolution.* (Boston: N. Hale and Gray & Bowen, 1829–30), 12 vols.

RDCW   Francis Wharton, ed., *The Revolutionary Diplomatic Correspondence of the United States* (Washington, D.C.: U.S. Government Printing Office, 1889), 6 vols.

REDX   *Early American Imprints, First Series, 1639–1800. Evans [microform]* (New York: Readex Microprint, 1983). Microfiche.

RHLL   James Curtis Ballagh, ed., *The Letters of Richard Henry Lee* (New York: Macmillan, 1911–14), 2 vols.

RJMP   James D. Richardson, *A Compilation of the Messages and Papers of the Presidents, 1789–1897* (Washington, D.C.: U.S. Government Printing Office, 1896–99), 10 vols.

RKLK   Charles R. King, ed., *The Life and Correspondence of Rufus King* (New York: G. P. Putnam's Sons, 1894–1900), 6 vols.

RWA   *Weekly Advertiser of Reading* (Berks County, Pennsylvania).

SCRT   *Report of the Trial of the Hon. Samuel Chase . . . Before the High Court of Impeachment . . .* (Baltimore: Samuel Butler and George Keatings, 1805).

SDAR   Daniel Sisson, *The American Revolution of 1800* (New York: Alfred A. Knopf, 1974).

SDBF   Rupert Furneaux, *Saratoga: The Decisive Battle* (London: George Allen & Unwin, 1971).

SDOP   Donald H. Stewart, *The Opposition Press of the Federalist Period* (Albany: State Univ. of New York Press, 1969).

SFAC   Benjamin Franklin Stevens, ed., *B. F. Stevens's Facsimiles of Manuscripts in European Archives Relating to America, 1773–1783* (London: Malby & Sons, 1889–1895), 24 portfolios.

SFP   Shaw Family Papers, Library of Congress.

SJPC   J. Paul Selsam, *The Pennsylvania Constitution of 1776* (Philadelphia: Univ. of Pennsylvania Press, 1936).

SJPF   Jeffery A. Smith, *Printers and Press Freedom* (New York: Oxford Univ. Press, 1988).

SJRH   John Jay Smith, ed., *Letters of Doctor Richard Hill and His Children . . .* (Philadelphia: privately printed, 1854).

SLFR   Laura Charlotte Sheldon, *France and the American Revolution 1763–1778* (Ithaca, N.Y.: Andrus & Church, 1900).

SRMG   George Richards Minot, *The History of the Insurrections in Massachusetts in the Year 1786 . . .* (Boston: James W. Burditt, 1810).

SSC   Simon Schama, *Citizens: A Chronicle of the French Revolution* (New York: Alfred A. Knopf, 1989).

SWHA   Helen Augur, *Secret War of Independence* (New York: Duell, Sloan & Pearce, 1955).

SWHP   J. Thomas Scharf and Thompson Westcott, *History of Philadelphia, 1609–1884* (Philadelphia: L. H. Everts, 1884), 3 vols.

TCER   Jacob E. Cooke, *Tench Coxe and the Early Republic* (Chapel Hill: Univ. of North Carolina Press, 1978).

TCPL   Dumas Malone, *The Public Life of Thomas Cooper, 1793–1839* (New Haven: Yale Univ. Press, 1926).

THRF   H. M. Tinkcom, *The Republicans and Federalists in Pennsylvania, 1790–1801* (Harrisburg, 1950).

TJAH   Claude G. Bowers, *Jefferson and Hamilton* (Boston: Houghton Mifflin, 1925).

TJJC   Chauncey Ford, ed., *Thomas Jefferson and James Thomson Callender 1798–1802* (Brooklyn, N.Y.: Historical Printing Club, 1897).

TJJM   James Morton Smith, ed., *The Republic of Letters: The Correspondence Between Jefferson and Madison 1776–1826* (New York: W. W. Norton, 1995), 3 vols.

TJMD   Dumas Malone, *Jefferson and His Time* (Boston: Little, Brown, 1948–1981), 6 vols.

TJMJ   James Thacher, *Military Journal During the American Revolutionary War from 1775 to 1783* (Boston: Richardson and Lord, 1823).

TJPB   Julian P. Boyd et al., eds., *The Papers of Thomas Jefferson* (Princeton, N.J.: Princeton Univ. Press, 1950–), 26 vols.

TJPM   Thomas Jefferson Papers Microfilm (Library of Congress).

TJWF   Paul Leicester Ford, ed., *The Works of Thomas Jefferson*. Federal Edition (New York, London: G. P. Putnam's Sons, 1904–5), 12 vols.

TJWL   Andrew A. Lipscomb and Ellery Bergh, eds., *The Writings of Thomas Jefferson* (Washington, 1903–4), 20 vols.

TMH   Hunter Miller, ed., *Treaties and Other International Acts of the United States of America* (Washington, D.C.: U.S. Government Printing Office, 1931).

TPAD   Gerard H. Clarfield, *Timothy Pickering and American Diplomacy, 1795–1800* (Columbia, Mo.: Univ. of Missouri Press, 1969).

TPHD   David Freeman Hawke, *Paine* (New York: Harper & Row, 1974).

TPKJ   John Keane, *Tom Paine: A Political Life.* (Boston: Little, Brown, 1995).

TPLW   Thomas Paine, *Letter to George Washington, President of the United States of America, On Affairs Public and Private* (Philadelphia: Benjamin Franklin Bache, 1796). REDX 30,951.

TPPM   Pickering Papers Microfilm, Massachusetts Historical Society.

TPTB   Benjamin Bussey Thatcher, ed., *Traits of the Tea Party: Being A Memoir of George R. T. Hewes, One of the Last of Its Survivors* (New York: Harper & Brothers, 1835).

TPW   Philip S. Foner, ed., *The Complete Writings of Thomas Paine* (New York: Citadel Press, 1969), 2 vols.

TYQ   Lyon G. Tyler, ed., *Tyler's Quarterly Historical and Genealogical Magazine* (Richmond, Va.: Richmond Press, 1919–1952), 33 vols.

UHRA   Jackson Turner Main, *The Upper House in Revolutionary America 1763–1788* (Madison: Univ. of Wisconsin Press, 1967).

W&A   George Gibbs, ed., *Memoirs of the Administrations of Washington and John Adams* (New York, 1907), 2 vols.

WBRA   Robert C. Alberts, *The Golden Voyage. The Life and Times of William Bingham 1752–1804* (Boston: Houghton Mifflin, 1969).

WCED   G.D.H. Cole, ed., *Letters from William Cobbett to Edward Thornton Written in the Years 1797 to 1800* (London: Oxford Univ. Press, 1937).

WCPM   George Spater, *William Cobbett: The Poor Man's Friend* (Cambridge, Mass.: Cambridge Univ. Press, 1982).

WCPW   William Cobbett, *Porcupine's Works* (London, 1801), 12 vols.

WCWR   Christopher Ward, *The War of the Revolution* (New York: Macmillan, 1952), 2 vols.

WDBF   William Duane, ed., *The Works of Dr. Benjamin Franklin* (Philadelphia, 1808–18), 6 vols.

WDBM   *Biographical Memoire of William J. Duane* (Philadelphia: Claxton, Remsen, and Haffelfinger, 1868).

WDCA   Allen C. Clark, *William Duane* (Washington, D.C.: W. F. Roberts, 1905).

WDGE   Elizabeth Duane Gillespie, *A Book of Remembrance* (Philadelphia: J. B. Lippincott, 1901).

WDKP   Kim Tousley Phillips, *William Duane, Radical Journalist in the Age of Jefferson* (New York: Garland Publishers, 1989).

WDLW   [William Duane,] *A Letter to George Washington, President of the United States: Containing Strictures on his Address of the Seventeenth of Sept. 1796, Notifying his Relinquishment of the Presidential Office,* by Jasper Dwight, of Vermont (Philadelphia: Benjamin Franklin Bache, 1796). REDX 31,315.

WDME   *Minutes of Examination, Taken in Short Notes—on the Trial of the Rioters, for a Riot and Assault on William Duane, on the 15 May, 1799—Trial 28 Apr., 1801* (Philadelphia, 1801?).

WDRP   William Duane, *The Revolutionary Part,* Vol. 4 (1798) of John Gifford, *The History of France, from the Earliest Time Till the Death of Louis Sixteenth . . . and Continued from the Above Period Until the Conclusion of the Present War, by a Citizen of the United States [William Duane]* (Philadelphia: Stewart & Rowson, 1796–98), 4 vols. REDX 33,796, 48,414.

WFST   Francis Wharton, ed., *State Trials of the United States During the Administrations of Washington and Adams* (Philadelphia: Carey and Hart, 1849).

WLFA   Leonard D. White, *The Federalists: A Study in Administrative History, 1789–1801* (New York: Free Press, 1948).

WPAE   Vincent J. Esposito, ed., *The West Point Atlas of American Wars* (New York: Praeger Publishers, 1959), 2 vols.

WWHJ   Edwin Wolf and Maxwell Whiteman, *The History of the Jews in Philadelphia* (Philadelphia: Jewish Publication Society, 1956, 1975).

YCJH   Henry P. Johnston, *The Yorktown Campaign and The Surrender of Cornwallis 1781* (New York: Harper & Bros., 1881).

YF   Thomas Condie and Richard Folwell, *History of the Pestilence, Commonly Called Yellow Fever, Which Almost Desolated Philadelphia, in the Months of August, September and October, 1798* (Philadelphia: Press of R. Folwell, 1798). REDX 35,335; 35,336; 36,287(#5).

[1] Detail, frontispiece (plate #2), BRP. William Birch etched his BRP engravings during 1798 & 1799 and appears to have sold some as individual prints early in 1799. See PG, Feb. 1, 1799.

[2] Detail, plate #12, BRP.

[3] Detail, plate #18, BRP.

[4] JA to Dr. Benjamin Rush, Apr. 12, 1809, JAWO, IX, 619.

[5] WDRP, 2.

[6] Detail, plate #19, BRP.

[7] GW to Benjamin Walker, Phil., Jan. 12, 1797, GWW, XXXV, 363–364.

[8] [Paul Wentworth], "Minutes respecting political Parties in America and Sketches of the leading Persons in each Province" [app. 1778] . . . The Endorsement . . . by the hand of Wm Eden. SFAC, V, 487. Like the memorandum from Rev. J. Vardill to William Eden, Apr. 11, 1778, "Sketches of American public Characters and Hints for the use of the Commissioners," SFAC, IV, 438, Wentworth's "Minutes . . ." was probably a briefing paper for the Carlisle Peace Commissioners who were sent to America to thwart a Franco-American alliance. See BSDR, 68 n.-69 n., BFAW, 580–583, 589–593.

[9] JA to Dr. Benjamin Rush, Apr. 12, 1809, JAWO, IX, 619.

[10] Detail, plate #8, BRP.

[11] AGA, May 12, 1800.

[12] Detail, plate #15, BRP.

[13] TJ to John Taylor, Phil., June 1, 1798, TJWF, VIII, 430, 432.

[14] See JAC, 231 ("Decidedly, some time after he became Vice President, Adams concluded that the United States would have to adopt a hereditary legislature and a monarch").

[15] See AGA, July 8, 14, Aug. 14, Sept. 27, 29, 1797, Mar. 30, 1798. Various people heard JA say Americans would not be happy without a king. SDOP, 490.

[16] JWM, 29, 63, BCMP, 192, JA to Jabez Bowen, June 26, 1789, JAPM, Reel 115.

[17] See AGA, Nov. 4, 1796, JWM, 30, JBZP, 46, JAPM, Reel 376, JA to Trumbull, Apr. 2, 1790, JAPM, Reel 115, and JA to Abigail Adams, May 19, 1789, JAPM, Reel 372.

[18] PG, May 14, 1798, has a detailed description of the cockade.

[19] Because this history depicts a radical 1790's Democratic-Republican point of view, your author has declined to use the narrative voice of the traditional historian (presumably impartial, implicitly omniscient, nearly anonymous, emotionally opaque) and has instead posited the *chooser-of-fact* to be William Duane, as he might narrate his life and times *"with the advantage of these intervening years."* Those who object to the anachronicity and other deficiencies of this choice may interpret the narrator's first-person/present-tense statements to be the author's third-person/past-tense statements about WD and his time (they are endnoted). WD's actual voice (as opposed to the narrative device) appears in Book Two and predominates in Book Three of this work, so WD's actual voice can be compared with your author's flawed, though useful, narrative device.

[20] Italicized sentence quoted verbatim from WD's letter to Stephen R. Bradley, Nov. 10, 1808, quoted in WDCA, 65–68.

[21] Detail, plate #20, BRP.

[22] The features of WD's life prior to his arrival in America are found in WDKP, 4–50, WDBM, 1–5, DAB, V, 467.

[23] Because the nation spoke and wrote of the paper as the *Aurora* or *Philadelphia Aurora* rather than as the *Aurora General Advertiser* (its masthead name), your author has frequently used the popular name when referring to the paper. For the history of the paper's masthead names, see BCAN, 891–892.

[24] TJ's words. TJ to James Monroe, Monticello, Oct. 19, 1823, TJWF, XII, 316.

[25] Detail, plate #9, BRP.

[26] AGA, Aug. 11, 1802, BFBS, 158.

[27] LTNA, II, 376.

[28] Detail, plate #20, BRP.

[29] N.H., Mass., R.I., Conn., Vt., N.Y., N.J., Pa., Del. , Md., Va., Ky., Tenn., N.C., S.C., Ga.

[30] *Philadelphia Monthly Magazine,* June 1798, 333–334.

[31] NJUV, 42, 44.

[32] Detail, plate #3, BRP.

[33] ANC, 5C, 2S, 961–962, MLA, 17–19, 27–29, 73–102, BFBT, 332, 362.

[34] BFBS, 135.

[35] ANC, 5C, 2S, 968.

[36] Detail, plate #22, BRP.

[37] ANC, 5C, 2S, 1034. See PG, Feb. 9, 14, 15, 16, 1798, TJAH, 360–361.

[38] BFBT, 331–332.

[39] AGA, Feb. 14, 1798.

[40] See BFBW, Pref.

[41] LTNA, II, 376.

[42] Detail, plate #22, BRP.

[43] *Philadelphia Monthly Magazine,* June 1798, 333–334.

[44] DMSM, 260–317.

[45] BFBB, 337.

[46] LTNA, II 379–380.

[47] DMSM, 316.

[48] See BFBP, 56–57, BFBT, 60–61.

[49] DMSM, 262–263.

[50] See AGA, Apr. 23, 1798.

[51] RHMP, I, 235, 239.

[52] TJ to Edward Rutledge, Phil., June 24, 1797, TJWF, VIII, 316, 318–319.

[53] Elizabeth Hewson to Thomas Hewson, June 5, 1797, HP, cited by BFBS, 147.

[54] AHO. See AHP, XXI, 121–144, JBZP, 75–85,168, TJMD, III, 326–328.

[55] *American Minerva* (N.Y.), May 14, 1797. The letter first appeared in the *Moniteur* (Paris) of Jan. 25, 1797. TJMD, III, 301–306, GWF, IV, 382.

[56] TJ to Philip Mazzei, Monticello, Apr. 24, 1796, TJWF, VIII, 235, 238–241. See TJMD, III, 267–268, xxiv, TCER, 376.

[57] ANC, 5C, 2S, 1200–1202.

[58] See SDOP, 609–612, 630–631.

[59] SDOP, 609–612.

[60] BFPP, 175.

[61] ITHP, 35.

[62] In general, see Joseph Moxon, *Mechanick Exercises on the Whole Art of Printing (1683–1684)* (London: Oxford Univ., 1958), Lawrence C. Wroth, *Benjamin Franklin: The Printer at Work* (N.Y.: privately, 1981), Lawrence C. Wroth, *The Colonial Printer* (Portland: Southworth-Anthoensen Press, 1938), Elizabeth Harris and Clinton Sisson, *The Common Press* (Boston: David R. Godine, 1978), Caleb Stower,*The Printer's Grammar* (London: Gregg Press, 1965), and Edward Grattan, *The Printer's Companion* (N.Y.: Garland, 1981).

[63] TJ to James Monroe, Mar. 8, 1798, TJWF, VIII, 380, 381.

[64] AGA, Aug. 4, 19, 1800. John Fenno's son, John Ward Fenno, denied JA helped. GUS, Oct. 14, 1800.

[65] Details of John Fenno's life are taken from John Hench,"Letters of John Fenno and John Ward Fenno," PAAS, Vol. 89, Part 1 (1979), 300–301. On Fenno being printer to the Senate, see AGA, June 19, 1798, Jan. 8, 1799.

[66] See TJMD, III, 142.

[67] JCPB, II, 148.

[68] AGA, May 8, June 18, Nov. 8, 1794, Jan. 15, 1795, BFBS, 118–119.

[69] WCPM, 17.

[70] WCPM, 68–69, BFBB, 282–283.

[71] PG, Mar. 4, 1797.

[72] BFWE, 269.

[73] BF published *Poor Richard's Almanacks* from 1733 to 1758. See PRA.

[74] BFPP, 72.

[75] AGA, Oct. 2, 1790.

[76] BF to Deborah Read Franklin, London, Aug. 14, 1771, BFPL, XVIII, 204–205.

[77] BF to Jane Mecum, Jan. 13, 1772, BFPL, XIX, 29.

[78] BF to Richard Bache, Passy, Nov. 11, 1784, BFSM, IX, 278–279.

[79] EHFJ, 6, as translated by FNE, II, 80.

[80] BFB to Margaret Markoe, May 2, 1790, BFBC, Film 1506, Reel 3. See BFBS, 102.

[81] SJPF, 111–112.

[82] TJ to Samuel Smith, Monticello, Aug. 22, 1798, TJWF, VIII, 443–446.

[83] James Monroe to Unidentified, Apr. 23, 1794, Simon Gratz Collection, Hist. Soc. of Penn., Case II, Box 16.

[84] E.g., AGA, Oct. 21, Dec. 29, 1795, Apr. 11, 12 & 16, 1796, Jan. 23, 1797.

[85] Benjamin Rush to JA, June 4, 1812, in A&R, 223.

[86] AGA, Jan. 2, 1793.

[87] AGA, Jan. 21, 1793.

[88] AGA, Feb. 16, 1793. See GUS, Feb. 23, 1793.

[89] AGA, Nov. 23, 1795.

[90] AGA, Sept. 11, 1795.

[91] AGA, Jan. 23, 26, Feb. 4, 1793.

[92] AGA, Dec. 7, 1792.

[93] AGA, Jan. 29, 1792. See also AGA, Nov. 23, 1795.

[94] AGA, Feb. 5, 18, 1793. See also AGA, Dec. 7, 1792.

[95] TJ to Edward Rutledge, Monticello, Nov. 30, 1795, TJWF, VIII, 199, 200.

[96] AGA, Aug. 22, 1795.

[97] AGA, Jan. 1, 13, 1796.

[98] AGA, Sept. 18, 1795. See AGA, Sept. 11, Oct. 16, Dec. 1, 1795.

[99] AGA, Nov. 2, Oct. 23, 27, 29, 30, 1795. See James Thomson Callender on same subject, JCHU, 247–248.

[100] AGA, Nov. 20, 1795.

101 AGA, Nov. 18, 1795. See AGA, Oct. 16, Nov. 26, 1795.

102 AGA, Oct. 21, 1795.

103 AGA, Sept. 24, 1795.

104 AGA, Dec. 29, 1795. See AGA, Dec. 21, 1796.

105 *Letters from George Washington to Several of His Friends, in June and July, 1776 . . .* (Phil.: Repub'd at Federal Press [by BFB],1795), 42. REDX 28,969. See AGA, Nov. 13, 1795.

106 James D. Tagg, "BFB's Attack on GW," PMHB, C (Apr. 1976), 194. See EMAF, 516.

107 GW to Gen'l Henry Lee, July 21, 1793, GWW, XXXIII, 23–24. See JABW, 53–55.

108 GW to Sec. of State, Mt. Vernon, July 18, 1796, GWW, XXXV, 143–144. See JABW, 53–55.

109 GW to Benjamin Walker, Phil., Jan. 12, 1797, GWW, XXXV, 363–364.

110 JA to Abigail Adams, Mar. 25, 1796, JAFW, II, 214, DMAF, 92. See JABW, 55–56.

111 GW to Alexander Hamilton, Mt. Vernon, June 26, 1796, GWW, XXXV, 101, 103.

112 Farewell Address (first draft), [May 15, 1796], GWW, XXXV, 51, 59. See BFBS, 145–146, AHWL, VIII, 203, JABW, 56–57. GWF, IV, 285 gives May 1 as date.

113 GW to Sec. of Treas., Mt. Vernon, July 6, 1796, GWW, XXXV, 125–126.

114 GW to Sec. of State Timothy Pickering, July 18, 1796, GWW, XXXV, 144–45.

115 GW's Farewell Address is dated the 17th but was first published in *Claypoole's American Daily Advertiser* (Phil.) on Sept. 19, 1796.

116 AGA, Mar. 6, 1797. See GWFS, VII, 439.

117 GW to Jeremiah Wadsworth, Mar. 6, 1797, GWW, XXXV, 420–421.

118 GUS, Mar. 7, 1797.

119 Benjamin Rush to JA, June 4, 1812, A&R, 223. See JABW, 57.

120 GW to Rev. William Gordon, Mt. Vernon, Oct. 15, 1797, GWW, XXXVI, 48, 50.

121 GW to Sec. of State, Mt. Vernon, Feb. 6, 1798, GWW, XXXVI, 155–156. See CRIS, 47.

122 TJMD, III, xxv, 332.

123 JCUS.

124 JCUS, 204–230. See JBZP, 162–163.

125 GUS, July 8, 1797. See JCUS, viii.

126 AHO. See TJMD, III, 328.

127 TJ to John Taylor, Oct. 8, 1797, TJWL, XVIII, 201–202. See JBZP, 169.

128 JCUS, 220.

129 JCSH, 100.

130 1757 ed., PRA, II, 338.

131 TPLW, 8, See BFB's approval of Paine's opinion, AGA, Dec. 22, 1796, and article to same effect, Sept. 24, 1795.

132 JA to Abigail Adams, Dec. 4, 1796, JAFW, II, 231, JA to Abigail Adams, Dec. 8, 1796, JAFW, II, 233–234.

133 James Monroe, *A View of the Conduct of the Executive, in the Foreign Affairs of the United States, Connected with the Mission to the French Republic, During the Years 1794, 5, & 6* (Phil.: BFB, 1797), REDX 32,491. See TJMD, III, 337–339.

134 AGA, Aug. 13, 1795 republished material sent with a June 23rd letter from Monroe to BFB, JMOW, II, 292–304.

135 Timothy Pickering obtained a copy of AGA. Pickering to Ed. Carrington, Dec. 9, 1797, TPPM. The disclosure persuaded GW to recall James Monroe. GW to Sec. of State, July 8, 1796, GWW, XXXV, 127–128 & 128n, TPAD, 55–5, BBMM, 9–79.

136 WDLW.

137 WDKP, 4, WDCA, 8.

138 WDKP, 5, WDGE. See AGA, May 18, 1799.

139 AGA, Mar. 13, 14, 1797. See also GUS, Mar. 12, 1797, BFBT, 284. Reply by Webster in *American Minerva* (N.Y.), Mar. 17, 1797. See also SDOP, 531.

140 See JAPW, xxvi, GWMK, 59. Historian Rupert Hughes held the same view. GWRH, III, 412.

141 The Jumonville event is well described in GWRH, I, 114–157, II, 106 ff. See GLBE, VI, 31, R. A. Brock, ed., *Dinwiddie Papers*, 2 vols. (Richmond: Virginian Hist. Collections, 1883), I, 120, 121, 151, 170.

142 PG, Apr. 10, 1798 reports Callender's relief application to the overseer of the poor.

143 JCHT, 29–37.

144 JCHT, 43–51.

145 See AGA, Aug. 11, 1802, BFBT, 402, PG, Apr. 24, 1798, GUS, Apr. 24, 1798, JCHT, 105, 107, 200.

146 JCHT, 63.

147 It is clear that TJ's and Thomas Leiper's relationships to Callender were as charitable as they were political. On TJ, see TJJC, 9, 11, TJMD, III, xxv-xxvi, 332, 469–470, TJ to Stevens T. Mason, Oct. 11, 1798, TJWL, X, 61–62, SDOP, 473, JAPS, II, 978. On Thomas Leiper, see *Richmond Recorder* (Richmond), May 26, Aug. 4, 25, 1802, TJ to Madison, Apr. 26, 1798, TJJC, 9, JCHT, 106.

148 1752 ed., PRA, II, 150.

149 RJMP, I, 264.

150 On use of "Peggy," see Mary Coxe to Mar-

garet Hartman Markoe, Phil., Nov. 22, [1789], BFBC, Film 1506, Reel 2.

[151] 1746 ed., PRA, I, 320.

[152] *Biographical Catalogue of the Matriculates of the College of the University of Penn.: 1749–1893* (Phil.: Society of the Alumni, 1894), 26.

[153] BFBS, 90, BFBT, 72–74.

[154] See letters from BFB to Margaret H. Markoe, Apr. 20, June 5, 15, 21, 27, Aug. 17, 18, 23, 27, Sept. 8, 15, 19, 23, Oct. 3, 4, 1791, in BFBC, Film 1506, Reel 2.

[155] BFBT, 73–78.

[156] BFB to Le Veillard, Apr. 6, 1792, *BF Papers,* Pierpont Morgan Lib., N.Y., quoted in BFBT, 77.

[157] SDOP, 198, TJAH, 273. BFBP, 115.

[158] Elizabeth Hewson to Thomas Hewson, June 5, 1797, HP, quoted in BFBS, 147.

[159] 1751 ed., PRA, II, 114.

[160] PG, Mar. 12, 1798.

[161] On Nov. 9, 1793 (just before Robespierre ordered his arrest), Médéric-Louis-Elie Moreau de St. Méry sailed from Le Havre with his wife and two children. DMSM, xv-xvi.

[162] DMSM, x.

[163] Frank Luther Mott says Volney's *Ruins of Empires* was America's only French best-seller during the eighteenth century. MFBS, 63, 305.

[164] PAPS, XXII, 168 (Moreau de St. Méry) & 246 (Volney).

[165] Democratic-Republicans generally viewed violence in the French Revolution as regrettable but necessary to end monarchy. On BFB's and AGA's views, see BFBT, 119, 312–313.

[166] 1750 ed., PRA, II, 98. On the use of terms "Jacobin," "Democrat," and "Anti-Federalist," see AGA, July 4, 1799.

[167] GW to David Stuart, Jan. 8, 1797, GWW, XXXV, 360. See WCPM, 74–75.

[168] On June 2, 1797, Congressman William L. Smith reported, "Porcupine is a great favorite at court," JABW, 91.

[169] Abigail Adams to Mary Cranch, Mar. 13, 1798, AANL, 142–143.

[170] JDBM, 11–25.

[171] *Notes, drafts, and fragments of Presidential messages and proclamations,* JAPM, Reel 387. See DAQW, 68–69, 399.

[172] Abigail Adams to Mary Cranch, Mar. 13, 1798, AANL, 142, 144. See JABW, 93.

[173] ANC, 5C, 1S, 430, DMAF, 135.

[174] DMAF, 135. See CRIS, 44, AGA, June 28, 1800.

[175] JCHT, 52.

[176] See adv. in AGA, June 14, 1798.

[177] MCA. Originally appeared as series of letters in *New-England Magazine* (July 1833–Dec. 1834), Vol. VI, 60, 93, 227, 306, 400, Vol. VII, 61, 145, 239, 320, 401, 481. See Edward Carlos Carter, *The Political Activities of Mathew Carey, Nationalist, 1760–1814* (Ph.D. Thesis, Bryn Mawr College, 1962) (Univ. Microfilms Int'l, 1964).

[178] Dr. James Reynolds is not the man of the same name with whom (and with whose wife) Alexander Hamilton had improper connections.

[179] JCPB, I, 37.

[180] JCHT, 76–77.

[181] Dr. James Reynolds is identified as the author of pieces which appeared in the AGA on Jan. 24 ("South Front Street"), 26 ("Thomas Pickering"), 29 ("James Reynolds"), Feb. 5, 27, 1798, charging Sec. of State Timothy Pickering with receiving gratuities for the issuance of passports. Timothy Pickering to BFB, Jan 25, 1798 and Timothy Pickering to Rev. John Clark, Jan. 26, 1798 TPPM, XXXVII, 264–266, Rawle to Pickering, Feb. 27, 1798, TPPM, XXII, 48.

[182] See WDKP, 47, 52, ITHP, 390, BCAN, 924, 955, WDBM, 5.

[183] [Abigail Adams] to [BFB], Mar. 17, 1798, BFBC, Film 1506, Reel 3.

[184] 1739 ed., PRA, I, 160.

[185] AGA, June 30, July 1, 2, 4, 5, 12, 15, 20, 24, 28, Aug. 2, 1791. The responses of "Brutus" appear in June 30, July 1, 2, 21, 24, 1791. See BFBT, 125, SDOP, 536, TJAH, 84–85.

[186] AGA, Oct. 29, 1796, SDOP, 536.

[187] AGA, Oct. 25, 1796.

[188] AGA, Nov. 11, 1796.

[189] AGA, Oct. 29, 1796.

[190] AGA, Oct. 18, 1796.

[191] AGA, Nov. 11, 1796. See JAWO, IV, 553.

[192] AGA, Nov. 16, 1796.

[193] AGA, Nov. 17, 1796.

[194] AGA, Nov. 4, 1796.

[195] 1736 ed., PRA, I, 88.

[196] ANC, 5C, 2S, 1271–1272, TJMD, III, 370.

[197] TJ to James Madison, Phil., Mar. 21, 1798, TJWF, VIII, 386–388. See also TJ to James Monroe, Phil., Mar. 21, 1798, TJWF, VIII, 388–389, and TJ to Edward Pendleton, Phil., Apr. 2, 1798, TJWF, VIII, 394–397.

[198] Abigail Adams to Mary Cranch, Mar. 20, 1798, AANL, 146–147.

[199] GUS, Mar. 22, 1798.

[200] TJ to James Monroe, Phil., Mar. 21, 1798,

TJWF, VIII, 388–389. In letters of this date to Monroe and Madison, TJ was correct that the constitution required Congress to declare war but incorrect that it required more than a majority vote.

201 TJ to James Madison, Phil., Mar. 21, 1798, TJWF, VIII, 386–388.

202 ANC, 5C, 2S, 1285–1296.

203 RJMP, I, 268–270. See BFBT, 344.

204 "Petition from the Quakers of Philadelphia to Congress," Mar. 23, 1798, *Logan Papers* (Hist. Soc. of Penn.) as cited in MRFC, 104.

205 WD gives the full story of his expulsion from the House in AGA, July 29, 1800. See also AGA Mar. 24, 1798, PG, Nov. 3, 1798.

206 The $800 figure is elsewhere in AGA, Mar. 24, 1798. WD identified as the author of this letter on the basis of *Carey's United States Recorder* (Phil.), May 3, 1798, which states: "In the Aurora of the 24th Mar. last, two essays treated mr. Harper with freedom and justice. At the bottom of one of them, the writer, mr. William Duane, gave notice, that his name, though not published, was left with the printer."

207 Abigail Adams to William Smith, Phil., Mar. 24, 1798, Smith-Carter Papers (MHS).

208 TJ to BFB, Apr. 22, 1791, TJPB, XX, 246. See BFBT, 101, 114.

209 TJ to GW, Monticello, Sept. 9, 1792, TJPB, XXIV, 351, 356.

210 TJ to James Madison, June 9, 1793, TJWF, VII, 373, 376. See JABW, 53, 57, GWF, IV, 46.

211 Benjamin Rush to JA, June 4, 1812, A&R, 223. See JABW, 56–57.

212 GW to Henry Lee, July 21, 1793, GWW, XXXIII, 23–24. GW then spelled BFB's name phonetically. See JABW, 53, 56.

213 JMOW, III, 106–115.

214 ANC, 5C, 2S. 3717.

215 ANC, 5C, 2S, 1319–1320, 1327–1328, 1333.

216 PG, Mar. 31, 1798. See AGA, June 14, 1800.

217 GLP, 46–47, 3–4.

218 GLP, 98.

219 GLP, 111–114.

220 GLP, 142.

221 GLP, 147.

222 ANC, 5C, 2S, 1336.

223 AGW, 103.

224 AGW, 103.

225 WCPW, III, 253.

226 AGW, 114.

227 It was reported in the gazettes, e.g. AGA, Apr. 6, Dec. 9, 1797, PG, Apr. 6, 12, 13, 1797.

228 AGA, Dec 9, 1797 ("Comm of Penn vs. C. Humphreys").

229 Sec. of State Pickering to M. Clement Humphreys, Phil., Mar. 29, 1798, ND, I, 47.

230 Detail, plate #29, BRP. On identification of shipyard as Humphreys', see S. Robert Teitelman, *Birch's Views of Philadelphia: A Reduced Facsimile of the City of Philadelphia—as It Appeared in the Year 1800* (Phil.: Univ. of Penn. Press, 1983), plate #29.

231 AGA, Apr. 6, 1797. See also AGA, Dec. 9, 1797 ("Comm of Penn vs. C. Humphreys"). PG, Apr. 6 ("Measure for Measure"), 12 ("Clement Humphries"), 13, 1797, BFBS, 159–160, BFBT, 328, Edmund Kimball Alden, "BFB," in DAB, I, 462–463, BFBW, pref., GUS, Aug. 9, 1798. See also *Papers of Joshua Humphreys* (Hist. Soc. of Penn.).

232 1736 ed., PRA, I, 88.

233 PG, Apr. 2, 1798, GUS, Apr. 3, 1798.

234 1754 ed., PRA, II, 224.

235 ANC, 5C, 2S, 1358–1359, 1364, 1366, AGW, 106.

236 Abigail Adams to Mary Cranch, Phil., Mar. 31, 1798, AANL, 150.

237 GUS, Apr. 4, 1798.

238 ANC, 5C, 2S, 1367, 1370–1371.

239 JMAW, VI, 311–314.

240 NJUV, 55.

241 NJUV, xix-xxv.

242 ANC, 5C, 2S, 1374–1375.

243 ANC, 5C, 2S, 536–537.

244 Abigail Adams to Mary Cranch, Apr. 7, 1798, AANL, 153–155. See JAPS, II, 958.

245 On AGA's revelation that Pickering's office was taking bribes, see AGA, Jan. 24 ("South Front Street"), 26 ("Thomas Pickering"), 29 ("James Reynolds"), Feb. 5, 27, 1798, Timothy Pickering to BFB, Jan 25, 1798 and Timothy Pickering to Rev. John Clark, Jan. 26. TPPM, XXXVII, 264–266, Rawle to Pickering, Feb 27, 1798, TPPM, XXII, 48. Pickering wrote about the whole matter to GW, Jan 27, 1798, TPPM, and GW responded to the Sec. of State, on Feb. 6, 1798, GWW, XXXVI, 155–157. See BFBT, 330.

246 PG, Apr. 21, 1798.

247 Timothy Pickering to Alexander Hamilton, Phil., Apr. 9, 1798, AHP, XXI, 408–409.

248 See ANC, 5C, 2S, 3336–3360.

249 JA to Alexander Hamilton, Apr. 5, 1798, W&A, II, 44–44.

250 PG, Apr. 13, 1798.

251 1733 ed., PRA, I, 7.

252 NJUV, 56–58.

253 1736 ed., PRA, I, 84.

254 1733 ed., PRA, I, 7.

255 ANC, 5C, 2S, 1402 ff.

256 Dunwoody's was at 285 High between 7th and 8th Streets. PDS, 49.

257 AGA, Aug. 15, 1798.

258 GUS, Apr. 13, 1798.

259 PDS, 140.

260 1751 ed., PRA, II, 124.

261 Anas, TJWF, I, 345–346.

262 PG, Apr. 14, 1798.

263 GW to Sec. of State, Mt. Vernon, Apr. 16, 1798, GWW, XXXVI, 248–249.

264 GUS, Apr. 18, 1798.

265 Abigail Adams to Mary Cranch, Apr. 17, 1798, AANL, 155, 156, JAPS II, 961.

266 ANC, 5C, 2S, 1427, FETT, 26, DMAF, 152.

267 See BFFC, 79–80, AANL, 164 n.

268 Anonymous to JA, Apr. 18, 1798, JAPM, Reel 388. See FETT, 26.

269 1742 ed., PRA, II, 228.

270 Distance indicated in BFBL, 67.

271 NJUV, 60–62, 308.

272 TJ to Madison, Apr. 19, 1798, TJWF, VIII, 409–411.

273 See GLM, 57–60, TJ to Samuel Smith, Monticello, Aug. 22, 1798, TJWF, VIII, 443–447.

274 GLM, 54.

275 1754 ed., PRA, II, 228.

276 ANC, 5C, 2S, 1484–1485, FETT, 155.

277 1745 ed., PRA, I, 300.

278 NJUV, 62.

279 PAPS, XXII, 270.

280 DMSM, 352.

281 DMSM, 350–351.

282 PAPS, XXII, 270.

283 1747 ed., PRA, I, 352.

284 Abigail Adams to Mary Cranch, Apr. 21, 1798, AANL, 157, 159.

285 GUS, Apr. 23, 1798. See AGA, May 3, Aug. 6, 1798. Cameron's is in PDS, 32.

286 AGA, Aug. 15, 1798.

287 GUS, Apr. 23, 1798.

288 PG, Apr. 25, 1798.

289 1736 ed., PRA, I, 81.

290 An account is in SWHP, I, 493.

291 ANC, 5C, 2S, 548, See FETT, Chapt. IV, SDOP, 465, TJAH, 374–375, DMAF, 165.

292 ANC, 5C, 2S, 1545, 1553, DMAF, 304.

293 Probably it was Callender. Fenno claims in GUS, Apr. 27, 1798 that BFB and Callender attended. In AGA, Apr. 30, 1798, BFB denies he was there and claims that Callender was not then very active at the paper.

294 DMSM, 345–347.

295 Abigail Adams to Mary Cranch, Phil. Apr. 26, 1798, AANL, 164–165.

296 "Hail Columbia," sung to the tune of the "President's March," served as America's unofficial national anthem until 1931. See Joseph Hopkinson, Song adapted to the President's March: sung at the theatre by Mr. Fox, at his benefit (Phil.: J. Ormrod, 1798), REDX 33,895, FETT, 8–9, JAPS, II, 962–963.

297 GUS, Apr. 26, 1798.

298 GUS, Apr. 26, 1798.

299 1739 ed., PRA, I, 155.

300 Abigail Adams to Mary Cranch, Phil., Apr. 26, 1798, AANL, 164–165. See Abigail Adams to Mary Cranch, Phil., May 26, June 23, 1798, AANL, 179, 195–196.

301 TJ to James Madison, Phil., Apr. 26, 1798, TJWF, VIII, 411–413. See FETT, 95, PMHB, LXXVII (1953), 3–23.

302 AGA, June 14, 1800.

303 Margaret Morris to Milcah Martha Moore, Montgomery, May 11, 1798, SJRH, 296. See BFBP, 103–104.

304 Abigail Adams to Mary Cranch, Apr. 27, 1798, Phil. AANL, 166.

305 ANC, 5C, 2S, 3722, DAQW, 90.

306 ANC, 5C, 2S, 3722.

307 Anonymous to JA, JAPM, Reel 388. Your author has dated this letter ten days after the Apr. 18 letter on the basis of Abigail Adams' statement: "Another Letter of the same purport was sent ten days after." Abigail Adams to Mary Cranch, May 10, 1798, AANL, 170–172.

308 1740 ed., PRA, I, 176.

309 Abigail Adams to Mary Cranch, Apr. 28, 1798, AANL, 167, FETT, 9, 191.

310 AGA, May 1, 1798, GUS, May 1, 1798, PG, Apr. 30, May 2, 1798. AGA, June 14, 1800, describes Relph's role.

311 According to WD, BFB got him to give up his $10-a-week salary sometime in May or June, so that BFB could hire James Thomson Callender, AGA, Aug. 11, 1802. BFBT, 402.

312 PG, Apr. 30, May 2, 1798. See AGA, June 14, 1800.

313 See AGA, June 14, 1800.

314 AGA, May 3, 1798.

315 PG, May 2, 1798.

[316] GUS, May 4, 1798, JAWO, IX, 186–187.

[317] See FETT, 8–9, JAPS II, 963.

[318] *Anas*, TJWF, I, 346.

[319] TJ to Madison, Phil., May 3, 1798, TJWF, VIII, 413–416. See NJUV, 68, 308, DMAF, 161.

[320] AGA, May 5, 1798.

[321] ANC, 5C, 2S, 1578.

[322] GUS, May 26, 1798.

[323] ANC, 5C, 2S, 3726.

[324] ANC, 5C, 2S, 3727.

[325] PAPS, XXII, 270–271.

[326] NJUV, 65–67.

[327] KMM, 182–183.

[328] GW to Sec. of State, May 6, 1798, GWW, XXXVI, 254.

[329] Abigail Adams to Mary Cranch, May 7, 1798, AANL, 169.

[330] GUS, May 7, 1798.

[331] PG, May 7, 1798.

[332] Abigail Adams to Mary Cranch, May 8, 1798, AANL, 169.

[333] 1740 ed., PRA, I, 186.

[334] JAWO, IX, 187–9.

[335] Abigail Adams to Mary Cranch, May 8, 1798, AANL, 169.

[336] AGA, May 9, 1798. See also NJUV, 67.

[337] BFBW, [i].

[338] NJUV, 67.

[339] Abigail Adams to Mary Cranch, May 8, 1798, AANL, 169.

[340] TJ to James Madison, May 10, 1798, TJWF, VIII, 417, 418. See AGA, June 14, 1800.

[341] To the people of Burlington County, N. J., [May 8, 1798], JAWO, IX, 191.

[342] ANC, 5C, 2S, 1631–1642.

[343] NJUV, 68.

[344] On this same day, William Cobbett published a pamphlet: William Cobbett, *Detection of a Conspiracy Formed by the United Irishmen, with the Evident Intention of Aiding the Tyrants of France in Subverting the Government of the United States of America* (Phil., 1798), REDX 48,395, WCPW, VIII, 220–225. See DMAF, 28, 150, TJAH, 375–376.

[345] TJ to James Madison. [Phil], May, 17, 1798, TJJM, II, 1049–1050.

[346] See W&A, II, 70–71, GLP, 150.

[347] Joseph Hopkinson, *What Is Our Situation And What Our Prospects? A Few Pages for Americans. By An American* (Phil., 1798), REDX 33,904. That this was sent to GW on May 9th, see GW to Joseph Hopkinson, Mt.

Vernon, May 27, 1798, GWW, XXXVI, 274–275.

[348] TJ to James Lewis, Jr., Phil., May 9, 1798, TJWF, VIII, 416–417.

[349] PG, May 10, 1798.

[350] AGA, Sept. 10, 1800.

[351] James Abercrombie, *A Sermon, Preached in Christ Church and St. Peter's, Philadelphia: on Wednesday, May 9, 1798* (Phil.: John Ormrod [1798]), REDX 33,263.

[352] David Osgood, *Some Facts Evincive of the Atheistical, Anarchical, and in other respect Immoral Principles of the French Republicans, stated in a Sermon Delivered on the 9th of May, 1798, the Day Recommended by the President of the United States for Solemn Humiliation, Fasting and Prayer.* (Boston: Samuel Hall, 1798), REDX 34,284. Reprinted in GUS, Aug. 21, 1798.

[353] Abigail Adams to Mary Cranch, May 10, 1798, AANL, 170–172.

[354] JCPB, I, 35. Callender described the leader of the plot to burn BFB's house on May 9 as "the attorney that fled for forgery." Your author has substituted the name Joseph Thomas to identify that person. See AGA, Aug. 6, 1798.

[355] AGA, Apr. 30, 1799.

[356] JCPB, I, 35.

[357] Margaret Morriss to Milcah Martha Moore, Montgomery, May 11, 1798, SJRH, 296. See BFBP, 103–104.

[358] JAWJ, 127, TJAH, 367.

[359] GUS, May 11, 1798.

[360] Abigail Adams to Mrs. Elizabeth Peabody, Phil., June 22, 1798, SFP.

[361] Abigail Adams to Mary Cranch, May 10, 1798, AANL, 170–172.

[362] "To the Printers of the Boston Patriot, Letter 1," JAWO, IX, 241, 279.

[363] JCPB, I, 35.

[364] AGA, May 21, 1798.

[365] To the citizens of Hartford, Conn., [May 10, 1798], JAWO, IX, 192.

[366] PG, May 23, 1798.

[367] TJ to James Madison, May 10, 1798, TJWF, VIII, 417, 418. See DMAF, 151.

[368] Abigail Adams to her sister, May 10, 1798, AANL, 172, FETT, 249.

[369] Eliz. Hewson to Thos. Hewson, May 10, June 20, 1798, HP, BFBT, 107.

[370] ANC, 5C, 2S, 1655–1656, 1678. See DMAF, 150, GUS, June 9, 1798, DAQW, 84.

[371] See GUS, May 11, 1798, AGA, May 14, 23, 1798.

[372] To the Citizens of Easton, Pa., *Columbian Centinel* (Boston), May 26, 1798, DMAF, 159.

[373] See GUS, May 11, 1798, AGA, May 15, 1798.

[374] Francis Von A. Cabeen, "The Society of the Sons of Saint Tammany of Philadelphia," PMHB, XXV (1901), 442–451; XXVI (1902), 346–347; XXVII (1903), 29–48, GLP, 150. See BFBB, 183–186.

[375] George Logan, *On the Natural and Social Order of the World, as Intended to Produce Universal Good; Delivered Before the Tammany Society, at Their Anniversary, on the 12th of May, 1798* (Phil.: BFB [1798]), REDX 34,011. Also, quoted in GLP, 151.

[376] ANC, 5C, 2S, 1727–1729. Two eminent historians have concluded that the army acts were to suppress democracy rather than to protect the country. AGHA, 170 and DMAF, 210. See ANC, 1631–1770, TPAD, 166–67.

[377] ANC, 5C, 2S, 1738–1739, 1744.

[378] ANC, 5C, 2S, 1744–1746.

[379] ANC, 5C, 2S, 1747–1748.

[380] ANC, 5C, 2S, 1752–1754.

[381] ANC, 5C, 2S, 1755.

[382] ANC, 5C, 2S, 1772, DMAF, 305.

[383] ANC, 5C, 2S, 559.

[384] TJMD, III, 374.

[385] Albert Gallatin to J. W. Nicholson, May 18, 1798, AGW, 107.

[386] DMAF, 222. See TJMD, III, 374–375.

[387] James Madison to TJ, May 20, 1798, JMAW, VI, 320–322.

[388] William Smith Shaw to Abigail Adams, May 20, 1798, JAPM, Reel 388. See FETT, 24.

[389] To the Young Men of Boston, Mass., [May, 22, 1798], JAWO, IX, 194–195.

[390] JCHU, 249.

[391] PG, May 26, 1798.

[392] Abigail Adams to Mary Cranch, May 26, 1798, AANL, 179–181.

[393] GW to Joseph Hopkinson, Mt. Vernon, May 27, 1798, GWW, XXXVI, 274–275.

[394] GUS, May 30, 1798.

[395] ANC, 5C, 2S, 3729–3733.

[396] To the Grand Jury for the County of Plymouth, Mass., [May 28, 1798], JAWO, IX, 195.

[397] AGA, June 9, 1798.

[398] TJ to James Madison, Phil., May 31, 1798, TJWF, VIII, 427–429.

[399] TJ to John Taylor, Phil., June 1, 1798, TJWF, VIII, 430–433.

[400] PAPS, XXII, 272.

[401] Abigail Adams to William Shaw, Phil., June 2, 1798, SFP.

[402] See Grenadiers adv., GUS, May 24, 1798.

[403] PG, May 26, 28, 1798.

[404] GW to Judge Alexander Addison, Mt. Vernon, June 3, 1798, GWW, XXXVI, 279–280.

[405] James Madison to TJ, June 3, 1798, JMAW, VI, 320–322.

[406] PG, June 7, 1798, CRIS, 39.

[407] See AGA, June 9, 1798. The Infirmary treated the doctors' threat of resignation as a resignation. JCPB, I, 37.

[408] See SWHP, I, 493, JAPS II, 969.

[409] GLP, 155.

[410] PG, June 7, 1798. See GUS, June 4, 1798.

[411] ANC, 5C, 2S, 1868.

[412] JCHT, 109, See GUS, June 6, 1798. See TJ to James Madison, Phil., June 7, 1798, TJWF, VIII, 433–434.

[413] 1739 ed., PRA, I, 156.

[414] YF, 36.

[415] PG, June 8, 1798.

[416] TJ to James Madison, Phil., June 7, 1798, TJWF, VIII, 433–434. See TJMD, III, 387.

[417] FETT, 160–161, DAQW, 87.

[418] FETT, 161, n. 6. See CFFR.

[419] Alexander Hamilton to Timothy Pickering, June 7, 1798, TPPM, XXII, 196.

[420] Italicized words in this paragraph are WD's. WDBM, 6. See WDKP, 54, Diary of William Wood Thackara (Hist. Soc. Penn.).

[421] BFB to unknown subscriber, June 8, 1798, BFBC, Film 1506, Reel 3.

[422] 1748 ed., PRA, II, 26.

[423] James Thomson Callender, *Sedgwick & Co. or A Key to the Six Per Cent Cabinet* (Phil., [at the office of the AGA], 1798), 35. REDX 48, 395. Pref. is dated May 22, 1798.

[424] Abigail Adams to Mary Cranch, June 8, 1798, AANL, 187–189.

[425] JMAW, VI, 323–325.

[426] 1749 ed., PRA, II, 64.

[427] GLM, 75–76.

[428] GLM, 57–60. See GUS, June 23, 1798.

[429] FETT, 206.

[430] ANC, 5C, 2S, 3737–3739.

[431] E.g. BFBW, 35–47, AGA, Mar. 26, Apr. 14, 25, 1798.

[432] AGA, Aug. 27, 1793.

[433] See WDRP, 553–576.

[434] BFBR, 46–47.

[435] JMOW, III, 125–136.

436 PMHB, XLVII, (1923), 359–360.

437 GUS, June 20, 1798.

438 GUS, June 21, 1798.

439 ANC, 5C, 2S, 3739–3742.

440 CRIS, 47–48, AALP, 350. See TJMD, III, 385.

441 1739 ed., PRA, I, 159.

442 ANC, 5C, 2S, 3425.

443 ANC, 5C, 2S, 1972–1973.

444 James Lloyd to GW, Phil., June 18, 1798, GW Papers (LC Microfilm), Ser. 4, Reel 112. See AGA, June 25, 1798, Time Piece (N.Y.), June 22, 1798, GUS, July 19, 1798, Albany Centinel (Albany, N.Y.), June 13, 29, 1798.

445 Abigail Adams to Mary Cranch, June 19, 1798, AANL, 193–194.

446 GUS, July 28, 1798.

447 Elizabeth Hewson to Thomas Hewson, June 20, 1798, BFBS, 158.

448 ANC, 5C, 2S, 2008, 2010, 2013–2014, 2016.

449 RJMP, I, 266.

450 TJ to James Madison, Phil., June 21, 1798, TJWF, VIII, 439–441.

451 JCHT, 106, 109.

452 ANC, 5C, 2S, 3743–3744. See DAQW, 96.

453 JA to GW, June 22, 1798, GW Papers (LC Microfilm), Ser. 4, Reel 112.

454 1748 ed., PRA, II, 20.

455 Abigail Adams to Mary Cranch, June 23, 1798, AANL, 196. See JAPS, II, 961.

456 GUS, June 25, 1798.

457 GUS, Aug. 2, 1798.

458 The sender, 28-year-old Louis Pichon, was working for the American section of the French Foreign Office and had worked as secretary to the French legation in Philadelphia. See BFBT, 377–386, 393 n. 42.

459 JCPB, II, 74–75.

460 Abigail Adams to Mary Cranch, June 25, 1798, AANL, 196.

461 GW to James Lloyd, June 25, 1798, GWW, XXXVI, 299. The dotted sections of this excerpt are illegible.

462 ANC, 5C, 2S, 3744–3746. See FETT, 61.

463 ANC, 5C, 2S, 3747–3748.

464 To the Students of Dickinson College, [June 25, 1798], JAWO, IX, 204–205, GUS, June 30, 1798.

465 AGA, Dec. 18, 1800.

466 1733 ed., PRA, II, 18.

467 AGA, June 27 & 30, 1798. BFBT, 387–388. Columbian Gazette (Boston), July 4, 1798, See BFBW, Pref., and Bee (New London, CT), July 4, 1798.

468 TJMD, III, xxvi, TJWF, VIII, xx.

469 See also PG, Apr. 16, 1798.

470 Italicized words in this paragraph are presumably WD's. AGA, Mar. 31, 1800.

471 See TJ to Samuel Smith, Monticello, Aug. 22, 1798, TJWF, VIII, 443, 446, Anas, TJWF, I, 353–354.

472 BFB to Louis Gabriel Cramer, June 27, 1798, BFBL, 70–71.

473 1737 ed., PRA, I, 105.

474 DMSM, 252.

475 DMSM, 252.

476 YF, 35.

477 YF, 35.

478 See GUS, Aug. 9, 1798, AGA, Aug. 10, 1978.

479 BFB's fourth son, Hartman, was born on Sept. 3, 1798.

480 Margaret Bache's brother responds,"You are certainly unhappy & I would advise you to come to us immediately." Fr[ancis] Markoe to Margaret H. Bache, Aug. 4, 1798, BFBC, Film 1506, Reel 3. See BFBT, 396, 403.

481 1740 ed., PRA, I, 180.

482 WWHJ, 31.

483 AGA, June 30, 1798. Opening date for Penn. Cir. Ct. from PDS, 21.

484 When Israel Israel was elected to the Penn. Senate in Oct. of 1797, PG called it a complete triumph of the Jews over the Gentiles. On Dec. 13, Penn.'s Federalist-controlled Senate called an investigation of his election and proceeded to expel him. PG, Oct. 10, 1797. See PG, Apr. 12, 15, 16, 1797, THRF, 176–177, 179. On the issue of his Jewish extraction, see WWHJ, 31, NJUV, 45.

485 See AGA, Aug. 22, 29, 1798.

486 Whether it was "Robert" Smith seems in some question. See GUS, June 30, July 3, 1798, FETT, 202, Massachusetts Mercury, July 6, 1798, BFBT, 387–389.

487 JCPB, I, 33.

488 WBRA , 341.

489 RJMP, I, 267, GWF, IV, 397.

490 DAQW, 343.

491 Thomas Day, An Oration on Party Spirit Pronounced Before the Connecticut Society of Cincinnati convened at Hartford . . . (Litchfield: T. Collier, 1798), REDX 33,612.

492 Theodore Dwight, Esq., An Oration Spoken At Hartford in the State of Connecticut on the Anniversary of American Independence, July 4, 1798 (Hartford: Hudson and Goodwin, 1798), REDX 33,655.

[493] Augustus Pettibone, *An Oration Pronounced at Norfolk on the Anniversary of American Independence* . . . (Litchfield: T. Collier, 1798), REDX 34,344.

[494] David B. Ogden, *An Oration Delivered on the Fourth of July, 1798* . . . (Newark: Jacob Halsey & Co., 1798), REDX 34,266.

[495] GUS, July 5, 1798.

[496] Abigail Adams to Elizabeth Peabody, Phil., July 7, 1798, SFP.

[497] PG, July 6, 1798.

[498] PG, Aug. 15, 1798.

[499] Stevens T. Mason to TJ, Phil., July 6, 1798, *TJ Papers*, (LC), CIV, 17825.

[500] ANC, 5C, 2S, 599. See DMAF, 162–163, 206, 343–348.

[501] James Lloyd to GW, July 4, 1798, *GW Papers* (LC Microfilm), Series 4, Reel 112. See DMAF, 199.

[502] GW to Pres. of the U.S., Mt. Vernon, July 4, 1798, GWW, XXXVI, 312–315.

[503] GW to Sec. of War, Mt. Vernon, July 4, 1798, GWW, XXXVI, 304–305. See TPAD, 168, 172, DAQW, 96–97.

[504] DAQW, 104.

[505] 1750 ed., PRA, II, 98.

[506] ANC, 5C, 2S, 2093–2101.

[507] ANC, 5C, 2S, 2107–2111.

[508] ANC, 5C, 2S, 2114

[509] GW to Sec. of War, Mt. Vernon, July 5, 1798, GWW, XXXVI, 318–320.

[510] ANC, 5C, 2S, 2118–2220.

[511] Abigail Adams to John Quincy Adams, Phil., July 20, 1798, JAPM, Reel 390.

[512] ANC, 5C, 2S, 3753–3754. See AALP, 350, DAQW, 100.

[513] ANC, 5C, 2S, 3752–3753.

[514] *Time Piece* (N.Y.), July 9, 1798, AGA, July 9, 1798, *Argus* (N.Y.), July 7, 1798, *Daily Advertiser* (N.Y.), July 7, 1798, FETT, 204–220, TJAH, 404–405.

[515] Timothy Pickering to Richard Harrison, July 7, 1798, TPPM, XXXVII, 315. See FETT, 211, TJAH, 404–405.

[516] ANC, 5C, 2S, 3754. See SDOP, 325, THRF, 183, DMAF, 305.

[517] *Bass vs. Tingey*, as reported in GUS, Aug. 20, Oct. 11, 1800, AGA, Aug. 22, Oct. 8, 1800.

[518] ND, I, 175–179, VII, 366.

[519] *Columbian Centinel* (Boston), July 14, Aug. 8, 1798, as quoted in ND, I, 176.

[520] ANC, 5C, 2S, 3757ff. See THRF, 215.

[521] GUS, July 12, 1798.

[522] ND, II, 363–364, GUS, Mar. 2, 1799.

[523] ND, II, 147–197.

[524] Abigail Adams to Mary Cranch, Phil., July 9, 1798, AANL, 199, 200.

[525] "Instructions of Sec. Stoddert to commander of U.S. Armed Vessels," July 10, 1798, ND, I, 187.

[526] By its own terms, the Sedition Act expired on Mar. 3, 1801, last day of JA's presidential term. See FETT, 130, 143.

[527] ANC, 5C, 2S, 3774–3776.

[528] JAWO, IX, 170–172, DAQW, 103, 410, BASN, 332.

[529] GW to JA, Mt. Vernon, July 13, 1798, GWW, XXXVI, 328. See JABW, 105.

[530] WDKP, 54.

[531] WDCA, 15. Cf. WDBM, 6 which says William John caught yellow fever.

[532] WDBM, 1.

[533] WDKP, 33.

[534] 1754 ed., PRA, II, 244.

[535] WDKP, 58, WDBM, 6–7.

[536] 1737 ed., PRA, I, 107.

[537] Callender found sanctuary in Loudon County, Va., at the home of Republican U.S. Senator Stevens Thomson Mason. James Thomson Callender to TJ, Rasberry Plain, Sept. 22, 1798, TJJC, 10. See TJ to James Monroe, Wash., July 15, 1802, TJWF, IX, 387–388.

[538] ANC, 5C, 2S, 3776–3777.

[539] See DMAF, 163–164, FETT, 441–442, DAQW, 100.

[540] JAWO, IX, 291.

[541] ANC, 5C, 2S, 3777–3785.

[542] DMSM, 253.

[543] ANC, 5C, 2S, 3785–3787.

[544] ANC, 5C, 2S, 619–624, 2186.

[545] FETT, 385–390.

[546] DMSM, 253.

[547] ANC, 5C, 2S, 622.

[548] ANC, 5C, 2S, 621–623.

[549] To the Freemasons of the State of Maryland, PG, Aug. 3, 1798.

[550] 1734 ed., PRA, II, 31.

[551] GUS, July 23, 1798.

[552] GLM, 75–76.

[553] GUS, July 24, 1798.

[554] 1740 ed., PRA, I, 184.

[555] PG, July 28, 1798. See WLFA, 42 & 42 n. (documenting JA's absences from Phil.).

[556] 1736 ed., PRA, I, 85.

[557] AGA, Aug. 2, 1798.

[558] AGA, Oct. 12, 1799. See Minutes of the U.S. Circuit Ct., Dist. of N. J., Oct. Sess. 1798, Records Group, 21 (Nat'l Archives), *Chronicle* (Newark, N.J.), Nov. 15, 1798, AGA, Aug. 2, 1798, as cited in FETT, 270–274, CRIS, 112–113.

[559] AGA, Oct. 12, 1799.

[560] PG, July 31, 1798.

[561] Sec. of the Navy to JA, Phil., July 30, 1798, ND, I, 255–256.

[562] Benjamin Stoddert to JA, Phil., Aug. 25, 1798, ND, I, 336.

[563] GW to Charles Carroll of Carrollton, Mt. Vernon, Aug. 2, 1798, GWW, XXXVI, 382, 384.

[564] AGA, Aug. 30, 1798.

[565] DMSM, 254.

[566] AGA, Aug. 30, 1798. See also the GUS, Aug. 9, 1798.

[567] See TJ's response, TJ to Samuel Smith, Monticello, Aug. 22, 1798, TJWF, VIII, 443–447.

[568] GW to William Heth, Mt. Vernon, Aug. 5, 1798, GWW, XXXVI, 388–389.

[569] JA to Benjamin Rush, Quincy, June 23, 1807, JAOF, 144, 148.

[570] YF, 46–47, 53.

[571] AGA, Aug. 10, 1798.

[572] GUS, Apr. 13, 23, 1798, AGA, Aug. 9, 15, 1798.

[573] Callender described the leader of the plot to burn BFB's house on May 9 as "the attorney that fled for forgery " and reported that the Federalist crowd concluded its activities by going "to serenade Liston's printer." JCPB, I, 35. See AGA, Aug. 6, 1798, Apr. 30, 1799.

[574] Carey is quoted in Earl Lockridge Bradsher, *Mathew Carey, Editor, Author and Publisher: a Study in American Literary Development* (N.Y.: Columbia Univ. Press, 1912), 11.

[575] AGA, Aug. 10, 1798.

[576] AGA, Aug. 9, 1798.

[577] GUS, Aug. 8, 1798.

[578] 1738 ed., PRA, I, 137.

[579] 1733 ed., PRA, I, 15.

[580] JBZP, 98–99.

[581] AGA, Aug. 10, 1798. See BFBT, 349, 366, BFBS, 161, JBZP, 184.

[582] GUS, Aug. 9, 1798.

[583] 1735 ed., PRA, I, 62.

[584] YF, 51.

[585] YF, 51.

[586] PG, Aug. 13, 1798.

[587] YF, 51.

[588] See FETT, 216–217, TJAH, 404–405.

[589] YF, 58.

[590] GUS, Aug. 20, 1798.

[591] To the Citizens of Harrison County, Va., JAWO, IX, 216, PG, Aug. 27, 1798. See DMAF, 144.

[592] Timothy Pickering to JA, Aug. 28, 1798, TPPM, XXXVII, 325.

[593] AGA, Aug. 30, 1798.

[594] YF, 94–95.

[595] DMSM, 255.

[596] AGA, Aug. 21, 1798. On the depth of the yellow fever problem, see BFBT, 396, SWHP, I, 459 n., TJAH, 380–381, TCER, 345.

[597] AGA, Aug. 24, 1798.

[598] Presumably GUS, July 28, 1798.

[599] TJ to Samuel Smith, Monticello, Aug. 22, 1798, TJWF, VIII, 443–447.

[600] IRPT, 295–299.

[601] ND, I, 331, VII, 366, 371.

[602] Richard Peters to Timothy Pickering, Belmont, Aug. 24, 1798, TPPM, XXXVII, 71.

[603] YF, 85–86.

[604] 1740 ed., PRA, I, 182.

[605] Timothy Pickering to William Rawle, Aug. 28, 1798, TPPM, XXXVII, 326.

[606] FETT, 216.

[607] AGA, Sept. 5, 1798.

[608] 1733 ed., PRA, I, 15.

[609] YF, 67–70.

[610] AGA, Nov. 9, 1798.

[611] AGA, Sept. 7, 1798, GUS, Sept. 6, 1798, See John Hench, "Letters of John Fenno and John Ward Fenno," PAAS, Vol. 89, Part 1 (1979), 301–302.

[612] ND, I, 377, II, 478 (map), VII, 371, DAQW, inside back cover.

[613] LTNA, II, 24–28.

[614] RWA, Sept. 15, 1798. See PG, Sept. 13, 1798.

[615] YF, 84.

[616] RWA, Sept. 15, 1798, quoted in Louis Richards, "Hon. Jacob Rush of the Pennsylvania Judiciary," PMHB, XXXIX (Jan. 1915), 65, 66. See AGW, 114.

[617] TCER, 346, FETT, 203, BFBT, 396.

[618] Will, Sept. 7, 1798, BFBC, Film 1506, Reel 3. See BFBS, 163.

[619] AGA, May 13, 1800.

[620] IRPT, 326.

[621] GW to William Jones and the Bd. of Manag-

ers of the Marine and City Hospitals, Sept. 10, 1798, GWW, XXXVI, 435).

622 *Independent Chronicle* (Boston), Sept. 17, 1798 reports that, "real friends of their country cannot but lament the loss of so valuable a citizen." BFBT, 398.

623 Elizabeth Hewson to Thos. T. Hewson, Oct. ? & 30, 1798, HP, BFBT, 396, 403 n. 5.

624 AGA handbill, Sept. 11, 1798. See BFBB, 356.

625 1757 ed., PRA, II, 355.

626 BF to BFB, Aug. 19, 1779, BFPL, XXX, 241.

627 Timothy Pickering to T. Williams, Trenton, Sept. 13, 1798, TPPM, IX, 315.

628 BFBS, 164.

629 GW to James McHenry, Sept. 30, 1798, GWW, XXXVI, 474. See DMAF, 215.

630 TJ to Stevens T. Mason, Monticello, Oct. 11, 1798, TJWF, VIII, 449–450. See SDOP, 472, JAPS, II, 978.

631 JA to Benjamin Rush, Quincy, June 23, 1807, JAOF, 144, 148.

632 Detail (cropping), *George Washington* (1776), by Charles Willson Peale (Brooklyn Museum, Brooklyn, N.Y.).

633 Doodle sketch of BF by BFB [1790], "Memorandum, No Date" Folder, Franklin Papers, Bache Collection (APS). Tentatively dated 1790 on the basis of Claude-Anne Lopez and Eugenia W. Herbert, *The Private Franklin: The Man and His Family* (New York: W. W. Norton, 1975), 140 (illus.). Cf. BFB's doodle sketches of BF in BFB's notes of debates in Congress, Mar. 7–17, Mar. 18–Apr. 10, 1796, BFBC, Film 1506, Reel 3.

634 BF to Robert Livingston, July 22, 1783, BFSM, IX, 62.

635 AGA, Oct. 29, 1796.

636 WD to Franklin Bache, Wash., Mar. 4, 1804, BFBC, Film 1506, Reel 3.

637 JA to Arthur Lee, Paris, Apr. 10, 1783, JAPM, Reel 108.

638 BFBR, 3, 65.

639 "Notes, drafts, and fragments of Presidential messages and proclamations," JAPM, Reel 387.

640 During the 1790's, Thomas Paine was known not only for his political writings during and after the American Revolution but also for his service as secretary to the Committee on Foreign Affairs of the Continental Congress during the revolution, viz. Thomas Paine, *The Writings of Thomas Paine, Secretary for Foreign Affairs to the Congress of the United States of America, in the Late War* (Albany, N.Y.: Charles R. & George Webster, 1792?) REDX 24,658 & 27,466. Paine served as secretary during 1777, while French arms were arriving to equip America's northern army under Gen. Horatio Gates. Paine was, therefore, well positioned to appreciate the dimensions of French aid.

641 WDRP, 545–555.

642 JA to Benjamin Rush, Mar. 19- Apr. 22, 1812, A&R, 211, 212–213.

643 Timothy Pickering to James Robertson, Salem, July 29, 1824, as reported in John Womack Wright, "Pickering's Letter on Washington," TYQ, VII (July, 1925), 16, 24–26.

644 ANC, 5C, 2S, 3776–3777.

645 James Monroe to TJ, Mar. 26, 1798, JMOW, III, 106–115.

646 BFB was born Aug. 12, 1769. BFB's college-age cousin, William Temple Franklin, also accompanied BF and would serve as secretary to the Paris commissioners.

647 JA to Abigail Adams, Phil., June 18, 1777, JAFC, II, 267–268.

648 BFBR.

649 GLBE, VI, 31–32.

650 GWRH, I, 113, GLBE, VI, 38–39, 52–53.

651 The Jumonville assassination and its aftermath are well described in GWRH, I, 114–157, GLBE, VI, Chap. 2.

652 GW to John Augustine Washington, June 28, 1755, GWPD, I, 321. ("The Genl. before they met in Council ask'd my priv'e Opinn concern'g the Exp'n . . . This was a scheme that took.") See GWRH, I, 205, 227–229, GWAC, 104.

653 GWRH, I, 197, 227–229. See GWAC, 102.

654 BFA, 159.

655 GW to John Augustine Washington, June 28, 1755, GWW, I, 241. See GLBE, VI, 82, 97.

656 GW's account is found in GWW, I, 151–152.

657 GWRH, I, 260.

658 GWKC, 147.

659 E.g., *Virginia Gazette* (Williamsburg, Va.), Sept. 3, Oct. 5, 1756. See GWKC, 222.

660 GWKC, 268.

661 Just a few months before marrying Martha, GW professed love to Sally Fairfax: "You have drawn me . . . into an honest confession of a Simple Fact—misconstrue not my meaning—'tis obvious—doubt it not, nor expose it—the World has no business knowing the object of my Love, declar'd in this manner to—you when I want to conceal it." GW to Sarah Cary Fairfax, Sept. 12, 1758, GWPD, VI, 10–13. See GWKC, 259.

662 MJTF, 64–65, GWMK, 108–120.

663 MJOR, 74–77, BSDR, 96–97, AGBE, 194–195.

664 See GWCA, 159–160, WDLW, 47.

665 MJOR, 82–89.

666 Adam Smith articulated the principles of mercantilism in his *An Inquiry into the Nature and Causes of the Wealth of Nations* (London: W. Strahan and T. Cadell, 1776).

667 On Hancock's smuggling, see JHHA, 45–47.

668 GW to William Crawford, Mt. Vernon, Sept. 21, 1767, GWPD, VIII, 26–29.

669 MJOR, 123–126, MJTF, 65.

670 Edmund S. Morgan and Helen M. Morgan, *The Stamp Act Crisis* (Chapel Hill, N.C.: Univ. of N. C. Press, 1953), 181, MJOR, 129–130, 144–145.

671 JADA, IV, 258, JAC, 49.

672 MJOR, 137–139.

673 MJOR, 143.

674 JCSH, 41. Radical Democrat-Republicans of the late 1790s, though passionately anti-British, fostered the suspicion that Federalists, particularly New England Federalists, really wanted independence to create their own monarchy and to establish themselves as a wealthy aristocracy, in short, to feather their own nests. See, e.g., JCUS, 270, TPW, II, 915–916.

675 JPBL, 78–83. Bernard Bailyn, *The Ideological Origins of the American Revolution* (Cambridge: Belknap Press of Harvard University Press, 1967) details the arguments.

676 MJOR, 231, 269–276, 287–295.

677 MJOR, 308–316.

678 MJOR, 76–77.

679 For GW's reaction, see GWAC, 159–160.

680 JHB, 282.

681 TPTB, 193, JHAH, 140–141.

682 MJOR, 359.

683 See RARW, 166.

684 From the late 1770s until 1796 when he came to America, WD worked for the *Clonmel Gazette* or *Hibernian Advertiser* in Clonmel, Ireland, for the *Bengal Journal* and the *Bengal World* in Calcutta, India, and the *Telegraph* and probably the *General Advertiser* in London, England. WDKP, 9–12, 21, 38.

685 As a weekly paper, the *Pennsylvania Gazette*'s masthead date means "the week ending Wednesday,—."

686 TPHD, 162.

687 BF to Richard Bache, London, Sept. 30, 1774, BFPL, XXI, 325–326. On the connection between Paine, BF, and BFB, see BFBT, 126–127.

688 "Crisis" (3d), TPW, I, 88 n. 7.

689 Thomas Paine to BF, Phil., Mar. 4, 1775, TPW, II, 1130–1131.

690 Paul Revere to Jeremy Belknap [ca. 1798], Revere Family Papers (MHS).

691 JAWO, II, 215–216, GWMK, 65.

692 MJTF, 36–37, TPAD, 8.

693 Italicized words from AGA, Apr. 11, 1800.

694 JCC, II, 26–27.

695 JCC, II, 24–25.

696 They were married on Sept. 1, 1730. BFCV, 93.

697 BFB was born Aug. 12, 1769. BFBT, 1.

698 MJTF, 90–91.

699 JA to Abigail Adams, Phil., May 29, 1775, JAFC, I, 207.

700 JCC, II, 91.

701 JADA, III, 321–323, MJTF, 61–62. See GWFS, III, 434–435, GWMK, 19, 84, 53–92.

702 JCC, II, 91.

703 JCC, II, 92–93.

704 JA to James Lloyd, Quincy, Apr. 24, 1815, JAWO, X, 162, 165–166.

705 BFBR, 30.

706 MJTF, 46–47, MJOR, 410–411.

707 JCC, II, 96–97.

708 MJTF, 48–52.

709 See Orlando W. Stephenson, "The Supply of Gunpowder in 1776," AHR, XXX (Jan. 1925), 271–281.

710 James Warren to JA, Watertown, June 20, 1775, JAPA, III, 37.

711 JCCS, I, 17.

712 JCC, II, 101.

713 GW to Pres. of Cong., Camp at Cambridge, July 10, 1775, GWPA, I, 85.

714 BFBR, 67.

715 BF to Mary Hewson, Phil., July 8, 1775, BFPL, XXII, 99–100.

716 JCC, II, 195–197. See FUMR, 80–83, BFWE, 238–239.

717 JCC, II, 199. Compare BF's plan in 1775 for a 125-member congress with the first U.S. House of Representatives fourteen years later which, despite the nation's population growth, had only 58 members. ANC, 1C, 2S, 1075.

718 Those who wanted the first U.S. House of Representatives to be larger (and voting districts to be smaller) feared that wealthy aristocrats would control large voting districts. See AFC, I, 43–44, V, 89–90, 192, 258, II, 235–

236, 268–269, 272–273, III, 158, VI, 154, BBDC, I, 320–322, 424–425, JPBL, 109.

[719] Gen. Orders, July 23, 1775, GWPA, I, 158.

[720] JA to Abigail Adams, Phil., July 23, 1775, JAFC, I, 252–253.

[721] GW to Pres. of Cong., Cambridge, Aug. 4, 1775, GWPA, I, 227.

[722] BF to Philip Schuyler, Phil., Aug. 10, 1775, BFPL, XXII, 160–161.

[723] Memorandum on the Use of Pikes, Aug. 26, 1775, BFPL, XXII, 182.

[724] GW to Richard Henry Lee, Cambridge, Aug. 29, 1775, GWPA, I, 374.

[725] Benjamin Rush to JA, Feb. 12, 1812, A&R, 206–207.

[726] BFPL, XXII, 181.

[727] GW to Pres. of Cong., Cambridge, Sept. 21, 1775, GWPA, II, 24, 28–29.

[728] JCC, III, 265.

[729] JCC, III, 266.

[730] JCC, III, 270–271.

[731] JCCS, I, 28.

[732] JCC, III, 484–485.

[733] JA to Abigail Adams, Oct. 29, 1775, JAFC, I, 318–319.

[734] GW to Pres. of Cong., Cambridge, GWPA, II, 349, 350.

[735] Abigail Adams to JA, Nov. 27, 1775, JAFC, I, 328–330.

[736] JADA, III, 358.

[737] GW to Pres. of Cong., Cambridge, Nov. 28, 1775, GAPA, II, 444, 446.

[738] GW to Joseph Reed, Cambridge, Nov. 28, 1775, GWPA, II, 448, 449–450.

[739] JCC, III, 392. See MJTF, 265, SWHA, 74–75, BSDR, 32.

[740] JCC, III, 400–401.

[741] GW to Pres. of Cong., Cambridge, Dec. 4, 1775, GWPA, II, 483, 486.

[742] BF to Joseph Priestley, Paris, Jan. 17, 1777, BFPL, XXIII, 237–238.

[743] BF writes Barbeu-Dubourg (French translator of BF's works) in Paris and Charles Willam Frederick Dumas (a paid American observer and agent) at The Hague. BSDR, 125–126.

[744] BF to Charles William Frederick Dumas, Phil., Dec. 9, 1775, BFPL, XXII, 287–290.

[745] BFPL, XXII, 311.

[746] GW to Pres. of Cong., Cambridge, Dec. 14, 1775, GWPA, II, 549.

[747] Richard Smith Diary, Dec. 18, 1775, LCCS, II, 494.

[748] JCC, III, 444–445.

[749] JCC, III, 446, 449.

[750] GW to Joseph Reed, Cambridge, Dec. 25, 1775, GWPA, II, 606, 607.

[751] Achard de Bonvouloir to Comte de Guines, Phil., Dec. 28, 1775, NDR, III, 279–285.

[752] JCC, III, 466. See BSDR, 34.

[753] Gabriel de Sartine to Comte de Vergennes, Versailles, Dec. 30, 1775, NDR, III, 465.

[754] See GW to Maj. Gen. Philip Schuyler, Camp at Cambridge, Aug. 20, 1775, GWPA, I, 331, 332, Instructions to Col. Benedict Arnold, [Cambridge, Sept. 14, 1775], GWPA, I, 457.

[755] Benedict Arnold to GW, Camp Before Quebec, Jan. 14, 1776, GWPA, III, 81–82.

[756] GW to Pres. of Cong., Cambridge, Jan. 4, 1776, GWPA, III, 18, 19.

[757] In general, see SWHA, 99–100, MJOR, 461–474, 492, TPHD, 39–41, 44. TPHD, 44 says pamphlet went on sale Jan 9.

[758] "Crisis" (3d), TPW, I, 88–89 n. 7.

[759] Thomas Paine to Hon. Henry Laurens, Phil., Jan. 14, 1779, TPW, II, 1160, 1163.

[760] See DERD 13 ("Thomas Paine . . . first identified the Revolution with democracy").

[761] TPW, I, 7,10,13, 16, 27.

[762] TPW, I, 27–29.

[763] William Temple Franklin confirmed this. BFWT, II, 13. See Benjamin Rush to James Cheetham, Phil., July 17, 1809, BRL, II, 1007, 1008, TPHD, 162.

[764] BFCV, 548.

[765] JADA, III, 330–332.

[766] GW to Pres. of Cong., Cambridge, Jan. 14, 1776, GWPA, III, 84–85.

[767] GW to Joseph Reed, Cambridge, Jan. 14, 1776, GWPA, III, 87–90.

[768] Caron de Beaumarchais to Louis XVI, [Jan. 22, 1776], NDR, III, 525–530. See RDCW, I, 369.

[769] Horatio Gates to Charles Lee, Jan. 22, 1776, quoted in TPKJ, 111.

[770] JADA, II, 227.

[771] GW to Pres. of Cong., Cambridge, Feb. 9, 1776, GWPA, III, 277, 278.

[772] GW to Joseph Reed, Cambridge, Feb. 10, 1776, GWPA, III, 286–287.

[773] BF to Charles Lee, Phil. Feb. 11, 1776, BFPL, XXII, 342–343.

[774] GW to Pres. of Cong., Cambridge, Feb. 18, 1776, GWPA, III, 335.

[775] BFBR, 6.

[776] GW to Pres. of Cong., Cambridge, Feb. 26, 1776, GWPA, III, 364–365.

[777] See SWHA, 119, 79, DNL, I, 268, BSDR, 23, 198.

[778] GWPA, III, 434.

[779] "Considerations on the Affair of the English Colonies in America," Versailles, Mar. 12, 1776, NDR, IV, 966–969. See SFAC, XIII, 1316.

[780] GW to Gov. Nicholas Cooke, Cambridge, Mar. 17, 1776, GWPA, III, 483.

[781] "A Letter to GW . . . ," TPW, II, 718–719.

[782] JA to Abigail Adams, Phil., Mar. 19, 1776, JAFA, 145–146.

[783] GW to Col. Joseph Reed, Cambridge, Apr. 1, 1776, GWPA, IV, 9, 11.

[784] FBRS, 70, quoting and translating DNL, I, 280–283. See JAPP, 153.

[785] JA to William Tudor, Apr. 12 1776, JAPA, IV, 118.

[786] *Pennsylvania Packet* (Phil.), Apr. 22, 1776, as cited by JAPA, IV, 68.

[787] John Adams, *Thoughts on Government: Applicable to the Present State of the American Colonies in a Letter from a Gentleman to His Friend.* (Boston, 1776), REDX 14,640, JAPA, IV, 88–89.

[788] DERD, 31–32.

[789] JA to Benjamin Rush, Apr. 12, 1809, A&R, 142, 144, JAOF, 375, 377.

[790] JADA, III, 333.

[791] Thomas Paine, "To the Citizens of the United States . . . Letter II," *National Intelligencer* (Wash.), Nov. 2, 1802, reprinted in TPW, II, 912, 915–916.

[792] Philip S. Foner, *The Life and Major Writings of Thomas Paine* (Secaucus, N.J.: Citadel Press, 1974), xiv, TPHD, 48.

[793] JAWO, III, 189.

[794] JA to TJ, Quincy, June 22, 1819, JATJ, II, 542.

[795] General Ct. to Mass. delegates, May 9, 1776, JAPA, IV, 180.

[796] JCC, IV, 342.

[797] JA to James Warren, May 12, 1776, JAPA, IV, 181–182.

[798] BSDR, 27.

[799] Quoted in JAPP, 141.

[800] JCC, IV, 357–358.

[801] JAWO, II, 510–511.

[802] JCC, IV, 427–429.

[803] JCC, IV, 429–431.

[804] JAWO, II, 510–511.

[805] JCC, IV, 432–433.

[806] DIMJ, 53.

[807] DIMJ, 70.

[808] DIMJ, 109, 118.

[809] JA to Benjamin Rush, July 20, 1811, A&R, 182–183.

[810] SJPC, 147.

[811] "A Serious Address to the People of Penn. on the Present Situation of Their Affairs," *Pennsylvania Packet* (Phil.), Dec. 1, 1778, as quoted in TPW, II, 277, 280. See BFPL, XXII, 512, which observes that BF "chaired the convention at a substantial proportion of its meetings."

[812] See BFSG, 22–32.

[813] See JADA, II, 247, BFPL, XXII, 536–538.

[814] Protest against the First Draft of the Articles of Confederation, BFPL, XXII, 571–574. See BFWT, II, 38–42.

[815] Lord Stormont to Lord Weymouth, Paris, July 31, 1776, SFAC, XIII, 1342.

[816] *Pennsylvania Archives*, 3rd Ser., X, 763, DERD, 267.

[817] Pierre Penet to BF, Nantes, Aug. 3, 1776, BFPL, XXII, 543–544.

[818] Abigail Adams to JA, Boston, Aug. 14, 1776, JAFC, II, 92.

[819] Silas Deane to Comm. of Secret Corres., Paris, Aug. 18, 1776, RDCS, I, 9, 30–31.

[820] JA to Francis Dana, Aug. 16, 1776, JAPA, IV, 466.

[821] Silas Deane to Comm. of Secret Corres., Paris, Aug. 18, 1776, RDCW, II, 112, 114.

[822] Caron de Beaumarchais to Comm. of Secret Corres., Paris, Aug. 18, 1781, RDCS, I, 35.

[823] Lieut. Col. Robert Hanson Harrison to Pres. of Cong., N.Y., Aug. 27, 1776, GWPA, VI, 140, 142. On Harrison, see GWPA, I, 78.

[824] GW to Pres. of Cong., Long Island, Aug. 29, 1776, GWPA, VI, 155–156.

[825] JA to William Tudor, Phil., Aug. 29, 1776, JAPA, V, 1–3.

[826] Gen. Orders, Hdqr., N.Y., Aug. 31, 1776, GWPA, VI, 171–172.

[827] GW to Pres. of Cong., N.Y., Aug. 31, 1776, GWPA, VI, 177–178.

[828] GW to Pres. of Cong., N.Y., Sept. 2, 1776, GWPA, VI, 199.

[829] JA to Samuel Cooper, Phil., Sept. 4, 1776, JAPA, V, 11.

[830] BF to GW, Phil., Sept. 8, 1776, BFPL, XXII, 593–594.

[831] JADA, III, 417–418.

[832] BFPL, XXII, 599. See MJTF, 129–131.

[833] GW to Pres. of Cong., Hdqr. at Col. Morris's House, Sept. 16, 1776, GWPA, VI, 313–314.

[834] BFBR, 6.

[835] JCC, V, 768–778.

[836] See BSDR, 46.

[837] JADA, III, 329.

[838] JAWO, II, 516. Also JADA, III, 337–338.

[839] WDBF, I, 367 (William Temple Franklin's words).

[840] PG, Mar. 31, 1779, SJPC, 186.

[841] PG, Mar. 26, 1777, SJPC, 215.

[842] Thomas Paine, *Constitutional Reform. To the Citizens of Pennsylvania on the Proposal for Calling a Convention,* TPW, II, 992–1002.

[843] Benjamin Franklin, *Queries and Remarks Respecting Alterations in The Constitution of Pennsylvania,* BFSM, X, 54, 56–58.

[844] Benjamin Franklin, *Queries and Remarks Respecting Alterations in The Constitution of Pennsylvania,* BFSM, X, 54, 58–60.

[845] JA to T. Pickering, E. Chester, Oct. 31, 1797, JAWO, VIII, 559–560.

[846] Benjamin Franklin, *Queries and Remarks Respecting Alterations in The Constitution of Pennsylvania,* BFSM, X, 54.

[847] Benjamin Franklin, *Queries and Remarks Respecting Alterations in The Constitution of Pennsylvania,* BFSM, X, 54–55.

[848] DERD, 216.

[849] SJPC, 190. Georgia emulated Pennsylvania in a unicameral legislature but required members to be Protestant and possess £250 in property (or 250 acres of land). For a comparison of the state constitutions, see William. C. Morey, "The First State Constitutions," *Annals of the American Academy of Political and Social Science,* Vol. IV (Sept. 1893), 201–232.

[850] JAFW, I, 168–169. See SJPC, 255–259. That John Adams was an American aristocrat, see RARW, 196.

[851] GW to Pres. of Cong., Col. Morris' on the Heights of Harlem, Sept. 25, 1776, GAPW, VI, 393, 394, 396.

[852] JA to Col. Tudor, Phil., Sept. 26, 1776, JADA, III, 437–439, 438n.

[853] JCC, V, 827. See BFPL, XXII, 624.

[854] See JADA, IV, 70, JAWO, I, 248.

[855] Richard Henry Lee to [TJ], Phil., Sept. 27, 1776, RHLL, I, 218–219.

[856] RDCW, I, 473.

[857] *Autobiography,* TJWF, I, 80.

[858] JA to Henry Knox, Phil., Sept. 29, 1776, JADA, III, 441–442.

[859] Comm. of Secret Corres. to William Bingham, Phil., Sept. 21st [-Oct. 1] 1776, BFPL, XXII, 615, 618–619.

[860] Comm. of Secret Corres. to Silas Deane, Phil., Oct. 1, 1776, BFPL, XXII, 639–645.

[861] JA to Gen. Parsons, Phil., Oct. 2, 1776, JADA, III, 444–445.

[862] Anthony Wayne to BF, Tyconderoga, Oct. 3, 1776, BFPL, XXII, 652–653.

[863] JA to Abigail Adams, Phil., Oct. 4, 1776, JAFC, II, 137–138.

[864] M. Garnier to Comte de Vergennes, London, Oct. 11, 1776, DNL, I, 615–616.

[865] Instructions to BF, Silas Deane, and Arthur Lee, Commissioners appointed by the Cong. of the U.S., Sept. 24–Oct. 22, 1776, BFPL, XXII, 625, 627–628.

[866] Comm. of Secret Corres. to Charles W. F. Dumas, Phil., Oct. 24, 1776, NDR, VI, 1407.

[867] Comm. of Secret Corres. to Captain Lambert Wickes, Phil., Oct. 24, 1776, NDR, VI, 1400–1401.

[868] Comm. of Secret Corres. to Commissioners in Paris, Phil., Oct. 24, 1776, RDCW, II, 178. See LWSR, 88–92.

[869] BFBT, 9, 23, SWHA, 127–128. See LWSR, Chapt. VI.

[870] BFWT, II, 46.

[871] Silas Deane to Comm. of Secret Corres., Paris, Nov. 6, 1776, RDCW, II, 190.

[872] GW to Pres. of Cong., Gen. Greene's Quarters, Nov. 16, 1776, GWW, VI, 284, 286–287.

[873] Nathanael Greene to Henry Knox, November 17, 1776, quoted in GWKB, 135–136, 136 n. 3.

[874] GW to John Augustine Washington, Hackensack, Nov. 19, 1776, GWW, VI, 243–246.

[875] See GWKB, 130, GWMK, 182–185, GWRH, III, 2.

[876] Col. Joseph Reed to Charles Lee, Hackensack, Nov. 21, 1776, LP, II, 293–294.

[877] GW to Pres. of Cong., Hackensack, Nov. 19 [-21], 1776, GWW, VI, 292, 295. See MJTF, 141–142.

[878] GW to Maj. Gen. Lee, Hackensack, Nov. 21, 1776, GWW, VI, 298.

[879] TPHD, 58.

[880] "A Letter to GW . . . " TPW, II, 691, 719.

[881] Timothy Pickering to James Robertson, Salem, July 29, 1824, as quoted in John Womack Wright, "Pickering's Letter on Washington," TYQ, VII (July, 1925), 16, 25.

[882] Charles Lee to Col. Joseph Reed, Camp, Nov. 24, 1776, LP, II (1872), 305–306.

[883] GW to Maj. Gen. Lee, Newark, Nov. 27, 1776, GWW, VI, 309.

[884] BFWT, II, 46–47.

[885] See SWHA, 146, LWSR, Chap. VI.

[886] Silas Deane to Comm. of Secret Corres., Paris, Dec. 3, 1776, RDCW, II, 210, 211.

[887] BF to Silas Deane, Auray in Brittany, Dec. 4, 1776, RDCW, II, 216–218.

[888] GW to Pres. of Cong., Trenton, Dec. 5, 1776, GWW, VI, 330–332.

[889] See GW to Pres. of Cong., Mr. Berkleys Summer seat, Dec. 8, 1776, GWW, VI, 335.

[890] MJTF, 144.

[891] BF to John Hancock, Nantes, Dec. 8, 1776, BFPL, XXIII, 31–33.

[892] GW to Lund Washington, Falls of Delaware, South Side, Dec. 10, 1776, GWW, VI, 345–346.

[893] LFCA, 79.

[894] Quoted in GWWF, V, 83 n.

[895] MJTF, 144. SWHA, 152.

[896] Silas Deane to Comm. of Secret Corres., Paris, Dec. 12, 1776, RDCW, II, 224.

[897] Charles Lee to Gen. Horatio Gates, Basking Ridge, Dec. 12/13, 1776, LP, II, 348.

[898] Caron de Beaumarchais, "A Faithful Statement of the good Offices of the Court of France Toward the Court of England, against her own Commercial Interests" [1779], SFAC, XXIII, 2008.

[899] GW to Council of Safety of Penn., Hdqr., Bucks County, Falls of Delaware, South Side, Dec. 15, 1776, GWW, VI, 376.

[900] GW to Lund Washington, Falls of Delaware, South Side, Dec. 10 [-17], 1776, GWW, VI, 345, 347.

[901] GW to John Augustine Washington, Camp, Near the Falls of Trenton, Dec. 18, 1776, GWW, VI, 396, 398–399.

[902] Thomas Paine's first "crisis" essay appeared in the *Pennsylvania Journal* and four days later as a pamphlet. TPHD, 61.

[903] TPW, I, 50.

[904] GW to Pres. of Cong., Camp, Above Trenton Falls, Dec. 20, 1776, GWW, VI, 400, 402, 404, 406.

[905] Lord Stormont to Murray Keith, Dec. 20, 1776, DNL, II, 103, partially quoted in PJFR, 219.

[906] Robert Morris to Commissioners at Paris, Phil., Dec. 21, 1776, RDCW, II, 231–235.

[907] Benjamin Rush to JA, Feb. 12, 1812, A&R, 206–207.

[908] BFPL, XXIII, 85 n.

[909] BFBR, 7.

[910] See MJTF, 155–158, 238, GWRH, II, 7.

[911] GW to Pres. of Cong., Hdqr., Newton, Dec. 27, 1776, GWW, VI, 441–443.

[912] Comm. of Secret Corres. to American Commissioners, Balt., Dec. 30, 1776, BFPL, XXIII, 96–98.

[913] JA to Edmund Jenings, July 18, 1780, JAPM, Reel 352.

[914] GW to Pres. of Cong., Pluckamin, Jan. 5,

1777, GWW, VI, 467–469. See MJTF, 159–160, GWRH, II, 16–17, 31–42.

[915] Quoted in GWWF, V, 149 n.

[916] Timothy Pickering to James Robertson, Salem, July 29, 1824, as reported in John Womack Wright, "Pickering's Letter on Washington," TYQ, VII (July, 1925), 16, 36.

[917] TJ to Samuel Smith, Monticello, Aug. 22, 1798, TJWF, VIII, 443.

[918] WDRP, 553–554.

[919] TPHD, 232–233, TPKJ, 322.

[920] WDRP, WDKP, 48.

[921] WDRP, 545–555.

[922] JAWO, I, 660. See CEFP, 93–94.

[923] BF to Comm. of Secret Corres., Paris, Jan. 4, 1777, BFPL, XXIII, 113–114.

[924] Jacques-Donatien Le Ray de Chaumont to BF, [before Jan. 4, 1777], BFPL, XXIII, 112.

[925] BFPL, XXIII, 112 n.

[926] BF, Lee, and Deane to Vergennes, Paris, Jan. 5, 1777, BFPL, XXIII, 122–123.

[927] [The American Commissioners]: Memoir [for Vergennes] [c. Jan. 8, 1777], BFPL, XXIII, 126–127.

[928] BF to Mary Hewson, Paris, Jan. 12, 1777, BFPL, XXIII, 155–156.

[929] Quoted in BFP, 49, and, with some variation, in BFFC, 61–62.

[930] BF, Lee, and Deane to Comm. of Secret Corres., Paris, Jan. 17, 1777, BFPL, XX, III, 194, 196.

[931] GW to Pres. of Cong., Hdqr., Morristown, Jan. 22, 1777, GWW, VII, 48, 49.

[932] Jonathan Williams, Jr., to American Commissioners, Nantes, Jan. 23, 1777, BFPL, XXIII, 225–226.

[933] BFPL, XXIII, 236 n.

[934] Jonathan Williams, Jr., to BF, Nantes, Jan. 25, 1777, BFPL, XXIII, 231–232.

[935] GW to Pres. of Cong., Morristown, Jan. 26, 1777, GWW, VII, 63, 67.

[936] GW to Maj. Gen. Philip Schuyler, Hdqr., Morristown, Jan. 27, 1777, GWW, VII, 68–69.

[937] BF to Joseph Priestley, Paris, Jan. 17, 1777, BFPL, XXIII, 237–238. Bracketed words replace the word "make" (which your author construes as camouflage for the French release of arms and ammunition for America).

[938] GW to Pres. of Cong., Hdqr., Morristown, Jan. 31, 1777, GWW, VII, 80–81. See GWRH, II, 73.

[939] Richard Bache to BF, Phil., Feb. 5, 1777, BFPL, XXIII, 279–281.

[940] Lambert Wickes to American Commission-

ers, Port Lewis, Feb. 14, 1777, BFPL, XXIII, 330.

[941] Sarah Bache to BF, Goshen, Feb. 23, 1777, BFPL, XXIII, 361–362.

[942] La Rochefoucauld to BF, before Feb. 24, 1777, BFPL, XXIII, 375 and 375 n.

[943] JAWO, IX, 622–623. See BFPL, XXII, 514.

[944] GW to New York Legislature, Mar. 1, 1777, GWW, VII, 215–216.

[945] GW to Gov. Trumbull, Hdqr., Morristown, Mar. 3, 1777, GWW, VII, 229, 230.

[946] GW to Pres. of Cong. (two letters), Hdqr., Morristown, Mar. 29, 1777, GWW, VII, 328–330.

[947] GW to Gov. Jonathan Trumbull, Hdqr., Morristown, Mar. 29, 1777, GWW, VII, 332, 334.

[948] GW to Gov. Nicholas Cooke, Hdqr., Morristown, Apr. 3, 1777, GWW, VII, 349.

[949] See MJTF, 208, 278–281, 505, SWHA, 137–140, MJSS, 21, BSDR, 37, 93.

[950] JA to Abigail Adams, Phil., Apr. 6, 1777, JAFC, II, 199–200.

[951] BF and Silas Deane to Comm. of Secret Corres., Paris, Mar. 12 [-Apr. 9], 1777, BFPL, XXIII, 466, 471–473.

[952] Comtesse Conway to BF, Apr. 14, 1777, BFPL, XXIII, 582.

[953] MJSS, 23–24.

[954] FBRS, 67.

[955] 1777 British pamphlet quoted in SLFR, 75–76.

[956] Abigail Adams to JA, Apr. 20, 1777, JAFC, II, 217–218.

[957] GW to Richard Henry Lee, Morristown, Apr. 24, 1777, GWW, VII, 462–464.

[958] Robert Gordon to John Robinson, Cork, Apr. 25, 1777, DRDK, XIV, 73.

[959] JA to James Warren, Phil., Apr. 27, 1777, JAPA, V, 173–174.

[960] Comm. of Secret Corres. to Commissioners at Paris, Phil., May 9, 1777, BFPL, XXIV, 46–47.

[961] BF, News from America [memorandum], Paris, May 12, 1777, BFPL, XXIV, 52–53.

[962] BF to Richard Bache, Passy, May 22, 1777, BFPL, XXIV, 63–64.

[963] American Commissioners in Paris to Comm. for Foreign Affairs [BF's handwriting], Paris, May 25, 1777, BFPL, XXIV, 73–76. See SWHA, 163–164.

[964] Abigail Adams to JA, May 28, 1777, JAFC, II, 248.

[965] Comm. of Foreign Affairs to Commissioners at Paris, Phil., May 30, 1777, BFPL, XXIV, 101.

[966] JA to Abigail Adams, Phil., June 18, 1777, JAFC, II, 267–268.

[967] GW to Chevalier D'Anmours, Hdqr., Camp at Middle Brook, June 19, 1777, GWW, VIII, 265, 266.

[968] TPW, II, 1132.

[969] William Carmichael to William Bingham, Paris, June 25 [-July 6], 1777, RDCW, II, 346–349.

[970] Lambert Wickes to American Commissioners, St. Malo, June 28, 1777, BFPL, XXIV, 232–234.

[971] Richard Bache to BF, Phil., July 1, 1777, BFPL, XXIV, 250–251.

[972] Lord Weymouth to Lord Stormont, July 4, 1777, quoted in SWHA, 185.

[973] Gen. Sir William Howe to Lord George Germain (No. 62), N.Y., July 7, 1777, DRDK, XIV, 129–130.

[974] Lord Stormont to Lord Weymouth, Paris, July 16, 1777, SFAC, XVI, 1575.

[975] Vergennes to Commissioners at Paris, Versailles, July 16, 1777, RDCW, II, 364.

[976] Lord Stormont to Lord Weymouth, Paris, July 16, 1777, SFAC, XVI, 1577.

[977] Lambert Wickes to Captain Henry Johnson, St. Malo, July 20, 1777, SFAC, XVI, 1583. See LWSR, 188–189.

[978] GW to Gov. Jonathan Trumbull, Coryell's Ferry on Delaware, July 31, 1777, GWW, VIII, 506–507.

[979] JCC, VIII, 604.

[980] JADA, III, 387.

[981] GW to John Augustine Washington, Germantown, near Phil., Aug. 5, 1777, GWW, IX, 20, 22.

[982] BFBS, 60.

[983] See JCC, VIII, 357, 357 n.-358 n.

[984] MJTF, 179–182, 190–191.

[985] GW to Pres. of Cong., Phil., Aug. 3, 1777, GWW, IX, 8–9. See GWRH, III, 133, 135–136, BARC, 335.

[986] Lieut. Gen. John Burgoyne to Lord George Germain (Private), Nearly Opposite to Saratoga, Aug. 20, 1777, DRDK, XIV, 165–167.

[987] GW to Pres. of Cong., Camp, at Cross Roads, Aug. 22, 1777, GWW, IX, 118–119.

[988] GW to Maj. Gen. Sullivan, Wilmington, Aug. 27, 1777, GWW, IX, 135.

[989] Quoted in GWRH, III, 139–140.

[990] Silas Deane to Robert Morris, Paris, Aug. 23, 1777. RDCS, I, 105–111.

[991] Paper by Comte de Vergennes, read to King of France, Aug. 23, 1777, SFAC, VII, 706.

992 GW to Pres. of Cong., Aug. 23, 1777, GWW, IX,127–128.

993 See MJTF, 200, MJSS, 26, GLP, 43.

994 JA to Abigail Adams, Phil., Sept. 2, 1777, JAFC, II, 336.

995 See MJTF, 202–203, HNYJ, I, 197, GWRH, III, 176, MSOH, 249.

996 GW to Pres. of Cong., Chester, Penn., Sept. 11, 1777, GWW, IX, 207.

997 Timothy Pickering to James Robertson, Salem, July 29, 1824, as reported in John Womack Wright, "Pickering's Letter on Washington," TYQ, VII (July, 1925), 16, 30.

998 HNYJ, I, 197.

999 GW to Pres. of Cong., Camp, Sept. 19, 1777, GWW, IX, 237, 238–239. See MJTF, 202.

1000 Timothy Pickering to James Robertson, Salem, July 29, 1824, as reported in John Womack Wright, "Pickering's Letter on Washington," TYQ, VII (July, 1925), 16, 25, 30–31.

1001 See MJTF, 204, TPHD, 68–70, GWRH, III, 183.

1002 Thomas Paine to BF, Yorktown, May 16, 1778, TPW, II, 1143, 1144.

1003 JADA, II, 264.

1004 Thomas Paine to BF, Yorktown, May 16, 1778, TPW, II, 1143, 1147.

1005 "Journal of Thomas Sullivan, H. M. Forty-Ninth Regiment of Foot," 132, in Hist. Soc. of Penn., as quoted in Henry Pleasants, Jr., "The Battle of Paoli," PMHB, LXXII (1948), 44, 45.

1006 JADA, II, 265.

1007 GW to Pres. of Cong., Camp, Near Potts Grove, Sept. 23, 1777, GWW, IX, 257–259.

1008 Elias Boudinot to Elisha Boudinot, Sept. 23, 1777, as quoted in GWKB, 195.

1009 Baron de K[alb] to Comte [de Broglie], Lancaster, Penn., Sept. 24, 1777, SFAC, VIII, 755.

1010 See Thomas Paine to BF, Yorktown, May 16, 1778, TPW, II, 1143, 1145, AGA, Aug. 29, 1804, TCER, 25–26 (which puts the occupying force at 3,000).

1011 GW to Pres. of Cong., Camp, Near Pennibacker's Mill, Oct. 5, 1777, GWW, IX, 308–310. See MJTF, 205–206, GWMK, 170–171, GLP, 44, TCER, 26–27, GWRH, III, 187–208.

1012 BFBR, 67.

1013 Minutes of Council of War at Saratoga, Oct. 12–15, 1777, DRDK, XIV, 212–215.

1014 Henry Laurens to John Laurens, Oct. 16, 1777, as quoted in GWKB, 67.

1015 MJTF, 208. See MJTF, 195, 212–213, SWHA, 137–140, BSDR, 37, 93.

1016 Orlando W. Stephenson, "The Supply of Gunpowder in 1776," AHR, XXX (Jan. 1925), 281.

1017 Orlando W. Stephenson, "The Supply of Gunpowder in 1776," AHR, XXX (Jan. 1925), 277–281.

1018 GW to Richard Henry Lee, Matuchen Hill, Oct. 17, 1777, GWW, IX, 387–389.

1019 SDBF, 272.

1020 "A Letter to GW . . . " TPW, II, 691, 720–721.

1021 GWRH, III, 228.

1022 GW to Landon Carter, Phil. Cty, Oct. 27, 1777, GWW, IX, 451, 453.

1023 Thomas Paine to Richard Henry Lee, Hdqr., fourteen miles from Phil., Oct. 30, 1777, TPW, II, 1138, 1140.

1024 GWRH, III, 251.

1025 Jonathan Dickson Sergeant to James Lovell, Nov. 20, 1777, as quoted in GWKB, 194.

1026 JCC, IX, 970–971.

1027 James Lovell to Horatio Gates, Nov. 27, 1777, Gates Papers (N.Y. Hist. Soc.), quoted in NGL, II, 7–8.

1028 GW to Thomas Conway, Nov. 9, 1777, GWW, X, 29, quotes the letter from Conway to Horatio Gates.

1029 JCC, IX, 975.

1030 JADA, IV, 3.

1031 JCC, IX, 1013–1014.

1032 Benjamin Rush to JA, Feb. 12, 1812, A&R, 206, 209.

1033 JCC, IX, 1023, 1026.

1034 BF, Deane, and Lee to Comm. of Foreign Affairs, Paris, Dec. 18, 1777, BFPL, XXV, 305–306.

1035 JCC, IX, 1035–1036.

1036 Penn. Archives: [1st ser.] Samuel Hazard, ed. (Phil.: J. Severns & Co., 1852–1856), VI, 104. The date of the remonstrance is surmised from its placement in the archives and from the action of the Continental Congress the next day.

1037 GW to Pres. of Cong., Valley Forge, Dec. 23, 1777, GWW, X, 192–194.

1038 Marquis de Lafayette to GW, Camp, Dec. 30, 1777, LFL, 14–16.

1039 Monsieur Gérard to [Comte de Vergennes], Jan. 1, 1778, SFAC, XXI, 1817.

1040 James Craik to GW, Port Tobacco, Maryland, Jan. 6, 1778, GWWS, V, 493–494.

1041 SWHA, 260–261.

1042 Louis XVI to Charles III, Jan. 8, 1778, RDCW, II, 467.

1043 Monsieur Gérard, Narrative of a Conference with the American Commissioners, Versailles, Jan. 9, 1778, SFAC, XXI, 1831.

1044 Anonymous (Benjamin Rush) to Patrick Henry, Yorktown, Jan. 12, 1778, GWWS, V, 495–496.

1045 BEJ, 73–76.

1046 Richard Bache to BF, Manheim 10 Miles wide of Lancaster, Jan. 31, 1778, BFPL, XXV, 551, 553.

1047 DJDH, 165–169.

1048 JCC, XI, 421–446.

1049 WDRP, 555.

1050 WDRP, 557.

1051 BFP, 121 ff.

1052 CMLV, I, 181.

1053 JADA, IV, 6–7.

1054 CMLV, I, 184–185. See BFFS, 124. For a different version, see HMP, III, 431. Though no dispositive evidence exists that Voltaire blessed BFB rather than William Temple Franklin, it would seem more reasonable for BF to request (even humorously) Voltaire's benediction for an eight-year-old child than for an eighteen-year-old man who was then secretary to the American legation. A rendering in *La Revue des Lettres et des Arts* (1889), reproduced in FNE, II, 78, affirms the image of a child rather than of a young adult.

1055 Lafayette to GW, Albany, Feb. 27, 1778, LFL, 31, 32.

1056 JADA, IV, 5–6.

1057 JCPB, II, 79.

1058 "To The Citizens of the United States," Letter VIII, TPW, II, 955–956, AGA, June 7, 1805.

1059 Lord George Germain to Lords of the Admiralty (Most Secret and Confidential), Whitehall, Mar. 21, 1778, DRDK, XV, 72–73.

1060 Secret Instructions for Gen. Sir Henry Clinton, St. James, Mar. 21, 1778, DRDK, XV, 74–75.

1061 M. d'Estaing à M. Gérard . . . Extraits de mes instructions du 27 mars 1778, DNL, III, 237.

1062 See MJTF, 316, SWHA, 282, MJSS, 59.

1063 King of France to Cong., Versailles, Mar. 28, 1778, RDCW, II, 521–522.

1064 BF to Richard and Sarah Bache, Passy, Mar. 31, 1778, BFPL, XXVI, 202–203.

1065 BF to Robert Livingston, July 22, 1783, BFSM, VIII, 62, IX, 62.

1066 JA to Dr. Benjamin Rush, Apr. 12, 1809, JAWO, IX, 619.

1067 Noted under Feb. 11, 1779, JAWO, III, 189.

1068 JADA, IV, 36–37.

1069 JADA, IV, 41–42.

1070 Noted under Feb. 11, 1779, JAWO, III, 190.

1071 JADA, IV, 48–49.

1072 JA to Abigail Adams, Passy, Apr. 12, 1778, JAFC, III, 9.

1073 DJFN, 112, MJSS, 57–58. GWKB,101 says fleet departed April 3.

1074 "Extracts of Letters from Paris . . . in the hand of Paul Wentworth," Apr. 16, 1778, SFAC, XXII, 1914.

1075 JADA, II, 302.

1076 JADA, IV, 69.

1077 BEJ, 77–81.

1078 MFDR, 565.

1079 JADA, IV, 79–81.

1080 [Virginia Delelgates in Cong.] to Gov. of Virginia, York, May 3, 1778, RHLL, I, 396–397.

1081 JCC, XI, 457–458.

1082 Gen. Orders, Hdqr., Valley Forge, May 5, 1778, GWW, XI, 353–354.

1083 From the *N.Y. Journal* (New York), June 15, 1778, as reported in MFDR, 578.

1084 "A Letter to GW . . . ," TPW, II, 691, 720.

1085 JADA, IV, 92.

1086 Thomas Paine to BF, Yorktown, May 16, 1778, TPW, II, 1143, 1151.

1087 JADA, IV, 118–119.

1088 JADA, IV, 120.

1089 JADA, IV, 120.

1090 JADA, IV, 121–123.

1091 Patrick Henry to Richard Henry Lee, Williamsburg, June 18, 1778, PHL, I, 564–565.

1092 GW to Pres. of Cong., Hdqr., 1/2 after 11 A. M., June 18, 1778, GWW, XII, 82–83.

1093 Gen. Sir Henry Clinton to Lord George Germain, N.Y., July 5, 1778, DRDK, XV, 159.

1094 GW to Pres. of Cong., English Town, July 1, 1778, GWW, XII, 139–146.

1095 LP, II, 435–436, as quoted in CLMS, 70–71.

1096 See CLMS.

1097 John Quincy Adams enrolled at Le Coeur's on Apr. 13th. JADA, IV, 57–58.

1098 JCC, XII, 908.

1099 JCC, VIII, 1034–1035.

1100 ALLR, I, 404–405.

1101 JA to James Warren, Passy, Dec. 5, 1778, JAWL, II, 73, 77.

1102 JA to Mercy Otis Warren, Passy, Dec. 18, 1778, JAPA, VII, 281, 282–284.

[1103] GWRH, III, 458. See GWF, II, 336 n, GWMK, 265.

[1104] JCC, XIII, 62–63.

[1105] JADA, II, 346.

[1106] JA to Samuel Adams, Passy, Feb. 14, 1779, JAPM, Reel 93.

[1107] JA to Abigail Adams, Passy, Feb. 20, 1779, JAFC, III, 175.

[1108] JA to Abigail Adams, Feb. 28, 1779 (2 letters), JAFC, III, 181–182.

[1109] JAPS, I, 426–431.

[1110] Gerard to Vergennes, Phil., Mar. 8, 1779, CGD, 563 (Dispatch 95), 565.

[1111] Gerard to Vergennes, Phil., Mar. 8, 1779, CGD, 568–570 (Dispatch 96).

[1112] BF to Jane Mecum, Passy, Apr. 22, 1779, BFPL, XXIX, 357–358.

[1113] BF to BFB, Passy, May 3, 1779, BFPL, XXIX, 413.

[1114] BF to David Hartley, Passy, May 4, 1779, BFPL, XXIX, 425–427.

[1115] JADA, II, 369. See JAC, 123–125.

[1116] BFB to BF, May 30, 1779, BFPL, XXIX, 578.

[1117] BF to Richard Bache, Passy, June 2, 1779, BFPL, XXIX, 599–600.

[1118] BF to Sarah Bache, Passy, June 3, 1779, BFPL, XXIX, 612–615.

[1119] JA to Edmund Jenings, L'Orient, June 8, 1779, JAPA, VIII, 78, 80.

[1120] Comte de Vergennes to Chevalier de La Luzerne, June 18, 1779, DJNM, 215–216.

[1121] JADA, II, 390–392.

[1122] GW to Pres. of Cong., Hdqr., New Windsor, July 21, 1779, GWW, XV, 447–448.

[1123] GW to Joseph Reed, Westpoint, July 29, 1779, GWW, XVI, 7–9.

[1124] GWWF, VII, 501 n.- 502 n.

[1125] JAPS, I, 434.

[1126] See BFBT, 30–31, BFBL.

[1127] BF to BFB, Passy, Aug. 19, 1779, BFPL, XXX, 241–242.

[1128] A&R, 145 n.

[1129] JA to Benjamin Rush, Apr. 12, 1809, A&R, 142, 145.

[1130] JA to Benjamin Rush, Braintree, Sept. 19, 1779, JAPA, VIII, 153.

[1131] JPJ, 148–163.

[1132] JCC, XV, 113.

[1133] JADA, IV, 178–180.

[1134] JADA, IV, 242–243.

[1135] Gen. Sir Henry Clinton to Lord George Germain, N.Y., Sept. 30 1779, DRDK, XVII, 229–230.

[1136] DNL, IV, 327 n.

[1137] See MJTF, 402–403, MJSS, 93, GWRH, III, 476, ODF, 68.-69.

[1138] Gen. Sir Henry Clinton to Lord George Germain, N.Y., Oct. 18, 1779, DRDK, XVII, 237.

[1139] JA prepared the first draft of the new Massachusetts state constitution. See Samuel Eliot Morison, "The Struggle over the Adoption of the Constitution of Massachusetts, 1780," *Proceedings of MHS*, L, 353, 356.

[1140] JAWO, IV, 220–266.

[1141] Oscar and Mary Handlin, eds. *The Popular Sources of Political Authority: Documents on the Massachusetts Constitution of 1780.* (Cambridge: Belknap Press of Harv. Univ. Press, 1966), 434, 437–438. The Constitutional Convention submitted its proposed constitution and the "Address" to Massachusetts towns on Mar. 2, 1780.

[1142] Samuel Eliot Morison, "The Struggle Over the Adoption of the Constitution of Massachusetts, 1780," *Proceedings of MHS,* L, 353, 389. See UHRA, 162–165.

[1143] JA to James Sullivan, Phil., May 26, 1776, JAPA, IV, 210.

[1144] JA to Benjamin Rush, Apr. 12, 1809, A&R, 142, 144.

[1145] TPHD, 102, 106.

[1146] JADA, IV, 191.

[1147] GW to Pres. of Cong., Hdqr., Morristown, Dec. 15, 1779, GWW, XVII, 272–273.

[1148] GW to Pres. of Cong., Hdqr., Morristown, Jan. 5, 1780, GWW, XVII, 355.

[1149] JA to Cong., Paris, Feb. 15, 1780, JADA, IV, 240.

[1150] JAWO, IX, 623. See JAPW, 105–106.

[1151] JADA, IV, 241.

[1152] JA to Comte de Vergennes, Paris, Feb. 12, 1780, JADA IV, 243–244.

[1153] Comte de Vergennes to JA, Versailles, Feb. 13, 1780, RDCS, IV, 363–364.

[1154] JADA, IV, 250–251.

[1155] JADA, IV, 251–252.

[1156] JADA, IV, 252.

[1157] JA to Comte de Vergennes, Paris, Feb. 25, 1780, JADA, IV, 253.

[1158] JA to James Lovell, Paris, Mar. 4, 1780, JAPM, Reel 96.

[1159] Instructions Delivered to M. de La Fayette [in the hand of M. de Vergennes], Mar. 5, 1780, DNL, IV, 314–315.

[1160] BF to GW, Passy, Mar. 5, 1780, BFSM, VIII, 27–29.

[1161] JCC, XVI, 263–265.

[1162] BF to Joseph Reed, Mar. 19, 1780, BFWS, VIII, 443, 445.

[1163] See MJSS, 115, PJFR 305, ODF, 70.

[1164] See DJFN, 191, MJTF, 513–518.

[1165] GWRH, III, 515–516.

[1166] GW to Marquis de Lafayette, Hdqr., Morristown, May 16, 1780, GWW, XVIII, 369–370.

[1167] GW to Joseph Reed, Morristown, May 28, 1780, GWW, XVIII, 434–435.

[1168] Chaumont to [unidentified] official of French Foreign Ministry, Passy, June 16, 1780, DJNM, 224–226. The "forty percent" figure is obviously mistaken.

[1169] BP, May 15, 1811, as reprinted in JAWO, I, 649, 654.

[1170] GW to Pres. of Cong., Hdqr., Springfield, June 20, 1780, GWW, XIX, 34–35.

[1171] Comte de Vergennes to JA, Versailles, June 21, 1780, JAWO, VII, 190–192.

[1172] JA to Comte de Vergennes, Paris, June 22, 1780, RDCW, II, 809–816.

[1173] JA to Comte de Vergennes, Paris, June 22, 1780, JAWO, VII, 193.

[1174] JA to Comte de Vergennes, Paris, June 22, 1780, JAWO, VII, 193.

[1175] BF to Comte de Vergennes, June 24, 1780, DJNM, 227.

[1176] Comte de Vergennes to JA, Versailles, June 30, 1780, RDCS, V, 232.

[1177] BP, May 15, 1811, as reprinted in JAWO, I, 649, 655.

[1178] Comte de Vergennes to BF, Versailles, June 30, 1780, DJNM, 227, 228–229. See RDCS, III, 152–153.

[1179] BP, May 15, 1811, as reprinted in JAWO, I, 649–651.

[1180] JA to Comte de Vergennes, Paris, July 1, 1780, RDCS, V, 233–234.

[1181] BP, May 15, 1811, as reprinted in JAWO, I, 649, 655.

[1182] GW to Fielding Lewis, Bergen County, Jersey, July 6, 1780, GWW, XIX, 129–132.

[1183] BFBR, 8.

[1184] BF to Comte de Vergennes, Paris, July 10, 1780, RDCS, V, 245–246.

[1185] See MJTF, xiii, 526, MJSS, 117–118.

[1186] GW to Comm. of Cooperation, July 13, 1780, GWW, XIX, 165, 166.

[1187] JA to Comte de Vergennes, Paris, July 13, 1780, RDCS, V, 247–259.

[1188] JA to Comte de Vergennes, Paris, July 17, 1780, RDCS, V, 266, 267.

[1189] JA to Edmund Jenings, July 18, 1780, JAPM, Reel 352.

[1190] Comte de Vergennes to JA, Versailles, July 20, 1780, RDCS, V, 278.

[1191] GW to Pres. of Cong., Hdqr., Prekeniss, July 22, 1780, GWW, XIX, 234–235.

[1192] Comte de Vergennes to JA, Versailles, June 25, 1780, JAWO, VII, 235–236.

[1193] JA to Comte de Vergennes, Paris, July 26, 1780, RDCW, IV, 7–10.

[1194] JA to Comte de Vergennes, Paris, July 27, 1780, RDCS, V, 301–303.

[1195] Comte de Vergennes to JA, Versailles, July 29, 1780, RDCS, V, 304–305.

[1196] Comte de Vergennes to BF, Versailles, July 31, 1780, RDCS, V, 305–306.

[1197] BP, May 15, 1811, as reprinted in JAWO, I, 649, 651–652.

[1198] JA left Paris on July 27th. JA to Pres. of Cong., Amsterdam, Aug. 14, 1780, JAWO, VII, 244.

[1199] BF to Samuel Huntington, Aug. 9, 1780, BFSM, VIII, 128.

[1200] JA to Mercy Warren, Quincy, Aug. 3, 1807, JAPM, Reel 118. See BP, May 15, 1811, as reprinted in JAWO, I, 649, 658.

[1201] Comte de Vergennes to Chevalier de La Luzerne, Aug. 7, 1780, DJNM, 232–233.

[1202] BF to Pres. of Cong., Passy, Aug. 9, 1780, RDCS, III, 161, 163–164.

[1203] BP, May 15, 1811, as reprinted in JAWO, I, 649, 653, 655–567.

[1204] BFB to BF, Dec. 21, 1779, BFB Papers (APS), as quoted in BFBT, 39.

[1205] Gen. Anthony Wayne to Robert Morris, York, Oct. 26, 1781, AWSC, 283.

[1206] Alexander Hamilton to James Duane, [Bergen County, N. J.], Sept. 6, 1780, AHP, II, 420–421.

[1207] WCWR, II, 728–730.

[1208] GW to Comm. of Cooperation, Hdqr., Orange Town, Aug. 17, 1780, GWW, XIX, 391.

[1209] GW to Pres. of Cong., Hdqr., Orange Town, Aug. 20, 1780, GWW, XIX, 402, 405.

[1210] GW to Comte de Guichen, Hdqr., Bergen County, Sept. 12, 1780, GWW, XX, 39–42.

[1211] GW to Pres. of Cong., Hdqr., New Bridge, Sept. 15, 1780, GWW, XX, 49, 51.

[1212] "Conference at Hartford," Sept. 22, 1780, GWW, XX, 76.

[1213] GW to Gov. Clinton [of N.Y.], Hdqr., Robinson's House, Sept. 26, 1780, GWW, XX, 93–94.

[1214] BF to John Jay, Passy, Oct. 2, 1780, BFSM, VIII, 142–143.

[1215] BF to JA, Passy, Ocober 8, 1780, RDCW, IV, 86–87. See JAPS, I, 480.

[1216] Marquis de Lafayette to GW, Light Camp, Oct. 30, 1780, LFSL, III, 211–212.

[1217] GW to Marquis de Lafayette, Hdqr., Oct. 30, 1780, GWW, XX, 266–267.

[1218] JCC, XVIII, 1079–1084.

[1219] Vergennes to Luzerne, Versailles, Dec. 4, 1780, RDCW, IV, 181–182.

[1220] JCC, XVIII, 1130.

[1221] GW to Gouverneur Morris, Hdqr., New Windsor, Dec. 10, 1780, GWW, XX, 457–458.

[1222] JCC, XVIII, 1141.

[1223] GWRH, III, 590–593.

[1224] Circular to New England States and New York, Hdqr., New Windsor, Jan. 5, 1781, GWW, XXI, 61–62.

[1225] Pres. of Cong. to JA, In Cong., Jan. 10, 1781, JAWO, VII, 353.

[1226] TJ to GW, Richmond, Jan. 10, 1781, TJPB, IV, 333–335.

[1227] GW to Lieut. Col. John Laurens, New Windsor, Jan. 15, 1781, GWW, XXI, 105–109.

[1228] GW to BF, New Windsor, Jan. 15, 1781, GWW, XXI, 100–101.

[1229] GW to Mrs. Sarah Bache, New Windsor, Jan. 15, 1781. GWW, XXI, 101–102.

[1230] Circular to New England States and New York, Hdqr., New Windsor, Jan. 22, 1781, GWW, XXI, 129–130.

[1231] GW to Inspector-Gen. von Steuben, Feb. 6, 1781, GWW, XXI, 192–193.

[1232] TPHD, 115.

[1233] "A Letter to GW . . . " TPW, II, 720.

[1234] BF to Comte de Vergennes, Passy, Feb. 13, 1781, RDCS, III, 186–188.

[1235] Comte de Vergennes to Chevalier de La Luzerne, Versailles, Feb. 19, 1781, DNL, IV, 583–584.

[1236] ANAM, II, 556, 558.

[1237] GWRH, III, 625.

[1238] Comte de Vergennes to Chevalier de La Luzerne, Mar. 9, 1781, DJNM, 236–237.

[1239] TPHD, 116.

[1240] As of Mar. 27, Laurens was still on the coast of France. See D. E. Huger Smith, ed., "The Mission of Col. John Laurens to Europe in 1781," S. Carolina Hist. and Geneol. Mag., I (1900), 34.

[1241] BF to Samuel Huntington, Passy, Mar. 12, 1781, BFSM, VIII, 217–219.

[1242] MJTF, 549–550, GWRH, III, 614.

[1243] John Laurens to Pres. of Cong., Passy, Mar. 20, 1781, RDCS, IX, 208–209.

[1244] John Laurens to Pres. of Cong., Phil., Sept. 2, 1781, RDCS, IX, 235–237.

[1245] GW to Benjamin Harrison, Hdqr., New Windsor, Mar. 27, 1781, GWW, XXI, 380–382. Harrison was speaker of the Va. House of Delegates.

[1246] GW to John Laurens at Paris, New Windsor, Apr. 9, 1781, GWW, XXI, 436, 438–439.

[1247] BF to William Carmichael, Passy, Apr. 12, 1781, BFSM, VIII, 236–237.

[1248] Comte de Vergennes to La Luzerne, Versailles, Apr. 19, 1781, DNL, IV, 588, 590.

[1249] Lafayette to GW, Alexandria, Apr. 23, 1781, LFM, I, 146.

[1250] GW to Lund Washington, New Windsor, Apr. 30, 1781, GWW, XXII, 14–15.

[1251] MJTF, 609, 609 n.

[1252] Comte de Vergennes to La Luzerne, Versailles, May 11, 1781, DNL, IV, 560.

[1253] BF to M. de Lafayette, Passy, May 14, 1781, RDCS, III, 209, 211.

[1254] "Substance of a Conference between Gen. Washington and Comte de Rochambeau at Weathersfield, 22 May, 1781," GWWF, IX, 251, 254.

[1255] GW To Chevalier de La Luzerne, Weathersfield, May 23, 1781, GWW, XXII, 103.

[1256] "A Letter to GW . . . " TPW, II, 691, 721.

[1257] Comte de Rochambeau to de Grasse, June 11, 1781, DNL, IV, 647, quoted and translated in MJSS, 152, and in GWRH, III, 640.

[1258] Gen. Sir Henry Clinton to Lieut. Gen. Earl Cornwallis, N.Y., DRDK, XX , 157–159.

[1259] Richard Henry Lee to Virginia Delegates in Cong., Chantilly, June 12, 1781, TJPB, VI, 90–92.

[1260] Autobiography, TJWF, I, 79.

[1261] TJMD, I, 354–358.

[1262] GW to Comte de Rochambeau, Hdqr., New Windsor, June 13, 1781, GWW, XXII, 207–209.

[1263] JCC, XX, 652–654. Instructions, JCC, XX, 651–652.

[1264] Quoted in MJSS, 152.

[1265] MJSS, 156, GWRH, III, 635.

[1266] See Gen. Sir Henry Clinton to Lieut. Gen. Earl Cornwallis, N.Y., June 11, 1781, DRDK, XX, 157–159 and Lieut. Gen. Earl Cornwallis to Gen. Sir Henry Clinton, Portsmouth, Virginia, July 27, 1781, DRDK, XX, 196–197.

[1267] James Lovell to JA, June 21, 1781, JAPM, Reel 355.

[1268] JCC, XX, 746–747.

1269 James Lovell to Abigail Adams, July 13, 1781, JAFC, IV, 173.

1270 GW to Richard Henry Lee, Camp, Near Dobbs Ferry, July 15, 1781, GWW, XXII, 382, 384.

1271 BFBR, 7.

1272 James Lovell to JA, Phil., July 21, 1781, LCC, VI, 151.

1273 GW to Comte de Grasse, Hdqr., Dobbs Ferry, July 21, 1781, GWW, XXII, 400–401.

1274 WPAE, I, Map 9.

1275 GW to La Fayette, Hdqr. near Dobbs Ferry, July 30, 1781, GWW, XXII, 432–433.

1276 MSOH, 259–260.

1277 "A Letter to GW . . . ," TPW, II, 718.

1278 GW to Pres. of Cong., Hdqr., Dobbs Ferry, Aug. 2, 1781, GWW, XXII, 445–447.

1279 BFBR, 9.

1280 MJTF, 594–595, MJSS, 165, GJAY, 113.

1281 BFB to BF, Geneva, Aug. 16, 1781, BFBC, Film 1506, Reel 1.

1282 GWD, II, 253–254.

1283 BF to JA, Passy, Aug. 16, 1781, JAWO, VII, 456.

1284 MJSS, 165.

1285 GJAY, 15, DJFN, 246, 246 n.

1286 JAC, 150, JAPS, I, 504–505.

1287 See JADR, 98.

1288 JA to Pres. of Cong., Amsterdam, Oct. 15, 1781, RDCW, IV, 779–780.

1289 JA to Abigail Adams, Amsterdam, Oct. 9, 1781, JAFC, IV, 224.

1290 JA to Pres. of Cong., Amsterdam, Oct. 15, 1781, RDCW, IV, 779–780. See JAC, 151–152.

1291 "A Letter to GW . . . ," TPW, II, 691, 721. See TPHD, 120, 151.

1292 GW to Superintendent of Finance, Chatham, Aug. 27, 1781, GWW, XXIII, 50, 52.

1293 TJMJ, 326–327.

1294 DFMC, 43.

1295 Gen. Anthony Wayne to Robert Morris, Williamsburg, Sept. 14, 1781, AWSC, 279, 280.

1296 Quoted in RDCS, XI, 463 n. -465 n.

1297 See MJTF, 607, MSOH, I, 263–265, GWRH, III, 649, ODF, 82.

1298 Gen. Sir Henry Clinton to Lord George Germain (No. 140), N.Y., Sept. 7, 1781, DRDK, XX, 222–223.

1299 Gen. Sir Henry Clinton to Lord George Germain (No. 141), N.Y., Sept. 12, 1781, DRDK, XX, 229–230.

1300 GWFB, 214.

1301 MJTF, 614. GJAY, 113. Historian Samuel Eliot Morrison placed GW's Yorktown army at 5,645. MSOH, 264.

1302 Lieut. Gen. Earl Cornwallis to Gen. Henry Clinton, Yorktown, Sept. 16, 1781, DRDK, XX, 231–232.

1303 DJFN, 246.

1304 Gen. Sir Henry Clinton to Lord George Germain (No. 142), N.Y., Sept. 26, 1781, DRDK, XX, 232–233.

1305 YCJH, 100, 112–117.

1306 GW to Pres. of Cong., Hdqr., Before York, Oct. 12, 1781, GWW, XXIII, 212–213.

1307 FFKL, 142.

1308 FFKL, 142.

1309 GJAY, 20–21, FFKL, 142–144.

1310 JA to Pres. of Cong., Amsterdam, Oct. 15, 1781, RDCW, IV, 776–779.

1311 GW to Pres. of Cong., Hdqr., Before York, Oct. 16, 1781, GWW, XXIII, 227–229.

1312 GJAY, 341.

1313 JA to Benjamin Rush, Dec. 4, 1805, A&R, 44–45.

1314 JA to Benjamin Rush, Jan. 26, 1806, A&R, 47–48.

1315 RANV, 140–141.

1316 MJSS, 180–181, PJFR, 394–395.

1317 GW to Pres. of Cong., Hdqr., Near York, Oct. 19, 1781, GWW, XXIII, 241–243.

1318 "A Letter to GW . . . ," TPW, II, 691, 721.

1319 Lieut. Gen. Earl Cornwallis to Gen. Henry Clinton, Yorktown, Oct. 20, 1781, DRDK, XX, 244–246.

1320 Gen. Anthony Wayne to Robert Morris, York, Oct. 26, 1781, AWSC, 283.

1321 MJTF, 614.

1322 MJSS, 182.

1323 Gen. Sir Henry Clinton to Lord George Germain (No. 145), *London* off Chesapeake, Oct. 29, 1781, DRDK, XX, 252–253.

1324 JA to Francis Dana, Amsterdam, Dec. 14, 1781, Dana Papers (MHS).

1325 BF to BFB, Passy, Jan. 25, 1782, BFSM, VIII, 372–373.

1326 BF to David Hartley, Passy, Feb. 16, 1782, BFSM, VIII, 381–382.

1327 MJTF, 617.

1328 BF to Lord Shelburne, Passy, Mar. 22, 1782, BFSM, VIII, 460–461.

1329 Lord Shelburne to BF, London, Apr. 6, 1782, BFSM, VIII, 461–462.

1330 JCCS, II, 415–416.

1331 Oswold to Shelburne, July 10, 1782, FC Lord John Russell, ed., *Memorials and Corre-*

spondence of Charles James Fox (London, 1853–1857), 4 vols., IV, 239–241. See BSDR, 207–208, MRPM, 287.

[1332] See TJMD, I, 399.

[1333] BSDR, 208.

[1334] See JAC, 161–163.

[1335] JA to Edward Jennings, Hague, July 20, 1782, JAPM, Reel 357.

[1336] Lord Shelburne to Richard Oswold, July 27, 1782, *Shelburne Papers* (William L. Clements Lib., Univ. of Michigan), LXXI, 165–169.

[1337] BF to Robert R. Livingston, Aug. 12, 1782, BFSM, VIII, 576.

[1338] BFB's Journal (translated into English by Margaret Hartmann Bache), Aug. 1, 1782–Sept. 14, 1785, BFBC, Film 1506, Reel 1.

[1339] BFBT, 33–34.

[1340] JA to Robert Livingston, Aug. 18, 1782; crossed-out portion in JA to John Trumbull, Jan. 23, 1795, De Coppet Collection, Princeton Univ. Lib. See MRPM, 304–305.

[1341] Thomas Townshend to Richard Oswald, Whitehall, Sept. 1, 1782, *Shelburne Papers* (William L. Clements Lib., Univ. of Michigan), LXXXVII,8 9.-96. See British Cabinet Meeting Minutes, Aug. 29, 1782, KGFJ,VI, 118, MRPM, 317–318.

[1342] JA to Robert Livingston, Hague, Sept. 6, 1782, JAPM, Reel 106.

[1343] Mathew Ridley to JA, Paris, Sept. 20, 1782, JAPM, Reel 358.

[1344] MRPM, 315–316.

[1345] JAC, 167, MJSS, 202. On Jay's approach to the negotiations, see DJDH,146.

[1346] Following Yorktown, French Admiral de Grasse returned to the West Indies and, on April 12, 1782, lost five ships-of-the-line and three thousand men to British Admiral George Rodney's fleet. See PJFR, 397–401.

[1347] Comte de Vergennes to Comte de Montmorin, Versailles, Oct. 2, 1782, BGH, III, 330–331. See BSDR, 243.

[1348] BSDR, 228.

[1349] RDCW, V, 805–807, MJTF, 639.

[1350] BFB to BF, Geneva, Oct. 15, 1782, BFBC, Film 1506, Reel 1.

[1351] JAC, 163.

[1352] JAC, 162.

[1353] JJPA, II, 448–449.

[1354] JADA, III, 37, JAGC, 166, JAPS, I, 537–539.

[1355] JADA, III, 38.

[1356] Mathew Ridley Diary (MHS), quoted in JADA, III, 40n.

[1357] JADA, III, 39.

[1358] JADA, III, 82.

[1359] JA to Sec. Livingston, Paris, Oct. 31, 1782, JAWO, VII, 652–654.

[1360] JADA, III, 46–47.

[1361] See MRPM, 298, 360. That Jay had a negative effect on negotiations, see MJTF, 628–632, 641.

[1362] JA to Sec. Livingston, Paris, Nov. 6, 1782, JAWO, VII, 659–660.

[1363] JA to Sec. Livingston, Paris, Nov. 8, 1782, JAWO, VIII, 3–4.

[1364] JA to Abigail Adams, Paris, Nov. 8, 1782, JAPM, Reel 359.

[1365] RDCW, V, 869.

[1366] JADA, III, 49–50.

[1367] *Letter from Alexander Hamilton, Concerning the Public Conduct and Character of John Adams Esq. President of the United States* [N.Y., Oct. 24, 1800], AHP, XXV, 169, 191.

[1368] JAC, 155.

[1369] See JAC, 155–157.

[1370] JADA, III, 53.

[1371] JADA, III, 64–65.

[1372] See MJTF, 630.

[1373] Vergennes to Luzerne, Nov. 23, 1782, as quoted in BSDR, 234 n.19.

[1374] BSDR, 232–233, 239.

[1375] JA to Robert Livingston, Paris, Dec. 4, 1782, RDCW, VI, 106. See JAC, 184.

[1376] John Jay to Robert R. Livingston, Paris, Dec. 12, 1782, JJPA, III, 6.

[1377] Comte de Vergennes to BF, Versailles, Dec. 15, 1782, RDCS, IV, 55.

[1378] BF to Comte de Vergennes, Passy, Dec. 17, 1782, RDCS, IV, 56–57.

[1379] Vergennes to La Luzerne, Versailles, Dec. 19, 1782, BFSM, X, 390–393.

[1380] BF to Samuel Cooper, Passy, Dec. 26, 1782, BFSM, VIII, 48–49.

[1381] JCC, XXIV, 4–6.

[1382] BSDR, 247.

[1383] BFB to BF, Geneva, Jan. 30, 1783, BF Papers (Hist. Soc. of Penn.).

[1384] JA to Robert Livingston, Paris, Feb. 5, 1783, JAPM, Reel 108.

[1385] JA to Thomas McKean, Paris, Feb. 6, 1783, JAPM, Reel 108. See JAC, 184n.

[1386] James Madison to TJ, Phil., Feb. 11, 1783, JMAP, VI, 220–221.

[1387] France: Feb. 25, 1783 (Ratified by the U.S. Oct. 31, 1783), TMH, II, 115, 118–120.

[1388] ODF, 90–91, MJSS, 202, 204.

1389 ODF, 91.

1390 JADA, III, 41 n.-43 n. See JAC, 181–182, JAPS, I, 549.

1391 JA to Samuel Osgood, June 30, 1784, JADA, III, 43 n.

1392 James Madison to Edmund Randolph, Phil., Mar. 18, 1783, JMAP, VI, 355.

1393 BF to Henry Laurens, Mar. 20, 1783, quoted in JADR, 134.

1394 JA to James Warren, Paris, Mar. 21, 1783, JAPM, Reel 108.

1395 Robert R. Livingston to Paris Commissioners, Phil., Mar. 25, 1783, RDCW, VI, 338–339.

1396 JA to Abigail Adams, Paris, Mar. 28, 1783, JAPM, Reel 360.

1397 JA to Gen. Warren, Paris, Apr. 9, 1783, JAPM, Reel 108.

1398 JA to Arthur Lee, Paris, Apr. 10, 1783, JAPM, Reel 108.

1399 JA to James Warren, Paris, Apr. 13, 1783, JAWL, II, 208–212.

1400 FNE, II, 171.

1401 JA to Abigail Adams, Paris, Apr. 16, 1783, JAPM, Reel 360.

1402 JCC, XXIV, 321.

1403 JADA, III, 117–118.

1404 JA to Robert R. Livingston, Paris, May 25, 1783 (unsent), JAPM, Reel 108.

1405 JCC, XXIV, 364.

1406 BF to BFB, Passy, June 23, 1783, BF Papers (Univ. of Penn.). See BFBS, 79.

1407 BFB to BF, Geneva, July 2, 1783, BFBC, Film 1506, Reel 1.

1408 JA to Robert Livingston, Paris, July 9, 1783, RDCW, VI, 529–530.

1409 BF to Robert R. Livingston, Passy, July 22, 1783, BFSM, VIII, 59–62.

1410 BFB to Mrs. [Sarah] Bache, July 27, 1783, quoted in in BFBT, 44.

1411 BFBT, 45. See BFPP, 9, 12.

1412 Definitive Treaty of Peace with Great Britain, Sept. 3, 1783 (ratified by the U.S., Jan. 14, 1784), TMH, II, 115, 152–153.

1413 GWAC, 173.

1414 JADA, III, 141–142.

1415 BP, Apr. 29, May 2, 1812, quoted in JADA, III, 143 n.-144 n. On the timing of JA's illness, JA writes that, as of Sept. 14, 1783, "I had been some days unwell, but soon fell down with a Fever." Diary, Paris, Sept. 14, 1783, JADA, III, 143.

1416 JA to Elbridge Gerry, Paris, Sept. 10, 1783, JAPM, Reel 107.

1417 BF to John Jay, Passy, Sept. 10, 1783, RDCW, VI, 686. BF sent identical letters of the same date to John Jay and JA.

1418 JA to Ben Franklin, Paris, Sept. 13, 1783, RDCW, VI, 696.

1419 Samuel Osgood to JA, Annapolis, Dec. 7, 1783, LCC, VII, 378, 383–384, 386.

1420 Letter from Alexander Hamilton, Concerning the Public Conduct and Character of JA . . . [N.Y., Oct. 24,1800], AHP, XXV, 169, 190–191.

1421 GW, Address to Cong. in Resigning His Commission, [Annapolis, Dec. 23, 1783], GWW, XXVII, 284–285.

1422 "A Letter to GW . . . ," TPW, II, 691, 718.

1423 JCC, XXVI, 22–23.

1424 BF to Mrs. Sarah Bache, Passy, Jan. 26, 1784, BFSM, IX, 161–162.

1425 MHCC. See BFCV, 710, BFWE, 326, BFFC, 80–82.

1426 See James A. Leith, "La Culte de Franklin en France Avant et Pendant la Révolution Française," AHFR , XLVIII, (Oct.-Dec.,1976), 543, 565.

1427 JAC, 194–195.

1428 JA to Arthur Lee, Hague, Apr. 6, 1784, ALLR, II, 250–251.

1429 Two drafts of letters (unsent) from JA to Samuel Osgood, Hague, Apr. 9, 1784, JAPM, Reel 362. The increasing type size is intended to mirror the size change in JA's handwriting.

1430 JCC, XXVI, 355–356.

1431 BF to Samuel Mather, Passy, May 12, 1784, BFWS, X, 82, 84–85.

1432 JAC, 195, TJAH, 98.

1433 Journal, BFBC, Film 1506, Reel 1.

1434 BF to William Strahan, Passy, Aug. 19, 1784, BFSM, IX, 259, 263–264.

1435 Journal, BFBC, Film 1506, Reel 1.

1436 Journal, BFBC, Film 1506, Reel 1. See BFPP, 9, 12.

1437 BF to Richard Bache, Passy, Nov. 11, 1784, BFSM, IX, 278–279.

1438 EHFJ, 6, as translated in FNE, II, 80.

1439 JA to Elbridge Gerry, Auteuil, Dec. 12, 1784, JAPM, Reel 107.

1440 JCC, XXVIII, 98.

1441 Elbridge Gerry to JA, N.Y., Feb. 24, 1785, JAPM, Reel 364.

1442 JCC, XXVIII, 134.

1443 Journal, BFBC, Film 1506, Reel 1. See Albert J. George, The Didot Family and the Progress of Printing (Syracuse, N.Y., 1961), 6–13.

1444 JA to Richard Price, Auteuil, Apr. 8, 1785, JAWO, VIII 232.

1445 Richard Price, *Observations on the Importance of the American Revolution, and the Means of Making it a Benefit to the World. With a letter to Price from Anne-Robert-Jacques Turgot* (London, 1784), 71-87, REDX 18,739.

1446 Anne-Robert Jacques Turgot to Dr. Richard Price, Mar. 22, 1778, reprinted in Bernard Peach, ed., *Richard Price and the Ethical Foundations of the American Revolution* (Durham, N. C.: Duke Univ. Press, 1979), 215–219.

1447 JAWO, IX, 623.

1448 JA to Elbridge Gerry, Auteuil, May 2, 1785, JAPM, Reel 364.

1449 Journal, BFBC, Film 1506, Reel 1.

1450 Journal, BFBC, Film 1506, Reel 1.

1451 Journal, BFBC, Film 1506, Reel 1.

1452 BF to Mr. and Mrs. Richard Bache, Passy, May 10, 1785, BFSM, X, 327–328.

1453 JAPS, II, 624–625.

1454 TJ to Rev. William Smith, Phil., Feb. 19, 1791, TJPB, XIX, 112–113.

1455 JA to Sec. John Jay, Bath Hotel, Westminster, June 2, 1785, JAWO, VIII, 255, 258.

1456 Journal, BFBC, Film 1506, Reel 1.

1457 Journal, BFBC, Film 1506, Reel 1.

1458 TJ to Rev. William Smith, Phil., Feb. 19, 1791, TJPB, XIX, 112–113.

1459 Journal, BFBC, Film 1506, Reel 1.

1460 JAWO, IX, 622–623. See BFPL, XXII, 514.

1461 WDBF, I, 367 n.

1462 On BFB and Rousseau, see BFBT, 130, 138.

1463 [Paul Wentworth], "Minutes Respecting Political Parties in America and Sketches of the Leading Persons in Each Province" [app. 1778] . . . The Endorsement . . . by the hand of Wm Eden. SFAC, V, 487.

1464 AGA, Oct. 29, 1796.

1465 JA to Benjamin Rush, Sept. 30, 1805, A&R, 39–40.

1466 WDRP, 558.

1467 FNE, II, 81.

1468 Thomas Paine to BF, N.Y., Sept. 23, 1785, TPW, II, 1250.

1469 Thomas Paine to Temple Franklin, N.Y., Sept. 23, 1785, TPW, II, 1251.

1470 BF to Thomas Paine, Phil., Sept. 27, 1785, BFSM, X, 467–468.

1471 TPHD, 162.

1472 BF to Mrs. Mary Hewson, Oct 30, 1785, Phil., BFSM, IX, 473–474.

1473 BF to Mrs. Mary Hewson, May 6, 1786, Phil., BFSM, IX, 510, 512.

1474 SRMG, 33–35.

1475 JA to Samuel Perley, June 19, 1809, JAWO IX, 623.

1476 JA to John Taylor, Quincy, Apr. 15, 1814, JAWO, VI, 486.

1477 See JAPP, 31, 38, JAGC, 212, JA to Benj. Rush, Braintree, Dec. 2, 1788, JAWO, IX, 556.

1478 *A Defence of the Constitutions of Government of the United States* . . . , JAWO, IV, 299–300.

1479 JAWO, IV, 358–359.

1480 JAWO, IV, 391–393.

1481 JAWO, IV, 397.

1482 JAWO, IV, 406.

1483 JAWO, IV, 414.

1484 JAWO, IV, 444–445.

1485 JAWO, IV, 553.

1486 TJ to William Short, Monticello, Jan. 8, 1825, TJWF, XII, 388, 394–395.

1487 John Jay to GW, N.Y., Jan. 7, 1787, JJPA, III, 226–227.

1488 BFCV, 743–744.

1489 "The Society for Political Enquiries," TPW, II, 41–43.

1490 JA to Samuel Perley, Quincy, June 19, 1809, JAWO, IV, IX, 621, 623–624.

1491 GLEF, 98–102, SSC, 237ff.

1492 *Autobiography,* TJWF, I, 106.

1493 Henry Knox to GW, Mar. 19, 1787, GWWS, IX, 237 n.-238 n.

1494 Abigail Adams to John Quincy Adams, London, Mar. 20, 1787, JAPM, Reel 369.

1495 BF to Duc de La Rochefoucauld, Phil., Apr. 15, 1787, WDBF, VI, 195–197.

1496 BF to Marquis de Chastellux, Phil., Apr. 17, 1787, WDBF, VI, 197–198.

1497 TPHD 173.

1498 BF to Francis Childs, Phil., May 8, 1787, BFSM, IX, 580–581.

1499 John Jay to JA, Off. of Foreign Affairs, May 12, 1787, JJPA, III, 246.

1500 FBRS, 192. See LFGB, 310, 314–315, CFR 13.

1501 SSC, 281–283.

1502 JMAD, I, 17–18.

1503 Thomas Paine to BF, Paris, June 22, 1787, TPW, II, 1262.

1504 CBCMP, 34–35.

1505 JMAD, I, 31.

1506 JMAD, I, 37–40.

[1506a] Benjamin Rush to Richard Price, Phil., June 2, 1787, BRL, I, 418.

[1507] JMAD, I, 41–46.

[1508] JMAD, I, 49–55.

[1509] BF, "Speech in a Comm. of the Convention," June 11, 1787, BFSM, X, 595–599.

[1510] JMAD, I, 111–120.

[1511] Alexander Hamilton's Notes [June 18, 1787], AHP, IV, 185–186.

[1512] TJ to William Short, Monticello, Jan. 8, 1825, TJWF, XII, 388, 392–394.

[1513] Anas, TJWF, I, 163, 179–180.

[1514] Thomas Paine to BF, Paris, June 22, 1787, TPW, II, 1262.

[1515] BF, "Proposal for Consideration in the Convention for Forming the Constitution of the United States," June 30, 1787, BFSM, X, 602–603.

[1516] BFBR, 34–35.

[1517] JAPS, II, 711.

[1518] John Jay to JA, N.Y., July 25, 1787, JJPA, III, 251.

[1519] BFB to BF, N.Y., Aug. 1, 1787, BFBC, Film 1506, Reel 2. See BFPO, 158–159.

[1520] JMAD, II, 363–368.

[1521] JMAD, II, 373–374.

[1522] BFB to R. Bache, N.Y., Aug 8, 1787, BFBC, Film, 1506, Reel 2.

[1523] BFB to BF, N.Y., Aug. 1, 1787, BFBC, Film 1506, Reel 2.

[1524] "BF's Speech at the Conclusion of the Constitutional Convention," BBDC, I, 3–4.

[1525] WDRP, 564.

[1526] JMAD, II, 577–583.

[1527] Remark to Gilbert Stuart in 1825, quoted by MSOH, 347.

[1528] Letter from "Z," in Independent Chronicle (Boston), Dec. 6, 1787, quoted in BBDC, I, 6, 8.

[1528a] The 17th Amendment (providing for direct popular election of U.S. senators) won't be adopted until 1913. The idea that, even with this change, the U.S. Senate would remain the handmaiden of aristocracy is a corollary of the anti-federalist fear that only wealthy aristocrats can win in larger voting districts (see anti-federalist arguments on the size of the House of Representatives, cited supra n. 718).

[1529] JA to John Taylor, Quincy, Apr. 15, 1814, JAWO, VI, 471–472.

[1530] JA to John Taylor, Quincy, Apr. 15, 1814, JAWO, VI, 470–471.

[1531] JA to John Taylor, Quincy, Apr. 15, 1814, JAWO, VI, 468.

[1532] JA to John Taylor, Quincy, Apr. 15, 1814, JAWO, VI, 473.

[1533] "Centinel" in the Independent Gazetteer (Phil.), Oct. 5, 1787, quoted in BBDC, I, 52, 54–61.

[1534] "A Letter to GW . . . ," TPW, II, 691–694.

[1535] "To the Citizens of Penn. on the Proposal for Calling a Convention" [1805], TPW, II, 992, 995, 1001.

[1536] TPLW, 9.

[1537] WD reports that, during the decade following publication of the Federalist Papers, Hamilton was thought to be their exclusive author. AGA, June 7, 1800.

[1538] PAFC, I, 186, AFC, III, 97.

[1539] BFBS, 90.

[1540] Independent Chronicle (Boston), Dec. 6, 1787, BBDC, I, 6–8.

[1541] Thomas Paine to George Clymer, Paris, Dec. 29, 1787, TPW, II, 1266.

[1542] Lafayette to Henry Knox, Paris, Feb. 4, 1788, Henry Knox Papers (MHS), Reel 23 (letter misdated on microfilm).

[1543] BF to Madame Brillon, Apr. 19, 1788, Phil., BFSM, IX, 643–645.

[1544] JAPS, II, 730–731.

[1545] Duc de La Rochefoucauld to BF, Paris, July 12, 1788, BFWS, X, 355, as quoted in J. Paul Selsam and Joseph G. Rayback, "French Comment on the Pennsylvania Constitution of 1776," PMHB, LXXVI (1952), 311, 325.

[1546] GW to Noah Webster, Mt. Vernon, July 31, 1788, GWW, XXX, 26–27.

[1547] JA to Benjamin Rush, Mar. 19- Apr. 22, 1812, A&R, 211, 212–213.

[1548] GLEF, 102.

[1549] TJ to James Monroe, Paris, Aug. 9, 1788, TJPB, XIII, 488, 489–490.

[1550] FNE, II, 81.

[1551] BF to M. Le Veillard, Phil., Oct. 24, 1788, BFSM, X, 673–674.

[1552] GLEF, 104–105.

[1553] BF to Mrs. Catherine Greene, Phil., Mar. 2, 1789, BFSM, X, 3, 4.

[1554] TJ to Francis Hopkinson, Paris, Mar. 13, 1789, TJPB, XIV, 649–651.

[1555] BFBR, 3.

[1556] Benjamin Rush to JA, Feb. 12, 1812, A&R, 206, 209–210.

[1557] JA to Benjamin Rush, Quincy, Apr. 22, 1812, JAOF, 375, 377.

[1558] John Hench, "Letters of John Fenno and John Ward Fenno," PAAS, Vol. 89, Part 1 (1979), 301–302.

[1559] JWMA, 3.

[1560] JWM, 10–13.

[1561] GLEF, 121.

1562 TJ to Lafayette, Paris, May 6, 1789, TJPB, XV, 97–98.

1563 JWMA, 40–41.

1564 JWMA, 46.

1565 JWM, 30.

1566 James Madison to TJ, N.Y., May 23, 1789, TJPB, XV, 147–148.

1567 Benjamin Rush to JA, Phil., June 4, 1789, BRL, I, 513–515.

1568 JA to Benjamin Rush, N.Y., June 9, 1789, JAOF, 36–38.

1569 WDRP, 8.

1570 JA to Benjamin Rush, N.Y., June 19, 1789, JAOF, 39–40.

1571 JA to Gen. Benjamin Lincoln, N.Y., June 19, 1789, JAPM, Reel 115.

1572 JA to Hon. Jabez Bowen, Richmond Hill, N.Y., June 26, 1789, JAPM, Reel 115.

1573 JA to Benjamin Rush, Richmond Hill, July 5, 1789, JAOF, 41–43.

1574 TJ to Thomas Paine, Paris, July 11, 1789, TJPB, XV, 266–268.

1575 DMSM, xii, GLEF, 135–137.

1576 WDRP, 17.

1577 SSC, 453–455.

1578 TJ to Thomas Paine, Paris, July 17, 1789, TJPB, XV, 279.

1579 JA to Benjamin Rush, N.Y., July 24, 1789, JAOF, 44–47.

1580 TJ to James Madison, Paris, July 29, 1789, TJPB, XV, 315–316.

1581 See FBRS, 269–270, 176.

1582 WDRP, 30.

1583 TJ to William Carmichael, Paris, Aug. 9, 1789, TJPB, XV, 236–238.

1584 WDGE, 22–23.

1585 WDRP, 38–39.

1586 SSC, 442. See Lafayette to TJ, Versailles, July 6, 1789, TJPB, XV, 249, GLEF, 143–145.

1587 WDRP, 39–40.

1588 TJ to James Madison, Paris, Aug. 28, 1789, TJPB, XV, 364–367.

1589 SSC, 458. On the choice between the JA and BF models in France, see Joyce Appleby, "America as a Model for the Radical French Reformers of 1789," William and Mary Quarterly, XXVIII (1971), 267–286.

1590 SSC, 458.

1591 JA to Count Sarsfield, N.Y., Sept. 16, 1789, JAPM, Reel 115.

1592 JWM, 155.

1593 GW to TJ, N.Y., Oct. 13, 1789, GWPB, IV, 174.

1594 BF to Samuel Moore, Phil., Nov. 5, 1789, BFSM, X, 63.

1595 "Queries and Remarks . . . " BFWS, X, 54, 58–60.

1596 BFAW, 780, 768.

1597 BF to David Hartley, Phil., Dec. 4, 1789, BFSM, X, 72.

1598 BFB to Margaret Markoe, Phil., Dec. 6, 1789, BFBC, Film 1506, Reel 2.

1599 DSFR, 167–168.

1600 JA to Benjamin Rush, N.Y., Feb. 2, 1790, JAOF, 54–55.

1601 ANC, 1C, 2S, 984.

1602 JWM, 191–192.

1603 JA to Francis Adrian Vanderkemp, N.Y., Feb. 27, 1790, JAPM, Reel 115.

1604 "To the Citizens of Pennsylvania on the Proposal for Calling a Convention" [1805], TPW, II, 992, 993, 998.

1605 Thomas Paine to Anonymous, Paris, Mar. 16, 1789 [sic], TPW, II, 1285–1286. This misdated letter is logically placed a year later. See TPHD, 202.

1606 JA to Francis Adrian Vanderkemp, N.Y., Mar. 27, 1790, JAPM, Reel 115.

1607 JA to Benjamin Rush, N.Y., Apr. 4, 1790, JAOF, 55–57.

1608 Benjamin Rush to JA, Phil., Apr. 13, 1790, BRL, I, 544, 546.

1609 BFWE, 347, BFBB, 117.

1610 BFB to Margaret Markoe, Phil., May 2, 1790, BFBC, Film 1506, Reel 2.

1611 BFPL, I, 109–111.

1612 ANC, 1C, 2S, 1534.

1613 TJ to William Short, N.Y., Apr. 27, 1790, TJPB, XVI, 387–388.

1614 TJ to Benjamin Rush, Wash., Oct. 4, 1803, TJWF, X, 31–32.

1615 "Discourses on Davila . . . " JAWO, VI, 225.

1616 Lettres d'un Bourgeois de New-Heaven à un Citoyen de Virginie, sur l'inutilité de partager législatif entre plusieurs corps. [Letters from a common citizen of New Haven to a Citizen of Virginia on the uselessness of dividing legislative power between several bodies], included in Filippo Mazzei, Recherches historiques et politiques sur les Etats-Unis de l'Amérique Septentrionale: où l'on traite des établissemens des treize colonies, de leurs rapports et de leurs dissentions avec la Grande-Bretagne, de leurs gouvernemens avant et après la revolution, &c. / par un citoyen de Virginie; avec quatre lettres d'un bourgeois de New Haven [Condorcet] sur l'unité de la législation, 4 vols. (Paris: Froulle, 1788), I, 267–371.

1617 "Discourses on Davila . . ." JAWO, VI, 224, 252.

1618 "Discourses on Davila . . ." JAWO, VI, 224, 399.

1619 Thomas Paine to GW, London, May 1, 1790, TPW, II, 1302–1303.

1620 WDRP, 62, See CFR, 152.

1621 JA to Thomas Brand-Hollis, N.Y., June 11, 1790, JAWO, IX, 571.

1622 Quoted in BFFC, 212–213, and in FBRS, 287.

1623 Louis-Guillaume Le Veillard to BFB, Paris, June 10, 1790, BFBC, Film 1506, Reel 2.

1624 TJ to Rev. William Smith, Phil., Feb. 19, 1791, TJPB, XIX, 112–113.

1625 LJLC, II, 34–35, as quoted in BFFC, 92.

1626 Gilbert Chinard, "The Apotheosis of Benjamin Franklin," PAPS, Vol. 99 (1955), 440, 463.

1627 Journal de la Société de 1789, June 19, 1790, as quoted in BFFC, 87.

1628 On Brissot's relationship to Franklin and America, see FBRS, 237–246.

1629 See FBRS, 237–247.

1630 J. P. Brissot de Warville, "Reflections on the Constitution of Pennsylvania" (1782), trans. by J. Paul Selsam, PMHB, LXXII (1948), 25–43.

1631 GLEF, 169.

1632 WDRP, 62–63.

1633 James A. Leith, "La Culte de Franklin en France Avant et Pendant la Révolution Française," AHFR , XLVIII, (Oct.-Dec.,1976), 543, 565.

1634 See Robert Morris to BFB, July 28, 1790, BFBC, Film 1506, Reel 2.

1635 AGA's original name was General Advertiser and Political, Commercial, Agricultural and Literary Journal. For the history of the paper's masthead names, see BCAN, 891–892.

1636 JWM, 349–350, 378.

1637 Gilbert Chinard, "The Apotheosis of Benjamin Franklin," PAPS, Vol. 99 (1955), 451–452.

1638 JWM, 379–380.

1639 TJ to Benjamin Rush, Wash., Oct. 4, 1803, TJWF, X, 31–32.

1640 TPHD 223–227.

1641 TPW, I, 298–301.

1642 TPW, I, 313–314.

1643 TPW, I, 338–340.

1644 TJ to Jonathan B. Smith, Apr. 26, 1791, TJPB, XX, 290.

1645 See TJPB, XX, 272.

1646 TJ to James Madison, Phil., May 9, 1791, TJPB, XX, 293.

1647 Tobias Lear to GW, May 8, 1791, GW Papers (LC), as quoted in TJPB, XX, 277.

1648 JAWO, VI, 272.

1649 Anas, TJWF, I, 163, 180.

1650 Thomas Paine to Messieurs Condorcet, Nicolas de Bonneville, and Lanthanas, Paris, June, 1791, TPW, II, 1315.

1651 GUS, July 20, 1791. The series was first published in the Columbia Centinel (Boston), June 8, 11, 15, 18, 22, 29, July 2, 9, 13, 20, 27, 1791. AGA carried "Publicola" series on June 30, July 1, 2, 4, 5, 12, 15, 20, 24, 28, Aug 2, 1791.

1652 CFR, 237.

1653 GLEF, 193.

1654 Séance du vendredi 7 octobre 1791. Correspondance patriotique, I (1791), 67, as quoted in BFFC, 87.

1655 TJ to Pres. of the U.S., Monticello, Sept. 9, 1792, TJPB, XXIV, 351, 354–355.

1656 TPW, I, 389.

1657 TPW, I, 410–413.

1658 TPW, I, 415.

1659 TJ to Lafayette, Phil., June 16, 1792, TJPB, XXIV, 290.

1660 TJ to Thomas Paine, Phil., June 19, 1792, TJPB, XX, 312.

1661 TPHD 257.

1662 See Thomas Paine, "Answer to Four Questions on the Legislative and Executive Powers," TPW, II, 521–534.

1663 WDRP, 194.

1664 SSC, 639–641, CFR, 291.

1665 Thomas Paine to Benjamin Mosley, Paris, Oct. I, I Year of the Republic, TPW, II, 1326.

1666 WDRP, 194.

1667 Thomas Paine, Address to the People of France, Sept. 25, 1792, TPW, II, 537–540.

1668 Thomas Paine, "An Essay for the Use of New Republicans in Their Opposition to Monarchy," TPW, II, 541, 543, 546–547.

1669 JA to Lafayette, Hague, May 21, 1782, JAWO, VII, 593.

1670 JAWO, IV, 358–359.

1671 Thomas Paine to William Short, Nov. 2, 1791, TPW, II, 1320.

1672 TPHD 266–267.

1673 LEV, 285–286, TPHD 267–270.

1674 As quoted in JCHU, 230–231.

1675 See The Whole Proceedings on the Trial of an Information Exhibited ex Officio by the King's Attorney-General Against Thomas Paine . . . Taken in Short-Hand by Joseph

Gurney (London: Sold by Martha Gurney, 1793), 71–73.

[1676] GLEF, 221–222.

[1677] BP, May 15, 1811, as reprinted in JAWO, I, 649, 660–663.

[1678] GLEF, 236.

[1679] JA to Abigail Adams, N.Y., Mar. 2, 1793, JAPM, Reel 376.

[1680] Tom Paine to Danton (undated), Danton Files, item #5, AF II 49, Dossier 380, Archives Nationales, Paris, cited and attributed in TPKJ, 357, 597, n.17.

[1681] JAWO, VI, 403. See JAPP, 167.

[1682] WDRP, 563. James Thomson Callender details the Democratic-Republican argument in JCPB, I, 95–108.

[1683] Willard Sterne Randall, *Thomas Jefferson: A Life* (New York: Henry Holt, 1993), 513–517. See GUS, Aug. 28, 1800.

[1684] AGA, Apr. 24, 1793. See TPHD 263–264.

[1685] French admirers often addressed BF as "Papa." BFLC. See, in general, James A. Leith, "La Culte de Franklin en France Avant et Pendant la Révolution Française," AHFR, XLVIII, (Oct.-Dec.,1976), 543–571.

[1686] R. R. Palmer observes,"The constitutions drafted in Pennsylvania in 1776, and in France in 1793, were, in their formal provisions, by far the most democratic of any produced in the eighteenth century." ADR, II, 219.

[1687] Detail, plate #12, BRP.

[1688] JA to Benjamin Rush, N.Y., June 9, 1789, JAOF, 36–38.

[1689] TJ to James Monroe, Monticello, Oct. 19, 1823, TJWF, XII, 316.

[1690] JA to Dr. Benjamin Rush, Apr. 12, 1809, JAWO, IX, 619.

[1691] WD to Franklin Bache, Wash., Mar. 4, 1804, BFBC, Film 1506, Reel 3.

[1692] James Madison to TJ, Wash., May 3, 1811, JMAW, VIII, 150–151. See WDCA, 53.

[1693] AGA, Oct. 2, 1790.

[1694] WD to Caesar Rodney, Oct. 13, 1798, Duane folder, General MS Collection, Columbia Univ. Lib., as quoted in BFBP, 113.

[1695] WD to Tench Coxe, Oct. 15, 1798, reprinted in Peter J Parker,"The Revival of the *Aurora*: A Letter to Tench Coxe," PMHB, 96 (Oct. 1972): 524–525. Sometime between the time BFB contracted and died of yellow fever, BFB wrote Tench Coxe, asking that the paper be continued for his "family, his country and mankind. " See Tench Coxe to Margaret Bache, Sept. 13, 1798, quoted in TCER, 346. BFB lost between $14,700 and $20,000 in the eight years he published the paper. See AGA, Aug 11, 1798, Apr. 23, 1800, Aug. 11, 1802. TCER, 345.

[1696] WDBM, 6.

[1697] WD's attraction to Margaret Bache is deduced from their later marriage.

[1698] Lyon's story is well told in FETT, 221–246.

[1699] SDOP, 616.

[1700] FETT, 188, 252.

[1701] "Capture of the Armed Schooner *Highlander*, Thomas M'Connell," ND, II, 6–7.

[1702] SDOP, 617–618.

[1703] FETT, 398–399.

[1704] See FETT, 257–262.

[1705] AGA, Nov. 13, 1798.

[1706] Quoted in GLM, 86 n. Pickering's account of the meeting is in "Report of the Secretary of State on the Transactions Relating to the United States and France . . ." Jan. 18, 1799, as printed in PG, Jan. 24, 1799.

[1707] KRW, 75–85, 96.

[1708] TJ to J. Cabell Breckinridge, Monticello, Dec. 11, 1821, quoted in KRW, 138–139.

[1709] GW, "Memorandum of an Interview," Nov. 13, 1798, GWW, XXXVII, 18–20.

[1710] GLM, 86–87.

[1711] FETT, 260–265.

[1712] GW to Alexander Spotswood, Phil., Nov. 22, 1798, GWW, XXXVII, 23–24.

[1713] JA to printers of the BP, JAWO, IX, 241, 244.

[1714] GLM, 85.

[1715] TJ to John Taylor, Nov. 26, 1798, TJWF, VIII, 479, 480.

[1716] WDKP, 26–28, citing John Shore (Lord Teignmouth), *The Private Record of an Indian Governor-Generalship: The Correspondence of Sir John Shore, Governor-General, with Henry Dundas, President of the Board of Control 1793–1798*, Holden Furber, ed. (Cambridge, Mass., 1933), 9–16, Sir John Shore to Henry Dundas, Jan 1794, Charles J. Shore (Second Baron Teignmouth), *Memoirs of the Life and Correspondence of John Lord Teignmouth*, 2 vols. (London, 1843), I, 275–282. *Calcutta Gazette* (Calcutta), Sept. 18, 1794, W. S. Seton-Kerr, ed., *Selections from the Calcutta Gazette, 1784–1823*, 5 vols. (London, 1864–1869), II, 393–394.

[1717] DMAF, 225.

[1718] RJMP, I, 271–273.

[1719] ANC, 5C, 3S, 2426–2427.

[1720] RJMP, I, 277.

[1721] GW to Sec. of War, Phil., Dec. 13, 1798, GWW, XXXVII, 32, 35.

[1722] ANC, 5C, 3S, 2445, 2447, 2450–2451, 2455.

[1723] GUS, Aug. 11, 1800.

[1724] Abigail Adams to William Shaw, Quincy, Dec. 20, 1798, SFP.

[1725] AGA, Dec. 24, 1798.

[1726] AGA, Dec. 24, 1798.

[1727] Abigail Adams to William Shaw, Quincy, Dec. 23, 1798, SFP.

[1728] KRW, 100–104.

[1729] GW to Marquis de Lafayette, Mt. Vernon, Dec. 25, 1798, GWW, XXXVII, 64–69.

[1730] GW to William Vans Murray, Mt. Vernon, Dec. 26, 1798, GWW, XXXVII, 71–72.

[1731] JA to Abigail Adams, Quincy, Dec. 31, 1798, JAPM, 392.

[1732] GUS, Jan 2, 1799.

[1733] AGA, Jan. 3, 14, 17, Feb. 18, 1799, June 11, Oct. 2, 1800, FETT, 242.

[1734] Hamilton to Dayton, 1799 [between letters of Dec. 28, 1798, and Jan. 6, 1799], AHWO, VI, 383–384, 387–388.

[1735] Timothy Pickering to Richard Harison, Esq., Dept. of State, Jan. 1, 1799, TPPM, XXXVII, 381.

[1736] Abigail Adams to William Shaw, Quincy, Jan. 3, 1799, SFP.

[1737] Pressmen and Compositors to Margaret Hartman Bache, Jan. 12, 1799, BFBC, Film 1506, Reel 3.

[1738] Margaret Hartman Bache to Pressmen and Compositors, [1799], BFBC, Film 1506, Reel 3.

[1739] The late Pressmen and Compositors to Margaret Hartman Bache, Jan. 15, 1799, BFBC, Film 1506, Reel 3.

[1740] Margaret Hartman Bache to Late Pressmen and Compositors of the AGA, Jan. 15, 1799, BFBC, Film 1506, Reel 3.

[1741] GW to Patrick Henry (Confidential), Mt. Vernon, Jan. 15, 1799, GWW, XXXVII, 87–89.

[1742] GUS, Jan 18, 1799.

[1743] GUS, Jan. 21, 1799.

[1744] GUS, Jan. 21, 1799.

[1745] GW to Rev. Bryan, Lord Fairfax, Mt. Vernon, Jan. 20, 1799, GWW, XXXVII, 91, 93.

[1746] Attribution to James Madison based on JMAP, XVII, 211–214, TJJM, II, 1073.

[1747] TJJM, II, 1073.

[1748] On the impact of the argument, see SDOP, 608–609.

[1749] TJ to Elbridge Gerry, Phil., Jan. 26, 1799, TJWF, IX, 15, 17–20.

[1750] ANC, 5C, 3S, 3795.

[1751] Alexander Hamilton to Theodore Sedgwick, N.Y., Feb. 2, 1799, AHP, XXII, 452–453.

[1752] TJ to James Madison, [Phil.], Feb. 5, 1799, TJJM, II, 1092–1093.

[1753] ANC, 5C, 3S, 2856–2857.

[1754] "Trial of Duane, Reynolds, Moore and Cuming . . . ," WFST, 345, 357–359.

[1755] Captain Thomas Truxton to Sec. of the Navy, U.S. Ship *Constellation* in sight of the Island of St. Christopher's, Feb. 10, 1799, ND, II, 326–327, VII, 365.

[1756] DAQW, 128–130, GUS, May 15, 1799.

[1757] "Trial of Duane, Reynolds, Moore and Cuming . . . ," WFST, 345, 358–359.

[1758] "Trial of Duane, Reynolds, Moore and Cuming . . . ," WFST, 345–388.

[1759] ANC, 5C, 3S, 2884.

[1760] AGA, Oct. 3, 4, 1799.

[1761] GUS, Oct. 3, 1799.

[1762] ANC, 5C, 3S, 2906–2907.

[1763] TJ to Archibald Stewart, Phil., Feb. 13, 1799, TJWF, IX, 40–41, 44.

[1764] DMAF, 229.

[1765] Italicized sentence from AGA, Oct. 2, 1800.

[1766] FETT, 242, AGA, Apr. 9, 29, June 10, 1799, Sept. 1, 1800.

[1767] JA heard of Talleyrand's willingness to negotiate not only from George Logan but also from Elbridge Gerry (one of JA's three original envoys), William Vans Murray (U.S. Minister at the Hague), American writer Joel Barlow, Boston merchant Richard Codman, and even from his diplomat sons, Thomas Boylston Adams and John Quincy Adams. See EMAF, 609–610, 614–618.

[1768] RJMP, I, 282–283.

[1769] See letter of James McHenry, Sec. of War, to Brig. Gen. William Darke, Dec. 18, 1798, GUS, Feb. 27, 1799.

[1770] PG, Mar. 19, 1799.

[1771] Abigail Adams to William Shaw, Quincy, Feb. 21, 1799, SFP.

[1772] GUS, Mar. 12, 1799.

[1773] "Trial of Duane, Reynolds, Moore and Cuming . . . ," WFST, 345–388. Wharton confuses the trial date with the date the verdict was rendered. See AGA, Feb. 22, 1799.

[1774] ANC, 5C, 3S, 2955.

[1775] Attribution based on JMAP, VI, 211–214.

[1776] ANC, 5C, 3S, 2985, 2992–2993, 3002.

[1777] RJMP, I, 284.

[1778] ANC, 5C, 3S, 3804–3805.

[1779] TJ to James Madison, Phil., Feb. 26, 1799, TJWF, IX, 59, 61.

[1780] ANC, 5C, 3S, 3808.

[1781] FETT, 253–254, SDOP, 476–477.

[1782] FETT, 254.

[1783] Abigail Adams to William Shaw, Quincy, Mar. 4, 1799, SFP.

[1784] GUS, Apr. 19, 1799.

[1785] JCSH, 120.

[1786] BFBR, 34–35.

[1787] BFBR, 38.

[1788] Speech in the Convention, BFSM, IX, 590, 592–593.

[1789] BF to Benjamin Vaughan, Passy, Mar. 14, 1785, BFSM, IX, 291, 296.

[1790] GUS, Mar. 14, 1799.

[1791] GUS, June 21, 1798.

[1792] GUS, Mar. 16, 1799.

[1793] Detail , *"Pennsylvania Drawn from the Best Authorities by Cyrus Harris—engraved by A. Doolittle,"* Jedidiah Morse, *The American Universal Geography* . . . (Boston: Thomas & Andrews, 1796), Part I, 533.

[1794] GUS, Apr. 1, 1799.

[1795] Capt. Thomas Truxton to Sec. of the Navy, Bassateer Road, Mar. 16, 1799, ND, II, 458, VII, 365.

[1796] GUS, Mar. 21, 1799.

[1797] AGA, May 24, 1799.

[1798] ND, III, 157, 494 (map), VII, 366.

[1799] AGA, May 24, 1799.

[1800] AGA, May 3, 1799.

[1801] "Trial of the Northampton Insurgents . . .," WFST, 458, 505–506.

[1802] "Trial of the Northampton Insurgents . . .," WFST, 458, 510–511.

[1803] "Trial of the Northampton Insurgents . . .," WFST, 458, 507–509.

[1804] Italicized words from AGA, Aug. 2, 1799.

[1805] FETT, 255.

[1806] TJ to Archibald Stuart, Monticello, May 14, 1799, TJWF, IX, 66–67.

[1807] That the units identified by GUS, May 15, 1799 were part of Macpherson's Blues, see PMHB, XLVII (1923), 359–360.

[1808] See AGA, May 3, 1798.

[1809] WDME, 14–15.

[1810] WDME, 6–7.

[1811] WDME, 4–5.

[1812] WDME, 11–13.

[1813] WDME, 6–7.

[1814] WD's testimony, WDME, 4–5.

[1815] WDME, 8–11.

[1816] WDME, 18–19.

[1817] AGA, May 21, 1799.

[1818] WDME, 19–20.

[1819] AGA, June 12, 1799.

[1820] GUS, May 18, 1799.

[1821] Detail, *William Duane* (1802), an engraving by St. Mémin, National Portrait Gallery, Wash., D.C. See AGA, Jan. 8, 28, 1799, Ellen G. Miles, *Saint-Mémin and the Neoclassical Profile Portrait in America* (Wash: Smithsonian Inst. Press, 1994), 87, 98, 293, 446–447.

[1822] See BFBP, 127, WDCA, 22.

[1823] This sentence verbatim from WD to Stephen R. Bradley, Nov. 10, 1808, cited WDCA, 65–68.

[1824] See AGA, June 21, 1799, quoting *Richmond Examiner* (Richmond).

[1825] Capt. Thomas Tingey to Sec. of the Navy, Ganges off St. Bartholemews, June 26, 1799, ND, III, 345–346, VII, 367.

[1826] TJ to William Green Munford, June 18, 1799, TJMD, III, 418.

[1827] GW to John Trumbull, Mt. Vernon, June 25, 1799, GWW, XXXVII, 247–249.

[1828] E. g., PG, Apr. 22, May 15, 1799.

[1829] For complete story, see TCPL.

[1830] GW to Gov. Jonathan Trumbull, Mt. Vernon, July 21, 1799, GWW, XXXVII, 312–314.

[1831] Timothy Pickering to JA, Phil., July 24, 1799, JAWO, IX, 3–4.

[1832] Timothy Pickering to William Rawle, Dept. of State, July 24, 1799, TPPM, XI, 486.

[1833] Timothy Pickering to William Rawle, Dept. of State, July 26, 1799, TPPM, XI, 495–496.

[1834] JA to T. Pickering, Sec. of State, Quincy, Aug. 1, 1799, JAWO, IX, 5.

[1835] T. Pickering to JA (Private), Phil., Aug. 1, 1799, JAWO, IX, 5, 7.

[1836] Elijah Griffiths to TJ, Aug. 4, 1799, *TJ Letters* (LC Microfilm). See WDKP, 95.

[1837] GW to Sec. of State (private), Mt. Vernon, Aug. 4, 1799, GWW, XXXVII, 322–324.

[1838] U.S. Circuit Court (3d Circuit). Copy of an Indictment. No I [-II]. In the Circuit Court of the U.S. [Phil., 1799], LOC. REDX 36,513.

[1839] GUS, Mar. 5, 1799.

[1840] GW to Maj. Gen. Charles Cotesworth Pinckney, Mt. Vernon, Aug. 10, 1799, GWW, XXXVII, 325–327.

[1841] GW to Sec. of War (Private), Mt. Vernon, Aug. 11, 1799, GWW, XXXVII, 327–328.

[1842] Timothy Pickering to Richard Harrison, Esq., Phil., Aug. 12, 1799, TPPM, XI, 599–600.

[1843] Timothy Pickering to Zebulon Hollingsworth, Esq. Dept. of State, Phil., Aug. 12, 1799, TPPM, XI, 603–604.

[1844] JA to Timothy Pickering, Sec. of State, Quincy, Aug. 13, 1799, JAWO, IX, 13–14.

[1845] GUS, Aug. 14, 1799, JBZP, 227–230.

[1846] Timothy Pickering to Thomas Nelson,

Esq., Dept. of State, Phil., Aug. 14, 1799, TPPM, XI, 611–612.

[1847] JA to T. Pickering, Sec. of State, Quincy, Aug. 16, 1799, JAWO, IX, 15–16.

[1848] GUS, Sept. 7, 1799.

[1849] See announcement in GUS, Sept. 2, 1799.

[1850] FETT, 398–400.

[1851] FETT, 390–398.

[1852] FETT, 385–386, 387n.

[1853] This issue of PG is dated "From Aug. 29 to Sept. 6, 1799."

[1854] TCPL, 103.

[1855] Timothy Pickering to William Rawle, Esq., Trenton, Sept. 20, 1799, TPPM, XII, 82.

[1856] FETT, 376–377.

[1857] "Keystone," see AGA, Oct. 8, 1803, HSKD, Chap. 1.

[1858] C. Lee, Att'y Gen'l to JA, Winchester, Oct. 6, 1799, JAWO, IX, 38.

[1859] FETT, 361–362, TJAH, 389–390.

[1860] GUS, Oct. 15, 1799, AGA, Oct. 17, 1799.

[1861] AGA, Dec. 24, 1799.

[1862] See THRF, 238.

[1863] AGA, Oct. 28, 1799.

[1864] See AGA, Nov. 1, 1800.

[1865] On the intimidating effect of the letter, see WCED, 121–122.

[1866] Date of Oct. 18 is approximate. ND, IV, 295, VII, 369.

[1867] See EMAF, 618, 635–639 which examines JA's diplomatic inertia.

[1868] Judge Peters to Timothy Pickering, Belmont, Oct. 23, 1799, TPPM, XXV, 259.

[1869] AGA, Aug. 16, 1800.

[1870] "Extract from a Pamphlet Addressed to the Electors of Pennsylvania," WCED, 121–122.

[1871] GW to William Vans Murray, Mt. Vernon, Oct. 26, 1799, GWW, XXXVII, 399–400.

[1872] Abigail Adams to William Shaw, East Chester, Oct. 28, 1799, SFP.

[1873] TJ to Charles Pinckney, Monticello, Oct. 29, 1799, TJWF, IX, 86–87.

[1874] "Trial of David Frothingham for a Libel on Gen. Hamilton," WFST, 648–651. Also, AHP, XXIV, 5–6, 6n.-7n.

[1875] FETT, 403–404.

[1876] AGA, Nov. 12, 1799.

[1877] ND, IV, 429–430, 463, 560 (map), VII, 364.

[1878] GW to Sec. of War, Mt. Vernon, Nov. 17, 1799, GWW, XXXVII, 428–429.

[1879] "Trial of David Frothingham for a Libel on Gen. Hamilton," WFST, 648–651, except your author sets the trial date as the 21st rather than the 16th per AGA, Nov. 25, 1799. See FETT, 400–417.

[1880] AGA, Dec. 6, 1799.

[1881] Abigail Adams to Mary Cranch, Nov. 26, 1799, AANL, 215–216.

[1882] GWWS, II, 2, GWMK, 267, 269–270, GWKB, 151–156. See Eugene E. Prussing, *The Estate of George Washington, Deceased* (Boston: Little, Brown, 1927), 148–149.

[1883] Detail, plate #11, BRP.

[1884] Queries and Remarks . . . , BFSM, X, 54, 57–58, 60.

[1885] Speech in a Comm. of the Convention, Jun. 11, 1787, BFSM, IX, 595, 596.

[1886] BF to M. Le Veillard, Phil., Oct. 24, 1788, BFSM, X, 673–674.

[1887] THRF, 238.

[1888] Calculation of electoral result based on 1799 county gubernatorial voting, as reported in AGA, Dec. 24, 1799, and the district plan of the Penn. Senate, as reported in AGA, Jan. 4, 1800.

[1889] James Monroe to TJ, Richmond, Jan. 4, 1800, JMOW, III, 169–170.

[1890] See Carl E. Prince, *New Jersey's Jeffersonian Republicans: The Genesis of an Early Party Machine, 1789–1817* (Chapel Hill: Univ. of N. C. Press, 1967), 60–61.

[1891] ANC, 6C, 1S, 28–29.

[1892] AGA, Feb. 25, 1800.

[1893] "Trial of James Thomson Callender for a Seditious Libel," WFST, 700.

[1894] JCPB, I, 18, 85, 86.

[1895] ANC, 6C, 1S, 47.

[1896] ANC, 6C, 1S, 49.

[1897] ANC, 6C, 1S, 53.

[1898] ANC, 6C, 1S, 62–63.

[1899] TJ to Samuel Adams, Phil., Feb. 26, 1800, TJWF, IX, 114.

[1900] ANC, 6C, 1S, 67.

[1901] ANC, 6C, 1S, 68, 85–86, 90.

[1902] Italicized words in this paragraph are from WD's announcement in AGA, Mar. 22, 1800.

[1903] Abigail Adams to Mary Cranch, Phil., Mar. 5, 1800, AANL, 236–237, 237–238 n. 3. Abigail Adams mistakenly wrote "1779" which your author has corrected.

[1904] ANC, 6C, 1S, 103–104.

[1905] ANC, 6C, 1S, 104.

[1906] Stevens Thomson Mason to James Madison, Phil., Mar. 7, 1800, JMAP, XVII, 371.

1907 *Anas,* TJWF, I, 353.

1908 ANC, 6C, 1S, 104–105.

1909 TJ to James Madison, Phil., Mar. 4 [-8], 1800, TJWF, IX, 118, 121–123.

1910 ANC, 6C, 1S, 106.

1911 A new Republican journal, the *American Citizen* (New York), succeeded Mrs. Greenleaf's *Argus.* SDOP, 30, FETT, 414–415.

1912 On August 18, 1800, "Burleigh" complained in the Connecticut, *Courant* (Hartford) that AGA was being "sent around the country *gratis."* SDOP, 637.

1913 AGA, Mar. 17, 1800.

1914 ANC, 6C, 1S, 110.

1915 ANC, 6C, 1S, 111–112.

1916 ANC, 6C, 1S, 112.

1917 ANC, 6C, 1S, 113.

1918 ANC, 6C, 1S, 116–117.

1919 ANC, 6C, 1S, 117.

1920 Thomas Cooper to TJ, Phil., Mar. 23, 1800, TJPM, XXII, 64.

1921 ANC, 6C, 1S, 118–119.

1922 AGA, Mar. 27, 1800.

1923 ANC, 6C, 1S, 121.

1924 ANC, 6C, 1S, 122–124.

1925 ANC, 6C, 1S, 126, 146.

1926 John Dawson to James Madison, Mar. 30, 1800, *Madison Papers* (LC), as quoted in WDKP, 88.

1927 Stevens Thomson Mason to James Madison, Phil., Apr. 2, 1800, JMAP, XVII, 376–377.

1928 TJ to James Madison, [Phil.] Apr. 4, 1800, JMAP, XVII, 378.

1929 FETT, 386–388.

1930 FETT, 383.

1931 TJ to L. W. Tazewell, Phil., Apr. 10, 1800, *TJ Papers* (MHS), Reel 5.

1932 See TCPL, 118–119, "Trial of Thomas Cooper for a Seditious Libel," WFST, 659–60.

1933 Italicized words from AGA, June 10, 1800.

1934 FETT, 379–381.

1935 AGA, Aug. 16, 1800. See *Examiner* (Richmond), May 2, 1800, Ebeling Collection, Houghton Lib., Harv. Univ.

1936 WD to James Thomson Callender, Apr. 17, 1800, *Examiner* (Richmond), May 2, 1800, Ebeling Collection, Houghton Lib., Harv. Univ.

1937 TJ to Edmund Pendleton, Phil., Apr. 19, 1800, TJWF, IX, 118n-119n.

1938 See WFST, 662–669, 676ff, FETT, 307–333, TCPL, 124–129.

1939 "Trial of Thomas Cooper for a Seditious Libel," WFST, 659, 671–673, 676–677.

1940 ANC, 6C, 1S, 678.

1941 Stevens Thomson Mason to James Madison, Phil., Apr. 23, 1800, JMAP, XVII, 381–382.

1942 "Trial of Thomas Cooper for a Seditious Libel," WFST, 659, 677, 679. Wharton misdates this hearing as on the 30th (see Mason's letter to Madison, Apr. 23, 1800, cited above).

1943 JA to Sec. of State and Heads of Depts., Phil., Apr. 23, 1800, JAWO, IX, 50–51.

1944 ND, V, 443, 550 (map), VII, 369.

1945 "Trial of Thomas Cooper for a Seditious Libel," WFST, 659, 679.

1946 AGA, Apr. 29, 1800.

1947 ANC, 6C, 1S, 691.

1948 "Trial of the Northampton Insurgents," WFST, 458, 544–545.

1949 "Second Trial of John Fries," WFST, 610, 612.

1950 "Second Trial of John Fries," WFST, 610, 622 n-623 n.

1951 "Second Trial of John Fries," WFST, 610, 633–634, 636.

1952 EMAF, 732, TJAH, 454.

1953 "Second Trial of John Fries," WFST, 610, 637–641.

1954 ABDM, II, 61.

1955 ABDM, II, 61–62.

1956 JAPS, II, 1027–1031, JAGC, 298.

1957 Abigail Adams to Mary Cranch, Phil., May 5, 1800, AANL, 250–252.

1958 See FETT, 359–373.

1959 "Trial of Anthony Haswell for a Seditious Libel," WFST, 684–686.

1960 Alexander Hamilton to John Jay, N.Y. , May 7, 1800, AHP, XXIV, 464–466.

1961 ABDM, II,61–62. See SDAR, 370.

1962 AGA, May 17, 1800, EMAF, 731.

1963 ANC, 6C, 1S, 713.

1964 WCPW, XII, 41.

1965 T. Pickering to JA, Dept. of State, Phil., May 12, 1800, JAWO, IX, 54–55.

1966 JA to Timothy Pickering, Phil., May 12, 1800, JAWO, IX, 55.

1967 TJ to James Madison, Phil., May 12, 1800, JMAP, XVII, 386–387.

1968 AGA, May 14, 1800.

1969 ANC, 6C, 1S, 1530.

1970 WCPW, XII, 44–45.

1971 JA to James Lloyd, Feb. 11, 1815, JAWO, X, 118.

1972 JCPB, II, 122.

[1973] ANC, 6C, 1S, 183–184.

[1974] JA to J. McHenry, Phil., May 15, 1800, JAWO, IX, 55.

[1975] JA to Att'y-Gen. and Dist.-Att'y of Penn., Phil., May 16, 1800, JAWO, IX, 56.

[1976] Speech in the Convention . . . , BFSM, IX, 590–592.

[1977] BF to Benjamin Vaughan, Passy, Mar. 14, 1785, BFSM, IX, 291, 292.

[1978] SDOP, 482–485, FETT, 344.

[1979] James Monroe to TJ, [May 25, 1800, Richmond], JMOW, III, 179–180.

[1980] TJ to James Monroe, Eppington, May 26, 1800, TJWF, IX, 135–138.

[1981] FETT, 345.

[1982] "Trial of James Thomson Callender for a Seditious Libel," WFST, 688, 695, 710, 718.

[1983] SCRT, 43.

[1984] SCRT, 43–44.

[1985] Gouverneur Morris to R. King, Morrisania, June 4, 1800, RKLK III, 251–252.

[1986] WCPW, XII, 42.

[1987] Italicized words from AGA, July 12, 1800.

[1988] AGA, June 30, 1800.

[1989] See AGA, July 29, 1800.

[1990] GUS, Aug. 1, 1800.

[1991] GUS, July 1, 1800.

[1992] E. g., PG, May 15, 1799.

[1993] Oliver Wolcott, Jr., to Alexander Hamilton, Wash., July 7, 1800, AHP, XXV, 15–16.

[1994] ND, VI, 128–129, VII, 366.

[1995] ND, VI, 172, 213, 566 (map), VII 366.

[1996] ND, VI, 195, 566 (map), VII, 367.

[1997] Alexander Hamilton to Oliver Wolcott, Jr., N.Y., Aug. 3, 1800, AHP, XXV, 54–55.

[1998] See WWHJ, 209.

[1999] W. Bingham to R. King, Phil., Aug. 6, 1800, RKLK, III, 284–285.

[2000] TJ to Philip Mazzei, Monticello, Apr. 24, 1796, TJWF, VIII, 235, 238–241. TJ drafted a constitution for Virginia, in 1776, which—though it included a single chief executive and a senate—embraced the same unicameral values as the Pennsylvania Constitution of 1776. TJ's final draft (3rd) called for a Virginia House of Representatives, annually elected by all taxpayers, which would itself choose both the state's executive (a one-year administrator without any veto power) and a senate with longer terms but whose 15–50 members would, as in the case of the Pennsylvania executive council, rotate from office one third at a time. Because TJ's executive and senate would be creatures of his House of Representatives,

they would serve the House of Representatives rather than any different constituent interest, such as wealth or property. See TJPB, I, 356, 358–359.

[2001] TJ to Jeremiah Moor, Monticello, Aug. 14, 1800, TJWF, IX, 142–143.

[2002] GUS, Aug. 30, 1800.

[2003] Oliver Wolcott, Jr., to Alexander Hamilton, Wash., Sept. 3, 1800, AHP, XXV, 104, 108.

[2004] WWHJ, 213.

[2005] AGA, Dec. 24, 1798.

[2006] JCSH, 224.

[2007] AGA, Mar. 4, 1801.

[2008] TJ to James Monroe, Monticello, Oct. 19, 1823, TJWF, XII, 316.

[2009] BF to David Hartley, Phil., Dec. 4, 1789, BFSM, X, 72.

[2010] TJ to Dr. Benjamin Rush, Monticello, Sept. 23, 1800, TJWF, IX, 146, 148–149.

[2011] BFCV, 774.

[2012] Thomas Paine to TJ, Paris, Oct. 1, 1800, TPW, II, 1406, 1407, 1410, 1412.

[2013] ND, VI, 422–423, 566 (map), VII, 366.

[2014] See AGA, Oct. 12, 1795, on constitution as a compromise.

[2015] TJ to John Taylor, Monticello, May 28, 1816, TJWF, XI, 527, 533.

[2016] TJ to Isaac H. Tiffany, Monticello, Apr. 4, 1819, TJPM, Reel 51, No. 162.

[2017] TJ to John Taylor, Monticello, May 28, 1816, TJWF, XI, 527, 531–532.

[2018] TCPL, 7, 136. See TJMD, III, 467–468.

[2019] ND, VI, 456–458, 566 (map), VII, 364.

[2020] Gabriel Duvall to James Madison, Annapolis, Oct. 17 1800, JMAP, XVII, 424.

[2021] FETT, 301.

[2022] ND, VI, 489, 525, 566 (map), VII, 368.

[2023] THRF, 246–247, DMAF, 256–258, 280.

[2024] *Letter from Alexander Hamilton, Concerning the Public Conduct and Character of John Adams, Esq. President of the United States,* [N.Y., Oct. 21, 1800] AHP, XXV, 169, 186–234. For info. on this letter's publication as pamphlet, see AHP, XXV, 173–178.

[2025] James Madison to TJ, Nov. 1–3, 1800, as quoted in AHP, XXV, 181.

[2026] JA to Abigail Adams, Wash., Nov. 2, 1800, JAPM, Reel 399.

[2027] THRF, 246–247, DMAF, 256–257.

[2028] JCPB, II, viii, 97–98.

[2029] THRF, 247–248.

[2030] O. Wolcott, Sec. of Treas., to JA, Wash., Nov. 8, 1800, JAWO, IX, 88–89.

[2031] SDOP, 601–602, JBZP, 207, W&A, II, 446–447.

[2032] Abigail Adams to Mary Cranch, Wash., Nov. 21, 1800, AANL, 256–258.

[2033] TJMD, III, xxx, 490.

[2034] "To the Citizens of Pennsylvania on the Proposal for Calling a Convention," [1805], TPW, II, 992, 998–999, 1006.

[2035] BFBR, 39.

[2036] ND, VII, 8, 312, 369, 462 (map).

[2037] TJ to Robert R. Livingston, Wash., Dec. 14, 1800, TJWF, IX, 150, 152–153.

[2038] TJ to John Breckenridge, Wash., Dec. 18, 1800, TJWF, IX, 156–157.

[2039] JA to Elbridge Gerry, Wash., Dec. 30, 1800, JAWO, IX, 577–578.

[2040] On BFB's views, see BFBW, 34–40, AGA, Jan. 29, 1795. On James T. Callender's, see JCPB , I, 10–11, II, 56, 89, 143–144, JCSH , 63, 83–89, JCHT, 86–90. On Thomas Paine's, see TPLW, 3–4, "To the Citizens of Penn. on the Proposal for Calling A Convention," TPW, II, 992–1007. On WD's, see [WD], *Experience the test of government in eighteen essays written during the years 1805 and 1806, to aid the investigation of principles, and operation of the existing constitution and laws of Pennsylvania.* (Phil.: WD, 1807), AGA, Feb. 18, 1800, Jan. 1, 1801, JA to Benjamin Rush, July 7, 1805, A&R, 29.

[2041] JCHT, 89–91 delineates the "radical" distinction.

[2042] See BFBT, 128, 138–140, AGA, Apr. 14, 1795, Feb. 18, 1800, WD to Franklin Bache, Wash., Mar. 4, 1804, BFBC, Film 1506, Reel 3.

[2043] See AGA, Feb. 2, 1801.

[2044] *Anas,* TJWL, I, 451–452. TJ places this conversation "about" Feb. 12 or 14.

[2045] MJFE, 236. Rep. James Bayard of Delaware broke ranks with his fellow Federalists to allow the vote for TJ. SDAR, 435.

[2046] AGA, Mar. 7, 1801.

[2047] AGA, Mar. 6, 1801. "Race"-street is a popular name for Sassafras-street, two blocks north of High. PDS, 7.

[2048] JA to Benjamin Stoddert, Quincy, Mar. 31, 1801, JAWO, IX, 582.

[2049] JA to Christopher Gadsden, Quincy, Apr. 10, 1801, JAWO, IX, 584.

[2050] TJ to WD, May 23, 1801, TJWF, IX, 255–258.

[2051] TJ to Abigail Adams, Wash., July 22, 1804, TJWF, X, 86n-88n.

[2052] JA to Thomas Boylston Adams, Quincy, Sept. 15, 1801, JAPM, Reel 401.

[2053] TJ to Attorney Gen. (Levi Lincoln), Wash., Oct. 25, 1802, TJWF, IX, 400–401.

[2054] William Plumer to Edward L. Livermore, Wash., Dec. 21, 1802, William Plumer Collection (LC), No. 165.

[2055] WD to Franklin Bache, Wash., Mar. 4, 1804, BFBC, Film 1506, Reel 3.

[2056] JA to Benjamin Rush, July 7, 1805, A&R, 29.

[2057] Margaret Hartman Duane to Peter Markoe, Phil., Mar. 10, 1807, BFBC, Film 1506, Reel 3.

[2058] TJ to William Wirt, Monticello, Mar. 30, 1811, TJWF, XI, 197 n.-198 n.

[2059] JA to Benjamin Rush, Dec. 4, 1811, A&R, 196–197.

[2060] TJ to James Monroe, Monticello, Oct. 19, 1823, TJWF, XII, 316. See SDOP, 634–640. Concerning AGA's credit for TJ's victory in 1800, see SDOP, 632–634.

[2061] Timothy Pickering to James Robertson, Salem, July 29, 1824, as reported in John Womack Wright, "Pickering's Letter on Washington," TYQ, VII (July, 1925), 16, 25.

[2062] Mason Locke Weems, *A history of the life and death, virtues and exploits, of General George Washington . . .* (N.Y.: Grosset & Dunlap, 1927) (Phil.: John Bioren, 1800). That Weems' clerical credentials and cherry tree account were fictitious, see Marcus Cunliffe, "Parson Weems and George Washington's Cherry Tree," *Bulletin of the John Rylands Lib.* (Manchester, Eng.), XLV (Sept. 1962), 71–96.

[2063] AGA, Aug. 30, 1799.

[2064] Napoleon had secretly acquired the land from Spain in Oct. 1801 (while America was waging its undeclared naval war against France).

[2065] *New York Times Co. v. Sullivan*, 376 U.S. 254, 273–274 (1964).

[2066] 1739 ed., PRA, I, 153.

[2067] JMAD, II, 583.

[2068] See BFPP, 121.

INDEX

(Note: Page numbers in *italics* indicate illustrations.)

Abercrombie, James, 115, 137, 623, 625, 687, 733, 840, 842, 847, 878
abolitionism, 497, 854
Academy of Sciences (France), 313, 356, 468
Adams (ship), 656, 718
Adams, Abigail, letters of, 40, 43–44, 47, 51, 61, 67, 76, 84, 88, 89, 92, 94, 95, 97, 108, 109, 111, 115–16, 117, 119, 132, 137–38, 145, 157, 164, 166, 179, 184, 186, 262, 284–85, 321, 323–24, 352, 411, 468, 555, 557, 565, 592, 600, 711, 721, 748, 783, 881–82
Adams, Abijah (journalist), 599, 625, 790
Adams, John (as ambassador to Great Britain), 435–36, 452, 454–55, 481, 510, 859–60
Adams, John (American Revolutionary era)
anti-French sentiments, 151, 238, 245, 273, 363–64, 366, 367, 369–70, 373–74, 381–82, 392, 393, 436–38, 454–55
as Boston Massacre defense attorney, 44–45
as British commerce treaty commissioner, 411, 423, 436, 445, 450
as British peace negotiator, 372–79, 387–400, 403, 406, 409–10, 414, 419–20, 423–50, 453–54, 888
as commissioner to France, 63, 151, 295, 310, 322, 324, 340, 348, 352–56, 359–74, 383–86, 391–92, 396–400, 406 (*see also heading* Adams (John)—

Franklin relationship *below*; *subhead* anti-French sentiment *above*
as Continental Congress delegate, 247, 253–54
and Declaration of Independence, 281–82
meeting with Howe, 288–89
motives for supporting, 111, 121, 279, 486–87
on Philadelphia evacuation, 334, 335
on poor troop discipline, 288, 294–95, 296
on Washington's command, 287, 288, 294–96, 320, 332, 335, 349–50
Adams, John (personal qualities), 97, 353, 391, 404, 406, 527
enviousness, 355, 356, 359–60, 439, 441, 442, 500, 507, 517, 535 (*see also* Adams (John)—Franklin relationship *below*)
as "His Rotundity," 3, 45, 732, 839
impressions of France, 353–64
lack of diplomacy, 392, 403, 411
on New England's superiority, 262
resentfulness, 359–61, 364–66, 372, 453, 517, 518
suspiciousness, 367–68, 437–38
vanity, 436, 453–54
Adams, John (personal relationships)
Bache and, 207, 237
Franklin and. *See* Adams (John)—Franklin relationship
on Hamilton, 420–21
on Jefferson, 281

Jefferson on, 501, 510
Logan and, 543–44, 562
Madison on, 436
Washington and, 189, 239, 242, 287, 288, 294–96, 320, 332, 335, 349, 476, 482–83
Adams, John (political views)
on American independence, 270
on American Revolution's historical misrepresentation, 500, 517–18
British government model, 486–87, 492, 532, 799
critique of, 714
on dangers of full equality, 504
on democrat vs. aristocrat, 215–16, 464, 864–65
"Discourses on Davila" articles, 503, 510, 723
and Divine Right, 282
Federal Constitution reflecting, 476
on Federalist self-destructiveness, 901
on forming state governments, 280
on French Revolution, 128, 129, 130, 137, 515
on French role in American Revolution, 238
on governmental structure, 276–79, 292–93, 298, 371–72, 374–76, 456, 457, 468, 799 (*see also* bicameralism; checks and balances; hereditary offices; unicameralism)
Hamilton's views vs., 473
on "ideology" terminology, 518
Jefferson on changes in, 510

Adams, John (continued)
on limited monarchy, 490,
500–501 (see also
monarchism)
and Massachusetts
constitution,371–72,374–
76, 453
on natural aristocracy, 464
on Paine's Common Sense,
270–71, 276–79, 352–53,
376
on Paine's Rights of Man,
510, 516
on Pennsylvania
constitution, 298, 318
on political parties, 188
on presidency, 477–78
on property ownership,
376, 490, 504, 901
"Publicola" articles, 860–
61
on republicanism, 177, 515
on revolutionary
movements, 516–18
on senatorial election, 477
Thoughts on Government
pamphlet, 277–78
on titles and pageantry, 488–
92
see also Defence of the
Constitutions of
Government of the
United States
Adams, John (as President)
Alien and Sedition Acts.
See Alien and Sedition
Acts
and black cockade, 113,
127
changes of principles, 90
deportation of French
emigrés, 194
dismissal of cabinet
officers, 783, 787, 788–
89, 793, 798, 802–3
Duane prosecution
continuance, 794, 809,
869, 870
Duane seditious libel
indictment withdrawal,
859–60, 870
example of seditious libel
against, 773
on foreign-influenced
threats, 101, 111, 118
and French treaty
abrogations, 185, 188–89,
523
Fries reprieve, 797, 798

"Hail Columbia" anthem,
90; 100–101
Hamilton pamphlet
criticizing, 873, 874, 881–
82
and Hamilton's adultery,
17, 18, 198–99
on inevitable conflict with
France, 102, 167
Jefferson as vice president,
562
on national unity, 121
naval vessel namesakes,
656
nepotism charges against,
37, 41–44, 47, 563
on Pennsylvania tax
rebellion, 609
political future, 702
prayer and fast day
proclamations. See Fast
and Prayer Day
on presidential reelection
loss, 894, 899 (see also
presidential election of
1800)
press mockery of, 820
proposed government-
owned newspaper, 776
refusal to reprieve Lyon,
562
resignation rumors, 47–48,
705, 712
rewards for Bache's
enemies, 56, 58, 73, 131,
145
Sedition Act. See Alien and
Sedition Acts
on seditious slander, 129
(see also seditious libel
prosecutions)
student demonstration
against, 179, 196
supportive events, 85, 90,
107–9, 179
suppression of political
opposition, 690, 695,
765, 768, 770, 804, 810
as war president, 737, 835
(see also war buildup)
and XYZ affair, 18, 19–20,
62–69, 71, 155, 160–61,
164
see also Alien and Sedition
Acts; congressional-
presidential relations;
war buildup
Adams, John (as Vice
President)

electoral votes, 484
on Franklinian democracy,
503
on French Revolution, 497
letter on British influence
in U.S. politics, 678, 683,
704, 708, 841, 859–60,
870, 872
testimony against Paine, 516
Adams (John)—Franklin
relationship
Adams commentary, 237–
38, 258, 313, 353–56,
359–61, 364, 367–70,
373, 393, 420, 425–27,
429–32, 438–42, 448–49,
452, 516–18, 521–22,
826, 874
on Franklin's celebrity,
208, 356, 517
on Franklin's conduct in
France, 359–61, 364,
365, 369
on Franklin's faults, 369–
70, 393
on Franklin's French
pronunciation, 355
on Franklin's historical
impact, 516–20
on suspected Franklin
intrigue, 367–68, 385
Adams' reaction to
Franklin's death, 502,
507
Adams' envy, 355, 369–70,
373–74, 379, 389–93,
425–27, 429–32, 436–42,
445–50, 452, 535, 825,
826, 874
Franklin's characterization
of Adams, 145, 237, 352,
405–6, 492
Adams, John Quincy, 37, 41–
44, 47, 348, 353, 363,
454, 511, 563, 860–61
Adams, Samuel, 254, 279,
365, 371, 745, 825, 858
Adams, Thomas (JA's son),
563, 902
Adams, Thomas (journalist),
196, 527–28, 556, 598–
99, 627, 639, 643, 694,
754, 880
Adcook, William, 459
Addis, Joseph, 851–52
Addison, Alexander, 138–39
Adrastes (ship), 194, 218
Age of Reason (Paine), 75,
148, 175, 622, 654, 858

Bache, Benjamin Franklin
(*continued*)
and schoolmate Adams (J.
Q.), 43–44, 353, 363
at university education,
460, 475, 480
Voltaire meeting, 348,
349
Bache, Deborah (BFB's
sister), 79, 906
Bache, Elizabeth (BFB's
sister), 79, 325, 346
Bache, Franklin (BFB's son),
37, 38, 903–4
Bache, Hartman (BFB's son),
226, 232
Bache, Louis (BFB's brother),
79
Bache, Peggy Markoe (BFB's
wife; later Duane), 173,
226, 231, 906
Aurora pressmen's
demands, 567–68, 569
Aurora reopening, 525,
538, 626, 748, 758
BFB courtship and
marriage, 37–38, 496–
97
and BFB's death, 232, 524
Federalist press ridicule of,
529–31, 537, 545, 554,
558, 569, 584, 620–22,
624, 626–29, 658, 660,
671, 672, 690, 830
marriage to Duane, 818–19,
820, 904, 906
Bache, Richard (BFB's
father), 26, 79, 83, 231,
248–49, 253, 317–18,
323, 325, 346, 351, 451,
454
Bache, Richard (BFB's son),
37
Bache, Sarah (BFB's sister),
79
Bache, Sarah Franklin (BFB's
mother), 26, 79, 253,
318, 325, 346, 364, 368–
69, 401, 448
Bache, William (BFB's
brother), 79, 136, 139,
143, 569, 571–73
Baker, Hillary, 159, 669, 672
Baldwin, Luther, 200–201,
532, 702, 790
Baldwin, Thomas, 812
Baltimore American, 652–53,
679, 695, 820
Bancroft, Thomas, 618

Barbary pirates, 61, 62, 69
Barbé-Marbois, Marquis de,
369
Barras, Comte de, 20, 413,
414, 417, 418, 421
Barry, John, 131, 199, 402,
801
Bastille, fall of, 491, 499,
503
Beale, Thomas, 486
Beaumarchais, Pierre-
Augustin Caron de, 272–
73, 285–86, 296, 306,
316, 319–20
Beckley, John, 211, 212
Bell, Robert, 267
Benjamin Franklin (ship),
137, 143, 163, 871
Bennington, Battle of, 328
bicameralism
Adams advocacy, 237, 292–
93, 371–72, 374–76, 463–
65 (*see also*
unicameralism)
arguments against, 292–93,
513, 731, 740–41, 753,
884, 894–95
British, 44, 731
as check on democratic
excesses, 883–84, 887
Federal Constitution
provision, 470, 476–77
Federalist championship of,
44, 45, 472
Jay advocacy, 465
Pennsylvania change to,
496, 499–500, 875, 883–
84
and presidential elector
selection, 732, 733, 734–
35
see also Congress, U.S.
Bill of Rights
articles, 174, 512, 593, 608,
849
Fenno (Jack Ward) attack
on, 600–601, 604–5
Jefferson championship,
483, 484, 493, 512
see also specific rights
Bingham, William, 176, 296,
789, 792, 833
Black, John, 555
black cockade, 3, 93, 105–8,
111–13, 117, 118, 120–
30, 138, 220, 811–12
Blank, Michael, 724
Bonaparte. *See* Napoleon
Bonaparte

Bon Homme Richard (ship),
372
Bon Père (ship), 616
Bonvouloir, Achard de, 265–
66, 275
Boston (ship), 866–67
Boston Commercial Gazette,
865
Boston *Independent
Chronicle,* 196, 527–28,
556, 598–99, 625, 627,
670, 689, 694, 754
Boston Massacre, 45, 246
Boston Tea Party, 247
Boudinot, Elias, 335, 345, 355–
56
Bowdoin, James, 465
Braddock, Edward, 243, 297
Bradford, Samuel, 527, 533,
541
Bradley, Thomas, 632
Brandywine Creek, Battle of,
332, 333, 363
Breckinridge, John, 537, 892
Breed's Hill, Battle of, 255,
256
Brennan, William, 907
Brent, Richard, 112
Brissot de Warville, Jacques-
Pierre, 477, 514, 515,
518
British Constitution. *See*
Constitution, British
British East India Company,
247
Broglie, Charles-François de,
321, 336
Brown, David, 533, 541, 617–
18, 630, 649–50
Brown, Moses, 870
Brown, Robert, 594
Bunker Hill, Battle of, 255,
256
Burgoyne, John, 328, 329,
337, 338, 339, 358
Burk, Christiana, 41
Burk, John Daly, 40–43, 76,
148, 184–86, 196, 197,
214–15, 223–25, 554,
555, 563, 654, 689
Burr, Aaron, 184, 485, 782,
889, 890
Bustletown (Pa.), 669, 672,
688

Cadwalader, Colonel, 300,
301, 309

French Revolution
(continued)
first days of, 491–92
Franklin as inspiration for,
505–6
Franklin on, 496
Jefferson and, 171, 491–95,
576
Lafayette command, 491
La Rochefoucauld on, 482
mob violence, 495
Paine and, 469, 499, 503–4,
511, 514–15, 518
"Publicola" criticism of, 44
Reign of Terror, 39, 76, 491
tricolor cockade, 491
see also War of the French
Revolution
Fries, John, 578, 605, 613,
617, 621–22, 625, 629,
639, 771, 779
conviction, 777, 789
death penalty, 781–82
presidential reprieve, 797,
798
Fries' Rebellion, 578, 605,
608–9, 611–19, 677, 702,
781–82
Frothingham, David, 715, 719–
20, 724, 754, 790, 869

Gabriel (slave), 853, 854, 855
Gage, Thomas, 247, 248, 252
Gallagher, James, Jr., 592–93
Gallatin, Albert, 54, 88, 156,
192
Cobbett's mockery of, 55–
56
as House Republican
leader, 55, 128
as object of Alien and
Sedition Act, 92
opposition to Alien and
Sedition Acts, 182–83,
594, 596, 597
opposition to provisional
army, 119, 125–26, 127
on publication of Alien and
Sedition Acts, 553
and Reading (Pa.)
reception, 229, 230
and war buildup movement,
54, 60, 72, 112, 192
Ganges (ship), 129, 131, 647,
828
Gano, Samuel, 61
Garrigues, Edward, 686–87

Gates, Horatio, 255, 273, 305,
309, 485
as Board of War president,
340, 343
Burgoyne surrender to,
338, 339, 412
Camden defeat, 394, 395
Northern Army command,
328, 329, 337, 338
and Southern Army, 380,
394
Washington and, 340, 343,
344, 345, 371
Gazette of the United States,
22, 23
as anti-immigrant, 40–41,
534, 536, 540, 542, 827
as anti-Semitic, 825, 832–
33, 836–37
continuance of, 792–93,
794
continuance of publication,
792–93
"Discourses on Davila"
articles, 503
Fenno death and successor,
234
Fenno (Jack Ward) control
relinquishment, 600–602,
801–2
Fenno (Jack Ward) farewell
editorial, 807
Fenno (Jack Ward) on sale
of, 774, 777–78
first issue, 486
front page, 24
incendiary song on Bache
and Franklin, 109–10
"Publicola" articles, 511
as quasi-official Federalist
newspaper, 23, 40
sale offer, 774, 777–78
warning to women in
politics, 538
Wayne ownership, 802
see also Fenno, John;
Fenno, John Ward;
Wayne, Caleb Barry
Geddes, Henry, 56
General Greene (ship), 129
Genêt, Edmond, 150–52, 279,
560, 667
George (ship), 393
George III, king of Great
Britain
Adams presented to, 454–
55
and American peace
negotiations, 427

British right to criticize,
532
Cobbett's support for, 25
colonial grievances petition,
248
and war to crush French
Revolution, 15, 76,
151
Gérard de Rayvenal, Conrad-
Alexandre, 285, 342–45,
352, 355
and American–British
peace negotiations, 429,
432
on American pro-British
faction, 366–67
Germain, George, 326, 329,
350, 361, 389, 417, 418,
423, 442
German immigrants
as Democratic-Republicans,
670
and Fries' rebellion, 618–
19, 622, 625, 779
and gubernatorial election,
666, 703
Germantown, Battle of, 336–
37, 855
Gerry, Elbridge, 19–20, 173,
282, 476
Gifford, John, 312, 542
Giles, William B., 611, 810,
878
Gordon, Robert, 322
Gordon, William, 803
Gossin, Jacob, 615
Grand Jurors (Pa.), 73–74,
78, 80
Grasse, François Joseph,
Comte de, 407–10, 412,
413, 416–18, 421–23,
483
Graves, Thomas, 416–19
Great Britain
Adams as first ambassador
to. See Adams, John
Adams' sympathies with,
111, 121, 799
American colonial policies,
244–48
American commerce treaty
commission, 445–46,
451
charged with influencing
American politics, 663–
64, 668, 670, 673–74,
680, 683, 704, 708, 718,
719, 790, 841, 859–60,
870, 872

Luzerne, Anne-César de la, 369, 373–74, 383, 391, 398, 403, 407, 415
Lyon, Matthew, 192
  Federalist press attacks on, 554, 555
  on House Speaker's press censorship, 49
  petition for presidential reprieve of, 562, 564, 590, 624
  physical assault on, 197–98, 203–4
  reelected to Congress, 560, 564, 580, 582, 594, 595
  second seditious libel indictment, 708
  seditious libel conviction, 526–28, 532, 533, 549, 564, 594, 618, 790, 880
  spitting fracas in House, 11, 13
  supporters' seditious libel indictments, 624, 699, 708, 713, 784, 805
  vote deciding Jefferson's presidency, 899

Maclay, William, 486–88, 495, 507, 508
Macpherson, William, 154, 570, 609, 612, 616–17, 623, 628, 629, 631, 643, 655, 728, 730
Macpherson's Blues
  Adams' praise for, 154–55
  anti-Bache actions, 103, 110–11, 113–14, 630
  attentions to Adams, 98, 107–9, 545
  Aurora ridicule of, 93, 197, 199, 202
  battalion orders, 631
  boisterous meetings of, 97, 99, 102
  cockade insignia. See black cockade
  disbandment, 809–14
  and Fast and Prayer Day, 113
  as federal army, 133, 609, 611
  formation of, 54, 60, 84
  and Fries' Rebellion, 612, 614
  Independence Day parades, 178–79, 655

meeting condemning, 61, 65
  mob violence by, 116–18, 778–79, 811
  pledge against foreign enemy, 101, 102
  Porcupine's Gazette defense of, 119–20
  reorganization of, 134
  and Silver Eagle cockade, 179
  under-voting-age members, 99–100, 113
  volunteer influx, 153
  and Washington's Philadelphia visit, 534, 535
Madison, James
  on Adams' character, 145, 436
  on Alien and Sedition Acts, 128, 732
  and American–British peace treaty, 437
  and American Revolution, 411
  on British influence on American press, 575, 582
  and Constitutional Convention records, 469–78
  on Duane's defense of liberty, 522
  and Duane Senate privilege case, 766, 767
  on executive branch powers, 470, 595–96
  on French war prospects, 139
  on Hamilton's attack on Adams, 874
  on mourning Franklin's death, 502
  presidency, 906
  on presidential title, 489
  Virginia Resolutions, 558
  on war powers, 62
Magill, Andrew, 555
Maillebois, Marshal de, 356
Marbois, M., 369
Marcus. See Gazette of the United States
Marignac, Gabriel Louis Galissard de, 393
Marine Corps, 188
Markoe, Francis, 173
Markoe, Peter, 38

Marshall, John, 19–20, 154, 164, 726–27
Marshall, Thomas, 275
Martin, Alex, 653
Mary John (ship), 37
Mason, George, 471, 476
Mason, John, 804–5
Mason, Stevens T., 180, 205, 213–15, 234–35, 532
  and Callender conviction, 810
  on Federalist stifling of free speech, 775
  and Senate contempt charge against Duane, 765, 767
  on Senate electoral choice bill, 750
Massachusetts
  Adams on natural inequalities in, 464
  and American Revolution, 249–59
  and British colonial policies, 152, 246, 247
  liberty poles, 533, 541, 618, 650, 658
  resolutions against merchant-ship arming, 59–61, 63, 75, 79
  sedition prosecutions, 533, 541, 598–99, 617–18, 649–50
  Shays' Rebellion, 460–62, 465–66, 468
  state government formation, 284–85, 321
  see also Constitution, Massachusetts
Massachusetts Senate, 375–76, 461
Massey, John, 631
Mather, Samuel, 450
Mathers, James, 792
Matlock, Timothy, 292
Maurepas, Comte de, 326
Maurepas, Madame de, 316
Mazzei, Philip, 17, 18–19, 72, 78, 178, 477, 836
McAdams, Thomas, 555
McCarney, Thaddeus, 593
McCauley, John, 631
McClenachan, Blair, 594
McConnell, Thomas, 529
McHenry, James, 68, 181, 234, 534, 612, 678, 718, 744, 772, 775, 879

property ownership
  Adams on protection of,
    376, 490, 504, 901
  British constitutional
    guarantees, 246
  as monarchy, 478
  as qualification for elective
    office, 371, 372, 475
  as suffrage qualification,
    375, 376, 838
property tax, 186, 608–9
proportionate representation,
  270, 278, 283, 472, 731
Prospect Before Us,
  (Callender), 737, 799,
  875
Prosser, Thomas, 853
Prosser slave rebellion, 853,
  854, 855, 857
provisional army. *See* army
"Publicola" articles, 44, 511,
  515, 860–61
public trial, right to, 160
"Publius." *See Federalist, The*
Putnam, Israel, 251, 255, 300

Quakers, 50, 53–55, 74, 688
Quartering Act of 1765, 245
quartering prohibitions, 512,
  608
  Federalist contravening of,
    619, 630, 631, 670
Quebec, Battle of, 264, 266–
  67
Quebec Act of 1774, 246
Quesnay, François, 517

Radcliff, Judge, 720
Randolph, Edmund, 437, 470,
  476
"Rat Catcher." *See* Duane,
  William
Rawle, William, 174, 175,
  664, 665, 670, 706
Read, Jacob, 773
Reading (Pa.)
  federal army harassment
    incidents, 615–16, 620–
    22, 629, 631, 643, 654
  Gallatin' travel through,
    229, 230
Reading Eagle, 620–22, 702
Reed, Joseph, 271, 276, 301–
  2, 303, 309, 370, 380,
  485

Reign of Terror (France), 39,
  76, 491
Relf, Samuel, 97, 107
religion. *See* atheism; Fast
  and Prayer Day; religious
  freedom; *specific
  religions*
religious freedom
  Adams' circumvention, 17,
    113, 375, 839
  Alien Act and, 216
  Aurora statement on, 846–
    47
  Bill of Rights on, 219, 512
  Declaration of
    Independence on, 282
  Federalist press against,
    175, 770
  French decree, 497, 511
  as inherent right, 829, 830
  Jefferson's statements on,
    218–19, 483, 484, 576,
    782, 801, 829, 839–41,
    846–47, 853–54
  New England
    Congregationalist
    circumvention, 839
  Pennsylvania state
    constitutional guarantee,
    286
  republicanism and, 836–37
  Vermont statute, 628
  see also Fast and Prayer
    Day
*Remarks Occasioned by the
  Late Conduct of Mr.
  Washington, President of
  the United States* (Bache
  pamphlet), 152
Renne, Joseph, 228
representation
  accountability and, 884
  Adams' view of, 277–78
  as British colonial issue,
    245–46
  as confederation issue, 283
  direct, 862–63
  Franklin/Paine advocacy of
    equal, 258, 270, 283–84,
    509, 731
  French Constitution (1793)
    on equal, 519
  proportionate advocacy,
    270, 278, 283, 472, 731
  see also elections; Electoral
    College
Reprisal (ship), 241, 299–
    300, 303, 304, 318, 327,
    330

Republican Blues, 139, 642–
  43, 647, 649, 655–56
republican government
  Adams on meaning of, 177,
    490, 500–501, 515, 535,
    685
  Adams seen as repudiating,
    510, 530
  Aurora defense of, 220, 221–
    22, 605
  Aurora on meaning of, 177
  Aurora on return of
    national belief in, 692,
    693–95, 704
  Aurora on trials of, 899–
    900
  Federalist press attacks on,
    604–6, 651–52
  Federalist press on
    delusions of, 757–58, 781
  France and, 514–15
  Hamilton's hostility to, 719
  Jefferson administration
    vow to establish, 902
  Jefferson on meaning of,
    630, 745, 862–63, 900
  Jewish rights under, 836–
    37
  long elective terms seen
    contravening, 884
  Paine outline of, 269–70
  presidential election of
    1800 as crucial to, 765–
    66
  Rush's defense of, 489
  Society for Political
    Enquiries supporting, 466
  Webster (Noah) on, 832
Republican Greens, 652, 655,
  656, 663, 677, 717, 718,
  772, 794, 822, 853, 854–
  55, 900
Republican Society of St.
  Tammany. *See* Tammany
  Society
Republicans. *See* Democratic-
  Republicans
Revere, Paul, 247, 249
revolutionary movements
  Adams on, 516–18
  see also American
    Revolution; French
    Revolution; Irish Revolt
Reynolds, James (securities
  speculator), 32, 33, 43,
  76
Reynolds, Dr. James
  ("Jimmy"), 112, 135,
  139, 143, 554, 555, 895

Washington, George
(continued)
Pickering on
indecisiveness, 302–3,
311
recruitment failures, 382–
83, 387, 394–95, 405,
411
Reed on indecisiveness,
301–2, 303, 309
Rush on weakness, 260,
309, 341, 345, 485
supporter's letter to, 344
Trenton and Princeton
victories, 309–11
as unifying popular symbol,
239, 240, 412
at Valley Forge, 341
Wayne on incompetence,
297–98
on Wayne's Stony Point
success, 370
and Yorktown, 394, 414,
416, 417, 419, 421, 482–
83
Washington, George (as
President)
anti-French actions, 17, 30,
34–35
Aurora criticism of, 28–32,
51, 152–53
British paid influences,
673, 678–79, 683, 704,
708, 718, 841–42
election, 484–85
Farewell Address, 31, 34–
35
inauguration, 487–88
Jay Treaty, 17, 30, 34–35,
38, 152
Jefferson and, 19, 51,
495
Monroe's critical book on,
34
Neutrality Proclamation
of 1793, 28, 152, 518–
19
as pro-monarchist, pro-
British, 18, 29–30, 473
refusal to seek third term,
31, 32
Washington, James, 243

Washington, Lund, 406
Washington, Martha, 73, 243,
726
Washington, D.C., 723, 774,
787, 795, 797, 801, 807,
874, 900
Adams (Abigail)
impressions of, 881–82
Adams' reception in, 808,
814, 815–16
British burning of, 906
first congressional session,
870
Washington [Pa.] *Herald of
Liberty,* 695
Watts, David, 685
Way, George, 641
Wayne, Anthony, 297–98,
334, 362, 370, 394, 416
Wayne, Caleb Barry, 802,
808, 812–13, 836
Weatherill, Samuel, 50, 53, 54–
55, 74
Webster, Noah, 218, 219, 482,
831–32
Weems, Mason Locke, 905
Wentworth, Paul, 456
West Indies, 150–52, 244,
407, 408 (*see also*
privateering)
West Point (N.Y.), 396, 441
Wharton, Robert, 563, 584,
587, 588, 681–82, 685
Whiskey Rebellion, 677
White, James, 627
Wickes, Lambert, 241, 299–
300, 303, 304, 318, 325,
327, 330
Wiley, Samuel, 555
William and Mary College,
154, 179–80, 196
Williams, David, 775
Williams, John, 54
Williams, Jonathan, 316
Williams, Steven, 59
Wilson, James, 470
Wolcott, Oliver, 48, 165,
166, 590, 618, 624, 644,
822
funds misuse charges,
808, 815–19, 821, 882,
888

Hamilton correspondence,
822, 831, 844
resignation and dismissals,
800, 823, 877
and treasury department
fire, 897
and war office fire, 877,
878, 879
Worrell, Isaac, 838–39

XYZ affair, 18–20, 56, 62–
69, 71, 86, 154, 155,
164
delegation's report, 155
and U.S. war sentiment, 70–
73, 82, 143, 173
Washington on, 74, 107

"Yankee Doodle" (song), 109–
10, 114, 169
yellow fever epidemic (1798),
141, 172, 207–33, 527,
531
yellow fever epidemic (1799),
684, 686–88, 690, 706,
721
yellow fever epidemic (1800),
829
Yorktown Campaign (1781),
406, 416–21
Cornwallis' defeat, 225
French bravery, 197
French casualties, 437
French fleet, 409, 416–19
French troops, 394, 415–
16, 418
Hamilton report on, 420
prelude to, 410, 413, 414
Washington reports on,
419, 420, 482–83
"Young Lightening-Rod." *See*
Bache, Benjamin Franklin
youth militia. *See*
Macpherson's Blues

Zeigler's plains, 707, 709

ABOUT THE AUTHOR

Les Gardner

Born in Boston in 1941, the son and grandson of printers, Richard Neil Rosenfeld is an independent scholar who lives in Chestnut Hill, Massachusetts. He holds degrees from Yale, Columbia, and Boston Universities, is a Councillor at the American Antiquarian Society, and is an Associate Fellow at Yale's Timothy Dwight College.

BEFORE THE CURTAIN RISES IN 1798

1754   America's French and Indian War begins. Britain wars with French Canada and its Indian allies.

1763   America's French and Indian War ends. Britain, the winner, obtains Canada from France.

1775   The American Revolution begins (April 19, Concord and Lexington).

1776   Declaration of Independence (July 4).

1778   America makes an alliance with France. France enters the war.

1783   The American Revolution ends. Britain recognizes the United States of America.

1787   Philadelphia convention drafts the U.S. Constitution.

1789   U.S. Federal Government begins operations (March 4).

        George Washington and John Adams elected as first U.S. President and Vice President (April 6).

        The French Revolution begins (July 14, Bastille Day).

1792   George Washington and John Adams elected to second term as President and Vice President.

1793   The French Revolution guillotines the French King (January 21).

        Britain goes to war against the French Revolution (February 1).

        George Washington proclaims American neutrality in the war between Britain and France (April 22).

        The Reign of Terror in France (September 1793–August 1794).

1795   George Washington signs the Jay Treaty with England.

1796   France refuses to receive a new American ambassador (December 11).

1797   John Adams becomes second U.S. President (March 4).

        John Adams nominates a three-man commission to negotiate with France (May 31).

        Adams' three-man commission arrives in France (October 4).

        No word from Adams' three-man commission in France (December 31).

AS THE CURTAIN RISES IN 1798

THE FEDERALISTS
Support a powerful federal government to lead the nation. Fear the French Revolution as an international threat.

THE REPUBLICANS
Fear a powerful federal government as a threat to liberty. Support the French Revolution for its opposition to monarchy.

Leading Federalist Newspapers

Gazette of the United States
  Publisher: John Fenno
  Wife: Mary Fenno
  Son: John Ward Fenno

Porcupine's Gazette
  Publisher: William Cobbett
  (a.k.a. Peter Porcupine)

Leading Republican Newspaper

Philadelphia Aurora
  Publisher: Benjamin Bache
  Wife: Margaret Bache
  Writer: William Duane
  Wife: Catherine Duane
  Son: William John Duane
  Writer: James T. Callender
  Writer: Thomas "Newgate" Lloyd

Federalist Leaders

John Adams, U.S. President (1797–)
  Wife: Abigail Adams
  Son: John Quincy Adams, U.S. Minister to Prussia
George Washington, private citizen, former U.S. President (1789–1797)
Alexander Hamilton, private citizen, former Treasury Secretary (1789–1795)

Republican Leaders

Thomas Jefferson, U.S. Vice President (1797–)
James Madison, private citizen, former Republican House Leader (1789–1797)
James Monroe, private citizen, former U.S. Minister to France (1794–1796)

Certain Federalists in the House

Jonathan Dayton, New Jersey, Speaker
Roger Griswold, Connecticut
John Allen, Connecticut
Harrison Gray Otis, Massachusetts

Certain Republicans in the House

Albert Gallatin, Pennsylvania, Republican House Leader
Matthew Lyon, Vermont
Edward Livingston, New York

Certain Federalists in the Senate

James Lloyd, Maryland
James Ross, Pennsylvania

Certain Republicans in the Senate

Stevens Thomson Mason, Virginia
John Langdon, New Hampshire

CERTAIN EUROPEAN REFUGEES IN AMERICA IN 1798

From Ireland: writers William Duane and Thomas "Newgate" Lloyd of the *Aurora*, editor John Daly Burk of the New York *Time Piece*. From Scotland: writer James T. Callender of the *Aurora*. From England: lawyer Thomas Cooper. From France: political philosopher Constantin-François Volney, scholar Médéric-Louis-Elie Moreau de St. Méry. From Poland: writer Julien Niemcewicz, General Tadeusz Kosciuszko.